Coastal Ecosystem Management

The Conservation Foundation

The Conservation Foundation is a nonprofit research and
communication organization dedicated to encouraging
human conduct to sustain and enrich life on earth.
Since its founding in 1948 it has attempted to provide
intellectual leadership in the cause of wise management
of the earth's resources. It is now focusing increasing
attention on one of the critical issues of the day—
how to use wisely that most basic resource, the land itself.

Coastal Ecosystem Management

A TECHNICAL MANUAL
FOR THE CONSERVATION
OF COASTAL ZONE RESOURCES

JOHN R. CLARK

The Conservation Foundation

A WILEY-INTERSCIENCE PUBLICATION

JOHN WILEY & SONS, New York • London • Sydney • Toronto

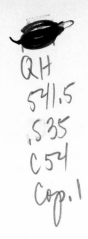
Published by John Wiley & Sons, Inc.

Library of Congress Cataloging in Publication Data:

Clark, John R.   1927–
    Coastal ecosystem management.

    "A Wiley-Interscience publication."
    Includes bibliographical references and index.
    1. Seashore ecology.   2. Coastal zone
management.   I. Title.

QH541.5.S35C54   639′.9′09146   76-40125
ISBN 0-471-15854-2

Printed in the United States of America

10 9 8 7 6 5 4 3 2 1

Preface

Environmental management is a form of art that prospers in direct proportion to the scientific knowledge on which it is based. While technical aspects vary somewhat from locale to locale, the practice of the art varies immensely. Mangrove coastlines are one thing, rocky shores another, but the ecological principles are the same. However, a management strategy that will work for an established seaport is only remotely similar to one designed for a developing recreational settlement on a remote piece of shore. The seaport case will test the manager's skills at accommodation, tradeoff, and balance. The remote settlement will test the manager's skill at creative environmental planning. The first draws more on political skills, the second more on technical skills.

This book conveys technical knowledge and methodology and therefore deals more with developing than with urbanized coasts. It focuses on county and municipal regulatory programs. Its advocacy is conservation of coastal resources and realization of the optimum carrying capacity of coastal ecosystems. Its viewpoint is that the simplest

and best management strategy is one that is based on understanding nature's systems and optimizing their functions. Its theme is planning, but planners are not the only audience. The book should be useful to officials of all levels of government and to professional ecologists, developers, lawyers, environmentalists, engineers, technical consultants, and students in many fields.

The complexities of natural systems can be dealt with easily enough by grasping a few basic ecologic principles—11 are presented in this book. The complexities of management can be simplified by founding programs on a few basic ecosystem management rules—this book offers 11.

To the extent that environmental management is built on predetermined guidelines and standards for accommodating development, the development review process becomes professional. This book focuses on the techniques for such accommodation and attempts to provide the basis for a professional approach. Because both planning and management have to go beyond generalities and deal with specific types of projects, it provides specific guidelines and implementation standards for 24 different development project types (Chapter 6).

The ideal backdrop for community coastal management is the Federal Coastal Zone Management Program. Under this program, state governments voluntarily participate and receive Federal funds to establish a statewide coastal management plan. The program requires conformance by local governments for participating states and may provide direct benefits including a state and federal approved management framework, technical assistance, and perhaps direct funding. Since this program requires the use of the existing tools and powers of local government for the most part, there will be little new in the way of demand for types of regulatory machinery. However, some restructuring will be needed.

A major viewpoint of this book is that all environmental requirements can be met with little added burden if existing development reviews are streamlined and if the new ones are integrated into a coordinated "one-stop" system. The object is to put the project proposer through a single coordinated review process rather than a long series of separate reviews. Therefore, we have concluded the descriptive part of the book (in Chapter 5) with suggestions for use of existing management tools and for integrating environmental controls into the existing land use and resource management programs of local government.

This is a technical reference book. Its credibility rests on the authority of the hundreds of technical references that are listed and on 41 contributions by specialists in a variety of technical fields (Chapter 7). An extensive technical supplement provides relevant numerical, graphic, tabular, technological, and descriptive data of use in resource inventory, environmental restoration, planning, management engineering, and environmental monitoring and enforcement.

JOHN R. CLARK

Washington, D.C.
January 1977

Acknowledgments

The preparation of this book was supported by grants from the American Conservation Association (New York), the federal Office of Coastal Zone Management (U.S. Department of Commerce), the Griffis Foundation (New York), and the Jesse Smith Noyes Foundation (New York). I am most grateful to the following officers of their respective organizations: George M. Lamb, Robert W. Knecht, Nixon S. Griffis, and Edith M. Muma.

An undertaking of this magnitude requires the vigorous support of scores of colleagues. Most are listed as authors of contributed articles; others include Joe C. Moseley, II, Marc Hershman, and Timothy Alexander. Lionel A. Walford started me on this path and, with support from The Conservation Foundation, directed photographers Michael P. Fahay and James Chess, who supplied many of the illustrations. I also want to thank my Conservation Foundation colleagues, Jack Noble and John Banta, whose help at crucial times was a godsend, and President William K. Reilly, whose patience with delays and mounting costs persisted to the end. To past President Sydney Howe and colleague William J. Duddleson I owe gratitude for originally inviting me to The Conservation Foundation to do this book. I am also most grateful to Roland S. Woolson, Jr., of John Wiley & Sons, editor and helmsman, who steered the book through its more perilous passages.

Among numerous research assistants, the following made outstanding contributions: Catherine Lochner, William MacKenzie, Trevor O'Neill, Paul J. Sarokwash, Ellen Thomas, Michael Walraven, Langdon Warner, Steve Wasserman, Claudia Wilson, and Steven Zwicky. The production of the entire manuscript was most competently supervised by Laura O'Sullivan, who was ably assisted by Elizabeth Schmid, Ann Thompson, and Jacqueline Virando.

Note. This book has been prepared with partial financial assistance from the Office Coastal Zone Management (National Oceanic and Atmospheric Administration, U.S. Department of Commerce). Statements regarding coastal resource management are the opinion of the author and do not necessarily reflect policy of the Office of Coastal Zone Management.

J.R.C.

Contents

Coastal Ecosystem Management

Introduction

It is not enough to think only of conserving what we have. Conservation must be part of a larger effort to create what we want. In a time of massive change, the task must be to maintain a creative balance between the forces of conservation and the forces of development. Only recently and in selected areas where people are applying new high standards to development is this balance becoming possible.

WILLIAM K. REILLY
The Use of Land, Thomas Y. Crowell Co.

The purpose of this manual is to reduce a vast stockpile of ecological data to a few simple principles and rules that can guide our use of coastal lands and waters. It is not within the scope of this manual to present extensive background data or to examine the merits of different opinions or scientific results. In many respects this is a preliminary effort in a new and undeveloped technical field.

We take the view that management of the coastal zone—coastal waters and shorelands—has as a fundamental goal the conservation of coastal ecosystems at the highest achievable carrying capacity, that is, ability to yield resources of value to man.

Our general theme is that coastal ecosystems can be maintained at high levels of health even while urbanization of the coastal zone increases, if there is effective planning. This will require foregoing many traditional economic ventures and community development programs. We believe that the trade-offs can be accomplished without serious penalty through innovative management programs.

Planning and advance goal setting are as essential for proper coastal zone management as for other critically important national programs. But coastal communities should not wait for the federal Big Brother to force the action. As stated by Alvin Toffler, in testimony before a U.S. Senate Subcommittee (December 15, 1975):

Failure to anticipate will lead to tragedy in America. By the same token, long-range thinking that is unconnected to the ideas, energy and imagination of our whole population, long-range thinking that is merely top-down, and not equally bottom-up, could also produce the end of democracy.

1

In this spirit we attempt to provide a comprehensive ecological background for local government decision-making and for building a management framework that will lead to the best achievable ecosystem function and the highest carrying capacity. How far short of this goal any management program falls must of necessity be decided by society, not by science. Although scientists can often state the conditions that are optimum for best ecosystem function, they are not specially equipped to offer advice on what constitutes socially acceptable or unacceptable levels of carrying capacity. In effect, ecological scientists can establish the criteria upon which to judge ecosystem condition and upon which public decision-making can proceed, but are not themselves qualified to make the decisions by virtue of their knowledge.

Whatever its specific goals may be, an environmental management program must embrace whole ecosystems. Any attempt to manage separately one of the many interdependent components of a complex ecosystem will probably fail. So will any attempt to control any one source of environmental disturbance to the system without controlling others. The ecosystem defined must embrace a complete and integral unit, one that includes a coastal water basin (or basins) and the adjacent shorelands to the extent that they have significant influence on coastal waters.

A program for conservation of coastal ecosystems should consist of four major elements: (1) protection of all ecologically vital areas; (2) elimination of all damaging discharges of pollution; (3) control of site alteration in the shorelands to maintain the optimum (natural) quality, abundance, and rate of flow of runoff from coastal watersheds into coastal water basins; and (4) control of excavation and alteration of the coastal water basins and their margins.

In the preparation of a management plan for any coastal area, it will be necessary to make a professional analysis of each coastal ecosystem to determine its values and vulnerabilities and to devise effective controls on potentially adverse activities. The framework for management analysis of an ecosystem must include not only a survey of natural systems and the important biota, but also knowledge of the major physical factors that affect the carrying capacity of the ecosystem and the ways in which these factors interact and in combination govern the life of the system.

Planning requires a system of identification and classification of general areas of critical environmental concern. These are areas within which human activities must be controlled (not necessarily prohibited) to protect the environment. Specific areas that are especially critical ecologically—vital areas—are to be designated for exemption from most uses within areas of concern. The whole of the typical estuarine basin— the estuary and its surrounding tidelands and wetlands—is an area of environmental concern. Coastal floodplains and coastal watershed drainage systems are also designated as areas of critical environmental concern because of their relation to coastal waters.

It is necessary to include the shoreland watershed adjacent to the coastal water basin for a very practical purpose: the flow of water from the land is a primary controlling factor on the condition of coastal ecosystems. Therefore maintenance of the quality and quantity of runoff through regulation of land-use practice is critical. This is a job for local governments, one that requires no new inventions or the fashioning of new tools. The regulatory machinery that is presently operating in the typical coastal community is sufficient to accomplish the local part of the job. Of course, a close integration with regional, state, and federal law, policies, and programs is necessary.

Ecologically, any development activity anywhere in coastal areas—watersheds, floodplains, wetlands, tidelands, or water basins— is a potential source of damage to the coastal waters ecosystem. The amount of damage that may result from any disturbance depends on the characteristics and vulnerabilities of the specific ecosystem involved. Development planning must recognize particularly that modification of the land area has a high potential for adverse effects on estuarine systems by altering runoff patterns and thereby reducing the capability of the land to store rainwater, to regularize its release from the watershed, and to cleanse it enroute to coastal waters.

Water system protection must first address the control of land modification activities, principally those associated with site preparation for development. It should become a standard management goal to maintain intact the natural pattern of freshwater inflow. Certainly, specific constraints should be imposed on project location, design, and drainage engineering throughout the coastal watershed, particularly in its water areas. These constraints should encourage, and in some cases require, the adjustment of traditional practices of residential development relative to density, project design, site preparation, drainage, and other factors. For example, the amount of impervious surface should be minimized and barren soils rapidly stabilized. Finished grades should be designed to direct water flows along natural drainage courses and through natural terrain where the vegetation can cleanse runoff waters. Watercourses (marshes, swamps, bogs, creeks) will have to be exempt from alteration. Moreover, major restoration should be undertaken for highly altered and damaged hydrological systems.

In planning for coastal land- and water-use management, it is necessary to identify, through impact assessment, the specific ecosystem hazards associated with specific types of utilization. Some types of use involve the construction of projects that will lead to gross disturbance of the ecosystem. Other uses may endanger ecologically vital areas or preempt space from them. Still others may cause day-after-day occupancy or operating disturbances lasting for the duration of their existence.

Ecosystems of the confined estuarine water basins are usually ecologically complex and exceptionally rich: "Characteristically, estuaries tend to be more productive than either the sea on one side or the freshwater drainage on the other" (E. P. Odum, *Fundamentals of Ecology*, W. B. Saunders Co.). On the other hand, estuaries are the most sensitive and stress-vulnerable coastal ecosystems of the confined water bodies—particularly those with poor circulation properties. Therefore development adjacent to estuarine waters will require exceptionally vigorous management. For this reason we have given a greater degree of attention to estuaries than to ocean water areas. However, we have also focused attention on the especially rich and vulnerable life systems of the ocean that require protection, such as coral reefs and kelp beds. Although we have not specifically addressed the Great Lakes, many of the principles applying to marine estuaries will be found to be relevant also to the ecosystems of the Great Lakes.

As a practical matter, we have had to recognize that the regulatory agenda must be considered in two management contexts: the ecological context, which reflects the permanent laws of nature, and the institutional context, which reflects the changeable laws and policies of man.

In addition to ecological concerns a major interest of coastal citizens is to acquire better control of growth through new approaches to public policy and law. Uncontrolled development has already undermined much of the value of coastal and estuarine resources and threatens vast damage to the remainder. The demand for permanent retirement and temporary recreational housing and for waterfront land investment opportunities has been intense. Developers have encouraged and then satisfied this demand and in so doing have created high capital and servicing costs. Tax rates have accelerated so that only the most expensive homes are actually paying their own way. The crux of the issue is whether, on the one hand, the governmental controls demanded over the use of private land can be tolerated politically and constitutionally, or whether, on the other hand, the lack of them can be tolerated economically and environmentally.

Even with regulations to provide ecological protection of critical areas, there may be need for a supplementary program of public acquisition to achieve other objectives. Since the supply of funds is always limited, acquisition priorities should be established. Acquisition is particularly needed to ensure public access to scenic, recreational, and other water-related resources. The highest priorities should go to acquisitions that provide access, enhance public recreation opportunity, provide views, or protect specific wildlife habitats. Acquisition priorities should be adjusted in any situation where environmental protection regulations cannot fully apply. In cases of prior irreversible commitment, for example, or adverse court decision, a "defensive" acquisition strategy might be employed which would prevent major ecological disruption and at the same time provide access to quality public recreation and scenic experience.

Starting with a foundation of fundamental ecological principles, we have developed for this manual a number of general management rules and suggested a variety of constraints on coastal development activities. These constraints are aimed at specific uses of coastal waters and shorelands, such as agriculture, marinas, or residential development. Chapter 7, a collection of articles by various specialists provides a detailed factual background, and an Appendix of tabular and graphical matter supplies useful technical data.

CHAPTER ONE

Ecology

Ecology is the science that treats the interrelations of living forms and their environments. The environment of any one species includes all the physical forces that influence it and all other species that affect it. The word "ecology," as we use it here, has the broad connotation of treating whole communities of life. Our discussion focuses on the *coastal waters ecosystem*—the basic functional geographic unit that embraces all of the life and physical components involved with a distinct coastal water basin. It also includes the stretch of shorelands that have immediate direct influence on the coastal water basin.

The ecosystem orientation toward management of the coastal zone stresses that, to be effective, the administrative area must be a coupled unit of coastal water basin and adjacent shorelands. The governing Ecological Principle is: *The carrying capacity of a coastal water basin is controlled by all factors that influence the function of the*

ecosystem of which the basin is a part (No. 1).

The essential qualities of a coastal ecosystem are features, processes (limiters), modulators, and characteristics. Features are the fixed physical objects, such as coral reefs, mud flats, or grass beds. Processes are the energy flows that "drive" the system, such as sunlight, water flow, or nutrient recycling; their rates of flow limit the productivity of the system. Modulators are the variable factors that limit carrying capacity on a short-term (often day-to-day) basis, for example, temperature, available mineral nutrients, dissolved gas concentration, or presence of toxic chemicals. Characteristics are the qualities that give each coastal water basin its distinctiveness, such as the species mix (the relative numbers of various species present), the general water condition, or the visual appearance of the basin (water and marginal area). An understanding of these factors is useful in devising ecosystem management programs. A system of evaluation and classification is required that can simplify the nearly limitless complexities of nature (see Chapter 3).

In this chapter we briefly describe some of the major features, processes, and modulators that control the carrying capacities of coastal water basins. This is not meant to be a comprehensive treatise on ecology; rather it is the briefest account possible of the essential properties of coastal ecosystems and the basic governing principles.

The shorelands regime (coastal watershed) is considered in regard to the aspects that have major influence on the function and carrying capacity of the coastal waters ecosystem (brackish to salty waters). The major focus is on the estuarine regime—the protected system of bays, lagoons, and other inner waters of the coastal zone—which is both the richest and the most vulnerable sector of the coastal waters. The seashore and ocean waters regime is given much less attention because it is both safer from disturbance by human society and of lesser interest to coastal management at the local level. Barrier islands are singled out for special attention because they have extraordinarily high resource values, because they are very vulnerable to ecological damage, and because the need for controls is so urgent.

THE GEOPHYSICAL SETTING

Coastal water ecosystems operate within the confines of existing geological structures, for example, deep rocky fiords, "drowned" river valleys, or shallow, marshy embayments between sand ridges (Figure 1.1). Similarly, systems in the shorelands operate within the geological confines of the watershed. The geological features themselves are modified over time by dynamic weathering forces—wind, water flow, erosion, waves, sedimentation—and by the effects of vegetation.

A wide ocean (continental) shelf is generally associated with extensive low-lying shorelands and a wide band of salt-marsh wetlands next to the coast, while a narrow shelf is associated with steep or mountainous shorelands. These associations and their characteristic ecosystems differ greatly from one coastal region to another.

Northern shores once covered by ice—New England, Puget Sound, and southeast Alaska—are sharply sculptured with generally steep shorelines marked by deep, heavily indented embayments, islands, steep rocky shores, and irregular bottom topography.[2]

The parts of the Atlantic and Gulf coasts that were unaffected by glaciation consist of relatively flat terrain in which wide coastal embayments and salt marshes are the predominant features. These are coasts that were formed primarily of sediments eroded from ancient mountains, and along which embayments and salt marshes form traps for sediments the rivers bring down to the shore. In time, deltas may be formed, stretching out into the sea. These coasts are characterized by great expanses of shallow water and aquatic vegetation. They have extensive sand dunes, and sandy ocean beachfronts are backed by well-developed estuaries (the protected waters of embayments, lagoons, and tidal rivers).

The constant input of sediments from erosion tends to fill up the estuarine basin. The most rapid sedimentation occurs in the inner, low-salinity portion of the estuary. Here salt water meets fresh, coalescing riverborne silts into larger, heavier particles that settle out as the estuary broadens and the flow slackens (Figure 1.2).

The form, or shape, of the estuarine water basin controls the ecological system largely through the secondary effects it exerts, that is, by influencing such factors as currents, temperature, vegetation, and flushing rate (the rate of replacement of the water in a basin). For example, the structure of a typical estuary sets up a pattern of currents that retains nutrients, sometimes called a

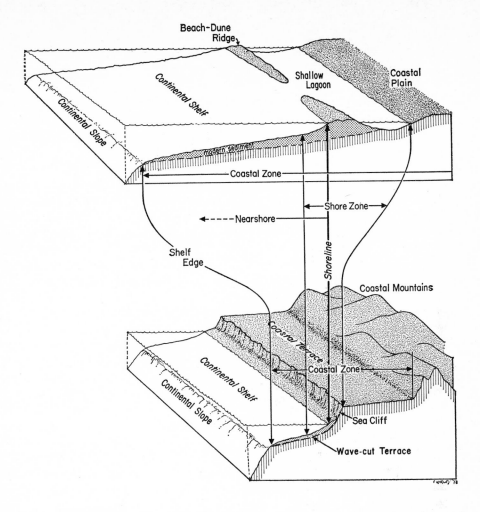

Figure 1.1   Wide-shelf plains coast (upper) characteristic of the U.S. east coast (trailing edge), and narrow-shelf mountainous coast (lower), characteristic of the U.S. west coast (collision edge). (SOURCE: Reference 1.)

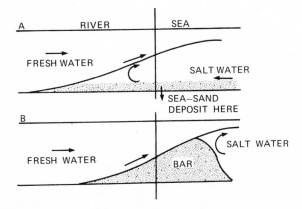

Figure 1.2   Formation of an estuarine sand bar. (SOURCE: Reference 3.)

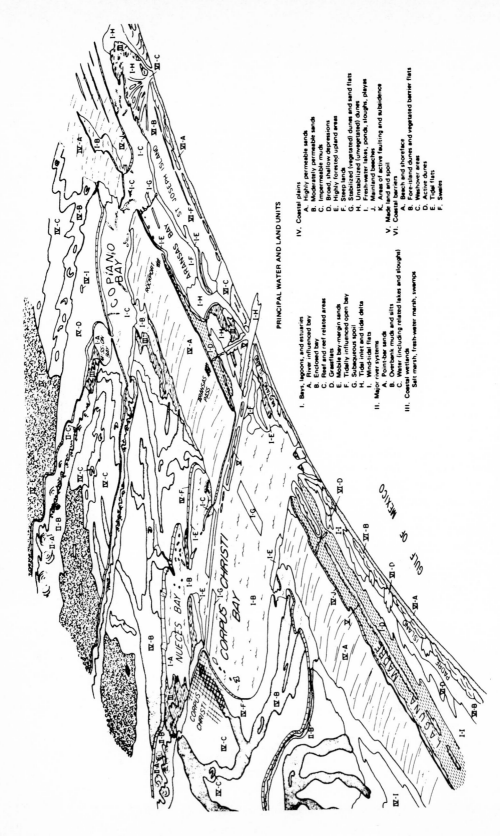

PRINCIPAL WATER AND LAND UNITS

I. Bays, lagoons, and estuaries
  A. River influenced bay
  B. Enclosed bay
  C. Reef and reef related areas
  D. Grassflats
  E. Mobile bay-margin sands
  F. Tidally influenced open bay
  G. Subaqueous spoil
  H. Tidal inlet and tidal delta
  I. Wind-tidal flats

II. Major river systems
  A. Point-bar sands
  B. Overbank muds and silts
  C. Water (including related lakes and sloughs)

III. Coastal wetlands
  Salt marsh, fresh-water marsh, swamps

IV. Coastal plains
  A. Highly permeable sands
  B. Moderately permeable sands
  C. Impermeable muds
  D. Broad, shallow depressions
  E. Highly forested upland areas
  F. Steep lands
  G. Stabilized (vegetated) dunes and sand flats
  H. Unstabilized (unvegetated) dunes
  I. Fresh-water lakes, ponds, sloughs, playas
  J. Mainland beaches
  K. Areas of active faulting and subsidence

V. Made land and spoil

VI. Coastal barriers
  A. Beach and shoreline
  B. Fore-island dunes and vegetated barrier flats
  C. Washover areas
  D. Active dunes
  E. Tidal flats
  F. Swales

Figure 1.3 Ecological subsystems (or environmental capability units) around Corpus Christi Bay, Texas, which include 34 distinct categories. Each will respond differently to similar environmental stresses. (SOURCE: Reference 4.)

8

"nutrient trap"; this condition is favorable to the development of a rich and varied community of coastal water life.

The effect on a coastal water ecosystem of any particular environmental disturbance depends partly on the geological form of the ecosystem basin and the ecological characteristics induced by that form. Furthermore, different subecosystems may be expected to react differently to a particular type of disturbance, depending on their forms (Figure 1.3).

The coastal waters of the United States may be conveniently divided into large biogeographical regions. These regions vary in such factors as climatic condition, the oceanographical characteristics of the seas that border them, and the way in which they are influenced by the type of land mass that lies behind them. Among climatic variables, temperature is often the primary determinant of the distribution of species of plants and animals throughout the coastal zone. Other significant climatic factors are the amount and the pattern of precipitation, of wind, and of sunlight. Large-scale oceanic forces that influence coastal ecosystems are prevailing wind and waves, permanent coastal currents, persistent coastal upwellings, massive oceanic currents, and other factors that vary from place to place along the coast. Most climatic and oceanic forces are beyond human control, but society can significantly control the ways in which the land surface influences coastal ecosystems.

ECOLOGICAL CONCEPTS

The biota of a coastal ecosystem includes a great variety of plants, birds, fish, mammals, and invertebrate organisms (Figure 1.4). In its natural condition the ecosystem is a balanced network of biotic relationships that is all too easily upset by pollution and other man-made disturbances. Fortunately, existing ecologic theory and knowledge are suf-

ficiently advanced to provide a basis for sound protection programs.

Within the subject matter of ecology there are a number of concepts that relate directly to protective management of coastal ecosystems. These concepts provide a framework for understanding how organisms interact with the forces and conditions of their environments and survive or suffer damage. The following discussion serves to explain briefly the more relevant of these concepts.

Carrying Capacity and Standing Crop

Carrying capacity is the limit to the amount of life that can be supported by a specified habitat; most narrowly, it is the number of individuals of a particular species. It is always used as a *potential*. The *actual* number (or mass) of species present in an area at any one time is the *standing crop*. In a wider sense carrying capacity expresses the total amount (numbers or mass) of beneficial life that an ecosystem or subsystem can support.

Thus, in the ecological sense, carrying capacity is the ultimate constraint imposed on the biota by existing environmental limits, such as the availability of food, space, or breeding sites, or by disease or predator cycles, temperature, sunlight, or salinity. The carrying capacity of a system can be markedly reduced by man-made disturbances that reduce available energy supplies or interfere with energy utilization.

The term "carrying capacity" is often used by planners in a more general, nonecological sense, for example, as an expression of the reasonable capacity of an area's resources to support human occupancy or activities. In addition the term has found use in social and economic sciences. Therefore it is always important to understand the specific context in which "carrying capacity" is used.

In the sense in which it is generally used in this book, *"carrying capacity" expresses*

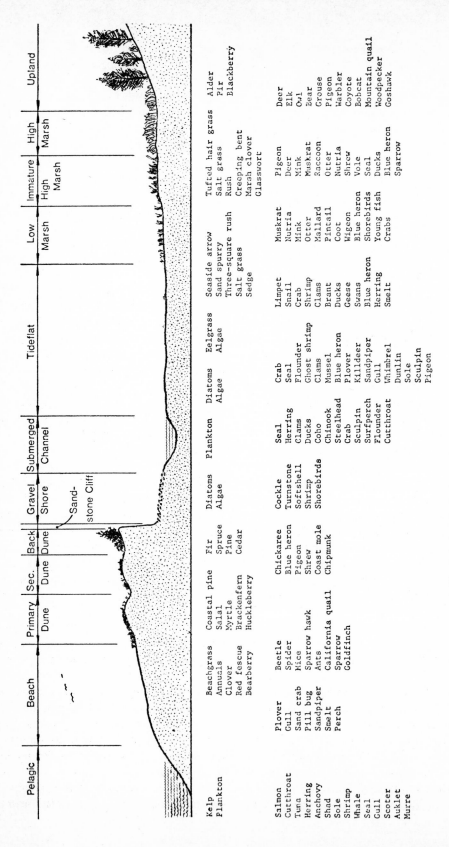

Figure 1.4 The biota of Siletz Bay, Oregon. (SOURCE: Reference 5.)

10

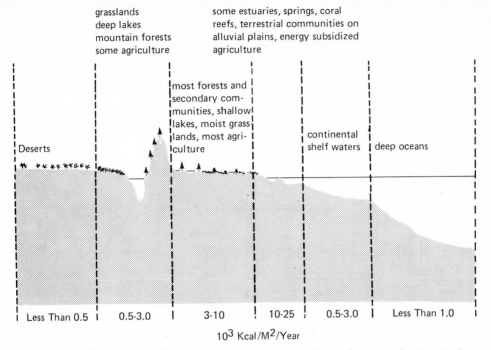

Figure 1.5   The world distribution of primary production in terms of annual gross production (in thousands of kilocalories per square meter) of major ecosystem types. (SOURCE: Reference 6.)

the potential of the ecosystem to provide products useful to human society. Thus it measures the condition of the natural resources base.

Productivity

The concept of *primary productivity* refers to the capacity of an ecosystem to produce basic plant material. Technically, primary productivity is the amount of energy converted from light, basic nutrients, and carbon dioxide to plant tissues, within a unit area during a unit of time, for example, as measured by the grams of carbon fixed per square meter per day. In terms of primary productivity, estuarine water bodies may produce 20 times as much as the deep sea and 10 times as much as either nearshore waters or deep lakes (Figure 1.5). Since primary productivity governs an ecosystem's total capacity for life, estuaries are generally more productive than the ocean.

Energy and Food

The immediate energy needs of coastal ecosystems are met in two ways: (1) from internal supplies that are recycled within the system, and (2) from external driving forces. Internally, the chain of life—food chain or food web—begins with energy assimilated by plants, or primary productivity, to create plant tissue (another form of energy), which is then available to animals as their basic foodstuff. The plants are eaten, are passed through the complex food web, and return as basic nutrients (page 13).

The major external driving forces of coastal ecosystems are tide, ocean currents, river inflow, wind, sunlight, and the basic inorganic nutrients (minerals) that nourish plants and animals (Figure 1.6). Because all animal food starts with plants, every organism ultimately depends on the major factors that limit the building of plant tissues, such as the external replenishment of

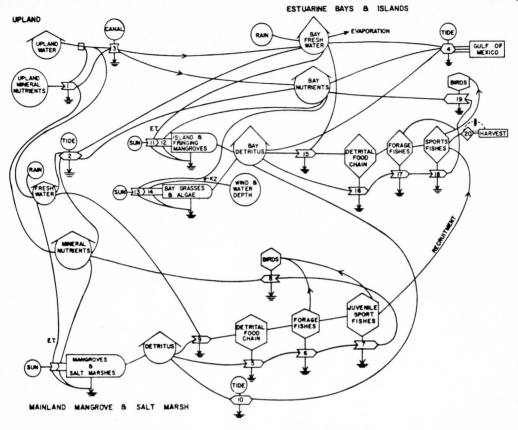

Figure 1.6   Estuarine ecosystem model, portraying food web and energy flows. (SOURCE: Reference 7.)

basic nutrients, the amount of carbon dioxide available, and access to sunlight. The governing Ecological Principle is: *The flow and amount of available energy controls life processes and limits the carrying capacity of the coastal ecosystem* (No. 2).

Food Chain

Animal life is nourished by plants that decay rapidly into small particles (detritus) after falling into the water. Colonies of microscopic life act upon these particles, and the resultant material is eaten by a wide variety of estuarine species such as oysters, shrimp, some fish, and myriad small crustaceans that serve as forage for birds and predatory fish.

Although some of the plant material

available in coastal waters is consumed directly by fish and shellfish, more often it is first eaten by zooplankton—tiny drifting animal life—which in turn become the food of fish, and they in turn are consumed by birds or people. This transfer of food energy from lower to higher forms up the *food chain* (or *food web*) involves a number of separate components.

The plants are the *producers*. Plant-eating animals (herbivores), called *consumers* (e.g., zooplankton, oysters), feed on phytoplankton (floating plant cells, algae) and, to a lesser extent, on larger plants. The *foragers* are those that prey directly on the consumers, and the *predators* are those that prey on the foragers. A few species, including the finest game fish, are superpredators that pursue and capture smaller predators

(Figure 1.7). Finally, there are the *decomposers*, bacteria that reduce dead matter back to basic minerals.

Many species change their feeding habits dramatically, utilizing different parts of the food chain as they grow from larvae to postlarvae to juveniles to adult fish. A sea trout might depend successively on crustacean larvae, copepods, small shrimp, bait fish, and eventually larger fish, crabs, and other invertebrates.

Storage

Storage is the capability of a natural system to store energy supplies in one or more of its component units. Theoretically, such a storage unit could be a stand of marsh grass, a fish school, a seed, organic sediment on the bottom, or phytoplankton in the water of a bay. However, when we use "storage" here we refer to the large, physically evident units. These units all gather and store a supply of energy that is a reserve against shortages. Thus they are exceptionally important stabilizers of carrying capacity.

Such estuarine plant communities as salt marshes, mangrove swamps, and eelgrass beds are particularly important as storage units. For example, marsh grass in its entirety—roots, leaves, flowers, stems—provides storage on which the estuarine food chain depends. The standing stock of grass, both living and dead, contains a large reserve of nutrient matter that is potential foodstuff for everything from bacteria to fish when

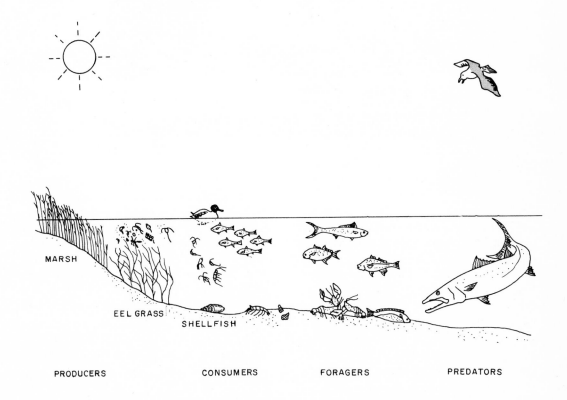

Figure 1.7 The food web, or food chain, in its basic form depicts the ecological system that supports fish, shellfish, and ultimately man. (SOURCE: Adapted from Reference 8.)

Figure 1.8   Coastal marshes serve as major storage units for nutrients that support the estuarine food chain. (Conservation Foundation photo by M. Fahay.)

carried by the tides into coastal water basins (Figure 1.8). Because the grass decomposes slowly, there is a ready supply of materials throughout the year. Storage in plant tissues is particularly important because the reserve of nutrients stabilizes the system and provides a buffer against irregular heavy demands or seasonal shortage periods (winter).

In addition, marshes have vast quantities of mineral nutrients stored in their soils that provide a readily available source of nourishment to the marsh grasses; for example, there is a sufficient reserve in some Georgia salt marshes to last for 500 years without renewal.[9] Renewal, however, is going on continuously.

Storage is nature's hedge against boom-or-bust fluctuations of abundance and scarcity. The result is a productive and stable ecosystem. The governing Ecological Principle is: A *high capability for energy storage provides for optimum ecosystem function* (No. 3).

In addition to the living components of the system, the storage protection principle applies also to certain nonbiotic, structural components of the environment that serve important ecologic functions. For example, sand dunes are, above all, giant storehouses of sand that function to resupply and stabilize beachfronts periodically torn away by violent storms (page 28).

Ecotone

An *ecotone* is the transition area, or border area, between two different ecological communities, as between a marsh system and a forest system (Figure 1.9). An ecotone combines the characteristics of the two communities it separates and often has an unusually high abundance and diversity of life. The ecotone thus serves a uniquely beneficial function to the ecosystem.

Succession

The ecological concept of *succession* refers to a sequence of species replacements in a particular area. The term is used to describe the changes in biota that take place in time—either those that occur over extended time because of long-term changes in environmental conditions, or those that occur rapidly to an area that has been disturbed

by some short-term event. In management one is most concerned with succession that follows a sudden change, either man-made or natural. An example of succession following man-made disturbance is the successive replacement of grasses by shrubs, and finally by trees, when wetlands are converted to dry lands by filling. An example of succession subsequent to a sudden natural event is the following sequence found on barrier beaches when bare sand is suddenly exposed by storms: sand → sparse grass → closed grass canopy → shrub savanna → closed shrub canopy → forest. The equilibrium plant community (here, the forest) is known as the *climax state*.

Diversity

Diversity is the variety of species present in an ecosystem. It is generally assumed that high diversity of species leads to better eco-

Figure 1.9   An ecotone is a biologically rich transition zone or border area between distinct natural communities; three shown above are (right to left): water-to-tideflat, tideflat-to-marsh, and marsh-to-forest. (Photo by author.)

system balance and provides greater resilience to catastrophic events, such as disease. Conversely, a low diversity (fewer species) indicates a stressed system or one that has been degraded, for example, by pollution. Ecologists have used the diversity index as a measure of the condition of an ecosystem as it may be affected by a variety of environmental disturbances.

FACTORS THAT LIMIT CARRYING CAPACITY

The carrying capacity of each coastal waters ecosystem is controlled by climatic, oceanic, and terrestrial factors that influence the condition of its waters and bottoms. A primary influence (and one that gives an ecosystem particular character) is the pattern of watershed drainage and freshwater inflow to its basin. Other important influences are the dynamic physical processes of tidal forces and currents. The biological needs of the system are supplied by constituents of the water—dissolved chemicals, suspended solids, and dissolved gases.

Water Circulation

The combined influences of freshwater inflow, wind, tidal action, and oceanic forces result in the specific pattern of water movement, or circulation, found in each coastal ecosystem. Circulation of water transports nutrients, propels plankton, distributes the suspended larvae of fish and shellfish, flushes away the wastes from animal and plant life, cleanses the system of pollutants, controls salinity, shifts sediments about, mixes the water, and performs other useful work. These considerations lead to a basic Ecological Principle: *The patterns of circulation within water basins govern the carrying capacities of coastal ecosystems* (No. 4).

In offshore ocean waters circulation patterns are dominated by large-scale forces that may have distant origins, such as massive currents like the Gulf Stream or the California Current.

In the nearshore waters more localized influences are important. Here, tide, wind, waves, and land runoff are the forces that control longshore currents, various reverse flows, eddies, and tide rips. Coastal upwelling occurs when the wind blows the surface layer away from the coast, causing the bottom layer of water to be moved shoreward, where it is forced up toward the surface. This process causes enrichment of water along the shore with nutrients brought up from the bottom.

In bays, tide is often the dominant force in water movement. Its amplitude (and therefore its strength in driving estuarine circulation) varies greatly with latitude and with certain ocean forces (Table 1.1). Amplitude varies within each system, decreasing inward from the ocean through the inlet to the head of the estuarine basin. It also varies with the shape, size, and even the bottom material of individual basins. Circulation forces tend to be greater, and flushing rates better, when tidal amplitudes are high.

In the confined basins of coastal lagoons, wind may be the dominant driving force, while in embayments and tidal rivers freshwater inflow may dominate (Figure 1.10).

Chemical Constituents

The chemistry of coastal waters is complex because of the number of elements and compounds present and the multitude of ways in which they are involved with the biochemical processes of the diverse biota. The activities of mankind complicate the chemistry and result in the addition of nutrient and other salts, trace metals, and toxic materials. Salinity, an important characteristic of coastal waters, is discussed in the following section.

Important chemicals in coastal waters fall into two classes: nutrients and trace elements. A supply of nutrients, added to the

Table 1.1   Typical tidal characteristics of the coastal zone of the United States (SOURCE: Reference 2)

Biophysical region	Type of tide	Tidal range (feet)			Maximum tidal flood	Current velocity ebb
		Mean	Spring	Diurnal[1]		
North Atlantic:						
Eastport, Maine (Bay of Fundy)____	Equal semidiurnal___	18.2	20.7	_____	3.5	3.5
Isle de Haut, Maine; (Penobscot Bay)_____do_____		9.3	10.7	_____	1.6	1.7
Portsmouth Harbor, N.H._____do_____		8.7	10.0	_____	1.4	2.1
Boston Harbor, Mass._____do_____		9.5	11.0	_____	2.0	1.5
Middle Atlantic:						
Dumpling Rocks (Buzzard Bay)_____do_____		3.7	4.6	_____	.9	1.3
The Narrows (New York Harbor)_____do_____		4.5	5.5	_____	2.0	2.3
Cape May Harbor, N.J._____do_____		4.4	5.3	_____	2.1	2.5
Virginia Beach, Va._____do_____		3.4	.1	_____	1.3	.9
Chesapeake Bay:						
Wolf Trap Light (lower bay)_____do_____		1.0	1.2	_____	1.8	2.2
Point No Point (midbay)_____do_____		1.3	1.5	_____	.5	.7
Chesapeake Bay Bridge, Maryland_____do_____		.8	.9	_____	.8	1.0
Washington, D.C. (Potomac River)_____do_____		2.9	3.3	_____	.7	.3
South Atlantic:						
Wilmington, N.C. (Cape Fear River)_____do_____		3.6	3.9	_____	2.0	1.7
Savannah River entrance, Georgia_____do_____		6.9	8.1	_____	1.8	3.0
Mayport, Fla. (St. Johns River)_____do_____		4.5	5.3	_____	2.5	3.5
Fort Pierce Inlet, Fla._____do_____		2.6	3.0	_____	3.0	3.5
Caribbean:						
Miami Harbor, Fla._____do_____		2.5	3.0	_____	2.2	2.4
Key West, Fla._____do_____		1.3	1.6	_____	1.2	2.0
San Juan, P.R._____do_____		1.1	1.3	_____	(2)	(2)
Christiansted, St. Croix_____	Diurnal_____			0.8	(2)	(2)
Gulf of Mexico:						
St. Petersburg, Fla. (Tampa Bay)_____do_____				2.3	.3	.3
Pensacola Bay entrance, Florida_____do_____				1.1	1.8	2.1
Barataria Bay, La._____do_____				.9	1.7	1.7
Aransas Pass, Tex._____do_____				1.7	1.6	1.0
Pacific Southwest:						
Sen Diego Bay entrance, California__	Unequal semidiurnal_	3.9	_____	5.6	1.2	1.4
Monterey Bay, Calif._____do_____		3.5	_____	5.3	(2)	(2)
San Francisco Bay entrance, California._____do_____		4.0	_____	5.7	3.3	3.9
Point Arena, Calif._____do_____		4.0	_____	5.8	1.3	1.3
Pacific Northwest:						
Humboldt Bay entrance, California_____do_____		4.5	_____	6.4	1.8	2.3
Yaquina Bay entrance, Oregon_____do_____		5.9	_____	7.9	2.8	2.6
Grays Harbor entrance, Washington_____do_____		6.9	_____	9.0	2.5	2.2
Puget Sound (Elliott Bay), Wash._____do_____		7.6	_____	11.3	(2)	(2)
Alaska:						
Juneau (Gastineau Channel)_____do_____		13.8	_____	16.4	2.3	2.3
Anchorage (Cook Inlet)_____do_____		25.1	_____	28.1	3.3	3.3
Goodnews Bay (Kuskokwim Bay)_____do_____		6.2	_____	8.9	2.6	2.4
Point Barrow_____do_____		.3	_____	.4	(2)	(2)
Pacific Islands:						
Honolulu, Hawaii (Oahu)_____do_____		1.2	_____	1.9	(3)	(3)
Hilo, Hawaii (Hawaii)_____do_____		1.6	_____	2.4	(3)	(3)
Apra Harbor, Guam_____do_____		(3)	_____	(3)	1.7	3.4
Pago Pago Harbor, American Samoa_____do_____		2.5	_____	4.0	(3)	(3)

[1] For an unequal semidiurnal tide, the diurnal range is the extreme range over the 2 sequential tides in slightly over 1 day.
[2] Weak and variable.
[3] No data.

system by natural processes (from runoff, rainfall, or ocean sources), keeps the system functioning optimally and enhances carrying capacity. The nutrients are vital to the whole chain of life in coastal waters because they are required by all plants, whether rooted plants or the suspended microscopic phytoplankton (floating plant cells, algae), and because the animal life is supported by the plants through the food chain (page 12).

Free nutrient chemicals (dissolved in the

water) are relatively scarce in the waters of a natural coastal ecosystem because they are taken up rapidly by the plant life present (page 673). The major plant nutrients are nitrate and phosphate, with the content of nitrogen in plant tissue higher than that of phosphorus.[9] In coastal waters (but not fresh waters) the amount of available nitrate (a form of nitrogen) is generally believed to be the nutrient factor that controls the abundance of plants.[11] The governing Ecological Principle is: *The primary productivity and carrying capacity of coastal waters are normally limited by the amount of available nitrogen* (No. 5).

Inorganic trace elements of importance in plant nutrition are iron, manganese, molybdenum, cobalt, and zinc. Other dissolved inorganic substances of importance are sulfate, carbonate, calcium, magnesium, sodium, and potassium. Certain organic substances may also be critically involved, such as vitamins, organic compounds of nitrogen, and simple sugars.

Salinity

The salinity of coastal waters reflects a complex mixture of dissolved salts, the most abundant being the common salt, sodium chloride. Salinity throughout the coastal ecosystem fluctuates with the amount of dilution by precipitation and by land drainage or river inflow. Typically, there is a gradient in salt content that starts with a value of about 35 ppt (parts of salt per thousand parts of water) offshore, drops to about 30 ppt in nearshore waters and in the seaward ends of estuaries, and then falls to less than 0.5 ppt at some distance up the tributary rivers. In estuaries, where more saline and heavier water is entering beneath fresher runoff water at the surface, a powerful two-layered circulation pattern is established (see Figure 1.10).

Some coastal species can tolerate a wide range of salinity, whereas others require a narrow range to live and reproduce successfully. Some species require different salinities at different phases of their life cycles, such as are provided by regular seasonal rhythms in salinity in estuaries from spring runoffs and summer drought.

Figure 1.11 shows the range of salinity tolerance characteristic of some estuarine plants and animals. Most of those with a narrow tolerance can nevertheless withstand short-term exposure to a much wider salinity

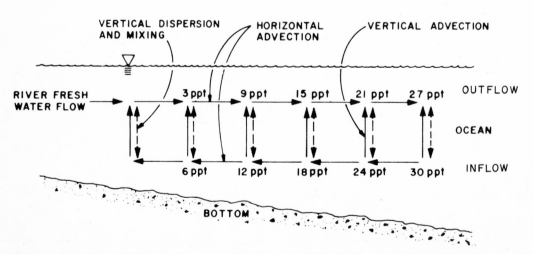

Figure 1.10   Salinity distribution in parts of salt per thousand of water (ppt) and flow pathways in a typical stratified estuary. (SOURCE: Reference 10.)

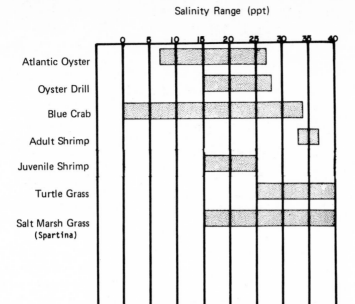

Figure 1.11   Salinity preference range for typical coastal species. (SOURCE: Adapted from Reference 2; data for juvenile shrimp, white and brown, added.)

range, depending on the rate of change. As with other environmental factors, coastal species have evolved over the years in harmony with their salinity environments and have become adapted to the natural regime. The governing Ecological Principle is: *Natural salinity patterns usually maximize the carrying capacities of coastal ecosystems* (No. 6).

Dissolved Gases in the Water

Of the various gases dissolved in coastal waters, those of greatest importance in the web of life are oxygen and carbon dioxide, both of which occur in small but vital quantities. Animals use oxygen and produce carbon dioxide. Plants use carbon dioxide and produce oxygen (on net balance). Therefore each form can benefit from the other's work—one's waste is the other's supply. There is a critical balance in the cycle between plants and animals that involves the continuous transfer of dissolved gases

across the water surface between the water and the atmosphere (Figure 1.12).

For optimum ecosystem function and maximum carrying capacity, coastal waters need an ample concentration of dissolved oxygen. Federal guidelines recommend a minimum of 6 ppm (parts per million) of oxygen and prescribe a minimum of 4 ppm.[12] The governing Ecological Principle is: *Ample supplies of dissolved oxygen are required for efficient ecosystem function and maximum carrying capacity* (No. 7).

Temperature

Temperature exerts a major influence on the coastal ecosystem. Both the occurrence of individual species and the mix of whole coastal water communities of life tend to vary from north to south with changing temperature (Figure 1.13). Many functions of aquatic animals are temperature controlled—migration, spawning, feeding efficiency, swimming speed, embryological de-

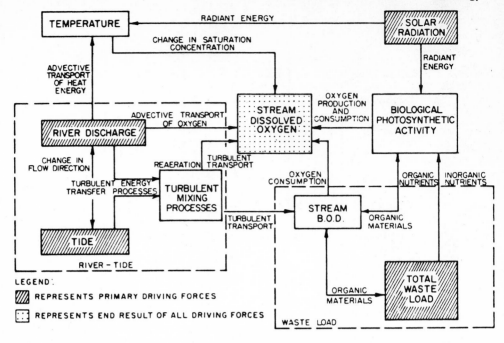

Figure 1.12   Factors affecting dissolved oxygen concentration in coastal waters. (SOURCE: Reference 2.)

velopment, and basic metabolic rate (which doubles with each increase of 10°C (18°F).[14] The biota is adapted to existing long-term patterns of seasonal temperature in such a complex manner that any significant change must be presumed detrimental in the absence of contrary evidence. The governing Ecological Principle is: *The naturally balanced temperature regime provides for optimum ecosystem function* (No. 8).

The Function of Light

Sunlight is the basic driving force of the ecosystem. It is the fundamental source of energy for the growth of vegetation, which in turn supplies the foundation of nourishment for all life in coastal waters. For the ecosystem to function well, sunlight must be able to penetrate the water to a considerable depth so as to foster the growth of the rooted plants and the phytoplankton that float beneath the surface (Figure 1.14). Estuaries are normally more turbid than ocean waters, being more silt laden and richer in nutrient-fostered phytoplankton.

Turbidity from suspended silt or from concentrations of organisms has a negative effect on plant growth in coastal waters. For this reason the growth of phytoplankton is self limiting; that is, as the plankton becomes denser, the water becomes more turbid and the penetration of light into the water decreases, inhibiting plant growth beneath a shallow surface layer of water. The governing Ecological Principle is: *Enhancement of light penetration increases ecosystem productivity and carrying capacity* (No. 9).

Light also affects the behavior of many animals. For example, because predatory game fish are visual feeders, they need light to see their prey and are aided in their feeding by good light penetration. Conversely, the tiny young stages of many coastal fish seek refuge in estuarine waters to escape predators, and turbidity may screen them from attack. Neither extremely clear not extremely murky water is the answer.

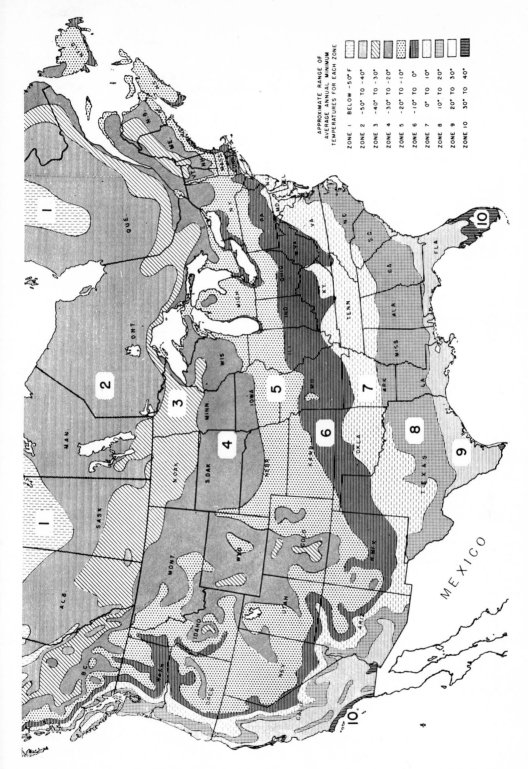

Figure 1.13 Ecologic temperature control zones that apply to coastal ecosystems. (source: Reference 13.)

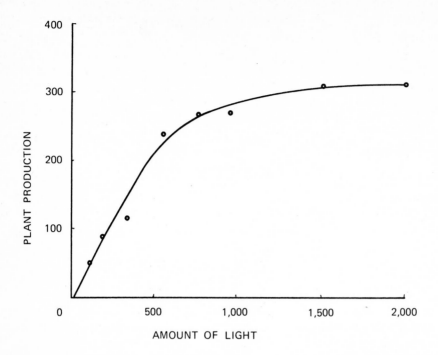

Figure 1.14   Relationships between plant production (gross primary production in milligrams O_2 per square meter per hour) and light intensity (in foot-candles); the carbon dioxide concentration was 6.6 milligrams per liter. (SOURCE: Reference 15.)

SHORELAND SYSTEMS

In the federal definition *shorelands* are the land areas that have "direct and significant impact on the coastal waters" (page 116, Chapter 3). More specifically, shorelands are defined here as all the lands of the *coastal watersheds*—the watersheds that drain directly into coastal water basins. They include the coastal floodplains that fringe the coast and lie just above the upper wetlands. These are land areas that strongly influence coastal ecosystems through the discharge of land drainage waters. They are, in turn, strongly influenced by coastal waters at their marginal floodplains. Also, certain areas of special ecological significance to coastal ecosystems lie along the lower edge of the shorelands, for example, sand dunes, which provide special habitats and structural support for the shoreline.

We do not treat the ecology of the shorelands per se in the following brief discussion. Rather, we consider only the ecological aspects of shorelands that have a direct and important influence on the functions and carrying capacities of the coastal water ecosystems.

Discharge Waters

Estuarine waters are a mixture of fresh water that flows in from the coastal watersheds and salt water that flows in from the sea. The functioning of the coastal water ecosystem is influenced by the intermixture of both these sources of supply and by the forces that drive the two water masses. In a way the two sources are in competition for the space within the enclosed estuarine basins.

The ocean source, with a giant reservoir of water and power behind it, pushes steadily inward against the often lighter and usually more variable force of the land source. Although the ocean flow is modified somewhat by tide levels, storms, and changes in inlet size, the freshwater flow from inland is considerably more variable because of seasonal changes in precipitation and runoff.

In the context of this competition, then, the ocean-water forces apply rather consistent pressure for estuarine space, while the land-water forces apply more fluctuating amounts of pressure. For this reason one looks to the land source—the watershed—for an explanation of intermittent, or seasonal, changes in such characteristics of the estuarine environment as salinity, circulation patterns, and water content. There is another reason to be concerned with the land sources—they are the ones we constantly alter and can most easily control.

Thus a primary determinant of coastal ecosystem function and carrying capacity is water from the land. The governing Ecological Principle is: *Water provides the essential linkage of land and sea elements of the coastal ecosystem* (No. 10).

Water moves seaward over the land by one or more of three types of flow: (1) channeled flow, (2) surface (sheet) flow, and (3) subsurface (underground) flow. Channeled flow is the water carried by open drainageways of all kinds—rivers, streams, creeks, swales, and gullies. Surface flow is the water that runs over the surface of land that is already saturated with water or is impermeable. Underground flow is the water that runs through subsurface aquifers.

Quality

The quality of the water that runs off the shorelands to the sea is a function of the amount of sediment, nutrients, minerals, organic matter, and other substances dissolved or suspended in the water and carried down rivers into the estuary. These materials have a strong influence on the coastal ecosystem because they affect such important carrying capacity controls as plant production, oxygen concentration, and the fallout of sediments in estuarine basins. Nutrients supplied naturally via runoff are an important part of the energy budget of many coastal ecosystems; this is particularly true of nitrogen, which is the key to the primary productivity of coastal ecosystems. Figure 1.15 shows how nutrients (ammonia, nitrate, and nitrite) and oxygen are related in the freshwater and brackish parts of a tidal river.

Volume

The freshwater discharge into each coastal ecosystem varies seasonally (Figure 1.16). Its volume influences the pattern of circulation of coastal waters by governing the rate of flushing of water basins and the strength of currents. In a stratified (two-layered) estuary the amount of runoff controls both the surface layer outflow and the bottom layer inflow (page 128).

The volume of the freshwater supply also governs the salinity of all coastal waters. Salinity influences the types of species and their abundance and therefore the whole distribution of life throughout coastal waters—fish, shellfish, plankton, plants, and bottom fauna. Normally there is a salinity gradient established in an estuary which fluctuates with the amount of river discharge. The location of the salt front, or of any specific salinity value, in the tidal river portion of a large estuary may vary by 10 to 20 miles up or down the river, depending on the amount of fresh water discharged upstream (Figure 1.17).

The situation concerning the effects of the volume of freshwater inflow on coastal systems may be summarized as follows[19]:

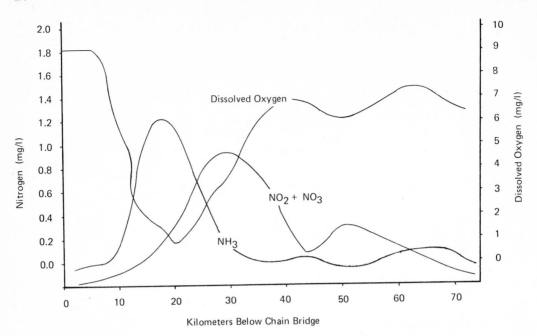

Figure 1.15   Ammonia (NH_3) and nitrate–nitrite concentrations (Aug. 19–22, 1968) and dissolved oxygen concentration (Sept. 22, 1968) at Chain Bridge, 5 miles upriver from downtown Washington, D.C. (SOURCE: Reference 16.)

1. Salinity is an important dominant factor in many estuarine system types, and the magnitude of freshwater input controls the salinity regime.
2. The main source of important nutrient materials for estuarine systems is the flow of water from the land.
3. Productivity in estuarine systems is dependent upon . . . organic matter brought into the system via freshwater input.
4. Both photosynthesis and respiration of the estuarine system are dependent upon inflowing materials from freshwater streams.

Rate of Flow

The timing (rate or schedule) of the flow of fresh water into coastal waters is governed by many of the same factors that govern volume. The timing of flow is important in its effect on the productivity, stability, and general health of the coastal ecosystem. The natural, preexisting rhythm of seasonal flow must be considered generally beneficial to the biota. Most species are tuned to this natural rhythm for critical

life functions—breeding, feeding, migration, and so forth.

The above considerations are the basis for the governing Ecological Principle: *The natural volume, rate, and seasonal pattern of freshwater inflow provide for optimum ecosystem function* (No. 11).

The detention characteristics of the terrain over which the runoff waters flow enroute to the river channel are important in governing the timing of flow, or the rate of delivery. For example, it may take from 3 to 4 months for rainwater that falls in the south central Florida area to move 60 to 80 miles south to reach the estuarine areas around Florida Bay.

Whereas rain moves directly into the hydrologic system as groundwater or surface runoff, snow and ice may remain for months, subsequently causing an influx of many months' precipitation when it melts.

Both the volume and the rate of flow are functions of factors such as the size of the watershed, the slope of the land, the soil

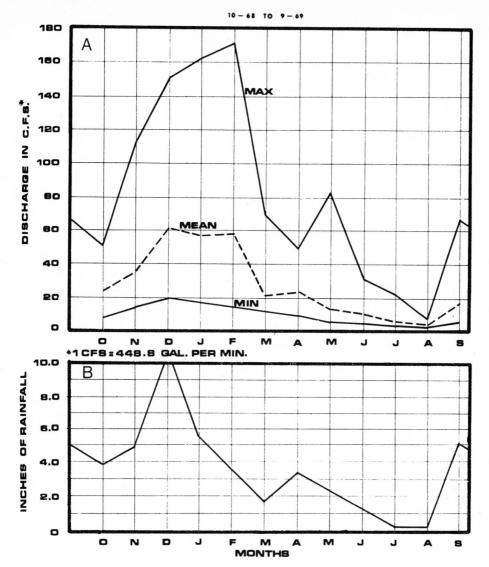

Figure 1.16 Mercer Creek, tributary to Lake Washington and Puget Sound (October 1968 to September 1969). A = stream discharge, B = monthly precipitation. (SOURCE: Reference 17.)

type, and the interplay between rainfall and the rate of loss to the atmosphere via evapotranspiration (water transpired by trees, shrubs, and plants, and evaporation); both of these vary seasonally in a more or less predictable manner (Figures 1.18 and 1.19). The annual variations in these factors cause ecologically important year-to-year differences in the volume and timing of flows to coastal waters.

Special Areas

Two types of areas of special significance to coastal ecosystems are found in shorelands: (1) all-water areas that make up the retention and direct drainage systems of the coastal watersheds, including drainageways and wetlands; and (2) the special ecological areas at the lower edge of the shorelands, such as sand dunes.

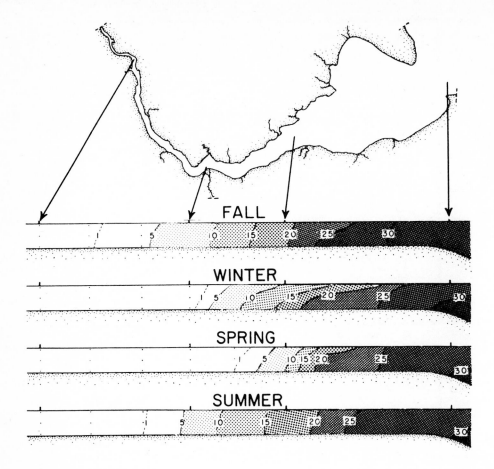

Figure 1.17   Salinity in the Delaware estuary varies seasonally according to the amount of freshwater discharge. Numbers refer to the salinity as amount of salts in parts per thousand of water (ppt). (SOURCE: Reference 18.)

Shoreland Water Areas

The watershed drainageways and other water areas throughout the shorelands that store runoff waters and deliver them directly to the coastal ecosystem are especially important elements. Included in shoreland water areas are (1) all the drainageways—creeks, streams, swales, sloughs, and other permanent or temporary surface channels—that direct flow into brackish or salt waters, and (2) all the connected freshwater wetlands that serve to detain and purify runoff waters (Figure 1.20). In addition to their intrinsic ecological values, these water areas (1) regulate the rate of runoff flow, (2) cleanse the runoff water by settling out suspended matter, and (3) take up dissolved contaminants (page 140).

Sand Dunes

The ocean beach is a physically harsh environment, and most animals that can withstand the high stress and constant motion of the beach sands are burrowing species—mole crabs, coquina clams, razor clams. Other species are temporary residents, such as the California grunion fish that nests on the beach. The beach is hardy and resistant

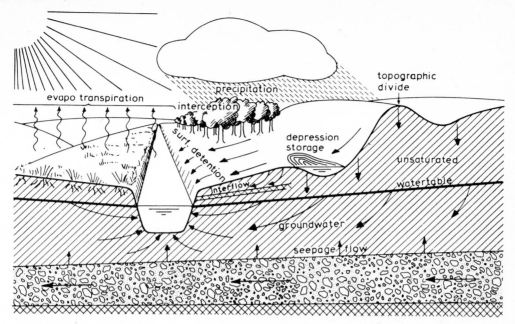

Figure 1.18   The riverine hydrologic cycle is controlled by many natural factors. (SOURCE: Reference 4.)

to ecological damage. However, this is not true of sand dunes.

Sandy ocean beaches are quite often backed by *sand dunes* (Figure 1.21), which, because of their extreme value for habitat and geological stability, are vital ecological areas. The following paragraphs (adapted from Frankenburg et al[9]) describe the basic characteristics and values of Atlantic dune systems:

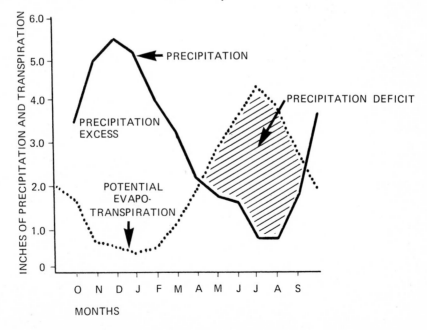

Figure 1.19   A typical pattern of precipitation and evapotranspiration (combined evaporation and transpiration) in western Washington State. (SOURCE: Reference 17.)

Figure 1.20 Freshwater wetlands, such as the cypress swamp, serve to purify and regularize the flow of land runoff into coastal water basins. (Conservation Foundation photograph.)

Dunes are waves of drifting sand, the height and movement of which are determined by the direction and intensity of the wind. The shifting dunes that normally lie directly behind the berm are most subject to stresses of wind and airborne salt [Figure 1.22]. Mild summer waves add sand to the berm, and prevailing onshore winds move it from the berm to the dunes. The berm moderates change by providing a reservoir of sand available to either dunes or beach as needed. In winter and during storms the berm may be completely reclaimed by the ocean, at which time the dunes must erode to replenish the lost sand.

The dunes are greatly influenced by the presence or absence of the associated plant community. Most shifting dune plants (sea oats, for example) are rapid growers and spread by forming runners. An important function of the plants is to impede the rate of sand movement. Since prevailing winds are onshore, shifting

dunes tend to move inland. Plants disrupt the smooth flow of air and allow the sand to settle out on the front or top of the dune, and it then stabilizes and its inland migration is slowed.

Countless shorebirds come to feed at the water's edge. The berms, sand dunes, and sand overwash areas behind the beach serve as nesting grounds for many of them. Coastal dunes and beaches provide habitats for chipmunks, woodchucks, and red foxes. These mammals prey on insect-eating shrews, bats, and mice.

The plant communities of the beachfront thrive on continuing natural disturbances, and the plant species living there are especially adapted for such stress. White-tailed deer and rabbits graze on dune grasses and succulent plants. Weasels, feeding mostly

Figure 1.21 The beach at Cape Hatteras, North Carolina, typical of the ocean beach environments, is a habitat of hardy and highly specialized species. (Photo by Joel Arrington for North Carolina Department of Conservation and Development.)

Figure 1.22 Large coastal dunes (background) in Texas, as elsewhere, are built from sand swept by the wind from the beach berm (foreground). (Photo by author.)

on mice and insects, also inhabit the dunes.[20]

ESTUARINE SYSTEMS

The richest part of the coastal zone is the estuarine sector—the protected waters of the bays, sounds, lagoons, bayous, and tidal rivers. Estuarine waters are also the most vulnerable to disturbance from uncontrolled activities in the coastal zone that pollute the waters and otherwise reduce the carrying capacities of coastal ecosystems.

Characteristics

The exceptional natural value of the estuarine type of system derives from a combination of physical properties that separately, or in combination, perform a unique set of functions beneficial to the biota. The more important of these properties are the following:

1. *Confinement.* This property provides shelter by protecting the estuary from wave action, enables plants to root and shellfish larvae to attach, and permits the retention of suspended life and nutrients.

2. *Depth.* Shallowness permits light to penetrate to plants over much of the bottom, allows the growth of marsh plants and tideflat biota, improves flushing, and discourages oceanic predators (which avoid shallow waters).

3. *Salinity.* Freshwater flow dilutes salt water and fosters an especially rich and varied biota, deters oceanic predators and encourages estuarine forms, and creates two-layer beneficial flow in some estuaries (see property No. 4).

4. *Circulation.* Freshwater outflow, tide, and salinity together create a beneficial system of water movement and transport for suspended life (particularly effective when stratified).

5. *Tide.* Tidal energy provides an important driving force; tidal flow transports nutrients and suspended life and dilutes and flushes wastes; tidal rhythm acts as an important regulator of feeding, breeding, and other functions.

6. *Nutrient storage and cycling.* The estuary has a high capacity for energy storage; marsh grass and submerged grasses convert and "bank" nutrients for later use; physical conditions promote the retention and rapid cycling of nutrients and the conversion of available nutrients to animal tissue.

Habitats

Estuarine habitat classes may be usefully categorized as the water masses, the basin bottoms, and the basin margins (inundated by coastal water at a frequency from semidaily to annually; see page 120). The most important of these habitats are identified as ecologically *vital areas* for management purposes (page 120). These vital areas that are part of the basin bottom or margin are easily located because they are physically identifiable, whereas those that are part of the water are more ephemeral and difficult to locate.

Shellfish Beds

Clams, oysters, and other valuable shellfish are not spread evenly over the bottom of estuaries but rather are concentrated in certain flats, banks, bars, or reefs. These *shellfish beds* are rather easily identified as vital areas and delineated in planning surveys (Figure 1.23).

Oysters, for example, are a food source for certain fish, birds, and mammals in shallow estuaries. Moreover, oyster beds provide an exceptional and unique habitat for a rich and diverse association of species that constitutes a major source of food for commercial and recreational fish and serves a vital role in assuring the integrity of the ecosystem. The vast production of oyster larvae provides an important source of microfoods for plankton feeders. The larvae are also important to the functioning of the ecosystem because large populations of oysters can filter a significant proportion of the water each day and in so doing remove suspended matter and thereby reduce turbidity.

Submerged Grass Beds

Although the species of grass may differ from region to region, *submerged grass beds* provide an ecosystem component of special value wherever they occur. They supply food to grazing animals and detrital nutrients to the water (tiny particles of plant stuff that float in the water). They add oxygen (during daylight hours) and stabilize bottom sediments. They provide nursery areas (vital places of refuge for young fish and other aquatic life forms). They attract a diverse and prolific biota and often create unique opportunities for the existence of certain species. For example, the tiny larval stages of estuarine scallops must attach to grass blades to survive, and therefore the species can exist only where there are grasses.

In certain estuaries submerged grass beds are potentially as productive of detrital nutrient as salt marshes. For example, in South Oyster Bay, Long Island, eelgrass grows in waters 6 to 8 feet in depth and covers about 60 percent of the bottom of the bay in stands of 1 to 6 tons per acre (dry weight)—the densest stands hold up to 14 tons per acre.[22]

In the Rookery Bay (Collier County, Florida) system, approximately 20 percent of the bottom of the open water area is occupied by submerged grasses. This area in total contains nearly as much fauna as the 80 percent unvegetated bottom area.[23] An essential role in grass bed productivity is played by rootless macroalgae (such as sea lettuce) that lodge in the grass beds.

In estuaries where marshes are reduced or absent, submerged grass beds may play the dominant role by providing the nursery areas, general habitat, primary productivity, and nutrient storage essential to proper

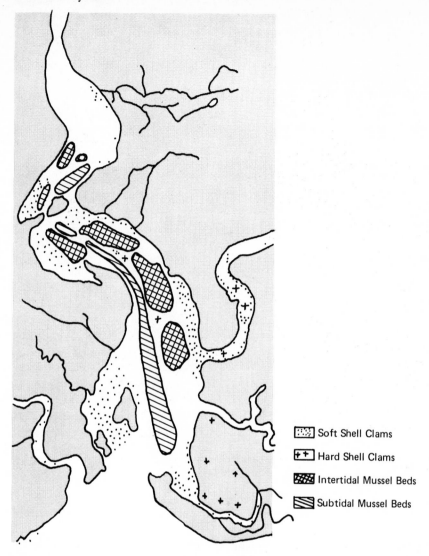

Soft Shell Clams

Hard Shell Clams

Intertidal Mussel Beds

Subtidal Mussel Beds

Figure 1.23 Major shellfish areas of the North River, Massachusetts, delineated in a planning survey. (SOURCE: Reference 21.)

function of the estuarine ecosystem and maintenance of a high carrying capacity.

The submerged grasses serve an important role in stabilizing the sediments in which they grow. They continue to collect and hold within their root structures the suspended particles that drop out as water slows in passing the bed. The grass bed itself may collect enough sediment to be beneficially elevated toward the surface and therefore closer to the source of light[24]—

an important factor in promoting growth of the grass (photosynthesis).

Eelgrass is the predominant species of the sea grass beds in estuaries of temperate latitudes, including most of the Pacific coast and the Atlantic coast south to Virginia. Widgeon grass also may be relatively abundant in temperate areas. In the South Atlantic and Gulf of Mexico areas, other species dominate, such as turtle grass and Cuban shoal weed (Figure 1.24).

Figure 1.24 Submerged beds of turtle grass (foreground in front of mangrove roots) provide essential habitat in subtropical estuaries. (Conservation Foundation photo by M. Fahay.)

Coastal Wetlands

All shoreline areas that are periodically (at least once a year) exposed and flooded by salt or brackish water through tide and normal storm action are part of the estuarine, rather than the shoreland, system. When these areas are vegetated marshes or mangrove swamps, they are referred to as *coastal wetlands*. They may be recognized by the types of grasses or other salt-tolerant plants that live there (page 142). Those above the high-water mark are referred to as *upper wetlands*; those below it, as *lower wetlands*.

The wetlands provide the essential habitat for many important estuarine species and serve other roles such as shore stabilization, flood control, and water purification. The vegetation plays the key role in converting inorganic compounds (nutrients) and sunlight into the stored energy of plant tissue. When the dead leaves and stems of the plants enter the water and are broken down by bacteria, they leave the storage component of the energy cycle and, as small particles of organic detritus, become the food of fiddler crabs, worms, snails, mussels, and the myriads of larval stages of fish and shellfish of estuarine waters (page 12). Upper wetlands vegetation often decomposes in place and is washed into the estuaries as dissolved basic nutrients.

The vegetation of the lower wetlands includes a wide range of salt-tolerant plants, the most prominent being salt grasses and red mangroves (Figure 1.25). The lower wetlands serve as the vehicle for the collection and storage of mineral nutrients washed down from the upper wetlands and from the shoreland watershed. The nutrients may be partially used and recycled within the lower wetlands system but are ultimately transported into coastal waters to provide basic nutrients for the food chain of coastal waters ecosystems. About half the plant tissue created in the grass marshes and mangrove swamps of the lower wetlands is flushed out into the estuary.[25]

Wetlands vegetation removes toxic materials and excess nutrients from estuarine waters. In addition, sediment and other inert suspended materials are mechanically and chemically removed from the water and deposited in the marsh or swamp, reducing the sedimentation of navigation channels and shellfish beds. The vegetation also slows the surge of floodwaters and may help to reduce the severity of flooding. Vegetation serves to stabilize estuarine shorelines and prevent erosion; for example, mangrove trees not only preserve shorelines, but ac-

tually can extend the land's edge by trapping sediments and building seaward.

Coastal upper wetlands are usually grass- or rush-vegetated high marshes or meadows, except in tropical regions, where they may be mostly swamps dominated by black and white mangroves. Some upper wetlands merge into freshwater wetlands, which serve, as upper wetlands do, to take up, convert, store, and supply basic nutrients to the coastal ecosystem, often via transfer through the upper (and lower) wetlands. Also, such adjoining freshwater wetlands often provide exceptional habitats for certain coastal birds and animals.

Although most experts agree that all existing coastal low marsh (lower wetlands; below high water) should be preserved, they are not unanimous about the preservation of all high marsh (upper wetlands; above high tide), (Figure 1.26). It would appear that the value of high marsh in providing detrital nutrients and certain types of habitat to aquatic species is often lower than that of low marsh. However, many

Figure 1.25 *Spartina* marshes are classified as vital habitat areas because they are components essential to the function of estuarine ecosystems. (Conservation Foundation photo by J. Chess.)

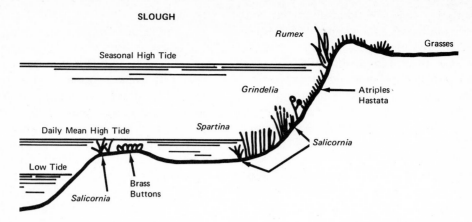

Figure 1.26   Typical northern California tidal slough; the area between daily and seasonal high tides is the upper wetland, an ecosystem component of important, yet unresolved, values. (SOURCE: Reference 26.)

experts have yet to study and come to appreciate high-marsh function in two important respects. First, as part of the hydrologic system high marsh serves to regulate the flow of runoff waters and to cleanse them of contaminants—a role of major importance, particularly for areas undergoing heavy development in the shorelands (page 85). Second, high marsh takes up nutrients from freshwater runoff and spring tide flows, stores them temporarily and then releases them in periodic pulses as dissolved nutrients. Such dissolved nutrients support phytoplankton (algae) and other important plants of the estuarine food chain.

Tideflats

Tidelands are normally vegetated with grasses or mangroves to the low-tide mark, below which they extend into tideflats, areas exposed on low-range tides as unvegetated expanses of mud or sand (Figure 1.27; also see Figure 1.9). These barren flats may extend above the low-tide mark and thus create a tideflat shoreline, where the tidelands area is unfavorable to the growth of grasses because of heavy tidal scouring or other factors. *Mud flats* or *sand flats* are often rich sources of basic nutrients for the ecosystem and feeding areas for fish at high

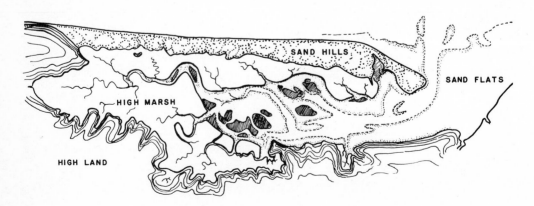

Figure 1.27   The Barnstable marsh (Cape Cod, Massachusetts). The dotted line indicates the extent of sand flats; the shaded areas are lower marsh. (SOURCE: Reference 27.)

tide or birds at low tide. In many estuaries they produce a high yield of shellfish or of baitworms for fishermen.

Recent research has shown that mud flats are important energy storage elements of the estuarine ecosystem. If the mud flats were not present, vital dissolved chemical nutrients (such as phosphates, nitrates, nitrites, and ammonia) would be swept out of the marshes with the ebbing tides, eventually depleting the energy supply to the marsh food chain. The mud flat serves to catch the departing nutrients and hold them until the returning tide can sweep them back into the marsh (Figure 1.28). There appears to be "an optimum balance between the proportion of marsh to mudflat area which is vital to the stability and the continued existence of both systems."[28]

Survival Strategies

Each species makes a unique demand on its environment, and the accumulated total of these demands gives the ecosystem its particular biotic character. It is important to recognize that each species has a distinct life pattern and set of strategies upon which its survival depends.

For example, the spotted weakfish, with its mottled pattern of coloring, is perfectly camouflaged for safety from predators so long as it lives among the submerged grasses of the Florida estuaries. It depends for its nourishment on the grass shrimp and small fish that occupy grass beds. If the grass beds were eliminated, the weakfish would have no place to hide or to feed and might either succumb to predators or desert the area.

Many plankton species have developed mechanisms to utilize the opposite flows of the two layers of stratified estuaries (page 128) for passive propulsion. (Plankton include all the multitude of tiny organisms that remain suspended in the water and swim weakly, if at all.) For example, to be propelled up the estuary, a plankter (plank-

Figure 1.28 Mud flats serve a vital function by retaining basic nutrients within the estuarine system. (Conservation Foundation photo by M. Fahay.)

ton organism) need only descend to the inward-moving bottom layer. On the other hand, to be propelled toward the sea, it need only move a few feet upward into the outbound surface layer.

Many forms migrate vertically every day—up each night and down each day—and are alternately carried inward by the bottom flow and then outward by the surface flow (Figure 1.29). By resting on or in the bottom when the tide ebbs and then rising when it floods, some gain a net movement inward that enables them to migrate from the ocean to the head of the estuary.

By this manner of strategic vertical movement, the organism can maintain itself in the most favorable part of the estuary. The result of the stratified circulation system, as we have observed it, is to allow plankton to concentrate most heavily in midestuary. For this reason and others the middle and inner parts of the estuary are the places where life abounds.

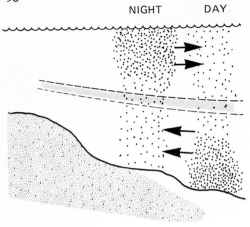

NIGHT   DAY

Figure 1.29   Strategic vertical shifts in the night and day distributions of estuarine zooplankton forms enable them to hold position in the estuary against tidal flows. (SOURCE: Reference 29.)

Wetlands–Estuary Relationships

Rooted plants are vital in the food system of estuaries, as previously discussed. In summary, as the major grasses die or the mangrove leaves fall into the water and begin to decompose, the decomposing plants create *organic detritus*, small organic particles that are spread by water flow throughout the ecosystem to become important nu-trient elements in the diet of many species (Figure 1.30). Beds of submerged grasses—eelgrass, turtle grass, widgeon grass—may also produce the valuable detritus.

In estuaries dominated by wetlands, much of the protein food of smaller aquatic animals is derived from digesting the bacteria and other microorganisms that live on the floating particles of organic detritus. The detritus is swallowed, the bacteria are digested, and the particles are passed back to the water, where new layers of bacteria form to nourish more animals. The essential ecosystem role of the bacteria is to continually decompose dead plants and animals and thus reduce their constituents to basic minerals (nitrates, phosphates, etc.), which provide the nutrient supply for a new cycle of plant life. There is a continuous loop (Figure 1.31).

Including wetlands, there are four basic sources of primary organic production (i.e., basic plant material that is the foundation of the food chain):

1. Stands of sea grasses and seaweeds.
2. Flats, banks, or shallow bottoms that are coated with algae.
3. Open-water areas containing large populations of phytoplankton.

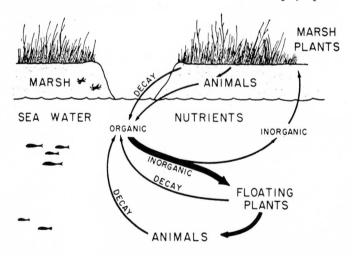

Figure 1.30   The marsh–estuarine nutrient exchange system is a continuous recycling process. (SOURCE: Reference 30.)

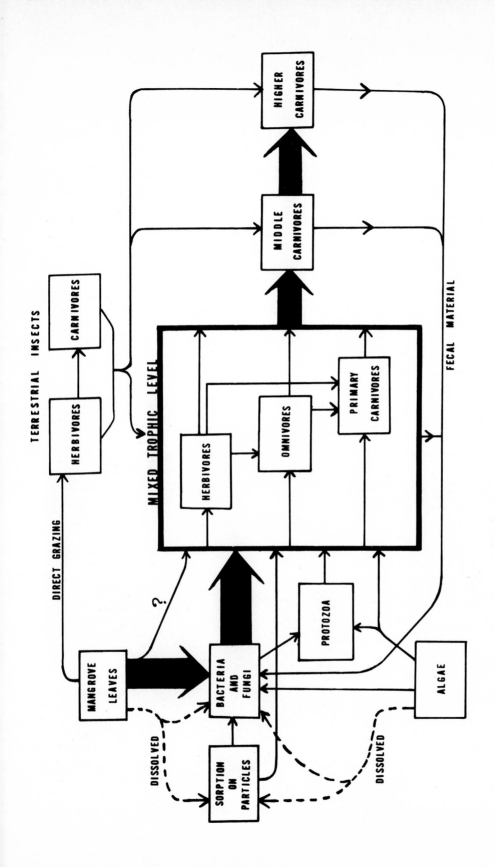

Figure 1.31 A conceptual model of the North River (Florida) food web, showing the most important flow of energy as a broad arrow, less important food chains as narrow arrows, and the pathway of dissolved leaf material as a dotted line. (SOURCE: Reference 31.)

37

4. Coastal marshes and the freshwater wetlands and drainages behind them.

The relative importance of these four
sources of organic production varies from
place to place, and in some estuaries and
lagoons one or more may be absent. The
importance of each of these four sources
to a given estuary or lagoon depends on the
specific form and amount of the organic
material produced therein. Sea grasses and
seaweeds usually contribute only modest
amounts to primary productivity, except in
certain estuaries with limited wetlands and
large stands of grass where they may be
principal sources of organic detritus entering
the food chain. Organic contribution by
mud algae is believed to be modest in a
majority of estuarine systems. The phytoplankton community in the open waters is
often quite important, and many species
may depend either directly or indirectly on
plankton as a principal food source.

The mangrove and marsh areas are often
most important. They contribute not only
to detritus feeders, but also to the phytoplankton by accumulating nutrient material
in upper wetlands and converting it into a
form that will nourish them, that is, into
dissolved nutrients such as nitrate (Figure 1.32).

The continuous uptake of detritus and
phytoplankton by zooplankton, shellfish, and
small fish is an effective method for storing
nutrients that might otherwise flow through
the estuary unused (page 88). Thus, in a
sense, the bodies of the organisms in the
food chain are energy storage units.

Figure 1.32   Red mangrove forests accumulate and store basic nourishment and provide it to the estuarine
food chain. (Conservation Foundation photo by M. Fahay.)

The life of the bottom, collectively termed the "benthos," is typically more abundant in estuaries than in either fresh waters or the ocean. This bottom community is critical, not only for its yield of shellfish but also as a major element in ecosystem stability and supply of forage for sport and commercial fish. The benthic species are highly diverse, including worms, lobsters, clams, oysters, shrimp, and fish. Many species forage about within the bottom sediments for their food. Others feed by filtering the water that passes by.

The tidal creeks that transect wetlands provide pathways for various fish and invertebrates to move into the marshes to feed, spawn, or seek sanctuary (Figure 1.33). Some species, such as the blue crab and various fish, actively move in and out of these tide marshes, whereas others, such as the copepods and the larvae of fish and in-

Figure 1.33 Tidal marsh creeks provide passage-ways for various fish and shellfish species to move into the marsh for feeding. (Conservation Foundation photo by M. Fahay.)

vertebrates, are passively carried in and out on the tides.

Flounder, shrimp, oysters, croakers, spot, and dozens of other coastal fish are supported on a diet of nutrients that originate with grasses in the marsh and shallow estuarine waters. Research has demonstrated that as the amount of marsh acreage increases the productivity of the fishery resource increases as well (judged by value per acre of fishable water). Decreases in fish production were shown to be directly proportional to the obliteration of marsh in a Florida estuarine area (mostly filled for real estate).[32]

Wetlands also supply the food base for mink, raccoons, nutria, land otters, and muskrats. Marsh grasses, such as three-square, cattail, and alligator weed, along with fish and invertebrate fauna, nourish these fur bearers. Emergent vegetation of cattails and bull-rushes provide housing materials and protection from predators.[33] Alligators are important reptiles of the coastal and adjoining freshwater wetlands, where the holes they dig for nests serve later as valuable habitats for other species. Also, the concentration of small life in and around the alligator holes attracts birds and mammals and provides them with a major source of food at various times of the year.[34]

Estuarine Dependence

Permanent residents of the estuary include a few important fish, such as the white perch and spotted sea trout. More species reside there only temporarily for spawning; for example, migratory sea fish such as weakfish, redfish, mullet, and black drum. Dozens of other species, including the majority of those that are important for commerce and sport, use estuaries as nurseries for their young or as feeding areas. This state of estuarine dependence has been summarized (by L. A. Walford and others) as follows:[35]

One group of migrant Atlantic fishes spends summer in the estuaries and winter off-shore

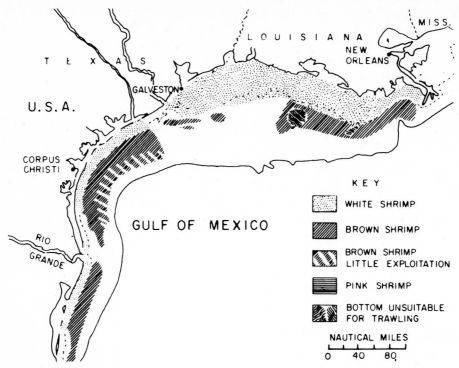

Figure 1.34   Shrimp fishing areas of the western Gulf of Mexico. (SOURCE: Reference 36.)

in deep waters; for example, croaker (hard-head) and spot (lafayette) do this. Others, such as the winter flounder, prefer deeper waters in summer and spend winters in the estuaries. Anadromous species such as salmon, shad, alewife (river herring), and striped bass come in from the ocean to go up the rivers for spawning. Catadromous species, such as the eel, live in fresh and brackish waters but spawn in the sea—but the young return to the estuaries and to fresh waters.

Some 60 to 70 percent of important coastal species of the Atlantic and the Gulf of Mexico are estuarine dependent (but considerably fewer Pacific species). Some important crustaceans are also involved in estuarine dependence patterns. As examples, life history profiles of two estuarine-dependent species, shrimp and striped bass, are discussed below.

Shrimp

Representative species of shrimp are found along all United States coasts. Many are commercially useful; all are essential to the food web. The penaeid shrimp of the South Atlantic and Gulf coasts (the brown, pink, and white) are the most valuable commer-cially (Figure 1.34). The various species appear to subsist on plant detritus and small crustaceans, worms, and various larvae. Although most species are oceanic residents as adults, the estuary fulfills two primary functions for certain of their life stages: (1) provision of adequate nourishment during a period of rapid physical growth, and (2) protection from predators.

The pink shrimp, abundant in the Gulf of Mexico, spawns offshore in water 100 to 150 feet deep. The larvae move and drift with currents toward the mainland for 3 to 5 weeks while passing through a series of developmental stages and growing to a size of about 0.5 inch. They enter the inlets, and within the estuary they grow rapidly, reaching commercial size in the next 2 to 4 months before returning to the sea to com-plete their life cycle (Figure 1.35). The closely related brown shrimp spawns offshore in depths of 150 to 230 feet. The young move inshore to remain for several weeks in the estuary. The other important Gulf of Mexico species, the white shrimp, inhabits water less than 100 feet deep and has a life cycle similar to that of the brown shrimp, although it resembles the pink shrimp in having a greater affinity for fresh water.[36]

Striped Bass

A single species, it occurs on the Atlantic coast from northern Florida to Canada, most abundantly from North Carolina to Massachusetts. Pacific striped bass are most abundant in the San Francisco Bay system, but some occur north to Oregon.

Along the Middle and North Atlantic coasts striped bass (also "stripers" or "rock-fish") live in bays, sounds, and tidal rivers, depending on season. Few ever travel more than 4 to 5 miles from shore. At their southern or northern extremes, Atlantic stripers seem to be wholly river fish. In the Middle Atlantic, populations winter in rivers and spawn there in the spring; the rest of the year they divide their time between ocean and estuarine feeding grounds. Distances traveled grow progressively longer with age. Stripers feed on a variety of prey found near shore, including fish, crabs, worms, and shrimp.

Striped bass breed along the Atlantic coast as far north as the Hudson, but not successfully to the north in New England rivers. They spawn in fresh or nearly fresh water of tidal rivers from April through June.[37] Details of the survival strategy of this species—a long pelagic larval life, congregation of small fish on shoals, winter

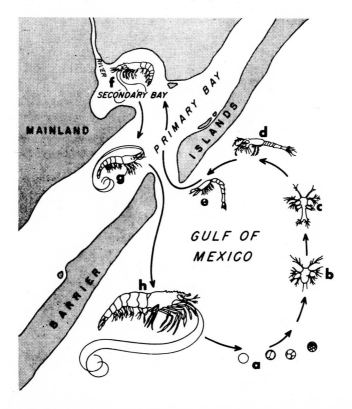

Figure 1.35 Typical life history of the Gulf of Mexico shrimp: (*a*) shrimp eggs, (*b*) nauplius larva, (*c*) protozoa, (*d*) mysis, (*e*) postmysis, (*f*) juvenile shrimp, (*g*) adolescent shrimp, (*h*) adult shrimp. (SOURCE: Reference 2.)

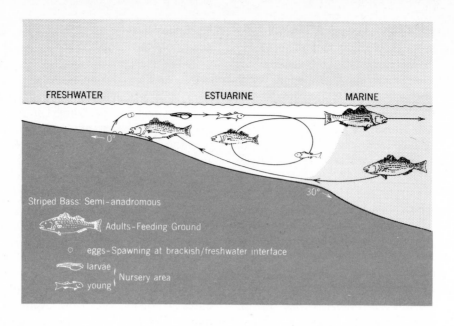

Figure 1.36   Life cycle of the striped bass shows extensive estuarine involvement. (SOURCE: Reference 29.)

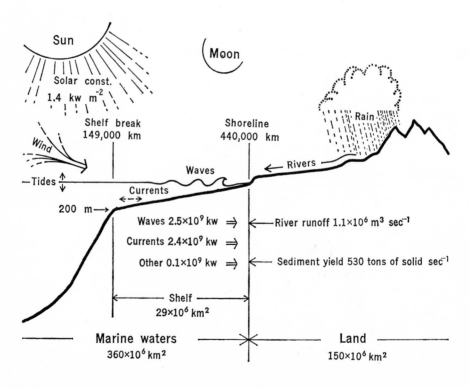

Figure 1.37   Budget of energy and land runoff in the coastal zone. Most of the energy in the nearshore zone (the territorial sea) comes from the open sea. (SOURCE: Reference 1.)

hibernation in the deeper water of estuaries, summer disperson, coastal migration—demonstrate the extensive estuarine involvement of the striped bass and its remarkable compatibility with the estuarine environment (Figure 1.36).

Striped bass from New Jersey, introduced into the San Francisco Bay region in 1879, bred successfully and have flourished there ever since. Like the Atlantic populations whence they came, they spawn in the spring and summer. Spawning occurs principally in the Sacramento and San Joaquin rivers (to a much lesser extent, it may occur also in rivers tributary to certain Oregon estuaries to which the bass have spread). As in the Atlantic, the young are waterborne for many weeks and then settle down to life in the upper estuary. They move toward bays as they grow older. The number of San Francisco Bay striped bass decreased to nearly half of the previous level through the 1960s, perhaps because of entrainment and death of suspended young stages in water diversions and power plants (page 452).[38]

NEARSHORE AND OCEAN SYSTEMS

Most of the deep part of the ocean is a biological desert. However, the territorial sea with the inner continental shelf and the band of nearshore waters, lying within the 3-mile territorial border, may be as rich as many estuaries, particularly along sheltered coasts. It is this coastal part, rather than the deep sea, that is of most concern to state and local governments in their environmental management programs.

The oceanic circulation type is characterized by vigorous currents, waves, and tides that effect rapid disperson and dilution. Storm forces push the sea onto the land, flooding its margin and restructuring sandy beachfronts (Figure 1.37). Oceanic circulation is ordinarily less complex than estuarine circulation except in areas near inlets. Inlet areas are most often estuarine in their ecologic character.

An effect of great importance is *upwelling*, a common occurrence along much of the oceanfront, where bottom water moves *inshore* to replace surface water pushed *offshore* by prevailing winds. Offshore, this upwelling brings nutrients from the deep ocean to the surface, where life blooms. Inshore, upwelling moves nutrient supplies shoreward along the bottom of the territorial sea and into the shore zone, where it causes rich biotic growth in the band of waters close to the beach. It also provides an important mechanism for suspended small life to be carried shoreward (by sinking or diving down) rather than to be swept out to sea.

Habitats

Whereas life of the deep ocean waters is thinly scattered except in scarce areas of richness, life on and over the continental shelf is generally more profuse and is concentrated in great abundance in many places such as current convergences, reefs, banks, and dropoffs, where there is a plenitude of nourishment and many agreeable habitats for shellfish, bait fish, other fish, marine mammals, and birds. Many nearshore and oceanic species resort to estuaries for breeding or for nurseries (page 140). Usually, the greatest abundance of life is in the territorial sea, within easy reach of the land and therefore under constant threat of pollution from the wastes of human society.

There are distinct areas that can be located and classified as ecological vital areas where life is highly concentrated—often within the territorial sea, sometimes beyond. Among such vital areas are shellfish beds (page 101), fishing banks, rock outcrops, deep holes, kelp beds, and coral reefs. Because of their particular importance to management programs, we have singled out the last two for special attention.

Kelp Beds

Stands of kelp are especially important components of certain coastal ecosystems, especially those of the partially sheltered waters of rocky Pacific shores (page 645), and should be classified as vital habitat areas. Kelp grows best in relatively cool waters where depths are less than 100 feet. The kelp bed breaks the force of the sea and provides a strip of quieter water between it and the shore. It provides food and a favorable habitat for many fish, as well as sheltered nursery areas for their young (Figure 1.38). Stands of kelp are a favored haunt of sea otters, which feed there on fish, crustaceans, and sea urchins.

Coral Reefs

These reefs are consolidated living colonies of microscopic organisms found in warm tropical waters (page 593). As the colonies grow, underwater reefs are formed by both the living organisms and the calcareous skeletons of preceding generations. Coral reefs are not only uniquely rich and beautiful but also highly sensitive to changes in their environment. A great variety of fish, shellfish, and smaller marine organisms depend on the coral reef habitat for shelter and food, making it the center of a productive and diverse biological community (Figure 1.39). The corals themselves depend on zooxanthellae, a type of algae, for their energy (via photosynthesis).

BARRIER ISLAND AND BEACH SYSTEMS

Much of the seacoast is fronted by elongated islands or peninsulas of sand. These *barrier islands* and *barrier beach strips* are mobile features that move about. They grow or shrink in response to storms and to fluctuations in sea level, currents, and sediment supply. The changes are the net result of

Figure 1.38 A representative kelp bed of the San Diego region. (SOURCE: Reference 39.)

erosion and deposition. The multiple rows of parallel ridges that form barrier islands are often visible in the patterns of vegetation (Figure 1.40). Major alterations in the shape and location of islands and barrier beaches are often the results of the formation or migration of inlets: "Inlet formation causes the island to widen; inlet migration widens the island over the distance of migration; the addition of new sand to the island gives it needed volume and elevation; and the sea level rise causes the shoreline to migrate or retreat landwards"[40] (Figure 1.41).

The perpetuation of barrier islands along high-energy coasts depends on perpetuation of the sand dune system. Dunes are the island's frontal defense against the forces of wind and waves because they store sand to replace that lost to big storms. They are

Figure 1.39   Coral reefs are biologically rich, beautiful, and critically important vital areas. (Photo by author.)

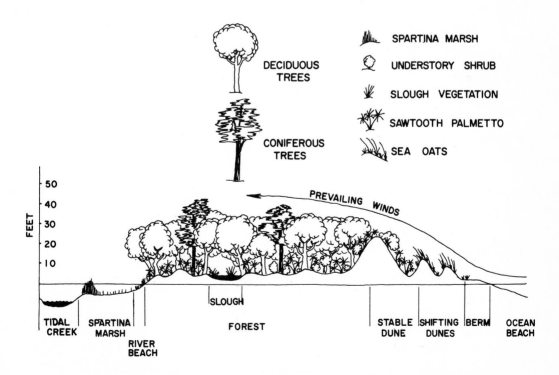

Figure 1.40   Hypothetical transect of a Georgia barrier island. (SOURCE: Reference 9.)

Figure 1.41   Barrier islands are mobile (Kewaydin Island, Florida). As sea level rises, they tend to move landward, changing the geometry of channels and inlets. (Photo by author.)

also the means by which islands move and grow. On the dune lines there is a succession of vegetation that changes from grasses on the frontal dune to forest communities on the back dunes. The vegetation promotes large-scale trapping of sand, whereby the reserves of the dunes expand; while the frontal dune remains fluid, the back dunes tend to become stabilized and rather permanent features of the landscape (page 96).

Water is a critical factor in the survival of island animals, and a variety of marshy sloughs provides for this need. Island sloughs may contain fresh or brackish water and range in area from a few square feet to hundreds of acres. They are characterized by fluctuating water levels.[9]

Fire is essential to normal Atlantic barrier island ecology. Mild (slow-burning) ground fires do not kill trees but simply burn away the accumulations of leaf litter on the ground. This burning stimulates the growth of grasses and annual herbs and keeps marshes and meadowlands open.

Barrier islands and barrier beaches typically support tidal marshes or mangrove swamps on the estuarine side (Figure 1.42). The characteristics and values of these coastal wetlands are described in detail elsewhere (page 000) as providing essential habitats for many forms of life, supplying basic nutrients to the coastal ecosystem, stabilizing the shore, absorbing floodwaters, and removing contaminants from the water.

From their natural systems, barrier islands derive an absolutely unique combination of values. They are the front line of storm defense for a thousand miles of United States coastline. They have scenic qualities of vividness, variety, and unity that are unparalleled elsewhere in the coastal zone. They offer broad sandy beaches and a score of other important recreational features. They provide habitats and food for hundreds of species of coastal birds, fish, shellfish, rep-

Figure 1.42   The protection afforded by barrier beaches allows mangrove forests to prosper in quiet estuarine waters (Sanibel Island, Florida). (Photo by author.)

tiles, and mammals. For example, 36 species of mammals are recorded from the Georgia barrier islands.[41]

There is a unity about the barrier island chain—a system of values that is tightly intertwined, with a natural flow between them. Sand, water, animals, and even plants (through seed transport) move from island to island and form a common pool for resource replenishment. The barrier islands are so special, and so fragile, that they require particular understanding and management attention.

SUMMARY OF ECOLOGICAL PRINCIPLES

1. The carrying capacity of a coastal water basin is controlled by all factors that influence the function of the *ecosystem* of which the basin is part.

2. The flow and amount of available energy control life processes and limit the carrying capacity of the coastal ecosystem.

3. A high capability for energy storage provides for optimum ecosystem function.

4. The patterns of circulation within water basins govern the carrying capacity of coastal ecosystems.

5. The primary productivity and carrying capacity of coastal waters are normally limited by the amount of available nitrogen.

6. Natural salinity patterns usually maximize the carrying capacity of coastal ecosystems.

7. Ample supplies of dissolved oxygen are required for efficient ecosystem function and maximum carrying capacity.

8. The naturally balanced temperature regime provides for optimum ecosystem function.

9. Enhancement of light penetration in-

creases ecosystem productivity and carrying capacity.

10. Water provides the essential linkage of land and sea elements of the coastal ecosystem.

11. The natural volume, rate, and seasonal pattern of fresh water inflow provide for optimum ecosystem function.

REFERENCES

1. Douglas L. Inman and Birchard M. Brush. 1974. "The coastal challenge." *Science*, Vol. 181, No. 4094, pp. 20–32.

2. U.S. Department of the Interior. 1970. *The National Estuarine Pollution Study*. U.S. Senate, 91st Congress, 2nd Session, Document No. 91–58. Superintendent of Documents, U.S. Government Printing Office, Washington, D.C.

3. H. Postma. 1967. "Sediment transport and sedimentation in the estuarine environment." In G. E. Lauff, Ed., *Estuaries*. American Association for the Advancement of Science, Publication No. 83, Washington, D.C., pp. 158–180.

4. National Science Foundation. 1973. "Managing coastal lands." *Mosaic*, Vol. 4, No. 3, pp. 26–32.

5. Howard, Needles, Tammen, and Bergendoff Co. 1975. *Wetlands Review of Siletz Bay, Oregon*. Preliminary Draft, U.S. Army Corps of Engineers, Portland, Oregon.

6. E. P. Odum. 1971. *Fundamentals of Ecology*. W. B. Saunders Co., Philadelphia.

7. M. R. Carter, L. A. Burns, T. R. Cavinders, K. R. Duggan, P. L. Fore, D. B. Hicks, H. L. Revells, and T. W. Schmidt. 1973. *Ecosystems Analysis of the Big Cypress Swamp and Estuary*. U.S. Environmental Protection Agency, Atlanta, Georgia.

8. M. Sosin and J. Clark. 1973. *Through the Fish's Eye*. Harper and Row, New York.

9. D. Frankenberg, L. R. Pomeroy, L. Bahr, and J. Richardson. 1971. "Coastal ecology and recreational development." In C. D. Clement, Ed., *The Georgia Coast: Issues and Options for Recreation*. The Conservation Foundation, Washington, D.C.

10. J. R. Clark. 1967. *Fish and Man: Conflict in the Atlantic Estuaries*. American Littoral Society, Special Publication No. 5, Highlands, New Jersey.

11. Richard B. Williams. 1973. "Nutrient levels and phytoplankton productivity in the estuary." In R. H. Chabreck, Ed., *Coastal Marsh and Estuary Management*. Division of Continuing Education, Louisana State University, Baton Rouge, Louisiana.

12. U.S. Environmental Protection Agency. 1973. *Proposed Criteria for Water Quality*, Vol. I. Washington, D.C.

13. Elbert I. Little, Jr. 1961. *Sixty Trees from Foreign Lands*. Agriculture Handbook No. 212, Forest Service, U.S. Department of Agriculture, Washington, D.C.

14. J. R. Clark. 1969. "Thermal pollution and aquatic life." *Scientific American*, Vol. 220, No. 3, pp. 19–27.

15. C. E. Warren. 1971. *Biology and Water Pollution Control*. W. B. Saunders Co., Philadelphia.

16. N. A. Jaworski, D. W. Lear, Jr., and O. Villa, Jr. 1972. "Nutrient management in the Potomac estuary." In G. E. Likens, Ed., *Nutrients and Eutrophication: The Limiting Nutrient Controversy*, Vol. I. American Society of Limnology and Oceanographic Special Symposium, pp. 259–263.

17. City of Bellevue. 1971. *Environmental Focus*. Planning Department, Bellevue, Washington.

18. Governor's Task Force. 1972. *The Coastal Zone of Delaware*. University of Delaware, College of Marine Studies, Newark, Delaware.

19. B. J. Copeland, H. T. Odum, and D. C. Cooper. 1972. "Water quantity for preservation of estuarine ecology." In *Conflicts in Water Resources Planning*. Water Resources Symposium No. 5, Center for Research in Water Resources, University of Texas, Austin, Texas.

20. Laurence B. White, Jr. 1960. *Life in the Shifting Dunes*. The Museum of Science, Boston, Massachusetts.

21. J. D. Fiske, C. E. Watson, and P. G. Coates. 1966. *A Study of the Marine Resources of the North River*. Massachusetts Department of Natural Resources, Monograph Series No. 3, Boston, Massachusetts.

22. F. A. Smith, L. Ortolano, R. M. Davis, and R. O. Brush. 1970. *Fourteen Selected Marine Resource Problems of Long Island, New York: Descriptive Evaluations*. Travelers Research Corp., Hartford, Connecticut.

23. Bernard Yokel. 1975. *Estuarine Water Quality*. Rookery Bay Land Use Studies, Study No. 3, The Conservation Foundation, Washington, D.C.

24. E. J. F. Wood, W. E. Odum, and J. C. Zie-

man. 1969. "Influence of sea grasses on the productivity of coastal lagoons." *Mem. Simp. Intern. Lagunas Costeras*, UNAM–UNESCO, pp. 495–502.

25. J. M. Teal. 1962. "Energy flow of the salt marsh ecosystem of Georgia." *Ecology*, Vol. 43, No. 4, pp. 614–624.

26. Harold B. Goldman. 1973. *Hayward Shoreline Environmental Analysis*. Hayward Area Shoreline Planning Agency, Hayward, California.

27. A. C. Redfield. 1959. "The Barnstable Marsh." In *Proceedings, Salt Marsh Conference*. Marine Institute, University of Georgia, Athens, Georgia, pp. 37–42.

28. Barbara L. Welsh. University of Rhode Island. Personal communication.

29. L. E. Cronin and A. J. Mansueti. 1971. "The biology of an estuary." In Philip A. Douglas and Richard H. Stroud, Eds., *A Symposium on the Biological Significance of Estuaries*. Sport Fishing Institute, Washington, D.C.

30. J. S. Rankin, Jr. 1961. "Salt marshes as a source of food." In *Connecticut's Coastal Marshes*. The Connecticut Arboretum, Bulletin No. 12, Connecticut College, New London, Connecticut.

31. William E. Odum. 1971. *Pathways of Energy Flow in a South Florida Estuary*. University of Miami Sea Grant Program, Sea Grant Technical Bulletin No. 7, Miami, Florida.

32. University of North Carolina Sea Grant Program. 1975. *Newsletter*, July, 1975, University of North Carolina, Raleigh, North Carolina.

33. R. H. Chabreck, Ed. 1967. "Fur production on Southeastern coastal marshes." In *Coastal Marsh and Estuary Management*. Division of Continuing Education, Louisiana State University, Baton Rouge, Louisiana.

34. Jean C. George. 1972. *Everglades Wildguide*. Natural History Series, National Park Service, U.S. Department of The Interior, Washington, D.C.

35. L. A. Walford, J. R. Clark, and D. G. Deuel. 1972. "Estuaries." In *Sport Fishing U.S.A.* U.S. Bureau of Sport Fishing and Wildlife, Washington, D.C., pp. 277–287.

36. U.S. Department of the Interior. 1968. A *Study of the Disposal of Effluent from a Large Desalinization Plant*. Office of Saline Water, R&D Progress Report No. 316, Washington, D.C.

37. J. R. Clark and S. E. Smith. 1969. "Migratory fish of the Hudson estuary." In G. P. Howells and G. J. Lauer, Eds., *Hudson River Ecology*. New York Department of Environmental Conservation, Albany, New York.

38. H. K. Chadwick. 1972. Letter from California Fish and Game Department to P. Issakson, New York Public Service Commission. In *Transcript of A.E.C. Licensing Board Hearings on Indian Point Nuclear Plant* No. 2 (unpublished).

39. J. C. Quast. 1968. "Some physical aspects of inshore environment, particularly as it affects kelpbed fishes." In *Utilization of Kelpbed Resources in Southern California*. Department of Fish and Game, Fishery Bulletin No. 139, Sacramento, California, pp. 25–35.

40. Orrin H. Pilkey, Jr., Orrin H. Pilkey, Sr., and Robb Turner. 1975. *How to Live with an Island, a Handbook to Bogue Banks, North Carolina*. North Carolina Department of Natural and Economic Resources, Raleigh, North Carolina.

41. Hans Neuhauser and W. Wilson Baker. 1974. "Annotated list of mammals of the coastal islands of Georgia." In A. Sydney Johnson, H. O. Hillestad, S. F. Shanholtzer, and G. F. Shanholtzer, Eds., *An Ecological Survey of the Coastal Region of Georgia*. National Park Service Monograph Series No. 3, Washington, D.C., pp. 197–209.

CHAPTER TWO

Managing for Optimum Carrying Capacity

Environmental management of coastal waters and shorelands has as its fundamental goal the maintenance of the carrying capacity of coastal ecosystems at the optimum level, which is normally construed as the highest possible level. In this context "carrying capacity" is understood to mean the capability of the resources of the ecosystem to sustain an *optimally balanced* resource base.

In this chapter we set forth principles to form the basis for managing coastal ecosystems for optimum carrying capacity. We also recommend criteria for the diagnosis and monitoring of ecosystem condition. Finally, we review the known major types of impacts that adversely affect coastal ecosystems and reduce their carrying capacities.

Development activity anywhere in coastal areas—watersheds, floodplains, wetlands, tidelands, or water basins—is a potential source of ecologic damage to the coastal waters ecosystem (Figure 2.1). Each type of residential, commercial, or industrial development has the potential for a particular combination of environmental disturbances. The amount of damage that results from any particular disturbance depends on the characteristics and vulnerabilities of the specific ecosystem involved.

Often the same qualities that make a coastal waters ecosystem so valuable also make it vulnerable to damage from pollution and other environmental disturbance. This is particularly true of estuarine ecosystems. Estuaries, surrounded by land on all sides, are easily accessible for urban or industrial development and for water-related human uses (Table 2.1). Use pressures are heavy in urban areas adjacent to estuaries, and the pollution potential is high. The confinement and the shallowness

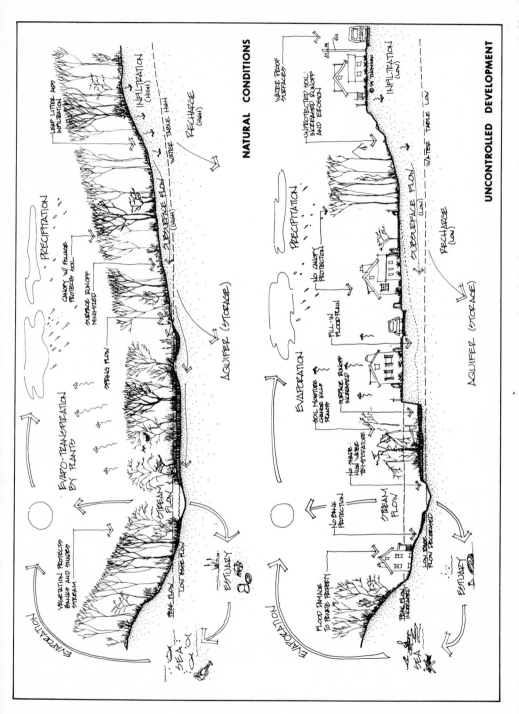

Figure 2.1 Development in the coastal watershed strongly affects coastal ecosystems through land runoff. (SOURCE: Reference 1; courtesy of S. Hamill of the Collins DuTot Partnership, Philadelphia, Pennsylvania.)

51

Economic and Population Growth	Some Major Resulting Agents of Modification		Identified Stressed Systems Related to These Activities	The Multiple-Stressed System: Ecology of The Future?	Some Components in the Resulting Multiple-Stressed System
1. Urban-Suburban Expansion in Response to Population Growth and Economic Opportunity	1. Waste Discharge	Municipal Industrial Agricultural	Sewage Wastes Seafood Wastes Pesticides Thermal Wastes Radioactive Wastes Papermill Wastes	Example of One Major Economic Component → Resulting Activities Waste Discharge	Development of Petrochemical Complexes
2. General Economic Growth Diversification, and Sophistication		Navigation		--Municipal --Industrial --Ships	Sewage Waste Dredging Spoil
3. Expansion of Specific Activities Related to the Estuarine Zone	2. Dredging	Mining and Processing Land Development	Dredging Spoil Phosphate Waste Destruction of Wetlands Altered Currents Salinities, etc.	Transportation Dredging and Filling	Impoundments Petroleum Stores Pilings
--Marine Fisheries				Population Growth and In-migration	Brine Pollution
--Civilian and National Defense Transportation	3. Physical Structures	Fresh Water Impoundment Diversion, etc. Piers, jetties, Hurricane Barriers, etc. Aids to Navigation	Impoundments Acid Waters Brine Pollution	Development of Secondary and Marginal Activities Shoreline Development, etc.	Petrochemicals Etc.
--Marine Mining and Processing					
--Outdoor Recreation					
--Waste Discharge					

Table 2.1   Impact of selected elements on coastal ecosystems (SOURCE: Reference 2)

of estuarine water basins allow pollutants to pervade their waters, particularly those that have poor flushing characteristics.

Vital areas are the physical elements of the coastal ecosystem that are essential to the survival and well-being of certain species, to the functioning of the entire ecosystem, and to the maintenance of optimum carrying capacity. A number of such vital areas have been described previously. Adverse impacts affecting vital areas are particularly damaging to the coastal ecosystem.

Much of the planning required to manage for optimum carrying capacity requires special ecological knowledge and skills that must be provided by experts in various biological and physical technical fields. The basic hydrologic forces at work in the shorelands are familiar to hydrologists, civil engineers, and planners (Figure 2.2), and understanding them requires little special knowledge. However, understanding the basic forces at work in coastal waters—tides, density layers, reversing currents—and the

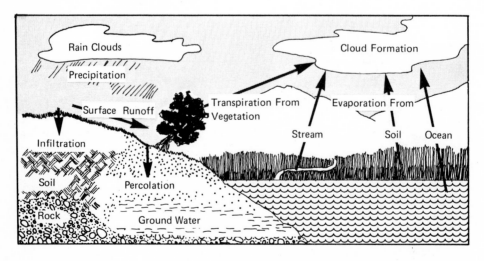

Figure 2.2   The coastal hydrologic cycle. (SOURCE: Reference 3.)

ways in which they react with the ecosystem does require special knowledge. Therefore expert assistance in the area of hydrography or oceanography will usually be required in coastal zone planning. In addition, water quality monitoring, ecosystem diagnosis, natural systems inventory, and other aspects may require that technical assistance be obtained.

THE ECOLOGIC BASIS OF MANAGEMENT

The complexity of biotic systems and the interrelatedness of their components mandate that each coastal water ecosystem be managed as a *whole system*. Neither piecemeal management nor treatment of single components or single species will succeed. Furthermore, the major external sources of influence on coastal water systems must be considered—shoreland watersheds, shoreline areas, and offshore waters.

To be effective for management purposes, each coastal ecosystem delineated for management must identify and include (1) a defined water basin (or series of interconnected basins), (2) all marginal (shoreline) transition areas, and (3) all shoreland watersheds that drain into the coastal basin. The ecosystem approach in coastal management is based on the following goal: *Each coastal ecosystem must be managed with respect for the relatedness of its parts and the unity of its whole.*

Coastal zone development planning must recognize particularly that modification of the land area entails a high potential for adverse effects on estuarine systems by modifying runoff patterns and thereby reducing the capability of the land to store and regularize the release of rainwater from the watershed and to cleanse it enroute to coastal waters.

A management program to protect and sustain a coastal ecosystem must be created to be compatible with ecological theory, as well as fashioned to the specific qualities of the ecosystem to be managed. Although standard ecological classification does not readily provide a useful management framework, one can work with ecological concepts and generally known relationships to devise a practicable system. Such a system identifies specific properties of the ecosystem and the combined effects—the interactions—of the various components. It also provides a basis for optimization of carrying capacity—the ability of the ecosystem to sustain resource values.

The productive capacity of any estuarine water body is governed by the interplay of the chemical, geological, physical, and biological factors that together govern its energy system and its carrying capacity. In the original scientific sense "carrying capacity" meant the potential *number of animals of a particular species* supported per acre (or other measure of size). However, we use the term here in a more current and general sense as the amount of recognized resource values that an ecosystem can supply. Each type of pollution, removal of habitat, interference with primary productivity, or other disturbance reduces carrying capacity in a specific way. A combination of disturbances causes a combination of carrying capacity reductions.

There are numerous components of the coastal water ecosystem that must be safeguarded—fringing vegetated water areas, estuarine bottoms, shellfish beds, and the breeding, nursery, feeding, and resting habitats of species. In addition basic dynamic processes must be maintained—water circulation, nutrient input, and sunlight penetration of water. Only after these vital basic processes and components have been identified, and their vulnerabilities to disturbances are known, can a comprehensive management program be developed.

In the following discussion we describe the major limiting factors that affect the total carrying capacity level of a coastal water system. Each of these factors has an

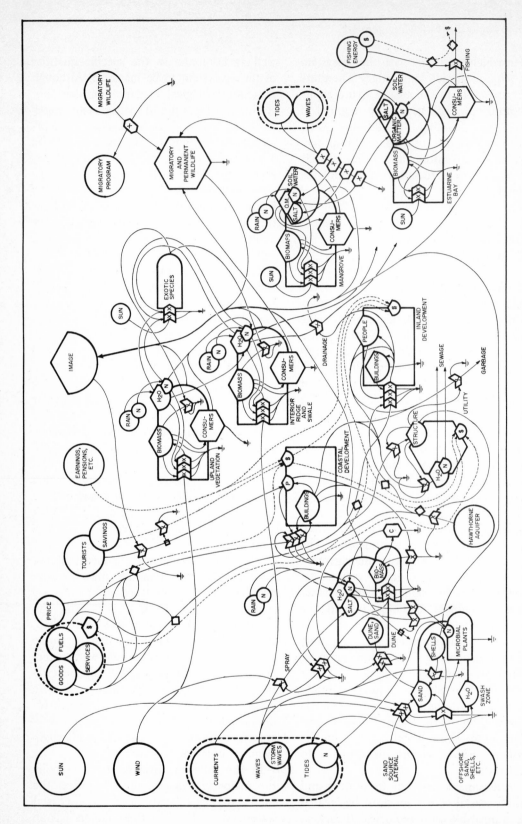

Figure 2.3 Regional model of Sanibel Island, showing main components that generate value and major flows of materials and energies that generate vitality. (SOURCE: Reference 5.)

optimum and an adverse level which should be learned. These two levels should be established and monitored (page 73) for each major component and process of the ecosystem and compared with the existing level of carrying capacity. The current condition can be determined from the criteria suggested in the section starting on page 65, and the effects of changes caused by ecological disturbances can be learned.

Basic Carrying Capacity Limiters

The fundamental suppliers of energy—light, water motion, and mineral nutrients—and their flows through the ecosystem and through the food chain should be identified and considered in management. Although the whole system that supports coastal resources and its relation to human life support systems is complex (Figure 2.3), the factors that principally govern the resource-carrying capacity of a coastal waters ecosystem can be reduced to a few simple "limiters" and modulators (Figure 2.4):

Limiters—Primary Supply Factors That Control Potential Primary Productivity:
   Nutrients (mineral)
   Gases (oxygen, carbon dioxide)
   Light (penetration controlled by turbidity)
   Storages (energy storage units)
   Reduction (bacterial decomposition)

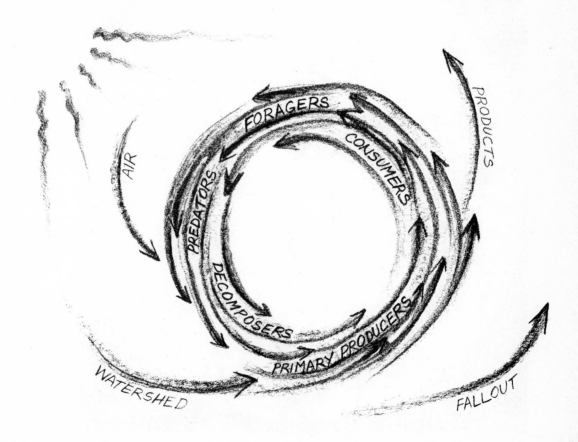

Figure 2.4 The energy that drives the biotic system of coastal waters may originate outside the system or recycle within it. (By C. Wilson, The Conservation Foundation.)

Modulators—Primary Variable Factors That
Govern Total Productivity:
   Temperature
   Salinity
   Habitat suitability (water and bottom
   quality)
   Pathogenicity (bacteria, viruses, fungi)
   Water circulation (wind, tidal, freshwater-
   driven)

The major factors that control the primary productivity of ecosystems (the plant
output)—light, oxygen, and mineral (in-

organic) nutrients—must be held at optimum levels to provide for highest carrying
capacity and for optimum ecosystem function in general (a high level of productivity
generally contributes to a high level of
carrying capacity).

The following are two examples of the
subjects that should be addressed in considering the existing condition of coastal
waters and the effects of man-made disturbances on coastal ecosystems: (1) water clarity—silt from soil erosion in shorelands
causes turbidity and blocks sunlight pene-

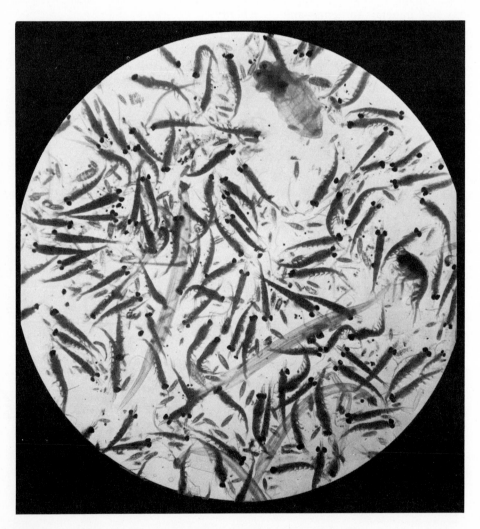

Figure 2.5 Zooplankton (small suspended animals) consume phytoplankton (algae) and become the food
of fish. (Conservation Foundation photo.)

tration to plants in the water (page 534), and (2) wetlands vegetation—coastal marshes adversely altered lead to loss of marsh grass acreage or to decreased vigor of remaining marsh area (which provides basic food for all animal life). In both examples the management purpose is to maintain the productivity of the energy system that converts sunlight to basic animal food by preventing blockage and by keeping the primary productivity units at maximum capacity.

These considerations lead to the following management goal: *To maintain an ecosystem at optimum function it is necessary to protect and optimize the sources and the flows of energy that power the system.*

Nutrients

All life of the estuarine ecosystem is supported by a food chain beginning with vegetation that includes large plants (mangroves, grasses), floating microplants, collectively called "phytoplankton," and bottom-growing microplants. Much of the animal life is nourished by wetlands detritus. These particles of plants (marsh plants and mangrove leaves) and the colonies of microscopic life on them are consumed by a wide variety of estuarine species, for example, oysters, shrimp, some fish, and a myriad of zooplankton (Figure 2.5) that serve as forage for birds and predatory fish. Disturbances that decrease the supply of natural nutrients to the wetlands plants that in turn supply the detritus are harmful to coastal ecosystems. (Wetlands also store and convert mineral nutrients to leaf detritus, and their decay reconverts the material back into minerals useful to phytoplankton.)

The plants are nourished by nutrient minerals dissolved in the water, particularly compounds of nitrogen (nitrates, ammonia) and phosphorous (phosphates). These nutrients are supplied from within the ecosystem through a continuous biochemical storage–release–cycling–restorage system. However, nutrients continuously trickle out of the system by various processes and are replaced by minerals in the inflow of land runoff and from other sources. It is essential to maintain these sources of nutrient replacement, without which the ecosystem would gradually become impoverished. This is best done by controls on watershed alteration to preserve or restore the natural quality, volume, and rate of flow of runoff. In this way a continuous supply of natural nutrients will be ensured.

Diversion of water from the watershed, channelizing rivers, clearing and surfacing land, or removal or alteration of wetlands may result in reductions of sources of dissolved nutrients to coastal waters or cause the inflow to move so quickly to sea that the ecosystem is unable to take up and store the nutrients. Hence a basic Ecosystem Management Rule is: *Reduction of the natural supply of nutrients to the coastal ecosystem by alteration of freshwater inflow should be avoided* (No. 1).

Conversely, the ecosystem may be unbalanced by an excessive supply of nutrient chemicals from shoreland watersheds due to septic tank leaching, discharge of sewage effluent or industrial organic wastes, contaminated land runoff water from fertilized farms or front yards, and so forth. An excessive supply of nutrient chemicals leads to eutrophication (over fertilization), an unbalancing of the natural species mix of the ecosystem, and general degradation of water quality. Rapid "blooms" of phytoplankton are followed by their mass death and decay. Waters may become turbid, estuarine bottoms fouled, and oxygen depleted. Particularly adverse are nitrogenous chemicals because these are the nutrients chiefly responsible for triggering phytoplankton "blooms" in estuarine waters.

In normally productive coastal waters a significant increase in nitrogenous compounds from sewage or crop fertilizers (particularly nitrates) will lead to adverse eutrophication. This leads to the following Ecosystem Management Rule: *Excessive discharge of nitrogenous compounds into confined coastal waters must be presumed to have adverse effects and should be avoided* (No. 2).

Since too much nutrient may be as bad as too little, the solution to the nutrient problem is to achieve balance. The balancing depends on a complex set of circumstances of supply, utilization, and recycling, but particularly on the *type* of nutrient. The right type in the right place at the right time of year is characteristic of ecosystems in natural equilibrium. In unnatural amounts and types, nutrients unbalance ecosystems and cause disequilibrium.

Gases

Of the various gases that are found dissolved in coastal waters, *oxygen* is of the most obvious importance to all fauna. Oxygen is needed to keep organisms alive and to provide for optimum ecosystem function and highest carrying capacity. Coastal waters need a high concentration (federal guidelines require a minimum of 4.0 ppm: page 70). Much of the available supply is produced by plants, which remove carbon dioxide from the water (in photosynthesis) and replace it with oxygen. Because the availability of carbon dioxide is not usually regarded as a limiting factor, the important gas to consider is oxygen.

The minimum amount of oxygen required for healthy ecosystem function is maintained by natural processes in undisturbed coastal waters (except some confined estuaries during warm seasons). But oxygen may fall to unhealthy levels when sewage and other wastes with high biological oxygen demand (BOD) pollute coastal waters and induce high bacterial action. The bacteria involved are common residents of coastal waters and are species that multiply rapidly to reach enormous abundance, thereby depleting the water of oxygen faster than it can be replaced by either plants or the atmosphere.

The whole ecosystem is degraded by inadequate oxygen (page 19). It is therefore essential to include considerations of dissolved oxygen in the coastal management program and to arrange controls for the maintenance of an optimum oxygen environment. This will normally mean concentrations much higher than the federal standard of 4 ppm. The goal should be to maintain oxygen at as near the saturation level as possible (Appendix, page 829) and never less than 6 ppm except when an extraordinary prevailing natural situation keeps the concentration lower. The appropriate Ecosystem Management Rule is: *Any significant reduction from the natural concentration of oxygen is presumed to be adverse and should be avoided* (No. 3).

Water Clarity

Sunlight is the basic force driving the ecosystem. It is the fundamental source of energy for plants, which in turn supply the basic food chain that supports all life. Sunlight must be able to penetrate coastal waters so as to foster the growth of both the rooted plants, such as sea grasses, and the suspended algae (or phytoplankton). Increased turbidity from the addition of excess suspended matter to the water reduces light penetration and depresses plant growth. Estuarine waters are normally more turbid (cloudy) than ocean waters, being both more laden with silt and more rich in suspended life.

In its undisturbed and virginal state the ecosystem responds and adjusts to the existing levels of turbidity caused by the suspended matter. The organisms in turn adapt to these levels, and the system comes into equilibrium. However, when the system is disturbed and degraded by a sudden addition of suspended matter, its carrying capacity is reduced and its general function declines below the optimum condition.

Increased turbidity may be caused by excavation in estuarine water basins or by the discharge of eroded soil with the runoff from shorelands. Other increases may be caused by excess nutrients derived from land runoff, sewage, or industrial waste discharges that stimulate algal growth and lead to clouding of the water. The excess suspended matter tends to settle out on shallow bottoms, where it may be readily resuspended by wind action or boat traffic.

Turbidity varies greatly with the seasons and with irregular environmental changes (freshets, winds, plankton blooms). Consequently, there is no one base turbidity value but rather a complex pattern of variation that characterizes an ecosystem. This pattern is difficult to pin down without extensive research. Therefore an appropriate management plan is to eliminate the sources of excess turbidity.

The overall solution is to maintain the natural condition of the environment by which the ecosystem has evolved and has naturally prospered. Therefore it is necessary to prevent the addition of unnatural amounts of silt that would block light penetration, or of nutrients that would stimulate excessive plankton growth and lead to the same condition (Figure 2.6).

Storage

There is an urgent need to understand the value of ecosystem storage elements because *storage components may appear as ecologi-*

Figure 2.6   Agricultural strip-cropping techniques help to prevent erosion, loss of soil to coastal waters, and resulting siltation and turbidity (Littleton, Maine). (Photo by G. S. Smith, U.S. Department of Agriculture, Soil Conservation Service.)

cal largesse and thus become victims of development. All components of the ecosystem that supply natural nutrients, convert them to useful form, or provide for their storage and flow to and through the ecosystem, such as wetlands, need protection from adverse change. Significant loss of nourishment to species of animal life undermines the whole system of life support in the estuary. Loss of sea grass beds, coral reefs, or kelp beds is similarly adverse. Tide flats contribute to primary productivity by the production of algae, which grow on their surface, and by storing and recycling nutrients.

One type of storage unit is a marsh, which stores excess nutrients in the system in plant tissue and then releases them periodically for recycling (Figure 2.7). Another completely different type is a dune, which stores sand against the time when storms rip

away the beach and sand must be resupplied. Whatever function they serve, the extreme value of storage units should be protected. The appropriate Ecosystem Management Rule is: *Storage components of ecosystems are of extreme value and should always be fully protected* (No. 4).

Ecosystem Modulators

A number of factors outside the direct energy path have strong effects on the biotic balance of ecosystems. The most significant of these indirectly modulating forces are temperature, salinity, habitat suitability (the condition of physical components, as well as water toxicity and repellence), and water circulation. Pathogenicity is also important, not only to ecosystem biota but also to human health.

Figure 2.7 Salt marshes serve as massive nutrient accumulation storage systems for coastal ecosystems (Charleston, South Carolina). (Conservation Foundation photo by M. Fahay.)

Temperature

The temperature of the water is a major control on life. Migration, spawning, feeding efficiency, swimming speed, embryological development, and basic metabolic rates of fish—all are controlled by temperature. The optimal temperature for the coastal water ecosystem depends on (1) the preferences of each of the individual species, and (2) the optimum functional balance of the system as a whole.

Temperature alteration, such as may be caused by power plant thermal effluents or changes in water flow pattern, is particularly critical to estuarine systems because life there is highly concentrated and because many important species resort to estuaries for certain key life functions (page 457).[6] An ecological system is in dynamic balance, and, as in a finely tuned automobile engine, any damage to a single component can disable or impair the efficiency of the entire system. The appropriate Ecosystem Management Rule is: *Significant alteration of the natural temperature regime of the coastal ecosystem is presumed to be adverse and should be avoided* (No. 5).

Salinity

Generally, there is a gradient in the salt content of coastal water that starts with high values along the outer coast, decreases inward through the estuary, and drops to near zero (less than 0.5 ppt) at some distance up the tributary tidal streams and rivers. Some coastal species tolerate a wide range of salinity, whereas others require a narrow range to live and reproduce successfully. Some species require different salinities at different phases of their life cycles, variations such as are provided by regular seasonal rhythms in the amount of runoff.

We have stressed that the health of the ecosystem depends on regularizing the inflow of runoff water, particularly that which enters via canals and creeks (page 22). Al-terations affecting freshwater inflow upset the natural salinity regime, disturbing the conditions to which the biota are naturally adapted (page 18). The volume of the freshwater supply also controls patterns of circulation. Moreover, any factor that affects circulation affects salinity through alteration of the volumes of salty ocean water entering estuaries and the ratio of dilution of fresh and salt water (Figure 2.8). The appropriate Ecosystem Management Rule is: *Any significant change from the natural salinity regime is presumed to be ecologically detrimental and should be avoided* (No. 6).

Chemical Suitability

Toxic substances added to coastal waters in significant quantity have obviously harmful effects (Figure 2.9). But protection of coastal water quality involves more than just avoiding lethal concentrations of toxic pollutants. There are definite lower limits of water quality below which mobile animals either desert an area, or survive in reduced health and abundance, failing to grow or reproduce properly. For example, sensitive oceanic migratory fish are particularly affected by chemical unsuitability of the water and typically abandon coastal areas with "bad" water. A variety of repelling substances come from industrial discharges or sewage effluent—heavy metals, oil, organic substances, and so forth. These repellents appear to be responsible for the virtual abandonment of many estuarine and near-shore ocean waters by water-suitability-sensitive sport fish species. The result is failure of a fishing area or depletion of the general carrying capacity of the ecosystem. Elimination of the discharge of repellent substances is essential in the restoration of many ecosystems to optimum function.

Physical Suitability

The accumulation of sediments on the bottom of an estuarine basin results in shoaling

Figure 2.8 Dams strongly alter the quality and rate of flow of fresh water to coastal ecosystems (Little River, Northport, Maine). (Conservation Foundation photo by M. Fahay.)

of the basin and has adverse effects on water quality, circulation, and general ecosystem function. Fine sediments on the bottom of the coastal basin trap pollutants and, when resuspended by wind, currents, or boat traffic, cause oxygen depletion, turbidity, and release of toxic substances and obnoxious gases. A heavy layer of fine sediment prevents occupancy by much of the normal bottom fauna and the rooting of sea grasses. Corrective measures require the control of (1) erosion from land clearing and site preparation in the watershed, (2) dredging activity and spoil disposal in estuarine basins, and (3) boat traffic (which resuspends sediments). The appropriate Ecosystem Management Rule is: *The discharge of suspensible solids to coastal waters is presumed to be adverse and should be avoided* (No. 7).

Water Circulation

The circulation of water through an estuary is a key ecologic factor. Water motion transports nutrients, propels plankton, spreads "seed" stages (planktonic larvae of fish and shellfish), flushes wastes from animal and plant life, cleanses the system of pollutants, controls salinity, shifts sediments, mixes water, and performs other useful work. Circulation strongly influences the abundance and the pattern of distribution of life in the coastal water basin, particularly the estuarine basin. Thus the entire dynamic balance of the estuary revolves around, and is strongly dependent on, circulation. The specific pattern of water movement found in any coastal basin is a result of the combined influences of freshwater flow, tidal action, wind, and, to a

Figure 2.9 Occasional massive fish kills occur when toxic wastes are discharged to coastal waters (Willapa Bay, Washington). (*Seattle Times* photograph.)

lesser extent, external oceanic forces. The configuration (depth and shape) and the condition of the bottom of the coastal water basin influence its circulation, as well as the quality of its waters and the health of its biotic system. Such projects as bridges, spoil piles, deep channels, and land fills can significantly affect circulation patterns. The appropriate Ecosystem Management Rule is: *Any reduction or blockage of water flow in or to an estuarine water basin is presumed to be adverse and should be avoided* (No. 8).

The rate or schedule of the flow of fresh water is important in its effect on the productivity, stability, and general health of the coastal ecosystem. Maintaining the original, natural rhythm or pattern of seasonal flow is generally beneficial to the ecosystem. Also related to volume of inflow are the amounts of pollution, sediment, nutrients, minerals, organic matter, and other substances dis-

solved or suspended in the water and carried down into the estuary, all of which affect the general function and the carrying capacity of the coastal water ecosystem.

Consequently, a fundamental goal of estuarine ecosystem management is to avoid changes in the system of land drainage and flow into coastal waters as far as possible. Uncontrolled development in estuarine watersheds creates adverse effects by reducing both the capability of the land to store and regularize the release of rainwater from the watershed and its capability to cleanse it of sediments, nutrients, and a wide variety of other contaminants. The total volume of fresh water reaching coastal waters may also be altered as land is covered with impervious surfaces. Installation of storm drain systems and excavation of drainage canals also unbalance flow patterns and delivery schedules and prevent recharge of ground water aquifers. Clearing and grading land have the

Figure 2.10   Estuaries are often damaged from circulation blockage by bridge crossings (Booth Bay Harbor, Maine). (Photo by author.)

same deleterious effects and also jeopardize the quality of the runoff water.

Projects that significantly alter the fresh-water flow pattern are presumed to be adverse, including control structures such as dams, impoundments, or canals. The same is true of land clearing and paving in the watershed, which lead to exaggerated flood-and-drought flow patterns.

In addition to freshwater inflow, the circulation of water in any coastal basin is affected by many factors that govern the relative influences of tide and wind (page 16). Where runoff is relatively low, wind and tide usually prevail as major circulation forces. Wind is often dominant in shallow lagoons, whereas tide is often dominant in bays and embayments (page 128). Tidal dominance is particularly to be expected when bays and embayments are relatively deep and the tidal amplitude is relatively

high (more than 2 feet). Whereas wind is little affected by human activity, tidal influence is quite alterable by changes in the form of the water basin from dredging or from the building of structures in estuaries. Therefore activities that may alter basins must be closely controlled (Figure 2.10).

Pathogenicity

The discharge of disease-carrying substances from sewage, land runoff, and other effluents and wastes has caused great losses of carrying capacity and ecosystem function. The well-known pathogens are bacteria and viruses that cause serious (and sometimes fatal) disease in human beings who eat shellfish that have become infested. The solution is to control and clean up sewage, septic tank, and stormwater runoff.

Less well known is nutrient stimulation,

by which natural pathogens in coastal waters are caused to bloom in great abundance by excessive nutrients from sewage, dredge spoils, and other sources. This stimulation appears to have caused widespread outbreaks of fish disease and to have started red tides (explosive growth of poisonous algae). The appropriate Ecosystem Management Rule is: *Any discharge of pathogens or toxic substances into coastal waters is adverse and should be avoided* (No. 9).

DIAGNOSIS OF ECOSYSTEM CONDITION

Major objectives of the coastal zone land and water environmental management program are to identify the sources of adverse impacts and to restore and maintain the quality of the coastal waters ecosystem. Therefore a valuable, if not essential, first step is to determine the presently existing condition of the ecosystem. It is of particular importance to identify and measure the disturbances that reduce the carrying capacities of coastal systems. The results will define the current status of the environment, identify the values that should be protected, and suggest an agenda for the restoration of damaged elements (Figure 2.11). Although a complete ecosystem diagnosis may be feasible only for advanced management programs, many of the simpler tests can be used in the most basic ones.

The same tests used for diagnosing the current condition of the ecosystem may be usefully employed to monitor the effects of the management system in operation and to detect problems that may develop later and require adjustments to the management program. In addition, tests of ecosystem condition find use in setting environmental standards—the specific requirements for control of potentially disturbing activity. Most of the existing quantitative ecosystem criteria concern water quality and the sources of water pollution. Simple, generally applicable tests of the ecological quality of basin margin areas and estuarine bottoms are presently scarce. Nevertheless, it should be quite possible to develop such criteria based on specific, expert knowledge of the local ecological system.

It is strongly recommended that the coastal zone management program start with a diagnosis of the existing condition of coastal waters ecosystems. Only with a measure of the relative ecological condition of the waters can one relate past practices to present states and proceed to formulate a management program to control adverse effects in the future. Otherwise the management controls may lack a firm basis of fact. It is a relatively simple job for a specialist in coastal ecology to conduct a preliminary reconnaissance survey of existing conditions to determine the basic needs of the program. Some suggestions of criteria to be used in such a survey are given in the following section.

Water Quality Criteria

Water pollution is largely controlled by a complex cooperative federal–state program. Under the 1972 Federal Water Pollution Control Act Amendments (page 193) the states may be authorized to implement and enforce federal water quality standards and effluent limitations. The water quality standards prescribed by the U. S. Environmental Protection Agency (EPA) under the Federal Water Pollution Control Act Amendments[8] make a useful set of guidelines for (1) local monitoring of ecosystem condition, and (2) establishment of legally enforceable performance standards. They provide an index to the success of local coastal zone land and water management programs that function in synchrony with the federal–state machinery for pollution control. A summary of typical "natural" water quality condition values is given in Table 2.2 (1968 data).

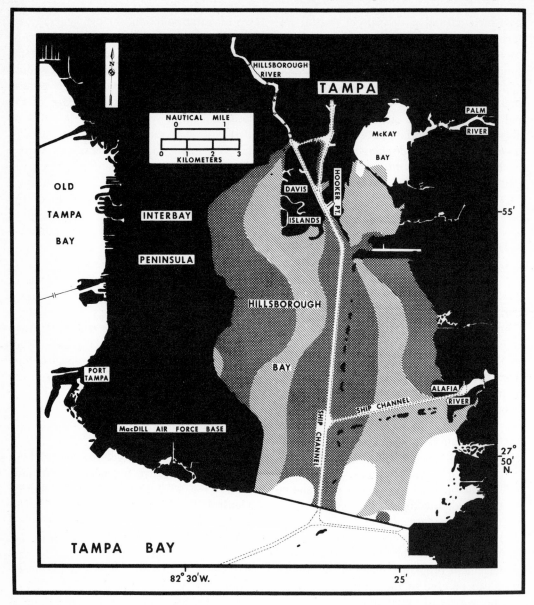

Figure 2.11 Ecological zones in Hillsborough Bay, Florida, based on the comparative diversity of mollusks
—healthy zone (unshaded); marginal zone (hatching); unhealthy zone (cross hatching)—August and
September 1963. (SOURCE: Reference 7.)

Numerical Standards

Quantitative standards are the most applicable ones for diagnosing ecosystem condition and for monitoring management programs, but qualitative and semiquantitative
criteria also have roles in coastal manage-

ment programs. Numerical EPA water
quality standards that apply to coastal areas
are discussed below, along with supplementary comments of our own. This information is meant to be illustrative rather than
definitive; it is necessary to contact the
office of the state department of pollution

Table 2.2   Natural ocean and river water quality typical of the estuarine zone (source: Reference 2)

Biophysical region	Ocean water quality						River water quality					
	Temperature (degrees Fahrenheit)	Disolved oxygen (P.P.M.)	pH	Salinity (Cl—) (P.P.M.)	Phosphate, phosphorus (P.P.M.)	Nitrate, nitrogen (P.P.M.)	Temperature (degrees Fahrenheit)	Disolved oxygen (P.P.M.)	pH	Salinity (Cl—) (P.P.M.)	Phosphate, phosphorus (P.P.M.)	Nitrate, nitrogen (P.P.M.)
North Atlantic:												
Summer	65	7.93	8.15	17,989	0.124	---	72	7.51	6.3	1.0	0.05	0.7
Winter	32	8.22	8.15	17,989	---	---	32	12.43	6.7	3.0	.06	.2
Middle Atlantic:												
Summer	73	6.34	7.62	17,385	1.053	0.280	71	7.60	7.6	9.5	.21	4.6
Winter	36	7.17	[1]	14,022	---	---	35	11.99	7.1	12.0	.03	1.1
Chesapeake Bay:												
Summer	80	6.60	7.66	10,266	1.425	.056	80	6.94	7.0	9.5	---	.6
Winter	38	8.13	7.53	7,922	.712	---	40	11.00	6.9	11.0	---	3.4
South Atlantic:												
Summer	87	6.66	8.17	19,723	.434	---	76	7.18	7.0	5.0	.14	1.5
Winter	50	6.74	8.00	19,839	1.084	---	55	9.16	4.9	6.2	.25	.5
Caribbean:												
Summer	87	6.70	8.10	19,723	.341	---	83	6.65	7.4	44.0	.12	---
Winter	71	6.33	7.99	19,906	.434	---	61	8.30	8.2	60.0	---	.7
Gulf of Mexico:												
Summer	87	6.52	8.03	19,424	.712	---	78	5.80	7.7	5.0	.00	.6
Winter	54	7.39	8.24	19,945	.372	---	57	8.99	6.8	6.0	---	1.2
Pacific Southwest:												
Summer	69	8.20	8.05	18,504	2.571	---	68	7.79	8.0	6.7	---	1.4
Winter	56	7.90	8.20	18,499	2.292	---	46	10.29	8.1	4.8	---	.9
Pacific Northwest:												
Summer	56	8.02	7.56	16,017	5.049	.812	74	7.29	7.5	3.0	.26	.3
Winter	45	8.76	8.33	14,770	6.721	---	46	10.29	7.9	2.0	.11	.3
Alaska:												
Summer	55	10.09	7.31	17,596	2.013	.042	52	9.23	7.5	3.2	[1]	.5
Winter	30	3.84	7.81	17,706	---	[1]	[1]	[1]	[1]	[1]	[1]	[1]
Pacific Islands:												
Summer	81	6.90	8.24	19,307	.898	[2]	[2]	[2]	[2]	[2]	[2]	[2]
Winter	73	6.97	8.23	19,396	.558	[2]	[2]	[2]	[2]	[2]	[2]	[2]

[1] No winter data available.

[2] No data available.

Note: Values estimated at 85 percent saturation.

Table 2.3 Coastal water quality criteria for toxic substances other than biocides (SOURCE: References 9 and 10)

SUBSTANCE	Maximum Acceptable Concentrations (96 hr LC_{50}) [1][2]	Maximum Acceptable Concentrations (Milligrams or Micrograms/liter) [2]	Minimum Risk Threshold (Milligrams or Micrograms/liter) [3]
Aluminum	1/100	1.5 mg/l.	0.2 mg/l.
Antimony	1/50	0.2 mg/l.	N.A. [4]
Arsenic	1/100	0.05 mg/l.	0.01 mg/l.
Barium	1/20	1.0 mg/l.	0.5 mg/l.
Beryllium	1/100	1.5 mg/l.	0.1 mg/l.
Bismuth	N.A.	N.A.	N.A.
Boron	1/10	N.A.	5.0 mg/l.
Bromine[5]	N.A.		N.A.
Cadmium[6]	1/100	0.01 mg/l.	0.2 ug/l.
Chromium[7]	1/100	0.1 mg/l.	0.05 mg/l.
Copper	1/100	0.05 mg/l.	0.01 mg/l.
Fluorides	1/10	1.5 mg/l.	0.5 mg/l.
Iron	N.A.	0.3 mg/l.	0.05 mg/l.
Lead[7]	1/50	0.05 mg/l.	0.01 mg/l.
Manganese	1/50	0.1 mg/l.	0.02 mg/l.
Mercury[8]	1/100	1.0 ug/l.	N.A.
Molybdenum	1/20	N.A.	N.A.
Nickel	1/50	0.1 mg/l.	0.002 mg/l.
Phosphorus	1/100	0.1 ug/l.	N.A.
Selenium	1/100	0.01 mg/l	0.005 mg/l.
Silver	1/20	0.5 ug/l.	N.A.
Thallium[9]		0.1 mg/l.	0.05 mg/l.
Uranium	1/100	0.5 mg/l.	0.1 mg/l.
Vanadium	1/20	N.A.	N.A.
Zinc	1/100	0.1 mg/l.	0.02 mg/l.
Cyanides[10]	1/10	0.01 mg/l.	0.005 mg/l.
Detergents	1/20	0.2 mg/l.	N.A.
Phenolics	1/20	0.1 mg/l.	N.A.
Phthalate Esters	N.A.	0.3 ug/l.	N.A.
PCBs[11]	N.A.	0.002 ug/l.[12]	N.A.
Sulfides[13]	1/10[12]	0.01 mg/l.[12]	0.005 mg/l.[12]

[1] The maximum acceptable concentration figures in this column are expressed as fractions of the 96 hr. LC_{50} for the most sensitive species in a given area. The 96 hr. LC_{50} is that concentration of a substance which kills 50 percent of the test species within 96 hours under standard bioassay conditions.

[2] Data are Environmental Protection Agency official criteria where available; National Academy of Sciences data used where EPA data not available.

[3] National Academy of Sciences data, for concentrations "below which there is a minimal risk of deleterious effects."

[4] N.A.—adequate data not available.

[5] The maximum acceptable concentration for free (molecular) bromine is 0.1 mg/l, for ionic bromate, 100 mg/l.

[6] In the presence of copper or zinc in concentrations of 1 mg/l or more, the minimum risk threshold should be lower by a factor of 10.

[7] In oyster growing areas, the minimum risk threshold should be lower.

[8] According to the National Academy of Sciences, "Fish-eating birds should be protected if mercury levels in fish do not exceed 0.5 mg/g. Since the recommendation of 0.5 mg/g in fish provides little or no safety margin for fish-eating wildlife (birds), it is recommended that the safety of the 0.5 mg/g level be reevaluated as soon as possible."

[9] 1/20 of the 20-day LC_{50}.

[10] Marine and estuarine acquatic and wildlife criteria not available; fresh water criteria are used (by EPA).

[11] According to the Environmental Protection Agency: "The maximum acceptable concentrations of PCB in any sample consisting of a homogenate of 25 or more whole fish of any species that is consumed by fish-eating birds and mammals, within the size range consumed is 0.5 mg/kg on a net weight basis."

[12] Data supplied by National Academy of Sciences.

[13] These concentrations are valid only if salt water pH is between 6.5-8.5.

Table 2.4   Coastal water quality criteria for manufactured biocides: recommended maximum concentrations of biocides in whole (unfiltered) water, sampled at any time and any place (milligrams per liter) (SOURCE: Reference 9)

Organochlorine Pesticides

Aldrin[1]	0.01	Endrin[1]	0.002
DDT[2]	0.002	Heptachlor[1]	0.01
DDE[2]	0.006	Lindane[2]	0.02
Dieldrin[1]	0.005	Methoxychlor[2]	0.005
Chlordane[2]	0.04	Toxaphene[2]	0.01
Endosulfan[2]	0.003		

Organophosphate Insecticides

Azinphosmethyl	0.001	Fenthion	0.006
Ciodrin	0.1	Malathion	0.008
Coumaphos	0.001	Mevinphos	0.002
Diazinon	0.009	Naled	0.004
Dichlorvos	0.001	Oxydemeton Methyl	0.4
Dioxathion	0.09	Parathion	0.0004
Disulfonton	0.05	Phosphamidon	0.03
Dursban	0.001	TEPP	0.4
Ethion	0.02	Trichlorophon	0.002
EPN	0.06		

Carbamate Insecticides

Carbaryl	0.02	Zectran	0.1

Herbicides, Fungicides and Defoliants

Aminotriazole	300.0	Diuron	1.6
Dalapon	110.0	2–4, D (BEE)	4.0
Dicamba	200.0	Fenac (Sodium salt)	45.0
Dichlobenil	37.0	Silvex (BEE)	2.5
Dichlone	0.2	Silvex (PGBE)	2.0
Diquat	0.5	Simazine	10.0

Botanicals

Allethrin	0.002	Rotenone	10.0
Pyrethrum	0.01		

[1] and [2]Maximum acceptable concentration in any sample consisting of a homogenate of 25 or more whole fish of any species that is consumed by fish-eating birds and mammals, within the size consumed on a net weight basis, expressed as ug/kg (EPA data available only for organochlorine pesticides). Note 1: 5 ug/kg. Note 2: 50 ug/kg.

control or the EPA for specific locally applicable standards:

1. *Toxic substances.* The maximum allowable concentrations of toxic substances as established by the EPA[9] following a National Academy of Sciences review in 1973 are summarized[10] in Tables 2.3 and 2.4.

2. *Pathogens.* The EPA standards (1973) for pathogenic organisms in swimming waters essentially prohibit concentrations higher than a log mean of 200 fecal coliforms per 100 milliliters of water. In non-

swimming waters the standards essentially permit concentrations to an average of 2000 per 100 milliliters. For shellfish waters the maximum permitted is a median of 70 MPN (most probable number per 100-milliliter sample). [There are no standards for viruses or other pathogens.]

3. *Oxygen.* The EPA standards (1973) suggest that dissolved oxygen concentrations be maintained at 6.0 ppm or higher. This seems like a reasonable normal minimum for a healthy ecosystem; lower values normally indicate adverse effects from unnatural causes. However, the standard recognizes that natural phenomena may cause the concentration to fall as low as 4.0 ppm. [No standards are available for carbon dioxide or other gases involved in ecosystem metabolism.]

4. *Temperature.* The EPA standards (1973) limit artificially induced increases in temperature to not more than 1.5°F in summer (June through August) or more than 4.0°F during the rest of the year.

General Standards

The following are useful nonquantified water quality criteria for which there is not a sufficient basis for numerical standards and therefore no EPA requirement for their observance.

1. *Nutrients.* Although no standards are available to evaluate the effects of nutrients that cause eutrophication (principally nitrogen, N), earlier EPA criteria (1968)[11] recommended prevention of releases that cause enrichment leading to any major change in the natural levels of flora (attached or floating plants, including phytoplankton), and one simply must conclude that eutrophication is evidence of ecological harm. [Numerical maxima have been recommended for certain areas, for example, from 0.3 to 0.5 ppm N for the Potomac River[12] and 0.1

to 0.2 ppm N for Hawaiian estuaries, depending on water class.[13]]

2. *Turbidity.* There are no national standards. The earlier EPA criteria (1968) recommend no discharge of substances that will result in turbidity levels deleterious to biota.[11] Also they state that turbidity levels less than a Secchi disc reading of 1 meter (3 feet) or the equivalent in Jackson turbidity units (JTU) "shall be regarded with suspicion." Since coastal waters have a natural content of organic and inorganic matter and a turbidity that varies greatly with the seasons and with irregular environmental changes, such as freshets, winds, and plankton blooms, it appears unreasonable to state a single base turbidity value that characterizes an ecosystem. There is, rather, a complex pattern of variations. [Certain states prohibit turbidity *increases* exceeding 50 JTU above natural levels. This may be feasible for naturally turbid waters but not for naturally clean ones; for example, in Oregon a *total* of 25 JTU is the maximum compatible with salmon migrations.[14] In Oregon, standards set for specific rivers may be stringent; for example, in the Willamette River in Oregon turbidities are not to exceed 5 JTU above natural background values except for certain short-term purposes authorized by the Oregon Sanitary Authority. For Hawaii it is recommended that visibility not be reduced by more than 5 to 20 feet, depending on water class, as measured by a Secchi disc.[13]]

3. *Circulation.* The earlier EPA criteria (1968) recommend that no activity be permitted which would change basin geometry or fresh water inflow so that the ecosystem is adversely affected.[11] [To this we would add a similar concern in regard to any interbasin transfer of incompatible estuarine waters.]

4. *Salinity.* The earlier (1968) EPA criteria recommend that no alteration in channels, basin geometry, or freshwater in-

flow be allowed that would cause a permanent change of more than 10 percent greater or lesser salinity than the existing natural level.[11] [These are important criteria but difficult to evaluate because they require determining the effects of (1) water flow far upstream in the freshwater sections of the rivers and their watersheds, (2) dredging to improve navigation, and (3) significant alterations of circulation caused by structures or modification of the bottom or shoreline of water basins.]

5. *Sedimentation.* No specific standards are available. [Any detectable shoaling of a water body is cause for concern because of the adverse effects of soil discharge, dredging, land erosion, and other factors.]

6. *Productivity.* No standards are available for primary productivity. Productivity measures are useful in diagnosing the condition of an ecosystem because they indicate the potential capacity to support life. By comparing the *actual* abundance of life with the *potential* abundance, one can determine whether the system is malfunctioning and needs attention. Because there are great difficulties in measuring the abundance of the variety of life forms in an ecosystem, ecologists often use "primary productivity" as a gauge of the total productivity of the system. Primary productivity measures the growth rates of plants, such as algae, seaweed, and marsh grasses (page 11). These values provide an index of the biotic *potential* or carrying capacity of an ecosystem. By an extension of this approach one can learn the sources of energy that fuel the ecosystem and the rates of energy flow through it, as well as diagnose the present condition of flows and determine whether some correctable blockage is interfering with energy flow and thus lowering carrying capacity. A loss of productivity is to be presumed adverse—vital productivity areas

require protection. For monitoring, rather accurate checks can be made on the crops of rooted plants, but plankton production is difficult to measure. [A detailed energy flow analysis requires highly specialized skills because the systems are so complex (as shown in Figure 1.6) and therefore may not be a practicable option for many management programs.]

7. *Habitat.* No specific standards are available on tolerable losses of habitat. Any loss of vital habitat area must be presumed to be adverse, not only of obvious entities such as coral reefs or grass beds, but of other important habitats (e.g., tideflats or certain submerged bottoms) as well.

8. *Biota.* No standards have been devised that are of general applicability, and the best general indicator of ecosystem quality may be the life itself. One can assume that any significant reduction in the abundance and diversity of species is *prima facie* adverse. Also, any shift in biotic communities from desirable to less desirable species should be considered adverse. Yet these biotic effects are often surprisingly difficult to pin down with hard and fast numerical indices. Changes in indicator species (see criterion No. 9) are sometimes recommended to avoid the complexities of measuring changes in the total biota of a coastal ecosystem.

9. *Indicator species.* An indicator species is one chosen to represent conditions in an ecosystem either because it is especially sensitive to change in the environment or because as an indicator of ecosystem condition, it is particularly easy to work with. An indicator species might be used in management to monitor the effects of pollution or other degradation of an environment by comparing the present standing crop of the species to the standing crop during a previous undisturbed condition, or to some specified standard. Certain invertebrate species of the bottom would be preferred indica-

tors because they stay in place and they are sensitive to disturbances. However, the pitfalls of this method of monitoring lie in sampling errors and in the difficulty of ascribing an observed change to a specific type of disturbance, for example, toxicity versus nutrient reduction.

Accurate quantitative sampling of aquatic *fauna* is difficult even for experts and usually may not be relied upon to accurately register moderate to small changes in species abundance. For example, an intensive investigation of the biota of Chesapeake Bay failed to provide any simple biotic tests of environmental conditions. The conclusion was that "simple, unequivocal standards . . . are not available" and, furthermore, those that have been used "can be interpreted only by comparative study and experienced judgment."[15] The idea is that trained scientists who have the opportunity to study and measure a variety of species are able to make a judgment of biotic conditions but can provide no single bellweather species, or set of species, that can be readily inventoried to provide a ready index of trends in carrying capacity. However, we believe that examination of the presence and condition of certain rooted aquatic plants represents a promising approach, and it would seem useful to explore the possibility of using such plant indicators in coastal zone ecosystem management programs. For example, the following associations between specific *rooted plants* and environmental conditions appear to provide useful indicators:[15]

Plant	Condition
Widgeon grass (*Ruppia maritima*)	Presence may indicate that turbidity conditions are acceptable.
Sea lettuce (*Ulva*)	Dense concentrations may indicate eutrophication due to

	sewage or other causes.
Water milfoil (*Myriophyllum spicatum*)	In fresher waters, presence is adverse (may indicate eutrophication).
Wild celery (*Vallisneria*) or pond weed (*Potamogeton*)	Presence may indicate good conditions.
Eelgrass (*Zoster maritima*)	In saltier waters, presence may indicate good conditions.

IMPACT ASSESSMENT

Beyond a general diagnosis of the condition of a coastal ecosystem, a management program must address the need for ascertaining, *in advance*, the likelihood of adverse impact of any significant potentially damaging project. Such advance study, including prediction of environmental impacts and exploration for alternative development solutions, is actually a requirement of federal law, under the National Environmental Policy Act of 1969 (page 160), for any land or water development enterprises that involve the federal government. In addition, many states now have statutory requirements for environmental review of major development projects, and some local governments also have impact review requirements (page 160). The concept of environmental impact assessment has now spread beyond statutory requirements into the environmental consciousness of society at large.

One important component of each local coastal zone management program should be an impact assessment process that would have the specific purpose of predicting the probability of significant adverse impact from any particular type of land use or construction activity. Such assessments would become part of standard community programs for land-use regulation and construction permitting.

It is possible to assess the degree of such ecological disturbances as changes in the flow rate of water, loss of wetlands vegetation, or discharges of sediment, nutrients, toxic substances, or thermal effluent (from factories or power plants). An analysis of such factors through environmental impact assessment is useful in determining necessary constraints on the siting, design, and construction of coastal development projects (Figure 2.12). Although it is possible to assess the nature and general consequences of such disturbances to the ecosystem, it is normally most difficult to quantify them for a benefit–cost analysis.

At the center of the impact assessment idea is a *presumption of adverse effects* for certain development programs identified as having high potentials for ecological harm. The term "adverse effects" may be defined as follows:[16]

Figure 2.12   Excavation of any kind in estuaries or along shorelines must be presumed to be significantly damaging to coastal ecosystems (Rumson, New Jersey). (Photo by author.)

Effects are considered adverse if environmental change or stress cause some biotic population or nonviable resource to be less safe, less healthy, less abundant, less productive, less aesthetically or culturally pleasing, as applicable; or if the change or stress reduces the diversity and variety of individual choice, the standard of living, or the extent of sharing of life's amenities; or if the change or stress tends to lower the quality of renewable resources or to impair the recycling of depletable resources.

Whether it is called "environmental impact assessment," "impact evaluation," "environmental effects analysis," or any other similar term, the concept is the same. We use the general term "impact assessment," by which we mean the evaluation of ecological effects (both negative and positive) and the determination of their impacts on human needs.

In impact assessment it often appears desirable to focus concern on *important species* or on subsystems rather than whole systems. One must be cautious of such selection, however, because it is easy to ignore certain species that are of value to the continued functioning of the whole ecosystem but not visibly important. One definition states: "A species, whether animal or plant, is 'important' if it is commercially or recreationally valuable, if it is rare or endangered, if it is of specific scientific interest or if it is necessary to the well-being of some significant species (e.g., a food chain component) or to the balance of the ecological system."[16]

A variety of approaches have been devised to assess the cause-and-effect linkage of human activity and environmental harm. We have taken the essential elements from this variety and melded them into a single process of impact assessment that should be useful for the purposes of coastal land-use planning and environmental management.

Disturbance and Impact Cycle

Impact assessment is the study of a cycle of events, linked in a chain of causes and effects that proceed from human needs. These needs lead to specific projects, which can

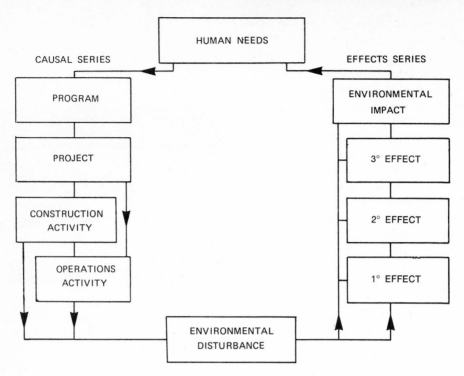

Figure 2.13   The impact cycle describes the pathways of cause and effect leading from development activities through ecosystem disturbances to detrimental impacts.

be categorized under broader programs. If a project leads to an environmental *disturbance* from some activity, it sets off a series of ecological effects. If these effects degrade the ecosystem, they cause an environmental impact that detracts from human needs. In short, projects that would backfire through the ecosystem can be identified and corrected at the start through effective impact assessment. Society is only now learning the wisdom of accurately predicting the long-term impact of activities that squander resources or despoil the environment.

The impact chart in Figure 2.13 shows how one can break down the cycle of causes and effects into a workable series of elements. These are defined as follows:

Human needs. The state of tension between what society has and what society wishes to have.

Program. A broad initiative taken to fulfill some human need or needs (housing, agriculture, recreation).

Project. One specific action taken under a program (housing subdivision, new farm, park).

Construction activity. An individual process involved in the construction of a project facility (has mostly short-term effects).

Operations activity. An individual process in the continuing operation of a project (has long-term effects).

Environmental disturbance. A perturbation; an alteration that disrupts an ecosystem.

Ecological effect. A reaction of an ecosystem to a disturbance.

Environmental impact. An environmental change that affects the fulfillment of a human need (adverse impacts lead to social detriment and interference with the fulfillment of other needs).

This impact structure is centered on human society. It is designed to accommodate the normal philosophy of community management that relates to the needs of people and to describe the sequence of events that result in predictable negative effects on the welfare of people. One can rightfully argue that a disturbance which degrades an ecosystem is adverse without any direct backfire involving the needs of people. However, we find it useful to "close the loop" and to construe *effects* as the *consequences to the ecosystem*, and *impacts* as the *consequences to the needs of society*, now or in the future.

The *causal series* of the impact cycle is sequential except that many programs cause minimal disturbances in the construction stage and substantial ones in the operational phase, for example, agriculture or logging. This case is shown by the causal pathway leading directly from project to continuing activity. Conversely, some programs lead to projects that cause major disturbances in the construction phase but not afterwards, for example, estuarine installation of a submerged pipe.

The *effect series* is made up of a number of effects that proceed from one to another, that interact or feed back. For simplicity we have shown only three stages of effects in Figure 2.13. At times the linkage may be longer and more involved. At other times it is so simple that the whole effect series is short circuited; for example, land clearing (construction) may lead directly to extensive freshwater dilution of an estuary from rapid stormwater runoff (disturbance) and cause a mass death of edible clams (environmental impact) that cannot survive the freshened water. Here the adverse impact, or detriment to mankind, is the loss of the clam resource.

Usually the sequence of effects between disturbance and impact has more similarity to a web than to a chain because of interactions and feedbacks. Often a profusion of effects leads directly from a single disturbance. Conversely, a number of separate disturbances may multiply a single effect. A typical array of effects is illustrated in Figure 2.14, where projects which require dredging are used as examples of activities that result in a complicated pattern of disturbances and effects.

Analysis and comprehension of this complex type of pattern may be difficult even for a knowledgeable scientist. Although such understanding may be required to solve certain local environmental management problems, much of the routine work of planning and ecosystem management can proceed at a simpler level. When more complex situations arise, it is important to recognize that detailed assessment of environmental impact is work for professional ecologists, who in turn will often need the assistance of engineers and other specialists (Figure 2.15).

The Impact Matrix

The matrix chart is a tool sometimes used in impact classification. It is of little use in case assessments because it relates only single pairs of variables and does not explain the mode of action of effects, the complex patterns of interaction, or the magnitudes of inputs. Its purpose is to provide a checklist, an analytical framework, or an organizing tool.

An example of a matrix display is given in Figure 2.16, which lists the probable effects of a project. A somewhat more sophisticated approach includes an evaluation system in which an index number in each cell of the matrix indicates the seriousness of the effect, say on a scale of 1 to 10.

The Elements of Assessment

To develop an adequate environmental data and information base for *large-scale projects* with potentially *serious adverse impacts*, we suggest that the ecological effects be determined in sufficient detail to make a thorough analysis for each of these: (1) the

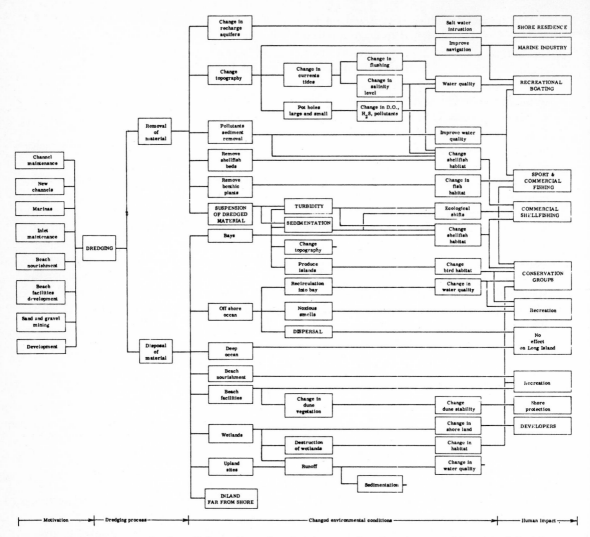

Figure 2.14   A typical effects linkage shows the disturbance web and environmental impacts of dredging. (SOURCE: Reference 17.)

project area, (2) the immediately adjacent ecosystem, and (3) the wider area ecologically affected by the project, for the following situations: (*a*) under optimal conditions (without any human interference); (*b*) as they presently exist, having been influenced by society; (*c*) as they will be affected by other activities occurring or expected to occur (cumulative impact); (*d*) as they will be affected by the project itself (e.g., by dredging, filling, or construction); (*e*) as they will be affected by each of the various

alternatives to the project, as proposed; (*f*) as they will be affected by combinations of secondary activities induced by the project or its alternatives (e.g., road construction and use, bridge construction, installation and maintenance of utilities, commercial activities, pest control operations, navigation and its maintenance).

The essential components of the ecosystems to be affected by any proposed project should be investigated to (1) determine their present status, (2) predict changes

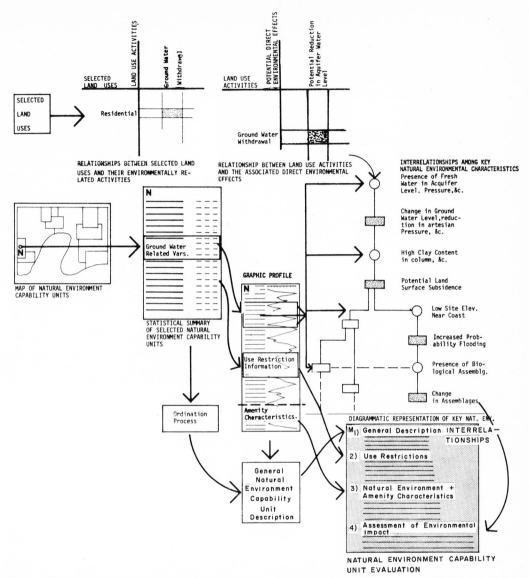

Figure 2.15   Diagrammatic representation of natural environmental capability. (SOURCE: Reference 18.)

that would be caused by *construction* of the proposed project, and (3) predict changes caused by *operation* (or occupancy) of the project.

The impact of the project on the full range of public benefits that depend on the natural values of an ecosystem should be estimated, along with the degree to which these values are to be diminished for the people who, to varying degrees, depend on

them—for example, the extent to which the food chain may be interrupted before the commercial and sport fisheries in the area become depleted. Of course, such a measurement should be based on the best scientific evidence and an objective appraisal of public needs, requirements, and desires. Whether the predicted level of impact is socially acceptable will be a policy decision that goes to the heart of the question of whether the

POSSIBLE USE RESTRICTIONS / ENVIRONMENTAL EVENTS	1. Aesthetics	2. Commercial Fishing	3. Mining	4. Mariculture	5. Transportation	6. Utilities	7. Recreation	8. Residential Construction	9. Preservation of Fish & Wildlife
1. BOD		●		●			●		●
2. Dissolved Oxygen		●		●			●		●
3. Nutrients		●		●			●		●
4. Pathogens		●		●			●		●
5. Floatables	●	●		●	●		●		●
6. Odors and Tastes	●	●		●			●		●
7. Color	●	●		●			●		●
8. Toxicity		●		●			●		●
9. Dissolved Salts		●	●	●			●		●
10. Suspended Solids	●	●		●			●		●
11. Radiological		●		●			●		●
12. Temperature		●		●		●	●		●
13. pH Buffering		●	●	●			●		●
14. Ground Water				●					●

(WATER QUALITY)

Figure 2.16   Matrix that relates selected human activities and water quality effects; dots in cells identify predicted interactions. (SOURCE: Adapted from Reference 19.)

public interest would be unduly threatened by a private action. The purpose is to look broadly at the functions and values of the ecosystems affected and to predict the consequences of any general degradation of these ecosystems on estuarine and ocean resources important to society.

Accumulated Effects

It is particularly important in impact assessment to predict the expected combination of past, present, and future effects so that approvals are not issued piecemeal upon the appearance of low impact of each single project under consideration. There should be an advance planning element in any impact assessment to ensure that addition of the effects of the present project to those of past and future ones does not, by accumulation, result in an unacceptable impact.

The following example of the effects of Watergate Village on the Back Creek–Spa Creek system (Annapolis, Maryland) puts the problem of accumulated effects into focus:[20]

The proposed facility itself would have negligible direct adverse effects on the Back Creek region, but viewed as an increment to the overall demands for development of the region the facility portends significant environmental degradation. There is evidence that storm-water run-off may be a major contributor to deterioration of water quality. The upper shore is probably as fully developed as it should be in view of its contribution to water pollution from storm drains; any increase in paved areas on the lower shore will lead to increased pollution unless alternative provision is made for disposal of storm run-off.

The growing boat population also poses a threat to water quality. At the present time approximately 1350 boats occupy and move about in a water area of 440,000 sq m or 326 sq m per boat. If 400 boats were added, the water area per boat would be reduced to 251 sq m . . . . Although it is true that boating might not result in discharge of any waste into the water, in fact it appears that it does. There are no effective prohibitions on the discharge of human wastes, and discharges of chemicals and oil regularly occur. Intensive boating on Spa Creek in Annapolis has contributed to persistent violations of the water quality criteria set by the state during the late spring and summer,[21] and there is every indication that more intensive boat usage, when combined with storm-water run-off, would have a similar impact on Back Creek.

Hence, when viewed as one increment to the overall development of Back Creek, the Watergate Village project would exacerbate two problems. First, if the number of boats moored in Back Creek continues to proliferate, the creek will be overcrowded. Lost-time costs will be imposed on the boaters, safety hazards will increase, and, in general, the quality of their recreational experience will be diminished. Moreover, if private mooring slips are permitted to proliferate, this will work at cross-purposes to provision of public access to Back Creek. Second, the increase in boat traffic, which the Watergate Village facility would occasion, would degrade water quality in Back Creek.

Regulatory agencies have ample powers to review the Watergate Village proposal and to determine whether it is in the public interest. Indeed the regulatory structure seems a labyrinth of duplicative and redundant decision making. At the federal level, the Corps of Engineers is charged with overall review of the project's acceptability, and the EPA and the Department of Interior have what often amounts to a veto on project approval. The state has authority to prohibit projects which will have a deleterious effect on wetlands or water quality. At the local level the city engineer is to assure that sediment resulting from construction is controlled and that the facility will be structurally sound; the port wardens are to preserve navigation and prevent boat-traffic congestion; and the City Council of Annapolis is to assure that the structure is compatible with the zoning plan for the city.

Notwithstanding the profusion of regulatory activity, the existing decision process seems inadequate to effectively evaluate the Watergate Village proposal. Present procedures are not well designed to permit analysis of the project as an increment to the overall development of Back Creek.

The type of accumulated water pollution effects that have resulted from contamination of land runoff is shown in Table 2.5. According to a study of this matter in Florida:[22]

The highest concentration of total dissolved metals . . . is adjacent to cultivated areas. . . . The severalfold increase in the metal content of the Barron River canal relative to the concentration levels in water from the undeveloped area suggests that heavy metals applied to farmed fields are introduced into the drainage

Table 2.5 Total dissolved-metal content of south Florida canal water (SOURCE: Reference 22)

Metal	Undeveloped area	Developed area	Developed undeveloped
Mn	4.2	29.0	6.9
Co	0.8	34.0	42.5
Cu	1.4	4.7	3.4
Zn	1.7	14.6	8.6
Cd	0.4	2.8	7.0
Pb	0.7	12.0	17.1

Table 2.6   Definition of planning subarea boundaries according to the potential geographical extent of the cumulative impacts (SOURCE: Reference 23)

Cumulative Impact Problems	Boundary Definition Criteria For Cumulative Impact Area
(1) Capacity of water and sewer systems	Jurisdictional boundary of water or sewer district and/or projected boundary of service area if existing available surface or groundwater reserves are developed
(2) Capacity of coastal highways	Existing highway service areas (Rts. 1 and 101); location of trip generation sources which are coastal dependent
(3) The quality of coastal estuaries in relationship to land use activities within the watershed	Major watershed boundary and sub-watershed boundaries (Central Coastal Commission)
(4) Scenic quality of coastal landscapes	Viewshed from existing coastal highways and/or lands with view of the ocean
(5) Socio-economic composition of communities and associated land uses	Jurisdictional boundaries and/or census tract boundaries (city, county) in urban areas; in rural areas, the edge of isolated communities defines a boundary or census tract
(6) Retention of coastal dependent and coastal related agriculture	Ownership boundaries of existing croplands and boundaries of potential croplands as shown on SCS Soil Surveys

system; thus the agricultural region constitutes a source of heavy metals for the Everglades estuaries to the south. All six metals studied are applied to farmed fields in pesticides and nutritional sprays, and in fertilizers to correct micro-nutrient deficiencies. Each of these metals is used in varying quantities, depending on the type of crop, season, disease, or deficiency to be corrected.

When viewed in the broader context of the needs for total coastal zone impact prediction, the problem becomes very complex indeed (Table 2.6). For example, the following six types of cumulative impact phenomena have been identified as problems of

sufficient magnitude and occurrence to require some measure of control by implementation of regional management in California:[23]

1. The capacity of water and sewage systems.
2. The capacity of coastal highways.
3. The ecological quality of estuaries in relationship to land-use activities within the watershed.
4. The scenic quality of coastal landscapes.
5. The socioeconomic compositions of communities and their associated land uses.
6. The retention of coastal-dependent and coastal-related agriculture.

DISTURBANCES FROM DIRECT DISCHARGE OF POLLUTANTS

The most damaging form of pollution is the chronic release of contaminants that insidiously degrade the coastal ecosystem. There may be no large fish kills or other dramatic evidence of harm, but only a pervasive and continuous degradation of the system manifested by an apparent and somewhat mysterious decline in its carrying capacity. The source will probably be liquid waste discharges from domestic waste products, industrial waste materials of all degrees of chemical complexity, cooling water with its thermal load, or organic waste. They alter carrying capacity of the coastal ecosystem in a great variety of ways.

The major sources of estuarine pollution have been summarized as follows:[2]

1. Those associated with the extent of development of the estuarine zone, including waste discharges from municipalities and industries, and land runoff from these as well as agricultural enterprises (Figure 2.17).
2. Those associated with particular activities of great pollutional significance, specifically dredging and filling, watercraft operation, underwater mining, and heated effluent discharges.
3. External sources having impact derived through flow regulation and upstream water quality.

In this brief section we review the effects of wastes from *point sources*, those collected and discharged from specific conveyances such as pipes or discharge canals. The more general diffuse sources of pollution are discussed in the following section on shorelands. As mentioned previously, the problems of point-source discharge are considered only superficially in this book because the requirements of the elaborate federal–state system for control of such pollutants are by now well known to most interested parties.

Figure 2.17 Drainage of agricultural land should be carefully managed to prevent pollution of coastal waters. (Photo by U.S. Department of Agriculture.)

Associated with the major metropolitan developments are large numbers of industrial complexes with their attendant waste products. Many of these *industrial wastes,* especially from the chemical industry, are of such a complicated nature that it is difficult both to identify them and to assess their effects on the receiving streams. Only 1000 of the more than 200,000 manufacturing plants in the coastal states account for 97 percent of the total liquid wastes discharged (1968 data).[2]

Among the waste products that are frequently introduced into the estuarine environment are some directly toxic to marine organisms. *Toxic materials* may exhibit a short, catastrophic impact or a more subtle long-term interference with growth and reproduction processes. The end result is to create a biological desert in which few organisms can prosper and the carrying capacity is greatly diminished.[2]

The salts of *heavy metals* are relatively soluble and stable in solution. Consequently, they will persist for extended lengths of time. Many of them are highly toxic to the aquatic biota, and since many marine organisms exhibit the ability to accumulate and concentrate substances within their cell structures, the presence of these metals from industrial waste discharge, even in small concentrations, can have deleterious effects.[2]

The addition of large quantities of *heat* from industrial cooling water constitutes a form of pollution that must be considered. The entire ecosystem may be stressed by thermal pollution (Figure 2.18).[2]

One of the major constituents of municipal sewage and many industrial wastes is *decomposable organic material.* Such materials consist primarily of carbohydrates from plants and paper, manufacturers' proteins from animal matter, and miscellaneous fats and oils. The decomposable organics are not

Figure 2.18   Thermal discharges from power plants unprotected by closed cycle cooling cause heavy stress to estuarine ecosystems (Moss Landing, California). (Photo by author.)

Table 2.7   Relative use of municipal treatment plants by major industrial categories (SOURCE: Reference 24)

Industries with Substantial Use of Municipal Plants(1)	Industries with Minimal Use of Municipal Plants (2)
Meat Processing	Mining (all types)
Dairy Processing	Petroleum & Gas Extraction
Canned and Preserved Fruits and Vegetables (3)	Sugar (except refining)
Grain Milling	Seafood Processing
Brewing	Iron and Steel
Textiles	Ferroalloys
Rubber Processing	Nonferrous Metals
Leather Tanning	Water Supply
Metal Finishing	Steam Electric Power

(1)   Generally more than 70 percent of plants or production capacity to municipal system.
(2)   Generally less than 10 percent of plants or production capacity to municipal system.
(3)   An estimated 40 percent of plants discharge to municipal system.

necessarily detrimental per se but exert a secondary effect by reducing the amount of dissolved oxygen in the water. The level of dissolved oxygen is one direct index of the health of the system. High levels are generally indicative of a healthy system that will support a diverse biota and multiple uses. The lower the concentration of dissolved oxygen, the lower the carrying capacity of the system becomes.[2]

Municipal wastes often contain significant amounts of industrial wastes, which may add to the variability and complexity of the wastes discharged (Table 2.7). Municipal waste discharges have four important effects on receiving-water quality: the depletion of dissolved oxygen, and the introduction of pathogenic organisms, settleable material, and inorganic nutrients.[2]

Occasionally, animals are killed by a sudden oxygen drop, but the usual effect is to impair their health or, if they are mobile, to drive them away. An example is the blockage of fish spawning migrations in the Delaware River, where greatly reduced oxygen near Philadelphia eliminated striped bass spawning (Figure 2.19). Occasionally,

whole areas of ocean coast can be affected by oxygen depletion, as exemplified by the southwest Florida situation of 1974:[26]

In brief, oxygen was depleted in bottom Gulf waters up to 8 km [5 miles] offshore the area from Boca Grande to Sarasota, Florida, in summer and fall of 1974. The initial external manifestation (mid-July) of this problem was abnormal crab behavior; unusually large numbers of crabs were noted swimming at the surface and crabs climbed on bathers, seemingly in an effort to leave the water. Minor crab kills occurred in late July and in August, and there were isolated reports of evacuations of crabs from the waters. A massive kill of marine fauna occurred off Sarasota on August 21st, encompassing many types of organisms including fishes, echinoderms, crustaceans, coelenterates, cephalopods, annelids and mollusks. Great numbers of distressed crabs, and fishes exhibiting signs of hypoxia, were concentrated at the shorelines in evacuation efforts.

One of the many unfavorable effects of municipal and some industrial wastes is the contamination of the receiving environment with bacteria, viruses, and other organisms of public health significance. *Pathogenic*

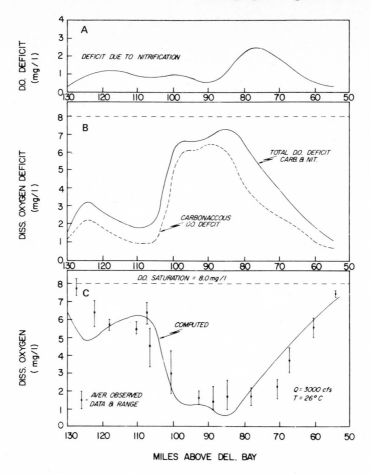

Figure 2.19 Delaware River. Oxygen deficit in the water results from excess discharges of nitrogen (A) and from excess nitrogen plus organic matter (B). The residual oxygen concentration (C) is far below the minimum federal standard for oxygen of 4.0 milligrams per liter or parts per thousand (ppt) of water along 30 miles of the river. (SOURCE: Reference 25.)

organisms, especially those from the intestines of warm-blooded animals, frequently persist for sufficient periods of time and distance to pose a threat to the health and well-being of unsuspecting water users. Secondary chances of exposure to these organisms exist through the contamination of shellfish which can be harvested for food.[2]

One of the greatest threats to the estuarine ecosystem is the ever-present chance for a *catastrophic oil spill* or release of other hazardous materials. The large volumes of petroleum and chemical products transported through the estuarine zone by ships, barges, pipelines, and railroads present a continuing opportunity for accidental bulk spills. The consequences of these spills depend on the amount and type of material released and the characteristics of the receiving water.[2]

The effect of any pollutant on an estuarine environment depends on where it goes, how strong it is, and how rapidly it is assimilated or flushed out of the environment. All of these conditions depend on water movement and circulation patterns, which are in turn governed by the relationship of tide and river flow to estuarine shape and size.[2]

Although estuarine water is in motion because of tidal action, the resultant flow may be mostly reciprocal, rather than directional, and the process of discharge to the ocean may be slow in nonstratified estuaries. Conversely, the subsurface landward flow of a stratified estuary may propel pollutants suspended in the lower layer toward the productive upper estuary. Management programs will often require specific studies by appropriate experts of the patterns of each water body, such as the details of flow pattern, velocity, and flushing rate.

From the preceding discussion it is apparent that particular characteristics of aquatic ecosystems govern their capacities to absorb impacts. Two important characteristics are (1) the *contamination potental*, the probability that pollutants discharged into any water body will accumulate to damaging levels: and (2) the *turbidity potential*, the probability that sediments deposited on the bottom will be resuspended by the action of boats (or natural forces) to cause turbidity or eutrophication. Both are controlled by water basin configuration (page 000). The contamination potential of a water body is a function of its capacity (length, width, and depth) and the rate of exchange (flushing) of its waters. The turbidity potential of a water body is a function of its depth (propwash effect), the thickness of the layer of sediments over the firm bottom, and the fineness of these sediments.

DISTURBANCES FROM SHORELAND WATERSHED DISCHARGES

A major source of disturbance of coastal ecosystems is alteration of the quality, the volume, and the rate (or schedule) of the flow of water discharged from coastal watersheds into coastal water basins. It is clear that the connection between shorelands and coastal water basins is primarily through the flow of runoff water.

Shorelands are defined as including all of the coastal watershed. A coastal watershed is a drainage basin immediately adjacent to coastal waters that is composed of lands all or some of which drain directly into coastal waters, and does not include lands of drainage basins that drain wholly into freshwater channels tributary to coastal waters.

Estuarine ecosystems extend landward to include any freshwater wetlands and drainage areas that provide storage and control systems that absorb the heavy seasonal rains and slowly release the accumulation in surface and subsurface flow through floodplains or wetlands and ultimately into open waters of the estuaries. Each section of the system filters physically and chemically, the water in transit, removing sediments, utilizing some of the nutrients, and finally releasing high-quality fresh water into the estuary at a reasonably uniform and seasonable rate that avoids the stress of rapid salinity change. Thus, in its unaltered state, the system is self-sustaining, providing for a cleansing of the water, a beneficial flow regime, and a suitable natural supply of nutrients into the rich estuarine zone.

Disturbances of the shoreland watersheds that significantly affect the *quality*, the *volume*, or the *rate of flow* of runoff coastal waters must be presumed to have the *potential* for adverse effects on coastal ecosystems. Such alterations of the pattern of freshwater inflow may interfere with a coastal ecosystem by causing changes in water circulation, flushing rate, salinity balance, sediment transport, or the natural supply of nutrients from upstream. These changes, in turn, affect the physical makeup of the estuarine zone and hence its plant and animal life.

A great variety of activities in the coastal watershed have the potential to seriously impair the quality of the freshwater discharge to the estuary. The quality of the watershed discharge may be degraded by runoff from land surfaces contaminated with a variety of industrial, agricultural, logging, commercial, or household residues; together,

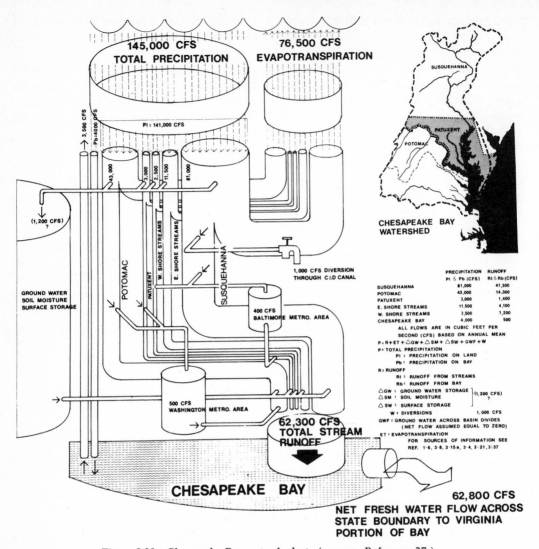

Figure 2.20   Chesapeake Bay water budget. (SOURCE: Reference 27.)

these diffuse sources are termed *nonpoint sources* (as opposed to point sources of pollution, which originate with piped or channeled discharges).

The most serious nonpoint pollution problems often result from persistent erosion of soil, from nitrogen fertilizers and biocides applied to the landscape, and from nitrogen and other nutrients and toxic substances in watershed discharges. Estuaries are the termini for coastal watershed drainage systems, and as such they tend to concentrate water-borne materials carried off the land. Although the national focus on pesticides has caused a marked shift away from the use of hard ones such as DDT, the dependence of agriculture on pesticides (including insecticides, fungicides, and herbicides) will not only continue but even increase in the future. However, there has been too little recognition of the serious harm done to coastal systems by runoff fertilizers and sediment.

Urbanization and water control projects (impoundment or diversion of water) for

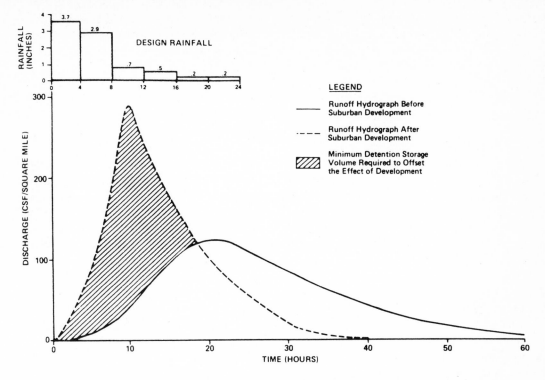

Figure 2.21   Typical storm runoff hydrographs, before and after development. (SOURCE: Reference 28.)

agricultural, domestic, or industrial use (Figure 2.20) often lead to an overall reduction of the freshwater input to an estuary and essentially shrink the size of its diluted brackish upper end—the biologically richest part—thus reducing its capacity to support life (page 18). Even if the volume of the freshwater input remains the same over the year, a significant change in the natural timing, or rhythm, of stream flow has adverse effects by disrupting salinity-related functions of species that are tuned to this rhythm, such as breeding, migration, defense against predators, and feeding (page 23).

Clearing coastal watershed lands of vegetation and covering them with impervious surfacing cause major disturbances in the quality, volume, and rate of flow of freshwater discharges into estuarine systems (Figure 2.21). Quality is lowered because clearing reduces the ability of watershed land surfaces to hold back runoff for cleansing

through soil infiltration and vegetative removal of contaminants. Paving and associated storm drains also short-circuit runoff, and the ensuing "surge" flows carry higher concentrations of contaminated sediment and other pollutants. In addition, paving and storm drains accelerate runoff and prevent soil infiltration and recharge of the groundwater aquifers that regulate the flow of runoff to streams, as well as filtering and cleansing the water as it slowly percolates through the soil toward the stream.

The total volume of fresh water delivered to the estuary may be increased if a lesser fraction is transpired by vegetation to the atmosphere or if a lesser fraction is evaporated to the atmosphere because the water moves to rivers faster over cleared land. The rate of flow of runoff may be altered by land clearing and paving, either by modifying surface runoff patterns or by reducing the capability of the land to store and regularize the release of precipitation, thus producing "surge" flows of water into the estuary. While a large, long-term increase in fresh water can overwhelm a small estuary, turning it into a virtual lake, even a small increase can disrupt the salinity balance of an estuary and the life processes of the organisms that depend on it. The higher the amounts of paved surface, the more rapidly the runoff surges into coastal waters. In typical single-family developments zoned at one dwelling unit per acre, impervious surface can run as high as 15 to 20 percent of the gross land acreage (with 5-acre single-family zoning the average will be 3 to 5 percent).

Except for certain flatlands, like the Florida Everglades, surface flow occurs only intermittently after rainfall. Problems with contamination of coastal waters from urban runoff typically start with surface flow over paved areas and other impervious surfaces. The best strategy for preserving the normal hydraulic regime is to permit this runoff water to flow through vegetation in order to stabilize its flow, to provide for natural removal of contaminants, and to enable it to percolate into the ground. This can be accomplished by appropriate land grading to control the surface water and to divert its flow through natural vegetated drainageways. Suitable vegetated buffer strips along the coastal shoreline provide for the cleansing of runoff water before it reaches coastal water basins, through vegetative "scrubbing" and infiltration through the soil.

The soil itself has a large capacity for water storage when its surface is vegetated, open, and permeable. It can then serve as a primary flow stabilizer. Underground water moves very slowly down to coastal waters, allowing time for removal of pollutants by natural purification. The benefit of this natural process is enhanced by minimizing any interference with the infiltration of water into the soil, such as occurs when the surface is covered with impervious materials.

Depending on the amount of intended development in a watershed area, additional buffer area width must be provided to offset the progressive effects of runoff contamination and unbalancing of rates and periodicity of runoff associated with increasing development. This leads to a basic management goal: *The higher the degree of development, the greater is the need to provide vegetative buffer areas along drainageways.*

The effects on coastal waters, especially estuaries, of drainage of shorelands must be emphasized in particular. When portions of the coastal watershed system are disrupted or short circuited by uncontrolled drainage or development, the natural flow pattern is disrupted, the water-cleansing function of the vegetation is eliminated, and freshwater flow into the estuaries occurs in surges. Not only do the resulting surge flows overburden estuaries with fresh water, but also at the

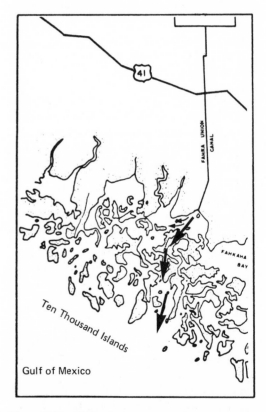

Figure 2.22 Fahka Union Bay and Canal, Collier County, Florida (main route of freshwater discharge shown by arrows). (SOURCE: Reference 31.)

same time they deprive land areas of water. Such alteration of seasonal discharges was observed to have six adverse effects on an estuary in Florida (Rookery Bay):[30]

1. Abrupt changes in salinity.
2. Increases in turbidity.
3. Increases in total phosphates.
4. Decreases in dissolved oxygen.
5. Dramatic increases in BOD.
6. Dramatic increases in coliform and fecal coliform bacteria count.

Alteration of the coastal watershed system may also reduce nutrient uptake. For example, a large canal in southwest Florida forces water so rapidly through Fahka Union Bay that the mangrove system has a reduced opportunity to assimilate the nutrients in the water and to store them for use at times of slow discharge (Figure 2.22). Because an unbalancing of the system is involved, one must start with a presumption that the natural condition is optimal and should be maintained unless there is substantial evidence to the contrary.

Any channelization and drainage of lowlands must be presumed to have negative effects on coastal living resources in the absence of contrary evidence. The value of coastal fisheries and recreational resources and the need to preserve coastal ecosystems mandate that drainage be controlled. It is recognized that this priority may foreclose the potential for agriculture, housing, and other uses in certain coastal areas unless technical solutions can be found. Attempts to find a technically suitable method for water balance restoration in large-scale agricultural drainage enterprises in North Carolina have not succeeded because of two problems: (1) colloidal substances released in dredging the drainage canals tend not to settle in treatment ponds, and (2) no economic way has been found of storing stormwater runoff to simulate the retention of the undrained soil in the interest of maintaining the natural salinity regime (Figure 2.23).

Channels that convey fresh water to coastal areas also may function in the reverse, that is, to convey salt water inland. The intrusion of salt water upstream in artificial canals often has serious adverse effects on inland systems, rendering the water unsuitable for native fish and wildlife. Seawater encroachment can contaminate human and agricultural water supplies, necessitating costly treatment or relocation of intake points. Increased salinity in the upstream environment results in increased corrosion and shorter life expectancy for engineering structures.

In respect to any proposed drainage schemes for the shorelands, it must be presumed that the natural pattern of drainage is the most favorable to the coastal ecosystem. The appropriate management goal is: *The system of land drainage in coastal watersheds should be retained in a form as near to the natural pattern as possible.*

Man-made lakes in the shorelands may precipitate serious pollution problems. Accumulated loading of the lakes in the interior wetlands from sewage wastes, fertilizer–pesticide runoff, and sediments will lead to gross pollution over a period of years and to rancidity of lake waters. Lake pollution is a delayed reaction problem whose true dimensions do not become apparent until several years after the lake is dug and its shores fully occupied.

DISTURBANCE OF COASTAL WATER BASINS

Coastal ecosystem management should be sensitive to the important effects of different patterns of circulation (page 128) and classes of water basins (page 125). Strong constraints on shoreland development and point-source discharges are imposed by the natural peculiarities of the different types. For example, any alteration that reduces water movement in an embayment with existing poor circulation and rate of flush-

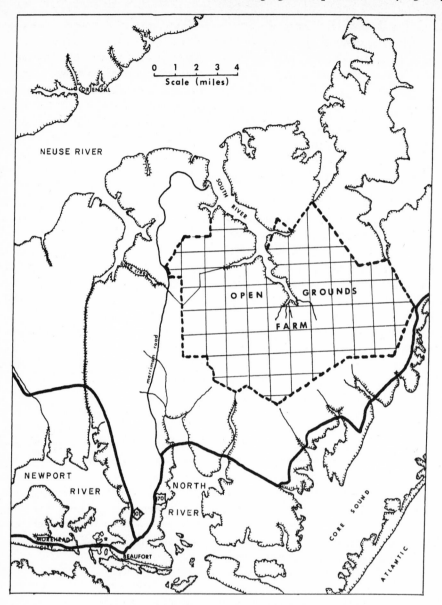

Figure 2.23 Unfortunate site of proposed 45,000-acre reclamation for crop and grazing land in North Carolina, which has been delayed because of expected problems of pollution and upset of the freshwater balance of the coastal ecosystem. (SOURCE: Reference 32.)

ing has a high potential for serious adverse effects (page 127).

The combined influences of freshwater flow, tidal action, wind, and oceanic forces result in the specific pattern of water movement or circulation found in the estuarine system. Tide is usually the dominant force

in water movement. Its amplitude varies within the system, decreasing inward from the ocean through the estuaries and into the tributaries. Water movement also varies with the shape, size, and even the bottom material of individual parts of the system. Circulation forces tend to be lesser and flushing rates poorer when tidal amplitudes are low and the basin is deep. Any disruption of flow that seriously reduces flushing allows a buildup of pollution and also may permit the salinity to increase to levels that will be adverse to the biota.

Flushing Rate Considerations

In *bays, embayments,* and *tidal rivers* with layered or stratified flow (page 000), the accumulation, concentration, and dispersal of pollutants are functions of the combined rates of flow of the two layers. Generally, the typical stratified estuary is less vulnerable to pollution than its opposite—lagoons and other estuaries of mixed or unstratified type—because flushing of pollutants is more rapid. However, the bottom flow can recycle pollutants that sink, sending them inward to the upper estuary. Also the saltier water moving inland at the bottom returns sediment toward the land, dropping it at the head of the estuary and thus causing shoaling and restriction of flow.

In estuarine *lagoons* (shallow basins with little freshwater inflow and restricted openings) wind is often the only force effectively driving circulation, in both the process of mixing and that of inducing currents. Lagoons are often poorly flushed and quite vulnerable to a buildup of contaminants and to other ecological disturbances.

In management programs, lagoons need a maximum of protective controls. These controls may include wide buffer strips above wetlands; no direct discharge of septic tank, sewage plant, or storm drain effluents; maximum safeguards against runoff of fertilizers, biocides, soils, and so forth; and restrictions on industrial activity. Boat traffic may have to be controlled to prevent turbidity from agitation of sediments, damage to grass beds, and boat pollution. Generally the size of the lagoon dictates the severity of controls, smaller lagoons requiring the most extensive restrictions.

Alteration of Basin Configuration

A number of projects and activities in the estuarine basin have the potential to significantly alter the natural pattern of circulation and flushing and would be presumed to be adverse, such as (1) restricting flow through inlets and passes by constricting them with bridges, causeways, or bulkheads; (2) impeding water flow with "spoil banks" of disposed dredged material; (3) diverting water flow by channel dredging; and (4) altering water flow patterns by the encroachment of bridges, piers, trestles, and fills into coastal waters (Figure 2.24). For example, the lengthening of the Sebastian Inlet jetty (Indian River area, Florida east coast) caused "a widespread change in the salinity period."[34]

Interruption of water circulation appears to be the most serious of the various effects from alteration of the water basin. The appropriate Ecosystem Management Rule concerning water basins is: *Any change in the configuration of the coastal water basin from structure or excavation that reduces water circulation is presumed to be detrimental and should be avoided* (No. 10).

Disturbance

The excavation of bottom material through dredging is performed to create and maintain canals, navigation channels, turning basins, harbors, and marinas. In addition dredging is used for laying pipeline and for obtaining material for fill or construction (Figure 2.25).

Dredge-and-fill activities adversely affect the coastal ecosystem in a variety of ways. Among the potential effects of dredging are the following: (1) to create short- and long-term changes in water currents, circulation, mixing, flushing, and salinity; (2) to add to water turbidity, siltation, and pollution; and (3) to lower the dissolved oxygen. Submerged bottoms and coastal wetlands and tidelands, along with their associated organ-

Figure 2.24   Bridge pilings that slow water flow adversely affect coastal ecosystems (Mobile, Alabama). (Photo by author.)

isms, are often obliterated by dredging. Dredging also produces spoil, which must be disposed of on some natural habitat, and filling requires that some natural area be dredged as a source of the fill material; thus such operations may cause a twofold destruction of habitat.

Uncontrolled removal, transportation, and deposition of sediment creates and disperses large quantities of silt and debris that settle on the bottom of coastal water basins.[36] Silty estuarine sediments act as a pollutant trap, or "sink." Many kinds of pollutants, including heavy metals and pesticides, are *adsorbed* onto the sediments. Dredging operations resuspend these in the water column, increasing the hazard of exposure to plants and animals. The silt suspension may also increase nutrient release, leading to eutrophic blooms. As silt deposits from dredging accumulate in the estuary, they form a "false bottom," characterized by shifting,

unstable sediments. These altered bottoms, fill deposits, and spoil areas may never be repopulated by the normal biota. For example, the larvae of some bottom-dwelling molluscs such as oysters and certain crustaceans will not settle on soft sediments.[37]

The kind of general ecological disruption that results from dredging in combination with other improperly controlled development activities is exemplified by the disturbance shared by the connecting estuaries—Back Bay and Currituck Sound—of Virginia and North Carolina. The bottoms of the two waterways (particularly Back Bay) became grossly blanketed with silt because of extensive erosion of nearby farmland channeled to the estuary by drainage canals and by dredging in the basin; as described in the following:[38]

There is no doubt, in my opinion, that major dredging activities in the Back Bay–Currituck

Sound area were instrumental in starting the chain of events resulting in excessive turbidities, silt deposits, and large, nonvegetated areas. The problem is complicated by the history of salt water, plant disease, and other factors.

Aside from the problems that turbidity causes in limiting sunlight, thus retarding photosynthesis by the plants, the deep silt deposits themselves are a principal limiting factor on aquatic growth. A seedling plant rooted in 2 to 3 inches of semiliquid silt has a very tenuous anchorage, and the frequent winds rarely enable any plants to secure their roots in the firmer subsoils beneath the silt in the large open water areas.

There is no doubt that these semiliquid silts are quickly resuspended after sufficient intensity and duration of wind. Once resuspended, many factors determine the duration of suspension. The frequency, direction, velocity, and dura-

tion of the wind, water temperature, CO_2 content, water salinity, rainfall, exposure to the site, depth of the water, currents, vegetation abundance, etc., all interact to determine degree and duration of turbidity.

Of all the forms of estuarine life affected by dredging, oysters are perhaps the most immediately vulnerable because they are sedentary creatures. The oyster chooses its home for life when it is a tiny larva, $\frac{1}{3}$ inch long. Oyster larvae hatch from floating eggs in early summer to drift about with the current until they find on the bottom a suitable firm object to which they attach themselves for the rest of their lives. A deposit of $\frac{1}{20}$ inch of silt on shell or rocks from dredging is enough to make attachment impossible for young oysters. And once they have found a clean solid surface for attachment,

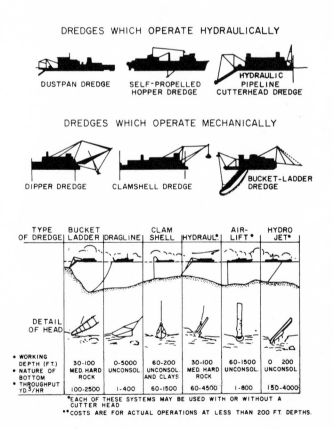

Figure 2.25   Basic dredge types and methods of marine ore exploitation. (SOURCE: Reference 35.)

Figure 2.26   Rocky oceanfronts are rugged and resistant to adverse impacts (California coast). (Photo by author.)

they have no chance at all to escape a dredge or a suffocating blanket of silt. The Chesapeake oyster industry has suffered more damage than any other: in 1880, 72 million pounds of oysters were harvested from Chesapeake Bay; by 1920 the yield had dropped to 31 million, and recently to around 8 million. This loss cannot be blamed entirely on siltation, of course.

Bottoms deepened by dredging below the depth of light penetration cannot support grasses or algae.[38] The stagnant waters in artificially deepened areas or man-made basins have reduced oxygen and act as sediment traps. These sediments lower water quality and productivity in three ways: (1) the area itself is unproductive; (2) low-quality water slowly leaches out, affecting neighboring waters; and (3) during storms large volumes of accumulated debris and anaerobic sediments may be flushed out,

causing a sudden reduction of water quality and consequent stress to surrounding organisms.[37]

Marginal Areas

Because basin margins vary so greatly in structure, widely different management problems are associated with different types.

Rocky oceanfronts are rugged and do not have delicate and easily damaged tidal areas (Figure 2.26). Sand beaches themselves are also tough and resilient and thus are damaged severely only by the removal of sand (page 142).

In contrast, the dunes lying just behind sandy beaches are fragile and easily damaged, and require extensive safeguards. When the dunes are damaged so that they erode away, the essential buffer is gone and the whole shore is threatened by each winter storm or hurricane, as explained in the following section on vital areas.

Estuarine shorefronts also require careful management. Much of the estuarine margins consist of vital areas such as wetlands and tideflats (see page 32), and many have seriously eroding banks.

DISTURBANCE OF VITAL AREAS

In the coastal ecosystem three types of ecologically vital areas can be identified—habitat units, productivity units, and structural units. Some vital areas fit only one category; others fit all three. This section is devoted to the major vulnerabilities of the important types of vital areas. It is clear that major damage to coastal ecosystems and severe reduction of carrying capacity can be expected to follow any significant loss or deterioration of vital areas.

Shoreland Vital Areas

The whole of the coastal watershed may be termed an environmentally critical area in some coastal management programs. In most of them it is anticipated that the drainage system and the floodplains would be so classified to provide special recognition that these are particularly sensitive areas. But there are areas that fall into a still higher priority because they are vital not only to the shorelands system but also to the coastal waters ecosystem. These vital areas include those that are essential to protecting the quality of the runoff—the freshwater wetlands, and those that are essential to preserving the structural integrity of the shoreline—the sand dunes.

Freshwater Wetlands

Central to the coastal watershed drainage system are the freshwater wetlands (Figure 2.27). They serve to detain and release run-

Figure 2.27 Freshwater wetlands in coastal watersheds are vital areas and should be protected to conserve coastal ecosystems (West Fremont, Maine). (Conservation Foundation photo by M. Fahay.)

off waters in an acceptable quality, volume, and rate of flow. This is their major value to coastal ecosystems. Although they serve a much wider use to the freshwater regime, we are concentrating here on the coastal waters ecosystem.

Freshwater wetlands are easily obliterated or seriously degraded by filling, by draining, and by diverting their water supply or lowering their water level. They are also lost through impoundment and use for dump sites. All such damaging activities have the potential to interfere with the function of coastal ecosystems and to reduce their carrying capacities.

The freshwater and coastal wetlands are interrelated in two ways. First, freshwater wetlands may lie directly behind and be continuous with coastal wetlands, draining directly into them. Second, while they may be removed from coastal wetlands, freshwater wetlands play an important part in conditioning the drainage flow from the coastal watershed to the estuarine basin. Furthermore, the vitality of a marsh or a mangrove swamp depends on the quality and quantity of freshwater inflow that it receives from the drainage of adjacent shorelands.

The natural drainage pattern fostered by freshwater wetlands is presumed to be beneficial, both in the manner by which waterborne nutrients are delivered to the estuary and in the volume and rate of the delivery. Development that eliminates freshwater wetlands and accelerates runoff results in surge flows that may bypass the marsh or mangrove swamp, carrying nutrients through the estuary too fast for them to yield their full benefit (see Figure 2.22).

Dune and Beach Ridge Systems

Dunes and lesser beach ridges serve as storage areas for sand to replace that eroded by waves or torn away by storms and thus to provide long-term stability to the shorefront (page 570). Because dune formations are fragile, activities of man that cause even slight alterations to them may lead to significant disruptions. Once the barrier dune is weakened, its valuable functions are impaired and it no longer serves its unique protective role.

The values and vulnerabilities of sand dunes may be summarized from Frankenburg et al[39] as follows:

The fragile network of vegetation growing on shifting dunes is adapted to withstanding the rigors of wind, sand, and salt but not human feet, vehicles, or grazing animals. When the mantle of vegetation is broken, the dune movement is accelerated to a point where plant growth cannot keep pace with the shifting sand. The result is a chain reaction which leads to erosion and loss of the shifting frontal dune.

Behind the shifting dunes are the stable dunes, characterized by heavier vegetation—perennial shrubs, trees, and vines. When prolonged drought, storms, or hurricanes periodically erode the shifting dunes, the stable dunes absorb the brunt of the physical forces.

When both shifting and stable dunes are destroyed by man, there is nothing left to stabilize the remaining sea of drifting sand but man himself.

Special risks are attached to development in any shoreland within reach of coastal storm or flood tides. On the open coast the risks are involved mostly with the direct onslaught of storm-driven waves. The sandy ocean beachfront is in dynamic equilibrium between two factors: (1) the erosive forces of storm winds and waves, and (2) the restorative powers of prevailing geological, oceanic, and meteorological actions (Figure 2.28). In response to the interplay of these forces, the whole system of beaches, barrier islands, and dunes shifts more or less continuously. The dunes play a key role.

The great development pressure on dunes and sandy shorefronts often creates a difficult land-use dilemma (Figure 2.29). Although these areas are most desirable loca-

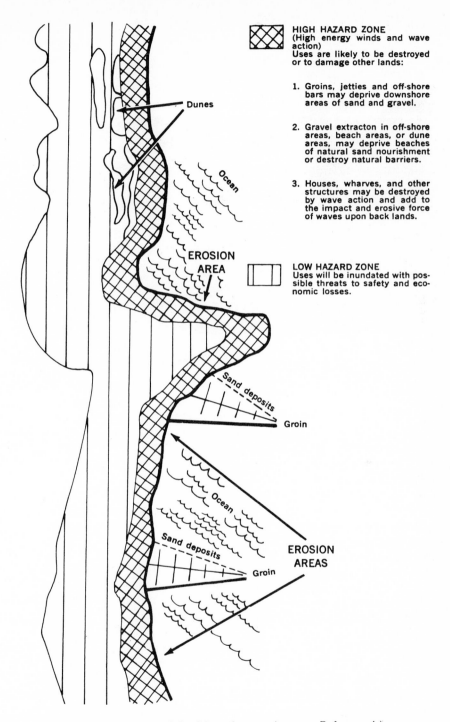

Figure 2.28   Coastal flood hazard zones. (SOURCE: Reference 4.)

97

Figure 2.29   Extensive foot traffic erodes vegetative cover, causing depletion of sand and shrinkage of dunes (Moss Landing, California). (Photo by author.)

tions for homes, they are at the same time environmentally sensitive, and any development of them may set off a chain reaction of events creating large-scale problems. In regard to this situation Frankenburg et al.[39] comment:

The destruction of buildings from tropical hurricanes and prolonged storms, from high seas and shifting sand, has occurred frequently in the past and will certainly occur in the future as long as people continue to build in dune areas. Even buildings on stable dunes are subject to periodic destruction, perhaps only once in fifty years. Conflict between man and nature only reaches intransigent proportions after the buildings are in place and the erosion has begun to occur. Then the disaster funds are called in, and the engineers attempt to stabilize with concrete and granite what the dunes achieved before, substituting seawalls for sea oats in the name of protecting human lives and property while further impairing the basic protective function of the sand dune system. What is so evident is that the trouble could

have been avoided in the first place. Permanent structures should be placed in permanent places, behind the stable dunes where mature trees indicate a permanent environment (Figure 2.30).

Coastal Wetlands

The coastal wetlands serve as an essential habitat, nutrient producer, energy storage unit, water purifier, sediment trap, aesthetic attraction, storm barrier, and shore stabilizer for the ecosystem. If the wetlands vegetation is eliminated, the biotic carrying capacity of the ecosystem is reduced—about 50 percent in a typical case. It is obvious that, as a coastal area becomes more occupied and its resources more heavily used, these benefits become more important. The appropriate Ecosystem Management Rule is: *The higher the degree of shorelands development, the greater is the need to preserve coastal wetlands* (No. 11).

The physical loss of coastal wetlands through filling has been cited frequently as a great detriment to coastal ecosystems because of the great variety of important purposes these wetlands serve. But there are a number of disturbances that significantly degrade coastal marshes and mangrove forests without physically removing or filling them. Ditching, draining, impounding, filling for causeways, or otherwise interfering with normal wetlands drainage has caused significant adverse effects on coastal eco-

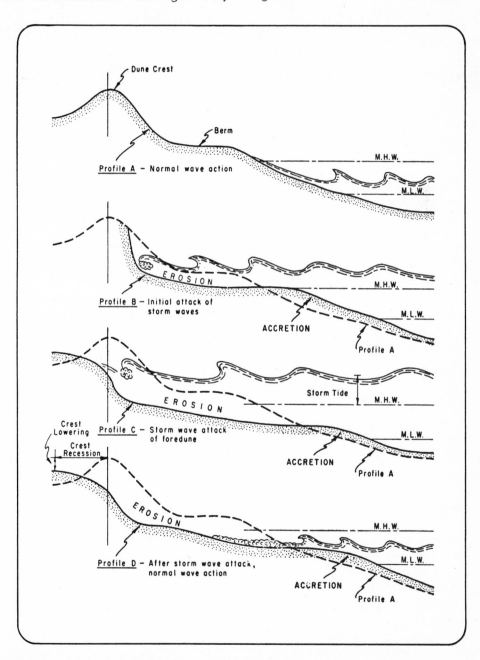

Figure 2.30   Schematic diagram of storm wave attack on beach and dune. (SOURCE: Reference 40.)

Figure 2.31   Roadway and rail line fills alter natural water flows through the marsh (Charleston, South Carolina). (Conservation Foundation photo by M. Fahay.)

system carrying capacity in many parts of the coast (Figure 2.31).

Although wetlands can assimilate a reasonable amount of contaminants, they do have a limit and so must be protected from gross pollution from both land runoff and estuarine sources, and in particular from oil and toxic substances. A polluted marsh is offensive to the senses, whereas a healthy one is an aesthetic resource. Also, nutrient pollution causes marshes to breed an abundance of mosquitoes and other pests.

Tidal Flats

Mud or sand flats are often unappreciated because their values are not visible. Growing evidence suggests, however, that tideflats contribute significantly to estuarine ecosystems (page 34). Therefore they should be protected, in so far as possible, as an integral and valuable part of the system. Changes in existing current flows, sedimentation, and the deposition of dredge spoil alter the bottom and have adverse effects on tidal flats. Pollutants such as sulfite waste liquor (from pulp mill effluent), heated effluents, and sewage are detrimental to tideflat communities. When polluted they may become odorous and unattractive. Consequently, although there is often community pressure to do away with tidal flats, the potential for

converting them to real estate or other economic use is low.

Submerged Grass Beds

Beds of submerged marine grasses are important elements of estuarine systems. They often provide a substantial amount of the primary productivity, nutrient storage, and nursery habitat available in shallow estuarine waters (page 30). They also stabilize bottom sediments and, in general, foster an abundance and diversity of life.

Marine grass beds are easily depleted, being especially vulnerable to pollution of all types, including heat discharged from power plants and the turbidity induced by them.[41] Turbidity from silt and eutrophication screens out light and prevents the growth of grass. Fine sediment (mud) often creates an unstable bottom condition in which the grasses cannot anchor their roots. Boat traffic over grass flats may compound the problem by stirring up the sediments and ripping up the plants.

Loss or degradation of grass bed areas is most detrimental to the ecological health of an estuary. Conversely, there can be too much grass. In estuarine waters that are highly polluted from sewage or urban runoff, grasses can become overdense and a nuisance to boaters, fishermen, and shore owners as they break loose and drift in clumps at the surface (as in Great South Bay, Long Island). Pollution control should provide a solution to overdense growths.

Kelp Beds

Stands of kelp provide critical nursery areas and general habitat for many marine species (page 645). Sewage discharges may be adverse to kelp because the ensuing water enrichment favors the food chain of sea urchins, and they in turn eat the kelp. Other potential dangers are chemical and thermal pollution and damage from boat propellers. Whether the routine harvest of kelp plants to produce algin and other salable chemical compounds is unduly adverse to the kelp bed ecosystem is the subject of a controversy as yet unsettled in California.

Shellfish Beds

Molluscan shellfish are important not only because they provide food but also because shellfish beds are essential elements in the functioning of the whole ecosystem (page 710). Many disturbances are harmful to oysters and other shellfish. For example, silt-laden waters are a harsh environment for their planktonic young stages, and layers of mud make an unsuitable bottom for most of them—even a thin veneer of silt over otherwise clean surfaces prevents oyster larvae from attaching. Freshwater deluges from urbanized coastal watersheds may kill or damage clams and other species.

Molluscan shellfish are notorious for filtering out of the water such harmful substances as bacteria, pesticides, and toxic metals and concentrating them in their tissues, thus often exposing the animals or people that eat them to potentially dangerous concentrations. For this reason about 2 million acres of United States estuarine shellfish beds have been closed to harvesting (page 714). A better solution than closing beds is to control the sources of pollution

to make the shellfish safe for human use and also to maintain the natural balance and general carrying capacity of the ecosystem.

Coral Reefs

Coral reefs provide shelter and abundant food for hundreds of species of fish and a wide variety of invertebrates. They serve many basic ecological functions as an essential element of tropical coastal ecosystems and provide a fundamental barrier to protect the tropical shoreline from storms.

The following impacts have been noted by coral reef expert R. E. Johannes (see page 593):

Suspended sediments, which reduce light penetration, inhibit coral growth. Sediments settling on corals may kill them within a few days if the blanket is thick enough. The planktonic larvae of corals and many other reef invertebrates cannot settle and colonize soft, shifting sediments. Dredging and coastal land filling associated with harbors, marinas, ship channels, etc., and sand removal for construction and beach replenishment have injured or destroyed hundreds of reef communities (Figure 2.32).

Figure 2.32 Silt from turbid or muddy waters caused by dredge-and-fill operations, if carried out to sea, can smother and kill coral reefs. (Conservation Foundation photo by M. Fahay.)

Sewage is probably the second worst form of pollution stress on reef communities (through accelerated effects of eutrophication and oxygen in tropic ecosystems and overgrowth of algae, which can smother corals). Another stress due to bad land management—accelerated runoff of freshwater—has sometimes lowered coastal salinities to the point where shallow reef communities have been completely killed within a few hours. Thermal effluent from power plants has killed corals and associated organisms in Florida, Hawaii, the Virgin Islands, Guam, and elsewhere.

The coral communities of the Florida Keys are at the northernmost extension of the range for coral reefs, and hence the activities mentioned above could place additional stresses on the reefs. Studies have revealed severe damages in certain coral communities of the Florida reef tract.[42] Most notable is the Hen and Chickens patch reef off Plantation Key, in which 82 percent of the reef-building corals are dead.

Breeding, Nursery, Feeding, and Wintering Areas

Many of the important coastal species concentrate in specifically defined areas for breeding. *Breeding areas* vary from species to species, ranging from treetop bird nests to spawning grounds at the bottom of estuaries. These all require special protection. Often the vital breeding areas are so limited in size that a major adverse effect could lead to elimination of much of the spawning and to the virtual demise of the stock breeding there.

Nursery areas are similarly essential and critical to the maintenance of the carrying capacity of a coastal system. Nursery areas are found in wetlands, grass beds, shallow estuarine areas, mangrove swamps, coral reefs, and other habitats (Figure 2.33). All can be degraded by pollution and physical alteration, as we seek to make evident throughout this book.

Figure 2.33   Red mangrove root systems are important nursery habitat for young fish (Eliot Key, Florida). (Conservation Foundation photo by M. Fahay.)

The special places where mobile species gather to feed, include, in addition to many of the fixed vital areas previously identified, a variety of other rich feeding spots in the coastal water basins. All these *feeding areas* are sufficiently important that their loss or degradation through pollution would reduce carrying capacity.

In northern latitudes certain aquatic species cease feeding actively in winter and retire to limited areas where they congregate for "hibernation." When concentrated in these special *wintering areas*, the species are especially vulnerable to environmental dangers—toxic substances, power plant effluents, and so forth (Figure 2.34). Some estuarine species spend the winter buried in specific parts of the bottom, where they can be destroyed by dredging activity or afflicted with bacterial infections acquired from polluted muds.

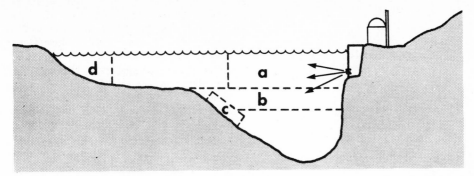

Figure 2.34 Profile of Hudson estuary at the Indian Point nuclear power station, showing areas involved with specific functions of striped bass: a = migration pathway, b = juvenile wintering area, c = adult and adolescent wintering area, and d = nursery area (summer). Arrows indicate discharge of warm effluent that attracts juvenile fish to plant intake in winter, where they are killed by suffocation against intake screens. (SOURCE: Adapted from Reference 43.)

SUMMARY OF ENVIRONMENTAL MANAGEMENT RULES

1. Reduction of the natural supply of nutrients to the coastal ecosystem by alteration of freshwater inflow should be avoided.
2. Excessive discharge of nitrogenous compounds into confined coastal waters must be presumed to have adverse effects and should be avoided.
3. Any significant reduction from the natural concentration of oxygen is presumed to be adverse and should be avoided.
4. Storage components of ecosystems are of extreme value and should always be fully protected.
5. Significant alteration of the natural temperature regime of the coastal ecosystem is presumed adverse and should be avoided.
6. Any significant change from the natural salinity regime is presumed ecologically detrimental and should be avoided.
7. The discharge of suspensible solids to coastal waters is to be presumed adverse and should be avoided.
8. Any reduction or blockage of water flow in or to an estuarine water basin is presumed to be adverse and should be avoided.
9. Any discharge of pathogens or toxic substances into coastal waters is adverse and should be avoided.
10. Any change in the configuration of the coastal water basin from structures or excavation that reduces water circulation is presumed detrimental and should be avoided.
11. The higher the degree of shorelands development, the greater is the need to preserve coastal wetlands.

REFERENCES

1. Samuel M. Hamill, Jr. 1974. *Environmental Profile and Guidelines*. Middletown Environmental Commission, The Township of Middletown, New Jersey.
2. U.S. Department of The Interior. 1970. *The National Estuarine Pollution Study*. U.S. Senate, 91st Congress, 2nd Session, Document No. 91–58. Superintendent of Documents, Government Printing Office, Washington, D.C.
3. City of Bellevue. 1971. *Environmental Focus*. Planning Department, Bellevue, Washington.
4. U.S. Water Resources Council. 1971. *Regulation of Flood Hazard Areas*, Vol. I, Parts I-IV. Washington, D.C.

5. Mark T. Brown. 1975. *An Energetic Analysis of Sanibel Island, Florida.* The Conservation Foundation, Washington, D.C.

6. J. R. Clark and W. Brownell. 1973. *Electric Power Plants in the Coastal Zone: Environmental Issues.* American Littoral Society, Special Publication No. 7. Highlands, New Jersey.

7. John L. Taylor, John R. Hall, and Carl H. Saloman, 1970. "Mollusks and benthic environments in Hillsborough Bay, Florida." *Fishery Bulletin;* Vol. 68, No. 2, pp. 191–202.

8. Federal Water Pollution Control Act Amendments of 1972. U.S. Public Law 92–500.

9. U.S. Environmental Protection Agency. 1973. *Proposed Criteria for Water Quality,* Vol. I. Washington, D.C.

10. National Academy of Science–National Academy of Engineering. 1973. *Water Quality Criteria.* Washington, D.C.

11. National Technical Advisory Commission. 1968. *Water Quality Criteria.* Report to the Secretary of the Interior, Federal Water Pollution Control Administration, Washington, D.C.

12. Norbert A. Jaworski, Leo L. Clark, and Kenneth D. Feigner. 1971. *A Water Resource—Water Supply Study of the Potomac Estuary.* U.S. Environmental Protection Agency, Technical Report 35, Washington, D.C.

13. Stephen V. Smith. 1974. *Environmental Status of Hawaiian Estuaries.* Diffuse Sources Branch, Office of Water and Hazardous Materials, U.S. Environmental Protection Agency, Washington, D.C.

14. George W. Gleeson. 1972. *The Return of a River: The Willamette River, Oregon.* Advisory Committee on Environmental Science and Technology and Water Resources Research Institute, Oregon State University, Corvallis, Oregon.

15. Andrew J. McErlean, Catherine Kerby, and Richard C. Swartz. 1972. "Discussion of the status of knowledge concerning sampling variation, physiologic tolerances, and possible change criteria for Bay organisms." In A. J. McErlean, C. Kerby, and M. L. Wass, Eds., *Biota of the Chesapeake Bay, Supplement: Chesapeake Science,* Vol. 13, December.

16. U.S. Atomic Energy Commission. 1972. *Guide to the Preparation of Environmental Reports for Nuclear Power Plants.* Washington, D.C.

17. U.S. Department of the Interior. 1968. *A Study of the Disposal of Effluent from a Large Desalinization Plant.* R&D Program Report No. 316, Office of Saline Water, Washington, D.C.

18. Rice Center for Community Design and Research. 1974. *Environmental Analysis for Developmental Planning, Chambers County, Texas. Technical Report, Vol. 1: An Approach to Natural Environmental Analysis.* Rice University, Houston, Texas.

19. Office of the Governor. 1973. "Bay and estuarine system management in the Texas coastal zone." In *Project Report Summaries,* Texas Coastal Resource Management Program, Division of Planning Coordination, Austin, Texas.

20. Garrett Power. 1975. "Watergate Village: a case study of a permit application for a marina submitted to the U.S. Army Corps of Engineers." *Coastal Zone Management Journal,* Vol. 2, No. 2, pp. 103–124.

21. N. Dimsdale. 1973. *SPA Creek Water Quality Study.* Final Report (Revised edition), Chesapeake Bay Foundation, Annapolis, Maryland.

22. G. J. Horvath, R. C. Harriss, and H. C. Mattraw. 1972. "Land development and heavy metal distribution in the Florida Everglades." *Marine Pollution Bulletin,* Vol. 3, No. 12, pp. 182–184.

23. Thomas Dickert, Jens Sorensen, and Robert Twiss. 1975. *Managing the Cumulative Impact of Cosatal Development.* Institute of Urban and Regional Development, University of California, Berkeley, California.

24. National Commission on Water Quality. 1975. *Staff Draft Report.* Washington, D.C.

25. Robert V. Thomann. 1972. "The Delaware River—a study in water quality management." In Ray T. Oglesby, Clarence A. Carlson, and James A. McCann, Eds., *River, Ecology and Man.* Academic Press, New York and London.

26. Patricia M. Bird. Mote Marine Laboratory, Sarasota, Florida. Personal communication.

27. J. J. O'Donnell. 1972. *Maryland Chesapeake Bay Study.* Maryland Department of State Planning and The Chesapeake Bay Interagency Planning Commission, Annapolis, Maryland.

28. Ronald L. Wycoff and R. David G. Pyne. 1975. "Urban water management and coastal wetland protection in Collier County, Florida." *Water Resources Bulletin,* Vol. II, No. 3, pp. 455–468.

29. D. R. Storm. 1973. *Hydrologic and Water Quality Aspects of the Tomales Bay Environmental Study.* Storm Engineering and Design Water Management, Davis, California.

30. John R. Clark. 1974. *Rookery Bay: Ecological Constraints on Coastal Development.* The Conservation Foundation, Washington, D.C.

31. M. R. Carter, L. A. Burns, T. R. Cavinders, K. R. Duggan, P. L. Fore, D. B. Hicks, H. L.

Revells, and T. W. Schmidt. 1973. *Ecosystems Analysis of the Big Cypress Swamp and Estuary.* U.S. Environmental Protection Agency, Atlanta, Georgia.

32. Richard S. Barber. Duke Marine Laboratory, Beaufort, North Carolina. Personal communication.

33. John L. Sincock, et al. 1966. *Back Bay–Currituck Sound Data Report. Environmental Factors, 1958–64.* U.S. Bureau of Sport Fisheries and Wildlife, Washington, D.C. (unpublished).

34. Samuel Snedaker. 1973. "Environmental experimentation, restoration and recovery of salt marshes." In *Salt Marsh Workshop and Conference.* Florida Coastal Coordinating Council and The Florida Institute of Technology, Melbourne, Florida.

35. John L. Mero. n.d. "Review of mineral values on and under the ocean floor." In *Exploiting the Ocean.* Marine Technology Society, Washington, D.C.

36. T. R. Hellier and L. S. Kornicker. 1962. "Sedimentation from a hydraulic dredge in a bay." University of Texas, Institute of Marine Science, Vol. 8, pp. 212–215.

37. Edward T. La Roe. National Oceanic and Atmospheric Administration, Washington, D.C. Personal communication.

38. Edward T. La Roe. 1973. "Effects of dredging, filling and channelization on estuarine resources." Presented at *Fish and Wildlife Values of the Estuarine Environment,* a Seminar Presented for the Petroleum Industry by the Bureau of Sport Fisheries and Wildlife, U.S. Department of the Interior, Atlanta, Georgia, June 13, 1973.

39. D. Frankenberg, L. R. Pomeroy, L. Bahr, and J. Richardson. 1971. "Coastal ecology and recreational development." In C. D. Clement, Ed., *The Georgia Coast: Issues and Options for Recreation.* The Conservation Foundation, Washington, D.C., pp. II-I to II-49.

40. U.S. Army Corps of Engineers. 1971. "Shore protection guidelines." *In National Shoreline Study,* Vol. 1. Superintendent of Documents, Government Printing Office, Washington, D.C.,

41. E. J. F. Wood, W. E. Odum, and J. C. Zieman. 1969. "Influence of sea grasses on the productivity of coastal lagoons." *Mem. Simp. Intern. Lagunas Costeras,* UNAM–UNESCO, pp. 495–502.

42. Florida Department of Administration. 1974. *Final Report and Recommendations for the Proposed Florida Keys Area of Critical State Concern.* Tallahassee, Florida.

43. J. R. Clark. 1972. "Certain effects of once-through cooling systems of Indian Point Units 1 and 2 on Hudson estuary fishes and their environment." Testimony before Atomic Energy Commission Licensing Board, October 30, 1972.

CHAPTER THREE

Classification and
Survey of Natural Systems

A thorough job of planning is the precursor to coastal environmental management. Planning is a process of analysis, a system of ordering relationships and interpreting data toward the formulation of a plan for action. Any such program of analysis requires as a first step that the subject material be identified, defined, and classified in categories with known attributes (Figure 3.1). In this chapter we attempt to classify and describe the major elements of the coastal ecosystem, as well as to provide related information applicable to natural resources that should be helpful in coastal environmental planning and in the administration of local management programs.

In this chapter we also advance the concept of *vital areas*, that is, elements of such importance to the functioning of the coastal ecosystem that they must be preserved as intact units by disallowing uses that would

alter them significantly. The vital areas are related to a broader system of resource capability designation that classifies ecologically sensitive broad areas as *areas of critical concern.*

NATURAL SYSTEMS SURVEY

The comprehensive planning and the specification of environmental controls that are required for effective ecosystem management must be done with full knowledge of the natural system and its elements. In planning programs the services of ecological specialists usually will be required to survey the soils, the waters, and the biota of both the shoreland and the coastal basin subsystems. Such surveys are necessary to establish the carrying capacity limits of the natural system and to reveal points of vulnerability of the eco-

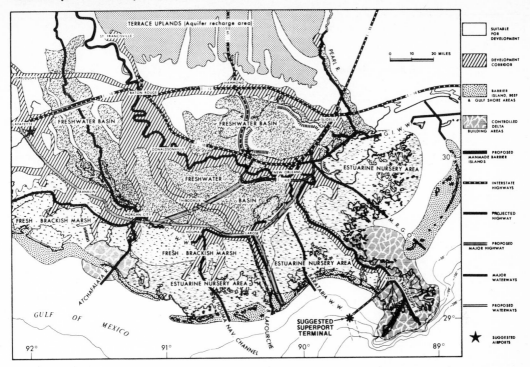

Figure 3.1 Proposed multiuse management plan for southeastern Louisiana. (SOURCE: Reference 1.)

system to adverse impacts of various kinds. This information may also be used as the basis for the selection of environmental standards to be used in defining permitted uses, identifying ecologically vital areas, and establishing a general strategy for development (Figure 3.2). It will also suggest the particular land-use control measures (e.g., designation of exempt vital areas) or performance standards (e.g., dredging limitations) needed to protect the ecosystem and to optimize its carrying capacity.

General Survey of Natural Systems and Resources

The principal items of natural systems interest are vegetation, soils, hydrology (water systems), geology, and topography. A survey of each of these should be included in the planning program. Inventories also may include identification and evaluation of such nonecological but natural factors as

scenic and recreational resources and natural hazard areas (Figure 3.3). The need for such surveys and the basic methods utilized are known to most professional planners and are not unique to coastal zone environments. It is our intent here only to emphasize the particular necessity of thorough knowledge of natural systems for coastal zone management and to provide concepts and definitions of natural elements in order to facilitate coastal planning activities.

The major natural systems elements of interest may be briefly described as follows:[4]

1. Topography—sometimes called "slope," "geography," "relief," or "physiography." A survey of the surface land forms (hills, mountains, ridges, valleys) (Figure 3.4), including a delineation of the surface relief by contour mapping.
2. Hydrology—sometimes called "water systems" or "drainage systems." A survey of the municipality's water systems (streams,

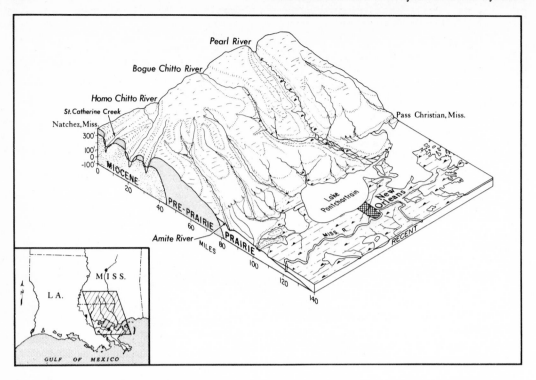

Figure 3.2   Geological setting of the New Orleans area. In contrast to the wetlands in the immediate vicinity of the city, Pleistocene terrace surfaces on the north shore of Lake Pontchartrain are well above sea level, naturally drained, and in general ideally suited for urban development. (SOURCE: Reference 2.)

rivers, ponds, lakes, swamps, bogs, oceans, and tidal marshes), including underground water supplies. Soils or subsurface geology may also be included. Since water is a necessity for life and can be a severe limiting factor to increased residential or industrial growth, it is a most important element in the natural systems and resource survey in all communities. In coastal communities it is usually the *most* important because of the critical role of water in governing ecosystems and limiting carrying capacity.

3. Soils—sometimes called "surficial geology." A survey of the soil properties in terms of intrinsic fertility for agriculture; ability to support structures; depth to water table; ability to absorb water, both natural and effluent, from septic systems; depth to bedrock; ability to support plant life other than crops. In coastal commu-

nities soils constitute a basic land suitability factor and a major control element on water systems.

4. Vegetation—a survey of the plant communities of the municipality in terms of their usefulness for soil and water retention and esthetics, and for basic information on wildlife populations. In coastal communities it serves as a basic indicator of vital areas and critical areas, and provides the framework for identification of separate elements of the ecosystem.

5. Geology—sometimes called "subsurface geology" or "bedrock geology" to differentiate from "surficial geology." A survey of the underlying rocks and parent materials of soils. This category can also include consideration of underground water supplies in terms of wells, aquifers, and aquifer recharge areas.

6. Valuable resources—a "catchall" survey

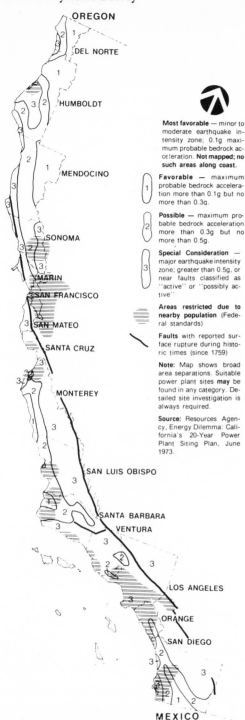

Figure 3.3   Optimum coastal areas for the licensing of nuclear power plants (based on seismicity and population). (SOURCE: Reference 3.)

that may include historic or cultural sites, areas of scenic interest, mineral deposits, or areas of national, state, or regional significance. In some cases where only one or two of these factors exist, they can be listed as separate categories. In the coastal zone this survey should include fish and shellfish resources, along with feeding, breeding, and wintering areas, and other places of special significance such as vital habitats, productivity, or structural areas.

7. Hazard areas—a survey of all natural hazard areas, such as those subject to earthquakes, mud and rock slides, flooding, high rates of erosion, and storm wave impacts.

Vegetation and Hydrology Survey

Plant and plant community types are the most reliable indicators of the natural characteristics that best identify many vital areas, for example, coastal marshes and mangrove swamps, freshwater wetlands, and submerged grass beds. In planning for a coastal zone environmental management program one should conduct a rather exhaustive survey of natural systems, including vegetation in drainageway corridors and in the floodplains, wetlands, tidelands, and bottoms (Figure 3.5).

Hydrologic factors control the abundance and diversity of plant life in coastal areas and therefore determine the natural patterns of vegetation. Topography, water quality, and soil condition are closely associated factors. Many aspects of coastal landuse management relate to the patterns of vegetation. On the one hand, certain *vital areas* are to be preserved because of the ecological value of their vegetation. On the other hand, patterns of vegetation are the key to identification of land and water capability types and therefore serve as a basis for land-use classification and suitability evaluation.

The survey of vegetation of shorelands

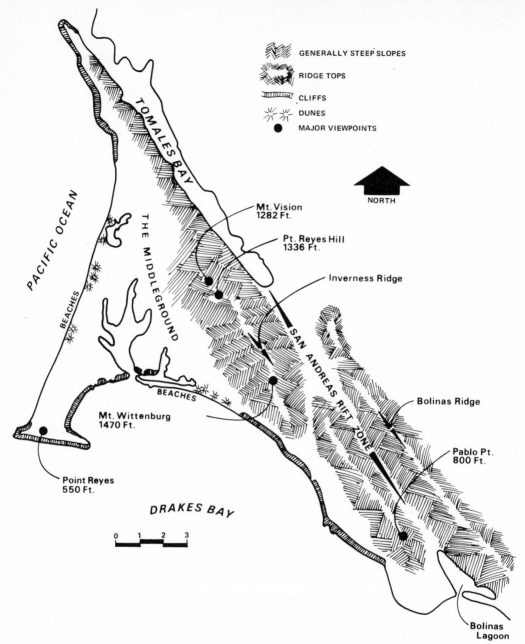

GENERALLY STEEP SLOPES
RIDGE TOPS
CLIFFS
DUNES
MAJOR VIEWPOINTS

NORTH

TOMALES BAY

PACIFIC OCEAN

THE MIDDLEGROUND

BEACHES

Mt. Vision
1282 Ft.

Pt. Reyes Hill
1336 Ft.

Inverness Ridge

SAN ANDREAS RIFT ZONE

BEACHES

Bolinas Ridge

Mt. Wittenburg
1470 Ft.

Pablo Pt.
800 Ft.

Point Reyes
550 Ft.

DRAKES BAY

0 1 2 3

Bolinas
Lagoon

Figure 3.4   Physiographic regions, Point Reyes, West Marin County, California. (SOURCE: Reference 5.)

and coastal water basins required for planning purposes can be facilitated by following the natural zonation of vegetation. At the basin margin zonation is governed by the joint influence of fresh and salt water—

tides are particularly important (various designations of tidal and stormwater levels are explained in Figure 3.6). The following is a convenient classification of natural vegetation (keyed to Figure 3.7):

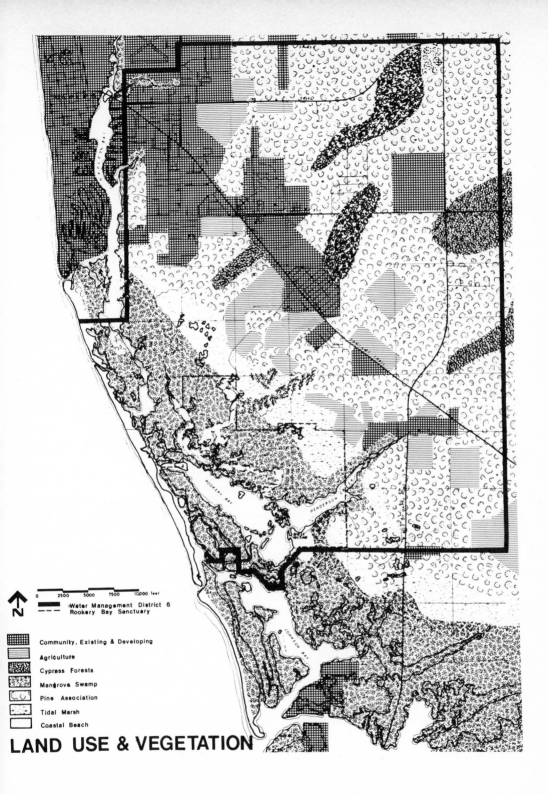

LAND USE & VEGETATION

Legend:
- Community, Existing & Developing
- Agriculture
- Cypress Forests
- Mangrove Swamp
- Pine Association
- Tidal Marsh
- Coastal Beach

Water Management District 6
Rookery Bay Sanctuary

0 2500 5000 7500 10000 feet

N

Figure 3.5 Water Management District No. 6, Collier County, Florida, with generalized patterns of vegetative cover and land use. (SOURCE: Reference 6.)

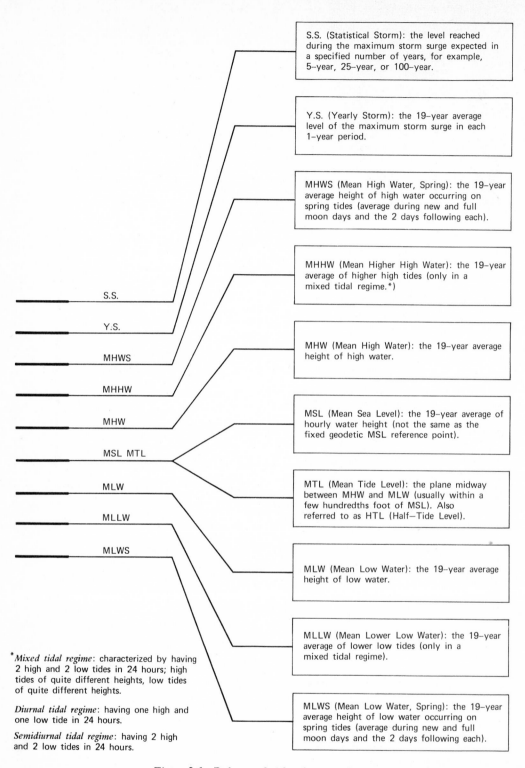

S.S. (Statistical Storm): the level reached during the maximum storm surge expected in a specified number of years, for example, 5-year, 25-year, or 100-year.

Y.S. (Yearly Storm): the 19-year average level of the maximum storm surge in each 1-year period.

MHWS (Mean High Water, Spring): the 19-year average height of high water occurring on spring tides (average during new and full moon days and the 2 days following each).

MHHW (Mean Higher High Water): the 19-year average of higher high tides (only in a mixed tidal regime.*)

MHW (Mean High Water): the 19-year average height of high water.

MSL (Mean Sea Level): the 19-year average of hourly water height (not the same as the fixed geodetic MSL reference point).

MTL (Mean Tide Level): the plane midway between MHW and MLW (usually within a few hundredths foot of MSL). Also referred to as HTL (Half-Tide Level).

MLW (Mean Low Water): the 19-year average height of low water.

MLLW (Mean Lower Low Water): the 19-year average of lower low tides (only in a mixed tidal regime).

MLWS (Mean Low Water, Spring): the 19-year average height of low water occurring on spring tides (average during new and full moon days and the 2 days following each).

S.S.

Y.S.

MHWS

MHHW

MHW

MSL MTL

MLW

MLLW

MLWS

*Mixed tidal regime: characterized by having 2 high and 2 low tides in 24 hours; high tides of quite different heights, low tides of quite different heights.

Diurnal tidal regime: having one high and one low tide in 24 hours.

Semidiurnal tidal regime: having 2 high and 2 low tides in 24 hours.

Figure 3.6   Reference heights for coastal waters.

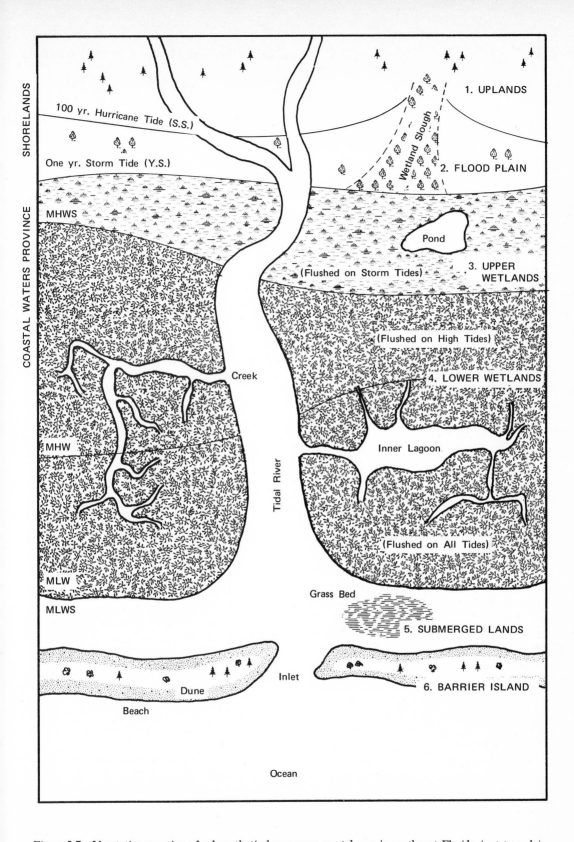

Figure 3.7   Vegetative zonation of a hypothetical mangrove coastal area in southwest Florida (not to scale).

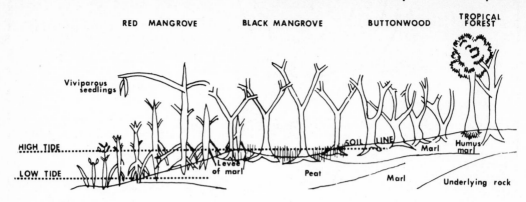

Figure 3.8   Diagrammatic cross section of a mangrove swamp. (SOURCE: Reference 7.)

Shorelands
  1. Upland vegetation
  2. Floodplain vegetation
Coastal waters province
  3. Upper wetland vegetation
  4. Lower wetland vegetation
  5. Submerged vegetation
  6. Barrier island vegetation complex

Each of these six classes may be further divided into categories representing recognizable vegetative subzones. For example, mangrove wetlands may contain separate red and black mangrove subzones (Figure 3.8).

For simplified planning purposes one may identify the general vegetative zones as they progress down the land–water gradient. But to meet legal requirements in management programs that involve use restrictions, a professional botanist will usually be called upon to identify the species of plants and to locate the boundaries between vegetative zones with precision.

In management, knowledge of vegetation may be essential because the presence of vegetative indicators on a parcel of land would trigger a special administrative review of a development proposal on the presumption that it could significantly alter a wetlands area. But it is also important to recognize that the vegetation is *in itself* valuable for the many functions described previously and requires protection for these values as well as its function as an indicator.

Survey with Color Infrared Photography

Usually, the most appropriate tool for vegetative survey is an aerial "color infrared" photographic survey of the whole area. Plant species, plant community characteristics, and vegetative condition can be determined from such a survey provided that sufficiently accurate field checks are made on the ground ("ground truth"). Marmelstein[8] has described the method as follows:

Color Infra-Red (CIR) photography is frequently used as a data source in coastal zone planning because its spectral sensitivity and scene rendition characteristics are such that it uniquely portrays significant features of this dynamic environment. CIR is a color reversal film which renders scene components in false color. It is filtered on exposure to eliminate blue sensitivity; CIR portrays scene components in three bands:

Green—rendered as blue in the processed print.
Red—rendered as green in the processed print.
Solar infra-red (reflected, *not* thermal)—rendered as red in the processed print.

For example, a scene component which is red in color to the eye is rendered in yellow on CIR, hence false color. Note also the film senses reflected solar radiation; it is *not* sensitive to nor does it display differences in temperature of the ground scene.

Two characteristics in particular make CIR valuable in the coastal zone. These characteristics are its ability to differentiate vegetative types and its ability to clearly define land/water boundaries. Furthermore, its lack of blue sensitivity results in better haze penetration than [is obtainable with] conventional color films, a clear advantage in the coastal zone. A disadvantage is the inability of CIR, when properly exposed for terrestrial or emergent scene components, to image submerged scene components.

Individual herbaceous green plants, plant associations, communities, etc., in vigorous growth are strong reflectors of solar infrared radiation and appear bright red on CIR films. The reflective characteristics in the solar IR and the green or chlorophyll band are strongly species, as well as vigor, dependent. Thus, with careful exposure and processing, an experienced interpreter can readily distinguish between plant communities as indicators of habitat types and soils/topographic differences. Furthermore, the rapid change in reflectance characteristics under physiological stress makes CIR an excellent tool for monitoring man-caused, or other, debilitating impacts on natural coastal plant communities.

The marked contrast in solar infra-red reflectance between most terrestrial scene components and open water makes CIR an excellent medium for differentiating land/water boundaries. Thus, this film is frequently used to define sinuous shorelines, etc., where vegetative cover does not obscure such boundaries. CIR flown across a tidal cycle can easily demonstrate tidal excursion in estuaries, an especially useful tool for productivity estimates in broad, shallow embayments. Reflectance characteristics of most soils, sands, muds, etc., versus water are such that water a few inches deep is all that is required to produce a sharp contrast at the boundary.

THE COASTAL ZONE

In general the coastal zone includes the parts of the continent under direct maritime influence. Its weather, vegetation, wildlife, and soils are obviously different to the senses from those of noncoastal areas. Even the smells and sounds are different near the shore. The coastal water basin and its biota are totally different in appearance. The water is salty and rises and falls with the tide. There is no mistaking the coastal zone. But when freedoms are restricted and legal issues are involved, an administrative definition is needed to designate a coastal zone with great specificity. This may be quite complicated.

The designation generally begins with a definition of the natural system and ends with boundaries set for administrative convenience. Typically, the extent of "coastal waters" is defined first, and then a strip of shoreland is added to embrace the interlocking land and sea elements of coastal zone management. The federal government has developed a process for such designation that local governments must follow if they (and their states) are participating in the federal coastal zone management program. The basic concepts and terminologies for definition of the coastal zone are presented in this section.

Coastal Waters

In the federal Coastal Zone Management Act of 1972 (P.L. 92–583) *coastal waters* are defined, in part, as "those waters adjacent to the shorelines which contain a measurable quantity or percentage of seawater" and which extend seaward to the outer limit of United States jurisdiction (Appendix, page 800). This is useful principally in establishing a boundary across open waters of tidal rivers, where fresh water meets salt water, and not for establishing a boundary along the shore where salt water meets the land.

"Measurable quantity or percentage of seawater" has no official or generally accepted administrative definition. The critical question is where one draws the line between ocean and fresh water in the tributaries and upper estuaries. The boundary between measurable and nonmeasurable amounts of seawater would occur in the vicinity of the "salt front," the somewhat arbitrary interface zone between seawater and undiluted fresh water. Here the vagaries of tide, runoff, and wind are such that this front is in constant movement and may vary up and down along a large tidal river basin for a distance of 10 to 20 miles or more. At any fixed point abutting this shifting front, the salinity may vary as much as 10 ppt (parts per thousand) or more from time to time.

For practical purposes of defining coastal waters, we recommend that a value of 0.5 ppt salinity be used as the least "measurable quantity or percentage of seawater" because it is the lowest value that consistently can be ascribed an important ecological meaning in most cases and because it can be detected by simple field equipment (this amount of salt is just above the taste threshold). In view of the larger problems of defining boundaries in this area of oscillating salinity, it would seem unreasonable to require the high level of accuracy that is available only with sophisticated laboratory equipment.

Boundaries

The federal Coastal Zone Management Act of 1972 requires participating states to identify the boundaries of the coastal zone (Appendix, page 800). In addition, the Act identifies the parameters that a state must use in identifying its boundaries by defining the coastal zone as the "coastal waters (including the lands therein and thereunder) and the adjacent shorelands (including the waters therein and thereunder), strongly influenced by each other and in proximity to the shorelands of the several coastal states, and includes transitional and intertidal areas, salt marshes, wetlands, and beaches"[9] (Figure 3.9).

The properties of the waters that characterize the watersheds and water basins of coastal ecosystems provide the best basis for the administrative definition. Because the

0.5-ppt salt front shifts up and down the estuary basin under the influence of wind, tide, and runoff, it is difficult to choose a fixed boundary for the inner edge of coastal waters. We expect that for practical reasons a fixed permanent boundary would be preferred for management, rather than a boundary that shifts with the position of the salt front. In choosing such a fixed management boundary we recommend that it be set at the point of maximum probable penetration of a "measurable quantity of seawater" (0.5 ppt) during the course of an average year. For practical purposes, as well as to avoid the complications of extraordinary events, the boundary might be set at the point above which the "measurable quantity of seawater" is found in the bottom waters less than 1 percent of the time during an average year's hydrologic cycle (or some other percentage that fits the particular case).

Another, and perhaps more satisfactory, method for fixing the inner boundary of

Figure 3.9   The transitional area between shoreland and coastal waters is often tidally flooded salt marsh (Charleston, South Carolina). (Conservation Foundation photo by M. Fahay.)

measurable salt is a biotic survey. The fixed (immobile) biotic community of tidal rivers and similar areas varies with the salt content of the water. The proportions of various species gradually shift from the sea toward the head of the estuary. At the point where the salt content falls below an average of about 0.5 ppt there is usually a sudden and dramatic change that signals the ecological boundary between the estuary and fresh waters—the ecological reference point above which there is no longer a measurable amount of salt at most times. This boundary is useful in setting the inner boundary of coastal waters because it integrates the effects of the whole range of variation in salinity on a long-term basis. Specifically, the boundary should be drawn at the point where the fixed biotic community shifts to over 50 percent endemic estuarine forms of life in any category (marsh grasses, molluscs, gastropods, nematodes, etc.). It is clear that the identifying biota should be those with extended life cycles (1 year or more) and those that are nonmobile. A more expanded special (perhaps regional) management area may be needed to protect the freshwater spawning areas of anadromous tidal fish such as striped bass, salmon, and shad.

States are permitted to delineate a planning area that is generally larger than the area ultimately identified as the coastal zone and encompasses it. This is suggested as a possible means of taking advantage of data, programs, and institutional boundaries (such as counties or areawide agencies) that cover geographical areas larger than the eventual coastal zone designation. It is also suggested as a means for taking into account existing developmental, political, and administrative conditions, as well as biophysical processes, that may be external to the coastal zone eventually selected for direct management control.[9]

According to the federal Office of Coastal Zone Management (OCZM), landward boundaries should be based upon "a determination of the inland boundary required to control shorelands, the uses of which have direct and significant impacts upon coastal waters, and including all transitional and intertidal areas, salt marshes, wetlands, and beaches." The regulations allow a boundary delineated by a strip of land of uniform depth (e.g., 1000 yards back from the shore) or by political boundaries, cultural features, property lines, or existing designated planning and environmental control areas, with the condition that any such boundaries refer to lands which have potential direct and significant impacts on coastal waters.[9] The state's offshore boundary is the edge of the territorial sea; the local community's boundary is that designated to it by the state.

In light of this situation the OCZM has determined that three types of approaches are acceptable for delineating a state's inland coastal zone boundary. However, we strongly urge that the boundaries of the coastal watershed be used as the primary inland boundaries of coastal management areas in which conservation of coastal water ecosystems is the goal (Figure 3.10). The three approaches suggested by the OCZM are as follows:[9]

1. *Biophysical.* A biophysical boundary can be defined in terms of natural features: biological, geological, physical, or a combination. These features can include drainage basins, floodplains, dune formations, ecosystems, and ridges of coastal mountain ranges. The use of a single biophysical feature for boundary delineation may not be adequate to ensure that all uses with direct and significant impacts on coastal waters are included. Often a combination of features may be most practicable.

2. *Biophysical as a base for administrative.* One method of circumventing some of the difficulties associated with a strictly biophysical boundary is the designation of an inland boundary along a set of existing, easily located lineaments that approximate natural features and include

Figure 3.10   All shorelands that drain directly into coastal waters are included in the coastal zone management area (Bolinas Bay, California). (Conservation Foundation photo.)

all necessary land areas. Once the appropriate biophysical delimiting features are identified, any number of political boundaries (county, township, municipal lines, etc.); cultural features (highways, roads, canals, etc.); existing designated planning areas (e.g., census enumeration districts); property lines; environmental control areas; and other such administrative or cultural features can be used as boundary lines. Boundaries designated in this manner should include the selected biophysical features and serve as adequate approximations of them.

3. *Multiple areas.* A multiple boundary permits communities to incorporate the provisions of existing statutory (state) programs and regulations. Multiple boundaries may delineate a combination of specific sections or zones of coastal land of different functions and resource bases, such as areas of critical concern ("particular concern" in the federal language), permissible uses, geological or biological features, air and water controls, and other functional bases. Multiple

boundaries can be designated on a basis of intensity of controls. The strongest and most direct control will normally be exercised in the zone or "tier" adjacent to the water's edge. Generally, but not always, the degree of control decreases in each succeeding zone landward. In any case the controls in a particular zone should be appropriate for existing planned or potential uses of the land and water within that zone. Examples of such multiple boundaries based on intensity of controls are the following: uniform distances measured horizontally from the shoreline, inland coastal county lines, and corporate limits of coastal communities.

This guidance offered to the states by the federal government should be heeded by communities in defining a coastal environmental management zone to provide for conformance between local and state purposes. Guidance should be obtained from the state coastal management office (Appendix, page 889).

THE SHORELANDS SUBSYSTEM

The coastal zone is logically separated into two major systems. They are distinct, but interlocking. As we have seen, the major connection is provided by water flow. One of these, the shorelands subsystem, is considered in this section; the other, the coastal waters subsystem, in the following section. We have identified them as *subsystems* to emphasize that it takes both to make up a complete coastal ecosystem.

Although the shorelands are ecologically complex and have high resource values, we are concerned here only with their interaction with coastal water systems and their influence on the carrying capacities of coastal ecosystems. Because this influence operates mostly through discharge of runoff water, coastal water concerns are specifically directed toward *coastal watersheds*, lands that drain directly into coastal waters (of more than 0.5 ppt salinity); these lands are defined as, and referred to as, the *shorelands*. Lands that drain wholly into fresh waters (less than 0.5 ppt salinity) tributary to tidal waters are not shorelands and would be excluded from the primary management area. However, to control significant discharge to coastal water basins via the freshwater tributaries it may be necessary to define a secondary management area, one that may involve upstream communities in a regional framework.

In the suggested context there are three elements of specific importance to be identified and surveyed: (1) all subwatersheds of the coastal watershed; (2) the complete water system of each subwatershed, including standing waters (ponds, lakes), natural detention areas (bogs, marshes), and drainage courses (streams, swales); and (3) all coastal floodplains (variations such as 100-year, 25-year, and 10-year levels may be needed for various management purposes), including high storm-hazard and erosion-hazard areas and structurally vital areas such as sand dunes. An important part of the survey and identification process for each of the three elements is to locate and evaluate all vital areas (habitat, structural, and productivity).

Although the survey elements recommended above emphasize only values that relate to coastal ecosystems, it is anticipated that many communities will wish to expand the program to identify areas of purely land-oriented interest, such as breeding areas, endangered species habitats, geological faults, and scenic vistas.

Coastal Watersheds

We have seen that coastal land- and water-use management has to recognize that water provides the essential linkage of land and sea elements of the coastal ecosystem (page 57). Thus water management in its many aspects is a primary consideration of the shorelands. We have defined "shorelands" to include all the terrain of the coastal watershed. Shorelands thus extend down to the upper boundary of the coastal water basin, which coincides with the inner boundary of the upper wetlands when such are present (page 131). This boundary also marks the lower edge of the coastal floodplain, which terminates where the coastal basin begins (page 120).

The shorelands (including floodplains) all have potential "direct and significant impact on the coastal waters" (as stated in the federal Coastal Zone Management Act) and must be included in the management program in order to protect coastal waters from pollution by sediment, nutrient, and toxic pollutants and to stabilize the volume and periodicity of the flow of fresh water into coastal water basins. There is an initial presumption of adverse impact of all land alteration in shorelands, and therefore all shorelands should be encompassed within the boundaries of the primary coastal zone management district. Subsequently, it may be discovered that portions of the defined shoreland area are not situated so as to

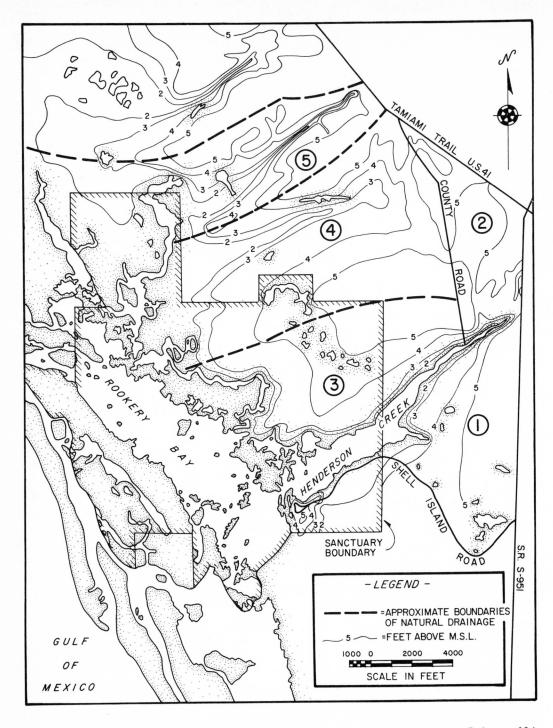

Figure 3.11 Drainage subbasins that drain into the Rookery Bay estuarine system. (SOURCE: Reference 10.)

have a significant influence (i.e., to cause significant disturbances) on coastal waters, because of topographic or drainage details. Such shorelands should require no special constraints for the protection of coastal waters and may be excluded from many of the special management requirements.

The methodology for identifying watersheds and drawing watershed divides in a shoreland area is essentially the same as for any other area. For effective environmental planning it is desirable to delineate the smallest identifiable drainage basins as sub-watersheds (Figure 3.11). Some of the flow may drain to channels, some to intermittent drainageways, and some directly to estuarine or ocean waters (Figure 3.12). We have indicated examples of drainage basin divides and resulting watershed areas in Figure 3.13.

It is recommended that all freshwater areas, including all drainageways through the coastal watershed, be identified as critical environmental areas (see page 134). They are integral parts of the greater coastal water system, and any disruption of them is presumed to be inimical to the functioning of the estuarine ecosystem. Also, it is recommended that the wetlands occurring within shoreline water areas be designated as vital areas, exempt from alteration (page 139).

The Coastal Floodplain

We have defined the coastal floodplain as the area that lies along the lower margin of the shorelands above the coastal wetlands or beaches and that is flooded with tidal waters at intervals of once per year or less (wetlands are flooded frequently—more than once a year, often daily). For general coastal zone management purposes the upper edge of the coastal floodplain is the 100-year mark (or 100-year storm-return interval), the point on the land that represents the furthest inland extension of floodwaters expected to occur once in 100 years. There

also may be a need to locate boundaries of other "statistical" floodplains; we have found it particularly useful to locate the 10-year and 25-year marks as an aid in designating buffer areas and in excluding or controlling certain uses.

Floodplain boundaries are set by various methods, none of which are particularly reliable for long storm-return intervals such as 50 or 100 years, because accurate historical records are not usually available (page 125). Nevertheless, this must be accomplished for a number of purposes in most coastal communities, and the information is necessary for coastal planning purposes.

Therefore it is convenient, if not necessary, to use the 100-year storm (Figure 3.14). Also, state floodplain management criteria may be based on this water level. However, as mentioned above, for specific environmental management purposes, it may be more appropriate to designate the 10-year, or other, statistical floodplain. The 1-year flood mark is of particular relevance because it marks the upper edge of the coastal wetlands. The choice will depend on the particular management goal under consideration and on land slope, drainage characteristics, soil type, and other variables.

The basic technique for delineating the coastal floodplain is to determine from available data the relation between forces that drive storms (hurricanes, nor'easters, etc.,), such as wind speed, and others that govern the moving impact of stormwaters, on the one hand, and those that govern storm surge elevation (that is, the height of the water during flooding), measured from a base point, usually mean sea level, on the other hand. The surge elevation can then be projected back onto the shoreland topography, and the line marking the penetration drawn along the appropriate land elevation line. The surge elevation will vary greatly from place to place along the shore, depending on the shore alignment; funnel-shaped configurations generally lead to the highest storm surges. Flood lines can be

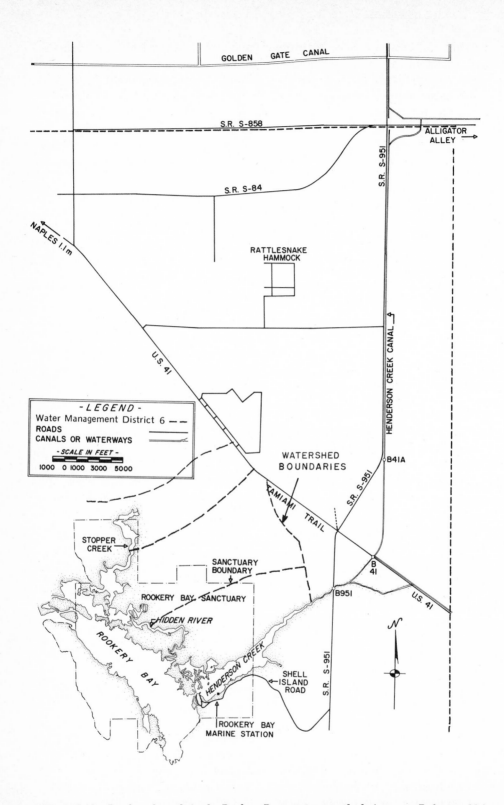

Figure 3.12   Roads and canals in the Rookery Bay system watershed. (SOURCE: Reference 11.)

122

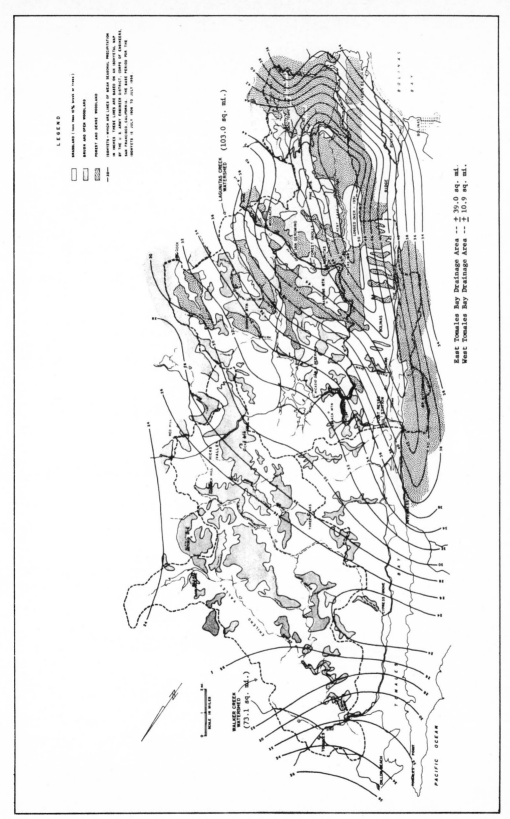

Figure 3.13 Watershed divides (dotted line), vegetation (shaded), and rainfall (line) for West Marin County, California. (SOURCE: Reference 12.)

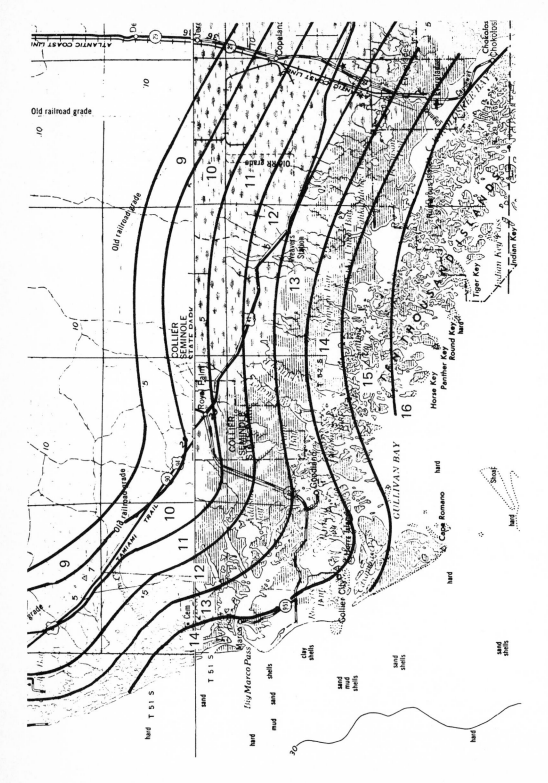

Figure 3.14 Preliminary predicted 100-year maximum flooding levels; numerals indicate heights above mean sea level. (SOURCE: Reference 13.)

mapped for storm surges for any probability of occurrence, for example, 10-year, 25-year, or 100-year (Figure 3.15). The federal government is responsible for locating the 100-year flood mark in all communities participating in the National Flood Insurance Program (page 173). The most difficult boundary location problems occur where inland floods and coastal floods intermix; there appears to be little or no theoretical base for predicting the high-water mark where the two coincide. Salt-tolerant vegetation, which is a good key to coastal floods of 1-year frequency, does not serve as a useful indicator of long-interval storms.

THE COASTAL WATERS SUBSYSTEM

The coastal waters subsystem can be conveniently categorized in three identifiable and functionally distinct *regimes*: the estuarine, the nearshore, and the oceanic regime. Each of these is discussed in this section.

Estuarine Water Regime

The term "estuary" has a variety of definitions, but, as used in this book, *an estuary is an enclosed coastal water body with a free connection to the sea and a measurable quantity of salt in its waters.* "Measurable" can be interpreted as greater than 0.5 ppt salinity (see page 119). We use this definition of estuary in preference to one which includes only enclosed water bodies that receive a "significant" freshwater input. The chosen definition includes all enclosed or "protected" coastal waters and avoids the problem of dealing with "lagoons" separately from estuaries because their rate of inflow from the land is low. Nevertheless, when it is necessary to make a distinction for management purposes (e.g., because of poor flushing) lagoons can be considered as one of the many different types of estuary.

Consequently, our definition agrees well with that of E. P. Odum[15] (as modified from D. W. Pritchard[16]): "a semi-enclosed coastal body of water which has a free connection to the sea; it is thus strongly affected by tidal action, and within it sea water is mixed (and usually measurably diluted) with fresh water from land drainage."

When we use the term "enclosed" to describe one property of the estuary, we do so in a relative sense, recognizing that the degree of enclosure is an important variable factor. The definition thus includes coastal water bodies ranging from very open bays with wide mouths to nearly landlocked salt ponds with very narrow water passages to the sea.

When it is important to distinguish between estuarine and open areas for planning or management purposes, we suggest the following "rule of thumb" based on the degree of enclosure: *An enclosed coastal water body, or estuary, is one that has a shoreline length in excess of three times the width of its outlet to the sea.*

The estuarine system includes the water basin (or basins) and the marginal areas found around the edge of the basin that are seasonally flooded by tides or storms. Water basins may be embayments, bays, sounds, fiords, lagoons, salt ponds, or tidal rivers. The fringing marginal area includes the tideflats and mud flats, the lower wetlands, the tidal salt marshes and mangroves, and the upper wetlands (high marsh flooded by spring tides) back to the limit of annual flooding (the 1-year flood mark), where the floodplain part of the shoreland starts (Figure 3.16).

Estuarine Water Basin Types

Coastal water basins occur in a nearly limitless variety of shapes and sizes, but the four types discussed below will cover most cases. The well-enclosed water bodies are normally distinct, readily recognized, and easily

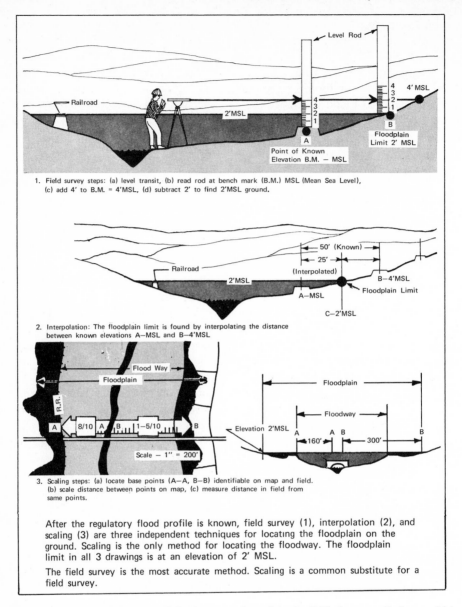

Figure 3.15 How floodplains and floodways are located in the field. (SOURCE: Reference 14.)

treated in management; however, sectioning the ocean waters into workable, distinguishable units may be quite difficult. The assistance of a trained ecologist will normally be required to both identify the water basins involved and to provide a detailed understanding of their functions and vulnerabilities. Estuaries are of particular management interest because of their exceptionally high

carrying capacities and their distressing vulnerability—they are classified in this book as *areas of critical environmental concern* (page 132). The four major basin types are as follows:

1. *Tidal river.* A tidal river is the lower reach of a river that enters the sea, often via an estuarine basin. The coastal seg-

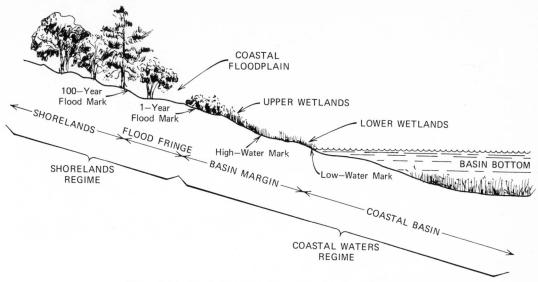

Figure 3.16   Typical profile of a vegetated coastal shoreline.

ment of the river—that of primary management interest—extends as far upstream as there is significant salt content in the water (0.5 ppt salinity). The boundary area is the *salt front* (page 35). The freshwater part (less than 0.5 ppt salinity) is normally excluded, even if it is tidally influenced, or is relegated to a secondary management district. Tidal rivers are normally well flushed by the combined, but opposing, actions of freshwater outflow and tide (see "Stratified estuarine circulation," page 128).

2. *Bay.* The larger, semi-enclosed, coastal water bodies are bays (here including sounds, to simplify classification). Many water bodies misnamed as "bays" are really embayments or lagoons. Such water basins should be classified in the management system proposed here in accordance with their natural characteristics, not their present colloquial designations. Bays are typically quite open to the sea, receive strong tidal flow, are well flushed through tidal exchange, and often receive considerable additional circulation driving power from freshwater inflow (see "Stratified estuarine circulation," page 128).

3. *Embayment.* Confined coastal water bodies with narrow restricted inlets and significant freshwater inflow are embayments. They usually have narrower inlets than bays and are generally shallower and smaller. Embayments usually have a relatively low tidal amplitude, and water circulation may be sluggish, resulting in a poor rate of flushing, unless the freshwater input is particularly high. In these respects and others they are intermediate between bays and lagoons.

4. *Lagoon.* Confined coastal water bodies with restricted inlets to the sea and with little freshwater inflow are termed lagoons. They tend to have sluggish water movement and to be especially vulnerable to pollution; thus their carrying capacities often have been severely reduced by human development around their shores (Figure 3.17). The aquatic communities of lagoons may be quite different from those of other basins because of higher and relatively constant salinity, somewhat higher and more constant pH, the dominant but variable role of circulation, the accumulation of organic sediments on their bottoms, and other factors.

Figure 3.17 Development must be severely limited in shorelands surrounding lagoons because they tend to be poorly flushed and susceptible to pollution (Sanibel Island, Florida). (Photo by author.)

Estuarine Circulation Types

Each of the three major estuarine water circulation types is controlled by a particular combination of tide, freshwater inflow, oceanic current, wind, or geological structure. Both the intensity of the stirring forces and the rate at which the water basins are flushed govern the productivity of estuarine ecosystems. The three major types of circulation are as follows:

1. *Stratified estuarine circulation.* The stratified system of circulation is typical of estuaries with a strong influx of fresh water. Stratified estuarine circulation is most commonly found in bays formed from "drowned" river valleys and in fiords and other deeper basins. It is the result of the intrusion of heavier salt water from the ocean (the "salt wedge") under the less saline and lighter outflow of water from the rivers. In this situation, common to deeper estuaries with high net movement of fresh water outward, the bottom water has a net movement inward, toward the upper estuary (Figure 3.18). This is referred to as *net flow*, where the oscillating tidal influence is discounted in order to detect the actual residual progress of the water in a particular direction. Under favorable conditions the two layers move at sufficient speeds, in opposing directions, to provide good circulation throughout much of the stratified estuary. The higher the rate of freshwater inflow, the higher the rates of both surface outflow and bottom inflow. The strength of the flow governs the position of the salt front (the boundary between coastal and riverine waters) and therefore the location of the most abundant populations of fish and microorganisms. The distinctive pattern of opposite flows at surface and bottom results in a net outward transport of surface organisms and a net inward transport of bottom organisms in stratified estuaries (see page 35).

2. *Nonstratified estuarine circulation.* In the mixed, or nonstratified, type of estuary, water movement is more sluggish and the flushing rate is lower than in the stratified type. Nevertheless there may be sufficient circulation to provide the basis for a high carrying capacity. Nonstratified estuarine circulation is common to shallow embayments and to bays lacking a good supply of fresh water from land

drainage. The flushing capability of the mixed estuary will depend principally on the particular combination of four variables: basin configuration, tidal amplitude, freshwater influx, and strength and direction of prevailing winds. The two-layered flow does not normally occur in lagoon-type systems or in shallow estuaries where the water is so readily and constantly mixed by wind and tide from surface to bottom that it cannot hold two separate layers.

3. *Lagoonal circulation.* Lagoonal-type circulation is characterized by low rates of water movement resulting from (1) a lack of significant freshwater input to the lagoon, and (2) a lack of strong tidal exchange because of the typically narrow inlet that connects the lagoon to the sea. Wind is often the main force that drives circulation. Lagoonal circulation is typical of highly enclosed lagoon-type basins that have too little force of net outflow (from freshwater input) to open a wide inlet.

In lagoon-type basin systems the major factor limiting biological productivity is often water circulation. Estuaries (usually lagoons) with lagoonal circulation are highly susceptible to pollution (page 127).

Nearshore and Oceanic Regimes

The *nearshore regime* includes all marine waters seaward of the estuarine boundary and shoreward of the territorial sea (nominally 3 miles distance from the shore). The terms "inshore" and "inshore waters" have such varied meanings that we have not tried to use them here in any specific sense. Either can be construed in general to include the estuaries and at least part of the nearshore zone.

The *oceanic regime* includes all waters seaward of the boundary of the territorial sea.

Exposed coasts are ocean shorefronts characterized by either solid rock formations or heavy deposits of sand (Figure 3.19). The

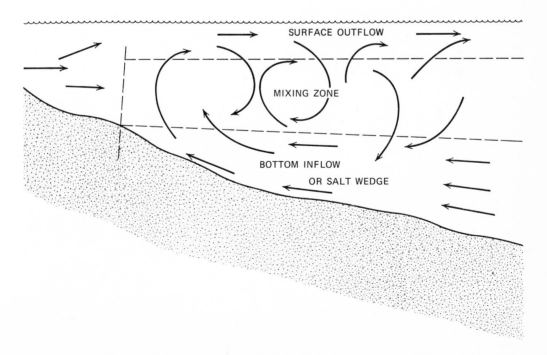

Figure 3.18   Circulation pattern in a typical stratified estuary. (SOURCE: Reference 17.)

Figure 3.19 The waters along exposed coasts usually are well mixed and less vulnerable to pollution buildup than the waters of estuaries (Oregon coast). (Photo by author.)

great capacity of the dunes and beach berms for storage of sand makes them the chief stabilizers of the sandy ocean beachfront. Water movement is usually strong, and mixing, dilution, and dispersal of wastes is rapid along exposed coasts.

Sheltered coasts occur in certain places along the ocean shorefront where the bottom slope is gradual and where offshore sandbars are thrown up by the force of waves, or coral reefs have built up in a barrier formation seaward of the shorefront. These sand or coral barriers provide a sheltered area inside the bar or reef where the ecosystem is in many ways characteristic of estuarine waters—marine grasses grow, shellfish prosper, and nursery areas for young fish are found. In addition, there are "low-energy" coasts (such as on the northwest Florida shore), where wave action is so reduced that, even without a pronounced offshore bar, the coast is sheltered in character,

the water is flushed more slowly, and semi-estuarine characteristics prevail.

Marginal Areas

At the margin of each estuarine and near-shore coastal water basin is a transitional area that is classified as part of the coastal basin, whether it is flooded daily by the tides or only yearly by a severe storm. This area is part of the *coastal waters* subsystem. It may be barren sand or rock or vegetated by coastal wetland plants (Figure 3.20). Most often, in protected estuarine areas it is vegetated except for the lowest elevations, which grade into tidal flats. But vegetation may be absent from most of the area on the exposed ocean coast, at least below the high-water mark.

The seaward boundary of the marginal area is the lowest elevation expected to be exposed at ebb tide during the course of a

Figure 3.20 The marginal areas surrounding an estuary that is flooded once a year or oftener are classified as part of the coastal basin (East Falmouth, Massachusetts). (Conservation Foundation photo by M. Fahay.)

year, and is thus below mean low water. This boundary may have little administrative significance, however, because the coastal water basin is normally in the public domain seaward from the mean low-water mark (from the mean high-water mark in some states).

The landward boundary of the marginal area of the coastal basin is the highest elevation expected to be flooded by coastal waters during the course of a year (see page 138). This boundary is extremely important administratively because it marks the upper boundary of the wetlands. All coastal wetlands are now strongly protected by federal regulations and often by state statutes or local ordinances (page 184).

A simpler and more reliable approach to locating the landward boundary is through the use of indicator plants (page 142). A biotic survey can determine the inner extent of saltwater influence—the line above which there is no "measurable" effect of saltwater inundation or penetration[18] (Figure 3.21).

Figure 3.21 Vegetation indicates the upper margin of the coastal water basin—the highest elevation of salt-tolerant wetlands vegetation, as shown by dotted line (Salisbury, Maryland). (Conservation Foundation photo by M. Fahay.)

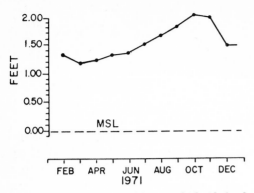

Figure 3.22   Average monthly mean high-tide levels for Gulf of Mexico, Collier County (Rookery Bay, 1971). (SOURCE: Reference 19.)

Although the concept remains the same, various terms are used for the three categories. They can be designated generically as *preservation, conservation,* and *utilization.*

As an example, the Florida Coastal Coordinating Council has defined the following use designations for statewide coastal land classification:[21] "preservation," no development suitable; "conservation," carefully controlled development suitable; "development," intensive development suitable. Six factors are utilized in selecting areas for these designations:

1. Ecological significance of the area and its tolerance to alteration.
2. Water classification of adjacent water bodies.
3. Soils suitability of the area.
4. Susceptibility of the area to flooding, both from storm surge and runoff.
5. Archaeological and historical significance of the area.
6. Unique environmental features that may warrant protection.

When the system was refined and adapted for Collier County, Florida (Water Management District No. 6 study), land was classified for "preservation," "conservation," or "development" according to the following categories (see also Table 3.1):[22]

a. *Preservation areas* are those that provide invaluable public benefits, such as recreation, aesthetics, economic value, and hurricane flood protection, and are intolerant of development. These are areas that it is recommended be preserved without any development and protected from degradation. "Preservation" areas include the waterways, mangroves, and marshes, which all form critical parts of the same productive and valuable coastal wetlands community. (Figure 3.24).

b. *Development areas* are those that, because of physiography, drainage, or other factors, are comparatively suitable for

There are many difficulties in locating the upper boundary by water level surveys. For example, the sea level is rising gradually along much of the United States coast—more than a foot per century in some areas. Often more troubling is the annual rhythm of rise and fall of sea level, whereby the sea level may be much higher in autumn, for example, than in spring (Figure 3.22). In addition daily and monthly cycles and irregularities are caused by wind variations, freshwater runoff, and other factors. There are also significant differences between the tidal responses of estuaries and those of the sea. A further complication is that the tide itself comes in three different modes (Figure 3.23).

AREAS OF ENVIRONMENTAL CONCERN

The planning framework for coastal management requires a system of classification and evaluation that embraces wide areas of environmental sensitivity, or *areas of concern,* as well as the smaller areas of concentrated ecologic value and particular essentiality to the ecosystem, the *vital areas.* A concept of designation of land by three broad use categories has arisen out of attempts to plan for the management of areas according to their ecological sensitivities.

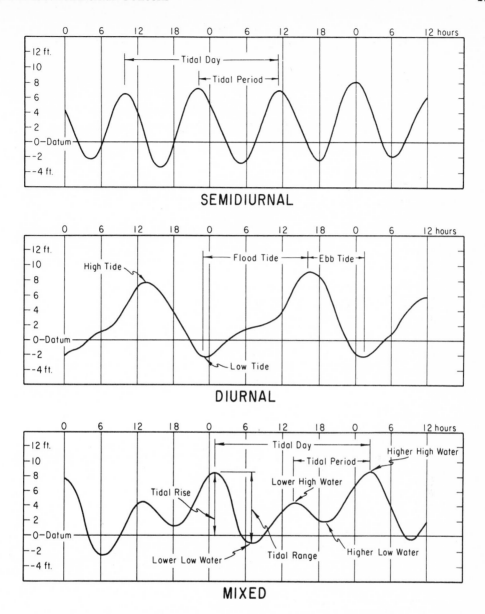

Figure 3.23 The three basic types of tides. (SOURCE: Reference 20.)

development, and that have a reduced ecological, recreational, and public importance. Lands that could be developed directly or with only minor alteration would be classified as "development."

c. *Conservation areas* include the remaining lands, those marginally suitable for development and possessing important

but noncritical ecological significance. These serve as a buffer between the preserved and the developed areas. They require special precautions when being developed. Because of flood and drainage problems, development in areas classified as "conservation" is generally very expensive, in terms both of initial cost and of

Table 3.1   Land-use constraints recommended for Collier County,
Florida (SOURCE: Reference 22)

PRESERVATION	CONSERVATION	DEVELOPMENT
No construction, development or land alteration	Limited development— homes on fill islands (upland clusters) or stilts. Maximum density 1 du/ 5 acre	Intense development
No roads	Roads parallel to water flow or raised (trestle)	Adequately culverted roads
No canals or dredging— maintain historic (natural) overland water flow	No canals or dredging— cypress slough used to receive, cleanse and disperse water	No canals longer than 800 yards—drainage into man-made retention ponds, eventually to sloughs
Low intensity recreation (hunting, fishing, individual camping)	Moderate intensity recreation, with realization that areas may be periodically flooded	Intense recreation
No waste disposal	No solid waste disposal, dumps or landfills. Sewage by approved system	No dumps. Approval of DPC for sewage and solid waste disposal
No water consumption	Water consumption not to exceed 150 gpd/acre	Water consumption not to exceed 1,800 gpd/acre
No removal of vegetation	Maximum 5% vegetation removed, except for exotics. Only native vegetation used for landscaping	Maximum 40% vegetation removed, except exotics. No melalogua or Brazilian pepper used

continuing maintenance costs. Developments in these areas pose potential hazards to both life and property and require the continual expenditure of public and private dollars to alleviate, prevent, or repair flood damage.

The concepts illustrated in the examples above are compatible with those of both *critical areas* and *vital areas*. The parallelism of these systems is shown in the following comparisons.

Vital areas or preservation areas: ecosystem elements of such critical importance and high value that they are to be preserved intact, exempted from any use that would alter them, and protected from harmful out-

side forces; normally encompassed *within* an area of environmental concern.

Areas of environmental concern or conservation areas: broad areas of environmental sensitivity (often containing one or more vital areas), the development or use of which must be carefully controlled to protect the ecosystem.

Utilization areas or development areas: areas where only normal levels of caution are required in utilization and in development activity.

Critical Areas

Areas of critical environmental concern constitute a planning classification within which

Figure 3.24   Mangrove forests, a vital part of the coastal basin margin, are normally preserved by exempting them from alteration in Florida. (Conservation Foundation photo by M. Fahay.)

human activities must be controlled, though not necessarily prohibited, to protect the environment. Smaller areas for complete preservation—vital areas—are to be designated within the areas of concern.

The areas of critical concern concept has developed concurrently in various federal and state land-planning studies over the past several years (Figure 3.25). Although it has been articulated in a variety of ways and has come to have a variety of implications, the basic concept remains the same—there are certain critical environmental areas that, because of their natural attributes, require special management attention. Most often these attributes are environmental, including natural hazards, although sometimes they may include cultural values (related to activities of mankind). Such critical areas are identified as those where uncontrolled devel-

opment might lead to significant adverse environmental impacts. Therefore some restriction on use and some control on activity are required.

Four examples of various applications of the areas of critical concern concept are as follows:

1. Florida Environmental Land and Water Management Act of 1972.[24] "Areas of critical state concern" include those containing, or having a significant impact on, environmental, historical, natural, or archaeological resources of regional or statewide importance, or those significantly affected by a major public facility or proposed area of major development potential.
2. California Coastal Zone Conservation Act of 1972.[25] "Areas of special biological

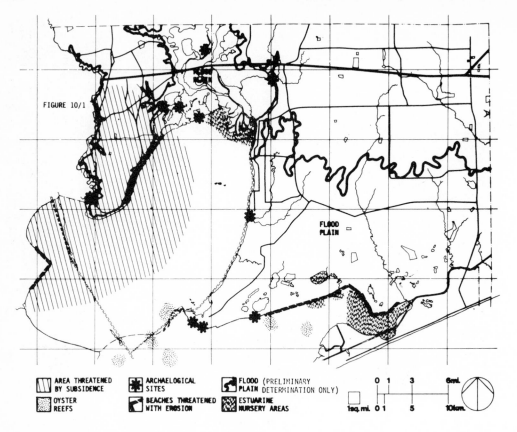

FIGURE 10/1

FLOOD PLAIN

AREA THREATENED BY SUBSIDENCE
OYSTER REEFS
ARCHAELOGICAL SITES
BEACHES THREATENED WITH EROSION
FLOOD (PRELIMINARY PLAIN DETERMINATION ONLY)
ESTUARINE NURSERY AREAS

0 1 3 6mi.
1sq. mi. 0 1 5 10km.

Figure 3.25 Sample mapping of "areas of critical environmental concern" (Trinity Bay area, Texas). (SOURCE: Reference 23.)

significance" are identified for protection without concern for economic values because they contain biological communities of such extraordinary, even though unquantifiable, value that no acceptable risk of change in their environments as a result of man's activities can be entertained.

3. U.S. Senate Hearings on Coastal Zone Management Act.[26] "Areas of critical environmental concern" include areas where uncontrolled development could (1) result in irreversible damage to important historic values, cultural values, aesthetic values, natural systems or processes, or (2) unreasonably endanger life and property as a result of natural hazards of more than local significance. Coastal area examples are:

a. Coastal wetlands, marshes, and other lands inundated by the tides.
b. Beaches and dunes.
c. Estuaries, shorelands, and floodplains of rivers, lakes, and streams.
d. Rare or valuable ecosystems.

4. North Carolina Coastal Zone Management Act of 1973.[27] "Areas of particular public concern" may include the following:

a. Marshlands and estuarine waters.
b. Areas with significant impact on environmental, historical, or natural resources of regional or statewide importance.

c. Areas containing unique or fragile ecosystems that are not capable of withstanding uncontrolled development.

d. Areas such as waterways and lands under or flowed by tidal waters or navigable waters, which the state may be authorized to preserve, conserve, or protect.

e. Areas such as floodplains, beaches, and dunelands wherein uncontrolled alteration or development increases the likelihood of flood damage and erosion and may necessitate large expenditures of public funds.

f. Areas significantly affected by, or having a significant effect on, existing or proposed major public facilities or other areas of major public investment.

The federal Coastal Zone Management Act uses the term "areas of particular concern" to embrace the areas requiring special management. The guidelines for the federal coastal zone program list the following representative factors as those to be taken into account when designating "areas of particular concern" as required by the Act:[28]

1. Areas of unique, scarce, fragile or vulnerable natural habitat, physical feature, historical significance, cultural value, and scenic importance.
2. Areas of high natural productivity or essential habitat for living resources, including fish, wildlife, and the various trophic levels in the food web critical to their well-being.
3. Areas of substantial recreational value and/or opportunity.
4. Areas where developments and facilities are dependent on the utilization of, or access to, coastal waters.
5. Areas of unique geologic or topographic significance to industrial or commercial development.
6. Areas of urban concentration where shoreline utilization and water uses are highly competitive.

Figure 3.26 Many beachfronts are extremely hazardous areas for occupancy because they are receding landward as sea level rises (Captiva Island, Florida). (Photo by author.)

7. Areas of significant hazard if developed, because of storms, slides, floods, erosion, settlement, etc. (Figure 3.26).

Areas designated for "particular concern" are scheduled to be preserved or restored for conservation, recreation, ecological, safety, or aesthetic purposes. There does not appear to be any intended differentiation between areas that are "vital" and areas that are "of concern" in the federal program. Such a differentiation is useful, however, in allowing more specificity of goals and more flexibility in management and is highly recommended. Therefore areas "of particular concern" under the federal coastal management program should be understood to mean general areas of critical concern. The term "vital areas" should be used for exceptionally valuable ecological areas within them.

Here we use the designation "areas of critical environmental concern" or, for brevity, simply "critical areas." Critical areas relating to the function of coastal ecosystems embrace (1) all drainageways throughout coastal watersheds, (2) all floodplains and beachfronts, and (3) all estuarine water areas, extending from the salt front (the 0.5-ppt line, page 127) seaward into ocean waters to the extent that estuarine influences prevail (page 116).

Shoreland water systems (lakes, ponds, marshes, creeks, swales, etc.) are critical areas because the coastal watersheds that drain through them have profound effects on coastal water ecosystems (page 134). Drainageways include all ponds, lakes, creeks, wetlands, natural swales, and other elements of the shorelands water system that detain, purify, or convey water from coastal watersheds to coastal water basins. For management purposes it may be useful to designate all of the most critical parts of the coastal watershed (those with high rates of erosion, major effects on drainage, etc.) as "critical areas" in which special attention is given to protection of the quality, volume, and rate of flow of the water draining from the shorelands into the coastal water basin (page 121).

Coastal floodplains have been described for classification previously. The floodplain is the part of the shorelands that has some probability of being inundated during storms (page 125). At such times it has a direct connection with coastal waters. As things work out ecologically, coastal floodplains are areas of critical environmental concern (at least to the 10-year level) and therefore require special programs of environmental management on their behalf to ensure that a high level of ecosystem vitality is maintained. Vegetated areas below the 1-year flood mark (wetlands) should be designated for more stringent control as vital areas.

The *beachfront* is also an area of critical concern from the most inland of secondary dunes to the furthest seaward extent of normal local government jurisdiction (page 144). Local jurisdiction normally extends a few hundred feet seaward of the beach and includes the submerged supplies of sand so important to the maintenance of beach stability (page 145). Within the beachfront zone the active dunes should be designated for more stringent control as vital areas.

Estuaries in their entirety should be designated as critical areas because of their high resource values and their extreme vulnerability. As we have seen, adverse use pressures are heavy in urban areas adjacent to estuaries and the pollution potential is high. The more urbanized an estuary is, the more it suffers from environmental stress. A particular estuary that we have studied in detail (Rookery Bay, Florida) holds the following variety of major resource values:[11]

1. A nutrient-rich saltwater nursery for fish and shellfish.
2. A protective habitat for various species of tropical wildlife, especially birds.
3. A natural assimilator and purifier of land runoff contaminants.
4. A unique locus for water recreation within a rapidly urbanizing area.
5. A natural buffer against shore erosion and storm floods for the urban area.
6. An accessible aesthetic resource of high value.

Thus there is persuasive opinion that estuaries and their surrounding tidelands should be designated as areas of critical environmental concern. It is particularly important that vital areas be encompassed within a broader area of critical concern. When moving water is involved, one cannot simply protect isolated vital areas within an ecosystem, such as grass beds or a coral reef, without regard for the condition of the surrounding waters. Such elements as these have been degraded extensively, or even destroyed, by disturbances originating in the water some distance away, for example, by sediment loading the water from dredging or by siltation of drainage courses in the shorelands by land clearing. Also, coastal aquatic species (clams, oysters, crabs, fish) roam about for feeding or spawning and their young often are carried widely by the currents before settling down.

VITAL AREAS

The inventory of vital areas should be accomplished early in the coastal zone planning program. Such areas should be identified, evaluated, and mapped for special protection. The vital areas of concern will most often be fixed ecosystem features of tangible physical character, such as coral reefs, submerged oyster beds, or cordgrass marshes, that remain essentially constant in location. (Figure 3.27). *Fixed vital areas* are readily located, surveyed, and mapped.

But there are other vital areas that are transient features of the water mass. These have specific attributes but not fixed boundaries. An example of a *transient vital area* is the salinity-controlled feeding area of young white perch, which may shift up or down the estuary 10 miles or more in response to river inflow (the zooplankton food of the perch lives within a restricted salinity).

Fixed vital areas, which are quite amenable to mapping, present little difficulty in administration, but transient ones may pose such problems that the concept would be used only in the most advanced management programs. In less comprehensive programs the water basin vital areas of estuaries could be protected to a degree by controls uniformly applicable throughout the estuarine *area of environmental concern* of which they are a part (page 134).

Transient vital areas are most often water masses of special ecological value that shift position with wind, tide, or river inflow. The services of a professional ecologist will normally be required to provide boundaries for transient areas that are of sufficient accuracy to serve regulatory needs. These areas

Figure 3.27 "Fixed" vital areas such as the salt marsh above can be readily identified and mapped (St. Simons Island, Georgia). (Conservation Foundation photo.)

do need recognition so that special efforts can be made to correct pollution impacts and to control dredging and other activities within their boundaries. Although transient vital areas may change location, their boundaries shift between known limits for the most part. Therefore it is possible to map out bounds that normally will encompass the full area for, say, 95 percent of the time. Such limits will be suitable for management purposes.

Vital Area Types

One can distinguish three types of vital areas. *Vital habitat areas* are those that chiefly provide general living space for particular species: coral reefs, for example. *Vital productivity areas* are those that chiefly supply nutrients to the system, for example, high marsh. *Vital structural areas* are those that physically protect the ecosystem through their structure: sand dunes, for example. Some areas serve a single vital

Figure 3.28 Lower wetlands and the surrounding shallows are important habitats for coastal life (Bear's Bluff area, South Carolina). (Conservation Foundation photo by J. Chess.)

function, whereas others serve two or perhaps all three functions.

Vital Habitat Areas

The following classes of vital areas provide high value for habitat in coastal ecosystems for a variety of animal species (Figure 3.28):

> Coral reefs
> Kelp beds
> Shellfish beds
> Grass beds
> Lower wetlands
> Breeding areas
> Nursery areas
> Wintering areas
> Migration pathways

Vital habitat areas are simply areas in which important species concentrate in high abundance during part or all of a year and without which their welfare and abundance would be greatly reduced. Many species are particularly vulnerable to damage when concentrated in their special feeding, breeding, nursery, or wintering areas or on migration pathways—these should all be located and mapped for protection as vital areas. Their identification and designation is usually a job for a zoological expert.

Vital Productivity Areas

The following classes of vital areas provide high values in the production and storage of primary productivity in coastal ecosystems:

> Coral reefs
> Lower wetlands
> Upper wetlands
> Tideflats
> Grass beds
> Kelp beds

Vital Structural Areas

The following classes of vital areas provide high value in establishing and maintaining the structural integrity of coastal ecosystems:

> Sand dunes
> Coral reefs
> Wetlands

These vital areas serve to protect the valuable estuarine and shoreland systems behind them from storm damage and erosion.

Freshwater Wetlands

Freshwater wetlands include vegetated areas that have saturated soils, are permanently flooded, or are flooded for a sufficient period each year to support communities (two or more species) of water-dependent freshwater plants (hydrophilic plants). These wetlands include marshes, cypress domes, swamps, strands, bogs, sloughs, vegetated natural swales, and all other similar natural elements (Figure 3.29). It is a rather routine task for a botanist to identify freshwater indicator plants, to evaluate freshwater area vegetation communities, and to locate boundary lines at the upper edge of freshwater wetlands (Table 3.2).

The freshwater wetlands of each coastal subwatershed, together with creeks, lakes, and streams, comprise a natural element that should be identified as an area of critical environmental concern and managed as an integral unit (Figure 3.30). Within the water areas the freshwater wetlands are identified as vital areas to be exempted from alteration.

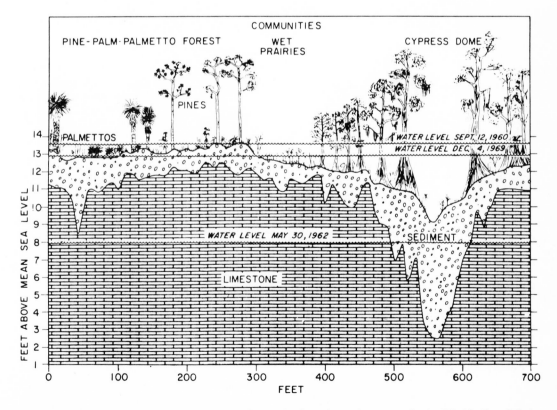

Figure 3.29   Cypress dome drainageway and adjacent lands under various water levels (Florida Everglades). (SOURCE: Reference 29.)

Table 3.2   Vegetative indicators of both saltwater and freshwater wetland areas in Collier County, Florida (SOURCE: Reference 11)

Marsh fleabane	*Pluchea foetida*
Sawgrass	*Cladium jamaicensus*
Arrowhead	*Sagittaria sp*
Pickerel weed	*Pontederia lanceolata*
Cattail	*Typha augustifolia*
Leather fern	*Acrostichum daneafolion*
Bald cypress	*Taxodium distichum*
Pond cypress	*Taxodium ascendens*
Sweet bay	*Magnolia virginiana*
Buttonbush	*Cephalanthus occidentalis*
Pond apple	*Annona glabra*
Popash	*Fraxinus caroliniana*
Willow	*Salix sp*
Glasswort	*Salicornia sp*
Saltwort	*Batis maritima*
Needlerush (black rush)	*Juncus roemerianus*
Seashore saltgrass	*Distichlis spicata*
Salt cordgrasses	*Spartina sp*
Wild Allamander	*Urechites lutea*
Rubber vine	*Rhabdadenia biflora*
Black mangrove	*Avicennia nitida*
Red mangrove	*Rhizophora mangle*
White mangrove	*Laguncularia racemosa*
Button wood	*Conocarpus erecta*

Vegetation will also be the key to the location of shoreland drainageways which are to be protected to preserve the quality, volume, and rate of flow of runoff waters that discharge to coastal water basins. For example, in Florida, cypress trees are a reliable indicator of wet ground drainage areas (see Figure 3.29). In each area there will be plant species known to professional ecologists that indicate drainageways.

The vegetative indicator system should identify not only the critical water areas as they exist presently but also, to some extent, those previously drained or otherwise degraded but restorable, because many of the plants from such areas remain even though they are no longer capable of reproducing.

Dunes and Beachfronts

The delineation of *dunes* is complicated by two principal factors. First, because they are often quite mobile and do not remain in place, they require a special approach in surveying and inventory. Second, dunes come in a variety of shapes and sizes; and when they are small, flat ridges, as they often are, they are not easily distinguishable from other parts of the beachfront (Figures 3.31 and 3.32). Dunes are most properly considered part of the shorelands (like floodplains), while the beach and associated berms are part of the coastal waters basin (being washed by tidewaters at least once per year).

Dunes and beaches require protective management and should be identified and classified for this purpose. The whole beachfront should be designated an area of critical environmental concern, from the inner edge of the active dune line to the seaward extent of local community jurisdiction. The dunes themselves are classified as vital areas.

The dune system to be designated as a

Figure 3.30 Shoreland streams and other drainage channels are areas of critical environmental concern that require protection in order to conserve coastal ecosystems (Charleston, South Carolina). (Conservation Foundation photo by M. Fahay.)

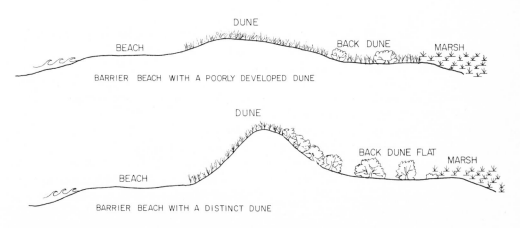

Figure 3.31 Cross sections of typical Rhode Island sand barriers showing the beach, undeveloped and developed dunes, the back dune, and the marsh. Developed dunes are usually densely vegetated by shrubs and small trees on the pond side. The primary dune vegetation is American beach grass. (SOURCE: Reference 30.)

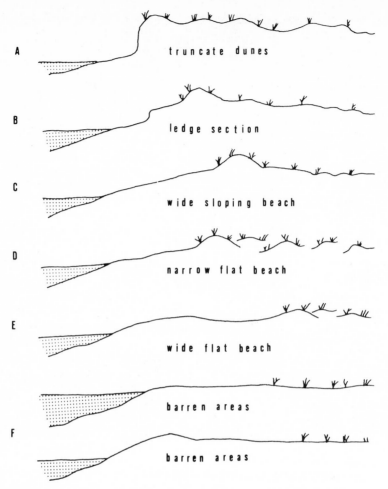

Figure 3.32 Diagrammatic cross sections of generalized beach types occurring on the barrier islands. (SOURCE: Reference 31.)

vital area should always include the frontal dune and all active secondary dunes. Basically it should be defined as extending from the "toe" of the frontal dune or beach ridge —the place where significant vegetation begins—to the back side of the most inland active dune. An "active" dune is one that is mobile, or in the process of visibly gaining or losing sand; such a dune is usually vegetated mostly with grasses rather than woody vegetation.

A *beach* may be defined as the unvegetated part of the shoreline formed of loose material, usually sand, that extends from the upper berm to the low-water mark. The

typical beachfront complex is composed of the following parts (Figure 3.33):

1. *Bar.* An offshore ridge that is submerged permanently or at higher tides.
2. *Trough.* A natural channel running between an offshore bar and the beach, or between offshore bars.
3. *Foreshore.* The part of the shore lying between the crest of the most seaward berm and the ordinary low-water mark; it is ordinarily traversed by the uprush and backrush of the waves as the tides rise and fall.
4. *Backshore.* The arm of the beach that is

usually dry, that lies between the foreshore and the coastline, and that is acted upon by waves only during storms and exceptionally high water.

5. *Berm.* A ridge or ridges on the backshore of the beach, formed by the deposit of material by wave action, that marks the upper limit of ordinary high tides and wave wash; berms have sharply sloping leading edges.

6. *Beach ridge.* A more or less continuous mound of beach material behind the berm that has been heaped up by wave action during extreme high-water levels (if largely wind built, usually termed "dunes," often vegetated).

7. *Dunes.* More or less continuous mounds of loose, wind-blown material, usually sand, behind the berm (often vegetated). The first layer dune is termed the "foredune," or the "frontal" or "primary" dune; those behind the frontal dune are called "secondary," "rear," or "back" dunes.

The anatomy of the beach remains generally constant, but its profile often shifts markedly with the seasons (Figure 3.34), particularly in response to winter storms. The berm-and-dune system acts as a buffer to the force of storm seas. As the dune is attacked by storm waves, eroded material is carried out and deposited offshore, where it alters the shore profile. Accumulating sand decreases the offshore beach slope (makes it more nearly horizontal), thereby presenting a broader bottom surface to storm wave action. This surface absorbs or dissipates, through friction, an increasingly large amount of destructive wave energy that would otherwise focus on the beach. It is the capacity of the berm-and-dune system to store sand and yield it to the adjacent submerged bottom that gives this system its outstanding ability to protect the shorelands. Low dunes have a lesser but nevertheless significant effect. Since storm resistance increases with dune height, all human uses of the barrier that devegetate, erode, or lower the dune expose the shorelands to increased storm damage.[30] An important exception is the overwash barrier beach, which functions in a different fashion (see page 573).

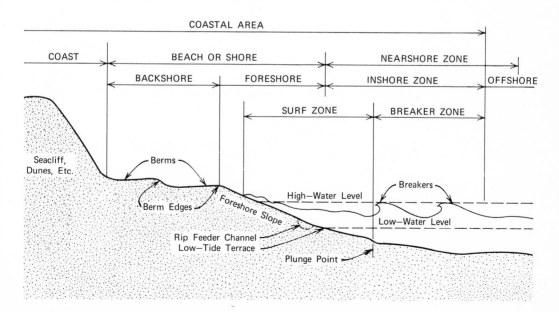

Figure 3.33 The anatomy of a typical beachfront. (SOURCE: Reference 32.)

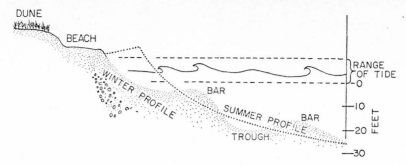

Figure 3.34 Typical winter and summer beach profiles. (SOURCE: Reference 30.)

Coastal Wetlands

In the profile of the shore landscape, coastal wetlands are recognized as areas subject to flooding by brackish or salty water and naturally vegetated with salt-tolerant plants (Figure 3.35). These plants occur in communities variously dominated by certain types of grasses, rushes, and other salt-tolerant species, including mangrove trees in subtropic and tropic areas. Soils may also be indicative of wetland areas, but they do not serve this role as readily or practicably as vegetation. The coastal wetlands are identified as vital areas because they play a valuable and critical role in the functioning of

coastal ecosystems and the maintenance of high levels of carrying capacity (Figure 3.36).

Because of the changing relative influence of various governing factors, there is a gradation in plant species from the lowest elevation of the wetlands up the slope to the upper boundary of the wetlands. It is relatively easy to find the point above which there is no significant growth of salt-water-tolerant plants. This will be the inner boundary of the coastal waters, as well as the wetlands, and approximates the annual flood mark or annual storm line—the point of the highest expected yearly storm surge, that is, the highest level to be ex-

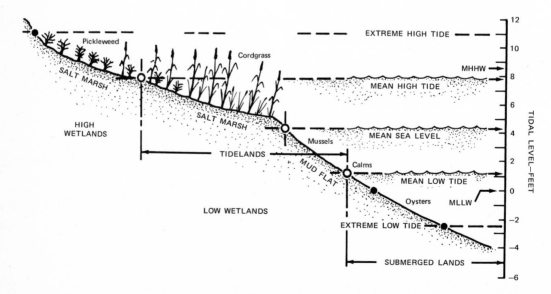

Figure 3.35 Profile of a California wetlands shoreline. (SOURCE: Reference 33.)

Figure 3.36 The soils around the fringes of coastal marshes support a variety of life that contributes to the food chain of the coastal ecosystem; the holes are burrows of fiddler crabs in a marsh near St. Augustine, Florida. (Conservation Foundation photo by M. Fahay.)

pected from normal storm action during the course of a year (see Figure 3.6).

The particulars of zonation vary from one coastal area to another, depending on the influence of a wide variety of natural conditions (see Figure 3.8). Professional assistance will be required in identifying, evaluating, and aligning boundaries (a general guide to indicator plants is given in the Appendix, page 896). Often the position of the boundary between the wetlands and the uplands will be controversial because any possible private property holdings below the boundary will be subject to strict controls on use.

It is convenient to distinguish between the *lower wetlands* (vegetated tidelands) and the *upper wetlands* because the two are often quite different in form, vegetation, and function, as well as in the application of environmental regulations. The lower wetlands extend from the low-water mark up to about the mean high-water mark. The upper wetlands extend from about the mean high-water mark up to the annual flood mark. (Figure 3.37).

The *upper wetlands* are naturally vegetated with salt-tolerant plants that prosper

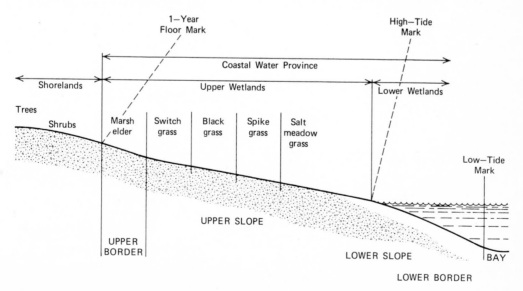

Figure 3.37 Vegetative zonation of a typical southern New England marsh shore. (SOURCE: Adapted from Reference 34.)

in the wet soils of the high marsh. Because they form the marginal zone of the estuarine water basin, when present, their landward edge is the boundary between the coastal waters province and the shorelands province. Immediately above the wetlands lie the floodplains, the lower, marginal zone of the shorelands. The line of demarcation between the two marginal zones—and therefore between shorelands and estuary—is readily identified by the sharp change in plant species near the high annual storm-water marks. (This transition zone is ecologically identified as an *ecotone*.) For example, the upper edge of the saltbush (*Iva frutescens*) clearly marks the boundary of coastal wetlands in many areas (Figure 3.38).

The lower wetlands extend down to the low-water mark from the high-water mark ("low-water mark" and "high-water mark" are used in a deliberately general sense because the exact tidal reference varies from place to place, and the boundary between upper and lower wetlands is more a zone than a line). The boundary between lower and upper wetlands is distinguishable by a change in species or in the *vigor* of species (height, color, size of leaf or blade). The lower wetlands are most often dominated by a species of *Spartina* grass, such as *alterniflora*, or of mangrove, such as *Rhizophora mangle*.

Tideflats

Tideflats may be defined as mostly unvegetated areas that are alternately exposed and inundated by the falling and rising of the

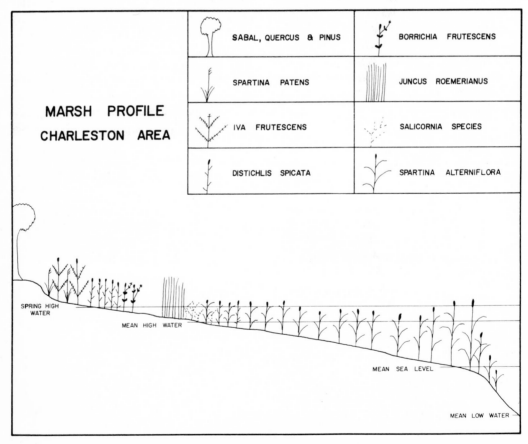

Figure 3.38   Typical transect of tidal salt marsh in Charleston Harbor estuary. (SOURCE: Reference 35.)

Figure 3.39   Tidal flats, which serve vital ecological functions, are easily classified and mapped (Ship Harbor, Maine). (Conservation Foundation photo by J. Chess.)

tide. They may be *mud flats* or *sand flats*, depending on the coarseness of the material of which they are made. They perform important functions for the estuarine ecosystem (Figure 3.39).

Submerged Grass Beds

Marine grasses grow in shallow waters in all latitudes where the currents are not too swift, wave action is low, and the bottom sediments are favorable. They occur on submerged bottoms in patterns of succession that are related to depth and other variables —salinity, temperature, turbidity, currents, and so forth. They prosper in the quiet, protected waters of healthy estuaries, often in "beds" that can easily be delineated in surveys for classification as vital habitat areas. Such grass beds are made of stands of various species of submerged sea grasses. They are normally found in shallow areas to a depth that light can readily penetrate and permit photosynthesis to occur under existing circumstances. They extend shoreward only to the point where a substantial disturbance from waves breaking on shore

begins—depths of a foot or more below mean low water.

Coral Reefs, Kelp Beds, and Shellfish Beds

Among the vital areas most readily located and mapped are coral reefs (page 44), kelp beds (page 44), and shellfish beds (page 30), but their identification and delineation is normally a job for a specialist. They have definite physical characteristics, and their boundaries can be readily determined. They tend to remain rather constant in size and position, except for certain shellfish beds on shifting bottoms.

Breeding Areas

Many far-ranging species tend to concentrate for spawning in specifically defined vital habitat areas. Breeding places vary from species to species. For example, salmon normally spawn only in specific shallow areas far up certain freshwater streams, where the right gravels are present for the depositing of eggs. On the other hand,

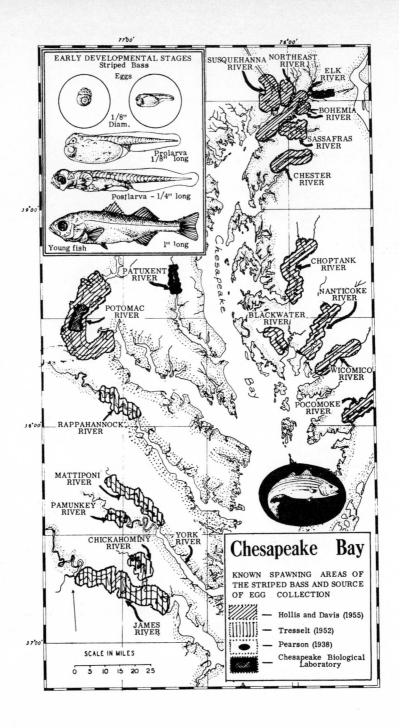

Figure 3.40 Range and location of spawning areas of striped bass in Chesapeake Bay, with illustrations of selected early development stages. (SOURCE: Reference 36.)

striped bass cast their eggs into the water of tidal rivers above the salt front, so that the tiny hatchlings drift down into brackish estuarine areas (Figure 3.40). It is common for young stages of many other coastal fish species to be planktonic, that is, to remain suspended and to drift with the currents for an extended period of time until they reach nursery areas (Figure 3.41). For example, winter flounder spawn mostly in deeper areas of the brackish upper ends of certain estuaries, and their young drift down into the bays.

Some important species of waterfowl (e.g., mallards and wood duck) and most wading birds also breed in limited coastal locations. Many seabird species breed in rookeries along the mainland shore or on isolated coastal islands. Seals also haul out for breeding at special coastal or island rookeries.

Nursery Areas

The young of many coastal species settle into special areas, called "nursery areas," when they are several weeks old. Here the young creatures prosper because the right food is available, predators are relatively scarce, and other conditions are most suitable for their survival (Figure 3.42). These productive nurseries should be identified and mapped as vital habitat areas requiring a maximum of protection from environmental disturbance. They may overlap with transient vital areas such as breeding areas or migration pathways. Nursery areas may be tidal creeks, shallows, grass beds, mangrove root areas, or open flats—all require special protection.

Many primarily oceanic fish are critically dependent on estuarine waters as nursery areas for their young. These fish—fluke, bluefish, menhaden, king whiting—spawn in the open sea like shrimp. Their tiny young, after hatching, drift and swim shoreward, passing through the inlets to find refuge and food in shallow estuarine waters.

A few important coastal fish are not oceanic migrants but live their whole lives within the estuaries; an example is the spotted sea trout of the South Atlantic. These year-round residents are completely dependent on the estuaries for all their survival needs. Their young also grow up in the shallow nursery areas.

The nursery area pattern of oceanic spawning fish, very common along the Atlantic and Gulf of Mexico coasts, is less common along the Pacific, where enclosed, warm, and shallow waters are scarce. However, there are important Pacific anadromous fish (species that spawn in rivers but live in the sea as adults) like salmon, shad, and Pacific striped bass, as well as estuary-spawning fish (e.g., the starry flounder), whose nursery areas require protection as vital habitats.

A detailed survey of nursery areas is required in coastal planning because there is a varied pattern of reproduction strategy among the various coastal species. For example, the young of striped bass drift downriver into estuarine nursery areas (Figure 3.43). On the other hand, Gulf of Mexico shrimp spawn in the ocean, but the young move to estuarine waters after they are hatched to spend several critical weeks or months (see Figure 1.35).

Feeding Areas

The feeding areas of mobile coastal species are often sufficiently circumscribed to be located, mapped, and protected as vital habitat areas. Waterfowl have definite and readily definable feeding areas in sloughs or marshes. Fish may also feed in certain areas, such as shellfish beds, grass beds, or coral reefs. Such ecosystem entities are vital habitat areas for reasons other than feeding, as we have seen. But there are other, not as well defined places that are restricted in extent and are important feeding areas, such as inlets or persistent tide rips, where baitfish gather to feed and game fish come to prey on them, or shallow bottoms, rich

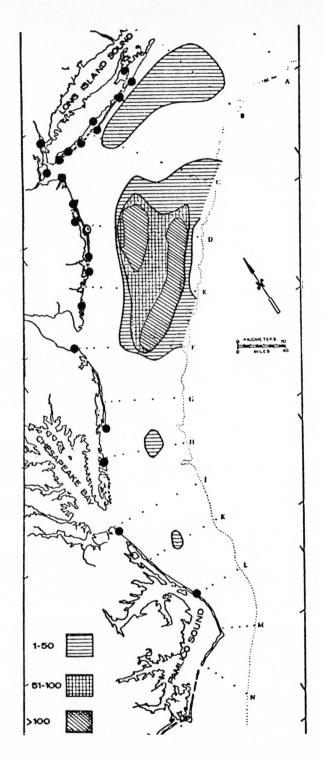

Figure 3.41 Offshore spawning areas of bluefish on the Atlantic Continental Shelf shown by shaded areas. Representative inshore nursery areas of bluefish, shown by dots. (SOURCE: Reference 37.)

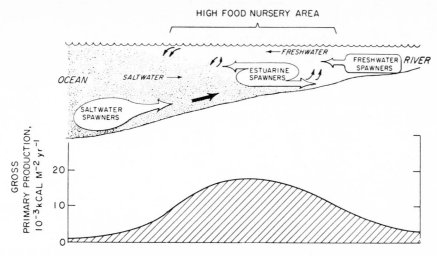

Figure 3.42   Primary productivity in various parts of a typical Atlantic estuary. (SOURCE: Reference 38.)

in bottom fauna, where diving ducks forage. These, too, need identification as vital habitats.

Migration Pathways

In their migrations, animals usually travel along particular pathways. Whereas the flyways of birds may be identified visually, the underwater pathways of fish are more difficult to locate. Fortunately these pathways are often fixed by various physical properties of the environment and remain essentially the same from year to year. Anadromous species, which travel from the ocean to spawn in rivers, often migrate along well-defined pathways—the shore edge, channel bottom, and so forth.

In a more general sense most inlets from the ocean to estuaries (and often the channels between estuarine basins) are routes of migration of fish, shrimp, or crabs and should be designated as vital areas safeguarded from pollution and other significant disturbances (Figure 3.44).

Wintering Areas

Most waterfowl species migrate from breeding places in the Far North to concentrated winter areas in more southerly regions, the majority in marshes or shallow bays along Atlantic, Pacific, and Gulf coasts (Figure 3.45).[42] For example, 2 million ducks, geese, coots, and swans winter on the salt marshes from New York to North Carolina. Many of the wintering areas of waterfowl are endangered and require preservation and protection.

Fish, too, may have special wintering areas. For example, after spending the warm seasons feeding along hundreds of miles of seacoast, much of the northern population of Atlantic striped bass seeks refuge in freshened upper estuaries (tidal rivers) for winter.

REFERENCES

1. Sherwood M. Gagliano and Johannes L. van Beek. 1975. "An approach to multiuse management in the Mississippi delta system." In Martha Lou Broussard, Ed., *Deltas, Models for Exploration*. Houston Geological Society, Houston, Texas.

2. Sherwood M. Gagliano. 1973. *Canals, Dredging, and Land Reclamation in the Louisiana Coastal Zone*. Hydrologic and Geologic Studies of Coastal Louisiana, Report No. 14, Center for Wetland Resources, Louisiana State University, Baton Rouge, Louisiana.

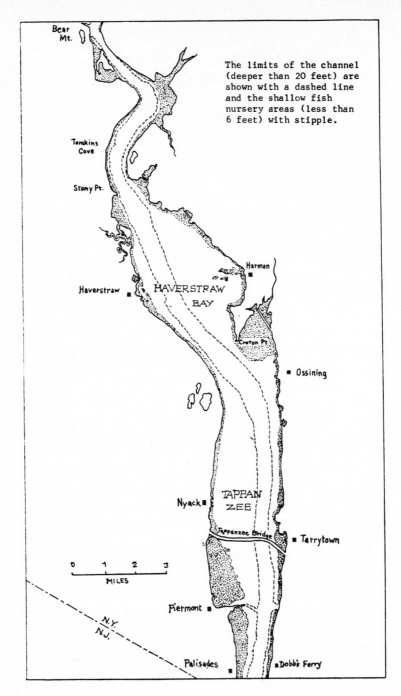

The limits of the channel (deeper than 20 feet) are shown with a dashed line and the shallow fish nursery areas (less than 6 feet) with stipple.

Figure 3.43 Primary shallow striped bass nursery areas in the Hudson estuary, New York. Significant spawning areas are found from Stony Point north some 75 miles up the river valley. (SOURCE: Reference 39.)

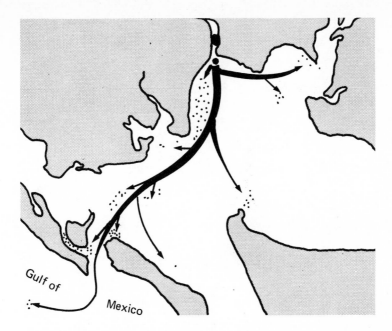

Figure 3.44   Outward migration of tagged brown shrimp from Galveston Bay, Texas. (SOURCE: Reference 40.)

3. California Coastal Zone Conservation Commissions. 1975. *California Coastal Plan.* Sacramento, California.

4. Richard E. Galantowicz. 1972. *The Process of Environmental Assessment—Options and Limits.* Part II: *Natural Resource Inventory for Municipal Fun and Profit.* North Jersey Conservation Foundation, Morristown, New Jersey.

5. National Park Service. 1975. *Preliminary Natural Resources Management Plan and Environmental Assessment, Point Reyes National Seashore, California.* Department of the Interior, Washington, D.C.

6. Albert R. Veri, Arthur R. Marshall, Susan Uhl Wilson, James H. Hartwell, Peter Rosendahl, and Thomas Mumford. 1973. *The Resource Buffer Plan: A Conceptual Land Use Study, Water Management District No. 6, Collier County, Florida.* Rookery Bay Land Use Studies, Study No. 2. The Conservation Foundation, Washington, D.C.

7. J. K. McNulty, W. N. Lindall, Jr., and J. E. Sykes. 1972. *Cooperative Gulf of Mexico Estuarine Inventory and Study. Florida: Phase I, Area Description.* National Oceanic and Atmospheric Administration Technical Report, National Marine Fisheries Service Circular 368, U.S. Department of Commerce, Washington, D.C.

8. Allan Marmelstein. n.d. Fish and Wildlife Service, Washington, D. C. Personal communication.

9. Paul R. Stang. 1975. "Inland boundaries of a state's coastal zone." In *Boundaries of the Coastal Zone.* Office of Coastal Zone Management, National Oceanic and Atmospheric Administration, Washington, D.C.

10. Bernard J. Yokel. 1973. *Estuarine Water Quality.* Rookery Bay Land Use Studies, Study No. 3. The Conservation Foundation, Washington, D.C.

11. John R. Clark. 1974. *Rookery Bay: Ecological Constraints on Coastal Development.* The Conservation Foundation, Washington, D.C.

12. D. R. Storm. 1973. *Hydrologic and Water Quality Aspects of the Tomales Bay Environmental Study.* Storm Engineering and Design Water and Waste Management, Davis, California.

13. Everett H. Ramey. 1974. Coastal Mapping Division, National Ocean Survey, National Oceanic and Atmospheric Administration, Rockville, Maryland. Unpublished communication.

14. ASPO Planning Advisory Service. 1972. *Regulations for Flood Plains,* No. 277. Chicago, Illinois.

15. E. P. Odum. 1971. *Fundamentals of Ecology.* W. B. Saunders Co., Philadelphia.

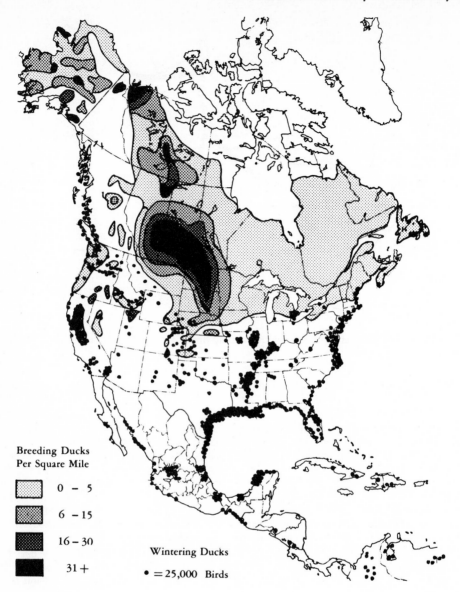

Breeding Ducks
Per Square Mile

- 0 − 5
- 6 − 15
- 16 − 30
- 31 +

Wintering Ducks

• = 25,000 Birds

Figure 3.45 Migratory ducks typically winter in certain places far to the south of their breeding areas. (SOURCE: Reference 41.)

16. D. W. Pritchard. 1967. "What is an estuary? Physical viewpoint." In G. E. Lauff, Ed., *Estuaries*. American Association for the Advancement of Science, Publication No. 83, Washington, D.C.

17. L. E. Cronin and A. J. Mansueti. 1971. "The biology of an estuary." In Philip A. Douglas and Richard H. Stroud, Eds., *A Symposium on the Biological Significance of Estuaries*. Sport Fishing Institute, Washington, D.C.

18. Eric M. Smith and Richard D. Wood. 1973. *The Salinity Gradient and Vegetation in the Saugatucket River Estuary*. Marine Technical Report Series No. 6, University of Rhode Island, Kingston, Rhode Island.

19. Thomas N. Lee and Bernard J. Yokel. 1973. *Hydrography and Beach Dynamics*. Rookery Bay Land Use Studies, Study No. 4, The Conservation Foundation, Washington, D.C.

20. U.S. Army Corps of Engineers. 1973. *Shore*

Protection Manual, Vol. III. U.S. Army Coastal Engineering Research Center, Vicksburg, Mississippi.

21. Florida Coastal Coordinating Council. 1972. *Florida Coastal Zone Management Atlas*. Tallahassee, Florida.

22. E. T. La Roe. 1974. *Environmental Considerations for Water Management District No. 6 of Collier County*. Rookery Bay Land Use Studies, Study No. 8, The Conservation Foundation, Washington, D.C.

23. Rice Center for Community Design and Research. 1974. *Environmental Analysis for Development Planning, Chambers County, Texas. Technical Report*, Vol. 1: *An Approach to Natural Environmental Analysis*. Rice University, Houston, Texas.

24. Florida Stat. Ann. 380. 012-100 (Supp. 1972).

25. California Pub. Res. Code 2700-27650.

26. U.S. Senate. 1971. *Coastal Zone Management Hearings*. Subcommittee on Oceans and Atmosphere of Commerce Committee. May 5, 6, and 11, 1971. (Ser. No. 92-15.)

27. North Carolina Coastal Zone Management Act of 1973.

28. U.S. Congress. The Coastal Zone Management Act of 1972. P.L. 92-583.

29. J. Klein, W. J. Schneider, B. F. McPherson, and T. J. Buchanan. 1970. *Some Hydrologic and Biologic Aspects of the Big Cypress Swamp Drainage Area, South Florida*. Open-file Report 70003, U.S. Geological Survey, Washington, D.C.

30. Stephen B. Olsen and Malcolm J. Grant. 1973. *Rhode Island's Barrier Beaches*, Vol. I: *A Report on a Management Problem and an Evaluation of Options*. Marine Technical Report Series No. 4, Coastal Resources Center, University of Rhode Island, Kingston, Rhode Island.

31. A. Sydney Johnson, Hilburn O. Hillestad, Sheryl F. Shanholtzer, and G. Frederick Shanholtzer. 1974. *An Ecological Survey of the Coastal Region of Georgia*. National Park Service, Scientific Monograph Series No. 3, Superintendent of Documents, U.S. Government Printing Office, Washington, D.C.

32. U.S. Army Corps of Engineers Division, Pacific Ocean Corps of Engineers. 1971. *Hawaii Regional Inventory of the National Shoreline Study*. Honolulu, Hawaii.

33. Harold B. Goldman. 1973. *Hayward Shoreline Environmental Analysis*. Hayward Area Shoreline Planning Agency, Hayward, California.

34. M. F. Roberts. 1971. *Tidal Marshes of Connecticut*. The Connecticut Arboretum, Report Series No. 1, Connecticut College, New London, Connecticut.

35. Office of Marine Conservation, Management, and Services. 1972. *A Study of the Charleston Harbor Estuary with Special Reference to Deposition of Dredged Sediments*. South Carolina Wildlife and Marine Resources Department, Marine Resources Center, Charleston, South Carolina.

36. R. J. Mansueti. 1961. "Effects of civilization on striped bass and other estuarine biota in Chesapeake Bay and tributaries." In *Proceedings, Gulf and Caribbean Fisheries Institute*, 14th Annual Session, Miami, Florida.

37. J. R. Clark. 1968. "Salt-water fish prefer estuaries." *In-Sight*. Bureau of Sport Fisheries and Wildlife, U.S. Department of the Interior, Washington, D.C.

38. W. L. Dovel. 1971. *Fish Eggs and Larvae of the Upper Chesapeake Bay*. National Research Institute, University of Maryland, Special Report No. 4, College Park, Maryland.

39. J. R. Clark. 1969. Testimony before U.S. House of Representatives, Committee on Merchant Marine and Fisheries, Subcommittee on Fish and Wildlife, June 24, 1969. Ser. No. 91-10: 11-26.

40. B. J. Copeland, H. T. Odum, and F. N. Mosely. 1974. "Migrating subsystems." In H. T. Odum, B. J. Copeland, and E. A. McMahan, Eds., *Coastal and Ecological Systems of the United States*, Vol. III. The Conservation Foundation, Washington, D.C.

41. J. P. Linduska, Ed. 1964. *Waterfowl Tomorrow*. Bureau of Sport Fisheries and Wildlife, U.S. Department of the Interior, Washington, D.C.

42. U.S. Department of the Interior. 1970. *National Estuary Study*. Fish and Wildlife Service, Washington, D.C.

CHAPTER FOUR

The Management Framework

In choosing strategies to protect its estuarine resources, each community should benefit fully from the actions of higher levels of government. The community should be aware of the important implications of federal and state actions and the opportunities therein to benefit the community. For one thing, the local unit of government should include, as a key element of a conservation strategy, actions to encourage careful local application of federal and state laws. For another, federal and state laws, carefully applied, can provide a considerable amount of the needed protection of local coastal areas and prevent some (though not all) of the local resistance that would otherwise occur with the application of purely local policies. In this section we discuss briefly the institutional setting for coastal ecosystem management and certain of the relationships among various levels of government, stressing the state and federal programs that are particularly relevant (Table 4.1).

The responsibilities of various levels of government may be clearly separate or perhaps combined or coordinate. On the one hand, the U.S. Environmental Protection Agency (EPA) delegates most implementation responsibility for water pollution to the states. On the other hand, the Federal Insurance Agency deals directly with local government. In between is the U.S. Army Corps of Engineers, a body that coordinates with state and local governments and normally requires approval from both before taking actions that affect local interest.

In this chapter we describe selected major elements of federal and state law, policy, and programs, and indicate where we believe they fit best into the overall management scheme. We include a discussion of the most salient federal laws, policies, and programs and their relation to state authorities. We *by no means* cover all relevant aspects, nor do we attempt to integrate all the concepts into a consolidated ecosystem conservation program.

Table 4.1 Permitting and review authorities of the federal government and the state of Florida (SOURCE: Reference 1)

	MAJOR RESPONSIBILITY							PRIMARY JURISDICTION										
	Land	Water	Air	Fish and Wildlife	People	Services	Planning	Upland	Below M.H.W.	Navigable Water	Wetlands	Submerged Lands	Coastal	Areas of Critical Concern	Parks and Recreation	Preserves	Sea Bed	High Seas
FEDERAL																		
National Marine Fisheries Service [1]		●		●					●	●		●						
Army Corps of Engineers [2]		●					○		●	●		●	●				●	
Environmental Protection Agency	●	●	●		●		●		●	●		●						
Department of Housing and Urban Development	●					●		●				●						
Bureau of Sports Fisheries and Wildlife [3]	●	●						●			●				●	●		
National Park Service [3]	●	●	●				○	●	●		●	●	●		●	●		
U.S. Geologic Service [3]		●					○		●	●		●						
Bureau of Outdoor Recreation [3]	●	●													●	○		
Federal Highway Administration [4]	●				●		●	●	○									
U.S. Coast Guard [4]		●					●		●	●		●	●					●
STATE																		
Administrative Commission [a]	●	●		●			●	●	●		●	●	●		●	●		
Division of State Planning [a]	●	●	●	●	●	●	●	○	○	●	●			●	○	○		
Division of Florida Land Sales [b]	●	●						●		●								
Coastal Coordinating Council	●	●		○		○	●	○	●	○	●	●				○		
Department of Commerce					●													
Department of Natural Resources	●	●	●	●	●	○	●	●	●	●	●	●	●		●	○		
Department of Pollution Control	●	●	●	○	●	○	○	●	●	●	●	●	●	●	○	○	○	
Department of State	○	○	○		●		●											
Department of Transportation	●	●	●		●	●	●	●	○	○								
Public Service Commission						●												
Trustees Internal Improvement Trust Fund	●	●		○			○	○	●	●	○	●	●	○				
REGIONAL																		
FCD	●	●				○	●	●	●	○		○	○	●				
Regional Planning Councils	●	●	●	●	●	●	●	●	●	○	●	○		●				
LOCAL (within political boundaries)																		
Municipal Commission	●	●	●	●	●	●	●	●	●	●	●	●	●	●	●	●	○	○
Planning Department	●	●	●	○	●	●	●	●	●	○	●	●	●	●	●	●		
Building and Zoning	●	●	●		●	●	●	●	●	○	●	●	●	●	●	●		
Pollution Control	●	●	●	●	●	○	●	●	●	●	●	●	●	●	●	●		

● Review and permit
○ Advisory
[1] Department of Commerce
[2] Department of Defense
[3] Department of Interior
[4] Department of Transportation
[a] Department of Administration
[b] Department of Business Regulation

The basic divisions of the coastal eco-system conservation program—shoreland, water basins, and water quality—are pre-sented in separate sections after a discussion of programs of general application to the whole coastal zone. These discussions show, on the one hand, how distinct the manage-ment authorities may be for each program division and, on the other hand, how well they can be combined into a coordinated local program based on the "single system" concept.

A separate section on ecosystem restora-tion clarifies the serious need to restore past damage and to develop better programs for resource protection in the future. Whereas *ecosystem conservation* principally involves the regulatory apparatus of governments, *ecosystem restoration* depends chiefly on the capital improvement apparatus.

PUBLIC ENVIRONMENTAL POLICY AND THE CITIZEN ROLE

A striking feature of the United States system of government is the degree to which citizens may become formally involved in public policies and actions. A broad format for participation details the rights and the responsibilities of citizens when they inter-vene on behalf of the public or some ele-ment of the public.

Both in the courts and in the legislatures there has been a growing trend toward ex-posing government and private actions to broad environmental scrutiny and toward providing direct citizen participation in the decisions of government. Although such policy slows down progress on the imple-mentation of projects, it has, in many cases, proved to be the only effective way to expose misdirected, faulty, or damaging actions. While some states and local govern-ments have adopted generic source legisla-tion to provide for effective agency and public environmental scrutiny, the major central source for national environmental policy is the National Environmental Policy Act.

National Environmental Policy

The *National Environmental Policy Act (NEPA) of 1969* (42 U.S.C. Section 4321 et seq.) is of great significance, although it does not control development activities di-rectly. Its major procedural requirement is that all agencies of the federal government consider environmental effects and include in every report on federal legislation and major federal agency activities significantly affecting the environment a detailed state-ment (called an "environmental impact statement") containing the following:

1. The environmental impact of the pro-posed activity.
2. Any adverse environmental effects that cannot be avoided upon implementation of the project.
3. Alternatives to the proposal.
4. The relationships between local short-term uses of the environment and the maintenance and enhancement of long-term productivity.
5. Any irreversible and irretrievable commit-ments of resources involved in imple-menting the proposal.

The NEPA process has as its major goal the enforcement of conscientious environ-mental planning by the federal agencies. An agency's duty is to consider all possible alternative methods to achieve its goals and to choose the approach that will reduce en-vironmental impacts to the minimum. How-ever, the process really achieves this goal only in enlightened departments of govern-ment, and too often the impact statement is simply an expensive rationale of past deci-sions made with little real concern for environment. A contributing problem is that department heads themselves decide whether an action is "significant" and whether preparation of a statement is required. The easiest course is to decide that no statement is needed and hence avoid making a record of the environmental consequences of a proposed action. Before completing the report the principal federal agency involved must obtain the comments of other federal agencies with jurisdiction in the area or with special expertise.

With all its faults the NEPA process has succeeded in fostering a much higher awareness of the needs for environmental protection. Because it is applicable to all federal permit actions, NEPA is often involved in the coastal zone. For example, both discharge permits, required by the EPA, and dredge or fill permits, required by the Corps of Engineers, must be considered as subject to NEPA provisions.

Opportunity for Direct Citizen Participation

Statutory provisions for direct citizen participation in government actions are provided more liberally in environmental affairs than in most other public program areas. One finds such provisions in major federal water pollution control laws, the *Coastal Zone Management Act*, and the *"Ocean Dumping" Act*, as well as NEPA. Statutory provisions for citizen intervention appear to have been necessary to make many public programs work.

For example, public participation in the NEPA impact statement process is superficially encouraged. Often agencies appear to desire the least possible involvement in their affairs by citizens. However, NEPA officially gives citizens the right to contest (standing to intervene) a government decision in formal hearings and in the courts. The legal intervention process has proved to be a most effective last resort in preventing collaboration between federal agencies and special interests on projects that would do serious damage to the environment.

In the Coastal Zone Management Act it is made clear that the vital decisions are not to be made by a small group of state planners alone. Too much is at stake. Throughout their planning process, states must actively involve local governments, regional bodies, federal agencies, private individuals, and various interested organizations. The decision-making process must provide adequate opportunities for any interested party to offer comments or suggestions on what direction the management program should take. Public hearings are required, and Chapter 3 contains specific suggestions for citizen participation in the development of the program.[2]

GENERAL COASTAL ZONE PROGRAMS

Legislation in a few states provides for comprehensive statewide or regional land-use planning. A more typical pattern may be seen in laws that protect particular resources of critical importance, such as fisheries, wetlands, and shorelands. Most relevant state programs are organized under the federal Coastal Zone Management Act, which provides opportunity, a source of authority, and a promise of funds for coastal zone planning and management. Many states are already quite aware of the need for ecosystem conservation; many have surveyed and identified systems in need of protection and restoration (Table 4.2).

The Federal Coastal Management Program

A national program under the Coastal Zone Management Act (CZMA) of 1972 is administered by the Office of Coastal Zone Management (OCZM) of the Department of Commerce. Its basic importance lies in its encouragement of and requirements for a comprehensive and unified consideration of land and water uses that is sensitive to maintaining coastal ecological integrity. Fundamentally, the OCZM provides funds for

Table 4.2   Summary of number of estuaries suffering recurrent environmental stresses in Hawaii, by island. Some fishing and recreational use occurs in most Hawaiian estuaries; the estuaries listed experience heavy use. The islands of Niihau, Lanai, and Kahoolawe do not have significant estuaries. (SOURCE: Reference 3)

Development	Kauai	Oahu	Molokai	Maui	Hawaii	Total
Water	12	6	0	8	3	29
Agricultural						
Sugar Cane	12	5	0	2	3	22
Pineapple	1	3	0	4	0	8
Taro	4	1	0	1	1	7
Ranching	14	7	1	6	0	28
Miscellaneous	0	1	0	0	0	1
Industrial						
Sugar Factory	1	1	0	0	1	3
Pineapple Factory	1	1	0	1	0	3
Petroleum Refinery	0	1	0	0	0	1
Thermal Discharge	1	2	0	1	0	4
Quarry	1	0	0	0	0	1
Miscellaneous	1	5	0	1	1	8
Urban						
Sanitary Sewage	2	8	0	1	1	12
Urban Cesspools	9	11	0	2	1	23
Estuarine						
Commercial/Military Harbor	2	3	0	1	1	7
Small Boat Harbor	2	5	0	1	1	9
Sewage Outfall	2	5	0	1	1	9
Fishing	2	2	0	0	1	5
Recreational	8	9	0	0	1	18
Number of Estuarine Systems	15	12	3	11	4	45

planning and plan execution by the state. It also provides funds for acquiring and operating "estuarine sanctuaries" and enables the state to require federal agencies to carry out their activities in compliance with the state's coastal policies ("federal consistency").

It is the stated purpose of the OCZM to "stimulate state leadership in planning and management of the coastal zone, and to bring into harmony the social, economic and ecological aspects of land and water use decisions of more than local significance." Furthermore, "through a series of incentives centered on a federal grants program and buttressed by technical assistance, the Act encourages a new partnership among various levels of government, through which each may exercise its unique management capabilities."[4] Federal guidelines set a framework for state coastal program development. Since the program lacks federal regulatory powers and financial "sanctions", its success depends on the voluntary participation of states and coastal communities, which must determine that the objectives of the national program are compatible with local managerial goals.

Three types of federal grants are offered to encourage coastal states and territories to implement comprehensive management programs. Initial grants are for program development—the planning phase. These may be followed by grants to implement a federally approved management program. To complement both planning and implementation, grants are available to help states establish estuarine sanctuaries as natural field laboratories to be used for education and research activities. All eligible Great Lakes and marine coastal states and territories (34) are participating in the program development phase (except for American Samoa).

Each governor designates a state agency responsible for administering the grant and completing the work plan. In its planning program the state must address six items:

1. Identification of the boundaries of the coastal zone.
2. An inventory and designation of areas of particular concern.
3. Broad guidelines on the priority of uses in particular areas, including specifically the uses of lowest priority.
4. A determination of permissible land and water uses that have direct and significant impacts on coastal waters.
5. The means by which the state proposes to control these uses.

6. The organizational structure that would implement the management program.

In addition, the states are required to undertake substantial consultations with federal, state, and areawide local agencies, as well as other interested parties. Specific requirements stemming from these tasks include adequate consideration of the national interest in facility siting (Figure 4.1), uses of regional (more than local) benefit, and incorporation of the federal water and air pollution control standards.

The Act specifies three optional types of controls to go into action when planning is completed (Section 306): (1) direct state regulation, (2) local regulation consistent with state-established standards, and (3) local regulation subject to state review. To secure federal approval for funding the management phase, the governor must have approved the program and the state must have developed the powers, arrangements, and authorities necessary to implement it.[4]

The OCZM gives wide latitude to each state to work out with its local units of government the specific arrangements, poli-

Figure 4.1 An important object of planning is to provide in advance for the siting of heavy industry facilities in the coastal zone (South Carolina). (Photo by author.)

Table 4.3 Requirements that are other than local in nature and in the siting of which there may be a clear national interest (SOURCE: Reference 5)

Requirements	Associated Facilities	Cognizant Federal Agencies
1. Energy production and transmission	Oil and gas wells; storage and distribution facilities; refineries; nuclear, conventional, and hydroelectric powerplants; deepwater ports	Federal Energy Administration, Federal Power Commission, Energy Research and Development Administration, Nuclear Regulatory Commission, Maritime Administration, Geological Survey, Department of Transportation, Corps of Engineers.
2. Recreation (of an interstate nature)	National seashores, parks, lakeshores, forests, large and outstanding beaches and recreational waterfronts; wildlife reserves.	National Park Service, Forest Service, Bureau of Outdoor Recreation.
3. Interstate transportation	Interstate highways, airports, aids to navigation; ports and harbors, railroads.	Federal Highway Administration, Federal Aviation Administration, Coast Guard, Corps of Engineers, Maritime Administration, Interstate Commerce Commission.
4. Production of food and fiber	Prime agricultural land and facilities; forests; mariculture facilities; fisheries.	Soil Conservation Service, Forest Service, Fish and Wildlife Service, National Marine Fisheries Service.
5. Preservation of life and property	Flood and storm protection facilities; disaster warning facilities.	Corps of Engineers, Federal Insurance Administration, NOAA, Soil Conservation Service.
6. National defense and aerospace	Military installations; defense manufacturing facilities; aerospace launching and tracking facilities.	Department of Defense, NASA.
7. Historic, cultural, esthetic and conservation values	Historic sites; natural areas; areas of unique cultural significance; wildlife refuges; areas of species and habitat preservation.	National Register of Historic Places, National Park Service, Fish and Wildlife Service, National Marine Fisheries Service.
8. Mineral resources	Mineral extraction facilities needed to directly support activity.	Bureau of Mines, Geological Survey.

cies, and procedures to carry out coastal management. Most of the job may pass to communities, or, alternatively, the state may retain much of the power, depending on the situation in the particular state. The OCZM is concerned mainly with the adequacy of program processes, rather than their specific substance. In short, the program does not set specific standards and goals to be achieved by the states. Rather, it relies on demonstration by the states that they have developed adequate levels of performance, capability, and authority to deal with coastal management problems.

The encouragement of the state to coordinate governmental levels—local to federal—during program development is intended to ensure that the dual intent of the law is met. The intent is that each coastal state establish a process for accomplishing the general goals of the Act, and that these state plans in their aggregate serve the interests of the nation.[4]

One of the more important facets of the national interest emphasized in the Act deals with the siting of facilities. The Secretary of Commerce, before approving a state management plan, must determine that the state has built into its program a process which "provides for adequate consideration of the national interest involved in the siting of facilities necessary to meet requirements which are other than local in nature" (Table 4.3). The purpose is to ensure that refineries, power plants, and other major (often unpopular or intrusive) facilities that may have national importance will be adequately considered and appropriately located.[4]

Federal guidelines encourage broad public involvement in all phases of the plan development at the state level. Federal program management is coordinated with the National Environmental Policy Act, and public hearings are held by the federal government before it approves a state management program. Reference to public involvement in coastal resources management implicitly means hearing diverse interests. The Act requires melding these views with "science and politics."[4]

The Act was passed primarily as an environmental protection measure. The congressional findings, the declaration of congressional intent, and the legislative history of the Act manifest a desire that decisions regarding the coastal zone give to ecological, cultural, historical (Figure 4.2), and aesthetic values a consideration at least equal to that accorded to the need for economic development.

The elements of the program of most direct environmental interest are the following:[6]

1. *Permissible uses.* Determination of land and water uses having a "direct and sig-

Figure 4.2 Historic, cultural, and aesthetic values are to be protected in coastal zone management, along with ecological values (ruins of the Dungeness mansion on Cumberland Island, Georgia). (Conservation Foundation photo.)

nificant" impact on coastal waters and identification of the uses that seem permissible. States should develop a method for ensuring that use decisions are made in an objective manner, applying the best available information concerning land and water capability and suitability. The development of *indices* for determining environmental and economic impact (beneficial, benign, tolerable, adverse) is suggested as an essential analytical step needed to give substance and clarity to the uses that are deemed permissible. When a state prohibits a specific use within the coastal zone, it must give its reasons.

2. *Areas of particular concern.* Inventory and designation of the following: areas of

unique, fragile habitat or of historical or scenic significance; areas of high natural productivity or essential habitat for living resources; areas of recreational value; areas where developments and facilities are dependent on utilization of, or access to, coastal waters; areas of unique geological significance; areas of urban concentration; areas of significant hazard from storms, slides, flood erosion, or subsidence; areas needed to protect, maintain, or replenish coastal lands, including coastal floodplains, aquifer recharge areas, sand dunes, coral and other reefs, beaches, offshore sand deposits, and mangrove stands (Figure 4.3).

3. *Areas of preservation.* A designation closely linked to the areas of particular

Figure 4.3 Salt marshes are among the vital areas suggested for protection under the federal Coastal Zone Management Program (South Creek, North Carolina). (Conservation Foundation photo by M. Fahay.)

concern. A state must establish standards and criteria for the designation of coastal areas intended for preservation or restoration because of their conservation, recreational, ecological, or aesthetic values. The fact that a state may be unable to proceed with the acquisition of certain of these properties because of temporary funding difficulties should not prevent the state from designating these areas in order of priority.

4. *Priority uses.* Priority guidelines indicating the degree of state interest in the preservation, conservation, and orderly development of specific areas throughout the coastal zone. This designation of priorities will provide the basis for regulating land and water uses in the coastal zone and serve as a common reference point for resolving conflicts. A state must show that a method has been developed for (1) analyzing state needs that can be met most effectively and efficiently through land and water uses in the coastal zone and (2) determining the capability and suitability of meeting these needs in specific locations of the coastal zone.

The OCZM requires that coastal management activities proceed within a precisely defined area called the "coastal zone." During the planning phase, states may use a larger "planning area," from which a more carefully delineated coastal zone is eventually carved. As was mentioned earlier in the chapter, the "coastal zone" is not defined according to standards a geographer or ecologist might establish for himself. By law the "zone extends inland from the shorelines only to the extent necessary to control shorelands, the uses of which have a direct and significant impact on coastal waters." Since the controls over land and water uses apply to uses having a direct and significant impact on the coastal waters, the definition of the coastal zone depends on the type of controls to be exercised, which, in turn,

depends on how a state defines "direct and significant impact" and "coastal waters." The CZMA provides little assistance regarding the meaning of "direct and significant impact," but "coastal waters" are "those waters, adjacent to the shorelines, which contain a measurable quantity or percentage of sea water, including but not limited to sounds, bays, lagoons, bayous, ponds, and estuaries" (waters in the Great Lakes area are defined separately). Although states are bound to follow this definition in delineating coastal zones for management purposes, the variety of interpretations available and of geographical forms in the coastal region indicates that "coastal zones" differ widely among the states, depending for the most part on the extent of management desired by the states as a matter of policy, rather than on clear biophysical factors.

Congress found that the key to more effective protection and use of coastal resources is "to encourage the states to exercise their full authority over the lands and waters in the coastal zone, and that this should include unified policies, criteria, standards, methods, and processes for dealing with land and water use decisions of more than local significance." Although the OCZM allows the state-developed program to be planned and implemented through its chosen agencies, which may include local governments, areawide agencies, regional agencies, or interstate agencies, the section of the Act that outlines general techniques for the control of land and water uses in the coastal zone requires *some degree of state involvement* in the decision-making. This is important since many of the uses contemplated to be covered under the CZMA have traditionally been overseen only by local government. Hence the CZMA is designed to bring higher levels of government into the decision-making process than have participated in the past. According to the CZMA, states must choose one of three alternative general techniques: direct state land- and water-use planning and regulation; state criteria and standards for local implementation; or state review of all plans, projects, or regulations to ensure consistency with the management program. This provision of the CZMA is potentially the strongest. When there is strict adherence by states, the *decision-maker* changes, not just the rules by which he makes the decision, and that decision-maker is further removed from the site of the particular use than has been the case in the past.

Other Federal Programs

The Endangered Species Act

The U.S. Fish and Wildlife Service has the prime responsibility for the *Endangered Species Act of 1973, Public Law 93–205* (16 U.S.C. Section 1531 et seq.). Other federal agencies with roles in the implementation of the Act include the Department of Commerce, the Department of Agriculture, and the Smithsonian Institution. The Fish and Wildlife Service determines whether species or groups of animals shall be added to or removed from the lists of endangered species and threatened species or changed in status from one category to the other.[7]

The Act provides for the conservation of all animal and plant species that are determined to be "endangered" or "threatened." Endangered species are those in danger of extinction throughout all or a significant portion of their range; threatened species are those likely to become endangered within the foreseeable future throughout all or a significant portion of their range. The official purposes are "to provide a means whereby the ecosystems upon which endangered and threatened species depend may be conserved, to provide a program for the conservation of such endangered and threatened species, and to take such steps as may be appropriate to achieve the purposes of the treaties and conventions. . . ." Congress notes in this Act that one of the unfortunate consequences of growth and develop-

ment in the United States and elsewhere has been the extermination of certain species and subspecies of fauna and flora; that such losses in species with educational, historical, recreational, and scientific value continue to occur; and that a key to more effective conservation of our native fauna which are endangered or threatened is to encourage and assist the various states in developing conservation programs for such wildlife.

The 1973 Act contains a habitat protection element (Section 6), which the Fish and Wildlife Service has been slow to implement. This element authorizes the Service (through the Interior Department) to identify habitats essential to the perpetuation of any of the endangered or threatened species and to require other federal agencies to restrain any actions that would degrade such habitats—including the granting of a federal permit needed by a private developer.

Planning

Since 1954 the federal government has had a grant program to aid local governments in the preparation of community master plans. Authorized by Section 701 of the Housing Act of 1954 is the Comprehensive Planning Assistance Program, often referred to as the 701 program. As initially enacted, the assistance program was for cities of under 25,000. By amendment the program was expanded to include cities, counties, metropolitan planning agencies, Indian tribes, interstate agencies, and the states. Under its auspices the federal government distributes grant money directly to city, county, metropolitan, regional, and state planning agencies. Funds for local planning assistance to smaller communities, however, are now channeled through state agencies. Under the Housing and Community Development Act of 1974, the emphasis of the 701 program has been changed from comprehensive plans to the recogntion of planning as a continuous process. The 701 program is coordinated with the CZMA program through the efforts of the Department of Commerce and the Department of Housing and Urban Development.

The *Federal Water Pollution Control Act Amendments of 1972* (33 U.S.C. Section 1251 et seq.) require, among other things, that states and regions engage in land-use planning to control the location of new sources of pollution, including those that pollute runoff waters and underground aquifers (33 U.S.C. Section 1288). Section 208 of the Act is aimed specifically at controlling all sources of water pollution, whether existing or potential sources, and point or nonpoint sources.

Water quality is affected, often very significantly, by land-use decisions. As a result, land-use issues can be expected to receive attention in the plan originating under Section 208. The program will undoubtedly provide impetus to existing public and private efforts to ensure that actions affecting land and resource utilization accurately reflect long-term public needs and desires. Section 208 planners are responsible for seeking the most effective ways to achieve water quality goals. There must be an examination of all the activities that result in water pollution and an analysis of alternative methods for reducing such pollution. Unlike previous federal water quality programs, Section 208 provides for management of nonpoint as well as point sources. To the maximum extent possible, the planning is to be on an areawide or regional basis. Section 208 requirements must be fulfilled either by the state or by a locally operated planning agency in a designated regional area, usually composed of numerous local jurisdictions.[8]

The state governor makes the final designation decision, and the state assumes responsibility for Section 208 planning in all nondesignated areas. In designated areas local governments must bear considerable responsibility for the direction and outcome of planning efforts. They are also responsible for devising a system for continuing financing of the program. Their individual actions—passage of sedimentation control ordinances, alterations in zoning laws, institution of drainage design standards and street sweeping routines, for example—will, in many cases, be critical to implementation of the plan. Local governments may assume significant portions of management agency responsibility. These responsibilities necessitate involvement of the local governments— and the individuals and interest groups they represent—from the earliest stages of plan development. As part of the Section 208 designation process, resolutions are obtained from local governments demonstrating their intentions to develop and implement areawide plans. This represents just one of several effective methods of focusing the attention of local governments on their responsibilities for the program's success.[8]

Additional Items

The *Interstate Land Sales Act of 1969* (15 U.S.C. Section 1701 et seq.) requires a developer of 50 or more lots to make a full disclosure of the subdivision's significant aspects. The *Land Use and Water Conservation Fund Act of 1965* (16 U.S.C. Section 460 L-4) provides federal grants for public acquisition of outdoor recreation areas. Section 22 of the *Water Resources Development Act of 1974* (Pub. L. No. 93-251, 88 Stat. 49) authorizes the Army Corps of Engineers to assist states in comprehensive planning for the Coastal zone. The *Clean Air Act of 1970* (42 U.S.C. Section 1857 et seq.) has land-use implications for the coastal zone, through provisions that require development to be controlled in order to avoid the significant deterioration of already clean air [42 U.S.C. Section 1857(b); 39 Fed. Reg. 42510 (1974); see *Fri v. Sierra Club*, 412 U.S. 541 (1973)] or, in polluted areas, to attain or maintain national air quality standards (42 U.S.C. Section 1857c-5; 40 C.F.R. Part 52.12).

SHORELANDS MANAGEMENT

Conservation of coastal ecosystems extends inland to embrace all of the coastal watersheds that make up a community's shorelands (page 119). Two elements are paramount in management: (1) water area conservation, and (2) land development control. Site preparation is the focus of management because it is the source of many major ecosystem conservation problems.

The basic theme of this section on shorelands management is that the natural system of water drainage and stream flow in coastal watersheds should be changed as little as possible from its original historic state. Clearing and developing land in the watersheds, if uncontrolled, can lead to serious disruption of coastal ecosystems and the resources they provide. The natural system usually accomplishes the job—con-

veying floodwaters, cleansing runoff, fostering wildlife, and generally benefitting man— more effectively and more cheaply, in the long term, than any artificial system (Figure 4.4). Normally the recommended alternatives are nonstructural substitutions—prevention instead of cure. Uncontrolled development activity anywhere in shoreland areas is a potential source of damage to coastal ecosystems.

For example, simply clearing the land of vegetation has many effects. One is a decrease in the ability of the watershed to hold back stormwaters (Figure 4.5). Another is an increase in the total volume of fresh water entering the estuary (page 546). Other alterations in flow are caused by water control activities such as excavation of drainage canals and by covering the land with impervious surfaces. In addition, installing storm drainage systems unbalances freshwater flow patterns and their timing

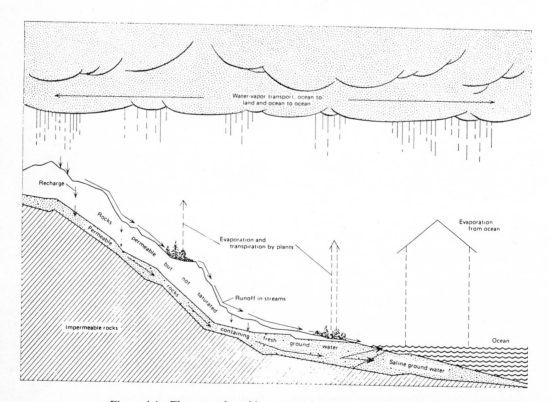

Figure 4.4   Elements of earth's water cycle. (SOURCE: Reference 39.)

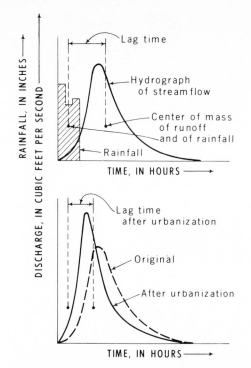

Figure 4.5 Sample hydrographs relating runoff to rainfall in urbanized and natural situations. (SOURCE: Reference 9.)

approaches are involved in the management program.

The discipline of *hydrology*, as it applies to the land surface, is well advanced, and *its principles* should be familiar to planners, water engineers, and ecologists. We can use these same principles to understand the factors that control land sources of water essential to coastal water systems. Use of hydrological principles in designing projects makes it possible to simulate closely the original patterns of freshwater supply to estuaries. This requirement represents a different concept in project design but nothing new or difficult in the way of engineering solutions that might prevent accomplishment of the following major Management Goal: *The original quality, volume, and rate of flow from coastal watershed into coastal waters should be preserved.*

Fulfillment of this goal will benefit the ecological condition of land areas and interior water areas as well as afford maximum protection to coastal ecosystem resources (Figure 4.6). For example, regularizing the runoff patterns will keep the volume and the delivery schedule of flow to coastal waters near the natural condition and thus promote optimum ecosystem function. Keeping water flow in its natural state will also ensure that such water will meet state and federal requirements and be of the best possible quality. (Exempting shoreland vital habitat areas from alteration when necessary and protecting them with marginal buffer areas will provide the essential spatial component to the shoreland program.)

Controls to prevent alteration of vital habitats and to protect the water runoff system will require an approach involving local review of development and the exercise of land-use powers by local government. Ecological constraints necessary for sound water management and conservation of coastal ecosystems will strongly influence site preparation for residential development. The activities affected include excavation, clearing, grading, paving, and the spatial ar-

and rate of delivery to the estuary. This leads to interference with normal salinity cycles in the estuary, with the recharge of freshwater aquifers, and with the water-cleansing processes of soil and vegetative cover. Finally, uncontrolled land clearing and construction greatly increases the amount of sediments, nutrients, and toxic substances carried down to estuaries with the freshwater runoff.

Shorelands areas may accommodate development at relatively high density if the original, historic, hydrological regimes throughout the land and water areas of the coastal watershed are protected so as to prevent significant adverse alteration of the shoreland water systems and thus the coastal water resources. It must be understood that the situation of the shorelands component of the coastal zone is totally different from that of the water basin and that different

Figure 4.6   Cypress sloughs are an essential ecological element of shoreland water systems in the south (Jamestown, Virginia). (Conservation Foundation photo by M. Fahay.)

rangements of a project. Significant amounts of land may be required for buffer strips, runoff detention areas, groundwater recharge, and other water protection measures.

In the pages immediately following, we discuss aspects of state and federal environmental laws, policies, and programs that have direct and specific relevance to shorelands controls, particularly land-use controls. In a later discussion we focus on the opportunities for local government to conserve coastal ecosystems through the use of existing regulatory tools. Since the shorelands program would be operated mainly through existing land-use controls, the bulk of the detailed discussion on shorelands development management is contained in the sections dealing with local government (page 233). We concentrate here on two federal programs—floodplain management and area-wide nonpoint pollution control.

Coastal Floodplain and Hazard Management

Coastal areas are often hazardous to occupy, being prone to flooding and wave damage during storms. In response to past high losses of life and property, state and federal governments have established regulatory programs to protect citizens from such hazards through floodplain management and property loss indemnification. Coastal communities have occasionally adopted special regulatory programs too. It is of paramount importance that there be coordination between the processes established for floodplain management and those set up for conservation of coastal ecosystems, since the elements of the two types of programs are remarkably parallel in many cases.

To conserve coastal ecosystems, development allowed in the floodplain should be under somewhat more stringent controls than that in the shorelands above them in order to prevent (1) erosion and general urban pollution, (2) diversion or disruption of natural drainage patterns, and (3) loss of critical habitat for coastal species. Such goals will usually require a lower density of occupancy and special constraints on landscaping, on waste disposal, on application of fertilizer and pesticides, and so forth.[10] These constraints are particularly important when the floodplain drains into a small embayment or lagoon with a restricted rate of flushing (page 127).

The National Floodplain Insurance Program (42 U.S.C. Section 4001 et seq.)

The *U.S. Flood Disaster Protection Act* (December, 1973) is destined to influence the course of coastal development in some communities through subsidized flood insurance that requires all participating communities to enforce land-use and construction standards. Although at present it appears to be merely an incentive program, it could become powerfully compelling in hazardprone coastal areas (Figures 4.7 and 4.8). According to the provisions of the law, all federal or federally related financing, including direct mortages or loans from any federal agency or from federally backed banks or lending institutions, will be cut off in communities that do not participate in the program. This includes most of the normal lending sources for residential purchase and construction. In practice, the program has enforced effective floodplain management only in willing communities so far, often those that see strong environmental benefits from its land-use provisions (Figure 4.9).

The basic purpose of the law is twofold—to provide compensation to victims of flood disasters, and to encourage effective floodplain management that will prevent or mitigate future disasters. But there is evidence that the first objective—availability of disaster relief—may militate against the second—sound floodplain management. According to H. Crane Miller:[13]

Recent studies for the New England River Basins Commission which focused on three Rhode Island communities indicate that in at least three localities flood insurance sustains and even increases already high demand and high priority values in coastal areas, substantially reduces financial risk of property owners from damage from hurricanes, and tends to act as a counterforce to effective coastal floodplain management.

Under the National Flood Insurance Program, organized under the Flood Disaster Protection Act, federally subsidized insurance against losses from flooding is available to coastal, riverline, and lacustrine (lake) communities that commit themselves to enact and enforce appropriate land-use and construction control measures (Table 4.4). These controls must be consistent with comprehensive criteria designed to (1) "constrict the development of land which is exposed to flood damage where appropriate, (2) guide the development of proposed construction away from locations which are threatened by flood hazards, (3) assist in reducing damage caused by floods, and otherwise improve the long-range management and use of floodprone areas." (See Appendix, page 790).

In addition to being areas of potential hazard to life and property, the coastal floodplains are areas of environmental concern that have limited carrying capacities and require special precautions to protect water systems (Figure 4.10). From the standpoint of environmental protection, adoption and enforcement of flood regulations sufficient to meet federal standards

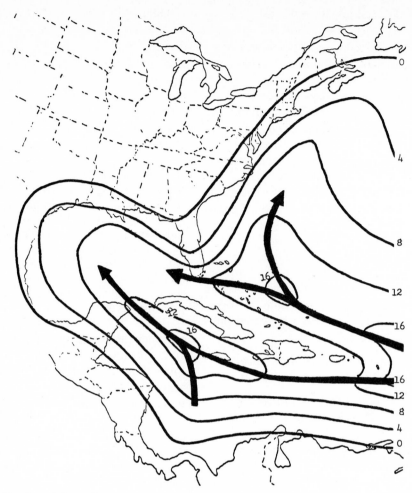

Figure 4.7   Number of times of passage in the past 100 years of an *extreme* hurricane (winds reaching more than 135 mph at some time during the storm's life cycle). (SOURCE: Reference 11.)

effectively supplement zoning or subdivision regulations designed to safeguard the coastal environment. The setbacks, building elevations, and fill prohibitions mandated by the National Flood Insurance Program all work powerfully to protect coastal ecosystems.

For example, a major provision of the Flood Disaster Protection Act in coastal areas is a required building setback for special erosion hazard areas "to create a safety buffer consisting of a natural vegetative contour strip" for receding shorelines. The Federal Insurance Agency (FIA) of the Department of Housing and Urban

Development (HUD) recommends that the buffer be used for agriculture, recreation, natural areas, open space, and related activities (page 790). Other provisions require administrative review of development proposals to ensure that the homes are properly built and anchored, that utility lines are installed to minimize flood damage, and so forth.

In communities conforming to the provisions of the Act, review of residential development proposals in coastal high-hazard areas should be painstaking. High-hazard areas are those subject to high-water

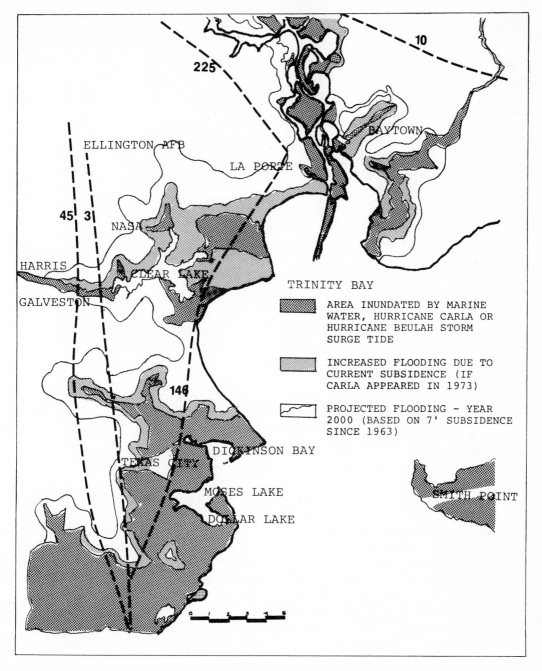

Figure 4.8   Inundation of the Galveston Bay shore (Texas) by Hurricane Carla (1961). (SOURCE: Reference 12.)

Figure 4.9   Foresighted communities can find in the National Flood Insurance Program means to prevent extreme ecological and safety hazards by discouraging the reckless placement of condominiums and other buildings on dunes and beach berms (Sanibel Island, Florida). (Photo by author.)

velocity during severe storms, that is, more than about 3 mph (Figure 4.11). The Act prohibits any structure planned for these areas to be elevated on fill: "the use of fill for structural support is prohibited within any designated high-hazard area." High-hazard areas of each community are designated by the FIA office of HUD and on boundary maps provided to the local government (Appendix p. 790).

Under the National Flood Insurance Program, residences *must* have their first-floor levels built above the 100-year flood height in all floodprone areas. These flood levels are computed for each coastal area by the FIA.

In local planning and floodplain management, it is necessary to use the 100-year flood level as the boundary of the special land-use management district, because FIA and state floodplain management criteria are based on this water level (pages 121 and

125). Designation of the 1-year and 25-year levels may also be desired locally for certain special environmental zones that would permit uses for agriculture, recreation, and open space (page 121).

Federal flood insurance incentives and restraints will definitely change the nature of coastal development in communities that cooperate fully with the federal program and further sound ecosystem management as well. It will no longer be reasonable to create lots from marshland by dredge and fill operations; massive Venetian-style, canalside home ventures such as those in Florida will no longer be feasible. Residential development will be shifted away from coastal flood hazard areas, and any structures built in such areas will largely be elevated on stilts (page 474) above flood levels to meet the provisions of the federal act (Figure 4.12). Other constraints preventing use of fill in coastal high-hazard areas and requir-

Table 4.4 How the national Flood Insurance Program works as amended by U.S. Public Law 93-234 (SOURCE: Reference 14)

Community	HUD	Chargeable or Subsidized Insurance	Actuarial or Unsubsidized Insurance
1. Writes to HUD, expressing interest in eligibility for flood insurance after which HUD sends forms and sample land use resolution; or	1a. Notifies community of tentative identification as containing one or more flood prone areas and sends application forms and sample land use resolution.	Not available	Not available
2. Community adopts initial land use measures and applies for eligibility.	3. Designates community as eligible for sale of subsidized insurance under Emergency Program within six working days after receiving completed application. HUD issues Flood Hazard Boundary Map delineating flood prone areas in community, then contracts with technical agency for rate study.	Available for all construction until date flood insurance rate map and elevation data for the area is published or until December 31, 1974, whichever is later.	
	4. Provides community with Flood Insurance Rate Map and 100-year flood elevation data. Community is given 6 months to adopt 100-year flood standard in its local zoning and building code ordinances.	Continues to be available for existing and new construction but not for buildings constructed within the hazard area after the Flood Insurance Rate Map publication date so long as it is published after December 31, 1974.	Available to all types of construction new or old.

Available Limits of Coverage	Subsidized Coverage	Total Coverage	Rates per $100 of Coverage (Subsidized Only)
Single family residential	$ 35,000	$ 70,000	.25
Other residential	100,000	200,000	.25
Nonresidential	100,000	200,000	.40
Contents, residential	10,000	20,000	.35
Contents, nonresidential	100,000	200,000	.75

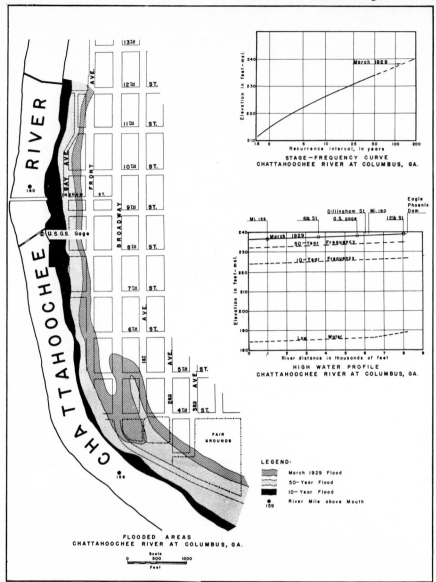

Figure 4.10   Sample riverine flood risk map (Chattahoochee River, Columbus, Georgia). (SOURCE: Reference 15.)

ing unoccupied setbacks along erosion prone coastal shores will also promote environmental goals.

State Regulations

Twenty-three states have some measure of state control over floodway or floodway fringe uses. State involvement has been necessary because local units of government have not adopted adequate floodplain controls and because they usually lack the technical expertise to map flood areas and administer controls. Regulation of the floodplain has been considered of statewide concern because of the multijurisdictional

Figure 4.11 Coastal "high-hazard zones" include exposed ocean beachfronts and their back shores for a considerable distance inland (Avon, New Jersey). (Photo by author.)

Figure 4.12 Structures elevated on pilings are protected against water rise, but not against wave action from storms in the "high-hazard zones" along the shoreline. (Photo by author.)

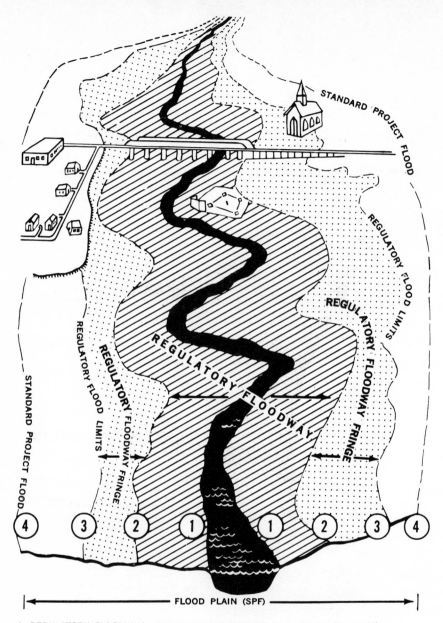

1. REGULATORY FLOODWAY—Kept open to carry floodwater—no building or fill.
2. REGULATORY FLOODWAY FRINGE—Use permitted if protected by fill, flood proofed or otherwise protected.
3. REGULATORY FLOOD LIMIT—Based on technical study—outer limit of the floodway fringe.
4. STANDARD PROJECT FLOOD (SPF) LIMIT—Area subject to possible flooding by very large floods.

Figure 4.13   Riverine flood hazard areas. (SOURCE: Reference 17.)

180

impact of floodplain and floodway uses. Floodway uses block channels, causing flood damage to upstream, downstream, or adjacent lands in other jurisdictions. State floodplain regulations include (1) dam permit and stream encroachment laws, (2) floodway regulations, and (3) floodplain regulations[16] (Figure 4.13).

COASTAL WATER BASIN PROTECTION

Three aspects of water basin condition that need major management attention are (1) changes in water circulation caused by alteration of basin configuration, (2) degradation of the general ecological condition of the bottom of the basin and its margins, and (3) loss of ecologically vital areas. Together these three aspects strongly govern the carrying capacity and the value of a coastal ecosystem to society.

Any excavation or construction in a coastal water basin bears the burden of presumption of adverse ecological effects. Changes in the shape of basins, release of sediments, deposit of spoil, or installation of structures—all have a potential for disturbance of coastal ecosystems (Figure 4.14). Alteration and degradation of vital areas also have a high disturbance potential, as discussed in a following section. Dredging activity appears to be the greatest single threat to coastal basins. For example, a whole estuarine system can be affected and its natural values seriously degraded by dredge-and-fill projects to create canalside residential lots (Figure 4.15).

Deposition of sediment, either silt fallout or spoil deposition from dredging, also has major adverse effects on coastal water basins (page 534). It can change the configuration of the basin and severely degrade the carrying capacities of large areas of estuarine bottoms (page 91). Furthermore, with loose

Figure 4.14 Marinas and the general associated commercial buildup have a strong potential for adverse alteration of the shoreline unless sited properly and designed and constructed according to appropriate standards (Merrimac River, Newburyport, Massachusetts). (Photo by author.)

Figure 4.15 Boca Ciega Bay, Florida, an estuary nearly obliterated by dredge-and-fill operations; bayfill areas (black) and proposed bayfill areas (shaded). (SOURCE: Reference 18.)

materials on the bottom, continuing resuspension by wind and tide causes increased turbidity. Therefore it is necessary to maintain strict controls on the sources of suspendible matter when navigational dredging is conducted in estuarine waters and when shorelands are being developed. Also suggested is the need for controls on boat size, speed, and traffic density in order to prevent continuing resuspension in shallow water areas. The Management Goal is: *Deposition of sediment or dredge spoil in estuarine basins is presumed to be adverse and should be avoided.*

The coastal water basin should be managed in relation to its circulation type, depth, form, and geology so that allowable water and land uses can be matched to its vulnerability to impact. The special vulnerabilities of water basins should guide policies for water traffic, waste disposal, navigation channel dredging, shoreland development, and so forth. Normally, the fundamental criterion will be the degree of water exchange or flushing rate of the water basin.

Circulation is controlled by the depth of the basin and channels, by the size of inlets or other constrictions, and by the general configuration of the basin. All these characteristics are subject to change by excavation (dredging), by filling (deposition), and by structures. Therefore excavation or major construction along the shoreline or within the water basin must be controlled to avoid significant adverse effects.

Controls on Alteration

The marginal wetlands are a functioning part of the coastal water basin subsystem and should be addressed as such. Prevention of alteration of coastal wetlands is important. The system of creeks that transect them and the existing patterns of tidal flushing should be maintained because tidal waters must have unrestricted entry to all marches and mangrove swamps (Figure 4.16). Such incursions as roads, canals, pipe-lines, drainage ditches, and transmission lines should be limited to the minimum in wetlands if the ecosystem is to function optimally (see "Vital Area Protection," page 251). Such facilities can usually be built above the wetlands, in the floodplains or adjacent uplands, and designed so as not to significantly obstruct or impede runoff water flow.

State Programs

The majority of coastal states have legislated some form of control over excavation, fill, and other alterations or uses of coastal water basins. The controlling agency may be a bureau of navigation or of environmental protection. These agencies levy royalties on sand and gravel or shell dredges or take leases on shellfish bottoms or riparian lands. They all work in close cooperation with the Corps of Engineers, often coordinating or combining the administration of permit reviews and approvals. By policy the Corps defers to the state (or local unit of government) in regard to the evaluation of permits and rejects permit applications not approved by local and state authorities.

U.S. Army Corps of Engineers

The Corps of Engineers has a major statutory responsibility to administer federal laws on the protection of the coastal zone. The Corps' basic authority over development of the coastal zone is the U.S. *River and Harbors Act of 1899.* Section 10 of the Act prohibits *without a Corps permit* any obstruction to or alteration of a navigable water of the United States. The types of activities that fall within Section 10 include the placement of structures such as piers or docks in navigable waters, dredging, filling, and excavation in such waters, as well as any other type of activity that would affect the course, location, condition, or capacity of such waters. "Navigable waters" has been broadly defined by the Corps to include al-

Figure 4.16   Roadways should be aligned to pass over high ground rather than wetlands, unless they are on piling-elevated causeways. (Photo by author.)

most every United States waterway, including those that are now or have been used for any type of interstate commerce, tidal waters, ocean waters, and any other waters that may affect interstate commerce, including adjacent wetlands.[19]

In 1972 Congress amended the Corps' responsibility with respect to dredging and filling and assigned to the U.S. Environmental Protection Agency (EPA) overview responsibilities under Section 404 of the *Federal Water Pollution Control Act Amendments of 1972.* The Corps permit for this type of activity now requires certain reviews, including notice and opportunity for a public hearing, and through court-enforced order (1975) the Corps is required to exercise permit authority over all wetlands. The Corps now takes a strong protective stance on any alteration that could degrade wetland values (Figure 4.17). (See

Appendix, page 761, for Corps regulations.)

The Corps applies a public interest review policy involving navigation, fish and wildlife, conservation, pollution, aesthetics, ecology, economics, general environmental concerns, historic values, flood damage prevention, land-use classification, recreation, water supply and quality, and the needs and welfare of the people. The policy precludes issuance of permits in valuable wetlands when the public interest dictates otherwise (i.e., the benefits from the wetlands alteration are outweighed by the loss to the wetlands resource). In making this public interest determination, Corps officials are required to consider *primarily* whether the proposed activity is dependent on the wetlands resource and environment and whether feasible alternative sites are available.[19]

The regulations of the Corps state specifically that wetlands are to be protected: "As

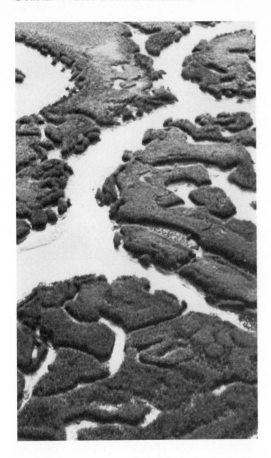

Figure 4.17 Coastal wetlands protection is now enforced under federal law by the U.S. Army Corps of Engineers, the U.S. Environmental Protection Agency, and the U.S. Fish and Wildlife Service (Georgia marshscape). (Conservation Foundation photo.)

environmentally vital areas, they constitute a productive and valuable public resource, the unnecessary alteration or destruction of which should be discouraged as contrary to the public interest." They further state: "Unless the public interest *requires* otherwise, no permit shall be granted for work in wetlands. . . ." Since the Corps has the major discretion in tidelands work for the federal establishment, one can assume that saline water areas will be altered only for public, rather than private, benefit. The test here is whether the public benefits of the proposed alteration outweigh the dam-

age to the wetland resources, and whether the proposed alteration is necessary to realize the benefit.

Corps procedures encourage public participation at various stages during the review of a permit application. Public notices that solicit comments on each permit application are widely distributed. In addition, the public is also encouraged to participate in public hearings on a particular activity and to comment on draft and final environmental impact statements prepared by the Corps during its decision-making process.[19]

The Corps has imposed on itself the same evaluation procedures and criteria and related public participation with respect to any of its own projects that involve the disposal of dredged material into United States waters or onto wetlands.

As a matter of policy, permits will not normally be issued when local or state authority is required and has been denied. Even if state or local authorization is not required, due consideration will be given to official local views.

Corps of Engineers–EPA Joint Controls

Section 404 of the 1972 federal Clean Water Act, which required a stricter permit system and guidelines to govern dredging and filling, directs primary attention toward preventing adverse effects in shellfish, fish, and wildlife habitats and recreational areas.

The rationale supporting extension of federal jurisdiction to *all wetlands* by Section 404 of the law is clear and simple. First, "navigable waters" are defined by law as "waters of the United States." Second, all coastal, estuarine, riverine, and lacustrine wetlands inundated by waters of the United States on a normally predictable basis (to the annual flood mark) are, therefore, themselves extensions and integral components of United States waters (as affirmed by a U.S. Court decision in 1975). Third, and most decisively, the value of wetlands as spawning and nursery areas for fish and

Figure 4.18   The U.S. Environmental Protection Agency has a firm policy to protect wetlands—including these mangrove forests—as ecologically vital areas. (Conservation Foundation photo by M. Fahay.)

aquatic life and as wildlife and recreational areas, as well as in the maintenance of water quality, is indisputable.

This section of the law is unique in that it makes an assessment of anticipated ecological consequences paramount to economics and navigation in granting final approval or disapproval of a dredge-and-fill project permit. This rationale represents a reversal of previous procedure; that is, it recognizes that, if the quality of coastal ecosystems is to be maintained, wetland resources must be preserved. As of 1975 the economic yardstick was no longer the decisive judgment factor.[20]

The Environmental Protection Agency was delegated ultimate authority to deny or restrict permitted actions destructive to wetlands under Section 404. The Agency's decision toward the preservation of such areas was adopted soon after receipt of this authority and is set forth in the Administrator's Decision Statement 4, "EPA Policy to

Protect the Nation's Wetlands," dated February 21, 1973 (Appendix, page 788). In this statement the importance of *all* wetlands, fresh- and saltwater alike, is recognized, along with their irreplaceability and man's dependence on them (Figure 4.18). This belief is reinforced by the statement of policy to protect all wetlands from abuse and destruction ". . . through waste water or nonpoint source discharges, and their treatment or control, or the development of waste water treatment facilities, or by physical, chemical, or biological means." When combined with the policies and responsibilities administered by the EPA under the 1972 federal Clean Water Act, this statement calls for the EPA to minimize alteration in the quality or quantity of the natural character of water inflow and withdrawals, to protect wetlands from adverse dredging and filling practices, siltation, or the addition of toxic materials arising from nonpoint source wastes and through construction activities, and to prevent violations of applicable water quality standards.

Applications for permits for the discharge of dredged or fill materials at specific disposal sites are reviewed with the EPA under Section 404(b) of the 1972 Water Act. Permits for ocean dumping must be evaluated under the standards established by Section 102(a) of the Marine Protection, Research, and Sanctuaries Act (page 196). An activity in the coastal zone of a state with a coastal zone management plan is to be evaluated in relation to the plan, and no permit is to be issued until compliance with the coastal zone management plan has been achieved (page 161).

In all permit cases the Corps must consult with the U.S. Fish and Wildlife Service (in accordance with the Fish and Wildlife Coordination Act, below). Great weight is given to the Service's views on the conservation of wildlife resources, and any unresolved objections in the local district are handled on a divisional or Washington level.

Role of the U.S. Fish and Wildlife Service

Under the *Fish and Wildlife Coordination Act* (1934, with amendments) each federal agency must submit its plans, if they would modify water bodies, for scrutiny by the U.S. Fish and Wildlife Service and by the state wildlife department, and full consideration must be given to their recommendations. To implement the provisions of the Fish and Wildlife Coordination Act and other acts affecting fish and wildlife resources, the Fish and Wildlife Service has published a set of guidelines (Appendix, page 775).

The stated objectives of the Service, in relation to dredge and fill and other coastal-waters-related activities, are "to protect and preserve fish and wildlife habitat, conserve fish and wildlife and related environmental resources, and protect public trust rights and use and enjoyment in and associated with navigable and other waters of the United States" (Figure 4.19). Other, more specific objectives include stopping and remedying all illegal activities damaging or posing a threat to the naturally functioning aquatic and wetland ecosystems or the dependent human uses and satisfaction, and insuring that work in navigable waters is truly desirable or necessary to the public health, safety, and welfare in the context of cumulative effects of other developments on the waterway and on related waterways.

The Fish and Wildlife Service actively discourages developments adversely affecting the nation's wetlands ecosystems and encourages the use of alternative upland sites. The Service provides to local government and citizens ecological advice on the formulation of federal plans and activities and technical guidance and assistance in regard to local management of waters and wetlands (see Appendix, page 775).

Area Acquisition and Designation Programs

There are federal programs authorized to purchase land in the coastal zones or to designate special areas or sites for a variety of natural, environmental, and recreational purposes: parks, seashores, wildlife refuges, educational, scientific, and wilderness areas, and historic and archaeological sites (Figure 4.20). Two recent programs of specific interest in respect to the conservation of coastal ecosystems are those establishing estuarine sanctuaries and marine sanctuaries.

Estuarine Sanctuaries

Authorized by the Coastal Zone Management Act, an estuarine sanctuary grant is made on a 50–50 percent matching basis. It enables a state to acquire estuarine water bodies and adjacent waters, wetlands, and uplands and to operate and maintain these areas for education and research in support of its coastal management efforts.

Figure 4.19   The U.S. Fish and Wildlife Service has been the nation's chief protector of the birds and wild-life of coastal wetlands and estuaries for several decades (Bear's Bluff, South Carolina). (Conservation Foundation photo by J. Chess.)

A limited number of sanctuaries are se-lected throughout the nation. The areas chosen are supposed to be representative of the nation's various ecosystem types, rather than being unique ecological areas. The criteria used in selection are based on eco-logical characteristics, size and selection of boundaries, cost, enhancement of noncom-petitive uses, proximity and access to exist-ing research facilities, availability of suitable alternative sites already protected, and lack of conflict with existing or potential com-peting uses in the area or nearby.

Unfortunately, the limited funds alloted to the program are used primarily to pur-chase lands adjacent to estuaries rather than to administer large estuarine areas as sanc-turies. There will be no more than one sanctuary for every two states. Therefore the program has little relevance to coastal communities.

Marine Sanctuaries

Under the Marine Protection, Research, and Sanctuaries Act of 1972 (or "Ocean Dump-

Figure 4.20   The federal government is the major source of funds for natural area acquisition in the coastal zone (Federal wildlife refuge on East River, Guilford, Connecticut). (Conservation Foundation photo by M. Fahay.)

ing" Act), the Office of Coastal Zone Management may designate as marine sanctuaries the areas of ocean waters seaward to the edge of the continental shelf, and other coastal waters where the tide ebbs and flows (plus the Great Lakes) that are necessary for the purpose of preserving or restoring the areas for their conservation, recreation, ecological, or aesthetic values (Figure 4.21). The state is given veto power over any OCZM determination within the territorial sea. After a marine sanctuary has been established, regulations are issued to control all activities within the area so as to preserve the sanctuary.

The law permits any area to be acquired and operated with full federal funding (when funding is necessary) and managed in a variety of ways through agreements with various federal or state agencies.

COASTAL WATER QUALITY PROTECTION

The carrying capacity of the coastal ecosystem is governed by the quality of its waters. A major factor affecting water quality is the discharge from point sources, particularly municipal sewage, industrial wastes, and thermal effluent. (Nonpoint sources, also very important, are discussed in the preceding section on shorelands, page 170). Point-source pollution control is the subject of a well-developed and very complex federal–state program; therefore it is only briefly

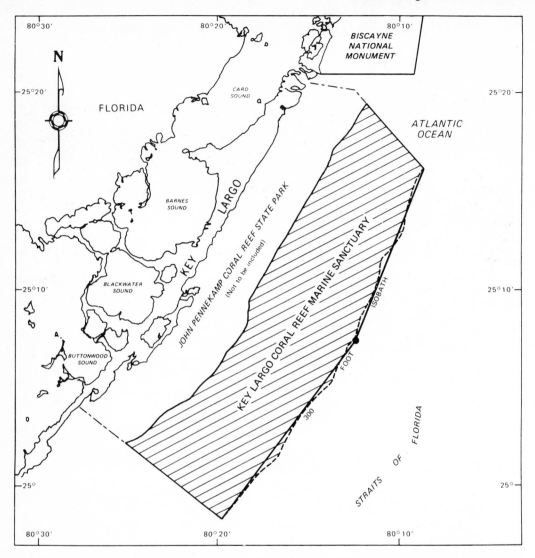

Figure 4.21   Key Largo Federal coral reef marine sanctuary adjacent to Florida State Park. (SOURCE: Reference 21.)

considered here. However, some general background information is provided on how certain circulation characteristics affect the control program on point-source pollution control (Figure 4.22).

Pollution Susceptibility

Active circulation and a good rate of flushing are usually considered beneficial because they provide rapid transport of nutrients and cleansing of the natural system, as well as performing other vital functions. To some extent, good flushing protects ecosystems stressed by development because it hastens the assimilation, dispersal, and dilution of pollution.

Lagoons

Because of very limited circulation of water and poor flushing, pollutants may easily

Figure 4.22 Human occupancy of estuarine margins normally leads to pathogen infestation of estuarine waters (Ducktrap River, Lincolnville, Maine). (Conservation Foundation photo by M. Fahay.)

build up and become pervasive in lagoons. Organic accumulation on the bottom is rapid in lagoons, and the eutrophication potential of the basin relatively great.

Embayments

These basins usually have low tidal action, and since the freshwater inflow is often not an adequate substitute, they may be easily polluted. Controls must be nearly as restrictive as those for lagoons, except for embayments characterized by unusually high rates of flushing. The vulnerability of the embayment is related to its size—the smaller ones are more valuable and require more severe restrictions for equivalent inlet width and freshwater flow.

Tidal Rivers

The tidal river basin may be a simple channel or a complex of tributaries, small associated embayments, marsh fronts, tidal flats, and so forth. It should be managed together with the bay or embayment into

which it discharges. These basins may be well flushed by the combined action of tide and freshwater outflow. The pollution damage potential varies in severity, depending on the degree of flushing and other natural factors.

Bays

Because bays are typically quite open to the sea and receive strong tidal flows, they are flushed more effectively than embayments or lagoons. The flushing action is augmented by river discharge, particularly when stratification is pronounced. Management needs are similar to those of lagoons and embayments, but controls usually can be somewhat less restrictive because of better circulation (Figure 4.23).

Sheltered Coast

In all sheltered coast areas, water movement is reduced and the effects of pollution are much increased as compared to waters of open ocean coasts. These sheltered coasts

Figure 4.23 Well-flushed northern embayments generally require less restrictive shoreland and pollution management than shallow southern lagoons (Bluehill Bay, Maine). (Conservation Foundation photo by J. Chess.)

should be managed separately from exposed coast systems. Management needs are similar to those of embayments.

Oceans

The management implication of the typically active oceanic circulation type is that the water itself is less susceptible to degradation from discharge of contaminants because water motion greatly reduces the chance for their accumulation. Moreover, usually pollution concentrations are more quickly dispersed in the oceans than in estuarine water basins.

Pollution Control

Disposal of liquid wastes to the estuarine environment is the major pollutional impact on coastal waters. This problem can be solved either by treating all wastes to such an extent that they do not reduce the ecosystem carrying capacity or else by entirely prohibiting their discharge to the environment.

Technology exists for the thorough treatment for nearly every kind of municipal and industrial waste, and there is no reason not to provide sufficient treatment to protect the environment from damage and to permit optimum ecosystem function. Treatment requirements for different wastes may vary from place to place according to local conditions, but damage to the environment and restriction of other uses can be prevented.

Water quality standards have been set and are now being implemented in all the coastal states. These standards and stringent effluent limitations are the foundations on which the effective control of estuarine pollution rests, and they provide the framework within which technical management can effectively operate.

Coastal wetlands serve to cleanse runoff waters and regulate their flow (page 33), and therefore they should be maintained as an essential component of the shoreline in developed areas. They should be designated for preservation and protected from degradation by pollution, drainage, channelization, or other disturbances. They should not be preempted for highways or pipeline routes, nor should their natural drainage be interrupted by canals or levees. After careful professional study of possible adverse effects, they may be used for "polishing" certain pretreated waste effluents.

Because the national pollution control program is so complex and omnipresent and because its requirements have so thoroughly infiltrated through state agencies to local governments, it is unnecessary to go into great detail on water pollution control in this book. Our purpose is rather to show how the pollution program integrates with a variety of other programs dealing with coastal environmental issues (Table 4.5).

EPA and the 1972 Water Act

In the Federal Water Pollution Control Act Amendments of 1972 (33 U.S.C. Section 1251 et seq.), Congress established as a national goal the elimination of discharges of pollutants into navigable waters by 1985. This will be achieved on an incremental basis. The "best available" control technology must be employed by 1977, but in the interim the most practicable means to ensure water quality through treatment must be employed. On or before July 1, 1983, water quality standards must be applied that provide for the protection and propagation of fish, shellfish, and wildlife, and that allow for recreation in and on the water. The Act requires the EPA to establish effluent limitations to achieve these results. States do the actual administration of the program after qualifying.

The federal program and its state counterpart programs also have significant coastal resource protection applications because they provide explicit standards and criteria for water quality. The National Pollution Dis-

Table 4.5 Coverage of pollution sources by the Federal Water Act of 1972, U.S. Public Law 92-500 (SOURCE: Reference 22)

Direct Coverage by PL-92-500			Exclusions	
Direct Coverage by NPDES	Controlled by Other Public Law 92-500 Programs	Indirect Coverage by NPDES	Dischargers Excluded from NPDES Coverage	Uncontrolled by PL 92-500
industrial dischargers	ocean dumping (Sec. 403)	combined sewers	storm sewer discharges	urban runoff
municipal treatment plants	marine sanitation dischargers (Sec. 312)	industrial pretreatment (Sec. 307)	small feed-lots	rural runoff
irrigation return flows	aquaculture (Sec. 318)	sludge disposal	small pre-treating industries	groundwater pollutants
large feed-lots	oil and hazardous materials (Sec. 311)		landfill or other solid wastes disposal systems	non-Federally funded land application projects
	dredging spoils (Sec. 404)		septic tanks, cesspools, & individual household systems	acid mine drainage
	Toxic substances (Sec. 307)			

charge Elimination System (NPDES) requires that industrial, municipal, and other point-source dischargers obtain permits for the discharge of any pollutants into the navigable waters of the United States.

As the principal enforcement vehicle for achieving national water quality goals established in the 1972 federal act, the Section 402 permit program has vast implications for development in the coastal zone. The application of stringent water quality standards to coastal development is likely to affect the potential siting, design, construction methods, and economics of such development.

Under the NPDES program, the discharge of pollutants from any point source into navigable waters requires a Section 402 permit. Discharges are not limited to effluent from municipal and industrial sources; the Act defines "pollutants" to include dredge spoil, rock, and sand. And "point source" encompasses "any discernible confined and discrete conveyance," including "any ditch, channel, conduit, or discrete fissure" (Section 502). These definitions directly apply the substantive provisions of the Act to dredging, filling, and other construction activities associated with many coastal development projects.

Assimilative Capacity

It is necessary, in conformance with the planning requirements of the EPA, to classify and rank basin waters according to the severity of pollution. This procedure entails delineating water segments, classifying them through a process involving assimilative capacity determination, and ranking them in the order of the severity of pollution problems associated with each.

A water segment is defined as a portion of the basin where surface waters have common hydrological characteristics, common physical, chemical, and biological aspects, and, thus, similar reactions to pollutants. These segments are to be classified

according to whether or not it is anticipated that water quality objectives will be met after application of 1977 effluent limitations established by the EPA. "Effluent-limited" segments are expected to meet the criteria, whereas "water-quality-limited" segments would not.

Assimilative capacity is an expression of the capacity of a water segment to accept waste loads that will not interfere with the attainment of receiving-water quality objectives. To determine the extent of removal of wastes from discharges, the total assimilative capacities of water-quality-limited segments must be estimated. Some can be expected to assimilate a limited amount of waste load, whereas others will tolerate little or no wastes.

This is a complicated process, and its terms are dictated by the state and the EPA; the intention here is merely to alert managers to the need for the basic classification. An example is given in Table 4.6 for the San Francisco area. Most simply, "water-quality-limited" segments are those already so degraded that they can receive no further discharges of certain wastes.

Environmental Pesticide Control Act of 1972

This Act provides that no person may sell or use any pesticide not registered with the EPA. Registration is granted if the labeling is correct and the product will perform its intended functions without unreasonably adverse effects on the environment. A state may regulate the sale or use of a pesticide, but its rules cannot allow any use prohibited under the Act, and stricter labeling and packaging requirements cannot be imposed.

Control of pesticide practice is complicated by the bewildering number of chemicals in use; a 1970 study identified 78 frequently used pesticides in the California coastal zone alone.[24] Because all pesticides must be examined and registered by federal and some state agencies before they can be

Table 4.6   Water segment classification, San Francisco Bay area (SOURCE: Reference 23)

Receiving water segment	Description	Classification	Category[a]
1	Pacific Ocean	Effluent limited	Z
2	Central San Francisco Bay	Effluent limited	Z
3	San Pablo Bay	Effluent limited	Y
4	Suisun Bay	Effluent limited	Y
5	Lower San Francisco Bay	Effluent limited	Y
6	South Bay	Water quality limited	X
7	Suisun Marsh	Water quality limited	Y
8	Napa River	Water quality limited	X
9	Petaluma River	Water quality limited	X
10	Sonoma Creek	Water quality limited	Y
11	Alameda Creek	Water quality limited	Y
12	Richardson Bay	Water quality limited	X
13	Tomales Bay	Water quality limited	X
	Other surface water segments[b]	Effluent limited	Z

[a] Categorization basis:

X – Present pollution problems anticipated to continue with conformance to 1977 federal limitations only.
Y – Future pollution problems may occur with 1977 federal limitations only.
Z – No pollution problems anticipated with conformance to 1977 federal limitations.

[b] Includes Coyote, Guadalupe, Walnut, Nicasio, and Pescadero creeks, as well as all fresh water impoundments.

used, the bases for general control mechanisms already exist at state and federal levels. But special community needs and problems may require additional constraints by local units of government.

The simplest management practices are to prevent accidental or deliberate introduction of pesticides into surface waters and to restrict the use of chemicals known to be toxic to estuarine organisms (Figure 4.24). Controlling soil erosion and storm runoff will also help to control the introduction of polluting pesticides into the ecosystem.

Ocean Dumping

The Marine Protection, Research, and Sanctuaries Act of 1972 regulates the transportation of material from the United States, or the dumping of material transported from outside the United States, if the dumping occurs in ocean waters over which the United States has jurisdiction or control. A permit must be obtained from the EPA. No permit can be issued for radiological, chemical, or biological warfare agents or any high-level radioactive waste. In reviewing applications, the EPA consults with such federal and state agencies as appears useful or necessary. However, the law is exclusive and all state laws are preempted. Provision is made for a citizen's suit after procedural requirements have been met. No permit is issued for dumping that violates applicable water quality standards.

Permits for the dumping of dredged material only are issued by the Corps of Engineers rather than the EPA. The "Ocean Dumping" Act also provides for the designation and protection of coastal waters of special importance. This aspect is discussed elsewhere (page 188).

Figure 4.24 Machine spraying of pesticides must be limited to sensible use, but it is less hazardous than aerial spraying, whereby accidental application to surface waters is a prevalent risk (near Charleston Beach, Rhode Island). (Conservation Foundation photo by M. Fahay.)

HARVESTABLE RESOURCES

It is customary for states to regulate inshore fisheries; the federal government usually has a peripheral role. Local governments sometimes regulate shellfish harvest and, less often, a herring run or other special situation. But local government plays a critical role in controlling access to recreational fishing via roads, parking lots, beaches, piers, and boat ramps.

Stronger roles for both federal and local governments should be considered if successful integrated programs of coastal fisheries management are to be implemented (Figure 4.25). We are not able to make specific recommendations to local governments for harvest management because there are few standard methods applicable to individual community programs. However, we will provide some general background information.

The states have a leading role in this regard, partly because fish migrate between local fishing areas. A species may breed in one bay, feed in another, and winter in a third place, making it impossible for any local government to act effectively. In addition, water moves from one locality to another, bringing one town's wastes to another's shores. Therefore the states are better equipped to deal with the management of fisheries. No state can do the whole job alone, however, because both fish and water can move from state to state. Hence there is clearly a federal management role in regard to coastwise migratory fish and to interstate environments. Interstate commissions have proved ineffective in coordinating the fishery management policies of individual states into successful integrated programs.

Traditional state fisheries management deals only marginally with the environment.

Figure 4.25   The harvest of sea fish must be allocated to a variety of competing uses by intelligent management. (Photo courtesy of Miami-Metro Department of Tourism and Publicity.)

Fishing regulations are usually aimed at allocating whatever fish there are to whichever fishermen are in the business. They limit the type of gear, size of fish, time of year, number of fish taken per day, and so forth. The process is a somewhat passive portioning out of the catch, usually without pretense of scientifically optimizing the yield from the ecosystems involved.

In state management the target is the species. Normally, rules are laid down for a particular species without regard for others that share the ecosystem—species that are prey, predator, competitor, or cooperator. The rules are applied through an often heavily politicalized process. If there is to be an effective strategy for comprehensive

management of harvestable resources, clearly defined goals are essential. These goals must be based on policies developed through the political process. Policy formation requires information on relevant ecological and cultural aspects, and this information is best developed in a comprehensive planning program.

Fishing results depend on the abundance of fish, which, in turn, depends on the carrying capacity of the coastal ecosystem. Carrying capacity itself, as pointed out previously, is governed by specific limiting factors. These limits, in turn, are depressed by adverse ecological impacts from development and human occupancy. Therefore coastal fisheries management must incorporate (and will ultimately depend on) management of whole ecosystems aimed at optimization of carrying capacity (Figure 4.26).

It is clear that management programs must include the protection of migratory species, particularly those whose life-styles are linked to estuaries, because it is there that the effects of pollution and other disturbances can be especially damaging. Management of such species is complex because it requires the coordination of programs between communities and between states.

An essential point is how necessary the estuarine system is to the survival of coastal migratory species. Without close study one might not even link such species as bluefish, mackerel, and channel bass to estuaries, or realize how very dependent the early lives of menhaden, striped bass, and croaker are on safe and healthy conditions in the brackish tidal rivers.

The estuarine-dependent species include those that spawn in the ocean, along the beaches, in the inlets, inside estuaries, and up the tidal rivers. The young of all these converge in the estuaries for food, refuge, and suitable water. Most estuarine-dependent fish are ocean or coastal migrants

that spend only part of their lives in the shallow estuaries. But this one period may be the most crucial time for the survival of the species. Three major categories of estuarine-dependent classes are shown below for sample species groups:[26]

Adults Found Mostly in the Estuaries, Some Only Seasonally:
> Flounder (winter flounder)
> Spotted trout
> Tarpon
> Croaker (hardhead)
> Snook
> Spot (lafayette)
> White perch*

Adults Found Partially in the Estuaries, Some Only Seasonally:
> Striped bass (rockfish)*
> Fluke (summer flounder)
> Porgy (scup)
> Weakfish (squeteague)
> Red drum (red fish or channel bass)
> Black drum
> Mullet

Adults Found along the Open Coast:
> Bluefish
> Tautog (blackfish)

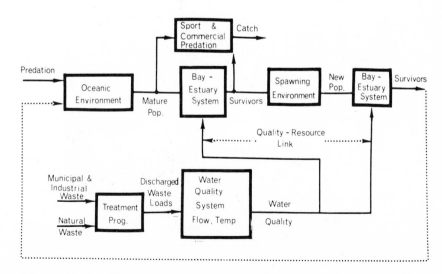

Figure 4.26 The pattern of life cycle dynamics of the shad. (SOURCE: Reference 25.)

King whiting (kingfish)
Alewife (river herring)*
Shad*
Atlantic mackerel
Menhaden (bunker, pogy)

*Anadromous species: living as adults in salt or brackish water but spawning in fresh or nearly fresh water.

The aim of one effective estuarine fisheries management program is to optimize the social benefits from the resource. This requires that goals and policies for management be based on a realistic evaluation of social, economic, and ecological factors. The following planning framework covers some of the major elements that might be considered:

1. *Access.* Provide a system that will guarantee an optimum pattern of fishing activity, including economic, sociological, and ecological considerations. Access means include beaches, bridges, piers, marinas, ramps, and charter boats. Demographic factors include geographical distribution, income level, and traditional use of resource (ethnicity, age, sex).

2. *Resource optimization.* Devise a system of estuarine resource management that involves both harvest control and ecosystem management. Harvest control in-

Figure 4.27 Coastal fisheries contribute to the economic strength and cultural diversity of seaside communities (crab trawlers, Aurora, North Carolina). (Conservation Foundation photo by M. Fahay.)

cludes bag limits, size limits, gear restriction, access limits, and closed areas and seasons. Ecosystem management includes control of chemical and industrial pollution, protection of ecologically vital areas, control of land clearing and site preparation in shorelands, maintenance of freshwater inflow, control of dredging and filling, and control of boat traffic.

3. *Allocation.* Plan for a balanced pattern of allocation of fish resources, including (*a*) competing user groups, such as commercial anglers, skin divers, and foreign fishermen; (*b*) various demographic elements (see item 1); (*c*) preferred sizes of the catch; and (*d*) preferred times and areas of fishing.

4. *Economics.* Examine commercial and recreational fisheries to determine the value of outputs for different patterns and use for different levels of production (Figure 4.27).

5. *Institutional.* Determine the optimum mix of federal, state, and local jurisdiction, and the best methods of implementation of management actions through existing or proposed legislation.

Such a planning exercise could be a joint effort of federal, state, and local governments. It should reveal the important current needs of ecosystem protection and other management actions. All possible actions should be taken immediately by existing authorities. There is reason to be optimistic that integrated environmental and harvest management can improve fishing, based on the general trend of improvement in fisheries that began in the late 1960s, quite possibly in response to pollution cleanup.

ECOSYSTEM RESTORATION

Coastal environmental management programs should, first, look at existing conditions in relation to past damage and explore needs and opportunties for restoration, and, second, look at needs and opportunities for controlling future activities. We make no attempt here to cover the subject of restoration. We present enough examples to make our point in the areas of drainage restoration, water basin restoration, and vital area restoration.

In many communities there will be opportunities for creative public works programs and private actions to restore and maintain damaged coastal ecosystems. *Restoration*, in the sense used here, includes steps that can be taken to rehabilitate damaged elements of the ecosystem, for example, marshes. The concept of *enhancement*, or improvement, relates to attempts to increase the productivity or habitat value of a natural system and thus to raise its carrying capacity. Single-purpose improvement projects may have vegetative effects on the ecosystem (e.g., impoundments for migratory birds) or contribute very little to its function (e.g., artificial reefs, which serve to attract rather than to generate life).

Restoration should be used to correct *past* problems or inadvertent damage, not for planned mitigation or compensation for a deliberate action that, it is predicted in advance, will have significant adverse effects on the environment. This must be stressed because (1) man's attempts to improve on natural ecosystems through engineering are normally failures, and (2) if valid improvement opportunities exist, they should be implemented in their own right.

Problems of Implementation

There are two major obstacles to implementation of coastal ecosystem restoration programs. The first is the lack of technical information and know-how by which to accomplish needed restoration activities. The second is the difficulty of raising the funds for capital improvements and for operations.

The lack of technical information will be

filled gradually over time as more attention is given to the subject. The problem of acquiring funds can be solved only by increasing the awareness of citizens and units of government concerning the necessity and value of restoration. However, planners should not be discouraged by an apparent shortage of funds and detailed technical information, but instead should include major restoration needs in the comprehensive plan. The community should be ready with well-established goals and clearly outlined restoration plans for the time when implementation becomes possible.

This approach is somewhat analogous to the concept of the individual nonconforming use, whereby a use problem is identified and designated for correction on an opportunistic basis. One can simply identify existing damaged environments that require correction with public funds as the opportunity arises. For example, a sediment-filled bay might be cleaned out in connection with a roadway crossing project, or a drained and dried marsh might be restored in connection with an open-water-marsh mosquito control project (page 666). Or perhaps the loss of breeding habitats for birds might be corrected by the creation of spoil islands in a navigational dredging project.

Shoreland Drainage Restoration

In many coastal communities uncontrolled drainage and diversion and local alteration projects have led to widespread adverse impacts on watershed drainage systems, which, in turn, have crippled coastal ecosystems. In low-lying coastal areas of Florida, Louisiana, and other states, watersheds have been altered, groundwater aquifers overpumped, and shorelands water systems and coastal ecosystems severely damaged. Occasionally, communities have attempted to control the damage or to restore these areas by limiting groundwater extraction or by building water control structures (Figure 4.28).

Correction of Flows

The increased flood volume and flood peaks caused by urbanization can be compensated for so that downstream flow is maintained (Figure 4.29). The first requirement is a thorough knowledge of the hydrology of the drainage basin involved and of associated factors such as seasonal precipitation, soils, slopes, vegetation, stream flows, and land-use patterns. From analyses of this information one can design the water project according to the specifications required for maintaining or restoring the pattern of flow.

Reservoir storage installed on a river reduces the magnitude of peak discharge by spreading the flow over a longer period of time. The provision of flood storage upstream, then, will decrease flood peaks and compensate for the increase caused by urbanization. This storage can be simulated by numerous smaller-scale adjustments to reduce peaks, such as the following suggestions for residential areas:

1. Drop inlet boxes at street gutter inlets.
2. Streetside swales instead of paved gutters and curbs.
3. Check dams, ungated, built in headwater swales.
4. Storage volumes in basements of larger buildings receiving water from roofs or gutters and emptying into natural streams or swales.
5. Off-channel storage volumes such as artificial ponds, foundations, or tanks.
6. Small reservoirs in stream channels such as those built for farm ponds.

The need to maintain the flow at some minimum level, even in drought periods, is a familiar concept. Some water control structures are advocated for this specific purpose: low-flow augmentation. The rule is that the minimum acceptable flow to the coastal ecosystem during dry season low flows is that which prevailed under natural conditions. The consequence may be that with-

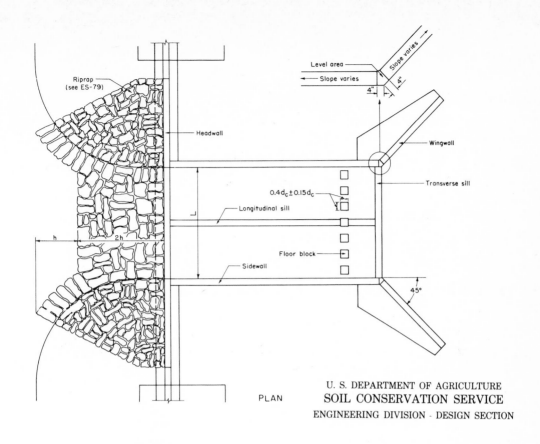

PLAN

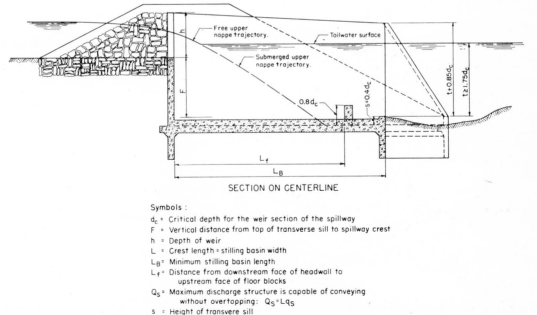

SECTION ON CENTERLINE

Symbols :

d_c = Critical depth for the weir section of the spillway
F = Vertical distance from top of transverse sill to spillway crest
h = Depth of weir
L = Crest length = stilling basin width
L_B = Minimum stilling basin length
L_f = Distance from downstream face of headwall to
upstream face of floor blocks
Q_S = Maximum discharge structure is capable of conveying
without overtopping: $Q_S = L q_S$
s = Height of transverse sill
t = Vertical distance from tailwater surface to top
of transverse sill

Figure 4.28   Drop spillway—hydraulic design, straight drop spillway stilling basin. (SOURCE: Reference 30.)

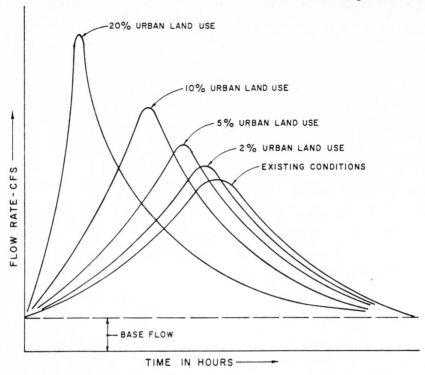

Figure 4.29   Typical flood hydrographs for various levels of urban land use. (SOURCE: Reference 27.)

drawal is curtailed in dry seasons if the storage reservoir holds less than enough water to meet both minimum ecosystem needs and the required withdrawal amount.

As an example the water program for Collier County, Florida, is aimed both at repairing damage to the shorelands and at improving and protecting estuarine water quality through a program of restriction and regulation:[28]

The water management program provides for major waterways in the upland areas to receive runoff from adjacent development. Development will be required to provide storm runoff detention areas, including lakes, which will retain storm water from the development area. The lake system will overflow into the major waterways, which will under normal conditions overflow into adjacent preservation zones. This will provide for the maximum nutrient intake from upland developments prior to runoff reaching the coastal wetlands. The major waterways would have water control structures within them which would be controlled so as to maintain groundwater tables at an elevation near ground surface during and immediately following the annual rainy season. Maintenance of a high groundwater table will minimize the impact of development upon terrestrial ecology, and will minimize irrigation requirements in developed areas. The runoff from the developed areas would be dispersed into the lower wetlands through the use of the spreader–interceptor waterways located along the upper wetland boundaries and through major slough areas [Figures 4.30 and 4.31].

The Sanibel Case[31,40]

Sanibel is a barrier island composed of two rows of parallel ridges of sand and shell. The two largest ridge systems run from one end of the island to the other—one on the landward side of the island and the other on the Gulf of Mexico side—and enclose a large, shallow central reservoir of fresh water received from the rain and stored in an un-

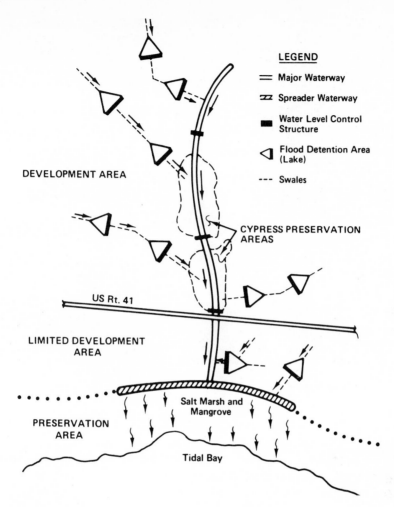

LEGEND

— Major Waterway

ᴢᴢ Spreader Waterway

▬ Water Level Control Structure

◁ Flood Detention Area (Lake)

--- Swales

DEVELOPMENT AREA

CYPRESS PRESERVATION AREAS

US Rt. 41

LIMITED DEVELOPMENT AREA

Salt Marsh and Mangrove

PRESERVATION AREA

Tidal Bay

Figure 4.30 Conceptual sketch of a proposed water management subsystem (Collier County, Florida). (source: Reference 29.)

usual wetlands system (Figure 4.32). This system is one of the four spatial elements that make up Sanibel's total ecosystem: beachfront, interior wetlands, mangrove forests, and upland areas. Each of these physical subsystems is a unique entity with water as the major force tying them together. A central slough, the Sanibel River, historically broke through the beach ridge when the water level was high (Figure 4.33). During the rainy season the water level would rise 5 to 6 feet above mean sea level (vs. 3 to 4 feet today) and commonly would break

through a low point in the beach ridge near the eastern end of the island.

The water table of the interior basin fluctuates according to rainfall, with the highest level in the fall at the end of the rainy season. The water table aquifer is comparable to a "leaky bathtub," with the sides made from two main sand ridges and the bottom from a layer of clay. This bathtub "leaks" salt water through "holes" in both the bottom and the sides (Figure 4.34). The high rate of loss of fresh water by evaporation and by transpiration of plants results

Figure 4.31　Continuing abuses have led to crisis-level water problems in Florida; sand bags and other stop-gap measures must be used to hold back water surges and restore water tables. (Photo courtesy of B. Yokel, Rookery Bay Marine Laboratory.)

in a decline in water table level during the dry season and an increase in salinity.

The lowering of the water table has had serious adverse effects on the interior wetlands system. Before the Sanibel River was channelized and two water control structures were installed, the water level fluctuated from slightly below mean sea level (MSL) to a maximum of 5 feet above MSL during occasional extreme rainstorms. With the water control structures now set at 2.0 feet above MSL, the water in the wetlands basin rarely rises above 3 feet, even at its farthest reaches to the west (Figure 4.35).

The increasing salt problem is caused principally by the unfortunate lowering of the water level in the interior basin. With the head pressure thus reduced, salt water penetrates through the sides and bottom of the basin because the tide level is greater than the interior water level. Irregular and

troublesome salt intrusion is caused by seawater overwash during heavy storms; this inundation reaches massive proportions during hurricanes, when the whole island typically goes underwater. When the island was in the undeveloped state, most of the salt water would run off in a rather short time; but now the hurricane surges fill up the man-made lakes, and the salt water, held there, intrudes deeply into the groundwater system.

Because of the lowered water table, hundreds of acres of the interior basin, particularly the high-ridge-and-swale wetlands, are no longer seasonally flooded. Changing vegetation patterns such as the invasion of local woody plants (e.g., saltbush) and exotics (e.g., Brazilian pepper) have displaced *Spartina* and are directly attributable to the reduction in water level.

The interior wetlands were altered for

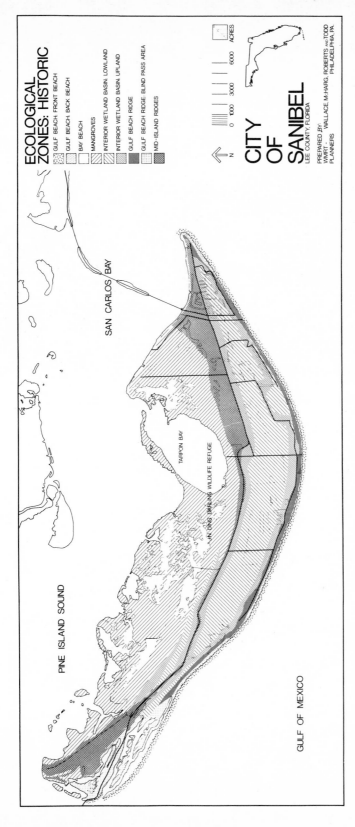

ECOLOGICAL ZONES: HISTORIC

GULF BEACH FRONT BEACH
GULF BEACH BACK BEACH
BAY BEACH
MANGROVES
INTERIOR WETLAND BASIN. LOWLAND
INTERIOR WETLAND BASIN. UPLAND
GULF BEACH RIDGE
GULF BEACH RIDGE BLIND PASS AREA
MID-ISLAND RIDGES

ACRES

0   1000   3000   6000

N

CITY OF SANIBEL

LEE COUNTY, FLORIDA

PREPARED BY:
WMRT - WALLACE, McHARG, ROBERTS AND TODD
PLANNERS   PHILADELPHIA, PA.

PINE ISLAND SOUND

SAN CARLOS BAY

TARPON BAY

J.N. DING DARLING WILDLIFE REFUGE

GULF OF MEXICO

Figure 4.32 "Historic" ecological zones of Sanibel Island, Florida. (SOURCE: City of Sanibel Planning Commission; courtesy of Wallace, McHarg, Roberts and Todd, Inc., Philadelphia.)

Figure 4.33 The Sanibel River is a somewhat brackish slough running through the Sanibel Island, Florida, interior wetlands system. (Photo by author.)

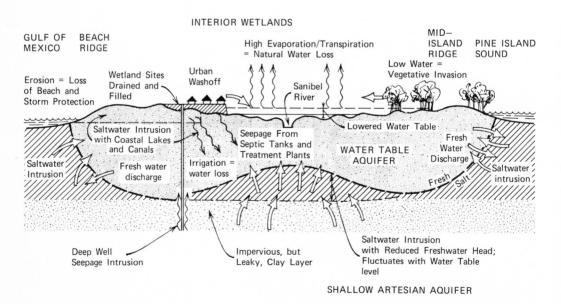

INTERIOR WETLANDS

GULF OF   BEACH
MEXICO   RIDGE

MID—
ISLAND   PINE ISLAND
RIDGE   SOUND

High Evaporation/Transpiration
= Natural Water Loss

Low Water =
Vegetative Invasion

Erosion = Loss
of Beach and
Storm Protection

Wetland Sites
Drained and
Filled

Urban
Washoff

Sanibel
River

Saltwater Intrusion
with Coastal Lakes
and Canals

Lowered Water Table

Fresh
Water
Discharge

Seepage From
Septic Tanks and
Treatment Plants

WATER TABLE
AQUIFER

Saltwater
Intrusion

Fresh water
discharge

Irrigation =
water loss

Fresh

Salt

Saltwater
intrusion

Deep Well
Seepage Intrusion

Impervious, but
Leaky, Clay Layer

Saltwater Intrusion
with Reduced Freshwater Head;
Fluctuates with Water Table
level

SHALLOW ARTESIAN AQUIFER

Figure 4.34 The hydrological system on Sanibel Island, Florida, has been greatly damaged by reckless development. (SOURCE: Reference 31.)

Figure 4.35 The primary water control structure for the Sanibel Island, Florida, interior wetlands–water storage area is designed to keep the water storage potential at optimum height; it has helped but is inadequate to fully accomplish the need. (Photo by DeWitt Jones, Captiva Island, Florida.)

mosquito control in the late 1950s. The purpose was to initiate a biological control system designed to nurture fish that feed on mosquito larvae. However, the system as executed has had a reverse effect, and the lowered water levels of the interior wetlands today have created a condition that discourages fish mobility and favors mosquito breeding because the control system was never completed as designed, has been disrupted by roadway blockages, and has had little maintenance since the early 1960s (Figure 4.36).

Because of these past abuses, there was an obvious need for restoration of Sanibel's interior wetlands as the first element of its environmental management program—a restoration program that would enable the wetlands to provide the additional benefits of conserving freshwater supplies, water quality, mosquito control, fire protection, vegetation, and wildlife habitat. The major components of the suggested restoration program were as follows:

1. Return the water systems (i.e., water levels, flows, etc.) as nearly to the preexisting state as possible and remove all significant existing obstacles to the passage of water in interior wetlands. Open up waterways and provide full and free flow of water, including stormwater.
2. Take all practical measures to prevent saltwater intrusion of interior wetlands.
3. Remove all exotic and adverse local vegetation that has invaded the wetlands during many years of abuse, utilizing mechanical removal, controlled burning, and other biologically acceptable techniques.

Figure 4.36 Roadways have disrupted the Sanibel Island, Florida, interior wetlands; culverting is inadequate to provide for water circulation in the wetlands and for stormwater relief because there are too few culverts and they were not placed at the right elevation. (Photo by author.)

Separate water management should be provided for each of the four major segments of the interior wetlands basin (Figure 4.37). In each segment the optimum level would be about 4 feet above MSL at seasonal maximum. It was recommended that two fixed sill structures be installed at the two discharge points, at 3 feet above MSL with options to 3.5 feet and 4 feet, the sills being designed to permit draining the system for occasional remedial flushing.

As the above constraints suggest, the natural characteristics of the Sanibel interior wetlands are such that preservation of their functional integrity precludes virtually any development within them. Any use of these wetlands would accordingly be oriented toward recreational purposes that would be enhanced by the installation of light-duty, elevated (pile-supported) structures such as blinds, catwalks, piers, and similar non-en-

closed recreational and access structures. If properly controlled in extent and design, these would not have a major detrimental effect on water systems and estuarine resources.

In 1976 the city of Sanibel developed a comprehensive plan with ordinances and a capital improvement program to implement the necessary restoration and conservation actions. This program was based on the Sanibel Planning Commission's considerations of the following: a survey of natural systems of the island (by The Conservation Foundation), a master plan formulated on carrying capacity limits (by Wallace, McHarg, Roberts, and Todd, Inc., Planners), and detailed performance standards (by Fred Bosselman of Ross, Hardies, O'Keefe, Babcock, and Parsons, Attorneys). The resulting management agenda calls for a complete revision of the old approach to resi-

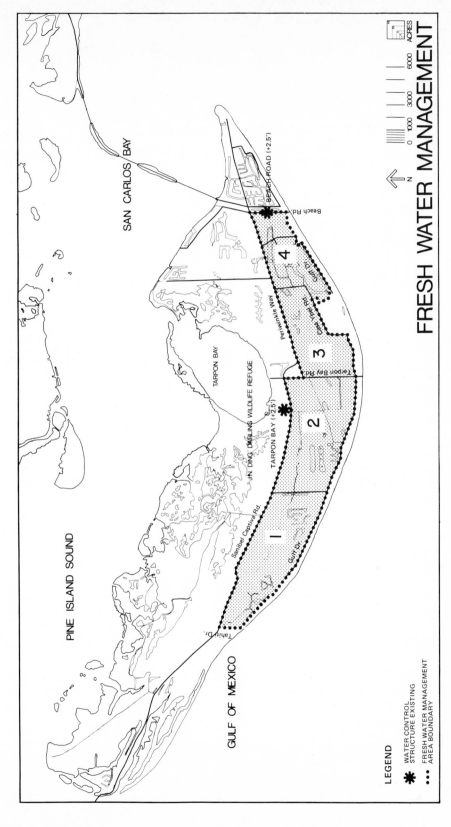

Figure 4.37 Four separate water management sectors suggested for the Sanibel interior wetlands—water storage basin. (SOURCE: City of Sanibel Planning Commission; courtesy of Wallace, McHarg, Roberts and Todd, Philadelphia: adaptation.)

211

dential development on Sanibel (the comprehensive planning for Sanibel is treated elsewhere; see page 271).

Coastal Water Basin Restoration

There are few coastal water basins in developed areas that do not need restorative attention. The major persistent problems are sedimentation (including organic ooze) and alteration of the basin configuration and circulation (vital areas are discussed elsewhere; see page 247).

Corrective Dredging

A majority of estuarine systems are impacted with polluted sediments. Poor farming practices have caused soil erosion, which has filled streambeds and covered wetlands and grass beds. In other areas, urban runoff has caused eutrophication and the buildup of organic ooze on the bottom. Corrective dredging to remove these sediments is very expensive and difficult to implement for ecological benefit to public waters. However, communities should inventory their coastal basins to identify those seriously degraded by sediment and then try to create an opportunity to deal with the worst of them.

One example of the opportunistic implementation of a plan prepared in advance is the restoration of Tillamook Bay, Oregon. The background is explained in the following account:[32]

Planning presumes the availability of a bank of hard data on biological stocks, historical uses, physical characteristics, etc. . . . Facts are not available . . . in some areas . . . but we can't wait. Make the necessary decisions on the basis of the best information—even if incomplete. Recognize that changes in the plan may be necessary when new data become available.

What are the opportunities to restore a dying estuarine ecosystem through selective dredging or current manipulation? Practically no attention has been given to opportunities to restore

an estuary that has been damaged. In Oregon, renovation and revitalization have been proposed for such estuaries as Tillamook, Nestucca, and Siletz Bays. A 1972 project by the U.S. Army Corps of Engineers in Tillamook Bay, which cleared the channels of the Wilson and Trask Rivers, may have successfully pioneered the concept of renovation. Large scale efforts are now needed.

The 1973 project mentioned above was made possible by massive flooding, which qualified the local area for federal disaster relief funds. By having the plan prepared ahead of time, the community was able to obtain and direct funds available on short notice to solve an environmental problem identified far in advance.

A large-scale plan for restoration of the heavily silt-polluted Back Bay–Currituck Sound estuarine system (Virginia and North Carolina) was proposed as the result of a special restoration study. The solution to the siltation problem lists a number of specific recommendations, including the following items:[33]

1. Limit dredging to essential projects, and conduct these in dormant vegetative periods, February and March.
2. Implement better soil conservation practices on adjacent farmlands.
3. Divert silt-laden runoff waters away from Back Bay via a canal along the shoreline.
4. Manipulate salt- and freshwater inflows to maintain a stable water salinity level high enough to flocculate silt, low enough to enhance the abundance of large-mouth bass, and of the right order to favor two plants that stabilize shorelines, sago pond weed and widgeon grass.
5. Construct bulkheads where necessary along the shore to prevent silt-laden water from running into the estuary.
6. Build a series of parallel sand fill strips 60 feet wide and 3 feet high strategically on the bottom of the bay to permit the rooting of plants and to lessen wave action and currents, which resuspend silt.

Although each of these suggestions appears to have merit, their implementation would be costly, requiring large expenditures of public money for engineering and construction. The restoration plan would appear to be feasible only as part of a large-scale interstate plan involving the use of all surrounding lands and connecting waterways.

Restoring Circulation

Lessons have been learned from storms and floods that accidentally improved circulation patterns in degraded areas. For example, on Long Island, New York, a storm opened an inlet on the east end of Fire Island and improved the tidal flushing of Moriches Bay, which had been heavily polluted by duck farm wastes; thereafter the ecosystem made a rapid comeback.[41]

A specific attempt at improving the tidal flushing of Pamlico Sound, North Carolina, was made by the Corps of Engineers in opening Drum Inlet on the Outer Banks. However, the relationship between incoming fresh water, tidal flushing action, and the concept of an inlet serving as a "release valve" for hydrological pressures was not then clearly understood, and Drum Inlet closed in again.

Tidal flushing and circulation were successfully improved in Laguna Madre, Texas. The dredging of the intercoastal waterway opened up this hypersaline lagoon (up to 70 ppt) and reduced salinity levels sufficiently (below 50 ppt) to greatly increase carrying capacity.

Improved understanding of tidal dynamics, storm actions, hydrostatic pressures, and beachfront geology will increase the likelihood of success in future programs for the correction of circulation deficiencies.

Innovative Engineering

There are many opportunities for creative engineering in water basins (Figure 4.38).

One such example is the combination use of *clean* spoil from channel dredging for estuarine breakwaters to protect marina sites. Properly designed, such islands allow adequate circulation around the marina area and create useful habitats as additional benefits (Figure 4.39).

Tens of millions of cubic yards of spoil are produced each year in dredging new channels and maintaining existing ones. The volume of maintenance spoil increases exponentially with design channel depth. Although much of this spoil is polluted or is useless muck, a considerable amount is clean and suitable for use in creative engineering projects. The most valuable opportunities appear to lie in the creation of artificial islands to increase breeding habitats for birds and to expand wetlands along the island fringe. If properly located and designed, such islands may increase ecosystem carrying capacity (Figure 4.40). The following criteria are suggested for the design of spoil islands:

1. Avoid all existing vital areas, including grass beds, shellfish beds, and wetlands.
2. Spoil should be coarse sand or other material not susceptible to rapid erosion; fine, organic sediments or polluted spoil should not be used.
3. The spoil island should be in a protected area away from heavily used boat channels to minimize erosion from boat wash.
4. The island should be vegetated with both upland plants and marsh grasses at the earliest possible time.
5. The island should be shaped so as to facilitate water movements, for example, elliptical in shape and parallel to water flows.

Dredge spoil islands permanently alter the natural system and must be planned with the utmost care (Figure 4.41). If the proposal is the basis for mitigation of deliberate degradation of other natural marsh or bird habitats, it should be viewed skeptically.

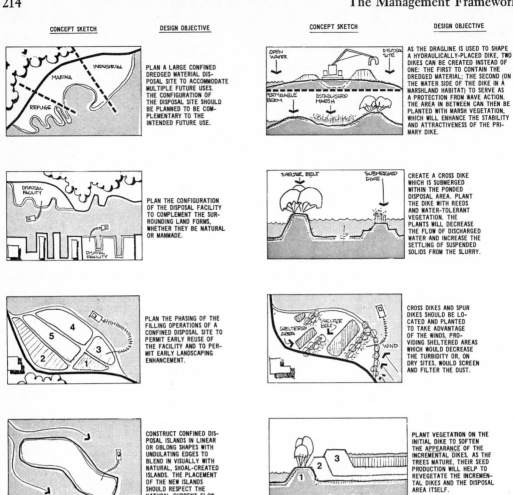

Figure 4.38 Dredge spoil disposal sites should be aesthetically as well as ecologically in harmony with the environment. (SOURCE: Roy Mann Associates, from Reference 34.)

Vital Area Restoration

Public awareness of the value of certain types of vital areas has been sufficiently high to foster a variety of attempts to rebuild, rehabilitate, or create natural units, particularly coastal marshes and dunes.

Marsh Restoration

Techniques have been developed for propagating salt-marsh grasses. Marsh grass plantings can be used to create marshes,[35] to stabilize dredge spoil (page 591), or to cre-

ate alternative "bulkheads" (page 592).

Marshes can be successfully restored by both the transplanting and the seeding of marsh grasses.[35,36] Transplants are more vigorous than seedlings and better able to survive on exposed sites and at lower elevations. Seeds can be easily harvested, stored for long periods of time under refrigeration, and planted by means of modified garden and farm machinery.

In the propagation of salt marshes by either seeding or transplanting, care must be taken in selecting or preparing sites that meet the requirements of the species used.

Figure 4.39   Clean sand dredge spoil can be used to build estuarine breakwaters and serve other useful purposes (Dinner Key Marina, Miami, Florida). (Photo courtesy of Miami-Metro Department of Publicity and Tourism.)

The interactions of such factors as tide range, elevation, slope, and salinity determine the species of plants present and influence their vertical zonation in marshes.

When planning marsh restoration, it is best to take elevation readings of the upper and lower limits of nearby natural marshes and plan to plant within this zone. In preparing a site, the area available for planting can be increased by making the slope as gentle as practicable without the ponding of water. The gentler the slope, the larger will be the alternately flooded and drained area.[35] High proportions of silt and clay are not suitable for conventional planting equipment. Dredged material that is composed mostly of sand has excellent physical properties. A list of guidelines for marsh construction is given in Table 4.7.

Dune Restoration

Private and public projects to restore and stabilize dunes should be encouraged. Simple structures such as snow fences and revegetation programs constitute inexpensive and effective methods to protect beaches. Such means enable individual property owners or community groups to build and rehabilitate sand dunes. Replacement dunes should be built above the high-tide line and on slopes that face the ocean. In some areas, in less than a year dunes 4 feet high or more may be built through the use of fencing, whereas in other places this growth may take several years. After dunes are constructed, they should be stabilized by vegetation to prevent them from being blown or washed away.[37]

Figure 4.40 Artificial islands of clean sand dredge spoil, if properly shaped, placed, and vegetated, offer ecological benefits to coastal ecosystems (Cape Fear, North Carolina). (Conservation Foundation photo by M. Fahay.)

Brush and discarded Christmas trees can be used to trap sand and build dunes by placing them in a fencelike structure. The material can be fastened to horizontal "rails" that are attached to posts. Or the pieces can be placed side by side in an upright position, like vertical fencing, and then partly buried in the sand. The butt ends should be inserted in a trench about 2 feet deep and firmly packed in place.[37]

Standard wooden snow fencing is ideal for collecting windblown sand for building dunes; it is readily available, can be handled easily, and can be erected in a short time. Wooden posts can be used to hold up the fencing; these should be spaced about 10 feet apart and driven into the sand to keep the fence from sagging or collapsing.[37] Straight fencing is recommended; zigzag or other fancy patterns have not proved more beneficial (Figure 4.42).

Dunes and sandy areas should be protected with a blanket of vegetation; this makes them more resistant to wind and water erosion. The best vegetation for use from Maine to North Carolina and in the Great Lakes area is American beach wetgrass (*Ammophila breviligulata*). Establishing and maintaining it is simple and relatively inexpensive. This perennial, native grass can tolerate sand blasting and deposition, strong winds, salt spray, occasional flooding, and droughty, infertile sand. Beach grass spreads by growing underground stems that form new plants for added protection. It can accumulate up to 4 feet of sand in a year's time. When this much sand or less is needed, beach grass can be used instead of fencing for dune building. In such cases it will also provide an immediate stabilizing cover. Beach grass should be planted in strips parallel to the shoreline. Throughout the rest of the southeast United States sea oats (*Uniola paniculata*) seems to be the best plant species for use in dune stabilization projects.[38]

Beach grass "culms" can be bought from commercial growers or obtained by thinning native stands; about 3000 are enough to stabilize an area of approximately 2000 square feet. In thinning, culms are pulled or dug from the sand, leaving a sufficient number of plants to prevent erosion. Culms can be safely taken only from back dunes or protected areas. Beach grass on public lands could be managed and supervised to make culms available to area residents. Areas to be thinned could be fertilized a year or two in advance in order to double or triple the number of culms available and to make them healthier, bigger, and easier to plant.[37] (Commercial sources of culms and other basic information are given by John A. Jagschitz and Robert C. Wakefield in

Figure 4.41 Successive stages in the formation of an artificial dredge spoil island near Fort Sumpter (Charleston, South Carolina). A. Charleston Harbor, April 1962. B. Charleston Harbor, October 1965. C. Charleston Harbor, March 1971—wide expanse of marsh inadvertently developed by disposal of dredged material. (Photos courtesy of U.S. Army Corps of Engineers.)

Table 4.7 Guidelines for siting, design, and construction of artificial marshes (SOURCE: Reference 36)

<u>Siting Considerations</u>

. Locate new marshes in low energy areas, such as,

   - in the lee of barrier beaches, islands and shoals;
   - in shallow water areas where wave energy is dissipated;
   - within the convex portion of river bends;
   - land extensions and embayments where marsh currently
       exists;
   - within zones of active deposition;
   - away from areas with long fetch exposure in the
       direction of prevailing winds;
   - away from major tidal channels and uncontrolled inlets;
   - away from headlands where wave energy is concentrated.

. Take advantage of high water energy areas (e.g., inlets)
   to obtain coarse grained materials, but only if the inlet
   will not become hydraulically unbalanced.

. Take advantage of on-going sedimentation processes, such
   as littoral drift for sand nourishment, to aid in
   stabilizing new marshes.

. Be aware of possible deflocculation effects when dredged
   sediments are obtained from highly saline areas and
   disposed in low saline areas.

<u>Design and Construction Considerations</u>

. Use available coarse grained material to protect exposed
   surfaces of the new marsh.

. Provide protection against wave erosion by creating a
   rim of coarse material on the windward face of the marsh.
   Design criteria of the rim are:

   - elevation above level of normal wave runup,
   - coarse material of substantial width.

. Plan the final grade of the protection rim or dike so that
   drainage of rain runoff and wave overwash will be towards
   the interior of the fill.

. Configure the marsh such that exposure to erosion forces
   is minimized.

. Plan for special action to repair storm damage during
   the initial period of marsh stabilization.

How to Build and Save Beaches and Dunes.[37]) (See Figure 4.43.)

REFERENCES

1. Albert R. Veri, William W. Jenna, Jr., and Dorothy Eden Bergamaschi. 1975. *Environmental Quality by Design: South Florida.* University of Miami Press, Coral Gables, Florida.

2. Natural Resources Defense Council. 1976. A *Citizens' Guide to Coastal Zone Planning.* New York (unpublished draft).

3. Stephen V. Smith. 1974. *Environmental Status of Hawaiian Estuaries, 1974.* Diffuse Sources Branch, Office of Water and Hazardous Materials, U.S. Environmental Protection Agency, Washington, D.C.

4. National Oceanic and Atmospheric Administration. 1975. *Considering Coastal Zone Management.* U.S. Department of Commerce, Washington, D.C.

Figure 4.42   Fencing and planting are major methods for dune rehabilitation. (Photo by author.)

5. *Federal Register*, Vol. 40, No. 6, Part 1, p. 1688 (January 9, 1975).

6. Mary Lee Strang. 1975. "Coastal zone management program." In *Current Focus*, April 1975. League of Women Voters, Washington, D.C.

7. Office of Endangered Species. 1975. *Liaison Conservation Directory for Endangered and*

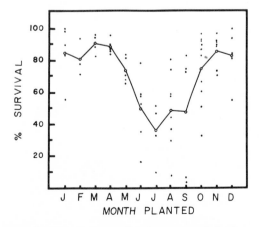

Figure 4.43   American beach grass, used in dune building along the Great Lakes and from Maine to North Carolina, should be planted from October through April. (SOURCE: Reference 37.)

Threatened Species. Fish and Wildlife Service, U.S. Department of the Interior, Washington, D.C.

8. Mark Pisano. 1976. "208: a process for water quality management." In *Environmental Comment*, January 1976. Urban Land Institute, Washington, D.C.

9. Luna B. Leopold. 1968. *Hydrology for Urban Land Planning—A Guidebook on the Hydrologic Effects of Urban Land Use.* U.S. Geological Survey, Geological Survey Circular 554, Washington, D.C.

10. Edward T. La Roe. 1973. "Effects of dredging, filling and channelization on estuarine resources." Presented at *Fish and Wildlife Values of the Estuarine Environment*, a Seminar Presented for the Petroleum Industry by the Bureau of Sport Fisheries and Wildlife, U.S. Department of the Interior, Atlanta, Georgia, June 13, 1973.

11. Don G. Friedman. 1975. *Computer Simulation in Natural Hazard Assessment.* Institute of Behavioral Science, the University of Colorado, Boulder, Colorado. Program on Technology, Environment, and Man, Monograph No. NSF-Ra-E-75-002.

12. Texas Coastal and Marine Council. Map prepared by the Bureau of Economic Geology, The

University of Texas at Austin, for the Texas Coastal and Marine Council.

13. H. Crane Miller. 1975. "Coastal flood plain management and the National Flood Insurance Program, a case study of three Rhode Island communities." In *Environmental Comment*, November 1975. Urban Land Institute, Washington, D.C.

14. Federal Insurance Administration. 1974. Washington, D.C.

15. Francis C. Murphy. 1958. *Regulating Flood-Plain Development*. Department of Geography Research Paper No. 56, The University of Chicago, Chicago, Illinois.

16. Eric Strauss and Jon Kusler. 1975. *Statutory Land Use Control Enabling Authority in the Fifty States*. U.S. Department of Housing and Urban Development, Federal Insurance Administration, Washington, D.C. (draft).

17. U.S. Water Resources Council. 1971. *Regulation of Flood Hazard Areas*, Vol. I, Parts I–IV. Washington, D.C.

18. John L. Taylor and Carl H. Saloman. 1968. "Some effects of hydraulic dredging and coastal development in Boca Ciega Bay, Florida." *Fishery Bulletin*, Vol. 67, No. 2, pp. 213–241. U.S. Fisheries and Wildlife Service, Washington, D.C.

19. William N. Hedeman, Jr. 1975. "The role of the Corps of Engineers in protecting the coastal zone." In *Environmental Comment*, April 1975. The Urban Land Institute, Washington, D.C.

20. D. B. Hicks, B. J. Carroll, and T. R. Cavinder. 1975. *Finger Fill Canal Studies Florida and North Carolina*. U.S. Environmental Protection Agency, Athens, Georgia. (draft)

21. National Oceanic and Atmospheric Administration. 1975. *Final Environmental Impact Statement, Key Largo Coral Reef Marine Sanctuary*. U.S. Department of Commerce, Washington, D.C.

22. National Commission on Water Quality. 1975. *Staff Draft Report*. Washington, D.C.

23. Regional Water Quality Control Board, San Francisco Bay Region (2). 1974. *Tentative Water Quality Control Plan, San Francisco Bay Basin (2)*. Oakland, California.

24. Gordon F. Snow. 1972. "Pesticides in the coastal zone." In *Agriculture in the Coastal Zone: Comprehensive Ocean Area Plan*, Appendix IV. Department of Navigation and Ocean Development, Sacramento, California, pp. 105–299.

25. Roberet V. Thomann. 1972. "The Delaware River—a study in water quality management."

In Ray T. Oglesby, Clarence A. Carlson, and James A. McCann, Eds., *River, Ecology and Man*. Academic Press, New York and London, pp. 99–129.

26. J. R. Clark. 1967. *Fish and Man: Conflict in the Atlantic Estuaries*. American Littoral Society, Special Publication No. 5, Highlands, New Jersey.

27. D. R. Storm, 1972. *Hydrologic and Water Quality Aspects of the Tomales Bay Environmental Study*. Storm Engineering and Design Water and Waste Management, Davis, California.

28. Black, Crow, and Eidsness, Inc. 1974. *Master Plan for Water Management District No. 6, Collier County, Florida*. Naples, Florida.

29. Ronald L. Wycoff and R. David G. Pyne 1975. "Urban water management and coastal wetland protection in Collier County, Florida." *Water Resources Bulletin*, Vol. 11, No. 3, pp. 455–468.

30. M. M. Culp and C. A. Reese. n.d. *Drop Spillways Engineering Handbook*, Section II. Soil Conservation Service, U.S. Department of Agriculture, Washington, D.C.

31. Albert Veri and Langdon Warner. 1975. *Interior Wetlands Water Quality Management*. The Conservation Foundation, Washington, D.C.

32. William Q. Wick. 1973. "Estuaries under attack." In *Water Spectrum*, Vol. 5(3), pp. 12–18. U.S. Army Corps of Engineers, Washington, D.C.

33. John L. Sincock, et al. 1966. *Back Bay–Currituck Sound Data Report. Environmental Factors, 1958–64*. U.S. Bureau of Sport Fisheries and Wildlife, Washington, D.C. (unpublished).

34. DMRP Work Unit 4A03. 1975. "Habitat development and reclamation on Nott Island." In *Dredged Material Research Notes–News–Reviews, Etc.*, July 1975. U.S. Army Corps of Engineers, Vicksburg, Mississippi.

35. W. W. Woodhouse, Jr., E. D. Seneca, and S. W. Broome. 1974. *Propagation of Spartina alterniflora for Substrate Stabilization and Salt Marsh Development*. U.S. Army Corps of Engineers, Technical Memorandum No. 46, Coastal Engineering Research Center, Fort Belvoir, Virginia.

36. Lynn E. Johnson and William V. McGuiness. 1975. *CEM Report 4165-519: Guidelines for Material Placement in Marsh Creation*. Center for the Environment and Man, Inc., Hartford, Connecticut (draft of final report).

37. John A. Jagschitz and Robert C. Wakefield.

1971. *How to Build and Save Beaches and Dunes: Preserving the Shoreline with Fencing and Beachgrass.* College of Resource Development, University of Rhode Island, Kingston, Rhode Island.

38. R. P. Savage and W. W. Woodhouse, Jr. 1968. *Creation and Stabilization of Coastal Barrier Dunes.* U.S. Army Coastal Engineering Research Center, Washington, D.C.

39. J. H. Feth. 1973. *Water Facts and Figures for Planners and Managers.* U.S. Geological Survey, Geological Survey Circular 601-1, Washington, D.C.

40. Wallace, McHarg, Roberts, and Todd. 1975. *Comprehensive Land Use Plan, City of Sanibel, Lee County, Florida.* City of Sanibel Planning Commission, Sanibel, Florida.

41. Arthur M. Reed and William G. Day, Jr. 1975. *Ship Behavior in Shallow Water with Particular Application to Ferry Operation on Great South Bay and Moucher Bay, Long Island, New York* (unpublished paper).

CHAPTER FIVE

Management Opportunities at the Local Level

An emerging new environmental concept is to consider the coastal zone as a single natural system and to integrate the three major elements of management—shorelands, water basins, and water quality—into a single coordinated program. This book is founded on the "single-system" concept, that is, the belief that the whole coastal zone must be managed as a single natural system. We recognize, however, that there may be sizable institutional and administrative hurdles to overcome in coordinating and reconciling the old authorities and adding the new ones.

In this chapter we suggest a framework for active ecosystem management at the local unit of government, much of which we have tested and found successful in our work with coastal communities. Some elements, however, are yet to be tried in comprehensive ecosystem management.

We make no claim to cover the subject comprehensively. Rather we select particular aspects of major significance in achieving coastal ecosystem conservation. However, enough basic ingredients and ideas are presented to provide the foundation for an effective local program.

ORIGINS AND AUTHORITIES

There is a prevailing general division of authority between federal, state, and local agencies that makes it possible to draw general conclusions about local management responsibilities. This we have done to the extent that is relevant to the issue at hand —the conservation of coastal ecosystems.

The various federal, state, and regional requirements for coastal zone environmental management can be administered by the local government in a coordinated system that also includes any additional community requirements. The basic constraints on development are set forth in Chapter 6 for each of 24 types of developmental projects. The general *guidelines* and specific *implementation standards* contain sufficient detail to provide the basis for a comprehensive ecosystem conservation program.

How the constraints might be worked into the administrative mechanism of local government in detail is a complex matter quite outside the subject of this book. Nevertheless, we have tried to be sufficiently aware of these mechanisms so that our recommendations are realistically achieveable. As a practical matter we have had to recognize that a regulatory agenda for coastal areas must be considered in two management contexts: the ecological context, which reflects the permanent rules of nature, and the institutional context, which reflects the changeable rules of mankind.

We have set high environmental goals for ecosystem conservation which only communities with deep convictions can be expected to reach within a reasonable amount of time. Obviously, the incorporation of all necessary constraints into the operating administrative mechanism of local government will take considerable time. Those that apply to public works or services may be more easily adopted than those that apply to private development, although the reverse may be true of some types of public projects.

Many of the environmental standards we recommend are familiar concepts. Those already in general use—erosion control methods, setbacks, sewage treatment—should be rather simple to implement. Other controls, such as protection of dunes, land application of sewage, and nonstructural protection of shorelines, may be innovative for many communities. These may be more difficult to implement.

Although coastal communities are strongly affected by federal and state environmental regulations, in a number of federal and state environmental programs all or part of the regulatory function is put into the hands of local government. In others the regulations are administered by the states or directly by the federal government (Figure 5.1). While many revelant regulatory programs involve land-use management, others of interest have such purposes as pollution control or water basin protection. It appears to us that the regulations required for the protection of coastal natural systems can be effectively incorporated into the existing structures of development control and of planning, without the need to create new local regulatory and administrative frameworks (Table 5.1).

According to land management experts, in recent years concern has increased among public officials and private citizens that land-use decisions are being made on the basis of expediency, tradition, and short-term economic considerations—in short, decisions are based on factors unrelated to sound land management policy. Rapid and continued growth or urban development, transportation systems, and large-scale industrial and economic expansion are all competing for additional land area. The Council of State Governments has said, "The fragmentation of governmental entities exercising land management powers and the increased size, scale, and impact of private action has created another crisis—a national land-use crisis."[3]

Levels of Authority

Federal

When the country was formed, the states retained the power to regulate land development within their boundaries. They delegated this authority to the localities. History has demonstrated that the federal government, under its various powers, can pass national legislation compelling some type of action at the state level. Federal coercion runs against the grain of American tradition,

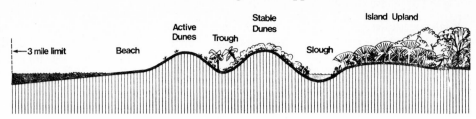

Regulations for Residential Development

* Permits for Activities in Navigable Waters

* State Ownership to High Water Mark, Unless Crown or State Grant

* State Permits for Alteration of Marshlands

* Environmental Protection Regulations

* Federal Legislation Protecting Historical and Archaeological Resources

* Cultural Resources on Submerged Lands Owned by the State are State Property.

* Beach and Sand Dune Protection Regulations

* Flood Plain Insurance Regulations

* Environmental Protection Regulations

* Zoning and Subdivision Regulations

* Septic Tanks and Private Wells

* Construction Codes

* State Land Sales Act

* Inter-State Land Sales Full Disclosure Act

* Federal Legislation Protecting Historical and Archaeological Resources

Figure 5.1   Summary of Environmental and Developmental regulations for coastal Georgia. (SOURCE: Reference 2.)

however, and that is the reason why the conventional approach to this type of problem has been for federal legislation to provide a vehicle for implementation.[3]

The vehicle for implementation in the area of land management has taken the form of financial inducements to encourage state, regional, and local actions, rather than direct federal involvement. These inducements consist of grant and loan programs that require planning as a precondition to the receipt of funds. One such is the Federal Coastal Zone Management Act of 1972 (page 800). Many other sources of federal authority affecting coastal ecosystem conservation are discussed in chapter Four.

Interstate

An Interstate compact is usually administered by a board, composed of appointees

of each governor involved, with specific responsibilities set forth in the legislation creating the compact for building and maintaining bridges and tunnels, operating parks and ports, or managing mass transit facilities. Although the use of the compact to solve interstate problems is on the increase, in some instances it has proved to be a cumbersome procedure. Identical forms of the agreement must be passed by all participating state legislatures. Thus, not only do the negotiations in setting up the proposal take years to complete, but also any subsequent amendment requires common passage. There is also the requirement of congressional approval of most interstate compacts.[3]

State

Subject to the United States Constitution, the states are the sources and the seats of sovereign power, such as the inherent pow-

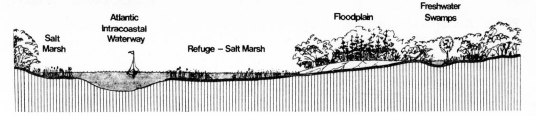

* Permits for Activities
  in Navigable Waters

* State Ownership to High
  Water Mark, Unless Crown
  or State Grant

* State Permits for Alteration
  of Marshlands

* Environmental Protection
  Regulations

* Federal Legislation Protecting
  Historical and Archaeological
  Resources

* Cultural Resources on Submerged
  Lands Owned by the State are
  State Property.

* Coast Guard Permits for Causeways
  or Bridges

* Flood Plain Insurance
  Regulations

* Environmental Protection
  Regulations

* Zoning and Subdivision
  Regulations

* Septic Tanks and Private
  Wells

* Construction Codes

* State Land Sales Act

* Inter-State Land Sales
  Full Disclosure Act

* Federal Legislation Protecting
  Historical and Archaeological
  Resources

ers of eminent domain, taxation, and police power. An extension of this is the authority to regulate land uses within state borders. Indeed, the Tenth Amendment to the Constitution has been generally interpreted to reserve to the states authority to regulate the use of virtually all state and private lands within their territorial boundaries. Land-use regulation has been approached primarily as a local government zoning problem for the last 50 years. However, when the recent dramatic changes in our metropolitan and rural areas are considered, the local zoning approach may no longer be sufficient to deal with contemporary land-use problems, as this quotation indicates:[3]

In attempting to cope with the myriad of problems, States have sought to regulate development by a variety of means. The States have come to realize that the dependence of local government on property taxes for support

has fostered an inherent conflict when they are petitioned by the developer. The resolution of this conflict of tax base versus social, environmental, or aesthetic interests of the region also has serious political ramifications. The fact that the decision-making power rests in local hands does not cause these problems; the defect is that the criteria for decision-making are exclusively local, even when the interests affected are far more comprehensive [Table 5.2 and Figure 5.2].

The ability to involve state (and regional) participation has the same common basis as the zoning laws—the police power. It is clear that the authority rests with the states to legislate for the promotion of the health, safety, and welfare of their citizens. There is no constitutional necessity for the delegation of all of the power to the local governments. The courts have consistently sustained a state's regulatory authority in the field of land management, even at the risk of cir-

Table 5.1   Relevance of local regulatory mechanisms to various environmental and non-environmental management elements, Nassau and Suffolk counties, New York (SOURCE: Reference 1)

L = Low M = Moderate H = High O = Technique not in use NA = Not applicable	Residential	Commercial	Industrial	Institutional	Utilities	Open Space	Wetlands	Flood plains	Beaches, Bluffs, and Dunes	Soils	Visual Character	Surface Fresh Water	Marine waters	Ground water
Comprehensive planning	H	H	H	H	H	H	H	H	H	H	H	H	H	H
Building permits	H	H	H	H	H	M	M	M	H	H	L	L	L	L
Zoning	H	H	H	H	H	m	H	H	H	H	H	H	M	H
Subdivision regulations	H	H	H	H	H	H	H	H	H	H	H	H	M	H
Site plan review	H	H	H	H	H	H	H	H	H	H	H	H	M	
Water supply regulations	H	H	H	H	H	H	H	H	H	H	NA	H	NA	H
Sewage regulations	H	H	H	H	H	H	H	H	L	H	L	H	H	H
Drainage regulations	H	H	H	H	H	H	H	H	M	H	M	H	H	H
Erosion control regulations	H	H	H	H	H	H	H	H	H	H	M	H	H	L
Development rights transfer	O	O	O	O	O	O	O	O	O	O	O	O	O	O
Acquisition	H	H	H	H	H	H	H	H	H	H	H	O	O	O
Utility location regulation	H	H	H	H	H	H	H	H	H	H	L	H	H	H
Tidal wetlands regulation	H	H	H	H	H	H	H	H	NA	H	H	L	H	H
Fresh water wetlands regulation	H	H	H	H	H	H	H	H	L	H	H	H	NA	H
Flood forecasting/warning	H	H	H	H	H	L	L	H	L	NA	NA	M	M	NA
Disaster assistance	H	H	H	H	H	H	H	H	H	M	NA	NA	NA	NA
Flood insurance	H	H	H	H	H	NA	H	H	NA	NA	NA	NA	NA	NA
Evacuation/relocation	H	M	L	L	M	H	H	H	H	NA	NA	NA	NA	NA
Floodproofing	M	H	H	H	H	NA	NA	H	NA	NA	NA	NA	NA	NA
Encroachment lines	O	O	O	O	O	O	O	O	O	O	O	O	O	O
Bulkhead lines	O	O	O	O	O	O	O	O	O	O	O	O	O	O
Water discharge permits	O	H	H	H	H	NA	NA	NA	NA	NA	NA	H	H	H
Ocean dumping permits	L	H	H	H	H	NA	NA	NA	NA	NA	NA	NA	H	NA
Sanitary landfill permits	H	H	H	H	H	H	H	H	H	H	H	H	H	H
Refuse incineration permits	H	H	H	H	H	NA	NA	NA	NA ,	NA	NA	NA	NA	NA

Table 5.2 Factors generating a need for state land resource management action (by percent of states expressing this factor in responses from 38 states replying to a Council of State Governments survey) (SOURCE: Reference 3)

A.	Lack of adequate provision for future needs of:	
	1. Agriculture	72
	2. Forestry	57
	3. Industry	70
	4. Business	48
	5. Residential communities	71
	6. Recreation	92
B.	Inadequate protection of:	
	1. Water supplies	79
	2. Wildlife	59
	3. Estuarine and marine fisheries	58
	4. Despoliation caused by poor mining practices	42
	5. Scenic areas	81
	6. Historic areas	60
C.	Rapid uncoordinated and piecemeal development	90
D.	To provide for proper development of "new towns"	69
E.	Lack of resources for adequate planning and zoning at the local level	74
F.	Parochial planning and zoning practices at the local level	79
G.	Lack of unified criteria upon which to measure developments proposed for critical areas	91
H.	Adverse developments contiguous to key public improvements and facilities	64

cumscribing the seemingly traditional rights of the landowner or local authorities. Therefore ample authority is vested in the states for the use of land management techniques. The question is mainly one of how to implement these techniques. To have each government level play an appropriate role appears to be one attractive alternative.[3]

Though the use of state power seems to have been mainly reactive, in recent years there has been a renaissance of state initiatives. Well over one-half of the states have approved measures dealing with basic environmental problems on numerous fronts, land management receiving the greatest attention. An array of statutes imposing controls on subdivisions, wetlands, natural areas, and strip mining has been passed. Other new statutes deal with air and water pollution control, solid waste disposal, dredging, and the protection of endangered species.[3]

The new initiatives mainly involve the reassertion by the states of their rights to regulate development, that is, the exercise of inherent sovereign police powers. These were powers that formerly may not have been exercised by anyone at the state or municipal levels. Many of these new state initiatives in regulatory matters have responded to this need for affirmative action. Innovative at-

Figure 5.2   Although planning is essential in most communities today, attractive and ecologically compatible waterfronts of the older seaside towns became so without the benefit of planning (Porpoise Point, Maine). (Conservation Foundation photo by M. Fahay.)

tempts to use or recover the power to manage development show that several states are now regulating large portions of their land and water areas. The first major exercise of the state police power through zoning occurred in 1961, when Hawaii enacted a comprehensive statewide zoning plan. The plan eventually set up four classifications of land within the state: agricultural, conservation, urban, and rural. Under this legislation the state determined the policy for development, allowing local input in the administration of the zoning program.[3]

Many states have reclaimed the authority over privately owned coastal wetlands and require state or coordinated state–local review and the approval of permits for any uses that may be potentially damaging to the coastal ecosystem. These programs have a variety of declared purposes, the most prevalent of which are to conserve fish and wildlife resources, to protect ecosystems, and to control development (Table 5.3).

Regional

Regional planning commissions exist in most metropolitan areas. They attempt to deal with the growth and development problems affecting the area they serve. Because of their voluntary nature, most have had little success in getting local governments to deal effectively with areawide problems other than roads, airports, and sewerage. Certain federal grant requirements impose many conditions before requests for grant-in-aid funds can be considered, including having the funding request reviewed by a metropolitan planning agency. Regional planning commissions face many problems fostered by local insensitivity. In addition, state government has created public authorities and special districts to handle areawide problems outside the existing local government structure. What this has done is to proliferate overlapping governments. The actions of these public authorities and special districts have tremendous impact on urban growth, but they do not always consider existing local plans in their expansion programs.[3]

Local

Control of the private use of land in the shorelands and the coastal water basin mar-

Table 5.3 Purposes of coastal-oriented environmental regulatory programs of certain states (SOURCE: Reference 4)

	1. Protect wildlife, fisheries	2. Protect ecosystems	3. Control development	4. Enhance aesthetics	5. Protect life, property	6. Enhance public recreation	7. Protect water resources	8. Conserve soil resources	9. Promote commerce	10. Protect navigability	11. Public access	12. Develop resource use
California	X	X	X	X	X	X		X			X	
Connecticut	X	X		X	X	X			X	X		
Delaware	X	X	X	X		X	X	X	X	X	X	
Georgia	X	X	X			X	X	X	X	X		
Maine	X		X	X	X		X					
Maryland	X	X	X	X	X	X				X		
Massachusetts	X			X								
Michigan	X	X	X			X		X				
Minnesota		X	X	X	X	X	X	X	X			X
Mississippi		X		X		X	X		X			
New Hampshire	X							X				
New Jersey	X	X	X	X	X		X		X			
North Carolina	X				X		X	X				
Rhode Island		X	X		X							X
Virginia	X	X	X	X	X	X	X	X	X	X		
Washington	X	X	X	X		X					X	
Wisconsin	X		X	X			X	X				
	14	12	12	11	10	10	9	9	7	5	3	2

Figure 5.3   Unsightly and ecologically destructive development can best be prevented by effective local land management practices (vicinity of Freeport, Texas). (Photo by author.)

gins is essential to the conservation of coastal ecosystems; therefore it is stressed repeatedly in this book. Clearly, the greatest power to affect land management rests at the local level of government. Therefore local government must recognize and uphold its responsibility if there is to be effective conservation. The job cannot be passed up to state and federal governments (Figure 5.3).

Often the tools are in the hands of the town, but in many areas of the United States the county provides the planning and zoning administration. The effectiveness of the process is dependent on the municipal or county administrative program, requiring the concerted effort and support of all officials and citizens. The legislative body, zoning administrative officer, board of appeals, planning departments, planning board, municipal or county attorney, and many other interested agencies must work in harmony.[3]

Floodplains

Enabling statutes in state law have, in most instances, delegated the enforcement of floodplain regulations to local general-purpose units of government (cities, villages, towns, counties, boroughs, and parishes). Local regulations have been adopted either as separate, free-standing ordinances or as part of broader zoning, subdivision control, and building code ordinances with special flood-related provisions. Coastal communities have special flood problems connected with ocean storms that require special mechanisms. Typical regulatory techniques authorized and applied to control floodplain uses include the following:[5]

1. *Zoning ordinances.* Floodplain zoning maps delineate the regulatory floodplain and, in some instances, floodway and coastal high-hazard areas. Zoning texts

establish minimum use standards, including (in most instances) very tight restrictions on building in floodway and coastal high-hazard areas and minimum flood protection elevations for structures and other damageprone land uses in outer flood fringe areas (Figure 5.4).

2. *Subdivision ordinances.* Flood-related subdivision controls typically require that subdividers install adequate drainage facilities and design water and sewer systems to minimize flood damage and contamination. They prohibit the subdivision of land that is subject to flooding unless flood hazards are overcome through filling or other measures. However, filling of actual floodways is prohibited. Subdivision ordinances require that subdivision plans be approved before the sale of land.

3. *Building codes.* A smaller number of local units of government have adopted flood-related building code provisions that typically establish minimum flood protection elevations and, in some instances, structural floodproofing requirements.

4. *Special codes and regulations.* In other cases, a mandatory state code may prevent local initiative. Special regulations pertaining to floodplain areas, including regulations for septic tanks, building setback lines along lakes and streams, wetland controls, and specific flood damage prevention ordinances, have usually been adopted pursuant to broader zoning enabling authority, special statutes explicitly authorizing such controls, or home rule powers.

Beach Access

An important part of each management program is to determine how public use and

Figure 5.4   Roadways built too close to the shore are periodically damaged by storm action; sand trucked away during cleanup is often a serious loss to the beach system (vicinity of Avon, New Jersey coast). (Photo by author.)

Figure 5.5 Beaches are key public recreational resources; they should be protected, and all citizens should be provided with ready access to them (Sanibel Island, Florida). (Photo by author.)

enjoyment of beach and tideland areas can best be secured (Figure 5.5). These areas may be owned by private individuals or various levels of government. Even when beaches are publicly owned, private developments bordering them may threaten public access. Acquisition of land or of user interests in land ("easements") may be a desirable, although expensive, approach. Alternatively, in areas about to undergo extensive development, the management program may make approval of a subdivision conditional on the developer's dedication of easements for beach access and use.[6]

There are other approaches as well. Under various common law doctrines, public recreational use of a privately owned beach over a period of years may be held to have established a public right to continue this use. An owner's acquiescence to long-term, open public use of his beach property, as if it were a public recreation area, is deemed to show

an intention to have the land dedicated for this use, regardless of the actual intent. In California, if the public used the beach for only 5 years at any time in the past, a new owner cannot revoke the effect of an earlier acquiescence. The ancient legal doctrine of "custom" provides another argument in support of public rights to a beach. Oregon's Supreme Court has held that the fact that dry sand beaches had been enjoyed by the public under claim of right since the beginning of the state's history was sufficient reason to prevent a resort owner from fencing off a beach.[6]

Large portions of the tideland beaches are now publicly owned. Moreover, privately owned tidelands and submerged lands have long been held subject to a public trust. This trust gives the public a continuing right to use the tidelands, not only for traditional purposes of fishing, navigation, and commerce, but also for recreational use in states where modern needs have been recognized. The scope of the public trust and its enforcement obligations vary from state to state. To utilize these doctrines, where available, the management program should provide for surveys of past public usage of beach areas and a program to assert the public's right to continued use of these beaches, through litigation where necessary.[6]

But the whole beach system must be carefully protected and its carrying capacity respected (Figure 5.6).

MANAGEMENT MECHANISMS

The various federal, state, and regional interests in coastal zone environmental

Figure 5.6 Beach and dune systems must be carefully managed to protect their values (Cape Cod National Seashore, Massachusetts). (Photo by author.)

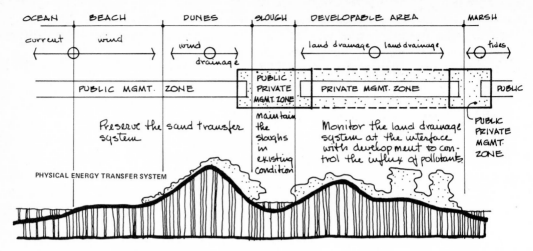

Figure 5.7 Sample management requirements and responsibilities: a typical barrier island coastal sector in Georgia. (SOURCE: T. Wilkinson for The Conservation Foundation.)

management can contribute to local government's community land use and environmental programs. The opportunities for coordination with state and federal programs and for innovation by local government depend on the political and legal structure of the local community. A "home rule" jurisdiction may have much greater freedom in designing a program to manage coastal resources than a small town with limited statutory authority to manage land use. Both legal and financial resources will depend on an individual community's circumstances. A given ecosystem objective may be attainable only through different technical and administrative arrangements in different localities.

The goal is for the ecosystem to continue to function optimally, and to achieve this objective there must be specific constraints on project location, design, and construction activity throughout coastal watersheds. Many of our recommended environmental standards are familiar concepts already in general use, implemented for erosion control, for setbacks, for sewage treatment, or for other purposes. They should be checked to see whether they meet our suggested criteria. Others, calling for land application of

wastes, protection of dunes, or nonstructural protection of shorelines, may be innovative for many communities and hence more difficult to implement.

Standard Mechanisms for Development Regulation

Before development and construction, the property owner must usually obtain approvals and permits from several governmental agencies. The particular approvals required vary with the type of development proposed, its location, and other factors. A review of all government regulations that may apply is absolutely essential for avoiding delays at later stages of planning and development (Figure 5.7). Governmental regulations that usually apply to residential development are summarized below.[2] All types of regulations may not apply to every proposed development.

Zoning Regulations

Zoning regulations are administered by local governments to ensure that various land uses are properly located in relation to each other and that adequate space in the community is provided for needed development. Effective zoning protects the investment of the landowner and makes the community a better and more pleasant place in which to live. A zoning ordinance identifies the permitted uses and density of structures permitted in each "zone" and is accompanied by a map showing the location of each zone in the community. A typical ordinance will include a separate zone for each of several types of residential, commercial, industrial, agricultural, and open-space uses. Special zones superimposed on the others establish added regulations, for example, in floodplains or aircraft flight paths. Zoning based on a comprehensive plan of the area is considered the most positive guide for development. The zoning ordinance and official map are the regulatory tools used to enforce the land-use plan.

Subdivision Regulations

Subdivision regulations are locally adopted controls, based on the police power authority of the state, which govern the process of converting raw land into building sites by dividing large parcels into two or more smaller lots ("subdivision"). Before a developer can improve or sell parcels of land, he must have a plat map approved by the appropriate local agencies. Subdivision regulations usually specify procedures for obtaining plat approval, as well as straight-forward minimum standards for the design of roads, parcel layout, utilities, sewage disposal, and other facilities. Often presubmission conferences on zoning permits involving a "sketch plan" are strongly encouraged by local planning offices to ensure that all factors are being considered by the developer. Official approvals of the preliminary plat and final plat should then follow.

Ideally the availability of utilities, such as sewage systems, water, gas, and telephone, is determined at an early stage. This information is provided by the planning department, planning commission, city or county engi-neer, and other offices. Subdivision regulations are meant to protect the consumer by ensuring that the lot for sale is buildable. Subdivision regulations also protect the developer against substandard competitors who may destroy the value of a well-planned subdivision by placing poor-quality development nearby.[2]

Construction Codes

Construction, or building, codes promote sound and safe construction by regulating the type of materials used and the manner of construction. Plumbing, electrical, and housing codes may exist in a community to protect the health and safety of occupants. Special standards for construction may be required by the U.S. Federal Housing Administration or the Veterans Administration, in order to qualify for mortgage insurance. Building codes are enforced through a system of permits and inspections. A person planning to construct a building or make major repairs must first submit plans and specifications to the local building inspector. Some states require that a registered architect prepare documents for buildings over a certain size. If a proposed structure meets the code requirements, a building or construction permit is issued. On-site inspections may then be made to ensure that construction is proceeding according to approved plans. After the successful completion of construction, occupancy permits are issued.[2]

Interrelation of Regulatory Mechanisms

Although zoning, subdivision controls, and building codes are meant to regulate different facets of land development or use, the distinctions are not always clear. "Zoning" is said to control the use of land; "subdivision regulations," the division of land for sale or building purposes; and "building codes," the design and materials used in building construction. This separation of

functions is to some extent artificial, however, since the "use" of land may be said
to encompass both sale and building construction. In addition, there are often some
overlap and considerable interrelationships
between regulations. For example, subdivision regulations typically require that all
proposed subdivisions comply with the use
standards of zoning, including minimum lot
sizes, fill and grading provisions, tree-cutting
regulations, and building setbacks.[5]

Nevertheless, despite some overlap, the
separation of control of zoning regulations,
subdivision controls, and building codes is
well established in the legal and planning
literature and in basic enabling statutes.
Zoning and subdivision regulations, often
authorized by separate enabling acts, are

sometimes administered by separate agencies.
In addition, the regulations differ in scope.
Zoning regulations are a broad tool pertaining to land use and may grant the administering agency substantial discretion in project review. Subdivision regulations, on the
other hand, usually are nondiscretionary,
setting minimum standards for the sale
of potential building sites.[5]

Certain aspects of zoning and building
codes are more closely allied in concept and
operation. Both zoning regulations and
building codes establish certain minimum
standards for building construction, although
zoning also regulates the type of use (e.g.,
residential, commercial). Typically, zoning
regulations specify bulk and density by setting permitted floor areas and building

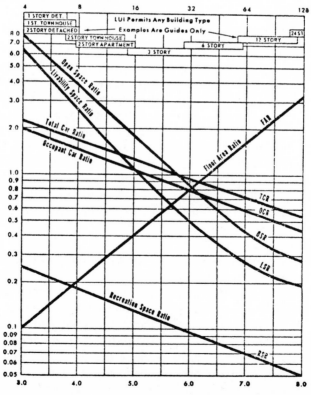

Figure 5.8   Land-use intensity for use in the design of planned developments; compares living units per acre
with acres per living unit. (SOURCE: Reference 8.)

heights for lots within a given zoning use district. In addition, zoning codes may indirectly affect design by specifying the type of use, and by regulating fill and grading, tree-cutting, sideyards, building setbacks, and other matters. Many communities have exercised direct zoning control over building design through the establishment of architectural or historic preservation controls. The building code controls the details of execution, with particular attention to safety from fire and to other health and safety concerns, such as hurricane resistance. Some states combine zoning and building code enabling statutes. However, most localities have separate building code and zoning enabling authorities.[5]

More recent innovations may combine zoning and subdivision types of review in special districts or for special sites where "flexible" standards are applied. These planned development provisions fall under many aliases: planned unit development (PUD), planned residential development (PRD), special treatment district, and so forth. They may permit a special review board to substitute new performance standards for all of the zoning ordinance requirements or, more typically, allow relaxation of individual lot size and density requirements to permit the clustering of buildings for site layout flexibility that is not possible when, for example, front yards must all be 60 feet and side yards 15 feet on minimum 1-acre lots. The device indicates one of the problems with traditional specification-type zoning standards. Though easy to enforce, they may stifle innovation for the developer who has a better idea, for example, grass gutters or permeable driveway surfaces.

Performance standards are requirements for meeting overall objectives in terms of density, drainage, green area, impervious surfaces, or any other aspect otherwise regulated by specification in a zoning ordinance (Figure 5.8). These standards usually require special reviews and are often difficult to

enforce. Also, unless carefully drawn, they may not give an applicant a clear idea of what is required. How new ecological standards are incorporated into zoning and subdivision ordinances will depend on the resources available for enforcement, the interest of citizen review boards, and the format of existing regulations.

Relation of Standard Mechanisms to Conservation

There is such variation from community to community in the administrative organization of land-use and development controls that we find it most reasonable to suggest requirements and leave it to local preference whether the particular item is incorporated in zoning, in site plan or subdivision review, or in building codes. In this section we outline major requirements that should be included in community development management in order to conserve coastal ecosystems and provide protection for coastal water-based resources.

Land Surface Alteration

Specific constraints are needed in regard to project location, design, and construction activity throughout the coastal watershed and for the application of strict performance standards. The amount of impervious surface should be minimized, and barren soils stabilized by replanting vegetative cover as quickly as possible after land clearing. Finished grades should be designed so as to direct water flows through natural terrain and along natural drainage courses, where the vegetation and soils can cleanse the runoff waters. Artificial storm drain systems should be eliminated whenever possible in favor of natural-type systems. Where used, artificial systems should be designed to harmonize with natural drainage patterns and to preserve the natural rate of flow.

Control of the quality, volume, and rate of flow of land runoff from shorelands into

Figure 5.9 Coastal ecosystem conservation requires standards for grading to avoid sediment pollution and disturbance of the watershed drainage system, including exemption from development of much wider buffers than the thin strip shown above (Avon, New Jersey). (Photo by author.)

coastal water basins is exercised mainly through site preparation constraints. Of particular concern are the activities involved in basic land clearing and the preparation of building sites. Coastal ecosystems can be protected through special application of the following standards:

1. Erosion standards. To prevent sedimentation, turbidity, and pollution from construction, logging, and agricultural activities.
2. Grading standards. To retain the beneficial effects of the natural drainage system and to control erosion (Figure 5.9).
3. Drainage standards. To require artificial storm runoff systems that best simulate the natural drainage system (Figure 5.10).
4. Excavation standards. To prevent surge runoff and general unbalancing of the water drainage system, to avoid stagnant

basins, and to protect runoff water quality.
5. Surfacing standards. To prevent unbalancing the drainage system by excessive paving and other impermeable surfaces (Table 5.4).

Areas Exempt from Development

A number of specific, identifiable land–water elements are so valuable in their natural states that they should ordinarily be fully protected and not altered by clearing, excavation, or building. Three major areas should be designated as exempt from typical development:

1. *Vital areas.* To protect from significant alteration areas essential to the proper functioning of coastal ecosystems (Figure 5.11).
2. *Drainageways.* To retain the benefits of

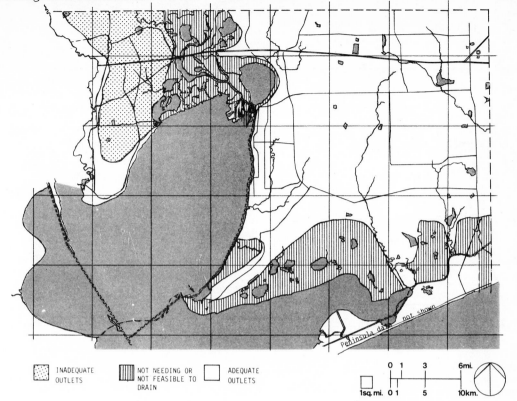

INADEQUATE OUTLETS

NOT NEEDING OR NOT FEASIBLE TO DRAIN

ADEQUATE OUTLETS

0 1 3 6mi.

1sq.mi. 0 1 5 10km.

Figure 5.10 Ecosystem conservation requires detailed knowledge of the coastal drainage systems (coastal watersheds) so that appropriate standards can be applied (vicinity of Trinity Bay, Texas). (SOURCE: Reference 9.)

the natural drainage systems of coastal watersheds.

3. *Buffers and setbacks.* To protect surface water quality, to stabilize shorelines, and to protect vital areas (Figure 5.12).

Siting Standards

Conserving coastal ecosystems often requires that certain structures or uses be located a specified distance from the water or that vital areas be designated as exempt from potentially altering uses, as shown in the following:

1. Industrial facility siting. To protect vital areas, water quality, shorelines, and water basins through the selection of alternative locations for potentially disturbing industry.

2. Residential and commercial siting. To protect vital areas, water quality, shorelines, and water basins through setbacks and special use standards.

Structural Standards

There are particular standards that should be applied to the design of structures and to construction activity in order to conserve coastal ecosystems. The following are two major approaches:

1. Elevation of structure. To protect vital areas and water quality through elevation of houses, piers, walkways, etc., on piling supports.

2. Construction constraints. To avoid soil erosion and eutrophication, toxification,

Table 5.4   Runoff ratings for selected land
uses (rating system: 1 = minimum impact;
10 = maximum impact; s.f.d. = single family
dwelling, s.f.a. = single family apartment;
p.u.d. = planned unit development. (SOURCE:
Reference 9)

LAND USE	PERCENT SITE RENDERED IMPERVIOUS	PERCENT SITE REQUIRED CLEARED	RATING
AGRICULTURAL			
crop and livestock production	0-5	100	3
timber production	0-5	100	3
RECREATIONAL			
inland	5-15	25-75	3
water related	25-50	50-100	5
RESIDENTIAL			
s.f.d. large lot	24	37	3
s.f.d. track house	36	70	5
s.f.d. high density	42	80	6
garden apartments	51	93	7
garden apartments high density	42	85	6
s.f.a. townhouse	45	91	6
s.f.a. rowhouse	56	93	7
mobile home park	28	54	4
p.u.d.	31	56	4
COMMERCIAL			
retail	100	100	10
office	50-100	80-100	8
INSTITUTIONAL			
all general facilities	25-100	50-100	4
INDUSTRIAL			
production	10-30	50-100	3
extraction	0-10	20-50	2
distribution	50-100	80-100	8
TRANSPORTATION			
roads	30-100	100	7
railroads	40	100	6
airports	2-40	3-100	4
UTILITY			
treatment plants	30-70	50-100	6
pipelines	0-30	100	4
landfill	0-10	100	3

and other disturbances of coastal waters
from disturbances caused by the construction process.

Waterfront Development

Special controls are required on waterfront
development to protect the shoreline and
water basins; three examples are as follows:

1. Shore alteration standards. To prevent
   alteration of the natural configuration of
   the shoreline.
2. Beach structure standards. To provide for
   the least ecological disturbance from private shore protection projects through
   careful engineering of jetties, groins, and
   seawalls (Figure 5.13).
3. Canal restrictions. To prevent damage to
   vital areas, shorelines, and water quality
   by restrictions on the excavation of canals
   in coastal floodplains and the margins
   of coastal water basins.

Roadway Constraints

It is necessary to plan thoughtfully for the
location, design, and construction of roadways in the coastal zone in order to protect
coastal ecosystems. Appropriate categories
are the following:

1. Location and alignment standards. To
   prevent damage to drainage systems, vital
   areas, and water quality.
2. Design standards. To provide for minimum interference with water flows, water quality, and vital areas.
3. Construction standards. To avoid water
   pollution and other disturbances.

Water Basin Protection

The water basins require a comprehensive
program of controls to protect their values
and productivity. Seven major requirements
are as follows:

Figure 5.11 Freshwater marsh systems in coastal watersheds are among the vital areas that should be fully protected to conserve coastal ecosystems (Kings Creek, vicinity of Jamestown, Virginia). (Conservation Foundation photo by M. Fahay.)

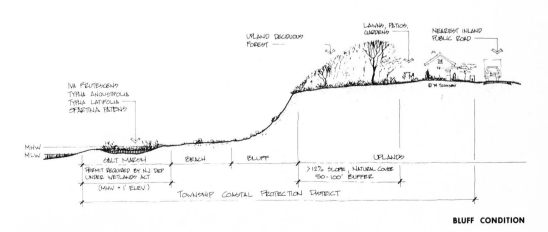

Figure 5.12 Provisions for ample buffer strips of natural vegetation and soil are necessary to conserve coastal ecosystems. (SOURCE: Reference 10; courtesy S. Hammill, The Collins Du Tot Partnership, Philadelphia, Pennsylvania.)

241

Figure 5.13 The Long Island beachfront is seriously degraded by inadequate land-use control and short-sighted development; the expensive groin system is an inadequate solution (West Hampton Beach, New York). (Photo by the U.S. Army Corps of Engineers.)

1. Channel standards. To control the depth and placement of channels to maintain water circulation, water quality, and vital areas.
2. Spoil disposal standards. To protect water quality, vital areas, and water basin configuration and bottom condition.
3. Fill standards. To protect vital areas, water quality, and basin configuration from adverse filling of land (Figure 5.14).
4. Structure siting standards. To protect water circulation and quality.
5. Inlet alteration standards. To maintain water circulation and prevent water quality degradation.
6. Mineral extraction standards. To protect basin configuration and water quality from strip mining activities.
7. Dredging operation standards. To protect water quality and other values.

Water Use and Control

Constraints such as the following on the use of freshwater resources in the coastal zone are necessary for a variety of purposes related to the conservation of coastal ecosystems:

1. Limitations on groundwater use. To avoid salt intrusion and land subsidence (Figure 5.15).
2. Limitations on surface-water use. To avoid the removal of suspended life and pollution of coastal waters.
3. Sewage system standards. To encourage beneficial use of domestic waste, to preserve vital areas, and to prevent toxic, nutrient, organic, and pathogenic pollution.
4. Marine waste standards. To prevent pollution from boat and marine wastes.

5. Solid waste standards. To prevent damage to vital areas and water quality (Figure 5.16).

Personal Activities Control

Certain restrictions on personal activities are necessary in a balanced conservation program, including these two types of controls:

1. Pollutant control. To avoid water pollution from excessive individual-homeowner use of chemicals such as fertilizers and biocides.
2. Traffic control. To prevent damage to water quality and vital areas from vehicles, boats (excessive speed), or foot passage (Figure 5.17).

Combination Reviews

There are now so many environmentally oriented state and federal regulatory pro-

grams affecting coastal communities and additions to local requirements that duplication, overlap, conflict, and confusion are avoidable only by structuring the framework of local ordinances and administrative review processes so that the various requirements of law and the various steps in the review process serve multiple purposes. Insofar as possible, applicants and petitioners should be required to respond to each substantive issue only once, and not numerous times for numerous regulations. For example, setbacks that are required to meet a number of regulatory purposes—for example, aesthetic enhancement, erosion control, avoidance of surface-water and groundwater pollution, noise abatement, beach stabilization—should be considered in one combined review, rather than in a separate review for each regulatory purpose.

Many communities have special-purpose "environmental impact assessment" require-

Figure 5.14 The filling of coastal marshes to create house lots is contrary to good ecologic practice (Stratford, Connecticut). (Photo by author.)

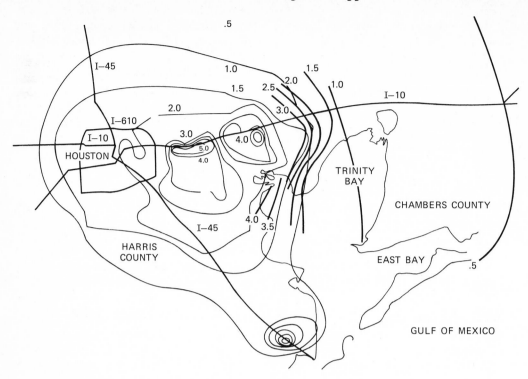

Figure 5.15   Shorelands in the Houston–Galveston Bay area have sunk as much as 8 feet in the past 30 years; communities such as Baytown are now under water during normal high tides and heavy rainstorms. (SOURCE: Reference 9.)

ments. Administrative processes for these should be combined with federal–state programs to the maximum extent possible.

Impact Assessment

It is most useful to require the developer of a project with a significant potential for adverse impact to conform to a formal review of environmental effects. Ordinances prescribing environmental assessments have been passed by many local jurisdictions. For example, in Collier County, Florida, a county ordinance requires an environmental impact statement to be submitted in conjunction with filing for rezoning petitions, subdivision proposals, or construction permits on developments involving more than 10 acres, 40 dwelling units, or 16,000 square feet of construction. The ordinance assures a careful review of major potential adverse

impacts and provides an additional mechanism to protect the county's wetlands, water systems, and estuarine resources.

It is quite practicable to establish, or to incorporate into existing subdivision or building permit reviews, a requirement for the assessment of the hydrological consequences of residential, commercial, industrial, or agricultural development in shorelands. When the consequence of private construction activity is a more rapid input of water volumes into streams, permits should be withheld until all feasible measures have been incorporated to reduce runoff volumes. Assessment reviews should also be required on the flooding consequences of all proposed public construction projects such as roads, bridges, culverts, or sewage systems. However, it should be realized that the program may be less than fully effective if restricted to a single coastal jurisdiction

Figure 5.16   Marshes should be exempt from dumping to prevent pollution and damage to coastal wetlands and estuaries (Bridgeport, Connecticut). (Photo by author.)

Figure 5.17   Boat speed should be controlled in shallow estuarine waterways to prevent continuous resuspension of silt deposits, as well as for safety (Savannah, Georgia). (Photo by author.)

when a coastal ecosystem receives a substantial amount of its freshwater input from a large river extending far inland. Such situations normally require management at a regional level.

Environmentally Nonconforming Uses

Nonconforming uses are uses that were ititiated before the adoption of an ordinance and that fail to conform to new zoning, subdivision control, or building code standards. Often communities provide at least minimal regulation of nonconforming uses by providing that nonconforming structures must be brought into conformity with regulations if destroyed, abandoned, or substantially modified or enlarged.[5]

General Coastal Application

The concept of nonconformance should be applied to coastal ecosystem conservation. The existence of poorly placed structures or other uses that do not conform to good environmental practice should not prevent the formulation of a proper management plan (Figure 5.18). Any such use should be identified as an *environmentally nonconforming use* and allowed to continue but be scheduled for removal or correction at the earliest opportunity. Expansion or improvement should not be allowed—only simple maintenance.

The opportunity for discontinuance may come at the point where the economic life of a structure ends, some natural disaster causes loss or extensive damage, or some public program enables the community to purchase the interest and end the use. Repair of minor damage would be permitted but not extensive rehabilitation or "substantial improvement." Some suitable insurance or loss control provisions may be necessary so that the owner can recover any fiancial loss on reversion of the use. The amount of improvement or of loss that is

considered "substantial" varies from locality to locality. The Federal Insurance Agency considers it to be "any improvement or repair of a structure, the cost of which equals or exceeds 50 percent of the market value of the structure before the improvement is started or the damage has occurred."[11]

Floodplains

As a practical matter, floodplain regulations have rarely been effectively applied to intensely developed areas because of political and planning considerations. Cost factors as well as equity considerations often require that wholly new uses be treated differently from existing uses. The existence of nonconforming uses in no way affects the designation of an area as a "floodplain," but the type and density of nonconforming uses may determine the reasonable use classification for the area and the most appropriate floodplain management technique. Such nonconforming uses are a major threat to floodplain management programs for several reasons:[5]

1. Nonconforming uses may be subject to severe flood losses.
2. Nonconforming uses may result in misguided political and economic pressures for structural protection through dams, dikes, levees, or flood control works, rather than for control of uses through regulation.
3. The failure to regulate nonconforming uses coupled with tight regulation of new uses may result in arguments of discrimination.
4. Nonconforming uses may establish a development pattern for an area, including the type of use, elevations for roads and sewers, and elevation of buildings, which may be difficult to modify through subsequent adoption of floodplain regulations requiring less intensive uses, higher road and sewer grades, and elevation of structures on fill.

Figure 5.18   Hurricane disaster traps, such as these structures on the Gulf of Mexico beachfront, should be designated as nonconforming uses and terminated at the earliest opportunity (Sanibel Island, Florida). (Photo by author.)

VITAL AREA PROTECTION

All three types of coastal ecosystem vital areas—*habitat units, productivity units,* and *structural units*—should be held exempt from alteration (Figure 5.19). The most important vital areas are often the combined units, those which include two or, at times, all three types. (Barrier islands are made up of such high proportions of vital areas that they are considered in detail as a special management case; see page 271.)

Regulatory Approach

Vital habitat areas are either fixed ecosystem features, such as salt marshes, or transient features without fixed boundaries, such as those with wind, tide, or river inflow. In either case the vital area is a critical element of the ecosystem, and its protection is essential. (A complete listing of vital area types is given on page 140 et seq.) The protective management of vital areas in the shorelands on the marginal areas of water basins (wetlands, tideflats) is rather direct and simple, technically because the principal method is simple exemption from an altering development. However, those that lie within the coastal water basins (shellfish beds, eelgrass beds) require somewhat more complex technical solutions to management needs (Figure 5.20).

Protective Actions

Vital areas should be designated as exempt from all but the most limited types of use, for example, light-duty recreation and other nonaltering uses. These areas should not

Figure 5.19   Cordgrasses give coastal marshes their extremely high value as vital areas. (Conservation Foundation photo by M. Fahay.)

be graded, cleaned, drained, dredged, or filled, and will require special care during site planning and preparation (page 98). They should also be protected from pollution and other external sources of disturbance. Ample precedent for such preservation is furnished by laws in several states that restrict the development of such vital areas as salt marshes and freshwater wetlands. In addition, many federal laws, policies, and programs provide for the preservation of wetlands (page 185).

Coastal wetlands protection is relatively simple when the wetlands involved are lower ones, below the high-water mark (in most states) and therefore in the public domain. However, in the case of upper wetlands private property is often involved, and

the owners may strongly object if they have plans for altering the areas for real estate or other purposes.

Vital Area Conservation Examples

Several examples of management problems with vital areas are discussed below to illustrate the need for vital area conservation.

Coral Reefs.   A much higher degree of protection than has been practiced in the past is necessary to preserve coral reefs. Sediment discharge from erosion, sewage pollution, chemical pollution, and urban runoff— all must be strictly controlled when reefs are significantly influenced by land drainage. Dredging in the vicinity of reefs may be particularly harmful because of the high incidence of silt fallout and sunlight screening caused by turbidity. Also, it must be concluded that any reduction of a coral reef structure decreases its function as a marine habitat, its scenic quality, and its role as a natural breakwater. Therefore removal of reef materials for commercial or personal purposes should not normally be permitted.

Grass Beds. Estuarine grass beds are vulnerable to turbidity, which screens out light and prevents the growth of the grass, and to fine sediments (mud), which create unstable bottom conditions wherein the grasses often cannot anchor. Heated power plant effluent destroys local grass beds. Boat traffic over grass flats may compound the problem by stirring up sediments and ripping out plants.

Shellfish Beds. Oyster and clam beds may be buried or dismantled by dredging.

Silt-laden waters are a harsh environment for their planktonic young stages, and layers of mud constitute an unsuitable bottom for their survival. Human activities that harm these beds and hinder their functions include those that cause erosion from upland, sediment from navigation dredging, oil spills, and industrial pollution.

Dunefronts. Clearly, the ocean beachfront is a risky place to maintain habitation. The costs in loss of property and life have been high for many beachfronts. Furthermore, the enormous private and public investments to stabilize and safeguard these inhabited beaches with structures have not often been rewarded with success. High-energy natural processes undermine the bulkheads, erode sand from behind the groins, and throw damaging breakers over the bulwarks.

Because dunes and other features are

Figure 5.20 Eelgrass beds are vital areas because they serve essential functions for the coastal ecosystems (Goose Cove, Annisquam, Massachusetts). (Photo by author.)

easily destroyed by man's activities, there are many constraints on their use and that of surrounding floodplains and shoreland. Vegetation must be kept intact, and all traffic, even foot traffic, should be strictly controlled or prohibited altogether. Highways should not be built adjacent to mobile dune fronts. Holding the beachfront in place by building protective structures as substitutes for dunes involves tremendous expense and usually is not permanently successful.

In summary, dunes are enormously valuable and exceptionally fragile. They should not be altered in any way. They should be set aside for complete preservation and encompassed by as broad a buffer area as necessary to allow for their movement and to protect them and the larger system of which they are an integral part.

In addition to the federal regulations (page 233), many states and local units of government have responded to this problem by establishing protection programs. For example, Texas has implemented a statute that prescribes the following:[12]

Sec. 4. PROHIBITED CONDUCT. (a) In any county in the area bounded on the south by the inlet known as Aransas Pass and on the north by the Texas–Louisiana state line, where a dune protection line has been established, it shall be unlawful for any person or association of persons, corporate or otherwise, to damage, destroy, or remove any sand dune or portion thereof on any barrier island or peninsula seaward of the dune protection line, or to kill, destroy, or remove in any manner vegetation growing on any sand dune seaward of the dune protection line, without first having obtained a permit as specified which authorizes such conduct (Figure 5.21).

(b) In any county in the area bounded on the north by the inlet known as Aransas Pass and on the south by the Mansfield Ship Channel, where a dune protection line has been established, it shall be unlawful for any person or association of persons, corporate or otherwise, to:

(1) excavate, remove, or relocate any sand

Figure 5.21   Texas is taking strong initiatives to protect its dune and beach systems. (Photo by author.)

dune or any portion thereof located seaward of such dune protection line so as to reduce the sand dune to an elevation less than the elevation, or elevations, shown on the Special Flood Hazard Map of such area promulgated by the administrator of the Federal Insurance Administration under and in accordance with the terms of the National Flood Insurance Act;

(2) kill, destroy, or remove in any manner any vegetation growing on any sand dune seaward of the dune protection line, without making provision for the stabilization of such dune by installation or construction of improvements or the replanting or resodding of vegetation thereon so as to maintain the dune at the minimum elevation set forth in Paragraph (1) above, without first having obtained a permit as specified hereafter which authorizes such conduct.

(c) In any county where a dune protection line has been established, it shall be unlawful for any person to operate a recreational vehicle on any sand dune seaward of the dune protection line.

Coastal Wetlands. Coastal shorelines with wetlands require special management consideration, not only to preserve the wetlands unit intact as a vital habitat area but also to control disturbances from adverse land-use practices in the floodplains and uplands above them. In many ways the wetlands are a vital component not only of the estuarine ecosystem but of the human community that surrounds them as well. The more intensely developed an area is, the more crucial the role of wetlands and the more urgent the need for their preservation through land-use control.

Appropriate local management programs can greatly reduce such adverse effects in shoreland watersheds, and even utilize the capacity of wetlands vegetation to receive urban runoff. Mangroves and marsh areas have the capacity to treat runoff waters, and possibly, under careful controls and with proper dispersal methods, pretreated effluents may be given a final polish within them. We have calculated from available information (in References 7, 25, and 26) that a marsh of 1000 acres may be capable of purifying the nitrogenous wastes from a town of 20,000 or more people.

Tidal marshes, bogs, and many other vital areas in coastal waters and shoreland areas are dependent for their viability on wet soils and regular flooding. If these areas are drained with excavated canals, their characters are completely changed and their values obviated. Therefore it is necessary to prohibit the excavation of any of these emergent vegetated water areas identified as vital areas (page 240) (Figure 5.22).

A possible protective strategy is to zone the wetlands of the community as a "vital area," subject to strict protective measures. In terms of permitted uses, densities, and alterations from site preparation and improvement, wetlands are normally unsuitable for development without major physical improvement to create buildable real estate. Therefore it is quite reasonable to identify wetlands as a "special district" when no other state or local protective regulations apply.

One such regulatory strategy has been implemented by ordinance in Collier County, Florida, where thousands of acres of mangrove and marsh were at stake.[13] *Special treatment* (ST) districts, or zones, were established in areas where the essential ecology could not be adequately protected under conventional zoning regulations. The purpose of the ST regulation is to protect and conserve areas of environmental sensitivity, while permitting types of development that will hold ecological alteration to acceptable levels. Areas of environmental sensitivity include mangrove swamp, coastal beaches, estuarine areas, cypress domes, freshwater marshes and tidal marshes, and natural drainage courses.

In developing the ST designation, the following provisions were incorporated into the final regulations:[13]

1. The ST designation must protect the environment from any use of development

Figure 5.22 Any excavation of wetlands must be presumed harmful to coastal ecosystems (Davis, North Carolina). (Conservation Foundation photo by M. Fahay.)

which will affect the environmental quality in a manner that is contrary to the health, safety, and well-being of the citizens of Collier County.

2. It must permit the reasonable use of the land consistent with its environmental constraints.

3. It must provide a means whereby lands which have special conditions and sensitive environmental character can be lawfully retained in their natural state without constituting a public taking requiring a large outlay of public funds for their actual acquisition.

4. It must provide a procedure whereby land having sensitive environmental qualities can be determined and so classified.

5. It must provide a procedure whereby each

use or development can be quantitatively reviewed to determine its effect on the environmental quality of the subject property as well as lands which it might affect.

6. It must conform to the policies of the Growth Policy and the goals and objectives of the Comprehensive Plan.

No lands designated as ST in Collier County may be cleared, altered, changed, or developed in any way until a permit has been obtained in the manner prescribed in the ST regulations. In essence, the ordinance works to prevent significant alteration of wetlands.

The ST designation was chosen to protect areas of environmental sensitivity because it had a better potential than any other suggestions that were advocated. The benefits of the ST zoning are listed as follows:[13]

1. It provides a lasting method for protecting and conserving areas of environmental sensitivity.
2. It encourages development consistent with the environmental quality of the property.
3. It "red-flags" areas of environmental sensitivity and puts the property owners on notice that such areas should be developed with care and restraint.
4. It is a rightful exercise of police powers and does not enter the area of "taking." This means that such lands do not have to be purchased in order to save them from destructive development.
5. It permits the transfer of development rights and thereby encourages development outside the areas of environmental sensitivity.
6. It encourages the donation of ST lands to the county or a private conservancy foundation after the development rights have been transferred. This eliminates taxes and encourages their protection in perpetuity.
7. It generates new taxes on the transferred development rights from lands which would not have been developed because of their physical limitations.

Community Acquisition Programs

Even with an optimal plan of regulations to provide ecological protection of critical areas, there may be a need for a supplementary program of public acquisition to achieve other objectives. Acquisition is particularly needed to ensure public access to scenic, recreational, and other water-related resources, and normally should not be required for environmental purposes when important water resources are at stake. In these cases regulation of land use should be acceptable.

There is such a variety of relevant state acquisition and designation programs that it is not possible to describe them here. Information can be readily obtained from any one of several state agencies, such as parks, environmental protection, or planning. Federal funds may also be made available through the Land and Water Conservation Fund, the Endangered Species Act, the Fish and Wildlife Act, the Migratory Bird Conservation Act, and other legislation. However, coastal water ecosystem protection is a central goal of only two federal programs.

It should be emphasized that the major scenic and public recreational values (and the incidental ecological and habitat benefits) of protected estuarine wetland marginal areas will be water resources oriented, and acquisitions will be limited principally to the saline water areas and a suitable buffer area. The land areas above the corridor and buffer can be fully developed for housing and other purposes, although general development restrictions will, of course, remain essential for these land areas.

The Collier County Case

Because acquisition of vital areas is often far beyond the means of a community, the local unit of government must rely on regulation of uses to provide the necessary controls. The local regulatory approach is supported by federal (and often state) regulatory programs. Collier County serves as an example. A comprehensive natural systems and planning study in 1974 showed conclusively that the county's shoreline fringe of some 100,000 acres of marsh and mangrove swamps should be preserved for its ecological benefit (Figure 5.23).

Collier County studied a number of approaches, and the following consideration of alternatives shows why the "ST" method was judged to be superior:[13]

1. Buy all areas of environmental sensitivity. This would protect such lands in per-

Figure 5.23   Collier County, Florida, has embarked upon a far-reaching management program aimed at preserving water systems and wetlands and conserving coastal resources and ecosystems. (Photo by author.)

petuity, but the county did not have the money for such purchase. It was estimated that about $0.5 billion would be required to purchase all areas of environmental sensitivity.

2. Purchase the development rights of areas of environmental sensitivity. No differentiation could be made between the cost of outright purchase of property and the purchase of development rights. Why would a property owner want to pay taxes on land that no longer could be developed? This approach was discarded as not much better than the first one.

3. Declare all lands of environmental sensitivity to be "preservation areas" and forbid their development. This approach is contrary to a property owner's right under the Constitution, which guarantees "nor shall private property be taken for public use without just compensation." The end result would be buying all such lands and not having enough money.

4. Grant tax forgiveness. This approach benefits the property owner without any guarantee that areas of environmental sensitivity will be protected beyond a time frame convenient to the owner. Such an approach is generally a tax forgiveness bonanza for the property owner with very little lasting benefit to the general public.

Acquisition funds, or tax-advantageous land donations, might be obtained from private sources. A combination of state–federal assistance, local initiative, assistance by national organizations, and private donations can make ambitious acquisition programs feasible.

Effect of Use Restriction

Vital areas may comprise a moderate part of the immediate coastal waters province in low-lying areas with rich aquatic ecosystems characterized by much vegetation, many shellfish beds, and so forth. For example, the estuarine water areas of the west coast of Florida are, on the average, about 50 percent coastal wetlands (mangrove, marsh, submerged grasses), as shown in Figure 5.24. Wetlands make up about 2.3 percent of the areas of all coastal counties.[15]

Areas of environmental concern constitute a larger, but not unreasonable, fraction of the available surface. For example, estuaries in their entirety are estimated to make up less than 10 percent of all the area (land and water) of the United States coastal counties.

Table 5.5 gives statistics for the Atlantic coast states (not available for Gulf or Pacific states) on the acreages of land, of water, and, for comparison of vital areas. Here it can be seen that wetlands comprise only about 1 percent of all state land and water areas. Of coastal waters alone, they make up 15 percent, of which about half, the tidelands, are presumed to be in the public domain (up to the high-water mark in most states). The 7 percent above high water—the wetlands—should be the only areas where a private landowner might be denied use by a management program.

Other vital areas that need protection constitute even less of total state areas; for example, oyster beds comprise about 0.5 percent of total lands, and coastal waters about 8 percent of the coastal waters province.

Redirecting Developments

In addition to land controls, it seems clear that all the vital areas of the coastal system must be protected in the formulation of a coastal environmental program. Vital areas include coastal freshwater wetlands—all marshes, cypress domes, sloughs, creeks, lakes, mangrove swamps or bays, and any other permanently or seasonally flooded areas, whether fresh- or saltwater (Figure 5.25). (Wetland and water areas that are not permanently flooded may be recognized by their characteristic vegetation; see Appendix, page 896).

The general case against industrial or commercial use of fragile wetland and water areas is so manifest that it scarcely requires justification. But the case against residential use may be equally compelling from the viewpoint of its potential for altering wetlands and damaging water systems and estuarine resources.

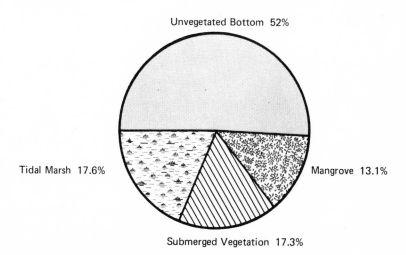

Figure 5.24 The percentages of mangrove swamp, tidal marsh, submerged vegetation, and unvegetated bottom in estuaries of the west coast of Florida are shown. (SOURCE: Reference 14.)

Table 5.5 Amounts of certain vital areas in the Atlantic Coastal Zone

State	Hard and Soft Clams[1] (Acres)	Oysters[1] (Acres)	Bay Scallops[1] (Acres)	Wetlands[2] (Acres)	Tidelands[3] (Acres)	Estuaries[4] (Acres)	Territorial Sea Area[5] (Acres)	State land Area[6] (Acres)
Me.	355,000	200	—	16,178	1,455	39,400	437,760	21,257,600
N.H.	5,000	2,000	—	5,285	375	12,400	24,960	5,954,560
Mass.	28,000	1,500	10,000	34,520	7,940	207,000	368,640	5,284,480
R.I.	22,000	1,000	4,000	1,360	645	94,700	76,800	776,960
Ct.	20,000	40,000	2,000	6,909	2,077	31,600	—	3,205,760
N.Y.	315,000	10,000	40,000	24,855	11,530	376,600	243,840	31,728,640
N.J.	300,000	60,000	1,000	150,440	20,870	778,400	249,600	5,015,040
Del.	15,000	20,000	—	49,578	43,756	395,500	53,760	1,316,480
Md.	250,000	326,000	—	117,840	15,890	1,406,100	59,920	6,769,280
Va.	300,000	384,000	—	44,950	86,100	1,670,000	215,040	26,122,880
N.C.	100,000	200,000	40,000	100,450	58,400	2,206,000	577,920	33,655,040
S.C.	2,000	20,000	—	91,000	345,000	427,900	359,040	19,875,200
Ga.	—	15,000	—	75,500	285,650	170,800	192,000	37,680,640
Fla.	1,000	15,000	—	134,600	158,200	1,051,200	1,113,600	37,478,400
Total	1,713,000	1,094,700	97,000	853,465	1,037,888	8,868,200	3,972,480	236,120,960

[1]Acreage of "important shellfish habitat," per reference 16.
[2]From page 4, reference 16.
[3]From page 4, reference 16.
[4]From page 30, reference 15.
[5]Coastline miles x 3, reference 1.7.
[6]Reference 17.

Figure 5.25   Estuarine and freshwater systems in the coastal watersheds are designated as critical areas, and fresh and salt marshes themselves as vital areas (Rye, New Hampshire). (Conservation Foundation photo by M. Fahay.)

We recommend that development location policy aim to concentrate development on drier land areas. Wetland areas should be designated for complete preservation because allowance for any major use would result in unacceptable alteration. This will bring the community program into agreement with federal (and often state) regulatory programs.

An integrated program to restrict development in water areas would redirect it to dry land sites, and would control site preparation of the land areas, including standards for excavation, drainage, grading, land filling, and paving, to ensure that water would leave any development site in the same condition in which it entered. It may be desirable to supplement the regulatory program by the purchase of some water-area parcels for public recreational and scenic purposes.

The regulation–redirection program leads logically to our recommendations that policies for the regulation of land areas and of wetlands and water areas be established and handled through the site plan review process according to a coherent set of development standards. For water areas we recommend a "no-alteration" use policy that can be also enforced through administrative interpretation of specific standards. These should provide for a variety of ecologically compatible, light-duty uses of wetlands and water areas, but not for the construction of permanent residential, industrial, or commercial structures. In effect, all uses should

Figure 5.26   Redirecting damaging residential development such as the above from wetlands and shorelines to areas further back in the shorelands is strongly recommended (New Topsail Beach, North Carolina). (Conservation Foundation photo by M. Fahay.)

be permitted that will not alter the form or ecological function of wetlands and water areas.

The no-alteration goal for wetland and water areas, along with drainage controls in land areas, would safeguard the water system and provide for the long-term protection of estuarine resources.

It is often not necessary, and sometimes not even desirable, to use a zoning approach because the application of standards with administrative review may be more flexible and it encourages positive innovation. An approach by standards may be extended immediately in local jurisdictions and without further survey because no mapping is required for its implementation—only the

application of standards through the locality's normal process of review of development applications. The plan controls to be used should provide the optimum protection consistent with reasonable private access and use, on the one hand, and the foreseeable degree of state and county commitment to preservation of water systems and estuarine resources, on the other (Figure 5.26).

Application of the "cluster" principle can also sometimes overcome owners' objections to a dry-land-only development policy. If a tract in single ownership contains large and accessible dry land areas, avoidance of wetlands and water areas may require no actual reduction in the number of dwelling units permitted.[18] Even in tracts where wetlands predominate, the total amount of permitted development can often be clustered on the remaining land portions through normal density realignment procedures.

Only a carefully applied process of administrative review can assure that the clustering of development satsifies both public and private objectives. With appropriate safeguards responsive to these administrative difficulties, however, cluster provisions offer a real opportunity. For the most part the clustering opportunity is greatest when tracts are sizable.

In some cases a combination of zoning with administrative review may be appropriate. Many local governments have taken this approach to protecting wetlands, waters, streams, and coastal resources. For example, as mentioned earlier, in Collier County, Florida, a county ordinance may establish a "special treatment" (ST) district, that is, a zone covering most marshes, swamps, and other intermittent water areas, wherein development is to be sharply curtailed to protect the county water sysem and estuarine resources (page 253). Development proposals must meet a number of environmental standards according to specific guidelines for permissible types of development. A provision is made in this ordinance for transfer of "residential density credit" out of ST areas to contiguous lands included in planned unit developments.[13]

Transfer Development Rights

The site transfer mechanism involved within land in common ownership, as provided in the cluster procedure, might be extended to transfer between owners through a system termed "transfer of development rights" (TDR). Advocates of the TDR approach stress that a property owner's customary right to develop a parcel of land at a prescribed number of units per acre could be transferred to another parcel of land by sale of the rights to another landowner who wishes to increase the density of development on his property beyond the prescribed number of units. The advantage to this exchange

Figure 5.27   Houses placed among the sand dunes are constantly in danger of destruction from storms and cause ecological and structural damage to the beachfront system (New Jersey). (Photo by author.)

would be to provide equity for the owner of undeveloped property who has a legitimate expectation of profit from the development of this property and whose hope of profiting is disrupted by new environmental restrictions on property use.

Although we believe that coastal communities may eventually find benefit from some form of TDR system, we cannot advocate its use because it has not yet emerged from the theoretical, untested stage. However, our concerns would not preclude a modification of the TDR idea to permit more flexibility than typical clustering does. Such a modification might be of use to provide additional immediate relief to property owners when new development standards would otherwise seriously reduce legitimate expectations. (See the Collier County case, page 253.)

Problems of Acceptance

The program that we recommend should guarantee reasonable use of private property, encourage thoughtful residential development, protect long-term property investments by protecting the resource base and by limiting hazard losses, cut public costs, provide maximum recreational and scenic experiences for citizens, and strengthen the tourist economy. It would accomplish these purposes by means of strategies to:

1. Induce a pattern of community development that follows natural constraints.
2. Protect water systems, water resources, wetlands, and estuarine resources.
3. Guarantee sufficient availability of wetlands and water areas for public access and recreational and scenic use.
4. Provide for optimum public safety from flood and other hazards (Figure 5.27).

We believe that coastal communities can afford to protect their wetlands, water areas, and water systems against destruction, and that it is, in fact, usually in their long-term economic interests to do so. However,

we also recognize that powerful objections to a strong program of protection will be raised in specific instances. Occasionally, it may well be necessary to permit noncompatible uses of minor water areas lest the entire scheme of protection be overwhelmed by accumulated opposition. But such instances must necessarily be infrequent; otherwise a comprehensive plan of protection could be dismantled piece by piece. In practice, deviations from the no-alteration policy in wetlands and water areas should be confined to the exceptionally rare case involving only a few acres.

Nevertheless, the adjustments to be made by property owners to achieve the program may stimulate a variety of objections, particularly the no-alteration strategy for wetlands and water areas that we have recommended. On the other hand, people concerned about protection of the ecosystem may find the no-alteration standards that permit light-duty use of wetlands insufficient on at least two grounds. First, they may doubt whether the standards will be effectively applied. They may question, for example, whether designers and contractors will cooperate in adhering to the protective purpose of the standards. They may also doubt the community's ability to enforce the standards, particularly those (such as the required replacement of damaged vegetation) that cannot be readily applied when project designs are reviewed. A further possible objection to the use standards—that even elevated "stilt" structures with low-density area land coverage may represent too much development—may be motivated by concern about the disruption of wetlands that even limited-scope and carefully controlled uses will create. Or (perhaps more likely) this objection may represent a conviction that conflict with other uses, such as wildlife habitat, estuarine resources, or simply aesthetics, makes virtually any development of wetland areas unacceptable.

Perhaps the most troublesome objections to a dry-land-only development policy arise

Figure 5.28   Exemption of vital areas, such as coastal marshes, from alteration may meet with objections from private owners and speculators because their market values will be reduced (Charleston, South Carolina). (Conservation Foundation photo by M. Fahay.)

because much of the water area is privately owned. Such objection is likely to focus on the seemingly sudden reversal of existing practice, including the prohibition against excavation of canals and filling of wetlands for urban development (Figure 5.28). Land speculators, builders, or lot owners intent upon building in exempted areas may find the virtual exclusion of residential development there inequitable.[18] Many owners of wetlands who expected to profit financially from the development of those areas can be expected to raise objections, before legislative bodies, administrative tribunals, and in the courts, to any proposed restriction of these expectations.

In the courts any proposal for water area preservation through a no-alteration policy risks an encounter with the "taking issue," an argument that regulation restricting the use of property in effect takes private property without compensation and thus violates the federal and state constitutions. Typically, the issue arises when a landowner argues that his property value has been affected by a land-use restriction. *The Taking Issue,*[19] a study of the interaction of land-use regulation and the Fifth Amendment ("nor shall property be taken for public use without compensation"), asserts that there is a powerful assumption which construes this Fifth Amendment language as the embodiment of any man's right to buy and sell land for a profit as he may choose, without regard to the commonweal. The reality, however, is a clear trend of judicial decisions that uphold the constitutionality of stringent land-use restrictions, especially when the protection of vital ecosystem elements is involved.

When land subject to regulation lies under water, any use may be further affected by the "public trust." This concept of "public trust" is a phenomenon of common law and dates back to the days when English monarchs first acknowledged significant rights in the public at large. Protection of these rights is never a taking of property, but rather an extension of the public's competing property interest—an interest that some states have found to be inalienable. The doctrine is complex, but there has been

an increasing willingness in the courts to reexamine the question of public trust when confronted by assertions that a restriction on land use constitutes a taking.

One of the most significant recent cases supporting local water area regulation occurred in Wisconsin, where the Supreme Court approved an ordinance based on state policy designed to prohibit alteration of certain (Marinette County, Wisconsin) wetlands. As a result a private owner was prohibited from continuing a waterfront fill program that he had begun on five of his waterfront lots. The Court stated as follows:

It seems to us that filling a swamp not otherwise commercially usable is not in and of itself an existing use, which is prevented, but rather is the preparation for some future use which

Figure 5.29   Long-range community plans to preserve shorelines and conserve ecosystems should include directing development away from shoreline transition areas (York, Maine). (Conservation Foundation photo by M. Fahay.)

is not indigenous to a swamp. Too much stress is laid on the right of an owner to change commercially valueless land when that change does damage to the rights of the public. The Justs [the complainants] argued their property has been severely depreciated in value. But this depreciation of value is not based on the use of the land in its natural state but on what the land would be worth if it could be filled and used for the location of a dwelling. While loss of value is to be considered in determining whether a restriction is a constructive taking, value based upon changing the character of the land at the expense of harm to public rights is not an essential factor or controlling.[20]

Protective regulations can often be strengthened, and objections to them lessened, by establishing supplementary development policies and requirements that provide positive alternatives. To increase the effectiveness of its wetlands and water area standards, for example, a community could supplement these standards with density allocations that would encourage development in appropriate land locations while discouraging or preventing it in inappropriate areas (Figure 5.29).

Recent actions of the federal and state governments promise to provide strong support for local protective regulations. As we have shown, these actions are severely restricting traditional development in the saline water areas; for example, federal flood protection policies may be expected to have increasingly constraining impacts in the future.

SPECIAL CASE: BARRIER ISLANDS AND BEACHES

The natural properties of barrier islands provide an absolutely unique combination of values. These islands are the front line of storm defense for a thousand miles of United States Atlantic and Gulf of Mexico coastline (Figure 5.30). They have scenic qualities—vividness, variety, and unity—unparalleled elsewhere in the coastal zone. They offer broad sandy beaches and a score of other recreational opportunities. They provide habitats and food for unique biotic communities—hundreds of species of coastal birds, fish, shellfish, reptiles, and mammals.

Natural Properties

There is a unity about the barrier island chain that is easily broken. The values of the islands are tightly intertwined, and there is a natural flow between them that must be preserved. The sand, the water, the animals, even the plants (through seed transport) move from island to island and form a common pool for resource replenishment. One island demolished by thoughtless development can break the flow and weaken the whole chain. Therefore preservation must be unified.

There are exaggerated problems of water supply and great difficulties with hydrological protection and restoration on barrier islands (page 44). They cannot be held in place easily with seawalls and groins because powerful oceanic and meteorological forces are at work to push them landward or to shift them along the beachfront. The great storms that sweep over them cannot be deflected.

Barrier islands have many unusual ecological quirks. One is that periodic natural fire is necessary for basic ecological purposes on the forested islands. It serves to resupply nutrients to the forest floor and to keep interior grassy marshes or meadows from becoming grown over. Today we extinguish these fires, and island forests are becoming choked with dense underbrush and highly inflammable leaf litter. When fire does start, the litter burns hot, killing trees that take years to replace. Neither the dense underbrush nor the uncontrolled fires are favorable for native wildlife, which ordinarily thrives on the grasses and insects associated with a fire-controlled ecosystem.[22]

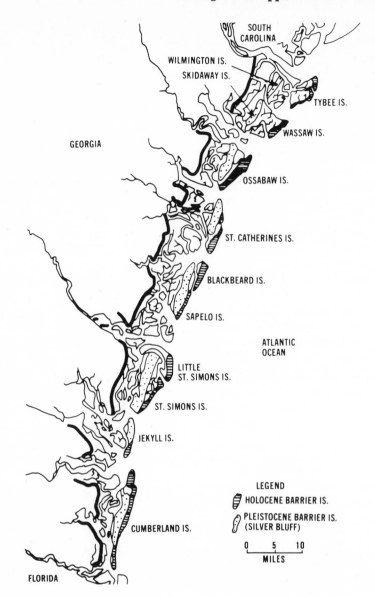

Figure 5.30 The coastal barrier islands of Georgia. (SOURCE: Reference 21.)

Needs for Protection

Barrier islands present a special area for environmental management because natural vulnerabilities are highly exaggerated on these exposed and fragile structures. The natural values are easily damaged. Human life and property are nowhere more severely threatened by storms than on these barrier strips; many occupied sand islands are *completely* inundated by seawater during the most intense hurricanes.

A generally poor understanding of the capacity of sand dunes to withstand alteration has frequently led to disastrous and expensive consequences on barrier islands. The ecosystem stability of the land and water areas behind the protective frontal line of dunes is dependent on (1) the capacity of the dunes to stop storm waves from cascading across the terrain, and (2) the ability of the dunes to hold the shore intact. Whereas the beach itself is tough, the dunes are fragile, and any alteration of them by construction, removal of sand, removal of vegetation, or traffic over them (even foot traffic) can lead to their demise.[23] Once the dunefront is degraded, the beach, as well as the backshore, is left without its main protective and restorative element (Figure 5.31).

With sand dunes or ridges bordering the ocean side and salt marshes or mangroves encompassing much of the estuarine side, barrier islands may be so narrow that these two types of vital habitat areas embrace most of their total area. The limited strip of buildable land in the middle may be further reduced by interior wetlands and sloughs (Figure 5.32). The preservation requirements are such that little, if any, suitable upland may be available for housing or other development on the narrower barrier islands.

Management

Because of the ecological fragility of the barrier islands, planning for their development must start with a thorough understanding of the natural systems, particularly water systems. A completely different approach to development controls must be evolved for barrier islands through exercise of local land-use authorities. Those islands are too ecologically sensitive and hazard-prone to be developed in accordance with the ordinary mainland rules.

Although narrow or unforested islands are not capable of sustaining urbanization, interior forest areas of the islands may be ecologically suitable for controlled human use because these areas are protected from wind and waves. Roads and buildings can be constructed if proper constraints are invoked,

Figure 5.31 Damaged dunefronts require extensive restoration; snow fencing is often used to trap sand and rebuild dunes (Avon, New Jersey). (Photo by author.)

Figure 5.32 The Sanibel River is central to the unusually well-developed interior freshwater system of Sanibel Island, Florida. (Photo by author.)

but only (1) if the island is not eroding and the building site is secure (Figure 5.33), (2) if the freshwater system is protected from saltwater intrusion (page 381) and pollution from runoff and sewage, and (3) if basic wildlife and other resources can be maintained (page 44).

Because of the numerous practical difficulties encountered, occupancy of barrier islands usually requires massive financial and administrative subsidy. Bridges, roads, sewers, beach protection, pest control, health and fire protection, and storm insurance are nearly always so costly that a disproportionate amount of public funds goes to support barrier island communities.

Case History: Rhode Island Study

An example of the type of management that is required for barrier beaches is the detailed set of recommendations for development control compiled for Rhode Island's barrier

beach environment[24] (by Olsen and Grant of the Coastal Resource Center of the University of Rhode Island). These are presented below in abridged form to provide an example without criticism or endorsement.

Building on Beaches

The beach is a hostile environment for the location of buildings. Normal tide fluctuations and periodic storm and hurricane flooding and wave damage threaten even the most substantial structures. The few buildings presently located on the beach proper appear to have found themselves stranded there as the dunes in which they had been built eroded back around them. Whether elevated on piles or stabilized by riprapping, they remain vulnerable to serious storm damage and are increasingly isolated from and unprotected by the dunes. Solutions are:

1. Prohibit further construction on the beach itself.
2. Remove existing violators to behind the dune.
3. Require public beach facilities built behind or on beaches without a dune to be elevated above 100-year flood levels and protected by a seawall.

Building on Dunefronts

The barrier beach and its sand dune are delicate natural features; the latter in particular is vulnerable to human damage. Damage is undesirable for more than aesthetic reasons. The beach dune acts as a buffer to the fury of storm seas. As the dune is attacked by storm waves, eroded material is carried out and deposited offshore, where it alters the underwater configuration of the beach. Accumulating sand decreases the off-shore beach slope (makes it more nearly horizontal), thereby presenting a broader bottom surface to storm wave action. This surface absorbs or dissipates through friction an increasingly large amount of destructive wave energy that would otherwise be focused on the shoreline behind the barrier.

The capacity of the dune for absorbing and moderating wave energy is not dependent on any ability to completely prevent breaching or flooding. Even in the process of being inundated and destroyed, as many are by hurricanes, the dune moderates back beach storm damage. This effect is less pronounced for low dunes, but nevertheless persists. Since storm resistance increases with dune height, however, all human uses of the barrier that devegetate, erode, or lower the dune expose the shoreline behind the barrier to increased storm damage.

Most of Rhode Island's barrier beaches

Figure 5.33 Sand passage across barrier islands is an essential process and should not be prevented; therefore such overwash areas of barrier beaches and islands as shown above cannot be subject to traditional development (Georgia). (Conservation Foundation photo.)

have a single line of low dunes runing parallel to the shoreline. In many areas these
dunes are so low as to be nearly undetectable; most others are of very modest height.
Management of the barrier dune is complicated by the frequent difficulty of defining
its extent. The back (pond side) slope of
many of the lower dunes is so gentle and
continuous as to prevent precise definition
of a base. It may, therefore, prove necessary
to arbitrarily establish this base from engineering survey data.

Rhode Island's barrier beaches are coming
under heavy developmental pressure. Increasing numbers of commercial, recreational, and, above all, residential structures
are being built, many on the dune. A developmental pattern common before the state's
low-lying beaches were swept clean by the
1938 and 1954 hurricanes is again establishing itself. Solutions are:

1. Discourage or prohibit all activities that
   weaken even the lowest of dunes.
2. Encourage all activities (private and public) that contribute to dune stabilization
   and natural regeneration.

Site Preparation

Construction typically requires that a level
building platform be prepared on the dune.
The dune crest is frequently lowered to provide such a platform and to improve the
view. Vegetative cover is often destroyed by
site preparation. Unstabilized sand is then
exposed to wind erosion, which in conjunction with lowering of the dune crest may
encourage the formation of blowouts. These,
in turn, increase the vulnerability of the
dune to storm damage and decrease its
value as a storm buffer. Solutions are:

1. Prohibit lowering of the dune crest to
   provide building sites.
2. Restrict construction to areas behind the
   dune line as defined by engineering surveys.

3. Prohibit all construction on the dune.
4. Where construction is permitted or already exists, require replanting of devege-
   tated areas.
5. Provide technical assistance and a convenient source of beach grass plantings
   to property owners.
6. Encourage   additional   stabilization
   through such methods as the installation
   of snow fencing.

Construction

Barrier buildings fall into two broad categories: those built on conventional solid
foundations and those elevated on stilts or
pilings. Windblown sand is accumulated by
porous barriers such as snow fencing and
beach grass. Solid objects, however, cause
minor accumulation on the upwind side and
erosive scour on the downwind side. Downwind erosion may, therefore, be expected
when solid foundation structures are built
on a dune. Solutions are:

1. Prohibit all construction on the dune.
2. If construction is permitted, discourage
   or prohibit solid foundations.
3. Require vegetative stabilization to trap
   moving sand.
4. Prohibit solid barriers or enclosures under
   elevated structures.

Life Support

There are great difficulties in providing human life support needs for barrier beach
areas, as compared to mainland areas.

Water Supply

Most structures will require a dependable
freshwater supply. This may be provided by
an on-site well or by a pipeline from an
external source. A pipeline, however, will be
vulnerable to shifting sands and storm
damage and may prove prohibitively expensive to maintain.

Barrier groundwater supplies are limited and respond to fluctuations in the level of the saltwater intrusion and consequent salt contamination of freshwater supplies. If groundwater levels are reduced below a critical point, stabilizing beach grass will sicken and die, exposing the dune to increased wind erosion and storm damage. Solutions are:

1. Provide piped water where possible. Towns should, however, be aware of the potential cost involved and may wish to charge barrier users for installation and maintenance.
2. Determine the minimum water table level necessary to sustain covering vegetation, and limit the withdrawal of water accordingly. This may require, in turn, a limiting of building density.

Sewage Disposal

There is no conclusive evidence that the disposal of domestic wastes through conventional septic systems now required by state and local health codes has any adverse effect on the dune itself. It might, indeed, be expected to provide additional nutrients to dune vegetation. When sufficient volumes of septic system effluent are introduced into the barrier marsh and pond, however, eutrophication may become a problem. Domestic wastes, if introduced in sufficient volumes, may in addition contaminate the limited ground water supply and thus pollute wells. Solutions are:

1. The construction of municipal sewer lines and treatment facilities is desirable. Lines may be vulnerable to storm damage, however.
2. Existing health department regulations should be rigidly enforced.
3. Additional treatment techniques such as aeration should be considered.
4. Residential density should be controlled when sewers are not provided.

Access Problems

A variety of unusual problems is encountered in providing access to barrier beaches —access by private persons to residences and businesses, and by the public to beach amenities.

Roadways

Safe, reliable, and convenient access routes must be provided to businesses, recreational facilities, and, most especially, homes located on Rhode Island's barrier beaches. Access is usually provided by a graveled or paved road open to conventional vehicles running the length of the barrier. When the access road is located behind the dune, it creates few natural problems. Even when unstabilized material is exposed, it is normally protected from wind and water erosion by the dune. When the dune is low, unstabilized, or blown out, however, the access road is vulnerable to drifting sand and storm washovers. Washovers may temporarily flood or completely wash out considerable lengths of road and thereby prevent escape during storm emergencies. Many of the deaths caused by the 1938 hurricane resulted from people being isolated in low-lying areas. Improved storm warning systems may prevent many such deaths, although residential use of areas subject to isolation and flooding remains undesirable.

The access road must be protected from storm damage if a safe emergency escape route is to be provided for barrier residents. Safe exit should be mandatory. Solutions are:

1. Elevating the road grade above hurricane flood levels.
2. Protecting exposed sections with riprapping or seawalls.
3. Preserving a vigorous natural dune.
4. Restricting or prohibiting outright the development of areas subject to isolation during extreme flood conditions.

5. Requiring mandatory evacuation of endangered areas during storm alerts.

Dune Traffic

Foot traffic across the dune is associated with the presence and use of homes, recreational facilities, or readily accessible open space. Vehicular traffic is common at public rights-of-way and along many stretches of undeveloped barrier, including conservation areas administered by the state and private groups.

Any access route across the dune line will become unstabilized and consequently vulnerable to erosion if it receives even occasional traffic. The natural vegetative cover of Rhode Island dunes is American beach grass. It is the primary stabilizing agent and is highly intolerant of foot and vehicular traffic. One or two passages by a vehicle or a dozen or so by foot over the same route in a

week's time will destroy most, if not all, of the grass along that route. Unless artificially stabilized, therefore, routes across the dune will be exposed to erosion. The public should be educated as to the value of the dunes and the need for any restrictions that are imposed. Solutions are:

1. Access across the dune should be restricted to stabilized paths or roadways. All other routes should be blocked off.
2. Foot traffic should be serviced by wood walkways, preferably elevated (Figure 5.34).
3. Vehicular traffic should be serviced by corduroy (wood) or paved roads.

Residential Development

This use in particular demonstrates a high probability of precluding other legitimate uses, and demand increases daily. The indi-

Figure 5.34 Elevated walkways are recommended to protect dunes. (Photo by author.)

vidual buyer requires only a small area, for which he is willing to pay a premium price. He seems willing to live in close proximity to his neighbors. He jealously protects his private rights. Solutions are:

1. Residential development should not prevent public access to the beach. Public rights-of-way should be provided at frequent intervals.
2. Residential density should be regulated with an awareness of the environmental capacity and the natural scenic beauty of an area.
3. Development of especially unique or valuable natural areas, wildlife habitats, or fragile natural environments should be prohibited.

Case History: Sanibel Island, Florida

Sanibel is a 12-mile barrier island in southwest Florida that spans the mouth of the Caloosahatchee River just offshore of its discharge to the Gulf of Mexico. Lying broadside to the path of seastorms and hurricanes, Sanibel is the major defense against battering storm waves and hurricanes in central Lee County. This stance also makes the Sanibel beach a depository of unparalleled diversity and abundance for tropic seashells that are cast up by passing storms.

For years the island was classified for development as though there were no special natural constraints. Sanibel was zoned for intensive development, with all that such zoning portends—condominiums, shopping centers, franchises, golf courses, and landing strips—a pattern for natural systems degradation that manifested a flagrant disregard of the quite apparent vulnerabilities of the delicately balanced island ecosystem (Figure 5.35).

On a few thousand acres of buildable land that the county zoned for construction of condominiums on frontal dunes and beach berms and for conversion of freshwater wetlands to golf estates, not only was nature's zoning violated profusely with such truly nonconforming uses, but also life and property were recklessly endangered through exposure to hurricane damage of nearly unimaginable proportions.

Finally, Sanibel voted to declare the island a free incorporated city to obtain the land-use controls needed to protect the priceless natural systems. On December 16, 1974, the new Sanibel City government took over and issued a moratorium on new development, and the island's 4000 residents began to replan its destiny. In March 1975 The Conservation Foundation was invited by island interests to assist in the environmental part of a major replanning.

We first proposed a series of separate natural systems surveys—hydrology, vegetation, soils, wildlife, energetics, beaches, coastal waters—and water quality studies. The second step was a diagnosis of the present condition of natural systems and natural resources. The third step was an integration of all information into a set of specifications for the city's planners—the planning firm of Wallace, McHarg, Roberts, and Todd.

Ecosystem Condition

Sanibel is but one of a hundred barrier islands thrown up by the sea along the coasts of our country. Yet this island is different. It is made up of rows and rows of parallel ridges of sand and shell, more than 100 altogether. The two largest ridge systems run from one end of the island to the other, one on the landward side, the other on the Gulf of Mexico. The center of the island is a large reservoir of fresh water received from the rains and stored within the soils of an unusual wetlands system. A fine ocean beach with a modest dune line edges the Gulf side, and a rich mangrove forest fringes the bay side.

We identified the four spatial elements that make up Sanibel's total ecosystem as follows: beachfront, interior wetlands, man-

Figure 5.35 Mangroves are a key element in the delicately balanced island ecosystem; they govern the carrying capacity of the coastal waters of Sanibel Island. (Conservation Foundation photo by M. Fahay.)

grove forests, and upland areas (Figure 5.36). Each of these physical subsystems is a unique entity with water as the major force tying the four together. Sanibel was created by ocean water currents. The ridges are a series of low sand dunes shaped by currents and changes in sea level.

Although these seperate subsystems are identifiable, the island functions as a single integrated ecosystem. The richness and beauty of Sanibel's natural systems are created out of the interaction of all the components reacting together in an extremely complex and delicate balance. Water is the integrating factor and the determiner of the ecosystem's vitality. The Sanibel ecosystem is a complex of components connected by interacting natural and human pathways of energy flow.

Twenty or more years ago, the low interior wetlands were open, grassy, and essentially treeless. Vegetation patterns were controlled by natural factors, including wind, altitude of the water table, salinity, and elevation of the land. Because Sanibel is an exposed barrier island with a freshwater table aquifer (periodically brackish), almost all plant species on the island are at least partially salt tolerant. The originl vegetative zonation of the interior wetlands was determined by a combination of natural water level and salt tolerance.

We soon realized that, if development had not yet come to Sanibel, the obstacles to habitation of the island might well be regarded as insurmountable because of high water tables, a high proportion of wetlands, extreme storm hazards, beach erosion poten-

Figure 5.36 Sanibel Island's major natural subsystems are the beach (upper), the interior wetlands (left center), the uplands (middle), and the mangrove wetlands (right). (Photo by author.)

tial, and absence of adequate water supplies. Because the natural amenity values are so high, however, Sanibel has experienced intensive development pressures and the sensible limits have already been exceeded in many parts of the island.

Over 1000 acres of the interior wetlands water storage area have been obliterated by development conversion since 1944. Moreover, the ecological health of the remaining 2400 acres has been drastically impaired by drainage for mosquite control and other excavations and by the introduction of exotic plants. The wetland system is also endangered by sewage, pesticides, and other water pollutants.

Also, accumulated loading of the manmade lakes in the borrow pits in the interior wetlands from sewage wastes, fertilizer–pesticide runoff, and sediments will lead to gross pollution over a period of years and to rancidity of the lake waters. Lake pollution is a delayed-reaction problem whose true dimensions will not surface until several years after the lakes are dug and their shores fully occupied.

The water of Sanibel was found to be salt polluted from four main sources of saltwater intrusion: (1) stormwater overwash and flooding, (2) saltwater intrusion through the semipermeable ridges that enclosed the interior basin, (3) upward leakage of saline water from the shallow artesian aquifer, and (4) overtopping of the water control structures by seawater and leakage around and through the structures.

Mangroves grow on the bay side of Sanibel Island and in the bayous at the west end. We found the mangrove communities, which play a critical ecological role, to be threatened primarily by physical alteration, although sediment and pollutants from projects in adjacent uplands can be detrimental. The greatest threat to mangrove function on Sanibel has been roadways and impoundments that restrict tidal flushing. A large tract of tidal mangroves was cut off from the sea by a boulevard and then killed during dewatering of an adjacent area in a dredge-and-fill project (Figure 5.37).

The condition of the beach and dune system reflects the high value of beachfront property. Development of the beach has centered on the dune system, the same sand

Figure 5.37 The type of large-scale clearing, excavating, and filling of the mangrove and interior wetlands for "golf estates" illustrated has degraded the natural system of Sanibel Island and the surrounding coastal ecosystems. (Photo by author.)

storage area that naturally stablizes the beach. Dunes have been flattened for landscape purposes and for foundations for large condominiums. In other areas the stabilizing vegetation has been destroyed by foot and vehicular traffic. With the dunes destroyed, the houses, hotels, and condominiums are totally exposed to damage by storm waves. The populations of wildlife species that depend on the beach environment have declined, some seriously.

The uplands have been greatly altered by the invasion of exotics. The new dominance of Australian pine and Brazilian pepper has altered historic wildlife patterns and lowered the productivity of the soils. Unaltered upland habitat was in very short supply.

Conclusions

We found that each type of residential development had the potential for a particular combination of environmental disturbances. The amount of damage to natural systems resulting from any disturbance depended on the characteristics and vulnerabilities of the specific subsystem involved. Three of the four subsystems that constitute most of Sanibel are far too vulnerable to withstand development, except for certain restricted examples. Therefore we advocated a strategy of protecting three natural zones—freshwater ponds–wetlands–streams (2400 acres), beaches–berms–dunes and mangrove forest (2800 acres)—and the plan was to redirect development to the higher sand ridges, the upland subsystem of the island. To accomplish this meant reversing some existing development privileges.

Protection of the three water-based subsystems included imposing controls on the fourth subsystem, the uplands, particularly controls on land modification activities associated with site preparation for development. The city was advised to impose specific constraints on project location, design, and drainage engineering throughout the uplands. These constraints encourage, and in some cases require, adjustment of traditional standards of residential development relative to density, project design, site preparation, drainage, and other performance factors.

A program of performance requirements was suggested (as a companion feature to the city's zoning program) which could be administered conveniently through the city's existing site plan review process. The development standards operate independently of traditional zoning maps and not only implement specific environmental objectives set out in regulations, but can also provide equity and predictability for developers in the approval process.

The following constraints were recommended as being necessary to carry out the plan for ecosystem resource conservation:

1. As a general rule, there should be no excavation in wetlands because the wet-land function would be disrupted—vegetation would be obliterated, water flow disrupted, soil layers destroyed, pollutable catchments formed, and drainage and drying out of wetlands facilitated. Accordingly, excavation should take place only for essential public purposes (e.g., mosquito control, wildlife enhancement) and should be limited to 10 percent of the area (Figure 5.38).

2. There should generally be no filling of wetlands. The soil cover would physically obliterate the wetlands and disrupt their function as completely as would excavation.

3. There should generally be no land clearing, grading, or removal of natural vegetation, since vegetation is a most important element of wetlands function. An exception should be made, however, to permit needed control and removal of noxious exotic plants. These should be removed mechanically or by controlled burning.

4. As a rule, discharge or release of pollutants into the wetlands should be pre-

Figure 5.38 All interior wetlands and water systems of Sanibel Island are scheduled for protection as vital areas by the land use management program enacted by the City of Sanibel on July 16, 1976. (Photo by author.)

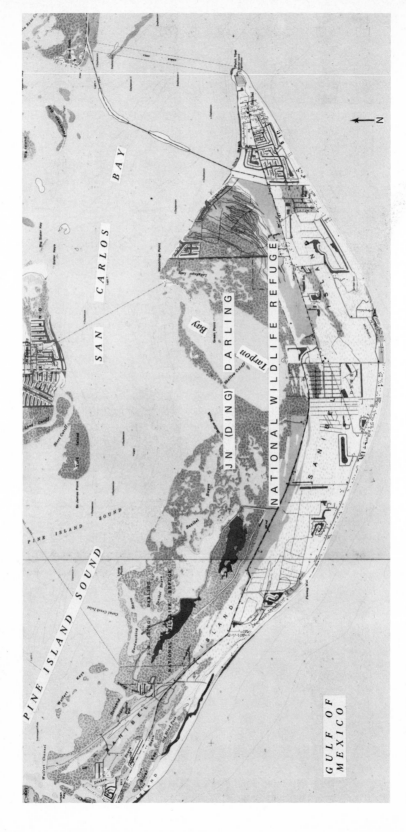

Figure 5.39 Sanibel Island in 1975. (SOURCE: The City of Sanibel Planning Commission; courtesy of Wallace, McHarg, Roberts, and Todd, planners).

vented. There may, however, be some
capacity for the wetlands to absorb certain storm runoff pollutants and thereby
to function as a "land treatment" system.
Any such pollutants should not exceed
the calculated receiving capacity of the
system and should not degrade surface
water or groundwater below allowable
standards.
5. There should generally be no solid-fill
roads or other structures in wetlands because they obstruct water flow. Also, fill
for any such structures must normally be
obtained by excavation, which is itself
damaging. Unavoidable roadways through
wetlands or over wetland swales should
be elevated on pilings rather than placed
on fill.

A set of formal performance standards
was prepared by the law firm of Ross,
Hardies, O'Keefe, Babcock, and Parsons to
be incorporated into the ordinances implementing the new land-use plan for Sanibel.

In addition to a conservation program,
we recommended a comprehensive program
for the restoration or repair of existing
damage to the natural systems. (Restoration is discussed in Chapter 4, page 201.)
The major elements of the recommended
program were water level restoration and
flood control in the interior wetlands basin,
drainage restoration in the mangroves, vegetation restoration in all four subsystems, and
beach profile restoration.

The series of maps from the resulting
Sanibel plan, prepared by the planning firm
of Wallace, McHarg, Roberts, and Todd,
in Figures 5.39 to 5.45 suggests the outlines
of the plan, as authorized by the Sanibel
Planning Commission (Duane White,
Chairman) and the City Council (Hon.
Porter Goss, Mayor).

After permitted uses were decided (Table
5.6) the planners were asked by the city to
allocate 2000 additional dwelling units,
equivalent to the maximum additional population the Planning Commission believed

Sanibel Island could accommodate in consideration of hurricane evacuation (over the
single bridge to the island) and the availability of services. The allocation was done
with respect for ecological sensitivity and
existing vested interests by the city (roads,
etc.) and private interests (parcel development commitments). Private lands were
then classified by zones of varying allowable
densities, from one dwelling unit per 40
acres (mangrove areas) to eight dwelling
units per acre (parts of beach ridge). (Separate performance standards were established
for each major type of ecological zone.)

REFERENCES

1. H. Crane Miller. 1975. *Management Techniques in the Coastal Zone.* Report to the
Nassau–Suffolk Regional Planning Board, Hauppage, New York.
2. Robert T. Segrest. 1975. *Building in the Coastal
Environment.* Resources Planning Section, Office
of Planning and Research, Georgia Department
of Natural Resources, Atlanta, Georgia.
3. The Council of State Governments. 1974. *A
Legislator's Guide to Land Management.* Lexington, Kentucky.
4. Steven Zwicky and John Clark. 1973. "Environmental protection motivation in coastal zone
land-use legislation." *Coastal Zone Management Journal,* Vol. 1, No. 1, (Fall, 1973), pp.
103–108.
5. Eric Strauss and Jon Kusler. 1975. *Statutory
Land Use Control Enabling Authority in the
Fifty States.* U.S. Department of Housing and
Urban Development, Federal Insurance Administration, Washington, D.C.
6. Natural Resources Defense Council. 1976. *A
Citizens' Guide to Coastal Zone Planning.*
7. R. R. Grant, Jr., and R. Patrick. 1970. "Tinicum Marsh as a water purifier." In *Two Studies
of Tinicum Marsh.* The Conservation Foundation, Washington, D.C.
8. J. Ross McKeever, Ed. 1963. *The Community
Builders Handbook.* Urban Land Institute,
Washington, D.C.
9. Rice Center for Community Design and Research. 1974. *Environmental Analysis for Development Planning, Chambers County, Texas.
Technical Report,* Vol. 1: *An Approach to Na-*

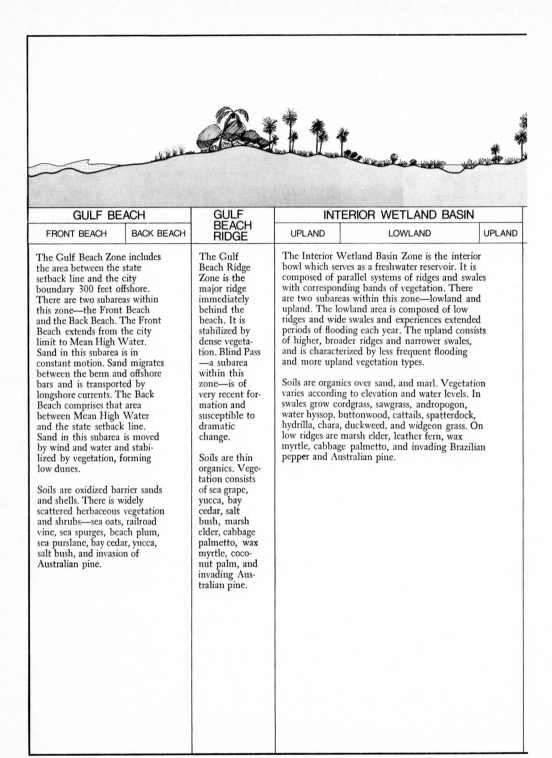

GULF BEACH		GULF BEACH RIDGE	INTERIOR WETLAND BASIN		
FRONT BEACH	BACK BEACH		UPLAND	LOWLAND	UPLAND

GULF BEACH	GULF BEACH RIDGE	INTERIOR WETLAND BASIN
The Gulf Beach Zone includes the area between the state setback line and the city boundary 300 feet offshore. There are two subareas within this zone—the Front Beach and the Back Beach. The Front Beach extends from the city limit to Mean High Water. Sand in this subarea is in constant motion. Sand migrates between the berm and offshore bars and is transported by longshore currents. The Back Beach comprises that area between Mean High Water and the state setback line. Sand in this subarea is moved by wind and water and stabilized by vegetation, forming low dunes. Soils are oxidized barrier sands and shells. There is widely scattered herbaceous vegetation and shrubs—sea oats, railroad vine, sea spurges, beach plum, sea purslane, bay cedar, yucca, salt bush, and invasion of Australian pine.	The Gulf Beach Ridge Zone is the major ridge immediately behind the beach. It is stabilized by dense vegetation. Blind Pass —a subarea within this zone—is of very recent formation and susceptible to dramatic change. Soils are thin organics. Vegetation consists of sea grape, yucca, bay cedar, salt bush, marsh elder, cabbage palmetto, wax myrtle, coconut palm, and invading Australian pine.	The Interior Wetland Basin Zone is the interior bowl which serves as a freshwater reservoir. It is composed of parallel systems of ridges and swales with corresponding bands of vegetation. There are two subareas within this zone—lowland and upland. The lowland area is composed of low ridges and wide swales and experiences extended periods of flooding each year. The upland consists of higher, broader ridges and narrower swales, and is characterized by less frequent flooding and more upland vegetation types. Soils are organics over sand, and marl. Vegetation varies according to elevation and water levels. In swales grow cordgrass, sawgrass, andropogon, water hyssop, buttonwood, cattails, spatterdock, hydrilla, chara, duckweed, and widgeon grass. On low ridges are marsh elder, leather fern, wax myrtle, cabbage palmetto, and invading Brazilian pepper and Australian pine.

Figure 5.40 Natural systems profile of Sanibel Island. (SOURCE: The City of Sanibel Planning Commission; courtesy of Wallace, McHarg, Roberts, and Todd, planners).

MID-ISLAND RIDGES	MANGROVES			BAY BEACH
	MANGROVES	TIDAL FLATS	MANGROVES	

The Mid-Island Ridges Zone comprises the major ridges along the central axis of the Island and includes the highest elevations. In most areas this zone divides the Bay-Mangrove watershed from the Interior Wetlands watershed.

Soils are thin organics. Vegetation is West Indian flora, cabbage palmetto, saw palmetto, seagrape, gumbo limbo, Jamaica dogwood, Florida privat, wild lime, strangler fig, wild coffee, myrsine, joewood, wax myrtle, sea oxeye, poison ivy, Virginia creeper, prickly pear cactus, bowstring hemp, and century plant. There is invasion of Australian pine, Brazilian pepper, and cajeput.

The Mangrove Zone includes all areas of red, black, and white mangroves, as well as the tidal flats and hardwood hammocks within them. Much of this zone, including all areas of red mangrove, is subject to daily tidal flooding. Other areas of the zone are subject to extended periods of flooding every year.

Soils are peat deposits and salt flats. Vegetation is mostly mangroves with hardwoods at higher elevations—red mangrove, black mangrove, white mangrove, buttonwood, seagrape, gumbo limbo, and palmetto. Vegetation responds to elevation and tidal patterns. Red mangroves predominate to the mean high tide line, and black mangroves predominate to slightly higher elevations above the mean high tide line.

The Bay Beach Zone extends from the city's boundary 300 feet into the bay to a setback line approximately 100 feet behind the Mean High Water Line. It is a lower energy beach than the Gulf Beach, and includes areas of marine grasses on the bay bottom. It includes both sand beach and mud beach.

Soils are muds, organic materials, and sands and shells. Vegetation on the sand beach is sea oats, railroad vine, sea spurges, beach plum, sea purslane, bay cedar, yucca, salt bush, and invading Australian pine. On the mud beach grow red mangroves, and on the submerged beach grow marine grasses.

279

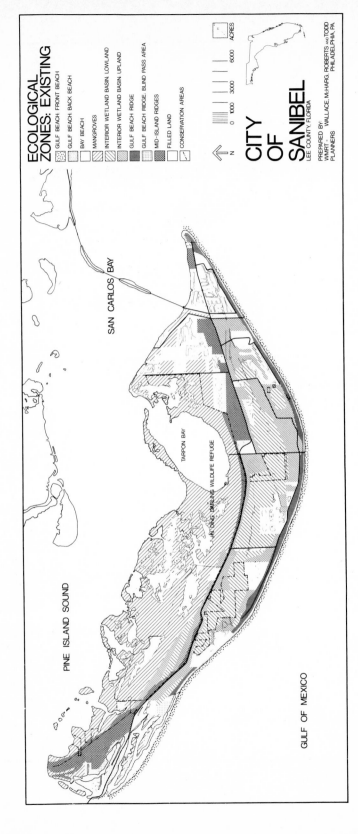

ECOLOGICAL
ZONES: EXISTING

- ▦ GULF BEACH FRONT BEACH
- ▨ GULF BEACH BACK BEACH
- ☐ BAY BEACH
- ▨ MANGROVES
- ▨ INTERIOR WETLAND BASIN LOWLAND
- ▨ INTERIOR WETLAND BASIN UPLAND
- ■ GULF BEACH RIDGE
- ▨ GULF BEACH RIDGE: BLIND PASS AREA
- ▦ MID-ISLAND RIDGES
- ☐ FILLED LAND
- ☐ CONSERVATION AREAS

☐ ACRES

0 1000 3000 6000

↑ N

CITY
OF
SANIBEL

LEE COUNTY, FLORIDA

PREPARED BY:
WMRT —   WALLACE, McHARG, ROBERTS AND TODD
PLANNERS   PHILADELPHIA, PA.

PINE ISLAND SOUND

SAN CARLOS BAY

TARPON BAY

"N DING DARLING WILDLIFE REFUGE

GULF OF MEXICO

Figure 5.41 Ecological zones of Sanibel Island. (SOURCE: The City of Sanibel Planning Commission; courtesy of Wallace, McHarg, Roberts, and Todd, planners).

280

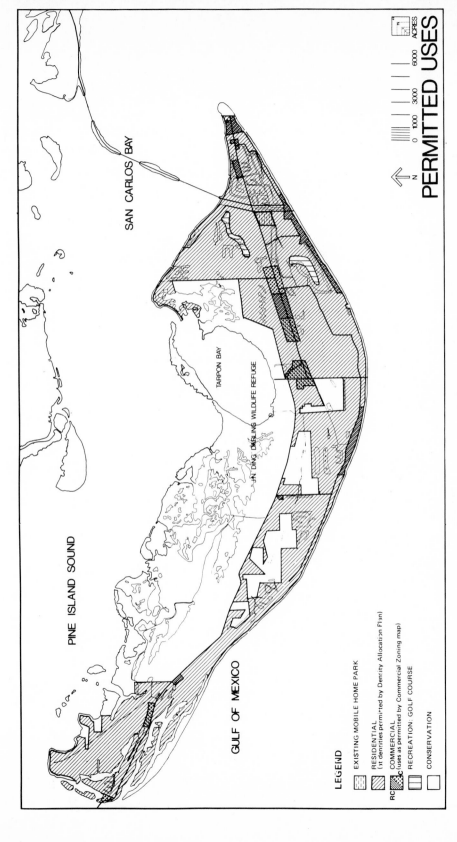

LEGEND

EXISTING MOBILE HOME PARK

RESIDENTIAL
(at densities permitted by Density Allocation Plan)

RC COMMERCIAL
(uses as permitted by Commercial Zoning map)

RECREATION: GOLF COURSE

CONSERVATION

PERMITTED USES

PINE ISLAND SOUND

GULF OF MEXICO

SAN CARLOS BAY

TARPON BAY

J.N DING DARLING WILDLIFE REFUGE

N

0 1000 3000 6000

ACRES

Figure 5.42 Permitted uses recommended for Sanibel Island by the new comprehensive plan. (SOURCE: The City of Sanibel Planning Commission; courtesy of Wallace, McHarg, Roberts, and Todd, planners).

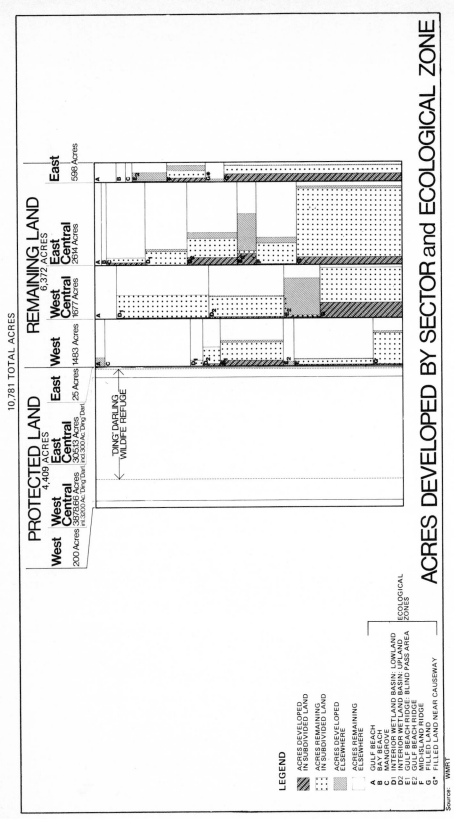

Figure 5.43 Land presently designated for protection for natural purposes (including the "Ding" Darling National Wildlife Refuge) and remaining land. (SOURCE: The City of Sanibel Planning Commission; courtesy of Wallace, McHarg, Roberts, and Todd, planners).

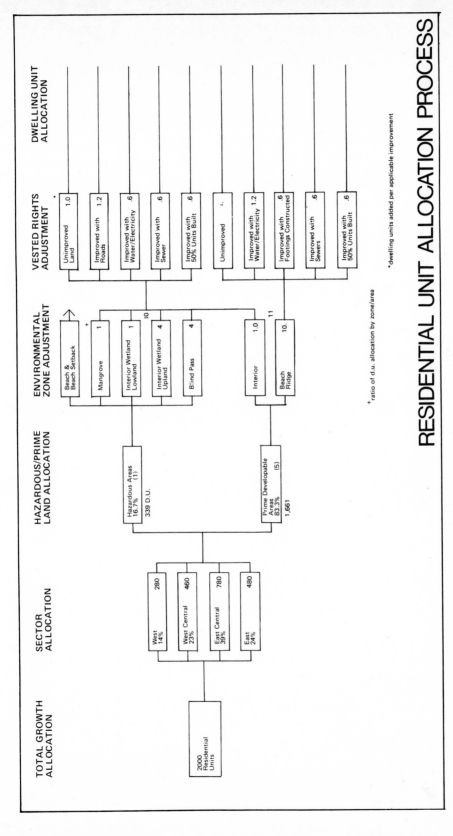

Figure 5.44 Scheme for allocating land uses in the city of Sanibel comprehensive plan; numbers in boxes are weighting valves. (SOURCE: The City of Sanibel Planning Commission; courtesy of Wallace, McHarg, Roberts, and Todd, planners).

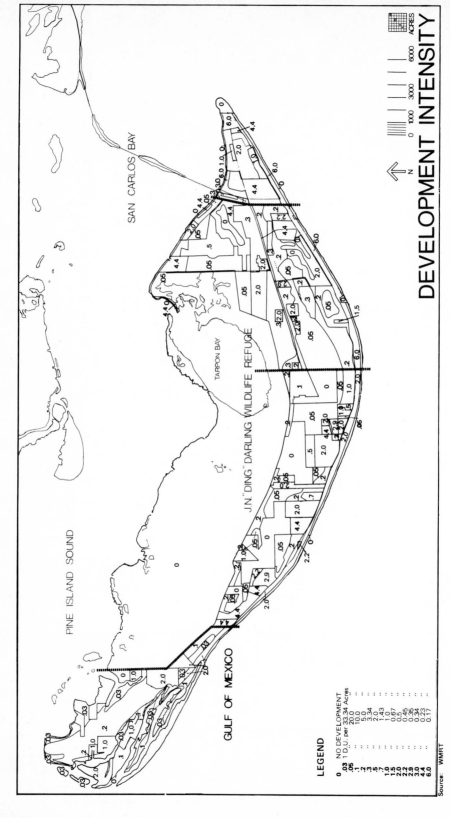

Figure 5.45 Dwelling unit density calculated for the city of Sanibel comprehensive plan. (SOURCE: The City of Sanibel Planning Commission; courtesy of Wallace, McHarg, Roberts, and Todd, planners).

Table 5.6 Permitted uses in the Sanibel comprehensive plan (* in designated areas only) (SOURCE: Sanibel Plan, The City of Sanibel Planning Commission, Sanibel, Florida)

ECOLOGICAL ZONES		PERMITTED USES
A	GULF BEACH	RECREATION & CONSERVATION ELEVATED WALKWAYS
B	BAY BEACH	RECREATION & CONSERVATION BOAT DOCKS AND MARINAS
C	MANGROVE SWAMP	RECREATION & CONSERVATION RESIDENTIAL
D1	WETLANDS: LOWLAND	RECREATION & CONSERVATION HORTICULTURE & AGRICULTURE RESIDENTIAL UTILITY FACILITIES
D2	WETLANDS: UPLAND	RECREATION & CONSERVATION HORTICULTURE & AGRICULTURE RESIDENTIAL EDUCATIONAL FACILITIES UTILITY FACILITIES COMMERCIAL DISTRICT
E1	GULF BEACH RIDGE: BLIND PASS AREA	RECREATION & CONSERVATION RESIDENTIAL PUBLIC FACILITIES RESTRICTED COMMERCIAL* COMMERCIAL DISTRICT*
E2	GULF BEACH RIDGE	RECREATION & CONSERVATION RESIDENTIAL HOTELS AND MOTELS RESTRICTED COMMERCIAL* RESTAURANTS MEETING HALLS PUBLIC FACILITIES ACCESSORY USES
F	MID ISLAND RIDGE	RECREATION & CONSERVATION RESIDENTIAL HOTELS AND MOTELS RESTRICTED COMMERCIAL* COMMERCIAL DISTRICT * RESTAURANTS MEETING HALLS PUBLIC FACILITIES ACCESSORY USES
G	FILLED LAND	RECREATION RESIDENTIAL HOTELS AND MOTELS COMMERCIAL DISTRICT *

tural Environmental Analysis. Rice University, Houston, Texas.

10. Samuel M. Hamill, Jr. 1974. *Environmental Profile and Guidelines.* Middletown Environmental Commission, The Township of Middletown, New Jersey.

11. U.S. Department of Housing and Urban Development. 1975. "Questions and answers: National Flood Insurance Program." In *HUD News,* March 10, 1975. Washington, D.C.

12. Texas Coastal and Marine Council. n.d. *Texas Coastal Legislation.* Austin, Texas.

13. Neno J. Spagna. 1975. "Can 'ST' save Collier's unspoiled lands?" In *Florida Environmental and Urban Issues,* Vol. II, No. 5. Joint Center for Environmental and Urban Problems, Florida Atlantic University, Boca Raton, and Florida International University, Miami, Florida.

14. J. K. McNulty, W. N. Lindall, Jr., and J. E. Sykes. 1972. *Cooperative Gulf of Mexico Estuarine Inventory and Study. Florida: Phase I, Area Description.* National Oceanic and Atmospheric Administration Technical Report, National Marine Fisheries Service Circular 368,

U.S. Department of Commerce, Washington, D.C.

15. U.S. Department of the Interior. *The National Estuarine Pollution Study.* U.S. Senate, 91st Congress, 2nd Session, Document 91–58. Superintendent of Documents, U.S. Government Printing Office, March 25, 1970.

16. G. Spinner. 1969. *Serial Atlas of the Marine Environment.* Folio 18: *The Wildlife, Wetlands, and Shellfish Areas of the Atlantic Coastal Zone.* American Geographic Society, New York.

17. Newspaper Enterprise Association. 1973. *The World Almanac.* New York.

18. Robert K. Davis and Robert M. Hirsch. 1973. *Economic Implicatoins of Land Development Alternatives.* Rookery Bay Land Use Studies, Study No. 11, The Conservation Foundation, Washington, D.C.

19. Fred Bosselman, David Callies, and John Banta. 1973. *The Taking Issue.* Superintendent of Documents, U.S. Government Printing Office, Washington, D.C.

20. *Just v. Marinette County,* 201 N.W. 2d 761, 770 (Wisc. 1972).

21. A. Sydney Johnson, Hilburn O. Hillestad, Sheryl F. Shanholtzer, and G. Frederick Shanholtzer. 1974. *An Ecological Survey of the*

Coastal Region of Georgia. National Park Service, Scientific Monograph Series No. 3, Superintendent of Documents, U.S. Government Printing Office, Washington, D.C.

22. D. Frankenberg, L. R. Pomeroy, L. Bahr, and J. Richardson. 1971. "Coastal ecology and recreational development." In C. D. Clement, Ed. *The Georgia Coast: Issues and Options for Recreation.* The Conservation Foundation, Washington, D.C.

23. Currituck County Planning Commission. 1972. *The Currituck Plan, Outer Banks Development Potential.* North Carolina.

24. Stephen B. Olsen and Malcolm J. Grant. 1973. *Rhode Island's Barrier Beaches:* Vol. I: *Report on Management Problems and an Evaluation of Options.* Marine Technical Report No. 4, Coastal Resources Center, University of Rhode Island, Kingston, Rhode Island.

25. A. E. Lugo. *Ecological Management of South Florida Range Ecosystems for Maximum Environmental Quality* (unpublished).

26. E. J. Heald and D. C. Tabb. 1973. *Applicability of the Interceptor Waterway Concept to the Rookery Bay Area.* Rookery Bay Land Use Studies, Study No. 6, The Conservation Foundation Washington, D.C.

CHAPTER SIX

Guidelines and Standards for Coastal Projects

In this chapter we recommend implementation standards for the management of specific coastal zone enterprises and projects. These are divided into 24 distinct types of projects that together represent the major development activities to be expected in the coastal zones of the United States. Each project type includes introductory material, followed by a series of implementation standards arranged under broad guidelines.

We have provided page citations for reference to other sections of the book where supporting or supplemental material may be found to develop the recommendations or provide a rationale for them. The reader is advised to refer to these other sections to gain a broad understanding of the ecologic basis for the recommendations, the appropriate planning response, or the complexities of implementation. Chapters 1 to 5 contain basic information on ecology, impacts, classification and survey, and government institutions, laws, policies, and programs. Chapter 7 and the Appendix provide a detailed technical basis for ecosystem conservation programs.

We wish to emphasize that our recommendations may challenge the machinery of local governments. None of the recommendations is beyond the possible, but many do test the will of the citizens of coastal communities to protect coastal resources and conserve coastal ecosystems. When such a commitment exists, however, the following information and recommendations should be of assistance in shaping a program for coastal ecosystem conservation.

Table 6.1 Demography and commitment of coastal county land to agriculture
(SOURCE: Reference 1)

Biophysical Regions and States	State Population Density (persons per sq. mile)	Population		Coastal Counties Population Density (persons per sq. mile)	Coastal County Land in Farms (%)
		Coastal Counties	Coastal* Urban Areas		
North Atlantic		3,258,798	3,541,000	292	17.6
Maine	31			61	21.6
New Hampshire	67			149	22.7
Massachusetts†	657			897	10.7
Middle Atlantic		22,387,123	20,852,000	1,165	28.1
Massachusetts†	657			719	16.2
Rhode Island	816			816	17.9
Connecticut	521			699	17.0
New York	351			5,009	4.5
New Jersey	806			962	17.1
Pennsylvania	251			2,091	26.4
Delaware	225			225	54.8
Maryland†	314			50	45.2
Virginia†	100			332	
North Carolina†	93			40	38.6
Chesapeake Bay		5,127,824	4,956,000	370	38.0
Maryland†	314			397	51.5
Virginia†	100			258	32.6
District of Columbia	12,442			12,442	
South Atlantic		2,202,669	1,659,000	89	31.5
North Carolina†	93			40	27.5
South Carolina	79			68	30.6
Georgia	68			92	15.9
Florida†	92			128	42.6
Caribbean		3,682,667	935,000		
Florida†	92			211	11.7
Puerto Rico	687			687	
Virgin Islands	133			133	52.2
Gulf of Mexico		5,833,149	3,109,000	121	49.1
Florida†	92			96	34.8
Alabama	64			129	
Mississippi	46			105	
Louisiana	72			119	
Texas	36			146	
Pacific Southwest		12,198,082	10,991,000	391	48.1
California†	100			391	48.1
Pacific Northwest		3,126,000	2,414,000	30	15.1
California†	100			27	20.0
Oregon	18			58	18.5
Washington	43			97	15.5
Alaska	0.4	168,721	85,531	0.5	<1.0
Pacific Islands		632,772	500,000		64.7
Hawaii	99			99	64.7
Guam	316			316	24.0
American Samoa	264			264	

*Based on standard metropolitan statistical areas (SMSA), except for Alaska, which are those communities with a population density of over 1,000 persons per square mile.
†States with area in more than 1 biophysical region.

1. AGRICULTURE

Much of the land in coastal counties of the United States is in agriculture (Table 6.1). Most of the crops grown there are not shoreland dependent and could be grown as well inland. A few crops, however, do benefit from or depend on direct proximity to the coastal area for suitable soil, humidity, temperature, rainfall, and other conditions, for example, salt hay and artichokes.

National policies directed at increasing food production in the coastal zone will have to reckon with potential conflicts between agriculture and coastal-water-based resources. Increasing agricultural production without improving environmental controls can heighten conflicts and lead to a reduction of the output from fisheries, shellfisheries, aquaculture, and other coastal resources. For example, during periods of short supply, high demand, and high prices for agricultural products, agency policies may encourage the use of coastal lowlands—low-lying, soggy land above the annual flood line—for cropland or livestock range. Often, draining such areas seriously stresses coastal ecosystems. Motivation for agricultural land drainage may be expected to continue, however, since about one-fourth of the inventory of United States cropland is excessively wet.[2] In addition to the environmental costs resulting from these attempts at reclamation, such ventures are financially risky and often lead to failure when the market shifts downward.

Major coastal ecosystem disturbances from shoreland agriculture in the United States include water pollution, alteration of the runoff water cycle, and loss of coastal wetlands. Sedimentation, nutrient enrichment, and inflow of toxic substances—the principal pollutants—are caused by soil fertilizers, animal wastes, and biocides carried into tidal waters with surface runoff and stream flow.[3] A relative ranking of total national sediment yields per year from seven source classes shows that cropland yields four times more

sediment to public waters than any other erosion source:[4]

Class	Rank
Cropland	200
Construction	50
Disturbed forests	40
Active surface mines	40
Abandoned mines	20
Grassland	10
Undisturbed forest	1

Cropland contributes about 45 to 50 percent of the total load of 4 billion tons of sediment generated per year in the United States. Construction contributes about 10 percent, and the other sources smaller percentages.

These eroded materials carry excess nutrients and toxic substances into water systems, causing water turbidity and the sedimentation of streams and bays. Many bays and harbors have been seriously degraded by sedimentation, and some require continuous dredging, at an annual cost to the nation of tens of millions of dollars.

Water pollution from agricultural activity is often diffuse (nonpoint) in nature and therefore difficult to identify and control, resulting in a near vacuum of federal and state regulatory policy. Modern farm practices that depend heavily on the use of fertilizers and biocides have greatly increased the potential for disturbance of coastal ecosystems. On the other hand, the accelerating cost of nitrogen fertilizers has decreased nitrogen use. Also, "hard" pesticides such as DDT have been essentially eliminated from agricultural use, and less damaging pesticides and new control techniques have been introduced. These trends in fertilizer and biocide practice should be encouraged because, in combination with improved soil conservation and pollution control techniques, they can significantly reduce adverse agricultural pollution effects on coastal waters.

Feedlots—often located along streams and

Figure 6.1   Uncontrolled feedlot waste runoff is a major source of water pollution (Gadsden County, Florida).
(Photo by John T. Barnes, U.S. Department of Agriculture, Soil Conservation Service.)

rivers that discharge into coastal waters—have for many years introduced animal wastes similar to untreated human sewage directly into surface waters (Figure 6.1). The Environmental Protection Agency (EPA) has identified these feedlots and other concentrated livestock operations as "point-sources" of water pollution.

Disruption of the natural runoff pattern—its quality, volume, and rate of flow—is caused by diking, drainage, irrigation works, and clearing of natural vegetation. Proximity to coastal waters and to tributary streams is a major factor controlling the severity of the impacts.

Reducing irrigation needs is often beneficial, because diversion of river water can alter the river flow rate or reduce water supply to coastal water basins, thereby upsetting salinity, nutrient, and circulation patterns (page 85). Irrigated U. S. land is expected to increase from about 40 million acres in 1970 to between 43 and 45 million in 1985. More efficient use of irrigation

water, however, could reduce gross water demands, thus lowering water requirements for projected irrigated acres in 1985 by 51.4 acre-feet annually.[2]

Agricultural use of land preserves the scenic and aesthetic values of open space in coastal areas. If, through proper management, significant environmental disturbances are eliminated, this is most desirable. Another advantage of encouraging coastal agriculture under proper control is the potential use of the higher parts of the floodplains for range and croplands rather than housing. The property damage and loss of life that could occur from flooding if such areas were urbanized are thus prevented.

The following guidelines on agriculture in the coastal zone are designed to suggest ways for making current agricultural practice as compatible as possible with the preservation of coastal ecosystems and with the perpetuation of coastal resources. They are based on two major premises: (1) fresh water should enter estuarine waters with a quality, volume, and rate of flow equivalent to those characteristic of the preexisting natural pattern, and (2) wetlands are vital habitat areas that require protection and should be exempted from cultivation, leveling, drainage, and impoundment and from roadways and structures (unless appropriately designed; see pages 98 and 498).

Coastal aquaculture is not discussed because it has shown little commercial promise so far as a result of negative food conversion efficiencies, general technical difficulties, confinement diseases, and local disinterest. It has been given a cool reception by coastal communities because of its potential for water pollution (from excrement)[5] and particularly for interference with the public use of estuarine waters (competition for bay area, shoreline sites, etc.).[6]

GUIDELINE.   Control of Agricultural Pollution

Control farm operations to protect coastal ecosystems from damage by fertilizers, biocides, sedimentation, and altered runoff.

Fertilizers, pesticides, herbicides, and other agricultural chemicals increase production efficiency and, in many ways, improve the quality of agricultural and forestry products. But these same chemicals, when used improperly, can pollute coastal waters. Conservation practices, including water management measures and soil erosion controls, are needed to alleviate pollution from contaminants carried into water bodies with sediment. Eutrophication (nutrient overfertilization from nitrates in runoff) and soil erosion have introduced vast layers of ooze (suspensible sediments) into the bottoms of many coastal water basins. Channelization and drainage of low-lying shoreland areas, particularly, cause the discharge of large quantities of fine silt into coastal waters.

The national campaign against pesticides has caused a marked shift away from the use of hard pesticides such as DDT. However, the dependence of agriculture on pesticides (including insecticides, fungicides, and herbicides) will continue and even increase in the future. Certain pesticides and other biocides have a well-documented potential to harm particular species of animals—fish, birds, and mammals—and to degrade ecosystems (Table 6.2). Although many states now require permits for the use of pesticides, control of pesticide practice is complicated by the bewildering number of chemicals in use; a 1970 study identified 78 frequently used pesticides in the California coastal zone.[6] All pesticides must be examined and registered by federal and some state agencies before they can be used. The basis for general control mechanisms may therefore already exist at the state and federal levels, but special local needs and problems may require additional constraints.

The simplest management practices are to prevent accidental or deliberate introduction of pesticides into surface waters and to restrict the use of chemicals known to be toxic to estuarine organisms. Controlling soil erosion and storm runoff will also help to prevent the introduction of polluting pesticides into the ecosystem.

Nitrogen is the key nutrient for algae production in brackish water. The system is therefore nitrogen sensitive; and when excessive amounts of nitrate from fertilizer runoff enter estuarine waters, eutrophication results. The resulting bloom of algae may occur well downstream after sufficient silt settles out to allow sunlight to penetrate deep enough to stimulate photosynthesis to an appreciable depth in the water column (page 20). There is a tendency on the part of many growers to overfertilize farmlands to be sure that a nutrient deficiency does not limit yields. The elimination of excessive application of nutrients is a primary measure recommended for the control of nutrient pollution.

Effective management of estuarine ecosystems requires regularizing the incoming freshwater supply, a dominant ecological

Table 6.2 Effects of common pollutants on bird life (SOURCE: National Commission on Water Quality, November 1975.)

PCB (poly-chlorinated biphenyl)	Decreased egg production Embryotoxic and/or mutagenic effects Altered parental behavior which reduces hatching success
Chlorinated hydro-carbons DDT, DDE, DDMU	Eggshell thinning Survival of young Altered adult behavior which reduces hatching success Affects salt gland, thyroid gland, adrenal gland
Chlorinated hydro-carbons Aldrin/Dieldrin	Survival of young Altered adult behavior which reduces hatching success
Chlorinated hydro-carbons Endrin, Chlordane, Heptachlor	Although not as well researched as the chlorinated hydrocarbons above, the effects are possibly similar
Chlorinated hydrocarbons Mirex	Survival of young may be affected with very high concentrations
Mercury	Affects the central nervous system Survival of young Decreased egg hatchability
Cadmium Lead	In high concentrations can result in death
Herbicides 2-4-D, 2-4-5-T	Indirect effect when habitat is destroyed Can have same effects of oil if sprayed in an oil solution
Oil	Direct effect through spills on both birds and habitat Affects hatching of eggs Prevents egg production Affects ability to survive in saline environments

element in the estuarine environment (page 23). To achieve this end, a number of water-related controls on agriculture are required for inland watersheds that discharge via rivers to distant coastal waters.

Drainage activities often significantly change the natural rhythm of flow, thereby altering the salinity of coastal waters and disrupting salinity-related functions of the species that are tuned to this rhythm. Because the estuarine ecosystem is so closely linked to salinity, the salinity pattern should be maintained as nearly as possible at natural levels by effective management of fresh water inflow. For example, because young shrimp in North Carolina need high salinity to flourish, large releases of fresh water from adjacent drained lands into their nursery areas, which lower the salt concentration, significantly increase mortality. Conversely, because young striped bass in the San Francisco Bay area need only moderately brackish water to survive well, low discharge of fresh water from the Sacramento River, because of upstream diversion for irrigation, leads to higher salinity downstream in the bay, reducing the survivability of young bass.

The following discussion deals with various measures that can be taken to prevent or control ecosystem disturbances. Practices that are primarily directed toward the control of erosion, the reduction of runoff, the management of fertilizers or animal wastes, and the management of pesticides are each dealt with under separate guideline and implementation sections. It should be recognized, however, that important interrelationships existing among the four groups of implementation practices may affect the choice of a particular method in a given situation. For example, the introduction of a minimum-tillage practice to control erosion may stimulate greater use of chemicals to control crop pests, so that the net benefit to the quality of the drainage streams may be less than expected.[9]

Implementation No. 1.   Soil Conservation in Agriculture

Conservation practices should be required to control cropland erosion and surface water runoff.

The key to the protection of coastal waters from runoff pollution by farmland is keeping the soil on the land. Good soil conservation practice also prevents the runoff loss of pesticides and phosphate fertilizers, which tend to adsorb to, and remain on, soil particles (page 595). Therefore soil conservation measures are of paramount importance in planning for land allocation, crop selection, tillage techniques, and water management. Advice and information on all aspects of soil conservation planning can be obtained from local Soil Conservation Districts or U.S. Soil Conservation Service regional agents (Appendix, page 879).

Table 6.3 provides a summary of soil erosion, sediment control, and water runoff practices necessary to protect farmlands and preserve the quality of aquatic ecosystems. In many situations erosion can be controlled with agronomical practices that make better use of crop residues or by improved crop systems, seeding methods, soil treatments, tillage methods, and timing of field operations. Generally, farming parallel to the field contours will reduce erosion. However, when slope length and steepness are great, or the area from which runoff concentrates is excessive, such control practices become ineffective and must then be supported by others, such as terrace systems, diversions, contour furrows, contour strip cropping (Figure 6.2), or water control.[9]

Direct surface runoff volumes can be reduced by measures that (1) increase infiltration rates; (2) increase surface retention or detention storage, allowing more time for water to infiltrate into the soil; or (3) increase the interception of rainfall by growing plants or residues. Infiltration rates, as well as detention storage, are raised by dense vegetation cover, increased mulch or litter, a high level of soil organic matter, good soil structure, and good subsurface drainage. Improvements in fertility levels and management practices that increase vegetative cover result in lower direct runoff. Surface storage can be substantially increased by contouring or contour furrowing, graded terracing, and level terracing.[9]

The advantages of no-till (Table 6.3, Practice No. 1) may be partially offset by problems that are inherent in minimum-

Table 6.3   Principal types of cropland erosion control practices and their highlights (SOURCE: Reference 8)

No.	Erosion Control Practice	Practice Highlights
E 1	No-till plant in prior-crop residues	Most effective in dormant grass or small grain; highly effective in crop residues; minimizes spring sediment surges and provides year-round control; reduces man, machine and fuel requirements; delays soil warming and drying; requires more pesticides and nitrogen; limits fertilizer- and pesticide placement options; some climatic and soil restrictions.
E 2	Conservation tillage	Includes a variety of no-plow systems that retain some of the residues on the surface; more widely adaptable but somewhat less effective than E 1; advantages and disadvantages generally same as E 1 but to lesser degree.
E 3	Sod-based rotations	Good meadows lose virtually no soil and reduce erosion from succeeding crops; total soil loss greatly reduced but losses unequally distributed over rotation cycle; aid in control of some diseases and pests; more fertilizer-placement options; less realized income from hay years; greater potential transport of water soluble P; some climatic restrictions.
E 4	Meadowless rotations	Aid in disease and pest control; may provide more continuous soil protection than one-crop systems; much less effective than E 3.
E 5	Winter cover crops	Reduce winter erosion where corn stover has been removed and after low-residue crops; provide good base for slot-planting next crop; usually no advantage over heavy cover of chopped stalks or straw; may reduce leaching of nitrate; water use by winter cover may reduce yield of cash crop.
E 6	Improved soil fertility	Can substantially reduce erosion hazards as well as increase crop yields.
E 7	Timing of field operations	Fall plowing facilitates more timely planting in wet springs, but it greatly increases winter and early spring erosion hazards; optimum timing of spring operations can reduce erosion and increase yields.
E 8	Plow-plant systems	Rough, cloddy surface increases infiltration and reduces erosion; much less effective than E 1 and E 2 when long rain periods occur; seedling stands may be poor when moisture conditions are less than optimum. Mulch effect is lost by plowing.
E 9	Contouring	Can reduce average soil loss by 50% on moderate slopes, but less on steep slopes; loses effectiveness if rows break over; must be supported by terraces on long slopes; soil, climatic, and topographic limitations; not compatible with use of large farming equipment on many topographies. Does not affect fertilizer and pesticide rates.
E 10	Graded rows	Similar to contouring but less susceptible to row breakovers.
E 11	Contour strip cropping	Rowcrop and hay in alternate 50- to 100-foot strips reduce soil loss to about 50% of that with the same rotation contoured only; fall seeded grain in lieu of meadow about half as effective; alternating corn and spring grain not effective; area must be suitable for across-slope farming and establishment of rotation meadows; favorable and unfavorable features similar to E 3 and E 9.
E 12	Terraces	Support contouring and agronomic practices by reducing effective slope length and runoff concentration; reduce erosion and conserve soil moisture; facilitate more intensive cropping; conventional gradient terraces often incompatible with use of large equipment, but new designs have alleviated this problem; substantial initial cost and some maintenance costs.
E 13	Grassed outlets	Facilitate drainage of graded rows and terrace channels with minimal erosion; involve establishment and maintenance costs and may interfere with use of large implements.
E 14	Ridge planting	Earlier warming and drying of row zone; reduces erosion by concentrating runoff flow in mulch-covered furrows; most effective when rows are across slope.
E 15	Contour listing	Minimizes row breakover; can reduce annual soil loss by 50%; loses effectiveness with post-emergence corn cultivation; disadvantages same as E 9.
E 16	Change in land use	Sometimes the only solution. Well managed permanent grass or woodland effective where other control practices are inadequate; lost acreage can be compensated for by more intensive use of less erodible land.
E 17	Other practices	Contour furrows, diversions, subsurface drainage, land forming, closer row spacing, etc.

294

Figure 6.2   Contour strip cropping reduces soil loss via runoff to coastal water basins. (Photo by U.S. Department of Agriculture, Soil Conservation Service.)

tillage systems. More herbicides and insecticides are usually required than with plow systems, and the plant residues left on the surface provide a source of nitrogen and phosphorous that can be leached out by surface waters. Thus an increase in runoff pollution by soluble chemical compounds may partially offset the reduction in sediment-transported compounds.[9]

Sod-based rotation (Practice No. 3) substantially reduces runoff over a long period.[9] It is preferred to continuous cropping because it can minimize the need for chemical fertilizers and pesticides, particularly if legumes (beans) or grasses are rotated with row crops.

Contouring (Practice No. 9) is a supporting practice that is widely recommended when drainage is not a problem. The crop rows follow the field contours across the slope, slowing runoff from the field and thereby reducing soil detachment and increasing infiltration. Contouring provides excellent control for moderate rainstorms. Contour farming reduces soil loss by 50 percent, and terracing (Practice No. 12) reduces it by 85 percent, as compared to straight-row farming,[10] especially on slopes of 2 to 8 percent.[9]

When there is a high potential for soil erosion and runoff of fertilizers and biocides directly into watercourses, close-growing crops instead of row crops that require extensive tillage should be used to protect water quality.[11] This is the strategy of strip cropping (Practice No. 11)—planting strips of close-growing crops or grasses between strips of tilled rows to serve as filter strips.

Grassed outlets (Practice No. 13) receive the drainage from contoured or graded rows or from terrace channels and remove it from the field, a highly effective erosion-control practice[7] (Figure 6.3) (See Appendix, page 847).

Figure 6.3   Farm layouts should include grassed outlets to receive field runoff (Denton, Texas). (Photo by James L. Coppedge, U.S. Department of Agriculture, Soil Conservation Service.)

Implementation No. 2.   Fertilizer Conservation in Agriculture

Fertilizer applications should be controlled to reduce their loss through runoff.

Because of the extensive use of nitrate fertilizers, attention should be given to controls on runoff from farmlands to estuarine coastal waters, since the nitrate form of nitrogen is quite soluble, is easily transported with surface water, and typically moves several hundred feet with the groundwater. Nitrogen controls are compatible with efficient farming practice because the farmer wishes to minimize loss of fertilizer for purposes of economy. Methods for holding fertilizer on the land parallel methods of erosion control; for example, 15 times as much nitrate may wash off fallow soil as sodded soil.

Nitrogen enters surface waters via storm water runoff or by leaching through the soil into the groundwater system. For example, in the delta waters of California, agricultural return flows are the primary source of nitrogen, contributing about 150,000 pounds daily.[12] Soil bacteria and plant root systems will remove significant quantities of nitrogen

if the groundwater can be filtered laterally through 150 to 300 feet (46 to 91 meters) of soil before entering water areas (page 503).

Many methods are available to avoid overuse of nitrogen fertilizer and to thereby reduce water pollution. Fertilizer should be applied only as actually needed. Recommendations based simply on standard "maintenance" or "balance" factors to replace the nutrients removed by the crop should be discouraged. Reliable soil tests are available for predicting fertilizer requirements in specific cases, particularly for phosphorus.[9] Recommended operational practices for reducing fertilizer loss and protecting coastal waters are summarized in Table 6.3.

It is well known that fertilizer nutrients, particularly nitrogen, are most efficiently used when the time of application coincides closely with the need of the plants (Table 6.4, Practice No. 2). Consequently, the ideal time to apply an "available nitrogen source" is at the period of greatest need by the plant. However, sources that require time for chemical conversion to an available form in the soil should be applied earlier. For example, nitrate—an "available source"—should be applied to corn about 3 to 4 weeks after emergence. This practice is generally known

Table 6.4   Principal types of nutrient control practices and their highlights (SOURCE: Reference 8)

No.	Nutrient Control Practice	Practice Highlights
N 1	Eliminating excessive fertilization	May cut nitrate leaching appreciably, reduces fertilizer costs; has no effect on yield.
	Leaching Control	
N 2	Timing nitrogen application	Reduces nitrate leaching; increases nitrogen use efficiency; ideal timing may be less convenient.
N 3	Using crop rotations	Substantially reduces nutrient inputs; not compatible with many farm enterprises; reduces erosion and pesticide use.
N 4	Using animal wastes for fertilizer	Economic gain for some farm enterprises; slow release of nutrients; spreading problems.
N 5	Plowing-under green legume crops	Reduces use of nitrogen fertilizer; not always feasible.
N 6	Using winter cover crops	Uses nitrate and reduces percolation; not applicable in some regions; reduces winter erosion.
N 7	Controlling fertilizer release or transformation	May decrease nitrate leaching; usually not economically feasible; needs additional research and development.
	Control of Nutrients in Runoff	
N 8	Incorporating surface applications	Decreases nutrients in runoff; no yield effects; not always possible; adds costs in some cases.
N 9	Controlling surface applications	Useful when incorporation is not feasible.
N 10	Using legumes in haylands and pastures	Replaces nitrogen fertilizer; limited applicability; difficult to manage.
	Control of Nutrient Loss by Erosion	
N 11	Timing fertilizer plow-down	Reduces erosion and nutrient loss; may be less convenient.

as "summer side-dressing"and is advantageous from an environmental point of view because it reduces nitrogen runoff.

The rotation of crops that require little fertilizer nitrogen (such as small grains or grasses) or those that require more (such as soybeans and other legumes) with crops requiring large amounts can reduce the amount of nitrogen available for leaching (Practice No. 3). Including a deep-rooted crop, such as alfalfa, in a rotation can also decrease nitrate leaching, because the plants can utilize nitrates from depths below the normal rooting zone. It is important to note that rotations often offer advantages for erosion and pesticide control, as well as for nutrient control.[9]

Animal wastes used as fertilizers (Practice No. 4) make nitrogen available over a longer period of time. Consequently, less nitrate is available at any one time for leaching. There are three major considerations in using animal wastes: (1) determining the amount of nitrogen in the waste actually being applied; (2) preventing loss of nitrogen before incorporation of the waste into the soil; and (3) determining the rate at which the nitrogen will become available for crop uptake. The rising cost of nitrogen fertilizer may increase farmers' interest in using manure.

Legumes (Practice No. 5) can supply substantial amounts of nitrogen to the soil. The quantity of nitrogen fixed will depend on the plant (amounts as high as 500 pounds per acre have been reported, but more commonly cited values range from about 80 pounds per acre for red clover to 200 pounds per acre for alfalfa). When legumes are used as the principal source of nitrogen for nonlegume crops, careful planning is required. If rotations are used, a 2- to 5-year cycle will help to supply nitrogen for subsequent crops and also allow economic benefit from the legume crop.[9]

The use of winter cover crops (Practice No. 6) such as small grains can reduce nitrate leaching in two ways. First, the cover crop extracts soil water during fall and spring so that less water is available for leaching. Second, the crop will utilize nitrate remaining from the preceding crops. Much of this nitrogen will become available to the succeeding crop after the cover crop is plowed under. Winter erosion is also decreased. In low-rainfall areas, however, the moisture used by the cover crop may decrease the yield of the cash crop.[9]

Implementation No. 3. Biocide Conservation in Agriculture

Biocide use should be managed so that runoff loss and direct application to water are minimized.

More than half a billion pounds of pesticides are used by agriculture in the United States each year. Pesticides are quite often applied at rates exceeding recommended levels. The more persistent organochlorine compounds and those containing heavy metals will remain on the vegetation and in the soil for extended periods of time. Runoff that moves fine-grained soils downstream takes the biocides with it. Loamy agricultural soil runoff is particularly capable of transferring these toxic substances to the coastal waters because they more readily adsorb to organic than to sandy soils.

A reduction in runoff of water and in soil losses due to erosion will reduce the loss of applied pesticides. Therefore practices that control runoff and erosion should always be considered in pesticide pollution control. In addition to these practices, a number of options exist that involve direct management of the pesticide itself. These can be used alone to provide the desired control, or can be employed in conjunction with runoff and erosion control measures.

A summary of improved pesticide use practices is given in Table 6.5. In relation to Practice No. 1, alternatives should be sought for the following pesticides, which are believed to be so toxic to marine organisms that their use in coastal watersheds should be discouraged (see Article 40, Chapter 7).

Organochlorines

Aldrin	DDT
BHC	Dieldrin
Chlordane	Endosulfan
Endrin	Methoxychlor
Heptachlor	TDE
Hexachlorobenzene	Perthane
Lindane	Toxaphene

Organophosphates

Coumophos
Dursban
Fenthion
Naled
Parathion
Ronnel

Pesticides that have low toxicity, are not persistent, and do not build up through food chains should be given preference. In an area of appreciable surface runoff but with little erosion hazard, pesticides that adsorb to soil should be favored over those that are readily dissolved in and move with the runoff water.

Crop rotation (Practice No. 3) is beneficial for pesticide conservation. In tests a potato–oats–sod rotation reduced runoff losses of organochlorine insecticides by as much as 40 percent, in comparison with losses from continuous potato production. In

Table 6.5   Practices for the control of pesticide loss from agricultural applications (SOURCE: Reference 8)

No.	Pesticide Control Practice	Practice Highlights
	Broadly Applicable Practices	
P 1	Using alternative pesticides	Applicable to all field crops; can lower aquatic residue levels; can hinder development of target species resistance.
P 2	Optimizing pesticide placement with respect to loss	Applicable where effectiveness is maintained; may involve moderate cost.
P 3	Using crop rotation	Universally applicable; can reduce pesticide loss significantly; some indirect cost if less profitable crop is planted.
P 4	Using resistant crop varieties	Applicable to a number of crops; can sometimes eliminate need for insecticide and fungicide use; only slight usefulness for weed control.
P 5	Optimizing crop planting time	Applicable to many crops; can reduce need for pesticides; moderate cost possibly involved.
P 6	Optimizing pesticide formulation	Some commercially available alternatives; can reduce necessary rates of pesticide application.
P 7	Using mechanical control methods	Applicable to weed control; will reduce need for chemicals substantially; not economically favorable.
P 8	Reducing excessive treatment	Applicable to insect control; refined predictive techniques required.
P 9	Optimizing time of day for pesticide application	Universally applicable; can reduce necessary rates of pesticide application.
	Practices Having Limited Applicability	
P 10	Optimizing date of pesticide application	Applicable only when pest control is not adversely affected; little or no cost involved.
P 11	Using integrated control programs	Effective pest control with reduction in amount of pesticide used; program development difficult.
P 12	Using biological control methods	Very successful in a few cases; can reduce insecticide and herbicide use appreciably.
P 13	Using lower pesticide application rates	Can be used only where authorized; some monetary savings.
P 14	Managing aerial applications	Can reduce contamination of non-target areas.
P 15	Planting between rows in minimum tillage	Applicable only to row crops in non-plow based tillage; may reduce amounts of pesticides necessary.

insect control, rotations suppress the build-up of resistance to insecticides and "break" the life cycles of certain insects that require specific host plants to survive.[9]

For certain insects the precise time of planting (Practice No. 5) influences the magnitude of crop infestation and thus the need for insecticide applications. For example, in northern states early-planted corn is less subject to attack by the corn earworm than later corn, but in southern states late planting deters the corn earworm and also white grubs and seed maggots.[9]

Eliminating excessive pesticide use (Practice No. 8) has many beneficial results. Most of the 300 million pounds of insecticides used annually in agriculture are applied on a routine schedule in anticipation of problems. If, instead, these insecticides were applied on a "treat when necessary" basis, it is esti-

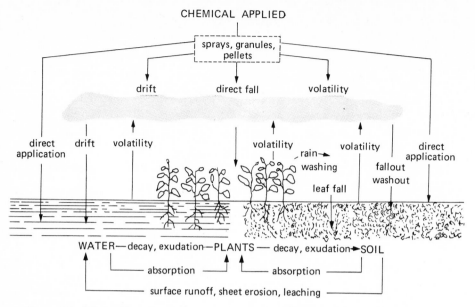

Figure 6.4   The cycling of toxic chemicals in the environment. (SOURCE: Reference 4.)

mated that treatments could be reduced by 35 percent.[13]

In normal practice, pesticides are often applied heavily in early spring, which coincides with the time when high rainfall and accompanying high runoff and sediment transport often occur (Practice No. 10). Since it is well known that losses of pesticide in runoff are relatively large only when rainfall occurs shortly after application, any

Figure 6.5   Pesticides carelessly sprayed directly over water are a great potential danger to water life. (Photo by Mark Twombly, *The Island Reporter*, Sanibel, Florida.)

Table 6.6   Drift pattern in relation to particle size (drift is the distance that a particle will be carried by a 3-mph wind while falling 10 feet) (SOURCE: Adapted from Reference 14)

Particle Type	Drop Diameter	Drift	
	Microns	Meters	Feet
Aircraft spray:			
Coarse	400	3	10
Medium	150	7	20
Fine	100	15	50
Air carrier sprays	50	50	180
Fine sprays and dusts	20	340	1,100
Usual dusts and aerosols	10	1,400	4,400
Aerosols	2	34,000	111,000

action taken to move the pesticide treatment away from peak runoff periods, while maintaining effectiveness, is advantageous.[9]

For pesticide control in runoff, an integrated program (Practice No. 11) that does not include chemical treatment would obviously be optimum, but this is rare. Some outstanding successes have been achieved with integrated programs, however. Programs now being studied give promise of overcoming very important pests, such as the cotton boll weevil and the bollworm.[9]

Biological methods (Practice No. 12) hold some promise for control of damaging insects and weeds. Although dramatic and advantageous results have been attained in a number of cases, biological control has not yet been used widely on crop pests. Methods include the use of sex attractants, insect growth regulators, sterilized male insects, insect pathogens (disease-causing agents), antifeeding compounds, and parasitic or predatory insects.[9]

In relation to aerial spraying (Practice No. 14), the application of pesticides or fertilizers to surface water areas, whether by wind drift or accidental direct spraying, should be avoided (Figure 6.4).

Aerial spraying or dusting of crops is frequently inefficient, with as little as 50 percent hitting the target. Depending on particle size, wind speed, and height of the airplane, pesticides are subject to considerable drift (Figure 6.5). Dusted and sprayed pesticides of small particle size can drift long distances, as shown in Table 6.6. Various emulsifiers and oils can be added to the spray to increase droplet size; however, drifting toxic pesticides can still be easily introduced directly into surface waters. Therefore aerial application of fertilizers and pesticides should be strictly controlled, or even prohibited, in areas adjacent to watercourses and estuarine water basins, where the risk of drift into surface water or accidental direct application is high. Prominent geographical features such as roads that are clearly visible from the air can be used as functional boundaries between safe zones and no-spraying zones adjacent to the water. Other farm practices, such as the washing of farm implements and spray equipment, also introduce pesticides and other toxic materials into surface waters.

It is necessary to control certain other chemicals used as biocides, such as zinc and copper, as well. For example, some coastal farmers apply copper as a biocide to soybeans and corn fields at rates of about 2.5 pounds per acre per year. This is sufficient to cause concentrations of 0.2 to 0.5 ppm in the runoff and make it toxic enough to cause serious ecological damage (page 740).

GUIDELINE.   Farm Layout Requirements

Include water quality and vital area protection in planning farm layouts.

The initial planning of farm layouts too often gives water quality considerations a low priority. This attitude has fostered a long history of sedimentation and pollution of watercourses and estuarine water bodies. Many United States estuarine basins have been heavily polluted, and a few nearly filled by sediment, from poor erosion control practices. Ecological damage has been so evident in past years that Louisiana, New York, North Carolina, and other states[15] have specifically identified agricultural runoff as a major "nonpoint" (diffuse) source of water pollution.

An effective means of retarding the impact of farm pollutants is to set all farms and feedlots back from the water edge by a buffer strip of natural vegetation. The strip should be wide enough that the natural filtration ability of soil and vegetation can cleanse the runoff water of significant con-

tamination. Coastal area planning should incorporate the buffer strip feature as part of the environmental control plan for agriculture. Moreover, the buffer strip has benefits other than runoff purification, for example, the stabilization of erodible banks by natural vegetation (Figure 6.6).

To the maximum extent possible, farmlands should be located out of the floodplain and away from tidal creeks, wetlands, and tidelands. Uncontrolled use of wetlands for agriculture has led to coastal ecosystem damage. Marshlands have been drained, impounded, and channelized, with adverse impacts on fisheries and recreational values (page 32). Agriculture is responsible for the obliteration of a high percentage of the coastal wetlands in the United States; for example, 53 percent of the wetlands in Maryland have been drained for agricultural operations.[14]

Attempts to reclaim lowlands ("excessively wet" land above the wetlands) for agriculture have led to the subsidence of large areas—more than a 13-foot drop in California and an 8-foot drop in Louisiana[17]—with concomitant financial disaster to the entrepreneurs. Experience, both in this country and abroad, shows that some types

Figure 6.6   Buffer strips of natural vegetation along the shoreline reduce water pollution from croplands. (Photo by author.)

of organic materials underlying coastal lowlands, when the latter are drained and used
for hay or grain crops, undergo decomposition and long-continued shrinkage. Gravity-
flow ditches become less and less effective
for drainage, necessitating the increased use
of pumps and dikes.[18]

In upland farms drainage should be arranged so that cropland runoff slowly filters
through a buffer area of natural vegetation
sufficient to remove contaminants and to
prevent runoff surges to the receiving public
waterways (page 239).

The major requirement is that neither
the water table nor the natural systems of
water drainage (including the alignment of
watercourses) be altered so that the timing
and the volume of flows are significantly
changed. The project design goal is to simulate the existing drainage so that the runoff
reenters public waters in its preexisting pattern of volume, quality, and rate of flow.

In any agricultural community one finds
numerous farms that are poorly planned in
relation to water protection. Correction of
the effects of any such "nonconforming
uses" may be required by state and federal
environmental regulations, perhaps subject
to local policy. When immediate correction
of such use would impose a severe burden
on the owner and it is therefore allowed to
continue, it should be identified as nonconforming and subject to correction when
the opportunity arises. Thus changes to
bring the use into conformance will be required if the farm is to be combined with
another, if its layout is to be revamped, if a
principal facility is to be rebuilt, or if flood
or storm damage requires major rehabilitation.

Implementation No. 1. Vital Area Protection in Agriculture

**All vital habitat areas should be identified
and exempted from agricultural use.**

The environmental management program of
the community should require that all vital
habitat areas, including wetlands, be identified and exempted from development (page
247). The wetlands exemption should include all fresh- and saltwater marshes, bogs,
swamps, natural swales, mangrove and cypress stands, and similar areas in coastal
watersheds (page 139). Wetlands should
not be converted to farmland or rangeland
by drainage or filling.

Wetlands also serve valuable functions in
the protection of water quality and water
resources when they are only irregularly
or seasonally flooded; examples are high salt-
marsh areas vegetated with salt-tolerant
plants that lie between the annual flood
mark and mean high water, and freshwater
shoreline areas up to the annual flood mark
that are vegetated with aquatic plants.

Although thousands of acres of wetlands
have been drained in the past to create
farmable land, with the encouragement of
the U.S. Soil Conservation Service and many
other agencies, state and federal laws and
policies are now increasingly limiting drainage and other physical alteration of wetlands.

The existing use of tidelands and wetlands
for agriculture is less common on the seacoast than inland, but there are some examples. In Louisiana and Texas levees are
often constructed as walkways for grazing
cattle to enter the marsh. In southern New
Jersey 10,000 acres of tidelands and wetlands
have been diked by salt-hay farmers. In
South Carolina dikes have been used to convert fresh tidal marshes to rice fields—once
for human use, now to attract waterfowl
for hunters. The purpose of dikes is to
stabilize the water flow; in New Jersey the
intent is to hold water out, and in South
Carolina to hold water in. In either case the
dikes obstruct the continuity from marsh to
estuary, blocking the passage of fish to the
marsh, and the flow of nutrients to the
estuary. Moreover, this diked land may no
longer function as useful waterfowl habitat.
As a result of diking, the 10,000 New Jersey
acres, 20,000 clapper rails lost breeding areas

Figure 6.7 Narrow buffer strips may be inadequate to prevent loss of soil to coastal waters from fields left bare in winter. (Photo by author.)

and 10,000 black ducks were denied wintering areas there.[17]

Implementation No. 2. Agricultural Land Setbacks

Croplands and rangelands should be set back from the water to provide a buffer area.

Setbacks should be required along all watercourses and coastal shorelines to separate tilled land from water bodies by a vegetated buffer area, or strip, of specified width (Figure 6.7). A major purpose of the buffer area is to remove contaminants and to retain and delay runoff water flow. Such buffers can consist of natural vegetation or of close-growing crops (grasses) that have matted root systems and require no fertilizers or pesticides.

The required buffer width varies with soil characteristics, slope, climate, time of har-

vest, amount of cultivated area, and type of vegetation in the filter strip. Also, buffer width depends on variations in the upland farm operation—type of crop, amount and type of fertilizer and biocide, tillage techniques, and so forth (page 378). For example, standard buffer widths recommended for Maine's coastal zone vary between 50 and 110 feet, depending on slope (Table 6.7). Although these may be sufficiently wide to

Table 6.7 Suggested buffer strip widths for the coastline of Maine (SOURCE: Reference 20)

Average Slope of Land Between Tilled Land and Normal High Water Mark (%)	Width of Strip Between Tilled Land and Normal High Water Mark [ft (m) along surface of ground]
0–4	50 (15)
5–9	70 (21)
10–14	90 (27)
15 and over	110 (34)

Table 6.8 Minimum filter strips for cropland water quality restoration recommended to the U.S. Agricultural Research Service (SOURCE: Reference 21)

Slope (%)	Slight Erosion [ft (m)]	Moderate Erosion [ft (m)]	Severe Erosion [ft (m)]
0	30 (9)	35 (11)	45 (12)
10	55 (17)	65 (20)	80 (24)
20	80 (24)	95 (29)	115 (35)
30	105 (32)	125 (38)	150 (46)

trap sediment, they should be increased to prevent nitrate pollution.

Guidelines developed for the U.S. Agricultural Research Service (Table 6.8) also suffer the drawback that they are primarily for sediment control. Therefore additional width would be required to provide for removal of nitrate and other agricultural chemicals.

The minimum fully safe setback for nitrate removal that will cover most soil, slope, and vegetative conditions is 300 feet (91.5 meters) (page 503). This width should be required unless thare is specific evidence that under the particular conditions at hand a lesser width will suffice to remove the nitrate (to the level officially required for tertiary sewage effluent). However, a plan to use any width less than 150 feet (45.7 meters) should be most rigorously supported with facts by the applicant (page 504).

Implementation No. 3. Lowlands Agriculture Controls

Farming in coastal lowlands should be restricted to operations not requiring drainage or heavy use of chemicals.

Restriction of certain farming operations is necessary in coastal lowlands to protect water quality and water resources. The extensive tillage, fertilization, and biocide application that typify modern agriculture are inappropriate in lower floodplains (10-year flood). When such areas are flooded, contaminants are washed into coastal waters or their tributaries, causing severe pollution. However, it should be possible to farm the lower floodplain successfully—where feasible on *undrained* lands—by thoughtful selection of crops and techniques. Many crops do not require extensive use of pesticides and fertilizers and do not create serious erosion problems. Grazing may also be acceptable in most areas, on either natural or improved pastureland (with "close-growing" crops).

Drainage of shoreland for conversion to crop or rangeland, however, should be avoided.

The drainage necessary to lower seasonally high water tables in lowlands causes damage to water quality and water resources that technology can rarely rectify economically. Channels excavated for drainage cause storm runoff waters to surge into coastal water basins and tributaries, disturbing the balance of coastal ecosystems (page 634). Further damage is done by the silt, pesticides, and fertilizers that channels convey directly into coastal waters and tributary streams. Most attempts to retain and to treat large volumes of such drainage water are unsuccessful. Much of the excessively wet land lies directly in coastal areas, particularly along the Middle Atlantic, Florida, and western Gulf of Mexico coasts (Figure 6.8). These are all areas that have extremely valuable fisheries and other coastal resources that need protection from disturbances caused by uncontrolled drainage.

Examples of practical and economic problems with drained lowlands (based on Louisiana experience) include:[22]

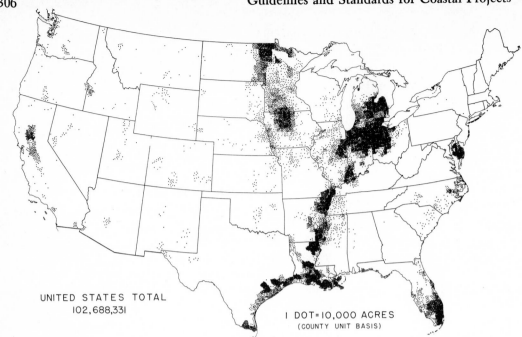

UNITED STATES TOTAL
102,688,331

I DOT=10,000 ACRES
(COUNTY UNIT BASIS)

Figure 6.8   United States agricultural land in drainage enterprises (one dot equals 10,000 acres or 4050 hectares). (SOURCE: Reference 16.)

1. *Acidity.* When thick organic soils are drained and oxidized to mineral soils, they are acidic with pH values of 3.7— toxic to some locally grown crops.
2. *Wetness and low permeability.* Excess moisture and lack of air in the root zone are problems in these soils. The very low permeability of the mineral soil, nearly level slopes, and high rainfall make wetness a limitation even under intensive drainage.
3. *Workability.* Poor soil structure is one of the serious problems affecting crop production in the marsh area. All marsh soils are very difficult and expensive to cultivate. Several years are required, especially on the peats, to obtain sufficient compaction to support normal types of equipment.
4. *Available plant foods.* Lack of balance in available nutrients causes poor quality in certain crops, for example, lodging of crops like rice and low sucrose content in sugarcane—conditions difficult to correct with fertilizers.

5. *Subsidence.* After drainage and initial air drying, peat shrinks to about two-thirds of its original volume. Cultivation and grazing compact the peat, causing further loss in volume. After the initial shrinkage, peat oxidizes and subsides approximately 1 inch per year regardless of use. In addition to man-made subsidence, geological subsidence is proceeding at various rates across the marsh area. These losses in elevation further complicate measures designed and installed to correct overflow and wetness. Subsidence from oxidization of organic matter can be slowed by controlling the water table to the highest feasible level while the soil is in use and by keeping the soil wet when not in use for crops or pasture.

A case in point is drainage to create agricultural lands and subsequent farming operations in the Pamlico Sound watershed, which threatens to significantly upset the natural drainage system and harm coastal resources. Channelization of 45,000 acres, by canals at 1-mile intervals with ditches in between, for the Open Grounds Farms has been shown by extensive research studies to pose a threat to the timing and flow rate of water that drains from the shorelands into the sound. Also, the introduction of colloidal silt from the sedimentary soils involved, which cannot be removed by settling ponds, has the potential to reduce water quality.[27] The overall effects would be to greatly reduce the production of young shrimp by the South River nursery grounds, to interfere with oyster beds, and to degrade the local fish nurseries.

The proposed First Colony Farms, located within the same estuarine system, threaten to intensify the problems. First Colony's

operations require an artificial drainage system capable of removing from its land area at least 1 inch of water each day to make the land suitable for corn and soybean production.[27] The combined effects of these drainage alterations are significantly hazardous to the coastal ecosystem (Figure 6.9).

Implementation No. 4. Upland Agricultural Control

Upland farm layout should be planned to minimize alteration of the natural drainage pattern and to prevent water pollution.

In upland and higher floodplain areas the farmer who uses good soil conservation prac-

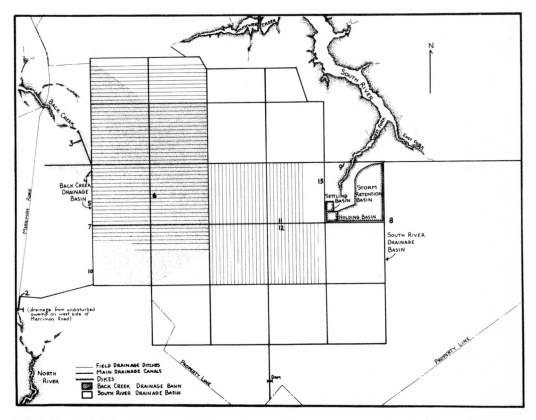

Figure 6.9 Under the conditions present at the proposed Open Grounds Farms site in North Carolina, detention basins are inadequate to correct erosion pollution because the runoff soil is virtually colloidal and remains suspended and would be carried into the South River. (SOURCE: Richard Barber, Duke Marine Laboratory, Beaufort, North Carolina.)

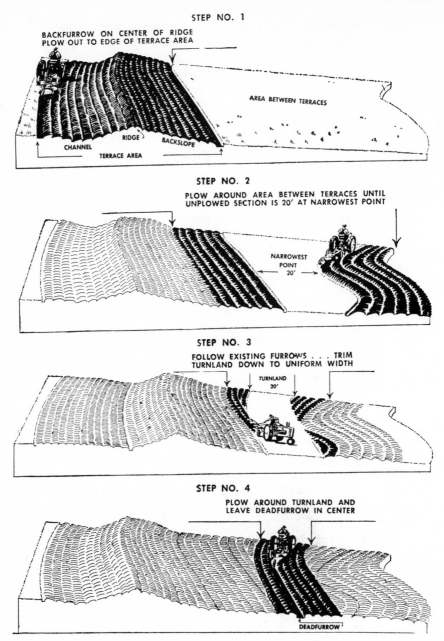

Figure 6.10   Methods for plowing terraced land. (SOURCE: Reference 21.)

tices should have little trouble in meeting most water pollution control requirements. Nevertheless, to be fully effective, the pollution control program must involve farm layout guidelines as well as operational control practices. Such methods as terracing (Figure 6.10) and contouring, which are of proved effectiveness, should be considered in planning the farm layout. Also, sediment control structures, including retention basins, impoundments, and sediment traps, should be laid out in the initial planning of the farm. The basic rule in layout is to plan land drainage so that runoff water is restored to its preexisting quality, volume, and rate of flow before release to public waters.

To summarize, after a setback has been established, farming activities on the remaining potential farmlands within the lower floodplain should be permitted so long as they do not involve heavy use of chemicals and are not conducive to erosion. Land drainage, however, should not be permitted. In the upper floodplain and uplands normal conservation safeguards for soil, water, and vegetation should be sufficient.

GUIDELINE. Feedlot Controls

Locate feedlots and other concentrated livestock operations on high ground and control waste discharge.

Since there are six head of livestock for each person in the country, feedlot and dairy wastes—principally urine and manure—are major potential sources of water pollution that cause eutrophication, oxygen reduction, and bacterial contamination of waters. Some waste equivalents are as follows: one cow produces wastes equivalent to six people; one hog, two people; and seven chickens, one person.[26] Animal wastes total about 1.4 billion tons annually in the United States. Detailed studies of the quantity and composition of wastes from feedlots are available from the U.S. Environmental Protection Agency (EPA).[22]

The dumping of animal wastes directly into surface waters is an obvious source of water pollution. But many wastes enter coastal ecosystems indirectly via stormwater runoff and subsurface ground water movement. Pollution from feedlot runoff has become so severe that the EPA now requires treatment of the runoff. State and federal guidelines also frequently recommend the "sealing" of feedlots with impervious floors to prevent groundwater pollution. Feedlot

runoff often carries 5000 ppm of biochemical oxygen demand (BOD) or 25 times the BOD of raw municipal sewage.

Water pollution from feedlots is now being regulated by federal (EPA) and state governments. Unlike many agricultural contaminants, pollutants from feedlots can be rather easily isolated (as a point source), making control and enforcement practicable. The EPA has developed effluent guidelines to aid in the elimination of direct discharge of animal wastes and the release of untreated runoff water. The EPA has defined a feedlot as a "concentrated, confined animal or poultry growing operation for meat, milk or egg production, or stabling, in pens or houses wherein the animals or poultry are fed at the place of confinement and crop or forage growth or production is not sustained in the area of confienement."[23] Examples include open lots, dairy barns, cowyards, racetrack stables, chicken houses, and duck farms.

The EPA requires that all feedlots be protected from the 25-year storm; that is, the facility should be located or floodproofed to the extent that storms up to this level will not wash wastes or untreated effluents into public waters. This problem is best solved by elevating feedlots above the floodplain.

Implementation No. 1. Feedlot Pollution Control

Stringent requirements for pollution control must be imposed on feedlots and other concentrated livestock operations.

No matter where a feedlot is located, some type of waste treatment system is required. Among the variety of mechanical and natural treatment methods available, land treatment and wastewater lagoons are the most widely used of the proved techniques. Ideally, treatment should be inexpensive and should use the surrounding land as a natural purification system. Waste treatment

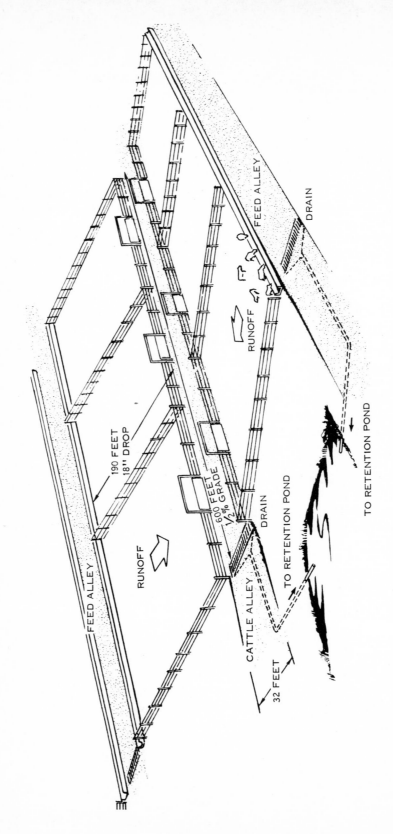

Figure 6.11 Open beef feedlot facilities should be designed to reduce water pollution potential to the minimum. (SOURCE: Reference 24.)

technology is rapidly expanding and is site specific; thus the advice of a specialist is necessary in choosing a system.

Retention lagoons, or ponds, provide waste treatment by bacterial decomposition (Figure 6.11). Such lagoons have been used successfully in curbing pollution from duck farms on Long Island, New York. North Carolina guidelines indicate that anaerobic lagoons 6 feet (1.8 meters) deep require from 110 square feet (33.5 square meters) of surface area per cow to 5 square feet (1.5 square meters) per chicken.[29] Costs can be lowered by following lagoon treatment with land application (page 513).

In land application, solid or liquid animal waste is applied to vegetated land, where it is cleansed by vegetation and by soil bacteria removing nitrogen, pathogenic bacteria, and other substances. Land application may involve either land treatment or land disposal. Land treatment implies that the water is to be recovered after purification (Figure 6.12);

land disposal, that the water enters the earth and, although not recovered, may serve a valuable purpose, such as the fertilization of cropland or rangeland.

State and federal agencies have set minimum standards for controlling water pollution from feedlots, including (1) no direct discharge of animal wastes, and (2) treatment of all effluent and polluted runoff.

Existing facilities must be capable of storing and treating feedlot wastes—with rainfall up to the amount delivered by the 10-year, 24-hour storm—using the "best practicable technology." By 1983 all waste treatment systems will have to handle the stormwater runoff from a 25-year, 24-hour storm, using the "best available technology." Individual states have developed specific guidelines for meeting these requirements.[20] The California State Water Quality Control Board recommends the following management techniques for livestock operations:[26] "routing of washwater and drain-

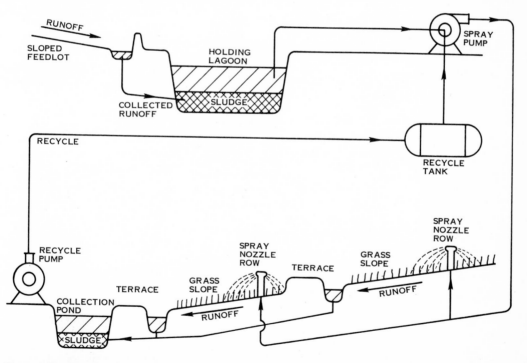

Figure 6.12 Spray irrigation purifies liquid feedlot wastes introduced into specially designed grassed slopes. (SOURCE: Reference 24.)

age to impervious areas, selecting more impervious soils, or paving, at manure storage areas, and applying manures and wastewaters on land at reasonable rates for minimal percolation."

Implementation No. 2. Feedlot Setback

Feedlots and other concentrated livestock operations should be located above floodplains.

The best approach to the protection of coastal ecosystems from feedlot pollution is to locate all feedlot operations above floodwater levels. Implementation of this location requirement would necessitate that all feedlots now in the 25-year floodplain be identified as nonconforming uses and terminated at a convenient opportunity in the future. An alternative, technological solution—to allow feedlots to be sited in the floodplain, with floodproofing to the 25-year flood level—would often be too expensive.

REFERENCES

1. U.S. Department of the Interior. 1970. *The National Estuarine Pollution Study.* U.S. Senate, 91st Congress, 2nd Session, Document No. 91–58. Superintendent of Documents, U.S. Government Printing Office, Washington, D.C.

2. Background data provided by U.S. Department of Agriculture. National Conference on Water, held at the Washington Hilton, Washington, D.C., 1975.

3. J. M. Laflen and W. C. Moldenhauer. 1971. "Soil conservation on agricultural land." *Journal of Soil and Water Conservation,* Vol. 26, No. 6, pp. 225–229.

4. U.S. Environmental Protection Agency. 1973. *Methods for Identifying and Evaluating the Nature and Extent of Non-point Sources of Pollutants.* Report No. EPA-430/9-73-014.

5. William E. Odum. 1974. "Potential effects of aquaculture on inshore coastal waters." *Environmental Conservation,* Vol. 1, No. 3.

6. Gordon F. Snow. 1972. "Pesticides in the coastal zone." In *Agriculture in the Coastal Zone: Comprehensive Ocean Area Plan,* Appendix IV. Department of Navigation and Ocean Development, Sacramento, California.

7. U.S. Environmental Protection Agency. 1975. *Control of Water Pollution from Cropland,* Vol. I: *A Manual for Guideline Development.* Office of Research and Development, Report No. EPA–600/2–75–026a, Superintendent of Documents, U.S. Government Printing Office, Washington, D.C.

8. U.S. Department of Agriculture. 1972. *North Atlantic Regional Water Resources Study,* Appendix L: *Water Quality and Pollution.* Forest Service and Soil Conservation Service, Superintendent of Documents, U.S. Government Printing Office, Washington, D.C., p. L–48.

9. Food and Agriculture Organization of the United Nations. 1965. *Soil Erosion by Water: Some Measures for Its Control on Cultivated Lands.* FAO Agricultural Development Paper No. 81.

10. U.S. Army Engineer District. 1974. *Environmental Working Paper, Port of Stockton to Port Edith.* U.S. Army Corps of Engineers, Sacramento, California.

11. Council for Agricultural Science and Technology. 1975. *Potential for Energy Conservation in Agricultural Production.* Council for Agriculture, Science, and Technology Report No. 40, Department of Agronomy, Iowa State University, Ames, Iowa.

12. U.S. Environmental Protection Agency. 1973. *Methods and Practices for Controlling Water Pollution from Agricultural Non-point Sources.* Report No. EPA–430/9–73–015.

13. John E. Hobbie, B. J. Copeland, and William G. Harrison. 1972. *Nutrients in the Pamlico River Estuary, N.C., 1969–1971.* Water Resources Research Institute, University of North Carolina, Raleigh, North Carolina.

14. Maryland State Planning Department. 1969. *Draft Report—Wetlands in Maryland,* Vol. II. Technical Report, Maryland General Assembly, Annapolis, Maryland

15. Floyd L. Corty. 1972. *Agriculture in the Coastal Zone of Louisiana.* Department of Agricultural Economics and Agribusiness, AEA Information Series No. 25, Louisiana State University, Baton Rouge, Louisiana.

16. Samuel P. Shaw and C. Gordon Fredine. 1971. *Wetlands of the United States.* U.S. Department of the Interior, Fish and Wildlife Service Circular 39, Superintendent of Documents, U.S. Government Printing Office, Washington, D.C.

17. Fred Ferrigno. New Jersey Division of Fish, Game; and Shellfisheries, Trenton, New Jersey. Personal communication.

18. Shoreland Zoning Project. 1972. *Suggested Interim Guidelines for Shoreland Zoning and Subdivision Control.* University of Maine, Orono, Maine.

19. John N. Holeman. Geologist (Sedimentation), Engineering Division, Soil Conservation Service, Washington, D.C. Personal communication.

20. Soil Conservation Service. 1966. *Louisiana Gulf Coast Marsh Handbook.* U.S. Department of Agriculture, Alexandria, Louisiana.

21. Paul Jacobson and Walter Weiss. 1952. Revised by R. C. Barnes, Jr., 1973. *Farming Terraced Land.* U.S. Department of Agriculture, Leaflet No. 335, Superintendent of Documents, U.S. Government Printing Office, Washington, D.C.

22. U.S. Environmental Protection Agency. 1972. *Cattle Feedlots and the Environment.* EPA Region X, Seattle, Washington.

23. U.S. Environmental Protection Agency. 1974. "Feedlots point source category, effluent guidelines and standards." *Federal Register,* Vol. 39, No. 32 (Feb. 14, 1974).

24. U.S. Environmental Protection Agency. 1973. *Development Document for Proposed Effluent Limitations, Guidelines, and New Source Performance Standards for the Feedlots Point Source Category.* Document No. EPA 440/1–73–004.

25. North Carolina Board of Water and Air Resources. 1972. *Tentative Guidelines for the Design, Installation and Operation of Animal Waste Treatment Lagoons.* North Carolina Agricultural Extension Service, Miscellaneous Extension Publication No. 89, Raleigh, North Carolina.

26. Regional Water Quality Control Board, San Francisco Bay Region (2). 1974. *Tentative Water Quality Control Plan, San Francisco Bay Basin (2).* Oakland, California.

27. North Carolina State University Task Force. 1974. *Report on Master Plan Preparation, First Colony Farms.* North Carolina State University, Raleigh, North Carolina.

28. John R. Clark. 1975. *Food Production in the Nation's Coastal Zone.* Working paper prepared for The Institute of Ecology, Founders' Conference, held in Morgantown, West Virginia, April 16–18, 1975 (unpublished).

29. National Commission on Water Quality. 1975. *Technical Environmental Volume.* Washington, D.C.

2. AIRPORTS

Airports for coastal cities have often been located in wetland areas. These low-priced sites offer flat, undeveloped land for landing strips, as well as unobstructed over-water landing approach paths. The use of these desirable sites for airports has led to the destructions of thousands of acres of wetlands by filling and the pollution of many bays from contaminated runoff.

In addition to destroying wetlands, ill-planned airport complexes have reduced the size of water bodies, blocked water circulation, and eliminated wildlife habitats. Degradation of water quality also has become a serious consequence of airports located on tidal water bodies. Discharge of airport stormwater runoff into estuarine waters pollutes them with sediments, organic matter, and toxic substances.[1] The problem is exacerbated in receiving waters that are inadequately flushed or in lagoons or confined bays, where dilution of pollutants is slow (page 127).

The magnitude of the ecological hazard is a function of the features of the particular coastal site where airport expansion or new construction is to take place. The original development of John F. Kennedy Airport in New York preempted 4500 acres of valuable marshland fringing Jamaica Bay[2] (Figure 6.13). An extension on landfill into Jamaica Bay and adjacent wetlands for a runway was permitted in 1962 (Figure 6.14). However, additional landfill expansion (see Figure 6.13) was denied in 1971 when a land-use study concluded that:

Any runway construction will damage the natural environment of [Jamaica] Bay and reduce its potential use for conservation, recreation, and housing. The degree of this impairment will be dependent upon the amount of Bay area taken for this airport extension. . . . A sufficiently large land taking . . . could cause major irreversible ecological damage to the Bay.[2]

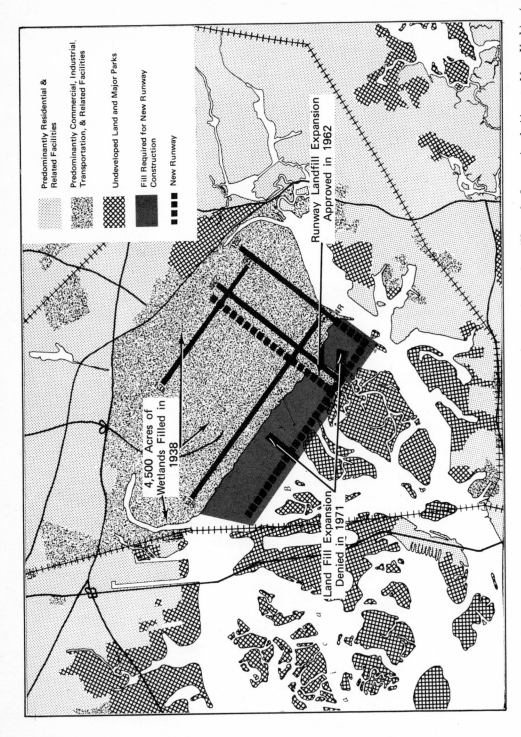

Figure 6.13 Extensive wetlands inventories have been obliterated at large coastal zone airport sites (Kennedy International Airport, New York). (SOURCE: Adapted from Reference 2.)

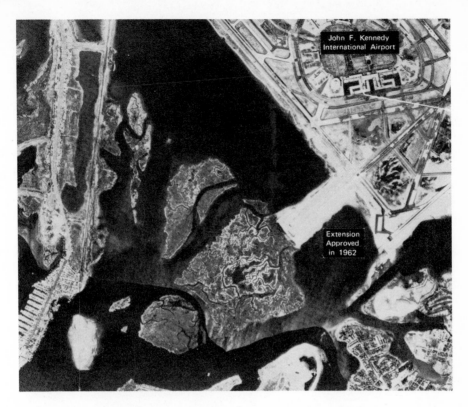

Figure 6.14   Extension of a landing strip at Kennedy International Airport, New York, blocked circulation in the Jamaica Bay estuary. (SOURCE: New York City Planning Commission.)

The potential environmental hazard from airport construction is further illustrated by a rejected proposal for a jetport in Florida. The construction of this facility, planned in the Big Cypress Swamp, was denied by the U.S. Department of the Interior on the following grounds: "Development of the proposed jetport and its attendant facilities will lead to land drainage and development for agriculture, industry, housing, transportation, and services in the Big Cypress Swamp which will inexorably destroy the south Florida ecosystem and thus the Everglades National Park."[3]

Although the more dramatic reports of potential damage originate from assessments of large urban airports, the cumulative effects of numerous small airports may be of greater concern in the future. For example, approval of a private plane airport planned for Fort Belvoir, Virginia, and designed to reduce pressure on Washington (D.C.) National Airport, was not granted because its location on a bay of the Potomac River would endanger bald eagle nesting in an adjacent 700-acre refuge.[4]

Fortunately, the past destruction of marshes and other vital areas may be minimized by locating new airports inland, away from vital areas and the lower coastal floodplain. This policy is in accord with the modern planning practice of siting major airports far outside of urban areas, for example, Dulles International Airport in Virginia. This planning concept is a result of the realization that airport expansion and new construction cannot continue indefinitely in large urban areas. Land and air space there is limited; many of these sites are already highly developed, particularly in the Boston–Washington corridor, the southern rim of the Great Lakes, the California coast from San Francisco to San Diego, and the east coast of Florida below Jacksonville.

The impacts of an airport are not confined to the immediate site. Airports and their access roads open new areas and often induce secondary residential, commercial, and industrial growth. As demands for municipal services such as sewer and water hookups, electricity, secondary roads, building lots, and other characteristic urban needs are fulfilled, environmental quality, particularly water quality, will be threatened. Air pollution, increased runoff, discharge of improperly or incompletely treated wastes, and disruption of natural drainage patterns must all be anticipated and their effects assessed.

Local authorities should attempt to revise airport plans that would cause major adverse impacts. Zoning and other means can be applied to locate secondary development elsewhere if it would contribute excessive amounts of pollutants to nearby water bodies or disturb vital habitat areas.

In summary, approval actions for airport projects should be taken only after careful examination has been made of all potential secondary development, and a strict procedure to control affected areas has been devised.

GUIDELINE.   **Restrictions on Airport Sites**

Design and locate airports so as to safeguard coastal ecosystems against pollution and the loss of vital habitat areas.

An early step in planning airports, as in any proposed project in the coastal zone, is to

Figure 6.15   Airports constructed in wetlands cause extreme ecological damage (new Marco Island Airport, Collier County, Florida). (Photo by author.)

refer to the inventory of identified vital habitat areas of the community (page 247). These are designated as off limits to development, including airports, because of the adverse effect on coastal ecosystems that would result (Figure 6.15).

To prevent polluted runoff from leaving the site untreated, it is necessary that airports include complete stormwater runoff management. All runoff water should be collected and restored by treatment to meet water quality standards before discharge to any coastal water area.

When siting an airport, careful thought must be given to long-range demands on the facility and to the question of whether future pressures for expansion can be met adequately. Once the site is selected and construction is completed, it may be tempting to expand into adjacent vital habitat areas initially intended for preservation.

It will be prudent to locate airports on land above the lower floodplain (10-year flood level) to avoid flooding and pollutant washoff, as well as to forestall the need for excavation in sensitive low-lying shorelands and wetlands. If an existing airport in the lower coastal floodplain must be expanded, steps should be taken to ensure that any major interference with vital areas is avoided, that all runoff and other waste water is adequately treated to prevent contamination of coastal water bodies, and that any secondary development related to the expanded facility is anticipated and considered in assessing the total impact of the project.

Implementation No. 1. Vital Area Protection in Airport Projects

Airport facilities should be designed to avoid encroachment on vital habitat areas and lower floodplains.

Neither wetlands nor lower floodplains (up to the 10-year flood level) should be used for airport development or expansion. Their

preservation will protect wetland areas and leave a buffer strip between the airport and water bodies to filter runoff water so that the direct washoff of pollutants will be eliminated during all but the worst floods.

To implement such policies, the California coastal plan recommends the following:[5]

Landfill and other land expansion of existing coastal airport facilities shall be permitted only if the applicant can demonstrate that (1) there is a need for expansion that cannot be met through more efficient use of existing facilities, or through other transportation systems; and (2) all other means of expanding have been evaluated and are unacceptable because of economic, environmental, and social costs.

Implementation No. 2. Airport Runoff

Stormwater runoff should be managed so as to avoid pollution of coastal water bodies.

Airports and airport facilities characteristically involve many acres of impervious paved surfaces that cause large-scale stormwater management problems (page 545). As rainwater or snowmelt runs off the runways, parking lots, roadways, and rooftops, it collects oils, jet exhaust particulates, and other airport-related pollutants. Specific water quality problems arise from aircraft washing, aircraft plant stripping, steam cleaning operations, the dumping of oily wastes, and fuel spills.[1] For example, Table 6.9 lists the concentrations of pollutants measured in a drainage canal at Oakland International Airport (California).

To avoid polluting adjacent coastal waters, airports should have complete runoff management facilities. The object is to collect, treat, and restore all stormwater to the same condition of quality, volume, and rate of flow that existed before construction of the airport. Treated runoff can be released into surrounding buffer areas for final polishing before it runs into a watercourse or seeps into the groundwater (see page 513).

Table 6.9   Runoff from coastal airports contains high
concentrations of pollutants (from drainage canal water at Oakland
International Airport)[1] (SOURCE: Reference 1)

PARAMETERS	CONCENTRATIONS
Total Solids (mg/l)	3600
Dissolved Solids (mg/l)	3400
Suspended Solids (mg/l)	200
Chemical Oxygen Demand (mg/l)	120
Nitrates (ppm)	4.5
Phosphates (ppm)	6.5
Color (color units)	510
Turbidity (Jackson turbidity units)	125
Lead (mg/l)	0.05
Zinc (mg/l)	0.05
Oil and Grease (mg/l)	9.0
Phenols (mg/l)	Trace
pH	8.0

Minimizing the amount of impervious surface through more efficient airport layout will guarantee a minimum of runoff water. For small private airports the use of porous materials for much of the parking lot surfacing may be practicable (porous surfacing can often virtually eliminate runoff). Problems arising from contamination of runoff can be reduced by keeping work areas clean and free of debris and polluting substances.

REFERENCES

1. Port of Oakland. 1974. *Metropolitan Oakland International Airport Master Plan Draft Environmental Impact Report Appendices*, Vol. II. San Francisco Bay Conservation and Development Committee, San Francisco, California.

2. James A. Fay, Chairman of Jamaica Bay Environmental Study Group. 1971. *Jamaica Bay and Kennedy Airport, a Multidisciplinary Environmental Study*, Vols. I and II. National Academy of Sciences–National Academy of Engineering, Washington, D.C.

3. U.S. Department of the Interior. 1969. *Environmental Impact of the Big Cypress Swamp Jetport.*

4. Donnel Nunes. "Airport plan perils eagle preserve." *Washington Post*, Aug. 6, 1973, p. 1.

5. California Coastal Zone Conservation Commissions. 1975. *California Coastal Plan*. San Francisco, California.

3. BEACHFRONT PROTECTION AND MANAGEMENT

Special risks are attached to development on the ocean beachfront, where buildings are directly in the path of storm-driven waves. Beaches and dunes shift with changes in the balance between the erosive forces of storm winds and waves, on the one hand, and the restorative powers of tides and currents, on the other. Consequently, along much of its length, the coast is a risky place to maintain habitation. The costs in property losses and human lives have been high. Furthermore, enormous sums of private and public money are spent to stabilize and safeguard inhabited beaches and are rewarded too rarely with success.[1]

Along much of the sandy shoreline of the United States the beach is receding because of a rise in relative sea level—more than 1 foot (30.5 centimeters) in the past 100 years in places along the Atlantic and Gulf of Mexico coasts.[2,3] As the sea level rises, the shoreline is forced inland and there is little to anchor it permanently in place. If left natural, beaches and whole barrier islands shift landward while still maintaining their equilibrium slopes as sea level rises (pages 44 and 96).

When sandy shores become occupied, roads are built, and investment capital is committed, it may seem desirable to retard the natural recession of the shore with sea-walls and groins. These structures serve only a temporary purpose, however, and, through a false sense of security, set the stage for a much larger-scale disaster than would occur without structural interference (Figure 6.16).

Ecologically, the beachfront is a unique environment occupied by animals adapted to the high stress and constant motion of the beach sands, for example, mole crabs, co-quina clams, razor clams, and other rapid-burrowing species. There are also many temporary residents, such as sea turtles and the grunion fish that come to nest on the beach. Countless shorebirds feed at the water's edge and nest on the upper beach areas, the sand dunes, and the sand over-wash areas behind the beach. The plant communities of the beachfront thrive on the continuing stress of natural disturbances, to which the grasses and other plant species living here are especially adapted. The vegetation plays a significant role in stabilizing the dune front, trapping and holding the sand blown up by the wind, and thereby allowing the dunes to build and stabilize.

The Government Role

Effective beachfront management requires closely coordinated federal–state–local participation in the planning and implementation of programs. Many communities have special boards or advisory groups to handle beachfront management problems. The most urgent task facing many communities is the formulation of a comprehensive beach-front management plan and the establishment of a regulatory program to protect

Figure 6.16 Bulkheads and seawalls on ocean beaches deflect wave energy downward and scour away beach sand, often causing serious erosion and permanent loss of beach. (Photo by author.)

beaches and to effect land-use controls in beach areas. Technical and financial assistance for local projects is often available through the state or, particularly, through the U.S. Army Corps of Engineers (see Appendix, page 877, for list of area offices).

Shoreline projects usually begin with a local request for help. Anyone can request information on combating erosion problems from the Corps of Engineers. Eroded public shores or shores damaged because of federal navigation projects are eligible for federal funds, as are private shores if public benefit will derive from their protection. Persons desiring information about beach erosion or assistance in combating it can usually secure better results if they work with the local agency concerned with shore protection because the local government must cooperate with the federal government and must share expenses for most projects.

The Secretary of the Army can authorize a beach erosion study if the project to be carried out is eligible for treatment as a "small-scale project" or if its purpose is to mitigate damages caused by a federal navigation project. For a larger-scale project, the study must be approved by Congress. Normally the elected federal representative of the locality desiring a study will request Congress to authorize it. The Corps' district engineer will hold a public hearing and examine problems involved in projects and causal factors. If the project seems to be desirable and local interests are willing to cooperate, the report on the study will recommend the adoption of the project. The report is reviewed by the Board of Engineers for Rivers and Harbors, the Chief of Engineers, the governors of affected states, and interested federal agencies. It is then submitted to Congress, which normally authorizes construction projects through the annual appropriations bill.

When funds are made available, the district engineer carries out the detail work essential to the construction of the project. He draws plans and consults with local interests, contracts for the construction, and generally undertakes its supervision. When the project is completed, he turns the project works over to the local interest for operation and maintenance.

The local government, as mentioned before, must cooperate and share costs with the federal government. The basic federal share is 50 percent of the construction cost for nonfederal public lands, 100 percent for federal public lands, and 100 percent for mitigation of damage caused by federal navigation projects. However, for certain projects involving nonfederal public shore parks and conservation areas that meet certain listed criteria, the Corps of Engineers may contribute 70 percent of the cost. The federal share of hurricane protection projects may also be up to 70 percent of the cost, exclusive of land cost. There are further provisions for the Secretary of the Army to reimburse local interests for expenses incurred on approved projects.

GUIDELINE.   Shore Protection

Develop a shore protection program aimed at preserving the beach profile in its present slope and configuration.

The natural beachfront has a standard structure. Its anatomy is known, and its parts are named (Figure 6.17).

The natural beachfront exists in a state of dynamic tension, continually shifting in response to waves, winds, and tide and continually adjusting back to equilibrium. Long-term stability is gained by holding the slope or profile intact through balancing the sand reserves held in various storage elements—dune, berm, offshore bar, and so forth. Each component of the beach profile is capable of receiving, storing, and giving sand, depending on which of several constantly changing forces is dominant at the moment. Stability is fostered by maintaining the storage capacity of each of the components at the highest level.

When storm waves carve away a beach,

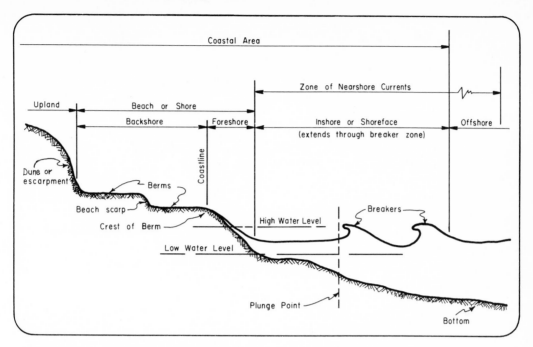

Figure 6.17   Standard beach profile—description and nomenclature. (SOURCE: Reference 4.)

they are taking sand out of storage (Figure 6.18). In the optimum natural state there is enough sand storage capacity in the berm or dune to replace the sand lost from the beach to storms. Consequently, the effects are usu-ally temporary, with the dune or berm gradually building up again (Figure 6.19).

Furthermore, the sand available to be relo-cated during storms serves a useful protec-tive service:[2]

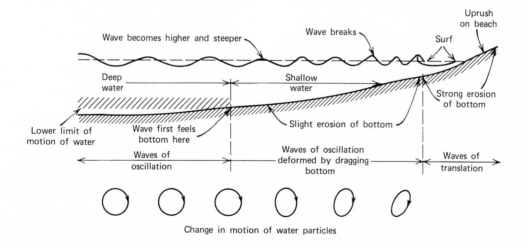

Figure 6.18   A wave generates strong erosive forces as it moves onto the shore. When it reaches a depth of about 1.3 times its height, the wave breaks. Breaking causes the water to travel forward as a foaming turbu-lent mass, which rushes up onto the shore. (SOURCE: Reference 6.)

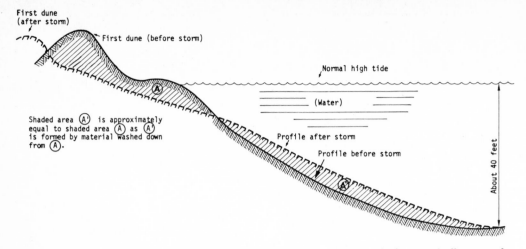

Figure 6.19 Storms cause a short-term change in the beachfront profile, which is gradually restored to equilibrium by natural processes. (SOURCE: Reference 7.)

As the dune is attacked by storm waves, eroded material is carried out and deposited offshore where it alters the beach's underwater configuration. Accumulating sand decreases the offshore beach slope (makes it more nearly horizontal), thereby presenting a broader bottom surface to storm wave action. This surface absorbs or dissipates through friction an increasingly large amount of destructive wave energy which would otherwise be focused on the shoreline behind the barrier.

If the dunes are bulldozed away, the berms built upon, or the shore bulkheaded, the reserve sand in storage will be reduced to a level no longer capable of replacing sand losses from severe storms. The beach system then becomes unstable, slumps in places, and attempts to reestablish its old equilibrium profile, or "angle of repose." But with less sand the equilibrium angle of repose can be established only at a position *inland* of the previous beach profile.[8] When this occurs, the beach cuts back into the land. The natural forces at work are immense, and the power of man to hold the beach at a higher than natural angle of repose to protect property is limited. Structural solutions are often ineffective and usually only temporary.

There are two possible solutions that

should be considered together. First, permanent development should be placed well inland of the active part of the shore, including receding shores that would be expected to become active in the future. Second, positive action should be taken both to prevent the removal of sand from *any* storage element and to prevent blocking the free transport of sand from any one storage element into the active part of the system.

The U.S. Army Corps of Engineers, which has the greatest expertise and capability for large-scale public works projects in the United States, has generally favored an engineering or structural approach to shore protection, but recently has taken more interest in long-term land-use controls and other nonstructural solutions.

Implementation No. 1. Structural Solutions to Beachfront Protection

Structures should be used for beachfront protection only to supplement a non-structural program.

Many experts advocate working with natural shore processes rather than fighting them. For example, they recommend maintaining the natural "overwash" environment of narrow barrier islands[9] by allowing storm surges to overflow these islands. In this fashion sand is deposited over the island rather than being carved away and carried out to sea by storm waves reflected back from sea walls and other structures. Although permanent development is not feasible on such overwash beaches, neither can a naturally receding beach be held forever with structures.

The solution is not to go exclusively with either structural or nonstructural techniques but to achieve a balanced plan emphasizing the nonstructural. Although it might be simplest to let nature take its course, extensive areas of the coast are already occupied and must somehow be maintained safely until setbacks and other protective land-use plans can be implemented. Yet even these systems should be allowed to remain as close to their natural dynamic states as possible. Some structural interference may be necessary, however, to stabilize inlets for navigation purposes.

Although beach nourishment (i.e., pumping sand onto beaches to stabilize them) is normally preferable to building fixed shore protection structures, close scrutiny must be given to nourishment projects because they require a large, continuing expenditure of tax money that must be justified as a public benefit. Nourishment projects should not become substitutes for balanced long-term beachfront management.

The principal shore protection structures include seawalls, revetments, groins, and breakwaters. Each serves a special purpose, and each affects beaches in a different manner (Figure 6.20).

A *seawall* is a solid barricade built at the water's edge to protect the shore and to prevent inland flooding. Seawalls are expensive and are usually suitable only for special situations, since they often compound shore erosion problems because in the long run they do not hold or protect the beach, the primary asset of shorefront property. In principle, the seawall is designed to absorb and reflect wave energy, as well as to hold fill in place and to raise the problem area above flooding elevations. Unfortunately, seawalls (including bulkheads and revetments) commonly accelerate the loss of sand as the wall deflects the wave forces downward into the beach deposit (Figure 6.21).[10] This causes the sand to erode away seaward of the footing and the beach to diminish or disappear. Often the seawall is undermined and collapses (Figure 6.22).

It can be estimated roughly that, for every 1 foot of wave height, storm forces have the potential to scour the beach to a depth of 2 feet (Figure (6.23).

The Corps of Engineers recommends protection on the upper part of the beach with seawalls to compensate for the natural protection lost when dunes have been destroyed. Extensive seawalls have been built as public works projects, principally in Massachusetts, Florida, Mississippi, Texas, and California (Figure 6.24). Seawall costs usually begin at around $200 per foot ($660 per meter) and may range considerably above $500 per foot (1973 dollars) for the heaviest structures built far from sources of materials.[4] Also, owners often armor their property with individual steel, timber, or concrete structures, which may evolve into one massive seawall.

A *revetment* armors the slope face of a dune or bluff with one or more layers of rock (riprap) or concrete (Figure 6.25). This protection dissipates wave energy with less adverse effect on the beach than occurs with a vertical seawall. Revetments usually cost about $75 to $150 per foot ($250 to $500 per meter) (1973 dollars) of shore protected, depending on strength needed, total length, and proximity to sources of construction material.[12]

A *groin* is a dam for sand, a structure built at right angles to the beach to interrupt longshore sand movement (littoral drift) and trap sand in order to stabilize or widen a beach. Groins are constructed of timber, steel, concrete, or rock (Figure 6.26). The trapping of sand by a groin is done at the expense of the adjacent downdrift shore.

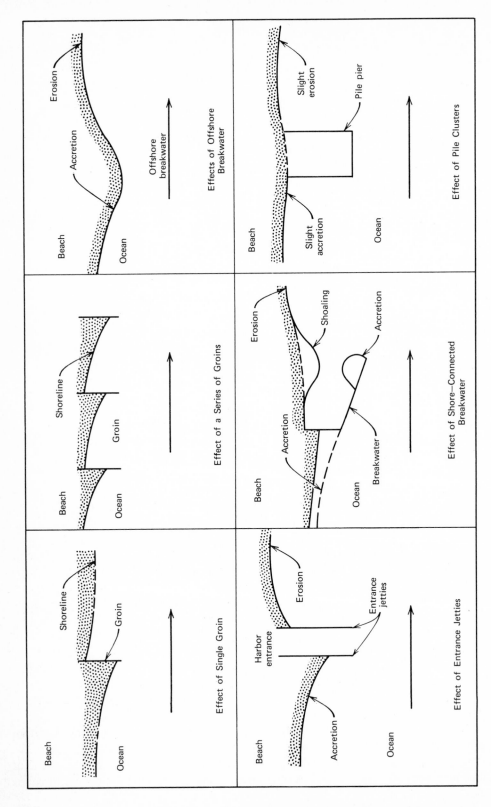

Figure 6.20 The effects of various structures on the transport of sand along ocean shorelines (littoral drift). (SOURCE: Reference 17.)

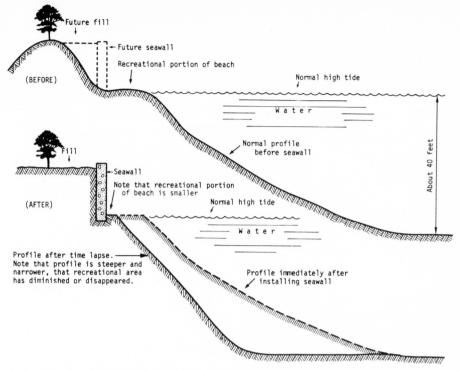

Figure 6.21 Decrease of beach area commonly occurs over time as wave energy is deflected downward by a seawall onto beach sand, rather than dissipating gradually over the beach and dune area. (SOURCE: Reference 7.)

Groins are effective only (1) when there is a significant volume of littoral drift, (2) when the drift carries coarse materials (greater than 0.2 mm), and (3) when the beach downstream from the groin can be sacrificed (the sand gained at one place is denied to another).[9] A row of parallel groins tends to force the littoral drift of sand offshore because much of the sand moves from tip to tip of the groin instead of moving along close to the beach, thereby causing sand starvation of the whole length of the beach (Figure 6.27).[8]

The Corps considers it ". . . desirable, and frequently necessary, to place sand artificially to fill the area between the groins, thereby ensuring a more-or-less uninterrupted sand supply to downdrift shores." Groin fields cost about $100 to $350 per foot ($330 to $1150 per meter) of shore protected, depending on such factors as ex-

posure to wave action, range of tide, and accessibility of building materials.[12] Beach fill required to prevent adverse effect on downdrift shores adds to the cost.[13]

Offshore breakwaters have been constructed to provide safe passage through inlets and to prevent sand blockage (Figure 6.28). Breakwaters have both benefiicial and detrimental effects on the shore. When placed on the updrift side of a navigation opening, a breakwater may impound sand, prevent it from entering the navigation channel, and afford shelter for a floating dredge that pumps the impounded material across the navigation opening back into the stream of sand moving along the shore.[4] An offshore breakwater stops wave action and creates a quiet water area behind it, which benefits navigation (Figure 6.29). However, in the absence of wave action to move the sand stream, sand is deposited and builds up

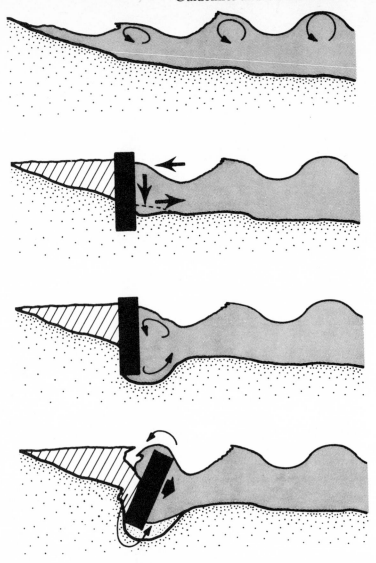

Figure 6.22 A naturally sloping beach dissipates wave energy, but a seawall or building foundation wall reflects the energy almost completely, creating a scouring action near the toe of the wall and causing the undermining and eventual collapse of the structure. (SOURCE: Reference 11.)

the shore seaward toward the breakwater. The buildup actually serves as a barrier to littoral sand drift and deflects the sand stream seaward, depriving the downdrift beaches of sand. Offshore breakwaters are also expensive; costs range from $200 to 500 per foot of shore protected.[12]

From these descriptions of structures it can be seen that various engineering ap-

proaches to shore protection have complex secondary effects. Often short-term solutions cause intensified long-term problems.[14] There are numerous examples of structures causing, or contributing to, destabilization of beaches. For example, Miami Beach has been all but eliminated by urban encroachment that led to extensive bulkheading and groin fields (Figure 6.30). To prevent such

Figure 6.23 Seawalls and oceanfront bulkheads cause scouring and loss of beach sand. (Photo by author.)

Figure 6.24 Curved concrete seawall with stone riprap at base to deter the scouring effect of waves on sand. (Photo by author.)

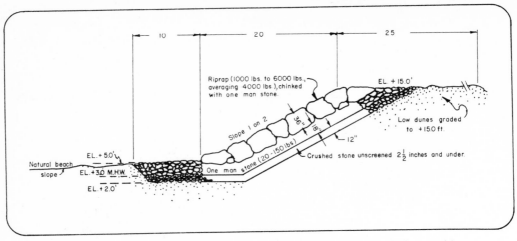

Figure 6.25   Stone revetment at Cape Henry, Virginia. (SOURCE: Reference 4.)

disasters it is necessary that a thorough study and comprehensive protection plan be developed before structures are authorized. Detrimental structures already in place should be considered as nonconforming, and a long-term strategy formulated to remove or replace them at the earliest opportunity.

Implementation No. 2.   Beach Nourishment

Sand for replenishing eroded beaches should be obtained from offshore deposits or from areas of active accretion.

Artificial beach nourishment is a desirable method of beach protection in many situations and is nearly always preferable to structural methods. However, it is still only a substitute for proper regulation of land use and beachfront activities.

Often a supply of sand of suitable quality (type and size) is not readily available; the grain size generally must exceed 0.25 millimeter to remain on the beach and therefore be useful for restoration. A minimum size as large as 0.4 millimeter may be required under unfavorable conditions.[15]

Unfortunately, the Corps of Engineers has

Figure 6.26   Groins may suffer heavy impacts from wave forces. (Photo by author.)

Figure 6.27   Groin fields are often ineffectual; deflection of sand offshore causes a net loss of sand to beach and recession of the beachfront (Westhampton Beach, Long Island, New York). (Photo by U.S. Army Corps of Engineers.)

too often regarded the beach sand stored in bays, lagoons, estuaries, and nearshore areas as a source of beach nourishment. With the recent awareness of the ecological sensitivity of estuarine ecosystems (and of the fact that estuarine materials are often too fine), however, estuarine and bay sources are usually not considered available for beach nourishment (page 626).

In the past, dune deposits have also been recommended by the Corps as a source of beach fill, although it warned that "these must be used with caution to avoid exposing the area to flood hazard."[4] In the light of present knowledge, any such removal of sand is known to threaten the beach profile because of the reduction of storage, whether taken from dunes, the beach itself, or from the longshore bar or nearshore submerged

bottoms. Therefore an erosion problem should not be solved by bringing sand from some other part of the same beach.

Since dunes, adjacent beaches, nearshore areas, and estuaries are generally considered off limits for sand removal, there are two appropriate sources of supply for beach nourishment: (1) the open ocean or broad non-estuarine bays beyond a depth of about 40 feet (14 meters),[16] or (2) around inlets or other areas of accretion, where the supply is constantly replenished by natural forces, particularly when navigation dredging is being done.

The feasibility of exploitation of offshore deposits has been established by the Corps of Engineers, but the technology appears to need improvement in order to make the method cost effective. According to the

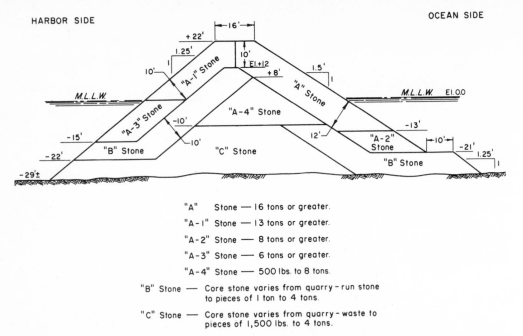

HARBOR SIDE
OCEAN SIDE

"A" Stone — 16 tons or greater.
"A-1" Stone — 13 tons or greater.
"A-2" Stone — 8 tons or greater.
"A-3" Stone — 6 tons or greater.
"A-4" Stone — 500 lbs. to 8 tons.
"B" Stone — Core stone varies from quarry-run stone to pieces of 1 ton to 4 tons.
"C" Stone — Core stone varies from quarry-waste to pieces of 1,500 lbs. to 4 tons.

Figure 6.28   Offshore breakwater at Marina Del Rey (Venice, California). (SOURCE: Reference 13.)

Figure 6.29   Offshore breakwaters stop wave action and create quiet water areas (Channel Islands Harbor, California). (Photo by U.S. Army Corps of Engineers.)

330

Figure 6.30   The groin system at Coney Island, New York, has contributed to the loss of large portions of the beach. (Photo by U.S. Army Corps of Engineers.)

Corps, "offshore sources will probably become the most important source when means for economic recovery become available."[4] It appears reasonable to assume that offshore sand exploitation will become a reality. Beyond a depth of 30 to 50 feet the sand reserve is generally independent of the sand reserves of the beach area, and therefore its removal should not upset the beach profile.

However, care must be taken during offshore dredging to avoid any vital habitat areas and to prevent excess siltation of the water. A University of Miami research team concluded that siltation is a potentially damaging factor along the southeast Florida coast.[11]

Siltation and induced turbidity may occur as a direct result of dredging, generally at and surrounding the dredging site, or from erosion of beach fill by waves, currents, or rain. Excessive silt may bury portions of reefs, suffocate fish by clogging their gills,

or settle out and smother bottom-dwelling life. The University of Miami team concluded that potential damage to coral reef communities is minimized when dredging is not done adjacent to reefs, when there is proper selection of equipment and care in dredging activities, and when rehandling of fill material between borrow areas and the beach is avoided.[10]

Beach fill for restoration can be expected to cost $50 to $400 per foot ($160 to $980 per meter) of shoreline filled (1973 dollars), depending on exposure, proximity of suitable fill-borrow sites, length of beach, and degree of restoration required. Because this approach affords only temporary protection (Figure 6.31), periodic nourishment may be required at intervals of 1 to 5 years at costs estimated to range from $5 to $15 per foot ($15 to $50 per meter) of shore per year, for straight beaches at least 2000 feet (600 meters) long. Retaining structures (groins) will add to the above costs.[4]

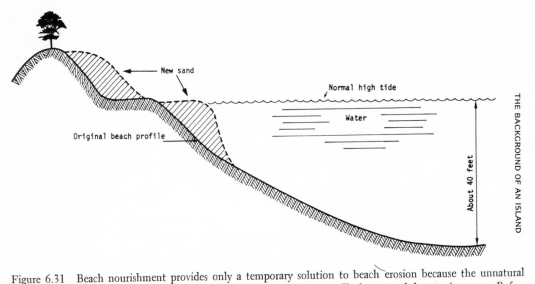

Figure 6.31   Beach nourishment provides only a temporary solution to beach erosion because the unnatural new slope will eventually be reduced to the original equilibrium profile by natural forces. (SOURCE: Reference 7.)

Implementation No. 3.   Inlet Stabilization

Inlet stabilization projects should be incorporated into the comprehensive shore protection program.

Inlets affect the stability of adjacent beaches by interrupting littoral drift and trapping sand. As sand moves into the inlet, the inlet narrows, causing acceleration of current velocity and thereby increasing the capacity of the current to suspend and to carry sand. On the flood tide, when the water flows in through the inlet, sand is carried a short distance inside and deposited. Such sand creates shoals in the landward end of the inlet, known as the *inner bar*. On the ebb tide the sand is carried a short distance out to sea and deposited on an *outer bar*. When this bar becomes high enough, waves break over it, causing sand to move toward the beach. The net result is the accumulation of sand on both bars and the starvation of downdrift beaches. However, this process reaches a state of equilibrium when the inlet bars are fully formed, after which natural bypassing will occur. When inlet channels are artificially deepened by

dredging, and the deposited sand is regularly dredged and hauled away, their capacity to store sand may be increased, thereby causing narrower beaches on the downdrift side of the jetty by reducing the supply of sand to these beaches.[4]

Jetties are structures developed to modify or control sand movement at inlets. They are constructed of steel, concrete, or rock, depending on foundation conditions, wave climate, and cost. Although jetties are similar to groins in that they dam the sand stream, they are usually considerably longer and larger, often extending seaward to a depth equivalent to the channel depth desired for navigation purposes.

Jetties not only stabilize the location of the channel by controlling sand movement but also shield vessels from waves. Adversely, sand is impounded at the updrift jetty and much is lost into deep water at the seaward end (Figure 6.32). The supply of sand to the shore downdrift from the inlet is thus reduced, causing erosion of that shore.[17] To eliminate undesirable downdrift erosion, some projects are provided with a bypass system for dredging the sand impounded by the updrift jetty and pumping it through a pipeline to the eroding beach. These bypass systems ensure a flow of sand to nourish the downdrift beach and prevent shoaling of the entrance channel (Figure 6.33). This may be accomplished in conjunction with an offshore breakwater.

A more recent development provides a low section or weir in the updrift jetty, over which sand moves into a predredged deposition basin (Figure 6.34). By dredging the basin periodically, deposition in the channel is reduced or eliminated. The dredged material is normally bypassed to the downdrift shore.

It is clear that both inlet deepening and inlet stabilization projects affect the sand supply moving along the beachfront and

that either can lead to a major imbalance of the beach system. Therefore inlet projects must be considered in the context of a comprehensive long-term plan for stabilization and protection of the beach system, which involves both land controls and engineered projects. Extensive information must often be compiled on ocean currents and their forces that affect the littoral transfer of sand (Figure 6.35).

Implementation No. 4.   Dune Restoration

Private and public projects to restore and stabilize dunes should be encouraged.

Two inexpensive and effective methods to protect beachfronts are simple structures,

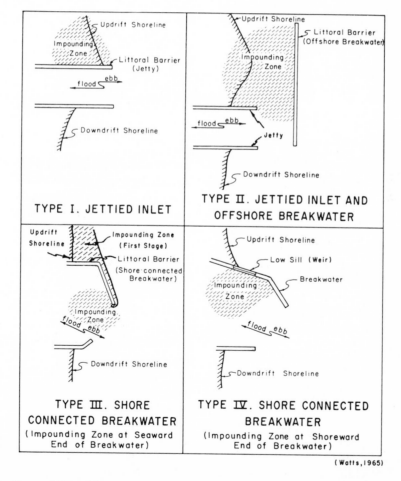

(Watts, 1965)

Figure 6.32   Types of littoral barriers where sand transfer systems have been employed. (SOURCE: Reference 13.)

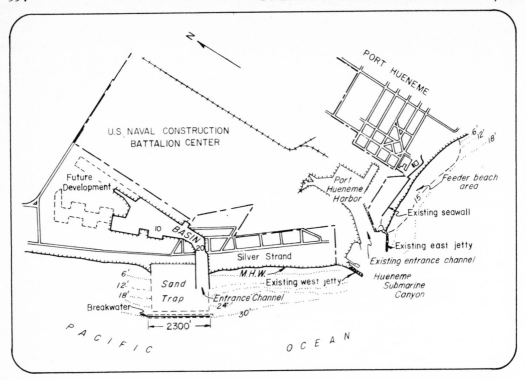

Figure 6.33   Sand bypassing at Channel Islands Harbor, California. Sand is periodically dredged from the trap and moved through a pipeline across both harbor entrances to the feeder beach on the far right. (SOURCE: Reference 4.)

such as snow fences, and revegetation programs (Figure 6.36). Such means enable individual property owners or community groups to build and rehabilitate sand dunes. Replacement dunes should be built above the high-tide line and on slopes that face the ocean. In some areas, in less than a year dunes 4 feet high or more may be built through the use of fencing, whereas in other places this amount of growth may take several years. The rate depends on the forces of wind that carry the sand onto the dunes. After dunes are restored, they should be stabilized by vegetation to prevent them from being blown away (page 215).[19]

Rehabilitation of damaged dunes to their natural condition is highly recommended, but artificially elevating them to unnatural heights to allow structures to be built on dangerous beachfronts is not recommended.[16] Under natural conditions dunes

and the whole beachfront are in a long-term equilibrium, a dynamic balance (page 96). Sand is sometimes lost and sometimes gained. Wind forces move the dunes about. Sometimes barrier islands are cut through by storms. This short-term mobility should be basic to the rationale of comprehensive community planning.

In many places, such as the North Carolina Outer Banks, the barrier islands are low, narrow, and geologically very active. On such islands occupancy should be limited to temporary structures and roads (page 263). In the past there were massive federal projects to maintain permanent development in these dangerous and unstable areas, but this approach is more or less discredited today. For example, the National Park Service has recently abandoned its long term efforts to build and maintain a massive series of artificially elevated dunes for pro-

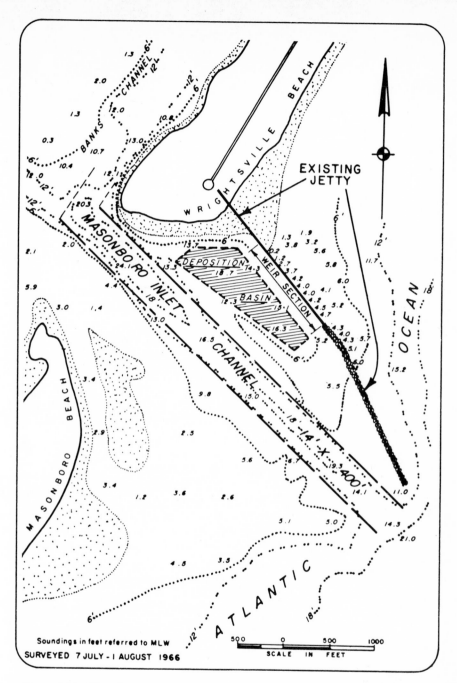

Figure 6.34   Masonboro Inlet, North Carolina, weir system. (SOURCE: Reference 4.)

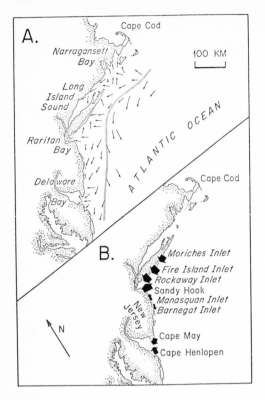

Figure 6.35 Littoral currents control the stability of ocean beaches. (A) General current flows along the northeast coast of the United States. (B) Detail of near-coast (littoral) currents. (SOURCE: Reference 18.)

tection of the Cape Hatteras area shores. (For details see Appendix, page 891).

GUIDELINE. Dune Protection

Implement regulations to protect the frontal dune system.

Dunes are waves of drifting sand, the height and movement of which are determined by the direction and intensity of the wind. The shifting dunes that normally lie directly behind the berm are the most susceptible to the stresses of wind and airborne salt. Mild summer waves add sand to the berm, and prevailing onshore winds move it from the berm to the dunes. The berm moderates winter losses by providing a reservoir of sand available to either dunes or beach as

needed. During storms most of the berm may be removed by the ocean, at which time the dunes slump onto the beach to replenish the lost sand.

The unaltered beach system can meet the challenge of periodic extreme storms. The initial stress of a storm is sustained by a broad beach; wave energy is rapidly exhausted as water flows between the dunes and across the islands. Very strong storm forces may succeed in eroding the beach face and the primary dunes, whereupon the secondary dune takes the brunt or, in a narrow overwash island, waves, sand, and shells may be carried completely across the island.[9] This is clearly no place to build a permanent structure.

The fragile network of vegetation growing on shifting dunes is adapted to withstanding the rigors of wind, sand, and salt, but not of human feet, vehicles, or grazing animals. When the mantle of vegetation is broken, the dune movement is accelerated to a point where plant growth cannot keep pace with the shifting sand. The result is a chain reaction that leads to erosion and loss of the shifting frontal dune.

In summary, dunes are enormously valuable and fragile. They should not be altered in any way. Dunes should be set aside for preservation and encompassed by as broad a buffer area as necessary to allow for their movement and to protect them and the larger system of which they are an integral part.

Implementation No. 1. Land-Use Regulations for Beachfronts

Land-use regulations should be implemented to prohibit development in the frontal dune and beach area.

To preserve the natural beach profile, roads, buildings, utilities, and other permanent structures should be prohibited in the frontal dune area. The mining of dunes for sand should also be completely banned.

Figure 6.36 Complex patterns of "snow fencing" are often used to rehabilitate dunes. (Photo by H. R. Slayback, U.S. Department of Agriculture, Soil Conservation Service.)

These measures will require a local land-use plan and adherence to federal flood insurance regulations. Technical expertise will be needed to identify unstable dune areas from storms and sea level rise. In all instances it should be realized that the dune system is the key to storm protection for shore areas and that both the berm and the frontal dune are inherently unstable and subject to frequent change.

Setbacks

The regulations promulgated by the U.S. Department of Housing and Urban Development (HUD) under the U.S. Flood Disaster Protection Act of 1973 specifically require communities to enforce land-use and building regulations in coastal "erosion-prone" areas. The purpose is to preserve the immediate shorefront, dunes, and upper beach[20] and to protect life and property. The HUD regulations for coastal erosion areas require a building setback to allow for a "safety buffer consisting of a natural vegetative or contour strip" between the beach and any structures. The buffer area is to be designated by HUD, not the community. The width of the buffer area should be based on the "useful life" of structures[6] and "the geologic, hydrologic, topographic, and climate characteristics of the community's land." Other HUD regulations (1) prohibit the use of fill in coastal "high-hazard" areas, those subject to storm-driven high-velocity waters, defined as having velocities in excess of 3 miles per hour (4.8 kilometers per hour); and (2) require houses to be built with the first floor above the 100-year flood height in coastal floodprone areas.

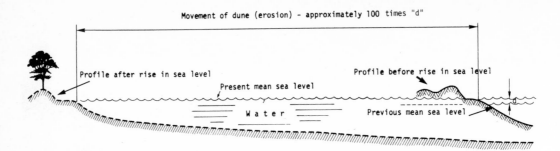

Figure 6.37   Recession of beachfront in response to a relative rise in sea level, with an average shore slope of 1 percent (Bogue Banks, North Carolina). The beach recedes a distance 100 times the increase in the height of sea level. (SOURCE: Reference 7.)

Many states and some communities already have dune setbacks or beach laws. For example, in Texas the state controls beach use up to "the line of vegetation."[21] In North Carolina, South Carolina, and Georgia, state law encourages communities to protect dunes with setback lines. The state of Florida is gradually establishing individually surveyed setback lines for each coastal community, based on topography, erodability, storm size, wave runup, vegetation, and other technical data, including beach slope.[22, 23] Until setback lines are designated for a Florida county by the state, builders are required to stay 50 feet (15 meters) back of the beach vegetation line (The setback may have to be greater for high-rise structures than for low ones because wind reflection from high structures can disturb the balance of dunes.) A setback line should be entirely landward of the shifting frontal dune system. Moreover, the line should be far enough landward to allow for predictable recession of the beach. We suggest that the beach and dune system be surveyed to establish a "50-year recession line"—the limit of expected recession and consequent landward movement of the frontal dune in a period of 50 years—to be designated as a setback line. This approach assumes a "useful length of life" of a structure of 50 years. For significantly receding beaches, new recession lines may have to be

established periodically. Buildings and other structures should be placed behind the 50-year recession line. Existing structures seaward of the recession line should be designated as non-conforming uses.

A recession line to govern the setback distances is important wherever a beach is receding significantly from erosive forces. The influence can be expected along most beaches during times of rising sea level because the effect of increased sea height is to force the beach inland as the shore profile adjusts to equilibrium (Figure 6.37). Many coasts of the world, including those of the United States, have been undergoing long-term increases in relative sea level. For example, the increase for United States coasts has averaged about 2 inches (5 centimeters) in the past 35 years, a rate of 0.5

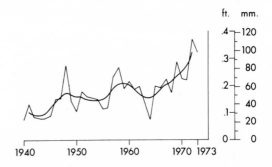

Figure 6.38   Average rise in sea level (series and curve) for the United States (except Alaska and Hawaii). (SOURCE. Reference 23.)

foot (15.25 centimeters) per century (Figure 6.38). This is sufficient to have caused serious recession along many miles of United States beachfront that have unfortunate combinations of slope and wave energy re-

Table 6.10   Apparent secular trends in sea level for the United States. Positive (rising) unless indicated by (−). (SOURCE: Modified from Reference 24)

Northeast Coast	Change in Sea Level	
	(cm/ decade)	(ft/ century)
Portland, Me.	1.62	0.53
Portsmouth, N.H.	1.65	0.54
Boston, Mass.	1.07	0.35
Woods Hole, Mass.	2.68	0.88
New London, Conn.	2.29	0.75
New York City	2.87	0.94
Sandy Hook, N.J.	4.57	1.50
Atlantic City, N.J.	2.83	0.93
Annapolis, Md.	2.87	0.94
Hampton Roads, Va.	3.20	1.05

Southeast and Gulf Coast	Change in Sea Level	
	(cm/ decade)	(ft/ century)
Charleston, S.C.	1.80	0.59
Fort Pulaski, Ga.	1.98	0.65
Fernandina, Fla.	1.25	0.41
Mayport, Fla.	1.55	0.49
Miami Beach, Fla.	1.92	0.63
Key West, Fla.	0.73	0.24
Pensacola, Fla.	0.40	0.13
Eugene Is., La.	9.05	2.97
Galveston, Tex.	4.30	1.41

West Coast	Change in Sea Level	
	(cm/ decade)	(ft/ century)
Juneau, Alaska	−13.05	−4.28
Sitka, Alaska	− 2.04	−0.67
Ketchinkan, Alaska	0.30	0.10
Seattle, Wash.	2.59	0.95
Astoria, Ore.	− 0.91	−0.29
Crescent City, Calif.	− 1.34	−0.44
San Francisco, Calif.	1.92	0.63
Los Angeles, Calif.	0.43	0.14
La Jolla, Calif.	1.92	0.63
San Diego, Calif.	1.43	0.47

gime. The particular sections of coast that have suffered much higher than average sea level increases have usually experienced the greatest recession of the beachfront. In some coastal areas, such as Galveston, Texas, recent rates of increase have been more than 1.4 feet (43 centimeters) per century (Table 6.10).

The combination of natural sea level rise and storm forces is sufficient to move whole barrier islands inland through a rollover process, that is, the washover of sand from the ocean beach onto the estuarine shore on the back side of the island (see page 572).[8]

Nonconforming Use

The existence of buildings and roads now in place that do not conform to good practice should not impede the development of a long-term shore protection program based on preserving the beach profile. These existing buildings, utilities, and roads should all be identified as nonconforming uses and be scheduled for removal or correction at the earliest opportunity (page 338). Expansion or improvement should be prohibited, and only basic maintenance should be allowed. When the structure is substantially damaged by storm or erosion, it should be moved to or rebuilt in a conformance area (Figure 6.39). Other opportunities for removal or correction may come at the end of the useful (economic) life of the structure or with community purchase of the interest. Suitable insurance or loss control provisions will be necessary to protect the owner's investment.

Implementation No. 2.   Dune Traffic Prohibition

Vehicle and foot traffic over the frontal dune system should be restricted.

Even slight alterations of dune formations, such as minor erosion or displacement of vegetation, may lead to significant disruption. Once the frontal dune is worn down by

Figure 6.39 Structures in beachfront hazard zones should be identified as nonconforming uses and terminated when significantly damaged by storm. (Photo courtesy of Frederick Wilson, Wilson Publishing Company, Wakefield, Rhode Island.)

Figure 6.40 Simple walkways over dunes protect the vegetation and help to stabilize beachfronts (Sanibel Island, Florida). (Photo by author.)

vehicles or foot traffic or by consequent loss of vegetation, it may be eroded by wind or wave action and no longer serve its unique protection role. Often the ridge of a dune is notched by a road or footpath, allowing erosive wind to funnel through the gap, causing a "blowout." During heavy winds and storms a blowout can split the dune and lead to a breakthrough that will divide a whole barrier island.

A shore protection plan should include regulations to preserve the frontal dune intact by controlling foot and vehicular traffic. Access to the beach should be limited to elevated steps and boardwalks over the dunes that allow unobstructed movement of sand beneath them (Figure 6.40), and foot traffic should be limited to these walkways. Fences should be erected to keep grazing animals off dunes. Vehicular traffic anywhere on the frontal dune system should be prohibited. Dune buggies, trail bikes, and other off-road vehicles should be restricted to the beach below the berm and to places where traffic will not interfere with other beach uses.

Vehicular access to the beach should be provided at points where dune crossing is unnecessary; temporary elevated roadways over the frontal dune may be acceptable in some circumstances.

Implementation No. 3. Beach Breeding Area Protection

Beach and dune breeding habitats should be identified and protected during critical seasons.

Many important birds, reptiles, and other animals use the dunes, berm, and open beach for nesting and breeding, as well as for feeding and resting. Areas that serve such important habitat functions should be protected, particularly breeding areas. For example, sea turtles come ashore during the spring and summer to lay their eggs above the high-water line. Terns and other seabirds frequently lay their eggs in the berm and other upper beach areas.

A survey of the nesting and breeding habits of local species that use the beach or dune is needed for the identification of specific nesting sites. Once identified, these critical habitat areas should be protected during the particular breeding and nesting seasons and regulations promulgated for keeping people out of these areas, as is practiced in England for tern protection.

REFERENCES

1. D. Frankenberg, L. R. Pomeroy, L. Bahr, and J. Richardson. 1971. "Coastal ecology and recreational development." In C. D. Clement, Ed., *The Georgia Coast: Issues and Options for Recreation*. The Conservation Foundation, Washington, D.C.

2. Stephen B. Olsen and Malcolm J. Grant. 1973. *Rhode Island's Barrier Beaches*, Vol. I: *A Report on a Management Problem and an Evaluation of Options*. Marine Technical Report No. 4, Coastal Resources Center, University of Rhode Island, Kingston, Rhode Island.

3. James P. Morgan. 1972. "Impact of subsidence and erosion on Louisiana coastal marshes and estuaries." In *Coastal Marsh and Estuary Symposium*, Louisiana State University, Baton Rouge, Louisiana.

4. U.S. Corps of Engineers. 1973. "Shore protection guidelines." In *National Shoreline Study*, Vol. I. Superintendent of Documents, U.S. Government Printing Office, Washington, D.C.

5. Lynn E. Johnson and William V. McGuinness, Jr. 1975. *Guidelines for Material Placement in Marsh Creation*. Dredged Material Research Program, U.S. Army Engineer Waterways Experiment Station, Vicksburg, Misissippi.

6. C. R. Longwell and R. F. Flint. 1962. *Introduction to Physical Geology*. John Wiley and Sons, New York. (As reprinted in Reference 5 above.)

7. Orrin H. Pilkey, Jr., Orrin H. Pilkey, Sr., and Robb Turner. 1975. *How to Live with an Island, A Handbook to Bogue Banks, North Carolina*. North Carolina Department of Natural and Economic Resources, Raleigh, North Carolina.

8. Paul J. Godfrey. 1970. *Oceanic Overwash and Its Ecological Implications on the Outer Banks of North Carolina*. U.S. Department of the Interior, National Park Service, Washington, D.C.

9. Robert Dolan. 1973. "Barrier islands: natural and controlled." In D. R. Coates, Ed., *Coastal Geomorphology*. State University of New York.

10. John R. Clark. 1974. *Coastal Ecosystems. Ecological Constraints on Coastal Development*. The Conservation Foundation, Washington, D.C.

11. Albert R. Veri et al. 1975. *Environmental Quality by Design: South Florida*. University of Miami Press, Coral Gables, Florida.

12. Michigan Department of Natural Resources. 1973. *Natural Resources: A Plan for Michigan's Shorelands*. Lansing, Michigan.

13. U.S. Army Corps of Engineers. 1973. *Shore Protection Manual*. U.S. Army Coastal Engineering Research Center, Vicksburg, Mississippi.

14. G. M. Silberhorn, G. W. Dawes, and T. A. Barnard, Jr. 1974. *Guidelines for Activities Affecting Virginia Wetlands*. Coastal Wetlands of Virginia. Virginia Institute of Marine Science, Interim Report No. 3, Gloucester Point, Virginia.

15. Louis Pinata. U.S. Army Corps of Engineers, District Engineer, New York, New York. Personal communication.

16. Robert Dolan, Paul J. Godfrey, and William E. Odum. 1973. "Man's impact on the barrier islands of North Carolina, a case study of the

implications of large-scale manipulation of the natural environment." *American Scientist*, Vol. 61 (March–April), pp. 152–162.

17. D. S. Davies, E. W. Axelrod, and J. S. O'Conner. 1974. *Erosion of the North Shore of Long Island*. Marine Sciences Research Center, Technical Report Series No. 18, State University of New York, Stony Brook, New York.

18. Robert H. Meade. 1969. *Sources of Sediments in Estuaries of the United States—A Summary of the Status of Knowledge*. Report to the Federal Water Pollution Control Administration, U.S. Geological Survey, Woods Hole, Massachusetts (preliminary unpublished manuscript).

19. John A. Jagschitz and Robert C. Wakefield. 1971. *How to Build and Save Beaches and Dunes*. Marine Leaflet Series No. 4, Agricultural Experiment Station Bulletin No. 408, University of Rhode Island, Kingston, Rhode Island.

20. Code of Federal Regulations. Title 24, Revised April 1973. Chapter X: Federal Insurance Administration; Subchapter B: National Flood Insurance Program, Section 1910.3.

21. Texas Coastal and Marine Council. *Texas Coastal Zone Legislation*. Texas Council on Marine-Related Affairs, Austin, Texas.

22. J. A. Purpura. 1972. "Establishment of a coastal setback line." In *Thirteenth International Conference on Coastal Engineering, 1972, Conference Abstracts*. The Canadian National Organizing Committee, Ottawa, Canada.

23. Steacy D Hicks and James E. Crosby. 1975. *An Average, Long-Period, Sea-Level Series for the United States*. National Oceanic and Atmospheric Administration, National Ocean Survey Program, Technical Memorandum No. 15, Rockville, Maryland.

24. S. D. Hicks. 1972. "On the classification and trends of long-period sea level series." In *Shore and Beach*, April 20–23.

4. BULKHEADS

A bulkhead is a vertical wall of wood, steel, or concrete, built parallel to the shoreline and designed to deflect waves and control erosion. The bulkheads discussed here are structures built to protect the shoreline from erosion, to serve aesthetic purposes, to provide boat-docking convenience, or to hold fill materials deposited for the conversion of low-lying land, wetlands, or water areas to real estate. We also include riprap (rock) walls and revetments used for the same purposes in protected and semiprotected waters (estuaries); these structures are assumed to have effects similar to those of bulkheads except as specifically differentiated in the following text. However, seawalls and other structures used on ocean beachfronts are discussed elsewhere (page 322).

Major environmental objections to bulkheading arise from the loss of coastal marsh and other vital habitat areas, the reduction in size of water bodies, the accompanying water pollution, and the interruption of the movement of fresh water into the estuary. The adverse impact is greatest when the outer periphery of a coastal marsh is bulkheaded and then covered with dredge spoil from the bay bottom or upland fill material in order to extend property lines to provide boat landings (page 473). In Maryland and Virginia alone, over 17 miles (27.4 kilometers) of new bulkheading and riprapping was constructed along Chesapeake Bay in 1973.[1]

The amount of vital marsh and tidal flat destroyed for real estate is often staggering. For example, 80 percent of the 300 square miles (780 square kilometers) of marshes and wetlands that rimmed San Francisco Bay has been converted or substantially altered.[2] Although the size of any one project may be modest, the accumulated losses and disturbances may be substantial.

Bulkheads to be built at or below the mean highwater line must always be approved by the U.S. Army Corps of Engineers (page 183). The Corps must consult with the U.S. Fish and Wildlife Service (and sometimes other federal agencies) concerning environmental effects (page 187). In most cases the Corps will act on a permit request only after the appropriate state authority dealing with navigational and/or environmental considerations has given its approval. The state agency often has strict environmental standards for bulkheads. Federal approval is necessary for any filling, dredging, or spoil disposal in the upper wetlands area (between mean high water and the annual floodmark; see page 183) but *not* for bulkheads per se.

Bulkheads for basic erosion control are normally acceptable provided that environmental safeguards and technical precautions are taken. But there are a number of uses for bulkheads that are unacceptable to the U.S. Fish and Wildlife Service and to many state review agencies. Bulkheads designed to allow marsh fill or water area reclamation will not receive permit approval. Aesthetic or cosmetic uses of wood or steel bulkheading are also discouraged. In addition, permits for bulkheads built as boat docks will be denied, since these structures have a much higher potential for adverse ecological impact than do pile-supported piers (page 449).[1,3]

In conformance with these federal guidelines bulkheads should be used only to protect unvegetated, eroding shorelines within the estuary. Bulkheads that are used to expand real estate acreage by filling or specifically to provide deep-water access for boats should be discouraged. If wetlands are found on the site, a bulkhead must be located at or above the annual flood line. If the shoreline is unvegetated, extension of the "toe" of the bulkhead below the mean low-water line should be permitted to prevent scouring and collapse of the structure. A Corps of Engineers permit will be required for any bulkhead below the mean high-water line and for all filling (but not necessarily for the bulkhead itself) below the annual flood line.

GUIDELINE. Bulkhead Location and Design

Locate bulkheads shoreward of all wetlands, and design them for ecological compatibility.

The most common types of protective structures in estuarine waters are wooden bulkheads and rock riprap structures. Wooden bulkheads are built of planking, pilings, and walers. They have a normal life span of 20 to 25 years, although some may last up to 50 years (Figure 6.41). For heavy-duty pur-

poses, interlocking sheet steel pilings or concrete slabs may be used where the shore is impacted by the full force of waves and boat wakes (Figure 6.42).

Riprap structures are usually built on a 2-to-1 slope and have extended lifetimes. They are constructed with the toe below the mean low-water line (Figure 6.43).

When the shore and the adjacent water body have a medium slope and are exposed to moderate wave energies, riprap may be preferred to concrete or timber structures. As long as the riprap is placed with a filter-cloth backing, it is ecologically more desirable than a vertical bulkhead because of its permeability. In its submerged lower parts, riprap also provides a greater surface area for the attachment of algae, barnacles, and other animals than the less biologically productive smooth, flat surface of a vertical bulkhead. Riprap can easily be built to conform to the natural configuration of the shoreline. Riprap structures are less expensive than concrete and are often comparable in price to wooden bulkheads.[1]

Although the details of construction and the variety of alternatives of design and location are extensive, the principles concerning shore and bank protection are relatively few and simple. First, whenever possible the existing shoreline should be preserved with natural erosion protection measures such as planted marsh grasses, rather than structures. Second, bulkheads should not distrupt the outward flow of ground water or runoff. Third, structures should not intrude into wetlands or other vital habitat areas; that is, they should be placed behind the line of annual flooding, which marks the inner edge of the coastal wetlands (page 247 et seq.).

Implementation No. 1. Natural Protection

Natural methods of erosion protection such as the planting of wetland vegetation should be encouraged.

In many cases eroded shores and banks can be stabilized by grading the shoreline and

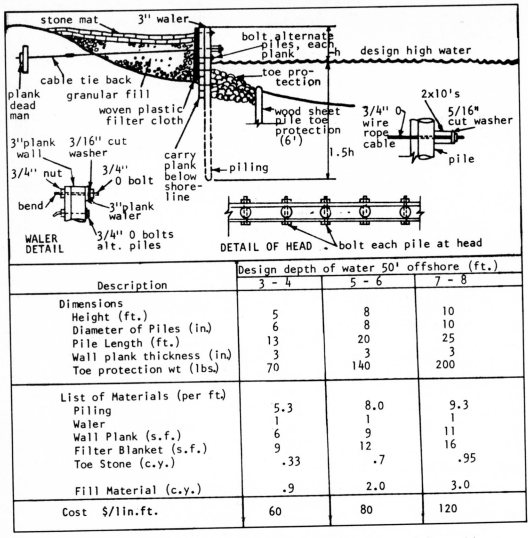

Description	Design depth of water 50' offshore (ft.)		
	3 - 4	5 - 6	7 - 8
Dimensions			
Height (ft.)	5	8	10
Diameter of Piles (in.)	6	8	10
Pile Length (ft.)	13	20	25
Wall plank thickness (in.)	3	3	3
Toe protection wt (lbs.)	70	140	200
List of Materials (per ft.)			
Piling	5.3	8.0	9.3
Waler	1	1	1
Wall Plank (s.f.)	6	9	11
Filter Blanket (s.f.)	9	12	16
Toe Stone (c.y.)	.33	.7	.95
Fill Material (c.y.)	.9	2.0	3.0
Cost $/lin.ft.	60	80	120

Figure 6.41   Design details of a typical wood sheet bulkhead. (SOURCE: Reference 1.)

planting salt-marsh grasses, mangroves, or other vegetation. This artificial marsh barrier is preferable to other types of shore erosion structures and should prove to be the least expensive. It has the added benefit of creating a more biologically productive shoreline, as well as one with higher natural aesthetic appeal.

In protected water bodies where erosion rates and wave action are low, an artificial marsh may be an effective method of shoreline protection, since wave forces are ab-

sorbed and sediments are trapped by the planted vegetation. Such use of planted marsh strips has been successful in the Middle Atlantic area (Figure 6.44).

In Florida, mangrove species lend themselves well to shoreline protection and may be incorporated into plans for the protection of private waterfront property.[6] Also, mangrove species imported from the continental United States (*Rhizophora mangle*) and from the Phillippines (*Bruguiera sexangula*) were introduced into the Hawaiian Islands

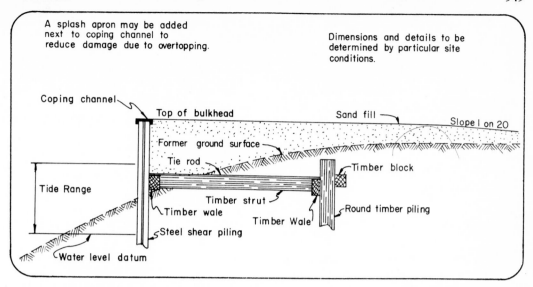

Figure 6.42 Typical sheet steel piling bulkhead. To protect coastal wetlands, bulkheads should be built at the annual flood mark, or above when the shore is vegetated. (SOURCE: Reference 4.)

for the purpose of erosion prevention. They have since become well established there and are extending their range naturally.[7]

Implementation No. 2. Location of Bulkheads

Bulkheads or similar protective structures should be built above the annual flood mark in wetland areas.

There are a number of reasons to require that bulkheads be built above the annual flood mark (Figure 6.45). By definition (page 147) coastal wetlands that should remain undisturbed lie below this level (Figure 6.46). In addition, bulkheads that extend into water areas often adversely alter water circulation, increase scouring of the bottom, reduce the surface area of the estuary, and preempt such vital habitat areas as tideflats and shellfish beds, in addition to marshes (Figure 6.47).

A permitted exception to the requirement of building bulkheads behind the annual flood line is the bare shoreline, one that has not supported vegetation and cannot do so in the future. Erosion is typically severe on

such shorelines, and stabilization is often clearly needed. It is recommended that bulkheads on bare shorelines not extend outward of the mean low-water mark. Furthermore, their use should be restricted to erosion control and not for the gain of real estate acreage at the expense of vital habitats or estuarine acreage.

Enforcing these requirements may change waterfront development patterns in many coastal areas; they will essentially limit the conversion of wetlands and estuarine bottoms to real estate. However, this is essential to other initiatives to preserve coastal ecosystems. In addition, they will inhibit the use of bulkheads as boat landings and encourage the construction of piers for this purpose (page 449).

Implementation No. 3. Permeable Bulkheads

Bulkheads should be designed to be permeable to groundwater and runoff.

A critical design feature to be incorporated in bulkheads is perforation to permit the natural flow of groundwater and runoff to

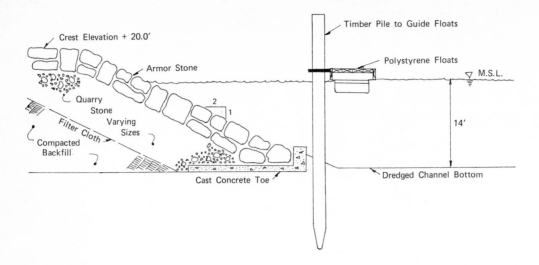

Figure 6.43 Section through riprap structure and floating dock; riprap permits the natural flow of groundwater to continue. (SOURCE: Reference 5).

Figure 6.44 Marsh grass buffer strip (shown 10 years after planting) controls shore erosion and eliminates the need for bulkheads. (Photo by Interstate Commission on the Potomac River Basin.)

Figure 6.45 Proper location of bulkheads above the annual flood line and behind marshes and other wetlands will preserve vital habitats while providing erosion and flood protection. (Photo by Thomas Barnard, Virginia Institute of Marine Science.)

Figure 6.46 The upper edge of the coastal wetlands is identifiable from debris and from vegetation that accumulates at the annual flood mark. The high marsh shown here (Wallop Island, Maryland) ends at the zone of saltbush (*Iva frutescens*) on the left. (Photo by author.)

347

Figure 6.47 Bulkheads should not be permitted to extend into marshes, tidelands, and estuarine areas to create real estate by shoreline filling (Melbourne, Florida). (Conservation Foundation photo by M. Fahay.)

pass through the structures. This supply of fresh water provides wetlands with waterborne nutrients. Also, the land above the bulkhead drains better, and soil erosion is reduced.

Wooden bulkheads should be built with "weepholes" backed with screen to allow water to pass through them. This design has the additional benefit that hydrostatic pressure from the groundwater head will be reduced, thereby decreasing the chance of structural collapse of the bulkhead.

Riprap is often the easiest and least costly technique for protection. This advantage is augmented by the high permeability of riprap and its other ecological advantages. Groundwater and runoff can move unimpeded through both the filter-cloth and the crushed-rock backings required for riprap structures (see Figure 6.43).

REFERENCES

1. Linda Gantt. *Ecological Considerations Regarding the Use of Bulkheads and Rip-rap in the Chesapeake Bay Estuary for Shore Erosion Control*. U.S. Fish and Wildlife Service Paper (unpublished).

2. U.S. Department of the Interior. 1970. *The U.S. Senate, 91st Congress, 2nd Session, National Estuarine Pollution Study*. Document No. 91-58. Superintendent of Documents, U.S. Government Printing Office, Washington, D.C.

3. U.S. Fish and Wildlife Service. 1975. "Guidelines for review of fish and wildlife aspects of proposals in or affecting navigable waters." U.S. Department of the Interior, *Federal Register*, Vol. 40, No. 231, Part IV (Dec. 1).

4. U.S. Corps of Engineers. 1971. "Shore protection guidelines." In *National Shoreline Study*, Vol. I. Superintendent of Documents, U.S. Government Printing Office, Washington, D.C.

5. Steven P. Giannio and Hsiang Wange. 1974. *Engineering Considerations for Marinas in Tidal Marshes*. College of Marine Studies, University of Delaware, Newark, Delaware.

6. T. Savage. 1972. *Florida Mangroves as Shoreline Stabilizers*. Florida Department of Natural Resources, Professional Paper Series No. 19, St. Petersburg, Florida.

7. H. T. Odum, B. J. Copeland, and E. A. McMahan. 1974. *Coastal Ecological Systems of the United States*, Vol. 1. The Conservation Foundation Washington, D.C. p. 369.

8. Courtland A. Collier. 1975. *Seawall and Revetment Effectiveness, Cost and Construction*. Report No. 6, Florida State Sea Grant Program, Gainesville, Florida.

5. DAMS AND WATER DIVERSIONS

Management of coastal ecosystems is largely a matter of maintaining the condition of the natural water system. To be effective, the natural pattern of freshwater input from rivers—a dominant ecological influence in much of the estuarine environment—must be preserved. Therefore management of the water supply to coastal basins must often extend to river segments upstream and to watersheds beyond the coastal district.

Dams (and the impoundments they create) are built to provide flood control, water supply, irrigation, hydroelectric power, recreation, and navigation benefits. To achieve these ends they store a given volume of water and regulate its release. Impoundments—reservoirs or artificial lakes created when dams or diversion projects block the flow of a river—vary in size from a few hundred acres to tens of thousands of acres. Water diversions reroute the water flow to areas outside the natural channel or even outside the watershed.

Dam and diversion projects involve the purposeful change of a stream's discharge pattern by altering one or more of its flow parameters: volume, rate, timing, direction, and quality. Such alterations of the pattern of freshwater input may interfere with a coastal ecosystem by causing changes in water circulation, salinity balance, sediment transport, flushing rate, or the natural supply of nutrients from upstream. Such changes affect the physical makeup of the estuarine zone, its energy flows and the plant and animal life.

Large water control projects have the potential for serious disturbance of coastal systems even when they are located well inland and upstream of tidal influence (Figure 6.48). For example, a proposal by the U.S. Army Corps of Engineers to construct a series of dams extending far up the Appalachicola River (Florida) was shown to have the potential to severely alter the salinity and temperature regime below the river mouth in Appalachicola Bay, to interrupt shad and striped bass migrations upriver, and to reduce the general productivity of Appalachicola Bay and its fisheries.[2]

Construction of dams in tidewater areas can have particularly severe effects on the productivity of coastal systems. In Texas the proposed 10-foot-high Wallisville Barrier Dam would cut Trinity Bay off from the Trinity River and would inundate 12,000 acres of productive coastal salt marshes with fresh water, cutting them off from the bay ecosystem. In its natural state the marsh is a nursery area for 59 estuarine-dependent species of fish and shellfish. Studies suggest that, by eliminating the marsh, the dam would cause an annual loss of 7 million tons of commercial fish, seriously reduce sportfishing, and generally interfere with the productivity of the estuary (see Article 10, Chapter 7).

Water control implements trap sediment. Even a small dike can trap an appreciable portion of a river's sediment; an impoundment that holds only 1 percent of the yearly flow of a river is capable of trapping nearly half its yearly sediment load. Although a river bed will tend to erode below an impoundment (in partial compensation for the lost sediment), the net effect is to decrease the overall amount of sediment carried downriver. In the larger rivers of Georgia and the Carolinas, the nutrient-rich sediment loads delivered to the estuaries are now only about one-third of what they were in 1910, mainly because of large numbers of dams built for hydroelectric power and, to a lesser extent, for flood control.[3]

GUIDELINE. Water Management Program Design

Design the water management program to preserve existing water quality, volume, and rate of flow.

The impacts of water control projects are as complex and interrelated as the coastal eco-

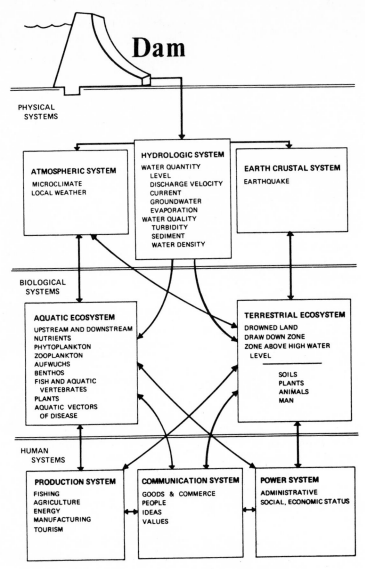

Figure 6.48 Dams have the potential for large-scale ecological disturbance. (SOURCE: Reference 1.)

systems they affect. Limiting adverse impacts requires designing, building, and operating a system that either maintains or simulates the natural characteristics of the freshwater supply to estuaries—the quality, volume, rate, and timing of the water flow. The approaches to the achievement of optimum freshwater flow should be both structural and nonstructural.

Alteration of estuarine salinity balance by an increase or reduction of fresh water is a matter of particular concern wherever it occurs. Estuarine waters are areas where seawater is continually diluted by fresh water from rivers and streams. The whole variety of estuarine life is adjusted to the pattern of decreasing salinity from the ocean through the bays and into tidal rivers. A long-term increase in fresh water, by input from another watershed (interbasin transfer), can overwhelm a small estuary, turning it into a virtual lake. A long-term net reduction in

fresh water essentially shrinks the most productive part of the estuary, the brackish
middle to upper part, and may seriously reduce its capacity to support life. Freshwater
reduction is usually irreversible when the
water is committed to other uses or basins.

Even if the volume remains the same over
the year, a significant change in the natural
timing, or rhythm, of stream flow disrupts
salinity-related functions of species that are
tuned to this rhythm, such as breeding,
migration, defense against predators, and
feeding. In short, the estuarine ecosystem is
closely tuned to a certain salinity pattern
that should be maintained by effective management of freshwater inflow (Figure 6.49).

Water management projects must provide for the survival requirements of fish and
other marine life. It is common for coastal
streams to have runs of anadromous fish
(fish that migrate in from the sea to spawn)
such as salmon, herrings, striped bass, and
shad. Alteration of the daily, seasonal, or
annual stream flow cycles may severely disrupt these movements. River structures that
block the migration routes of anadromous
fish seriously interfere with their breeding
potential. For example, over 60 percent of
the river line spawning grounds for salmon
and steelhead in the Pacific Northwest has
been cut off by the construction of high
dams. Moreover, hydroelectric dams may
destroy large numbers of the newly spawned
fish moving downstream to the ocean as they

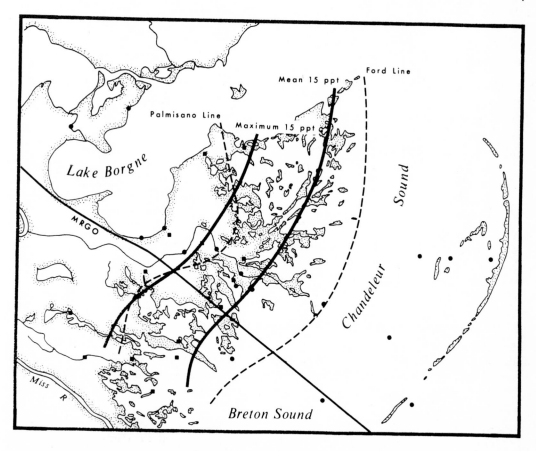

Figure 6.49   The proposed minimum inshore (Palmisano) and maximum offshore (Ford) 50 percent dilution lines of seawater with fresh water (dotted), and the historically observed 50 percent dilution lines
(15 ppt = 15 parts per thousand of salt in water). (SOURCE: Reference 4.)

pass through the turbines (Article 10, Chapter 7).

Impoundment-caused loss of sediment to the estuarine zone has two potentially serious consequences. First, the dynamic balance of ocean beaches may be upset by loss of the sand supplied to them by rivers; the result is that the beach diminishes and the shoreline recedes (page 634). Furthermore, a valuable nutrient supply to coastal waters may be trapped with sediments behind the dam, thus reducing potential overall productivity. For example, blockage of nutrients by the Aswan Dam in Egypt so diminished the productivity of the eastern Mediterranean Sea that the Egyptian sardine fishery was ruined; output dropped by about 18,000 tons annually (Article 10, Chapter 7).

Implementation No. 1. Nonstructural Freshwater Management

Nonstructural solutions for controlling freshwater flow should be used to the maximum extent possible.

In developing water resources, alternative management provisions should be found whenever possible for water diversions that have a significant adverse impact on coastal ecosystems. Interbasin transfers—diverting water from one channel of a basin and transferring it to another—are particularly disturbing because they may deprive the first ecosystem of needed freshwater inflow and may oversupply the second. For example, a proposed expansion of a large diversion and interbasin transfer project on the Sacramento River was found likely to cause intrusion of salt water far up the Sacramento–San Joaquin delta area and reduction of the San Francisco Bay flushing rate.[5] The project would deplete San Francisco Bay striped bass stocks in two ways: (1) removal of masses of suspended striped bass larvae with the river water, and (2) reduction of the brackish nursery area. Some combination of these effects had already reduced the striped

bass population in the bay 50 percent by the early 1970s.[6] Diversions, to be acceptable, should normally take place upstream from spawning and nursery areas of estuarine-dependent fish, and the water should also be returned to the river above such areas.

Both federal and state laws require that fish, wildlife, and other environmental values be thoroughly considered and provided for in the planning and execution of public water control projects. Depending on jurisdiction, regional river basin commissions, water and sewer authorities, public utility commissions, and county and municipal agencies are all involved in planning or permit processes for water control works. They can also be moved to use their respective influences in seeing that the quality, volume, and flow rates of watercourses are maintained.

In all water management programs, planning and design of the dam or diversion should be based on a thorough knowledge of the hydrology of the drainage basin involved. Data should include precipitation patterns, soils, slopes, vegetation, stream flows, and land-use patterns. From analysis of this information, the existing natural conditions, alternative options, and control measures can be determined for maintaining or restoring the stream flow pattern.

Nonstructural maintenance of the integrity of natural stream flows stresses the achievement of water control by means other than dams. All proposals for water control structures must be scrutinized closely, and the effects on coastal ecosystems assessed for all upstream water control and diversion projects. In some cases impoundment or diversion of water may be found to be unnecessary or not in the public interest when environmental effects are taken into account. Structural projects should be avoided when suitable alternatives are available. For example, the need for dams as flood control measures can be reduced by prescribing land uses that retain flood volumes and protect water quality for floodplain areas (page 202).

Figure 6.50   Water control structures can restore watershed discharges to nearly the original flow rates. (Photo by B. Yokel, The Rookery Bay Marine Laboratory.)

As much floodplain land as possible, including cropland, should have constant plant cover growth to reduce runoff volumes by soaking up excess waters, and to protect soils from erosion.

When structural projects are necessary, every attempt should be made to correct existing ecosystem imbalances. For example, flows from altered watersheds—where land clearing, paving, and agriculture have reduced the ability of the land to retain water and release it slowly—typically have exaggerated high and low peaks that the water control project can reduce. In these watersheds the structural project should take the opportunity to recreate the flow conditions that prevailed before watershed alterations, perhaps by using a series of dams, control gates, or regularly timed water releases (Figure 6.50).

For guaranteeing the delivery of fresh water to the estuary and preventing wide oscillations in the salinity levels, (1) the unnatural surge peaks should be reduced by storage, and (2) the minimum flow in the dry season should not be allowed to fall below the level of the dry-season low flows that prevailed under natural conditions. Although most important fish and shellfish can tolerate a marked change in salinity for a period of minutes or hours, they cannot survive a major change for more extended periods of time. Species with strong swimming ability can avoid unfavorable zones and seek preferred salinities elsewhere in the region (if available), but sessile forms, such as oysters, cannot avoid adverse conditions. Consequently, if the salinity of an area (such as a mixing zone) is shifted outside the tolerance range of the indigenous species, these species will be eliminated from the area under consideration.[7] As a rule, the salinity should not be allowed to vary more than ± 10 percent from the natural regimen; otherwise the production of valuable bottom organisms, such as oysters and clams, will greatly diminish.[8]

Flow maintenance is also important to migrating fish so that they are not stopped by an insufficient water level in the river basin. Withdrawal from the storage impoundment may need to be curtailed in dry seasons if it holds less than enough water to meet both minimum ecosystem needs and desired withdrawal amounts.

River structures that block the migration routes of anadromous (and catadromous) fish seriously interfere with their breeding potentials. For example, a dam on the lower Susquehanna River (Maryland) blocked shad from going upstream to spawn and has cut back the spawning area of striped bass.[9] Before such dams are approved, fish passages (ladders) of proved effectiveness should be designed for installation. Dams also interfere with the movements of marine fish species, such as croaker, menhaden, sea trout, and spot, which migrate inshore to spend a few months in the lower, tidally influenced reaches of coastal rivers where food is plentiful and predators scarce. It is important that dams, intakes, and the like not be built across these tidal reaches.

REFERENCES

1. Karl F. Lagler. 1973. "Ecological effects of hydroelectric dams." In *Impact of Water Resources Development*. Environment Information Center, New York.

2. Robert J. Livingston. 1975. *Resource Management and Estuarine Function with Application to the Appalachicola Drainage System (North Florida, U.S.A.)*. Florida State University, Tallahassee, Florida.

3. J. R. Schubel and Robert H. Meade. *Man's Impact on Estuarine Sedimentation* (unpublished manuscript).

4. Sherwood M. Gagliano, Phillip Light, and Ronald E. Becker. 1973. *Controlled Diversions in the Mississippi Delta System: An Approach to Environmental Management*. Hydrologic and Geologic Studies of Coastal Louisiana, Report No. 8, Center for Wetland Resources, Lousiana State University, Baton Rouge, Louisiana.

5. Robert M. Hagan and Edwin B. Roberts. 1972. "Ecological impacts of water projects in California." *Journal of the Irrigation and Drainage Division*, ASCE, Vol. 98, No. IRI, Proc. Paper 8780.

6. H. K. Chadwick. 1972. Letter from California Fish and Game Department to P. Issakson, New York Public Service Commission. In *Transcript of A.E.C. Licensing Board Hearings on Indian Point Nuclear Plant No. 2* (unpublished).

7. U.S. Atomic Energy Commission. 1973. *General Environmental Siting Guides for Nuclear Power Plants* (draft).

8. National Technical Advisory Commission. 1968. *Water Quality Criteria*. Report to the Secretary of the Interior, Federal Water Pollution Control Administration, Washington, D.C.

9. Eugene Cronin. 1967. "The role of man in estuarine processes." In G. H. Lauff, Ed., *Estuaries*. American Association for the Advancement of Science, Publication No. 83, Washington, D.C.

6. ESTUARINE FLOOD PROTECTION

Growth trends in coastal land use and marine resources use in the United States have been accompanied by serious impacts on natural systems, including systems needed for sound coastal floodplain management. There are high concentrations of people living in coastal areas. Well over half of the United States population now lives in counties, cities, towns, and villages within 50 miles of the seacoast. Where such population concentrations occur, there is high demand for coastal properties.

Management goals for the protection of life and property against coastal storms and flooding are remarkably similar to those for the conservation of coastal environments and natural resources. Both are concerned primarily with water systems and water-based biophysical resources. Effective community programs of coastal floodplain management should include recognition of the compatibility of floodplain management goals with those for the management of environment and natural resources.

Estuarine flood protection, as it is discussed here, includes programs for shorelands adjacent to estuarine water bodies— bays and other enclosed basins where tidal inundation from rising water level, rather than wave action, is the principal threat.

The special problems of storm protection on open ocean beaches, where wave velocity and erosion are the principal threats, are considered in the section on beachfronts (page 318).

Many natural factors contribute to serious coastal flooding problems, including barometric pressure, shoreline configuration, tides, winds, and water depths. Storm-caused sea level rises are associated with such severe weather disturbances as hurricanes and winter "northeasters." The frequency of such storms is surprisingly high in many areas. For example, between 1900 and 1960 Florida alone experienced 117 severe tropical storms, 43 of which reached hurricane force (winds exceeding 74 mph). Of the 60 years between 1900 and 1960, only 11 were without hurricanes or severe tropical depressions; the longest continuous period with no hurricane was 4 years.[1]

The danger to life and property from estuarine flooding is exacerbated by the intensity of development in the coastal zone. Mounting flood losses can be expected when new residential, commercial, and industrial uses are located in floodprone estuarine shoreland sites. To illustrate the danger of flooding, a U.S. Army Corps of Engineers study reported that 75 percent of all loss of life in Florida hurricanes has been due to tidal inundations. Moreover, very few Florida coastal communities were located on land high enough to escape partial flooding during a severe hurricane. The study found that a 10-foot storm tide would flood 50 percent of the coastal areas developed on land less than 20 feet above sea level—and in the Florida Keys would flood 90 percent of the land area.[2] Furthermore, because of the unusual absence of major hurricanes in the late 1960s and early 1970s a false sense of security has led to the construction of many new homes in floodprone estuarine areas.

It has become increasingly evident in recent years that the means of preventing flood losses lies in nonstructural floodplain management rather than in the construction of flood control structures. Structural solutions have been the core of the federally directed flood protection program since 1936. The failure of this program to protect the nation from flood losses is apparent from the accelerating annual cost of federal disaster relief—from $52 million in 1953 to $2.5 billion in 1973.[3] About 85 percent of those expenditures resulted from flood losses.

Much of the loss of life and property is attributable to the false confidence inspired by control structures that ultimately failed. The complacency that these structures stimulate gives strong impetus to development in floodprone areas which otherwise might be left uninhabited.

The trend now is toward floodplain management systems that discourage occupancy of floodprone areas, and control land use and construction in ways to protect life and property without reliance on structures. In general, areas that are flooded every few years should be reserved for uses which do not expose life and property to risk. Some recommended uses include recreation, open space, wildlife habitat, shelter belts, buffer strips, nonresidential recreational structures, and scientifically controlled silviculture (Figure 6.51).

The Government Role

Regulation of the use of floodplain lands is a responsibility of state and local governments. A variety of means is available to guide and regulate people's use of floodplains to lessen the adverse effects of floods. These may include establishment of floodplain zoning ordinances, subdivision regulations, and building codes. The following example of recommended potential types of control is given for the purpose of critical evaluation.

1. Building codes that specify construction standards to withstand wind stresses and anchoring to prevent flotation, define minimum flood protection elevations for

Figure 6.51 Lower floodplain areas should be left undeveloped as shoreline buffer strips. (Photo from New Jersey Department of Environmental Protection.)

coastal structures (Figure 6.52), and establish structural floodproofing standards.

2. Zoning regulations that define minimum protection elevations for buildings and services in coastal low-hazard areas, and stringently restrict uses in coastal high-hazard areas subject to severe erosion or wave action damage.

3. Subdivision regulations that prohibit subdivision of coastal flood- and erosion-hazard areas unless the flood threat is overcome and the lands are suitably conditioned through placement of fill for building sites, bulkheading, construction of seawalls, construction of erosion control structures, or other techniques (see page 233).

4. Miscellaneous regulations such as dune protection ordinances, ordinances to protect natural storm beaches (see page 240), ordinances controlling seawall construction and bulkheading (see pages 240 and 342), ordinances defining structural setbacks from the water line, special coastal conservancy zoning, and sanitary codes.

The engineering solutions listed in the above—seawalls, anchoring, erosion control structures—are typical of approaches to flood protection that often lull property owners and community officials into a false sense of security while possibly actually heightening the risk from large storms. The nonstructural solutions listed above, such as zoning and setbacks, are better approaches in most situations (page 234).

For bringing future order to floodprone estuarine shorelands already endangered by occupancy, nonconforming use regulations are an important long-term tool. Under this plan each nonconforming structure is phased out at an opportune time. This concept also may be applied to purposes other than estuarine shorelands flood protection, for example, beach and dune protection (page 338).

It is clear that the building codes and regulations typically in use throughout the nation do not contain the necessary special requirements, limitations, or design and construction restrictions to provide flood protection for structures located in flood-hazard areas and susceptible to flood damage. This general shortcoming has been verified in a review of the subject by the U.S. Army Corps of Engineers.[5] One result is that the National Flood Insurance Program, as revised by the Flood Disaster Protection Act of 1973, directs the Department of Housing and Urban Development (HUD) to require that communities implement effective building standards as a condition for flood insurance eligibility.[1] The HUD program also requires each community with floodprone land to establish a minimum floodplain management program aimed at decreasing flood losses—reduced occupancy of flood prone areas is one goal of the program. If appropriate controls are not implemented by the community within a reasonable time, federal or federally related sources of all building or development funds to the community can be withheld for all construction in floodprone areas, including most mortgage loans from banks.

Flood insurance, not previously available from private insurance companies, is made available by the National Flood Insurance Program at reasonable rates through a joint government–industry program. To receive this low cost protection for life and property, communities must adopt floodplain man-

Figure 6.52   Houses in coastal floodplains must be elevated above the 100-year flood level. (Photo by author.)

agement regulations consistent with federal criteria to reduce or avoid flooding in connection with future construction in floodplain areas.[1] Although local communities should be encouraged to set even higher standards, they may not establish lesser ones if they wish to participate in the federal program. For details on the National Flood Insurance Program see Appendix, page 790.

In no small measure the importance of the indemnification, financing, and flood-plain management requirements could strongly influence the course of coastal zone development. Through combinations of economic incentives and disincentives, and through the minimum floodplain management requirements for maintaining community eligibility, the National Flood Insurance Program stands as a strong potential force to reduce ever-mounting property losses from coastal storm and flood damage by using environmentally sound management techniques.

There is, however, some evidence that the availability of flood insurance in coastal areas may work as a counterforce to sound floodplain management.[6] Studies for the New England River Basins Commission show that flood insurance reduces the financial risk of property owners from storm flood damage.[7] Banks that formerly took no mortgages on shorefront risk properties now appear willing to assume equity positions of 70 to 80 percent.[6] As a result development has accelerated in many coastal areas, increasing the threat of both flood damage and adverse environmental impact to dunes and wetlands resulting from physical intrusion, excavation, and artificial fill.

GUIDELINE. Integrated Flood and
Ecosystem Management

Combine and integrate estuarine floodplain management and ecosystem management programs.

Many federal, state, and local programs for floodplains and coastal environment protection are closely related to the goals of the National Flood Insurance Program. These include wetlands management, surface and groundwater quality, construction and operation of sewage treatment facilities, coastal excavation and filling, coastal zone management, power plant siting, and endangered species. Many of our coastal states have enacted regulatory measures relevant to coastal floodplain management and environmental protection programs (see Chapter 5, page 230).

Because the approaches to flood protection and to environmental management are so closely in accord with one another, local officials should make every effort to integrate ecosystem protection measures with provisions for protection against floods. Many coastal communities will recognize the advantage of coordinated management responses to floodplains and environment; and once they have information and methodologies readily and economically available to them, they can plan and implement such management programs (page 230).

Nassau and Suffolk counties, New York, may serve as a model to suggest the relevance of 25 regulatory techniques to conditions found on Long Island, most of which are directly germane to coastal floodplain management. Zones of concern for which definitions and regulations are given under the authority of the Flood Disaster Protection Act include the following:

1. "Erosion areas" or "erosion prone areas," which include the "land area adjoining the shore of a lake or other body of water which due to the composition of the shoreline or bank and high-water level or wind-driven currents is likely to suffer flood-related erosion damage."

2. "Coastal high-hazard areas," meaning "the portion of a floodplain having special flood hazards that is subject to high velocity waters, including hurricane wave wash and tsunamis."

3. "Floodplains" or "floodprone areas," including "any normally dry land area that

is susceptible to being inundated by water from any source."

It is the third of these, floodprone areas, that form the particular subject of this discussion. The land-use requirements and structural standards for flood protection in these areas are remarkably similar to certain requirements for coastal ecosystem protection.[9] For example, the lower floodplains are areas of critical ecological concern wherein certain activities have high potentials for pollution of coastal waters. Also, the wetland parts of the floodplains are vital habitat areas that should be preserved. For the protection of life and property, flood regulations would exclude much development in such areas and would require special structural adaptations for any buildings that might be put there (Figure 6.53).

If, as consistently recommended herein, the use of wetlands is limited to light-duty recreational structures elevated above flood heights, such structures can easily conform to the management standard of the National Flood Insurance Program that every residential or nonresidential structure be elevated so as to raise the lowest floor to a level equal to or above the level of the 100-year flood. In estuarine shoreland areas this would be normally accomplished by elevating houses on pilings. This measure is consistent with good wetlands management practice, since it minimizes the possibility of interference with surface water and groundwater flow and makes excavation for fill unnecessary.

When development has already encroached upon floodprone estuarine shorelands, any structures now in place that do not conform to good practice should be designated as "nonconforming" uses. Their existence should not stand in the way of formulating a proper long-term floodplain management plan (see page 357). Any structures identified as nonconforming would be scheduled for removal or correction at the earliest opportunity. Expansion or major rehabilitation would not be allowed; only maintenance would be permitted. The opportunity for discontinuance might come when the economic viability of a structure ended or when public or private financing enabled the community to purchase the interest and end the use. Occupancy certainly would be discontinued after a major storm disaster that caused extensive damage (amounting to 50 percent or whatever standard percentage loss of value was used by the community for such purposes). A suitable arrangement for indemnification of loss would be necessary to protect the owner's investment. (A sample nonconforming use regulation appears on page 843 of the Appendix.)

Implementation No. 1. Estuarine Shoreline Setbacks

All structures on estuarine shores should be set back of the annual flood line.

Flooding of low-lying coastal lands becomes a problem only when man occupies them. In fulfilling the urge to live as close to the water as possible, we have been forced, as a nation, to cope with loss of life and property by storm and flood forces and to recognize the need for limitations on shoreline development. In addition to life and property risks, development in these areas has also resulted in major degradation of coastal water bodies and ecologically vital habitat areas. To minimize both of those losses, a setback line for future development should be established behind the annual flood mark (at the highest level to which the water may be expected to rise during a year), which forms the inner edge of estuarine wetlands (page 147). The setback line should be drawn at least as far inland from the present annual flood mark as one can predict it will rise on the land in the next 50-year period (a nominal length of economic life projection for structures) because of rising sea level or land subsidence (see page 338 for a detailed analysis).

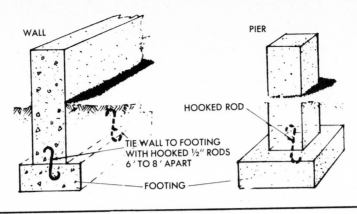

WALL

PIER

HOOKED ROD

TIE WALL TO FOOTING
WITH HOOKED ½" RODS
6' TO 8' APART

FOOTING

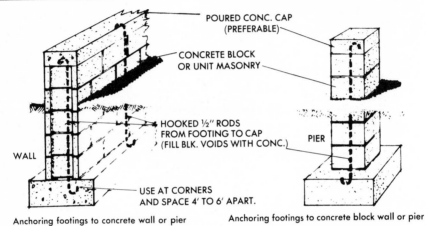

POURED CONC. CAP
(PREFERABLE)

CONCRETE BLOCK
OR UNIT MASONRY

HOOKED ½" RODS
FROM FOOTING TO CAP
(FILL BLK. VOIDS WITH CONC.)

PIER

WALL

USE AT CORNERS
AND SPACE 4' TO 6' APART.

Anchoring footings to concrete wall or pier   Anchoring footings to concrete block wall or pier

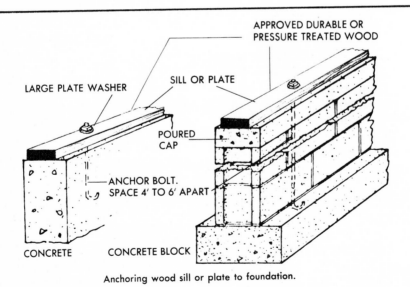

APPROVED DURABLE OR
PRESSURE TREATED WOOD

LARGE PLATE WASHER

SILL OR PLATE

POURED
CAP

ANCHOR BOLT.
SPACE 4' TO 6' APART

CONCRETE   CONCRETE BLOCK

Anchoring wood sill or plate to foundation.

Figure 6.53 Proper foundation anchorage is essential for buildings in floodprone areas. (SOURCE: Reference 10.)

360

Figure 6.54 The requirement for piling supports has generated a variety of designs in single-family homes. (Photos by author.)

Figure 6.55 Condominiums, motels, and hotels also must be elevated above the 100-year flood height. (Photo by author.)

Implementation No. 2. Elevation of Structures in Floodplains

Elevate all structures placed in estuarine floodplain areas above the 100-year flood level.

For coastal communities to comply with regulations established for the National Flood Insurance Program, they must "require new construction and substantial improvements of residential structures within the area of special flood hazards for which base flood elevations have been provided to have the lowest floor (including basement) elevated to or above the level of the 100-year flood. . . ."[1] This requirement is consistent with coastal wetlands protection to the extent that it minimizes interference with water flows and obviates the need for excavation. As discussed elsewhere in this book (page 99), all excavation and fill in wetlands should be prohibited. Also, wetlands construction should be restricted to light-duty structures not used for permanent occupancy; the wetlands should not be significantly altered.

Piling-supported structures are a familiar feature in many coastal areas and provide proved protection against flood damage (Figures 6.54 and 6.55), especially when tie-downs are installed (Figure 6.56). The additional cost over that of grade-level construction is estimated (in certain parts of Florida) at 7 to 10 percent.[12] However, the cost for additional dirt fill to reach the regulated height, if this were permitted, could run from 5 to 10 percent. Moreover, the ground level area under the first floor has value for car parking and the storage of boats and implements.

Implementation No. 3. Estuarine Flood Control Structures

Areawide flood protection structures are to be avoided.

Current approaches to flood protection are to discourage the occupany of threatened zones and to require safety standards in the design of the individual structures. Nevertheless, because many homes already in coastal areas are subject to flood damage, areawide engineering solutions will still be sought, such as sealing off whole bay systems or building massive artificial barrier dune structures. Such structural solutions have been discredited because of their expense, their potential for ecological damage, their failure to accomplish long-term protection from tidal inundation of estuarine shorelands, and the false sense of security they afford, which encourages the occupancy of hazardous shore areas.

An example of the extent of structural requirements for coastal flooding hazards is the Corps of Engineers plan for the south shore of Long Island.[13] The plan would require, among other elements, a 4350-foot wall across the mouth of Jamaica Bay, with a 300-foot gate for boat passage that could be

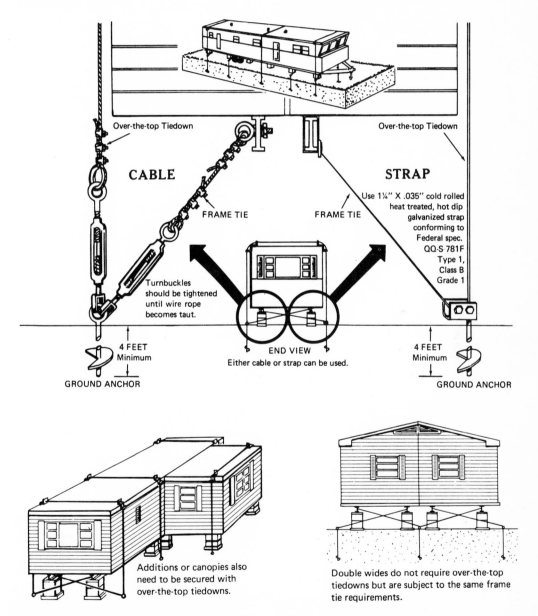

Figure 6.56 Tie-down arrangements are necessary for mobile homes in storm prone areas. (SOURCE: Reference 11.)

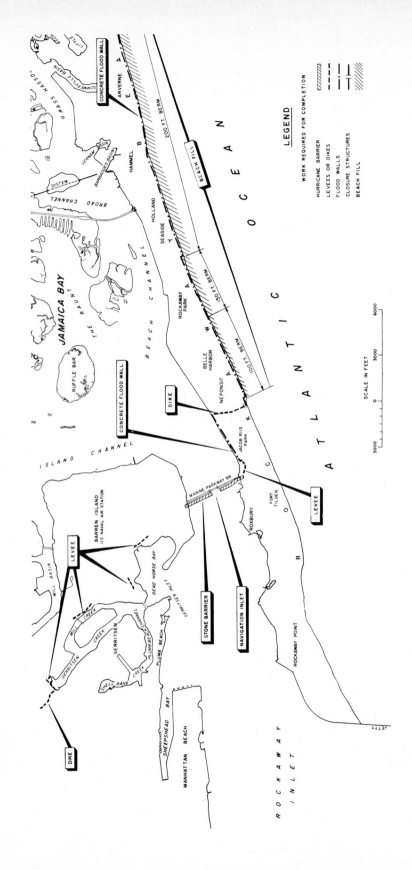

Figure 6.57 Structural flood control plan for Long Island (by U.S. Army Corps of Engineers) includes a mammoth gate across Rockaway Inlet, New York). (SOURCE: Reference 14.)

364

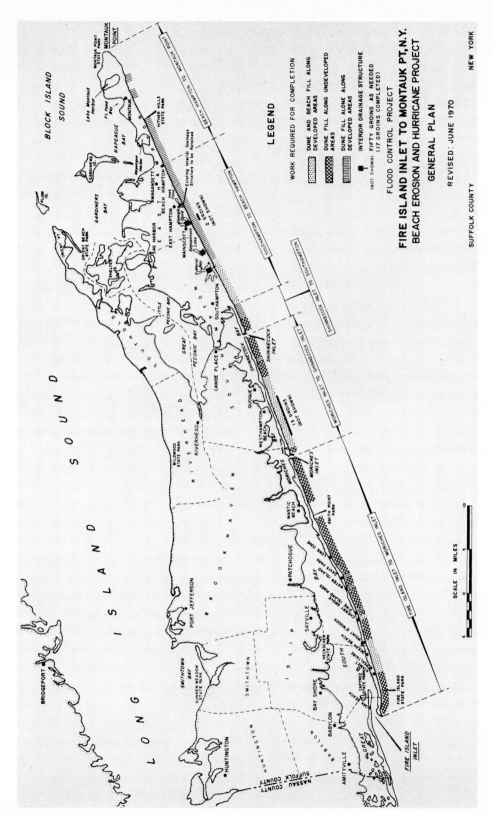

Figure 6.58 Structural beachfront stabilization plan for Long Island (by U.S. Army Corps of Engineers) includes 75 miles of 20-foot-high artificial dunes. (SOURCE: Reference 14.)

365

closed in the event of a storm (Figure 6.57). With such a small opening available for water exchange, the health of the whole estuarine ecosystem would be jeopardized by blocking the tidal circulation. Another element calls for the construction of a massive 20-foot-high dune line extending from "Fire Island Inlet to Hither Hills State Park at Montauk" —75 miles of artifical structure. Such a high dune would be most difficult to maintain over the years, and the feeling of safety it would afford might actually encourage occupancy and thus increase the hazard from the severest storms that could breach the dune line and flood the estuary (Figure 6.58).

Such major structural solutions should be discouraged. It is barely conceivable that there may be some situation in which they are necessary as a last resort after all other flood protection management approaches have been thoroughly examined and proved ineffectual.

REFERENCES

1. U.S. Department of Housing and Urban Development. 1975. "National Flood Insurance Program proposed criteria." *Federal Register*, Vol. 40, No. 59 (March 26).

2. W. M. Partington and W. R. Barada. 1973. "Florida hurricanes." *ENFO News*, July 1973. Florida Conservation Foundation.

3. Natural Resources Defense Council et al. 1975. "Federal flood control programs are failing to prevent flood losses—federal flood control projects can increase flood losses." *NRDC Leaflet*, Washington, D.C.

4. U.S. Department of the Interior. 1972. *Regulation of Flood Hazard Areas to Reduce Flood Losses*, Vol. 2, Part V-VI. U.S. Water Resources Council, Superintendent of Documents, U.S. Government Printing Office, Washington, D.C.

5. U.S. Army Corps of Engineers. 1972. *Flood Proofing Regulations*. Superintendent of Documents, U.S. Government Printing Office, Washington, D.C.

6. H. Crane Miller. 1975. "Coastal flood management and the National Flood Insurance Program." In *Environmental Comment*, November. Urban Land Institute, Washington, D.C.

7. Philip B. Cheney and H. Crane Miller. 1975. *The Application of Nonstructural Measures to Coastal Flooding*. Report to the New England River Basins Commission. Cheny, Miller, Ellis, and Associates, Inc., Washington, D.C.

8. H. Crane Miller. 1975. *Management Techniques in the Coastal Zone*. Report to the Nassau–Suffolk Regional Planning Board, Hauppage, New York.

9. John Clark. 1974. *Rookery Bay: Ecological Constraints on Coastal Development*. The Conservation Foundation, Washington, D.C.

10. U.S. Forest Service. 1965. *Houses Can Resist Hurricanes*. U.S. Forest Service Research Paper FPL 33.

11. U.S. Department of Defense. 1972. *Protecting Mobile Homes from High Winds*. TR-75, Defense Civil Preparedness Agency, Washington, D.C.

12. Albert R. Veri et al. 1973. *The Resource Buffer Plan: A Conceptual Land Use Study*. Rookery Bay Land Use Studies, Study No. 2. The Conservation Foundation, Washington, D.C.

13. U.S. Army Corps of Engineers. 1971. *National Shoreline Study*, Vol. 1: *North Atlantic Region*.

14. Gilbert K. Nersesian. 1973. "Federal beach erosion control activities on Long Island." In *Proceedings of the Seminar on Dredging and Dredge Spoil and Coast Stabilization and Protection*. Nassau–Suffolk Regional Planning Commission.

7. EXTRACTIVE INDUSTRIES

Mineral resources other than oil and gas extracted in tidal rivers and coastal waters and on the continental shelves of the open sea—sand, gravel, shells, salt, phosphate, and hard minerals—are of great economic value. These substances are found in surface and subsurface deposits and in solution in the water.

Surface deposits in the estuarine zone typically are of loose materials that can be extracted by dredging. Sand, gravel, and shell are the most commonly excavated materials in this category and are usually of low unit value, with transportation costs determining the feasibility of the mining operation. The surface deposits represent the most widely exploited group of mineral

Figure 6.59 Phosphate strip mine on the Pamlico River, North Carolina. (Conservation Foundation photo by M. Fahay.)

resources within the coastal waters today, with the major exception of petrolelm.

Subsurface deposits are costly to extract since the expense increases proportionately to depth and distance from shore. Subsurface resources can be classified as either unconsolidated materials (phosphate) or consolidated materials (hard rock and metals). Potential methods of recovery vary from drilling, to strip mining, to using cofferdams, or to extending underground mines from adjacent land areas. Strip mining for phosphate in the southeastern states is the largest of these industries (Figure 6.59).

Aqueous deposits include minerals found in solution in seawater, as well as the water itself. The principal minerals extracted in the United States are chlorides (including common salt), magnesium compounds, metals, and bromine. Evaporation and chemical processes are the main methods of extraction.

Disturbances caused by extractive activities have physical, chemical, and biological effects on coastal waters. Local governments must give consideration to the potential for environmental impact of extractive activities. Mining in wetlands, tidal rivers, and estuarine waters may cause serious adverse effects associated with excavation, extraction of the raw materials, transporting them ashore, and processing them. The most severe environmental impacts result from (1) disruption of vital habitat areas in estuaries, and (2) degradation of water quality. The massive disruption that would accompany estuarine strip mining appears to hold the greatest future threat to coastal ecosystems. Improperly located, designed, or operated onshore facilities also pose major threats. Detailed information is given by Riggs (Article 14, Chapter 7).

GUIDELINE. Extractive Industry Controls

Control the location and operation of extractive industries to avoid damage to coastal ecosystems.

Extraction has to take place where the minerals occur. The potential environmental and pollution problems associated with the extraction, preparation, and transportation of minerals are often exceedingly high. Extraction is frequently a messy operation capable of physically, chemically, and biologically disrupting and/or modifying coastal systems. Effects may be direct or indirect, temporary or permanent, and of varying degrees of severity, depending on the resource itself and the methods of extraction and processing. In addition, the onshore satellite industries that develop in the coastal zone often have a greater cumulative pollution potential than the extractive industry itself (page 388).

Construction industries use enormous amounts of sand and gravel (or aggregate), both of which are available at the bottoms of tidal rivers, estuaries, and the nearshore ocean. About 90 percent of the sand and gravel sold is used for making concrete. As construction needs increase the demand for sand and gravel and as the sources on land near urban areas become depleted, coastal deposits become more attractive. Powerful hydraulic suction dredges make estuarine mining practicable and profitable. Sand can be dredged for less than $1.00 per yard and sold for $2.00 to $3.00 per yard (1971 dollars). Costs of transportation from dredge to construction site govern profit.[1]

Industry sources report that presently held land reserves for sand and gravel production may be exhausted in 20 years.[1] The implication is that the demand on coastal sources in proximity to fast-growing urban areas will accelerate. At the present time about 100 million tons or roughly 10 percent of commercial sand and gravel comes from submerged coastal beds.[1]

Oyster shell strip mining poses serious ecological problems in the estuarine environment. There are large deposits of oyster shell in shallow bottoms from North Carolina to Texas, as well as in San Francisco Bay, that are used for making cement, for poultry grit, for soil conditioner, and for other products requiring a high calcium content. In San Francisco Bay, oyster shells

and mud are dredged together and both used to make concrete. Clam shell is sometimes dredged for roadway surfaces but is too dense for conversion to calcium products.[2]

The major problem with shell mining is the pollution resulting from turbidity and resuspension of sediment (page 627) when the overburden is dredged and discharged into the water, and as mud is washed from the shell.

The high potential for adverse environmental effects makes shell dredging a dubious enterprise. It has little economic or public value and entails great risk of public detriment. Private property rights are not usually involved since shell bottoms are public domain. Partly because of growing environmental objections, extractors have often disguised commercial coastal sand mining as public-benefit dredging for navigation improvement. Shell dredging should be discouraged, and alternative sources found to meet the demand for calcium products.

Extraction of hard minerals from bedrock and placer deposits in coastal waters is not now significant. However, there is a potential for gold, titanium, zirconium, tin, chromium copper, zinc, and nickel mining by various techniques. For example a copper–zinc mine is operating in Penobscot Bay, Maine; a titanium recovery operation, in the marshland area of Toms River, New Jersey; and a barite mine, at Castle Island, Alaska.[3] Such operations can create numerous pollution problems and disturbances and should be prohibited when vital habitat areas are involved, large amounts of process water are required, or pollutants are discharged.

Concentration of salt and other minerals from seawater has been a small industry with few plants, limited to a handful of coastal states, Texas and California in particular. The related desalination process for providing freshwater supplies for municipal use is more widespread; in 1967 there were 286 freshwater conversion plants in the country.[2] Desalination is an expensive process, however, and generally feasible only in island areas.

Implementation No. 1. Dredge and Strip Mining Control

Estuaries and vital habitat areas should be exempted from dredge and strip mining.

Aggregate

The same sort of potential for ecological disruption exists for sand and gravel mining as for any other dredging operation—turbidity, sedimentation, loss of productive bottom, and a diminishing of plant life, shellfish beds, and fish stocks (page 422). In addition saltwater intrusion may be encouraged and circulation characteristics adversely altered as channels are widened or deepened (page 479). When excavation leaves holes in the estuarine bottom, foul conditions result from the reduction of oxygen (page 479).

The simplest and environmentally safest way to avoid any threat of disruption would be the elimination of all sand and gravel dredging from estuaries and careful control of offshore mining. There could be exceptions at specific estuarine sites where sand is continuously piling up because of the action of water currents, and can therefore be regarded as a renewable resource. However, these shoals may be productive clam beds or serve as rich feeding areas for fish, for example, at the mouth of Sandy Hook Bay, New Jersey. When some removal of sand and gravel from estuaries is permitted, the decision as to how much and from where should be made on ecological grounds, according to an environmentally sound plan. Production costs in dredging will usually be higher, and the profit correspondingly less, when public benefit and environmental protection are safeguarded than when dredging is unrestricted.

Ongoing sand, gravel, and shell dredging and estuarine strip mining operations that are not in conformance with ecological requirements should be terminated as rapidly as possible, that is, as soon as existing leases, licenses, or other commitments expire or can be terminated. In the interim phase-out period operations should be controlled according to the best available technology and new locations outside of estuarine areas developed.

A potential hazard is mining too close to shore. When sand is removed close to a beach and the equilibrium of the slope is upset, the beach slumps away into the sea (page 425). Offshore mining should be conducted outside the active surf zone (in depths greater than 30 to 40 feet) in places of low biological activity (Figure 6.60).

A promising alternative to mining in ecologically sensitive estuaries is to dredge sand and gravel offshore on the continental shelf.[4] Surveys of the Atlantic coast show that an enormous supply is available offshore.[4] Moreover, new methods and equipment that are required for feasible offshore mining are under development. Definite ecological hazards exist, however, so offshore mining will have to be closely controlled to prevent water pollution, general ecosystem deterioration, damage to shellfish beds, and disruption of the feeding, spawning, and nursery areas of fish and other marine life.

Shell

Oyster shell is usually mined with a hydraulic suction dredge fitted with a rotating cutter head, which loosens and breaks up clusters of shells from the reef. Usually the dead oyster reefs are buried under a layer of mud eroded from the land. Extreme disturbances occur when the overlying mud sediment is stripped off the shell reef and spreads through the water (Figure 6.61). Although there are extensive local disturbances of the bottom, experts disagree on the extent of temporary and permanent ecosystem damage that is caused. Turbidity in the area of shell dredging may be 10

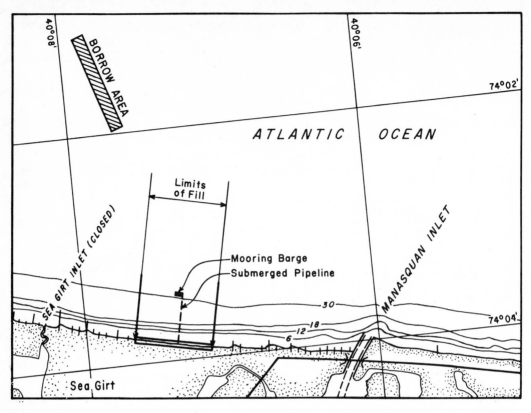

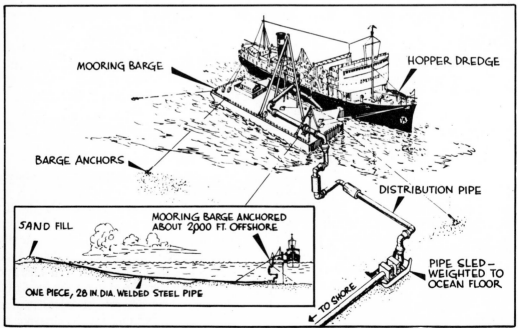

Figure 6.60 Offshore sand mining for beach nourishment (Sea Girt, New Jersey). (SOURCE: Reference 5.)

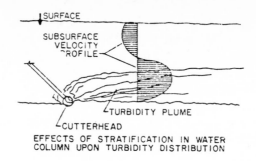

EFFECTS OF STRATIFICATION IN WATER
COLUMN UPON TURBIDITY DISTRIBUTION

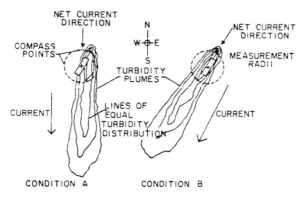

CONDITION A   CONDITION B

Figure 6.61 General description of the spread of sediment and the turbidity introduced by dredging. (SOURCE: Reference 6.)

times higher than that caused by currents, wind, or boat traffic. Shell dredging also leads to "density" mud flows that cover and suffocate the bottom life in their path. These mud flows may extend 1500 to 2000 feet from the dredge.[7] Other potential effects from shell dredging include serious reduction of dissolved oxygen in the dredged area, eutrophication, and alteration of current flows due to changed basin shape.

To prevent gross pollution it is often recommended that dredges remain 1200 feet away from live oyster reefs and other vital areas.[2] But in Mobile Bay, Alabama, where 20 miles of trench is dredged and 2 million cubic yards of shell removed per year, currents from winds of 12 to 15 mph were observed to create a turbidity plume visible for 1.5 miles behind a dredge. National Aeronautics and Space Administration aerial photographs showed a plume 20 miles long

and 0.5 mile wide at slightly higher winds.[7] Clearly a 1200-foot buffer would not be adequate protection under these conditions. The most appropriate solution is to eliminate strip mining for shell in estuaries unless it is shown that particular public benefits will be achieved as a result of the operations.

Phosphate

Strip mining of phosphate for fertilizer in coastal waters poses special ecological problems. For example, in a 9000-acre tract adjacent to the Pamlico Estuary, North Carolina, that is leased from the state, cofferdams and pumps are used to expose phosphate deposits 100 feet deep. The ecological hazards are turbidity, sedimentation, and particularly the eutrophication that results when there is sufficient nitrogen in the water to combine with the excess phosphate released by the constant pumping of water from behind the cofferdam (Figure 6.62). The bottom of the Pamlico River is covered with a thick layer of semicolloidal, fluidized silt that supports little useful life and, when stirred up into the water, has serious adverse effects. Yet this is as well controlled and as carefully run a mining operation as one might find.

Florida's Peace River has been badly altered and polluted by inland phosphate strip mining. Georgia, however, rejected a bid for large-scale coastal phosphate mining because it would obliterate thousands of acres of marshland.[3] Again, because of the high potential for ecological damage, coastal deposits should not be mined.

Implementation No. 2. Evaporation Process Controls

Desalination and salt recovery operations should be controlled to prevent water pollution and drainage damage to vital habitat areas.

Desalination, the process of extracting salts from seawater, is an expensive way to produce drinkable water and is generally practicable only in island areas such as the Florida Keys and the Caribbean. The major disturbances from the processing of seawater are thermal pollution and high salinity discharge into coastal waters. In distillation processes the effluent temperature can be 12 to 15°F higher than the receiving waters.[8] Increases in temperature can endanger fish and other marine life. Saline-water conversion plant effluents also contain dissolved substances at higher concentration levels than are present in the influent water, as well as other chemicals added in the process.

Table salt, magnesium, bromine, sodium, calcium, and other minerals are extracted from seawater by evaporation and processed for commercial use. In San Francisco Bay,

for example, thousands of acres of marshland have been converted into salt ponds for the processing of seawater. Salt ponds are created by diking off marshland and permitting seawater to enter through tidal gates. The seawater is collected and held in a series of concentrating ponds, generally 400 to 500 acres, and the brine is moved from pond to pond over a period of 4 to 5 years. Magnesium compounds, gypsum, bromine, and bittern (the product of salt recovery) are also processed. After evaporation and crystallization the crude salt is broken up and transported for further processing.

The major environmental disturbance from salt extraction is the preemption of valuable marshland. The productivity of the coastal waters is decreased, and food webs are broken (page 98). Salt ponds in any marsh areas so affected should be identified as nonconforming uses and returned to their original condition as soon as opportunity permits. In the meantime, pollution caused by runoff of concentrated brine wastes into coastal waters must be avoided.

REFERENCES

1. Frank T. Manheim. 1972. *Mineral Resources off the Northeastern Coast of the United States.* U.S. Geological Survey, Geological Survey Circular No. 699, Washington, D.C.

2. Bostwick H. Ketchum, Ed. 1972. *The Water's Edge: Critical Problems of the Coastal Zone.* The Massachusetts Institute of Technology Press, Cambridge, Massachusetts.

3. S. A. Feitler. 1974. "Mineral resources of the coastal zone." In R. H. Chabreck, Ed., *Coastal Marsh and Estuary Management.* Division of Continuing Education, Louisiana State University, Baton Rouge, Louisiana.

4. John Schlee. 1968. *Sand and Gravel on the Continental Shelf off the Northeastern United States.* U.S. Geological Survey, Geological Survey Circular No. 60, Washington, D.C.

5. U.S. Army Corps of Engineers. 1973. *Shore Protection Manual.* U.S. Army Coastal Engineering Research Center, Vicksburg, Mississippi.

6. Richard F. Dominguez and David R. Basco.

Figure 6.62   Phosphate strip mining is a hydraulic process in which large volumes of polluted wastewater are discharged to coastal waters after passage through large settling basins (Pamlico River, North Carolina). (Conservation Foundation photo by J. Chess.)

1971. "Muddy aspects of water quality affecting dredges." In *World Dredging and Marine Construction*, Vol. 7, No. 14.

7. U.S. Army Corps of Engineers. 1973. *Final EIS Permit Application by Radcliff Materials, Inc.*

8. U.S. Department of the Interior. 1969. *Disposal of the Effluents from Desalination Plants into Estuarine Waters.* Prepared by the Dow Chemical Company.

9. H. B. Goldman. 1967. *Salt, Sand, and Shells; Mineral Resources of San Francisco Bay.* San Francisco Bay Conservation and Development Commission, San Francisco, California.

8.   FOREST INDUSTRIES

Forest growth forms the principal cover that protects the headwaters of streams, prevents soil erosion, and stabilizes runoff and stream flow. Natural forests maintain high surface-water quality and stabilize flows into coastal waters. Forest ecosystems provide habitats for deer, elk, and other game and also contain streams used by anadromous fishes (salmon, shad, etc.) for spawning. Uncontrolled logging in coastal watersheds has a high potential for disruption of the complex and delicate forest ecosystem, causing immediate and long-term impacts on water quality. Well-planned and properly managed logging operations, on the other hand, can minimize adverse impacts on stream and coastal waters.[1]

Commercial timber harvesting is a major activity in many coastal states. The primary harvesting areas for commercial timber in coastal areas are found in the Pacific Northwest and the southeastern states.[2] When harvesting activity in these areas takes place in the coastal watersheds, controls are required to prevent damage to coastal ecosystems from the erosion of soil and nutrients and from the imbalancing of the runoff cycle. Erosion control and buffer strips around water areas are major requirements, particularly when hydrogeological conditions are adverse to water quality control, as in the Pacific coastal watersheds.

Tree harvest is often a prelude to a complex cycle of conversion of forest land to residential use—level land is clear-cut and drained, first for pine monoculture, later for agriculture, and finally for housing subdivisions. Logging operations include the following processes: (1) construction of logging roads, (2) harvest (cutting) of timber, (3) transportation of logs, (4) disposal of logging debris (slash), (5) reforestation and maintenance of logging areas, and (6) use of biocides to control forest pests.

The principal forest harvesting (cutting) methods are (1) clear-cutting, in which whole stands of trees are completely harvested (Figure 6.63); and (2) selective (or partial) cutting by various techniques, whereby certain trees are selected for cutting according to plan. About 50 percent of all wood removed from commercial forest lands is removed by clear-cutting.[2] Factors influencing the use of a particular harvesting

method include cost, volume of timber, topography, location of the harvesting area, erosion potentials, wildlife habitat requirements, and fire, insect, and disease hazards.

Clear-cutting involves the clearing of all trees. Patches, strips, or an entire watershed may be clear-cut, thus increasing the potential for erosion, sedimentation, and disruption of the runoff cycle until the cover is reestablished (page 377). Uncontrolled clear-cutting also has been shown to cause debris jams and to increase stream temperature by eliminating tree shading.[2] Although clear-cutting does not always increase the hazards of erosion, in all cases it increases the quantity of loose debris.

Selective cutting often appears to have a lower potential for damage to coastal ecosystems. This method involves the removal of mature trees singly or in small groups at varying intervals. It encourages a continuous establishment of natural reproduction and the maintenance of a mixed-age stand. If properly managed, selective cutting often reduces the potential for erosion and sedimentation typical of clear-cut areas by leaving a viable forest ecosystem.

Advocates of clear-cutting cite as major economic advantages that it facilitates harvesting on steep slopes, minimizes the need for roads and disturbances, and provides desirable replacement growth by favoring light-demanding trees like pines. Also, clear-cutting is often justified in areas prone to wind gusts or areas where partial cutting would prevent the regeneration of shade-intolerant species. Unfortunately, however, the profit-maximizing factors involved in clear-cutting sometimes conflict with protection of the environment.

There are a number of examples of bays impacted with sediments from the erosion of deforested areas in Pacific coastal areas (e.g., the Eel River–Humboldt Bay system in California) and of streams degraded for salmon spawning by siltation and heating from removal of shade trees along stream banks (Figure 6.64). In southeastern coastal

Figure 6.63 Clear-cut areas yield a high soil runoff initially but eventually become stabilized by revegetation. (Photo by F. Lee Kirby, U.S. Forest Service.)

Figure 6.64   The Eel River (California) is heavily impacted by sediment from uncontrolled logging and regularly floods riverside communities. (Photo by author.)

areas, deforestation has at times led to accelerated sedimentation of bays and to imbalance in the cycle of freshwater inflow to bays. Also, loss of detrital inputs from harvested deciduous forests may be ecologically adverse. For example, leaf matter from deciduous trees that grow along the Appalachicola River (Florida) accumulates downstream in Appalachicola Bay, where it provides a significant source of nutrition (as it decays) for the bay's shrimp and oyster fishery populations, the mainstay of Franklin County's economy.[3] Uncontrolled deforestation would reduce the supply of leaf detritus.

Uncontrolled logging practices have disrupted the hydrologic cycle in many forest ecosystems. Specific harvesting practices such as clear-cutting can greatly increase total yearly water outflow from a watershed by up to 5 area-inches (12.7 area-centimeters) by reducing the transpiration potential of forests.[4] More importantly, clear-cutting can cause storm flow discharges nine times the level of those from an undisturbed watershed (Figure 6.65).

Joint planning for logging operations involving local government and private timber interests and including public participation can minimize the impacts on water resources and coastal ecosystems. A logging plan pro-

vides specifically for (1) well-designed, well-located and well-maintained logging roads, (2) appropriate harvesting (cutting) methods, (3) appropriate methods for transporting logs, (4) buffer strips to be left along streams, and (5) precautions for protecting water quality during logging and restoration of the logging area.[1]

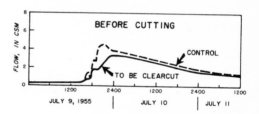

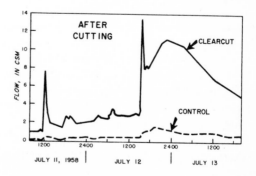

Figure 6.65   Sample storm hydrographs of clearcut and control watersheds before and after treatment. (SOURCE: Reference 4.)

Table 6.11   Relative erosion hazard of logging areas in relation to site factors (SOURCE: Reference 5)

Site Factor	High Erosion Hazard	Moderate Erosion Hazard	Low Erosion Hazard
Parent rock	*Acid Igneous* Granite, diorite, volcanic ash, pumice, some schists	*Sedimentary and Metamorphic* Sandstone, schist, shale, slate, conglomerates, chert	*Basic Igneous* (Lava rocks) Basalt, andesite, serpentine
Soil	Light-textured, with little or no clay	Medium-textured, with considerable clay	Heavy-textured, largely clay and adobe
Mantle stability	Unstable mantles	Mantles of questionable stability	Stable mantles
Slope	Steep (over 50%)	Moderate (20–50%)	Gentle (0–20%)
Precipitation	Heavy winter rains or intense summer storms	Mainly snow with some rain	Heavy snow or light rain
Vegetation and other organic matter on and in soil	None to very little	Moderate amounts	Large amounts

GUIDELINE.   Watershed Runoff Control

Control logging activities so that watershed runoff water is maintained at the preexisting quality, volume, and rate of flow.

Controls on inland forest harvest should have as a goal that rivers enter coastal areas with the quality of the water and its volume and rate of flow unaltered (page 170). There may be a high potential for damage to coastal ecosystems via river flow from areas many miles inland through increased sedimentation, eutrophication, and alteration of runoff cycle. To control this may require a system of regional management whereby coastal communities can exert some influence on the preservation of upstream watersheds.

Major natural factors contributing to impacts from logging on the quality and flow of runoff water include (1) steepness of slopes, (2) stability of soil, (3) rate of vegetative recovery after logging, and (4) climatic factors (Table 6.11). The relation

between topography and rainfall is especially important. Potential disturbances from uncontrolled logging operations may include (1) erosion and sedimentation, (2) detrital nutrient and chemical runoff, (3) disruption of the hydrologic cycle, (4) toxic runoff, and (5) thermal pollution. In addition, biocides used to control forest pests—insecticides, fungicides, herbicides, and rodenticides—can pollute forest streams and the coastal waters they enter, particularly when they are deposited directly on water surfaces through careless application.

A few sections of coastal forest are situated so as to have such a high potential for environmental damage during and after harvest that there may be no feasible way to harvest them and still safeguard water resources and coastal ecosystems. Such areas can serve an economic function by conversion to light-impact recreational use. Hiking, primitive camping, and fishing require minimal facilities and should have only a slight impact on the ecosystem.

Uncontrolled logging operations that leave

organic debris and litter—foliage, branches, bark, rotten material, roots, and waste wood —scattered about stream watersheds have a potential for adverse impact. In Douglas fir forests (Pacific coast), for example, the average weight of logging wastes may be about 40 tons per acre (90 metric tons per hectare). Proper disposal of the slash (organic debris) in logging operations is necessary to prevent accumulation of decomposing debris in streams and consequent degradation of water quality. Debris dams due to waste slash from cutting often clog streams, causing blockage of flow and increased erosion and deposition. Logging slash left in streams often creates migration barriers that, in one west coast case study, caused a 75 percent decrease in spawning salmon.[5] High-flood-hazard areas can be designated, avoided, and protected. Debris can be reduced by salvage, prelogging programs, and satisfactory stream clearance.

Watershed restoration is necessary to reclaim and improve land that has been logged. Restoration programs (1) reestablish vegetative cover and renew the forest hydrologic balance, (2) conserve soil resources by reducing soil erosion and providing soil stability, (3) deter runoff and reduce damage from floods by lowering stream flow peaks, (4) minimize the sediment carried into streams, and (5) enhance aesthetic considerations and recreational uses in the area. Seeding and planting native vegetation stabilizes disturbed areas. A restoration program will also provide for vegetation to be established on such disturbed areas as roads, skid trails, landings, and firelines.

Streamside buffer strips of existing vegetation are effective in the trapping of sediment, the purification of storm runoff, and the maintenance of bank stability, as well as in providing wildlife habitat. If properly planned, buffer strips can filter out most pollutants resulting from logging operations and can be the key to protecting the freshwater supply to an estuary.

Implementation No. 1. Erosion Control

Strict erosion control standards should be required in all phases of coastal logging operations.

Increased erosion of mineral soil is normally the most serious disturbance caused by logging operations. Therefore strict soil erosion control in watersheds draining directly into coastal waters is the principal safeguard required to avoid adverse impacts from logging. Stormwater runoff from poorly managed cutting areas carries mineral and organic sediments into watercourses flowing to the coast (Table 6.12). Also, excessive quantities of plant material (leaves and twigs) may be carried downstream, contributing to eutrophication problems in coastal waters.

In clear-cut areas, terracing, composting, mulching, and fertilizing accelerate the establishment of planted species and, by aiding the restoration process, reduce sediment output (Table 6.13). Skid trails and roads

Table 6.12 Maximum turbidities under four cutting practices on the Fernow Experimental Forest in West Virginia (SOURCE: Modified from Reference 5)

Quality of Logging Operation	Cutting Practice	Maximum Turbidity (ppm)
Very poor	Commercial clear-cut	56,000
Poor	Diameter limit	5,200
Good	Extensive selection	210
Very good	Intensive selection	25
Undisturbed	(Control watershed)	15

Table 6.13 Influence of forest cover on control of sediment yield by erosion (Potomac watersheds) (SOURCE: Modified from Reference 2)

Land Area with Forest Cover (%)	Sediment Yield [metric tons/sq km/yr (tons/sq mi/yr)]	
20	140	(400)
40	70	(200)
60	31.5	(90)
80	15.75	(45)
100	7.7	(22)

should also be immediately reseeded to speed the restoration process. Erosion control practices established during logging must be continued until the original quality, volume, and rate of flow of runoff water have been restored.

It is often reported[2] that the major adverse effects of logging are associated with transporting logs from the cutting areas to processing areas, particularly with logging roads. Transport from staging areas requires skid trails and roads to move logs to a loading area, where they are transported by water, truck, or railroad.

Logging roads are usually considered to be the most significant persistent source of soil erosion. Studies by the U.S. Forest Service have shown that as much as 90 percent of the sediment produced from "timber sales" areas comes from logging roads.[5]

With proper location, design, construction, and maintenance of main roads, secondary roads, spur roads, and skid trails, soil erosion and related runoff problems in forest watersheds can be significantly reduced. In locating roads, consideration should be given to soils, gradient, topography, and systematic layouts. Where possible, roads should be located on natural benches, ridge tops, and lower slopes to avoid cutting and filling and thus minimize disturbances of the terrain. Roads should be located on stable areas well away from streams, marshes, ponds, natural drainage

channels, and the bottoms of narrow canyons (Figure 6.66). Retaining walls or riprap should be required when necessary to increase the stability of fill embankments. Proper maintenance requires cleaning of drainage diversions and replanting where lost ground cover needs to be replaced. Roads should be set back at least 100 feet (30.5 meters) from streams to provide sufficient buffer area for vegetation and soil to filter sediment from surface runoff before it leaches into streams.

Bridges, causeways, and culverts should be located so as to minimize bank disturbance.

Roadside ditches and culverts should be designed for a minimum slope of 1 percent. They should include sediment catchment basins.[1] Stream flow should be diverted around construction sites whenever possible.

Skid trails can be planned to incorporate dips, water bars, and cross drains to prevent water accumulations. These drainage structures should be close together so that collected water can be diverted easily into vegetated buffer areas. To prevent silt-laden waters from draining into streams from roads, gravel surfacing may be required. Application of chemical dust inhibitors that could wash into receiving waters should be discouraged.

Proper disposal of slash (organic debris) from logging operations is necessary to protect water quality and wildlife habitat. Slash should be disposed of away from all water areas inland of the protective buffer strip.

Implementation No. 2. Buffer Strips in Logging

Buffer strips of natural vegetation should be required along coastal water bodies and tributary watercourses.

Many state and local authorities currently require that logging plans submitted to them for approval include buffer strips along all watercourses. Buffer or filter strips, like

Figure 6.66 Logging roads placed alongside streams lead to major disturbances in water quality and water flow (Dismal Creek, tributary to the Umpqua River and Winchester Bay, Oregon). (Photo by U.S. Forest Service.)

coastal wetlands, trap and filter out sediment and protect water from degradation. They are especially helpful between streams and logging roads.

In San Mateo County, California, the required protective strip of vegetation must have "sufficient filter capacity to effectively remove waterborne sediment."[6] On the federal level both the Environmental Protection Agency and the U.S. Forest Service encourage the use of buffer strips (also called "filter strips"), and guidelines on their width and location have been published.[1]

The dimensions of a buffer strip depend on slope, wind exposure, rainfall, type of vegetation, proximity to the coast, and type of timber harvest. A buffer strip of natural vegetation should start at and extend inland

from the water's edge along the shoreline of all streams and watercourses. Clear-cutting, tree farming, and general intensive monocultural logging practices should be avoided in buffer areas adjacent to coastal water bodies and tributary streams. However, selective cutting of mature trees within the buffer areas should normally be encouraged so long as the vegetative ground cover is preserved and logging roads or skid trails are prohibited.

Trimble and Sartz[7] recommend a minimum buffer strip of 25 feet (7.6 meters) plus 2 feet (0.6 meter) for each 1 percent of slope between surface water and logging area (Table 6.14). The U.S. Forest Service suggests the following formula for determining ideal buffer width: width = 4

Table 6.14 Recommended widths for filter (buffer) strips (derived for higher-slope harvest areas) (SOURCE: References 5 and 7)

Slope of Land (%)	Width of Filtration Strip (ft)
0	25
10	45
20	65
30	85
40	105
50	125
60	145
70	165

feet (1.2 meters) × (percent slope) + 50 feet (15.2 meters).[5] Recent federal guidelines for logging in the Pacific Northwest recommend a minimum buffer width of 75 feet (22.4 meters), increased proportionally to the peculiar problems imposed by local terrain.[1] Generally, if the terrain is steep, the potential for erosion is moderate to severe, and large-scale clear-cutting is to be used, then the buffer strip must be substantially wider than the recommended minimum.

Buffer strips also provide a canopy for forest streams. Harvesting (cutting) to the edge of forest streams exposes the water to direct heating by the sun, causing recorded increases in water temperature of up to 16°F (8.9°C)[1] (Figure 6.67). Such increases produce temperatures known to be damaging to resident fish species and to the spawning of anadromous coastal fish that breed in forest streams. Research has shown that a buffer strip 80 feet (24.4 meters) wide will provide ample shading for streams.[2]

In summary, a buffer strip of unaltered forest or a restricted cutting area should be required for all coastal water bodies and tributary watercourses, including all fringing wetlands. The buffer should be as wide as is feasible but not less than 75 feet (22.9 meters)unless there are overriding special reasons to the contrary.

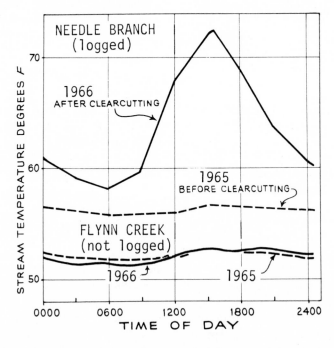

Figure 6.67   Water temperature in Needle Branch in Oregon varied by only 2°F during an average summer day before the trees were removed by the clear-cut logging method but varied 15°F after clear cutting. (SOURCE: Reference 1.)

REFERENCES

1. U.S. Department of the Interior. 1970. *Industrial Waste Guide on Logging Practices*. Federal Water Pollution Control Administration, Northwest Region, Portland, Oregon.

2. U.S. Environmental Protection Agency. 1973. *Processes, Procedures and Methods to Control Pollution Resulting from Silvicultural Activities*. Office of Air and Water Programs, Superintendent of Documents, U.S. Government Printing Office, Washington, D.C.

3. Robert J. Livingston. 1975. *Resource Management and Estuarine Function with Application to the Appalachicola Drainage System (North Florida, U.S.A.)*. Paper presented at The Estuarine Pollution Conference, Pensacola, Florida, U.S. Environmental Protection Agency.

4. K. G. Reinhart, A. R. Eschner, and G. R. Trimble, Jr. 1963. *Effects on Streamflow of Four Forest Practices in the Mountains of West Virginia*. U.S. Forest Service Research Paper NE-1, U.S. Department of Agriculture, Upper Darby, Pennsylvania.

5. U.S. Environmental Protection Agency. 1975. *Forest Harvest-Regeneration Activities and Protection of Water Quality*. EPA Region X, Seattle, Washington (draft).

6. Board of Supervisors, County of San Mateo, California. Ordinance No. 2143: Regulation of Timber Harvesting.

7. G. R. Trimble and R. S. Sartz. 1957. "How far from a stream should a logging road be located?" *Journal of Foresty*, Vol. 55, No. 5, pp. 339–341.

9. GROUNDWATER EXTRACTION

Groundwater resources are under growing pressure from coastal communities as shoreland aquifers are increasingly pumped for industrial and domestic water use. In southern California, Florida, New Orleans, and Long Island the groundwater aquifer has already been overpumped and has become contaminated by saltwater intrusion. Some coastal areas are close to running out of uncontaminated groundwater because of saltwater intrusion. With as little as 2 percent contamination by salt water, a drinking water supply is classified as unfit according to federal potable water standards.

The big users of groundwater in coastal areas are municipal water suppliers and industry, with very little employed for irrigation anywhere along the coast. The time has passed in most developed areas where such uses can go unmanaged. Public regulation of groundwater resources is urgently needed in many communities to prevent disastrous contamination and depletion or costly subsidence of land. For example, in Long Island overpumping for municipal supplies and industrial operations caused the freshwater head to drop as far as 35 feet (10.7 meters) below sea level. The resulting intrusion of seawater forced Long Island communities to limit water use and eventually to abandon many supply wells.[1] Along California's populated coast there has been seawater intrusion in at least 12 localities; 7 others are known to be threatened, and 15 others are regarded as potential intrusion sites.[2]

Subsidence of the surface results because the land loses the subsurface support provided by groundwater. The San Joaquin Valley and Long Beach, California, have had serious subsidence problems.[3] In the heavily industrialized areas around Galveston Bay, Texas, particularly at the southern end of the Houston ship channel, extensive land subsidence caused by excessive industrial groundwater withdrawal has occurred at an increasing rate since the 1940s (Figures 6.68 and 6.69) and is predicted to continue. The bay area land has sunk as much as 8 feet (2.4 meters) below sea level.[4, 6] This subsidence has drastically increased the flooding danger and made the area especially vulnerable to hurricane disaster. Structural solutions have been attempted. Dikes have been built and pumps installed to help ward off flooding problems (Figures 6.70 and 6.71). Unfortunately such structural protection measures treat only the "symptoms" of unmanaged groundwater pumping—the increase in relative sea level and flooding—and do not solve the problem.[4] It should be noted that land subsidence is also caused by the settling of soft subsoil when struc-

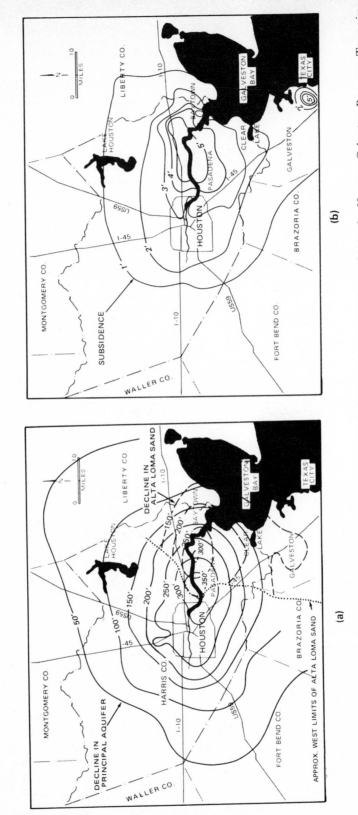

Figure 6.68 Overpumping of groundwater caused extreme groundwater level decline (a) and subsidence (b) in the Houston–Galveston Bay area, Texas, in the period from 1906 to 1964. (SOURCE: Reference 4.)

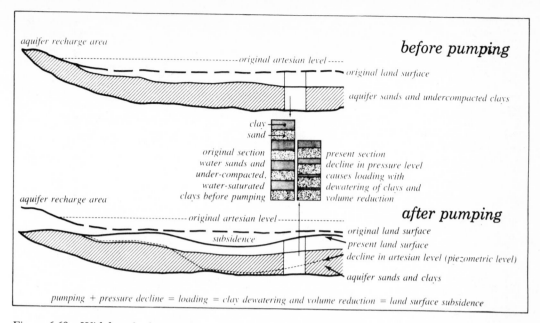

before pumping

aquifer recharge area

----------original artesian level----

original land surface

aquifer sands and undercompacted clays

clay
sand

original section
water sands and
under-compacted,
water-saturated
clays before pumping

present section
decline in pressure level
causes loading with
dewatering of clays and
volume reduction

after pumping

aquifer recharge area

----------original artesian level----

original land surface

subsidence

present land surface

decline in artesian level (piezometric level)

aquifer sands and clays

pumping + pressure decline = loading = clay dewatering and volume reduction = land surface subsidence

Figure 6.69 Withdrawal of water from the aquifer reduces piezometric pressure, dewaters the clays and causes them to compact, and results in a subsidence of the land surface (Houston, Texas). (SOURCE: Reference 5.)

Figure 6.70 In Seabrook, Texas, land subsidence from overpumping of groundwater for industrial use has caused the bay shore to sink and home sites to be flooded. (Photo by author.)

Figure 6.71 Water must be continually pumped from flooded home sites behind dikes near Baytown, Texas; overpumping of groundwater aquifers caused the land to sink. (Photo by author.)

tures are built on "reclaimed" wetlands (page 472). Clearly, a stringent water management program is needed to maintain the water table and to protect additional land areas from exposure to hazard.

GUIDELINE.   Groundwater Withdrawal Controls

Include controls on groundwater withdrawal in a comprehensive water management program.

The solution to protecting groundwater and land resources from seawater intrusion and land subsidence is sound and comprehensive water management. A total management program provides for groundwater, surface water, and reused water supplies to be inventoried and utilized in a coordinated plan of "conjunctive" management. In one California case where extensive withdrawal caused saltwater intrusion in the fresh water supply, a water control program was implemented that reduced the harmful amounts withdrawn and allocated the water resources according to historical uses.[7] The California Coastal Plan recommends comprehensive watershed management for the coastal communities, to be coordinated at local, regional, and state levels.[8]

The recharge potential of groundwater aquifers should also be protected in the management program. Aquifers are naturally recharged by rain percolating downward from the land surface or laterally from a lake or stream. In most cases the aquifer will be recharged when the permeable formation is near the land surface (Figure 6.72). The area of recharge, where rainwater or seepage actually enters the aquifer, may be a long distance from the wells, thereby requiring regional management. Impervious surfacing, removal of vegetation, and land drainage in recharge areas divert waters that otherwise would filter into groundwater aquifers. These adverse effects should be controlled by relevant land-use controls.

Each community must know the extent of its groundwater, the source of replenish-ment of aquifers (recharge areas), the potential for contamination and depletion, and the possibilities for reclaiming wastewater and minimizing unnecessary water consumption. With this information at hand, the limits of use can be determined, and an effective comprehensive plan formulated.

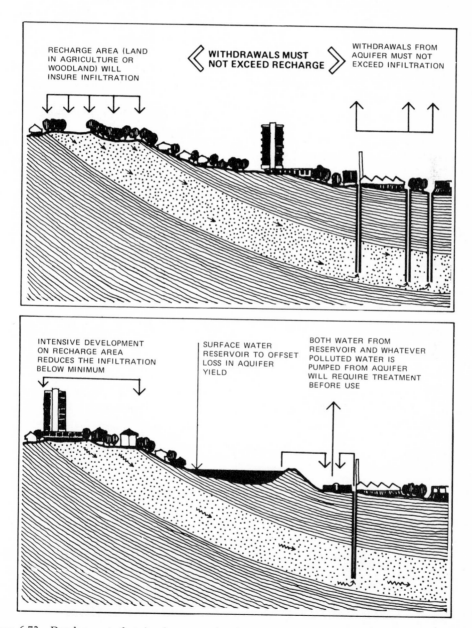

Figure 6.72 Development that involves extensive nonpermeable land surfacing reduces the groundwater head, thus encouraging saltwater intrusion in areas near the shore. (SOURCE: Adapted from Reference 9.)

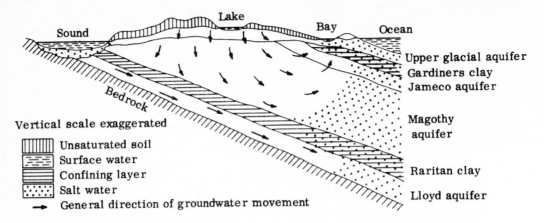

Figure 6.73   A typical profile of aquifers of Long Island, New York. (SOURCE: Reference 10.)

Implementation No. 1.   Withdrawal Control

Groundwater withdrawal should be controlled to prevent saltwater intrusion and land subsidence.

Surface aquifers vary in level with seasonal changes in rainfall, sometimes rising above the land surface and flooding it, but usually remaining below at a depth of several inches to many feet. There may also be a number of deeper confined aquifers, which are separated from each other and the surface aquifer by more or less horizontal layers of impermeable rock or clay (Figure 6.73). Typically the confined aquifers are sloped seaward with fresh water flowing out of them

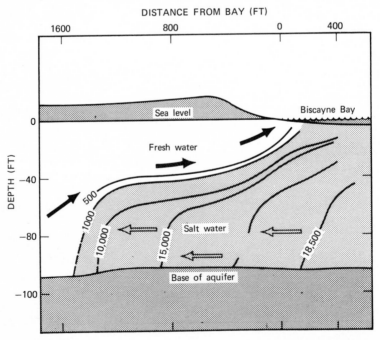

Figure 6.74   The pattern of saltwater intrusion (salinities in parts per million) of the Biscayne aquifer in the vicinity of Miami, Florida. (SOURCE: Reference 11.)

where they intercept the seafloor. The head pressures on the aquifer normally prevent salt water from intruding into the fresh water (page 639), but overpumping may cause intrusion if the water is drawn from either surface or deeper aquifers (Figure 6.74). If a confined aquifer is overpumped, the head pressure will fall and the result is the same: salt water will intrude.

To prevent saltwater contamination of groundwater supplies and land subsidence there must be comprehensive management based on a thorough understanding of the groundwater system—its supply limitation, its replenishment rate, the present and anticipated future demands, and any special pertinent characteristics. Assistance in determining these parameters may be obtained from U.S. Geological Survey offices located in all states.

Physically, groundwater management should include the entire aquifer system of a basin, since pumpage in any one area ultimately can affect a very large portion of the aquifer. Statewide and regional cooperation may be needed for adequate management. The patterns and schedules of recharge and extractions of water would be regulated. For example, the management program would specify the number and location of wells, together with their pumping rates and annual limitations on total extractions. Upper and lower groundwater levels would also be defined. Water quality objectives would be set, and sources and causes of pollution carefully controlled. Artificial recharge using storm flows, imported water, or reclaimed water could be involved, as in the plan suggested for Long Island, New York (Figure 6.75).

Ideally, groundwater use should be managed in conjunction with surface-water use.[7] Under such conjunctive management groundwater would be pumped during periods when surface-water supplies were limited. At other times, when surface-water supplies were greater, groundwater supplies would be pumped less or not at all, and would be recharged both naturally and artificially. Such a combined water source system should provide a larger, surer, and more economic water supply than would be available from either source individually.

Generally, conjunctive water management can be effectively accomplished at the local or regional government level, operating within a framework of powers and duties established by state statutes. The state laws and regulations would protect groundwater aquifers from injury and authorize enforcement both by individual property owners who are damaged and by public officials and management districts charged with the responsibility of managing groundwater and surface-water resources.

REFERENCES

1. Louisiana Water Resources Research Institute. 1968. *Salt-Water Encroachment into Aquifers.* Proceedings of the Limited Professional Symposium, May 4–5, 1967, Bulletin No. 3, Louisiana State University, Baton Rouge, Louisiana.

2. U.S. Environmental Protection Agency. 1973. *Identification and Control of Pollution from Salt Water Instrusion.* Office of Air and Water Programs, Superintendent of Documents, U.S. Government Printing Office, Washington, D.C.

3. William H. Wintz, Jr., Raphael G. Kazmann, and Charles G. Smith, Jr. 1970. *Subsidence and Ground-Water Off-take in the Baton Rouge Area.* Louisiana Water Resources Research Institute, Bulletin No. 6, Louisiana State University, Baton Rouge, Louisiana.

4. A. Frank Marshall, Jr. 1973. "How much more will Houston sink?" *The Slide Rule,* Vol. 33, No 2 (February). Houston Engineering and Scientific Society, Houston, Texas.

5. W. L. Fisher. 1973. "Natural hazards in land use." *TSNL Review,* Vol. 1, No. 1. Texas System of Natural Laboratories, Inc., Austin, Texas.

6. Texas Department of Public Safety. 1974. *If a Hurricane Strikes. . . .* Division of Emergency Services, Hurricane Awareness Program Bulletin, Austin, Texas.

7. David Seckler, Ed. 1971. *California Water.* University of California Press, Berkeley, California.

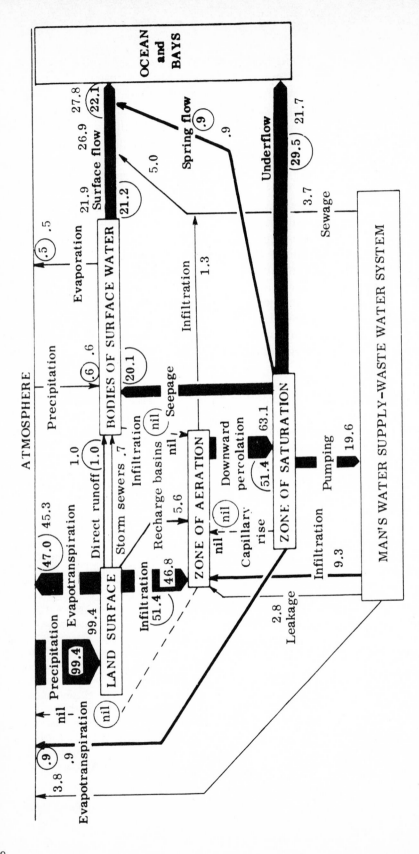

Figure 6.75 Flow diagram of the hydrological system, water budget area, for Long Island, New York. Numerical entries represent average flows in percentages of total precipitation; "nil" indicates negligible amounts. Encircled numbers depict the natural system; the other numbers represent the system as influenced by man. (SOURCE: Reference 12.)

8. California Coastal Zone Conservation Commission. 1975. *California Coastal Plan.* San Francisco, California.

9. Joachim Tourbier. 1973. *Water Resources as a Basis for Comprehensive Planning and Development of the Christiana River Basin.* Prepared for the U.S. Department of the Interior. Water Resources Center, Newark, Delaware (final report).

10. W. V. McGuinness, Jr., and R. Patchai. 1972. *CEM-4103-456: Integrated Water Supply and Waste Water Disposal on Long Island.* The Center for the Environment and Man, Inc., Hartford, Connecticut.

11. U.S. Department of the Interior. 1973. *Resources and Land Information for South Dade County, Florida.* Geological Survey Investigation I-850, Superintendent of Documents, U.S. Government Printing Office, Washington, D.C.

12. U.S. Geological Survey. 1968. *An Atlas of Long Island's Water Resources.* Prepared in cooperation with the New York State Water Resources Commission, Bulletin 62.

10. HEAVY INDUSTRY

In recognition of a high potential for adverse impact, restrictions on the location of heavy industry have been imposed by a number of coastal states. For example, the Coastal Zone Act of Delaware, passed in 1971,[1] "seeks to prohibit entirely the construction of new heavy industry in its coastal areas, which industry is determined to be incompatible with the protection of the natural environment in those areas." Furthermore, "control of industrial development other than that of heavy industry in the Coastal Zone of Delaware through a permit system at the state level is called for." The Act lists the following factors to be considered in reviewing permits for the "other than" heavy industry category:[1]

Environmental impact, including but not limited to, probable air and water pollution likely to be generated by the proposed use under normal operating conditions as well as during mechanical malfunction and human error; likely destruction of wetlands and flora and fauna; impact of site preparation on drainage of the area in question, especially as it relates to flood control; impact of site preparation and facility operations on land erosion; effect of site preparation and facility operations on the quality and quantity of surface, ground, and subsurface water resources, such as the use of water for processing, cooling, effluent removal, and other purposes. . . .

In 1973 the state of New Jersey enacted the Coastal Area Facility Review Act,[2] in which it is declared that "the coastal area, and the State will suffer continuing and ever-accelerating serious adverse economic, social, and aesthetic effects unless the State assists . . . in the assessment of impacts stemming from the future locating and kinds of facilities within the coastal area, on the delicately balanced environment of that area." The Act mandates that the builder(s) of any facility constructed in the coastal area of the state apply for and receive a permit issued by the commissioner of the State Department of Environmental Protection. Included in the definition of "facilities" are industrial plants involved in electric power generation, incineration of wastes, paper production, agrichemical production, inorganic acid and salt manufacture, mineral product production, food and food by-product production, chemical processing, storage, and metallurgical processing.

An act similar to that of New Jersey was enacted in Maine in 1970 under the title "Site Location of Development Act." Under this Act a permit is required from the State Department of Environmental Improvement to assure that developments that substantially affect the environment are sited so as to reduce the potential for adverse effects on the natural environment.[3]

Such legislation is often stimulated by the threat of decentralization, that is, location of major new industrial complexes outside present ports and centers of industry.[4] Suitable coastal sites are growing scarce and expensive, and meeting pollution standards and other constraints is becoming more difficult.

Figure 6.76   Industry siting policies vary greatly from state to state. Above, the Maine side of the Piscataqua River estuary is developed very little, whereas the New Hampshire side (Portsmouth) is committed to a variety of heavy industry. (Conservation Foundation photo by M. Fahay.)

In addition to such state facility-siting regulations, numerous federal environmental programs and local planning requirements and land-use programs are involved (Figure 6.76). The complexities of siting are so great that within the limitations of this book it is possible only to briefly summarize the major considerations.

In general, the coastal zone is attractive to five major types of industry:[5]

1. Industries that benefit from location near low-cost water transportation and inland transportation systems.
2. Industries that derive power from water or use water for process or cooling purposes.
3. Industries that are beneficially located near centers of population but do not have direct dependence on, or need for, water or water access.
4. Marine transportation industries.
5. Industries that depend directly on the marine environment for raw material for commercial activity (including energy sources such as gas).

The coastal counties have had concentrated within them 40 percent of all manufacturing plants in the United States, closely paralleling coastal population distribution (Table 6.15). Over half of all plants in the coastal counties and one-fifth of all manufacturing plants in the United States have been located in the Middle Atlantic coastal region.[6]

Communities considering industrial development options tend to view new plant payrolls and property taxes as an added economic benefit, and commercial interests sense the potential for increased profits. But the commitment of coastal lands for heavy industry sites may engender a wide variety of environmental problems with impacts that extend considerably beyond the direct, localized impacts of the plant. For example,

Table 6.15 Extent of industrial development in the marine coastal zone (SOURCE: Modified from Reference 6)

Biophysical Regions	Total Number of Plants	Number of Large Plants*	Major Water Use Plants in the Coastal Zone				Density of Industrial Development (number of plants per mile of tidal shore-line)
			Paper and Allied Products	Chemical and Allied Products	Petroleum and Allied Products	Primary Metals Industries	
North Atlantic	8,617	2,933	132	88	13	60	0.7
Middle Atlantic	65,000	21,847	761	840	78	532	2.7
Chesapeake Bay	5,186	2,064	86	127	13	41	0.4
South Atlantic	2,695	693	40	59	12	10	0.07
Caribbean	2,554	654	18	16	5	9	0.2
Gulf of Mexico	6,980	2,013	70	192	62	61	0.1
Pacific Southwest	27,508	7,633	240	332	54	286	2.5
Pacific Northwest†	7,584	1,804	76	55	14	47	0.4
Total coastal zone	126,124	37,641	1,423	1,709	251	1,046	
Total United States	306,316	98,661	3,526	3,977	689	3,585	

*More than 20 employees.
†Excluding Alaska.

a new factory may require dredging a deep-water channel, which raises a number of ecological problems (page 422), or increased pressure on land and air transportation links may require expansion of highways and of airports, each with its own potential for ecological disruption (pages 484 and 313). Expansion of utilities and services such as sewage treatment, water supply, and electricity may also place an added strain on available resources and on natural systems. A factory may attract housing projects, shopping centers, and other community development. Also, it may attract other industry. Not only does this impose higher costs on the community for more streets, police and fire protection, schools, and other essential services, but also the overall environmental and service costs (police, fire, school, roads) placed on the community will be far greater than those due to the factory itself, so that planning decisions relating to industrial siting must include the secondary development such industry will induce.

GUIDELINE.   Controlling Industrial Pollution

Direct heavy industry away from ecologically sensitive areas.

The choice of location for heavy industry depends to some degree on the extent of effluent discharge and the anticipated degree and type of waste treatment. Although industrial wastes have heavily damaged estuarine and nearshore ecosystems in the past, recent federal water pollution control legislation administered by the U.S. Environmental Protection Agency (EPA) holds promise of preventing or greatly reducing damage in the future. The new federal and state regulations are so comprehensive, and the criteria and mechanisms so detailed and complex, that we shall touch only on major points here.

Although pollution matters will be controlled through the federal–state permit program, local authorities will have an essential role through controlling land use. By using established local land-use control mechanisms, communities can influence the type and location of industrial development, and hence the type and location of waste discharges to local waters, as well as encroachment into vital habitat areas.

Implementation No. 1. Committed Areas as Industry Sites

Waterfront-dependent heavy industry should be located, to the maximum extent possible, in areas presently committed to industrial use.

The recent trend toward locating new industrial complexes in less developed coastal locations means that more and more of the nation's remaining unpolluted estuaries are being threatened by encroachment and contamination. To site industry properly and to maintain the natural values of coastal water bodies, it is often desirable for communities to cooperate through some type of regional planning authority which can assist industries in the selection of sites that will involve a minimum of adverse ecological effects.

In some coastal areas that have undergone intensive development, a few locations ideally suited for industrial use still remain. These prime locations should be identified, inventoried, and reserved as important industrial resources. Many such sites in growing metropolitan areas, such as the San Francisco Bay region, have been and continue to be taken over by housing and commercial establishments, which have no waterfront-dependent needs. To ensure that prime industrial shorelands are available when needed for industrial use, special land-use controls may have to be applied, restricting the development of these areas to waterfront-dependent industry.

It also may be desirable to direct new industrial development to areas that have already been modified and disturbed through existing industrial development or other land alteration (Figure 6.77). If industrial development must occupy new areas, ecologically viable areas should be avoided. A

Figure 6.77 New industry should be directed to areas of existing intense industrial development whenever feasible (Corpus Christi, Texas). (Photo by author.)

Figure 6.78 A buffer area of natural vegetation is required to provide both purification of contaminated runoff from paved surfaces and a visual screen (Georgetown, South Carolina). (Photo by author.)

prime example of a site that has already been disturbed and has had its environmental value reduced is a shoreline location which has been used as a dredge spoil disposal area and subsequently has had little ecological value. Such sites, which have had their ecological functions obliterated, may safely be developed for industrial use, provided that any adjacent vital areas are preserved intact.

It should be noted that problems arise with expanding in committed areas that are designated by the EPA as presently air pollution impacted and where new industry is essentially banned to prevent further air quality degradation.

There are many reasons to locate an industry back from water bodies and to provide for a buffer strip of natural vegetation between the facility and the water's edge (page 88). The vegetated area provides a visual screen, a purification system for storm runoff, and a protective buffer for the eco-logically sensitive shoreline, especially the fringing wetlands (page 239) (Figure 6.78). The setback should be placed above the annual flood line (which marks the upper edge of wetlands) and should provide a buffer wide enough to cleanse the maximum storm runoff it might receive in the 5- or 10-year rainstorm (page 304). Floodplain management and floodproofing requirements must also be considered (page 230; Appendix, page 790).

Implementation No. 2. Industrial Waste Disposal Control

Heavy industry should be located where waste discharges present the least ecological threat.

The Federal Clean Water Act of 1972 has as a goal the elimination of all discharge of polluting substances to United States waters by 1985 (page 193).

Federal and state regulations pursuant to the Act should correct pollution problems of the past, as explained below:[9]

The effects of all of these forms of [industrial] pollution can be eliminated by the application of existing waste treatment technology and recognition of the characteristics of the estuarine environment which is the final disposal point of the treated waste discharge. Even estuaries which are heavily polluted now can be reclaimed if the wastes entering them are adequately treated.

The wastewaters from industries sited in coastal areas have potential impacts on coastal ecosystems. These impacts range from relatively minor disturbances (such as temporary, localized turbidity increase) to major disruptions (major water pollution) caused by discharge of toxic chemicals. The origin, characteristics, and treatment and disposal methods for wastes from 34 types of industry are described in the Appendix (page 835). Water quality guidelines for industrial pollutants developed by the EPA and the National Academy of Sciences are listed on page 68.

Thermal pollution must also be considered, along with the uptake of large quantities of cooling water. Both pose a major threat to free-floating planktonic forms of life, including larval and juvenile species of important commercial and sport fish and crustaceans (see page 452 for details).

Current federal law prohibits the discharge of toxic industrial wastes into streams, estuaries, or nearshore waters; nor should they be dumped offshore unless toxic or otherwise harmful components are at or below expected allowable concentrations. Cleaning up industrial effluents sufficiently to meet state-federal criteria requires advanced treatment systems (Table 6.16).

In locating a new industry it will be necessary to ensure that its treatment needs are incorporated into the community's long-term plan for environmental protection. For example, since the constituents of industrial effluent are usually quite different from those of domestic sewage, separate private systems may have to be constructed by industry, and planned for accordingly. When discharge into the municipal collection network is allowed, private pretreatment units will probably be necessary to reduce the industrial waste flow to domestic strength before discharge, in order to protect the municipal facilities and the receiving waters (page 553).

Industrial facilities with difficult discharge problems, such as food-processing, petrochemical, wood pulp, and steel processing plants, should not be located on confined estuarine waters (page 523). Moreover, tidal streams, dead-end harbors, small lagoons, and similar small or poorly flushed water bodies should be completely avoided because of their extremely limited capacity to accept and assimilate even small amounts of contaminants (Figures 6.79 and 6.80).

REFERENCES

1. Delaware House of Representatives. 1971. 126th General Assembly, 1st Session. "Coastal Zone Act," *Laws of Delaware*, Chapter 175, Vol. 58.

2. New Jersey Senate and General Assembly. 1973. "Coastal Area Facility Review Act" New Jersey P.L. 1973, Chapter 185.

3. Harriet P. Henry. 1973. *Coastal Zone Management in Maine: A Legal Perspective*. State Planning Office, Augusta, Maine.

4. U.S. Fish and Wildlife Service. 1970. *The National Estuary Study*, Vol. 5. U.S. Department of the Interior, Washington, D.C.

5. Bostwick H. Ketchum, Ed. 1972. *The Water's Edge: Critical Problems of the Coastal Zone*. The Massachusetts Institute of Technology Press, Cambridge, Massachusetts.

6. U.S. Department of the Interior. 1970. *The National Estuarine Pollution Study*. U.S. Senate, 91st Congress, 2nd Session, Document No. 91-58. Superintendent of Documents, U.S. Government Printing Office, Washington, D.C.

7. San Francisco Bay Conservation and Development Commission. 1968. *Waterfront Industry*. San Francisco, California.

8. Federal Water Pollution Control Act Amendments of 1972. U.S. Public Law 92-500, 92nd Congress, Oct. 18, 1972.

Category	Parameters Controlled by 1977	Additional Parameters Controlled by 1983
Canned and Preserved Fruits and Vegetables	BOD, TSS, Fecal Col., pH, O&G	none
Inorganic Chemicals	TSS, and pH for all subcategories; plus for specified products: Ammonia, COD, BOD, Heavy Metals, Fluoride, Iodate, Sulfur, Sulfite, Sulfide, O&G, Total Organic Carbon, Cyanide	none[1]
Iron and Steel	TSS, O&G, pH, Cyanide, Phenols, Ammonia, Heavy Metals	Sulfides, Fluoride, Nitrates, Manganese
Metal Finishing	Heavy Metals, TSS, pH, Cyanide, Fluoride, Phosphorus	All other process water pollutants[2]
Organic Chemicals	BOD, TSS, pH for all subcategories; plus for specified products: Phenols, Cyanide, Heavy Metals	COD
Petroleum Refining	BOD, COD, TSS, O&G, pH, Phenols, Ammonia Sulfides, Chromium	none
Plastics and Synthetics	BOD, COD, TSS, pH for all subcategories; plus for specified products: O&G, Heavy Metals, Phenols	none
Pulp and Paper	BOD, TSS, pH	color
Steam Electric Power	TSS, O&G, pH, Polychlorinated Byphenols, Chlorine, Heavy Metals	Heat,[2] Additional Heavy Metals
Textiles	BOD, COD, TSS, Fecal Col., pH, Phenols, Sulfides, Chromium	color

(1) The 1983 limitations correspond to complete elimination of discharge of the pollutants limited by 1977 for selected processes within the industry.

(2) The 1983 limitations for these parameters correspond to complete elimination of discharge of process-water pollutants.

Table 6.16 Industrial pollutant parameters controlled by effluent limitations either promulgated or under consideration by the U.S. Environmental Protection Agency (SOURCE: Reference 10)

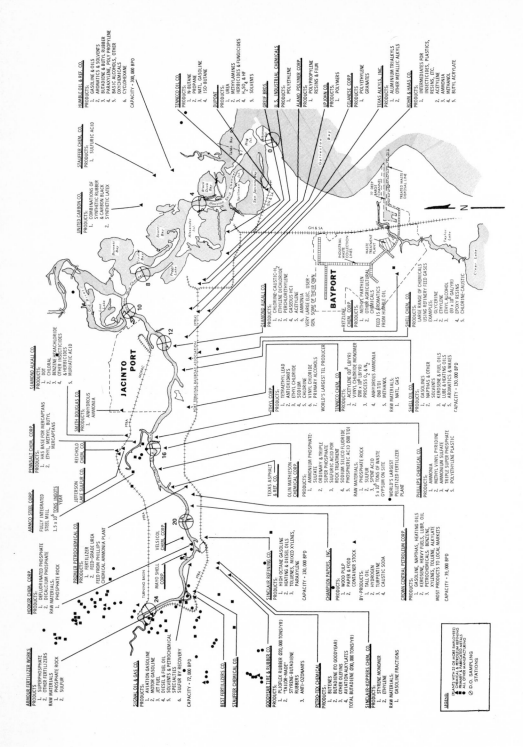

Figure 6.79 Pollutant buildup has deprived Houston ship channel waters of oxygen, turning the channel into a biological desert from Jacinto Port west. (SOURCE: Reference 11.)

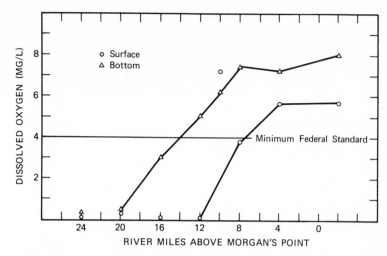

Figure 6.80 Discharge from heavy industry has severely depleted the oxygen supply in river water along the Houston ship channel. (SOURCE: Modified from Reference 11.)

9. T. A. Wastler. 1968. "Municipal and industrial wastes and the estuaries of the South Atlantic and Gulf coasts." In *Proceedings of the Marsh and Estuarine Management Symposium*, Louisiana State University, Baton Rouge, Louisiana, July 19-20, 1967.

10. National Commission on Water Quality. 1975. *Staff Draft Report*. Washington, D.C.

11. Roy W. Hann. 1969. *Management of Industrial Waste Discharges in Complex Estuarine Systems*. Estuarine Systems Projects, Technical Report No. 1, Environmental Engineering Division, Texas A & M University, College Station, Texas.

11. LAND DRAINAGE

Artificial drainage of shorelands is a common practice in low-lying coastal areas. It is accomplished by excavation of canals or ditches to lower the water-table excess surface water from wet areas. The purpose is to provide high-water-table land suitable for uses that require drier land. By its nature artificial land drainage within a coastal watershed alters a vital element of coastal ecosystems—the natural drainage system—and requires careful control to ensure coastal ecosystem protection.

This section concerns artificial drainage of lands for agriculture and forestry and for home, commercial, and industrial sites. Discussed elsewhere is land drainage for flood control (page 354) and mosquito control (page 413).

Coastal ecosystems extend landward from an estuarine basin to include the coastal watersheds, which provide storage and control systems to absorb the heavy seasonal rains and slowly release the accumulation via drainage through wetlands and salt marshes into the open waters of the estuaries. Each section of the system physically and chemically filters the water in transit, removing sediments, utilizing some of the nutrients, and finally releasing fresh water of improved quality into the estuary at a reasonably uniform rate that avoids stressing estuarine function by rapid salinity change. Thus, in its unaltered state, the system is self-sustaining, providing for a cleansing of the water, a beneficial flow regime, and a suitable natural supply of nutrients into the rich estuarine zone.

When portions of this system are removed or short-circuited by drainage canals or land development, the natural flow pattern is disrupted, the water-cleansing function of the vegetation is eliminated, and freshwater flow into the estuaries occurs in surges. In periods of heavy runoff, the canals can swiftly and suddenly pour huge quantities of unfiltered, poor-quality fresh water into an estuary.[1] Not only do these surge flows overburden the estuary with fresh water but also the rapid runoff often contains suspended sediments that produce a variety of negative impacts on the receiving estuary (page 293). Moreover, artificial drainage may cause subsidence of organic soils, requiring the canals to be dug deeper and pump stations to be installed to keep the area dry.

In addition to altering water flow, land improvement projects are often accompanied by a large increase in "nonpoint-source" pollutants. Newly tilled or logged land (page 293) and construction areas (page 537) are erosion-prone and produce large amounts of sediment. Farming operations yield pesticides (page 298), fertilizers (page 296), and animal wastes (page 309) that often are conveyed in channeled runoff directly to estuarine waters.

The following estuarine disturbances are typical of runoff short-circuited by artificial drainage:[2]

1. Abrupt changes in salinity.
2. Increases in turbidity.
3. Increases in nutrients (nitrogen).

4. Increases in biochemical oxygen demand (BOD).
5. Increases in coliform and fecal coliform bacteria count.
6. Decreases in dissolved oxygen.

Because of these potential adverse ecological consequences, projects that require the drainage of wet areas for development should generally be avoided and more appropriate alternatives should be explored (Figure 6.81).

When a land drainage project has been authorized and an irreversible commitment to development has been made, strict controls should be imposed on the design of the drainage facilities. Such measures might include the use of water control structures to hold back the runoff in times of high rainfall and to provide for the settling of suspended solids or other necessary on-site treatment of the runoff water before its release to public waters (Figure 6.82).

The federal government has recognized the value and sensitivity of coastal wetlands and other vital areas through regulations that protect these areas from alterations such as ditches and canals used in land drainage (page 98). However, alteration of the water

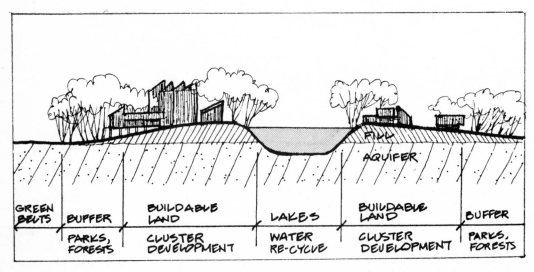

Figure 6.81   When used properly, fill can create dry land in shorelands and avoid alteration of the natural drainage system. (SOURCE: Reference 3.)

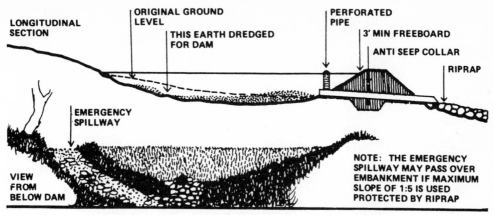

SEDIMENT BASIN CONSTRUCTION — EARTH-FILL DAM

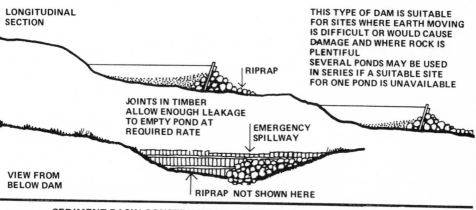

SEDIMENT BASIN CONSTRUCTION — TIMBER FRAME & RIPRAP DAM

Figure 6.82   Water control structures are often necessary to protect watershed runoff water from pollution. (SOURCE: Reference 4.)

runoff from shorelands can have significant effects on the health of a coastal ecosystem, for example, when runoff from a poorly controlled drainage project flows into an estuarine area at unnatural rates, carrying a high load of contaminants.

GUIDELINE.   Preservation of Natural Water System

Maintain the quality, volume, and rate of flow of coastal watershed drainage systems.

Full protection of the quality, volume, and rate of flow of the watershed drainage sys-

tems of shorelands will greatly benefit the environmental condition of land areas, interior water areas, and estuarine resources. This can be accomplished as follows: (1) prohibit drainage of wetlands, or (2) when drainage is necessary in shoreland areas, require that the artificial drainage system regularize the runoff patterns so that the volume of flow and the delivery schedule of runoff to coastal waters are maintained in the natural preexisting state. These precautions will also help to ensure that water delivered to the estuary meets prescribed state and federal requirements.

Figure 6.83 Drainage projects degrade the basic ecological function of wetlands. (Conservation Foundation photo by M. Fahay.)

Implementation No. 1. Wetlands Drainage Constraints

Wetland areas should not be drained.

Wetlands, tidal marshes, bogs, and many other vital habitat areas in coastal water and shoreland areas are dependent for their viability on wet soils and regular flooding. If such an area is drained with excavated canals its character is usually completely changed and its value obviated (Figure 6.83). As explained elsewhere (page 98), the greatest damage to vital areas occurs from excavation for draining, grading, and filling. Prohibition of these activities is a major aspect of the controls on site preparation in water areas (page 538).

The regulations of the U.S. Army Corps of Engineers (*Federal Register*, July 25, 1975, Vol. 40, No. 144) state specifically that wetlands are to be protected: "As environmentally vital areas, they constitute a pro-

ductive and valuable public resource, the unnecessary alteration or destruction of which should be discouraged as contrary to the public interest." And further: "Unless the public interest requires otherwise, no permit shall be granted for work in wetlands. . . ."[5] Since the Corps has the major federal discretion (with the Environmental Protection Agency) for control of wetlands development, one must assume that wetland areas may be altered only for public, never for private, benefit.

Implementation No. 2. Shoreland Drainage Constraints

Systems for the artificial drainage of shorelands should be designed to ensure that water leaves the project area in the quality, volume, and rate of flow prevailing in the natural drainage system.

The health of the coastal ecosystem depends on regularizing the inflow of runoff water, particularly that which enters via canals and creeks. Surge flows of existing drainage canals should be controlled by the use of spreader canals and the restoration of the pattern of land drainage as nearly as possible to the natural condition (Figure 6.84). Strong controls must also be exerted on drainage plans for new developments.[6] By slowing the flows during wet periods and increasing them during dry periods, wide oscillations in salinity and circulation of water in the inner reaches of an estuary are prevented.

The quantity and rate of water flow from uplands into estuarine waters are prime determinants of an estuary's salinity balance, upon which many species, such as shrimp and oysters, are dependent (page 23). Certain species of shrimp have special salinity requirements for breeding success. If too much fresh water from accelerated land drainage dilutes their estuarine nursery area (page 40), the shrimp population will decrease and shrimp fishing will be poor. For

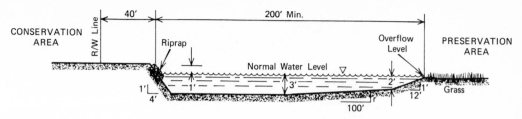

Figure 6.84 Spreader canals are useful in rehabilitating shoreland drainage by detaining land runoff water and dispersing it into other natural areas such as high marsh. (SOURCE: Reference 1.)

this reason the state of North Carolina is discouraging the artificial drainage of coastal lowlands, which would cause exaggerated flows of fresh water into shrimp nursery areas.[7]

The proposed First Colony Farms, located in the center of North Carolina's estuarine system, threatens to intensify the problems. First Colony's operations require an artificial drainage system capable of removing from its land area at least 1 inch of water each day to make the land suitable for corn and soybean production. The combined effects of these drainage alterations alone are significantly hazardous to the coastal ecosystem.

The canals used in land drainage operations to convey fresh water to coastal areas may function in the reverse, that is, to convey salt water inland. The intrusion of salt water upstream in artificial canals often has serious adverse effects on inland systems, rendering the water unsuitable for native fish and wildlife. Seawater encroachment can contaminate human and agricultural water supplies, necessitating costly treatment or relocation of intake points. Increased salinity in the upstream environment also results in increased corrosion and shorter life expectancy for engineering structures. The construction of barriers (sills or weirs) across drainage canals near their point of entry to the estuary to prevent saltwater inflow provides only a partial solution because a sill low enough to provide drainage is usually not effective against a massive inflow of saline water during storm tides (Figure 6.85).

It is difficult to find ecologically accept-able methods for shoreland drainage that are, at the same time, workable and cost efficient. But when they can be designed to provide the necessary function and remain environmentally compatible they should be encouraged. The principle for low-lying lands is: New drainage facilities should be designed to closely approximate the natural system of water drainage and to maintain the water table as nearly at its historic level as possible.

Artificial drainage facilities should release water from a developed area in a manner approximating the natural local surface flow regime by the use of either (1) a spreader pond or performance-equivalent structure on site, or (2) an adequate natural retention or natural filtration and flow area, such as a grassy swale or vegetated buffer strip (page 812).

Drainage facilities should be designed to maintain natural groundwater levels through the use of high-level weirs or performance-equivalent structures or systems (Figure 6.86).

Canals should have gently sloping sides (preferably not greater than 6:1 and never greater than 4:1). They should also be the minimum depth necessary to maintain reasonable flow and to keep down cattails and other rooted weeds (minimum 3 to 4 feet; 0.9 to 1.2 meters). They should normally be no deeper than 7 or 8 feet (2.2 to 2.5 meters).[1] Canals excavated in the uplands should be completely stabilized with vegetation before runoff is allowed to be released through them to adjacent public waters.

Modifications to existing faciliites should

Figure 6.85 Combined water control structure at Beach Road, Sanibel Island, Florida. (A) Water level control (foreground) for interior wetlands and automatic water level recorder (background) operated by U.S. Geological Survey. (Photo by author.) (B) Flap valve on outlet pipe prevents saltwater entrance during high tides. (Photos by Dewitt Jones, Captiva, Florida.)

Figure 6.86 Water control structures are essential to preserve groundwater levels in many areas (Titusville, Florida). (Photo from Brevard County, Florida, Mosquito Control.)

be encouraged to raise the groundwater table, to limit saltwater intrusion, or in other ways to benefit the water system and estuarine resources. Improvements to existing systems should be mandatory in any modification or expansion work.

Although the federal government has regulations covering the alteration of wetlands and water areas, state and local governments hold the broad responsibility for adoption and implementation of development controls in the shore uplands. Therefore local community jurisdictions must rely on their own programs of development and drainage standards in order to protect their coastal resources.

It is quite practicable to establish, or to incorporate into existing subdivision or building permit reviews, a requirement for analysis of the hydrological consequences of residential, commercial, and agricultural development in a coastal watershed.[7] When the consequence of private construction activity will be a more rapid input of water

volumes into streams, local authorities should not approve the permit in question until all stipulated measures have been incorporated to stabilize runoff quality, volume, and rate of flow (page 237).

REFERENCES

1. Black, Crow, and Eidsness, Inc. 1974. *Master Plan for Water Management District No. 6, Collier County, Florida.* Report to Collier County Water Management District No. 6, Gainesville, Florida.

2. John Clark. 1974. *Rookery Bay: Ecological Constraints on Coastal Development.* The Conservation Foundation, Washington, D.C.

3. University of Miami. 1971. *An Environmental Land Planning Study for South Dade County, Florida.* Division of Applied Ecology. Coral Gables, Florida.

4. Joachim Tourbier and Richard Westmacott. 1974. *Water Resources Protection Measures in Land Development—A Handbook: Water Resources as a Basis for Comprehensive Planning and Development of the Christina River Basin.*

A Prototype Project, Phase II. Water Resources Center, University of Delaware, Newark, Delaware.

5. U.S. Army Corps of Engineers. "Permits for activities in navigable waters or ocean waters." *Federal Register*, Vol. 40, No. 144 (July 25, 1975).

6. Michael R. Carter et al. 1973. *Ecosystems Analysis of the Big Cypress Swamp and Estuaries.* U.S. Environmental Protection Agency, Region IV, Atlanta, Georgia.

7. The Conservation Foundation. 1975. *Sanibel Natural Systems Study, Preliminary Summary of Findings and Recommendations.* Washington, D.C.

12. MARINAS

Any stretch of seacoast that is within commuting distance of a populated area and has a modicum of sheltered water attracts boating enthusiasts. This demand is reflected in new coastal residential developments catering to second-home buyers, which rarely fail to include some form of marina services in their plans. Many coastal communities see marinas as potential sources of income, both from the facility itself and from adjacent development. However, these benefits must be weighed against potential adverse impacts of marinas and marina activities.

As environmental and other constraints increase, the large centralized marina emerges as a better alternative than a collection of numerous smaller dock sites. The significant determinants of the environmental impact of a marina include its location, site preparation and construction methods, modifications required to make the site practicable (such as drainage or landfill), design details of the facility, and the extent of dredging required for access canals. With reasonable environmental controls on location, design, and operations, marina and harbor development can continue to benefit communities with minimal damage to coastal ecosystems.

When deciding on the location of a large marina, it will be necessary to consider sites within the context of an overall community master plan. Only in this way can a site be selected that will have the proper blend of minimal environmental degradation, community access, and use of existing public utilities. The consequences of poor marina siting are too serious to be left to chance or the discretion of the private entrepreneur. At stake is not only the natural environment but also orderly community development involving roads, utilities, services, and induced secondary development.

The necessity for recognizing the influence that a marina may have on surrounding development is illustrated in the extreme by Marina Del Rey in Los Angeles, California, now one of the largest marinas in the world (Figure 6.87). Before development the marina area was 1513 acres of salt marsh and farm and residential land. The marina was first designed to serve recreational boating interests, but the land-use scheme was changed to a high-density residential development because of the county's need to pay back revenue bonds that boat-slip rental fees alone could not cover. By 1971 this "recreational boating facility" contained 4500 apartment units, plus supporting restaurants and shopping areas, with a value exceeding $105 million (a further $60 million complex was under construction). All this required greatly expanded public utilities, road surfaces, and parking areas, and a demand for services not foreseen in the original marina development plan.[1]

Marinas are traditionally defined as waterfront facilities for recreational boating,[2] but the range of services provided at the newer marinas stretches this definition considerably. A modern marina is a big operation. Facilities include advanced sewage treatment plants, engine repair shops, fuel depots, restaurants, stores, and docking for massive numbers of boats. Each of these marina services has the potential for polluting the water and altering coastal ecosystems.

Figure 6.87   Marina Del Rey near Los Angeles, California, exemplifies the type of high-density development that may be induced by urban marinas. (Photo by author.)

GUIDELINE.   Water Pollution

Marinas and small-boat harbors should be planned to minimize the risk of water pollution.

Potential damage to the natural system from induced secondary development around marinas may include contamination of surface water and groundwater from inefficient sewage treatment procedures, interruption of groundwater recharge and saltwater intrusion, water pollution by surface runoff, erosion and sedimentation resulting from failure to properly revegetate or drain cleared surfaces, and loss of vital habitat areas.

Marinas in tidal creeks or estuarine water bodies with restricted natural flushing rates are particularly troublesome environmentally because the water body is unable to rid itself of marina-source contaminants, including heavy metals and hexane extractables (Figure 6.88). In addition, breakwaters, jetties, and other structures required to protect the marina from wave action may interfere with tides and currents, further reducing the flushing rate.

The demand for storm protection and ease of navigation frequently results in excessive channel dredging, breakwaters, groins, jetties, and the digging of dead-end canals

Figure 6.88   The open entrance and piling–supported piers of this marina allow for circulation of tidal waters. (Photo courtesy of Miami–Metro Department of Publicity and Tourism.)

to create more boat landings (Figure 6.89). These structures alter water movement, creating stagnant sinks for pollutants, and often cause off-site erosion. All such alterations have the potential for serious degradation of the quality of coastal waters.

When a marina site requires excavation for utilities, building foundations, fill, or canals, the potential for erosion and sedimentation in nearby waters is increased. Increased stream flow resulting from rainwater runoff from cleared and surfaced areas causes erosion, sedimentation, downstream flooding, and the introduction of high nutrient loads into estuarine waters.

Ancillary marina facilities—parking areas, boat storage, housing, repair yards, and so forth—should be situated above the wetlands and, where possible, out of the coastal floodplains so as to displace the effects of surfacing and clearing and the runoff pollution potential to less sensitive areas. An internalized drainage system to collect and restore water runoff and other liquid waste should

always be installed. Sewage facilities should be designed to meet the maximum capacity of boat slips. Construction on the waterfront, such as docks, piers, and walkways, should be elevated on pilings, not placed on landfill. Marina space should be allocated so that larger boats with deeper draft are kept in deeper water while smaller boats can be located closer to the shoreline in shallow water.

Other results of construction activity adjacent to streams or coastal waters are the degradation of water quality resulting from spillage of concrete and asphalt waste, sanitary debris, fuels, grease, or oil, which may enter nearby water bodies directly through runoff or may contaminate groundwater supplies. Even when a marina is adequately designed and located, there are many requirements for pollution safeguards during its operation.

In summary, coastal ecosystem disturbances are associated with (1) the continuing influence of bank- and shore-protective devices on fresh water stream flow and coastal water patterns; (2) the release of pollutants, such as gas and oil, from marina supply sources and from operating boats; (3) water turbulence and sediment suspension by boat traffic; (4) the disruption of the longshore movement of beach sand replenishment; (5) the deposition of silt and sand on bottom areas and submerged vegetation and shellfish; (6) the stimulation of eutrophic conditions due to inadequate flushing combined with over-enrichment by marina-based nutrient contaminants; (7) erosion scouring along the outer rim of bulkheads, jetties, or breakwater structures; (8) reductions in dissolved oxygen caused by fouling communities on the undersurface of floats, on wooden pilings, and on boat bottoms; (9) the toxicity associated with motor exhausts; (10) concentrations of toxic copper in marina-area water from boat antifouling paint; (11) the reduction of habitat suitability for wildlife and waterfowl due to increased noise and human activity; and (12) turbidity and possible release of heavy metals and pesticides during dredging and subsequent maintenance.

Implementation No. 1. Marina Location

Marinas should be located on water bodies where there is a high rate of flushing.

Marinas should be located near tributary mouths or on larger water bodies that are characterized by strong currents and water movement. This prevents stagnant water and the accumulation of pollutants introduced into marine waters by sewage effluent, land runoff, antifouling paints, and other sources.

Any marina design that would create stagnant water areas, such as dead-end channels or confined basins, should be avoided (Figure 6.90). Box-cut dredged channels become sediment traps for dead and decaying organic material. These accumulated materials exert a strong oxygen demand on overlying waters, depleting dissolved oxygen and causing anaerobic (without oxygen) conditions. There may be periodic mortalities of benthic organisms and a serious reduction of fish.[3] Jetties and breakwaters that limit water movement in enclosed marinas cause static conditions, with virtually no flushing action to remove accumulated debris and other pollutants.

Figure 6.89 Excavation of dead-end canals to create marinas should be discouraged in favor of less environmentally damaging approaches. (Conservation Foundation photo by M. Fahay.)

Figure 6.90   The narrow entrance and confined space in this marina limit the cleansing action of tidal flushing. Ideally, marina sites should have a turnover, or water replacement, time of 2 to 4 days. (Photo by author.)

Another problem with poorly flushed marinas and dead-end canals is foul odors from decaying algae. Hydrogen sulfide, a by-product of bacterial decomposition, emanating from canals in Florida has turned white paint black on nearby homes. Also it has caused fish kills, both by its poisonous effect on marine life and by contributing to the reduction of oxygen in overlying waters.[3]

To prevent stagnation, marinas should be located and designed so that the adjacent water has a rapid "turnover time." Generally, turnover time can be defined as the number of days or hours required for tidal action or river flow to replace the water of a bay or tributary with new water from another source. Only if good tidal flushing is maintained will water quality remain high. This requirement means that many small tributaries, and confined stagnant water areas in general, will be off limits for marina sites.

When considering tributaries of larger bays for marina locations, the flushing time

of the tributary, as well as that of the main bay to which it is attached, must be used in the calculation of flushing time. In the absence of specific information to the contrary, a maximum turnover time of 2 to 4 days should be safe as a design criterion. Normally, a period of more than 10 days should be considered an unacceptable turnover time.

Implementation No. 2.   Circulation Enhancement for Marinas

Marina access channels should be designed to maximize circulation and avoid dead spots.

Since alteration of the shore configuration and excavation of dead-end canals should generally be avoided in new marina construction, the requirement to design channel systems for rapid flushing applies mostly to the restoration and rehabilitation of existing marinas. However, there may be instances in which new marinas might include some excavation in shorelands where circulation enhancement could be implemented.

Rehabilitation includes two possibilities for circulation enhancement. First, dead-end, box-cut channels can be opened up by connection to other channels or to open water so as to achieve flow flushing. Second, the channels can be redesigned to a simulated "dendritic" system—decreasing channel cross sections and water depths, which will increase water velocity and improve the flushing action in a similar fashion.

The dendritic system is patterned after the natural system of dead-end tributaries in estuaries and marshes, whereby the cross section becomes progressively smaller as the head of the tributary is approached (Figure 6.91). The decreasing cross-sectional area of waterways permits water velocities to remain constant throughout the system despite the progressively smaller volumes of water. A large entrance channel should taper to a pro-

portionately shallower and narrower channel at the head of the marina, and the smaller side channels should also decrease in width and depth. In cross section the channels should be smooth, and deep holes and other dead spots should be avoided.

A marina redesigned in this fashion will have greatly improved flushing action. A strategy of reallocation of berths will be necessary to put the smallest craft at the channel heads.

Implementation No. 3.   Waste Control in Marinas

Marina designs must incorporate facilities for the proper handling of sewage, refuse, and wastes.

Sewage from boats has forced the closing of productive shellfish beds near marinas and small-boat harbors because of bacterial contamination. For example, the state of Virginia automatically requires the closing of

Figure 6.91   A marina designed to simulate the dendritic pattern of natural waterways, with channels that are progressively narrower and decrease in depth from the entrance, similar to the marsh depicted, will maintain current velocity and increase flushing at the channel's head. (Conservation Foundation photo by M. Fahay.)

shellfish beds around marinas immediately after they are established. The state recommends the following:[4]

Number of Boats	Condemned Area (all directions)
1– 50	⅛ mile (⅕ km)
51–100	¼ mile (⅖ km)
100+	½ mile (⅘ km)

Discharge of untreated sewage into surface waters from boats is now usually prohibited in marina areas. To prevent bacterial contamination of shellfish and eutrophication of estuaries, federal and many state regulations require pump-out facilities for the treatment of sewage from boats. All marine toilets must be self-contained with the sewage retained and pumped ashore for treatment.

A storm sewer that drains into the head of a poorly flushed marina basin may cause pollutants such as heavy metals, pesticides, oil, and road dirt to reach unacceptable levels. Also, silting will increase, accelerating the frequency of maintenance dredging. To avoid this, runoff water should be appropriately managed as discussed elsewhere (page 237).

Antifouling paints and outboard engine exhausts are other sources of pollution in marinas. Outboard engines leach oil and gasoline into the water, and their exhaust contains carbon monoxide, which can build up to damaging levels (page 243). Copper, lead, and other toxic substances leach into the water[5] and (principally in large, poorly flushed marinas) may reach levels harmful to shrimp, phytoplankton, and other marine life.

GUIDELINE. Shoreline Alteration

Marinas and small-boat harbors should not alter the existing shoreline configuration or degrade vital habitat areas.

Marinas must be designed for minimum interference with vital habitat areas such as wetlands and shellfish beds. Essential shoreline structures should be placed so as to preempt a minimum of these areas and to require no dredging or filling of wetlands. Marinas should be located so as to minimize the severe environmental impacts that result from required channel and basin dredging. Marinas should not be sited so as to require the excavation of man-made canals, particularly dead-end canals that have restricted flushing capacity. Locating marinas as far as possible in places that provide natural protection and accessibility greatly minimizes environmental impact, as summarized by S. W. Hole:[6]

Other than . . . small-boat docks, few mooring facilities occur without rather massive changes to the shore system and these changes can significantly affect the water system. Storm runoff that originally reached the water as gradual overland flow causing neither erosion of the banks nor a significant change in water quality can become pointed, orders of magnitude larger, and cause significant changes in water quality. Parking lots and roofs of covered dry storage and many other things contribute to these changes. Diversion, relocation, polishing, or other methods of treatment of storm water may be needed unless the effects are acceptable.

Banks that were once naturally stable become unstable as a result of the use of the area and changes in upland and bank vegetation that occur. Then too boats create waves and this, as a pratical matter, can cause problems. Special planting and lining of banks too steep for the natural soils with stone often has helped reduce the effect of boat traffic.

When the natural bank has been replaced with vertical seawalls, the problems of wave reflections from natural causes may be so severe that the area is simply not an acceptable anchorage site. In other instances, because of wave reflection from boat traffic, conditions may so develop that the area becomes unacceptable. Frequently, in the latter instances and occasionally in the former, lining the seawalls with rubble may reduce the problem to acceptable levels. This treatment of the wall also reconstructs to a certain degree the natural sloping bank, pro-

Figure 6.92   Offshore mooring of watercraft is recommended to avoid the ecological disturbance caused by construction of shoreline docking facilities (South Freeport, Maine). (Conservation Foundation photo by M. Fahay.)

viding thereby a gradual transition from upland to deeper waters.

In our work we find that as much attention must be paid to effects of upland change as to the work over and in the water.

Implementation No. 1.   Reducing Shoreline Alterations for Marinas

Marinas should be planned so as to minimize the extent of excavation, shoreline alteration, and disturbance of vital habitat areas.

The configuration of the shoreline is governed by natural process and factors—tides, littoral drift, sea level, and geological forma-

tion. Generally, changes in the natural configuration have adverse effects, for example, wetlands filling, bulkheading, and canal excavation (and subsequent maintenance). Marinas should therefore be designed to avoid significant shoreline alteration.

To eliminate channel excavation, piers should extend out to naturally deep water, be built on pilings, and connect to land above the annual flood line. Floating docks should be planned wherever possible (page 449). Offshore moorings or onshore dry storage for boats will reduce the size and cost of a marina's piers and docks and should be used whenever feasible (Figures 6.92 and 6.93).

Figure 6.93   Offshore mooring is recommended to avoid dead-end canal dredging and other environmental disturbances (Dinner Key Marina, Miami, Florida). (Photo courtesy of Miami–Metro Department of Publicity and Tourism.)

In the past, coastal wetlands have appeared to be the logical place to build marinas and small-boat harbors. Tidal wetlands were cheap, easily available, and in prime locations. As recently as the early 1960s, marina builders were advised as follows:[2]

One kind of site that can be recommended for consideration as the future home for the marina is the so-called useless swamp or salt marsh. These areas, prior to improvement, are usually too low and too soft for practical land usage and at the same time are seldom covered by sufficient water for even a rowboat. By dredging one part and filling another, a well-balanced, valuable and usable area is obtained at moderate cost that will meet all requirements for the marina.

Increasingly strict state and federal controls on dredge-and-fill operations in wetlands will limit marina construction in the future (page 251). Recommendations for locating marinas in tidal marshes and compensating for this disturbance by creating new, artificially planted marsh on dredge spoil islands elsewhere[7] should be regarded skeptically, as the productivity of the artificially altered area is questionable. The public benefits of a healthy, natural tidal marsh to fish and wildlife, recreation, and flood protection are too great to allow its destruction (page 98). It is frequently possible to avoid vegetated shorelines and to design marina piers and docks to extend over a wetland on pilings to deeper water (page 589).

The construction of groins, bulkheads, and jetties alters the sand transport patterns along the shore. In coastal waters such structures may also interfere with tides and currents and thus modify flushing rates, temperatures, and salinity ratios. These changes will, in turn, influence the availability of oxygen and nutrients to the biota. Similar changes are likely with breakwaters.

Particularly damaging are shoreline protection structures in the transition zone of estuaries, including the intertidal and adjacent shallow subtidal areas. Bulkheading

here eliminates the shallow intertidal zone, thus destroying an area of high productivity and an important shallow-water habitat for aquatic animals (page 343).[8]

Many of the supporting facilities related to marinas and small-boat harbors can be located inland, with only minimal alteration of the shoreline for boat docks and piers. When the opportunity exists, inland storage of small boats should be included. Regulations for the protection of wetlands in Georgia include the following requirements:[9]

All (marina) plans should be minimum in size and include only those facilities requiring a waterfront location. Supporting marina facilities, such as storage yards, repair shops, retail stores, restaurants, etc., should not be located in marshlands.

The location of the marina and the extent of its ancillary services will be the principal determinants of the amount and kind of associated construction activity. If the site requires clearing for buildings and parking lots, the available habitat will be reduced and the possibility of erosion and sedimentation in nearby water bodies increased. The amount of land to be cleared will depend on three factors: (1) the condition of the land at the outset, (2) the range of services offered by the marina, and (3) the water surface area encompassed by the marina. A minimum-service marina will require a land-to-water surface ratio of about 1 : 1.[10]

REFERENCES

1. George P. Schultz et al. n.d. *Marina Del Rey Study, Working Paper IB: The Development of the Marina, Coastal Zone Planning and Management Project.* University of Southern California Sea Grant Program, Los Angeles, California.

2. Charles A. Chaney. 1961. *Marinas: Recommendations for Design, Construction and Maintenance.* National Association of Engine and Boat Manufacturers, Inc.

3. William Barada and William M. Partington.

1972. *Report of Investigation of the Environmental Effects of Private Waterfront Canals.* Florida Conservation Foundation, Winter Park, Florida.

4. Kenneth L. Marcellus, George M. Dawes, and Gene M. Silberhorn. 1973. *Local Management of Wetlands, Environmental Considerations.* Applied Marine Science and Ocean Engineering of the Virginia Institute of Marine Science, Special Report No. 35, Gloucester Point, Virginia.

5. Scott W. Nixon, Candace A. Oviatt, and Sharon L. Northby. 1973. *Ecology of Small Boat Marinas.* University of Rhode Island, Marine Technical Report Series No. 5, Kingston, Rhode Island.

6. Stanley W. Hole. Stanley W. Hole and Associates, Inc., Consulting Engineers and Architects, Naples, Florida. Personal communication.

7. S. P. Giannio and H. Wang. 1974. *Engineering Considerations for Marinas in Tidal Marshes.* College of Marine Studies, University of Delaware, Newark, Delaware.

8. William E. Odum. 1970. "Insidious alteration of the estuarine environment." *Transactions of the American Fisheries Society,* Vol. 99, pp. 836–847.

9. State of Georgia, Department of Natural Resources. "Rules and regulations for Coastal Marshland Protection Act." *Georgia Laws, 1970,* p. 939, and as amended.

10. Walter Isard. 1972. *Ecologic–Economic Analysis for Regional Development.* The Free Press, New York.

13. MOSQUITO CONTROL

Salt marshes and mangrove areas that lie above mean high water are well known as potential mosquito-breeding areas. In these high-marsh wetland areas salt-marsh mosquitoes lay their eggs on damp soil. Development is completed in a few days, but hatching is dependent on a periodic tidal flood or rainstorm.[1] Salt-marsh mosquitoes do not breed in low-marsh areas, which are flooded by daily tides.

Large amounts of tax dollars are spent annually to control insect populations; in 1971, $38 million was expended by 191 publicly funded mosquito abatement districts. The states of California and Florida accounted for the largest expenditures, $10 and $11 million, respectively.[2]

Partial draining of salt marshes with grid-pattern ditching and channels running directly to the estuary was a prevalent method of controlling salt-marsh mosquitoes (Figure 6.94) for several decades up through the 1940s.[3] The idea was to dry up the surface of the marshes rapidly and thus prevent water from remaining in surface depressions longer than a few days (a week at most), thereby preventing mosquito larvae from hatching. This method was partially successful for controlling mosquitoes, but surface dewatering proved to be damaging to the marsh ecosystem.

From the late 1940s into the 1950s the use of DDT to kill mosquito larvae became common. By the mid-1950s however, DDT had fallen into disrepute because it proved harmful to a wide spectrum of animal life, including the natural predators and parasites that control mosquitoes. Moreover, many strains of mosquitoes developed a genetic immunity to the compound. Eventually the sale of DDT was banned by federal regulations, and other pesticides came into common use. By the late 1960s about 2 million acres of salt marsh and tidelands were chemically treated annually to control insects such as flies, gnats, and mosquitoes.[4] By 1970 ecologic and health problems were associated with the use of other chlorinated pesticides (e.g., aldrin, endrin, heptachlor, and dieldrin),[5] and steps to limit the production and/or use of all of these have since been taken. Fortunately, they have been used to only a limited degree to combat salt-marsh mosquitoes.

Because of the increasing resistance of mosquitoes to pesticides and because of public concern about pesticides and grid ditching of marshes, experts have given more attention to alternative systems for controlling mosquitoes. These systems require water management, particularly stabilization of water levels in the marshes to interrupt the

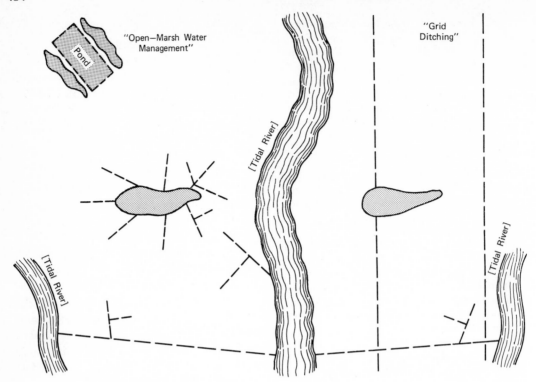

Figure 6.94   A comparison of two management techniques for mosquito control—the efficient open marsh water management system (left side) and the outdated grid ditching system (right side)—on portions of a hypothetical marsh. (SOURCE: Adapted from a drawing by Fred Ferrigno, New Jersey Division of Fish, Game and Shell Fisheries.)

breeding cycles of mosquitoes, and improved channelization methods to encourage access by predatory fish to the mosquito larvae. Modern water management methods, if correctly implemented, may have minimal adverse impacts on wetlands and on coastal ecosystems.[6, 7]

Nearly 200 organized mosquito control districts have been established in the United States. Often they have separate taxing powers and operate with considerable independence from the local political apparatus. However, they are usually under considerable direct public pressure during the mosquito season, and most staffs attempt to maintain high visibility in their activities to mollify the citizenry. Unfortunately, the labor and money put into water management on the marshes often go unnoticed,

whereas fogging trucks and helicopters gain wide public exposure.

GUIDELINE.   Water Management

Use appropriate water management techniques to control salt-marsh mosquitoes.

A range of water management methods provides effective control of salt-marsh mosquitoes with minimal environmental disruption. Although at the outset water level management may cost more than direct control by pesticides, it provides long-term solutions that are often cheaper over a number of years. In addition to providing effective mosquito control, water management can enhance the flow of water through the marsh, increase marsh productivity, and provide

Figure 6.95 Open-marsh water management provides the necessary mosquito control, eliminates insecticides, and increases wildlife utilization. (Photo by Jerome Carrol, U.S. Fish and Wildlife Service.)

habitat for waterfowl (Figure 6.95).[8] (Article 22, Chapter 7.)

Water management includes (1) impoundments, whereby marshes are surrounded with dikes to control the water level (Figure 6.96); and (2) open-marsh water management, whereby a connected system of ponds and open channels is developed to provide habitats for mosquito-eating fish and give them access to all temporary standing water areas (Figure 6.97).

Water management for mosquito control is based on two natural factors: (1) salt-marsh mosquitoes must have periodic fluctuations in water level to breed; and (2) if certain species of fish have access to breeding waters, they will devour large quantities of larvae. For example, a mosquito fish (Gambusia) may eat as many as 580 mosquito larvae per day.[10] Water management attempts to keep water levels stable or to open salt marshes with channels so that fish have access to all ponds and other water-collection places.

Open-marsh water management requires considerable planning, surveying, and engineering, as well as biological study by entomologists and wildlife biologists.[11] Yet the cost appears to be justified by the result: effective, long-term control of mosquito breeding. Of all possible mosquito control methods, the open-marsh system interferes least with normal wetland function.[14]

Although open-marsh water management is generally preferred to impoundments, there are exceptions because of tidal conditions or the need for waterfowl habitat. Limited use of pesticides for short-term relief of extra-heavy outbreaks may be justified. Adult mosquito poisons are effective for 1 day; larval mosquito poisons, for several days.[13]

Implementation No. 1. Open-Marsh Management

Open-marsh water management should be used as the primary means of salt-marsh mosquito control

The dominant United States salt-marsh mosquito species (Aedes) share a common basic life history and ecology. Eggs are laid singly on the moist, organic soil of the marsh, usually where there is vegetative cover and never in flooded areas or open waters. Development of the eggs does not occur until the soil is flooded by higher tides or rainwater, whereupon the larvae hatch within hours and begin rapid development. A regular flooding cycle is necessary for successful breeding—from 4 to 10 or more days of flooding (for larval development) in standing water, followed by a period of at least 4 to 10 days of absence of standing water (for egg laying for the next brood). Within 7 to 15 days (at summer temperatures) the new hatch is ready to lay eggs. Only the females bite, since the blood is used for generating a new batch of eggs. (See Article 22, Chapter 7.)

The cycle of flooding required for mos-

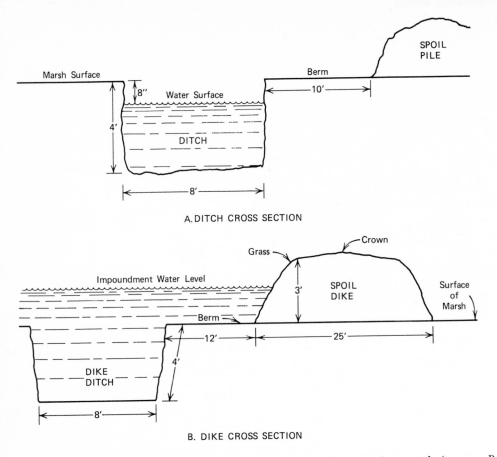

A. DITCH CROSS SECTION

B. DIKE CROSS SECTION

Figure 6.96 Schematic ditch, dike, and impoundment cross sections for mosquito control. (SOURCE: Reference 9.)

Figure 6.97 In open-marsh water management pond radials provide access for killifish from open waters to surrounding mosquito breeding depressions. (Photo by Fred Ferrigno, New Jersey Department of Environmental Protection.)

quito production is not present in low marshes or tidal marshes, which are flushed by tides every day. But this cycle is present in the high marsh—the upper wetlands, or back portion of the marsh—which is flooded only by rain, storms, or spring tides. When the floodwater is retained in isolated pockets (ponds, salt pannes, and other depressions) for periods of 4 to 10 days or more, a high potential for mosquito breeding is created. For effective control one need only connect the isolated pockets to the natural drainage system of the marsh with properly designed, "selective" channels. These provide access to all potential breeding areas for mosquito-eating minnows such as killi-

fish and mosquito fish (Figure 6.98; also see Figure 6.97). The system must also include sufficient deeper, permanent water areas, where the fish can reside during lower water periods.

A rotary ditcher or the equivalent is effective for digging the channels in grassy marsh areas (Figure 6.99). Such machines disperse the channel spoil evenly over the marsh rather than dumping it in piles, which may impede tidal flow.[11] Connector channels, or radials, also facilitate the transport of suspended organisms and nutrients between marsh and estuary and improve the function of the coastal ecosystem. If done correctly, they are of great value in mosquito

Figure 6.98 Selective channels connect upper marsh ponds—prime mosquito breeding sites—to permanent residence areas of mosquito-eating fish. (Conservation Foundation photo by M. Fahay.)

Figure 6.99 A rotary ditcher is used to dig channels through grassy marsh because it dispenses channel spoil evenly. (Photo courtesy of Quality Marsh International Corporation, Thibodaux, Louisiana.)

water level management because they eliminate the routine need for insecticides, as has been demonstrated in Cumberland County, New Jersey.[11] This approach is called "open-marsh water management."[14]

In such water level management the channels should be dug only to the depth and width necessary to connect the isolated pockets to the water system. Weirs at strategic heights (between mean high water and mean sea level) built across the channels may be helpful in maintaining the water table. A variation of this technique is practiced in Louisiana, where weirs (low dams) are used to hold the water level in tributary creeks and ponds to a minimum during neap (low-range) tide periods for combined ecological management and boat access by trappers, with incidental benefits for mosquito control.

The open-marsh water management approach is now feasible throughout most of the salt marshes of America, but its technology has yet to be adapted to the mangrove tidelands of Florida.[15] Figure 6.100 shows

water management methods recommended for various elements of marshes.

There remain many thousands of acres of salt-marsh wetlands in the Middle Atlantic region and New Jersey that have been seriously degraded by ditching and draining. They can be rehabilitated through modern water management methods in which an appropriate system of connector channels would be created to replace the ditches. The old ditches would be connected to the system only if they are active mosquito breeders or lead to breeding places; those that have silted in and become revegetated would be left to fill in naturally.[16]

Implementation No. 2. Mosquito Impoundments

The use of impoundments to control salt-marsh mosquitoes should be restricted to circumstances where open-marsh water management is not effective.

The purpose of impounding salt marshes for mosquito control is to hold a body of

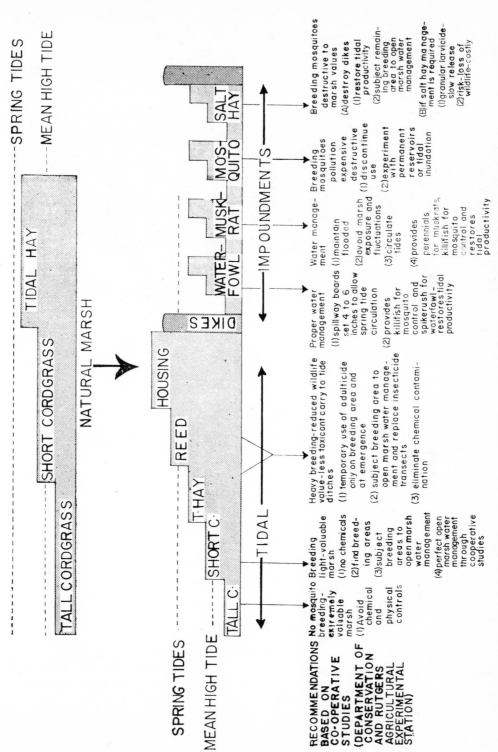

Figure 6.100 Recommended marsh management for mosquito control based on the ecology of specific marsh elements. (SOURCE: Reference 8.)

Figure 6.101   When marsh flooding for mosquito control is necessary and appropriate, impoundments should be opened for free water exchange during the nonbreeding season; the section illustrated here is essentially closed and has debilitated the mangrove forest ("Ding" Darling Refuge, Lee County, Florida). (Photo by author.)

standing water over a marsh in order to eliminate breeding potential (Figure 6.101). Impoundments may also enhance the diversity and abundance of birds.[17] But by altering the marsh to an impounded water body, much of its important natural value may be lost; organic detritus is not produced in a permanently impounded marsh to enrich the estuary, nor can estuarine fishes enter for feeding or protection. For these reasons, M. W. Provost, a leading authority on impoundments for mosquito control, advocates releasing the water and allowing the area to dry or to be flushed with regular tidal flow whenever there is "no adult on the wing." (See Article 22, Chapter 7.)

Because of the adverse effects caused by marsh alteration, impoundment should be allowed only in situations where open-marsh management is not feasible, for example, where there is insufficient tidal amplitude to energize the flow of water through the connector channels (e.g., in the southeastern states). And, as discussed, impoundments for salt-marsh mosquito control should be designed for closure only during breeding (warm) months and opened to tidal action during the rest of the year.[18] In North Carolina the cost for impounding a "typical salt marsh" was $35 per acre (1970 dollars).[9]

Implementation No. 3.   Pesticide use for Mosquito Control

Restrict the use of pesticides to the application of short-duration compounds for urgent situations.

The use of pesticides in mosquito control should be limited to real needs. Larvaciding is generally considered to be more efficient than spraying against adult mosquitoes, but caution is required in applying pesticides directly to water, as is done with larvacides.

Adulticides should be applied shortly after emergence, when adult mosquitoes are still concentrated near their source areas and before they have dispersed: "Only as a last resort should adulticides be used over great acreage for dispersed or migrating adult mosquitoes."[19] Ground-level application, typically from truck-mounted foggers, may keep the pesticides confined closer to the application area than is possible with aerial fogging.

Products such as Abate (for larvae) and malathion and dibron (for adult mosquitoes) are in most common use today; they are believed to be relatively benign and short lived in the ecosystem.[20] Nevertheless, the misapplication of these organophosphate chemicals has been shown to have potentially lethal effects on fish, shrimp,[6] and warm-blooded animals.[5] Consequently, even these chemicals are often held in reserve to combat only massive outbreaks.

REFERENCES

1. Ann K. Robas. 1970. *South Florida's Mangrove-Bordered Estuaries: Their Role in Sport and Commercial Fish Production.* University of Miami, Sea Grant Information Bulletin No. 4, Coral Gables, Florida.

2. D. V. Debord, G. A. Carlson, and R. C. Axtell. 1975. *Demand for and Cost of Coastal Salt Marsh Mosquito Abatement.* North Carolina Agricultural Experiment Station, Technical Bulletin No. 232, Raleigh, North Carolina.

3. W. S. Bourn and C. Cottam. 1950. *Some Biological Effects of Ditching Tidewater Marshes.* Fish and Wildlife Service, Research Report No. 19, U.S. Department of the Interior, Washington, D.C.

4. Phillip A. Butler. 1967. "Pesticides in the estuary." In *Proceedings of Marsh and Estuary Management Symposium*, Louisiana State University, Baton Rouge, Louisiana, Thomas J. Moran's Sons, Inc.

5. U.S. Department of the Interior. 1972. *Fish, Wildlife, and Pesticides.* GPO 917-905. Superintendent of Documents, U.S. Government Printing Office, Washington, D.C.

6. A. Bodola. 1970. "An evaluation of the effectiveness of natural pools, blind sumps and champagne pools in reducing mosquito production on a salt marsh." In *Proceedings of the 57th Annual Meeting, New Jersey Mosquito Extermination Association*, Atlantic City, New Jersey.

7. Anthony J. Taormina. *Total Management for Resource Values of Long Island's Tidal Wetlands.* New York State Department of Environmental Conservation, Division of Fish and Wildlife, Albany, New York.

8. F. Ferrigno, L. G. MacNamara, and D. M. Jobbins. 1969. "Ecological approach for improved management of coastal meadowlands." In *Proceedings of the 56th Annual Meeting, New Jersey Mosquito Extermination Association*, Atlantic City, New Jersey.

9. D. Boseman. 1974. "Impoundment." In R. C. Axtell, Ed., *Training Manual for Mosquito and Biting Fly Control in Coastal Areas.* University of North Carolina Sea Grant Program, Raleigh, North Carolina.

10. George Campbell. "Fish that feed on mosquito larvae." In *The Island Reporter*, May 2, 1975, Sanibel, Florida.

11. F. Ferrigno, Patrick Slavin, and D. M. Jobbins. n.d. *Salt Marsh Water Management for Mosquito Control.* New Jersey Division of Fish, Game and Shellfisheries, Trenton, New Jersey.

12. F. Ferrigno. 1970. "Preliminary effects of open marsh water management on the vegetation and organisms of the salt marsh." In *Proceedings of the 57th Annual Meeting, New Jersey Mosquito Extermination Association*, Atlantic City, New Jersey.

13. American Cyanamid Company. 1967. *Technical Information: Abate Mosquito Larvacide and Insecticide.* Princeton, New Jersey.

14. F. Ferrigno and D. M. Jobbins. 1968. "Open marsh management." In *Proceedings of the 55th Annual Meeting, New Jersey Mosquito Extermination Association*, Atlantic City, New Jersey.

15. M. W. Provost. n.d. "Salt marsh management in Florida." In *Proceedings of the Tall Timbers Conference on Ecological Animal Control by Habitat Management*, Tall Timbers Research Station, Tallahassee, Florida.

16. F. Ferrigno. New Jersey Division of Fish, Game and Shellfisheries. Personal communication, April 2, 1975.

17. M. W. Provost. 1969. "Ecological control of salt marsh mosquitoes with side benefits to birds." In *Proceedings of the Tall Timbers*

*Conference on Ecological Animal Control by
Habitat Management,* Tall Timbers Research
Station, Tallahassee, Florida.

18. M. W. Provost. 1968. "Managing impounded
salt marsh for mosquito control and estuarine
resources conservation." In *Proceedings of the
Marsh and Estuarine Management Symposium,*
Louisiana State University, Baton Rouge, Louisiana, July 19-20, 1967.

19. New Jersey Agricultural Experiment Station–
Cook College. 1975. *Insecticides for Mosquito
Control in New Jersey.* Rutgers University, New
Brunswick, New Jersey.

20. D. L. Coppage and T. W. Duke. n.d. "Effects
of pesticides in the estuaries along the Gulf
and Southeast Atlantic coast." In *Proceedings
of the 2nd Gulf Coast Conference on Mosquito Suppression and Wildlife Management,*
New Orleans, Louisiana, October 20–22, 1971.

14. NAVIGATION DREDGING AND SPOIL DISPOSAL

Dredging is done to create and maintain
canals, navigation channels, turning basins,
harbors, and marinas, as well as to lay pipeline and to obtain material for fill or construction. However, the following discussion
is concerned primarily with dredging for
navigation purposes and with the disposal of
the dredged materials or spoils. The specific
problems related to filling wetlands and
tidelands with dredged spoils to create salable real estate are discussed elsewhere (page
464), as are the problems involved in dredging ditches for mosquito control (page 413)
and in land drainage enterprises (page
400). One must presume that some adverse
ecologic effects will be associated with any
excavation or construction in a coastal water
basin. Elimination of vital habitat areas,
water quality degradation, and alteration of
circulation all have potentials for damage
to coastal ecosystems. In fact, dredging
activity poses the greatest single threat to
many coastal ecosystems.

Dredging projects in the coastal zone are
diverse in purpose and severity of effects.
The major potential adverse environmental
effects are (1) increased turbidity (page

58), (2) sediment buildup (page 91), (3)
reduction of oxygen content (page 58),
(4) disruption and removal of productive
estuarine bottom and the life it contains,
(5) creation of stagnant deep-water areas,
(6) disruption of estuarine circulation (page
62), and (7) increased upstream intrusion
of salt water and sediments.

These problems can be avoided for the
most part through careful planning and
attention to the natural processes at work
in coastal ecosystems and to the probable
effects of dredging. The first approach in
planning is to search for alternative solutions that eliminate the need for channels
and save money. Projects that are essential
to the public and for which there are no
alternative solutions should be minimized in
extent, designed with care, and built under
stringent environmental controls.

The Federal Role

Any nonfederal dredging operation, whether
a public work or private enterprise, requires
permit approval from the U.S. Army Corps
of Engineers, and usually also from the state
authorities that have jurisdiction over dredging operations. The U.S. Environmental
Protection Agency (EPA) assists the Corps
in environmental consideration of permit
applications, as do the U.S. Departments of
Interior and Commerce. The Corps has
operated a permit program for dredge-and-
fill activities in all United States "navigable"
waters since early in the twentieth century
(see page 183).

Before planning any type of dredging
activity, it is necessary to contact the state
dredging authority or the district office of
the Corps of Engineers (Corps offices are
listed in the Appendix, page 877). The complex federal regulations contain stringent
guidelines for dredging projects that provide
for the issuance of public notice and for
public comments on economics, navigation,
conservation, aesthetics, historic value, fish
and wildlife values, flood damage prevention,

recreation, land use, water supply, water quality, and general environmental concerns. The major federal enabling act is Section 404 of the Federal Clean Water Act (1972), which authorizes the Secretary of the Army, acting through the chief of engineers of the Corps, to issue permits, after notice, for the discharge of dredged materials into navigable waters at specified disposal sites. The selection of disposal sites for dredge spoil is governed by guidelines developed by the administrator of the EPA in conjunction with the Secretary of the Army. Section 103 of the Federal "Ocean Dumping" Act (1972) authorizes the Secretary of the Army to issue, after notice and opportunity for public hearing, permits for the transportation of dredged materials for the purpose of dumping them into ocean waters. Furthermore, under both the Federal Clean Water Act and the "Ocean Dumping" Act, the administrator of the EPA can prohibit or restrict the use of any defined area as a disposal site whenever he finds, after notice and opportunity for public hearing, that the discharge of such materials into such areas will have an unacceptable adverse effect on municipal water supplies, shellfish beds, fishery areas, and wildlife or recreational areas. Furthermore, in evaluating permits for transporting dredged material for dumping into ocean waters, the Corps of Engineers will specify the dumping site, using the recommendations of the EPA (see Appendix, page 769).

The total program for regulating nonfederal dredging and filling activities (including spoil disposal) involves all ocean and estuarine waters; all lakes, rivers, and most other watercourses; and most wetlands, including both freshwater wetlands (bogs, marshes, swamps) and coastal wetlands (salt marshes, mangrove swamps) extending up to the limit of annual flooding (the 1-year flood mark, page 127).

In addition to its regulatory (permit) responsibility over nonfederal dredging projects, the Corps of Engineers itself dredges enormous volumes of material annually in the construction and continual maintenance of navigable waterways, harbors, and ports, the Intracoastal Waterway, flood protection projects, and beach restoration and enhancement. The Corps spends over $150 million yearly just to maintain United States navigable waterways.[1]

Any large-scale dredging operations conducted by the Corps of Engineers must be authorized by Congress. Briefly this process involves (1) project formulation by local authorities, (2) congressional authorization for the Corps to make initial and detailed studies, (3) congressional project authorization, (4) congressional appropriation for project funding, and (5) periodic congressional appropriation of funds to carry out maintenance dredging.

Large tax-supported dredging projects are popular "pork-barrel" items, for which justification in terms of public need is often marginal at best. The public value of each proposed project should be rigorously scrutinized because the potential for ecologic loss to coastal waters is very high. In addition, the justification for private projects should also be closely investigated. In many past instances an oversize private dredging project proposed for navigation has been exposed as a cover for mining operations designed to recover sand and gravel, or as justification for a landfill project.

GUIDELINE. Dredging Project Design

Design navigation dredging projects so as to avoid erosion, water pollution, circulation change, and disturbance of vital habitat areas.

Dredging for navigation improvement creates complex environmental management problems. In large part, the solution lies in correct choice of location and design of the channel system, choice of dredge type, and performance controls. The degree of success with which the problems are solved or minimized will depend on the plan selected for the physical configuration and layout of the dredging. The selection process by which the most appropriate plan is chosen should consider all ecological aspects involved in channel development and subsequent maintenance dredging in coastal waters, including the following disturbances:

1. Removal of the bottom habitat of important organisms.
2. Creation of new deep-water areas that may affect animal and plant populations.
3. Increased upstream intrusion of salt water (and the chemical, physical, and biological conditions coincident with it).
4. Alteration of water circulation and drainage patterns.

In particular, dredging plans must recognize and reflect the need for constant periodic maintenance dredging after completion of the initial work on the project. In many cases the frequency and amount of subsequent maintenance dredging will impose a limit on the feasibility of the original project, because of the expense or difficulty involved in locating adequate spoil disposal areas.

A proposed port expansion project for the city of Georgetown, South Carolina, represents a case in point. Although the city wanted to expand and deepen its port facilities to accommodate new industry in the area, the large quantities of dredge spoil generated by the maintenance dredging necessary to sustain adequate water depths posed a major obstacle in 1975. The existing

Figure 6.102 Industrial port development in Georgetown, South Carolina, has been slowed because available spoil disposal areas have nearly reached their maximum capacity. (Photo by Robert H. Dunlap, Jr., South Carolina Wildlife and Marine Resources Department.)

spoil areas, located on lower wetlands (before they were recognized as vital habitats), were filled nearly to capacity with maintenance-derived spoil. Because of Corps policies prohibiting the use of coastal wetlands for spoil disposal, similar disposal areas were unavailable, and new disposal sites meeting environmental and economic constraints were difficult to locate in the Georgetown area. Inability to find a suitable site of sufficient capacity to handle the long-term disposal needs (up to 2.8 million cubic yards per year)[2] was largely responsible for the virtual abandonment of the proposed project (Figure 6.102).

Implementation No. 1. Navigation Channel Location

Navigation channels should be so located as to protect vital habitat areas and to prevent erosion of shorelines.

One of the most obvious effects of channel dredging is the direct removal of vital habitat areas such as grass beds, shellfish beds, coral reefs, and other productive marine habitats. To a large extent avoidance of vital habitats can be realized by limiting dredging to existing natural estuarine channels. Therefore an important part of planning should include the identification of all vital habitat areas in the water body involved (page 247). The project safeguards for these vital habitats should include a surrounding protective buffer strip of several hundred (or thousand, in some cases) feet, from which dredging should be excluded.

Channels dredged into shallow-water areas should be limited to the minimum depth needed for small boats, with a requirement of restricting larger boats to the deeper portions of the estuary (page 409). A maximum channel depth of 4 to 6 feet (1.2 to 1.8 meters) below mean low water is preferable. This practice lowers the amount and cost of initial dredging and decreases the frequency of maintenance dredging operations. In addi-

tion many environmental impacts associated with the creation of areas too deep to permit the light penetration necessary to stimulate benthic plant life are avoided. Conversely, a minimum channel depth is required to prevent excess turbidity due to resuspension of silt by prop wash from fast-moving boats; this minimum depth can be decreased by limiting the speed of boats.

Channels dredged too close to the shore in shallow-water areas often result in severe shoreline recession (Figure 6.103), both from channel slumping and from direct erosion of banks. The presence of a channel may increase the frequency and speed of boat passage and thus the intensity of boat wake impact on the shore. In addition, the deepening of the shoreline will cause higher wave impacting, decreasing the dissipation effect that shallower water bottoms have on incoming waves.

A major environmental impact associated with dredging in shallow-water areas is disruption of natural water circulation patterns. The effects are particularly severe when channel cuts are made across low marshes in an attempt to straighten winding creeks and rivers. A common effect is the alteration of sedimentation patterns with the natural filling of the cut-off oxbow bend.

Serious intrusion of salt water can be caused by dredging deep channels up tributary rivers or into shorelands. The resulting chemical and physical changes in the water and alteration of circulation patterns unbalance the ecosystem. Again such impacts can be avoided by using natural channels and by restricting shallow waterways to shallow draft boats.

Implementation No. 2. Navigation Channel Dimensions

Navigation channel dimensions should be kept to the minimum size.

The adverse environmental impacts associated with many navigational dredging proj-

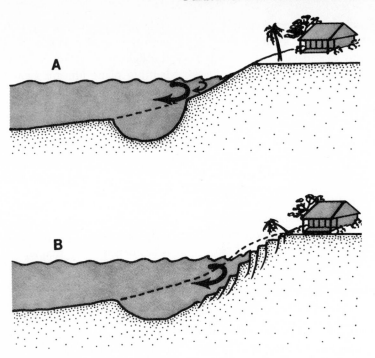

Figure 6.103   Channel cuts located too close to the shoreline (A) can cause slumping and erosion of the shore (B). (SOURCE: Reference 3.)

ects can be reduced greatly by minimizing the length, width, and depth of the channels. In general, a navigation channel needs to be no wider than about three or four times the width of the largest vessel for which it is designed. Similarly, operable channels do not need to be more than about 3 feet (0.9 meter) deeper than the deepest draft vessel at low water, provided that traffic moves at low speeds. In many cases it is not unusual to add to this depth an additional foot (0.3 meter) or so to accomodate siltation or slumping and to reduce the frequency of maintenance dredging.

The effects of channel edge slumping must be taken into account. The amount of slumping and thus the residual slope of the channel sides will be a function of the sediment particle size, local current velocities, and other factors. To avoid excessive slumping of the adjacent bottom into the channel and the high expense of maintenance dredging, channel sides should be dredged out to a stable slope during the initial operation. Slopes should not normally be cut greater than 1:5 for sand bottoms and 1:10 for mud bottoms, the exact cut depending on the specific geohydrological conditions. Excessively steep channel edges may lead to the unexpected loss of adjacent vital habitat areas, such as shellfish or grass beds.

Deep harbor entrance channels often have complex ecologic side effects. For example, deep channels may increase the inward flow of water along the bottom, accelerating sedimentation. Such acceleration increases the inward transport of materials from down harbor or from the ocean, as exemplified by the problems of Savannah Harbor, where channel deepening resulted in increasing deposits of ocean-originated sediment.[4]

Additional problems are created by imbalances in water circulation resulting from major channel deepening, as demonstrated by the Sacramento River delta navigation project. The channel deepening in this project was shown to greatly increase the subsurface flow of salty water up the channel with resulting saltwater intrusion.[5] Such a change in salinity shifts and disrupts the nursery areas of striped bass (page 41).

Once physical design features have been worked out, special consideration is needed to ensure that the environmental impact of the actual dredging operation is minimized. Proper management of the dredging operation is aimed primarily at controlling the effects from the reintroduction into the water column of polluted bottom sediments.[6] Major problems are increased water turbidity and the release of large quantities of trapped nutrients, organic materials, and toxic pollutants in the spoil (Figure 6.104).

Although these conditions are temporary, lasting for the period of dredging and a few days after its completion, the environmental impacts created during the work periods are of sufficient magnitude to require that steps be taken to eliminate or control their extent. Included in the short-term effects that may

be expected are clogging of the gills of aquatic organisms with silt; reduced light penetration; eutrophication; depletion of dissolved oxygen content (page 58); and uptake by organisms of heavy metals, pesticides, or other toxic substances stirred up by the dredging. These accumulate in their tissues to extremely high concentrations.

Recurrent objections to dredging activities are largely related to turbidity and sediment buildup. In an attempt to contain turbid water near the dredge site, preventative "silt curtains" or "diapers" have been developed (Figure 6.105). These vertical barriers or floating "screens" have been used around both dredging and spoil disposal operations with only limited success, since they cease to function in moderate- to high-velocity currents or in cases where there is wave action from wind or boat traffic. Worse, silt curtains are often brought in simply to placate the authorities by dredge operators who make no real effort to keep them functioning.

Figure 6.104 Sediment stirred up by dredge-and-fill operations (light area in photograph) may smother and kill coral reefs. (Photo from U.S. Geological Survey, Miami, Florida.)

Figure 6.105 Turbidity screens and other silt-trapping devices are often ineffective, as illustrated by the turbidity cloud moving with water currents (from left to right) unhindered by the screen. (Photo by E. T. LaRoe, National Oceanic and Atmospheric Administration.)

Implementation No. 3. Restricted Periods for Dredging

Dredging operations should be suspended during critical periods of fish migration and breeding.

Dredging may be much more adverse at one time of year than another. For example, a dredge-induced turbidity barrier to anadromous fish would be critical during their migration season. A section of highly cloudy water can effectively hinder these species in trying to reach their breeding grounds and thus reduce their breeding success. Consequently, dredging operations along migration routes should be suspended during known periods of migration and spawning of such species as salmon, striped bass, and oysters.

Dredging should also be curtailed near known nursery areas during periods when the young of a species are passing through critical development stages there. During this time, poor water quality created by dredging operations reduces the survival of vulnerable larval and juvenile populations.

As a specific example of this kind of restriction, the U.S. Fish and Wildlife Service has required a cessation of dredging and spoil disposal activities in shallow areas of low salinity in Chesapeake Bay during the period from April to August, when the embryonic and larval fishes and shellfish are most vulnerable to death or debilitation. They also recommend that extensive alterations in channel areas in the bay be avoided from November to January, when postlarval and young fishes are found in these deeper areas. The months of February, March, September, and October appear to be the times during which the least damage to fish eggs, larvae, postlarvae, and young would be expected.[7]

Implementation No. 4. Dredge Type Selection

Dredge types should be selected that will minimize operational environmental disturbances.

Because dredging has a high potential for reducing water quality, proper environmental control strategy involves choosing the dredge that, for the job at hand, produces the least ecosystem disturbance. The five common kinds of dredge rigs are described in Table 6.17.

In addition to the suction (hydraulic) and mechanical dredges, a third group should be identified that combines these two categories and is termed, appropriately, "suction/mechanical" dredges. This type is simply a modification of the pipeline or hopper dredge whereby a cutterhead or rotating bit is attached to the mouth of the suction line to loosen compacted sediments and rock.

Of these three types of dredging mechanisms, the suction dredge (Figure 6.106A) appears to be the least likely to cause signifi-

Table 6.17   Five common types of dredge rigs: the first three (dipper, ladder, and bucket) are mechanical dredges; the last two (pipeline and hopper), suction or hydraulic dredges (SOURCE: Reference 9)

Dipper Dredge—The dipper dredge is basically a power shovel mounted on a barge. The barge (which serves as the work platform for the shovel) uses three spuds (two spuds at the forward end and a single spud at the stern) to provide stability during dredging operations. The dipper dredge is capable of excavating from 3 to 10 cubic yards of hard material per cycle. It can remove blasted rock or loose boulders. The dredged material is discharged within the reach of the dipper boom. The digging boom limits the depth of excavation to not more than 60 feet.

Ladder Dredge—The ladder dredge uses an endless chain of buckets for excavation. The dredge is mounted on a barge which is stabilized by side cables during the dredging operation. The ladder dredge is capable of excavating from 1 to 2 cubic yards of hard material per bucket. It can remove blasted rock or loose boulders. The excavated material is dumped from the buckets into chutes or onto belts and is discharged over the side of the barge. The design of the ladder limits the depth of excavation to not more than 100 feet.

Bucket Dredge—The bucket dredge is basically a crane mounted on a barge. The bucket (clamshell, orange-peel, or dragline) can be changed to suit the job conditions and material to be removed. The barge (which serves as the work platform for the crane) uses either spuds or anchor lines to provide stability during dredging operations. The bucket dredge is capable of excavating moderately stiff material in confined areas. It is generally not used for large scale projects. The excavated material is dumped within the reach of the boom.

Pipeline Dredge—The pipeline dredge is the most versatile and widely used dredge. It can handle large volumes of material in an economical fashion. Using a cutterhead the dredge can excavate material ranging from light silts to heavy rock. It can pump the dredged material through floating and shore discharge lines to remote disposal areas. Pipeline dredges range in sizes (as measured by the diameter of the pump discharge) from 6 inches to 36 inches. The depth of excavation is limited to 60 feet. The rate of dredging will decrease with (1) difficulty in digging, (2) increase in length of discharge pipe and (3) increase in lift to discharge elevation.

Hopper Dredge—The hopper dredge is a self-propelled vessel designed to dredge material hydraulically, to load and retain dredge spoil in hoppers, and then to haul the spoil to a disposal area or dump. Loading is accomplished by sucking the bottom material through a drag-head into the hoppers while making a cut through the dredging area. The quantity of volume pumped during a loading operation depends primarily upon the character of the material and the amount of pumping time involved as well as the hopper capacity and the pumping and propulsive capability of the dredge. The loaded dredge proceeds to the disposal area where the dredge spoil is discharged through gates in the bottom of the hoppers.

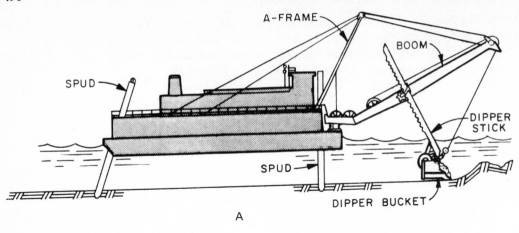

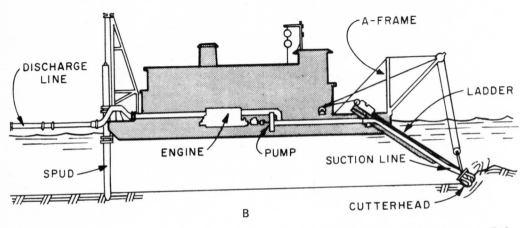

Figure 6.106 (A) Bucket (mechanical) dredge, and (B) suction (hydraulic) dredge. (SOURCE: Reference 9.)

cant environmental impacts at the point of dredging. Suction dredging, suitable only for removal of loose material, produces the least turbidity if properly operated.[1] Unfortunately, however, the suction dredge, commonly used in dredging navigation channels, has a high potential for ecologic disturbance at the terminus of the pipeline, where the spoil (a slurry of about 20 percent sediment and 80 percent water) is discharged (Figure 6.107). The effects may be severe if the spoil contains a high proportion of contaminants: organic matter, nutrients, toxics, and fine sediments.

The mechanical dredge (Figure 6.106B) is less desirable from an environmental point of view because material is washed freely from the bucket as it is raised from the bottom. This increases turbidity, which can in turn depress dissolved oxygen, release toxic chemicals, reduce light penetration, clog the gill structures of organisms, and destroy microorganisms. However, mechanical dredges are less expensive to operate, do not require pipelines, and are more versatile, being designed to cut into compacted sediments better than suction dredges.[10]

The cutterhead dredge appears to be the type of operation with the most potential for creating adverse environmental impacts. These dredges are perhaps the most versatile of all but are expensive to operate.[2] Unfor-

Figure 6.107 Hydraulic dredge spoil, discharged as a slurry of about 80 percent water, has a high potential for water pollution. (Conservation Foundation photo by J. Chess.)

tunately, because of the manner in which they operate, turbidity clouds can be generated in the vicinity of the cutterhead, thereby significantly decreasing ambient water quality.

GUIDELINE. Spoil Disposal Constraints

Control dredge spoil disposal to protect vital habitats and estuarine water quality.

The Army Corps of Engineers has recorded annual dredging quantities currently averaging about 80 million cubic yards of spoil in new dredging activities and about 300 million cubic yards in maintenance activities.[1] The disposal of these materials along the coast has important environmental effects separate from the effects of the dredging operation itself (Table 6.18). Considerable ecologic damage often occurs when dredge spoil is dumped on productive estuarine bottoms or deposited on vital habitats such as wetlands, tidelands, and shellfish beds. Before any disposal of dredge spoil, an inventory should be taken of all vital habitat areas, and these areas should be excluded from consideration as disposal sites.

Table 6.18 Critical and vital areas eliminated by dredging and spoil disposal in the Texas coastal zone (data to 1966) (SOURCE: Reference 4)

Type of Habitat	Channel Area (acres)	Spoil Area (acres)	Total Area (acres)
Open estuary	7,590	30,320	37,910
Tideflats	920	3,920	4,840
Vegetated tidelands	6,980	23,000	29,980
	15,490	57,240	72,730

The Corps of Engineers presently disposes of approximately 65 percent of the dredge spoil it produces directly into the water. A variety of potential adverse environmental impacts is associated with this open-water disposal of dredged materials. Short-term adverse effects include increased turbidity, sediment buildup, oxygen depletion, and the release of toxic pollutants. Long-term effects include changes in water circulation, accumulation of deposits that may prevent recolonization by benthic species, and subsequent resuspension of polluting substances by boats, wind, and currents. Currently about 34 percent of all spoil deposited in open water is considered polluted, based on present criteria.[10]

Stringent state and federal regulations and the increasing values placed on intertidal wetlands have made the practice of spoil disposal on estuarine marsh and mangrove areas impracticable. In addition, environmental considerations have fostered a new trend away from open-water disposal and toward land and contained disposal.[1] The problems of site acquisition for land disposal are difficult nationwide, but because of disadvantages in land characteristics, spoil volumes, land use, and other factors they are most acute in the southeastern United States.[1]

Land disposal of dredge spoil offers the possibility of preventing adverse environmental impacts that cannot be controlled in open-water disposal. Matters of concern include (1) the quality of the water effluent separated from the spoil, (2) the potential loss of wetlands and other vital areas to be used as disposal or fill sites, and (3) possible alterations to the natural drainage patterns of wetland or upland areas used for disposal.

The land area required for spoil disposal is often extensive. The local community or private sponsor of any new nonfederal project that will require the disposal of dredged material has the responsibility for locating a suitable disposal area. Even for projects that are Corps conducted and require federal funding, the local community shares the responsibility for locating suitable spoil areas. To ensure the availability of adequate ecologically acceptable disposal sites the sponsor is required to acquire spoil disposal areas for both project construction and long-term maintenance disposal.

Implementation No. 1.   Habitat Protection in Spoil Disposal

Alternative methods should be used to avoid disposal of spoil in open estuarine waters or on vital areas.

Broadcasting spoil into estuarine waters is particularly damaging to water quality and bottom life. Two such methods used in navigational channel dredging are (1) sidecast disposal, in which the spoil from a suction dredge is discharged directly overboard at the dredge site; and (2) agitation dredging, whereby the spoil from a hopper dredge is pumped directly into the water so as to be dispersed widely by current action.[8] Such overboard discharge methods cause widespread pollution when the spoil consists of fine silts. When the bottom is coarse and clean—that is, consists of sand or gravel without much clay, mud, or organic matter —overboard disposal may be acceptable, provided that the spoils do not contain toxic pollutants and are not deposited in ridges that significantly impede water flow (Figure 6.108).

Habitat creation and enhancement through regulated spoil disposal offers a potential solution. It is possible to create marshes from clean dredge spoil[11] (Figure 6.109). Islands of spoil can absorb large volumes of materials and become desirable habitats for shorebirds.

As other solutions become more expensive, long-distance pipeline or rail transport moves closer to the realm of economic reality. The possibility of long-distance pipeline transport of spoil to rehabilitate strip mine areas has been seriously explored.[1] Large central disposal sites serving multiple projects appear to offer distinct advantages, because long-

Figure 6.108 Clean, coarse sand is the best building material for spoil islands (Cocoa Beach, Florida). (Conservation Foundation photo by J. Chess.)

distance pipeline transport to inland sites is more feasible when the number of separate containment facilities is reduced.

Another alternative to protect estuarine ecosystems involves disposal of spoil in the ocean by hopper dredge, barge, or possibly pipeline. There are important differences in opinion as to the environmental impact of deep-water ocean disposal of various types of waste. In regard to dredged materials, it appears that ocean disposal is acceptable for relatively unpolluted spoil, if the site is sufficiently far offshore to ensure against currents carrying the spoil back onto the beaches or into the estuaries. Ocean disposal is presently limited principally by the high cost of transport.

Another possibility is disposal on existing spoil banks. The past practice of dumping spoil on marsh areas has left many spoil banks, which have already destroyed the ecologic value of these areas. Continued disposal on these banks will not increase the loss of vital habitats if the dewatering is properly controlled. Control in this instance must be directed toward preventing the de-struction of healthy adjacent habitat areas by spillover or mud waves and toward governing the content of the water runoff.

Major drawbacks to inland disposal include the difficulty of securing the large areas needed for the facility and the access easements. In urban situations the only available sites with sufficient acreage may be those that are assigned to open space, recreation, or natural areas. Also, severe problems of polluted water runoff can be anticipated for upland disposal sites.

Introducing a relatively high-salinity efflu-ent into a lower-salinity or freshwater envi-ronment surrounding an inland disposal area would be ecologically troublesome. Saltwater intrusion into groundwaters could also occur, contaminating local aquifers used for pot-able water supply. Because of the great ex-pense of desalinization treatments, it might be necessary to pipe discharge water back to the estuary from which the spoil was dredged. Most problems could be mitigated however, by appropriate systems of controls.

Evaluation of sites proposed for confined disposal facilities must be rigorous. Inade-

Figure 6.109 With proper dikes and management for spoil "dewatering," artificial islands offer an opportunity for the creation of valuable new estuarine island habitat providing the dredged material is clean and nonpolluting (New Topsail Beach, North Carolina). (Conservation Foundation photo by M. Fahay.)

quate environmental considerations may result from the intense need for disposal sites in marshy areas. Disposal areas should be located inland well away from the estuary whenever possible and in places where their presence will not interfere with vital habitat areas. In no instances should wetlands be used.

Implementation No. 2. Pollution Control in Spoil Disposal

Handling, dewatering, and disposal of spoil should be controlled so as to prevent water pollution.

Disposal of polluted spoil poses a significant threat to estuarine areas. Consequently, dredge spoil should be routinely analyzed to determine (1) whether sediments contain pollutants, and (2) if so, the degree to which they are polluted. Any spoils found to be polluted should be disposed of in confined areas, not in open coastal waters.

There are several methods of treating spoil to remove contaminants and to improve the quality of effluent from dewatering operations at disposal sites. The major pollution problems with spoil are generally the highly organic, petrochemical-laden silts and clays mixed with domestic sewage sludge that are found on the bottoms of urban harbors. Treatment methods include flocculation, filtration, aeration, incineration, chemical processes, and sewage plant treatment. These are all very costly.

Table 6.19 Criteria of the EPA for determining acceptability of dredged spoil disposal to the nation's waters (1970 version) (SOURCE: Reference 1)

Use of Criteria

These criteria were developed as guidelines for FWQA evaluation of proposals and applications to dredge sediments from fresh and saline waters.

Criteria

The decision whether to oppose plans for disposal of dredged spoil in United States waters must be made on a case-by-case basis after considering all appropriate factors; including the following:

(a) Volume of dredged material.

(b) Existing and potential quality and use of the water in the disposal area.

(c) Other conditions at the disposal site such as depth and currents.

(d) Time of year of disposal (in relation to fish migration and spawning, etc.).

(e) Method of disposal and alternatives.

(f) Physical, chemical, and biological characteristics of the dredged material.

(g) Likely recurrence and total number of disposal requests in a receiving water area.

(h) Predicted long and short term effects on receiving water quality. When concentrations, in sediments, of one or more of the following pollution parameters exceed the limits expressed below, the sediment will be considered polluted in all cases and, therefore, unacceptable for open water disposal.

Sediments in Fresh and Marine Waters	Conc. % (dry wt. basis)
*Volatile Solids	6.0
Chemical Oxygen Demand (C.O.D.)	5.0
Total Kjeldahl Nitrogen	0.10
Oil-Grease	0.15
Mercury	0.001
Lead	0.005
Zinc	0.005

*When analyzing sediments dredged from marine waters, the following correlation between volatile solids and C.O.D. should be made:

$$T.V.S.\% \ (dry) \ = \ 1.32 \ + \ 0.98(C.O.D.\%)$$

If the results show a significant deviation from this equation, additional samples should be analyzed to insure reliable measurements.

The volatile solids and C.O.D. analyses should be made first. If the maximum limits are exceeded the sample can be characterized as polluted and the additional parameters would not have to be investigated.

Dredged sediment having concentrations of constituents less than the limits stated above will not be automatically considered acceptable for disposal. A judgement must be made on a case-by-case basis after considering the factors listed in (a) through (h) above.

In addition to the analyses required to determine compliance with the stated numerical criteria, the following additional tests are recommended where appropriate and pertinent:

Total Phosphorus	Sulfides
Total Organic Carbon (T.O.C.)	Trace Metals (iron, cadmium, copper, chromium, arsenic, and nickel)
Immediate Oxygen Demand (I.O.D.)	Pesticides
Settleability	Bioassay

The first four analyses would be considered desirable in almost all instances. They may be added to the mandatory list when sufficient experience with their interpretation is gained. For example, as experience is gained, the T.O.C. test may prove to be a valid substitute for the volatile solids and C.O.D. analyses. Tests for trace metals and pesticides should be made where significant concentrations of these materials are expected from known waste discharges.

The EPA guidelines for acceptability of dredge spoil disposal are given in Table 6.19. The seven parameters mentioned in criterion (h) can be divided into two categories, based on their effects and manner of association with the bottom sediments. The first category includes volatile solids, chemical oxygen demand, oil and grease, and total Kjeldahl nitrogen, typical of materials such as organic oozes and sewage sludges that, when dredged and spoiled in open waters, can exert a strong short-term oxygen demand. The second category consists of the heavy metals, including mercury, lead, and zinc, that are either physically or chemically sorbed or bound within the sediment matrix and that have long-term effects. Associated PCBs and pesticides may also have long-term effects.

A major problem in handling polluted spoils involves the contaminants carried by the effluents from the dewatering process. Despite the high cost of dikes and water control structures, disposal of spoil in estuarine containment areas is common. Containments range in size from less than 10 acres to over 4 square miles and have life expectancies from less than 1 year to over 100 years.[1] Nearly all containment areas are enclosed by dikes and equipped with height-adjustable spillways to accommodate varying filling rates. Containment areas include a detention capability for the removal of suspended matter by settlement.[12] Although the effluent is somewhat improved before it flows over the spillways, a higher level of treatment is often required before discharge when polluted spoil is involved. From Table 6.20 it is possible to compute flows from pipelines of various sizes and therefore to determine the required size of the detention facility.

Experience has shown that polluted fine sediments accumulate on the surface in containment areas for maintenance dredging spoils. To prevent these fines from washing back to the estuary with runoff from rainstorms, it is necessary to keep the spillways (stop logs, return weirs) in place and functioning after the dredging has terminated or else to cover the areas with a layer of clean, coarse fill.[13]

Table 6.20   Discharge rates for hydraulic dredge pipelines (SOURCE: Reference 11)

Pipeline Diameter (in.)	Discharge Rate (for Flow Velocity of 12 ft/sec*)	
	(cu ft/sec)	(gal/min)
8	4.2	1,880
10	6.5	2,910
12	9.4	4,220
14	12.8	5,750
16	16.5	7,400
18	21.2	9,510
20	26.2	11,740
24	37.7	16,890
27	47.6	21,300
28	51.3	23,000
30	58.9	26,400
36	84.9	38,000

*To obtain discharge rates for other velocities multiply the discharge rate in this table by the velocity (ft/sec) and divide by 12.

REFERENCES

1. M. B. Boyd, R. T. Saucier, J. W. Keeley, R. L. Montgomery, R. D. Brown, D. B. Mathis, and C. J. Guice. 1972. *Disposal of Dredge Spoil; Problem Identification and Assessment and Research Program Development.* U.S. Army Engineer Waterways Experiment Station, Technical Report No. H-72-8, Vicksburg, Mississippi.

2. Henningson, Durham, and Richardson. 1975. *Preliminary Feasibility Study for Sampit River Channel Development.* Prepared for the city of Georgetown, South Carolina.

3. Albert R. Veri et al. 1975. *Environmental Quality by Design: South Florida.* University of Miami Press, Coral Gables, Florida.

4. C. Chapman. 1968. "Channelization and spoiling in Gulf coast and South Atlantic estuaries." In *Proceedings of the Marsh and Estuarine Management Symposium,* Louisiana State University, Baton Rouge, Louisiana, July 19-20, 1967.

5. David McCulloch and John Conomas. U.S. Geological Service. Personal communication, 1974.

6. U.S. Geological Survey. 1973. *Resource and*

Land Information, South Dade County, Florida. U.S. Department of the Interior, Geological Survey Investigation I-850.

7. National Resources Institute. 1970. *Gross Physical and Biological Effects of Overboard Spoil Disposal in Upper Chesapeake Bay.* U.S. Bureau of Sports, Fisheries and Wildlife, Washington, D.C.

8. J. L. Machemehl. 1971. *Engineering Aspects of Waste Disposal in the Estuarine Zone.* Conference on Dredge and Fill Legislation, East Carolina University, Regional Development Institute.

9. U.S. Army Corps of Engineers. 1969. *Dredging and Water Quality Problems in the Great Lakes: Summary Report.* Buffalo District, New York.

10. J. Harrison, R. L. Montgomery, and F. H. Griffis, Jr. 1974. *Problem Identification and Assessment for the Corps of Engineers Dredged Material Research Program.* U.S. Army Engineer Waterways Experiment Station, Miscellaneous Paper D-74-12, Vicksburg, Mississippi.

11. L. E. Johnson and W. V. McGuinness, Jr. 1975. *CEM Report 4165-519: Guidelines for Material Placement in Marsh Creation.* Center for the Environment and Man, Inc., Hartford, Connecticut (draft of final report).

12. U.S. Environmental Protection Agency. 1971. *Water Quality Considerations for Construction and Dredging Operations.* Water Quality Office, Southeast Region.

13. Larry E. Shanks. U.S. Fish and Wildlife Service, Department of the Interior, Bay St. Louis, Mississippi. Personal communication. 1975.

15. OIL AND GAS INDUSTRIES

All phases of oil and gas production—extraction, transport, and refining—can cause serious environmental impacts on coastal waters. Moreover, hazards to marine and shore life can be expected to increase as technological improvements permit oil extraction to take place at greater and greater depths—up to 300 feet in the Gulf of Mexico, California, and Alaska, with a growing capability to drill in the deeper waters of the outer continental shelf (Figure 6.110).

The major potential environmental disturbances in the extraction and processing of oil and gas are (1) pollution by oil spills from blowouts, pipeline ruptures, and transport accidents; (2) preemption or destruction of vital habitat areas (e.g., shellfish beds, wetlands) and energy flows; (3) general disruption of the coastal environment (e.g., from channel dredging); and (4) primary and secondary environmental and socioeconomic impacts from a wide variety of associated onshore facilities.

Control of oil production in coastal marshes and estuaries has been less than effective, and control of onshore-facilities development has been almost nonexistent. All phases of production and transport have the potential for serious environmental impacts on coastal waters. Oil extraction in estuarine wetland areas and near coastal waters is the most dangerous in terms of the risk to coastal ecosystems (Figure 6.111).

Although the disturbance of coastal ecosystems to date has been caused chiefly by oil and gas operations in the coastal zone, the operational scene is rapidly shifting to the outer continental shelf (outside the territorial sea, bounded by the 3-mile limit) (Figure 6.112). Development of outer continental shelf oil and gas resources is a complex industrial process that requires extensive advance planning and coordination of all phases from exploration to processing and shipment. Each of dozens of components linking development and production systems has the potential for adverse environmental effects on coastal water resources, and it is necessary to understand these probable effects in sufficient detail so that methods can be devised to minimize environmental damage. With sufficient advance knowledge, both industry and public authorities can assess the environmental acceptability of each of hundreds of options for linking the components of the system and thereby choose the approach that will best protect fish and wildlife resources from adverse impacts, including the probable secondary effects from onshore facilities.

Any decision on whether a community

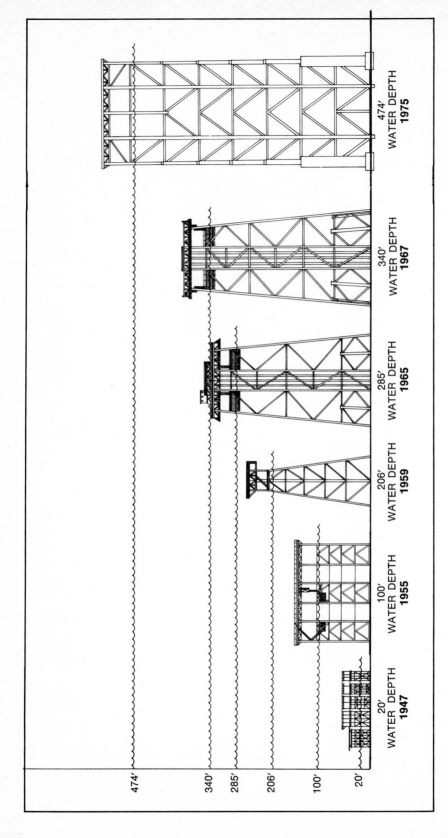

Figure 6.110 Continual technological improvements over the years have permitted the oil industry to extend drilling operations to deeper and deeper waters. (SOURCE: Reference 1.)

Figure 6.111 Oil derricks are a familiar sight in the estuaries of Texas. (Photo by author.)

should cooperate with a proposed onshore site must include full consideration of the secondary development it will induce, including the effects of industrial and urban expansion on the aquatic and coastal ecosystems and on coastal resources, such as endangerment of vital habitat areas, wetlands, rookeries, threatened-species habitats, surface waters, and aquifers.

Information concerning the natural resource base is required in sufficient detail to allow planners to assess the effects of both primary developments, such as oil extraction operations, onshore fabrication plants, storage yards, crew bases, pipelines and landfalls, tank farms, and refineries, and secondary developments, including highways, schools, and shopping centers. Additional information will be needed on the location, size, time of construction, life of the facility, manpower requirements, demand on public services (water, roads, sewage system, utilities, etc.), and anticipated special pollutants or problems such as the effect on ground-

water resources of saltwater intrusion from the uptake of groundwater by refineries and satellite industries. All required information should be supplied by the industry involved or by responsible federal or state agencies.

First, the community must determine whether it is a likely location for the development of onshore facilities to support ocean exploration and production. Second, it will be necessary to determine the probability that any type of onshore support facility will be built. Third, the full range of expected community impacts must be predicted, including environmental, social, and economic factors such as coastal resource uses (land and water), ownership patterns and land values, employment income tax generation, costs of compliance with present or potential local constraints, changes in the distribution of resources among social groups, and effects on existing sociological patterns. Factors influencing land, water, and air capability and suitability for the development of onshore facilities should be

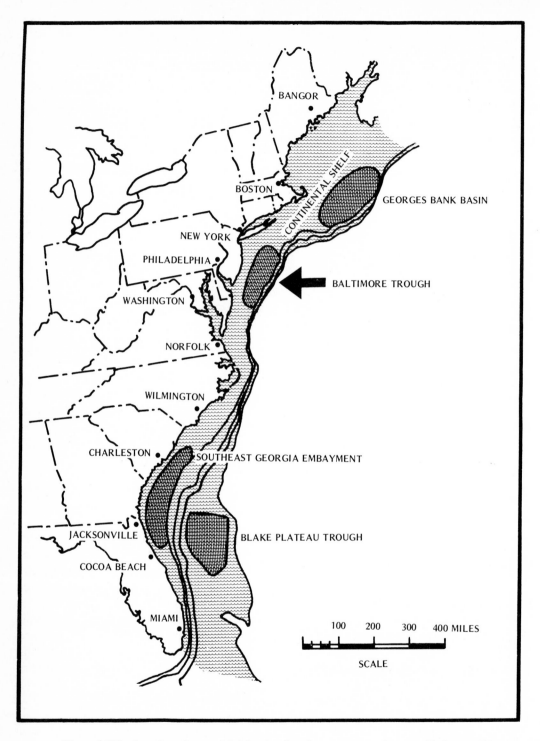

Figure 6.112 Location of potential Atlantic oil and gas resources. (SOURCE: Reference 2.)

identified and analyzed to determine methods for their optimum use. Such analysis should include the scope and type of onshore facilities and the land, water, and human resources needed for development. Furthermore, it is necessary to predict the timing of events that require community action so that the review process can proceed in an orderly fashion.

GUIDELINE. Control of Oil and Gas Development

Control oil and gas development so as to minimize environmental disturbances from offshore, inshore, and onshore activities.

Disturbances caused by the extraction, transport, and refining of oil and gas have the potential for serious environmental damage to coastal waters and marine life. To anticipate specific environmental impacts, it is necessary to understand the five phases of oil and gas development and the ensuing onshore facility requirements. The five phases include (1) geophysical exploration, (2) exploratory drilling, (3) field development, (4) production, and (5) transportation to refineries onshore. These are described in detail in the Appendix (page 906).

Preexploration

Geophysical exploration includes all activities, except drilling, used to locate and describe geological formations that may contain petroleum hydrocarbons. Magnetic and gravity surveys are used to describe relatively large areas.[3] Seismic profiling, bottom sampling and coring provide more detailed geological information on particular areas (Figure 6.113). Unless very extensive oil and gas resources exist in an area, no permanent onshore support facilities are needed by geophysical contractors.[2]

Exploration

Drilling is conducted to determine whether commercial quantities of oil and/or gas are present at a given site. Semisubmersible or jack-up drill rigs are most commonly used, though barges and drill ships are occasionally employed in shallow and deep water, respectively (Figure 6.114). These are all mobile and can be brought from long distance, thus avoiding the need for construction of these structures near the potential field.

Semisubmerisble floating drilling rigs are most likely to be used in the mid-Atlantic, since they are designed for rough-water operation. Their working decks cover 2 acres; they drill to depths of 30,000 feet and can operate in waves of 40 to 80 feet. The rigs are supported by supply boats carrying equipment and supplies from shore and by helicopters carrying relief crews.[5] Onshore support facilities for offshore operations normally consist of primary staging areas and coastal supply bases, from which workers, equipment, and supplies are shuttled to and from the mobile drilling rigs.[2] For the most part environmental impacts during this phase will be relatively minor, as most areas have existing harbors that are near enough to potential fields to fulfill the requirements.

Field Development

If oil or gas is located in commercial quantities, field development begins with the drilling of delineation wells to determine field configuration and capacity. A production platform is obtained and emplaced, development wells are drilled (sometimes more than 40 holes per platform), a transportation link to a processing facility is established, and the drill rig is removed from the production platform. The production equipment and other related devices constructed and installed include "Christmas trees," a complex arrangement of valves that control product flow and facilitate the reworking of a well. Processing units are built offshore for separating sand, water, and gas from oil and onshore for stripping heavier fractions from oil, and finally, the mainte-

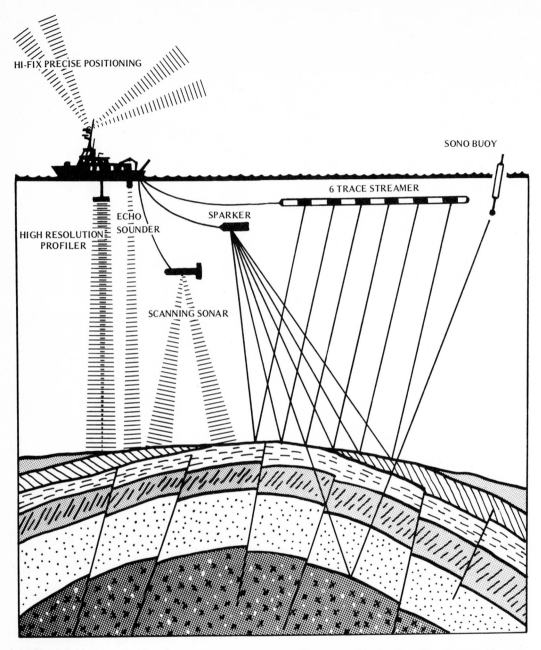

Figure 6.113 A variety of methods are used in geophysical survey exploration for oil and gas on the outer continental shelf. (SOURCE: Reference 2.)

nance operations that keep the wells flowing are set up.[2]

It is during this period that construction activity reaches peak levels as a variety of onshore support facilities is developed— tanker terminals, pipelines, storage yards, crew bases, gas-processing plants, platform fabrication plants, tank farms, refineries, and port facilities for supply vessels—each of which poses potential disturbance to coastal ecosystems.

Production

In the production phase, oil is extracted, separated, metered, and pumped to offshore storage tanks, to shore by pipeline, or to tankers for transport ashore. Gas is separated, dehydrated, pressurized, metered, and pumped ashore by pipeline. The life of a well varies between 20 and 40 years. By the production phase most onshore facilities will have been constructed, and environmental impacts will be attributable primarily to oil spills and persistent leakage. Oil spills resulting from blowouts, pipeline ruptures, and collision are the most serious distur-

bances in coastal areas caused by oil extraction and transportation processes. Oil spills can cause severe damage to water quality, waterfowl, fish, and marine organisms.

Transportation

The impacts of transportation are associated with the expansion of port facilities, oil pollution, and the laying of pipelines. Pipe sections (generally greater than 12-inch diameter) are welded together on a barge and allowed to sink under their own weight to the seafloor. In water depths less than 200 feet the pipeline is buried by water jet excavation. As the pipeline comes ashore, it is buried deeply enough to avoid its being exposed by storms. Onshore pipelines are buried in trenches.[2]

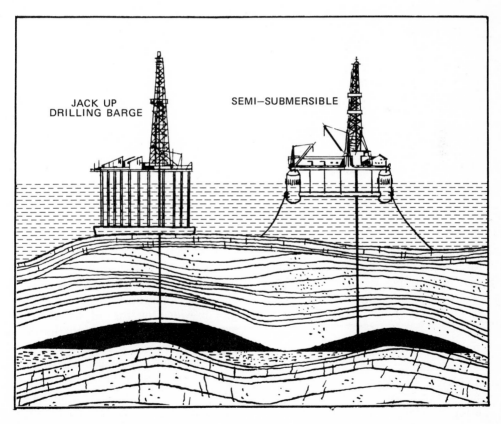

Figure 6.114   Both semisubmersible and jack-up rigs are in use for oil and gas exploration on the outer continental shelf. (SOURCE: Reference 4.)

Figure 6.115 Massive industrial complexes often build up around onshore petroleum facilities (New Orleans vicinity, Mississippi). (Photo by author.)

In inshore areas pipeline construction requires dredging, often including wide barge canals for the laying of equipment. These canals, usually dredged to 40 feet in width, often traverse and cut through marshlands and estuaries, where they disrupt coastal ecosystems (page 479).

Altogether, collisions, storms, accidents, and pipeline ruptures result in the release of over 100,000 tons (metric) of oil each year.[6]

Refining

Approximately 60 percent of the refining capacity of the United States is concentrated in four coastal states—Texas, Louisiana, California, and New Jersey. Improperly located refineries and related facilities can have serious impacts on coastal water, air, and aesthetic resources. For example, a 100,000 barrel-per-day refinery will require at least 4 million gallons per day of fresh water and will release almost 60,000 pounds per day of pollutants into water. Such burdens can easily overtax local services.

A major onshore environmental impact of petroleum facilities is associated with induced development. Employment opportunities provided by the oil industry attract many people, thus increasing the demand for public facilities (roads, hospitals, schools, etc.), housing, and small business. In addition, the presence of the oil industry attracts other industries, including manufacturing and petrochemical complexes, thus placing a further stress on local resources (Figure 6.115).

Implementation No. 1. Oil Pollution Prevention

Oil and gas operations should be controlled to minimize the risk of oil pollution.

Oil and gas are discharged into the environment at all points from wellhead to ultimate destination on land. In the transportation system small-volume spillage occurs routinely, particularly at transfer points between different components of the system (e.g., terminal–tanker, refinery–pipeline). Moreover, accidents, human errors, and equipment failures can cause large spills at any time.[7] Consequently special efforts should be made to keep transfer points out of environmentally vital water areas.

Other sources of pollution contributing to coastal ecosystem degradation are vessel deballasting and bilge pumping, and detergent and chemical cleanup techniques. Nearshore and estuarine areas are vulnerable to offshore spills through wind, ocean current, and tidal transport of oil shoreward. Efforts to clean up these pollutants with chemical applicants, themselves pollutants, may also be detrimental to coastal plants and animals by placing additional stresses on the ecosystem.

Most oil spilled into water initially floats at the surface. However, wind and water forces effectively distribute spilled petroleum hydrocarbons into all components of the marine and coastal environment, including the water column, sediments, the atmosphere, and the organisms present in the marine and coastal ecosystems.

Petroleum discharge from persistent leaks, seeps, runoff ashore, or dramatic large spills along the coast is acutely toxic to virtually all marine and coastal organisms—waterfowl, mammals, fish, shellfish, reptiles, plankton, and so forth.

In addition to direct kills of organisms, the major adverse environmental effects of direct oil pollution of coastal waters are (1) disruption of the physiological and behavioral patterns of feeding and the reproductive activities of aquatic species; (2) changes in physical and chemical habitats, causing exclusion of species and reduction of populations; and (3) stresses on the ecosystem from decomposition of refinery effluents, resulting in altered productivity, metabolism, system structure, and species diversity.

Although ocean oil and gas extraction technology is improving rapidly, environmental protection technology is lagging behind in many areas. Until such technology has achieved proved effectiveness, stringent controls on operations must be imposed in granting permits for oil and gas ventures. In addition, consideration must be given to the outright prohibition of drilling in vital marine areas, or areas where the risk is high for wind and tide to carry a possible spill onto a vital area.

Implementation No. 2. Oil Industry Impacts on Coastal Waters

Control of dredging and other activities in coastal waters by oil industries should follow standards set for all development.

Oil drilling and related onshore development frequently threaten vital habitat areas. The total effect of dramatic major spills appears to have been of lesser consequence than the impact of associated activities—refineries, the dredging of barge canals through marshes, and the construction of shore facilities such as tank farms, transfer facilities, workships, piers, and equipment storage yards.

For example, the dredging of channels, canals, and ditches for tanker traffic, pipelines, and onshore rig fabrication sites creates both short- and long-term environmental effects. The potential exists for damaging coastal ecosystems by uncontrolled dredging and other activities. Modified estuarine circulation and salinity regimes could result, along with benthic habitat destruction.

The requisite controls may be found else-

Table 6.21   Possible employment–population impact in middle Atlantic states from outer continental shelf oil and gas development (for Baltimore Trough fields) (SOURCE: Reference 2)

	1976	1977	1978	1979	1980
Rig buildup	3	6	12	19	21
(60 men/rig)	180	360	720	1,140	1,260
Direct support					
(multiplier of 2)	360	720	1,440	2,280	2,520
Total offshore operations	540	1,080	2,160	3,420	3,780
Indirect support					
(multiplier of 3.0)	1,620	3,240	6,480	10,260	11,340
Total petroleum-based employment	2,160	4,320	8,640	13,680	15,120
Total population (multiplier of 4)	8,640	17,280	34,560	54,720	60,480

where in this book for each specific type of activity.

Implementation No. 3. Oil Industry Onshore Impacts

In assessing the effects of coastal oil and gas development the full range of direct and indirect environmental, social, and economic effects of onshore facilities must be determined.

The greatest impacts from coastal and offshore oil and gas development can be expected to occur onshore in association with support facilities and with onshore processing and refining activities. Refineries must be located so as not to obliterate wetlands or degrade water quality during the construction and operational phases. In operation they require large quantities of water for both cooling and processing purposes. Cooling water is used to reduce the heat generated during refinery operation; it does not come into direct contact with the petroleum and is not thereby contaminated. However, it does present potentially significant thermal pollution problems and directly kills organisms sucked in with the cooling water. Saltwater intrusion of aquifer may be caused by the overpumping of groundwater to supply refinery processes.

The predictable impact of onshore facilities includes the secondary development induced by the presence of industry. For example, a petroleum facility may attract related industries (e.g., petrochemical industries), often requiring a local work force expansion of 3.5 times the work force for the oil facility, to which one must add the full induced population (Table 6.21).

The "typical petrochemical complex" will require 20 million gallons per day of water and will produce an approximate load of 125,000 pounds per day of air pollution and approximately 120,000 pounds per day of water pollutants. Equivalent estimates of the electrical load, water demand and waste load generated by the induced population can be derived from planning estimates of state and county agencies.[2]

Petroleum-induced growth may fundamentally alter the socioeconomic status of an area through changes in population and land use. In the Kenai area of Alaska, for example, the population almost doubled in 5 years (8000 to 14,000) and tax-supported services increased from $6 million to $24 million.[2] Community expansion generates new housing projects, shopping centers, and other ancillary development on surrounding lands.

The major land commitments for direct support activities are needed for steel fabrication (platforms, etc.), storage (tanks, warehousing, etc.), and transportation (helicopters, supply ship wharfage, crewboat docks, ship repair). Pipeline corridors to transport oil or gas, however, are not great land users, and unless they transect vital habitat areas are relatively benign. When the pipeline is buried in the right-of-way, the land is restored and quickly revegetated, just as in the case of existing lines that distribute gas and other materials and services. For ship operations and platform construction, there will be pressure for land near

navigable water, and this pressure could lead to the filling or dredging of thousands of acres of wetlands.[2]

Any onshore facilities proposal that would preempt vital habitat areas, pose a significant pollution threat, disrupt drainage water flows, reduce natural productivity, or otherwise degrade coastal ecosystems should be regarded critically. Consequently, assessment of coastal oil activities should include a searching review of impacts. Much of the coastline is clearly unsuitable for onshore facilities for oil and gas development, and many refinery proposals have been disapproved because of probable adverse effects on the environment and for other reasons (Table 6.22). A smaller fraction will be

Table 6.22   Refineries planned but not constructed (SOURCE: Reference 8)

Company	Location	Size (barrels/day)	Final Action Blocking Project
Shell Oil Co.	Delaware Bay, Del.	150,000	State reacted by legislature passing bill forbidding refineries in coastal area.
Fuels Desulfurization*	Riverhead, L.I., N.Y.	200,000	City council opposed project and would not change zoning.
Maine Clean Fuels*	South Portland, Me.	200,000	City council rejected proposal.
Maine Clean Fuels*	Searsport, Me.	200,000	Maine Environmental Protection Board rejected proposal.
Georgia Refining Co.*	Brunswick, Ga.	200,000	Blocked through actions of Office of State Environmental Director.
Northeast Petroleum	Tiverton, R.I.	65,000	City council rejected proposal.
Supermarine, Inc.	Hoboken, N.J.	100,000	Withdrawn under pressure from environmentalist groups. Considering site near Paulsboro, N.J.
Commerce Oil	Jamestown Island, R.I. Narragansett Bay	50,000	Opposed by local organizations and contested in court.
Steuart Petroleum†	Piney Point, Md.	100,000	Withdrawn under pressure from environmentalist groups.
Olympic Oil Refineries, Inc.	Durham, N.H.	400,000	Withdrawn after rejection in local referendum.

*Maine Clean Fuels and Georgia Refining Company and subsidiaries of Fuels Desulfurization and the refinery in question are the same in each case, so the capacity in B/D is not additive, but the incidents are independent and additive.
†Again being introduced.

capable of supporting some development with rigid environmental safeguards.

REFERENCES

1. J. Ray McDermott & Co., Inc. 1975. *The Jaramac*. New Orleans, Louisianna.
2. Joel M. Goodman. 1975. *Decisions for Delaware: Sea Grant Looks at OCS Development*. Marine Advisory Science, University of Delaware Sea Grant Program, Newark, Delaware.
3. Francis Marion. 1975. "Hunting the Atlantic with 500-pound air guns and a 2–½-mile snare." *Mobil World*, Vol. 41, No. 9, pp. 7–10.
4. Shell Oil Company. *Shell's Wonderful World of Oil*. Publication No. 5-1845-3-74.
5. Office of Technology Assessment. 1975. *Proposed New Energy Technologies off the Shores of New Jersey and Delaware*. Superintendent of Documents, U.S. Government Printing Office, Washington, D.C.
6. U.S. Department of Commerce. *Final Environmental Impact Statement*. Maritime Administration, Tanker Construction Program, NTIS Report No. EIS-7307-F, p. IV–4.
7. E. T. LaRoe and P. Stang. 1975. *Coastal Management Aspects of OCS Oil and Gas Developments*. National Oceanic and Atmospheric Administration, Office of Coastal Zone Management, Washington, D.C.
8. Federal Energy Office. 1974. *Trends in Refinery Capacity and Utilization*. Superintendent of Documents, U.S. Government Printing Office, Washington, D.C.

16. PIERS AND DOCKS

Most construction projects in United States coastal waters include landing facilities for family boats. Because of the popularity of boating and the convenience of docking the family boat at one's own property, most applications for permits to district offices of

Figure 6.116 Boat landings built on piers or floating docks are preferred to bulkhead or canalized landings (Georgia). (Conservation Foundation photo.)

the Corps of Engineers are for piers and docks for recreational craft.

The Corps has the final word on approving pier construction, and a boat owner must in every case apply to the Corps for a permit.[1] The state or local government may also have regulations governing piers or incidental work such as the dredging of access channels.

Piers, floats, and piling-guided floating docks are definitely preferred over filling and bulkheading to gain recreational access (Figure 6.116). There is no reason why any such structure should cause major environmental disturbance if sufficient thought is given to design, location, and construction. Generally, environmental safeguards are consistent with navigational safeguards.

GUIDELINE.   Water Area Encroachment of Piers

Limit the encroachment of recreational boat landing facilities into wetlands and coastal waters.

The Corps of Engineers limits the encroachment of piers into coastal waters to prevent interference with navigation. For example, the Baltimore District Office of the Corps has generally not approved piers that extend within 15 feet of navigation channels and has limited the length of all piers to less than one-third of the width of the watercourse.[2] State and local jurisdictions often require or recommend similar or more restrictive limits; for example, a model ordinance drafted for southern Maine would restrict encroachment to a maximum of 10 percent of the width of a watercourse.[3]

Recently the Corps of Engineers has begun to impose environmental constraints on piers in addition to the navigational constraints it has traditionally used.[4] Many states also impose environmental requirements. The thrust of these restrictions is (1) to reduce the potential blockage of water flow and decrease in flushing that would be caused by structures, (2) to mini-

mize their encroachment into coastal water areas, and (3) to eliminate as much dredging as possible (see also page 404).

Implementation No. 1.   Water Flow Protection in Pier Design

Piers should be built on pilings rather than solid fill.

To minimize disruption of water flows and alteration of wetlands, the following general limitations for pier construction have been applied by federal, state, and local authorities:

1. Solid-fill structures extending into water areas are discouraged in most states, except where winter ice conditions preclude piling-supported piers. Whether the filling and bulkheading are specifically for boat landing or are part of a general landfill and property extension, the encroachment onto the natural shoreline is generally considered to have an adverse effect on coastal ecosystems (page 000). Solid-fill structures tend to adversely alter water flows by restricting flow through narrow channels, thus blocking the flow path of water and creating eddies and turbulent backwaters, which increase localized sedimentation. Therefore the use of floating docks or pile-supported piers is required or recommended by the U.S. Department of the Interior[4] and many states (e.g., Washington[5] and South Carolina[6]), in order that water movement under the structures will be facilitated and alteration minimized (Figure 6.117). When structures are placed over a marsh, they should be sufficiently high above the marsh to allow sunlight entering from the sides to sustain the aquatic ecosystem underneath.

2. In construction of boat landings care should be taken to prevent pollution of coastal waters by silt and associated contaminants. For example, driving piles is preferred over jetting them in. Jetting

Figure 6.117 Floating docks are preferred because they require minimum disturbance of the estuarine bottom and the shoreline configuration (Moss Landing, California). (Photo by author.)

Figure 6.118 Communal neighborhood boat landings are encouraged to reduce the proliferation of individual piers (Charlestown Pond, Rhode Island). (Photo by author.)

tends to force silt into the water, which adversely affects water clarity, reduces dissolved oxygen, and often smothers bottom organisms.

3. To the extent possible, boat landings should be located in areas that have minimal dredging requirements because dredging causes a number of major adverse disturbances to coastal ecosystems (page 422). Boat landings should be encouraged where it is feasible to build pile-supported piers out to reach suitably deep water. It may be necessary to limit the use of a pier to shallow draft boats to eliminate dredging requirements, and to accommodate larger boats at deeper-water marinas nearby.

Implementation No. 2. Shared Docking Facilities

Proliferation of individual piers should be discouraged in favor of mooring buoys and shared community landings.

Federal and state authorities commonly discourage the proliferation of private piers by encouraging communities to build neighborhood boat-landing facilities. A dense accumulation of individual piers can cause a major obstruction of water flow along the shoreline, as well as significantly litter and pollute the water (e.g., by accumulation of oil and gasoline from leaks and spills). The community solution advanced by the Corps of Engineers—to "encourage cooperative or group use facilities in lieu of individual proprietor use facilities"—suggests that a few neighbors get together and build a communal boat landing instead of each family constructing its own pier (Figure 6.118). This could save considerable money and result in better facilities, as well as benefiting the coastal environment. Community piers are now standard in new waterfront subdivisions in the state of Washington.[5] Another suggested alternative is to encourage the use of "dry storage"—pulling boats out

on the land between uses—rather than the proliferation of piers.

We believe that the constraints listed in the above implementations should be more than sufficient to protect coastal waters from adverse impacts due to private boat landings. However, the potential adverse effects of boat operation on coastal ecosystems (pollution, stirring up the bottom, etc.) discussed in another section (page 404) should be considered in reviewing plans and permit applications for boat landings, particularly in relation to boating density, depth of waterway, condition of bottom, and currents and flushing rate of basin. Many a waterway is reaching the limit of its capacity to handle boat traffic. Individual permits should be approved only in the context of a plan that considers total future accumulated effects, including the capacity of the water system to handle the traffic and the capacity of the shoreline and water basin to absorb the impacts of noncontrollable waste discharges.

REFERENCES

1. U.S. Army Corps of Engineers. "Permits for activities in navigable waters or ocean waters." *Federal Register*, Vo. 40, No. 144, Part IV (July 25, 1975).

2. Garrett Power. 1975. "Watergate Village: A case study of a permit application for a marina submitted to the U.S. Army Corps of Engineers." *Coastal Zone Management Journal*, Vol. 2, No. 2, pp. 103–124.

3. Southern Maine Regional Planning Commission and the State Planning Office. 1973. Model Zoning Ordinance, State of Maine.

4. U.S. Fish and Wildlife Service. 1975. "Guidelines for review of fish and wildlife aspects of proposals in or affecting navigable waters." U.S. Department of the Interior, *Federal Register*, Vol. 40, No. 231, Part IV (Dec. 1).

5. Department of Ecology, State of Washington. 1972. *Final Guidelines Shoreline Management Act of 1971.*

6. Marine Resources Division. 1974. *Guidelines for Coastal Wetlands Developments.* South Carolina Wildlife and Marine Resources Department, Charleston, South Carolina.

17. POWER PLANTS

In the past, power plant siting has been mostly a concern of local authorities, although many states have power of condemnation to acquire land for power plants and transmission systems, or have become involved in other ways. Recently, much of the power of decision on power plant siting has passed to the federal government for the highly regulated nuclear reactors and for certain aspects of the larger "fossil fuel" plants as well. The growing national problem of energy supply will encourage increased federal involvement in the future, perhaps including implementation of national policies on siting that override local interests. Nevertheless the local community will have considerable political influence and a high stake in the outcome of siting issues. Therefore local interests must understand the full range of possible environmental, social, and economic consequences of power plants. It must be understood that the environmental damage that may accrue to a neighboring community from a badly located power plant may outweigh any tax revenue or other benefits to the community that has the plant.

We have learned lessons from environmental mistakes made in the past regarding large steam-powered electric plants. There are good and bad places to put steam plants; there are good and bad ways to design steam plants; and there are good and bad ways to operate steam plants. The same lessons hold whether the steam plant is fired by oil, coal, gas, or nuclear power. The sources of damage are well known.

Both fossil-fuel and nuclear-fired electric generating plants operate on the same general principle. Steam is produced from water by burning the fuel substance and is used to power a turbine, which turns an electric generator. The spent steam is condensed, and the water returned to be revaporized into steam to start the cycle anew. The steam condenser is cooled with water that is either drawn continually from a natural water body or recirculated through a closed-cycle cooling system.

Thermal pollution is not always the leading cause of damage to aquatic ecosystems, as was once believed. Very often a greater threat is the high death rate of organisms suspended in the water and drawn into power plants with the cooling water (Figure 6.119). The potential for environmental damage from massive entrainment and death of these organisms—fish, plankton, and larval stages of shellfish—is of such magnitude that it has caused a sweeping change in policies governing the design and location of power plants in the coastal zone.[1]

The following basic criteria provide considerable protection for aquatic resources in power plant siting and design. First, *open-cycle* systems are acceptable for sites on the open ocean coast provided that certain precautions are taken. Second, *closed-cycle* cooling should be used whenever a steam plant is located on an estuarine water body such as a tidal river, bay, or lagoon.

Vital habitat areas should be protected against preemption or degradation. Also, in siting power plants, one must consider not only the effect of the plant itself but also the aggregate environmental effects of other development attracted to a new industrial zone created by the presence of the plant, access roads, and so forth (See "Industry Siting," page 391).

GUIDELINE. Locational Constraints on Power Plants

Locate power plants so as to avoid damaging vital habitat areas.

Broad estuarine marshscapes offer attractive sites for nuclear plants, because the price of marshland is low, cooling water is available, and a degree of seclusion is possible (Figure 6.120). However, this siting con-

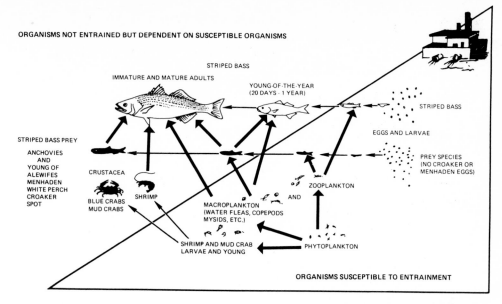

ORGANISMS NOT ENTRAINED BUT DEPENDENT ON SUSCEPTIBLE ORGANISMS

STRIPED BASS
IMMATURE AND MATURE ADULTS

YOUNG-OF-THE-YEAR
(20 DAYS - 1 YEAR)

STRIPED BASS

EGGS AND LARVAE

STRIPED BASS PREY

ANCHOVIES
AND
YOUNG OF
ALEWIFES
MENHADEN
WHITE PERCH
CROAKER
SPOT

PREY SPECIES
(NO CROAKER OR
MENHADEN EGGS)

CRUSTACEA

ZOOPLANKTON

BLUE CRABS
MUD CRABS

SHRIMP

AND

MACROPLANKTON
(WATER FLEAS, COPEPODS
MYSIDS, ETC.)

SHRIMP AND MUD CRAB
LARVAE AND YOUNG

PHYTOPLANKTON

ORGANISMS SUSCEPTIBLE TO ENTRAINMENT

Figure 6.119 Potential power plant impacts on striped bass and associated food items. (SOURCE: Reference 1.)

flicts with state and national initiatives for protection of these vital areas. Siting in the lower floodplain (up to the 10-year flood mark) should also be discouraged for many ecologic and pragmatic reasons; this area is recommended as a buffer zone where development should be strictly limited (page 172).

Excavation, dredging, and other potentially disturbing activities should be closely controlled during construction to prevent damage to vital areas (page 237).

Implementation No. 1. Vital Area Protection in Power Plant Siting

Power plants should be located away from vital habitat areas.

Power plants should be excluded from vital areas, and from sites where cooling water would be withdrawn from or discharged into vital areas.

Wetlands should not be used as power plant sites, nor should wetlands be ditched or otherwise altered in power plant construc-

tion. Wetlands play an especially key role in estuarine ecosystems. Grassy marshes and mangrove swamps are crucial to the ecological functioning of the estuaries that they border and therefore require special protection. Many coastal states have passed laws to protect wetlands or wetland areas (page 251).

Within estuaries there are also numerous submerged habitat areas that are critical to the vitality of the estuarine ecosystem (page 30) and are easily overlooked in siting consideration. It is not likely that a generating station would be built out in the open water where these submerged habitats are found, but intake structures may easily impinge on them and cooling water may draw from or discharge into them. These vital habitat areas include ecologic elements such as breeding places, fish migration pathways, and shellfish beds (page 30). They occur to a lesser extent in the ocean than in estuaries, but those in the ocean should also be zoned for protection, for example, kelp beds along the Pacific coast. Therefore the

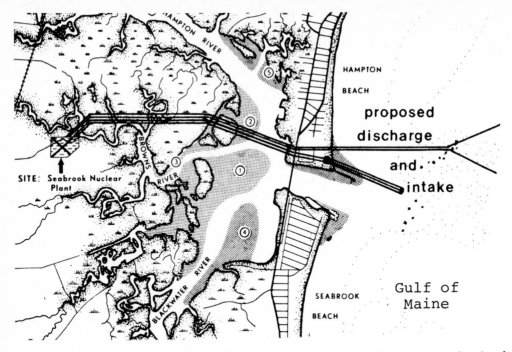

Figure 6.120 The initial plan for the Seabrook–Hampton plant on the New Hampshire coast, locating the nuclear reactor and generator complex within a 4000-acre vital marsh habitat; later the utility was required to drill discharge and intake lines (18-foot diameter) through deep granite bedrock to avoid disrupting the marsh with surface pipeline excavation. (SOURCE: Reference 2.)

biotic survey that precedes any site selection action must identify and exempt submerged vital areas as sites for power plant intakes or discharges.

GUIDELINE. Power Plant Cooling System Safeguards

Locate, design, and operate power plants so as to avoid adverse effects from withdrawal and discharge of cooling water.

Most power plant problems for the aquatic environment are caused by the condenser cooling system, particularly the form popular in the past, called "open cycle" or "once through." This cooling system draws massive quantities of water from an adjacent lake, river, or estuary. The natural waters of these confined basins and the suspended life in them are seriously threatened by their passage through the steam cooler and by the addition of chemicals (Figure 6.121). Much of the entrained life is killed or damaged. Fish are often attracted plantside in winter by the heated effluent water and are suffocated on the intake screens. The entire aquatic ecosystem may be degraded by thermal pollution.

The areas of greatest environmental threat are the enclosed waters—estuaries, bays, lagoons, and tidal rivers—which are of critical environmental concern because of their high productivity and the abundance and diversity of life that they support. These areas, which require the highest degree of protection, are also the most attractive as power plant sites for many practical and strategic reasons and therefore the most threatened.

The principal criteria for locating power plants in the past have been (1) cooling water availability, (2) fuel availability, (3)

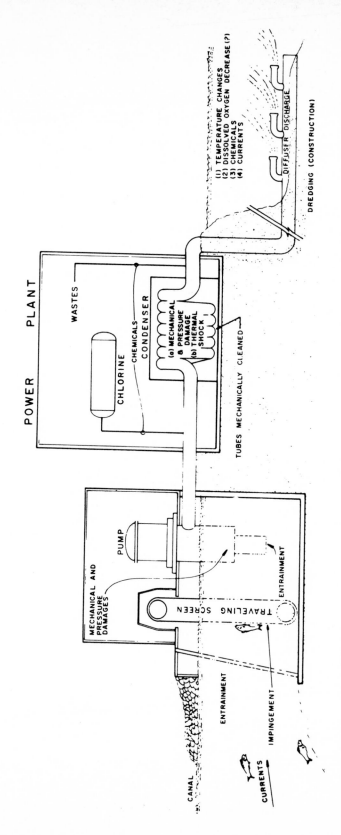

Figure 6.121 Schematic representation of the proposed condenser cooling system of the Shoreham nuclear power station and sources of potential biological damage. (SOURCE: Reference 3.)

land suitability, (4) engineering feasibility, (5) cost of land, (6) transmission of power to market areas, and (7) for nuclear plants, nuclear safety. Aquatic resources and ecological considerations have often been ignored, resulting in much serious damage to natural systems. Electric power production can be harmonized with environmental protection in coastal areas if certain traditional practices are modified to respect resource and ecological needs.

The major solutions are to (1) locate power plants along the open coast, where there is deep water nearby for strategic placement of intake and outlet structures if open-cycle cooling is to be used; and (2) reduce the volume of cooling water used by plants on estuaries by requiring closed-cycle systems, which recirculate cooling waters, rather than open-cycle systems, which continuously withdraw from and discharge into the environment large volumes of water.

Implementation No. 1. Ocean Coast Siting of Power Plants

Open-cycle cooling should be restricted to open coast or offshore ocean sites.

When open-cycle plants are permitted on the ocean coast, intakes, outlets, and other submerged structures must be designed with care to prevent entrainment, entrapment, and impingement of aquatic life.

To minimize adverse aquatic impact the first requirement for selection of an ocean coast site should be a broad survey to locate all vital habitat areas (page 247), both permanent (e.g., kelp beds) and intermittent (e.g., fish migration pathways). Such areas should be classified as off limits for power plant intakes and effluent discharges, and a location selected from among those that serve no vital function.

The second requirement is that the cooling system be designed for minimal disturbance of coastal ecosystems. Specifically, the following should be required: (1) limit the

discharge of chemicals, (2) provide for minimal disruption of natural water flow, and (3) locate cooling water intake and outlet for minimal effect on biota.

Implementation No. 2. Estuarine Siting of Power Plants

Open-cycle cooling should be prohibited for all power plants located on or adjacent to enclosed water bodies.

A large nuclear generating unit of around 1000 MW^e (megawatts electricity) with once-through cooling is typically fitted with a row of six 140,000 gpm (gallons per minute) pumps, each mounted within a separate intake chamber. In front of the pumps are various screens and other devices to protect the cooling system from damage caused by floating debris. A typical screen is made of sections of 3/8–inch mesh mounted on drums, so that it may be rotated for cleaning when debris or dead fish accumulate and reduce the flow of water through it. The number of fish impaled on these screens has exceeded five million in a few weeks' time at estuarine-sited power plants with the old open-cycle cooling.

The amount of water required for open-cycle cooling of steam condensers is a function of certain design features that govern the rate of heat transfer to the water. With a typical modern nuclear plant of 1000-MW^e capacity, fitted with open-cycle cooling, water goes through the plant in less than 1 minute, and its temperature is raised by 10 to 34°F (5.6 to 19°C) before being discharged directly back into public waters (Figure 6.122). Diesel fuel plants are more efficient than nuclear plants and discharge about one-third less waste heat. Whereas a fossil fuel plant might require about 600 gpm of cooling water per megawatt electricity produced, a nuclear plant might require 900 gpm.

Inside a large (1000-MW^e) nuclear plant the cooling water passes through a manifold

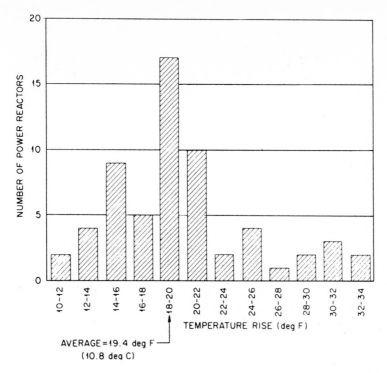

Figure 6.122 Design temperature rises through condensers of 67 nuclear power plants. (SOURCE: Reference 4.)

of 35,000 1-inch metal tubes, each about 50 feet (15.2 meters) long. The tubes are surrounded by the steam that is to be condensed. As the cooling water traverses the tubes, it cools the steam, gains heat, and then flows via a junction box out a conduit back to the source water body. Once back in the source body, the heated water may rise, sink, or remain suspended, depending on the relative densities of effluent and receiving waters (Figure 6.123).

This heated effluent from open-cycle power plants adversely affects the natural patterns of life and the behavior of all aquatic species and thus is called "thermal pollution." How pervasive this pollution may be and how damaging depends on the size and flushing characteristics of the public water basin that is threatened with pollution. For example, five proposed electric plants would raise the temperature of the Hudson estuary by 4 to 5°F (2 to 2.8°C)

over a range of 35 miles—a sufficient rise to kill striped bass at certain embryonic stages.[2] Where water is shallow and protected by sand bars, as on the sheltered coast of western Florida (Figure 6.124), grass beds are exposed to extensive damage from temperature buildup.

The temporary shutdown of power plants has caused severe cold-shock kills of fish in discharge-receiving waters in winter. Coastal species often linger in the warm effluent plume, during their winter southern migration, unaffected by the changing season. When the heat source is suddenly cut off, the fish are subjected to rapid and sometimes lethal temperature drops.

The major source of disturbance associated with open-cycle cooling is entrainment, whereby aquatic forms drawn in with the cooling water are exposed to heat, turbulence, abrasion, and shock. The effects are especially direct and severe when plants are

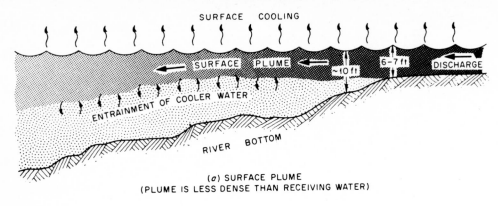

(a) SURFACE PLUME
(PLUME IS LESS DENSE THAN RECEIVING WATER)

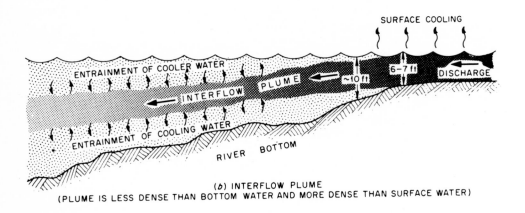

(b) INTERFLOW PLUME
(PLUME IS LESS DENSE THAN BOTTOM WATER AND MORE DENSE THAN SURFACE WATER)

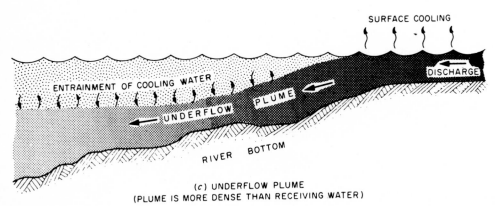

(c) UNDERFLOW PLUME
(PLUME IS MORE DENSE THAN RECEIVING WATER)

Figure 6.123 Discharge plume conditions for a low-salinity upper estuary in northern latitudes. (SOURCE: Reference 5.)

located in estuarine spawning and nursery areas of fish and shellfish. For example, 30 percent or more of the annual brood of an estuarine-spawning fish can be killed by the operation of one 1000-MW[e] plant on the Hudson estuary.[7]

Power plant cooling systems tend to become internally fouled with aquatic life. The chemical treatment for cleaning is a periodic dose of hypochlorite (chlorine), which poisons fouling organisms and, unfortunately, much of the other life in the water that is passing through at the time. Moreover, large amount of hypochlorite may be needed for plants with once-through cooling. Even with closed-cycle systems, chemicals should be used sparingly in treating the cooling water and should be replaced where possible by mechanical or thermal systems of cleaning and balancing.

The open-cycle cooling system has recently become less environmentally feasible because of the increasing size of plants, coincident with more limited supplies of

water available for plant cooling. Also there is an increased awareness of potential damage to the aquatic environment. Consequently, a majority of steam-powered plants now in planning for inland or estuarine sites are designed to operate with closed-cycle cooling systems that do not require massive use of water and instead transfer the waste heat to the air. However, capital and operating costs are higher. Closed-cycle systems may have natural draft cooling towers, forced (mechanical) draft cooling towers, cooling ponds, or spray canals (Figures 6.125 and 6.126).

The required precaution of closed-cycle cooling may demand a greater immediate

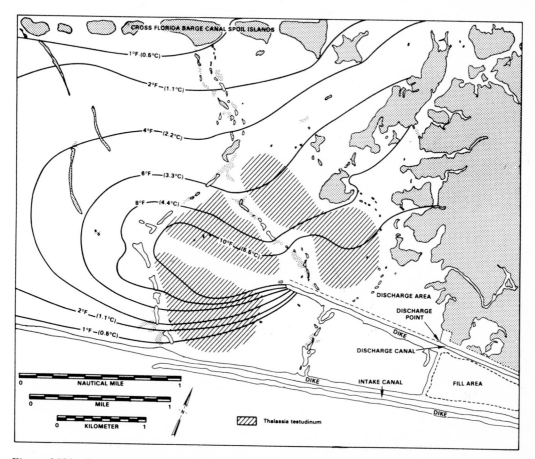

Figure 6.124 Predicted temperature increments above ambient [at 3 feet (0.9 meter) below the surface, average for full tidal cycle] for a power plant at Crystal River, Florida (shaded areas are grass beds). (SOURCE: Reference 6.)

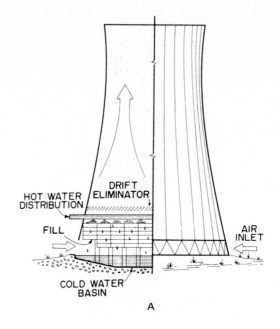

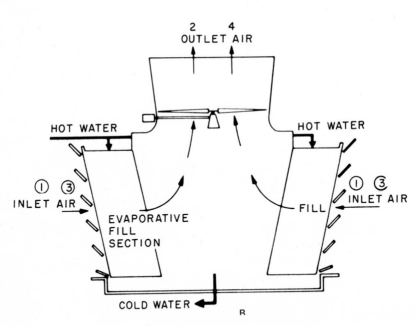

Figure 6.125   Cooling towers for power plant closed-cycle condenser cooling: (A) natural draft tower; (B) mechanical draft tower. (SOURCE: Reference 8.)

expenditure of fiscal resources but over time should result in a worthwhile economy through protection of aquatic resources. Advanced engineering has produced satisfactory closed-cycle cooling systems that utilize only 2 to 4 percent as much water as is used by fully open-cycle systems. Consequently, the closed-cycle alternatives consume only 1/25

Figure 6.126 Spray canal system at Pittsburg steam plant (Sacramento–Joaquin delta, California) minimizes salt spray problems from air-cooled systems (however, note the unfortunate location in the coastal lowlands–wetlands area). (Photo courtesy of Pacific Gas and Electric Company, San Francisco, California).

to 1/50 of the marina biota destroyed by once-through plants. Another advantage is that they discharge a similarly small fraction of heat and chemicals into public waters.

A closed-cycle system is not expensive if designed into the plant at the outset. However, backfitting such systems into existing plants is more expensive than designing them into new plants. Typical capital costs for cooling systems for 1000-MW^e nuclear plants are as follows:

Once-through	$3–5 million
Wet towers	$8–13 million
Dry towers	$25 million

Both short-chimney mechanical draft towers and high-chimney natural draft towers are available market items. There are two

possible drawbacks to the cooling towers. First, their appearance may be a deterrent. Mechanical draft towers rise 70 feet (21.3 meters) or so from the ground and have an industrial look. Natural towers rise 400 feet (122 meters) or more from the ground; and, although they have a pleasant hyperbolic geometry, they clash with natural features and in most settings protrude above the skyline. They may be not worse than smokestacks, but in a nonindustrialized area cooling towers, like smokestacks, may be a significant aesthetic intrusion.

Second, towers emit a plume of vapor that may detract from the natural beauty of an area and under certain conditions could lead to some fogging, icing of roads, and undesirable salt fallout in the neighborhood of the plant. However, recent studies have shown the salt fallout problem to be localized to the immediate vicinity of the plant. The drift from high natural draft towers can be expected to carry somewhat into local surroundings, however, if the towers are not equipped with drift eliminators.

"Spray ponds" appear to be a better environmental choice than towers because they are at ground level and do not cause significant salt drift beyond the plant site.

REFERENCES

1. State of Maryland. *Record of the Maryland Power Plant Siting Act*, Vol. 1.
2. J. R. Clark and W. Brownell. 1973. *Electric Power Plants in the Coastal Zone: Environmental Issues*. American Littoral Society, Special Publication No. 7, Highlands, New Jersey.
3. U.S. Atomic Energy Commission. 1972. *Final Environmental Statement—Shoreham Nuclear Power Station*.
4. C. C. Coutant. 1971. "Effects on organisms of entrainment in cooling water: steps toward predictability." *Nuclear Safety*, Vol. 12, No. 6, pp. 500–607.
5. U.S. Atomic Energy Commission. 1972. *Final Environmental Statement—Surry Power Station Unit 1*.

6. U.S. Atomic Energy Commission. 1972. *Draft Environmental Statement—Crystal River Nuclear Station Unit 1.*

7. D. L. Ray, Chairman of the U.S. Atomic Energy Commission. 1973. Letter (Dec. 5) to U.S. Senator A. Ribicoff.

8. T. D. Kolflat. 1973. *Cooling Towers—State of the Art.* Paper given at U.S. Department of the Interior–Atomic Industrial Forum Seminar, Washington, D.C., February 13-14, 1973.

18. RESIDENTIAL DEVELOPMENT

Coastal zone property suitable for development has become scarce and demand has increased, forcing up prices. Regulatory programs that limit its uses have added to these trends. Increased demand for coastal residential sites often conflicts with the environmental controls required for the protection of coastal ecosystems and their scenic qualities.

Such conflicts can be resolved through the use of appropriate regulatory tools: plan reviews and permits, development performance standards, and zoning. Many states and some local communities require developers to explore the probable environmental impacts of proposed residential subdivisions and report on them. Environmental appraisal is becoming a routine part of subdivision review in some coastal communities. This section outlines development criteria and suggests standards to guide local officials in protecting the coastal environment as they review plans for residential development.

The environmental review of residential development applications in coastal areas must include the full range of commercial, recreational, and other types of development induced by increased occupancy. A coastal residential community requires roads, marinas, storm drain systems, parking lots, waste treatment facilities, and so forth, and each of these has the potential for disturbance of coastal ecosystems. Although the following discussion concentrates on development on the scale of larger subdivisions, small projects, including individual homesites, should also conform to the basic controls.

Natural hazards to life and property are related to habitation of coastal floodplains. Development risks result from the direct onslaught of storm-driven waves on the open coast and storm-induced high waters in estuaries. The construction of housing in flood and coastal storm hazard areas has resulted in loss of life and property during storms and obliteration of dune lines and other critical natural areas. The severity of the damages and the financial losses suffered by residents in these areas led to the establishment of the National Flood Insurance Program (page 173).

Large-scale housing projects for both "primary home" and "second home" developments have had pronounced adverse effects on coastal water resources and ecosystems over the years (Figure 6.127). Uncontrolled development throughout shoreland watersheds has caused widespread soil erosion, sedimentation, and contamination of coastal waters. In addition the disturbance of watersheds by construction and paving has led to rapid stormwater runoff, floods, and the unbalancing of coastal ecosystems (Figure 6.128). Hurricane Agnes in 1972 provides a dramatic example of how upstream development exacerbates storm runoff, causing flooding, widespread destruction of private property, and massive disruption of coastal ecosystems. Prevention of this damage requires controls on site preparation and construction throughout the coastal watershed.

The dredging, filling, and canal excavation for waterfront homesite preparation that have been popular in many areas have led to the ruin of estuarine systems. New state and federal environmental policies clearly identify estuarine areas as requiring a high degree of protective action.

Federal water quality legislation seeks to eliminate pollutant discharge into United States waters, especially estuaries. Nevertheless, local governments still retain the broad

Figure 6.127   Large-scale waterfront developments have a wide range of potential adverse impacts on coastal ecosystems (Morehead City, North Carolina). (Conservation Foundation photo by M. Fahay.)

responsibility for the adoption and implementation of coastal residential development controls. Rather than relying on the new state and federal initiatives, local governments must establish their own programs of development and drainage standards if they are to protect their coastal resources and ecosystems.

The water areas include all creeks, lakes, marshes, cypress domes, mangrove swamps, sloughs, bays, and any other permanently or seasonally flooded areas, whether fresh or salt water. Vital habitats among the water areas—such as watershed drainageways, wetlands, productive tideflats, and sand dunes—are irreplaceable and essential components

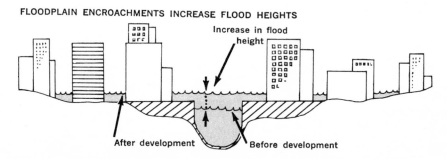

Figure 6.128   Urbanization inland of the coastal zone will induce storm runoff, increasing flooding in coastal areas. (SOURCE: Reference 1.)

of the coastal ecosystem and therefore should be kept in an unaltered state. The planning framework requires a system of inventory and classification that embraces specific vital habitat areas, as well as wide areas of special environmental sensitivity, often known as "critical areas" (page 134).

GUIDELINE. Residential Development Review

Review all residential development and construction applications in shorelands for compliance with ecosystem protection requirements.

The subdivider's responsibility for water management in the shorelands can be expressed clearly in one statement: *Ensure that water leaves the subdivision in as nearly as possible the same quality, volume, and rate of flow that prevailed before development.* This policy will ensure the least possible disruption of coastal ecosystems. As long as these water and soil rules are adhered to, a developer can proceed without interference insofar as effects on coastal ecosystems are concerned. The success of the coastal community's environmental management program will depend on the success of measures taken to preserve and restore the natural level of water quality and the pattern of water flow. The community's economic future, too, may be served by restoration and preservation of the natural water runoff system. These systems play a vital integrating role that maintains an uncontaminated and ample freshwater supply and provides storm and flood protection.

Artificial draining of land to dry it up for residential development has adverse effects (page 397). Coastal ecosystems and estuarine resources are absolutely dependent on the inflows of inland water and are highly sensitive to alteration in the quality, volume, and rate of these flows. When portions of this system are removed or short circuited by

drainage canals, the natural flow pattern is disrupted, the water-cleansing function of the vegetation is eliminated, and freshwater flow into the estuaries occurs in surges. Since the paved surfaces and reduced vegetation will increase stormwater runoff and the chance of downstream flooding, specific provisions must be included to reduce the threat of flooding to life and property.

Water supply needs, solid waste and sewage disposal, private land care, and water diversions will affect the groundwater and surface-water systems, and their impacts must be thoroughly considered.

With about 1 million acres of land cleared for development each year in the United States, soil loss and consequent sedimentation of estuarine waters constitute a major problem throughout the coastal zone. Soil erosion control should concentrate on (1) attempting to keep the soil in place, and (2) where soil is disturbed, preventing it from leaving the subdivision. Both of these efforts require water management because water, rather than wind, is the principal eroding force in most coastal areas.

The principal purpose of this section is to review the standards for development management found in other sections of this book and suggest how they may be combined into an integrated residential development program for regulation of coastal areas.

Implementation No. 1. Vital Areas

Vital areas should be exempt from residential development.

Many components of the coastal ecosystem are of critical importance to certain species or to the functioning of the entire ecosystem (page 140). These vital areas should be designated as exempt from all but the most limited types of use, for example, light-duty recreation and other nonaltering uses (Figure 6.129). These areas should not be drained, excavated, or filled, and will require special

Figure 6.129   Small-boat landings adjacent to marinas and accessways on pilings can be built with little effect on coastal ecosystems (Lee County, Florida). (Photo by author.)

care during site planning and preparation (page 247). They should also be protected from pollution and other external sources of disturbance. Ample precedent for such preservation is furnished by the laws in several states that restrict development in coastal freshwater wetlands and that preserve streams and stream banks. Many federal laws, policies, and programs provide for the preservation of wetlands (page 183 et seq.).

Designated vital areas that should not be converted to residential use or otherwise atlered include creeks, streams, swales, and other watershed drainageways; marshes, bogs, sloughs, and other freshwater wetlands; tide-flats and sand dunes; coastal marshes and mangrove swamps; productive sand flats; submerged grass beds; oyster beds; and nursery areas. All vital areas should be identified and delineated on the community master land-use map, including any requirement for buffer strips (Figure 6.130). Land designated for such exemption would have low value

for residential use. The recorded inventory and mapping should serve to avert conflict over no-alteration constraints on vital areas because all land purchasers will know of the restrictions before they buy the property.

Although restrictive performance standards are intended to modify existing land-clearing, site preparation, and construction practices, their application will incidentally modify existing location practices; for example, it will shift conflicting uses away from the ecologically sensitive water areas.

When a parcel in private ownership purchased for residential development includes a substantial amount of exempted vital area such as wetlands, some compensation may be arranged by allowing the developer to build at higher densities on the upland parts of the property.[2,3] Such density-compensated transfers of development—clustering, or utilization of a formal process of transfer development rights or density credits—may be useful as a specific management tool in moving

Figure 6.130 A wide buffer strip of native vegetation between residential developments assists in purifying urban runoff before it reaches coastal waters (Cape Elizabeth, Maine). (Photo by author.)

development from vital habitat areas to higher ground in shorelands, while maintaining the desired density (page 259).

Implementation No. 2.   Water Runoff

Residential development should be fully controlled to prevent degradation of the quality, volume, and rate of flow of the natural drainage system of the watershed.

A program designed for protection of coastal and estuarine resources must recognize the critical role of water flows in integrating the total ecosystem, from the watershed through the estuarine system and into the ocean. The water system and related ecosystem elements must be protected from destructive modification. To accomplish this, new approaches to land and water management are required, which should focus on ecological systems and encourage the use of development performance standards as a complement to traditional zoning and ad hoc administrative review procedures.[4]

The coastal water basin—bay, lagoon, or tidal river—is but one part of a larger integral ecosystem, essentially water based, and

extending from the beaches and bays inland to the farthest reach of the watershed that drains into it. Therefore mangament for each basin must extend inland to include all related wetlands and water areas.

Site preparation should be the focus of protective water management programs (page 533). For example, simply clearing the land of vegetation has many effects. One is a decrease in the ability of the watershed to absorb stormwaters (page 87). Another effect is an increase in the total volume of fresh water entering the estuary due to (1) decreased transpiration to the atmosphere because of reduced vegetation, and (2) decreased evaporation to the atmosphere because of the increased rate of water movement over cleared land (page 87). Other alterations in flow are caused by water control activities such as excavation of drainage canals and by the use of impervious surfacing materials over large areas of land (page 87). In addition, installation of storm drain systems usually interrupts freshwater flow patterns, and in turn alters their timing and rate of delivery to the estuary (page 552). This leads to interference with normal salinity cycles in the estuary, the recharge of freshwater aquifers, and the water-cleansing processes of soil and vegetative cover (page 550). Finally, uncontrolled land clearing and construction greatly increase the sediment load in the runoff from any construction site (page 552).

Development standards can operate independently of traditional zoning maps. Well-conceived standards not only implement the specific environmental objectives set out in regulations, but also provide equity and predictability for developers in the approval process. An effective program can be administered conveniently through the existing site plan review process, which was set up to ensure conformity with zoning and subdivision regulations or planned unit development provisions. Specific technical considerations are outlined below.

Runoff Water Control

The development plan should clearly indicate any expected land and water alteration and explain how the developer will ensure that water will leave the project area in virtually the same quality, volume, and rate of flow that prevail in the undeveloped state. Each project component should show proof that these water drainage characteristics will be maintained both during construction and after completion. The emphasis should be on controls during site preparation—land clearing, grading, and surfacing (page 237). The basic requirement is as follows: *All subdivisions should be designed to retain within their boundaries the maximum expected rainfall and to release it at a natural rate and in acceptable quality.* For example, in an area of Collier County, Florida, where the 25-year return maximum rainfall is 8.2 inches in 24 hours (30,000 cubic feet per acre), the capability for artificial detention and release at the natural rate should be about 15,000 cubic feet of rainwater per acre (4 inches of rainfall) or more for most sites.[5] Greater artificial detention—up to 20,000 or more cubic feet per acre—must be encouraged

when the soil or surface is particularly impermeable. If properly designed, 6000 square feet per residential unit of functioning vegetated surface over which runoff flows, or a permanent retention basin that can accommodate an equivalent volume, should be adequate for water quality restoration (Figure 6.131).

The development review process must consider the long-term effects of the design of the proposed project as well as the immediate effects of the construction activity.

Drainage of Wetland

The ecological consequences are usually too severe to allow drainage of wetlands—land too wet during parts of the year to be suitable for homesites (page 146). When there is a present strong development commitment to a wetlands owner that cannot be reversed, strict constraints should be imposed on the project, including the design of the drainage facilities for flood protection and ecological purposes (page 230).

Erosion Control

Soil disturbance is inevitable in site preparation for residential development. Control measures are required to prevent sedimentation and water pollution. Loss of soil from the project site by erosion and water transport should be eliminated, and any exposed soil promptly stabilized by revegetation (page 537). Development plans should ensure that soils exposed during site alteration will be trapped through catchment ponds or performance-equivalent structures or systems in order to prevent erosion of soil from the construction site or the discharge of any other polluting substance (page 537).

In general, disruption of the vegetation cover should be limited to the smallest work area practicable, and revegetation and stabilization of disturbed areas should be accomplished at the earliest possible date (page 537).

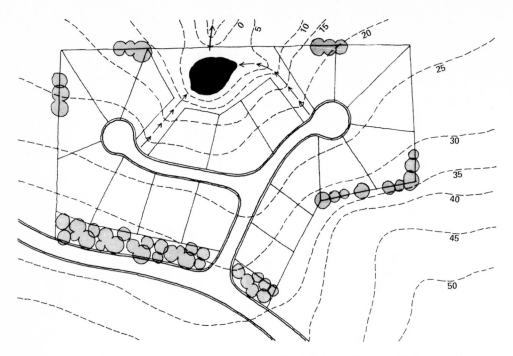

Figure 6.131   Runoff detention basin in a small subdivision. (SOURCE: Reference 6.)

Impervious Surfaces

Rooftops, paved roads, parking lots, and sidewalks in residential developments adversely alter the quality, quantity, and rate of flow of runoff from any watershed and thus should be minimized (page 547). It is recommended that the least possible land area of any subdivision be covered with impervious surface (normally, not more than 10 percent of the gross area). The purpose is to maintain the pattern of natural infiltration and to prevent excess runoff and lowered water quality. Performance-equivalent substitutes that allow a higher percentage may be satisfactory if they result in the collection, treatment, and release of runoff in a manner approximating the natural condition.

To minimize the percentage of impervious surface, alternatives to traditional paving practices should be encouraged. In suburban developments, porous surfaces can be used for driveways, sidewalks, play areas, patios,

and low-activity roads. In second-home developments these surfaces are particularly appropriate throughout the community because of lighter use patterns.

Storm Sewers

Self-contained soil infiltration systems and grassed drainageways are generally practicable and cost-effective substitutes for storm sewers (page 549). When storm sewers are necessary a decentralized pattern of small separate systems is recommended; they incorporate natural restoration techniques such as land application (page 549).

Groundwater

Aquifers are sensitive to water withdrawal, paved surfacing, water diversion, and pollutants introduced into the water system by any kind of development. Standard reviews of proposed residential development should include measures for aquifer protection (page 381). The domestic water supply needs of any proposed residential development should be included in the plan, and the development approved only if its requirements fall within the limits of the available fresh groundwater supply (Figure 6.132).

Water diversion caused by paved surfaces and altered water drainage may reduce the amount of recharge that would replenish the groundwater aquifer under natural conditions (page 384). Protection of ground water recharge areas from these diversions is therefore a necessary component of coastal housing development (page 384). Septic tanks (page 502) and dumps (page 527) pose major threats to groundwater quality through leaching, and both should be set back from open-water areas and prohibited where there is a high water table (page 504).

Sewage

Where feasible, septic tanks should be permitted in coastal residential developments, unless there is a proved need for central sewage systems (page 502). However, poorly designed septic tank systems and sanitary landfills leach chemical contaminants to the groundwater system. To avoid groundwater pollution, septic systems should not be used where there is a high water table [closer to the surface than 10 feet (3 meters), page 504]. They should be located a safe distance back from the water's edge (normally, 150 feet or more behind the annual flood mark) to avoid damage to coastal ecosystems by pollutant leaching through the groundwater (page 504).

Central sewage systems should include land treatment and disposal of effluent whenever possible (page 513). Outfalls of standard secondary treatment plants should not discharge to estuarine waters (page 516). Residential development plans should incorporate, to the maximum extent possible, systems that utilize wastes through constructive recycling practices (pages 506 and 524).

Figure 6.132   Land subsidence occurs in areas with clay subsoils where the groundwater supply has been overpumped, usually for industrial use; in the scene depicted here dikes and automatic pumps have been installed to rectify the situation (Baytown, Texas). (Photo by author.)

Figure 6.133 Shoreline dumps are ecological as well as aesthetic and health threats and should be prohibited (Cape Kennedy, Florida). (Conservation Foundation photo by M. Fahay.)

Solid Waste Disposal

The state and federal wetlands protection laws require that solid waste landfills not pre-empt vital habitat areas (page 529). Such landfills should be set back from the water's edge and located in appropriate upland sites, where they will not pollute surface waters or groundwaters (Figure 6.133).

Residential Land Care

To protect coastal waters from the home-owner's use of biocides and fertilizers, tradi-tional practices must be changed. Application of these chemicals can be avoided or greatly reduced by voluntary homeowner action, by regulating the use or sale of some products, and by substituting improved products (page 243). Moreover, their appli-cation should be controlled in respect to conditions of soils, slopes, erosion patterns, and water runoff, proximity of coastal water, and vegetation in flow course.

Natural local vegetation should be used for landscaping. Native vegetation is ad-justed to the local environment (soils, water cycles, nutrients, insect pests, etc.) and does not require the often expensive, destructive, and polluting maintenance (watering, fertilizing, spraying) that introduced plants normally need. Furthermore, the native wildlife is adapted to utilize native vegetation (for cover, nesting, food, etc.), and therefore loss of the natural vegetation reduces wildlife habitat.[7]

During development it will often be necessary to implement a setback provision, whereby a buffer strip is required between the defined edge of a water body or wetlands and the developed land area. Uses permitted within the buffer strip will be limited to those that do not alter or pollute water or wetlands (page 275).

GUIDELINE. Waterfront Residential Development Review

Establish a special review process for waterfront and floodplain residential development and construction proposals.

The special environmental problems of residential developments in waterfront and floodplain areas demand special precautions

in planning and constructing such developments. The problems specific to these areas have been recognized for many years by a number of states and communities through establishment of special zoning or performance standards for development in coastal areas. The Federal Coastal Zone Management Act[8] (page 161) provides further inducement for statewide controls on coastal development, including special considerations for shoreline areas. The Federal Flood Disaster Protection Act[9] requires special land-use management and development control programs in coastal floodprone and storm hazard areas (Figure 6.134).

Every coastal community that has not already done so should establish special land-use allocations and regulations and systems of review for waterfronts and floodprone areas, including subdivision reviews, building codes, zoning actions, and other land- and water-use control programs, to take into account the unique coastal conditions and problems of these areas.

The environmental disturbances typical of development anywhere in the coastal zone are applicable also to waterfront develop-

Figure 6.134 Each community should have firm prohibitions to prevent structures from being built on dunes or beach berms, where they cause rapid depletion of beach sand and they will be massively damaged in storms (Sanibel Island, Florida). (Photo by author.)

Figure 6.135 A canalized development behind a barrier beach sets the stage for extensive damage to the natural system and for high risk of damage to life and property from hurricanes (North Carolina). (Conservation Foundation photo by M. Fahay.)

ment. In addition, the following may occur: (1) short circuits of natural drainage flows (caused by dredged channels), (2) saltwater intrusion of groundwater (due to canals) (page 381), and (3) increases in the tidal prism (from canal excavation and navigation channel deepening in the adjoining water basin) (page 423). Further ecosystem disturbance results from bulkheading and other attempts at landfill or erosion prevention along occupied shorelines (page 342). Additional problems of waterfront occupancy arise from natural storm and flood hazards (page 354), the lack of suitable soils for foundations or drainage, and the shortage of freshwater supplies (page 381) (Figure 6.135).

The proximity of waterfront subdivisions to the shore also means that polluted runoff goes directly to the coastal water basin with little time for natural purification through vegetation and soil. Waterfront land clear-

ing and site preparation cause direct discharge into coastal waters of polluting sediment and nutrients that can drastically reduce water quality. Serious and often irreversible pollution also may result from sediments dispersed in channel-dredging operations. Therefore buffer areas are mandatory (page 239), and special provisions must be made to handle land grading and drainage during site preparation (page 237).

Waterfront development by dredging wetlands, tidelands, and estuarine bottoms and using the "spoil" to fill and elevate the land is the most disturbing of all types of coastal residential development, particularly when canals are dredged and the dredge spoil is plied on adjacent wetlands or low lands to gain elevation and to create lots for canalside homes (Figure 6.136). The canals collect pollutants, become foul, and contaminate estuarine waters; septic tanks cannot normally be used because nitrogen (page

503) and other substances are introduced into the canal waters so rapidly (in 4 to 60 hours) that there is inadequate time for purificating action. Further ecosystem disturbance may result from bulk-heading and other attempts to hold the fill and prevent erosion (page 342).

The planning stage of a waterfront development provides an excellent opportunity to ensure that access to the public shoreline is facilitated. In California, shoreline developers must provide off-street public parking facilities along the coast sufficient to accommodate the anticipated needs of shore visitors.[11]

Special efforts will be needed to preserve the drainage systems of floodplains because these areas have high water tables and direct hydraulic connections to coastal waters (page 354). The lower floodplain (10-year) can serve as a buffer area to protect vital water areas that lie along the shoreline,

such as wetlands and tidal flats. The floodplain filter or buffer strip protects the wetlands and tidelands from runoff surge and heavier loads of sediment and other pollutants than they can assimilate (Figure 6.137).

All existing residential development should be brought into conformance with the community plan. Therefore nonconforming uses should be identified and terminated or altered to conform as opportunity permits. There will be many existing structures in floodprone areas and along waterfronts that do not conform to new setback standards. These residential developments should be identified as *environmental nonconforming uses* and allowed to continue, but be scheduled for removal or correction at the earliest opportunity (page 246). Expansion or improvement should not be allowed. The opportunity for discontinuance may come when the economic life of a building ends or fire, flood, or other natural disaster damages

Figure 6.136 Massive dredging of wetland canals for fill to elevate canalside lots on the Florida Gulf coast has been stopped in most areas to protect wetlands and water quality. (Photo by author.)

Figure 6.137 A buffer strip of natural vegetation should remain between houses and the water to provide shore stability, flood protection, water purification, and other values. (Photo by author.)

the structure. Extensive rehabilitation should not be permitted. Suitable insurance or loss control provisions will be necessary so that the owner can recover any financial loss.

Implementation No. 1. Floodplains and Hazard Areas

Residential development proposed for floodprone areas must be specially controlled and must comply with federal flood insurance criteria.

The open ocean coast is often a hazardous place to maintain habitation. The ocean shoreline is in dynamic equilibrium between two factors: (1) the erosive forces of storm winds and waves, and (2) the restorative powers of prevailing geological, oceanic, and meteorological actions. In response to the interplay of these forces, the whole system of beaches, barrier islands, and dunes shifts continuously (page 569), jeopardizing all permanent structures built in these areas (Figure 6.138). In addition, shoreline areas are most vulnerable to ocean storms and hurricanes, and costs in loss of life and property during storms and hurricanes have been high for many developed and occupied beachfronts (page 562).

Attempts to stabilize and safeguard inhabited beaches with structures have required enormous private and public investments and have not often been rewarded with success. The structures interefere with the natural shore-rebuilding process and may even accelerate shore erosion (page 320).

They should therefore be considered only when necessary, and designed with great care (page 322).

Estuarine areas do not receive the wave pounding that ocean beaches do, but they often suffer persistent erosion, particularly shores characterized by earth banks. The preferred means of handling the problem is a construction setback; protective structures are a second choice. A setback on estuarine shores has the advantage of allowing the area between the bank and the building to be left as a naturally vegetated buffer for the cleansing of runoff waters (page 359) and for shore stabilization and scenic purposes (Figure 6.139). When riprap or bulkheads are required (page 322), they should be built at or above the mean annual flood line, behind the line of vegetation (page 343).

The most recent legislation under the National Flood Program—the U.S. Flood Disaster Protection Act (December 1973; Appendix, page 790)—will strongly influence the course of coastal development by enforcing standards for home and commercial structures in flood-threatened areas through the inducement of subsidized flood insurance, which requires all participating communities to enforce land-use and construction standards. Although this program may appear to be merely an incentive one, it is also powerfully compelling (page 173).

Federal flood insurance restraints may completely change the nature of coastal development in some areas. For example, it will no longer be reasonable to elevate lots out of mangrove swamps by dredging and filling operations when storm tide flooding reaches 10 or 15 feet above mean sea level because residences *must* have their first habitable floor levels built above the 100-year flood height (page 176).

Review of residential development proposals in coastal high-hazard areas should be detailed, as these areas are subject to high water velocity during severe storms (about 3 mph or more) (Figure 6.140). The Flood Disaster Protection Act prohibits any structure planned for these areas to be elevated on fill: "the use of fill for structural support

Figure 6.138   Structures built directly on the beachfront with no protection will be virtually destroyed by a large hurricane; bulkheads only add to the danger by eroding the beach. (Photo by author.)

Figure 6.139   Use of a grassy slope is better ecological practice than construction of a bulkhead to protect the shore. (Photo by author.)

is prohibited within any designated high hazard area." When feasible, *all* construction should be set back of the coastal high-hazard area, leaving a safety buffer of natural vegetation (see Figure 6.40).

Another major provision of the Act for coastal areas is a required building setback for special flood-related *erosion hazard areas* "to create a safety buffer consisting of a natural vegetative contour strip." The Department of Housing and Urban Development recommends that the buffer be used for agriculture, recreation, a natural area, open space, and related activities (page 176). Other provisions require administrative review of development proposals to ensure that the homes are properly built and

anchored, that utility lines are installed to minimize flood damage, and so forth.

Implementation No. 2.   Waterfront Residential Development

Special constraints should be imposed on waterfront development to preserve shoreline configuration, protect vital areas, and avoid water pollution.

Special waterfront development problems involve such items as marinas, piers, seawalls, direct groundwater and surface-water pollution of coastal waters (e.g., leaching of septic tanks), and canal perforation of the shoreline. A special review process should be established for waterfront developments to incorporate consideration of these special problems, including those discussed below.

Beach Protection

Any residential plan that requires beach stabilization measures should be given the closest scrutiny (page 318). All housing should be set back from hazardous, erodible ocean beaches. Further protection should be provided by dune and berm management employing sand fences, dune grass planting, and so forth (page 215). Bulkheads, jetties, groins, and other structural protection techniques should be avoided (page 322). Beach protection programs necessary for existing waterfront development should be incorporated in a comprehensive, coordinated plan and not left up to individual waterfront residents (page 320). The review process for

waterfront residential development must include consideration of its unique problems, in addition to nearly every general environmental aspect of coastal zone management.

Dredging

Excavation along and adjacent to shorelines has a high potential for adverse effects on coastal ecosystems.[12] Channels, canals, and ditches—for boat traffic, inland or wetland drainage, and shoreland construction—alter natural water flow patterns, preempt vital areas, and pollute coastal waters[13] (page 422) (Figure 6.141).

Federal and many state programs now protect wetlands from on-site dredge and fill (page 238). However, uncontrolled dredging activity in adjacent open-water areas for fill or navigational purposes degrades submerged vital areas such as grass beds and oyster reefs,

Figure 6.140   The extreme in hazardous development—the next severe hurricane will remove these houses. The row of groins along the beach represents a futile effort to hold the barrier island beach (Captiva Island, Florida). (Photo by author.)

Figure 6.141   Alteration of the shoreline by dredging should be discouraged. (Photo by author.)

and special precautions must be taken to prevent the loss of these submerged vital areas. Turbidity, sedimentation, oxygen reduction, and other disturbances due to dredging (page 422) can be controlled by local government action if included in the development review process. Every permit application should first be checked for alternative solutions that eliminate the need for dredging or filling and that minimize environmental degradation. Dredging creates complex management problems, the solutions to which lie in correct choices of location, design, and performance controls. Any dredging and spoil disposal in navigable waters ultimately requires a permit from the U.S. Army Corps of Engineers and usually from the state first (page 183).

Boat Facilities

Marinas, docks, piers, and other recreational and water access facilities along the shoreline pose threats to vital habitat areas, beach stability, water circulation, and water quality (pages 404 and 448). Therefore control of these facilities should be adequately provided for in the review of plans for waterfront residential development. Many states encourage centralization of marinas (public, commercial, or cooperative) to avoid numerous individual docks and piers (page 451).

Well-flushed water areas with steep shores provide the most ecologically favorable marina sites (page 407). All waterfront facilities that extend into water areas should be built on elevated pilings rather than solid fill (page 449). Excavation of canals and boat basins into shoreland areas (including floodplains) is to be avoided for a variety of reasons (page 451). Ancillary marina facilities, such as parking and boat storage areas, housing, and repair yards—facilities that are not absolutely water side dependent—are to be situated above the wetlands, as far as possible out of the coastal floodplain (Appendix, page 412).

The wide variety of navigational dredging projects makes it difficult to suggest specific constraints for this activity, but a few general rules can be applied and enforced in the permit review process (page 422):

1. Dispose of dredge spoil in upland areas or deep ocean sites rather than wetlands or estuaries.
2. Design boat channels for the minimum dimensions required (page 425).
3. Locate necessary channels a sufficient distance from shorelines to avoid inducing shore erosion (page 425).

Setbacks

Regardless of the type of development, a buffer strip of unaltered land should be required between the water's edge and a stipulated setback line (page 239). A setback distance of 150 feet in common use for the protection of streams and other water areas should be sufficient (page 503). The purpose of a buffer zone is to intercept water runoff and to provide for purification of the water by soil infiltration and vegetative "scrubbing" before it enters any water areas (page 535). A wide buffer is particularly important in areas where the ground surface slopes steeply from land to water and the transition zone does not include a wide margin of vegetation (page 535).

Roadways

The nearer roadways are to water, the greater is their potential for adverse impacts. Location is the most critical aspect of roadway planning (page 486). Roadways should be located so that they conform to existing topography. They should not be constructed in vital habitat areas. Roadways crossing wetlands and other water areas, including all surfaces intended for vehicular passage, should be elevated on open pile supports installed over existing grades (page 493).

Plans should avoid the location of bridges and causeways across wetlands, tidelands, and water basins. Roadways should not impinge on floodprone areas except under strict environmental constraints. Roadway design should not require landfill, nor should it impede the natural water flow (page 493).

Implementation No. 3. Canal and Fill Projects

Excavation and fill to create canalside waterfront homesites should be prohibited.

Neither excavation nor filling of wetlands is an acceptable activity (page 81). Nor is canal dredging to drain lowlands to be encouraged (page 98). These constraints together virtually eliminate further canal and fill projects along bay shores to create buildable land for homesites (Figure 6.142). The following paraphrase from an EPA report summarizes the situation.[3]

Two methods of canal development are prevalent throughout the southeastern U.S. One method, utilized extensively in the Carolinas and the northern Gulf coastal area, is the excavation of creeks or the creation of a totally new watercourse. Branching from such channels may be a "perimeter" canal along the marsh upland or a series of extensive canals through the uplands. This method of development often results in adverse ecological consequences affecting both wetlands and water quality. The second method of development, employed extensively in the Florida peninsula and Keys, is the excavation of canals within wetlands. The spoil is used to cover adjoining wetlands and raise elevation for the purpose of residential development. Environmental alteration and destruction resulting from this type of development are absolute and represent a twofold threat to the survival of existing coastal ecosystems.

Canal systems excavated in lowlands are incongruent with the function of the natural system. The purpose is to excavate channels to accelerate dewatering of wetlands, providing fill and waterfront property for residential development. The depth of the channels is primarily governed by fill requirements and not navigational needs. In light of the natural conditions, the function of the canal systems is not analogous to [that of] tidal creeks, rivers, and marshes. For instance, the deep canals accelerate runoff, lower freshwater aquifers, disrupt nutrient inputs to the vegetative food chain, deny the hydraulic buffering effect of the shallow flats, and probably provide sinks for nutrients and dense saline waters [Figure 6.143].

Canalside housing projects affect the ecosystem adversely in three major ways: (1) water quality, (2) habitat, and (3) ecosystem productivity. These three basic factors are further affected by replacement of

Figure 6.142 Massive excavation of mangrove forest and replacement with artificial canals and filled land have caused extreme damage to estuarine resources (Marco Island, Collier County, Florida). (SOURCE: Deltona Corporation, Miami, Florida.)

Figure 6.143 Creation of homesites by dredging artificial canals from wetland shores is ecologically destructive (Louisiana). (Photo by author.)

Figure 6.144   Canalside lots on long, artificial dead-end canals dug out of the mangrove forest at Marco Island, Collier County, Florida, have caused harmful loss of wetlands and serious water quality degradation. (Photo from Marco Island Development Corporation.)

the natural system by bulkheaded dead-end canals (Figure 6.144).

Water Quality

Sediment and other settleable substances resulting directly from dredging and associated activities for canalside developments form objectionable deposits (Figure 6.145; page 91)[14] that have an adverse effect on valuable marine bottoms such as grass beds and communities of marine organisms (Figure 6.146). Of particular concern are the proposed artificial waterways, whose depths in most instances greatly exceed natural depths. Labyrinthine dead-end channels serve as traps for silt and organic ooze, accumulating deep beds of anaerobic materials (page 92). These cause persistent lowering of oxygen to unacceptable levels. During storms such sediments partially flush out into estuarine waters, causing stress through the reduction of dissolved oxygen levels.

Deleterious and/or toxic substances discharged from storm sewers or overtopping seawalls and discharges from other sources often contain excessive loads of dissolved nutrients, pesticides, fungicides, herbicides,

Figure 6.145 Dredge-and-fill activities to create canalside homesites often cause widespread sediment pollution. (Conservation Foundation photo by M. Fahay.)

heavy metals, and mineral and organic residues. Nutrients from lawn fertilizers are a recognized threat to bays and estuaries when housing areas adjoin such waters. The nutrients stimulate the growth of algae to the extent that the original plant–animal balance is affected. Many of the pesticides, fungicides, herbicides, and heavy metals are accumulative in marine plants or animals and therefore, even at low levels, pose a

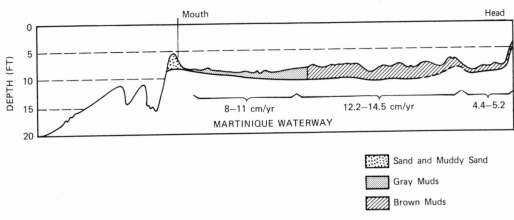

Figure 6.146 Sediment accumulates rapidly in canals dug for canalside housing projects, causing unacceptable water quality. (SOURCE: Reference 16.)

hazard to plant and animal life and to human health (page 186).

Oxygen levels are depressed to low values in artificial canals where fine sediments accumulate and water becomes stagnant (e.g., 0.5 pound of grass clippings per day can contaminate a 100-foot length of canal, reducing oxygen from 4.5 to 3.8 ppm).

Habitat

When habitat is reduced, existing species populations are first crowded and then dispersed by the effects of such reduction. Wetlands are vital habitat areas, particularly critical to ecosystem productivity, that require full protection, as we have pointed out repeatedly in this book. Dredge-and-fill projects for canalside homesites, by their very nature, obliterate or disable wetlands[17] as well as tidal flats, sea grass beds, and estuarine bottom habitat. The damage is high because much of this habitat serves as critical breeding and nursery areas for fish, shellfish, and water birds.

Productivity

Wetlands, tidelands, and sea grasses provide a critical link in the basic food chain energy system, assimilating, converting, storing, and transferring nutrients (page 32). Wetlands themselves typically provide about half the basic nutrients for estuarine life systems (page 33). When the productivity components are eliminated or short circuited, estuarine ecosystems are seriously degraded (page 98).

REFERENCES

1. U.S. Water Resources Council. 1971. *Regulation of Flood Hazard Areas to Reduce Flood Losses*. Vol. 1, Parts I-IV. Superintendent of Documents, U.S. Government Printing Office, Washington, D.C.

2. John Clark. 1974. *Rookery Bay: Ecological Constraints on Coastal Development*. Rookery Bay Land Use Studies, Final Report. The Conservation Foundation, Washington, D.C.

3. D. B. Hicks, B. J. Carroll, and T. R. Cavinder. 1975. *Finger-Fill Canal Studies, Florida and North Carolina*. U.S. Environmental Protection Agency, Surveillance and Analysis Division, Athens, Georgia (preliminary draft).

4. Albert R. Veri, A. R. Marshall, S. U. Wilson, J. H. Hartwell, P. Rosendahl, and T. Mumford. 1973. *The Resource Buffer Plan: A Conceptual Land Use Study*. Rookery Bay Land Use Studies, Study No. 2. The Conservation Foundation, Washington, D.C.

5. Black, Crow, and Eidsness, Inc. 1974. *Master Plan for Water Management District No. 6, Collier County, Florida*. Report to the Collier County Water Management District No. 6, Gainesville, Florida.

6. Joachim Tourbier. 1973. *Water Resources as a Basis for Comprehensive Planning and Development of the Christina River Basin*. Prepared for the U.S. Department of the Interior. Water Resources Center, University of Delaware, Newark, Delaware (final report).

7. Edward T. LaRoe. 1974. *Environmental Considerations for Water Management District 6 of Collier County*. Rookery Bay Land Use Studies, Study No. 8. The Conservation Foundation, Washington, D.C.

8. Coastal Zone Management Act of 1972. 92nd Congress, S. 3507, Public Law 92-583.

9. Flood Disaster Protection Act of 1973. 93rd Congress, H.R. 8449, Public Law 92-234.

10. William Barada and William M. Partington, Jr. 1972. *Report of Investigation of the Environmental Effects of Private Waterfront Canals*. Environmental Information Center, Florida Conservation Foundation, Winter Park, Florida (unpublished report).

11. Francis J. Burgweger, Jr. 1975. "The California Coastal Zone Conservation Act of 1972: A sampling of developers' problems." *Environmental Comment*, No. 20, April. Urban Land Institute, Washington, D.C.

12. C. Chapman. 1968. "Channelization and spoiling in Gulf coast and South Atlantic estuaries." In *Proceedings of the Marsh and Estuarine Management Symposium*, Louisiana State University, Baton Rouge, Louisiana. July 19-20, 1967.

13. John Clark. *The Environmental Impact of the Proposed Seabrook Nuclear Power Plant*. Testimony before the New Hampshire Bulk Power Supply Site Evaluation Committee, February 8, 1973.

14. Virginia K. Tippie. 1975. *Sedimentary Processes in Coastal Canals of Southwest Florida.* Unpublished master's thesis, University of Rhode Island, Kingston, Rhode Island.

15. John L. Taylor and Carl H. Saloman. 1968. "Some effects of hydraulic dredging and coastal development in Boca Ciega Bay, Florida." *Fisheries Bulletin*, Vol. 67, No. 2, pp. 233–241. U.S. Fish and Wildlife Service, Department of the Interior, Washington, D.C.

16. H. R. Wanless. 1974. *Sediments in Natural and Artificial Waterways, Marco Island Area, Florida.* University of Miami Scientific Report No. 74032, Miami, Florida.

17. Franklin C. Daiber et al. 1974. *Ecological Effects upon Estuaries Resulting from Lagoon Construction, Dredging, Filling and Bulkheading.* Report to the Division of Fish and Wildlife, Department of Natural Resources and Environmental Control, State of Delaware; Project F-25-R, College of Marine Studies and Department of Biological Sciences, University of Delaware, Newark, Delaware.

19. ROADWAYS AND BRIDGES

The protection of water resources and coastal ecosystems must be given high priority in locating and designing road systems. In the absence of environmental safeguards, coastal area roadways not only alter the lands in the road right-of-way and induce new forms of land use along the road corridor, but also, through pollution and interruption of water flows, may reduce the quality of coastal ecosystems.

There is a wide freedom of choice for road system routing outside of the central urban area. Roadways and bridges can be controlled by applying the highest standards of protection of water resources and natural systems. Too often planners have tried to overcome natural obstacles rather than seeking imaginative solutions by working with the natural systems. Cost considerations have often been given higher priority than environmental protection. For example, in crossing wetlands areas, roadway designers often have been persuaded to economize and choose solid-fill causeways in preference to ecologically protective elevated structures (Figure 6.147).

Presently the cost efficiency of the solid-fill approach appears to be declining, partly because of the increased values placed on the ecologic functions of wetlands and partly because of the increased costs of fill. Together these factors have significantly

Figure 6.147 Seventeen miles of U.S. Interstate Highway 10 is elevated over the Atchafalaya Basin in Louisiana to protect wetlands and allow for passage of floodwaters. (Photo by author.)

changed the benefit–cost balance between solid-fill and elevated roadways. In addition, stringent new federal and state policies on spoil disposal (e.g., under Section 404 of the 1972 Federal Clean Water Act) have further restricted the use of solid fill because of a growing scarcity of suitable sites for the disposal of spoil (marsh-muck) removed before fill can be placed.

Although the direct effects of roadway systems on coastal waters and shorelands are of great concern, often the indirect effects of induced development that typically follow new route construction have a greater impact on coastal ecosystems. Even if the highway itself is designed for minimum impact, the urbanization that this system generates may be the factor that ultimately degrades a marsh or a bay. A major road system generates commercial, industrial, and residential areas. Any of these may induce potentially detrimental activities and effects such as filling or draining of wetlands, bulkheading, stormwater runoff, and sewage pollution.[1]

The necessity of predicting these induced effects is well established in modern planning methodology. The means by which to assess their accumulated impacts can be found throughout this book. In a comprehensive assessment it is necessary to analyze the impacts on water resources and ecosystems from the following five general categories of roadway programs: the location of the system, the design of the system, the construction and maintenance of the system, the use of the system, and the impact of development induced by the system.

The results of this ecological analysis should be included in a land-use study that evaluates all possible transportation corridors in a particular coastal area. In many cases there will be little real justification for road and bridge access to a location under consideration,[2] and alternative modes of travel will give a more acceptable environmental, social, and economic balance.

Commercial development in coastal regions has created a high demand for new and improved roadways in these areas. Many of these highways have caused significant deterioration in the environmental quality of coastal vital habitat areas, particularly wetlands and sand dunes. Unfortunately, the severity of environmental impacts resulting from locating highways in vital areas has gone largely unrecognized and unheeded in the past and is only now beginning to be acknowledged. Consequently, insufficient attempts have been made to divert roadways away from vital areas such as wetlands. In fact, highway planners have often been *attracted* to wetland areas because of their low purchase prices and because of the scarcity of higher, drier land.

Wetlands nevertheless present major ecological and economic constraints on roadways and urbanized development.[1] The surface and subsurface hydrology of wetland areas presents engineering difficulties to coastal road system development that can be resolved only by costly construction methods. Moreover, the disruption of the natural soil and foundation condition of the wetland zone that results from such construction can cause severe adverse effects on the coastal ecosystem. For example, the construction of an interstate highway in the Louisiana coastal zone has had a wide variety of adverse environmental impacts (Table 6.23).

When the method of construction is to dig out (or "muck" out) existing deep layers of organic muck and replace it with a different type of base, there may be an alteration of the subsurface drainage pattern, for example, if excavation cuts through the soil beneath a surface aquifer and allows contamination of the clean water by intrusion from a lower, salt-intruded or otherwise polluted body.

A roadway often forms a virtual dam, an effective barrier to sheet water flow of low-lying wetland areas in the shorelands, and concentrates the flow into a few channels leading to culverts beneath the road. This can lead to flooding on the "high" side and drying out on the "low" side. The solution

Table 6.23   Stress levels imposed by various roadway project activities: L = low, M = medium, H = high, T = temporary (SOURCE: Modified from Reference 12)

Source of Disturbance	Habitat Loss	Drainage Pattern Alteration	Runoff Storage Flow Destabilization	Ground Water Alteration	Segmentation or Habitats	Disrupting Faunal Movements
Highway on embankment	H	H	H	H	H	H
Highway on structure	M	L	-	-	M	M
Construction canal (open with spoil banks)	H	H	H	H	H	H
Construction canal (backfilled)	M	L	M	H	M	T
Interchanges on embankments	H	H	H	H	H	H
Interchanges on structure	M	L	-	-	M	M

is an elevated causeway that allows water to flow beneath it, or an extensive, well-planned system of collection above and redisbursement of water below. In areas where the roadbed crossing a water area is raised on piles, drainage may be blocked if continuous lateral spoil banks are left after construction.

Alignment is the most critical aspect of roadway planning. Roadways should not be located in vital habitat areas. Nor should they impinge on floodprone areas except under strict environmental constraints. The nearer a roadway is to water, the greater are its pollution potential and habitat alteration impact.

GUIDELINE.   Roadway Location

Locate road systems to avoid impingement on vital habitat areas or interference with surface-water or ground water flow.

A major adverse environmental effect of highway location in water areas of the coastal zone has been the replacement of extensive marsh and mangrove wetland areas

with the roadbed or with dredge spoil mucked out for the roadbed. A second major effect is the disruption of normal circulation patterns, both tidal and land drainage. Roadways built parallel to the coastline and through coastal zone water areas have often acted as dams to fresh water draining down toward the sea or as blockages to tidal flows within estuaries (Figure 6.148). A third major impact is the creation of mud waves undulating out from and parallel to the highway fill. These waves of mud are created by the pressure of the roadbed on organic soils. Marshes over 100 yards (9.14 meters) away from roads often have been buckled and disrupted by mud waves.[3] These effects have had pronounced negative environmental impacts on the productivity of affected estuaries.

All roadways in coastal areas should be located so that they conform to existing topography and require a minimum of alteration of soils and vegetation. Groundwater is most important for slowing water drainage, holding soil, and generally maintaining unpolluted land runoff and must be protected.

Major highways with unrestricted access and an extensive induced development corridor can be particularly damaging to coastal areas. A major environmental problem involves the effects of roads that are partly devised to "open up new territory" for development. In such cases, unless a complete projection of land-use effects is available so that an imaginative approach to environmental design can be devised, significant environmental deterioration will ensue (Figure 6.149). To hinder ecologically damaging development, zoning regulations are helpful, where appropriate, to control the kind and extent of development that often ensues when roads "open up" new areas. Another alternative means of control is to permanently restrict access to and from roads when they pass through ecologically sensitive and vital areas.[1]

In locating a roadway network it is necessary to consider the land and its resources as a total natural system. Land-use planning then aims at identifying and setting priorities for various uses and amenities and concurrently assessing environmental and cultural effects. Factors demanding consideration include community, institutional, and residential values; the value of land for recreation; surface-water and groundwater values; and wildlife and fisheries resource values. With these values considered, roadway location can then be best determined to simultaneously serve the purposes of preservation of natural systems and need for urban expansion.[1]

Figure 6.148   Solid-fill causeways across estuaries block tidal circulation essential to proper ecosystem function. The small bridged section (upper right) does not permit adequate water passage (near Cape Fear, North Carolina). (Conservation Foundation photo by M. Fahay.)

Figure 6.149 Community land-use planning must be coordinated with bridge and roadway planning to avoid environmentally destructive development of barrier islands induced by new major access routes (Sanibel Island, Florida). (Photo by author.)

Implementation No. 1. Vital Area Avoidance in Roadway Location

Roadway systems should be located so as to avoid vital habitat areas.

Roadways, including viaducts, bridges, and causeways, have a potential for the preemption and disturbance of vital habitat areas. Coastal zone environmental planning programs require that all vital habitat areas (e.g., wetlands and dunes) within each subwatershed of a planning district be identified and designated for special protection. This information will be available to highway planners and should be consulted before locational choices are made (Figure 6.150).

By locating major roadways upland of the lower coastal floodplain, the need for bridges and causeways across wetlands and water basins is minimized and the environmental damage potential reduced (Figure 6.151).

It is U.S. Department of Transportation policy to "avoid, to the fullest extent practicable, drainage, filling, or interference with wetlands or the water sources supplying them."[4]

South Carolina state guidelines recommend that major highways be located inland from wetland areas. They further state that "existing shoreline roads should not be expanded, but reserved for slow-moving recreational traffic."[5]

One proposed plan for expansion of the Texas coastal highway system is to locate a new major highway parallel to the coastline, ranging from 25 to 75 miles (40 to 120 kilometers) inland; this would avoid the need to cross bays, marshlands, and dunes. Access to beach areas would be provided by spurs or feeder roads perpendicular to the coast, which would connect the inland freeway with the coastline roadway network.[6]

Dunes serve as a useful example of a vital area that needs protection in roadway planning. Alignments in or along the edges of

Figure 6.150 To protect wetlands a new, wider crossing was shifted to the higher land to the right of the old crossing (Seattle, Washington). (Photo by author.)

Figure 6.151 Water circulation is blocked by solid-fill roadbeds across the path of wetlands water flow (Knott's Island, North Carolina). (Conservation Foundation photo by M. Fahay.)

Figure 6.152   Roadways that crowd dunelines lead to deterioration of both dunes and roadways. (Photo by author.)

shifting dunes and beach ridges may result in serious impacts. In many areas rising sea levels are causing gradual landward recession of the beachfront and dunes (page 339). Roadways built directly behind the dune arrest this free movement and lead to deterioration of both dunes and roadway (Figure 6.152). As the dune pushes landward, it begins to cover the pavement but the accumulated sand is removed by roadway maintenance crews. As the dune continues to move, it must narrow and diminish in volume by the amount of sand it loses. Eventually storms cut through the depleted dune, damage the road, and endanger lives by flooding storm evacuation routes.

Bulkheads and other emergency measures may serve to hold receding beachfronts as stopgap solutions only; eventually the roadway has to be moved inland. A better choice is to align the roadway inland in the first place after careful calculation of the recession rate of the beach. Roadways should be located sufficiently landward of the existing dune line to permit natural sand movement for the expected life of the roadway. A sufficient setback is also required to prevent encroachment onto the dunes by development attracted to the area by the newly created highway access; dune deterioration is not only a direct result of the roadway, but is due also to induced development adjacent to roadway corridors. Additional problems are caused by increased use of off-road vehicles, such as dune buggies.

No standard setback footage to ensure adequate protection of the dunes can be recommended. The designation of a setback should depend on local conditions and should be based on a life-of-economic-use projection; 50 years is appropriate for many structures (page 338). For example, by using this estimate the inner location of the dune line 50 years in the future is designated as the seaward limit for the construction of any permanent structures, including roadways (page 337).

In recession areas only temporary, lightly surfaced roads should be permitted where active dune movement is present or expected. In no case should a frontal dune be altered or crossed.

Barrier islands are particularly vulnerable to the landward stresses of wind and water forces, and shift constantly in response to them. Therefore bridges essential for connecting barrier islands to each other and to the mainland should be positioned perpendicularly to the main coastline, to accommodate the islands' inevitable changes of position (Figure 6.153).

Implementation No. 2. Floodplain Roadway Alignment

Grade-level roadways across the lower floodplain should be located parallel to the path of water flow.

The ecological precept that water flows must not be obstructed is a governing factor in the location and design of road systems in coastal areas. The general flow of water that drains the land is normally perpendicular to the coastline, and structures built in floodprone areas parallel to the coast tend to block this flow. The natural flow to the coast is interrupted with consequent severe adverse impacts, for example, altered estuarine salinity balance. Moreover, water impounded landward of the road may flood

Figure 6.153   Bridge connections over inlets should be designed with respect to the manner in which the inlets shift with rising sea level and changes in ocean currents (Captiva–Sanibel Bridge, Florida). (Photo by author.)

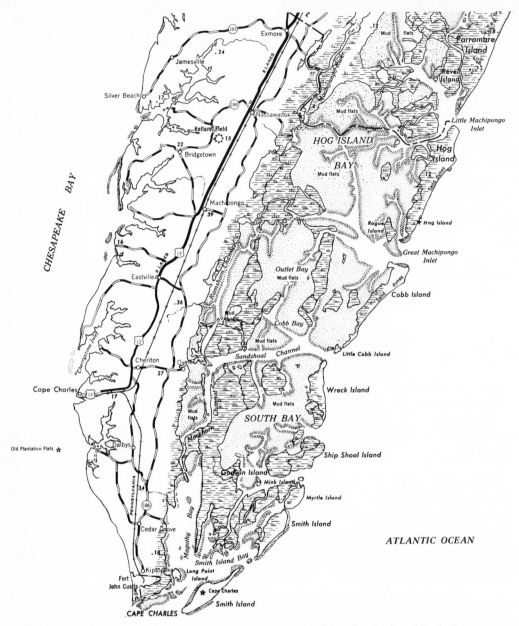

Figure 6.154 Major roadways should be located away from low-lying shorelands, while feeder routes to the shore should lie parallel to water flows (Northhampton County, Virginia). (SOURCE: U.S. Geological Survey "quad" map.)

large areas of vegetation. Only a slight shift in water elevation is required to greatly disrupt the upstream ecosystem.

Spurs and feeder roads that provide access to the coast from major highways

should generally be aligned perpendicularly to the coastline to minimize interference with natural water circulation patterns (Figure 6.154). Unless placed on elevated pilings, roadways in the lower floodplain should be located parallel to land drainage flow and tidewater movement (Figure 6.155). Only essential service roads should be allowed to run parallel to the coast, and these should be provided with sufficient water passes and culverts to provide as nearly natural a pattern of runoff and tidal flow as possible. Bridges and pile-supported causeways can be incorporated into the design plan to reduce interference with tidal creeks, overland flow, and natural transport of sand along the shore (page 495).

All secondary roadways in floodprone areas should follow the same principle— location parallel to the water flow. To further minimize ecologic disturbance, the location of the roadway network should be thoughtfully worked out in the planning stage to ensure efficient use of the roads and to avoid unnecessary surfacing.

Figure 6.155   Feeder routes to the shoreline (upper left) should be parallel to water flow patterns through floodplains or wetlands. (Conservation Foundation photo.)

GUIDELINE.   Roadway Design

Elevate roadways over water areas and otherwise design them to avoid alteration of vital habitat areas and to minimize disruption of water flows in water areas and floodplains.

The adverse ecologic impacts of solid-fill causeways are exemplified by degraded marshes and choked-off bays and tidal tributaries in coastal areas around the country.

The construction of a number of highways through marsh areas has effectively separated the upper reach of a tributary stream of wetland from the lower reach, completely altering the circulation patterns of the entire marsh system. The blockage has prevented the normal circulation of waters and exchange of nutrients and organisms and lowered the productivity of the coastal system.[7] The effects of such high "dams" could be minimized if pilings and piers had been used instead of solid-fill causeways to allow water circulation to continue. However, the extensive use of construction channels for barge access to construction sites has further

changed water flow patterns, even when the completed highway is elevated.

Proposed federal floodplain regulations prohibit in any floodway "fill, encroachments, and new construction and substantial improvements of existing structures, which would result in any increase in flood heights within the community during the recurrence of the 100-year flood discharge."[8]

To meet these regulations, coastal causeways and bridges must be elevated and otherwise designed to avoid interference with flood water flows to the 100-year flood level (Figure 6.156).

Implementation No. 1.   Roadway Elevation

Causeway design should elevate the roadway on pier or piling supports and avoid the need for solid fill.

Even when culverts are incorporated into roadway design, solid-fill causeways have the potential for a number of adverse environ-

Figure 6.156 Railroad crossings should be elevated when they pass over marshes and floodplains to prevent interference with marsh function and water passage. (Photo by author.)

mental effects. Any type of solid-fill causeway can disrupt the natural tidal flow in an estuary sufficiently to upset the delicate salinity balance essential for the survival of many estuarine organisms. Besides obstructing tidal flushing, causeways also act as water barriers during severe storms and hurricanes. For example, a water pileup in the late 1960s killed all of the ground-nesting birds in the Pelican Island National Wildlife Refuge.[3] Buildup of sediments and

pollutants behind causeways has also caused the closure of shellfish areas in Indian River, Florida. Also, solid-fill construction usually requires extensive dredging for fill and the excavation of construction access canals, which result in additional loss of wetlands and tidelands, soil discharge into the estuary, disruption of water flows, mud waves, and so forth.

When it is imperative to plan a causeway through a wetland, tideland, or open-water

Figure 6.157 Elevated roadbeds allow circulation of estuarine waters, as well as sunlight penetration to the vegetation below. (Conservation Foundation photo by M. Fahay.)

area, the roadbed is to be elevated by the use of pile supports rather than fill (Figure 6.157). This is in agreement with South Carolina guidelines, which recommend "where coastal wetlands cannot be avoided [in roadway routing], bridging should be used to the maximum extent possible to create road beds, rather than filling and embankment."[5]

Solid-fill causeway construction and barge-access canal excavation often create a spoil disposal problem, particularly when excess dredging occurs. Vital habitat areas are not suitable disposal sites, and acceptable sites that are easily accessible are becoming scarce. The remaining alternatives are to transport spoil either well inland or to the ocean (page 431). To minimize disposal problems, roadway designers should anticipate and eliminate whenever possible any requirement for dredging.

The design goal set here is to avoid placing fill in water and wetland areas. This is easily met on crossings over open water, where bridges are normally a routine requirement (Figure 6.158). It is also easily met when the cost of "mucking out" and replacing the soft sediments with firm fill is greater than the cost of constructing an elevated structure. The costs of elevated structures, which minimize the use of fill, have been comparable with those of solid-fill causeways when there is about 10 to 12 feet (3 to 3.7 meters) of "muck" and usually have been lower when deeper trenches are required.[9] According to a recent Louisiana study, elevated structures may become a cost-effective alternative to solid-fill causeways in only 3 feet (0.9 meter) of muck.[10] Also, the time period to reach the 95 percent compaction point, required before road pavement can be laid, increases exponentially with any depth increase past 10 feet.[9]

When abutments or fill areas must impinge on water areas, it is necessary to reduce the encroachment to the minimum (Figure 6.159). To meet federal flood protection regulations, the cross-sectional area of a waterway should in no case be reduced to less than that which can adequately pass the 100-year maximum flood waters, that is, the bridge should not raise the floodwaters more than 1 foot above the natural flood level. The basic circulation pattern of the wetlands or tidal marshes should be preserved by appropriate use of

Figure 6.158 Bridge designs should minimize obstruction of water flow (Bahia Honda Bridge, Florida, Keys). (Photo by author.)

Figure 6.159   Bridge abutments that encroach on watercourses reduce water flow and degrade coastal eco-systems (Merrimac estuary, Massachusetts). (Photo by author.)

Figure 6.160   Roadway culverts should be designed to permit water passage at the natural rate (Sanibel Island, Florida). (Photo by author.)

Figure 6.161   Bridges should be designed for minimal structural interference with water flow (Louisiana). (Photo by author.)

culverts under filled causeways where the roadway routing crosses upland tributaries (Figure 6.160).

When building a causeway over wetlands, construction activity should take place on the causeway structure and off the wetlands to the maximum extent possible; that is, heavy equipment needed to place the roadway pilings—cranes, dredges—should be operated from the roadbed. This topside construction approach is recommended to avoid the need for barge canals.

Structures over the water should be designed to maintain the natural water flow and circulation regime.[6] As far as possible, bridge design should minimize the number and size of support members, such as piers and pilings, and streamline their form (Figure 6.161). The same holds true for redesigning an existing bridge crossing.

Poorly designed and constructed bridges act as partial barriers to natural water flow. For example, the piers supporting the Great South Bay Bridge on Long Island, New York, slow water flow and deflect it toward the open center span (Figure 6.162). A federal study concluded that restricted circulation west of the bay bridge was a contributing factor to the degradation of water quality in the area.[11] In many urbanized bays, impairment of water circulation by bridges results in a buildup of pollutants to adverse levels, as well as shoaling problems.

Bridges should be designed so as not to impair tidal flow in respect to volume, velocity, or direction. Abutments should be built back from the water edge, and clear spans used rather than piers. Most simply, the cross-sectional area of a watercourse should not be reduced by abutments, support piers, pilings, and so forth. It may be necessary at times to enlarge the watercourse before

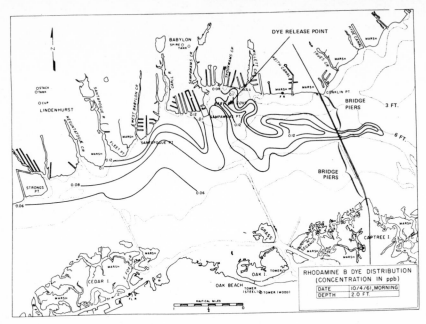

Figure 6.162   Dye releases indicate that water passage is virtually confined to the small open section of the causeway (Great South Bay, New York). (SOURCE: Reference 11.)

construction in order to finish with the original cross-sectional area.

GUIDELINE.   Roadway Construction

Utilize construction and maintenance methods that do not alter wetlands, intertidal marshes, or other vital areas and that do not adversely affect water quality or water flow.

Construction of roadway systems in coastal shorelands and over water areas is accompanied by a variety of potential environmental problems.

The disturbances from highway construction in wetlands, intertidal marshes, and other ecologically vital areas hold a great potential for environmental disruption even if roadways are properly designed. During construction builders sometimes deposit excess fill and spoil on marsh areas in order either to dispose of such materials or to create a storage area for heavy equipment and supplies.[2] Similarly, builders sometimes wish to construct access roads through water areas. Such practices must be avoided, however, as they preempt marsh habitats, disrupt water flow, and degrade water quality.

Massive losses of vital water areas due to spoil disposal have accompanied many highway projects. For example, it has been calculated that each 100-foot section of Interstate 95 on the Georgia coast required 2.4 acres of spoil area when the disposal site was diked and 0.84 acre when it was not[12] (Table 6.24). Moreover, extensive pollution and sedimentation have occurred from the water draining from undiked spoil areas.

When barge access is cut alongside a bridge construction project across a waterway, a trench 12 feet (3.7 meters) or deeper is created between the banks of the waterway (Figure 6.163). Since this channel is usually perpendicular to water flow, it becomes a repository for silts, sediments, and organic pollutants. The resultant conditions produce many of the adverse effects of stagnant holes (page 422) and dead-end canals (page 479).

Table 6.24   Marsh areas required for disposal of unsuitable materials by different techniques in Georgia (SOURCE: Reference 12)

```
Undiked Disposal Area^1/
     Length of highway right-of-way                        11,400 ft.
     Spoil volume excavated                               614,000 cu. yd.
     Waste disposal area                                       71 ac.
          Spoil volume per 100 feet highway                 5380 cu. yd.
     Actual spoil area per 100 feet highway                  0.62 ac.
     Adjusted spoil area per 100 feet highway^4/             0.84 ac.


Diked Disposal Area^2/
     Length of highway right-of-way                         3800 ft.
     Spoil volume excavated                               287,900 cu. yd.
     Waste disposal area                                       89 ac.
          Spoil volume per 100 feet highway                 7580 cu. yd.
     Actual spoil area per 100 feet highway                   2.5 ac.
     Adjusted spoil area per 100 feet highway                 2.4 ac.


Side Cast Spoil Disposal^3/
     Length of highway right-of-way                         5640 ft.
     Spoil volume excavated                               519,000 cu. yd.
     Waste disposal area (64 acres additional right-of-way,
                         40 acres diked disposal)            104 ac.
          Spoil volume per 100 feet highway                 9200 cu. yd.
     Actual spoil area per 100 feet highway                   1.8 ac.
     Adjusted spoil area per 100 feet highway  (.8 acres forms
                         part of highway slope;  .6 acres is
                         diked spoil area)                    1.4 ac.
```

[1] I-95 construction at Ogeechee River on Chatham-Bryan county line (completed).

[2] I-95 construction at N. Newport River.

[3] I-95 construction at Satilla River (estimate).

[4] assuming a trench width of 140 feet and an average removal depth of 14 feet, spoil removal for 100 feet of highway is 7250 cubic yards. Adjusted spoil area per 100 feet of highway equals actual spoil area per 100 feet highway x (7250 cubic yards/ actual spoil volume per 100 feet highway).

Implementation No. 1. Roadway Construction Activities Control

Construction operations should adhere to all requirements for water quality and general ecological protection of coastal waters.

In shorelands, roadway construction, operation, and maintenance activities should be controlled to prevent erosion and sedimentation, obstruction of groundwater recharge, alteration of stream flow, and increased pollution and eutrophication of coastal waters. Construction activities of concern are excavation of borrow material, cuts, and fills; land clearing, grading, and recontouring;

Figure 6.163 Barge access channels and spoil mounds preempt wetlands and interfere with their natural circulation (New Topsail Beach, North Carolina). (Conservation Foundation photo by M. Fahay.)

and stream channelization or realignment (page 240). The California Coastal Plan[13] recommends:

Road construction shall eliminate or minimize adverse impacts on sandy beaches; environmentally sensitive areas, including but not limited to coastal wetland or estuarine areas, historic or acheological sites; and other significant man-made resources. Mitigation measures shall be employed in planning, design, and construction of new or expanded roadways, including minimizing interference with natural drainage patterns and the need for cutting, filling, and grading for roadway construction. . . .

An inspection system should be established to ensure that proper environmental safeguards are used during construction, that they function properly, and that they perpetrate no unnecessary environmental disturbances. After the construction activity is completed, the area should be restored to its original state by removal of spoil banks and other construction debris that will adversely affect environmental quality.

In many coastal areas extensive filling of many spoil disposal sites and protection of others by wetland laws has made spoil disposal sites scarce. Roadway spoil will normally have to be transported inland or out into the ocean to ecologically less sensitive disposal sites. (Table 6.24 shows the acreages of marsh required for spoil disposal in several roadway projects.)

Figure 6.164 Retention basins (lower left) are often used to catch and hold roadway runoff. (Photo by author.)

Construction supply storage areas must be moved above the annual flood mark, and equipment access roads should be placed only in the actual roadway corridor.

Effects related to the day-to-day use and maintenance of roadways are usually of secondary impact but can be significant in certain situations. Continuing disturbances occur because of altered runoff from road surfaces and improperly graded or vegetated adjacent slopes; soil erosion; and the introduction of deicing salts,[14] herbicides, and the runoff of street surface contaminants into nearby watercourses (see page 728).

A most difficult long-term problem involves storm drainage runoff. Traffic generates a continual supply of pollutants, ranging from rubber particles to wasted fuel and oil to lead and chemical agents. This "road dirt" becomes concentrated in water draining from the road surface; and if this runoff goes directly into coastal water areas, these pollutants harm coastal life.[1] Runoff should be managed by natural means to the maximum extent possible with vegetated buffer strips (page 238) located along the roadsides. Drainage collection systems will be necessary to collect runoff and channel it to retention ponds, buffer areas, or other treatment facilities where "road dirt" can be filtered out (Figure 6.164).

Implementation No. 2.   Roadway Construction Scheduling

Schedule construction phases to avoid critical periods of breeding, feeding, and migration of coastal species.

Even with the most environmentally protective approach, significant temporary adverse effects can result. Therefore it will be necessary to avoid causing temporary disturbances during seasons of critical migration, breeding, feeding, and other functions of aquatic life. For example, silt may interfere with oyster breeding, and therefore excavation should not be conducted during late spring and summer, when oysters spawn. The seasonal cycles of important aquatic life are known to ecologists and fish and wildlife biologists, and their advice should be sought before any roadway or bridge construction in wetlands or estuaries is undertaken.

REFERENCES

1. Coastal Environments, Inc. 1973. *Environmental Considerations, Interstate I-410.* Report prepared for Louisiana Department of Highways, Baton Rouge, Louisiana.

2. Department of Transportation. 1974. *Draft Environmental Impact Statement for Proposed Fixed Highway Bridge across Station Creek, Mile 2.6, Beaufort County, S.C., for Access from St. Helena Island to a Planned Residential Development on St. Phillips Island.* DOT/U.S. Coast Guard, October 10.

3. Larry Shanks. U.S. Fish and Wildlife Service, Department of the Interior, Bay St. Louis, Mississippi. Personal communication.

4. U.S. Department of Transportation. 1975. *Preservation of the Nation's Wetlands.* Order 5660.1 (5-21-75), Washington, D.C.

5. Marine Resources Division. 1974. *Guidelines for Evaluating Coastal Wetland Developments.* South Carolina Wildlife and Marine Resources Department, Charlestown, South Carolina.

6. Texas Transportation Institute. 1973. *Transportation in the Texas Coastal Zone.* Division of Planning Coordination, Office of the Governor, Austin, Texas.

7. B. J. Copeland. 1974. "Impoundment systems." In H. T. Odum et al., *Coastal Ecological Systems of the United States,* Vol. III. The Conservation Foundation, Washington, D.C.

8. Department of Housing and Urban Development. 1975. "National Flood Insurance Program, proposed criteria." *Federal Register,* Vol. 40, No. 59 (March 26).

9. William Taylor. Taylor, Wiseman and Taylor, Moorestown, N.J. Personal communication.

10. R. M. Pope and J. G. Gosselink. 1973. "A tool for making management decisions in the coastal zone." *Coastal Zone Management Journal,* Vol. 1, No. 1, pp. 65–74.

11. U.S. Department of the Interior. *The National Estuarine Pollution Study.* U.S. Senate, 91st Congress, 2nd Session, Document No. 91-58. U.S. Government Printing Office. Washington, D.C.

12. J. G. Gosselink et al. n.d. *Spoil Disposal Problems for Highway Construction through Marshes.* The Institute of Ecology, University of Georgia, Athens, Georgia.

13. California Coastal Zone Conservation Commissions. 1975. *California Coastal Plan.* San Francisco, California.

14. Highway Research Board. 1973. "Environmental degradation by de-icing chemicals and effective countermeasures." Nine reports in *Highway Research Record*, No. 425, National Academy of Sciences, Washington, D.C.

20. SEPTIC TANK LOCATION

Septic tanks and related systems for underground disposal of household sewage are major potential sources of pollution when they are placed near water bodies.

In low-lying areas with naturally high water tables, liquid waste from septic systems may saturate the soil and then rise to flow over the surface of the ground and into coastal waters. This pollution potential is exacerbated in floodprone areas, where high tides and storms periodically raise the water table even higher and completely saturate the soils. These conditions weigh heavily against the use of septic tanks in floodplains and in favor of central sewage systems. However, if the necessary water and soil requirements can be met in the coastal zone, and if septic systems are properly maintained and operated within their physical capacities (Table 6.25), they should be adequate

Table 6.25 Liquid capacity of tank (gallons) (Provides for use of garbage grinders, automatic clothes washers, and other household appliances.) SOURCE: Reference 1.

Number of Bedrooms	Recommended Minimum Tank Capacity	Equivalent Capacity per Bedroom
2 or less	750	375
3	900	300
4[a]	1000	250

[a]For each additional bedroom, add 250 gallons.

for their purposes and central sewage systems will not be needed. A proper septic system injects effluent into the ground with no harmful effects and with all the benefits of simplicity and economy.

Because the primary ecological hazard of septic tank systems is water pollution, the following guideline and implementation standards are designed to prevent contaminants, particularly nitrogen wastes, from polluting the water.

GUIDELINE.   Septic Tank Constraints

Locate and maintain septic tank systems so as to avoid water pollution.

A septic system is a microcosm of a land sewage treatment system (page 513). Wastewater from one or several homes flows into a concrete septic tank, where the solids settle to the bottom to be decomposed by bacteria into organic matter. Nutrients are released during this partial solids digestion and flow into drainage areas through subsurface tiles to percolate through ground for removal. The nutrients are often taken up locally by trees and shrubs, or are adsorbed to soil particle surfaces. Periodically the resulting sludge in the bottom of the tank must be removed and disposed of.

There are three major problems relating to septic tanks in coastal areas: (1) wastes leached into coastal waters when septic tanks are located too close to the shore, (2) tidally induced high water tables that provide direct and rapid flushing of drain fields into coastal waters, and (3) inadequate drain field components or soil absorption characteristics that cause tanks to overflow, particularly during rainstorms, and to pollute coastal waters. The solution to these problems lies in proper location of septic tanks in relation to water.

How well a septic tank sewage disposal system works depends largely on such factors as soil permeability, groundwater level, stratigraphy, the distribution of soil types,

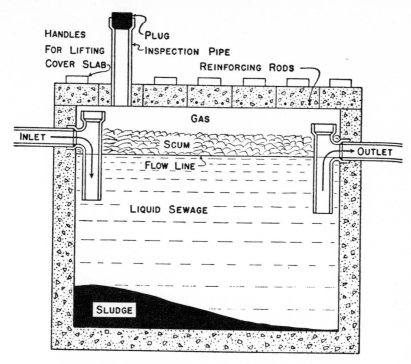

HANDLES FOR LIFTING COVER SLAB

PLUG

INSPECTION PIPE

REINFORCING RODS

GAS

INLET

SCUM

OUTLET

FLOW LINE

LIQUID SEWAGE

SLUDGE

Figure 6.165   Typical septic tank detail. (SOURCE: Reference 4.)

and slope.[2] Because shoreline soils typically have poor percolation and drainage characteristics and shallow water tables—often less than 5 feet (1.5 meters)[3] soils in shoreline areas typically impose severe septic tank limitations.

The septic system has two main components—a tank and an absorption field (Figure 6.165). The tank is a chamber for the primary treatment of household sewage. The drainage field functions to provide final purification within the soil. If the distance between the septic system and the water is insufficient, the liquid waste leaching through the soil is inadequately treated. Consequently, it reaches the water basin in contaminated condition, polluting the water with a variety of substances, the most troublesome of which are nutrients, particularly nitrogen compounds. Nitrate (NO_3), which is particularly mobile in groundwater, is the probable cause of most estuarine eutrophication.

Implementation No. 1. Septic Tank Setbacks

The disposal or absorption field of a septic tank system should be set back at least 150 feet (46 meters) from the annual high-water line.

After extensive review of the facts, U.S. Geological Survey hydrology expert L. B. Leopold concluded that "for soil cleansing to be effective, contaminated water must move through unsaturated soil at least 100 feet (30 meters)"; that "... it might be advisable to have no source of pollution such as a seepage field closer than 300 feet (90 meters) to a channel or watercourse"; and that even this setback does not prevent dissolved materials such as nitrates from enriching the water and thus potentially creating a biotic imbalance through eutrophication.[5] The issue is most complex, and therefore the U.S. Environmental Protection

Agency has no national standard for the amount of nitrate allowed in coastal waters. But one may consider a concentration higher than 0.5 ppm as potentially adverse; this is the limit recommended for the Potomac River.[6]

Local regulations have typically required the absorption fields of septic tanks to be set back a minimum of 50 feet (15 meters) from the edge of the water—stream, lake, open ditch, or other water body into which unfiltered effluent could escape.[1] Some states (e.g., Maine and Wisconsin) require a 100-foot (30-meter) minimum setback from surface water areas. The purpose of the setback is to allow for removal of pollutants, particularly coliform bacteria and other waterborne pathogenic organisms, from the wastewater through soil purification before it reaches the adjacent water body via the groundwater. However, it has been shown rather clearly that, although these setbacks may be sufficient to remove pathogens, they are not adequate for the removal of certain dissolved pollutants, particularly nitrates.[7] Consequently many urbanized estuarine water bodies have become highly eutrophic and degraded from septic tank leaching and overflow (combined with runoff of fertilizer).

Nitrate is particularly troublesome, as it is extremely soluble and mobile in groundwater. Scientific studies have shown that the nitrate form of nitrogen is commonly found in high concentrations (up to 40 ppm) at distances of 100 feet from septic systems.[7] Other studies have shown unacceptable amounts of nitrate at 150 feet.[7, 8] Consequently a setback distance at least 150 feet inland of the annual flood line is required to minimize nitrate pollution.

A setback of 300 feet should be safe unless local soil and groundwater conditions are particularly unsuited for nitrate removal, in which case a greater distance is required. Therefore a setback of 300 feet should be required whenever possible. When lot lengths, streets, or other practical difficulties

interfere, a lesser setback may be allowed, provided that soil and water table conditions permit. At less than 150 feet, however, the danger of excess nitrogen reaching the waters and causing estuarine pollution is unacceptably high.[7] Therefore a setback of 150 feet should be required unless specific studies show the local soil and groundwater situation to be peculiarly well suited to nitrate removal. The strictest setback standards should be applied when habitation is denser than one two-bedroom dwelling unit per acre and particularly when an apartment, country club, or other high-density structure is involved. Although there may be pollutants other than nitrate (e.g., sulfur or chlorides) in septic system effluents that would adversely affect coastal waters, these should also be adequately controlled by the setbacks we have recommended.

These setback standards, which provide for nitrate removal, are particularly important for coastal waters, because nitrogen is normally the controlling nutrient in brackish and salt water and is particularly critical to ecological balance.

Implementation No. 2.   Water Table Limitations on Septic Tanks

Septic tank systems should be installed only when the highest annual groundwater level is at least 4 feet (1.2 meters) below the absorption field.

If the groundwater beneath the septic tank absorption field rises to the level of the discharge pipes, the saturated soils cannot absorb the effluent. In addition, the groundwater may become grossly polluted. In the worst situations the unpurified effluent may even rise to the surface, where it will drain directly into an adjacent water body. This problem arises particularly in shoreline areas, where tidal movement raises groundwater levels. Consequently it is recommended that the drainage pipes of the absorption field be placed at least 4 feet

(1.2 meters) above the highest expected annual groundwater level.[2]

Similarly, there should be a minimum of 4 feet of soil material between the bottom of the absorption field trenches and any subsurface rock formation or other impermeable stratum. Shallower soil depths will permit incompletely treated effluent to percolate down to the impermeable stratum and flow horizontally into adjacent water bodies.

Implementation No. 3. Soil Limitations on Septic Tanks

Septic tank systems should be installed only when soil characteristics are suitable.

A major consideration governing septic tank efficiency is the rate at which effluent moves into and through the soil. The amount and type of gravel, sand, silt, and clay influence this rate, and movement is faster through sandy and gravely soils than through clayey ones. Soil permeability for septic tanks should be moderate to rapid, allowing a percolation rate of at least 1 inch (2.5 centimeters) per hour.[2]

Serial distribution of the effluent is advisable when absorption fields are characterized by variation in soil types.[2] Serial distribution is an arrangement of components—absorption trenches, seepage pits, or seepage beds—such that each has the capacity to retain the wastewater before it flows into the succeeding component, and to disperse it over the total effective absorption area.[1] Before issuing a permit for a septic tank system, an on-site soil survey should be conducted by an appropriate local authority (U.S. Department of Agriculture or Soil Conservation Service, local soil conservation district, or state agricultural experiment station).

Properly spaced septic tanks on slopes of less than 15 percent usually do not create serious problems if soil properties are adequate for sewage absorption; however, on steeper slopes, controlling the downhill flow

of the effluent may be difficult. Steep slopes can allow improperly filtered effluent to reach and contaminate receiving waters. Consequently installation of septic tanks on shorelines with slopes greater than 15 percent should normally be prohibited.[2]

Several other precautions should also be observed. Overflow pipes, which convey sewage directly to the water basin when the septic tank fills, should be prohibited. Seepage pits should be discouraged in favor of septic drainage fields. Finally, septic tanks and similar private sewage treatment facilities should be inspected on a regular basis by the local health department to ensure proper working order and adequate treatment.

REFERENCES

1. U.S. Department of Health, Education and Welfare. 1972. *Manual of Septic Tank Practice.* Public Health Service, Superintendent of Documents, U.S. Government Printing Office, Washington, D.C.

2. W. H. Bender. 1971. *Soils and Septic Tanks.* Soil Conservation Service, Agricultural Information Bulletin 349, U.S. Department of Agriculture, Washington, D.C.

3. H. B. Goldman. 1974. *Hayward Shoreline Environmental Analysis.* Hayward Area Shoreline Planning Agency, San Francisco, California.

4. National Association of Counties/Research Foundation. *Community Action Program for Water Pollution Control.* Washington, D.C.

5. Luna B. Leopold. 1968. *Hydrology for Urban Land Planning—A Guidebook on the Hydrologic Effects of Urban Land Use.* U.S. Geological Survey, Geological Survey Circular 554, Washington, D.C.

6. Garrett Power. 1975. "Watergate Village: A case study of a permit application for a marina submitted to the U.S. Army Corps of Engineers." *Coastal Zone Management Journal,* Vol. 2, No. 2, pp. 103–124.

7. Martha Ketelle. 1972. *Physical Considerations for the Location of Septic Disposal Systems.* An Inland Lake Renewal and Shoreland Management Demonstration Project, University of Wisconsin Extension, Madison, Wisconsin.

8. Roger A. Minear and James W. Patterson. n.d.

Septic Tanks and Groundwater Pollution. Department of Environmental Engineering, Illinois Institute of Technology, Chicago, Illinois.

21. SEWAGE TREATMENT SYSTEMS

Sewage is any waste material carried by sewers. As such, it often contains, in addition to household domestic wastes, wastes from industries, institutions, and commercial establishments and runoff from streets and highways. The accumulation of these wastes presents a real threat to the coastal ecosystem if they are not properly collected, treated, and disposed of.

For many years it was standard practice across the United States to dispose of treated sewage effluent by discharging it into a nearby water body with little consideration of the water's capacity to accept pollutants. Many coastal water basins receive sewage that contains greater concentrations of nutrients, organic matter, toxic substances, and pathogenic organisms than

they can safely assimilate.[1] For example, sewage discharge to estuarine waters is responsible for the contamination and subsequent closing of over 2 million acres of commercial shellfish beds in the estuaries of the United States,[2]—44,000 acres in North Carolina alone[3] (Figure 6.166). The potential 1975 catch from shellfish beds closed in that one year would have been in excess of 700 million pounds and would have been worth more than $100 million.[5] Inadequately treated sewage has also caused oxygen reduction, toxification, and other degradation of hundreds of estuarine water bodies in the United States.

Five major pollution problems from inadequately treated human wastes are (1) hazard to human health from pathogens in coastal waters and in shellfish, (2) aesthetic offenses, (3) oxygen reduction of coastal waters from biological oxygen demand (BOD) loading, (4) eutrophication (overfertilization) of coastal waters from release of dissolved nitrates, and (5) poisoning of coastal waters by pesticides, heavy metals,

Figure 6.166   Urban pollution contaminates shellfish beds (Boca Ciega Bay, Florida). (SOURCE: Reference 4.)

Figure 6.167   Tidal flood heights at the sewage treatment plant on Skillman Street in Roslyn, New York. (Photo from New York District, U.S. Army Corps of Engineers.)

and other toxins. Of these the most insidious is eutrophication, caused mainly by nitrate pollution (whereas phosphates may be the principal nutrient pollutant in fresh waters).

Land application methods for effluent and sludge, tertiary treatment of coastal discharge, and water purification and reuse are treatment options that avoid direct nitrate pollution of estuarine water bodies and help to prevent future shortages of fresh water and arable land. In many circumstances these methods are economically and technically feasible, are ecologically acceptable, and meet federal and state waste treatment and pollution regulations.

Because it is most efficient to operate a sewage collection system by gravity flow, coastal treatment plants often have been built in floodplains along coastal water courses or on wetlands. There the land was available and cheap, and the effluent could be simply disposed of into the adjacent waters. This had led to flooding of the plant sites during high-water stages and to the obliteration of wetlands (Figure 6.167).

Because sewage systems require massive capital investments and have a strong influence on residential and commercial development trends, the plan for a complete municipal sewage facility is frequently a land-use plan for the community. Sewers running through vacant lands may create a great pressure for the development of these lands whether or not the community has planned for it. Therefore sewage systems must be part of a long-term realistic, comprehensive community plan.

Federal Program

Sewage treatment and disposal are regulated in a complex federal–state program established by the Federal Clean Water Act.[6] The Environmental Protection Agency (EPA) administers the Act, but management of the program is in the hands of the states. When qualified by the EPA to administer provisions of the National Pollution Discharge Elimination System (NPDES), a state is delegated the authority to regulate the discharge of effluents and to issue permits. Every municipal sewage treatment disposal system requires a permit under the NPDES program. In addition to the regulation of discharge through state permits, the federal program provides direct grants to communities for the construction of sewage facilities. Since federal funds are inadequate for all needs, each state establishes priorities for construction aid to communities, depending primarily on four criteria:

1. The severity of pollution problems.
2. The population affected.
3. The need for preservation of high-quality waters.
4. National priorities as determined by the administrator of the EPA.

Details of the more important provisions of the federal program are as follows:[7]

1. The NPDES permits not only specify required effluent limitations, but also set all conditions of compliance with 1977 and 1983 standards. By July 1, 1977, all publicly owned treatment works must meet effluent limitations based on secondary treatment as designed by the administrator of the EPA. The parameters described for secondary treatment include BOD, suspended solids, fecal coliform bacteria, and pH. All municipal wastewater facilities must apply "best practicable" waste treatment technology by 1983.
2. The Act specifies that, whenever secondary treatment as defined by the EPA is not sufficient for the "attainment or maintenance of water quality," the administrator shall impose stricter effluent limitations. Before this is done, the EPA is required to issue a public notice and to hold a public hearing on the proposed limitations within 90 days. The public hearings must consider the social, economic, and environmental consequences of the limitations.
3. The EPA regulations require the state to divide all basin waters in the state into

two different types of segments—water-quality-limited and effluent-limited segments. Water-quality-limited segments are these basin segments that are already polluted to the extent that water quality standards cannot be achieved by the imposition of effluent limitations. Effluent-limited segments are the segments that either currently meet water quality standards or will meet standards with the imposition of 1977 effluent limitations. This simply means that sewage treatment facilities located on water-quality-limited segments will be subject to stricter effluent limits.

4. Any industry discharging into a publicly owned municipal wastewater facility will have to meet applicable "pretreatment standards for introduction of pollutants into treatment works."[8] Waste treatment facilities that serve industrial users will be required to charge fees that will recover from these users their respective shares of the capital and operating costs.
5. The federal program encourages the conducting of waste treatment management on an areawide basis so as to provide control and treatment of all point and non-point sources of pollution. Waste treatment planning is more than selection of the most cost-effective method of sewage treatment; it is one of the most important planning decisions that a community makes. Growth patterns will be largely determined by the capacity of the wastewater facility to handle additional waste and by the location of sewer lines. Moreover, the quality of the effluent will do much to determine the biological stream quality and the adequacy of a community's water supply.
6. The EPA is required to encourage revenue-producing waste treatment facilities. Among issues to be considered are the recycling of waste through the production of agricultural and silvicultural products, the reclamation of wastewater, the contained disposal of waste, and the disposal

of sludge—all, of course, without environmental hazard. The EPA is required to
encourage the integration of sewage treatment with facilities to dispose of other
municipal and industrial wastes, including solid and thermal wastes. It is also
required to encourage the integration of
waste treatment facility planning with
the recreation and open-space requirements of an area.

7. Every organization that has been authorized as the planning agency for an areawide waste treatment mangement plan
shall "have in operation a continuing
area-wide waste treatment management
planning process." The EPA is not allowed to approve any grants "for construction of a publicly owned treatment
works within such a designated area
unless such works are consistent with
applicable area-wide waste management
plans," once they are approved.

GUIDELINE. Vital Area Constraints on Sewage Systems

**Locate sewage treatment plants, outfalls,
pipe systems, and storm sewers so that they
do not disrupt vital habitat areas.**

Along the water's edge, wetlands often have
been the most easily available area for the
location of treatment facilities and the least
expensive, even when the problems and costs
of filling and general site preparation are
considered. In addition, the collection mains
(trunk mains) have often been routed
through wetlands, where inexpensive land is
available and wastewater can flow easily by
gravity to the treatment plant.

The use of wetlands as sites for sewage
plants is now generally considered environmentally unacceptable because wetlands are
vital habitat areas (page 32). This constraint applies also to excavation for pipelines in most cases. Therefore federal and
state agencies will normally refuse to issue
the required permits (page 185).

In reviewing applications for facility construction grants EPA policy is to require full
protection of wetlands. Specifically, the EPA
requires the following in its "Policy to Protect the Nation's Wetlands"[8] (see Appendix, page 788):

In compliance with the National Environmental Policy Act of 1969, it shall be the
policy of this Agency not to grant Federal
funds for the construction of municipal waste
water treatment facilities or other waste-treatment-associated appurtenances which may interfere with the existing wetland ecosystem
except where no other alternative of lesser
environmental damage is found to be feasible.

The EPA defines the wetland ecosystem as
follows: "marshes, swamps, bogs and other
low-lying areas, which during some period
of the year will be covered in part by natural non-flood waters."

In addition to wetlands, other types of
vital areas require protection. Not only
should such areas be reserved for essential
ecological purposes, but also they should be
protected from alteration of water flow,
trenching, disposal of construction wastes,
and other disturbing effects.

Implementation No. 1. Vital Area Avoid-ance in Sewage System Placement

**Select routes for collector systems and sites
for sewage treatment facilities that avoid
vital habitat areas.**

Wetlands and other coastal vital areas require identification at an early stage in
community planning so that they can be
adequately safeguarded, not only in relation
to sewage systems but also for the purpose
of controlling all development (page 139).
Once these are identified, an informed site
selection that avoids vital areas can be made
for sewage collection and treatment systems
(Figure 6.168). Among the more important
vital areas to be identified are coastal wetlands; dunes; freshwater creeks, sloughs,
bogs, and marshes; breeding and feeding

Figure 6.168 Dredging ditches through coastal marshes for sewer trunk lines may significantly interfere with marsh functions. (Photo by author.)

areas of coastal birds and mammals; and endangered species habitats (page 140).

GUIDELINE. Sewage Treatment and Disposal

Take immediate action to upgrade municipal sewage treatment and disposal systems to federal effluent standards.

Central municipal sewage treatment facilities have the potential for protection of coastal waters if properly designed and operated. If not, they may only accomplish a transfer of major pollution from dispersed sources to a concentrated point source in coastal waters. Most existing sewage systems must be upgraded to meet the minimum requirements for the protection of coastal ecosystems.

The confinement and shallowness of typical estuarine water basins allow pollutants to pervade their waters because they tend to have poor flushing characteristics. The longer that discharged sewage effluent remains concentrated in an area, the more pronounced will be its effects.

Urban storm sewers are sometimes separate and sometimes combined with sanitary sewer systems. In a separate system, one set of sewer lines carries household and industrial wastes, and another carries stormwater runoff. Stormwater is generally permitted to enter receiving waters untreated. In a combined system, both sanitary sewer pipes and storm drains are connected to a large interceptor line. During a rainstorm, when the flow to the sewer system is greatest, varying amounts of raw sewage and stormwater may be detoured past the sewage treatment facility, which does not have the capacity to handle the increased flow, and discharged to coastal waters with no treatment whatsoever. Generally, separate systems are preferred (page 552).

Two basic levels of waste treatment are in common use—primary and secondary. In primary treatment solids are usually screened or allowed to settle and are removed from the water. As sewage enters a plant for primary treatment, it flows through a series of screens that removes the larger objects (sticks, rags, etc.). After it has been screened, it is passed through a grit chamber and then a sedimentation tank for removal of sand grit and similar small particles (Figure 6.169).

In secondary treatment wastes are further purified through the use of biological processes. The two principal types of secondary treatment are trickling filters and activated sludge processes, in which up to 90 percent of the organic matter is removed. The treated effluent usually goes to a nearby water body, while the sludge is removed by treatment to landfill or to an incinerator.

Chlorination, a process in which chlorine

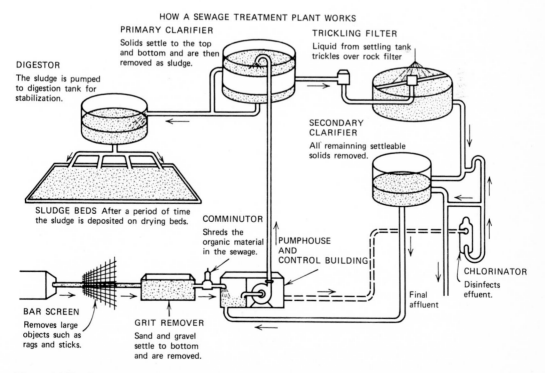

Figure 6.169   Components and processes of a secondary sewage treatment plant (Salt Lake City). (SOURCE: Reference 9.)

gas is fed into the effluent, is a final step taken in either primary or secondary treatment for the purpose of destroying disease-causing bacteria. Chlorination may kill over 99 percent of the harmful bacteria in sewage effluent.[10]

As summarized in an EPA report, municipalities that discharge effluent into estuarine-related water bodies "must be committed to ever-increasing demands to provide the maximum amount of treatment, certainly secondary and possibly tertiary, to preserve and protect the sensitive and important estuarine and nearshore coastal waters."[11] This is a particularly important warning because secondary treatment does not efficiently remove nitrogen. It is clear that nitrogen is the controlling nutrient of estuaries and that eutrophication is caused by nitrate excess.[12,13] Because of the sensitive nature of estuaries and the nitrogen content of secondary treatment effluent, sewage treatment plants should be designed so that effluent is

not discharged into typical estuarine water bodies without further purification.

Nitrification–denitrification is a presently available advanced, or tertiary, method for removing nitrogen from effluent. Tertiary treatment will remove a high proportion of the nutrients, allowing the effluent to be safely discharged into all but the most confined estuarine waters. A very advanced waste treatment system can provide an effluent of sufficient quality for the recharging of aquifers in areas where water shortages present a problem.[14]

The soil and land surface can handle a wide range of pollutants normally found in the wastewater of municipal, agricultural, and industrial producers. The use of land treatment offers a workable solution to the oxygen reduction and overfertilization that result when sewage effluent is discharged into a water body. In a properly integrated land-use plan, sufficient naturally or artificially vegetated land is set aside to purify

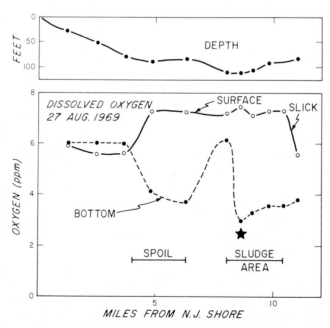

Figure 6.170 Many square miles of the ocean bottom off Sandy Hook, New Jersey, are so blighted with pollution from New York City sludge and harbor dredge spoil dumping that the dissolved oxygen level sinks below the absolute minimum threshhold for the support of marine life in deposition areas. (SOURCE: Reference 17.)

the effluent, removing the organic (BOD) content and the inorganic (phosphate and nitrate) nutrients in passing across vegetated terrain and through the soils. Golf courses, farms, timber land, or natural meadow and marshland buffer areas can be used for this purpose.

Sludge removed in sewage treatment may also be reintroduced to the ecosystem through land application. Biologically digested sludge can be used as a soil enricher for agricultural and recreational lands, as well as for the reclamation of areas imbalanced by strip mining. Dried or dewatered sludge has a special utilization in the production of certain crops, where the slow release of mineral nitrogen by the sludge is more beneficial than conventional intensive nitrogen fertilizer applcation.[15] The cost of recycling sludge in these ways may be less than the cost of sludge incineration that meets federal air pollution laws. Incineration of dewatered sludge releases pollutants into the air and creates a massive ash disposal problem, since 35 percent of the dried sludge is noncombustible.[15] Ocean sludge disposal may lead to a total degradation of the valuable bottom life community in the vicinity of the dumping site[16] and is generally unacceptable (Figure 6.170).

In cases where land application and advanced treatment are impractical, the use of ocean outfalls offers a sewage treatment option that, if properly designed and located, is relatively compatible with ocean ecosystems (but is not acceptable for estuarine ecosystems). Ocean pitfalls for secondary or primary effluent must be considered on a case-by-case basis, with a wide range of geological, hydrological, and biological factors being taken into account. The use of ocean outfalls can be supported in circumstances where ocean dispersion is great enough to dilute toxic and hazardous effluent pollutants.[18]

In nonheavily developed areas, with proper soil and location, septic tanks are an advantageous way of handling wastes and returning them to the earth (page 502).

Implementation No. 1. Land Application of Sewage Effluent

Land application of treated sewage effluent should be used whenever practicable.

An effective alternative to dumping sewage effluent into coastal water bodies is land application (treatment and disposal) of wastewater. The feasibility of this approach is demonstrated by the more than 500 municipalities in the United States that use some form of land application for disposal or treatment of wastes.[19] Land application of sewage effluent after conventional secondary treatment (or tertiary where necessary) is often recommended by the EPA. The 1972 Federal Clean Water Act advocates grants for "waste treatment facilities which encourage the development of systems that provide for total recycling and the reclamation of wastewater."[6]

In the land application system, wastewater is applied by spray irrigation or overland flow to a land surface, where it is cleared by biological, chemical, and mechanical processes and/or filters through the soil as it travels over a vegetated surface. Finally, it either filters into the groundwater or is collected for discharge to a water body, depending on the system used. Land *disposal* implies complete dissipation of effluent into the earth. Land *treatment* is a substitute for tertiary treatment and as such is designed to remove a significant percentage of polluting nitrogen and phosphorus from secondary-treatment effluent and also to eliminate waterborne pathogens, which typical secondary treatment fails to remove.[20]

Three basic approaches to land application are infiltration–percolation (disposal), irrigation (disposal, treatment), and overland flow (treatment)[19] (Figure 6.171 and Tables 6.26 and 6.27).

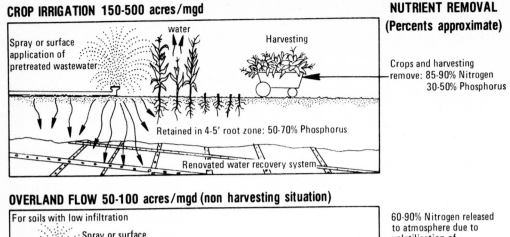

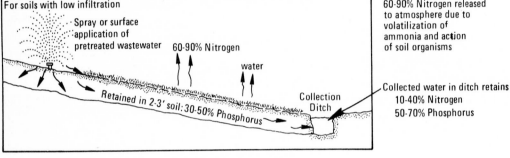

Figure 6.171   The three drawings above compare land application methods to renovate pretreated wastewater. (SOURCE: Reference 5.)

Irrigation appears to be a reliable land application technique with respect to long-term use and removal of pollutants from the wastewater. It is sufficiently developed so that general design and operational guidelines can be prepared from current technology. Criteria for determining the feasibility of land application by irrigation are given in Table 6.28 for various conditions.

At Pennsylvania State University crop irrigation studies have shown that, when sewage effluent is applied to agricultural lands, nitrogen is removed by crop uptake and that nitrate does not move into the groundwater.[27] This constructive use of nitrogen should be encouraged as an alternative to disposal in coastal waters, where nitrogen is a troublesome eutrophication

Table 6.26   Comparison of irrigation, overland flow, and infiltration–percolation of municipal wastewater (SOURCE: Reference 21)

Objective	Type of approach		
	Irrigation	Overland flow	Infiltration-percolation
Use as a treatment process with a recovery of renovated water[a]	0-70% recovery	50 to 80% recovery	Up to 97% recovery
Use for treatment beyond secondary:			
1. For BOD$_5$ and suspended solids removal	98+%	92+%	85-99%
2. For nitrogen removal	85+%[b]	70-90%	0-50%
3. For phosphorus removal	80-99%	40-80%	60-95%
Use to grow crops for sale	Excellent	Fair	Poor
Use as direct recycle to the land	Complete	Partial	Complete
Use to recharge groundwater	0-70%	0-10%	Up to 97%
Use in cold climates	Fair[c]	- -[d]	Excellent

a. Percentage of applied water recovered depends upon recovery technique and the climate.

b. Dependent upon crop uptake.

c. Conflicting data--woods irrigation acceptable, cropland irrigation marginal.

d. Insufficient data.

agent. An example of practical application is a large-scale system designed for Muskegon County, Michigan, which partially treats the effluent and sprays it on farmland to fertilize crops. Any runoff from the fields is collected in storage basins for reuse or recharging of the groundwater supply. The system features a storage element that can accumulate 8 months of runoff for application during a 4-month growing season.[23]

Overland flow appears to be currently useful for industrial as well as municipal wastewater treatment.[24] In an *optimum* treatment system with appropriate slopes (3 to 6 percent) and vegetation (e.g., canary grass), 130 acres (53 hectares) may handle the municipal wastes of 10,000 people.[25] Package plants, designed to treat the wastes of small 50- to 150-unit developments, may be particularly amenable to this type of soil and vegetative restoration.

It is important to note that the land treatment process is not yet thoroughly understood in all its applications. Unanswered questions remain in regard to the long-term ability of land *treatment* to remove nitrates. Land *disposal* should accomplish nitrogen removal more effectively, provided that the treatment system can be shown not to pollute aquifers or surface waters. Infiltration–percolation is presently a feasible method of land disposal, but criteria for site selection, groundwater pollution control, and management techniques for high-rate systems need further development.[21]

Sound planning for land application re-

Table 6.27 Comparative characteristics of irrigation, overland flow, and infiltration–percolation systems (SOURCE: Reference 19)

| Factor | Type of Approach | | |
	Irrigation	Overland flow	Infiltration-percolation
Liquid loading rate[a]	0.5 to 4 in./wk	2 to 5.5 in./wk	4 to 120 in./wk
Annual application	2 to 8 ft/yr	8 to 24 ft/yr	18 to 500 ft/yr
Land required for 1-mgd flow	140 to 560 acres plus buffer zones	46 to 140 acres plus buffer zones	2 to 62 acres plus buffer zones
Application techniques	Spray or surface	Usually spray	Usually surface
Soils	Moderately permeable soils with good productivity when irrigated	Slowly permeable soils such as clay loams and clay	Rapidly permeable soils, such as sands, loamy sands, and sandy loams
Probability of influencing ground-water quality	Moderate	Slight	Certain
Needed depth to groundwater	About 5 ft	Undetermined	About 15 ft
Wastewater lost to:	Predominantly evaporation or deep percolation	Surface discharge dominates over evaporation and percolation	Percolation to groundwater

a. Irrigation rates of 4 in./wk are usually seasonal; yearly maximum loads of 8 ft/yr would average about 2 in./wk.

quires close contact with state pollution officials and the local EPA regional office. For example, certain aesthetic and public health problems must be resolved in choosing a land application system.[25,26] Existing local and state regulations may have to be revised in order to facilitate land application, and some change effected in misinformed negative opinion.[27] The status of progress in this area should be checked with state pollution officials.

To establish an effective land application system it may be more efficient to strategically locate a number of small treatment facilities than to provide for high-capacity central treatment facilities. This arrangement could help to keep wastewater discharge at manageable quantities and reduce the extent of the collection system and the size of the trunk lines.

Implementation No. 2. Sewage Treatment for Estuarine Disposal

Tertiary treatment should be required for sewage effluent to be discharged into typical estuarine waters.

Unfortunately, secondary-treatment plants remove no more than half of the nitrate and phosphate nutrients in sewage (Table 6.29). The effluent is typically discharged with nitrate values as high as 15 to 50 ppm, which may be 1000 times greater than the natural levels of healthy coastal waters.[4] Excessive discharge of effluent with such a high concentration of nitrate causes eutrophication (overfertilization) of confined and poorly flushed estuarine waters. This results in a damaging overgrowth of algae and can bring about high turbidities, reduced dis-

Table 6.28 Site selection factors and criteria for effluent irrigation (SOURCE: Reference 19)

Factor	Criterion
Soil type	Loamy soils preferable but most soils from sands to clays are acceptable.
Soil drainability	Well drained soil is preferable, consult experienced agricultural advisors.
Soil depth	Uniformly 5 to 6 ft or more throughout sites is preferred.
Depth to groundwater	Minimum of 5 ft is preferred. Drainage to obtain this minimum may be required.
Groundwater control	May be necessary to ensure renovation if water table is less than 10 ft from surface.
Groundwater movement	Velocity and direction must be determined.
Slopes	Up to 15 percent are acceptable with or without terracing.
Underground formations	Should be mapped and analyzed with respect to interference with groundwater or percolating water movement.
Isolation	Moderate isolation from public preferable, degree dependent on wastewater characteristics, method of application, and crop.
Distance from source of wastewater	A matter of economics.

solved oxygen content, and the formation of layers of noxious organic matter on estuarine basin bottoms from the fallout of dying algae. In cases where excessive nitrogen values are present in estuaries or tidal rivers, (e.g., the lower Potomac River), sewage effluents have generally been the primary cause of eutrophication.[12]

The content of typical secondary-treatment effluent is shown in Table 6.30. Since it is the general goal of the federal pollution program administered by the EPA to require only secondary treatment of sewage, large amounts of remaining nitrate will still be released with the effluent in expanding urban areas. Thus there is a high potential for widespread eutrophication when secondary effluent is discharged into estuarine waters. The nutrients remaining after conventional secondary treatment will have to be removed by an additional process before discharge of the effluent to typical estuarine waters.

In addition to the nitrogenous substances, secondary sewage effluent also contains concentrations of other substances that can

Table 6.29 Average efficiency of primary and secondary sewage treatment plants (SOURCE: Reference 28)

	Removal efficiency of treatment	
	Primary	Primary Plus Secondary
Biochemical oxygen demand	35%	90%
Chemical oxygen demand	30%	80%
Refractory organics	20%	60%
Suspended Solids	60%	90%
Total nitrogen	20%	50%
Total phosphorus	10%	30%
Dissolved minerals	—	5%

pollute estuarine waters, including oxygen-depleting organic matter (BOD substances); heavy metals, pesticides, and other toxic substances; and viruses, bacteria, and other pathogens. Treatment methodology and discharge strategy must include the removal or immobilization of any such harmful substances. It is important to recognize that, although chlorination of secondary effluent may kill a high proportion of bacteria, there is no certainty that it immobilizes viruses, which are the agents for serious diseases such as hepatitis and polio. Also, chlorine is itself a toxic and highly polluting substance.

Under the 1972 federal program, the EPA must require secondary treatment for all sewage effluent by July 1, 1977, and "best practicable" treatment by 1983. In addition, better than secondary treatment will be required in cases where, with secondary, the receiving waters would fall below established minimum water quality standards (pag 195) or where presently the waters are so degraded that they do not meet the minimum

standards. Therefore it may be assumed that tertiary treatment will be required by the EPA for most typical estuarine disposal because the assimilative capacities of estuaries are so low that most would be (or are presently) overwhelmed by discharge from secondary-treatment plants.

Tertiary treatment requires moving beyond the simple mechanical and biological methods employed in primary and secondary treatment to incorporate more advanced techniques, such as coagulation–sedimentation, adsorption, electrodialysis chemical oxidation, nitrification–denitrification or a combination of these[10] (Figure 6.172). A properly designed and operated tertiary sewage treatment system that would permit discharge of an effluent of acceptable quality into estuarine waters would combine many of the methods mentioned above. For example, a series of steps might include the conventional primary treatment for removal of large solids, a secondary step that would eliminate decomposable impurities through

Table 6.30 Typical content of secondary treatment effluents (in milligrams per liter) (SOURCE: Reference 29)

	Concentration (mg/l)	Average increment added during water use (mg/l)
Gross organics	55	52
BOD & COD	25	25
Sodium	135	70
Potassium	15	10
Ammonium	20	20
Calcium	60	15
Magnesium	25	7
Chloride	130	75
Nitrate	15	10
Bicarbonate	300	100
Sulfate	100	30
Silica	50	15
Phosphate	25	25
Hardness (as calcium carbonate)	270	70
Alkalinity (as calcium carbonate)	250	85
Total dissolved solids	730	320

biological processes, coagulation–sedimentation to remove suspended solids, carbon adsorption to remove dissolved organic matter, electrodialysis to remove salts, biological denitrification to remove nitrogen, and finally chlorination to kill pathogenic organisms.[10]

Implementation No. 3. Ocean Outfalls

Ocean outfalls should be located at the greatest practicable distance from shore and designed to provide maximum dispersal of the effluent.

Ocean dispersal of treated sewage may be feasible if properly done. We find no facts to substantially challenge the properly designed and controlled ocean discharge of sewage effluent, provided that high concentrations of toxic substances are absent.

The principal advantage of the ocean as a disposal site is a reduction of costs, compared to the advanced treatment required

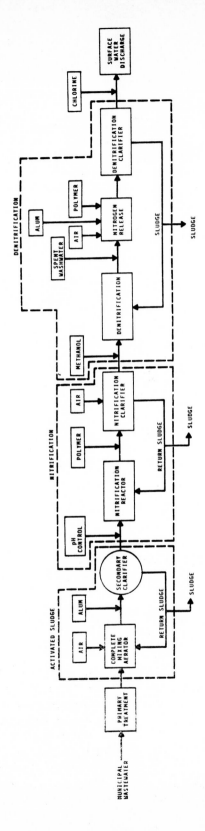

Figure 6.172 Advanced wastewater treatment: biological–chemical method employing activated sludge treatment with alum addition and nitrification–denitrification. (SOURCE: Reference 31.)

FLOW	INCREASE IN ANNUAL TREATMENT COST DUE TO CONVERSION FROM SECONDARY TO ADVANCED WASTEWATER TREATMENT	ANNUAL COST PER MILE OF SEWAGE OUTFALL (For secondary treatment effluent)	COST-EFFECTIVE OUTFALL LENGTH (Cost equal to cost of advanced treatment for same volume of wastewater flow)	
Million gallons per day	Dollars	Dollars/mile	Miles	Kilometers
1	178,500	30,800	5.8	9.3
10	712,000	131,000	5.4	8.7
100	4,560,000	256,000	17.8	28.6

Table 6.31 Length of ocean outfall for secondary-treatment effluent that can be constructed at cost of conversion to advanced wastewater treatment (SOURCE: Adapted from Reference 32)

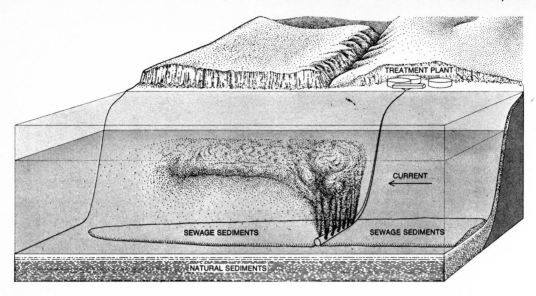

Figure 6.173 Idealized oceanic disposal system for a California coastal sewage treatment plant. Effluent from the plant flows a distance of 2 to 5 miles through an outfall pipe that is 6 to 12 feet in diameter. For about 0.25 mile at its end the pipe has numerous 6-inch discharge ports. The liquid material that it discharges rises to the thermocline (the boundary between deep, cool water and the warmer surface layer) and moves with wind and tide. (SOURCE: Reference 34.)

for disposal in estuarine waters (Table 6.31).[1] The ocean rapidly disperses and dilutes the effluent because of its volume and mixing capabilities, thus reducing the potential for ecologic damage. The location and physical configuration of ocean effluent outfalls should be determined by depth, distance from shore, circulation and mixing features of the particular ocean location, and factors influencing interactions of wastes with the environment.[33] But it must be clearly understood that high concentrations of sewage released at a single point anywhere in the ocean may overwhelm its assimilative capacity and cause extensive local damage, particularly to bottom life (see Article 11, Chapter 7).

In California, where the oceans are deep, outfalls are located generally from 2 to 7 miles offshore, at depths of 100 to 200 feet. Because conditions there are conducive to rapid mixing, and therefore rapid diffusion of effluent, the discharge of secondary effluent appears acceptable (Figure 6.173).

Nevertheless, the concentrations must be kept within reason. For example, the large volumes discharged from Los Angeles sewage outfalls have caused extensive damage, including reduced abundance and diversity of bottom life, sickness in fish (particularly fin rot), interference with breeding, and long-term loading of the ocean floor with DDT (about 200 tons total).[35] Another major effect has been the accumulation of fine sediment, which apparently smothers both plants and animals. The extensive kelp forests that grew in the area 20 to 30 years ago are now virtually gone, and attached plants or animals are scarce at depths greater than about 30 feet, where fine sediment blankets the bottom. Inshore, large numbers of sea urchins (perhaps partly nourished by organic material in the sewage) keep much of the bottom grazed clean of plant life.[36] Wider dispersal of the effluent could minimize this type of damage.

The Atlantic coast presents a generally different situation with a lowered potential for ocean discharge because of the relatively shallow water over the broader continental shelf, which extends to a hundred miles or more offshore at its widest. Conditions along much of the Atlantic coast do not provide sufficiently rapid dispersal and dilution of effluent to justify the discharge of large amounts of secondary effluent nearshore. However, there happen to be certain stretches of shore where currents are strong enough and nearshore water deep enough to provide the needed volume of water and mixing potential.

An issue open to resolution is whether certain deep bays and sounds should be classified as "oceans" and thus as acceptable receiving waters for secondary effluent. As secondary treatment does not remove all bacteria and is of very uncertain value in terms of virus removal, outfalls in bays and sounds could endanger recreational and shellfishing waters. Also toxic substances and nutrients released into such water bodies may reach unacceptable concentrations and cause extensive damage. This decision will depend wholly on local conditions affecting dispersal, dilution, and assimilation of pollutants.[11] However, this type of disposal should be a last-ditch choice when all other options—land application, ocean disposal, and tertiary treatment—cannot be proved feasible.

Implementation No. 4. Selective Wastewater Treatment

Stormwater and industrial sewage collection and treatment systems should be separated from sanitary sewage systems to the maximum extent possible.

Normally, it is not practicable to include stormwater with the sanitary sewage system. If, to save expense, inadequate capacity is provided, most plants are overwhelmed during heavy storms with the result that volumes of untreated sewage overflow to coastal waters. This results in a high degree of pathogen contamination of shellfish, over-

fertilization of waters, oxygen reduction, and contamination by toxic substances. The additional plant capacity required to effectively handle the large amounts of water received during peak storms is enormous and entails great capital expense. A solution often recommended is to plan for separate collection and treatment of storm runoff waters, which may be more heavily polluted with nutrients, organic waste, oil, and other toxic substances than sewage (page 552).

Because the composition of industrial wastewater is typically different from that of domestic sewage, treatment methods for the two types may differ significantly. Therefore some pollutants in raw industrial wastewater that are discharged into municipal collection lines may pass through municipal treatment facilities unchecked. In some cases industrial sewage so discharged contains sufficient biocidal substances to reduce the efficiency of municipal facilities to purify domestic sewage (Table 6.32). (see Appendix, page 838).

To avoid any complications that might arise from trying to treat both types of sewage with a single facility—which could require costly modifications of locally operated sewage treatment plants—systems should be designed so that each type can be treated separately from the other. The design requirements of individual industrial wastewater treatment facilities will vary greatly, depending on the type of industry and the kinds of pollutants involved, and may be significantly different from those of typical municipal sewage treatment plants.

In instances where a design commitment already made prevents separating industrial and domestic sources, industrial wastewater should be pretreated to remove all pollutants that would not be completely eliminated at the municipal plant or that might interfere with the treatment process.[37] Safeguards are required to ensure that raw or improperly treated industrial wastes are not accidentally discharged into municipal lines.

Table 6.32 Effects of industrial wastes on municipal treatment plants (SOURCE: Reference 5)

Type of Effect	Waste Characteristic	Potential Industrial Discharger
Damage to Structures	Acids Solvents Strong Alkalies	Chemicals* Petroleum Refining Textiles
	Large Solids	Essentially all
	Excessive flow	Essentially all
Reduced Treatment Performance	Excessive variability	Food Processing (seasonal)
	Toxics	Textiles Chemicals* Petroleum Refining Leather Tanning Metal Finishing
Pollutant Not Amenable to Treatment	Non-degradable organics	Pulp and Paper Chemicals* Textiles Petroleum Refining
	Inorganic salts (including metals)	Metal Finishing Chemicals* Iron and Steel Textiles Petroleum Refining

*Includes Inorganic and Organic Chemicals and Plastics and Synthetics

Implementation No. 5. Sewage Sludge Disposal

Sewage sludge should be recycled through land application where practicable.

Nearly all of the basic wastewater treatment processes, including clarification, biological filtration, activated sludge, and chemical precipitation, convert pollutants into a concentrated form called "sludge." As wastewater treatment systems become more complete, both in municipalities and in industry, the column of sludge produced and the concentration of undesirable impurities in it will dramatically increase.[38] All this sludge must be treated so that it can be disposed of easily and economically without further pollution of water, air, or land.

The basic aim of sludge treatment is to reduce volume and destroy or stabilize sludge solids before final disposal. There are two basic pathways through which the sludge can be processed.[38] The first method involves either concentration, digestion, and land application or dewatering and disposal. Sludge concentrators and thickeners increase the solids concentration from 1 to 4 percent. The sludge is then subjected to anaerobic digestion, which makes it easier to dewater and converts some of the organic matter to gaseous end products. This digested sludge can then be used as a soil conditioner and fertilizer alone or in combination with secondary sewage treatment effluent.

An alternative option in the first method involves further dewatering by drying beds, filters, or centrifuges. The dried sludge can then be applied as fertilizer–conditioner or disposed of in landfill. Ocean dumping of sludge is now severely limited and closely regulated by the EPA, since it has been shown to have deleterious effects on the bottom life surrounding dumping sites. Landfill disposal of sludge cakes is a waste of a valuable resource—the concentrated sludge nutrients—and is impracticable in areas where landfill space is scarce. The use of sludge to fertilize and condition recreational areas, agricultural fields, and strip-mined land is highly recommended. An existing drawback is the presence of residual concentrations of toxic metals and pathogens in the sludge. However, soil and crop management practices allow modification of environmental conditions detrimental to plants or animals;[15] such control options are absent in ocean disposal and incineration practices.

A second overall treatment plan utilizes heat drying and combustion to handle the dual tasks of volume reduction and solids destruction. Heat drying can be used to produce sludge cakes[39] for fertilization or landfill, but is usually a preliminary step to incineration. Operational costs for incineration are high compared to those for other sludge disposal methods. Moreover, sludge incineration presents other disadvantages, such as air pollution, ash disposal, and operational problems due to flue gases.

REFERENCES

1. U.S. Department of the Interior. 1970. *The National Estuarine Pollution Study*. U.S. Senate, 91st Congress, 2nd Session, Document 91-58. Superintendent of Documents, U.S. Government Printing Office, Washington, D.C.

2. U.S. Department of the Interior. 1968. "Aquatic living commercial resources," Issue Support Paper No. 70-7. In *Estuarine Research and Management*. Washington, D.C.

3. I. E. Gray. 1974. "Worm and clam flats." Chapter C-6 in H. T. Odum, B. J. Copeland E. A. McMahan, Eds., *Coastal Ecological Systems of the United States* (4 vols). The Conservation Foundation, Washington, D.C.

4. J. K. McNulty, W. H. Lindall, Jr., and J. E. Sykes. 1972. *Cooperative Gulf of Mexico Estuarine Inventory and Study. Florida: Phase I, Area Description*. National Oceanic and Atmospheric Administration Report, National Marine Fisheries Service Circular No. 368, U.S. Department of Commerce, Washington, D.C.

5. National Commission on Water Quality. 1975. *Staff Draft Report*. Washington, D.C.

6. U.S. Senate. 92nd Congress, S.2770. Act to Amend Federal Water Pollution Control Act. P.L. 95-500, Oct. 18, 1972.

7. The Conservation Foundation. 1974. *Water Quality Training Institute Manual*, (funded under a grant from the U.S. Environmental Protection Agency). Washington, D.C.

8. U.S. Environmental Protection Agency. 1973. EPA *Policy to Protect the Nation's Wetlands*. Administrator's Decision Statement No. 4, Washington, D.C.

9. National Association of Counties/Research Foundation. *Community Action Program for Water Pollution Control*. Washington, D.C.

10. U.S. Environmental Protection Agency. 1971. A *Primer on Waste Water Treatment*. Water Quality Office, U.S. Superintendent of Documents, Government Printing Office, Washington, D.C.

11. U.S. Environmental Protection Agency. 1974. *Secondary Treatment of Municipal Ocean Discharges*. Task Force Report—(draft). Office of Water Programs Operations, U.S. Environmental Protection Agency, Washington, D.C.

12. Donald M. Martin and David R. Goff. n.d. *The Role of Nitrogen in the Aquatic Environment*. No. 2, Department of Limnology, Academy of Natural Sciences of Philadelphia, Philadelphia, Pennsylvania.

13. Michael A. Champ. 1975. *Nutrient Loading in the Nation's Estuaries. A Report to Congress.* American University, Washington, D.C.

14. Program for Water Reclamation and Groundwater Recharge. 1973. *Santa Clara County Flood Control and Water District Environmental Impact Statement.*

15. T. D. Hinesly. 1973. "Sludge Recycling: The Most Reasonable Choice?" *Water Spectrum,* Vol. 5, No. 1. Office of the Chief of Engineers, Department of the Army, Washington, D.C.

16. National Research Council, Committee on Oceanography. 1970. *Waste Management Concepts for the Coastal Zone, Requirements for Research and Investigation.* National Academy of Sciences–National Academy of Engineering, Washington, D.C.

17. U.S. Army Corps of Engineers. 1973. *Ocean Dumping in the New York Bight.* Technical Memorandum No. 39, Coastal Engineering Research Center, Washington, D.C.

18. Dean F. Bumpus, W. R. Wright, and R. F. Vaccaro. 1971. "Sewage disposal in Falmouth, Mass.: Part II, Predicted effect of the proposed outfall." *Boston Society of Civil Engineers Journal,* Vol. 58, pp. 278–320.

19. Charles E. Pound and Ronald W. Crites. 1973. *Wastewater Treatment and Reuse by Land Application, Vol. 1: Summary.* Prepared for the Office of Research and Development, U.S. Environmental Protection Agency, Washington, D.C.

20. E. J. Heald and D. C. Tabb. 1973. *Applicability of the Interceptor Waterway Concept to the Rookery Bay Area.* Rookery Bay Land Use Studies, Study No. 6, The Conservation Foundation, Washington, D.C.

21. U.S. Environmental Protection Agency. 1975. *Evaluation of Land Application Systems.* Washington, D.C.

22. Richard E. Thomas. 1973. "Land disposal, II: An overview of treatment methods." *Journal of Water Pollution Control Federation,* July, 1973, pp. 1476–84.

23. Soap and Detergent Association. 1972. "Increasing land disposal of wastes shows problems as well as merits." In *Water in the News.*

24. U.S. Environmental Protection Agency. 1974. *Feasibility of Overland Flow for Treatment of Raw Domestic Wastewater.* National Environmental Research Center, Corvallis, Oregon.

25. Michael R. Stevens. 1972. *Green Land—Clean Streams.* Center for the Study of Federalism, Temple University, Philadelphia, Pennsylvania.

26. U.S. Environmental Protection Agency. 1975. "Land treatment of municipal wastewater effluents." In *Technology Transfer,* October, EPA-335. Washington, D.C.

27. Belford L. Seabrook. 1973. "Land application of wastewater with a demographic evaluation." In *Proceedings of the Joint Conference on Recycling Municipal Sludges and Effluents on Land,* Chicago, Illinois. July 9-13.

28. American Chemical Society, Committee on Chemistry and Public Affairs. 1969. *Cleaning Our Environment, The Chemical Basis for Action.* Washington, D.C.

29. L. W. Weinberger, D. G. Stephan, and F. M. Middleton. 1968. "Solving our water problems—water renovation and reuse." *Annals of the New York Academy of Science,* Vol. 136, Art. 5, p. 131.

30. R. Alderson. "Effects of low concentrations of free chlorine on eggs and larvae of plaice, *Pleuronectes platessa.*" In *Marine Pollution and Sea Life,* Food and Agriculture Organization of the United Nations, Fishing News (Books), Ltd.

31. Council on Environmental Quality–U.S. Environmental Protection Agency. 1974. *Municipal Sewage Treatment.* Washington, D.C.

32. Erman A. Pearson. 1975. *Estuarine Wastewater Management.* Paper presented to The Estuarine Pollution Conference, Pensacola, Florida, February. U.S. Environmental Protection Agency, Washington, D.C.

33. National Academy of Sciences–National Academy of Engineering. 1970. *Waste Management for the Coastal Zone: Concepts for the Assessment of Ocean Outfalls.* Washington, D.C.

34. Willard Bascom. 1974. "The disposal of waste in the ocean." *Scientific American,* Vol. 231 (August 1974).

35. D. R. Young et al. 1975. "Pollution inputs and distributions off Southern California." Preprint of paper from *Proceedings of the 169th National Meeting of the American Chemical Society, at Special Symposium on Marine Chemistry in the Coastal Environment,* Philadelphia, Pennsylvania, April 8-10. Southern California Research Project.

36. John Clark. 1974. *Coastal Ecosystems: Ecological Considerations for Management of the Coastal Zone.* The Conservation Foundation, Washington, D.C.

37. U.S. Environmental Protection Agency. 1973. *Pretreatment of Pollutants Introduced into Publicly Owned Treatment Works.* Office of Water Program Operations, Washington, D.C.

38. R. H. Marks, Ed. 1967. "Waste-water treatment." *Power* (special report), June, New York.

39. Craig Claiborne. 1976. *The New York Times. Personal communication.*

22. SOLID WASTE DISPOSAL

About 8.6 pounds (3.9 kilograms) of solid waste is collected per day for each person in the United States (1972 data). About 8 percent of it goes to 300 municipal incinerators in the United States. More than 90 percent is taken to some 12,000 land disposal sites. Hog feeding and composting account for relatively small fractions of the solid waste disposal load. Of the 300 incinerators only about 30 percent have adequate air pollution control devices. Of the 12,000 land disposal sites only about 6 percent are acceptable sanitary landfills, defined as having daily cover, no open burning, and no water pollution problems.[1]

There is a high demand for disposal in shore areas because the coast is so highly populated—60 million people live within 5 miles of the United States seacoast. Much of the waste is destined, not for proper landfills, but for disposal in wetlands and other inappropriate places. Wetlands disposal once seemed logical because such space was cheap, available, and normally thought of as "wasteland." This attitude has since changed, however, because of the recognition of marshes, bogs, swamps, and other wetlands as vital habitats essential to the proper functioning of natural water systems (page 98). Through the 1960s, 9000 acres of marshland from Maine to Delaware was lost to disposal sites alone.

In addition to their direct loss from filling with solid wastes, wetland and lower flood plain dump sites have high potentials for causing water pollution. In these areas there is a high rate of leaching of toxic chemicals, nutrient chemicals, and dissolved organic matter from the town dump into the groundwater, combined with the washoff of the same pollutants during rainstorms and flooding. Coastal waters may be adversely affected by the downstream flow of polluted water from dump or landfill sites located far inland on coastal tributaries.

New state and federal laws protecting wetlands and other water areas require that communities find alternative pollution-free sites for waste disposal. The most suitable alternative is transporting refuse out of the coastal zone to an inland site.[2] In the San Francisco Bay region, for example, refuse is trucked inland over 30 miles to landfill operations in the city of Mountain View.[3]

Recent creative approaches to solid waste management emphasize recycling and reusing the materials or burning them for electric power rather than burial. One such approach reported by the American Chemical Society[1] involves cost recovery through composting since the compost itself is sold and materials such as paper and rags may be salvaged and sold. The concept can also be applied to refuse incineration by using the heat produced to generate steam. There is very little evidence to suggest that cost recovery will be a panacea. The importance of the concept lies in the recognition that municipal refuse can be treated as an asset, rather than a nuisance, even though no net profit is realized.

In the following discussion we emphasize the importance of the location and design of sanitary landfills to protect vital habitat areas and to prevent water pollution. Both aims are covered by relevant federal and state laws, which should be thoroughly investigated in relation to rehabilitating or abandoning old sanitary landfill sites or locating new ones. For example, coastal wetlands are protected through programs of such federal agencies as the U.S. Corps of Engineers, the U.S. Environmental Protection Agency (EPA), and the U.S. Fish and Wildlife Service. Many states also have wetlands protection laws. Water pollution programs are principally based on standards established by the EPA under a 1972 act of

Congress and implemented locally by state pollution control authorities.[2]

By whatever means or for whatever purpose, ocean dumping of solid waste is regulated by a permit system established in the Federal "Ocean Dumping" Act (properly the Marine Protection, Research, and Sanctuaries Act of 1972) and the Federal Clean Water Act (particularly the Federal Water Pollution Control Act Amendments of 1972), both administered by the EPA. Their object is to prevent or strictly limit the dumping into ocean waters of any materials that would adversely affect either human health, welfare, and amenities or the marine environment, ecological systems, or economic potentialities.[4] Ocean dumping is a complex matter and is of little interest to other than large cities; therefore it is not discussed here in detail. However, one potential use of solid waste of interest to many communities is the building of new coastal

habitat areas, such as artificial fishing reefs from junk cars (Figure 6.174).

Because of the complexities of existing environmental requirements, a local government will find it necessary to thoroughly reexamine solid waste disposal management and then devise a system that will satisfy a broad range of future community needs.

We make the basic assumption that dumps will generally be phased out in favor of modern sanitary landfills designed to meet agency standards (Figure 6.175). We also assume that wetlands and/or floodplains will no longer be acceptable as sites for waste disposal.

GUIDELINE.   Sanitary Landfill Location

Locate solid waste disposal areas so as to prevent the pollution of coastal waters.

The town dump is being replaced by the sanitary landfill to solve both health and

Figure 6.174   Certain types of solid waste can be used to build offshore artificial fishing reefs and to serve other beneficial purposes. (Photo by Richard B. Stone, National Marine Fisheries Service.)

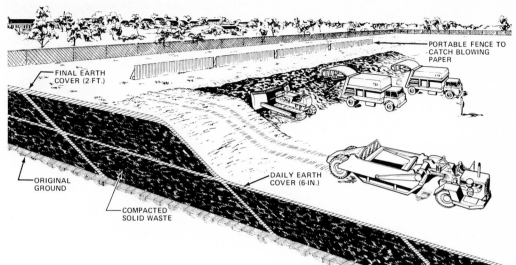

FINAL EARTH
COVER (2-FT.)

PORTABLE FENCE TO
CATCH BLOWING
PAPER

ORIGINAL
GROUND

DAILY EARTH
COVER (6-IN.)

COMPACTED
SOLID WASTE

Figure 6.175 Area method of landfill: the bulldozer spreads and compacts solid wastes; the scraper covers waste each day; the portable fence catches blowing debris. (SOURCE: Reference 5.)

environmental problems. However beneficial this trend may be, it is important to control the location of landfills and the way in which they are operated. Controls are needed mainly to solve two major problems associated with poorly planned coastal landfills—obliteration of vital habitat areas, and pollution of water.

The aim of solid waste disposal processes is to convert the waste to a less offensive form and to reduce its volume so that it can be disposed of more readily. Sanitary landfilling can increase the density of municipal refuse from about 7 to 20 cubic yards per ton (5.4 to 15.3 cubic meters).

According to the American Chemical Society report:[1]

Incineration can reduce the volume 80 to 85 percent if the refuse is uncompacted and about 95 percent if cans and similar material are compacted. In composting, the organic matter in the refuse is reduced about 40 percent in weight by biological degradation and marketed as compost. If the uncomposted residue is used in landfill, the process achieves an overall volume reduction similar to that of incineration.

In summary, the following procedures are useful in reducing the total volume of wastes and consequently the extent of landfill: (1) mechanical compaction of wastes, (2) incineration with control of air pollutants, (3) hauling to inland sites ($5 per ton or $5.50 per 1000 kilograms at distances less than 50 miles or 80 kilometers),[2] (4) reuse of economically recoverable wastes, and (5) reduction of sources of waste.

Implementation No. 1. Vital Area Protection in Solid Waste Disposal

Vital habitat areas should not be used as landfill sites.

The value and importance of vital habitat areas are discussed in many places throughout this book (page 95). To realize its best use, a vital habitat area must be allowed to exist in a state as near its natural one as possible and should be designated only for uses that depend on its natural qualities and at the same time preserve them (page 247). Sanitary landfills achieve neither of these goals. They pollute and unnecessarily pre-

Figure 6.176   Pollution of estuarine waters will occur when dump sites are located adjacent to surface water bodies. (Conservation Foundation photo by J. Chess.)

empt coastal vital habitat areas; wetland vital areas are particularly susceptible. To safeguard them and to protect adjacent water bodies from the polluting effects of solid waste disposal, refuse to be buried should be transported to landfills located inland above the floodplain.

The numerous existing dumps improperly located in vital areas, within floodplains, or at the water's edge (Figure 6.176) should be identified as nonconforming uses (page 247). Such nonconforming dumps should be removed with dragline or power shovel or sealed up and revegetated at the earliest opportunity. Remedial action is complete only after the area has been freed of pollution leaching, suitably revegetated, and

graded so that it can regain its marshland functions.[6]

Implementation No. 2. Soil and Water Constraints on Sanitary Landfills

Sanitary landfills should be located in areas of suitable water characteristics and soil permeability.

Typical components of solid wastes collected in urban communities are shown in Table 6.33. Groundwater or infiltrating surface water moving through these solid wastes produces a solution, called a "leachate," which contains dissolved and finely suspended solid matter and microbial waste

Table 6.33   Sample municipal refuse composition (United States east coast) (SOURCE: Reference 7)

Weight per cent

Physical		Rough Chemical	
Cardboard	7%	Moisture	28.0%
Newspaper	14	Carbon	25.0
Miscellaneous paper	25	Hydrogen	3.3
Plastic film	2	Oxygen	21.1
Leather, molded		Nitrogen	0.5
plastics, rubber	2	Sulfur	0.1
Garbage	12	Glass, ceramics, etc.	9.3
Grass and dirt	10	Metals	7.2
Textiles	3	Ash, other inserts	5.5
Wood	7		100.0
Glass, ceramics, stones	10		
Metallics	8		
Total	100		

products. The leachate may leave a landfill in the surface runoff water or percolate through the soil and rock underlying the landfill and enter the water table aquifer.[8] In either case, if leachate from a landfill is intermittently or continuously in contact with groundwater or surface-water sources, the water becomes polluted,[3] with potentially serious consequences for human health, general water quality, and coastal ecosystems (Figure 6.177). For example, recently landfill leachate has been identified as a major source of polychlorinated biphenyl (PCB) pollution of coastal waters: the non-biodegradable PCBs from discarded electrical transformers and capacitors enter natural food chains, causing a wide range of serious systematic disorders in animals and human beings.

Modern engineering requirements require

Figure 6.177   Leachates from improperly designed sanitary landfills pollute groundwaters and estuaries. (SOURCE: Reference 8.)

Table 6.34   Generalized analyses of various liquid wastes (in parts per million) (SOURCE: Reference 9)

Constituents	Landfill Leachate Less than 2 yrs old	6 yrs old	17 yrs old	Raw Sewage[1]	Slaughter-house[2] wastes
BOD*	54,610	14,080	225	104	3,700
COD†	39,680	8,000	40	246	8,620
Total Solids	19,144	6,794	1,198		2,690
Chloride	1,697	1,330	135		320
Sodium	900	810	74		
Iron	5,500	6.3	0.6	2.6	
Sulfate	680	2	2		370
Hardness	7,830	2,200	540		66
Misc. Heavy Metals	15.8	1.6	5.4	1.3	

[1]Data provided by the Metropolitan Sanitary District of Greater Chicago.
[2]Data from the files of the Illinois Department of Public Health.
*Biological oxygen demand.
†Chemical oxygen demand.

the control of leachate production and its movement away from the landfill site. This is accomplished by reducing the amount of surface water and groundwater entering the fill area to the minimum and controlling the leachate runoff from the fill. As shown in Table 6.34, the typical leachate contains greater concentrations of pollutants than either raw sewage or slaughterhouse wastes.

The movement of leachate from a waste disposal site is governed by the physical environment. When the wastes are deposited above the water table, both chemical and biological contaminants in the leachate move downward through the surficial soils (zone of aeration) at a rate dependent in part on the properties of the soils. The chemical contaminants, being in solution, generally tend to travel faster than suspended biological contaminants. Particulate biological contaminants are largely filtered from the percolating leachate. The chemical contaminants, however, may be carried rapidly by the leachate water to the hydraulics of the system. Thus the potential for water pollution depends on the mobility of the contaminant, its accessibility to the groundwater reservoir, and the hydraulic characteristics of that reservoir.[8]

In areas of high rainfall, the pollution potential from leachates is greater than in less humid areas. In semiarid areas there may be little or no risk of pollution because all water is either absorbed by the refuse or is

held as soil moisture and is ultimately evaporated. In areas of shallow water table, where refuse is in constant contact with the groundwater, leaching is a continual process, producing maximum potential for groundwater pollution.[8]

In summary, the water pollution potential of leachate varies with the characteristics of the leached refuse, the distance it travels to and with the groundwater, and the characteristics of the soil it passes through. All of these factors are site specific and should be considered together.

To avoid leachate pollution, the landfill should be located well above the groundwater table, where soils are of optimum permeability and texture. It is advisable to secure soil analyses and hydrological recommendations from the U.S. Geological Survey or Soil Conservation Service or from a state technical assistance agency.

At the minimum we recommend a distance of 10 feet (3 meters) between the lowest layer of deposited refuse and the seasonal high groundwater table,[10] to provide sufficient protection of groundwater quality. This distance will have to be increased even further when soil and refuse characteristics are inappropriate. To further safeguard against leachate infiltration of the groundwater, clay (or a suitable equivalent) should be used to seal the walls and bottom of the prepared fill site.[11]

In many cases poor landfill or dump siting

has created severe water pollution problems because refuse was deposited in the path of surface-water drainage flows. In existing situations of this type, mangement of surface-water flow is necessary to minimize runoff to and into the deposited waste by rerouting it around the landfill area.

Proper water management is effected by diverting surface water flow via channels, diversion ditches, culverts, grading, and other similar drainage techniques. A less desirable option, which is sometimes necessary, is to collect the leachate for treatment near its exit point from the landfill. When there is serious existing leakage of contaminant, the polluted groundwater to be treated should be intercepted as near the fill site as possible, before it causes widespread contamination of the aquifer and pollutes the surface bodies that it enters. Existing landfills with pollution problems that are not correctable in any practical sense should be identified as nonconforming uses (see page 000) and either removed or sealed up and properly revegetated at the earliest opportunity.

In summary, landfill sites should always be out of the path of natural drainageways, above the lower coastal floodplain (above the 10-year flood level), and away from surface water bodies. We recommend a minimum distance of 1000 feet (300 meters) from surface water and 1 mile (1.6 kilometers) from municipal wells.[10]

REFERENCES

1. American Chemical Society. 1969. *Cleaning Our Environment: The Chemical Basis for Action.* Report by the Subcommittee on Environmental Improvement, Committee on Chemistry and Public Affairs, Washington, D.C.

2. U.S. Environmental Protection Agency. 1971. *Recommended Standards for Sanitary Landfill Design, Construction, and Evaluation, and Model Sanitary Landfill Operation Agreement.* National Solid Waste Management Program, Washington, D.C.

3. American Chemical Society 1972. *Sanitary Landfill: Alternative to the Open Dump.* Reprinted from *Environmental Science and Technology,* Washington, D.C.

4. U.S. Congress. Marine Protection, Research and Sanctuaries Act of 1972. Public Law 92-532: 86 STAT 1052, Oct. 23, 1972.

5. Thomas J. Sorg and H. Lanier Hickman, Jr. 1970. *Sanitary Landfill Facts.* U.S. Department of Health, Education, and Welfare, Public Health Service, Bureau of Solid Waste Management, Superintendent of Documents, U.S. Government Printing Office, Washington, D.C.

6. Dirk R. Brunner, S. Jackson Hubbard, Daniel J. Keller, and James L. Newton. 1971. *Closing Open Dumps.* U.S. Environmental Protection Agency, Solid Waste Management Office, Washington, D.C.

7. E. R. Kaiser, 1967. "Refuse reduction processes." In *Proceedings of the Surgeon General's Conference on Solid Waste Management for Metropolitan Washington.* U.S. Public Health Service Publication No. 1729, Superintendent of Documents, U.S. Government Printing Office, Washington, D.C.

8. William J. Schneider. 1970. *Hydrologic Implications of Solid Waste Disposal.* U.S. Geological Survey, Geological Survey Circular No. 601-F, Washington, D.C.

9. George M. Hughes and Ken Cartwright. 1972. *Scientific and Administrative Criteria for Shallow Waste Disposal.* Reprint from *Civil Engineering-ASCE,* Vol. 42, No. 3.

10. E. J. Wingerter. 1972. *Sanitary Landfill—A Survey of State Land Disposal Regulations.* National Solid Wastes Management Association, Technical Bulletin, Vol. 3, No. 3. Washington, D.C.

11. U.S. Environmental Protection Agency. 1973. *Processes, Procedures and Methods to Control Water Pollution from Subsurface Excavations* (draft). Office of Water Program Operations, Water Quality and Non-Point Source Control Division, Washington, D.C.

23. TRACT AND SITE PREPARATION

A program for the protection of coastal resources and ecosystems must provide controls on alterations of the land surface, particularly those related to development site preparation. These controls may often require an adjustment of customary practices of residential development.

Coastal ecosystems extend landward to include the watersheds of the freshwater systems that flow into coastal basins. The natural storage-and-release mechanisms of these watersheds absorb the heavy seasonal rains and slowly release the accumulated water through inland wetlands drainageways and salt marshes, and ultimately into the open waters of the estuaries. Each section of the system filters the water in transit physically and chemically, removing sediments and assimilating nutrients. Finally the watershed releases fresh water into the estuary at a modulated rate that avoids the stress of rapid salinity change. Thus, in its unaltered state, the storage-and-release system is self-sustaining, providing for a cleansing of the water, a beneficial flow regime, and a suitable natural supply of nutrients into the rich estuarine zone.

Site preparation for development and construction in coastal watershed areas requires some degree of land clearing, grading, surfacing, or similar land alteration. These processes remove natural ground vegetation and expose soils to the erosional forces of wind and water. The unprotected soils are eroded and washed into tributaries or directly into coastal waters, where they degrade water quality and interfere with normal biological processes. Not only are water basins impacted with sediment but also water transparency is decreased, blocking light penetration and inhibiting the growth of algae and bottom plants.

Customary site preparation processes have frequently altered existing water and drainage systems adversely by filling in or draining marshes, bogs, and swamps, and by diverting, obliterating or channelizing natural drainageways. Site grading often disrupts the flow systems of small subwatersheds which can then no longer detain runoff before it enters coastal waters or tributaries and remove sediments and otherwise purify it (Figure 6.178).

In general, shoreland developments should be regulated so that the amount of imper-

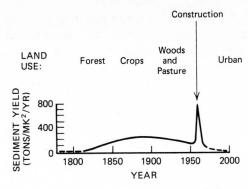

Figure 6.178 Schematic representation of changes in sediment yield accompanying changes in land use in a fixed area of the Maryland piedmont. (SOURCE: A. Wolman, Chesapeake Bay Institute.)

vious surface is minimized and barren soils are rapidly stabilized. Finished grades should be designed to direct water flows along natural drainage courses and through natural terrain, where the vegetation can cleanse runoff waters. The appropriate local authority should prevent any significant alteration of the terrain or its wetlands.

GUIDELINE. Erosion Control on Construction Sites

Exercise strict controls on erosion during site preparation and construction.

The following discussion of erosion controls and land drainage assumes that the construction site has already been properly selected to avoid vital areas, floodprone areas, steep slopes, and similar ecologically hazardous sites, that if modified, could adversely affect coastal ecosystems. It also assumes that local soil and groundwater conditions and other limitations have been examined.

Runoff flow from construction sites often carries sediments, toxic materials, nutrients, coliform bacteria, and other undesirable matter in quantities that will pollute the coastal waters it enters (page 546). This flow should be managed with appropriate erosion controls and land drainage techniques in order to protect coastal ecosystems from harmful pollutants. Construction sites have a higher potential yield of sedient runoff from erosion than sites involved in any other major land activity, as shown in the following representative data:[2]

Activity or Use	Sediment Produced (tons/sq mi/yr)
Construction	48,000
Cropland	4,800
Grassland	240
Forest	24
Disturbed forest (not clear-cut)	24,000
Active surface mines	24,000
Abandoned mines	2,400

Techniques for erosion and sediment control can be divided into three functional types: (1) trapping of eroding sediments with vegetated buffer strips and sediment detention ponds; (2) diversion of runoff away from likely erosion areas through grading, diversion cuts, and lined channels; and (3) prevention of soil movement and erosion, including the use of such methods as reseeding, mulching, and the placement of netting over exposed soils. The Maine shoreland guidelines require diversions, silting basins, terraces, and other methods to trap sediments in order to control sedimentation from filling, grading, lagooning, or dredging in coastal watersheds.[3]

Frequently, site preparation for large housing developments and industrial parks involves the clearing of unnecessarily large amounts of land. A useful erosion control method is to remove a minimum of existing vegetation, as suggested in the Maine guidelines.[3]

Implementation No. 1.   Detention Basins and Buffer Strips

Buffer strips of natural vegetation and artificial detention systems should be used to control erosion.

Vegetated buffer strips and artificial control systems such as sediment basins can provide sound erosion control for on-going construction operations. They can also be used successfully after construction if other soil stabilization techniques fail to provide adequate erosion control. (Figure 6.179).

Vegetated buffer strips should be planned for all watercourses and shorelines in order to trap sediment and other pollutants. They should be incorporated into the development plan and remain unaltered after construction is complete. Their width should be determined according to the slope of the land, the severity of the erosion problem, and the existing vegetation type (page 304).

Sediment basins (Figure 6.180) detain runoff and trap sediment, thus preventing increased turbidities in adjacent water bodies. They should usually be considered as temporary structures.[5, 6]

Care must be taken with water pumped from pits to facilitate excavation. For example, a tract of about 70 acres of tidal mangroves (Sanibel, Florida) was killed by flooding during the dewatering of an adjacent area in a dredge-and-fill project because it was closed off by a roadway and could not drain properly. Although larger culverts were installed under the roadway after the kill and 40 acres were replanted with mangrove seeds in a restoration attempt, most of the tract remained effectively dead and deprived of adequate tidal circulation several years later, with minimal chances for return to good function (Figure 6.181).

Implementation No. 2.   Runoff Diversions in Site Preparation

Construct runoff diversions in conjunction with sediment removal methods to minimize the extent to which exposed soils are eroded.

A useful method of erosion control is diversion or channeling of runoff away from exposed soils. Small parallel diversions or troughs can be cut across long slopes to

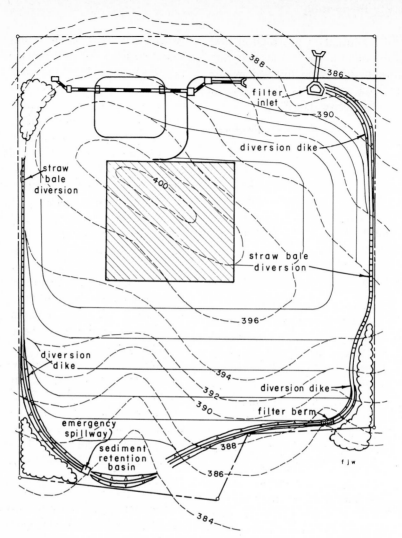

Figure 6.179   A sample sediment and erosion control plan. (SOURCE: Reference 4.)

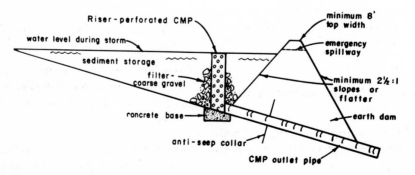

Figure 6.180   Temporary retention (detention, sediment) basins prevent serious water pollution from eroded soil. (SOURCE: Reference 4.)

536

Figure 6.181 A 70-acre coastal mangroves wetlands tract (above and right of cleared area) killed by flooding with fresh water from dewatering excavations (Sanibel Island, Florida). (Photo by author.)

intercept the downward flow of water. Bench terraces can also be constructed across a slope to achieve the same purpose on steeper grades. These diversions can divert water either into sediment basins or into vegetated buffer strips, where any accumulated sediments can be removed.

Grassed waterways (swales) can also be used effectively in certain situations. Such channels can be most effective in removing moderate amounts of sediment. In addition, grass protects the channel against erosion by reducing the velocity of the water at the soil surface. The most suitable grasses to use are those that produce a dense uniform cover near the soil surface, are long lived, provide protection during all seasons of the year, and are able to withstand the impact of sediments (Table 6.35).

Implementation No. 3. Soil Stabilization

Ground surfaces should be stabilized immediately after any action that destroys the natural vegetational cover and leaves soils exposed to erosion forces.

Once site alteration has commenced, im-

mediate steps should be taken to stabilize barren soils. Many state and local development regulations require immediate restabilization of cleared areas. Three common methods used are revegetation, mulching, and sodding (Figure 6.182).

Plant cover is easy to establish and maintain in locations that have fertile soils and moderate slopes (not exceeding 33 percent, a slope of 3 : 1). If construction is delayed on a site that has been cleared and graded, temporary cover crops can be used to protect the site against erosion; rapidly growing plants, such as small grains and grasses, are best.[6]

Immediate mulching and reseeding of bare earth can eliminate significant soil loss (Table 6.36). Generally mulch is applied at rates of 1 to 2 tons per acre.[5] Jute netting can be applied to soils to protect newly seeded areas until vegetation becomes established. Alternatively, it can be used to hold down mulch and repair diversions and outlets where gullies have cut channels; cotton or paper netting can also be used.[6] Jute netting is particularly well suited, however, as it can withstand the higher flow velocities

Table 6.35 Relations between types of vegetation and permissible channel velocities for vegetated runoff channels. (SOURCE: *Reference* 6)

| Cover | Slope Range (Percent) | Permissible Velocity[1] | |
		Erosion Resistant Soils (fps)	Easily Eroded Soils (fps)
Reed canarygrass	0-5	7	5
Tall fescue	5-10	6	4
Kentucky bluegrass	Over 10	5	3
Grass-legume mixtures[2]	0-5	5	4
	5-10	4	3
Red fescue	.0-5[3]	3.5	2.5
Annuals[4] Sudangrass, small grain (rye, oats, barley)	.0-5	3.5	2.5

[1]Velocities may exceed five (5) feet per second only where good vegetative cover and proper maintenance can be obtained.

[2]Do not use on slopes steeper than 10 percent, except for side slopes in a combination channel.

[3]Do not use on slopes steeper than five percent, except for side slopes in a combination channel.

[4]Annuals -- Use as temporary protection until permanent covers are established.

associated with ditches, steep slopes, and similar areas where the establishment of vegetation is difficult.[5]

GUIDELINE. Preservation of Natural Drainage

Preserve wetlands and other components of the natural drainage system of the area under development.

In planning a site for development it is necessary to preserve existing components of the natural water system. Many communities realize the need for controls on site preparation and require strict erosion controls aimed at protecting vital areas and preventing siltation of streams and water basins. Yet the need for specific regulations to protect the natural water system is often not appreciated. Performance standards for site prepa-

ration should include measures to protect wet areas from being drained or otherwise altered.

Drainage of wetlands and other vital habitat areas should be prohibited (page 247). Nor should areas that are regularly flooded or have permanent or periodic high water tables be drained. Drainage of such upland areas for agriculture, homes, or commercial sites is potentially damaging to coastal ecosystems by reducing the capability of the land to retain, purify, and gradually release floodwater (page 85).

During planning it should be recognized that on-site detention of stormwater is a necessary ecologic safeguard for all residential and commercial developments. Retention can be accomplished by installing either detention ponds or infiltration enhancement devices such as "French drains" (page 551). Nonpermeable surfacing should

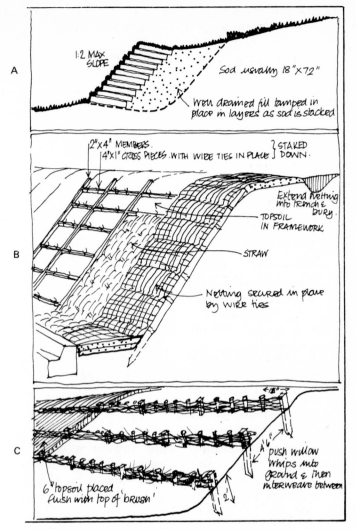

Figure 6.182   Three techniques for protecting a steep slope from soil erosion: (1) sod, (2) straw mulch and netting supported by a timber frame, (3) willow whips woven between stakes. (SOURCE: Reference 7.)

be kept to a minimum, and casual (unsurfaced) roads should be required to the maximum extent possible. For example, blacktop parking lots and hard-surfaced roads and driveways adjacent to water bodies should be discouraged in favor of any of a wide variety of available permeable surface materials (page 548). To provide sufficient filtration and purification of runoff water from developed areas, a buffer strip of natu-

ral soil and vegetation must be required around all open-water areas (page 239).

Implementation No. 1.   Restriction on Land Drainage

Drainage of high-water-table areas should be discouraged.

In shoreland areas with high water tables, excavation should be limited to borrow pits

Table 6.36 Effectiveness of planting and mulching for soil erosion control during site preparation (Fairfax County, Virginia) (SOURCE: Reference 8)

KINDS OF GROUND COVER	SOIL LOSS REDUCTION RELATED TO BARE SURFACES (percent)
Vegetative Stabilization*	
Permanent grasses	99
Ryegrass (Perennial)	95
Ryegrass (Annual)	90
Small Grain	95
Millet & Sudangrass	95
Field Bromegrass	97
Grass Sod	99
Non-Vegetative Stabilization	
Hay (4485 kg/ha; 2 tons/acre)	98
Small Grain Straw (4485 kg/ha; 2 tons/acre)	98
Corn Residues (8970 kg/ha; 4 tons/acre)	98
Wood Chips (13,455 kg/ha: 6 tons/acre)	94

* Based on fully established stand

or ponds, artificial lakes, or other containment works specifically designed to preserve the natural water system. Such artificial basins should be shallow and have gently sloping sides (not steeper than 6 : 1). Water quality degradation in these man-made lakes can increase over time, often accelerating as adjacent lots are occupied. The lakes gradually accumulate pollutants and sediments and can become grossly polluted if not properly design and maintained (Figure 6.183).

Lakes should be deep enough to provide at least 4 feet of water at the lowest water stage. This will ensure that rooted aquatics such as cattails do not take over. Lakes should be shallow enough, however, to permit the maintenance of acceptable water quality through wind turnover. This generally means that they should be no deeper than 7 or 8 feet below seasonal high water (Florida conditions). At greater depths wind turnover is unlikely to prevent an accumulation of polluting substances in the deeper water at the bottom, which degrade water quality below federal standards (e.g., less than 4.0 ppm dissolved oxygen normally violates federal standards).

All artificial basins should be surrounded by a buffer strip of vegetation for restoration of runoff water quality; the width should be not less than 50 feet (15.2 meters) normally, but where soil and vegetation conditions are unfavorable or fertilizer use is heavy, a buffer of up to 150 feet (45.7 meters) of water may be necessary. Furthermore the edge configuration of lakes should provide for acceptable wildlife habitat without an overgrowth of cattails.

In southern Florida, where much of the land either has seasonally high water tables or virtually becomes wetland during flooding, high-density clusters on fill islands with

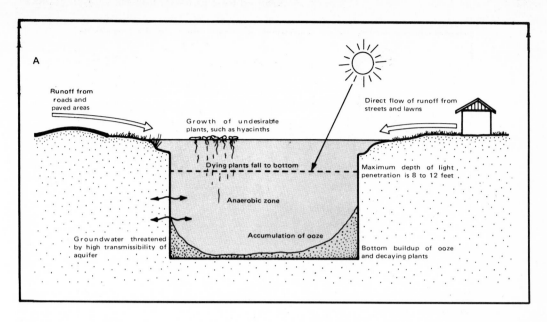

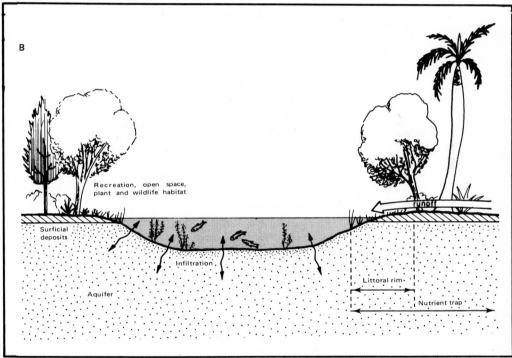

Figure 6.183 (A) Improperly designed artificial lakes and borrow pits become polluted in a few years; light cannot penetrate to the bottom, resulting in an anaerobic zone of accumulated ooze where oxygen falls to substandard levels. (B) Lakes created by properly designed shallow borrow pits can function as natural systems. Depth is limited so that the optimum amount of light can penetrate to encourage bottom vegetation. (SOURCE: Reference 9.)

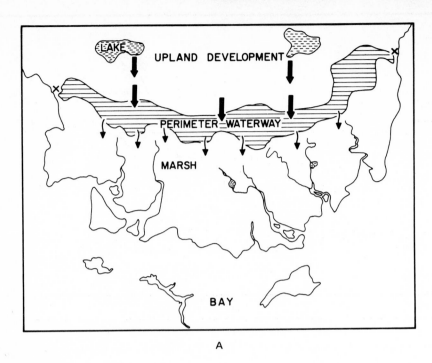

A

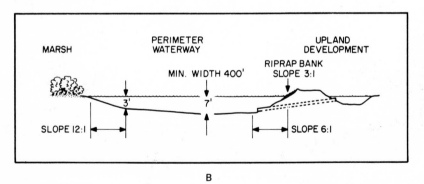

B

Figure 6.184   The perimeter, or interceptor, waterway concept. The purpose is to provide a source of land-fill and a method for detention and redistribution of runoff water into coastal marshes: (A) plan view, (B) cross section. (SOURCE: Adapted from Reference 11.)

central runoff purification ponds (made from construction borrow pits) may be an alternative to artificial land drainage through grids of canals. Such drainage canals lower the water table generally, whereas cluster islands disturb only a small area.[9] Another concept is the perimeter, or interceptor, waterway (Figure 6.184), basically a borrow

pit designed to become a canal that detains and purifies upland runoff before it discharges to coastal waters.[11] This idea has merit if no vital habitat area such as wetlands are preempted and if the water quality of the waterway can be maintained on a long-term basis. It is essential that such waterways be placed behind the 1-year flood level, which marks the inner edge of the coastal wetlands.

In many coastal areas massive amounts of land have been drained in past years, and high priority should be given to remedying this damage through restoration programs. In general, all existing artificial land drainage facilities should be redesigned to closely approximate the natural system of water drainage and to maintain the water table as close to its historic level as possible. This can be done through partial or complete refilling of canal sections, installing elevated sills or weirs (page 202), and redesigning the edge configuration.

Implementation No. 2.   Use of Private Wetlands

Wetlands should be allocated for purposes that require only light-duty structures.

Wetlands simply do not have the carrying capacity that land areas have for supporting commercial and industrial activities or urban occupany (page 247). Controls for wetlands should be developed that will allow the widest variety possible of environmentally compatible uses. A few simple standards should serve to adequately control development in privately owned wetlands.

Excavation, grading, and filling should be prohibited in wetlands for any purpose other than the installation of pile supports for permitted elevated structures. As explained in detail in various other sections of this book, the greatest damage to wetlands occurs with excavation, grading, and filling. Prohibition of these activities is the most important aspect of the controls on site preparation in water areas that we have recommended.

It should be the public policy of each coastal community to ensure that wetlands remain functionally intact. This applies to the inland swamps, bogs, and drainage courses of coastal watersheds as well as to salt marshes and mangrove forests—all are vital habitat areas of the coastal zone (Figure 6.185). Whatever use is made of privately owned wetlands, they should not be

Figure 6.185   All freshwater and saltwater marshes are essential ecological units and should be exempt from alteration of any kind (Charleston, South Carolina). (Conservation Foundation photo by M. Fahay.)

altered in ways that will degrade their natural function. The following constraints are necessary to carry out the policy:

1. As a general rule, there should be no excavation in wetlands because the wetland function would be completely disrupted; vegetation would be obliterated, water flow disrupted, soil layers destroyed, pollutable catchments formed, and drainage and drying out of wetlands facilitated. Accordingly, excavation should take place only when required for essential public purposes (e.g., mosquito control, wildlife enhancement) and should be limited to a small percentage (perhaps 10 percent) of the area.

2. There should generally be no filling of wetlands. The soil cover would physically obliterate the wetlands, change elevation, alter the water regime, and generally disrupt their function as completely as would excavation of them.

3. There should generally be no land clearing, grading, or removal of natural vege-vegetation, since vegetation is a most important element of wetlands function. An exception may be made, however, to permit needed control and removal of invader plants (page 209).

4. As a rule, discharge or release of pollutants into the wetlands should be prevented. There may, however, be some capacity for the wetlands to absorb certain storm runoff pollutants and thereby to function as a "land treatment" system. Any such pollutants should not exceed the calculated receiving capacity of the system and should not degrade surface water or groundwater below allowable standards.

5. There should generally be no solid-fill roads or other structures in wetlands because they obstruct water flow. Also, fill for any such structures must normally be obtained by excavation, which is itself damaging. Unavoidable roadways through wetlands or over wetland swales should

be elevated on pilings rather than placed on fill (page 493).

As the above constraints suggest, the natural characteristics of wetlands are such that preservation of their functional integrity precludes virtually any development within them. Any use of these wetlands should accordingly be oriented toward recreational purposes that would be enhanced by the installation of light-duty, elevated (pile-supported) structures such as boathouses, boat shelters, fences, duck blinds, footbridges, observation decks, and similar nonenclosed recreational and access structures, none of which should be designed for permanent occupancy. If properly controlled, these should not have a major detrimental effect on water systems and estuarine resources. Nevertheless, even these should be designed and built to cause minimum impact from shading, water flow interruption, site disruption, and so forth. They should be elevated above the 5-year flood mark and should have very low ground coverage (perhaps about 0.5 percent). Any area disrupted for the installation of facilities should be fully restored to its natural condition of grade, vegetative associations, and soils immediately after project completion.

Crossing water areas during construction with heavy grading and construction equipment should be permitted only when there is no alternative. When crossing is unavoidable, culverts and bridges should be used to minimize degradation of the water system.

REFERENCES

1. Robert H. Meade. 1969. "Errors in using modern stream-load data to estimate natural rates of denudation." *Geological Society of America Bulletin*, Vol. 80.

2. Midwest Research Institute. 1973. *Methods for Identifying and Evaluating the Nature and Extent of Non-point Sources of Pollutants*. EPA Con. No. 68-01-1839.

3. University of Maine. 1972. *Interim Guidelines*

for *Shoreland Zoning and Subdivision Control.* Shoreland Zoning Project, Assisted by Department of Environmental Protection and State Planning Office, Augusta, Maine.

4. U.S. Department of Agriculture. 1975. *Guidelines for Soil and Water Conservation in Urbanizing Areas of Massachusetts.* Soil Conservation Service, Amherst, Massachusetts.

5. U.S. Environmental Protection Agency. 1973. *Comparative Costs of Erosion and Sediment Control, Construction Activities.* Office of Water Program Operations, Report No. EPA-430/9-73-016, Superintendent of Documents, U.S. Government Printing Office, Washington, D.C.

6. U.S. Department of Agriculture. 1972. *Minimizing Erosion in Urbanizing Areas: Guidelines, Standards and Specifications.* Soil Conservation Service, Madison, Wisconsin.

7. J. Tourbier and R. Westmacott. 1974. *Water Resources Protection Measures in Land Development—A Handbook: Water Resources as a Basis for Comprehensive Planning and Development of The Christina River Basin.* A Prototype Project, Phase II. Water Resources Center, University of Delaware, Newark, Delaware.

8. U.S. Environmental Protection Agency. 1973. *Processes, Procedures, and Methods to Control Pollution Resulting from all Construction Activity.* Office of Air and Water Programs, Report No. EPA-430/9-73-007, Superintendent of Documents, U.S. Government Printing Office, Washington, D.C.

9. Albert R. Veri et al. 1975. *Environmental Quality by Design: South Florida.* University of Miami Press, Coral Gables, Florida.

10. John Clark. 1974. *Rookery Bay: Ecological Constraints on Coastal Development.* Final Report, Rookery Bay Land Use Studies. The Conservation Foundation, Washington, D.C.

11. Durbin C. Tabb and Eric J. Heald. 1973. *The Coastal Interceptor Waterway.* University of Miami Sea Grant Program, Sea Grant Coastal Zone Management Bulletin No. 4, Miami, Florida.

12. Durbin C. Tabb, Eric J. Heald, and R. G. Rehrer. 1973. *Innovations in Coastal Management.* University of Miami, Coral Gables, Florida.

24. URBAN RUNOFF

An acre of land in the United States receives, on average, about 1 million gallons of precipitation each year. Around one-third of this is given off to the atmosphere in evaporation and transpiration; the remainder eventually finds its way to a watercourse and thence to the sea. Coastal waters are strongly influenced by this runoff and by its content and rate of discharge.

In a developed, or developing, area the amount of runoff increases proportionately with the extent of impervious surfaces and rooftops (Figure 6.186). In heavily urbanized areas (e.g., Philadelphia), as much as 55 percent of the total rainfall may leave as

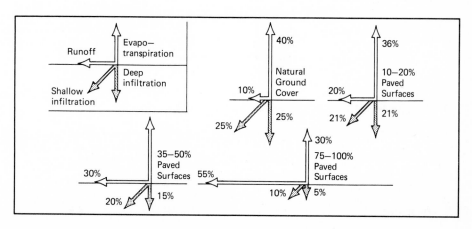

Figure 6.186 Typical hydrograph changes due to increasing the area of impermeable paved surfaces (roofs, etc.) in a developing area. (SOURCE: Reference 1.)

runoff, while only 15 percent filters into the soil, and 30 percent evaporates or is transpired by plants.[1] This increase in runoff frequently will raise the historical peak flood levels of a river basin.

Runoff from urbanized areas has the potential for serious adverse effects on the quality of coastal waters. Urban runoff may have higher chemical and biochemical oxygen demands (COD and BOD) and greater concentrations of various pollutants than domestic sewage[2-4] (Table 6.37). Sources of contamination include street litter, household refuse, automobile drippings, pet wastes, spillage from bulk chemical storage, and exposed dirt piles at construction sites (Table 6.38).

Shellfish beds adjacent to urban areas are inevitably closed by public health officials because of high levels of coliform bacteria introduced into coastal waters by runoff and sewage effluent. Runoff alone is often severe enough to drive the coliform count above the national health standard of 70 MPN (most probable number per 100 milliliters of sample water). For example, on Long Island, New York, local officials are gradually realizing that, despite plans for a billion-dollar sewage treatment plant, productive shellfish beds will remain closed because of bacterial contamination from urban runoff.[5]

Historically, rainfall in urbanized areas has been considered a nuisance, and the resulting runoff removed as quickly as possible. In the coastal zone, standard practice has been to pipe runoff directly into surface waters with little or no treatment. Natural subsurface purification is therefore bypassed by channeling contaminants directly into the estuary.

In the natural system, water passes over vegetated land as overland flow or through the soil in the groundwater. Pollutants are removed biologically by microorganisms or plants; physically by filtration, absorption, or deposition; and chemically by oxidation and other reactions. Purification continues in streams and drainageways by the same processes. Natural watercourses tend to meander through coastal watersheds and floodplains, thus slowing the passage of water to the sea and allowing greater oppor-

Table 6.37   Calculated quantities of pollutants that would enter receiving waters (hypothetical city: streets = 4000 curb-miles, cleaned each 5 days; population = 100,000; area = 14,000 acres, 75 percent residential, 5 percent commercial, 20 percent industrial; sewage = 12 million gpd) (SOURCE: Reference 3)

	STREET SURFACE RUNOFF (following 1 hr storm) (lb/hr)	RAW SANITARY SEWAGE (lb/hr)	SECONDARY PLANT EFFLUENT (lb/hr)
Settleable plus Suspended Solids	560,000	1,300	130
BOD$_5$	5,600	1,100	110
COD	13,000	1,200	120
Kjeldahl nitrogen	800	210	20
Phosphates	440	50	2.5
Total cell form bacteria (org/hr)	4000×10^{10}	$460,000 \times 10^{10}$	4.6×10^{10}

Table 6.38   Sources of pollutants in urban runoff (SOURCE: Reference 4)

Dustfall and rainfall	Suspended solids (particulates), nitrogen, sulfur, acid, pesticides
Vegetation	Oxygen-demanding substances, nutrients
Animal droppings	Bacteria, oxygen demanding substances
Fertilizer usage	Nutrients
Pesticide usage	Pesticides
Erosion at construction sites and other pervious areas, and in drainage channels	Suspended solids
Motor vehicles	Suspended solids, lead, oil and grease
Snow and ice removal	Dissolved solids, chloride, suspended solids, toxic compounds (e.g., sodium ferrocyanide)
Weathering of paving materials	Suspended solids

tunity for natural purification. Meandering watercourses are also conducive to streamside vegetation, which aids greatly in purification.

Unless there is evidence to the contrary, any change in the natural pattern of land drainage should be presumed to have adverse effects on water quality. Such changes include filling or devegetation of drainageways, alteration of natural land grades, straightening or channelization of watercourses, land clearing, and land surfacing (page 85). Therefore shoreland management should respect the principle of retaining the system of land drainage in as nearly the natural pattern as possible (page 85). The goal in the management of urban runoff should be restoration of the water cycle to the preexisting state so that water leaves an altered area in virtually the same quantity, and rate of flow.

GUIDELINE. Impervious Surface Constraints

Limit impervious surfacing to the minimum possible.

Paved surfaces should be reduced to the minimum in coastal areas. When impervious paving cannot be avoided, natural drainage should be protected and storm runoff quickly incorporated back into the natural system.

Paved surfaces often channel off stormwater runoff, intercepting downhill drainage and bypassing the natural purification system of soil and vegetation. Seepage into subsurface aquifers is blocked, and rainfall moves directly into surface waters. Among the continuing effects of paved surfaces are (1) sedimentation, resulting from the erosion of soil by runoff from impermeable surfaces; (2) reduction in groundwater recharge due to increased impermeable surface area

Figure 6.187 Uncontrolled storm runoff from commercial parking lots is a major source of pollution in adjacent streams of coastal watersheds (Monmouth County, New Jersey). (Photo by author.)

and channelization of runoff; and (3) addition of pollutants such as lead, zinc, and oil to coastal waters (Figure 6.187).

In response to the national effort to control water pollution much attention is being given to the control of stormwater runoff and to new methodology combining engineering and land-use allocation. One such control technique, permeable surfacing, will be of use in suburban developments, second-home developments, and recreational areas.

In suburban development permeable surfaces often can be used successfully for driveways, sidewalks, play areas, patios, and certain neighborhood roads. In second-home developments the use of such surfaces is appropriate throughout the community because of mild weather during use periods and generally lighter traffic. Moreover, the cost to the community of an expensive storm sewer system can be eliminated. The ecologic benefits are particularly important for recreational home developments and seasonal facilities, such as beach areas and marinas, which are adjacent to the shoreline, where the risks from runoff pollution may be highest.

Implementation No. 1. Permeable Surfaces

Development should be planned to utilize permeable surfaces wherever feasible.

Because of the high water pollution potential from runoff of impermeable surfaces such as concrete and asphalt, these paving surfaces should be employed only when expected heavy-duty use requires them. Arterial roads with heavy automobile and truck traffic will probably require traditional paving materials. However, secondary roads, parking lots, and sidewalks that are used only seasonally can utilize permeable surfacing. For example, shopping center parking lots in some beach resorts can be paved with gravel or other porous materials, with only the entrances, exits, and loading area built of asphalt or concrete.

A variety of alternative paving techniques and materials is available. Some of these are of proved effectiveness, whereas others are still in development and have yet to be fully tested. There will be some applications in which construction costs can be reduced over those for the traditional paving approach. In other cases the total dollar costs, including maintenance, may be higher, but environmental costs will be sufficiently reduced to make the trade-off worthwhile.

Gravel, crushed rock, or crushed shell is the simplest form of permeable paving.[1] It is inexpensive, widely used, and acceptable for driveways and many other surfacing needs. Gravel can be used throughout the coastal watershed for parking lots, driveways, and secondary roads. Crushed stone, because its shape and larger size limit compaction, may be suitable in soft muddy areas or on sites prone to erosion or high water flows.

There are other suitable paving materials made of concrete, brick, and metal. Examples range from lattice concrete blocks to standard paving bricks with corner lags to control spacing to perforated bricks.[1] Porosity varies with the subsoil and the amount and type of subsurface gravel. Lightly used roads and driveways can be stabilized by utilizing buried porous paving slabs instead of standard asphalt or cement.

Porous asphalt must be considered experimental. Research has shown "porous asphaltic concrete containing 55 percent asphalt by weight and aggregate graded to allow water flow of 76 inches (193 centimeters) per hour to be optimal porous road material."[1] But plugging of the pores of the surfacing by dirt particles and ice is a major drawback. Therefore large-scale use of porous asphalt cannot be recommended until the product is further developed. For diagrams and technical information on permeable paving materials see Appendix, page 863.

GUIDELINE.   Natural Simulation

Design storm drainage projects to simulate the natural pattern as nearly as possible and to reduce the need for storm sewer systems.

The typical storm drainage system is designed to short-circuit the natural process. Runoff water is diverted to street drains, then to collection pipes and trunks, and fi-

nally to outlets that discharge into the nearest watercourse. Alternatively, the system is combined with the sewers, and stormwater is carried to the sewage treatment plant. Chemical or mechanical treatment of stormwater is often prohibitively expensive. Also, treatment plants rarely can handle the runoff from severe storms and are forced to release untreated overflow water. In both storm sewer systems and treatment plants, all possibility for purification and detention of stormwater by natural processes is removed. Natural purification by vegetation and soils is more efficient and far less expensive than these artificial measures.

For protection of coastal waters the best stormwater system is one that most nearly simulates the natural system, that is, one that has features to detain storm runoff and to provide the maximum of infiltration for natural purification. The ideal would be to preserve and utilize existing natural drainageways—creeks, sloughs, swales, and so forth.

The Soil Conservation Service has summarized some of the many techniques available for controlling runoff and thus simulating the natural rate of release (Table 6.39). Although many of these techniques may be unsuitable for wide application because they are experimental or do not fit local circumstances, they suggest the variety of alternative solutions available. The use of self-contained soil infiltration systems appears particularly promising for individual units in new developments (page 551). Also, vegetated depressions and drainageways appear to constitute practicable and inexpensive solutions for small or individual units. For large communities detention basins are appropriate (page 552).

Implementation No. 1.   Natural Restoration of Runoff Flow

Stormwater runoff should be diverted and dispersed into areas of natural vegetation and soils wherever feasible.

Thoughtful control of runoff should be prac-

Table 6.39 Measures for reducing and delaying urban storm runoff (SOURCE: Reference 6)

Area	Reducing Runoff	Delaying Runoff

Large flat roof	1. Cistern storage
	2. Rooftop gardens
	3. Pool or fountain storage
	4. Sod roof cover
		1. Ponding on roof by constricted down-spouts
		2. Increasing roof roughness
		   a. Rippled roof
		   b. Graveled roof

Parking lots	1. Porous pavement
	   a. Gravel parking lots
	   b. Porous or punctured asphalt
	2. Gravel beds or cisterns beneath parking lots in high-value areas
	3. Vegetated ponding areas around parking lots
	4. Gravel trenches
		1. Grassy strips on parking lots
		2. Grassed waterways draining parking lot
		3. Ponding and detention measures for impervious areas
		   a. Rippled pavement
		   b. Depressions
		   c. Basins

Residential	1. Cisterns for individual homes or groups of homes
	2. Gravel driveways (porous)
	3. Contoured landscape
	4. Groundwater recharge
	   a. Perforated pipe
	   b. Gravel (sand)
	   c. Trench
	   d. Porous pipe
	   e. Dry wells
	5. Vegetated depressions
		1. Reservoir or detention basin
		2. Planting a high delaying grass (high roughness)
		3. Gravel driveways
		4. Grassy gutters or channels
		5. Increased length of travel of runoff by means of gutters, diversions, etc.

General	1. Gravel alleys 2. Porous sidewalks 3. Mulched planters	1. Gravel alleys

ticed in coastal communities. Runoff should be restored as nearly as possible to the preexisting, natural pattern of quality, volume, and rate of flow. A useful approach is to arrange to collect and detain stormwater and to release it at the predevelopment rate of flow onto vegetated land of sufficient capacity to assimilate pollutants and restore water quality (page 85). Land preparation for developments would include grading requirements to enhance natural-type flow.

Runoff waters from developed areas should be diverted through vegetated areas into natural drainageways. The natural system will function very effectively and be virtually cost free in a coastal community set back from the water's edge by a buffer area, which will serve as a filter and runoff purifier between the community and the coastal waters. Such a system will function without a stormwater treatment facility in a coastal community of moderate density if it is included in the original planning.[7] In densely developed communities it will be necessary to incorporate impoundments or ponding areas into the system to make up for the reduction in natural storage capacity caused by devegetation, paving, and buildings.[8]

Communities that are already in advanced stages of development may find a partial solution in diverting storm runoff through remaining natural areas of appropriate slope and soil type, where purification will occur. If the appropriate natural conditions do not prevail, it is possible to design and construct a sloped and vegetated surface for efficient land treatment (page 847).[9]

There are many design techniques for returning rainfall to the soil, based on collection of water and seepage through gravel into the groundwater. In coastal areas it has become customary to require that stormwater be detained and pretreated, that is, within the project boundaries.

Runoff can be held on-site in any combination of the following:

1. Gravel-filled channels.
2. Gravel-filled seepage pits.
3. Runoff retention ponds.

At minimum, the capacity of the system should equal the anticipated rainfall from the most severe storm that can reasonably be expected in a 10-year period (standard urban storm drainage systems are often designed to handle a 25-year storm).

Seepage beds, often called "Dutch drains," are gravel-filled ditches that dispose of stormwater by ground infiltration before any concentration of the runoff (Figure 6.188). They can reduce total runoff volume and diminish local flood peaks in any area where

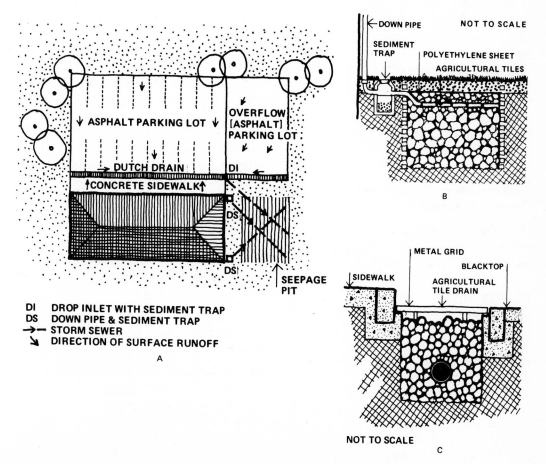

DI DROP INLET WITH SEDIMENT TRAP
DS DOWN PIPE & SEDIMENT TRAP
→— STORM SEWER
↘ DIRECTION OF SURFACE RUNOFF

Figure 6.188 Sample infiltration system for runoff water shows: (A) plan; (B) seepage pit, detail section; (C) Dutch drain, detail section. (SOURCE: Reference 1.)

soil porosity is at least 0.12 foot (3.7 centi-meters) per day. Dutch drains can eliminate the need for storm sewers and thus result in cost savings; the cost of excavation, materials, and paving for an average drain is $15.00 per cubic yard ($20 per cubic meter) of stored water (1972 dollars).

Like seepage drains, seepage pits are usually gravel-filled structures that collect runoff and allow percolation into the soil (see Figure 6.188). Seepage pits, however, hold the runoff long enough to allow concentration before release. As a result, they are more likely to become clogged with sediments than are Dutch drains. A properly designed seepage pit (also called a "dry well") will maintain infiltration at predevelopment levels and enhance the local water supply, provided that soil porosity is at least 0.15 foot (4.6 centimeters) per day. It can be located centrally in parking lots and other large paved areas; an overflow storage system can use part of the paved area as a detention basin.[1]

For further technical information on Dutch drains and seepage pits see Appendix, pages 857 and 859.

Implementation No. 2. Detention and Dispersal of Stormwater

Delay stormwater runoff with detention systems for dispersal and release at a flow simulating the predevelopment state.

In extensively developed areas, large-scale storm sewer systems often collect runoff and pipe it either (1) directly into coastal waters or (2) into the municipal wastewater treatment plant (combined system). The direct discharge (no-treatment) alternative (1) creates high peak flow surges of fresh water to the coastal basin with adverse effects on the ecosystem (page 87). On the other hand, the combined treatment alternative (2) may lead to flow surges that overwhelm the treatment system and lead to discharge of raw sewage and stormwater to

the coastal basin (page 511). Thus neither method is satisfactory.

An acceptable alternative is to retain collected stormwater and delay its release to approximate the predevelopment rate of flow as closely as possible (Figure 6.189). Retention facilities should be of sufficient capacity to absorb the maximum amount expected (Figure 6.190). Where possible, stormwater should be introduced into the soil for restoration to acceptable quality and quantity. A combination of such runoff retention ponds with seepage structures is advisable whenever possible.

Large trunk lines that channel collected runoff into surface waters are a major potential ecological danger in storm sewer systems.[11] These large pipes are point sources of pollution, and future U.S. Environmental Protection Agency (EPA) regulations may require treatment of this stormwater in aggravated cases.[12]

An alternative approach to central storm sewer systems is a decentralized pattern of numerous smaller systems that incorporate natural restoration techniques such as land treatment (page 513). Diversion of runoff through grassed swales to aquifer recharge areas (including wetlands) should be used to the fullest extent possible. Small detention basins built throughout the drainage area could serve as playgrounds, parking lots, and woodland areas, as well as for the temporary storage of water. These small subsystems should be designed to handle at least the 10-year storm.

GUIDELINE.   Artificial Treatment of Runoff

Plan for separate collection of storm runoff for utilization where possible and for separate treatment where not.

The pollution effects from storm drain discharges can be mitigated by installing a treatment plant to remove contaminants—this may be required by the EPA in some

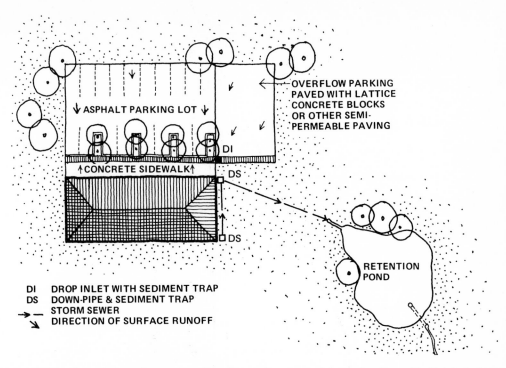

Figure 6.189 Retention ponds store runoff and can often be used in conjunction with Dutch drains and seepage pits. (SOURCE: Adapted from Reference 1.)

cases.[12] Because urban runoff flow is sporadic, an efficient treatment system requires high storage capacity in order to avoid building the huge-capacity plant required to treat peak runoff flows spontaneously. Also, it will be desirable (and in some cases necessary) to isolate industrial areas or others of unavoidably high runoff pollution potential—"hot spots"—and provide for pretreatment of the storm runoff before it enters the regular system.

Runoff from a paved area should be restored to the same quality, volume, and rate of flow as exist in the natural system. Chemical or mechanical treatment of stormwater should be avoided when natural purification by vegetation and soils is a realistic alternative. The natural approach has many secondary benefits (page 513), including cost reduction.

More frequent and effective street cleaning can significantly reduce the pollution load of urban runoff.[3] Improvements in street cleaning techniques should be aimed at picking up a far larger proportion of fine solids; this can be achieved by the wider use of vacuum sweeps. Broader concrete gutters will also lead to greater street cleaning efficiency.[1] Another alternative is to utilize urban runoff water as a resource, instead of considering it a waste, where this approach is cost efficient. It is estimated that the use of stormwater could provide for half the water demands of certain communities if the water were pretreated to acceptable standards.[2]

Implementation No. 1. Separate Systems

The stormwater collection and treatment system should be separated from the sanitary system whenever feasible.

Combining the stormwater and sewage systems for convenience and economy is not

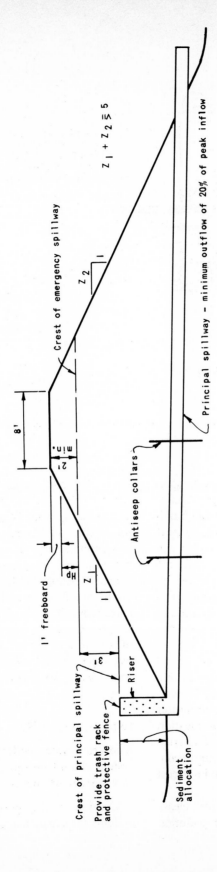

Figure 6.190 Large, well-engineered detention pond and sediment basin dam; note outlet pipe with riser, gravel core filter, and seepage-path cut-off collars on outlet. (SOURCE: Reference 10.)

usually acceptable; the lesson to be learned from existing combined systems is that they are generally not capable of handling the combined load during runoff surges. A treatment plant of sufficient capacity to handle the peak storm flow along with the sewage load may be uneconomical unless the water following the heavily polluted "first flush" of a rainstorm is diverted away from the treatment facility. Also, the treatment required for sewage may be quite different from that required for stormwater because the contaminant concentrations are different (page 523). The best solution is to separate the two functions and optimize each for its specific purpose.

Modification of existing systems in urban areas with combined collection and treatment of sanitary wastes and stormwaters to achieve separate stormwater treatment is difficult and very expensive. In either restoration or planning for a new system, substantial savings can be realized by designing the separate stormwater system to route to treatment only the initial, highly polluted first flush increment of runoff—the first half inch or so which contains most of the pollutants. For example, over 85 percent of the BOD may occur in the first $\frac{1}{3}$ to 1 inch of rainfall.[13] A key to the success of this approach is a high storage capacity for the first flush water so that it can be routed for treatment at a delayed, slower rate.

Seattle's Metro sewer system includes oversized pipes to store the fluctuating quantities of stormwater for later release as the capacity of the treatment plant allows.

Implementation No. 2.   Storm Runoff from Concentrated Sources

Specific concentrated sources of runoff contamination should be located and isolated for special treatment.

Storm runoff from heavily industrialized sites, such as those occupied by petroleum refineries, slaughterhouses, gas stations, and chemical plants, contains quantities of wastes not found in residential areas. In one study runoff from industrial areas contained 2800 pounds of contaminants per road curb-mile. Residential areas, on the other hand, contributed 1200 and commercial areas 290 pounds per curb-mile.[1] Industry also surfaces more land than commercial or residential development and further aggravates runoff problems (Table 6.40).

The presence of toxic metals in industrial runoff poses a special treatment problem, as their presence can reduce BOD removal by killing bacteria in the activated sludge, anaerobic digestion, and nitrificaton–dentrification types of sewage treatment. Information on the concentrations at which these metals interfere with these important methods of secondary and tertiary wastewater treatment can be found in the Appendix, page 838.

Special management is required for these

Table 6.40   Percent of impervious surface for various densities of urban occupancy (SOURCE: Reference 14)

Land Use	% Impervious
Low Density Residential	20 – 30
Medium Density Residential	25 – 35
High Density Residential	30 – 40
Business – Commercial	40 – 90
Light Industrial	45 – 65
Heavy Industrial	50 – 70

areas of concentration. Separate collection and treatment, or pretreatment, is advisable. Chemical precipitation (flocculation) in a package plant can be used effectively to treat these metals before they reach the main municipal sewage treatment plant.[15]

REFERENCES

1. Joachim Tourbier and Richard Westmacott. 1974. *Water Resources Protection Measures in Land Development—A Handbook: Water Resources as a Basis for Comprehensive Planning and Development of the Christina River Basin.* A Prototype Project, Phase II. Water Resources Center, University of Delaware, Newark, Delaware.

2. C. W. Mallory. 1973. *The Beneficial Use of Storm Water.* Prepared for The Office of Research and Monitoring, U.S. Environmental Protection Agency, Washington, D.C.

3. J. D. Sartor and G. B. Boyd. 1972. *Water Pollution Aspect of Street Surface Contaminants.* U.S. Environmental Protection Agency, Environmental Protection Technical Series, Report No. EPA R2-72-081, Washington, D.C.

4. Black, Crow and Eidsness–Jordan, Jones, and Goulding. 1975. *Study and Assessment of the Capabilities and Cost of Technology for Control of Pollutant Discharges from Urban Runoff* (draft).

5. Anonymous. 1974. "The Great South Bay." *Newsday: A Special Report,* Garden City, New York, June 9.

6. U.S. Department of Agriculture. 1975. *Urban Hydrology for Small Watersheds.* Soil Conservation Service, Technical Release No. 55, Washington, D.C.

7. Albert R. Veri et al. 1971. *An Environmental Land Planning Study for South Dade County, Florida.* Center for Urban Studies, University of Miami, Coral Gables, Florida.

8. Roy Burke, III. 1971. *A Survey of Available Information Describing Expected Constituents in Urban Surface Runoff; with Special Emphasis on Gainesville, Florida.* Occasional paper, University of Florida, Department of Environmental Engineering, Gainesville, Florida.

9. R. Michael Stevens. 1972. *Green Land—Clean Streams.* Center for the Study of Federalism, Temple University, Philadelphia, Pennsylvania.

10. U.S. Department of Agriculture. 1972. *Minimizing Erosion in Urbanizing Areas.* Soil Conservation Service, Madison, Wisconsin.

11. S. R. Weibel. 1969. "Urban drainage as a factor in eutrophication." In *Eutrophication: Causes, Consequences, Correctives.* National Academy of Sciences, Washington, D.C.

12. U.S. Congress. Federal Water Pollution Control Act Amendments of 1972. P.L. 92-500, 92nd Congress, S.2770, Oct. 18, 1972.

13. Anne M. Vitale and Pierre M. Sprey. 1974. *Total Urban Pollution Loads: The Impact of Storm Water.* Report submitted to the Council on Environmental Quality. Enviro Control, Inc., Rockville, Maryland.

14. Cudworth and Bottorf. 1969. *Effects of Urbanization on Storm Runoff.* Presented to Water Management Subcommittee, PSIAC. U.S. Army Corps of Engineers, South Pacific Division.

15. U.S. Environmental Protection Agency. 1971. *A Primer on Waste Water Treatment.* Superintendent of Documents, U.S. Government Printing Office, Washington, D.C.

CHAPTER SEVEN

Contributed Articles

This chapter presents 41 articles written by specialists with a great variety of expertise in coastal ecosystems management. Although these articles contain technical details in many areas of special interest, they do not cover the whole field. The extensive reference lists provided in preceding parts of the book, however, should lead the reader to sources of information that we may have missed here. We are deeply grateful for the efforts of our colleagues in providing this fund of special knowledge.

1. AESTHETICS AND PERCEIVED VALUES

Dr. Ervin H. Zube
Director, Institute for Man and Environment
Universtiy of Massachusetts
Amherst, Massachusetts

Aesthetic values are those that enhance one's sensory satisfaction—that contribute to one's derivation of pleasure from the environment. They contribute to a sense of well-being—to the quality of life. And they are usually associated with healthy well-managed environments.

Aesthetic perception encompasses visual, olfactory, auditory, and tactile sensory modes. The major emphasis in coastal zone planning and management programs, however, is usually placed on the visual mode, the mode that man tends to rely on most. Key elements of aesthetic evaluation are (1) the identification and description of visual coastal landscape characteristics, (2) the ranking of related aesthetic values or preferences, and (3) the prediction of the probable visual impact of construction projects and land-use changes.

A number of basically similar techniques have been developed that are applicable to the coastal zone for the identification and description of the visual landscape. The state of the art is such, however, that general-purpose, reliable models are not available for predicting aesthetic values and preferences, particularly as they relate to the impact of proposed construction projects and changes in land-use activities. The subjective nature of aesthetic values, coupled with the growing importance attached to them by the public, requires that any ranking of aesthetic values and preferences be based on measurement of the public's perceptions. Professional or expert judgments are important both for identifying and describing landscape characteristics and for judging the probable visual impacts of construction projects and land-use changes. The relationships between these identified characteristics and aesthetic preferences, and between the probable impacts of proposed projects and aesthetic preferences, however, need to be determined by measurement of the public's aesthetic preferences.

The perception of the aesthetic impacts of proposed construction projects and land-use changes, in the human observer, through the interaction of the proposed project or change and the existing coastal landscape. In other words, the impact will be influenced by the perceived appropriateness and congruence of that which is being proposed with that which exists and by the respective values attached to the proposed project and the existing environment.

Characteristics of existing coastal landscapes that can influence the aesthetic impact include the degree of visual exposure or enclosure provided by the existing landform and vegetation; the degree of naturalness or man-madeness of the landscape; the amounts of open and developed land; the size and type of existing developments; the height and density of existing vegetation and the related capacity for screening and blocking objects and views; the number, location, and magnitude of vista and viewpoints; the kind and location of unique or rare natural and cultural features and man-made artifacts; and the kind and location of misfits—objects and areas that are perceived to detract from aesthetic quality.

At the broadest level of generalization, *all* of the coastal zone is, or has the potential of being perceived as, a resource of aesthetic value. Land–water edges have universally attracted people and been identified as environmental amenities. Water is a singularly important resource contributing to aesthetic landscape preferences. Within this zone of land–water edges however, some sections are

perceived as of higher value than others. Aesthetic values are not uniform throughout the coastal zone.

Some examples of more highly valued areas are reasonably well known and serve as aesthetic benchmarks. They are exemplified by unique or dramatic undeveloped natural landscapes such as are found in sections of the northern coast of California and in portions of the rocky coast of Maine. They are also exemplified by the juxtaposition of historic villages and coastal landscapes such as are found on Cape Cod, and by the abundance of wildlife in salt marshes. Although these exemplary benchmarks represent only a small fraction of the coastal zone, they indicate some of the physical components and characteristics to be considered in the visual analysis of the coastal landscape. Also, they indicate the importance of both man-made and natural components of the coastal zone, the significance of artifacts and cultural features as well as ecological elements, and the diversity of settings that are perceived to be of very high value.

Physical components and landscape characteristics that help to describe the coastal landscape, that may influence aesthetic preferences, and that relate to the probable visual impacts of proposed construction projects and land–use changes are both natural and man-made. Principal among the natural components are the following:

1. The landform or profile of the immediately adjacent land, such as gently sloping sand or stone beaches, dunes, estuaries, wetlands, islands, and bluffs or headlands, which help to define the character of the landscape and determine an observer's elevational position.
2. The configuration of the land–water edge: concave, focusing visual attention inward on a central point; convex, radiating views to numerous points of the compass; or straight and linear.
3. The vegetative cover: sparse and/or low vegetation, affording uninterrupted views in all directions, progressing to dense, high vegetation that screens and/or buffers both vision and sound.
4. The quality of the water—its movement rate and breadth, sound, color, and odor.
5. The existence of dramatic, rare, or unique

natural features such as high rocky cliffs or island wildlife habitats.

Principal among the man-made components are these three:

1. The character and image of the landscape as exemplified in such terms as the following: *urban*, with highly intensive uses of the land, including many large structures; *suburban*, with more extensive use of the land and mostly one-story structures; *rural*, with a mixture of villages and open land; and *open land*, consisting of natural and agricultural areas.
2. The extent to which man's activities on the coastal landscape and the resulting transformation of it enhances, limits, or denies visual and physical access to the shoreline.
3. The existence of dramatic, rare, or unique man-made artifacts and cultural features, individually and collectively, such as lighthouses, fishing villages, historic urban waterfronts, and waterfront promenades and parks.

These man-made components also describe areas of social activity that may be strong indicators of perceived responses. They may be indicators of the aesthetic expectations of most users. They may influence perceived values by their cognitive association with previous experiences in environments with similar visual characteristics.

Classifying the coastal zone according to its dominant visual characteristics, as has been done for Long Island Sound and the California coastal zone, provides a systematic approach to inventory and description, a basis for comparative judgments of aesthetic preferences for different sections of the coast, and a baseline against which probable visual impacts can be assessed. Such classification also provides a means for facilitating communications about the coastal landscape by defining each section of the coast in terms of its dominant physical components and visual characteristics. General approaches to classification are frequently based on landform (e.g., beach, dune, estuary, wetland, island, bluff, or headland) and the nature and intensity of man's transformation of the landscape (e.g., urban, suburban, village, open, or natural). Further refinement is obtained by including the configuration of the land–water edge, the nature of the vegetative cover, and the existence of dramatic, rare, or unique natural features and/or man-made artifacts (Figure 1).

Important criteria for a systematic approach to the *identification* of visual characteristics are (1) the system is as objective as possible; (2) the system includes the full range of physical components from natural to man-made; (3) the system is suitable for the scale of the planning activity (e.g., local or regional); and (4) the system is replicable. The *evaluation* or ranking of aesthetic preferences should be (1) as objective and free of the planner's or manager's biases as possible, and (2) based on perceptual responses of user populations.

Techniques used for evaluation—for eliciting user perception of varying environmental settings—include (1) rank ordering, on a scale of highest to lowest aesthetic preference, of a series of coastal landscapes that are representative of the different classifications; (2) the use of semantic scales for describing and evaluating samples of each identified landscape, such as beautiful–ugly, noisy–quiet, and unpleasant odor–pleasant odor; (3) the sorting of photographs representative of the range of coastal landscapes into groups of equal aesthetic quality; and (4) paired comparison, whereby samples of each coastal landscape are compared on the basis of aesthetic preferences to every other coastal classification. These techniques provide a means of identifying the sections and characteristics of the coast that are deemed to be of highest aesthetic value and of ascertaining the extent of interperson and intergroup (e.g., user population) agreement on perceived values.

Man-induced change (construction projects) in the coastal zone influences a range of environmental values involving multiple modes of perception. The introduction of new or enlarged transportation facilities such as airports and highways or of heavy industrial complexes can significantly alter ambient sound, both quantitatively—loudness—and qualitatively—noisiness. The loudness or noisiness of new sounds may not only exceed the previous ambient levels, but may also mask previously

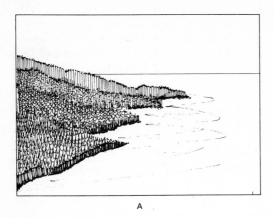

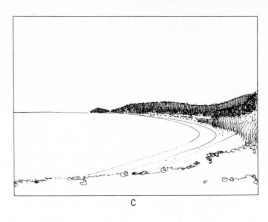

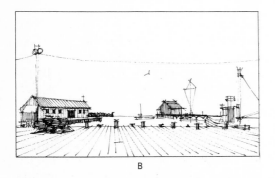

Figure 7.1.1 Landscape classification characteristics: (A) land form and vegetative cover, (B) man's transformation of the landscape, (C) configuration of the land–water edge, (D) man-made artifacts. (Drawings by Stephen Wing.)

heard pleasant sounds. Highway alterations that provide for increased capacity and speeds can raise noise from the level of 60 dBA to 70 dBA or greater—a tenfold increase in the perceived level, an increase that in some areas can mask the sound of surf breaking on the shore. Changes also occur in the perceived olfactory environment with the introduction of fumes from highways, factories, food processing plants, and liquid and solid waste disposal facilities. For most such olfactory and auditory impacts there is also an associated visual object: a highway, a building, or a

smokestack. Thus, even though there may be temporal variations in the emission of the olfactory or auditory stimulus, there probably is also a constant visual reminder to reinforce the perception of change in environmental quality.

Characteristics of proposed construction projects or land–use changes that may influence the perceived impact include the scale of the project, the compatibility or contrast of activities generated by the project with existing activities, and the contextual relationship of the new components with existing ones. An important question is: Are they different from an addition to or an extension of existing components? Details of materials, forms, colors, and textures may also influence the perceived aesthetic impact.

The impact of scale is a function of the size of the area subjected to development or change, for example, the length and width of the area to be clear-cut in a logging operation or the acreage to be subdivided for housing. It is also a function of the three-dimensional mass of objects being placed in the landscape, for example, the mass of a 500-foot-high cooling tower for a nuclear power plant (Figure 2) or a one-story interpretive center for a national seashore park. Compatibility or contrast of activities includes the visual consequences of the dynamics of use, such as more cars or more people, and of the physical facilities required to accommodate them.

The magnitude and the affective nature of the impact will also be influenced by the probable location of the majority of those who will view the development—will they be near to it or far away from it, will they be viewing it from a stationary or mobile position, will they be above it, below it, or at the same elevation? In the case of olfactory perception, location in reference to prevailing winds, upwind or downwind, is an important consideration. Additional factors include the expected number of viewers and the prevailing climatic conditions during the most probable viewing times (e.g., rain, fog, sunshine, etc.).

The probability of major aesthetic impact, either negative or positive, is highest when (1) the development is located in an exposed position—a location not screened by topography or vegetation, an area visible to large

Figure 7.1.2   The scale of smokestacks at a nuclear power plant (Biscayne Bay, Florida) contrasts strongly with their flat estuarine environment. (Conservation Foundation photo by M. Fahay.)

numbers of people, and an area visible from both land and water, as exemplified by a location on a ridge line or shoreline; (2) the scale of the development dominates the existing environment—a 500-foot cooling tower on low undulating or rolling hills or on sand dunes, or a 200-acre subdivision and shopping center adjacent to a 50-acre village; (3) the form of the development is in strong contrast with existing forms—transmission lines or highway cuts in hilly and mountainous areas or a high-rise structure in a village of one- and two-story buildings; (4) the character of the environment changes; for example, as a result of suburban or commercial development, the environment is perceived as becoming significantly more man-made, or as farming declines an agricultural area "reverts to nature"; and (5) the development intrudes on or destroys a dramatic, rare, or unique natural feature or cultural artifact.

REFERENCES

R. B. Litton, R. J. Tetlow, J. Sorenson, and R. A. Beatty. 1974. *Water and Landscape: An Aesthetic Overview of the Role of Water in the Landscape.* Water Information Center, Inc., Port Washington, New York.

U.S. Environmental Protection Agency. 1973. *Aesthetics in Environmental Planning.* Socioeconomic Environmental Study Series, U.S. Government Printing Office, Washington, D.C.

U.S. Environmental Protection Agency. 1974. *Promoting Environmental Quality Through Urban Planning and Controls.* Socioeconomic Environmental Study Series. U.S. Government Printing Office, Washington, D.C.

E. H. Zube, R. O. Brush, and J. G. Fabos. 1975. *Landscape Assessment: Values, Perceptions and Resources.* Dowden, Hutchinson and Ross, Inc., Stroudsburg, Pennsylvania.

2. BEACHFRONT PROTECTION—I

Dennis W. Berg
U.S. Army Corps of Engineers
Washington, D.C.

The imminent loss of a home or valuable property of unusual beauty or particular economic resource to the ravages of an ocean storm will often incite the immediate correction of nature's "mistake" by man. Too often, though, nature's "mistake" is actually the process of equalizing man's "improvement" of the coastal zone. For those who are concerned with man's use of the coastal zone there is a requirement to understand the processes that are constantly occurring and to use this knowledge in assisting, rather than "correcting," nature.

During the early history of the United States, natural beach processes continued to mold the shore as in ages past. As the country developed, activity in the shore area was confined principally to harbor areas. Between the harbor areas the shore developed slowly as small, isolated fishing villages. As the national economy developed, however, improvements in transportation brought more people to the beaches, and the fishing villages gave way to massive and permanent types of resorts.

Numerous factors control the growth of development at beach areas, but undoubtedly the beach is the resort's basic asset. The desire of visitors, residents, and industries to find accommodations as close to the ocean as possible has resulted in man's encroachment on the sea. In their eagerness to be as close as possible to the water, developers and property owners often forget that land comes and goes, and that land which nature provides at one time may later be reclaimed by the sea. There are also numerous places where the beach has been gradually widened by natural processes over the years; lighthouses and other structures that once stood on the beach are now located hundreds of feet inland. Yet once the seaward limit of a development is established, this line must be held if large investments are to be preserved. This type of encroachment has resulted in great monetary losses because of storm damage and the ever-increasing costs of protection.

BEACHES AND DUNES

The ocean shoreline is nature's defense against the attack of storms, waves, and currents. The first of these defenses is the sloping nearshore underwater bottom that dissipates the energy of waves by causing them to break. This breaking of waves in turn creates the next line of defense against the uprush of the following waves. Beyond this ridge, or berm crest, lies the flat beach berm that is reached by only the largest storm waves.

Winds blowing across the beach foreshore and berm move sand along the beach and often inland to form dunes. Various forms of vegetation are nourished in these dunes and help in stabilizing the location of the dunes, which are the final natural protection line against the attack of waves. Coastal dunes are also a reservoir of sand against the onslaught of the largest storm waves, which erode the dunes but provide additional sand to the beaches in self-defense.

Along portions of our coast an additional form of natural protection of mainland communities is available in the barrier beaches. These beaches, essentially long, narrow islands or spits built parallel to the shoreline by wave action and changes in sea level, are backed by shallow lagoons of varying width and provide protection to the mainland during the most severe storms. Even when these barrier beaches cannot absorb the complete energy of a storm and the dunes are eroded or breached, the major damage is the cutting of an inlet which permits sand to enter the lagoon, protecting the mainland from the major damages of eroding storm waves.

Barrier islands are separated from each other by inlets, which are relatively narrow channels of water connecting the ocean with the lagoons and bays. Inlets may be created by storms and serve as storage depots for sand eroded from the barrier beaches.

Beaches and the nearshore underwater bottom are usually composed of sand, small, resistant rock particles that have been transported to the shore from eroding uplands by rivers and streams. Some sands are derived from the erosion of rocky headlands and carried alongshore by litteral forces. This transport of sand along the shore is a continuous process, and large volumes of sand are moved along the coast each year.

However, because the main force providing energy for this movement is the waves that strike the shoreline and because the strength of the waves varies with time as well as the

direction from which they approach the shoreline, the movement of sand along the coast varies in volume on a daily basis and in direction.

WATER IN MOTION

Other than tides, the principal waves of the oceans are those generated by the winds blowing over the water surface. Wind waves may vary in size from ripples to giants 60 feet or more in height. As previously noted, such waves are the major forces moving sand alongshore and cause most of the damage to our seacoasts. Another type of wave, which fortunately does not occur frequently, is a tsunami, a wave created by earthquakes or other large disturbances on the ocean bottom; such waves have caused spectacular damage in the past and are commonly known as "tidal waves."

Wind waves are usually described by their height, length, and period. Wave height is the vertical distance from the top of the crest to the bottom of the trough between crests. Wave length is the horizontal distance between successive crests. Wave period is the time required for successive crests to pass a given point.

When waves move over the water, only the form and energy of the waves move forward. Advance of the wave form causes oscillatory motions of the individual water particles. In deep water these particles describe circular orbits with each particle returning to its original position after passage of the wave. In shallow water the orbital motion flattens, and at the bottom there are merely horizontal oscillations to and fro as the wave form passes. Wave characteristics—height, length, and period—are determined by the fetch (the distance the wind blows over the sea in generating the waves), the speed of the wind, and the length of time that the wind blows. Generally, the longer the fetch, the stronger the wind is; and the longer the time that the wind blows over the water, the larger the waves will be. Waves of many heights, lengths, and periods are generated by the wind simultaneously as it blows over the sea.

If winds of a local storm blow toward the

coast, the waves upon reaching the shore will be rather steep and the wave length some 7 to 20 times the wave height. When waves are generated by a distant storm, they travel through hundreds or even thousands of miles of calm area before reaching the shore. Under these conditions the waves age or decay and have lengths 30 to 500 times the wave height; these are called "swells" or "ground swells."

A current is a flow of water from a higher water level area to a lower one, in an ocean or other body of water. Some causes of differences in the elevation of the water in the oceans are the ordinary tides, the blowing wind, waves breaking on a beach, and streams that flow into the ocean. Changes in water temperature cause changes in water density and produce currents such as the Gulf Stream.

The wind creates currents because, as it blows over the surface of the water, it produces a "stress" on the surface water particles and starts these particles moving in the direction in which the wind is blowing. Thus a surface current is created. When such a current comes to a barrier, such as a coastline, the water tends to pile up against the land. In this way "wind tides" or "storm surges" are created by the wind. In violent storms such wind surges may raise the sea level as much as 20 feet. Storm surges may also be increased by the funneling effect in converging estuaries.

Waves create a current known as the "long-shore current" when they approach the beach at an angle. As they break on the beach, they set up a current that moves parallel to the shore in shallow water. The longshore current is frequently noticeable to swimmers and bathers in the surf when they find themselves being moved slowly along the beach. Under certain conditions this current may turn and run out to sea in what is known as a "rip current," which transports sediment seaward and when strong enough may endanger swimmers by carrying them seaward to deeper water rather unexpectedly.

The rivers and streams that flow into the ocean are currents themselves, and they carry the sediments that have been eroded from the land.

The tides are a rise and fall in the water level. If the water level is to rise and fall at any particular place, then water must flow into and out of the area, forming a current. The most important currents that the tides generate are those at inlets to lagoons and bays or at entrances to harbors. At most such places, the water flows in when the tide in the sea is rising (flood tide) and then flows out as the tide in the sea falls (ebb tide).

BEACH DYNAMICS

The sediments of a beach are determined by the forces to which the beach is exposed and the type of material available at the shore. Most beaches are composed of very fine to very coarse sand. This sand is supplied to the beaches by the streams and by the erosion of the shores by waves and currents. Fine silts and clays do not usually remain on exposed beaches because the waves create turbulence in the water and the fine materials are kept in suspension in the shore area. It is only after moving away from the beaches into quieter or deeper water that these fine particles settle out and deposit on the bottom. Many beaches along the New England coast are composed of rather large stones, frequently called "shingle" or "gravel." Some beaches on water bodies where wave action is very mild are composed of mud. Grasses usually grow in the mud; thus these shores are marshes.

The characteristics of a beach are usually described in terms of the average size of the sand particles that make up the beach, the range and distribution of sizes of those particles, the elevation or width of berm, the slope or steepness of the foreshore, and the general slope of the inshore zone fronting on the beach. Generally the larger the sand particles that make up the beach, the steeper the beach will be. Beaches with gently sloping foreshores and inshore zones usually have the finer or smaller sizes of sand.

The primary agent causing onshore, offshore, and alongshore movement of sand is the breaking wave or "breaker." As a wave moves onto the shore, it finally reaches water which is so shallow that the wave collapses, or "breaks." Breaking results in a sudden dissipation of the energy of the wave, which causes a great turbulence in the water and stirs up the bottom materials. After breaking, the water travels forward as a foaming, turbulent mass, expending its remaining energy in a rush up the beach slope; then, falling under the influence of the force of gravity, the water runs back down the beach slope to the sea.

Wind waves affect the beaches in two major ways. Short, steep waves, which usually occur during a storm near the coast, tend to erode a beach. However, when the local weather is fair, the long swell that comes ashore from distant storms tends to rebuild the beaches. On most beaches there is a constant change due to the erosion by local storms followed by gradual rebuilding by swells from distant storms. A series of violent local storms in a short time can result in severe erosion of the shore, if there is not enough time between them for swells to rebuild the beaches. Alternate erosion and accretion is seasonal on some beaches; the winter storms erode the beach, and the summer swells rebuild it. Beaches may also follow long-term cyclic patterns. They may erode for several years, and then accrete for several years.

The longshore current is very important in coastal processes because it carries sand that has been stirred into suspension by the turbulence of the breaking waves. The sand moved in this way is known as "littoral drift."

The direction and force of the wave attack determine the direction and magnitude of the littoral transport at a given time. For instance, on a coast facing to the east, violent storm waves from the northeast would produce a high rate of littoral transport toward the south. Conversely, mild wave action out of the southeast would result in a much smaller rate of littoral transport to the north. However, if the southeast waves existed for a much longer time than did the northeast waves, the effect of the southeast waves might well be more important in moving sand than that of the northeast waves. In reality, most shores show changes in the direction of littoral transport as the weather patterns change. Most shores, however, consistently have a net annual littoral transport in a single direction. Determining the direction and the average net annual amount of the littoral drift is important in developing shore protection plans.

The average annual net rate of littoral transport at a given place is fairly regular from year to year unless man changes the shore, and eliminates or reduces the supply of sand. The average annual rate varies considerably from place to place and depends on the local shore conditions and alignment, as well as the energy and direction of wave action in the area.

Inlets have important effects on adjacent shores by interrupting the littoral transport of sand and trapping the littoral drift. As the littoral drift moves into the inlet, it narrows the inlet. Increased tidal currents caused by the construction then pick up the littoral drift from the inlet. On the ebb current the sand is carried a short distance out to sea and deposited on an outer bar. When this bar becomes large enough, the waves begin to break on it, and this sand again begins to move along the bar toward the beach. However, on the flood tide, when the water flows through the inlet into the lagoon, the littoral drift in the inlet is carried a short distance into the lagoon and deposited. Such sand creates shoals in the landward end of the inlet, known as "middle ground shoals" or "inner bars." Later ebb flows may bring some of the material in these shoals back to the ocean, but some is always lost from the littoral drift stream and thus from the downdrift beaches. In this way inlets frequently store sand and cause narrower beaches by reducing the supply of sand to these beaches. Also, by temporarily interrupting the transport of sand, inlets may cause alternate periods of erosion and accretion on the downdrift shores.

Hurricanes or other severe storms moving over the ocean near the coast will change beaches drastically. Such storms generate large, steep waves. These waves take sand from the beach and carry it offshore; they move much more sand than do ordinary waves. In addition, the strong winds of the storm often create a storm surge. This surge raises the water level and exposes higher parts of the beach not ordinarily vulnerable to waves. Structures inadequately protected and located too close to the water are then subjected to the forces of the waves and are often completely destroyed. Low-lying areas next to the ocean or lagoons and bays are often flooded by such storm surges, which are especially damaging if they occur at the same time as high tide.

The berm, or berms, of the beach are built naturally by waves to an elevation approximating the highest point reached by normal storm waves. Although berms tend to absorb the major forces of the waves, overtopping permits waves to reach the dunes or bluffs in back of the beach and to damage unprotected man-made features.

When storm waves erode the berm and carry the sand offshore, the protective value of the berm is reduced and large waves can overtop the beach. The width of the berm at the time of a storm is thus an important factor in the amount of upland damage the storm can inflict.

In spite of the changes in the beach that result from storm wave attack, a gently sloping beach of adequate width and height is nature's most effective method of dissipating wave energy.

Although a beach may temporarily be eroded by storm waves and later restored by swells, and erosion and accretion patterns may occur seasonally, the long-range condition of the beach—whether eroding, stable, or accreting—depends on the rates of supply and loss of littoral material. Erosion or recession of the shore occurs when the rate of loss exceeds the rate of supply. The shore is considered stable (even though subject to storm and seasonal changes) when the rates of supply and loss are equal. The shore accretes, or progrades, when the rate of supply exceeds the rate of loss.

SHORE PROTECTION

While the sloping beach and beach berm constitute the outer line of defense to absorb most of the wave energy, dunes are the last zone of defense in absorbing the energy of storm waves that succeed in overtopping the berm. Although dunes erode during severe storms, they are very often substantial enough to afford complete protection to the land behind them. Even when breached by the waves of an unusually severe storm, dunes gradually rebuild naturally to provide protection during future storms.

Continuing encroachment on the sea with man-made development has very often taken place without proper regard for this protection provided by dunes. Great dune areas have been leveled for real estate developments, and because such developments were left unprotected, severe damage has resulted during storms. Dunes are frequently lowered to permit easy access to the beach. This allows stormwaters to flood the area behind the dunes. When there is inadequate dune or similar protection against storm waves, the stormwaters may wash over low-lying land, moving or destroying everything in their path. Sometimes those waters cut new inlets through barrier islands.

Where beaches and dunes serve to protect the shore developments, additional protective structures may not be required. However, in some localities where development encroaches onto the beach and into the sea, storm waves overtop the beach and damage backshore structures. Measures designed to stabilize the shore fall into two general classes: (*a*) a structure to prevent waves from reaching erodible materials; and (*b*) an artificial supply of sand to the shore to make up for a deficiency in sand supply through natural processes, with or without structures such as groins to reduce the rate of loss of littoral material.

Separate protection for short reaches of eroding shores (as an individual lot frontage) within a larger zone of eroding shore is difficult and costly. Such protection often fails at the flanks as the adjacent unprotected shores continue to recede. Partial or inadequate protective measures may even accelerate the erosion of adjacent shores. Coordinated action under a comprehensive plan that considers the erosion processes over the full length of the receding shore segment is much more effective and economical.

Bulkheads, Seawalls, and Revetments

Protection on the upper part of the beach, fronting backshore development, is required as a partial substitute for the natural protection that is lost when the dunes are destroyed. Shorefront owners have resorted to armoring of the shore by wave-resistant walls of various types. A vertical wall in this location, sometimes known as a "bulkhead," serves as a secondary line of defense in major storms. Bulkheads are constructed of steel, timber, or concrete piling. For ocean-exposed locations bulkheads do not provide a long-lived permanent solution, because eventually a more substantial wall is required as the beach continues to recede and larger waves reach the structure.

Unless combined with other types of protection, the bulkhead eventually evolves into the massive seawall capable of withstanding the direct onslaught of the waves. Extensive seawall structures have been built principally in Massachusetts, Florida, Mississippi, Texas, and California. Seawalls may have vertical, curved, or stepped faces. Although seawalls may protect the upland, they do not hold or protect the beach, which is the greatest asset of shorefront property. In some cases the seawall may even be detrimental to the beach in that the downward forces of water, created by the waves on striking the wall, rapidly remove sand from the beach.

A revetment armors the slope face of a dune or bluff with one or more layers of rock or concrete. This protection dissipates wave energy with less damaging effect on the beach than results from waves striking vertical walls.

Breakwaters

Beaches and bluffs or dunes can be protected by an offshore breakwater that prevents waves from reaching the shore. However, offshore breakwaters are more costly than onshore structures and are seldom built solely for this purpose. Offshore breakwaters are constructed mainly for navigation purposes. A breakwater enclosing a harbor area provides shelter for boats. Breakwaters have both beneficial and detrimental effects on the shore. All breakwaters reduce or eliminate wave action and thus protect the shore immediately behind them. Whether the breakwater is offshore or shore-connected, the elimination of wave action reduces littoral transport, obstructing the free flow of sand along the coast and starving the downstream beaches. At a harbor breakwater the sand stream generally can be restored by pumping the sand through a pipeline from the side where sand accumulates to the starved side. Even without a shore arm an offshore breakwater stops wave action and

creates a quiet water area between it and the beach. In the absence of wave action to move the sand stream, the sand is deposited and builds the shore seaward toward the breakwater. The buildup actually serves as a barrier and completely dams the sand stream, depriving the downdrift beaches of sand.

Although this type of construction is generally detrimental to downstream beaches, there is one case in which it may be used to aid the beach processes. When placed on the down-drift side of a navigation opening, a breakwater impounds sand, prevents it from entering the navigation channel, and affords shelter for a floating dredge to pump the impounded material across the navigation opening back into the stream of sand moving along the shore.

Groins

Long ago investigators noted that obstructions on a beach, such as logs or wrecks, would trap sand moving along the beach and cause the beach to widen. Such observations led naturally to devising the groin, a barrier-type structure that extends from the backshore into the littoral zone of sand movement. In earlier times, before the current extensive development of upstream river basins and major portions of the seacoast, the natural supply of beach sand was plentiful, and in many instances groins succeeded remarkably well. This led to further, excessive and indiscriminate use of groins. They often were installed without considering all the factors pertaining to a particular problem.

The basic purpose of a groin is to interrupt alongshore sand movement, to accumulate sand on the shore, or to retard sand losses. The trapping of sand by a groin is accomplished at the expense of the adjacent downdrift shore unless the groin or groin system is filled with sand to its entrapment capacity. To reduce the potential for damage to property downdrift of a groin, some limitation must be imposed on the amount of sand permitted to be naturally impounded on the updrift side. Since more and more shores are being protected and less and less sand is available as natural supply, it is now desirable (and frequently necessary) to place sand artificially to fill the area between the groins, thereby ensuring a more or less uninterrupted sand supply to downdrift shores.

Groins have been constructed in many ways, using timber, steel, concrete, or rock, but can be classified into such basic physical categories as high or low, long or short, and permeable or impermeable. A high groin extending through the zone of breaking for ordinary or moderate storm waves initially entraps nearly all of the sand moving along the shore within that intercepted area until the areal pattern or surface profile of the accumulated sand mass allows sand to pass around the seaward end of the structure to the downdrift shores. A low groin (top profile no higher than that of desired reasonable beach dimensions) functions like a high groin, except that appreciable amounts of sand also pass over the top of the structure. A permeable groin permits some of the wave energy and moving sand to pass through the structure.

Experience has shown that a short groin in a heavy drift area may fill quickly and have a limited effect on adjacent beaches. High groins, particularly if they extend beyond the breaker zone for most waves, adversely affect downdrift shores long after their updrift-side impounding capacity is reached. This is caused by diversion of littoral drift offshore beyond the end of the groin, where its subsequent movement deprives downdrift beaches of an adequate supply of nourishment. The accreted sand adjacent to the updrift side of a long groin may result in such a different shore alignment from that of the natural ungroined shore that sand movement along that alignment by waves is retarded for many years. Short groins and groins that have an appreciable degree of permeability do not cause a pronounced setback in the shore immediately downdrift of them, as the littoral transport of sand over and through these structures allows a more continuous supply to the downdrift area.

Present knowledge of sediment transport by waves and currents does not permit satisfactory determination of the optimum degree of permeability for the proper functioning of permeable groins. Impermeable groins can be more readily designed to serve the desired purpose, and they are more widely used. But groins of any type should not be built unless properly designed for the specific site. In particular, the effects of the contemplated groins on adjacent beaches should be studied by an experienced engineer.

Jetties

Another structure developed to modify or contral sand movement is the jetty. This structure is generally employed at inlets in connection with navigation improvements. When sand being transported along the coast by waves and currents arrives at an inlet, it flows inward on the flood tide to form an inner bar, and outward on the ebb tide to form an outer bar. Both formations are harmful to navigation through the inlet and must be controlled to maintain an adequate navigation channel. The jetty is similar to the groin in that it dams the sand stream. Jetties are usually constructed of steel, concrete, or rock. The type depends on foundation conditions, wave climate, and economic considerations. Jetties are considerably larger than groins, since jetties sometimes extend from the shoreline seaward to a depth equivalent to the channel depth desired for navigation purposes. To be of maximum aid in maintaining the channel, the jetty must be high enough to completely obstruct the sand stream.

Jetties aid navigation by reducing the movement of sand into the channel, by stabilizing the location of the channel, and by shielding vessels from waves. Adversely, sand is impounded at the updrift jetty, and the supply of sand to the shore downdrift from the inlet is reduced, thus causing erosion of that shore. Before installation of a jetty, nature supplies sand by transporting it across the inlet intermittently along the outer bar to return to the downstream shore.

To eliminate undesirable downdrift erosion, some projects provide for dredging the sand impounded by the updrift jetty and pumping it through a pipeline to the eroding beach. This ensures an uninterrupted flow of sand along the shore to nourish the downdrift beach and also prevents shoaling of the entrance channel.

Beach Restoration and Nourishment

Beach structures, when properly used, have a place in shore protection. But research has shown that the best protection is afforded by using methods as similar as possible to natural ones. In other words a greater degree of effectiveness is obtained by the type of protection provided by nature, which permits the natural processes to continue unhampered. To simulate natural protection, dunes and beaches are rebuilt artificially. Sand from sources behind the beach or offshore is placed on the shore. To ensure continued stability of the beach, material is placed periodically to make up deficiencies in the natural supply. This is most economical for long beaches as the increase of supply benefits the entire beach.

Coastal engineers can now determine the dune and beach dimensions required to protect against storms of any given intensity. Dune heights sufficient to prevent overtopping by waves and dune widths adequate to withstand the erosion of a given storm can be determined. Also, beach dimensions, including height and width of berm and characteristics of sand required to maintain beach slopes, can be designed to withstand storms of a specified degree of severity. Sometimes structures must be provided to protect dunes, to maintain a specific beach shape, or to reduce nourishment requirements. In each case the cost of such structures must be weighed against the added benefits they would provide. Thus measures to provide and keep a wider protective and recreational beach for a relatively short section of an eroding shore will require excessive nourishment without supplemental structures such as groins to reduce the rate of loss of material from the widened beach. A long, high terminal groin or jetty is frequently justified at the downdrift end of a beach restoration project to reduce losses of fill into an inlet and to stabilize the lip of the inlet.

3. BEACHFRONT PROTECTION—II

Joseph M. Colonell
Civil Engineering Department
University of Massachusetts
Amherst, Massachusetts

Beaches are the line of confrontation between land and water masses. It is on the beaches that the seemingly boundless energy of the waves must ultimately be expended. The capability of a beach to resist the endless attack by waves is determined by its ability to remain in equilibrium with the various forces that act upon it.

Although beaches vary widely in composition and appearance around the world, the principles that govern their behavior remain the same. Most United States beaches are composed of coarse, light-colored sands that are the result of the weathering of granitic rocks into their two major constituents—quartz and feldspar.[1] However, in this general discussion the term "sand" may be considered to apply to almost any beach material.

The most significant feature of any beach is its transient nature. Untold quantities of sand are carried in nearly perpetual motion on and off the beach and along the shoreline in a continual response to the forces exerted by waves, currents, and the wind. Although the visible response of the beach to these forces is by no means insignificant, the major part of the sand movement occurs beneath the water surface. It may be said that, in addition to water, the existence of a beach depends on the continued presence of three elements:

1. A supply of beach material (usually sand).
2. A shoreline area in which it moves.
3. A source of energy to move it.

Because the beach is sensitive to the disturbance of any of its three essential elements, particular vigilance must be exercised over any activity or natural occurrence that has the capability to alter the delicate balance among them.

As waves travel toward a shoreline, their characteristics are significantly and progressively altered as they pass through water that has a depth less than one-half their length. The process by which waves are slowed, shortened, and steepened, as they travel into progressively shallower water, is called "shoaling." Typically, shoaling does not occur uniformly along a wave front, so that, as the wave speed decreases in accordance with the shorter wavelength, the wave front bends as a result of the variations in speed along the front. This combination of shoaling and wave front bending is called "refraction" and, for purposes of analysis, is regarded as analogous to its optical counterpart in the refraction of light rays.[2] To estimate the onset of shoaling, it is useful to know that the length (in feet) of a wave in "deep" water (i.e., before shoaling) is approximately five times the square of the wave period (in seconds).

The result of wave refraction is a tendency for the wave fronts to become aligned with the shoreline; however, in most cases the refraction is incomplete, and the waves break before the fronts become parallel to the shoreline. The net effect of this is to cause a portion of the wave energy to be transmitted in a direction parallel to (or along) the shoreline, while the remainder is expended directly upon the beach. The latter expenditure of wave energy serves to move sand on and off the beach, while the former establishes the transport of sand along the beach in what is known as the "longshore" current. Clearly, any change in the incoming wave conditions must result in an alteration to the longshore current, which in turn affects the rate at which sand is transported along the beach.

The processes that disturb the equilibrium of a beach can be classified as either natural or man-made. Natural causes are conveniently grouped according to their time scales:

1. Short-term (measured in hours or days). Individual storms can often be the predominant natural factor in determining the condition of a beach, especially in the northeastern United States.[3] Tsunami (seismic sea waves) provide rare and usually catastrophic alteration to the equilibrium of a beach.[4]
2. Intermediate-term (months). Seasonal variations in wave energy can produce significant alterations to beach equilibrium, especially on the United States Pacific coast. The different beach conditions are often referred to as the "summer" and "winter" beach profiles, the former being the result of the lower, shorter waves typical of summer conditions, while the latter are produced by the higher, longer waves of the winter season.[5]
3. Long-term (years or decades). Fluctuations in mean sea level over periods of only a few years have been blamed for some long-term alterations to beach equilibrium. Similarly,

the slow but definite rearrangement of bottom sediments by storm waves and tidal currents can alter bathymetry to the extent that significant changes occur in the behavior (i.e., refraction) of waves approaching the shoreline.[6]

Man-made disturbances to beach equilibrium are usually the result of construction activity within the coastal zone; however, the equilibrium of some beaches is so delicate that it can be upset just by heavy usage for recreational purposes (e.g., by dune buggies and other vehicles). Construction activities that can be especially disruptive to beach equilibrium include the following:

1. Dredging (for any purpose) and spoil disposal.
2. Navigation channel or canal development.
3. Installation of offshore structures, either bottom-fixed or floating (e.g., towers, islands, docks, and breakwaters).
4. Installation of structures on or attached to the beach (e.g., walkways, launching ramps, piers, jetties, and groins).

In all of these examples, whether natural or man-made, a disruption to beach equilibrium will occur if one or more of the three elements essential to the preservation of that equilibrium is altered. The disruption will generally occur in the following way(s):

1. The supply of beach material (sand) is altered. If the supply is reduced, the beach can respond only by eroding until a new equilibrium level is established—in the extreme case the beach can virtually disappear; if the supply is somehow enhanced, the beach will widen (i.e., "accrete") until equilibrium is established once again.
2. The shoreline area in which the sand travels is altered. Just as a river needs a channel in which to flow, the sand that forms beaches requires the byway that is known as the "shoreline." If the shoreline is interrupted by a structure or altered by excavation or dredging, it must be expected that the flow of sand will be interrupted. The consequence is usually an accumulation of sand on the updrift side of the structure or within the excavation and at least temporary starvation of the beach on the down-

drift side due to elimination of the sand supply to it.

3. The source of energy for the system is altered. There are several ways in which this disruption can occur. Sometimes only subtle changes in offshore bathymetry can produce marked variations in the energy of the waves that impinge along a shoreline.[7] Such changes can occur naturally or can be the result of excavation or deposition of dredge spoil. If the waves are interrupted during their travel toward the shore, similar variations in the energy level can occur. Complete interception of the waves, as might occur at a breakwater, results in a wave "shadow" at the beach and a consequent loss of energy there to sustain the longshore current. As noted previously, any alteration to the incoming waves is manifest as an alteration to the longshore current that serves to transport sand along the beach.

Because beaches are attractive for a wide variety of recreational purposes, there is an understandable desire to build on or near them. When such building is permitted, efforts to protect the resulting investments have typically manifested themselves in the construction of concrete or rubble shore protection structures. All too often, however, these structures fail to accomplish their intended purpose, or they necessitate corrective action elsewhere on the coastline because of their disruption of the beach equilibrium.

For many years the accepted way to control beach erosion was to build groins, that is, low dams of rocks or wood piling that extend a few hundred feet out from the beach face to catch the passing sand. Considerable experience with groins has shown that, although they can be constructed to hold sand, they provide only a local and temporary solution to a beach erosion problem. There is no escape from the fact that, if no action is taken on an erosion problem, everyone along the shore shares the erosion. However, if one part of the shore is "protected," for example by a groin, the remainder of the shore must provide the necessary sand. And if the sand supply is diminishing, the result is a more aggravated situation than would exist if there were no "protection."

Another engineering solution to shoreline erosion that has received widespread application is beach "nourishment." This solution requires the supplying of sand by artificial means to a beach system that, for whatever reason, has suffered a reduction (or even elimination) of its natural supply. If the reduction is due to natural causes, any effort to maintain the beach is probably futile; if it is due to man-made disruption of the equilibrium, man must become involved in the system to the extent that he has disrupted it and he must provide sand and often the energy to keep it moving. For either case beach nourishment presents a costly and inadequate solution.

The only solution to shoreline protection that seems truly acceptable from a long-term viewpoint is that employed by the people of the Netherlands to secure their coastline.[8] The Dutch rely on the natural sand dunes as their primary (or outer) defense against the sea, and on dikes, which are actually substitute dunes, for their secondary (or inner) defense ring. The manner of construction and maintenance of these defenses is such as to ensure their natural state, which is sufficiently flexible and resilient to absorb all but the severest forces of wind and waves.

The key to Dutch success in maintaining their coastal protection lies in the management of their dune and dike system.[9] Although intensive recreational usage is permitted on the beach, absolutely no passage, breaching, or building on the dunes is permitted. Limited recreation and building are permitted in the trough between the primary and the secondary dune (or dike). The backdune area is recognized as the most suitable for development. This strategy of encouraging the coastline to persist in its natural state serves to maintain the optimum protection afforded by nature.

With greater understanding of coastal processes has come the realization that the best strategy of beach protection is one that involves little or no intervention in the natural system. To achieve the goal of a harmonious existence with the coastal environment, man must accept the natural variability of shoreline features and limit his activities accordingly to those that do not alter the overall equilibrium of the beach.

REFERENCES

1. Willard Bascom. 1964. *Waves and Beaches*. Anchor Books, Doubleday and Company, Garden City, New York.

2. J. M. Colonell, S. C. Farrell, and V. Goldsmith. 1973. "Wave refraction analysis: Aid to interpretation of coastal hydraulics." In *Hydraulic Engineering and the Environment*. American Society of Civil Engineers, New York, 131–140.

3. M. O. Hayes and J. C. Boothroyd. 1969. "Storms as modifying agents in the coastal environment." In M. O. Hayes, Ed., *Coastal Environments: NE Mass. and N.H.* Department of Geology, Contribution No. 1-CRG, University of Massachusetts, Amherst, Massachusetts, 290–315.

4. J. A. Roberts. 1964. "The reshaping of South Beach, Crescent City, California, after the tsunami of 27–28 March 1964." In *Proceedings of the Beach Erosion Control Conference*. California State Department of Water Resources, Sacramento, California.

5. F. P. Shepard. 1969. *The Earth Beneath the Sea*. Atheneum Press, New York.

6. P. Bruun and F. Gerritsen. 1960. *Stability of Coastal Inlets*. North-Holland Publishing Company, Amsterdam.

7. V. Goldsmith and J. M. Colonell. 1970. "Effects of nonuniform wave energy in the littoral zone." In *Proceedings of the Twelfth Conference on Coastal Engineering*, Vol. 2. American Society of Civil Engineers, New York, 767–785.

8. J. H. van Veen. 1955. *Dredge, Drain, Reclaim —The Art of a Nation*. Trio Printers, Ltd., The Hague.

9. I. McHarg. 1972. "Best shore protection: Nature's own dunes." *Civil Engineering—ASCE*, September, 66–70.

4. BEACHFRONT PROTECTION—III

Robert Dolan
Department of Environmental Sciences
University of Virginia
Charlottesville, Virginia

Patricia Dolan
Coastal Research Associates
Charlottesville, Virginia

Beach erosion in the United States is now a serious national problem. About half of our shorelines are subject to erosion, and several coastal areas require continuous beach restoration programs. Nevertheless, the shore zone remains one of the most desirable settings for recreational, residential, and commercial development and competition for the remaining; undeveloped land has increased in recent years. Planners and decision-makers responsible for the management of shoreline resources must have a basic understanding of the nature of the inshore zone and ready access to reliable information.

On the basis of our experiences, we believe that William R. Vines's statement concerning the management of shoreline resources is appropriate:

In no other resource-management field is there more misconception, mysticism, and generally confused thinking than in beach erosion control. The problem is often approached on an emotional rather than a scientific basis. Amateurish schemes for erosion control abound. The reason for the uncertainties about how to deal with erosion is that erosion control is far from an exact science. The professionals in the field are quick to announce that, although there is a large pool of scientific information on beach erosion, techniques for restoring and protecting eroding beaches must be substantially improved.

Beaches are constantly changing natural systems. Even a stable beach undergoes constant change with periods of erosion balanced by periods of deposition. "Stable" does not mean permanent, nor does it imply that the beach is fixed; rather, what is meant is that the natural processes are balanced over a long period of time.

This balance is delicate and can easily be upset. Beach stability is determined by (1) the amount and type of materials making up the beach, (2) the intensity of the natural forces responsible for change, and (3) the stability of sea level.

Beaches recede when the capacity of the wave forces to transport sand exceeds the amount of sediment supplied to the system. The greater the deficiency of sand, or the greater the capacity of the wave forces, the more rapid the rate of sediment transport and, at times, of erosion. A variation in any of three factors—energy, sediment, or sea level—can alter the balance of erosion and deposition. Beach erosion is a natural process and becomes a serious problem only when man's structures are placed in the path of shoreline recession.

The "natural condition" for beaches and barrier islands is simply a wide range of sand-deposit responses to various wave conditions. Like river systems, in which streams adjust in cross section to accommodate the water flow, beaches adjust in cross section to accommodate wave runup. During winter storms, when the wave runup of the surf zone can be high, the active beach expands, landward and seaward during the summer, when the runup is generally low, the active beach zone contracts.

Most of the time this process of beach-profile expansion and contraction is of minor significance, geographically or economically, because it is confined to the central part of the active zone, where little change in the sand deposit is involved. Under these conditions the cross section required to accommodate the wave runup is similar to the stream cross section at low-river stage. In the river system the flow is confined within the stream banks most of the time, so that the stream bed can easily accommodate the discharge. In the beach system the berm serves as the topographic constraint for wave runup most of the time.

During such extreme storm conditions as hurricanes or severe winter northeasters, the beach cross section makes major adjustments to lengthen the distance of the runup and thus dissipate the increased energy. In the offshore region this results in an extension of the zone of shoaling and breaking waves be-

yond the outer bar. At the landward end of the profile, if the increased energy level is high enough, the wave runup extends into the zones normally associated with the sand dunes and adjacent sand flats.

Man's most ambitious and extensive efforts to stabilize beaches and barrier islands have focused on the areas that are only occasionally penetrated by storm surge, have terrains suitable for permanent development, and are amenable to simple modification. The active beach does not fit any of these criteria, but dune and sand-flat areas can, to some degree, be controlled, although intuition suggests that, by stabilizing, the dunes are a response element of the system and not a forcing element.

The rationale behind the construction and stabilization of barrier dunes is that the dunes confine the upper limit of the wave uprush within the "swash zone" and prevent the undesirable effects of overwash and channel development. For permanent stabilization this requires a beach system that is stable through time; however, erosion of beaches and barrier islands is now a well-understood geological process. To reiterate, beach stability for any period of time is a function of sea level, wave energy, and the amount of sedimentary material supplied to the coast. If the sea level rises or the amount of material required to sustain the system is reduced, the entire beach system migrates landward with areas of backshore becoming foreshore and areas of dunes becoming backshore. If the dune areas are stabilized, the new system cannot adjust to changes that occur in the beach itself (Figure 1). In other words, when the sea level rises

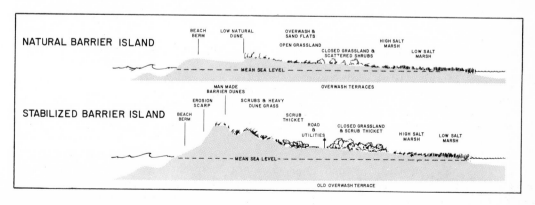

Figure 7.4.1   Natural barrier islands are resilient and well adapted to withstand storm impacts.

and the beach zone shifts landward, the dunes must also shift or the beach zone of the system is reduced in width, the energy-dissipation process is changed, and the entire system is forced out of equilibrium.

The unaltered beach or barrier island can withstand periodic extreme storms because no permanent obstructions lie in the path of the waves and surge and the broad beaches sustain the initial stress of an extreme storm. When no resistance is provided by impenetrable landforms or man-made structures, water flows harmlessly between the dunes and across the islands, dissipating wave energy (Figure 1). The combination of high tides and high waves can erode the beach face and frontal dunes, carrying sand and shell inland across the island and into the marshes.

A steadily rising sea level (about 1 foot during the last century) along the mid-Atlantic beaches has resulted in increased wave energy reaching the frontal dunes and in further overwash and buildup in the interior sand flats and the marshes. The net effect of this natural process has been a gradual westward movement of the beaches and islands. Even inlets opened during severe storms have resulted in sand moving inland to be deposited along the inner margins of the barrier islands.

Most erosion problems along the middle Atlantic coast can be traced back to the early development of beach-front property during the 1920s, 1930s, and 1940s. As the coast and beaches were stabilized, the "line of development" soon became a "line of defense." Further private and public development contributed directly to increased pressure to protect this line.

Along the coast of North Carolina the initial concept of management was to create a continuous line of high barrier dunes approximately 500 feet inland from the active shoreline (Figure 2). The WPA–CCC labor force of the 1930s was used to construct sand fences out of millions of locally cut scrubs and trees. These fences disrupted the winds blowing across the beaches and adjacent sand flats, causing fine sands to drop near the fences. As the sand accumulated, forming dunes, more fences were constructed at higher and higher levels, trapping large masses of wind-blown sand. Soon roads and utility lines ap-

peared, followed by subdivisions. Unfortunately, sea level has continued to rise since the 1930s, and the shoreline has receded hundreds of feet. Since the dunes are now disappearing rapidly under the direct attack of waves, other methods, including fixed structures and beach nourishment, are being explored.

The ideal solution to the beach-erosion problem would be (1) to plan all developments well inland from the high-water line and (2) to design all structures so that periodic severe-storm surges can occur without major damage. The life expectancy of any development should be planned according to its location; buildings placed near the upper limit of the storm-surge zone should not be designed to last for decades. However, since these ideal conditions seldom exist, and, as we have indicated, conditions along the shoreline change, what alternatives are available?

Shoreline-protection schemes fall into four categories. Protection may be designed (1) to stabilize sand, including dune and dike construction, and to use plants to trap sands moved by winds; (2) to construct breakwaters, seawalls, bulkheads, sandbags, or revetments; (3) to inhibit currents that transport sand with jetties and groins; and (4) to actually replace lost sand through beach nourishment.

SAND STABILIZATION

Wind flow across the beach can be modified to accumulate sand at predetermined locations; however, such works cannot prevent shoreline recession. At best, sand dunes can only stall the inland penetrations of storm surge.

SEAWALLS AND BREAKWATERS

Seawalls and breakwaters are massive, expensive structures to be used only after all other means of protection prove impracticable (Figure 3). These structures are designed to absorb and to reflect wave energy and, in the case of the seawall, to elevate the problem area above the high-water line. Breakwaters, seawalls, bulkheads, and revetments do not prevent the loss of sand in front of the structures; in fact, they commonly accelerate the

Figure 7.4.2 Massive artificial barrier dunes were built along the North Carolina Coast in the 1930s; above views to the north from Hatteras Lighthouse: A = 1933; B = recently.

loss because the wall deflects the wave forces downward into the beach deposit.

GROINS

Groins are damlike structures built perpendicularly to the beach to trap sand transported along the shore by littoral drift processes (Figure 4). These structures should be used only when there is littoral drift sediment of at least sand size (0.20 millimeter and larger) and when the shore downbeach is expendable.

Because of their limitations, groins are often more expensive and less effective than a well-planned beach-nourishment program.

BEACH NOURISHMENT

For more than a century man has built jetties, groins, seawalls, and other structures in a futile effort to trap sand and to protect beaches. These structures, designed to alter the energy flow and to interfere with the natural equilibrium of the beach, only cause fur-

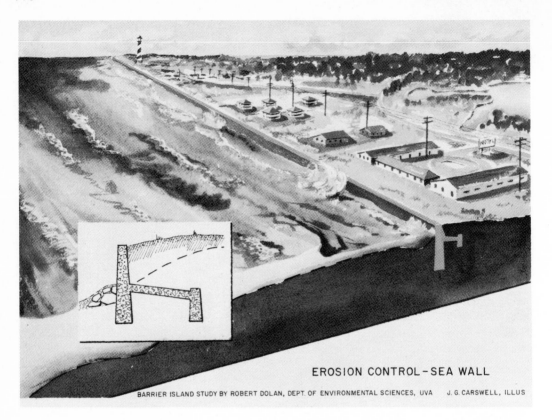

EROSION CONTROL – SEA WALL

BARRIER ISLAND STUDY BY ROBERT DOLAN, DEPT. OF ENVIRONMENTAL SCIENCES, UVA   J. G. CARSWELL, ILLUS

Figure 7.4.3   Seawalls and breakwater structures are last resorts to be used only when nonstructural approaches fail.

ther problems. It is now clear that the best method of beach restoration does not alter the natural processes. Rebuilding beaches artificially (beach nourishment) by replacing sand lost to the system permits the natural process to continue unhampered. This artificial beach nourishment provides (1) a beach suitable for recreational purposes, (2) an effective check on erosion in the problem area, (3) a supply of sand to adjacent beaches, and (4) an economical answer to beach erosion if large quantities of sand are available. Moreover, since no permanent structures are required, no major management commitment is necessary; if beach nourishment does not produce the desired result, the project may be discontinued (Figure 5).

The major limitation of artificial nourishment is that large quantities of sand of compatible type and size must be available near the problem beach. Nourishment sand can be dredged from sounds or bays immediately inland from the beach or transported from other inland sources. With the present concern about estuarine ecology, estuarine sources are generally no longer available; and sound materials are usually not compatible with beach sand. Consequently sand for large beach-restoration projects of the future will probably come from offshore or from coastal inlets (Figure 6).

Material added to the subaerial beach as nourishment must become part of the natural onshore–offshore sediment-exchange process. Within a short period of time after a nourishment program, the original mass of sand should be undetectable on the subaerial beach. This would indicate that the sand added to the beach system has been redistributed by natural onshore, offshore, and alongshore processes.

Any form of beach restoration is expensive. Groins may cost $500,000 each; seawalls, $200 to $500 a foot. The cost of sand used for beach nourishment can range from about $1.50 to 2.00 a cubic yard for sand pumped by a dredge over a short distance to as much as $5.00 a cubic yard if the sand is truck hauled (1975 prices).

In attempts to stabilize beaches and to protect coastal property, tens of millions of dollars of private and public funds have been spent over the past two decades. Available methods of stabilizing beaches are limited, and the best method (beach nourishment) leads directly to serious economic and sometimes environmental problems. The U.S. Army Corps of Engineers completed a study (1973) in which the initial cost of restoring the average 50-foot beach front lot along the North Carolina coast was estimated at around $20,000, with an additional $1000 to $2000 a year to maintain stability. Investments of this magnitude obviously limit beach erosion control projects to coastal areas where man's confrontation with the sea has implications of national significance. The best land utilization couples man's works with nature; it does not confront nature. If we continue to pursue a course of "man against the sea," we are almost certain to lose. Instead, we must strive to maintain the delicate balance that now exists but can so easily be disturbed. Only the application of an equation that recognizes and balances the forces of both man and nature can be effective.

C. S. Schuberth (1971) has stated:

If man wishes to build his works on the fringes of such a battle ground (the coast), he must understand that the rules of this ancient battle require the beach, the berm, and the dunes to shift constantly before the assault of the sea. If man tries

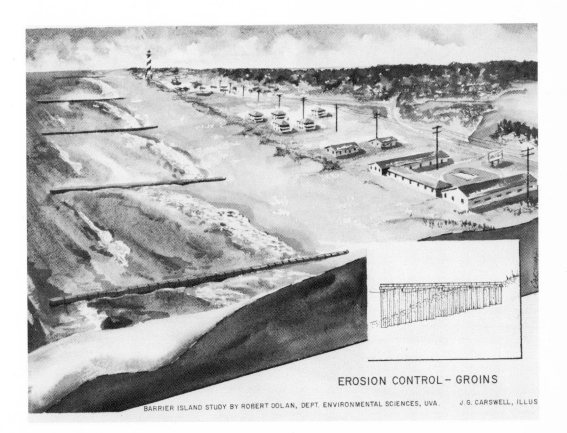

EROSION CONTROL — GROINS

BARRIER ISLAND STUDY BY ROBERT DOLAN, DEPT. ENVIRONMENTAL SCIENCES, UVA.   J.G. CARSWELL, ILLUS.

Figure 7.4.4 Groins, built to trap sand, are an expensive way to hold sand on beaches.

EROSION CONTROL - NOURISHMENT

BARRIER ISLAND STUDY BY ROBERT DOLAN, DEPT. OF ENVIRONMENTAL SCIENCES, UVA   J. G. CARSWELL, ILLUS

Figure 7.4.5 Beach nourishment is a nonstructural process of restoring a shore profile by pumping sand onto beaches; A = sand deposits, B = resulting beach condition.

Figure 7.4.6 Sand for beach nourishment should come from offshore or from inlets, rather than from estuaries.

to change these rules, he can only fail; and in his failure he may even undermine the fragile hold of these outposts against the powerful sea.

REFERENCES

Willard Bascom. 1964. *Waves and Beaches.* Anchor Books, Doubleday and Company, Garden City, New York.

D. W. Berg and D. B. Duane. 1968. "Effect of particle size and distribution on stability of articially filled beach, Presque Isle Peninsula, Pennsylvania." In *Proceedings of the 11th Conference on Great Lakes Research*, pp. 161–178.

T. W. Bilhorn, D. W. Woodard, L. C. Otteni, B. E. Dahl, and R. L. Baker. 1971. *The Use of Grasses for Dune Stabilization along the Gulf Coast with Initial Emphasis on the Texas Gulf Coast.* Gulf Universities Research Corporation, Report No. 114, Galveston, Texas.

Per Bruun. 1962. "Sea level rise as a cause of shore erosion." *Journal of the Waterways and Harbors Division—ASCE*, Vol. 88; pp. 117–130.

J. M. Caldwell. *Shore Erosion by Storm Waves.* U.S. Army Corps of Engineers, Beach Erosion Board, Miscellaneous Paper No. 59.

John M. Darling. 1968. *Surf Observations along the United States Coasts.* U.S. Army Corps of Engineers, Coastal Engineering Research Center, Miscellaneous Paper No. 1–68.

John M. Darling and D. G. Dumm. 1967. *The Wave Record Program at CERC.* U.S. Army Corps of Engineers, Coastal Engineering Research Center, Miscellaneous Paper No. 1–67.

M. M. Das. 1972. "Suspended sediment and longshore sediment transport data review." In *Proceedings of the 13th Conference on Coastal Engineering*, Vancouver, B.C., Vol. I, pp. 1027–1048.

R. G. Dean. 1942. "Storm characteristics and Effects." In *Proceedings of the Seminar on Planning and Engineering in the Coastal Zone.* Coastal Plains Center for Marine Development Services, Wilmington, North Carolina.

R. Dolan. 1972. "The barrier dune system along the outer banks of North Carolina: A reappraisal." *Science,* Vol. 175, pp. 286–288.

R. Dolan. 1972. *Beach Erosion and Beach Nourishment: Cape Hatteras National Seashore, North Carolina.* National Park Service Dune Stabilization Study, Natural Resource Report, No. 4.

R. Dolan. 1973. "Barrier islands: Natural and controlled." In Donald R. Coates, Ed., *Coastal Geomorphology,* State University of New York, Binghamton, New York.

R. Dolan and Paul Godfrey. 1972. *Dune Stabilization and Beach Erosion: Cape Hatteras National Seashore, North Carolina.* National Park Service Dune Stabilization Study, Natural Resource Report No. 5.

R. Dolan and Bruce P. Hayden. 1974. "Adjusting to nature in our national seashores." *National Parks and Conservation Magazine,* 9–14.

R. Dolan, John Fisher, Bruce P. Hayden, and Paul Godfrey. 1973. *A Strategy for Management of Marine and Lake Systems within the National Park System.* National Park Service Dune Stabilization Study, Natural Resource Report No. 6.

R. Dolan, Paul Godfrey, and William E. Odum. 1973. "Man's impact on the barrier islands of North Carolina." *American Scientist,* Vol. 61, No. 2, pp. 152–162.

P. S. Eagleson and R. G. Dean. 1960. "A discussion of 'Supply and Loss of Sand to the Coast' by J. W. Johnson and M. Asce." *Journal of the Waterways and Harbors Division—ASCE,* Vol. 86 (WW2).

R. O. Eaton. 1950. "Littoral processes on Sandy coasts." In *Proceedings of the 1st Conference on Coastal Engineering,* pp. 140–154.

B. O. Gage. 1970. *Experimental Dunes of the Texas Coast.* U.S. Army Corps of Engineers, Coastal Engineering Research Center, Miscellaneous Paper No. 1–70.

C. J. Galvin, Jr. 1970. "Wave climate and shore processes." In Arthur Ippen, Ed., *The Water Environments and Human Needs.* The MIT Press, Cambridge, Massachusetts.

R. T. Giles and O. H. Pilkey. 1965. "Atlantic beach and dune sediments of the southern United States." *Journal of Sedimentary Petrology,* Vol. 35, No. 4, pp. 900–910.

Paul J. Godfrey and Melinda M. Godfrey. 1973. "Comparison of ecological and geomorphic interactions between altered and unaltered barrier island systems in North Carolina." In Donald R. Coates, Ed., *Coastal Geomorphology.* State University of New York, Binghamton, New York.

V. Goldsmith, J. M. Colonell, and P. W. Carbide. 1972. "Forms of erosion and accretion on Cape Cod Beaches." In *Proceedings of the 13th Conference on Coastal Engineering,* Vancouver, B.C., Vol. II, pp. 1277–1291.

Bruce Hayden and R. Dolan. 1974. "Impact of beach nourishment on distribution of *Emerita Talpoida,* the common mole crab." *Journal of Waterways and Harbors, Coastal Engineering Division—ASCE,* Vol. 100 (WW2), pp. 123–132.

Bruce Hayden and R. Dolan. 1974. "Management of highly dynamic coastal areas of the National Park Service." *Coastal Zone Management Journal,* Vol. 1, No. 2, pp. 133–139.

M. O. Hayes. 1964. *Hurricanes as Geological Agents: Case Studies of Hurricanes Carla, 1961, and Cindy, 1963.* Bureau of Economic Geology, Report No. 61, University of Texas, Austin, Texas.

S. D. Hicks. 1972. "On classication and trends of long period sea level series." *Shore and Beach,* Vol. 40, No. 2, pp. 20–23.

J. W. Johnson. 1956. "Dynamics of nearshore sediment movement." *American Association of Petroleum Geologists Bulletin,* Vol. 40, No. 9, pp. 211–2232.

J. W. Johnson and M. Asce. 1959. "The supply and loss of sand to the coast." *Journal of the Waterways and Harbors Division—ASCE,* Vol. 85, pp. 227–251.

S. Judson. 1968. "Erosion of the land, or what's happening to our continents." *American Scientist,* Vol. 56, No. 4, pp. 356–374.

W. C. Krumbein. 1957. *A Method for Specifications of Sand for Beach Fills.* U.S. Army Corps of Engineers, Beach Erosion Board, Technical Memorandum No. 102.

J. R. Mather, H. A. Adams III, and G. A. Yoshioka. 1964. "Coastal storms of the eastern United States." *Journal of Applied Meteorology,* Vol. 3, No. 6, pp. 693–706.

J. W. Pierce. 1969. "Sediment budget along a barrier island chain." *Sedimentary Geology*, Vol. 3, pp. 5–16.

R. P. Savage and W. W. Woodhouse, Jr. 1968. "Creation and stabilization of coastal barrier dunes." In *Proceedings of the 11th Conference on Coastal Engineering*, Vol. I, No. 2, pp. 671–700.

C. J. Schuberth. 1970. "Barrier beaches on eastern North America." *Natural History*, June–July, pp. 46–55.

Francis P. Shepard and Harold Wanless. 1971. *Our Changing Coastlines*. McGraw-Hill Book Company, New York.

G. Soucie. 1973. "Where the beaches have been going: Into the ocean—ironically hastened by man-made remedies." *Smithsonian*, Vol. 4, No. 3, p. 54.

G. Soucie. 1974. "Here today, gone tomorrow." Audubon, Vol. 6, No. 1, p. 70.

D. R. Stoddart. 1969. "World erosion and sedimentation." In Richard J. Chorley, Ed., *Water, Earth, and Man*. Metheun & Company, Ltd., London.

W. F. Tanner. 1961. "Mainland beach changes due to hurricane Donna." *Journal of Geophysical Research*, Vol. 66, No. 7, pp. 2265–2266.

U.S. Army Corps of Engineers. 1973.. *Shore Protection Manual*, Vols. I–III. U.S. Army Coastal Engineering Research Center, Vicksburg, Mississippi.

U.S. Army Corps of Engineers. 1971. *National Shoreline Study*. Great Lakes Region Inventory Report.

Limberios Vallianos. 1970. "Recent history of erosion at Carolina Beach, N.C." In *Proceedings of the 12th Conference on Coastal Engineering*, Vol. II, pp. 1223–1242.

William R. Vines. 1969. *Surface Waters, Submerged Lands, Waterfront Lands*. Part I: *Comprehensive Inventory and Analysis*. Palm Beach County Area Planning Board, West Palm Beach, Florida.

F. M. Watts. 1956. *Behavior of Beach Fill at Ocean City, N.J.* U.S. Army Corps of Engineers, Beach Board Technical Memorandum No. 77.

M. Gordon Wolman and John P. Miller. 1960. "Magnitude and frequency of forces in geomorphic processes." *Journal of Geology*, Vol. 68, No. 1, pp. 54–74.

R. Dolan and Paul Godfrey. 1973. "Effects of hurricane Ginger on the barrier islands of North Carolina." *GSA Bulletin*, Vol. 84, pp. 1329–1334 (April).

5. BOUNDARIES, OWNERSHIP, AND JURISDICTIONAL LIMITS IN THE COASTAL ZONE

Marc J. Hershman
Institute of Marine Studies
University of Washington
Seattle, Washington

Managing the use of coastal lands and waters requires knowledge of the rights and duties of different owners, users, and regulators. Before determining the rights and duties of individuals in developing or conserving particular areas, it is necessary to know the precise geographic area in which owners and users have an interest. The types of rights and duties one may exercise within a particular area depend on both ownership and regulatory jurisdiction. Boundaries are the limits of the ownership and jurisdictional areas expressed in geographical or subject matter terms specific enough so that the limits can be readily determined by reference to a map or chart or to physical characteristics of the land or water area. Legal boundaries may be ambulatory or changing, as when expressed with reference to a tidal or vegetation line, or fixed, using natural or artificial survey markers.

In the coastal zone there are many overlapping jurisdictions, each of which has a separate set of boundary delineation issues. For example, a private owner near a beach needs a precise line to mark how far seaward his land extends, either to protect his private property or to determine development rights without encroaching on public lands. Federal jurisdictional interests extend inland to different points depending whether water quality or navigation is at issue. Boundaries separating state or federal government agencies' regulatory areas within the coastal zone often present problems. For example, the division between adjacent states or counties in water areas and the separation of federal and state submerged lands are frequently issues in the courts. This paper presents the key aspects of boundary determination and jurisdiction in general terms.

WHERE DOES STATE OWNERSHIP OF LAND END AND PRIVATE OWNERSHIP BEGIN?

Determining public and private ownership of land and waterbottoms in shoreline and coastal regions is difficult. Historically, in the United States the public owned the land covered by water frequently enough to inhibit private cultivation and occupation, and its sale was restricted by a right of public use. Normally "high-water mark" or similar terminology has been used to describe the dividing line between public and private interests as various states refined this definition. Because of the variations in the height of water due to tides and storms, it has long been a challenging technical and legal problem to determine the precise dividing point for this traditional definition of the boundary between privately owned and public land. Sale of public land is also possible; and in some cases restrictions relating to residual public rights have been critical to coastal management, since they define who the manager is, and what the rights of nonowners are in the use of the land. An important additional question is how to determine water elevations so that a series of marks on the ground where the water intersects the land can provide a precise demarcation of the boundary similar to descriptions of property boundaries in upland areas. (Tidemarks are discussed more fully below.)

Three zones of land are important to the question of ownership: submerged land, tidelands, and uplands. These zones are divided by reference to a tidal plane that intersects the land at certain points (see Figure 1).

Private ownership normally prevails in the upland area and extends to the high-water boundary. The state owns the submerged lands and tidelands and can determine the disposition of these lands. In some states grants to private individuals give title to land to the low-water boundary. In some cases these grants have been determined to be limited, and certain public rights of use and enjoyment in the tideland regions have been preserved under a "public trust" concept. Some states have granted away submerged lands in the past. Many states have forbidden, by amendments to their constitutions, any further sale of state tidelands or submerged lands.

A vexing problem is the legal demarcation of the tidal boundary. Along much of the Atlantic and Gulf coasts, the slope of the nearshore areas is 1–500 or less, so that a difference of 1 inch in the tidal plane can result in a boundary displacement of over 40

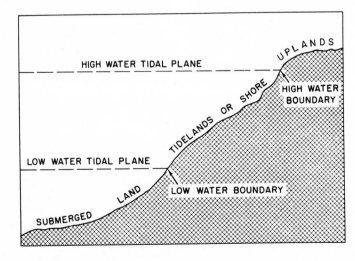

Figure 7.5.1   The intersection of the tidal plane with the shore defines the tidal boundary. (SOURCE: After Reference 7.)

feet. Thus differences in tide level that are inconsequential for navigation purposes become crucial in boundary problems.

Legal difficulty in the tidemark problem has been increased because courts use such modifiers as "ordinary," "mean," and "usual" interchangeably when referring to tide water marks. The National Bureau of Standards has regarded "ordinary" as the equivalent of "mean," and this view is generally recognized as accurate by the courts. The mean or ordinary high-tide line or mark does not refer to a visible line on the shore such as a line of foam or debris, but rather is a line ascertained from the mean rise of the tide outside the nearshore zone and projected horizontally to the shore, irrespective of the runup or wash of the waves.

Physically, the line cannot be calculated based on first principles. Rather, tidal lines are predicted on the basis of past observations of water level. Apparent water level varies not only from the tides, but also from other causes, including wind, barometric pressure, river discharge, wave runup, seawater density, ocean currents, long-term climatic changes, and geological processes.

The majority of courts that have dealt with the problem of what or where mean high tide is have based their decisions on the existence of the 18.6-year tidal cycle, and the Supreme Court of the United States has utilized this test on at least two occasions; however, some states have used the 19-year cycle. Unfortunately, records of sufficient duration are available for only a small number of stations located around United States coastal waters; the large majority of tidal stations have only a few days of observations available. By comparing observations sufficient accuracy is obstained for navigation purposes, but errors of 1 or more vertical inches may occur at remote stations. It is particularly difficult to extrapolate coastal data into estuaries, where basin configuration, wind, and river flow affect water levels. Any plane other than mean sea level (e.g., mean high or low tide) depends on the tidal range, which varies much more with location than does mean sea level, another complicating factor. Recognizing that the needed data are not always available, a few courts have declared that the full tidal cycle need

be used only when possible, or that a considerable or reasonable period is adequate.

Tidal lines are ambulatory—they change gradually over time (e.g,, because of sea level rise)—and most state and federal laws require the legal boundary to conform to this gradually changing line. The erosion or accretion of open coast at an average rate of a foot per year is quite common, but the rates for spits and headlands may be considerably greater. Cape Henlopen, Delaware, for example, is growing at about 80 feet per year. These average rates are often masked, however, by the much greater short-term effects of individual storms. Almost all states and the federal courts recognize that boundaries do not shift when changes are abrupt, such as the sudden shift of a stream to a different course, or when they result from deliberate dredge or fill activities. Jurisdictions differ on the boundary consequences when natural changes are induced by artificial structures, such as accretion and erosion occurring when jetties are constructed at inlets.

Because of the changing nature of boundaries, the date at which a boundary is measured is a difficult problem, for example, in cases where private ownership of uplands is set at the high-water mark as of the date a state was admitted into the Union, or as of the date of a particular court case or statutory enactment that adjusts rules for determining boundaries. The existence of accurate surveys of coastal lands and waters as of those dates is crucial to a clear determination of property rights.

Attempts in Florida and other states are under way to deal with the determination of tidal boundaries. One proposal would replace the changing tidal line with fixed "bench marks" at 1-mile intervals, significantly closer than in the past, allowing land surveyors to determine boundary lines accurately without the necessity of measuring tide elevations at each point along the coast. Property disputes could be resolved once the bench marks are placed. Aerial photographs of mean high tides could be drawn on charts by established photogrammetric techniques to provide more accurate lines for planners and managers. A further development likely in the future is a requirement under state law that these techniques be used to aid in the planning of proposed land-use and land-acquisition programs.

Ownership of uplands by private persons does not necessarily mean uncontrolled discretion in determining the uses of land. In coastal areas public interests are given considerable protection through planning, zoning, and special-purpose regulations that a state or local government may implement under its constitutional "police" powers. These governmental controls are limited, however, through the protection given a private property owner by the United States Constitution against unreasonable governmental restriction of private property rights.

Because of the legal and technical differences among states in regard to tidal boundary problems, readers are referred to specific offices of state government, typically the state land office or the state attorney general (land or natural resources division) for further information on these problems.

(References 2, 3, and 7 apply to this subsection.)

WHAT ARE THE OVERRIDING FEDERAL INTERESTS IN COASTAL LANDS AND WATERS, AND HOW FAR INLAND DO THEY EXTEND?

The United States Constitution states that Congress can regulate commerce among the several states. Since early commercial trade and transport in this country was by boat, the U.S. Supreme Court established the principal that "navigable waters" were a vital avenue of commerce, to be regulated by Congress, not the several states. The Court has ruled that federal jurisdiction extends to the ordinary high-water mark of all navigable waters of the United States.

"Navigable waters" are all waters that are in fact navigable, regardless of whether they are influenced by the tide, are landlocked or open, or are salt or fresh. Waters are navigable when they are, in their ordinary condition, used or susceptible to use as highways for commerce, over which trade and travel are or may be conducted in the customary modes of trade and travel on water. The test of navigability is not destroyed because a watercourse is interrupted by occasional obstructions, nor need navigation be open at all seasons of the year or at all stages of the water. Included are waters that were once navigable in fact but are no longer, and waters that are not now navigable but that may be made navigable through reasonable improvements.

Up until 1972 the U.S. Army Corps of Engineers and the U.S. Coast Guard were the primary federal agencies responsible for regulating activities on navigable waters that might affect interstate commerce, or other federal interests expressed in congressional legislation, such as protection of the environment. All activities or works in navigable waters needed a permit before they could begin.

In 1972 the Federal Water Pollution Control Act Amendments (FWPCA) contained a definition of "navigable waters" that expanded the term for water pollution control purposes to mean "waters of the United States." Section 404 of that Act requires regulation of dredged spoil disposal jointly by the U.S. Environmental Protection Agency (EPA) and the Corps of Engineers. Since almost all activities affecting navigable waters regulated by the Corps of Engineers involve some aspect of dredged spoil disposal, the new definition has resulted in considerable expansion of federal regulation in coastal areas. The new definition of "navigable waters" to mean "waters of the United States" eliminates the requirement that "navigability" be shown before federal jurisdiction is assumed. The regulation of coastal activities by the Corps of Engineers and the EPA when dredged spoil disposal is involved under Section 404 of the FWPCA extends beyond traditional authority to include the following:

- Coastal wetlands, mud flats, swamps, marshes and shallows that are adjacent to other navigable waters and are periodically inundated by brackish or saline water and characterized by salt or brackish water vegetation.
- Artificially created channels and canals used for recreational or other navigational purposes connected to other navigable waters.
- Tributaries of navigable waters.

• Freshwater wetlands, marshes, shallows, and swamps that are contiguous or adjacent to navigable waters and support freshwater vegetation.

These overriding federal interests are not "ownership" interests but are jurisdictional rights that the federal government assumed to protect water quality as required under federal law. Ultimately, the authority is derived from the United States Constitution, which grants Congress the authority to regulate interstate commerce. Thus, in the control of land and water use in coastal areas, the rights of the owner of the land, either a private owner or a public body, must be viewed in the context of other subject-oriented jurisdictions, such as the Water Pollution Control Act, that affect the particular physical resources of the site in question.

(References 1 and 4 apply to this subsection.)

HOW FAR SEAWARD DOES THE STATE'S JURISDICTION EXTEND

At one time the question of whether the federal or state government was the owner of tidelands and submerged lands was important, but it has now been settled in most respects.

Since early in the nation's history the U.S. Supreme Court has said that the state owns the tidelands and submerged lands beneath the navigable waters within the state. Earlier in this century a question arose as to the ownership of submerged lands offshore from a coastal state. In 1947 the U.S. Supreme Court decreed that the federal government had paramount rights in the submerged lands off a state's coast seaward of the ordinary low-water mark and outside inland waters. However, as a result of pressure from the states to have ownership rights over the mineral-rich offshore submerged lands, Congress enacted the Submerged Lands Act in 1953. This act allowed every coastal state to extend its boundaries to 3 geographical miles from its coast, potentially up to 3 marine leagues (10.6 miles) from the coast in the Gulf of Mexico, and to the international boundaries in the Great Lakes. The act relinquished to the states the interest of the United States in the lands beneath such waters. The United States reserved only such rights as were necessary for the regulation and control of commerce, navigation, national defense, and international affairs. The federal government also retained all rights in outer continental shelf lands seaward of the state's boundaries.

The Submerged Lands Act states that the boundary limit separating state from federal submerged land is 3 miles seaward of the coastline (or 3 marine leagues in the Gulf of Mexico). The act defines the coastline as "the line of ordinary low water along that portion of the coast having contact with the open sea and the line marking the seaward limits of inland waters." To determine the "line of ordinary low water" from which the state's seaward boundary will be measured, the U.S. Supreme Court adopted the international rules for drawing a baseline found in the Convention on the Territorial Sea and the Contiguous Zone. The Court recognized that under these rules the baseline for measuring the seaward boundary will be ambulatory as a result of erosion, accretion, and, potentially, man-made features. However, the Court reasoned that any inconvenience caused by an ambulatory coast could be resolved by legislation or agreement between the parties concerned.

There are still some unresolved questions on the location of the coastline and hence the precise location of the division between state and federal offshore lands. There are also unresolved questions regarding the lateral boundaries between adjacent states in offshore waters. New developments in the International Law of the Sea and the greater use of offshore submerged lands may result in congressional action sometime in the future to vary further this division of ownership between the states and the federal government.

(References 1, 4, and 7 apply to this subsection.)

HOW ARE BOUNDARIES BETWEEN ADJOINING STATES, OR BETWEEN LOCAL GOVERNMENTS OR SPECIAL AGENCIES, DETERMINED?

When two states conflict on the issue of the boundary separating them, the question has normally been resolved in one of three ways: Congress determines the boundary by federal law: the states agree on the boundary and enter into an interstate compact that Congress must approve; or the U.S. Supreme Court decides the boundary issue after taking evidence and studying the legal, historical, and technical information presented to it. Many disputes between states arise when a water body separates the states, and the Supreme Court has often had to resolve these disputes.

Within a state the jurisdiction of a local government, special agency, or district is almost always set out in the legislation establishing the jurisdiction of the governmental subunit in question. The jurisdictions of counties and cities vary considerably from state to state but can almost always be found by reference to the statutes and court decisions of the particular state. For example, in the state of Washington counties surrounding Puget Sound extend to the middle of the water bodies in the sound. In Louisiana, however, not all parishes (counties) along the coast have been given jurisdiction to the limit of the state's jurisdiction in the territorial sea—their control stops at the shoreline. Jurisdiction of the five parishes surrounding Lake Pontchartrain is uncertain; there exist numerous claims and counterclaims by the parishes on their authority to control causeways crossing the lake, shell removal from the lake bottom, and criminal activities occurring on boats moored at various places along the lake. State law must be consulted for a resolution of these types of issues.

WHAT ARE SOME RULES FOR DETERMINING JURISDICTIONAL BOUNDARIES FOR COASTAL MANAGEMENT PURPOSES?

States have enacted a great deal of legislation dealing with the regulation of aspects of coastal zone, shoreline, and wetlands use. Techniques for determining the area to be regulated have varied a great deal. Typical of the features used to designate landward boundaries are the following: linear measurement inland from the coastline; physical features such as marshes, swamps, floodplains, tidal

waters, estuaries, beaches, islands, and soil types; vegetation; elevation; and political boundaries or roads and highways. These boundary limits have varied because the interest to be regulated varied. For example, when shorelands are to be managed, a linear distance inland has been used to mark the boundary. When wetlands are to be conserved, vegetation has often been used to define the area. In the case of more comprehensive coastal management statutes, broader coastal areas have been defined by reference to political jurisdictions, elevations, and roads and highways.

A "second generation" of coastal management statutes and programs is possible under the Federal Coastal Zone Management Act of 1972. Under the Act the state must develop and apply a procedure for identifying the boundaries of the coastal zone subject to the management program. At a minimum this procedure should result in a determination of the inland boundary required to control "shorelands the uses of which have direct and significant impacts upon coastal waters." "Uses" are land and water uses and include existing, projected, and potential uses.

In reviewing jurisdictional boundaries for government management, it is important to recall that they may be geographically based by reference to charts and maps (to the middle of a water body, or "to the limit of the state's jurisdiction") or may be designated by reference to specific subjects (discharge or deposits in water, or salt-resistant vegetation), and both are legally valid. Such jurisdiction may apply irrespective of ownership (within constitutional limits) and may include a large number of separate areas. The most efficient way to determine applicable jurisdictions for a given property parcel is to review ownership *and* resources, especially the following: periodically submerged land, endangered species, salt-tolerant vegetation, barrier dunes, commercial or sport fisheries, and the like, both on the property and immediately adjoining it. The longer the list of resources in the vicinity, the higher is the likelihood of state or federal jurisdictional interests, in addition to traditional local building and setback controls.

(References 1 and 6 apply to this subsection.)

REFERENCES

1. R. Adams, M. Hershman, W. McIntire, and K. Midboe. 1976. *Rationale for Determining Louisiana's Coastal Zone Boundary*. Louisiana State University, Sea Grant Program, Baton Rouge, Louisiana.

2. J. Bockrath and D. Polis. 1974. "Tidemarks," in personal communication to the author, 7 pp.

3. C. Corker. 1968. "Where does the beach begin?" 42 *Washington Law Review* 33.

4. Commission on Marine Science, Engineering and Resources, 1969. "Developing law in the coastal zone." In *Science and Environment*, Chapter 8, pp. III-107–III-131.

5. F. E. Maloney and R. C. Ausness. 1974. "The use and legal significance of the mean high water line in coastal boundary mapping." 53 *North Carolina Law Review* 185.

6. J. M. Robbins and M. J. Hershman. 1974. "Boundaries of the coastal zone: A survey of state laws." *Coastal Zone Management Journal*, Vol. I, pp. 305–331.

7. A. Shalowitz. 1962, 1964. *Shore and Sea Boundaries* (2 vols.). Superintendent of Documents, U.S. Government Printing Office, Washington, D.C.

6. CONSOLIDATION OF FINE-GRAINED SOILS

Joseph F. Wiseman
Taylor, Wiseman and Taylor
Mt. Laurel, New Jersey

Fine-grained soil deposits of silt, clay, and peat are of widespread occurrence in all of the coastal plain states. The location of fine-grained soils in the littoral zone is a function of wave action, contributions of sediments from rivers and other sources, and recent geological history. Fine material is found at or near the surface along the coasts of Georgia, and western Florida, on the Gulf coastal plain, and in large bays such as Chesapeake Bay and Long Island Sound, where the annual mean breaker height is below about 1 foot. On the other hand, fine sediments are rarely found along the Pacific coast, where the annual breaker height exceeds 2.5 feet.[1]

Tidal flats and marshes behind barrier islands contain vast amounts of fine-grained soils, a great deal of which is organic. Deposits can vary from a few feet to over 20 feet in thickness. As the barrier islands are eroded and the active sand beach is pushed back, the former tidal flats may outcrop along the shore.

Lowlands between terraces and mature stream valleys within the coastal zone commonly contain freshwater marshes and swamps with fine-grained soil deposits. These deposits are usually relatively shallow.

Any change in the stresses acting on a soil mass will result in a change in the volume of the soil mass and will alter its properties. An increase in load will generally cause a decrease in the permeability and an increase in strength of the soil. If the change in volume becomes significant, it may affect the adequacy of structures founded on or in the soil mass.

Volume changes in granular soil occur rapidly and are usually of minor magnitude. However, volume changes in fine-grained soils can be significant and can occur over a long period of time. If the compression is due solely to the reduction of void spaces between soil particles and the rate of compression is governed by the resistance to flow of the water within the voids, the process is called "primary consolidation." The rate of primary consolidation is proportional to the square of the longest drainage path that a particle of water must travel to reach a free draining surface. If the compressible soil has a drainage surface at the top and bottom, the drainage path is one-half the thickness of the deposit. Experience with a variety of doubly drained New Jersey muck deposits indicates that the time (in days) required to reach 90 percent primary consolidation is equal to approximately 6 times the square of the thickness of the compressible layer (in feet). The total settlement that will occur is proportional to the increase in load and the thickness of the deposit. Methods for estimating the amount and rate of consolidation are presented in numerous soil mechanics textbooks.[2, 3] In many soil deposits, particularly organic ones, consolidation due to deformation of the soil skeleton itself may be significant. This process is referred to as "secondary conpression." At present there is no generally accepted method of estimating this effect.[4]

Construction activities, within the coastal

zone, in areas underlain by fine-grained soil have high potentials for adverse effects on the coastal ecosystem. The adverse impact of development and related construction is discussed in many other articles of this publication. This article will deal only with some of the problems that can be encountered and the controls that should be imposed when construction activities must take place in coastal areas containing significant deposits of fine-grained soil. Some of these activities may include highway or rapid transit construction, the installation of electric transmission towers or pipelines, and housing developments.

Highways and rail lines parallel to shorelines should be located above the coastal zone to minimize the impact on wetlands and tidal bodies of water. An example of this is the Garden State Parkway, which is constructed in the upper reaches of the coastal zone and crosses only a few deeply penetrating tidal estuaries. (The state of New Jersey uses the parkway to delineate a large portion of the coastal area along its eastern coast that is regulated by the Coastal Area Facilities Review Act.) However, it may be necessary to traverse the wetlands to provide access to existing development along the barrier islands such as Atlantic City, New Jersey. These crossings should be kept to a minimum width by using barrier dividers rather than wide medians. The elevation of the roadway should be kept to a minimum consistent with local flood levels to reduce the width of embankments.

When roadways or railroads are constructed over fine-grained soil deposits, the compressible material must be removed or stabilized, or the loads must be transferred, by means of piles or piers, through the weak and compressible soils to a firm substratum. Failure to do so will result in long-term settlement problems that will require constant maintenance and possibly create a flood hazard. Uneven settlements can result in the disruption of roadside utilities because of the tilting of poles or the fracturing of pipes. If high embankments are constructed, there is also the danger of rapid shear failure, which will cause sliding of the embankment into the meadow and the creation of mud waves beyond the toe of the embankment, thereby raising the elevation of wide areas of tidal flats and inhibiting the normal tidal action.

The most common method of stabilizing embankment foundations is to totally remove the unsuitable material beneath the embankment. In areas of shallow muck the width of the excavation normally does not exceed the width of the embankment. As the depth of the muck increases, however, the width of the excavation may exceed the width of the embankment in order to ensure lateral stability.

Low fills over shallow deposits of organic material with proper erosion control and adequate waterway opening have the least adverse impact on wetlands since damage can be confined to the location of the embankment itself. Fill for such embankments should be placed by truck from upland borrow areas. Hydraulic dredging of organic material, down to firm bottom, can be permitted with proper control of runoff from an upland disposal site.

Low fill over shallow deposits of organic material can also be placed without removal of the compressible soils if adequate time is permitted for the settlement to occur before paving or utility installation commences. The time required to achieve the anticipated primary consolidation can be shortened by the application of a surcharge. A surcharge is additional fill that is placed above the design grade of the proposed embankment. Although the time required to reach a given percentage of consolidation is independent of the applied load, the settlement at a given time is altered because the total settlement increases with increase in load. For example, if 50 percent consolidation occurs under the surcharge load in a given time, it could be equivalent to 90 percent of the consolidation that will occur under the design load. When the ultimate settlement due to design height is achieved, the overload is removed and settlement ceases. There is also evidence that surcharges can be effective in controlling secondary compression.[5]

Sand drains have been used to stabilize embankments more rapidly in areas of deep muck. This method requires that the entire load of the embankment be carried by the underlying muck. Since this is an inherently unstable condition for high embankments, wide counterbalances must be constructed beyond the toe of the slope to ensure stability. Thus the area of marsh permanently covered by the construction can be considerably wider than the required embankment. Surcharges are commonly employed with sand drains, thereby necessitating even wider counterbalances.

When the level of the roadway must be raised to provide navigational clearance or the depth of compressible material becomes great, the width of the embankment greatly exceeds the roadway width. When this width becomes excessive, the roadway should be carried on pile- or pier-supported bridges or causeways to minimize meadow disruption.

With the advent of offshore electric generating stations it will be necessary to construct additional transmission towers in the coastal zone. These should be constructed along or adjacent to existing rights-of-way whenever possible. Abandoned railroads have been utilized by power companies for some time.

When new alignments through wetlands are imperative, the structures should be pile supported to eliminate any dredging. Construction equipment, personnel, and structural units should be delivered to the tower sites by helicopter so that there is no environmental damage between sites.

Construction of residential developments in coastal wetland areas has been largely stopped by federal and state legislation because of its degrading influence on these vital areas. However, there are still many areas of former wetlands that were filled in the past for lagoon-type developments or as dredge spoil areas. The existing fill may range from several to perhaps 15 feet above the normal high tide. Since permits for construction in these areas can still be obtained, great care must be taken in the development of such sites to overcome the detrimental effects of compression of the underlying fine-grained soils.

Since most existing fills are presently below the flood hazard level, additional material must be placed to raise the street and lot elevations to prevent frequent flooding. Before further construction is permitted, tests must be conducted to determine how much, settlement will occur, and at what rate, when the required additional fill is placed. After the site has been graded, settlement platforms should be installed to determine the rate and amount of settlement actually taking place.

The construction of houses, utilities, and roads cannot be started until the settlement platform readings indicate that the area has stabilized. Construction before this time could create problems due to (1) the reduction of street grades, which will result in drainage problems; (2) the reduction of sanitary sewer grades, thereby reducing pipe capacities and causing stoppages; and (3) the settlement of lots below the flood hazard level.

In addition to raising the site to the proposed grade, additional fill is required to account for the anticipated settlement. Surcharges should also be employed to hasten primary consolidation, reduce secondary compression, and preload the building sites to account for the settlement due to the load of the structure.

If buildings are to be constructed on pile foundations before settlement of the site is complete, the piles must be designed to withstand the additional load imposed by friction between the settling fill and the pile. Since it is not usually economical to design piling for residential structures to withstand this additional load, construction should not be permitted until settlement has ceased.

REFERENCES

1. U.S. Army Corps of Engineers. 1973. *Shore Protection Manual.* U.S. Coastal Engineering Research Center, Ft. Belvoir, Virginia.

2. K. Terzaghi and R. B. Peck. 1948. *Soil Mechanics in Eingeering Practice.* John Wiley and Sons, New York.

3. J. E. Bowles. 1968. *Foundation Analysis and Design.* McGraw-Hill Book Company, New York.

4. G. A. Leonards. 1962. *Foundation Engineering.* McGraw-Hill Book Company, New York.

5. G. A. Leonards and B. K. Ramiah. 1959. *Time Effects in the Consolidation of Clay: Symposium on Time Rates of Loading in Testing Soils.* American Society of Testing Materials, Special Technical Publication No. 254.

7. CONSTRUCTIVE USE OF DREDGE SPOIL

Robert J. Reimold
Marine Resources Extension Center
University of Georgia
Brunswick, Georgia

By removing sediment from waterways or other aquatic systems and moving it to other land or water and discharging it, dredging is conducted to maintain, improve, or extend navigable waterways, or to provide natural resource construction materials. It involves all the components of natural systems as they are influenced by construction projects. In most instances this dredging results in environmental impact and sometimes in significant environmental disturbance.

Dredge spoil management refers to the problems associated with developing methods to reduce to a minimum, or eliminate where possible, the adverse effects on the environment. There are two general categories of disposal, open-water and land disposal.[1]

With open-water disposal, resuspension of large volumes of sediment occurs over a relatively short period of time. In contrast to this, natural processes are continually resuspending bottom sediments. In many instances the two processes are similar, but the range and intensity of the effects are often increased by open-water dredge spoil disposal. This type of disposal results in sediment deposition that frequently changes reproductive geographical locations, reduces species diversity, and changes or eliminates the vegetative cover of the submerged aquatic plants. The increased turbidity (usually short-lived) decreases light and consequently biological productivity. Finally, the open-water method frequently changes water chemistry by adding toxic substances to the system. This occurs from the shift in redox potential of the chemicals in the substance due to dredging. When these chemical pollutants are resuspended (via the dredging), there is grave concern as to how they will alter biological communities and, ultimately, man.

Land disposal has been developed to overcome the possible problems associated with open-water spoil disposal. Land disposal most often means disposal in wetlands, marshes, or swamps, as opposed to fast land such as pine forests or pasture land. A conflict arises over where the spoil should be placed (if land disposal is chosen), since these wetlands and marshes are among the most biologically productive systems known to man. These marshes, which serve as breeding areas, zones of maximum biological productivity, and nurseries, are only marginally understood by scientists. Although intuition has suggested certain rela-

tionships between the productivity and the wealth of biological life, and between the nursery concept and the fisheries production of the nearshore coastal zone, scientific experiments to document these associations are in their infancy.

Land disposal raises several concerns related to the possible pollution of groundwater reservoirs. Land disposal also alters vertical elevation and, consequently, vegetation patterns, and these modifications can create significant changes in drainage patterns and other hydrographic features. These hydrographic and vegetative alterations in turn create changes in the wildlife use of the area.

If dredged spoil could be used advantageously, it might acquire a new name, "dredged material." Already this is applicable in some instances. When dredging yields natural resources for construction, there is little concern over dredged material management since the material is commercially valuable. On the other hand, muck, clay, silt, and other pedeologic assemblages are not marketable commodities and constitute a problem in terms of disposal. Here is where dredge spoil can be considered as dredged material if useful alternatives can be found.

The most promising management concept for dredged material centers on the creation of artificial habitat. In potential open-water disposal sites it is essential to determine the baseline conditions of the location. These will quantify sediment compositional and distributional data, which will be indicative of prevailing energy regimes. These factors govern the pattern and rate of spoil disposal. The new concepts in this type of disposal[2] rely on the premise that natural sediment distribution and processes are suggestive of the prevailing natural geological phenomena. These long-term trends are more indicative of the feasibility of environmentally compatible dredged material disposal than are short-term intensive site observations. The major considerations in open, shallow-water disposal center on substrate sedimentary processes, including physical aspects, biological phenomena, and chemical equilibria.

The placement of open-water dredged material in certain locations results in substrate enhancement. In one instance where the undisturbed substrate was coarse sand and gravel and the benthic community diversity was low, the placement of soft clay on the bottom resulted in a rich species diversity due to communities that recolonized the area. In this instance the new benthic fauna and flora were more productive and more diverse than the original community. Another management scheme for open-water disposal involves the creation of suitable shellfish habitat; coarse material is distributed on the bottom to provide attachment areas for shellfish larvae. Open-water dredged material has also been disposed to create artificial fishing reefs. By the use of newly dredged material, the substrate properties of a previous disposal site can be altered to favor the growth of suitable benthic communities.

In respect to deep-water dredged material disposal, there are many opposing views at present. Some scientists favor such areas (over 15,000 feet deep) for disposal of many types of wastes (excluding radioactive material). They suggest that the deep oceans are natural sinks which are not active in food chains. The opposing view is that no material should be dumped in the ocean until more relevant research information is available.[2]

In land and wetland disposal, artificial habitat creation affords the most useful alternative with the minimum environmental impact. Spoil islands have been created in the past at random. Some have ended as favorable habitats; others have resulted in a biological deserts. Upland spoil islands creatively constructed so as to optimize appropriate factors will become naturally colonized with terrestrial vegetation and ultimately provide desirable habitats for terrestrial wildlife. Such an island can be constructed with diversified habitats, such as small water impoundments within the artificial island, to attract not only game but also waterfowl. Other land spoil can be deposited to create fish hatcheries or even access areas (boat ramps, parking areas, picnic areas) for recreational development.

The shortcomings of "island" construction are twofold. One disadvantage is that often biological recolonization occurs before the island has served its maximum usefulness as a site for dredged material disposal. In some instances bird populations have invaded a partly filled spoil disposal area, and conservationists have requested that further filling be terminated to prohibit damage to this new temporary habitat. The second factor opposing this type of disposal is that certain ecological and economic assessments must be made to decide whether the "island" to be created is more valuable (economically and ecologically) than the natural undisturbed system (e.g., old field communities, hardwood forests, benthic sea grass communities, or alpine tundra ecosystems).

Habitat creation in wetlands affords possibilities of creating high fast ground in place of marsh, creating low wetlands in place of submerged habitat, or slightly elevating existing wetlands. Since significant areas of marshes have been lost to dredge-and-fill operations in our nation's coastal zone, the creation of additional marsh is very desirable in some areas. It has been demonstrated that transplantation of marsh vegetation on diked spoil disposal areas has stabilized the substrate and created new marsh. In creating these new marshes, the major emphasis (in research) is now being directed toward enhancing the physical and chemical properties of the substrate and placing the material at a suitable elevation to enhance natural processes of revegetation and rehabitation by other marsh organisms. Newly developed agronomic techniques are already available for the rapid production of marsh plant seeds and seedlings for recolonization. Although the propagation techniques are economically feasible, the actual transplanting and seeding of dredged material is very time consuming and expensive. Current research is investigating means of temporarily diking intertidal mud flats so that dredged material may be deposited there and stabilized until a new marsh can be created. The U. S. Army Corps of Engineers Dredged Materials Research Program is investigating the feasibility of saltmarsh habitat creation in several areas around the country, including the northeastern Atlantic seaboard; the James River, Virginia; Buttermilk Sound, Georgia; Bolivar Peninsula, Texas; and the mouth of the Columbia River, Oregon. These studies are aimed at evaluating total habitat development and establishment.

On the negative side it is of merit to consider that today the disposition of dredged material for environmentally compatible habitat construction entails the high initial cost of dredging (as compared with old established disposal practices), and that the benefits of habitat creation will not always produce tangible results (as measured by today's economic scale).

Another use of dredged material has been land development on landfill operations. Most major ports of the world are constructed (at least in part) on dredged material. Many other developments such as airports, golf courses, recreational facilities, and housing developments have also been constructed on dredged material. In the future, part of this abuse to the environment can be avoided by long-range planning for siting as much development as possible away from wetlands. Also, part of the materials accumulated through maintenance dredging of ports should be used to elevate (vertically) the current industrial development rather than to expand it. This would afford even greater storm and hurricane protection for industry located along the water's edge. If true long-range planning were used, industrial port development would not be permitted on dredged material until it had reached an elevation suitable for development without additional storm protection needs.

Dredged material can also be used creatively to buffer subsidence and erosion. Changes in sea level, compaction of sediments, nearshore water currents, and other mechanisms are responsible for erosion at the land–water interface. In general, accretion is not taking place and coastal wetlands are not being formed, with the exception of the Mississippi delta. In most cases the marshes are simply existing at a finite level or are eroding. A similar situation exists in beaches where wave and storm energy continually move and redeposit sediments. Dredged materials, of proper grain size, are excellent for the nourishment of these areas.

Dredged material also can be moved to distant locations (up to 100 miles) by the slurry system (transport of liquidized spoil). Since this is economically feasible (when environmental considerations are included), the dredged material can be used for landfill operations at considerable distances away from the dredging site. Areas such as abandoned strip mines (for coal, phosphates, and other

minerals) will serve as suitable disposal areas. One possible use of mine pits filled with dredged materials is the creation of additional agricultural land. In addition to new land creation, some dredged material can be creatively used to alter the organic content, water retention capacity, or soil fertility and thus actually increase the agronomic productivity of some lands. Of particular importance is the limited use of this management technique when saline dredged material is involved. Often the salt problems and redox potentials prohibit this type of disposal from being beneficial.

The best source of information relating to past as well as present and future dredged material management practices is the U. S. Army Corps of Engineers, Waterways Experiment Station, Dredged Materials Research Program (Vicksburg, Mississippi). The Corps is conducting a long-term program related to dredged material and open-water disposal, land disposal, productive use of dredged material, disposal area reuse and multiple use, and development of new treatment techniques and equipment, as well as new dredging and disposal techniques. It has prepared a comprehensive document[3] that identifies management problems associated with dredged material, as well as new research needed for better decision-making.

Indeed, dredge spoil management has a wide spectrum of possibilities. With long-range planning, more knowledge of the natural system, and better assessment of ecological and economic considerations, dredged spoil need no longer be considered as harmful "dredged spoil" but rather as creative "dredged material" which can actually enhance the environmental attributes of the system.

REFERENCES

1. J. W. Morton. 1973. A Selected Bibliography on Dredging and on the Disposal of Dredge Spoils. Cornell University, Ithaca, New York, 23 pp.
2. Woods Hole Oceanographic Institution–U.S. Army Engineers, New England Division, 1971. Proceedings of the Ocean Disposal Conference, Woods Hole, Massachusetts, Feb. 23, (unpublished).

3. M. B. Boyd, R. T. Saucier, J. W. Keeley, R. L. Montgomery, R. D. Brown, D. D. Maethis, and C. J. Guice. 1972. *Disposal of Dredge Spoil.* U.S. Army Waterways Experimentation Station, Technical Report No. H-72-8, Vicksburg, Mississippi, 121 pp.

8. CORAL REEFS

Dr. R. E. Johannes
Department of Zoology
University of Georgia
Athens, Georgia

Coral reefs are among the most biologically productive, taxonomically diverse, and esthetically celebrated communities in the world. While their massive geological presence provides extensive wave protection along tropical coastlines, their biological productivity yields seafood to man in areas where terrestrial protein sources are often inadequate. These communities are also the main focus of skin diving, sport fishing, and shell collecting in the tropics, and, as such, constitute a vital stimulus to the tourist industry. The gross production of calcium carbonate in the skeletons and shells of reef organisms ranges between 100 and 500 tons per acre per year; fragmentation and transport of this material create and nourish most tropical sand beaches. In the United States and its territories, coral reefs are found in Hawaii, southern Florida, Puerto Rico, the U.S. Virgin Islands, American Samoa, Guam, and around more than 2000 islands of the U.S. Trust Territory of the Pacific.

Accelerated sedimentation due to bad land management and dredging is probably responsible for more damage to reef communities than all other forms of human insult combined. Growth in reef corals is mediated by light-requiring algae called zooxanthellae, which live within the tissue of the coral animal. Suspended sediments that reduce light penetration, therefore, inhibit coral growth.

Sediments settling on corals may kill them within a few days if the blanket is thick enough. The planktonic larvae of corals and many other reef invertebrates cannot settle and colonize soft, shifting sediments. Thus, in sheltered areas where currents are not strong enough to remove the sediments, recolonization is prevented indefinitely, even when additional sediment input is eliminated.

In the most extensive coral reef complex in Hawaii—Kaneohe Bay, Oahu—the bottom depth has decreased by an average of 6 feet in recent years as a result of very poorly regulated land clearing in the adjacent watershed. Complete and sometimes irreversible destruction of reef communities has resulted. An opaque red halo of suspended sediment extends around parts of Hawaii and much of Puerto Rico after heavy rains. The resulting damage is often obvious to the most casual underwater observer.

Dredging and coastal land filling associated with harbors, marinas, ship channels, etc., and sand removal for construction and beach replenishment have injured or destroyed hundreds of reef communities. The deleterious effects of sedimentation may last longer than those of any other form of man-made stress. Continual resuspension of sediments originating from dredging in the vicinity of coral reefs has been observed many years after dredging ceased.

Sewage is probably the second worst form of pollution stress on reef communities. Although the respiratory rates of tropical organisms are higher than those of temperate species, the dissolved oxygen levels in the water are lower. Tropical organisms thus live, on the average, closer to their lower oxygen limits. Consequently oxygen-consuming substances in sewage (as well as in suspended sediments) bring about proportionately more stress, per unit introduced, in tropic than in temperate waters.

In addition, dissolved nutrient levels are generally much lower in the tropics. Thus the introduction of sewage that would raise nutrient levels by, say, 30 percent in temperate waters may raise them by as much as 1000 percent in the vicinity of a coral reef.

Sewage pollution brings about reductions in the diversity of species of corals and other reef organisms. This is often accompanied by the overgrowth of algae. In Kaneohe Bay, Hawaii, which is a victim of sewage as well as sediment pollution, a single species of alga that is normally a minor component of most tropical reef communities has completely overgrown entire patch reefs. Corals are literally engulfed by the alga, and the coral skeletons are then dissolved away by some unknown process. This alga, *Dictyosphaeria cavernosa*, is now the single most abundant benthic organism in the bay.

Another stress due to bad land management —accelerated runoff of fresh water—has sometimes lowered coastal salinities to the point where shallow reef communities have been destroyed in a few hours. Exposure of corals to fresh water will kill them within 30 minutes.

Thermal effluent from power plants has killed corals and associated organisms in Florida, Hawaii, the Virgin Island, Guam, and elsewhere. Since tropical organisms live closer to their upper temperature limits than temperate organisms, it takes smaller heat increments to injure or kill them.

Several sets of both laboratory experiments and field observations provide no conclusive evidence that oil *floating above* reef corals damages them. However, extensive mortalities of other reef invertebrates and fish have occurred as a result of oil spills. In addition, in regions where corals are exposed to the air on low spring tides, floating oil will come into direct contact with them. Tissue death ensues in the areas of the coral where oil adheres. In some areas where chronic low-level oil spills occur, some reef fish can no longer be eaten because of their oily flavor.

Very little research has been done on the impact of industrial pollutants in reef communities. But because of higher water temperatures and high concomitant metabolic and chemical reaction rates in the tropics, the toxicity of such pollutants is probably higher, at comparable concentrations, than in temperate waters. However, for the same reasons, the concentration of the pollutant may be expected to diminish more rapidly with time and distance from the source.

Among heavy metals, copper appears to be the most toxic in effluents from power and desalination plants. Chlorine, used sporadically in massive doses to remove fouling from industrial outfalls, can be hazardous to reef biota. Chlorinated hydrocarbons have been shown to bring about increased respiration and to decrease photosynthetic rates in reef corals.

Coral communities recover less rapidly from severe stress than their temperate counterparts. Because many temperate marine species often reach full size and maturity in 2 or 4 years, temperate coastal marine communities may recover from heavy stress within this time span. Many corals, on the other hand, live and grow for several decades or more. Corals are so central to the integrity of the reef community that when they are killed the migration or death of many other reef animals ensues. It often takes badly damaged coral reef communities several decades to recover completely under the most favorable circumstances.

The problems of managing coral reef fisheries are much greater than those encountered in typical temperate coastal regions. The unparalleled numbers of species involved, the fact that the biology of most of them is very poorly understood, and the miniscule budgets of most tropical fisheries units all conspire to make optimum resource use in these areas exceedingly difficult. Overfishing is a chronic problem. The use of explosives and poisons such as household bleach to kill fish is facilitated by the clarity of reef waters and has reached plague proportions in many areas.

Considerable public concern has been voiced in the past few years concerning the effects of commercial and recreational collection of shells, corals and aquarium fish on reef communities. There is no reason why these communities cannot support such activities, just as they support seafood fishery. However, some areas have clearly been overharvested. Unfortunately almost no research has been done on these problems to provide us with a clear idea of just how much of these activities coral reef communities can tolerate.

REFERENCES

R. H. Chesher. 1975. "Biological impact of a large-scale desalination plant at Key West, Florida." In E. J. F. Wood and R. E. Johannes, Eds., *Tropical Marine Pollution.* Elsevier Scientific Company, Amsterdam.

R. E. Johannes. 1975. "Pollution and degradation of coral reef communities." In E. J. F. Wood and R. E. Johannes, Eds., *Tropical Marine Pollution.* Elsevier Scientific Purchasing Company, Amsterdam.

R. E. Johannes and S. B. Betzer. 1975. "Marine communities respond differently to pollution in the tropics than at higher latitudes." In E. J. F. Wood and R. E. Johannes, Eds., *Tropical Marine Pollution.* Elsevier Scientific Publishing Company, Amsterdam.

9. CROPLAND POLLUTION CONTROL

Robert D. Hart
Nonpoint Sources Branch
U.S. Environmental Protection Agency
Washington, D.C.

Of the 916 million hectares (2.264 billion acres) of land in the United States, approximately 167 million hectares (412 million acres) are used for crop production activities.[1] Although the most important output of these production systems is food and fiber in sufficient quantity to satisfy the needs of the entire country, there are also undersirable outputs that pollute the nation's waters. Crop production systems may have a significant impact on coastal ecosystems, even if they are located many miles away.

A crop production system consists of agricultural materials such as seed, fertilizer, pesticide, land, and machinery organized into a system that will convert solar energy into crop yield. Water is an important input into crop production systems. Unfortunately, water is also a significant output. With the exception of wind erosion and pesticide drift from aerial application, almost all agricultural pollution is associated with runoff from land being used for agricultural purposes.

When the runoff from a crop production system is intermittent and diffuse, the resulting pollution can be defined as nonpoint source pollution, as opposed to pollution from point sources, which are described in Public Law 92-500 as "any discernible, confined and discrete conveyance."[2] The effluent from a nonpoint source is almost impossible to monitor, making it very difficult to relate nonpoint pollution to specific water quality problems. The U.S. Environmental Protection Agency, under the authority of Section 208 of Public Law 92-500, is encouraging state and local planning agencies to control nonpoint source pollution as part of areawide and statewide planning programs.[3] When these planning agencies identify and assess their nonpoint source problems, crop production systems will probably be found to be significant contributors to local water quality degradation.

Nonpoint source pollutants from crop production systems include sediments, nutrients, and pesticides. The pollutants may reach a watercourse by runoff of surface water or through infiltration and percolation to subsurface water.

By volume, sediment is the most important agricultural nonpoint source pollutant. The process of erosion has been identified as the single most significant reaction that directly affects the coastal environment.[3] Although sediments result principally from the erosion of soils, they may also include crop debris, which may place an oxygen demand on receiving waters during their decomposition.

Nutrients may be transported from the crop production system either in a water-soluble form or adsorbed on sediment. Nitrogen and phosphorus are the most important nutrients affecting water quality. These nutrients occur naturally as components of the soil, but in crop production systems are usually supplemented by fertilizer application. Nitrogen in nitrate form may be leached from the soil and be carried into the groundwater or may be removed by the runoff. Nitrogen in organic forms may be associated with soil particles and plant debris and be removed by sediment transport processes. Most of the phosphorus removed from the crop production system is associated with sediment transport processes, although some movement of soluble phosphorus in runoff does occur. The impact of these nutrients on coastal ecosystems can be enormous. It has been estimated that the Hudson River estuary receives 5 to 10 times more nutrients than it is capable of assimilating.[4]

Pesticides may be water soluble and move with percolating water and runoff, or may be adsorbed on soil particles and moved through sediment transport processes. The predominant mode of transport depends on the chemical compound in question. There have been many investigations dealing with the movement of pesticides in runoff from treated land, and nearly all conclude that the total amount of pesticide that runs off is usually less than 5 percent of the quantity applied, except when heavy rainfall occurs shortly after application.[5] Although the concentration of pesticide in receiving water is indeed low, there is little doubt that pesticides are significant pollutants in terms of impact on coastal zone ecosystems.

The elimination or reduction of nonpoint source pollution from crop production systems that have an impact on coastal zone ecosystems can best be approached in terms of source management. The alternative to this approach, the installation of treatment plants between the source and the ecosystems that is receiving the pollutants, would be prohibitively expensive. Source management involves integrating water-quality-related management practices into the crop production management practices presently being used.

A crop production system can be visualized as a cropping system with inputs and outputs (Figure 1). The inputs are from natural sources such as solar energy, precipitation, and soil nutrients, as well as from human activities such as the application of fertilizer and pesticides, planting, and harvesting. Cropping systems involve the spatial and sequential arrangement of crop plant populations. The out-

puts from the cropping systems include crop yield, runoff water, and nonpoint source pollutants.

Some examples of agricultural pollution abatement management practices are classified under input, cropping system, and output categories and listed in Table 1. There are, of course, many other management practices that could be listed. These practices are outlined in greater detail in publications from the Soil Conservation Service of the U.S. Department of Agriculture and the U.S. Environmental Protection Agency (EPA).[6]

Analysis of the effectiveness of pollution abatement practices is complicated by the variability in local conditions and the inherent complexity of crop production systems. It is obvious that a management practice that is effective in controlling one pollutant may not affect, or may even increase, another pollutant. For example, decreasing fertilizer application could result in increasing the time before a crop has a closed canopy, and this in turn could cause greater erosion and sediment loss. One method of analyzing and predicting the effectiveness of different management practices is to use computer simulation models.[7] Models that can be used for this purpose are currently being developed by the Southeast Environmental Research Laboratory of the EPA in Athens, Georgia.

Most analyses of the effectiveness of pollution abatement practices have emphasized the effect of the different practices on erosion, although the general relationship between quantity and timing of fertilizer application has been studied.[8] The U.S. Department of Agriculture has used a soilloss equation that pre-

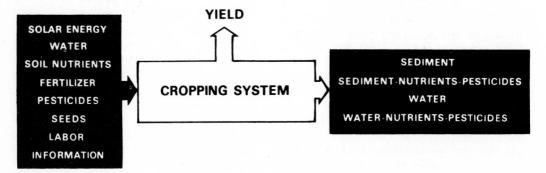

Figure 7.9.1 Crop production system.

Table 7.9.1 Examples of agricultural pollution abatement management practices

<u>Input Management</u>

    1.   Quantitative reduction in fertilizer and pesticide application.

    2.   Better timing of fertilizer and pesticide application.

    3.   Use of less persistent pesticides

    4.   Diversions

<u>Cropping System Management</u>

    1.   Miniumum tillage practices

    2.   Crop rotation

    3.   Strip cropping

    4.   Contouring

<u>Output Management</u>

    1.   Terraces

    2.   Debris basins

    3.   Drop spillways

    4.   Sod flumes

dicts soil loss per unit area of farmland when factors relating to rainfall, soil erodibility, slope length, slope gradient, cropping management, and erosion control practices are known.[9] The numerical values for the cropping management practices are between 0.0 and 1.0, with the high value arbitrarily assigned to continuous fallow land, tilted up and down the slope. The numerical value assigned to a cropping system in the soilloss equation is a measure of its effectiveness in reducing erosion, with a low value indicating effective control.

Some examples of different management practices and their effectiveness are listed in Table 2. This table is included for illustrative purposes only, since the actual value that would be used in calculating soil loss from a crop production system must be weighed against the effectiveness of a particular man-agement practice. Cost–effectiveness, the ratio of the cost to the owner of the crop production system to the effectiveness of the management practice in controlling pollution, can be visualized by plotting cost and effectiveness on a graph. In Figure 2 the effectiveness, which is assumed to be inversely related to soil loss in tons per acre per year, of five erosion control practices is plotted against the cost of implementing the practices in the corn belt of the United States.[10] In analyzing the cost–effectiveness of these selected management practices, it is obvious that conservation tillage is the most cost–effective, since the farmer actually made more money using this practice. However, if it were determined that a soil-loss limit of 7 tons per year was required in order to meet water quality goals, then strip cropping might be selected as the most cost–effective

Table 7.9.2 Effectiveness in erosion control of selected pollution abatement management practices applied to a corn production system

Cropping System	Effectiveness
Continuous Fallow	1.00
Conventional management	.50
All crop residue left on field	.40
Corn-wheat rotation	.30
Chisel planting in shredded stalks	.20
No-till planting in shredded stalks	.10

management practice, even though terracing and contour farming would also meet these limits. It can be seen from the graph that for only $1 more per acre soil loss can be decreased from seven to three by choosing strip cropping over contour farming. It must be emphasized that the cost–effectiveness of a particular management practice will vary with local conditions.

In the above discussion the cost and effectiveness of different management practices were considered on the assumption that they are applied individually. The practices can, however, be applied to a crop production system in combination. For example, better timing of fertilizer application, conservation tillage, and terracing can all be integrated into the management of a crop production system at the same time.

The EPA in its nonpoint source program is encouraging state and local planning agencies to apply pollution abatement practices to nonpoint sources of pollution.[11] After determining water quality goals and the cost–effectiveness of technically feasible management practices, and giving due consideration to the local socioeconomic environment, the "best management practices" can be selected.

The abatement of nonpoint source pollution from crop production systems does not stop with identifying pollutants, setting water quality goals, and selecting best management practices. The institutional arrangements that can result in the integration of the abatement practices into the crop production system must be identified and pursued. Success in the re-

duction of agricultural pollution will depend on the cooperation of the agricultural community. The Soil Conservation Service has been working with local soil and water conservation districts, irrigation districts, resource districts, and other local groups with similar functions for many years. Institutions that can also provide technical assistance in the selection of best management practices include local land grant universities and the extension services. The availability of economic incentives and legal sanctions to encourage the application of best management practices will vary among states and localities.

Summary

Sediment, nutrients, and pesticides are agricultural pollutants that have significant impacts on coastal ecosystems. When these pollutants enter a watercourse in an intermittent and diffuse manner, as in runoff and percolating water from cropland, they are defined as nonpoint source pollutants.

The abatement of nonpoint source pollution from crop production systems requires a systems approach. Pollution abatement practices should be selected by considering their effectiveness in controlling pollution and the cost to the owner of the crop production system of implementing the practices. The best pollution abatement management practice or combination of management practices should then be integrated into the crop production system.

At present, crop production systems are managed with the primary objective of maxi-

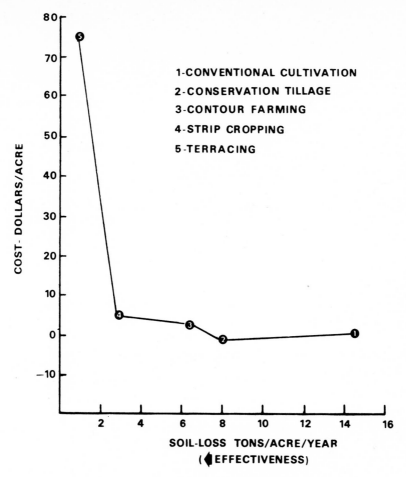

Figure 7.9.2   Cost-effectiveness of selected management practices.

mizing short-term economic gain. A secondary objective of minimizing nonpoint source pollution from the crop production system must be coupled to the primary objective. It is the task of the local planning agency to provide the economic incentive and, if necessary, legal sanction to ensure that water quality and the protection of coastal zone ecosystems are considered by the owners of crop production systems.

REFERENCES

1. U.S. Environmental Protection Agency. 1973. *Methods for Identifying and Evaluating the Nature and Extent of Nonpoint Sources of Pollutants.* Report No. EPA 430/9-73-014, Washington, D.C.

2. U.S. Environmental Protection Agency. 1972. Federal Water Pollution Control Act Amendments PL 92-500, Oct. 18.

3. B. H. Ketchum. 1972. *The Water's Edge: Critical Problems in the Coastal Zone.* The MIT Press, Cambridge, Massachusetts.

4. Agricultural Research Service, U.S. Department of Agriculture, and U.S. Environmental Protection Agency. 1975. A *Manual for Guideline Development,* Vol. 1, (draft copy).

5. U.S. Environmental Protection Agency. 1973. *Methods and Practices for Controlling Water Pollution from Agricultural Nonpoint Sources.* Report No. EPA 430/9-73-015, Washington, D.C.

6. H. P. Nicholson. 1975. "The needs for water quality models on agricultural watersheds." *Journal of Environmental Quality*, Vol. 4, No. 1, pp. 21–23.

7. U.S. Environmental Protection Agency. 1971. *Management of Nutrients on Agricultural Land for Improved Water Quality*. 13020 DPB 08/71, Washington, D.C.

8. W. H. Wischmeier and D. D. Smith. 1966. *Predicting Rainfall-Erosion Losses from Cropland East of the Rock Mountains*. Agricultural Research Service, Handbook No. 282, U.S. Department of Agriculture.

9. U.S. Environmental Protection Agency. 1975. *Cost Effectiveness of Agricultural Nonpoint Source Water Pollution Control* (draft copy). Submitted by Development and Resources Corporation.

10. U.S. Environmental Protection Agency. 1975. *Water Strategy Paper—A Statement of Policy form Implementing Certain Requirements of the 1972 Federal Water Pollution Control Act Amendments*. Washington, D.C.

10. DAMS, IMPOUNDMENTS, RESERVOIRS

Brent Blackwelder
Washington Representative of the
Environmental Policy Center and
Chairman of the Board of the
American Rivers Conservation Council
Washington, D.C.

Dams are constructed on large rivers and tiny streams; some are built high in mountainous areas, others close to the coastline. Dams are designed to serve one or more of the following purposes: flood control, water supply, hydroelectric power, irrigation, recreation, navigation, fish production, and augmentation of stream flow. They vary in size from small structures 10 feet high to giant ones more than 500 feet high that impound millions of acre-feet of water.

Reservoirs or artificial lakes are formed as dams block the flow of a river and create impoundments that vary in size from a few hundred acres to tens of thousands of acres. The level at which the reservoir is normally maintained is called the "normal pool." The area occupied by the reservoir when the dam holds back flood waters is called the "flood pool." The normal pool of Shelbyville Reservoir in Illinois is 11,000 acres, but its flood pool occupies about 25,000 acres.

The environmental effects of dams vary considerably, depending on the size and location of the project and the manner in which it is operated. In this respect dams are unlike channelization, which inevitably has adverse environmental effects as well as severe negative impacts. Few human actions can have such far-reaching ecological effects as the construction of a gigantic hydroelectric dam.

In fact, the construction of a dam can have a variety of environmental impacts long before it is completed and the reservoir fills with water. As the site for the dam is cleared of vegetation and large quantities of earth are excavated to prepare the foundation, soil erosion can cause sedimentation of the river downstream from the dam site. Air pollution can result from construction activities at the dam site from the burning of timber cleared away from the area to be inundated by the reservoir. In addition, there are environmental impacts associated with obtaining the energy and materials required for construction of the dam. Recent studies on energy show that building dams uses more energy per dollar spent than almost any other type of activity or program funded by the federal government.[1]

In turning a portion of a river into a lake, a dam produces major hydrological changes from which stem important biological, geological, and social changes. First, the natural flow patterns of the river are altered. For example, normal low flow periods, common in the late summer and fall, may be reduced or eliminated if releases of water are made from the reservoir at these times. Dams built for irrigation purposes can result in dramatic reductions in stream flow as water is withdrawn from the reservoir and used for irrigation purposes. On the other hand, dams are sometimes built to augment the flow of a river for navigation or other purposes during low flow periods.

By preventing seasonal flooding, dams can adversely affect species that spawn at flood stage. Some dams are built primarily for irrigation purposes, and significant amounts of water taken from these reservoirs for agriculture are consumed and are not returned to the river for uses downstream. In fact, so much water can be diverted that streams are dried up. There is concern about estuaries along the Texas Gulf coast should upstream dams now being considered for irrigation purposes siphon off large amounts of water. The entire character of the coastal zone will be altered if the estuaries are deprived of vital freshwater flows.

Other important hydrological changes involve water chemistry, water quality, and temperature, which can undergo major modifications depending on the type of land and vegetation inundated by the reservoir and the depth of the reservoir. For example, one fear expressed about the proposed Applegate Dam in Oregon is that it would inundate arsenic deposits which would have adverse impacts on water quality. Dams can bring about major changes in water temperatures both within the reservoir and downstream from the dam site.

Releases made from the base of dams draw the coldest layer of water from the reservoir, and this cold water can produce changes in the downstream ecosystem. Sometimes cold-water fisheries can be created below dams where there were none before. However, cold releases, particularly in the summer, can produce changes in the native fish populations and can do damage to the natural aquatic life not accustomed to sudden changes in water temperature or able to withstand them. If releases are made from oxygenless zones in the reservoir or from zones laden with hydrogen sulfide, the result can be to make large stretches downstream from the dam uninhabitable to fish.

When a dam is built, a river ecosystem with its fishery is converted into a lake ecosystem with a lake fishery. Some species formerly present in the river can survive in slack water conditions; others cannot and disappear. Species of fish adapted to lake conditions expand their populations, whereas those adapted to river ecosystems decline. The type of fishery that evolves after a dam is built varies considerably, depending on a number of conditions. Cold-water impoundments (those created by dams on cold-water streams) tend to be relatively unproductive or infertile from a

biological standpoint. Warm-water impoundments have greater rates of biological productivity and can be built for the specific purpose of raising certain commercial species of fish like catfish. Whether trees and other vegetation are cleared away from the area to be inundated or are left there can have major effects on water quality in the reservoir and on the type of fishery and aquatic life emerging in the reservoir. Trees left in reservoirs become habitats for game fish like bass.

In some reservoirs where trees have not been cleared, the flooded vegetation decomposes, releasing nutrients into the reservoir, sometimes in enormous quantities. These nutrients serve as food for aquatic plants which rapidly multiply, and the reservoir may become eutrophic, resulting in major changes in its ecosystem. A reservoir may also become eutrophic from excessive amounts of nutrients from upstream farm feedlots or from sewage discharges that enter the reservoir. It is predicted that the proposed Tocks Island Dam on the Delaware River and the LaFarge Dam in Wisconsin will develop eutrophic conditions from nutrients entering the reservoirs.[2]

Water quality is degraded when unstable or easily erodible soils are inundated by the dam. Various types of clays form colloidal suspensions that do not settle out. Imigrant Lake in Oregon is a turbid impoundment as a result of unstable soil conditions, and it releases turbid waters downstream into the Rogue River. Bank slumpages from hillsides along the reservoir create adverse turbidity.

In contrast to muddying a river, a reservoir can turn a brown stream into a blue–green one, as Egypt's famous Aswan Dam has done to the Nile and navigation dams have done on the Arkansas River. Dams create slack water and thus allow silt and sediment to precipitate out. The reservoir water becomes clear, and the downstream releases in turn are also clear.

As a dam blocks the flow of a stream, the water becomes slack and sediment being carried in the river drops to the bottom of the reservoir. All reservoirs will eventually fill up with silt, but the time required depends on a number of factors such as the size of the reservoir and the type of farming, mining, and forestry practices upstream from the lake, as well as the presence or absence of urban sprawl in the upstream watershed. The Mono Reservoir in California filled with silt in less than 20 years, as did Lake Austin in Texas. Even large reservoirs can fill rapidly with silt as a consequence of poor upstream land practices. For example, Fishtrap Lake in Kentucky has experienced extensive siltation as a result of coal mining activities and may last only several decades.[5]

Important downstream changes occur when a dam turns a muddy river into a clear one. Clear water has a greater tendency to erode soil and to pick up what could be termed its missing silt load. As a result, erosion downstream can be greatly aggravated. The clear release of Colorado River water below Hoover Dam resulted in excessive erosion and extensive sedimentation in the town of Needles, greatly exacerbating flood problems there. The clear waters of the Nile River are causing severe erosion downstream from the Aswan Dam and along the Mediterranean coastline.

Although dams are designed to prevent or reduce downstream flooding, there are cases in which downstream flooding has been aggravated. In the Carlyle Dam in Illinois, the downstream channel is inadequate to handle releases from the dam, and farmers downstream are confronted with flooding problems and wet conditions throughout a large portion of the year. Similar problems have occurred with Libby Dam in Montana, and Congress has authorized payments to downstream farmers damaged by the increased flows occasioned by this dam. By arresting the seasonal flooding patterns of rivers, dams can alter the fertility of soil in the downstream flood plain and can produce drastic changes in the coastal zone at the mouth of the river. The Aswan Dam on the Nile stopped the seasonal flooding that over the centuries had deposited rich silt on farmland. Egyptians are now turning to heavy use of artificial fertilizers, which have many associated environmental costs. Runoff of these fertilizers into rivers can result in water pollution from excess nitrates and phosphates. Because the Aswan Dam blocked the flow of nutrients downstream and altered conditions in the Nile delta, Egypt's sardine fishery was ruined, declining by about 18,000 tons annually.

Dams serve as barriers to the passage of fish and other aquatic life and can result in serious losses of diadramous fish. Over 60 percent of the riverine spawning grounds for salmon and steelhead in the Pacific Northwest have been cut off by the construction of high dams with no provision for fish passage. Dams not only serve as obstacles to upstream migration but also can result in high mortality rates to fingerling fish moving downstream to the ocean if they pass through turbines in dams producing hydroelectric power.

In the Pacific Northwest a particularly serious problem called "nitrogen poisoning" is caused by dams in the Columbia River basin. Salmon and steelhead are believed to experience something akin to the "bends" suffered by deep-sea divers; this is caused by nitrogen supersaturation, which occurs as water spilling over dams puts excess quantities of nitrogen and oxygen gas onto water droplets. Then, as the water droplets plunge to the bottom of the river, high pressures force the gas into solution with the water. Salmon and steelhead pick the gas up through their gills; and, as they surface, the water pressure decreases and the gases expand, often with fatal results. High mortality rates of salmon and steelhead have been attributed to gas supersaturation.[3]

Construction of dams in coastal areas for navigation projects can alter the character of coastal marshes. For example, the Wallisville Barrier Dam, a dam less than 10 feet high now being built across Trinity Bay, Texas, as part of the Trinity River Canal project, would inundate 12,000 acres of productive coastal marshland and create a shallow freshwater impoundment. This marshland serves as a prime nursery ground for shrimp, crabs, menhaden, and 56 other estuarine-dependent species. Studies suggest that by eliminating this marsh the Wallisville Dam will cause an annual loss of 7 million tons of commercial fish.

Although the level of natural lakes varies from a high in the spring to a low in the late summer and fall, impoundments generally fluctuate much more. If a dam is operated for hydropower production, these fluctuations may occur daily. The reservoir level can be greatly lowered if summertime releases are made to augment navigation or for other purposes. The drawdowns of water in a reservoir produce a zone generally called a "mud flat," which can be an impediment to recreational uses. The fluctuation of a reservoir affects the type of vegetation that can grow along the shoreline. It can also have a great impact on the fishery resources of the lake. As the reservoir is drawn down, small fishes and motile invertebrates are concentrated in a smaller area of water, exposing them to dangers of increased predation. These effects are reflected throughout the food chain.

The actual way in which a dam is operated can have important consequences for the aquatic ecosystem downstream. Some dams that are operated as peaking power facilities cause profound changes in a stream as flows are practically cut off during weekend periods of light electricity demand. Then during the week surging volumes of water are sent down the stream as the dam is used to meet a peak demand. Operation of a dam in this manner eliminates aquatic habitat and fish populations. On the other hand, dams can be operated in a way that will benefit fish populations, for example, by providing optimal water levels for spawning.

One of the major justifying purposes of some Corps of Engineer dams has been improved water quality from low flow augmentation. Conservationists criticized this as pollution dilution and argued that polluters should be forced to clean up their wastes at the source and not rely on upstream dams to flush out these wastes. Now the Environmental Protection Agency has the authority to determine whether water quality improvement may be included as a project purpose in a federal water resources project.

The creation of a reservoir causes significant changes in the terrestrial ecosystem. As the reservoir fills with water, plants, animals, and organic soil components are drowned and wildlife habitat is eliminated. Inundation of river valleys or canyons often destroys ecologically critical areas, including habitats for endangered species. Examples of projects that threaten endangered species are the Tellico and Duck River dams in Tennessee, the Wallisville Dam in Texas, the Meramec Park Dam in Missouri, the LaFarge Dam in Wisconsin, and the Tennessee–Tombigbee Waterway in Mississippi and Alabama. Wildlife

losses from the Corps's Dworshak and Libby dams in the Northwest have been serious, and the Corps is now seeking congressional aid to mitigate these losses. The proposed Tocks Island Dam on the Delaware is expected to eliminate over 50,000 mammals.[6] Rare forms of plant life can also be eliminated by dams, as they would be by the Red River Gorge Dam in Kentucky.

Impoundments can inundate areas of special geological significance, archaeological importance, or historic interest. Marmes Rockshelter in eastern Washington, where archeologists discovered the oldest known human skeletal fragment in North America, was inundated by Lower Monumental Dam on the Snake River. Tellico Dam, now under construction in Tennessee, will inundate the ancient Indian village from which the state derives its name. The proposed Meramec Park Dam in Missouri would inundate over 100 caves, including Onondaga Cave, rated as one of the nation's most beautiful by top speleologists.

There is some evidence that certain large dams—those that are more than 300 feet high and impound more than 1 million acre-feet of water—can cause earthquakes, even in areas not known to be previously earthquake prone.[7] The most famous case is that of the Koyna Dam in India, which caused a quake killing 177 persons and injuring 2300. Although present evidence is inconclusive about the precise relationship between dams and earthquakes, the question is receiving serious study and attention. Numerous shocks were recorded after the filling of Lake Mead on the Colorado River.

Although many of the adverse environmental effects of dams cannot be prevented, some can be mitigated or reduced in severity. Here are some of the major ways of lessening adverse impacts. Fish ladders can be installed to facilitate the passage of fish. Release gates can be designed in dams to allow water to be let out from different depths in the reservoir so that the temperature can be controlled at an appropriate level for downstream aquatic life.

Releases can be timed to benefit fish migrations or to avoid interfering with spawning activities. Wise land use upstream can prevent farm runoff and reduce the threat of eutrophication in the reservoir. It can also reduce the sediment load deposited in the dam and prolong the life of the reservoir. To mitigate the destruction of wildlife lands, land suitable for wildlife management can sometimes be acquired elsewhere and developed for this purpose. Although this technique can lessen the extent of the loss, usually the land inundated is the prime habitat, and suitable replacement cannot be found to compensate for the destruction.

REFERENCES

1. Bruce Hannon and Roger Bezdek. 1974. "Energy, manpower, and the highway trust fund." *Science*, Vol. 185, pp. 669–675.

2. See comments of the U.S. Environmental Protection Agency and the Council on Environmental Quality on the environmental impact statements for these projects.

3. See U.S. Environmental Protection Agency, *Nitrogen Supersaturation in the Columbia and Snake Rivers*, Seattle, Washington, July 1971. Also see National Marine Fisheries Service, U.S. Department of Commerce, *Summaries of Studies of Measures Taken by the Corps of Engineers to Reduce Losses of Salmon and Steelhead in Columbia and Snake Rivers*, Seattle, Washington, September 1971.

4. R. T. Baldauf. 1970. *A Study of Selected Chemical and Biological Conditions of Lower Trinity River and Upper Trinity Bay*. Water Resources Institute, Technical Report No. 26, Texas A&M University, College Station, Texas.

5. *Adverse Effects of Coal Mining on Federal Reservoir Projects*. Hearings before the Subcommittee on Conservation and Natural Resources of the House Committee on Government Operations, Oct. 25, 1973.

6. Figures on wildlife losses from Dr. L. M. Rymon: *Public Works for Water and Power Development and Atomic Energy Commission Appropriations*. 1975. House Appropriations Committee, Part 7, "Testimony of Members of Congress and Other Individuals and Organizations."

7. National Academy of Sciences–National Academy of Engineering. 1972. *Earthquakes Related to Reservoir Filling*. Washington, D.C.

11. DISCHARGE OF SEWAGE

J. Kneeland McNulty
Middle Atlantic Coastal Fisheries Center
Sandy Hook, New Jersey

The discharge of sewage into coastal waters is a major environmental problem of our time because of the great quantities being discharged and the substantial cost of reducing its harmful effects to acceptable levels. Sewage endangers human health, offends the senses, and disrupts and sometimes kills marine life. Sewage is by definition any waste material carried by sewers, and as such it often contains wastes from industries and small businesses such as garages, as well as runoff from streets and highways, in addition to household wastes. Its major constituent is dissolved and particulate organic matter containing rich populations of microbes, some pathogenic to man. It commonly contains ammonia nitrogen, phosphate phosphorus, oil and grease, detergents, phenols, cyanide, arsenic, and trace metals—cadmium, chromium, copper, iron, lead, manganese, mercury, nickel, silver, and zinc—in concentrations that vary with the source of the waste. Runoff into sewers from landscaped areas contains DDT, other pesticides, and herbicides.

Over 8 billion gallons of municipal sewage are discharged each day to the nation's coastal waters, about one-half receiving secondary treatment (Table 1). Greater New York City alone accounts for nearly 2 billion gallons per day, a quantity roughly double that of the entire California coast from San Francisco to San Diego, and about 10 times that of the southeast Florida coast from Palm Beach to Miami. (Figure 1)

Three levels of sewage treatment—primary, secondary, and tertiary—are recognized, although tertiary treatment is still basically in the pilot-plant stage of development. Primary treatment removes much floating and solid materials by skimming, screening, and sedimentation. Secondary treatment eliminates nearly all remaining solid materials by sedimentation and biological treatment, but it does not remove considerable quantities of dissolved phosphates, nitrates, organic materials, and trace metals; some metals are removed quite effectively, whereas others exhibit small or no re-

Table 7.11.1 Municipal waste discharges in the coastal zone, including estuaries[1]

Region[2]	Total volume of Municipal wastes (mgd) [3]	Percent of sewered population with secondary treatment 1968[4]
North Atlantic	550	25
Middle Atlantic	3500	60
Chesapeake Bay	640	90
South Atlantic	370	75
Caribbean	160	--[5]
Gulf of Mexico	760	75
Pacific Southwest	1900	35
Pacific Northwest	390	50
Alaska	13	25
Pacific Islands	85	25
Total	8300	50

[1] Source: U.S. Department of the the Interior, 1970. National Estuarine Pollution Study. U.S. Government Printing Office. See p. 257.

[2] North Atlantic: Canadian border to Cape Cod.
   Middle Atlantic: Cape Cod to Cape Hatteras excluding Chesapeake Bay.
   Chesapeake Bay: Chesapeake Bay systems inland of Cape Charles and Cape Henry.
   South Atlantic: Cape Hatteras to Fort Lauderdale, FL.
   Caribbean: Fort Lauderdale to Cape Romano, FL, plus Puerto Rico and Virgin Islands.
   Gulf of Mexico: Cape Romano to Mexican border.
   Pacific Southwest: Mexican border to Cape Mendocino.
   Pacific Northwest: Cape Mendocino to Canadian Border.
   Alaska: Alaska.
   Pacific Islands: Hawaii, Guam, American Samoa.

[3] Based on 150 gallons per capita per day of total population in coastal counties plus a few noncoastal counties, 1965. (See source)

[4] Data from U.S. Department of the Interior, Federal Water Pollution Control Administration, 1969. Cost of Clean Water.

[5] Not available.

duction. Tertiary treatment removes phosphates, nitrates, and other dissolved materials chemically. Much sewage discharged to coastal waters receives little treatment beyond comminution and maceration, which reduces the size of solid particles but does little to remove bacteria and viruses. Chlorination of effluent is commonly employed to kill pathogenic organisms. The extracted solid material (sludge) is burned, spread on land, buried, or dumped at sea. Roughly 70 percent of the nation's sludge dumping at sea by barge is done off metropolitan New York City. Pumping of sludge through pipes well offshore is practiced in southern California.

The degree of treatment is important ecologically. If untreated, sewage discharged in water bodies causes bacterial and viral contamination, high turbidity, accumulation of sludge, depletion of dissolved oxygen, eleva-

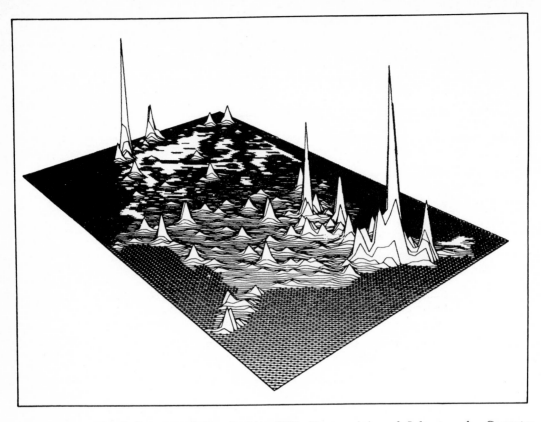

Figure 7.11.1 United States population densities, 1970. (By permission of Laboratory for Computer Graphics and Spatial Analysis, Graduate School of Design, Harvard University.)

tion of plant nutrients, and accumulation of toxicants when present. If given proper secondary treatment, the discharged effluent's addition of plant nutrients is of primary concern unless sludge containing toxicants and undecomposed organic material is dumped or pumped into the environment. In this case the concerns are much the same as if untreated sewage were being discharged. In practice, however, treatment plants frequently operate below design capability; virtually all effluents exhibit some or all of the characteristics of untreated sewage at times. For example, if storm sewers discharge to a treatment plant, the high flow of water through the plant during heavy rains precludes complete design treatment.

The ultimate goal of the Federal Water Pollution Control Act Amendments of 1972 is to eliminate the discharge of pollutants to the nation's waters by 1985. The bill calls for

"best practicable" treatment by 1983. A second, intermediate goal is that all sewage treatment plants attain a minimum of secondary treatment by July 1, 1977. A central problem in implementation is that estimates of the total cost to attain nationwide secondary treatment have increased dramatically since the bill was written, while at the same time yearly expenditures have risen very little. The Act authorized federal grants totaling $18 billion for municipal waste treatment plants on the basis of a needs survey conducted while writing the bill. Subsequent annual surveys increased this estimate to $60 billion in 1973, and $114 billion in 1974. Actual expenditures for sewage treatment were about $3.2 billion in 1972 and about $3.5 billion in 1973, the last year for which figures are available.

The very low incidence of disease traceable to either bathing in polluted water or eating contaminated shellfish attests to the effectiveness of the controls exercised by public health agencies in the United States. But the fact that disease incidents do occur from time to time indicates that control could be improved. Pathogenic microorganisms of primary concern include the Salmonellae (typhoid), *Shigella* species (dysentery), *Leptospira* species (jaundice), and the intestinal viruses, including the virus of infectious hepatitis. Fortunately, most pathogenic organisms die in reasonable time in the hostile environments of sewage systems and coastal waters. Water and the meats of molluscan shellfish are tested routinely for numbers of the coliform group of bacteria, which serve as rough indicators of the presence of pathogens associated with fecal material of human origin. Testing directly for human pathogens is seldom attempted because the procedures are complex and few laboratories possess the necessary equipment and trained personnel.

Standards for waters in which molluscan shellfish are harvested are more stringent than those for bathing and swimming waters. General agreement has not been reached in the United States or internationally through the World Health Organization on uniform standards applicable to coastal bathing and swimming waters because of the difficulty encountered in demonstrating direct correlation of coliform bacterial levels with epidemiological evidence. Standards are set by state and local public health agencies. In contrast, uniformly strict standards are maintained for the coastal waters of the United States from which molluscan shellfish are harvested, because oysters, clams, and mussels can filter bacterial and viral pathogens from coastal waters and concentrate them. Many examples exist of disease attributable to eating contaminated shellfish. For example, in Italy in 1973, 70 confirmed cases of cholera including four deaths were linked to eating mussels contaminated by *Vibrio cholerae.* Approximately 20 percent of America's shellfish-producing areas are closed because of pollution and patrolled to prevent harvesting.

The aesthetic value of coastal water is universally acknowledged and is increasingly a strong motivation for pollution abatement. Community disgust has frequently polarized to bring about improvement. For example,

even though other values were involved, cleaning up the Thames River, England, over the past 15 years at a cost of $500 million reflects the determination of Londoners to have a river and an estuary they could enjoy and be proud of. The elimination of untreated sewage from northern Biscayne Bay, San Diego Bay, and Lake Washington reflects similar determination on the part of the residents of Miami, San Diego, and Seattle, respectively. In the New York metropolitan area, oil slicks mark areas of recent sludge dumping, and solid objects from sewage sludge litter bathing beaches, to the dismay of sport fishermen and people using the beaches.

Sewage discharge is mixed, diluted, and removed by water movements. The longer it remains in an area, the more pronounced are its effects. Water movement flushes rivers, estuaries, and shelf areas, the rate of flushing depending basically on the relation of the rate of inflow (hence outflow) and the volume of the body of water being flushed. Flushing time varies widely. For example, flushing time in the inner New York Bight and on the continental shelf shoreward of sewage outfalls off southeastern Florida is about 1 week, whereas in several estuaries it is considerably greater. Flushing time is 10 to 21 days for Raritan Bay (high river flow), about 25 days for Long Island Sound, 33 to 87 days for Delaware Bay (high river flow), and about 52 days for the Bay of Fundy. The foregoing estuarine figures are based on the parts of bays that flush most completely. Other parts flush less efficiently with the result that pollutants tend to accumulate in particular local areas.

Sewage exerts separate but interrelated effects on the three biological components of coastal ecosystems: the plankton (suspended plant and animal life), the benthos (bottom-dwelling life), and the nekton (swimming life). The effects of sewage effluent are complex because it contains both dissolved and particulate constituents, both growth-stimulating and lethal or debilitating substances, and both biodegradable and persistent materials. Particulate material is of concern because oxygen is utilized in its biodegradation and because metals and other persistent toxicants are adsorbed to it. Most particulate material is slightly more dense than seawater and gradually settles to the bottom. While settling, it reduces light penetration and serves as food for bacteria and filter-feeding organisms. Once on the bottom it becomes incorporated into sediments, where it continues to serve as food for bacteria and filter-feeders, and for deposit-feeding invertebrates as well. Dissolved oxygen is removed from the water and utilized during the entire process, often to an excessive degree. The U.S. Environmental Protection Agency (EPA) has recently determined that reduction of dissolved oxygen to a level below 4 ppm can be expected to change the kinds and abundance of populations of aquatic life. This concentration is used by the EPA as the minimum allowable level.

The net effect of sewage is to stimulate the population growth of both phytoplankton (plant plankton) and zooplankton (animal plankton). It does so by providing dissolved fertilizing compounds of nitrogen and phosphorus, which the phytoplankton take up when light and other conditions are favorable. Because the zooplankton feed on the phytoplankton, they too increase. This growth-stimulating process is frequently excessive, resulting in an overabundance of phytoplankton, known as a "plankton bloom." If, as often occurs, cloudy weather develops, or the supply of nutrients becomes depleted, the phytoplankton suddenly die, and with them the zooplankton. The decomposing plankton settle to the bottom, where they deplete the available dissolved oxygen, often resulting in reduction of oxygen concentration below that required by other organisms, including fish. Fish kills frequently result.

Research of recent years is demonstrating that the relatively minute phytoplankton (nannoplankton) are favored over larger phytoplankton (e.g., diatoms) by the fertilizing effects of coastal pollution. For example, duck farm wastes emptying into Moriches Bay, Long Island, New York, resulted in excessive abundance of the minute *Nannochloris atomus* at the expense of a normally occurring larger diatom on which the oysters were feeding. Serious damage to the valuable oyster fishery occurred because of an unusually low nitrogen-to-phosphorus ratio, indicative of fecal pollution, which was associated with the species shift. Similar examples of species imbalance

have continued to be demonstrated elsewhere. Work in the New York Bight and elsewhere has shown that nitrogen is the growth stimulant, rather than phosphorus.

The stimulating effects of added nitrogen and other nutrients are, however, counterbalanced to some degree by decreased transparency near outfalls (which limits light penetration and reduces photosynthesis) and by the lethal or debilitating effects of toxicants that kill or inhibit plankton. The toxicants include heavy metals, phenols, and arsenic, which depress the growth of phytoplankton and small zooplankton. Most marine animals have planktonic eggs and larvae that are more vulnerable to toxicants, than the older individuals.

The pattern of the distribution of the benthos (bottom animal life) with distance away from untreated sewage and sludge deposits is well documented. Benthic macroinvertebrate populations (larger invertebrate bottom life) are commonly reduced in the immediate vicinity of outfall pipes or sewage sludge dump sites, increased along the periphery, and finally returned to normal beyond the periphery (Figure 2). Particulate material of the type in sewage sludge constitutes food for the benthos. Unusually large populations of bottom-dwelling invertebrates occur where prevailing currents carry food to the animals, oxygen is ample, and sediment is suitable (Figure 3). Close to outfalls or within sewage sludge dump sites, depressed populations are associated with low dissolved oxygen and accumulations of toxicants such as heavy metals.

Crustaceans that move across the bottom over and around sewage sludge deposits are vulnerable to environmental stress. For example, diseased and dead crabs, *Cancer irroratus*, have been found at the New York Bight sludge dump site. Their shells had necrotic lesions, the gill chambers were partially filled with sludge sediments, and the gills were heavily fouled with sediments. Other large crustaceans showing pathogenic symptoms have also been sampled at this site.

The relation of nekton (free-swimming animals) to sewage and sludge is documented to a lesser degree than that of plankton and benthos, largely because fish and other swimming life can avoid polluted areas and because

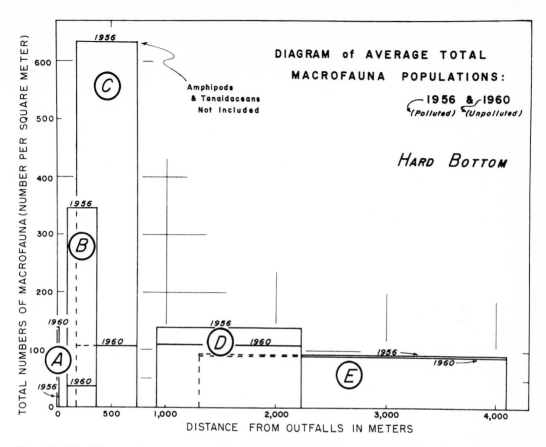

Figure 7.11.2 Diagram of average numbers of bottom-dwelling macroinvertebrates screened from Biscayne Bay sediments at various distances from outfalls before and after sewage pollution abatement. (From J. K. McNulty, *Effects of Abatement of Domestic Sewage Pollution on the Benthos, Volumes of Zooplankton, and the Fouling Organisms of Biscayne Bay, Florida*, Studies in Tropical Oceanography, No. 9, 1970. By permission of University of Miami Press.)

sampling them is difficult. Evidence exists, however, that sewage-tolerant species replace less tolerant species in polluted areas, that some bottom-dwelling fish avoid sludge-covered areas, and that the incidence of disease is relatively high in sewage-polluted waters. For example, the incidence of fin rot disease is higher in fish of the inner New York Bight than in those of adjacent unpolluted coastal waters. Fish afflicted with fin rot, also called "fin erosion," have fins partially or totally missing. The disease is also known from sewage-polluted areas of Narragansett Bay (Rhode Island), the Irish Sea and southern California (particularly in the area affected by discharge from the Los Angeles White Point

sewer plant). Infected species include the Dover sole of California (*Microstomus pacificus*), winter flounder (*Pseudopleuronectes americanus*), summer flounder (*Paralichthyes dentatus*), bluefish (*Pomatomus saltatrix*), and weakfish (*Cynoscion regalis*) of the northeastern United States; and plaice (*Pleuronectes platessa*) of the Irish Sea. Although the search for exact causes continues, both bacteriological and toxic metal associations have been implicated so far.

In summary, sewage pollution of coastal waters is a major environmental problem because sewage endangers human health, offends the senses, and disrupts and sometimes kills marine life. Sewage restricts or prohibits food

Figure 7.11.3 Diagram of the macroinvertebrates screened from hard-bottom (sandy) sediments of Biscayne Bay 185 to 740 meters from raw sewage outfalls before and after sewage pollution abatement. (From J. K. McNulty, *Effects of Abatement of Domestic Sewage Pollution on the Benthos, Volumes of Zooplankton, and the Fouling Organisms of Biscayne Bay, Florida*, Studies in Tropical Oceanography, No. 9, 1970. By permission of University of Miami Press.)

production, recreational use, and general enjoyment of coastal waters. Although abatement nationwide is falling short of the scheduled goals of the Federal Water Pollution Control Act Amendments of 1972, important local improvements continue to be made.

12. DREDGING—ECOLOGICAL IMPACTS

Dr. Edward T. LaRoe
Office of Coastal Zone Management
National Oceanic and Atmospheric
  Administration
Washington, D.C.

Dredging, the excavation of bottom material, and filling, the deposition of materials onto the bottom, are construction techniques used widely in the coastal zone. *Dredging* may be performed to create and maintain canals, navigation channels, turning basins, harbors, and marinas; to lay pipeline; and to obtain a source of material for fill or construction. *Filling* relates to the deposition of dredged materials, either for the specific purpose of creating real estate or for disposal of the by-product (dredge spoil) produced during dredging.

The wide-scale practice of dredging and filling, especially to create fast land, dates from only the early 1900s; the first large-scale landfill project began in Orchard Beach, New York, in 1937. Since that time, however, a significant share of the nation's biologically important estuarine habitat has been altered by dredge and fill. In 1967 the U.S. Department of the Interior reported that the nation had lost 7.7 percent of its important fish and wildlife estuarine habitat. This loss varies significantly among the states, with California having destroyed 67 percent of its estuaries,

New York 16 percent, and New Jersey 13 percent. More recently, it was estimated that 23 percent of United States estuaries have been severely modified, and 50 percent moderately so.

The primary incentives to dredge and fill are financial. Estuarine and offshore dredging is an inexpensive and frequently convenient source of sand and aggregate, which can be used for fill, beach restoration, and construction. Filling bay bottom, submerged lands, and tidal marshes is also an inexpensive method of creating valuable new real estate. Dredging navigation channels and harbors, whether by private industry or as a public works project, is also in response to financial benefits. Although the economic gains from such projects may be quite large, especially in relation to the investment, they are also frequently of benefit to only a small segment of the population. Until recently, however, the great loss of public resources which they may cause has been generally ignored.

Dredge and fill activities adversely affect the estuarine system in a variety of ways. They can create short- and long-term changes in water currents, circulation, mixing, flushing, and salinity; add to the water turbidity, siltation, and pollution; and lower the dissolved oxygen. The effects are frequently synergistic, creating severe stress on the estuarine environment which leads to an imbalance and unstable conditions. As a result, the rich estuarine benefits are reduced or destroyed. The most obvious effect of dredge and fill is the direct destruction of habitat. Submerged bottoms or coastal wetlands, along with their associated organisms, are directly destroyed by these processes. These activities assume special significance because of the great importance of submerged coastal lands and benthic organisms. In addition, dredging produces spoil, which must be disposed of, and filling requires some area to be dredged for a source of fill material; such operations cause a twofold destruction of habitat that extends beyond the area of primary concern.

In addition to the direct loss of habitat that accompanies dredge and fill, the removal, transportation, and deposition of sediment create and disperse large quantities of silt and debris. The larger sediment particles quickly settle out of the water column, but the finer particles can be carried for extensive distances —over 0.5 mile—before settling out. In such fashion the effects of dredge and fill can extend far beyond the project boundaries. Moreover, the finer sediments are easily resuspended by tidal and wind currents, and the silt-related effects are therefore extended in time or duration as well as in area.

Suspended silt creates a number of adverse environmental impacts. As it settles, it physically smothers bottom-dwelling plants and animals; while suspended it can actually smother fish by clogging their gill structures. The fish and other mobile organisms not killed are usually driven from the area. The behavior of remaining organisms can be severely modified. High turbidities reduce vision and can mask odors, both important to the survival of many fish. Suspended silt can clog the feeding mechanism of filter feeders; some species, such as oysters, cease feeding under turbid conditions. This retards growth and weakens the health of the animal.

Estuarine sediments generally have a very high organic content which could result in anaerobic conditions, leading to the development of toxic hydrogen sulfide deposits. Marine grasses keep the upper sediments aerobic by absorbing oxygen from the water and passing it, via their root systems, into the sediments. Coarse sediments that promote interstitial water circulation also aid in aeration of the subsurface layers. This aerobic state is necessary for the development of a healthy, productive bottom community. Fine sediments created by dredging can seal the bottom, reducing interstitial circulation. Once the bottom is sealed and the grasses are destroyed, the upper sediments can turn anaerobic, further adding to the difficulty of reestablishing the valuable bottom fauna and flora.

By increasing turbidity, the silt, which is suspended during dredge-and-fill operations or is subsequently resuspended by water currents, decreases light penetration into the water. This in turn reduces photosynthesis (which is related to light intensity) and results in decreased productivity and a lowered dissolved oxygen concentration. These effects, coupled with the release of anaerobic (reduced) sediments and the increased biochemical oxygen demand (BOD) placed on the water column by the organic matter suspended in the sediments, can significantly and seriously depress the dissolved oxygen in the vicinity of dredge, fill, and channelization activities.

Estuarine sediments also act as a pollutant trap or sink. Many kinds of pollutants, including heavy metals and pesticides, are adsorbed onto the sediments. Dredging operations resuspend these in the water column, increasing the hazardous exposure to plants and animals. The silt suspension can also increase nutrient release, leading to eutrophic blooms.

The conditions that result from dredge-and-fill activities create other long-term problems beyond the immediate and direct impact. Under normal conditions, for example, marine grasses and tidal marshes provide a number of benefits in addition to their enormous contributions of productivity and of habitat. They stabilize the exposed and submerged soils, preventing erosion. Destruction of the vegetated bottoms and replacement with denuded unconsolidated sediments—dredged bottoms, cut channels with barren banks, and spoil or fill deposits, for example—induce future erosion, creating an extended problem of high turbidities that depress life.

In addition to physically stabilizing or binding the soil, wetland and submerged vegetation provides a natural filtration system that removes silt, debris, and particulate matter and serves to maintain water quality. Tidal and submerged vegetation, its associates, and the organic material it produces also adsorb chemical pollutants, including dissolved nutrients and organic compounds such as hydrocarbons. This filtering process is dependent on the slow flow and extended contact of the water mass with the vegetation. The destruction of marshes, mangroves, and sea grasses by dredge and fill results in the loss of these natural purifying systems.

Once vegetation and filtering systems have been destroyed, conditions in broad areas of an estuary can become unstable. As erosion continues, turbidity increases, dissolved oxygen decreases, and adjacent bottom plants and animals are destroyed; greater stress is placed on the remaining estuarine areas. If sufficiently stressed, they too can become barren, adding to the decay a new source of erosion and silt

and a new oxygen sink, and in a cyclic fashion conditions progressively deteriorate.

As silt deposits accumulate in the estuary, they form a "false bottom." Characterized by shifting, unstable sediments, the dredged bottoms, fill deposits, or spoil areas are only slowly, if at all, recolonized. The larvae of many bottom-dwelling animals, such as oysters, snails, and crustaceans, will search for hard bottoms and will fail to settle on soft, unconsolidated sediments. A veneer of silt over a hard bottom will prevent many forms from settling. Even some burrowing animals will refuse to settle on dredged bottoms because the fine sediments do not permit adequate oxygen exchange and may interfere with feeding and tube or burrow building.

The physical alterations associated with dredge and fill can also adversely affect the environment. For example, dredging and channelization result in deepened areas or depressions in the bottom. One simple but frequent result is that the deepened bottoms may be below the depth of light penetration. This acts to prevent recolonization by grasses or algae and is a permanent effect.

Depressions—either basins or channels—as well as areas of fill or spoil banks can result in long-term changes in currents and water circulation. These may affect the mixing and flushing of estuarine waters, eventually causing changes in water temperature, salinity, dissolved oxygen, sediment accumulation, and ultimately productivity.

In contrast to the generally mixed water masses in shallow estuaries, the water below the rim ("sill depth") of dredged basins or borrow pits tends to have restricted circulation and hence a reduced oxygen content. On a large scale spoil banks and fill deposits can act as a dam, restricting water flow and tidal exchange. This can be especially damaging if one portion of an estuary is isolated from another by long, uninterrupted spoil banks, created frequently by channel construction or by "finger fill" projections. Altered in this fashion, large portions of estuarine areas can be degraded or removed as productive units from the total system.

The stagnant waters in artifically deepened areas or man-made basins also act as sediment traps. The sediment settling in these basins usually becomes anaerobic. Such sediments reduce water quality and productivity in three ways: the area itself is unproductive; low-quality water slowly leaches out, affecting neighboring waters; and during storms large volumes of accumulated debris and anaerobic sediments may be flushed out, causing a sudden shock to water quality and surrounding organisms.

Dredged channels themselves act in a number of adverse ways. They, too, may change water flow characteristics. This can greatly disturb water quality, especially the important freshwater—saltwater balance. In natural conditions, estuaries are fed by overland freshwater runoff across the marshes, mangroves, and wetlands, and by freshwater input from rivers and creeks. The natural system is one of moderate and gradual changes, which encourage a steady state of high productivity. Dredged channels can greatly modify this overland and riverine flow. By diverting overland flow from coastal wetlands and by bypassing the river meanders, channels rush fresh water to the estuary, delivering it in surges following rains. Because runoff drains away so rapidly, the period or duration of freshwater inflow is greatly reduced, and the natural system of moderate change is replaced by one of sudden extremes. Also, the zone of brackish water mixing—the most productive zone biologically—is reduced.

In addition to increased drainage, dredged channels also provide an avenue for saltwater intrusion. Lying almost undiluted below the freshwater strata, tongues of dense salt water may extend up dredged channels for several miles inland. Overdrainage caused by channels can also lead to salt water intrusion by lowering the freshwater head and by reduction of the hydroperiod. Increased salinites in marsh and wetland communities may lower their biological productivity; coastal groundwater reserves may also be contaminated.

Diversion of water from overland flow across coastal marshes by dredged channels reduces the productive nutrient input from those marshes. It also removes the water from the filtering effect gained by contact with the vegetation, and in its place imposes a new stress on water quality and productivity—the septic canal.

The resultant effect of dredge and fill activities is the accumulation of a series of stresses which may result in loss of biological productivity, diversity, and value; the increase of trash or unwanted species; the loss of desirable species; and ultimately the destruction of the biological system.

Federal law assigns primary regulatory and permitting authority for dredge and fill activities in navigable waters to the U.S. Army Corps of Engineers, under the overview of the U.S. Environmental Protection Agency (EPA). The permit process provides for the issuance of a public notice and for public comments, which may be made on all relevant factors, including economics, navigation, conservation, aesthetics, historic value, fish and wildlife values, flood damage prevention, recreation, land use, water supply, water quality, general environmental concerns, and, in general, the needs and welfare of the people. The Fish and Wildlife Coordination Act requires that the Corps of Engineers consult with representatives of the Fish and Wildlife Service (Interior) and the National Marine Fisheries Service (Commerce) and satisfy the EPA with regard to potential effects of dredge-and-fill activities on fish and wildlife resources. In addition to requirements for dredge and fill, a variety of agencies may exercise some degree of control or permitting authority.

In addition to its regulatory role, the Corps of Engineers is also directly responsible for conducting most of the coastal dredge and fill in the United States. As an agency, it dredges enormous volumes of material annually in the construction and continual maintenance of navigable waterways, harbors, and ports, the Intracoastal Waterway, and flood protection projects, as well as for beach restoration and enhancement. The Corps of Engineers spends over $100 million yearly just to maintain United States navigable waterways.

REFERENCES

1. Mark F. Godcharles. 1971. *A Study of the Effects of a Commercial Hydraulic Clam Dredge on Benthic Communities in Estuarine Areas.* Florida Department of Natural Re-

sources, Technical Series No. 64, St. Petersburg, Florida.

2. Edward T. LaRoe. 1972. "Horse Creek—effects of dredge and fill activities in the Cocohatchee River." *Florida Naturalist*, Vol. 45, No. 6, pp. 166–169.

3. A. R. Marshall. 1968. "Dredging and filling." In *Proceedings of the Marsh and Estuarine Management Symposium*, Louisiana State University, Baton Rouge, Louisiana, July 19-20, 1967.

4. Edwin B. May. 1973. "Extensive oxygen depletion in Mobile Bay, Alabama." *Limnology and Oceanography*, Vol. 18, No. 3, pp. 353–366.

5. Thomas Savage. 1972. *Florida Mangroves as Shoreline Stabilizers*. Florida Department of Natural Resources, Professional Papers Series No. 19, St. Petersburg, Florida.

6. James E. Sykes and John R. Hall. 1970. "Comparative distribution of mollusks in dredged and undredged portions of an estuary, with a systematic list of species." *Fishery Bulletin*, Vol. 68, No. 2, pp. 299–306.

7. John L. Taylor and Carl H. Saloman. 1968. "Some effects of hydraulic dredging and coastal development in Boca Ciega Bay, Florida." *Fishery Bulletin*, Vol. 67, No. 2, pp. 213–241.

8. U. S. Army Corps of Engineers. 1973. *Dredged Materials Research*. Miscellaneous Paper No. D-73-1.

9. U. S. Department of the Interior, Fish and Wildlife Service. 1970. *National Estuary Study*. Washington, D.C.

10. U. S. Committee on Merchant Marine and Fisheries. 1967. *Estuarine Areas*. Report No. 989 to the 90th Congress, 1st Session, House of Representatives.

13. ESTUARINE CIRCULATION

James P. Schweitzer
Associate Professor of
Marine Sciences and Education
Louisiana State University
Baton Rouge, Louisiana

NOTE. Adapted from LSU Marine Science Teaching Aid, Issue No. 6, Center for Wetland Resources, Louisiana State University, Baton Rouge, Louisiana, April 1975.

If a marine biologist, a geographer, and a physical oceanographer each were asked to define the term "estuary," the three definitions might differ considerably. The biologist would want to emphasize that estuaries provide living organisms with widely varying salinity conditions. The geographer would stress the fluvial, marine, and sedimentary processes at work in a drowned river mouth. The physical oceanographer's attention would be drawn to the interplay of river flow, tidal fluctuations, and the density distribution.

Dictionaries also differ in their definitions of an estuary. According to the *Concise Oxford Dictionary*, an estuary is "the tidal mouth of a large river." *Webster's Seventh New Collegiate Dictionary* defines an estuary as "a water passage where the tide meets a river current." *Webster's Third New International* gives three definitions, one of which is "a drowned river mouth caused by the sinking of the land near the coast."

A good working definition of an estuary, if not satisfactory to everyone, is "an embayment of water at the margin of the sea in which there is a considerable mixture of salt and fresh water." An estuary should have these three features:

1. It is coastal.
2. It involves the mixing of two kinds of water, seawater and fresh water, which have essentially different salinities.
3. Its circulation is strongly influenced by the presence of boundaries.

However defined, estuaries are important for a number of reasons. As biological habitats they tend to be enormously productive, in both the variety and the volume of organic material. Many estuaries have economic importance in that they are portals of commerce; they provide a protected anchorage for ships and direct access to up-stream river ports. Estuaries tend to be very active geological environments because the dynamic processes of the sea meet frontally with the processes of the land augmented by the flow of river water and sediment.

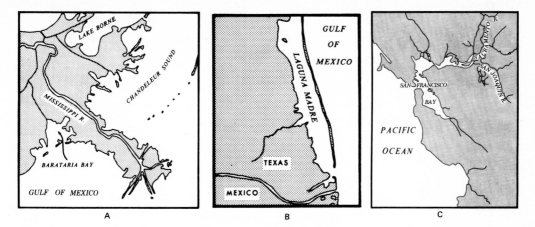

Figure 7.13.1   (A) Mississippi River delta, a coastal plains, drowned river valley estuary, and Barataria Bay, a bar-bounded estuary; (B) Laguna Madre, an "estuary in reverse"; (C) San Francisco Bay, a tectonic estuary.

KINDS OF ESTUARIES

Estuaries may result from the drowning of a river valley (a coastal plains estuary), the drowning of a glacial valley (a fiord), the occurrence of an offshore barrier (a bar-bounded estuary), or some tectonic process (a tectonic estuary or bay).

The coastal plains estuary most closely conforms to the classical estuaries defined by physical geographers and oceanographers. Many estuaries of the eastern United States are of the coastal plains type. These include the Chesapeake and Delaware bays and the estuaries of the Hudson, Savannah, and Mississippi rivers. In Europe the Po, Rhine, Danube, Thames, and Seine rivers all terminate as coastal plains estuaries. Additional examples include the Si Kiang (China), the Murray (Australia), the Niger and the Nile (Africa), and the Amazon (South America).

All fiords have been gouged out by glaciers. They tend to be deep and narrow and are characteristically u-shaped in cross section. Often they have shallower sills resulting from accumulated moraine deposits. The largest fiords occur in Scandinavia, British Columbia, and Chile.

Bar-bounded estuaries result from the development of an offshore barrier, which may be a beach strand, a line of barrier islands, reef formations, a line of moraine debris, or the subsiding remnants of a deltaic lobe. Albemarle and Pamlico sounds in North Carolina (see map, Figure 2E) and Mississippi Sound (Figure 2F) and Barataria Bay (Figure 1A) along the Gulf of Mexico are bar-bounded estuaries. Long Island Sound resembles both a coastal plains and a bar-bounded estuary. Its circulation is complicated by the fact that most of its fresh water is introduced by several rivers near the eastern (open) end of the estuary. Laguna Madre, along the Texas–Tamaulipas coasts, is similar to a bar-bounded estuary (Figure 1B). Its scant freshwater inflow and its excessive evaporation, however, create salt concentrations higher than those of normal seawater, thus making Laguna Madre an "estuary in reverse."

The fourth category of estuaries includes those resulting from tectonic processes but may also serve as a catchall for estuaries not clearly included in the other divisions. San Francisco Bay as a whole may be a tectonic estuary because it probably resulted from slippage along fault lines, although the San Joaquin–Sacramento River delta complex may be of the coastal plains type (see Figure 1C).

The foregoing classification of estuaries, based on geological origin, is useful, but the physical oceanographer needs to study and compare estuaries on the basis of such physical

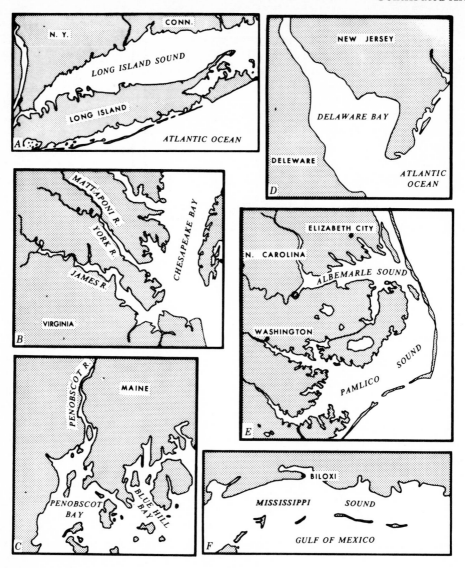

Figure 7.13.2   (A) Long Island Sound, (B) Chesapeake Bay, (C) Penobscot Bay, (D) Delaware Bay, (E) Albemarle and Pamlico sounds, (F) Mississippi Sound.

processes and parameters as density distribution, rates of water and salt exchange, and circulation patterns. The intent of this article is to review briefly and nonmathematically some of the physical aspects of estuaries, especially the circulation patterns. The concepts treated here are based primarily on the work of D. W. Pritchard and others at the Chesapeake Bay Institute of The Johns Hopkins University.[1, 2]

CAUSES OF CIRCULATION

In 1951 the American oceanographer Henry Strommel suggested that the major forces that cause circulation in estuaries could be used as a unifying principle in classifying estuaries. These forces are (1) the wind, (2) the tidal flow, and (3) the river flow. Most bar-bounded estuaries are wind-dominated; principally, it is the wind that mixes and moves water about in such estuaries. On the other hand, river flow controls the mixing and movement of water in the Mississippi delta, decidedly a river-dominated estuary. Other estuaries, notably the James River (Virginia) and the Penobscot River (Maine), are tide-dominated.

Clearly no estuary is entirely dominated by any single major cause of circulation. In every estuary all three of the driving forces exert their influence. Thus every estuary has a pattern of circulation which has been brought about by a dynamic balance unique to that estuary in both time and geometry. In view of the wide range of possible circulation patterns in nature, there must be a continuous sequence of circulation patterns rather than a few discrete varieties.

Obviously the same causes that mix and move water in an estuary also mix and distribute salt. Thus the distribution of salt, relatively easy to measure, is both an indicator and a result of the circulation pattern for a given estuary.

A SEQUENCE OF ESTUARINE TYPES

Over the years D. W. Pritchard and his co-workers have devised a classification of estuarine types based on circulation and salt distribution. The system works extremely well when it is applied to the classical coastal plains–drowned river valley estuary. Such an estuary more nearly conforms to an idealized shape, which involves a long embayment with increasing seaward depth and width. Tectonic and bar-bounded estuaries, and even fiords,

often depart radically from the shape and physical dimensions of the idealized coastal plains estuary. In many instances their circulation is so heavily influenced by their physical geography that they do not fit any scheme of classification yet devised.

Although Pritchard's classification of estuarine types is intended to be a continuum, he has identified four major groupings:

A. Highly stratified estuary.
B. Partially stratified estuary.
C. Vertically homogeneous estuary.
D. Sectionally homogeneous estuary.

Highly Stratified Estuary (Type A)

Consider Figure 3, which illustrates an idealized coastal plains estuary. A river bed extends from above sea level and slopes downward to below sea level. Let us suppose that there is no wind, no tide, and no river flow. Seawater has invaded the riverbed up to a "fall line," where the riverbed is at sea level. The shape of the salt water in the riverbed resembles a wedge. There is a sharp division between the river water above and the salt water below. The boundary separating the fresh and the salt water is known as a halocline.

The static model suggested cannot exist in nature because of gravity, wind, tidal movements, river flow, and the mixing of water across density boundaries. But the model is useful in that it serves as one extreme in our continuum of estuarine types. Now we can subject our model to the first change. We will allow the river to flow normally.

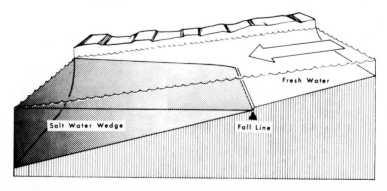

Figure 7.13.3 An idealized coastal plains estuary. (SOURCE: Adapted from Reference 3.)

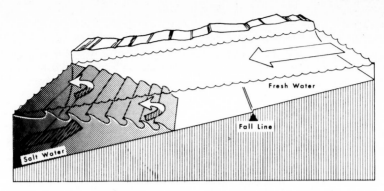

Figure 7.13.4   A highly stratified estuary (Type A). (SOURCE: Adapted from Reference 3.)

With the addition of river flow several things happen. First, the river flow creates both pressure and shear forces, which tend to push the wedge of salt water seaward beyond the fall line. The salt water wedge now slopes upward in the seaward direction. The less dense river water overrides the salt water and spreads outward in a thinner and thinner layer toward the open end of the estuary.

Even if the river did not flow, there would be some mixing, due to diffusion of salt and fresh water across the halocline, which in turn would become somewhat blurred. As the river flow is introduced, the landward edge of the saltwater wedge is pushed seaward, and the amount of diffusion across the halocline increases.

If the river flow is increased even more, the halocline becomes unstable. The first indication of instability occurs as internal waves form along the halocline (see Figure 4). The formation of these internal waves is somewhat analogous to the transfer of energy from the wind to the surface of the sea in the wave-building process. The internal waves are subject to the laws governing all waves; this means that the waves will break under conditions of instability. As the internal waves along the halocline break, volumes of salt water become entrained in the flow of fresh water above.

In 1949 G. H. Keulegan conducted experiments in a flume, using fluids of different densities.[4] He was able to reproduce the conditions found in a highly stratified estuary. As he reduced his "river flow," there was almost no mixing between the fluids he used. When he increased his river flow, however, large internal waves began to form and break along the interface between the fluids. Curiously, Keulegan's waves always broke upward and never downward. This upward breaking of the internal waves in an actual highly stratified estuary causes the movement of salt always to be upward. Thus the river water becomes increasingly saline as it moves seaward, but the lower layer of water retains its original salinity. The continued loss of salt water from the lower to the upper layer requires weak currents of salt water flowing in from the sea along the bottom of the estuary to replace salt water lost to the upper layer.

The highly stratified estuary occurs under conditions involving a large river flow, a relatively small flow resulting from tides, and a relatively small ratio of width to depth. A major characteristic of such an estuary is a division between fresh and salt water that is rather sharply defined in the vertical direction. These conditions are found at the mouths of the Po, the Danube, and the Mississippi rivers. The Mississippi River estuary in places may be as deep as 30 meters, but the transition from entirely fresh water to undiluted seawater may occur in a zone no thicker than 1 meter.

Partially Stratified Estuary (Type B)

In the partially stratified estuary (see Figure 5) the primary agent of mixing is no longer shear along the halocline but rather a turbulence resulting from tidal currents. Internal waves along the halocline in the highly stratified estuary (Type A) have resulted in the addition of salt water to the upper layers of fresh water,

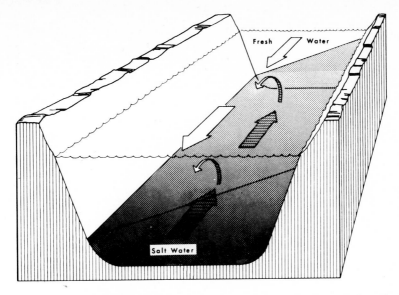

Figure 7.13.5   A partially stratified estuary (Type B). (SOURCE: Adapted from Reference 3.)

causing an increasing salinity in the surface waters at the seaward end of the estuary. Under the conditions described in the Type A estuary, uniformity of salinity existed throughout the volume of salt water below. When tidal movements are added to the Type A estuary, however, a general mixing of water occurs at all levels. Not only is salt water added to the upper layer, but also fresh water is introduced to the lower level.

Essentially, the difference between Type A and Type B estuaries is that the effects of tidal currents and turbulence are added to the conditions that prevailed in the Type A estuary. Even though mixing occurs at all levels, there is still a degree of stratification in the Type B estuary, as the name implies.

The transition from Type A to Type B can be accomplished either by decreasing the flow of river water or by increasing the turbulence due to tidal currents. It should be emphasized that it is not the absolute magnitudes of river flow and tidal flow that are important. Rather, it is their relative sizes that determine the classification of an estuary.

No sharp halocline is likely to exist in the Type B estuary; there is, however, a faint boundary between the fresher water above the saltier water below. This faint horizontal boundary separating layers of various salinities will not be level from one side of the estuary to the other. The outward-flowing fresh water will tend to hug the right side of the estuary (looking seaward), whereas the incoming layer of salt water will tend to favor the estuary's left bank.

Both of these tendencies are the result of the Coriolis effect, which influences all currents. Because of the rotation of the earth, currents in the northern hemisphere tend to veer to their right, whereas in the southern hemisphere the apparent deflection is to the left. Thus in the northern hemisphere the halocline in an estuary will tend to slope upward from the right bank to the left, whereas in the southern hemisphere the halocline will tend to slope downward from the right to the left bank.[5]

Some of the tributaries of the Chesapeake Bay, notably the James River estuary, as well as the entire Chesapeake Bay itself, show the essential characteristics of the partially stratified (Type B) estuary. The Savannah, the Charleston, the Hudson, the Merrimac (Connecticut), and the upper reaches of the Delaware estuary are additional examples of the Type B estuary.

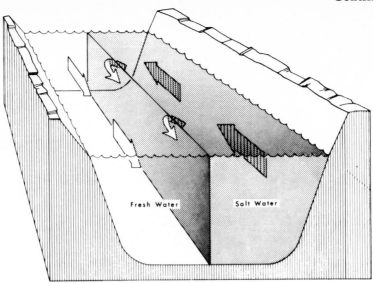

Figure 7.13.6   A vertically homogeneous estuary (Type C). (SOURCE: Adapted from Reference 3.)

Vertically Homogeneous Estuary (Type C)

The transition from the Type A to the Type B estuary involved a relative decrease in river flow, an increase in tidal flow, and an increase in the width-to-depth ratio, that is, the width increased but the depth became shallower. If all these trends are continued even further, a transition will occur from the partially stratified (Type B) estuary to the vertically homogeneous (Type C) estuary.

The vertically homogeneous estuary (see Figure 6) differs from the partially stratified estuary in that mixing results from a tidal turbulence so vigorous that virtually all vestiges of a horizontal halocline are destroyed. In such a situation the boundary between fresh and salt water is vertical. At any point in the estuary, the salinity will be constant from top to bottom, but where there will be a markedly different salinity in the water from side to side (due to the Coriolis effect) and, of course, from end to end, where the salinity increases. Again, the less dense fresh water is concentrated on the right side of the estuary, looking seaward, as is characteristic of estuaries in the northern hemisphere.

The open end of the Delaware Bay, the wider reaches of the Raritan estuary (in New

Jersey), and the Piscataqua estuary (in New Hampshire) show the essential characteristics of the vertically homogeneous (Type C) estuary.

Sectionally Homogeneous Estuary (Type D)

The sectionally homogeneous estuary approaches the opposite extreme along the continuum begun with the estuarine model suggested in Figure 3. In this case we envision an estuary (see Figure 7) in which the tidal movements are so large that they overwhelm the effects of the river flow. In the extreme case of tidal dominance there will be variation of salinity from top to bottom or from side to side. There will be, however, a gradual increase in salinity longitudinally in a seaward direction.

How can an estuary permanently maintain a salt distribution that is homogeneous in any cross section? What mechanisms are capable of moving salt up the estuary against a small but inevitable river flow? Clearly, the landward-flowing layers of salt water and the vertical mixing processes operating in Types A and B estuaries do not work here because there are no layers of salt water.

There are several processes working together

that can transport salt against the net movement of water in an estuary, which over the long haul must be seaward. One of these is molecular diffusion, the result of the random motions of molecules. As an example of molecular diffusion, sugar added to a cup of tea soon sweetens the tea even without stirring. It is unlikely that molecular diffusion alone, however, could maintain the salt balance in an estuary unless it was augmented by other processes.

Eddy mixing, or turbulence, is another process that disperses dissolved materials in the sea. Eddy mixing is somewhat similar to molecular diffusion except that volumes of fluid larger than molecules are exchanged in the mixing process. Eddy mixing occurs at virtually all times and places in the sea. It is nearly always a far more important mixing process than molecular diffusion.

It may be unlikely that even molecular diffusion and eddy mixing added together can maintain the salt balance in an estuary unless they are complemented by some additional mechanism such as the rhythm of the tides. Once or twice daily, in obedience to gravitational forces centered in distant celestial bodies, the estuary swells in size as waters from the sea surge inland. Then, in a matter of a few hours, the waters retreat. Again and again the tide replays its unending drama. How can the cyclic movements of the tidal currents help maintain the salt balance in an estuary?

Consider Figure 8, which pictures a tide-dominated river during four stages of the tidal cycle. In the first frame (time or $t = 0$), the tide is at a high-water slack. A dye that has been added midstream has diffused across the river and has invaded a small embayment (A) in the right bank. At $t = 1$ the ebbing tide carries the dye seaward, but some of the dye remains entrapped in embayment A. At $t = 2$ the tide is at a low-water slack. The dye front is abreast with and has partially diffused into another embayment (B). At $t = 3$, the tide is at flood. Notice that traces of the dye escaping from embayment A have been carried upriver beyond the point where the dye was introduced into the river. From this process it is easy to see that salt, as well as a dye, can be moved upstream in an estuary whose banks are irregular or indented.

Experiments similar to the one discussed

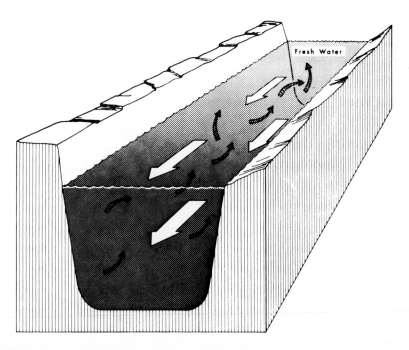

Figure 7.13.7   A sectionally homogeneous estuary (Type D). (SOURCE: Adapted from Reference 3.)

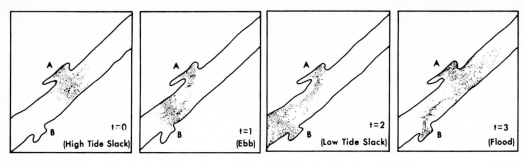

Figure 7.13.8   A tide-dominated estuary during four stages of the tidal cycle.

above have been performed on the Mattaponi River, a small tributary of the Chesapeake's Virginia side.[6] The dye was spread across a stretch of the Mattaponi in which, unlike the estuary in the foregoing description, there were no significant irregularities along the banks. Although the dye was moved seaward with ebbing tidal current, it left trails along both banks. These trails of dye then diffused toward midstream, only to be carried upriver on the returning tidal flood (see Figure 9).

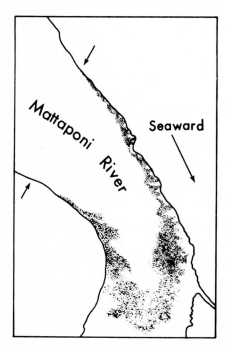

Figure 7.13.9   Dye is added to river between arrows. Ebbing tide leaves trail of dye along banks. Dye trails then diffuse toward midstream and are carried upstream on next tidal flood.

The Mersey River (near Liverpool, England) resembles the Type D estuary, at least during some phase of its tidal cycle. It seems that a completely sectionally homogeneous estuary is extremely difficult to find in nature. Perhaps the Type D estuarine model is useful only as idealization. We must await the time when some investigator locates and describes a strictly sectionally homogeneous estuary. Perhaps some of the larger tidal creeks in a coastal salt marsh would be likely places to look.

REFERENCES

1. W. M. Cameron and D. W. Pritchard. 1963. "Estuaries." In M. N. Hill, Ed., *The Sea*, Vol. 2. Interscience Publishers, New York.

2. D. W. Pritchard. 1960. "Estuarine oceanography." In *McGraw-Hill Encyclopedia of Science and Technology*. McGraw-Hill Book Company, New York.

3. Jerome William. 1962. *Oceanography: An Introduction to the Marine Sciences*. Little, Brown and Company, Boston, Massachusetts.

4. G. H. Keulegan. 1949. "Interfacial instability and mixing in stratified flows." *Journal of Research of the National Bureau of Standards*, Vol. 43, pp. 487–500.

5. J. P. Schweitzer. 1973. *As the World Turns: The Coriolis Effect*. Center for Wetland Resources, LSU Marine Science Teaching Aid, Issue No. 3 of a series, Louisiana State University, Baton Rouge, Louisiana.

6. Blair Kinsman. 1965. Notes on (24) 626: Lectures on Estuarine Oceanography delivered by D. W. Pritchard, Oct. 3 through Dec. 14, 1960 (unpublished notes distributed to students of the course at the Chesapeake Bay Institute and

Department of Oceanography, The Johns Hopkins University, Baltimore, Maryland).

14. EXTRACTIVE INDUSTRIES

Stanley R. Riggs
Department of Geology
East Carolina University
Greenville, North Carolina

This article considers all known mineral resources, excluding petroleum, that presently occur or may occur in the future within the estuaries, the nearshore continental shelf waters, and the adjacent land areas within the continental United States exclusive of the Great Lakes. Also, it does not directly consider the consequences of dredging, particularly as related to channel and harbor dredging and maintenance.

The extractive industries include all forms of recovery of natural minerals from the sediments and rocks of the earth's crust and from the water column comprising the oceans and estuaries. More specifically this topic covers (1) breaking the surface soil in order to facilitate or accomplish the extraction of natural minerals, (2) all activities or processes involved in the extraction of natural materials from their original locations, and (3) any preparation and treatment of these natural materials required to make them suitable for use. This broad array of activities associated with the mineral extraction industries ranges from the exploration and mining activities, to the processing and treatment plants, to the complex transportation systems involving pipelines, channels, and harbors. The potential conflict with other coastal uses and the potential impact of these activities on the deliberate balances of the fragile and limited estuarine zone have given rise to a dilemma that is slowly growing to prohibitive proportions.

Various geologists have projected that the major mineral reserves in the United States, which are presently derived from land, will be exhausted by the year 2000.[1] Future resources will come from the coastal areas and the continental shelves. Since the shelves are geologically nothing more than submerged portions of the continent, it is possible to assume that their mineral potential should be roughly comparable to that which has already been found on land.[2]

To date only a very small percentage of the coastal and shelf environments have been explored for anything other than possible petroleum. If the major thrust for the future mineral resources is on the continental shelf, then the coastal zone will play an ever-increasing role in the extractive industries. This role will include some mining itself, but probably of greater significance will be the critical part the estuaries will play in supporting the massive transportation system and processing plants necessary for the offshore extractive industries.

At the present time it is nearly impossible to describe accurately or completely the location and size of existing extractive industries in the coastal zone, to say nothing about the mineral reserves. In fact, the mineral resource potentials of the estuaries and continental shelves, with few exceptions, are at best only superficially known. The reasons for this are as follows: (1) the geological and mining agencies that monitor these industries have not differentiated and do not at present differentiate the extractive operations that are related to the coastal zone from those of any other region; (2) the same agencies generally are not able to relate production statistics for competitive reasons, and rarely do they have access to good reserve information if it is even known; and (3) detailed geological investigation, exploration, and research in the coastal zone is extremely expensive and technologically difficult, and generally constitutes a relatively "new" science. Recent inquiries underscore both the lack of knowledge of the resources and the meager effort to monitor any existing mineral extraction within or adjacent to the estuaries or the offshore areas.

Consideration of estuarine and offshore mining must deal with the potential, since the present mineral production from below the sea is limited to only a few commodities, the major one being petroleum. However, present economic and technological restraints, which are the major limiting factors in mining the seafloor, are rapidly being overcome by current efforts within the swiftly changing field of offshore petroleum exploration and develop-

Table 7.14.1   Categories of extractive resources and their development potentials within the coastal zone

RESOURCE CATEGORY	EXTRACTIVE RESOURCES	RESOURCE POTENTIAL		
		Past or Current Production	Near Future	Long Range
SURFACE DEPOSITS				
Unconsolidated to Partially Consolidated Sediment	Total sediments	***	***	***
	Shell gravels	**	**	**
	Quartz and rock gravels	*	**	***
	Light mineral sands	*	*	*
	Heavy mineral sands	**	**	**
	Salt	*	*	*
	Clay minerals	*	*	*
	Phosphate	*	**	***
	Peat	*	*	*
Consolidated Rock	Rock aggregate	NP	*	**
	Limestone	NP	*	*
SUBSURFACE DEPOSITS				
Pumpable Materials Gas and Fluids	Oil	***	***	***
	Natural gas	***	***	***
	LPG	***	***	***
	Geothermal energy		*	**
Soluble Solids	Sulfur	**	***	***
	Potash	*	**	***
	Salt	*	**	**
Slurry Solids	Phosphate	NP	***	***
	Glauconite	NP	*	*
	Sand	NP	*	**
Partially Consolidated to Consolidated Rocks	Phosphate	NP	**	***
	Fuels (coal, uranium, etc.)	NP	**	***
	Metals (gold, silver, copper)	NP	**	***
AQUEOUS DEPOSITS	Chlorides	**	*	*
	Magnesium	***	***	***
	Bromine	***	*	*
	Fresh water	*	***	***
	Other materials	NP	*	**

KEY: NP - No known production
      * - Minor source or potential
    ** - Moderate source or potential
   *** - Major source or potential

ment. These advances include (a) a rapid annual increase in the number of holes drilled, (b) an expansion into deeper waters further from shore, (c) a complementary increase in the size and capabilities of offshore drilling rigs, and (d) an increasing sophistication of underwater operating facilities and pipeline systems. As the petroleum industry continues to expand its exploration and operations into coastal and offshore areas, there will be an increase in the discovery and recovery of associated minerals that can be obtained by pumping and solution mining. Such minerals as sulfur and potash occur in salt domes, which are major petroleum reservoirs. The sophisticated technology necessary for the exploration and mining of other types of mineral deposits from the seafloor will quickly follow.

Most extractive industries, whether in, adjacent to, or distantly remote from an estuarine system, will have some impact on the coastal zone. Since most of the drainage systems off the land end ultimately in the estuaries, the drainage network funnels a great variety of contaminants into the coastal system. These contaminants are derived from a multitude of sources, including the extractive industries, agriculture, and urban and industrial wastes. Consequently, coal becomes part of the sediment load entering the Potomac River, dissolved phosphorous enriches the water of the Pamlico River in North Carolina, and dissolved metals reach San Francisco Bay from the mines in the Sierras. On the other hand, no two extractive industries will have similar effects or degrees of impact. For example, a sand and gravel quarry adjacent to an estuary can be completely sealed so that no sediment reaches the estuarine waters, while a mercury mine many miles from the estuarine zone may contribute minute but lethal concentrations of dissolved mercury to the bottom muds. Unless the extractive industry is directly within the estuary, the processing plants and allied industries utilizing the recovered commodity will often have a greater potential or actual long-term pollution effect on the estuarine system than will the mechanical or the chemical extraction in an adjacent land of offshore area.

The economic value and demand for a given commodity are determined by the (a) specific qualities of the material, which in turn determine the technological uses; (b) availability and concentration of the material, (c) cost of recovering and processing the commodity (d) cost of transporting the ore for processing, as well as the distance to markets; and (e) time delays resulting from possible restraining orders, hearings, and court litigations. A knowledge of these parameters is essential before the formulation of any local or regional land- and water-use management plans involving the continued development of our coastal zone. However, the economics of a given mineral resource may change dramatically in response to new technological advances or the discoveries of new ore deposits, or as industrial and social demands change through time. Such changes can have drastic effects on the

same management programs that define land and water uses.

As we begin to go to the sea for more of our mineral resources to offset dwindling onshore supplies, spiraling prices, and the increasing need for national independence, new pressures will develop. These new pressures, when combined with the existing pressures of a general growing technology and ever-expanding population, can only have *significant* increased pollution impact on an already environmentally overstressed coastal system. The coastal counties of the United States contain only a small percentage of the land area; however, they carry a relatively large percentage of the population and the manufacturing plants in the United States, and they continue to grow. Thus the human dilemma also continues to grow—the need to protect a delicately balanced natural system, on which man is dependent, and at the same time to dramatically increase its use and modication for materials on which man is also dependent.

The extractive industries that occur either within the estuaries, on the nearshore continental shelf, or in adjacent land areas can by divided into two main categories: surface and subsurface deposits (Table 1). Each category of deposit has its own types of materials and problems associated with their recovery. A third group, the aqueous deposits, or minerals extracted from seawater, is not discussed here.

SURFACE DEPOSITS

The natural materials occurring within or constituting the surficial deposits of the estuarine zone are extremely varied not only in composition but also in potential use (Table 2). In general, the materials in this category are unconsolidated or poorly consolidated sediment that is capable of being dredged directly without the problems of removing overburden sediments or breaking up consolidated materials. These materials are generally renewable only over extended periods of time. Under local high-energy conditions, and if there is an adequate source and supply, some sediment deposits can be rapidly renewed; examples of such deposits are sands and gravels associated with inlets, nearshore shoals and capes, and river mouths. For the

Table 7.14.2   Utilization of surficial sediment deposits

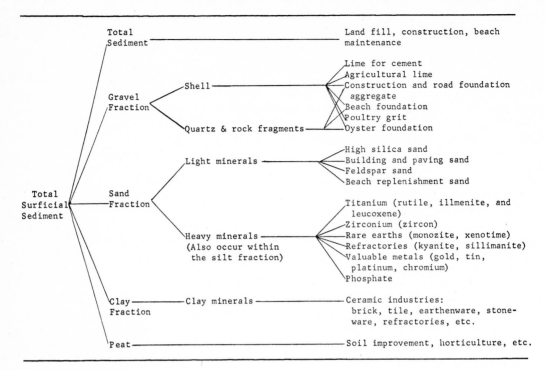

most part the deposits considered here are low-value commodities (the exceptions being some of the heavy minerals; Table 2) that require very modest, if any, beneficiation or preparation before use. Also, because of this low unit value, the commodities have limited and often local markets that are dictated by the very high transportation costs. Consequently, most operations are very small scale, low budget, and temporary, depending on the highly variable local markets and economies.

The surface deposits represent the most widely exploited group of mineral resources within the coastal waters today, with the major exception of petroleum. They include the following commodities: sand and gravel, shells, heavy and light minerals, clay, peat, and total sediment for landfill.

Sand and Gravel

The rising demand for sand and gravel is reflected in the total United States consumption, which accelerated from 500 million tons in 1954 to 980 million tons by 1970, with a projection of 1670 million tons by 1985 and 2530 million tons annually by 2000.[3] The rate of consumption of sand and gravel during 1970, which amounted to 5 tons per capita, was greater than that of any other mineral commodity except water. Although most of this sand and gravel comes from the land, sand and gravel probably represent the most important commodities recovered from the coastal zone in terms of both volume and value. However, since no records are kept of production in the estuarine zone, the values commonly cited are highly suspect. Nevertheless, the explosive urban and industrial growth in the coastal areas, which demand an ever-increasing amount of construction aggregate, is rapidly depleting the known land supplies in nearby areas or is burying them in their urban sprawl. Since most of the cost of these essential low-unit-value commodities involves transportation, a proximal location to the market is essential. As transportation costs rise and land supplies dwindle, the extensive and high-quality deposits of submarine sand and gravel occurring in the coastal zone become increasingly attractive.

It has been estimated that sand deposits cover about 50,000 square miles of the Atlantic shelf and areas about half as large on both the Gulf of Mexico and Pacific shelves.[4] Extensive gravel deposits have been outlined north of Barmount Bay off the New Jersey coast,[5] within Massachusetts Bay and the Gulf of Maine, and on the Florida shelf.[6] Apparently, the offshore sand and gravel industry is still in its infancy and will grow and develop extremely rapidly because of the abundance of suitable deposits in shallow water near markets and the relative ease with which materials can be recovered, classified, and transported by barge.[4] This will be particularly true in the Boston to Norfolk megalopolis.

In addition to the massive needs of aggregate for the construction industries, another important use is emerging for the submarine sands and gravels. During 1973 millions of cubic yards of sand were pumped from the beach at Cape Hatteras, North Carolina, to nearby beaches by the National Park Service. This major effort to replenish 2.2 miles of lost beach with sand is only temporary, since shoreline recession in this area has averaged 9 meters per year for the past 100 years.[7] This is becoming an ever-increasing problem around the entire country as the rate of shoreline development spirals. The U.S. Army Corps of Engineers estimates that about 7 percent of the United States shorelines are experiencing critical coastal erosion, and an additional 36 percent slight to moderate erosion.[8]

Shell

Shell aggregate is commonly dredged from shallow estuarine waters and adjacent land areas in several portions of the United States coastal zone. The shell, which is dominantly from old oyster reefs, is primarily used for aggregate in road building and concrete and for the manufacture of Portland cement and lime; small amounts are used for miscellaneous markets such as poultry grit and cultch material for modern oystering.

The largest production of shell comes from the Gulf coast states, including Texas, Louisiana, Mississippi, and Alabama, with lesser amounts from Florida and California. Some minor production has come from the Middle Atlantic states of Virginia, Maryland, and New Jersey. The state of North Carolina is presently carrying out a shell survey within some of the estuaries. Extensive shallow Pleistocene oyster reefs and marine shell beds underlie the estuaries and the mainland areas adjacent to the estuaries in northeastern North Carolina.[9] Since extensive limestone deposits outcrop along most of the North Carolina coast, the muddy shell deposits are only locally mined for landfill purposes. Most of the Middle and South Atlantic coastal states have a similar geological setting, and the need for and probability of developing the estuarine shell resources in these areas is minimal. The North Atlantic states have only minor shell deposits because of the occurrence of extensive glacial sand and gravel deposits throughout the coastal zone.

In contrast to the Atlantic coastal plain, the Texas coastal zone has limited limestone, gravel, and crushed stone reserves to supply the needs for constructional aggregate, cement, and the large chemical–industrial complexes. These massive needs are supplied largely by the extensive shell dredging industry in the shallow Trinity, Galveston, and San Antonio bays, about 75 percent of current production coming from the latter. The shell occurs as distinct reefs either at the bay bottom, where they support living oysters, or buried at varying depths within the bay muds. In 1971 production began to fall off considerably, because of both rapidly diminishing reserves and increasing environmental pressures.

Heavy and Light Minerals

Many of the sand resources of the coastal area contain varying concentrations of heavy and light minerals that have significant economic value. The heavy minerals (those with high specific gravities) include the titanium and refractory minerals, zircon, monazite, and the less common minerals such as gold, tin, platinum, chromium, and diamonds (Table 2). These minerals occur concentrated in placer deposits in drowned river channel deposits, modern beaches, and old beaches on both the adjacent coastal plain and continental shelf that were formed during fluctuations in the sea level. These minerals are commonly mined from similar types of deposits on the land, but rarely have they been successfully mined in the offshore zone. In spite of the lack of past economic development of these coastal deposits within the United States, heavy minerals are extremely popular and have been and are presently being extensively studied in the marine sediments in most coastal states. Some of these metals, such as gold, tin, platinum, and chromium, will probably be dredged from the United States seafloor in the near future simply because they are in considerably short supply. The Pacific shelf has known deposits of gold off California and Oregon, chromium off Oregon, and gold, tin, and platinum off the Alaskan coast.

The light minerals (those with average or less than average specific gravities) include pure quartz or high-silica sand and feldspar-rich sands which can be used as a source of potash (Table 2). Both of these commodities are of considerably less value than the heavy metals and are very abundant on land; consequently, economical extraction of these commodities from the sands in the marine environment probably lies sometime in the future.

Clay

Clay is another low-unit-cost commodity critical to the construction industries and therefore related to the metropolitan markets; thus transportation costs and land values are again the critical parameters. Since clay deposits are extremely common and widespread on the land, there is little need to develop submarine clays. Nevertheless, clay is a major sediment type that is being deposited in the modern estuaries as well as occurring in the older Pleistocene sediments.[9]

Peat

Extensive peat deposits commonly occur in the protected estuarine intertidal salt marshes and freshwater swamps. These low-energy transitional zones from water to land represent areas of rich organic growth that produces the thick peat accumulation of partially decomposed organic matter. The peat is used in horticulture for soil improvement; however, this market

is both local and somewhat limited. Consequently, most peat extractive industries are very small operations.

Total Sediment

Probably the most common form of extractive industry in the estuaries is the dredging of sediment for adjacent landfill and shoreline modification purposes, in which case the sediment itself has a low unit value. This whole category seems to comprise a gray zone that nobody claims, acknowledges, or considers as a legitimate part of the mineral industries within any of the coastal states. This total sediment dredging includes everything from landfill itself to beach replenishment, ditching for mosquito control, drainage of marshes for agriculture and logging, stream channelization, harbor development, and finally channel dredging and maintenance. This extractive industry represents by far the greatest volume of material extracted directly from the estuaries. As a result, it probably has a far greater pollution impact on the estuaries than all other forms of mineral extraction.

The pollution effects resulting from the extraction of surface sediments by mine dredging are no different from those caused by conventional channel and harbor dredging. In fact, the latter probably represents by far the single most important form of "estuarine mining" that takes place in our coastal waters. The subject of channel dredging is treated in considerable depth elsewhere (page 91). In general, the pollution effects from the extraction of mineral resources from surface sediments can be summarized as follows:

1. Since there is often little processing other than washing and sizing, surface sediment operations generally contribute minimal amounts of dissolved metals and substances to the coastal waters.
2. Extraction operations of surface sediments on the land areas adjacent to the estuaries can generally be carried out in shallow closed systems so that little deleterious sediment escapes into coastal waters and there is minimal impact on the groundwater system of the region.

3. Extraction operations within estuarine waters can produce vast amounts of sediment and have a dramatic impact on the physical–chemical character of the estuaries. More specifically, these effects include the following:

   a. Large amounts of sediment will be suspended, producing increased water turbity. This tends to decrease organic productivity by affecting light penetration and the resulting photosynthesis. More importantly, however, these increased suspended sediments can drastically change the bottom sediment patterns and the resulting benthic floral and faunal populations. In a study of the nearshore area off Pinellas County, Florida, the high amount of organic-rich suspended sediments derived from landfill dredging in Boca Ciega Bay had a drastic effect on the nearshore environments around John's Pass.[9] The suspended sediments in the murky estuarine waters are pulled out of suspension primarily by "filter-feeding benthic organisms (mostly polychaetes) and excreted as fecal pellets, which then accumulate in extensive ephemeral deposits."[9] The resulting pelletal muddy sand populated by polychaetes is rapidly displacing the "more desirable" populations, including the beautiful and extensive "sponge gardens" and associated invertebrate and fish populations that occur throughout this nearshore area.

   b. The removal of materials from the estuarine bottoms and the disposal of spoils produce great modifications of the bottom topography. Such changes have dramatic effects on the rest of the estuarine system, which includes the circulation system and the resulting water chemistry (salinity, dissolved oxygen, etc.) produced by that particular circulation system. The deepening of the water and the steepening of slopes will also increase wave-induced erosion of the adjacent estuarine shorelines.

   c. In addition, these extraction processes produce temporary disruption of the productive habitat and often a permanent change in the type of habitat. For example, generally a greater area will have deeper water and steeper slopes after dredging than existed before dredging, thereby producing a net loss of the more productive shallower water environments. This will result in major changes to the biological population inhabiting the area, as well as a loss of the shallow breeding grounds.

4. Most operations to extract surface sediments on the continental shelves could probably be carried out with a smaller immediate and less far-reaching pollution impact on the estuaries than direct estuarine mining itself. However, since there are so many variables, such as geographical location, character of the sediment, local current system, and energy levels, each specific circumstance must be considered independently.

Thus the extraction of surficial deposits in the estuarine zone has extremely variable effects on the estuarine system. Exploitation of land deposits adjacent to the estuaries should be allowed to develop fully in order to supply the local needs, however, but with strong controls on handling and discharging surface waters, effluent control, and reclamation. Exploitation of the vast potential resource wealth in the offshore area should also be encouraged, but, again, only with strong controls that allow each deposit or operation to be evaluated independently. On the other hand, extraction of the surface deposits within the estuary itself should not be allowed. The resources in the surficial deposits are usually stimulated by local economic development and are absorbed into the local urban development and do not spawn significant new industrial and economic development. Also, most often these commodities can be replaced with other low-unit-cost alternative materials, including natural, man-made, and waste products. The short-term gains associated with low-unit-value materials cannot justify the increased pollution and modification problems in an already highly stressed system that plays an important role in the productivity of the oceans.

Table 7.14.3   Relationship of types of mineral resource to the general resource values and cost of production within the coastal zone

RESOURCE CATEGORY	EXAMPLES	MINING METHOD	PRESENT STATUS	VALUE	COST
SURFACE DEPOSITS Unconsolidated to Partially Consolidated Sediment	Sand, gravel, shell, etc.	Dredge	Abundant Production	General increase in value of the resources available for exploitation	General increase in cost of exploration and exploitation
Consolidated Rock	Crushed rock and limestone	Explosives and dredge	No Production (only for channel dredging, pipe- lines, etc.)		
SUBSURFACE DEPOSITS Pumpable Materials Gases and Fluids	Oil, gas, LPG	Drill hole (pumping)	Very Abundant Production		
Soluble Solids	Sulfur, potash	Drill hole (solution mining)	Abundant Production		
Unconsolidated Sediment	Phosphate	Dredge (island dam- ming and open pit)	No Production (technology being developed)		
	Phosphate	Drill hole (slurry mining)	Moderate Production		
Consolidated Sedimentary and Crystalline Rocks	Coal, iron, oil shales, metals (gold, silver, copper, etc.)	Hard rock underground mining methods	No Production (technology avail- able for working from adjacent land areas or artifi- cial islands)		

SUBSURFACE DEPOSITS

The extraction of natural materials from the subsurface is a much more expensive operation and requires more sophisticated technology and equipment than the extraction of surficial materials. Consequently, the types of materials that can profitably be recovered from the sub- surface are the "glamor" commodities, includ- ing fuels, metals, and higher-unit-cost non- metallic resources (Table 3). The deeper in the ground or the further to sea one has to go to recover these commodities, the higher the cost and the more "glamorous" the material has to be. Also, the technical problems and the cost of recovery increase dramatically as we move from materials that can be pumped to the surface, to unconsolidated sediments, to consolidated rock (Table 3).

Pumpable Materials

The materials included here are the soluble solids, which include sulfur, salt (NaCl), and the various potash minerals. (Gas, oil, LPG, groundwater, and geothermal energy are con- sidered elsewhere in this book.) All three of these materials are associated with evaporite deposits and the resulting salt domes, which are in themselves a very important reservoir trap for petroleum. Since salt domes com- monly occur in the coastal zone and on the continental shelves, and because exploration for and development of offshore petroleum are increasing rapidly, the future increased extraction of these commodities in coastal areas is fairly certain.

Presently, sulfur is the only soluble solid being produced from the coastal zone in the United States. Currently known deposits of sulfur occur in the Texas and Louisiana es- tuarine zone, with present production coming from only one offshore area in Louisiana. Sulfur is extracted from many wells located on fixed, above-water platforms utilizing the Frasch method of solution mining; the sulfur is then pumped through heated pipelines to proces- sing plants on land.

The pollution problems associated with solution mining in the coastal zone can be summarized as follows:

1. The problems of leaks, breaks, and effluent (hot water, brines, drilling mud, etc.) associated with solution mining and pipeline operation.
2. The problems resulting from the operation and maintenance of the massive equipment associated with drilling, pumping, and transportation.
3. By far the most important problem, particularly with petroleum—the allied industries that are established in nearby coastal waters.

Unconsolidated to Partially Consolidated Sediments

This category includes any mineral resource that occurs in the subsurface in soft or unconsolidated sediments that are diggable. The major resources that presently fit into this category are phosphate and, possibly, coal and oil shale. Coal is mined from below coastal waters in many places around the world; however, in the United States the underwater coal potential does not appear to be very great, and oil shale is probably down the road some. On the other hand, both the Atlantic and Pacific coastal waters have vast phosphate reserves; these occur primarily in the subsurface, with only small surface concentrations.

The outer coastal plains, estuaries, and near-shore shelf areas of North Carolina, South Carolina, Georgia, Florida, and California have tremendously large and extensive beds of phosphorite sediments that occur under from 10 to several hundreds of feet of overburden sediments. In Beaufort County, North Carolina, the Pungo River Formation is presently being strip-mined directly on the banks of the Pamlico River estuary. Three million tons of phosphate has been produced annually for the past 8 years from a 50-foot bed below 90 feet of overburden. The operating company controls 30,000 acres, which contain over 2 billion tons of phosphate reserves. The existing phosphate mining operation has had a very small direct nutrient impact on the adjacent estuaries. The addition of phosphorus in the estuary result-

ing from the adjacent phosphate mine has been irregular and small, producing only slightly higher concentrations than normal. The periods of high photosynthesis within the estuary are a direct function of nitrate fluctuations coming from upstream, and not the phosphorus. Surprisingly, there appears to have been only a minor effect on the major freshwater aquifer, which directly underlies the phosphate bed, due to the need for heavy pumping to dewater the large open-pit mine.[10]

Similar extensive subsurface deposits of phosphorite occur in the coastal areas extending from Charleston, South Carolina, to south of Savannah, Georgia. The California continental shelf also has extensive deposits of phosphate sediments.

Exploitation of the unconsolidated sediments from the subsurface generally represents tremendous earth-moving operations utilizing open-pit strip-mining techniques with massive equipment. Vast acreages are involved in both recovering the extensive beds of reserves, and treating and disposing of the waste materials. It has been demonstrated in North Carolina that such operations can safely take place on the lands adjacent to the estuaries with only very minimal pollution and direct environmental impact on the estuaries. However, similar mining operations in central Florida, 20 to 50 miles inland from the coastal zone, have been extremely damaging to the estuaries; upon occasion the wall of a "slimes pond" will fail, sending million of tons of mud downstream.

Similar types of mining operations are technically feasible within the estuarine waters; the shallow waters can be filled, or even diked and drained, allowing for either open-pit dry mining or underwater dredge mining. However, because of the extremely large land requirements, the vast amounts of earth movement, and the problems associated with the resulting waste materials, there is a tremendous permanent modification of the estuarine environment and system. Also, there is a great potential for massive estuarine damage resulting from broken dikes during major storms and storm tides. Offshore mining of these deep phosphate reserves is technologically and economically questionable at the present time.

Consolidated Rock

Because of the high cost of hardrock mining in the subsurface, the only potential mineral resources that can be economically considered in this category are the "glamor" metals (gold, silver, copper, lead, zinc, etc.) and the fuels such as coal and radioactive minerals. Since the continental shelves are merely the submerged portions of the continents, they can be expected to contain mineral resources similar to those of the continents. For example, a copper and zinc deposit below the tideflats of Penobscot Bay in Maine was originally mined from three underground shafts.[11] More recently, a 90-acre salt marsh was dammed and drained for a short-lived open-pit operation. The environmental pollution problems included saltwater encroachment into the freshwater aquifer, silting and water turbidity, and heavy metal contamination in the estuary, not to mention habitat loss.

Technology presently exists for mining below the estuary from shafts on the mainland or from man-made islands within the estuary. This would allow for the use of the same mining techniques as are employed on land.[2] To date, this technology has not been put into operation in the nearshore ocean environments, but its use is not too far in the future.

The potential impact on the estuaries of subsurface hard rock mining on land is extremely variable and is only partially dependent on the proximity of the mining to the estuary. Regardless of its location, resulting heavy metal contamination of the estuarine waters and bottom muds is common. On the other hand, operations that are in close proximity to the estuarine system could have a more direct impact on both the groundwater and estuarine waters.

Impacts resulting from subsurface mining within the estuary and nearshore environments are probably not as great as those from surface mining in the same areas would be. This type of extractive operation would cover smaller areas, move smaller volumes of material, and would not be directly connected with the water column, so that it generally would be a cleaner operation. The major impact would be associated with the barge transportation of the ore and the necessary processing plants located on the nearby coastal area. The potential chemical and sediment pollution resulting from hard rock metal beneficiation plants and smelters is generally very great.

CONCLUSIONS

The relationship between mineral resource utilization and the coastal system is presently producing, and will continue to produce, a dilemma with respect to estuarine pollution. This basic dilemma will only continue to increase, since our growing technological society is totally dependent on a myriad of basic mineral resources that are the raw materials for the technical machine. The value of and the demand for any of these basic resources are dictated by the industrial technology and economic considerations at any given time, both of which are highly changeable and volitile controls. Extraction of minerals has to take place where the minerals occur; the location of resources cannot be legislated or decreed. Since the coastal zone contains a myriad of potential resource commodities necessary for our technological society, and since these commodities have economic value, society demands exploitation. Even though there is considerable mineral resource potential within the coastal zone, there is a dramatic lack of information pertaining to the occurrence, distribution, and concentration of specific materials. This essential information is prerequisite to any form of coastal zone management.

The potential environmental and pollution problems associated with the extraction, preparation, and transportation of resources, operations that are prerequisite to their use, are often exceedingly great. The processes of extraction of these resources are often messy operations that are capable of physically, chemically, and biologically disrupting and/or modifying the fragile coastal and estuarine system. The resulting effects may be either direct or indirect, local or broad scale, temporary or permanent, and they may be of varying degrees of severity, all depending on the commodity itself and the methods of extraction and processing. In addition, a myriad of satellite industries develop in the coastal zone in response to a given extractive industry; often these industries have a greater potential cumulative impact on estuarine pollution than does the extractive industry itself. Moreover, some extractive and satellite industries are not compatible with other legitimate uses of the estuarine system.

For some resources there are alternative sources from which the necessary raw materials can be supplied, and for many others substitute materials that can be made available or developed. This is particularly true of the low-unit-cost aggregate materials. Other materials, however, do not have alternative sources or substitutes. Consequently, attitudes toward and the necessity for the recovery of mineral resources within the estuaries and offshore areas vary between the two opposite extremes of complete abstinence and complete development.

The estuarine system of the United States occupies a very narrow transitional zone between the land area and the continental shelf; the total area extent of this system represents an extremely small but manifestly important percentage of the United States. The estuaries, for the most part, are the terminal mixing basins of the freshwater drainage systems off the land with the ocean's waters. Therefore they receive the cumulative residue, waste, pollution, and sediment resulting from all man's and nature's activities within each drainage system that is funneled into the estuaries. In addition, the social, industrial, and demographic evolution of the United States has developed (and it appears that it will continue to develop in the future) with disproportionate concentrations within the coastal zones. This continual encroachment and the mounting intensity of development and use of the estuarine zone have produced a highly stressed system that is resulting in major and potentially devastating changes within this fragile and important transitional area.

However, the question of mineral extraction from within the estuaries themselves should be seriously reevaluated. The age-old question of which is the most valuable to man elicits the honored response: "It's a case of the old trade-off game." But, as man's needs grow, the trade-offs grow too, and rather soon we're "trading off the trade-off." Man can no longer

afford this sort of approach to the continued development of some small part of the system that in its totality is a critical resource with well-defined limits. The need is to start evaluating the natural systems, upon which man is so dependent, from a long-term basis of interdependence, and not from the immediate short-term dollar value point of view. One must approach the continued use and development of the estuaries as a question involving a single complex interacting ecosystem that has finite limits—and these limits must be defined now.

Development of the mineral resources on the adjacent lands and the offshore continental shelf areas should be encouraged with the proper setback lines from the shore, environmental controls, and a viable monitoring system. The situation is so urgent in certain areas as to require a moratorium on extraction until the foregoing safeguards are met.

REFERENCES

1. J. R. Moore. 1972. "Exploitation of ocean mineral resources—perspectives and predictions." *Proceedings of the Royal Society of Edinburgh*, Vol. 72, pp. 193–206; Sea Grant Reprint No. WIS-SG-73-333.

2. V. E. McKelvey. 1968. "Minerals in the sea." *Ocean Industry*, Vol. 3, No. 9, pp. 37–43.

3. M. J. Grant. 1973. *Rhode Island's Ocean Sands: Management Guidelines for Sand and Gravel Extraction in State Waters*. Sea Grant Program, Marine Technical Report No. 10, University of Rhode Island, Kingston, Rhode Island.

4. W. B. Pings and D. A. Paist. 1970. "Minerals from the oceans—Part I." *Mineral Industries Bulletin*, Vol. 13, No. 2, pp. 1–18. Colorado School of Mines, Golden, Colorado.

5. J. Schlee. 1968. *Sand and Gravel on the Continental Shelf off Northeastern United States*. U.S. Geological Survey, Geological Survey Circular No. 602.

6. J. B. Rigg. 1974. "Minerals from the sea." *Ocean Industry*, Vol. 9, No. 4, pp. 213–219.

7. R. Dolan, P. J. Godfrey, and W. E. Odum. 1973. "Man's impact on the barrier islands of North Carolina." *American Scientist*, Vol. 61, No. 2, pp. 152–162.

8. U.S. Army Corps of Engineers. 1971. *National Shoreline Study* (including the report on the

national shoreline study, nine regional inventory reports, shore protection guidelines, and shore management guidelines). U.S. Government Printing Office, Washington, D.C.

9. S. R. Riggs and M. P. O'Connor. 1974. *Relict Sediment Deposits in a Major Transgressive Coastal System*. East Carolina University, Sea Grant Publication No. UNC-SG-74-04, Greenville, North Carolina.

10. J. E. Hobbie, B. J. Copeland, and W. G. Harrison. 1972. *Nutrients in the Pamlico River Estuary, North Carolina, 1969–1971*. Water Resources Research Institute, Report No. 76, University of North Carolina, Raleigh, North Carolina.

11. P. A. Smith. 1972. "Underwater Mining—Insight into Current United States Thinking." University of Wisconsin, Sea Grant Publication No. WIS-SG-72-330, Madison, Wisconsin.

15. FRESHWATER DISCHARGE

Charles R. Chapman
U.S. Fish and Wildlife Service
Washington, D.C.

Freshwater inflow alteration is the modification by man of freshwater tributary flow destined for and received by estuaries. Historically, tributary flow varied appreciably with changing climatic conditions and other natural events. Most estuarine organisms are attuned to such natural variations in tributary inflow, particularly seasonal variations; even severe conditions eventually will reverse. Man-induced freshwater inflow alterations, which result mostly from diversion, impoundment, and consumption, however, tend to simulate permanently the more adverse and severe natural excursions. Many organisms cannot adjust to the stresses of such a permanently changed environment. Specific alterations can include larger or diminished volumes of inflow, changes in seasonal runoff cycles, a changed inflow site, or any combination of these.

That estuaries need fresh water is inherent in virtually all of the definitions that have been advanced. The key is that seawater is measureably diluted with fresh water drained from the land to create a brackish condition. Should an estuary be deprived of its tributary

fresh water so that marine waters prevail, it would become a coastal lagoon. Conversely, should tributary freshwater inflow become so excessive as to preclude a brackish condition, a freshwater lake would be created regardless of its proximity to the ocean. Neither coastal lagoons nor freshwater lakes are nearly as productive as estuaries, particularly of living resources valuable to man.

The circulation patterns in estuaries, based on the inflow of fresh water and the tidal intrusion of marine waters from the ocean, react in a rather predictable manner, depending on basin configuration and stresses from temperature and wind.[1] Thus estuaries frequently are referred to in relation to their freshwater–saltwater balance as stratified, well mixed, or partially stratified or partially mixed. Significantly, however, it is where moderately large rivers and streams meet the sea that the most unique circulation patterns occur. In the deeper estuaries a typical "salt wedge" moves upstream along the bottom, and a nearly freshwater layer moves seaward on the surface. The more saline water in the bottom layer (wedge) mixes constantly into the outward-flowing surface layer, which becomes saltier seaward in a horizontal gradient. It is important to note that the saltwater bottom current brings with it marine minerals that mix with nutrients drained from the land. The greater the flow of tributary runoff (within reason), the greater will be the flow of the saltwater wedge inland. Should tributary runoff be curtailed, so would much of the supply of marine minerals as well as of land-drained nutrients.

The well-mixed estuaries, on the other hand, typically are rather large and shallow with a small tidal range and moderate to large inputs of tributary fresh water. Wind action frequently dominates circulation, and waters are well mixed surface to bottom, so that vertical stratification does not occur.

Depending on the amount of freshwater tributary runoff received, such estuaries are stratified horizontally; salinity is negligible at the mouth of the tributary stream and increases gradually seaward, reaching near sea strength at the junction with the ocean. These estuaries are subject to large seasonal variations in salinity throughout in direct relation to changes in river flow, seasonal winds, and tides.

Between the salt wedge or well-stratified estuary and the well-mixed estuary every combination and variation of type occurs. An estuary may be stratified during periods of high river flow and well mixed at other times. Moreover, an estuary may be well mixed in its uppermost shallow reaches and stratified near the ocean or in deeper channels. The common denominator for all these variations, however, is the inflow of tributary fresh water. Basin configuration and wind, tide, and climate can be considered constants and not controllable.

The productiveness of an estuarine system is an expression of its energy input, and the conversion of this energy to other forms (i.e., food) is essential to the total life complex of the system. Much of this energy input derives from the freshwater tributary inflow.

Some forms of aquatic life are tolerant of large salinity ranges from practically fresh water to marine. Other forms can live and reproduce only if the salinity range is narrow. Still other animals require different salinities during different stages of their development.

Fortunately, typical estuaries are characterized by well-defined salinity gradients between headwater and ocean. They possess wide ranges of brackish conditions that can accommodate, simultaneously, at high density many different estuary-dependent species of aquatic life. It is essentially the freshwater tributary inflow that makes this possible.

The inflow of tributary fresh water to an estuary, in addition to bringing nutrients, creating a brackish salinity gradient, and contributing to circulation, does much more. At times it brings with it excessive amounts of sediment that increase turbidity, sometimes severely so for extended periods. Incoming waters frequently are polluted, but in other circumstances the inflow helps to dilute wastes in the estuary or to flush them out. As noted earlier, excessive flooding with fresh water can render an estuary unfit for most, if not all, marine organisms. Furthermore, the fresh water received by an estuary eventually is flushed to the ocean, where it continues to have a decided, but less concentrated, influence over large areas for some time.

The value of freshwater inflow to an estuary is enormous. It contributes significantly to the high productivity of estuaries, which in turn is reflected in the production of fish and wildlife resources and plants of value to man, more acceptable water for industry, and many forms of recreation.

In 1972, 63.5 percent of the 4.7 billion pounds of commercial fish caught by American fishermen consisted of species that were estuarine dependent or associated.[2] Some regional catches, such as those from the Chesapeake Bay, South Atlantic coast, and Gulf of Mexico, were more than 90 percent estuarine dependent. Furthermore, almost 65 percent of the estimated 817.3 million marine fish caught by saltwater anglers in 1970 was estuarine dependent or associated.[3]

Signicantly, it has been shown that brackish estuaries with decided salinity gradients are more productive of fishery resources of value to man than high-salinity estuaries and coastal lagoons, such as the Laguna Madre in Texas.[4,5]

Furthermore, it is the tidal marshes that serve at the base of the food chain for most of the more productive estuaries through the organic material (detritus) they contribute.[6] Substantial portions of such estuaries consist of tidal marshes, coastal wetlands, and streams that feed into the marshes and estuaries. The tidal marshes proper are dependent in great part for their high biological productivity on nutrients from inland and upland sources delivered by the freshwater inflow systems.

Tidal marshes also provide excellent cover (habitat) for the young of estuary-dependent fishery resources and for all life history stages of many wildlife species. In addition, the marsh vegetation helps to weaken the onslaught of storm-generated waves and acts as a reservoir for coastal stormwaters, so that the land proper and man's nearby developments are protected.

Even more striking, however, is the ability of estuary–tidal marshes to accomplish waste treatment through the "tertiary" stage of nutrient removal and assimilation. This valuable contribution, unaided by man, is free and has always been taken for granted, or its value has not been recognized. Artificial tertiary treatment of wastes is extremely costly. It has been estimated that an acre of estuary–marsh is capable of doing $14,000 worth of waste treatment work each year at a daily loading of 19.4 pounds of biochemical oxygen demand (BOD), assuming a cost of $2.00 per pound of BOD for tertiary treatment.[7] And it is the freshwater tributary inflow carrying land-derived nutrients that makes much of this possible through the growth of marsh vegetation.

A recent study to calculate the value of estuaries and marshes demonstrated their versatility and importance. The four levels selected for monetary evaluation—(1) by-product yield (fisheries, etc.), (2) potential for aquaculture, (3) waste assimilation, and (4) total life support value as a function of primary production —were calculated to be worth $7100 per acre per year. The income-capitalized value would be $142,000 per acre.[8]

Similarly, it has been calculated that marshes and estuaries of Florida are worth $2.0 billion each year to the state's economy in terms of direct expenditures for recreation and the wholesale value of commercial fish.[9] This value can continue only if a highly productive and high-quality coastal environment is maintained, and, of course, tributary freshwater inflow is a key factor.

Alterations may take the form of reduced or increased freshwater inflow. The runoff (inflow) discharge cycle may be modified, and the point (river mouth) at which fresh water discharges into an estuary may be changed. Furthermore, all possible combinations of these alterations occur.

Reduction in tributary flow probably is the most severe of the various alterations, although changes in runoff cycles certainly can be disruptive. Only very few increases in overall flow have been noted. Any major alteration in natural tributary inflow to estuaries, however, will have an impact of some kind, either good or bad, depending on individual circumstances. Usually, a reduction in tributary inflow will result in lowered productivity of an estuary, and, of course, the degree of decline will dictate its severity. Reduced inflow usually will result in a loss of land-derived nutrients, as well as marine minerals. The naturally established salinity gradient will be altered, and marshes will diminish or change to a less desirable high-salinity type. Likewise, reduced tributary inflow will prevent adequate dilution or flushing of wastes and make it more difficult to maintain desirable water quality. Overall, the habitats of fish and wildlife resources and their production will diminish, waste treat-

ment ability will decline, and the utility of the water for recreation and industry will be impaired.

A similar threat also can occur with changing runoff cycles even though the total volume of water received may not change appreciably. Salinity gradients may be disrupted at critical times for both plants and animals so that overall productivity may still decline. Dilution of waste will be intermittent, as will the ability to assure adequate water quality continuously. Such a feast-or-famine situation probably will be as damaging as a reduction in total inflow.

Changes in the point of discharge in an estuary can also be serious. Even though a new gradient may be established in another location, the discharging waters usually are of poorer quality, and, of course, the original area will receive less tributary fresh water.

Freshwater inflow to estuaries can be altered for a variety of reasons and purposes. Many times it is altered deliberately to serve an assumed higher value or purpose. Frequently, however, freshwater inflow is altered inadvertently, or even accidentally, without knowledge of or concern for the values to be sacrificed or traded.

Deliberate alterations usually are made to permit the use of tributary freshwater inflow for other purposes. These include—but not in priority order—water for drinking, industry, agriculture, recreation, water quality maintenance, waste dilution, aquatic resources, navigation, domestic uses, power production, and aquaculture, as well as control of water to prevent flooding. The means to accomplish such alterations may be (1) diversion, (2) direct consumption, and (3) storage for control or later use.

Diversion may be accomplished for the following reasons: (1) supplying water-deficient areas for any use, (2) contributing to a local water supply system, usually for consumptive use, (3) flood control, (4) recreation, (5) navigation, (6) water quality maintenance or improvement, and (7) fish and wildlife resources.

Consumptive use may be provided through direct withdrawal or accomplished after storage or diversion but usually is for (1) drinking, (2) domestic use, (3) industry, and (4) agriculture. Evaporation and seepage take their toll; and even where a large share of the withdrawn water is returned, its quality is usually much lower (i.e., it becomes polluted through use).

Storage for later use is accomplished usually by upstream reservoirs so that water supply is reduced and/or the flow characteristic is changed. Storage can provide a means for direct withdrawal for use, for diversion to other areas, or merely for retaining water for hydroelectric power, downstream flood control, or navigation. The utility of the water does not change except that the volume usually is reduced by evaporation and seepage. Temperatures also may be altered through impoundment, and sediment and nutrients trapped. Periodic or intermittent increased downstream flows can be provided for (1) water supply withdrawal, (2) navigation, (3) dilution of wastes, (4) recreation, (5) power, (6) maintaining downstream quality, (7) aquatic resources, and (8) legal reasons.

Unintentional alterations result from the side effects of an activity or program intended for another purpose. Whether inadvertent or accidental, however, the impact is the same as follows deliberate alteration or withdrawal for immediate use or for diversion. Unintentional alterations most frequently result from (1) land clearing, (2) paving, (3) watershed abuse (i.e., poor agricultural practices), (4) navigation channels, (5) flood control, (6) draining wetlands, and (7) road construction. There are, of course, many other factors that contribute to freshwater inflow alterations, including the natural forces of earthquakes and landslides, and the relatively short-term changes in climatic cycles, particularly as reflected by wind, temperature, and precipitation.

Just how extensive and serious is the problem of freshwater inflow alteration to the nation's estuaries and coastal zones? Although several investigators have discussed inflow alterations as a local or regional problem,[4,5,10] only the National Estuary Protection Act Study[11] has attempted to assess the problem and its ramifications on a national level. This study found that the problem of freshwater inflow alteration, although not a source of concern for all estuaries, was sufficiently serious to warrant special study and consideration. Of the 10 biophysical regions identified and assessed, the diversion of tributary fresh water destined for estuaries was found to be a great problem (on a rating scale of "none," "small," "moderate," and "great") in 6 regions: the Middle Atlantic, Caribbean (which included south Florida), Gulf of Mexico, Pacific Southwest, Pacific Northwest, and the Pacific islands. It was a small problem in the Chesapeake Bay, South Atlantic, and Alaska regions, and no problem at all in the New England region.

The problem of controlling tributary flow (through impoundment) destined for estuaries also was assessed in the National Estuary Protection Act Study. It was considered to be a great problem in 5 of the 10 regions, a moderate problem in 2 regions, a small problem in 2 other regions, and no problem in 1 region: Alaska. Significantly, the National Estuarine Pollution Study[12] found that on the Atlantic coast alone, 30 dams on major estuary-terminating streams provided for more than 10 million acre-feet of storage, which could be released, diverted, or used directly. In 1963 more than 20 million gallons of water each day was needed for cooling, and nationally almost 5000 industrial plants were considered to be major users of fresh water destined for estuaries. The greatest number of these plants (2892) was located on the Atlantic coast; 1104 were on the Pacific coast; and only 385 were on the Gulf of Mexico coastal area.

At the present, the problem of diverting fresh water destined for estuaries probably is most severe in Florida Bay and the famous Ten Thousand Island Region, located adjacent to the Everglades, the Mississippi River delta estuary–marsh complex of Louisiana, most of the Texas estuaries, and San Francisco Bay.[13] The problem of changes in tributary runoff cycles is evident for most of our estuaries because upstream impoundments have been build on virtually all major coastal terminating streams. As yet, however, the problem of changing freshwater discharge sites is relatively small in comparison to diversions and changes in discharge cycles. And, of course, the problem of reduced water quality, even though it is an inflow alteration problem and not discussed herein, is universal and extremely serious, as indicated by the large national effort in behalf of pollution abatement and control.

Measures necessary to control or correct freshwater inflow alterations, although very evident, have not been successful in most cases. Meaningful success to ensure that tributary inflow to estuaries will not be adversely altered has not been achieved because the true value of such discharge has not been generally recognized. In only a very few cases has the value of tributary fresh water for estuaries been calculated or demonstrated in relation to planned use for other obvious needs. It has only been very recently that the hard, cold facts of the natural values of tributary fresh water for the coastal zone have started to emerge. Unfortunately, for the most part such benefits are recognized only by a minority group without sufficient authority to force a real comparison of alternatives for water-use values, much less the long-range planning needed to ensure the maintenance of natural coastal ecosystems. For too long it has not been realized or recognized what natural values are sacrificed when tributary fresh water is committed to other uses or other areas or is evaporated or lost; it is extremely difficult to recover or to replace so that fresh water can once more flow to an estuary.

The problem of freshwater inflow alteration can be solved only when it is recognized that estuaries must have fresh water of good quality and that the values and benefits so derived may in many cases be equal to, or even exceed, the ones that such water would have if it were impounded, diverted, and/or consumed for other uses. It is necessary, therefore, to determine how much fresh water is essential for each of our most valuable estuaries, when it should be received, and what its quality must be. It is equally important, however, to document what values and benefits accrue by providing such water to the coastal zone and what values and benefits will be lost if it is not provided.

REFERENCES

1. L. Eugene Cronin and Alice J. Mansueti. 1971. "The biology of the estuary." In A *Symposium on the Biological Significance of Estuaries,* Houston, Texas, Feb. 13, 1970. The Sport Fishing Institute, Washington, D.C.

2. U.S. Department of Commerce. 1973. *Fisheries of the United States, 1972.* National Marine Fisheries Service, Current Fisheries Statistics No. 6100.

3. U.S. Department of Commerce. 1973. *1970 Salt-Water Angling Survey.* National Marine Fisheries Service, Current Fisheries Statistics No. 6200.

4. Charles R. Chapman. 1966. "The Texas basins project. In A *Symposium on Estuarine Fisheries.* American Fisheries Society, Special Publication No. 3.

5. Charles R. Chapman. 1971. "The Texas water plan and its effects on estuaries." In A *Symposium on the Biological Effects of Estuaries,* Houston, Texas, Feb. 13, 1970. The Sport Fishing Institute, Washington, D.C.

6. E. P. Odum and Armando de la Cruz. 1967. "Particulate organic detritus in a Georgia salt marsh–estuarine ecosystem." In G. Lauff, Ed., *Estuaries.* American Association for the Advancement of Science, Publication No. 83, Washington, D.C.

7. D. C. Sweet. 1971. *The Economic and Social Importance of Estuaries.* U.S. Environmental Protection Agency, Water Quality Office, Washington, D.C. (unpublished).

8. James G. Gosselink, Eugene P. Odum, and R. M. Pope. 1973. *The Value of the Tidal Marsh.* Urban and Regional Development Center, Work Paper No. 3, (prepublication draft), University of Florida, Gainesville, Florida.

9. John L. McQuigg. 1971. *The Economic Value of Florida's Estuarine Areas.* Estuarine Seminar, May 6, 1971, Pine Jog Environmental Sciences Center, West Palm Beach, Florida (unpublished).

10. S. M. Gagliano, N. J. Kwon, and J. L. Van Beek. 1972. *Deterioration and Restoration of Coastal Wetlands.* Coastal Resources Unit, Center for Water Resources, Hydrologic and Geologic Studies of Coastal Louisiana, Report No. 9, Louisiana State University, Baton Rouge, Louisiana.

11. U.S. Department of the Interior. 1970. *The National Estuary Protection Act Study* (8 vols.). Report to the Congress of the United States by the Fish and Wildlife Service.

12. U.S. Department of the Interior. 1969. *The National Estuarine Pollution Study,* Vols. I-III. Report to the Congress of the United States by the Federal Water Pollution Control Administration.

13. Charles R. Chapman. 1973. "The impact on

estuaries and marshes of modifying tributary runoff." In *Proceedings of the Second Symposium on Coastal Marsh and Estuarine Management*, Louisiana State University, July 17–18, 1972. Division of Continuing Education, Louisiana State University, Baton Rouge, Louisiana.

16. GROUNDWATER

Grant E. Kimmel
John Vecchioli
U.S. Geological Survey
Mineola, New York

Natural processes such as the rise and fall of sea level, long-term climatic trends, and rock erosion and deposition cause groundwater conditions to change very gradually over thousands or millions of years. In contrast, activities of man may greatly alter coastal groundwater systems during very short periods of time, measured in years or decades. Human activities that tend to change the coastal groundwater system include (1) withdrawal of groundwater; (2) any land-use practice, such as the construction of impervious surfaces (pavements and rooftops); (3) incidental recharge of aquifers by leaky water and sewage systems; (4) excavation of ship channels and drainage canals; and (5) application of chemicals and disposal of liquid and solid-waste material on or beneath land surfaces.

Coastal hydrogeological environments vary widely. Bedded deposits of seaward-dipping unconsolidated or poorly consolidated sediments extend along the Atlantic and Gulf coastal plains from Long Island, New York, to Mexico and occur in discontinuous areas along the west coast of the United States. Water in these rocks moves through interstitial openings whose volume is commonly 10 to 40 percent of the rock mass. Very large volumes of fresh water may be in transient storage; for example, Long Island's main groundwater system contains an estimated 60 trillion gallons of fresh water.[1] In contrast, the northeastern coast of North America and some localities on the west coast are underlain by dense rocks in which fractures and joints are the principal openings for water movement. These less permeable

rocks generally contain much less water than sediments do. A third major hydrogeological coastal environment is that of cavernous and highly permeable consolidated rocks such as those that underlie some volcanic islands (Hawaiian Islands) or karstic (limestone) areas (Puerto Rico, Florida, Yucatan peninsula, Mexico). In these cavernous rocks water may move rather rapidly wherever there is an interconnecting network of very large openings.

Whatever the geological environment, water flows through the rocks in the direction of decreasing head. A groundwater system begins in an area of recharge (high head), extends through a region of flow, and ends in an area of discharge (low head). In a coastal area this system can be either local, where all three segments of the flow system are at or near the coastal environment, or regional, where the area of recharge may be many miles from the coast. The two systems, however, share common areas of discharge near, at, or seaward of the shoreline.

Two examples of groundwater flow system in a coastal environment are shown in Figure 1. The unconfined system is typical of an offshore bar or an island in which the top of the zone of saturation is an unconfined free surface, or water table. The confined system is one in which low-permeability confining beds separate and impede the movement of water between aquifers. In a confined system water flows downward through confining beds in recharge areas and upward through confining beds in discharge areas near the shoreline. Pollutants infiltrating to the groundwater system tend to move through the system along the groundwater flow paths from the point of introduction to the area of discharge (Figure 1). If not removed by interactions with the rock matrix, these constituents may be discharged with the transporting groundwater at or near the shoreline.

As the density of seawater is about 1.025, fresh water tends to float on and to override the seawater in deposits near coasts (Figure 1). Under static or nonflowing conditions, a head of 1 foot of fresh water above sea level causes fresh water to displace seawater to a depth of 40 feet below sea level; however, the seaward flow of fresh water and the small amount of mixing at the interface cause the

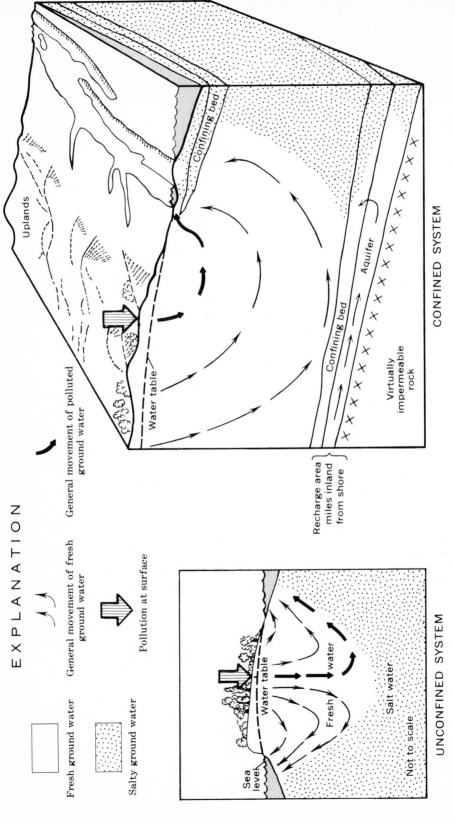

EXPLANATION

Fresh ground water

Salty ground water

General movement of fresh
ground water

General movement of polluted
ground water

Pollution at surface

Not to scale

Uplands

Water table

CONFINED SYSTEM

Confining bed

Confining bed

Aquifer

Virtually
impermeable
rock

Recharge area
miles inland
from shore

Sea level

Water table

Fresh water

Salt water

UNCONFINED SYSTEM

Figure 7.16.1   Coastal groundwater systems, showing the relationship of fresh water to salt water and the movement of polluted water. (SOURCE: Modified from Reference 1.)

fresh water to occur farther seaward than it would under static conditions.

The interface between salt water and fresh water under natural conditions is not a sharp surface but rather a zone of mixing, often called the "zone of diffusion." Mixing is caused by tidal ground water movements transmitted into the aquifer from the ocean and by seasonal fluctuations in freshwater head. The thickness of the zone of diffusion is variable: in Florida it has been estimated to be several tens of feet;[2] on Long Island, New York, several hundreds of feet.[3]

Saltwater intrusion, a common alteration of coastal groundwater systems, is the advance of salt water into aquifers that previously contained fresh water. Intrusion is brought about by changes in the head relations between fresh water and interconnected bodies of salt water, such as the ocean and its arms, or with other aquifers or parts of the same aquifer containing salt water. Urbanization may reduce the amount of precipitation that, under natural conditions, would replenish the aquifer and maintain the head and seaward flow of fresh water. The pumping of fresh water from a coastal aquifer system may also reduce or even reverse the seaward-sloping, natural hydraulic gradient. Concomitantly, the seaward flow of fresh water necessary to maintain the natural position of the saltwater interface may be reduced or reversed, and salt water may encroach into the freshwater part of the aquifer.

Saltwater intrusion also can develop because of, or be accentuated by, construction work that provides artificial direct access between saltwater and freshwater bodies. Excavation of drainage canals and the deepening of ship channels or marinas in the coastal zone may cut through protective clay beds, exposing the previously confined freshwater aquifer to seawater. Improperly constructed wells or abandoned wells with deteriorated casings may permit movement of salt water from either surface bodies or salty groundwater zones to fresh groundwater zones.

The extraction of groundwater in a coastal zone enables man to harvest and use some of the seaward discharge of fresh groundwater, a resource that, in effect, otherwise would escape to the sea. Large-scale withdrawals (many millions of gallons per day) of groundwater have supplied major coastal cities such as Atlantic City, New Jersey; Savannah, Georgia; Miami, Florida; Houston, Texas; and many smaller towns for many years without any serious saline contamination of the well supplies by encroachment of salt water. Carefully managed extraction can provide for a readjustment of the saltwater interface to a new static position landward of its natural position but seaward of supply wells. However, because as little as 2 percent of seawater mixed with fresh water can render the water unpotable, saltwater intrusion is a permanent concern to water supply systems in coastal aquifers. Notable occurrences of intrusion in the United States include those in California, Florida, Hawaii, New York (Long Island), and Texas.

The risk of saltwater intrusion can be evaluated only after studying the hydrogeology of the coastal groundwater system and determining the values for the various components of the system's hydrological budget, such as rates of recharge to and discharge from the system.

The amount of natural subsurface freshwater discharge to the sea must be known before limitations on extraction can be assessed. Theoretically, any extraction of groundwater from a coastal system will cause a readjustment of the saltwater interface landward. The speed and the extent of intrusion depend on the magnitude and location of the extraction in relation to the size and shape of the groundwater system and the natural rate of seaward freshwater discharge. In general, if extraction is dispersed so as to minimize the lowering of groundwater levels near the coast and does not exceed the amount of natural subsurface discharge of fresh water, a new equilibrium position for the interface will eventually be established. However, if extraction exceeds the natural freshwater discharge, continual mining of fresh groundwater will occur, and the salt water will continue to intrude indefinitely, until extraction is reduced.

Saltwater intrusion can be controlled by the following methods:[4]

1. *Control of pumping draft.* By limiting withdrawals and (or) careful emplacement of pumping wells within the coastal basin, the effect of the intrusion on available groundwater supplies can be minimized.

2. *Artificial recharge.* By augmenting natural recharge to an aquifer, the freshwater head and the seaward flow of fresh water can be sustained. Artificial recharge can be accomplished by spreading water on the surface if the aquifer to be protected is unconfined, or by injecting water through wells if the aquifer is confined. Waters that have been used for artificial recharge include water imported from another basin, storm runoff, and wastewater.

3. *Freshwater pressure ridge.* By artificially recharging the aquifer along a line adjacent and parallel to the coast, a freshwater pressure ridge can be maintained high enough above sea level to prevent encroachment of salt water beyond the hydraulic barrier.

4. *Pumping trough.* By constructing and pumping a line of interceptor wells adjacent and parallel to the coast, the encroaching salt water can be prevented from moving farther inland toward supply wells. Vertical encroachment of salt water from deep saltwater-bearing parts of an aquifer upward to freshwater zones can be prevented through the use of interceptor wells.

5. *Subsurface barrier.* By placing an impermeable barrier in the aquifer between salt water and fresh water, encroachment of the salt water can be prevented.

Other alterations that may result from a reduced freshwater head in shallow groundwater (water table) include (1) a reduction in dry-weather flow of streams, (2) a decline in the levels of lakes, and (3) an increase in the salinity of brackish surface-water bodies, such as marshes, estuaries, and bays, to which fresh groundwater discharges.

In deep confined aquifers a reduction of the freshwater head is commonly accompanied by compaction, principally of fine-grained beds (clay or silt) interlayered with the aquifers. Compaction of these beds may cause damaging subsidence of land surfaces—a few to more than 10 feet—as has been observed in such widely separated coastal areas as the Santa Clara Valley, California; the upper Gulf coast region, Texas; Venice, Italy; and Tokyo, Japan.[5]

Many activities of man can alter the quality of groundwater in ways other than by saltwater intrusion. Disposal of solid or liquid wastes on or beneath the land surface can add chemical contaminants to the groundwater reservoir. Some of these contaminants persist over long periods of time and long distances of travel, and are eventually discharged with the groundwater into streams or coastal waters. Chemical reactions between wastes, or leachates from them, and the aquifer can add other objectionable constituents to groundwater. Seemingly innocuous practices such as the salting of road surfaces in winter or the recharge of clean, heated, industrial cooling water to the ground can alter groundwater quality, at least locally, by increasing the salinity or the temperature of the groundwater, respectively. On the other hand, microbial contaminants often do not travel beyond a few hundred feet from the point of entry into porous-rock aquifers but can proceed for much longer distances in cavernous or fissured-rock aquifers.

Because of the great number of contaminants possible and the diverse ways with which they may be introduced into the groundwater system, each potential groundwater pollution hazard needs to be evaluated in terms of the longevity of the contaminant, its harmfulness, its quantity of concentration, its point of entry into the groundwater flow system, and the local and regional hydrogeology. In general, disposal of contaminant-producing wastes in aquifer-recharge areas (areas of high head) should be avoided. Recharge areas are generally upland areas in which the aquifer either occurs at the land surface or is directly overlain by a permeable surficial formation.

The history of groundwater development on Long Island, New York, provides examples of several of the alterations that can occur in a coastal groundwater system.[1] Large concentrated withdrawals of groundwater on the western end of Long Island caused the freshwater head to drop to as much as 35 feet below sea level, and the resulting widespread saltwater intrusion caused the abandonment of many supply wells. The combination of urbanization, large-scale pumping, and sewering has reduced groundwater discharge to streams to the extent that some previously perennial streams now flow only intermittently. In addition, because of the widespread contamination of the shallow groundwater by wastes, the dissolved-solids concentration of groundwater discharging to the streams and bays is greater than it was previously. Locally, the temperature of groundwater has risen as much as 8°C (15°F) because of the return of heated water used for industrial cooling and air conditioning. Some of these alterations to the groundwater quality can be remedied, but the flushing of contaminants by the generally slow-moving groundwater requires a long period of time.

REFERENCES

1. Philip Cohen, O. L. Franke, and B. L. Foxworthy. 1968. *An Atlas of Long Island's Water Resources*. New York Water Resources Commission, Bulletin No. 62.

2. F. A. Kohout and Howard Klein. 1967. *Effect Of Pulse Recharge on the Zone of Diffusion in the Biscayne Aquifer*. Symposium in Haifa (Israel), March 1967, International Association of Scientific Hydrology, Publication No. 72.

3. N. J. Lusczynski and W. V. Swarzenski. 1966. *Salt-water Encroachment in Southern Nassau and Southeastern Queens Counties, Long Island, New York*. U. S. Geological Survey, Water-Supply Paper No. 1613-F.

4. D. K. Todd. 1959. *Ground Water Hydrology*. John Wiley and Sons, New York.

5. J. F. Poland. 1972. "Subsidence and its control." In T. D. Cook, Ed., *Underground Waste Management and Environmental Implications*. American Association of Petroleum Geologists, Memoir No. 18, pp. 50–71.

6. Task Committee on Saltwater Intrusion of the Committee on Ground-Water Hydrology of the Hydraulics Division. 1969. "Saltwater intrusion in the United States." *Journal of the Hydraulics Division-ASCE*, Vol. 95, No. HY5.

17. HYDROGEN SULFIDE GAS

David A. Bella
Department of Civil Engineering
Oregon State University
Corvallis, Oregon

Under certain conditions, bottom deposits within estuarine systems can release free sulfides. These free sulfides may build up to high concentrations (100 milligrams per liter) within the interstitial waters of the deposits and may be released to the overlying waters. Hydrogen sulfide may also be released to the atmosphere, particularly from deposits that are tidally exposed. The presence of free sulfides is manifested most noticeably by the strong "rotten egg" odor of hydrogen sulfide. Deposits that contain free sulfides usually can be clearly identified by the presence of this odor when the deposits are disturbed.

High concentrations of free sulfides within the deposits and the release of these sulfides to the overlying water and atmosphere can be environmentally significant for a number of reasons; among these are the following:

1. Free sulfides, particularly hydrogen sulfide, are toxic at low concentrations to a wide variety of organisms.[1-6]

2. The release of free sulfides can lead to a decline in the aerobic zone of the deposit and a lowering of the dissolved oxygen concentrations within the overlying waters, particularly in the interfacial regions. In addition, if bottom deposits are physically disrupted, a reduction of dissolved oxygen within the water column because of the chemical oxidation of the total sulfides may occur.

3. The release of hydrogen sulfide to the atmosphere can cause an air pollution problem. Not only does hydrogen sulfide have an undesirable odor, but it is also toxic. Moreover, the release of hydrogen sulfide from tidal flat areas may cause a significant input of atmospheric sulfur.[7]

Organics within a bottom deposit are decomposed primarily by bacteria. Oxygen that is dissolved in the water is used by these bacteria as a hydrogen acceptor. This oxygen must diffuse into the deposits from the overlying waters. Usually, except for relatively clean sands, the dissolved oxygen within the interstitial waters of the deposits is depleted within a very short distance from the surface. Thus the availability of dissolved oxygen for bacterial decomposition of organics is often limited to the surface regions of a deposit (several millimeters or less). This aerobic region (containing dissolved oxygen) can often be identified by its lighter (frequently brown) color.

Below this aerobic region bacterial decomposition of organics will usually rely on sulfates as hydrogen acceptors.[8,9] This process is called "sulfate reduction." Sea water contains high concentrations of sulfates (about 2600 milligrams per liter). Estuarine waters, which are mixtures of seawater and freshwater runoff, also contain high concentrations of sulfates, roughly in proportion to their salinities. The sulfates will diffuse into the bottom deposits. As a result of bacterial sulfate reduction, sulfates are reduced to hydrogen sulfide, which is found in solution as part of the pH-dependent system

$$H_2S \leftrightharpoons HS^- \leftrightharpoons S^{2-}$$

In the present discussion all components of the above relationship will be defined as "free sulfide." At a pH of 6.5 to 7.0, the free sulfide is divided approximately evenly between H_2S and HS^-, with S^{2-} negligible. Free sulfides are also produced during anaerobic putrefaction of sulfur containing amino acids, but this process is usually of negligible importance in marine environments.[3,10]

Free sulfides form insoluble compounds with heavy metals, particularly iron. Free sulfide quickly reacts with available iron within the deposits to form ferrous sulfide, FeS, which gives benthic deposits their characteristic black color.[11] The input of iron into the deposits results primarily from the deposition of insoluble inorganics that contain ferric oxides and other insoluble forms of iron.[12] Not all of this iron, however, is available to react with the sulfides.

Free sulfide concentrations within benthic deposits will remain at low levels (generally well below 1 milligram per liter) when available iron is present. If available iron is sufficiently depleted, however, free sulfides within the anaerobic regions of deposits will increase and may then diffuse to the aerobic regions of the deposits and into the overlying waters. Physical disruption of bottom deposits may also lead to the release of free sulfides within the deposits to the overlying waters.

Free sulfides are oxidized within the aerobic regions of the deposits and within aerobic

waters. This reaction is extremely complex and appears to be catalyzed by the presence of metallic ions.[13] Within oxygenated seawater, the half-life of sulfide has been reported to vary from 10 minutes to several hours.[10,14]

When the amount of organics deposited to the bottom is high, the free sulfides produced through bacterial sulfate reduction may exceed the available iron. Then free sulfides will build up within the deposit, rather than forming insoluble ferrous sulfide, and may then cause the problems previously described.

Human activities can significantly contribute to the release of free sulfides.[15] The release of domestic and industrial organic wastes will contribute in the manner described above. Dikes, docks, and other structures that tend to cut off estuarine areas can result in a high settlement of organics within these areas. In addition, such areas may experience a high rate of algal growth. Within diked or partially diked tidal flat areas, algal mats may grow on the mud surface. The organics produced by such algal growth may be decomposed in part by sulfate reduction, and free sulfides may be released.[16]

Control of free sulfide release is achieved principally by the control and treatment of domestic and industrial organic wastes. Dredging may be used to remove high organic deposits containing free sulfides; however, such dredging is only a temporary treatment of a symptom and should not be considered a substitute for waste treatment. In addition, structures such as dikes, which tend to isolate portions of estuaries and disrupt the natural flow patterns, should be kept to a minimum.

REFERENCES

1. P. I. Colby and L. L. Smith, Jr. 1967. "Survival of walleye eggs and fry on paper fiber sludge deposits in Rainy River, Minnesota." *Transactions of the American Fisheries Society*, Vol. 96, pp. 278–296.
2. R. E. Dimick. 1952. *The Effects of Kraft Mill Waste Effluents and Some of Their Components on Certain Salmonoid Fishes of the Pacific Northwest*. National Council for Stream Improvement, Technical Bulletin No. 51, pp. 1–23.

3. T. Fenchel. 1969. "The ecology of marine microbenthos. IV: Structure and function of the benthic ecosystem, its chemical and physical factors and the microfauna communities with special reference to the ciliated protozoa." *Ophelia*, Vol. 6, pp. 1–182.

4. E. P. Haydu, H. R. Amberg, and R. E. Dimick. 1952. "The effect of kraft mill waste components on certain salmonoid fishes of the Pacific Northwest" *Tappi*, Vol. 35, pp. 545–549.

5. M. V. Ivanov. 1968. *Microbiological Processes in the Formation of Sulfur Deposits.* Translated by S. Nemchonok; edited by Dr. E. Rabinovitz. Israel Program for Scientific Translations, Jerusalem, Israel, 297 pp.

6. J. A. Servizi, R. W. Gordon, and D. W. Martens. 1969. *Marine Disposal of Sediments from Bellingham Harbor as Related to Sockeye and Pink Salmon Fisheries.* International Pacific Salmon Fisheries Commission, Report No. 23.

7. W. W. Kellogg, R. D. Cadle, E. R. Allen, A. L. Larus, and E A. Martell. 1973. "The sulfur cycle." *Science*, Vol. 175, No. 4022, pp. 587–596.

8. L. G. M. Baas Becking and E. J. F. Wood. 1955. "Biological processes in the estuarine environment. I: Ecology of the sulfur cycle." *Proceedings of the Koninklijke Nederlanse Akademie van Wetenschappen Amsterdam*, Vol. 58, pp. 160–181.

9. A. E. Ramm and D. A. Bella. 1974. "Sulfide production in anaerobic microcosms." *Limnology and Oceanography*, Vol. 19, No. 1, pp. 110–118.

10. J. D. Cline and A. Richards. 1969. "Oxygenation of hydrogen sulfide in seawater at constant salinity, temperature and pH." *Environmental Science and Technology*, Vol. 3, No. 9, pp. 838–843.

11. R. A. Berner. 1969. "Migration of iron and sulfur within anaerobic sediments during early diagenesis." *American Journal of Science*, Vol. 267, pp. 19–42.

12. R. A. Berner. 1967. "Diagenesis of iron sulfide in recent marine sediments." In G. Lauff, Ed., *Estuaries*. American Association for the Advancement of Science, Publication No. 83, Washington, D.C., pp. 268–272.

13. K. Y. Chen and J. C. Morris. "Oxidation of aqueous sulfide by O_2: General characteristics and catalytic influence." In *Proceedings of the 5th International Water Pollution Research Conference*. Pergamon Press, Oxford, England (in press).

14. H. G. Ostlund and J. Alexander. 1963. "Oxidation rate of sulfide in sea water: A preliminary study." *Journal of Geophysical Research*, Vol. 68, pp. 3995–3997.

15. D. A. Bella. 1972. "Environmental considerations for estuarine benthal systems." *Water Research*, Vol. 6, pp. 1409–1418.

16. D. A. Bella, A. E. Ramm, and P. E. Peterson. 1972. "Effects of tidal flats on estuarine water quality" *Journal of the Water Pollution Control Federation*, Vol. 44, pp. 541–556.

18.   KELP FORESTS

John S. Pearse
Valrie A. Gerard
Division of Natural Sciences
University of California
Santa Cruz, California

Kelp forests are complex marine communities that occur along rocky coasts of most temperate regions of the world. Several species of large brown algae, belonging to the order Laminariales and commonly known as "kelps," dominate the appearance of these forests and often form dense mats, or "kelp beds," on the sea surface. Species composition varies in different parts of the world. Along the shores of the North Atlantic (New England, Canada, northern Europe), the major kelps are several species of the genus *Laminaria*. The dominant plants in the kelp forests along western North American shores and those of the southern hemisphere (Australia, New Zealand, South America, South Africa) belong to the genus *Macrocystis*, the giant kelp. Giant kelp forests are especially productive and diverse, and the following discussion will deal mainly with those of western North America, particularly California.

Giant kelp forests have a well-defined physical structure, comparable to that of terrestrial forests (Figure 1). Much of this structure is defined by the form of the giant kelp. The full-grown diploid plant (sporophyte) can be divided into several discrete parts: the holdfast, fronds, and sporophylls. The holdfast is composed of numerous, closely entwined, rootlike haptera which grow downward among crevices and interstices on available substrates to anchor

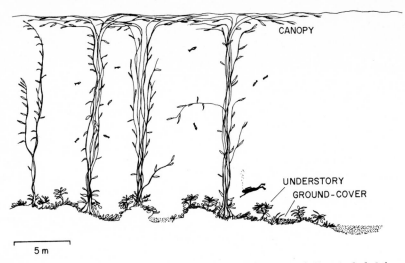

Figure 7.18.1   A typical central California kelp forest. Silhouette of diver included for scale.

the plant. The fronds grow upward to the sea surface and may attain lengths of more than 30 meters. Each frond consists of an axial stipe and numerous blades (sometimes over 200 per frond), each with a basal, gas-filled bulb, or pneumatocyst, and a leaflike lamina. The apical blade of each frond includes a meristem, which produces new blades. If broken off or removed in harvesting, it cannot be regenerated; although the frond may continue to elongate, no new blades can be added. Elongation of the stipe between the blades allows the frond to increase as much as 0.5 meter per day in length. New fronds are produced from meristematic regions just above the plant's holdfast. The sporophylls are specialized laminae that form a bushy clump within the first meter above the holdfast. Large numbers of haploid flagellated spores are released from the sporophylls, and most settle within a few meters of the parent plant. These spores develop into microscopic, multicellular gametophytes which produce eggs or sperms. Fertilized eggs develop into the large sporophytes, and the life cycle requires a minimum of 1 year for completion. New fronds reach the sea surface within 3 to 5 months, and the average life span of a frond is about 6 months. An individual plant may live for several years and may have up to 200 or more fronds at one time.

The floating fronds of the giant kelp and several other species of kelps with pneumatocysts (e.g., feather boa kelp, *Egregia*; bull kelp, *Nereocystis*; elk kelp, *Pelagophycus*) form a dense canopy at the sea surface. Although the entire plant has the capacity to photosynthesize, in a well-developed kelp forest over 90 percent of the primary production can occur in the canopy, within 1 meter of the sea surface, when nutrients are not limiting. Sometimes during summer months in southern California, the water is stratified and nutrients become limiting near the surface. In such cases maximum production by giant kelp plants occurs in nutrient-rich water below the thermochine, as much as 6 meters below the surface. Photosynthates are translocated downward to the lower portions of the plant, including the holdfast, sporophylls, and juvenile fronds. Only a small percentage of the light penetrates the canopy, and the interior of the forest is rather dimly lighted. Below the canopy there is often much open area, because the larger individual giant kelp plants are usually well spaced (about two to three plants per 10 square meters in a typical forest).

Many kinds of apparently shade-tolerant plants form several subcanopy layers, including the understory algae, the ground-cover algae, and the algal-invertebrate turf. The understory layer is composed of several kinds of algae with blades supported on stiff, woody stipes, a meter or so above the bottom. These include the kelps *Laminaria, Eisenia,* and *Pterygophora,* and other brown algae, such as *Cystoseira.* Diverse smaller species of foliose and encrusting red and brown algae make up the ground-cover layer and, with various sessile invertebrates (sponges, cnidarians, barnacles, vermetids, bryozoans, and ascidians), often form a close turf.

The structural diversity characteristic of most giant kelp forests provides a wide variety of habitats for many different kinds of animals. The spaces among and below the floating fronds of the canopy are occupied by fish and crustaceans (mysids and shrimp), and are especially important refuges for larval and juvenile fish. The surfaces of the fronds support an abundant sessile fauna, including hydroids and bryozoans, as well as motile animals, such as isopods, copepods, and snails. Many diverse motile and sessile animals inhabit the understory and ground-cover layers, form the algal-invertebrate turf, and occupy crevices and sediment pockets in the bottom substrate. The kelp holdfasts also harbor a rich and varied fauna.

In addition to the characteristic physical structure of giant kelp forests, there is a trophic and energetic structure that ties most of the organisms in the community into a food web. Most of the primary production of the forest occurs in the canopy of the giant kelp itself. Measurements in central California suggest net production levels of about 2-3 kilograms of dry weight per square meter per year, comparable to levels in tropical rain forests. There can be little question that kelp forests are among the most productive systems in the world.

A small part of the net primary production of kelp forests is consumed directly by grazing animals (e.g., snails and isopods), but most of it becomes algal drift and detritus when parts of the plant are broken or sloughed off. Algal drift and detritus probably form the main food source for many drift feeders (e.g., spider crabs, snails, abalones, sea urchins, bat stars) and suspension feeders (e.g., sponges, ascidians, bivalves, vermetid snails, tubiculous worms). However, much of the algal drift and detritus may be transported out of the forest by water currents. This material probably forms an important food source for animals outside the kelp forest, including those on beaches, within

mud and sand bottoms, and in deeper offshore water. The dependence of these communities on a kelp forest energy source needs critical study, and the destruction of kelp forests may have profound effects far outside the forests.

The primary consumers of the kelp forest, including grazers, drift feeders, and suspension feeders, support a variety of secondary consumers: predaceous cnidarians, sea stars, snails, crustaceans, fish, and, in parts of the Northeast Pacific, sea otters. Many of these animals and others (e.g., birds, pinnipeds, human beings) prey largely upon other secondary consumers and therefore constitute the apices of the complex kelp forest food web. Primary and secondary consumers may regulate, and be regulated by, the densities of their food species. Selective grazing by different herbivores prevents the monopolization of bottom substrate by a few species of algae, while predation on grazers may prevent overgrazing. These regulatory links in the food web are poorly understood at present and need detailed study, but, as discussed below, human overexploitation of some species may affect many other species.

Kelp forests are a hindrance to some human activities. Forests that grow in harbors and on breakwaters are minor nuisances to boaters and swimmers, because kelp fronds entangle objects passing through the canopy. Drift kelp often accumulates as large piles of offensive, rotting seaweed wrack on beaches, and heavily used beaches must be raked and cleaned. These hindrances to human activities, however, are rarely serious or worth the expense of limiting kelp forests.

Direct human uses of kelp forests include harvesting, commercial and sport fishing, recreational diving, and wildlife watching. As part of a multimillion dollar industry, kelp fronds are harvested, and the alginic acid is extracted for use in numerous industries, including ice cream, dairy food, beverage, pharmaceutical, cosmetic, paint, rubber, ceramics, textile, and paper. Kelp also has served as a source of potash and fertilizer and may find future application as fuel and livestock food.

Kelp forests are inhabited by numerous animals that are fished for commerce and for sport, including many kinds of fish, crabs, spiny lobsters, abalones, and sea urchins. Furthermore, the exquisite beauty of many of the plants and animals in kelp forests make these forests among the most popular areas in the world for recreational scuba diving and photography. Kelp forests are also popular sites for watching marine birds, pinnipeds, and, along the central California coastline, sea otters.

Human activities can threaten kelp forests either by direct overexploitation of various species or by the indirect effects of urbanization and other forms of coastal disturbance. Kelp harvesting off southern California has continued for over 50 years and is managed largely from past experience. Canopies are harvested up to three times each year by barges that cut the fronds 4 feet below the surface. After cutting, more light penetrates into the forest and undamaged, juvenile fronds grow upward to replace the canopy in 3 to 5 months. In this way canopy cutting may enhance photosynthesis in the kelp forest. However, in turbid waters, where light penetration is low, canopy removal can reduce the photosynthetic activity of the plants, and canopy regrowth may be slow. Moreover, in turbid waters canopy cutting may reduce the amount of organic material reaching the holdfast and lower parts of the plant. Successive canopy-cutting experiments in central California resulted in reduced holdfast growth and premature loss of plants during storms.

Kelp canopy harvesting may also adversely affect other plants and animals in the forest. Many of the canopy dwellers are disrupted or destroyed by harvesting, including snails, isopods, and crabs, which may be important food items for other animals, and juvenile fish, which use the canopy as a refuge. Increased light in the forest as a result of canopy removal may enhance the growth of some algae at the expense of others, including juvenile kelp plants. Furthermore, since each kelp forest is subject to natural fluctuations in density and composition and to a unique set of physical parameters (light, turbidity, bottom substrate, sedimentation, water movement, and storm exposure), these factors should be studied and understood, as well as the effects of harvesting, before the intensity and frequency of canopy cutting are determined.

Other species within kelp forests may also be overexploited, with effects reaching far beyond these particular species. Sea urchins, for example, are mainly algal drift feeders, but when numerous they heavily graze attached algae, including giant kelp. Areas with large numbers of sea urchins are typically devoid of most large algae. Overexploitation and the near extermination in the nineteenth century of the sea otter population off western North America removed a major predator of sea urchins and apparently has resulted in large, relatively barren, sea-urchin-dominated areas now present along much of that coast. Off southern California, where kelp canopy harvesting is commercially important, sea urchins are treated as pests, and their numbers are controlled by divers armed with hammers or by lime (CaO). Off the coast of northeastern North America, overexploitation of lobsters, also predators on sea urchins, similarly may have resulted in excessive numbers of sea urchins and overgrazing of the *Laminaria* forests there.

Not only may overexploitation of predators lead to excessive numbers of grazers and to overgrazing, but also overexploitation of competitors at the same trophic level may result in profound changes in kelp forests. Abalones, for example, may compete for space or food with sea urchins, and intensive abalone fishing during the past 25 years off southern California may have contributed to the high numbers of sea urchins there. These and other complex interactions require further study and understanding before large-scale management plans are formulated.

Coastal urbanization and land disturbance effects that may have adverse impacts on kelp forests include increased nutrient levels, turbidity, and sedimentation from land runoff and sewage outfalls. Increased turbidity may depress the growth of understory algae, including juvenile kelp plants. A major effect of large sewage outfalls, particularly the Los Angeles County outfall off the Palos Verdes peninsula, has been the accumulation of fine sediment (leptopel) which apparently smothers both plants and animals. The extensive kelp forests that grew in the area 20 to 30 years ago are now virtually gone; few attached plants or animals occur at depths greater than about 10 meters, where fine sediment blankets the bottom. Inshore, large numbers of sea urchins (perhaps partly nourished by organic material in the sewage) keep much of the bottom grazed clean of algae.

Most kelp forests are restricted to cold temperate shores, and kelp plants cannot tolerate high temperatures. The giant kelp plants in southern California do poorly at temperatures above 20°C, and during the late 1950s summer surface sea temperatures exceeded this value. These high sea temperatures, perhaps in concert with excessive sea urchin grazing and increased turbidity and sedimentation from outfalls, apparently led to extensive reduction of local kelp forests. Kelp forests in the vicinity of electrical power plants using seawater as a coolant can also be expected to be adversely affected by sea temperature increases.

Attempts are presently being made to establish kelp forests in entirely new areas or to reestablish them in areas where they formerly thrived (e.g., off the Palos Verdes peninsula). Railroad cars, automobiles, tires, cinder blocks, and other objects have been placed on sandy bottoms to form artificial reefs with promising results in terms of algal and fish production. Techniques for reestablishing former forests include controlling grazers (sea urchins and some fishes) and transplanting adult or juvenile sporophytes, or gametophytes. Temperature-tolerant strains of giant kelp are also being grown for possible use around electrical power plant sites. These techniques hold promise for sound management of at least the dominant plants in the giant kelp forests of California. However, much more needs to be known about the effects of harvesting, species interactions, sedimentation, sewage discharges, increased water temperature, and other factors, as well as about natural fluctuations and community ecology, before kelp forests can be practically and predictively managed. They are, after all, among the most complex marine ecosystems known.

NOTE. Some information used in this summary is the result of research sponsored by the National Oceanic and Atmospheric Administration, Office of Sea Grant, U.S. Department of Commerce, under Grants No. USDC 2-35208 and No. 04-3-158-22.

REFERENCES

A. R. O. Chapman. 1974. "The ecology of macroscopic marine algae." *Annual Review of Ecology and Systematics*, Vol. 5, pp. 65–80.

D. J. Jones. 1973. "Variation in the trophic structrue and species composition of some invertebrate communities in polluted kelp forests in the North Sea." *Marine Biology*, Vol. 20, pp. 351–365.

K. M. Mann. 1973. "Seaweeds: Their production and strategy for growth." *Science*, Vol. 182; pp. 975–981.

D. J. Miller and J. Geibel. 1974. *Summary of Blue Rockfish and Lingcod Life Histories; a Reef Ecology Study; and Giant Kelp, Macrocystis pyrifera. Experiments in Monterey Bay, California*. California Department of Fish and Game, Fish Bulletin No. 158.

W. J. North, Ed. 1971. "The biology of the giant kelp beds (*Macrocystis*) in California." *Nova Hedwigia*, Vol. 32, pp. 1–600.

W. J. North and C. L. Hubbs, Eds. 1968. *Utilization of Kelp-Bed Resources in Southern California*. California. Department of Fish and Game, Fish Bulletin No. 139.

State Water Quality Control Board, Sacramento, California. 1964. "An investigation of the effects of discharged wastes on kelp." Publ. No. 26, 124 pp.

19. LAND TREATMENT OF SEWAGE EFFLUENT

Joseph J. Salvatorelli
Taylor, Wiseman and Taylor
Mt. Laurel, New Jersey

We have reached that period in time when the pollution control methods of the past are not adequate for present and future needs. With the development of each new treatment process we have delved more deeply into the impacts of pollution on our environment and the disturbances it causes, and have come to a better realization of the far-reaching problems of pollution control management. Many successful treatment processes have been developed to meet the requirements of the time; however, our need for higher-quality discharges has become increasingly evident as we study further the more subtle effects of these discharges on our environment. Even with the use of the highest level of efficiently performing biological waste treatment (tertiary treatment), these discharges contain contaminants such as nutrients, heavy metals, pathogenic organisms, suspended solids, and toxic chemicals that can be detrimental to our environment.

When these discharges enter a river or tributary having assimilative and renovative capacity, because of its length, volume of flow, and turbulent flow characteristics, the discharges may be acceptable. Unfortunately, most rivers and tributaries in the coastal zone do not have these characteristics. The distance traveled is short before they reach areas of recreational use and marine life propagation. Their flows can be quiescent and often subject to tidal backup. These conditions may dictate a fourth level of treatment to remove contaminants. However, a viable alternative to AWT is land treatment of sewage effluent. In the immediate coastal areas, ocean outfalls have been considered an acceptable disposal alternative, but land disposal provides numerous advantages related to coastal region water resources.[1]

1. A large percentage of the treated wastewater is returned to groundwater resources and also serves as a deterrant to saltwater intrusion.
2. Land disposal offers the flexibility of retrieving the treated water for transfer to other critical areas.
3. Land disposal can provide for the irrigation of marginal lands or forested land, creating better havens for game life.
4. Utilization on land insures that there will be no adverse affect on any marine life or recreational use of shore waters.
5. Land disposal can provide that measure which will ensure open-space areas, when land disposal as a means of pollution control is integrated into other publicly funded projects to serve multiple purposes.[2]

Taking large quantities of water from underground supplies, using it, and then discharging it into rivers, streams, and the ocean continually depletes our groundwater supply. Similarly, taking large quantities of water from surface and underground supplies, using it, and then piping it long distances downstream to treatment plants deprives others of the potential use of the reclaimed water. Land treatment can provide a means of recycling water locally by recharge of underground stores, which in turn recharge streams and rivers.

Land treatment of sewage effluent is the application of pretreated (usually by secondary treatment) sewage on land, using the earth cover and the earth mantle as a means of providing tertiary and advanced wastewater treatment. There are various physical concepts of applying sewage on land for treatment; however, in process theory two basic principles are used:

1. Low-rate land treatment: using application rates of up to 6 inches per week.
2. High-rate land treatment: using application rates of up to 150 inches per week.

Applying wastewater to land for treatment is not a new or unusual approach to pollution management. Land disposal of wastewater dates back many centuries, and some of the systems in the United States began operation before the turn of the twentieth century. The 1972 Inventory of Municipal Waste Facilities listed 571 systems in operation, serving a population of 6.6 million persons.[3] Other surveys have indicated that this number is probably low.

The Flushing Meadows project near Phoenix, Arizona, which used high-rate land treatment, was started in 1967.[4,5]

Full-scale studies at Pennsylvania State University, using spray irrigation, started in 1962 and have been in operation for more than 10 years.[1] As early as 1955 spray irrigation and overland flow were used for the disposal of food processing wastewater at Campbell Soup Company plants in Napoleon, Ohio; Sumter, South Carolina, and Paris, Texas.[6,7,16] Seabrook Farms, New Jersey, used spray irrigation for the disposal of vegetable and fruit processing wastes in the early 1950s.

The use of infiltration or percolation lagoons and basins as a method for land treatment of sewage effluent is generally classified as a high-rate concept. Management is extremely important to successful operation of infiltration

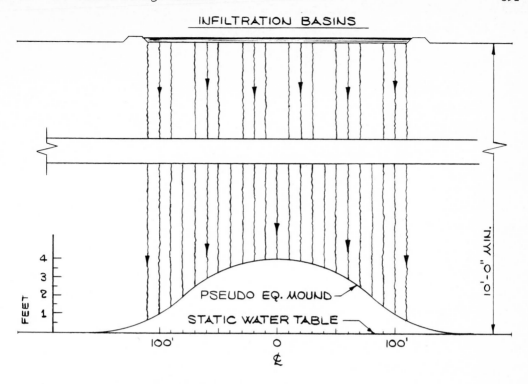

Figure 7.19.1 Typical groundwater mounding.

lagoons. Initial rates as high as 420 inches per week have been reported but could not be sustained on a continuous basis. Depth to groundwater table is critical. Groundwater table mounding under infiltration lagoons of 6 to 8 feet is not unusual when high rates are used. Figure 1 illustrates a typical groundwater mounding profile. When the mound nears the basin bottom, the infiltration rate can be reduced. Soil clogging also reduces the infiltration rate.[8,9] Suspended matter can physically clog the soil pores at the surface and also by penetration into the lower levels, and such clogging has been shown to be a function of particle size distribution. Clogging can also be caused by chemical interaction, biological growth, and algae.

Successful operation can be obtained only by periodic charging of the basins and then allowing them to empty and dry for a resting period.[10] Drying of the soil and bottom deposits and reoxygenation of the soil have been found to restore the infiltration rates. The sustained infiltration rates and nitrate removal of grass-covered basins are higher than those of bare soil basins. Signfiicant reduction of total nitrogen and phosphorus can be achieved. Short cycles of wetting and drying (2 days wet, 3 days dry) can achieve complete oxidation of nitrogen to nitrates. Longer cycles (14 days wet, 7 days dry) can achieve 90 percent removal of total nitrogen, and even longer cycles may result in still higher removals. Anaerobic conditions in the latter portion of the 14-day period in the presence of organic carbonaceous material produce the condition of biological denitrification, liberating nitrogen as a gas. Although consideration has been given to the addition of organic carbons to the wastewater to support denitrification, no data are available on such studies.

Absorption sand beds are another effective means of providing land treatment of sewage effluent and are also considered high rate. On the basis of the intermittent sand filter concept, a sand bed is intermittently dosed with sewage effluent, which is allowed to percolate through the bed directly into the ground

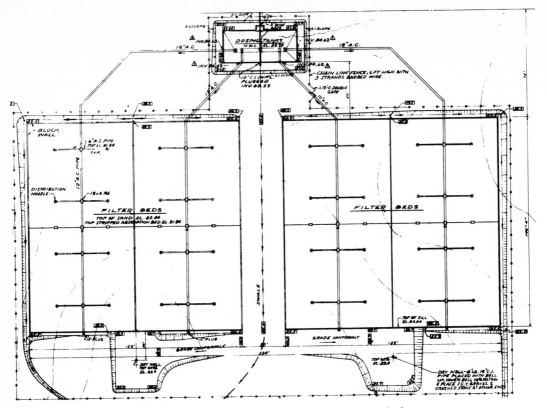

Figure 7.19.2   Layout of typical ground absorption beds.

beneath. Application rates of 80 inches per week can be used. Alternating wetting and drying is extremely important, and only a trace of chlorine is permissible. An aerobic biological mass is created in the surface layer of sand, which reduces the suspended solids and converts nitrogen to nitrates. Nitrates and phosphates are removed by soil mechanisms of chemical interaction, adsorption, and ion exchange and also by organic denitrification in the saturated soil zone. Beds are dosed with 4 to 6 inches of sewage in 15 minutes, which is allowed to percolate completely into the bed and then to dry. Air is drawn into the bed as the water level falls, reaerating the 2-foot-deep sand bed. Drying cycles are 8 to 16 hours. Depth to groundwater table must be a minimum of 10 feet from the level at which sewage percolates into the ground. Groundwater mounds of 3 to 6 feet are not unusual.

Nitrate levels of 25 to 30 ppm and phosphate levels of 3 to 4 ppm can occur beneath the bed area; these reduce to acceptable levels within 200 feet of the bed area. When grass is allowed to grow on the bed and is cut regularly, removing clippings, the removals of nitrate and phosphates are increased. Figure 2 is an example of a ground absorption bed layout which has been in successful operation for 3 years.

Furrowing and overland flow have also been used for land treatment of sewage effluent.[7,11] Control is difficult, and this method is used most often when soil percolation rates are poor.[19] Some preparation of the site is required, and the distances to drainage ditches, streams, and other waterways are important. Erosion should not occur in a properly operating system. Some of the water is lost by evapotranspiration in the process. Only a few of these systems have been installed, chiefly for food processing wastewater, and few data have been reported. The process is most effective in the removal of pollutants when there is a ground cover of grass, crop, and vegetative litter. Application rates of 5 to 6 inches per week are possible.

Spray irrigation is probably the most widely used and the most successful, from the standpoint of effluent renovation, of all the methods of land treatment of sewage effluents. Spray irrigation of grasslands, wooded areas, fodder crops, parks, and golf courses has been used with great success. Application rates are related to the irrigation tolerance level of the ground cover crop[18] or vegetation, rather than to the percolation rate of the soil. Soil percolation rates should not be too high, since effluent must be retained within the soil mantle for a sufficient period to allow renovation by the root growth and soil mechanisms. Renovation should occur in the earth mantle before reaching the groundwater table. The higher the application rate, the deeper the wave front of nitrogen and other pollutants will penetrate. In the Pennsylvania State University studies the nitrate penetration was 17 feet after 6 months of application at the rate of 6 inches per week applied in a single day. Rates of 1 to 4 inches per week applied at the maximum rate of 0.25 inch per hour, with cycling to provide drying rest periods, were capable of removing from the effluent up to 82 percent nitrates, 95 percent ABS, and 99 percent phosphates.[1] Spraying was done on reed canary grass, silage corn, and forestlands.

Spray irrigation land treatment has been termed the "living filter" process.[20] The soil mantle functions as a physical, chemical, and biological filter to remove solids, nitrates,[17] phosphates, ABS, bacteria, and some heavy metals. Cover vegetation utilizes these elements, stored in the soil, for growth and when harvested removes them completely from the immediate environment, in essence for recycling.[14,15] Oxygenation of the soil to maintain aerobic conditions is important in the management plan. However, anaerobic conditions developed in the saturated soils in the presence of organic carbons can promote denitrification.[12]

The tendency is to design spray irrigation systems with movable piping for flexibility and economy. It has been found, however, that undue reliance on the operator of such systems for proper placement and cycling has caused system failures. Fixed piping systems that are not too rigid and have the capability of rearrangement and the use of simple cycling control systems are preferrable.

Spray irrigation can be utilized as an all-year disposal method, provided that ground cover is properly selected. Spraying in forests can be done throughout the winter if precautions are taken against such problems as ice damage, wind throw, and bark damage. In cold climates there will be periods of hard freeze when spraying cannot be accomplished without heavy runoff. Holding lagoons must be provided to store effluent during this period so that spraying can be curtailed until soil percolation returns. Figure 3 illustrates a layout of a typical spray irrigation system with holding lagoons.

Land treatment of effluent is not a panacea for sewage treatment. Rather, it is a viable alternative in pollution management and should be considered with all other sewage treatment alternatives.[13] It is relatively difficult to evaluate since it involves many more disiplines than the engineer or environmentalist has heretofore had to consider in sewage treatment. The tendency has been a failure to consider many intangible environmental values in land treatment when comparing the various alternatives.

In considering land treatment each case must be studied with care. Such things as climate, geology, groundwater quality and level, plant life, wildlife, soil consistency, absorption, and percolation, and wastewater character must all be considered.

Extreme care must be exercised when the geology shows a thin earth mantle overlying rock, particularly carbonate or fractured geological formations. Although most bacteria will not travel more than 200 feet in soil, in such geological formations they can travel much further. When employing land treatment in forest areas, consideration must be given to possible timber use; investigations have shown effects on the wood properties of trees to be used for timber or paper raw product. Herbaceous vegetation exhibits a change of species from arid types to varieties favoring a moist, shaded environment.

Land treatment areas should be buffered, and the use of shallow, potable water wells prohibited in the immediate area. Ground-

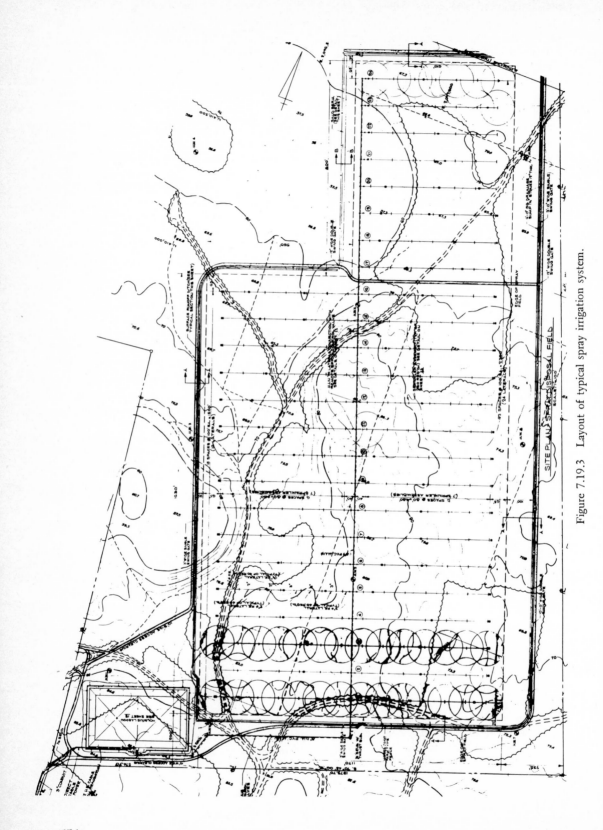

Figure 7.19.3   Layout of typical spray irrigation system.

water-monitoring wells should be placed within the disposal area and completely surrounding it, located 100 to 200 feet from the outer edges.[14] These should be sampled and tested regularly to evaluate the system performance and make adjustments in rates to achieve the treatment required.

Disposal systems involving small quantities of effluent are ideally suited to land treatment. As disposal quantities become larger, the application of land treatment becomes more critical. Adequate study of each case is mandatory. Necessary safeguards and provisions for monitoring the effects on soil and groundwater must be designed into the system. Land disposal has been used successfully for many years, and with the addition of present-day technology and further research presently under way it should be considered a viable alternative to tertiary or advanced wastewater treatment.

REFERENCES

1. W. E. Sopper, L. T. Kardos, et al. *Recycling Treated Municipal Wastewater and Sludge through Forest and Cropland*. The Pennsylvania State University Press, University Park, Pennsylvania.

2. W. K. Davis. 1973. "Land disposal. III: Land use planning." *Journal of the Water Pollution Control Federation*, Vol. 45, No. 7 (July).

3. R. E. Thomas. 1973. "Land disposal. II: An overview of treatment methods." *Journal of the Water Pollution Control Federation*, Vol. 45, No. 7 (July).

4. H. Bouwer, R. C. Rice, and E. D. Escarcega. 1974. "High-rate land treatment. I: Infiltration and hydraulic aspects of the Flushing Meadows project." *Journal of the Water Pollution Control Federation*, Vol. 46, No. 5 (May).

5. H. Bouwer, J. C. Lance, and M. S. Riggs. 1974. "High-rate land treatment. II: Water quality and economic aspects of the Flushing Meadows project." *Journal of the Water Pollution Control Federation*, Vol. 46, No. 5 (May).

6. L. C. Gilde et al. 1971. "A spray irrigation system for treatment of cannery wastes." *Journal of the Water Pollution Control Federation*, Vol. 43, No. 10 (October).

7. L. C. Gilde. 1973. "Land treatment of food processing wastewaters." *Journal of the Irrigation and Drainage Division—ASCE*, September.

8. R. C. Rice. 1974. "Soil clogging during infiltration of secondary effluent." *Journal of the Water Pollution Control Federation*, Vol. 46, No. 4 (April).

9. J. de Vries. 1972. "Soil filtration of wastewater effluent and the mechanism of pore clogging." *Journal of the Water Pollution Control Federation*, Vol. 44, No. 4 (April).

10. C. W. Fetter, Jr., and R. G. Holzmacher. 1974. "Groundwater recharge with treated wastewater." *Journal of the Water Pollution Control Federation*, Vol. 46, No. 2 (February).

11. R. E. Thomas et al. 1970. "Hydrology of spray-runoff wastewater treatment." *Journal of the Irrigation and Drainage Division—ASCE*, September.

12. J. C. Lance. 1972. "Nitrogen removal by soil mechanisms." *Journal of the Water Pollution Control Federation*, Vol. 44, No. 7 (July).

13. K. A. Godfrey, Jr. 1973. "Land treatment of municipal sewage." *Civil Engineering*, September.

14. U.S. Environmental Protection Agency. 1973. *Proceedings of the Conference on Land Disposal of Municipal Effluents and Sludges*, Rutgers University, New Jersey, March 12–13. Report No. EPA 902/9-73-001.

15. Association of State Universities and Land Grant Colleges. 1973. *Proceedings of the Joint Conference on Recycling Municipal Sludges and Effluents on Land*, Champaign, Illinois, July 9–13.

16. G. R. Vela and E. R. Eubanks. 1973. "Soil microorganism metabolism in spray irrigation." *Journal of the Water Pollution Control Federation*, Vol. 45, No. 8 (August).

17. J. R. Tilstra, K. W. Malueg, and W. C. Larson. 1972 "Removal of phosphorus and nitrogen from wastewater effluents by induced soil percolation." *Journal of the Water Pollution Control Federation*, Vol. 44, No. 5 (May).

18. D. C. Baier and W. B. Fryer. 1973. "Undesirable plant responses with Sewage irrigation." *Journal of the Irrigation and Drainage Division—ASCE*, June.

19. E. Sepp. 1973. "Disposal of domestic wastewater by hillside sprays." *Journal of the Environmental Engineering Division—ASCE*, April.

20. R. R. Parizek et al. *Wastewater Renovation and Conservation*. Pennsylvania State University Study No. 23, University Press, University Park, Pennsylvania.

20. LIFE IN THE BOTTOM —MEIOBENTHOS

Cathy Kerby
Oceanographic Sorting Center
Smithsonian Institution
Washington, D.C.

In the early 1900s biologists discovered a unique fauna occupying the interstitial water in marine, estuarine, and freshwater sediments.[1,2] This fauna, variously referred to as "interstitial fauna," "mesopsammon," "meiofauna," or "meiobenthos," moves along the water–sediment interface and through the microchannels formed by sediment grains, in contrast with larger benthic organisms—the "macrobenthos"—which displace the sediment.[3,4] Thus this fauna is distinguished, if not defined, by its size. Meiobenthic invertebrates generally are between 0.062 and 1.0 millimeter in their greatest dimension, whereas macrobenthos generally is larger than 1.0 millimeter. A third category, "microbenthos," consists predominately of bacteria and small protozoa and generally is less than 0.06 millimeter.[5,6]

Immature life history stages may be classified as temporary meiobenthos; permanent meiobenthos consists of a distinct faunistic assemblage of small metazoans that differ considerably from macrobenthos.[5]

Most invertebrate phyla are represented in interstitial habitats. The meiobenthos includes taxa commonly of small body size (e.g., nematodes), whose structural organization preadapts them to this special habitat (e.g., tardigrades). Qualitatively and quantitatively the important groups of permanent meiobenthos can be ranked in the following order: Nematoda, Copepoda, Turbellaria, Gnathostomulida, Annelida, and Ostracoda.[5,7,8] In other instances, taxa such as crustaceans, coelenterates, echinoderms, and bryozoans are represented in the meiobenthos by small, morphologically aberrant forms, sometimes of entirely new structural types.[1,9–11]

Meiobenthos inhabits sediments composed of shell, gravel, sand, and mud.[12] The size of the sediment particles, their shape, the degree of packing, and the amount of shifting of sediment particles all influence the availability of interstitial space, as well as the porosity and the permeability of sediment to water.[12] If the pores are not completely filled with water, the living space available may be limited. Meiobenthos usually occupies only sediments containing water saturation of at least 10 percent.[12] Segregation of surface layer particles depends on water movement, mineral composition, wind, exposure, and so forth.

Ecological factors affecting the interstitial habitat act, not individually, but in combination with one another. It is known that meiobenthic organisms react to temperature, salinity, oxygen, and light gradients and that they perceive pore space, gravity, currents, and chemical substances produced by their own species.[14] These factors determine in part their composition, abundance, and distribution.[13]

Meiobenthos is subjected to temperature variations as a result of seasonal changes, time of day, weather, and geographical locality.[12,15] Vertical stratification of temperature is not uncommon; for example, a gradient decrease of at least 10°C within the upper 2 centimeters of sediment is known to occur. However, there is little change of temperature below 20 centimeters.[13] These organisms are also subjected to salinity fluctuations. Many species are both eurythermal and euryhaline; but when other ecological conditions are satisfactory, they migrate vertically in order to maintain optimal temperature and salinity conditions.[11–13]

The availability of oxygen present within a sediment affects meiobenthic distribution. Broadly speaking, the abundance of oxygen in the interstices decreases from the edge of the water to the shore and from the sediment surface to greater depths.[16,17] The abundance of oxygen depends on the permeability of sediments to water.[12] Species dependent on oxygen consumption cannot vertically migrate to depths where oxygen is lacking.[16,17] Facultative, anaerobic species, for example, some gnathostomulids, prefer to live in the deep, H_2S-rich layers.[18,19]

The presence of organic detritus in the interstices is advantageous in that it serves as a food source for meiobenthos and disadvantageous in that it clogs the pores and thereby limits the available space and the water retention capacity. It is present in small quantities in sandy areas but is more abundant in fine, muddy sediments.[12,13]

Meiobenthic habitats in the estuaries and coastal regions of the open ocean are numerous. A specific interstitial brackish water fauna inhabits the coastal subsoil water (in a sandy beach, the narrow zone of brackish water formed by the contact and resulting mixture of fresh water from the land and salt water from the sea). Organisms such as hydrozoans and polychaetes are known to live in this habitat.[1,9,12,20]

Meiobenthos living in intertidal sand is found as deep as 1 meter below the surface. The interstitial space in this habitat is extensive, and drainage is relatively good. The animals therefore can migrate vertically in order to maintain optimal salinity, temperature, and oxygen conditions.[5] Coarse boreal beaches are populated by fewer organisms than finer ones. Beach stability appears to play a dominant role in biomass control.[21] On exposed sand in temperate regions, meiobenthic populations greatly outnumber the macrobenthos. On the other hand, the meiobenthos and macrobenthos coexist in large numbers on tropical beaches.[22]

In intertidal muddy deposits meiobenthos generally is restricted to the upper few centimeters. Distribution is controlled by the reduced oxygen abundance resulting from poor drainage and by the interstitial space reduction due to compaction of the particles.[5]

It appears that meiobenthic organisms in the subtidal zone are confined to the superficial layers, but data are sparse.[5] Meiobenthic populations in the subtidal region are from 30 to 190 times more numerous than the macrofauna. They are most abundant in soft mud in deep water.[5]

Sufficient data are not yet available for comparison of macrobenthos with meiobenthos. However, macrobenthos is known to affect meiobenthos by predation, probably by competition, and by physical disturbance of the habitat. On the other hand, meiobenthos appears to flourish better than macrobenthos in environmental stress areas, such as exposed beaches and organically poor deep-water deposits.[5]

The maximum body size of meiobenthos is limited by the availability of interstitial space.

The largest protozoan and the smallest metazoan are found here. Elongated, flat, and broad body shapes are dominant. Vermiform-shaped bodies, which are prevalent, are considered the best suited to this habitat.[1]

Meiobenthic organisms have undergone other morphological changes in order to adapt themselves to the environment in which they live. Mechanical protection is a necessity for many of these fragile species. In some, the body wall is reinforced by cuticular scales, spines, spine-scales, or epidermal spicules. In others with thin body walls, a marked ability to contract provides this protection. A characteristic feature of many meiobenthic species is the ability to adhere. Adhesive glands, often located on the epidermis, and gripping structures, such as claws and hooks, are used for this purpose. Interstitial organisms often possess static sense organs.[1]

The continuous movement of sediment particles in many habitats often makes the ability to move a necessity for meiobenthos. Locomotion is primarily by swimming, ciliary gliding, writhing, and crawling. A few semisessile and sedentary forms have been found, but survival is dependent on the presence of a relatively stable sediment, satisfactory water circulation, and a suspended food supply.[1]

To understand the role of the meiobenthic species in the ecosystem, it is necessary to place them accurately within the food web.[1,5] Although additional information is needed on population size and fluctuation, distribution, food sources, and utilization by predators, some generalizations can be made.

The density of meiobenthic populations is often high. In the intertidal zone the number of individuals ranges from 11,000 to more than 16,000,000 per square meter, with sheltered areas supporting the higher densities. In the subtidal zone the number ranges from 4000 to 3,200,000 per square meter, with abundance declining as depth increases. In both zones softer deposits are generally the richest.[5] Population fluctuations are dependent on reproductive cycles, physical forces affecting the sediment, seasonality, and the hydrography of the overlying water column, such as the presence of a thermocline.[23] These fluctuations occur more frequently in the intertidal than in the subtidal zone.[5]

The main predators of meiobenthos are small fish, such as juvenile flatfish, and other meiobenthic organisms, such as nematodes, turbellarians, and tardigrades. Both hard- and soft-bodied organisms are consumed by predators, but less is known about the consumption of soft-bodied forms. The effect of predation on meiobenthic populations is not yet known.[5] In addition, meiobenthos is consumed, but not necessarily digested, by macrobenthic deposit feeders.[3]

The basic food sources of meiobenthos are dead organic matter, in the form of detritus and fallen plankton, and live matter, in the form of fauna, microflora, and bacteria.[3,5] Microflora, such as diatoms and peridineans, lie free in the interstices or encrust the sand grains.[3] Four meiobenthic feeding types are recognized; (1) predators; (2) diatom and epigrowth feeders, including the browsers, puncture-suckers, pump-suckers, and sand-lickers; (3) detritus eaters; and (4) suspension feeders, found only in semisessile or sedentary forms.[1] Meiobenthos is known to feed directly on bacteria, but the extent to which it depends on them for a food source is not known.[1,5]

Meiobenthic organisms appear to be at the top of the food chain since a large proportion of them seem free of predation by animals at higher trophic levels. In some localities they may even compete with macrofauna for food. It is known that they play an important role in nutrient recycling.[1]

Meiobenthic species are important also in the chemical processes occurring in the sediments. They increase the rate of transport of different substances from one depth to another, they help to control the population density of microbenthos, and they contribute to the mineralization of organic substances.[18]

Eggs of meiobenthic organisms are, or become, sticky soon after spawning and adhere immediately to the substratum.[1] In many species larval stages are reduced, and the pelagic stage in particular is suppressed.[3] In other species direct development is not uncommon. Brood protection and viviparity are widespead.[1] Observations of meiobenthic species indicate that generation times, from egg to egg production, are about 1 month and that two to four generations are produced annually.[1,5]

This timing is dependent on environmental factors such as food, temperature, and predation.[5]

The development, morphology, and biology of meiobenthos appear designed to ensure that an organism remains in the interstices of the locality inhabited by its parents. Cosmopolitan species and high global similarity are nevertheless prevalent.[24] Most contemporary methods of dispersal are restricted to short range.[3,24] Slow speciation coupled with geological dispersal by continnental drift provides the best explanation of world wide distribution.[24]

Only a few studies have been made on the effects of pollution on meiobenthos. In macrobenthos severe pollutional effects are detected by density reductions, and less severe effects by changes in species composition.[25] It is not unusual for large changes in species diversity of meiobenthos to occur over small changes in the substratum. Diversity indices are therefore not a sensitive tool for assessing pollution effects on meiobenthos.[5] Estuarine meiobenthic species appear the most resistant to stress, probably because they are already physiologically tolerant of environmental variations.[25] Some species are capable of either cryptobiosis or encystment during natural ecological stresses.[26] Although significant differences in the abundance of meiobenthos have been noted in polluted and unpolluted regions, it has not been possible to show direct cause-and-effect relationships.[27] Laboratory studies indicate that various pollutant chemicals affect species synegistically.[28]

In summary, the great abundance, adaptation to a wide variety of habitats, and diverse morphology of meiobenthos suggest that these organisms play a complex and signicant role in the ecology of the coastal environment.

REFERENCES

1. B. Swedmark. 1964. "The interstitial fauna of marine sand." *Biological Review*, Vol. 39, pp. 1–42.

2. R. W. Pennak. 1968. "Historical origins and ramifications of interstitial investigations." *Transactions of the American Microscopical Society*, Vol. 87, No. 2, pp. 214–218.

3. P. J. S. Boaden. 1964. "Grazing in the inter-

stitial habitat: A review." In D. J. Crisp, Ed., *Grazing in the Marine Environment*, Blackwell Publishers at Oxford. 322 pp.

4. E. Kirsteuer. 1971. "The interstitial nemertean fauna of marine sand." In N. C. Hulings, Ed., *Proceedings of the First International Conference on Meiofauna*. Smithsonian Contributions to Zoology, No. 76; pp. 1–205.

5. A. D. McIntyre. 1969. "Ecology of marine meiobenthos." *Biological Review*, Vol. 44, pp. 245–290.

6. N. C. Hulings and J. S. Gray. 1971. A *Manual for the Study of Meiofauna*. Smithsonian Contributions to Zoology, No. 78, pp. 1–84.

7. W. Noodt. 1971. "Ecology of the Copepoda." In N. C. Hulings, Ed., *Proceedings of the First International Conference on Meiofauna*. Smithsonian Contributions to Zoology, No. 76, pp. 1–205.

8. A. D. McIntyre. 1971. "Observations on the status of subtidal meiofauna research." In N. C. Hulings, Ed., *Proceedings of the First International Conference on Meiofauna*. Smithsonian Contributions to Zoology, No. 76, pp. 1–205.

9. C. Clausen, 1971. "Interstitial Cnidaria: Present status of their systematics and ecology." In N. C. Hulings, Ed., *Proceedings of the First International Conference on Meiofauna*. Smithsonian Contributions to Zoology, No. 76, pp. 1–205.

10. J. S. Gray. 1971. "The meiobenthic Bryozoa." In N. C. Hulings, Ed., *Proceedings of the First International Conference on Meiofauna*. Smithsonian Contributions to Zoology, No. 76, pp. 1–205.

11. B. Swedmark. 1971. "A review of Gastropoda, Brachiopoda, and Echinodermata in marine meiobenthos." In N. C. Hulings, Ed., *Proceedings of the First International Conference on Meiofauna*. Smithsonian Contributions to Zoology, No. 76, pp. 1–205.

12. L. W. Pollock, 1971. "Ecology of intertidal meiobenthos." In N. C. Hulings, Ed., *Proceedings of the First International Conference on Meiofauna*. Smithsonian Contributions to Zoology, No. 76, pp. 1–205.

13. B. Jansson. 1971. "The 'Umwelt' of the interstitial fauna." In N. C. Hulings, Ed., *Proceedings of the First International Conference on Meiofauna*. Smithsonian Contributions to Zoology, No. 76, pp. 1–205.

14. J. S. Gray, 1967. "Substrate selection by the archiannelid *Protodrilus rubrophoryngeus*."

Helgolaender Wissenschaftlische Meeresuntersuchungen, Vol. 15, pp. 253–269.

15. O. Kinne. 1963. "The effects of temperature and salinity on marine and brackish water animals. I: Temperature." *Annual Review of Oceanography and Marine Biology*, Vol. 2, pp. 281–339.

16. B. Jansson. 1967. "The availability of oxygen for the interstitial fauna of sandy beaches." *Journal of Experimental Marine Biology and Ecology*, Vol. 1, pp. 123–143.

17. R. W. Pennak. 1951. "Comparative ecology of the interstitial fauna of fresh-water and marine beaches." *Annals of Biology*, Vol. 27, pp. 449–480.

18. T. Fenchel and B. Jansson. 1966. "On the vertical distribution of the microfauna in the sediments of a brackish-water beach." *Ophelia*, Vol. 3, pp. 161–177.

19. T. M. Fenchel and R. J. Riedl. 1970. "The sulfide system: A new biotic community underneath the oxidized layer of marine sand bottoms." *International Journal on Life in Oceans and Coastal Waters*, Vol. 7, No. 3, pp. 255–268.

20. W. Westheide. 1971. "Interstitial polychaeta." In N. C. Hulings, Ed., *Proceedings of the First International Conference on Meiofauna*. Smithsonian Contributions to Zoology, No. 76, pp. 1–205.

21. J. S. Gray and R. M. Rieger. 1971. "A quantitative study of the meiofauna of an exposed sandy beach, at Robin Hood's Bay, Yorkshire." *Journals of the Marine Biological Association of the U.K.*, Vol. 51, pp. 1–19.

22. A. D. McIntyre. 1968. "The meiofauna and macrofauna of some tropical beaches." *Journal of Zoology (London)*, Vol. 156, pp. 377–392.

23. B. C. Coull. 1969. "Hydrographic control of meiobenthos in Bermuda." *Limnology and Oceanography*, Vol. 14, pp. 953–957.

24. W. Sterrer. 1973. "Plate tectonics as a mechanism for dispersal and speciation in interstitial sand fauna." *Netherlands Journal of Sea Research*, Vol. 7, pp. 200–222.

25. J. S. Gray. 1971. "The effects of pollution on sand meiofauna communities." *Thalassia Jugoslavica*, Vol. 7, No. 1, pp. 79–86.

26. R. P. Higgins, 1972. "Tardigrada of the Chesapeake Bay." In McErlean, Kerby, and Wass, Eds., Biota of the Chesapeake Bay. *Chesapeake Science*, Vol. 13 (Supplement), pp. S1–S197.

27. J. C. Makemson, 1973. "Oxygen and carbon dioxide in interstitial water of two Lebanese sand beaches." *Netherlands Journal of Sea Research*, Vol. 7, pp. 223–232.

28. J. S. Gray and R. J. Ventilla. 1971. "Pollution effects on micro- and meiofauna of sand." *Marine Pollution Bulletin*, Vol. 2, pp. 39–43.

21. MANGROVE SWAMPS

Lawrence A. Burns
Center for Wetlands
University of Florida
Gainesville, Florida

Mangrove swamps dominate tropical and subtropical shorelines throughout the world. Within the geographical zone defined by the 25° north and south latitude lines, the mangrove swamp forest ecosystem occupies about 75 percent of the coastal fringe. The distribution of mangroves is geographically limited by winter frosts, for although species sensitivities may vary somewhat, mangrove trees cannot survive air temperatures much below 25°F (−4°C).[1] The largest and best-developed mangrove forests of the United States occur in south Florida, where they play an ecological role analogous to that of salt marshes in the temperate zone.

"Mangrove" is a term denoting any salt-tolerant intertidal tree species, primarily represented in Florida by four species (red, black, and white mangroves, and buttonwood) of three separate plant families. Black mangrove is the most extensively distributed mangrove species in Florida, and can be found from St. John's County on the east coast to Louisiana. Red mangrove is less widely distributed, reaching its northern limit in Volusia County on the east coast and in Levy County on the west, at about 28° north. White mangrove and buttonwood show distributional ranges much the same as that of red mangrove. Two additional mangrove species, one of which is a naturalized import from Polynesia, are restricted to the Florida Keys.

General distributional maps and species ranges are somewhat misleading as to the relative importance of mangrove communities in Florida's coastal zone. On the northwest coast, black mangrove occurs mostly as scattered shrublands, and the coastal zone community is dominated by cord grasses and black rush marshes. On the eastern Atlantic shore, mangroves are entirely lacking on high-energy beaches fronting the ocean, but well-developed communities occur behind barrier islands and on the shores of protected coastal lagoons.

Large mangrove swamp forests are only found in south Florida and are especially extensive along the protected southwest coastline. In south Florida, mangrove forest occupies about 3.6 percent of the total area and some 8.3 percent of the forested land area of the region.[1]

Mangrove trees are of direct economic importance in many tropical countries as timber, charcoal, tanbark, source materials in the textile industry, and indirectly as a fisheries resource. In the United States the primary benefits to man have derived from the mangrove's ecological role in the coastal wetland ecosystem. These benefits can be broadly summarized as follows:

1. Mangroves protect the shoreline from major erosional damage due to tropical storms. The mangrove fringe occupies the portion of the coastal zone most at risk when hurricanes come ashore along the Florida coast. For example, most of the economic damages attributable to a hurricane that crossed the northwest coast of Florida in the fall of 1975 were sustained in a zone extending only 100 yards inland of the normal tide line. This instance clearly indicates the advantages of discouraging major economic development in the coastal fringe. First, damage to coastal mangroves is repaired naturally, without major assistance from organized human society. In addition, the mangrove forest may exert a breakwater effect in absorbing most of the energy of storm-driven wave action, thus helping to protect housing and service structures further inland. Although mangroves do not "build land" in the sense inadvertently implied by earlier authors, they exert an important stabilizing effect on areas where they are able to grow. The state of Florida has conducted several studies on the feasibility of planting mangroves to stabilize dredging spoil and other disturbed soil areas in the coastal zone, and mangroves

were introduced into Hawaii for the specific purpose of beach erosion control.

2. The mangrove ecosystem is a major nursery ground for many economically important animals, including commercially harvested fish such as mullet and sea trout, sports fish (snook, tarpon, etc.), and shrimp. Part of this benefit derives from the protection of the juveniles from predation that is afforded by brackish water conditions, but the primary production of the plant community itself is also of great importance. The detrital food chains that support fisheries production are fueled by the food-generating activities of mangroves.

3. Mangrove swamps also have economic value in that they support and make possible the sports fishery, the hosts of spectacular wading and fishing birds, and the feeling of wild country that engenders interest and return visits from vacationers. The uniqueness of the Florida mangrove wilderness in Everglades National Park was one of the prime reasons for establishing the park.

The mangrove ecosystem, like any other ecosystem, is far from being a simple sum of component animal and plant populations that exist independently of events in surrounding physical and ecological systems. The mangrove swamp is an "open system," continually adjusting to changes in the system environment. To understand the ways in which man's activities affect mangrove swamps, we must make the connection between the ways in which the ecosystem responds to its environment, and the ways in which the activities of man change that environment and induce later changes in the biological community. In other words, the detrimental effects of man's activities on the ecosystems we depend on for life support can be minimized only when we have some ability to successfully predict the environmental costs and net benefits of the array of development alternatives that are available.

Each of the benefits listed above accrues from special properties of the mangrove ecosystem, and each is sensitive to pressures from industrial society. Some important environmental variables that exercise controls on mangrove swamps, and that may be impacted by human activities, are briefly discussed below.

The coastal sedimentation environment is important in determining where mangroves can grow.[2] The net of prop roots and trapped debris of the mangrove fringe acts as a sedimentary weir, slowing water movement and allowing any load of entrained particles to settle out of the water column. Beyond this effect, however, mangroves obviously have no ability to "build land" in any concrete sense. Thus mangroves are generally found only on low-energy, accreting shorelines and are largely absent from eroding shorelines, although they may help to stabilize marginal shoreline dynamics. For this reason one might suspect that beach erosion control works (jetties, groins, etc.) may reduce local sand transport sufficiently to cause shrinkage of contiguous mangrove swamps.

Although tolerant of high-salinity conditions, mangroves appear to reach their best development in polyhaline (estuarine) situations. A study conducted by the Environmental Protection Agency in southwest Florida[3] showed that maximum net primary production occurred in the mid reach of the study zone under the most strongly polyhaline conditions (Table 1). Net production, which represents the organic fuel available to dependent wildlife and fishery food chains, declined both toward the ocean front and toward freshwater marshes. It appears that competition for space and nutrients may limit the landward extension of mangrove forests, while salt stress may suppress maximum productivity under fully marine or hypersaline conditions. In this case modication of estuarine salinity patterns by upland drainage and other surface-water control structures may have profound effects on the mangrove community and its associated fisheries. Community net production under fully marine conditions in the study cited above amounted to only 64 percent of polyhaline values, and this drop probably indicated a similar decline in the carrying capacity of the area for wildlife.

Thus accelerated transport of upland fresh water to the lower estuary, bypassing coastal swamps and marshlands via dredged waterways, may have several adverse side effects. Pollutional loadings are not cleansed by passage through marshes and swamps, sharp salinity shocks are imposed on the lower estuary, the

Table 7.21.1   Community metabolism of mangrove forest in southwest Florida (Ten Thousand Island Region) (SOURCE: Adapted from Reference 3)
GPP stands for gross primary productivity (i.e., total carbon fixation); NPP, for net primary productivity, the net fixation of organic materials for growth of the forest and support of dependent food chains; R, for respiration, the quantity of carbon released by the plant community in the course of maintenance metabolism. Metabolism units are in grams of carbon fixed (or released) per square meter of forested land surface per day.

Station	Surface Water Chloride		Community Metabolism		
	mean	range	GPP	NPP	R
	(ppt)		(grams carbon/m^2/day)		
Upper Estuary	4.7	0.4	10.3	6.6	3.7
Middle Estuary	12.7	8.8	11.8	7.5	4.3
Lower Estuary	16.0	2.0	13.9	4.8	9.1

productivity and carrying capacity of the mid-reach estuary decline, and freshened water conditions that protect juvenile fish, shrimp, and so forth from predation are destroyed.

The causes of the decline in community vigor with loss of a polyhaline environment are not, at this writing, completely clear. The most plausible explanation appears to involve an interaction of water chemistry with the physical energies of tidal water movement within the mangrove forest. Tidal movement of water, alternately draining and reflooding the intertidal zone, may serve to replenish the soil solution from which mangroves derive their water supply. This renewal cleanses the soil of accumulated salts and toxic sulfur compounds and renews the supply of inorganic nutrients for further photosynthesis. Briefly, the availability of freshened water for such injection into the soil system will enhance forest productivity by reducing salt stress and salt inhibition of production. More precisely, the soil solution salt content determines the osmotic pressure gradient between the soil water and the plant vascular system, which partially controls the rate at which water can be supplied to leaf tissues to support transpiration water losses. When this water supply is deficient, the leaf stomata close to reduce the rate of water export; this also lowers the uptake of gaseous carbon dioxide from the air and thus reduces productivity. In addition, glandular excretion of excess salts from mangrove leaves requires an expenditure of energy that would otherwise be available for tissue growth.

Mangrove forests are of considerable importance to the integrity of coastal zone ecosystems where they occur. As already discussed, these areas are breeding, feeding, and nursery grounds for substantial populations of spectacular wading and fishing birds and sport and commercial fish, and help to protect the coastal zone from devastation by tropical storms and hurricanes. The mangroves themselves are the primary food-producing agents in tropical estuarine ecosystems, producing as much as 80 percent of the total organic materials available to the aquatic food chain.[3] The transport of mangrove-derived organic mate-

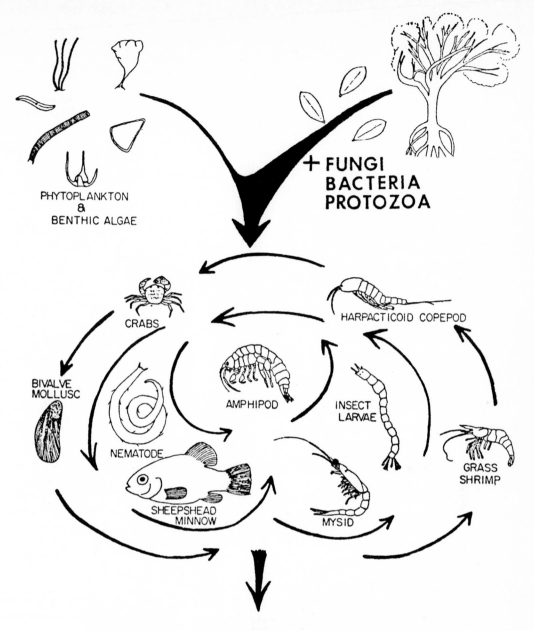

PHYTOPLANKTON
&
BENTHIC ALGAE

+ FUNGI
BACTERIA
PROTOZOA

CRABS

HARPACTICOID COPEPOD

BIVALVE
MOLLUSC

AMPHIPOD

INSECT
LARVAE

NEMATODE

GRASS
SHRIMP

SHEEPSHEAD
MINNOW

MYSID

2ND CONSUMERS

Figure 7.21.1 Detrital food chain based on red mangrove detritus. The cyclical pattern of this food chain arises from the multiple reuse of detritus commonly found in detritivore populations. The basic food source for macroscale animal life is the fungi, bacteria, and protozoan populations that develop on the surface of decaying leaf litter. The animal populations digest the microorganisms from the litter surfaces and grind up the detritus into many smaller fragments, producing a greatly increased surface area per unit volume of original material. After passage through the animal's gut, the macerated plant debris is returned to the environment. Facilitated recolonization by microbes and further breakdown of the plant remains take place, and the cycle begins again. (SOURCE: Reference 5.)

rials into the estuary and the patterns of utilization of these materials by estuarine animals have been amply documented by E. J. Heald[4] and W. E. Odum,[5] respectively (Figure 1). Considerable recent controversy has arisen, however, over the relative roles of the several species of mangroves in this process. The drainage basin studied by Heald and Odum was dominated by red mangroves with about a 1 percent admixture of white mangroves; no black mangroves were present. The spatial zonation usually seen in areas of mixed swamp forest is schematically depicted in Figure 2.

The fact that intact black mangrove leaves are rarely observed floating in the estuary suggests that export of organic matter from black-mangrove-dominated forest zones may be predominantly in a dissloved or very finely divided form. Whether such dissolved organic materials play a substantial role in the estuarine ecosystem is an open question. Finely divided particles in transit through detrital food chains are usually exceptionally rich in protein,[4] and dissolved compounds may serve regulatory roles within the system.[6] However, it should be emphasized that such possibilities are currently pure conjecture.

The internal ecological relations of the black mangrove zones of south Florida coastal forests have been examined by Tabb et al.,[7] especially in terms of *in situ* fish production. These authors conclude that events in this zone, although partially isolated from interchange with the lower estuary, are as important as red

mangrove production in supporting estuarine animal populations. The black mangrove swamps and high marshes of Everglades Park are nursery grounds for tarpon, snook, and other juvenile marine fish that derive their nutrition and growth from a detrital food chain based on a feeding sequence with black mangrove debris as the primary source material. This food chain proceeds through the feeding of mosquito and tendipid midge larvae on detrital materials, and heavy predation of killifish, mosquito fish, and other "forage" fish on these insect larvae (Figure 3). Seasonal dry-downs of these marshes concentrate forage fish in pockets within the marshes, which are then intensively utilized by wading birds during the rookery season. During high-water periods or storm floods, considerable quantities of nutrients, including large numbers of fish, are transported out of the marsh, providing a seasonal pulse of food nutrients to the lower estuary.

This chain of events is strikingly similar to the ecological relationships existing in freshwater marsh areas of south Florida and suggests that black mangrove swamps are intermediate in character between red mangrove swamps, regularly washed by tide waters, and uplands completely isolated from marine influences. If this view is correct, the snook and tarpon are in a sense Florida's version of an anadromous fishery, with all the protection problems such an analogy implies. Preservation of the essential characteristics of this system can be accomplished only by careful con-

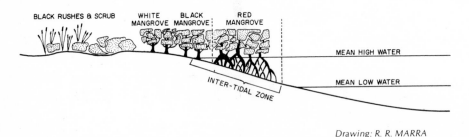

Drawing: R. R. MARRA

Figure 7.21.2 Diagrammatic and highly idealized scheme of mangrove zonation, indicating the general relation of tidal levels and ground elevation to the spatial distribution of vegetation communities in the coastal fringe. (From Ann K. Robas, *South Florida's Mangrove-Bordered Estuaries: Their Role in Sport and Commercial Fish Production*, Sea Grant Information Bulletin No. 4, December 1970, University of Miami Sea Grant Institutional Program.)

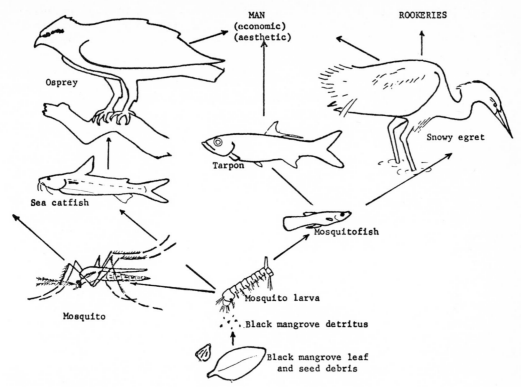

Figure 7.21.3 Food chain in black mangrove zone, emphasizing mosquitoes as primary detritivores. This diagram also shows the subsequent links in the consumer food chain leading to fisheries and bird life. (SOURCE: Reference 7.)

trol of freshwater drainage. The natural seasonal freshening accelerates the productivity of the swamp forest, creates physical conditions that exclude predators, and permits the development of the food chains that support estuarine-dependent fish and bird rookeries.

REFERENCES

1. J. H. Davis. 1943. *The Natural Features of Southern Florida, Especially the Vegetation and Everglades.* Florida Geological Survey, Geological Bull. No. 25.
2. D. W. Scholl. 1963. "Sedimentation in modern coastal swamps, southwestern Florida." *American Association of Petroleum Geologists Bulletin*, Vol. 47, pp. 1581–1603.
3. M. R. Carter, L. A. Burns, T. R. Cavinder, K. R. Dugger, P. L. Fore, D. B. Hicks, H. L. Revells, and T. W. Schmidt. 1973. *Ecosystems Analysis of the Big Cypress Swamp and Estuaries.* U.S. Environmental Protection Agency. Region IV, S.A.D. Atlanta, Georgia, EPA Report No. 904/9-74-002.
4. E. J. Heald. 1971. *The Production of Organic Detritus in a South Florida Estuary.* University of Miami, Sea Grant Technique Bulletin No. 6.
5. W. E. Odum. 1972. *Pathways of Energy Flow in a South Florida Estuary.* University of Miami, Sea Grant Technical Bulletin No. 7.
6. D. H. Janzen. 1974. "Tropical blackwater rivers, animals, and mast fruiting by the Diperocarpaceae." *Biotropica*, Vol. 6, pp. 69–103.
7. D. C. Tabb, B. Drummond, and K. Kenny. 1974. *Coastal Marshes of Southern Florida as Habitat for Fishes and Effects of Changes in Water Supply on These Habitats.* University of Miami, Final Report to U.S. Department of the Interior, BSFW Branch of River Basins, Contract No. 14-16-0004-56.

22. MOSQUITO CONTROL

Maurice W. Provost
Florida Medical Entomology Laboratory
Vero Beach, Florida

Mankind has been pestered by mosquitoes and has fought them as best he could far back into prehistory. But it was not until he learned that they alone transmitted such diseases as yellow fever and malaria that organized efforts at mosquito control came into being. This was at the very beginning of the twentieth century, and only a few years after it had been reported that a little kerosene on water could kill mosquito larvae and pupae. Now, three-quarters of a century later, mosquito-borne diseases of many kinds have long been under siege and greatly reduced, chemical control of mosquitoes has become a very intricate science, and control organization is a widespread and complex endeavor demanding the best efforts of highly trained career people. In the United States today, some 260 organized mosquito control districts expend over 50 million tax dollars annually, and probably half or more of this operation is in the coastal zone.

Salt-marsh mosquitoes of the genus *Aedes* usually dominate the coastal zone mosquito fauna so thoroughly that other species are ignored in this article; most are not restricted to this terrain in any event. The five salt-marsh *Aedes* species in America share essentially the same basic life history and ecology. Eggs are laid singly on the moist, organic soil of the marsh, seldom where there is no vegetative cover and never on free water. In a few days the fully developed larva is ready to hatch but will do so only when covered by tidewater or rainwater; unflooded, it will survive unhatched for months. After hatching, the larval and pupal stages together last from 7 to 15 days at summer temperatures. The newly emerged females mate, feed on nectar, and disperse widely in the first few days of adulthood; they then settle down to biting, blood being necessary for ovarian development, and laying eggs. There may be up to four biting and egg-laying cycles, each lasting 5 to 7 days, but the first one is the only one for the overwhelming majority. Egg hatching and adult production occur in large, synchronized broods, of which there may be several a year, depending on tide and rainfall patterns.

The salt marshes of America are unevenly distributed and are characterized by different geographical species of certain dominant plant genera,[1] but they have much in common with respect to mosquito ecology. The salient points are that a low marsh and a high marsh are present and that periodicity of submergence and emergence varies over the marsh profile. The low marsh is flooded by tide almost daily. Cordgrass (*Spartina alterniflora*, east coast, and *S. gracilis*, west coast) dominates the low marsh everywhere but in south Florida, where the red mangrove (*Rhizophora mangle*) is preeminent. On the coastal plain marshes of the Southeast the black rush (*Juncus roemerianus*) may cover extensive areas from low to high marsh. The high marsh is flooded only by the year's highest tides or, in Florida, only by summer and fall tides. From New England to Texas the predominant plants of the high marsh, sometimes called the "salt meadow," are the salt meadow grass (*Spartina patens*) and the saltgrass (*Distichlis spicata*). These grasses give way to glassworts (*Salicornia perennis*, east coast; *S. pacifica*, west coast) in central Florida and in California, and to black mangrove (*Avicennia nitida*) and saltwort (*Batis maritima*) in south Florida. The relationship of all these salt-marsh plants to tide levels has been well documented.[2-4]

The developmental stages of the salt-marsh mosquito dictate that water must stand on the marsh a minimum of 4 to 10 days to produce a brood of adults. When these adults are laying their eggs, a week or so after emergence, there must not be any water over the ground for another 4 to 10 days if a sizable egg deposit is to eventuate and develop to the resting stage. What this means is that salt-marsh mosquitoes cannot breed under conditions of daily tide floodings, for example, on the low marsh, whereas the high marsh is their domain *par excellence*. Tide floodings of the high marsh, with retention of water in depressions for many days, are what produces mosquitoes. Such floodings twice a month may result in some mosquito broods, while tide floodings separated by a month or more are sure to produce mosquitoes. A series of monthly floodings will pyramid broods into calamitous populations. Mosquito production on the salt marsh can therefore be prevented by so altering the high marsh that (1) water never stands on it, (2) surface water where ground is vegetated never lasts for more than 2 or 3 days, or (3) water covers the ground completely whenever there are gravid mosquitoes about. The first option is chosen when marshes are hydraulically filled, the second when they are ditched, and the third when they are impounded and flooded. The alternative to these marsh alteration techniques is "temporary" mosquito control, or letting production proceed but attempting to kill the aquatic stages or the adult mosquitoes.

Before elaborating on salt-marsh mosquito control practices, it is well to consider the value of the habitat involved. It may be shocking to hear values as high as $83,000 an acre[5] placed on "unimproved" salt marsh because prevailing economic thought places no value on work performed by nature for man. In this case the work performed gratis has been brought to light only in the past two decades. In the 1950s it was learned that estuaries were essential nursery areas for many of the more important marine fisheries, for example, commercial shrimp, blue crab, mullet, snook, weakfish, and tarpon. In the 1960s it was learned that estuaries were detritus ecosystems dependent on leaf fall grasses and mangroves as essential nutrient sources, while also relying on the "nutrient trap" functioning of salt marshes to prevent open estuarine waters from becoming grossly polluted. Confronted with this new knowledge, no one could regard salt marshes as wasteland any longer, and mosquito control had to reevaluate its operations on the tidelands.

Once the basic biology of salt-marsh mosquitoes was made known,[6] immobilizing the salt marshes began. Extensive salt-marsh ditching began in New Jersey in 1912, and by the late 1930s thousands of miles of hand-dug ditches gridded nearly all the marshes north of Chesapeake Bay and many in Florida and California. Conflicts with wildlife interests developed, largely because the ditching was done indiscriminately.[7] After the World War II interlude, conflicts flared again when widespread use of DDT as a larvicide was added

to the concerns of the conservationists. Although collaborative research had begun in the late 1930s, the culmination of peace efforts had to wait until 1959, when a symposium of leaders held in Washington led to the establishment of the National Mosquito Control–Fish and Wildlife Management Coordination Committee.[8] Counterpart committees formed at regional and state levels have helped to maintain liaison ever since.

In the meantime research and experimentation on managing salt marshes for several purposes had expanded greatly, especially in New Jersey, Delaware, and Maryland. Although DDT was eminently effective as a larvicide, its lethality to many important nontarget organisms in the estuarine ecosystem aroused conservationists almost from its first use. Fortunately for the environment, mosquitoes soon developed a marked resistance to DDT and its related compounds, so that by the mid-1950s larviciding salt-marsh mosquitoes had greatly abated. This gave increased impetus to control by habitat manipulation: canaling, impounding, and semi-impounding. By this time the awakening concern for the tideland habitat was able to impose needed constraints on such work, however, and the new day of multipurpose salt-marsh management was dawning.

Hydraulic filling is the ultimate salt-marsh mosquito control, but it exterminates the habitat. Only in Florida was it practiced on any scale. From 1953 to 1968 three mosquito control districts owned dredges and filled, in all, about 3000 acres. The practice was halted because it was too expensive and was subject to a variety of public criticism. It was environmentally destructive beyond the mere filling of marshes, as it entailed all the well-known undesirable effects of estuarine dredging.

Ditching the salt marsh has often been done in a manner harmful to its resident biota,[7] but this is now known to be remediable. The aim instead should be open marsh water management,[9] in which channels are dug only where needed to connect mosquito-breeding depressions to tidewater or to ponds, while permanent ponds and pools are saved and isolated from the channel (see Figure 1). This method is expensive, requiring a great deal of preliminary inspection and engineering

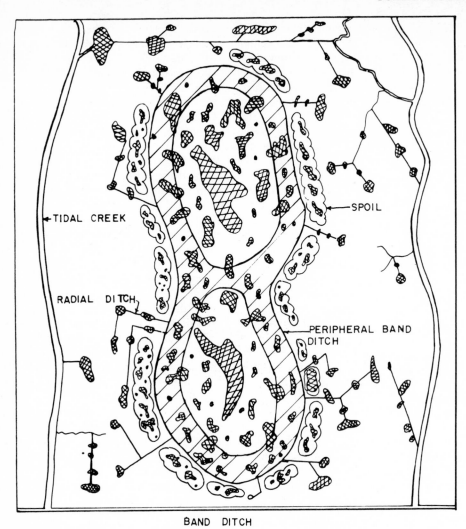

←TIDAL CREEK

SPOIL

RADIAL DITCH

PERIPHERAL BAND
DITCH

BAND DITCH

Figure 7.22.1   Open marsh water management plan to eliminate mosquito breeding in many depressions (cross-hatched) by ponding (hatched) and ditching. (SOURCE: Reference 9.)

work. It is a far cry from the simple grid system of ditching both high and low marsh so commonly practiced in the past. It has already been shown that open marsh water management effectively controls mosquito breeding without harming the vegetation, while increasing the populations of many important marsh organisms.[10, 11] It has the great advantage of maximizing the effectiveness of mosquito-eating minnows (*Fundulus, Cyprinodon, Gambusia*, etc.) and facilitating the transport of all life forms and nutrients between marsh and estuary. This management

method is feasible now throughout the grass salt marshes of America, but its technology has yet to be adapted to the scrub and mangrove tidelands of Florida.[12] Dragline channeling of salt marshes is a well-developed procedure that need not ever, of itself, harm estuaries.

Impounding and flooding salt marshes has been practiced for waterfowl, muskrat, and other wildlife management purposes in many states, but its benefits to mosquito control are only incidental, however real. Impounding for the sole purpose of preventing salt-marsh mosquito breeding has been practiced mostly in Florida, where it has incidentally enhanced bird usage of the marsh.[13] Since the mosquitoes breed mostly between June and October, it should be possible, with adequate water control structures, to impound and flood the marsh only during those months and to let tidewater circulate freely during the rest of the year.[14] The possibilities of the technique to achieve mosquito suppression while allowing the tidelands to function as necessary elements of the estuarine ecosystem are thought to be great, though awaiting further investigation.[12] The impoundment of Gumbo Island

in the Banana River, Florida, was designed for seasonal management to eliminate mosquito breeding, which occurred heavily throughout the 102-acre island (see Figure 2). After 3 years of operation and no mosquito production, there has been no kill whatever of even such vulnerable plants as black mangrove, saltwort, and salt grass, which dominate the habitat. From experience in other states as well as in Florida it appears that salt-marsh mosquito control by impoundment should be limited to tidelands with insufficient tide interval to properly energize a channel system.

Of the 7 million acres of salt marsh in the

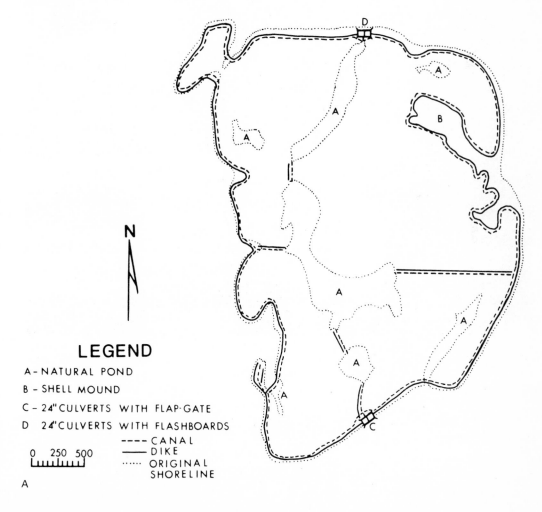

LEGEND

A - NATURAL POND

B - SHELL MOUND

C - 24" CULVERTS WITH FLAP-GATE

D   24" CULVERTS WITH FLASHBOARDS

```
                    ---- CANAL
0   250  500        ——— DIKE
Luuuluuul           ····· ORIGINAL
A                         SHORELINE
```

Figure 7.22.2   Seasonal impoundment on Gumbo Island, Florida: (A) Preliminary plan. (SOURCE: Reference 12.) (B) Completed impounding. Water management devices: (a) spillway, low, grassed-over section

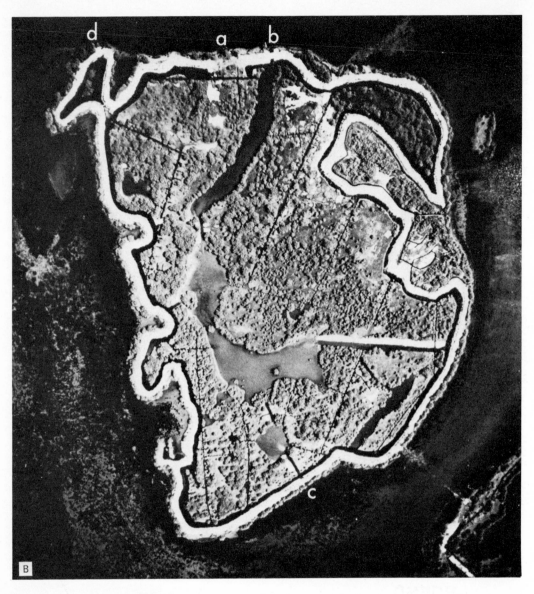

of dike; (*b*) culverts with flash boards; (*c*) culverts with flap-gate; (*d*) electric pump, served by underwater cable. (Photo courtesy of National Aeronautics and Space Administration.)

United States, between 80 and 90 percent have never received insecticides for the control of mosquitoes. During the heyday of DDT use, only the Middle Atlantic states, Florida, and California were organized for salt-marsh mosquito control. Today, when control has extended to Texas, Louisiana, Georgia, and the Carolinas, larviciding has been curtailed everywhere, especially on the salt marsh. All the larvicides of choice are now infinitely less toxic to estuarine life and less persistent in the environment. The most popular are oil and surfactant combinations and Abate, a short-lived organic phosphate insecticide that is the least toxic to estuarine fish and invertebrates of all such preparations that have been synthesized. Consequently, the threat to estuarine biota from chemical mosquito control should be minimal at present.

In summary, the control of salt-marsh mosquitoes need not now or hereafter be damaging to the estuarine ecosystem. Although environmental malpractice may still occur and many errors of the past await correction, the means are available to control these mosquitoes with impunity to the environment if only the necessary sophistication and funds are recruited for the purpose. This is particularly reassuring because salt-marsh mosquities, which reach extraordinary numbers when allowed to breed, are the least likely of all species to be controlled any time soon by the most environmentally acceptable methods of the future, such as genetic control.

REFERENCES

1. V. J. Chapman. 1960. *Salt Marshes and Salt Deserts of the World.* Interscience Publishers, New York.

2. N. Taylor. 1938. A *Preliminary Report on the Salt Marsh Vegetation of Long Island, New York.* New York State Museum, Bulletin No. 316, pp. 21–84.

3. H. Kruz and K. Wagner. 1957. *Tidal Marshes of the Gulf and Atlantic Coasts of Northern Florida and Charleston, S. Carolina.* Florida State University Studies, No. 24, Tallahassee, Florida.

4. H. P. Hinde. 1954. "The vertical distribution of salt marsh phanerograms in relation to tide levels." *Ecological Monographs,* Vol. 24, pp. 209–225.

5. J. G. Gosselink, E. P. Odum, and R. M. Pope. 1974. *The Value of the Tidal Marsh.* Center for Wetland Resources, Sea Grant Publication No. LSU-SG-74-03, Louisiana State University, Baton Rouge, Louisiana.

6. J. B. Smith. 1904. *Report of the New Jersey State Agricultural Experiment Station upon the Mosquitoes Occurring within the State, their Habits and Life History, Etc.* Macbrellish and Quigley, Trenton, New Jersey.

7. W. S. Bourn and C. Cottam. 1950. *Some Biological Effects of Ditching Tide Water Marshes.* Fish and Wildlife Service. Research Report No. 19, U.S. Department of the Interior, Washington, D.C.

8. P. F. Springer and R. L. Vannote. 1961. "Activities of the National Mosquito Control–Fish and Wildlife Management Coordination Committee" *Mosquito News,* Vol. 21, pp. 158–160.

9. F. Ferrigno and D. M. Jobbins. 1968. "Open marsh water management." In *Proceedings of the 55th Annual Meeting, New Jersey Mosquito Extermination Association,* pp. 104–115.

10. A. Bodola. 1970. "An evaluation of the effectiveness of natural pools, blind sumps and champagne pools in reducing mosquito production on a salt marsh." In *Proceedings of the 57th Annual Meeting, New Jersey Mosquito Extermination Association,* pp. 45–56.

11. F. Ferrigno. 1970. "Preliminary effects of open marsh water management on the vegetation and organisms of the salt marsh." In *Proceedings of the 57th Annual Meeting, New Jersey Mosquito Extermination Association,* pp. 79–94.

12. M. W. Provost. 1973. "Salt marsh management in Florida." In *Proceedings of the Tall Timbers Conference on Ecological Animal Control by Habitat Management,* pp. 5–17.

13. M. W. Provost, 1969. "Ecological control of salt marsh mosquitoes with side benefits to birds." In *Proceedings of the Tall Timbers Conference on Ecological Animal Control by Habitat Management,* pp. 193–206.

14. M. W. Provost. 1968. "Managing impounded salt marsh for mosquito control and estuarine resource conservation." In *Marsh and Estuary Symposium,* Louisiana State University, Baton Rouge, Louisiana, July 19–20, 1967.

23. NOISE AND DISTURBANCE

Ian C. T. Nisbet
Massachusetts Audobon Society
Lincoln, Massachusetts

Noise affects animals in two ways: by masking sound signals used for communication, and by conveying signals of danger. The seashore is a naturally noisy environment, and many coastal animals have loud or shrill voices well adapted for communication through background noise of wind and surf. These animals are usually little affected by an added background of continuous man-made noise, for example, from boat motors or road traffic. However, loud or unpredictable sounds, such as gunshots, explosions, or noises emanating from rapidly approaching boats and aircraft, are often very disturbing. Sonic booms and helicopter motors seem to be particularly alarming, especially to birds.

Noise in the coastal zone also has serious direct impacts on human beings who live or seek recreation there. Continuous noise or intermittent loud noise imposes a physiological stress that may result in adverse health consequences after long exposure. Although many individuals can tolerate noisy environments and some deliberately choose crowded resort areas, many others seek solitude and quiet when they visit the coast for recreation; these persons are adversely affected by noise from vehicles, boats, and aircraft. Since noisy human activities preempt quiet ones, there is a good case for zoning the coastline to maintain certain quiet areas for those who need them. This would require control over the use of motor vehicles, hunting, and other noisy activities. In some states vehicle access to the shoreline is locally restricted; however, there are very few fully protected wilderness areas along the coasts of the United States, and even these may be disturbed by motor boats and aircraft.

Among the wild animals most disturbed by noise are colonially nesting seabirds. Gunshots, explosions, or low-flying aircraft make them fly up in panic, sometimes tipping eggs or young out of nests or exposing them to predation by other birds. Sonic booms have similar effects: in one reported case a series of low-level supersonic flights is believed to have caused complete breeding failure in a large tern colony. Although birds and mammals may thus be affected severely by irregular human activity, they have remarkable abilities to adapt to *predictable* disturbance. Birds readily habituate themselves to vehicular traffic; they can often be approached closely in boats or automobiles, and sometimes nest unconcernedly beside highways or railroads. They can also adapt to predictable noises, and locally nest freely in front of foghorns or close to airport runways.

Colonies of seabirds—and of mammals such as seals and sea lions—are disturbed by human intrusion, whether casual or taking the form of deliberate molestation. Birds such as least terns, black skimmers, and plovers, which nest on sandy beaches, are especially vulnerable because of the intense human activity there. However, even birds and mammals nesting on remote islands can be seriously affected by occasional visits at critical times, such as the periods of birth or hatching. If birds are kept off their nests for even an hour in very cold weather or under a hot sun, their eggs or young may die. Consequently, one picnicking party in a seabird colony on a hot afternoon can have drastic effects on breeding success.

Many birds and mammals can also adapt to human visits to their colonies on foot, provided that they are never molested. If visitors appear at regular times and follow prescribed routes around or through the colonies, many birds and mammals learn within a few seasons that the visitors present no danger, and they will allow very close approach. Under careful management such colonies can be important educational resources or even tourist attractions. Outstanding examples are the colonies of terns on the Farne Islands in England, of gulls at Jones Beach, Long Island, and of elephant seals at Ano Nuevo State Park, California. However, before a colony can be managed in such a way, it requires careful study. Colonies on remote islands are subject to infrequent visits, so that the animals have little chance to adapt. Moreover, some species may prove to be intolerant of disturbance and can be protected only by prohibiting access. Other species will require careful management, including posting and fencing of colonies, marking of access paths, control of visitors' behavior, and restriction on access at critical periods in the breeding cycle. In most cases a full-time warden is required if a colony is to be protected completely against irresponsible individuals.

Although birds and mammals are generally most vulnerable when breeding, they are also subject to disturbance at other times of year. Many shorebirds and herons, for example, use estuaries and marshes for feeding and rest on islands, beaches, or salt marshes at high tide. They may be adversely affected or even driven away altogether if continually disturbed. Therefore provision of local sanctuaries free from disturbance is desirable in areas of intense human activity.

Little is known about the effects of boat traffic and underwater noise on marine animals. Propellers of large ships generate much underwater noise at low frequencies, which may interfere with communication by whales. Smaller boat motors and propellers are also very noisy and may well affect animals, such as porpoises, certain fish, and shrimps, which use sound for communication. Every fisherman knows that an approaching motor boat may scare fish away.

As human activity in the coastal zone increases, the number of quiet, undisturbed places available for peaceful recreation and for colonially breeding animals is dwindling. Therefore greater control over noise and human activity is urgently needed. The activities of the armed forces, including the Coast Guard, are a major source of noise in the coastal zone and should be carefully reviewed and curtailed.

At the level of regional planning, major noise-generating facilities such as airports, highways, and railroads should be sited in such a way as to minimize their impacts on residential and recreational areas. Sonic booms, if permitted at all, should be strictly limited to corridors where they will have no adverse impact on human beings or animals. More coastal wilderness areas are badly needed.

At the state level noise regulations are needed not only for off-the-road vehicles, but also for boat motors, which are characteristically very noisy. At the local level zoning and control of motorized vehicles should be used to preserve peaceful areas. Local control should be considered over the use of motor boats, light aircraft, and helicopters, whose pervasive effect is very disturbing.

24. NUTRIENTS IN ESTUARIES

Lawrence R. Pomeroy
Department of Zoology
University of Georgia
Athens, Georgia

Nutrients are substances essential to the growth of aquatic plants, microscopic floating and bottom-dwelling algae, and macroscopic sea-

weeds and grasses. Nutrients include both the essential elements, such as nitrogen, phosphorus, iron, and a considerable number of others, and organic compounds, such as vitamins, which may be required by some species. These nutrient substances occur naturally in all waters, and plants will not grow without them. In some estuarine and coastal waters one or more nutrients are present in limiting concentrations, and in such situations the addition of more of the limiting substance will lead to changes in the amount or the mix of species in the living communities. In other estuaries all essential nutrients are present in relative abundance, and the living communities are limited primarily by the amount of sunlight or by the amount of space in which to grow.[1-3] In predicting the results of man's alterations to estuaries it is important to distinguish between these two possible states, as well as intermediate ones.

As a first approximation in distinguishing between nutrient-rich and nutrient-limited estuaries a useful key is water turbidity. Turbid waters are usually nutrient rich, whereas clear waters are likely to be low in nutrients. Water turbidity may be the direct result of dense populations of microscopic phytoplankton, but more often it is caused primarily by suspended clays and organic particles that have signicant amounts of phosphate, ammonia, and other nutrients absorbed on their surfaces.[4]

In deep embayments, varying from Chesapeake Bay to Olso Fjord, it is possible to have a two-layered system.[5] The lower water layer is sometimes rich in nutrients, originating partly from organic pollution. Since the lower layer is salty and more dense, it mixes relatively slowly with the upper layer, which is more brackish. The effect of the large reservoir of nutrients in the lower layer may be relatively minor so long as the upper layer is thick and stable enough to minimize mixing and prevent the supply of excess nutrients to algae near the surface. Seasonal mixing, as density of the upper layer changes with temperature, may result in temporary eutrophication and algal blooms.

Human activities alter the nutrient contents of estuaries and some coastal waters. Municipal sewage, even after secondary treatment, contains large amounts of phosphate, ammonia, nitrate, vitamin B_{12}, and other growth-promoting substances.[6] Other sources of sewage, such as ships, are also significant when their density is high. Suspended soils eroded from construction sites bring substantial quantities of nutrients with them into estuaries. Their potential impact as causes of eutrophication is often as great as the damage done by covering and smothering bottom communities. Special industrial processes, such as phosphate mining or processing near coastal plain rivers or estuaries, can introduce large amounts of nutrients into estuarine water.[7-9]

Shallow, turbid estuaries with bottom sediments made up of clays, fine sand, and organic material are naturally rich in nutrients and naturally eutrophic systems. These biologically productive systems support important finfish and shellfish populations and are important as nursery grounds for juvenile fish, partly because they produce abundant food for growing organisms. The high productivity is dependent on natural reservoirs of nutrients in the sediments of the bottom, including the sediments of intertidal salt marshes or mangrove swamps. These natural reservoirs of nutrients are in equilibrium with the estuarine water, but they contain much higher concentrations of nutrients than the water does because of the sorptive properties and humic organic materials of clays and because microbial processes in the sediments convert deposited organic matter into available inorganic nutrients.[4]

Additions of nutrients to shallow, turbid estuaries already rich in nutrients may have relatively little effect, but this cannot be taken for granted. It has been shown that additions of nitrate or ammonia to coastal waters, estuaries, and salt marshes stimulates the growth of plants signicantly.[2,10,11] Moreover, a relatively small increase in productivity may have a profound effect on the living communities of estuaries that are already naturally eutrophic. High natural productivity means high rates of respiration in the water. In summer the oxygen concentration in tidal creeks in salt marshes along the east coast of the United States naturally drops to very low values at night.[12,13] If the oxygen concentration were

driven lower or kept low for longer periods as a result of either organic pollution or enhanced eutrophication, entire populations of fish and shellfish could be killed. This type of fish kill is a common phenomenon in polluted rivers, and there are indications that it has occurred in some estuaries.

Estuaries frequently have been used as dilution sinks for treated and untreated sewage and industrial wastes.[5,14-17] There is much current interest in the capacity of estuaries and their associated marshes to assimilate wastes. Research now in progress should help us to define the limits of acceptable estuarine pollution, but it is apparent that such limits already have been exceeded in a number of urban areas. Sometimes the specific effects of excess nutrients may be obscured by other kinds of pollution. For example, in such grossly polluted waters as Galveston Bay and New York Harbor, toxic pollutants probably have diminished biological activity and reduced the complexity of the communities that survive there. Such enriched but toxic systems represent a special problem of increasing frequency.

Estuaries and embayments with clear water, which are naturally deficient in nutrients, are radically changed by even small additions of nutrients. A now classic case of eutrophication of a clear water embayment is Kaneohe Bay, Hawaii. Kaneohe Bay originally contained extensive coral reefs and is a tourist attraction. It has been receiving treated sewage and substantial amounts of silting from construction on the hillsides overlooking the bay. Coral populations within part of the bay have been buried in silt or covered over by rapidly growing algae and worm populations. Although corals still survive in the outer bay, they are being progressively eliminted.[18] Comparable problems, primarily associated with industrial wastes,[19] have been reported in New Caledonia.

Coastal and ocean waters are less vulnerable to damage by wastes because of their larger scale and volume. However, local areas of the continental shelf have been polluted significantly by the continuing dumping of municipal and industrial wastes in a limited area.[20-24] Some continental shelf waters are flushed rather slowly, although we are likely to think of them as simply a part of the ocean. Eutrophication around major sewer outfalls that extend into shelf waters is well documented. Its extent and its impact depend on both the volume of nutrients introduced and the rate of mixing and water movement away from the outfall.

A probable but poorly understood example of eutrophication in coastal waters, on a relatively large scale, is the so-called red tide on the west coast of Florida. Although it is probable that the red tide is a phenomenon of the eutrophication type, we know that it is not a simple case of excess inputs of nitrogen or phosphorus. Red tides were rare before 1942, and their appearance as a regular phenomenon coincided with a rapid increase in population on the Florida west coast. Red tides in Florida are characterized by massive populations of a specific organism, *Gymnodinium breve*, which produces toxins and causes extensive fish kills. A dinoflagellate, *G. breve* has complex nutrient requirements, including vitamin B_{12}.[25]

Another troublesome dinoflagellate is *Gonyaulax*. It is not always toxic to fishes or to shellfish that ingest it, but shellfish that have fed on *Gonyaulax* are highly toxic to man. *Gonyaulax* occurs naturally along the west coast of the United States, including Alaska, and of Canada in amounts that usually make shellfish dangerous to eat at certain times of year. *Gonyaulax* also occurs on the east coast of the United States, but until 1973 it did not appear in sufficient numbers to make shellfish poisoning a serious problem. We cannot be certain that this recent increase in *Gonyaulax* in New England waters and the resulting bans on eating shellfish are the result of man-made eutrophication but if poisonous shellfish appear in subsequent years, the possibility of a man-induced cause must be considered.

If we compare estuaries that have been drastically modified by human activities with those on which man has had little impact, it is evident that a high intensity of human use makes estuaries less pleasing and reduces the diversity of resources obtainable from them.[26] There are conflicts between potential uses of estuaries, and nutrients are a major source of conflict. Estuaries are often used as economically desirable sinks for both urban and industrial wastes. All estuaries have limited capacities to assimilate wastes, and some have very little capacity in this regard. One of the end results of waste assimilation is eutrophication with the set of problems it entails.[27-29] Eroded earth from agricultural, industrial, or highway earth-moving operations can make its way into estuaries from the coastal plain and even the piedmont, as well as from the immediate shores of the estuary. Again, estuaries have different capacities to assimilate an input of sediments, and in those with clear water small inputs may be a significant cause of eutrophication.

Because of the range of sensitivity to nutrient addition of different estuaries and coastal waters, each case requires individual assessment, but we have had enough experience with a range of coastal waters to warrant some generalizations. The shallow, highly turbid estuaries of the Middle and South Atlantic coasts of the United States are probably the most tolerant of additions of dissolved nutrients and sediments that carry nutrients. When there are extensive salt marshes in a natural state, they will add substantially to the capacity of the estuary to assimilate nutrients without deleterious changes.[4,10,11,30] However, it is clear that in the New York Bight and in some other areas the limits of tolerance have been exceeded.

The clear water estuaries of subtropical Florida and of the Pacific Northwest are more vulnerable to eutrophication than are turbid estuaries. Most vulnerable of all are the tropical, coral reef systems of Hawaii and the Florida Keys.[14,31]

Damage from excessive nutrients can be prevented or sometimes reduced by determining the optimum nutrient concentrations for a given body of water, and identifying and reducing sources of nutrients that will introduce an excess. These include both raw and treated sewage, a variety of organic and inorganic industrial wastes, and sediments from erosion of the land. Although some estuaries naturally contain an abundance of nutrients and are highly productive, it does not follow that enrichment by man of estuaries and coastal waters that are naturally impoverished of nutrients will result in high productivity of fisheries and aesthetically pleasing waters. Instead, enrichment from pollution usually results in the growth of noxious organisms and the reduction of dissolved oxygen concentration, altering the system in ways that are generally undesirable from man's viewpoint. Nor can any single nutrient be singled out as the key pollution problem in estuarine and coastal waters. Since the ratio of nitrogen to phosphorus usually is low in coastal waters,[2] there may be a more dramatic response to additions of available nitrogen. However, it is generally advisable to preserve the natural concentrations and the existing nitrogen-to-phosphorus ratio whenever possible.[27] Technological developments that would permit the use of nutrients from sewage to produce commercially valuable fish and shellfish are being attempted,[32] but they are not yet ready for application.

Because estuaries vary so widely in their circulation patterns and flushing rates, sweeping regulations covering an entire state or the nation ought to be worded in terms of prohibiting any actions that will result in undesirable effects, such as eutrophication or fish kills. Since actual causes of eutrophication will vary, a regulation that limits the input of any specific nutrient will be of limited value and indeed may work hardship without achieving a worthwhile result. It should be kept in mind that estuarine and coastal zone problems often are watershed runoff problems. For this reason regulations that control activities in the water or around the immediate shoreline may not always be sufficient. Nutrients and other materials may be carried into the coastal zone from a considerable distance away in a large watershed.

REFERENCES

1. R. B. Williams. 1973. "Nutrient levels and phytoplankton productivity in the estuary." In R. H. Chabreck, Ed., *Coastal Marsh and Estuary Management*. Division of Continuing Education, Louisiana State University, Baton Rouge, Louisiana, pp. 59–89.

2. J. H. Ryther and W. M. Dunstan. 1971. "Nitrogen, phosphorus and euthrophication in in the coastal marine environment." *Science*, Vol. 171, pp. 1008–1013.

3. L. R. Pomeroy. 1970. "The strategy of mineral cycling." *Annual Review of Ecology and Systematics*, Vol. 1, pp. 171–180.

4. L. R. Pomeroy, L. R. Shenton, R. D. H. Jones, and R. J. Reimold. 1972. "Nutrients and eutrophication." In G. E. Likens, Ed., *Nutrient Flux in Estuaries*. American Society for Limnology and Oceanography, Special Publication No. 1, pp. 274–291.

5. H. Stommel and H. G. Farmer. 1952. *On the nature of Estuarine Circulation, I–III.*" Woods Hole Oceanographic Institute, Technical Report, Refs. 52–51, 52–53, and 52–88.

6. H. P. Jeffries. 1962. "Environmental characteristics of Raritan Bay, a polluted estuary." *Limnology and Oceanography*, Vol. 7, pp. 21–31.

7. J. E. Hobbie. 1970. *Phosphorus Concentrations in the Pamlico River Estuary of North Carolina*. Water Resources Research Institute, Report No. 33, University of North Carolina, Raleigh, North Carolina, 44 pp.

8. B. J. Copeland and J. E. Hobbie. 1972. *Phosphorus and Eutrophication in the Pamlico River Estuary, N.C., 1966–1969—a Summary*. Water Resources Research Institute, Report No. 65, University of North Carolina, Raleigh, North Carolina.

9. J. E. Hobbie, B. J. Copeland, and W. G. Harrison. 1972. *Nutrients in the Pamlico River Estuary, N.C., 1969–1971*. Water Resources Research Institute, Report No. 76, Universty of North Carolina, Raleigh, North Carolina.

10. I. Valiela and J. M. Teal. 1973. "Nutrient limitation in salt marsh vegetation." In R. J. Reimold and W. H. Queen, Eds., *Ecology of Halophytes*. Academic Press, New York.

11. I. Valiela, J. M. Teal, and C. D. Van Raalte. 1972. "Nutrient and sewage sludge enrichment experiments in a salt marsh ecosystem." *INTECOL Symposium on Physiological Ecology of Plants and Animals in Extreme Environments*, Dubrovnik.

12. D. Frankenberg and S. Shimmel. 1975. "Estimates of grass primary production in the Duplin River, Georgia, based on diurnal oxygen changes." Bulletin of the Georgia Academy of Science, Vol. 33, pp. 195–200.

13. D. Frankenberg and C. W. Westerfield. 1968. "Oxygen demand and oxygen depletion capacity of sediments from Wassaw Sound, Georgia." *Bulletin of the Georgia Academy of Science*, Vol. 26, pp. 160–172.

14. Paul De Falco, Jr. 1967. "The Estuary, septic tank of the megalopolis." In G. H. Lauff, Edr., *Estuaries*. American Association for the Ad-

vancement of Science, Publication No. 83, Washington, D.C., pp. 701–703.

15. J. N. Smith. 1972. *The Decline of Galveston Bay*. The Conversation Foundation, Washington, D.C.

16. B. H. Ketchum. 1950. "Hydographic factors involved in the dispersion of pollutants introduced into tidal waters." *Journal of the Boston Society of Civil Engineers*, Vol. 37, pp. 296–314.

17. B. H. Ketchum. 1951. "The flushing of tidal estuaries." *Sewage and Industrial Wastes*, pp. 198–208.

18. S. V. Smith, K. E. Chave, and D. T. O. Kam. 1973. *Atlas of Kaneohe Bay: A Reef Ecosystem under Stress*. University of Hawaii, Sea Grant Program, Publication No. TR-72-01.

19. M. Wijsman-Best. 1974. "Habitat modification of reef corals (Faviidae) and its consequences for taxonomy." In *Proceedings of the 2nd International Symposium on Coral Reefs*, Brisbane, Vol. 2. pp. 217–228.

20. E. A. Pearson, Ed., 1959. *Waste Disposal in the Marine Environment*. Pergamon Press, New York.

21. D. W. Hood. 1971. *Impingement of Man on the Oceans*. John Wiley and Sons, New York.

22. M. G. Gross, J. A. Black, R. J. Kalin, J. R. Schramel, and R N. Smith. 1971. *Survey of Marine Waste Deposits, New York: Metropolitan region*. Marine Science Research Center; Report No. 5, State University of New York, Stony Brook, New York, 72 pp.

23. R. C. Dugdale, J. C. Kelley, and Th. Becacos-Kontos. 1971. *The Effects of Effluent Discarge on the Concentration of Nutrients in the Saronikos Gulf*. Food and Agriculture Organization Conference on Marine Pollution, Rome. Fishing News (Books) Ltd., London, England.

24. R. C. Dugdale and T. Whitledge. 1970. Computer simulation of phytoplankton growth near a marine sewage outfall. *Revue Internationale d'oceanographie Medicale*, Vol. 17, pp. 43–52.

25. Karen A. Steidinger. 1973. "Phytoplankton ecology: A conceptual review based on eastern Gulf of Mexico research." Chemical Rubber Company, Critical Reviews in Microbiology, Vol. 3, No. 1, pp. 49–68.

26. H. T. Odum, B. J. Copeland, and E. A. McMahan. 1974. *Coastal Ecological Systems of the United States* (4 vols). The Conservation Foundation, Washington, D.C.

27. Federal Water Pollution Control Administration. 1968. *Water Quality Criteria*. Report of the National Technical Advisory Committee to the Secretary of the Interior. Washington, D.C., 234 pp.

28. J. P. Barlow, C. J. Lorenzen, and R. T. Myren. 1963. "Eutrophication of a tidal estuary." *Limnology and Oceanography*, Vol. 8, pp. 251–262.

29. J. H. Ryther. 1954. "The ecology of phytoplankton blooms in Moriches Bay and Great South Bay, Long Island, N.Y." *Biological Bulletin*, Vol. 106, pp. 198–209.

30. S. W. Nixon and C. A. Oviatt. 1973. "Ecology of a New England salt marsh." *Ecological Monographs*, Vol. 43, pp. 463–498.

31. E. J. Ferguson Wood and R. E. Johannes, Eds. *Tropical Marine Pollution*. Elsevier Scientific Publishing Company, Amsterdam.

32. E. J. Kuenzler and A. F. Chestnut. 1971. *Structure and Functioning of Estuarine Ecosystems Exposed to Treated Sewage Wastes*. Institute of Marine Science, University of North Carolina, Annual Report to National Oceanic and Atmospheric Administration, 1970–1971.

25. PLANKTON RESOURCES

H. Perry Jeffries
Graduate School of Oceanography
University of Rhode Island
Kingston, Rhode Island

Roughly translated, *plankton* means "wanderer." Planktonic organisms live precariously above the bottom, suspended in the water, and at the mercy of currents, unable to direct their motion in a level direction. They are so diverse in form and function that generalizations are more misleading than useful. Among the plankton the plants are called "phytoplankton," and the animals "zooplankton." The resource manager needs an understanding of these organisms somewhere between "plankton are the base of the food chain" and graduate course work. This article attempts to provide a useful outline of subgroups within the plankton, show how the seasons control production and indicate where such considerations are important in estuarine management.

In the ocean there are three major groups of organisms: plankton, benthos, and nekton. No one category is exclusive, and all are functionally related. Benthic animals live on the bottom, but they usually have planktonic larval stages. So do many fishes before the time when their larvae metamorphose and join the nekton (creatures capable of directed movement in a three-dimensional environment). Functionally the system is tied together in such ways as planktonic plants utilizing the dissolved wastes of fish and benthic animals, a process that, in shallow water at least, serves to lessen the huge effect of nutrient limitation.

All phytoplankton are algae, and except for *Sargassum* weed only the single-celled forms are represented. Compared with the seed-bearing plants of fresh waters and land, algae are structurally simple, but from this simplicity there arise diverse metabolic capabilities and a photosynthetic potential that yields far more organic matter than is broken down upon death and decay.

An ecologist usually divides the phytoplankton into diatoms and flagellates. A diatom's cell wall consists of two siliceous cylinders that fit together like a pill box. Several algal classes comprise the flagellates. Using one or more whips, they move over short distances in the water column.

In contrast to the phytoplankton's limited taxonomic range, the zooplankton have representatives from phyla. These small organisms —the chief converters of plant to animal tissue in the sea—are separated into (1) the *holoplankton*, animals spending their entire life cycle above the bottom; (2) the *meroplankton*, larval stages that develop into benthos or nekton; and (3) the *tychoplankton*, a numerically insignificant group of organisms occasionally swept off the bottom by currents. The term "neuston" refers to small organisms found at the surface.

More than half, and usually about three-quarters, of the total zooplankton consists of holoplanktonic copepods. These small crustaceans reach several millimeters in length after 12 developmental stages. Many species feed by filtering the phytoplankton with a remarkable set of appendages, whereas others feed on one another.[1] For only brief periods during summer is the dominance of copepods interrupted by larval molluscs, crabs, and shrimp of the meroplankton.

Compared with land, the oceanic environment is physically stable. Consequently marine organisms have simpler regulatory structures than their terrestrial and aquatic counterparts. It follows that when the oceans do change the biological consequences are severe.

Most planktonic organisms are small, and their life cycles are shorter than the period of environmental change. Accordingly entire communities rise and fall several times a year. As shown in Figure 1, the annual cycle starts in winter, when surface waters are rich with inorganic nutrients supplied in land runoff or mineralized in nature from the remains of past generations. The phytoplankton do not respond immediately, however; growth is delayed until day length and sunlight increase. Vernal warming also causes thermal stratification in the water column and algae are retained in the upper layers, whereas previously there was a greater tendency for them to sink into darkness.

With restraints on primary productivity removed, what follows is one of the earth's most dramatic natural phenomena: the winter–spring diatom bloom of temperate waters. Diatoms divide several times each day. Within a few weeks abundance increases 50-fold, from roughly 200 to 10,000 cells per milliliter. A fine net towed through the water comes up caked with algae, giving off a sweet aroma similar to that of fresh apples or new-mown hay.

Growth cannot be sustained for long at such a high rate. The first limitation to take effect is nutrient depletion. In Long Island Sound nitrate drops from over 15 micromoles per liter to below the limits of measurement, while phosphate, which was over 2 micromoles per liter before the bloom, decreases by at least one-half.[2] Furthermore light does not penetrate with the same intensity as it did before the bloom. Most diatoms range from only 10 to 100 microns in diameter, but the light scattering by these specks should be obvious when we realize that there are as many as 4500 cells in every drop of water.

Production does not collapse completely during spring because algae have flexible chemical activities. Even though diatoms have reduced the concentrations of nutrients available for algal growth, environmental conditions now favor flagellates. Perhaps flagel-

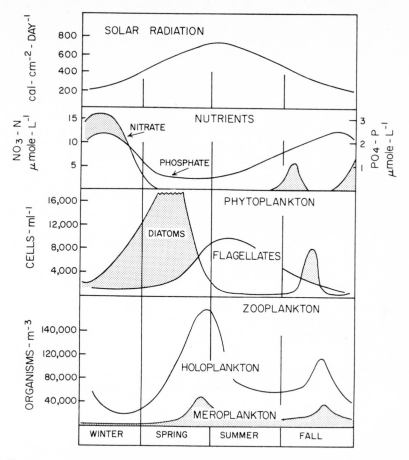

Figure 7.25.1 Responses of phytoplankton and zooplankton to seasonal changes in the physical–chemical environment of coastal waters. Simplified from various descriptions of patterns along the Rhode Island to New Jersey coast.

lates are better able than diatoms to utilize in warm water the organically bound nutrients released by animals and produced during early stages of mineralization by microorganisms. At least one flagellate species releases a substance into the water that inhibits diatoms. Finally flagellates have a greater surface area relative to cell volume, an adaptation for the absorption of nutrients in low concentration.

Grazing by copepods, each organism filtering 100·milliliters or more of seawater per day,[3] also limits the spring diatom bloom. Adult *Acartia tonsa*, the major summer species in temperate estuaries, achieves an abundance greater than 2000 per cubic meter;[4] therefore, if each adult ingests the phytoplankton from only 25 milliliters per day, this species

alone is able to consume up to 5 percent of the crop every day. Immature copepods also feed, and their total density in Raritan Bay New Jersey, has exceeded 200,000 per cubic meter.[5] Nor is grazing is limited to the holoplankton. On the bottom a single mollusc filters and removes the phytoplankton from up to 25 liters daily. Larval molluscs, crabs, and fish, which abound in the meroplankton following the diatom bloom, also require a daily ration of phytoplankton.

Zooplankton populations grow rapidly, but by late spring predation and diminishing food supplies take effect. Adult copepods, which previously subsisted on phytoplankton, sometimes consume their own young.[6] During summer, predatory jellies (ctenophores) and various jellyfish have been known to decimate an entire zooplankton community.

With grazing pressure reduced and some nutrient mineralization having occurred in late fall, diatoms bloom again. This increase is less intense and not as regular as the winter–spring bloom; but when it does occur, zooplankton respond shortly thereafter, although with less intensity than seen earlier in spring.

Thus far we have observed bursts of growth in spring and fall and the creation of an uneasy situation at each of two levels, wherein nutritional limitation on one side is countered by a tremendous reproductive potential on the other. The balance is constantly shifting within and between animal and plant components because of seasonal change and cyclical forces that develop among competing populations. The overall effect is instability, a chief characteristic of planktonic communities. But the instability is predictable, happening year after year in much the same manner. Other communities dependent on plankton for food have therefore been able to develop relatively stable populations over geological time. Spawning, growth, and migration among these larger and generally more advanced species in the benthos and nekton are timed with respect to the predictable vagaries of plankton production.

Because man adds nutrient-rich wastes to a nutrient-limited system, he disrupts the very base of control and balance within the ever-vulnerable plankton. Obviously the consequences are grave once the plankton's ability to process pollutants has been exceeded. The effect, when it comes back to act on our economy, may be magnified as each component of the ecosystem becomes involved.

The Raritan estuary serves as a good example of plankton dynamics. Two major estuaries meet the ocean at the apex of the New York Bight. The Hudson and East rivers discharge through the Narrows between Staten Island and Brooklyn; immediately to the south lies the funnel-shaped Raritan (Figure 2). Historically these estuaries have been a major access to the world's most sociologically and technologically diversified area. Massive efforts to understand and control pollution date back to the 1800s. One of the most important attempts—a trunk sewer serving portions of the Raritan Valley—began operation

in early 1958. After primary treatment the effluent is released in the head of Raritan Bay. Plans are now being made to expand collection and treatment, with the expectation that effluent will increase from 80 to 240 million gallons a day in a space of 35 years. Decisions involving huge expenditures are based on uncertain levels of understanding plankton production and its control. The principles and problems that one faces in an analysis of the situation are certainly not unique to the Raritan and may prove useful in application to other areas.

The first question one askes about the plankton of Raritan Bay is, "Why in an estuary so heavily polluted do we observe phenomena that are in accord with what we find in unpolluted estuaries?" Although the summer phytoplankton is dominated by an indicator of sewage pollution (*Nannochloris*, a minute green alga), diatoms bloom during winter–spring in the manner described above for all temperate coastal waters, albeit more intensely and for a longer period in the Raritan.[7] Moreover diatom species replace one another in familiar patters.[8]

Events occurring in the Raritan's zooplankton, even before trunk sewer operation, correspond with those of nearby estuaries. Two calanoid copepods dominate the holoplankton throughout most of the year: *Acartia tonsa* during summer–fall and *A. clausi* during winter–spring. Large, integrative processes, such as temperature–salinity relationships during the replacement of *A. clausi* by *A. tonsa* in late spring, take place in the Raritan in the same manner as in other estuaries from Narragansett Bay, Rhode Island, to the York River, Virginia.[4] The Raritan is also "normal" with respect to the distribution and abundance of the copepod genus *Eurytemora*.[5]

If abnormalities are to be found in the Raritan's plankton, they are in the meroplankton.[9] Clam larvae are less abundant in the Raritan than in other estuaries. Late appearance in late spring may be due to inhibitors produced by algae during the extremely intense and long-lasting diatom bloom. Barnacle nauplii, the immature stages of another group of benthic filter feeders, also appear rather late in the Raritan. Polychaete larvae are delayed, but once reproduction starts they

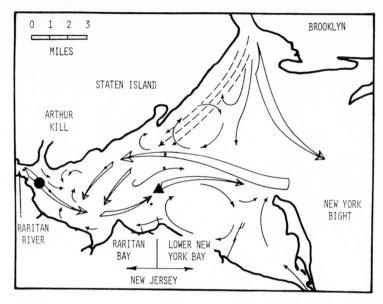

Figure 7.25.2 Net currents in the Raritan estuary, location of old outfall ●, location of a proposed, midbay outfall ▲. (SOURCE: Reference 11.)

become excessively abundant, perhaps because the adult worms are deposit feeders, and they find an abundance of food in the rich, organic sediments of the bay. Scarcity of crab larvae is another characteristic of the Raritan. The meroplankton presumably mirror processes affecting benthic communities, which appear more vulnerable to factors arising from pollution than do the holoplankton.

The Raritan's ecological system must have, therefore, a capacity for processing huge amounts of waste, which, expressed as biochemical oxygen demand (BOD), represents a daily input exceeding 0.25 million pounds.[10] Fundamental to the process is the sluggish but efficient current system, in a simple, funnel-shaped basin. As shown in Figure 2, seawater entering the bay from the New York Bight is deflected to the right or Staten Island shore.[11] Well into the bay, the floor current thrusts southward, across the Raritan River discharge from the previous ebb tide, thereby exerting a "milking action" that hastens ebb flow along the bay's southern shore. In effect, waste materials from the head of the bay become entrained in a fast current that increases in volume as it goes toward the ocean. During wet seasons river discharge flows over the more

saline bottom water as the system adjusts to high runoff. Wastes are flushed seaward even faster than would be expected. Flows are weakest during dry summers; but because replenishment and renewal occur year round, the waters do not become a rich organic soup.

The broken lines and eddies in Figure 2 south of the Staten Island–Brooklyn Narrows indicate flow from the Hudson that is partially blocked by shoals just inside the mouth of the estuary. Perhaps on a phase of each tide—and certainly during spring runoff—waters emanating from New York Harbor cross the shoals. Pollutants are now in position to be forced throughout the Raritan on successive flood tides. Here is an example of one estuary fertilizing another with nutrient-rich pollutants.

After the completion of initial cleanup efforts in the Raritan valley, the zooplankton changed significantly. In comparison with the summer before trunk sewer operation, the holoplankton increased more than twofold; larvae of the soft clam, *Mya arenaria*, appeared in numbers up to 79,300 per cubic meter, whereas the year before there had been none; larvae of the hard clam, *Mercenaria mercenaria*, increased 50-fold in the mouth of the

Raritan River; and eggs of the menhaden, *Brevoortia tyrannus*, increased at least twofold. In the vicinity of the outfall of the treatment system, near the head of the bay, 1000 menhaden eggs per cubic meter occurred; before operation of the primary treatment system no more than 164 per cubic meter were found, and these appearances were limited to the downbay portion.

Much of the increase that accompanied cleanup, both in the holoplankton and in the meroplankton, may be attributed to natural, annual variation. Certain aspects, however, such as the 50-fold increase in *Mercenaria* larvae in the mouth of the Raritan River, indicate an improved environment. Another sign was the irregular behavior of both the plant and animal plankton during the preceding summer, when chlorophyll *a* disappeared for 1 week, dropping from a characteristically high Raritan Bay level of 40 micrograms per liter. *Acartia tonsa* disappeared at the same time, first in the head of the bay, then a week later in the midbay area. In the northern sec-

Table 7.25.1   Method of calculating the volume of mixed water moving seaward daily in the midbay area that transports 1 day's contribution of river water.
Approximate dilution of effluent delivered at 908.4 × 10⁶ liters per day (240 million gallons per day) by seaward-moving water, assuming that complete mixing and seaward transport ≫ effluent flow.

Variable	Unit	Summer	Winter
S	o/oo	26.5	18.5
σ	o/oo	29.0	26.0
F		0.0862	0.2885
R	10^6 1/day	733.5	4,890.2
V	10^6 1/day	8,509.3	16,950.4
E	10^6 1/day	908.4	908.4
V_s	10^6 1/day	9,417.7	17,858.8
D		0.096	0.051

a.   Determine fraction fresh water, F.

$$F = (1 - S/\sigma)$$

S = salinity at mid-bay

σ = salinity of source seawater

b.   Determine volume moving seaward daily, V

$$V = \frac{R}{F}$$

R = river flow

c.   Determine total seaward flow, V_s

$$V_s = V + E$$

E = effluent flow

d. $D = \dfrac{E}{V_s}$

D = dilution

Table 7.25.2 Concentrations of nutrients (in micromoles per liter) in sewage effluents after various levels of treatment

Treatment	PO_4-P	NH_3-N	$(NO_3+NO_2)-N$
Primary[a]	587	1,785	14
Secondary[b]	100	1,532	11
Advanced[a]			
nitrification, PO_4 removal	65	143	1,142
denitrification, PO_4 removal	65	143	143

[a]. J. Coleman, personal communication.[13]

[b]. S. Nixon, personal communication.[14]

tor the collapse of the populations was less severe, possibly because Staten Island waters were isolated from toxic substances released upbay and carried seaward by the net ebb drift down the New Jersey shore. The plankton recovered rapidly, but variations of such scope were not seen the following summer, when the treatment plant was operating.

From the plankton biologist's point of view, management and planning require difficult decisions, such as the following:

1. Where should a new outfall required to release additional loads and meet new regulations be located so that dispersal is maximized without causing an alteration of the salinity gradients that control landward penetration of coastal species?
2. To what extent should treatment be increased to regulate excess nutrients, trace metals, and substances suspected of inhibiting algal growth?
3. If fisheries are to be encouraged, what effect does nutrient enrichment have on the kinds of species that are available as food?

Several options for treatment and release may be proposed. From intuition alone, one soon gets the feeling that certain options should be eliminated or at least ranked on a conflict scale. Before making a final decision,

we may need experts to simulate flows, mixing, dispersal, uptake, and regeneration by computer modeling. At the beginning, however, useful calculations can be made by anyone, with data that are often readily available. All that is needed are (1) salinity and river flow, (2) nutrient and trace metal concentrations in sewage effluents, and (3) acceptable levels for nutrients and trace metals in marine waters. We assume that (1) a simple determination of the volume of mixed water moving seaward daily[12] at the outfall site is valid for present purposes, and (2) the effluent is mixed completely with water ebbing from the bay. The options considered are for a midbay outfall discharging 240 million gallons a day of either secondary or tertiary effluent.

From the seaward flows calculated in Table 1, we see that dilution of bay water (D) with sewage effluent during summer would be only half that occurring in winter. A management problem is identified immediately. During low river flow, gravitational forces tend to spread the less dense mixture formed in the head of the bar across the bay's surface. Consequently the amount of water ebbing along the southern shore—a convenient access for sewage dispersal—is decreased out of proportion to the decrease in river discharge. Several conditions have now been met for the development of potentially dangerous red tides. These huge

Table 7.25.3   Concentrations and standards for trace metals and nutrients in marine waters; composition of sewage effluent, Muncie, Indiana; and California effluent quality requirements, not to be exceeded more than 50 percent of the time.

Substance	A Sea water	B[b] Permissable level	C Deleterious effects	D Toxic effects	E Secondary effluent	F California requirement
Metals: µg/1						
Aluminum	1	1,500	--	--	--	--
Arsenic	2	50	10	2,000	--	10
Cadmium	0.1	100	0.2	10,000	--	20
Chromium	0.5	100	10	1,000	50	5
Copper	0.7	50	10	100	80	200
Iron	3	300	--	--	550	--
Lead	0.03	50	10	100	170	100
Manganese	0.3	100	20	320	80	--
Mercury	0.02	100	0.1	100	--	1
Nickel	(2)[a]	100	2	100	110	100
Selenium	0.1	10	5	--	--	--
Silver	0.01	0.5	1	--	--	20
Zinc	(3)[a]	100-200	20	10,000	240	300
Nutrients: µmole/1						
Ammonia	1-7	28.6				
Nitrate	5	--				
Phosphate	0.3-0.5	--				

[a]Analytical accuracy in doubt.   [b]Provisional.

Columns

A   Metals: P. G. Brewer via S. Pietrowicz, personal communication;[15] nutrients: Kester and Courant (1973); nitrate and phosphate, coastal waters; ammonia, Narragansett Bay.[16]

B   Environmental Protection Administration, October 1973 (provisional).[17]

C   Ketchum (1975).[18]

D   National Estuarine Pollution Study (1969).[19]

E   Craddock (1973).[20]

F   Finishing Highlights, June 1973, p. 35.[21]

algal blooms are usually produced during summer by flagellates that require organically bound nutrients. Occurrences are well known in the Raritan estuary.[8]

Multiplying the concentrations of nutrients and trace metals in sewage plant effluent (Tables 2 and 3) by the dilution factors de-termined above, we can make a rough calculation of the enrichment in the water moving seaward at midbay. Although the results shown in Table 4 are intended for preliminary comparison of outfall sites and treatments, they reveal major problems. Ammonia, ranked second with respect to conflict, in the ebbing

Table 7.25.4 Nutrient and trace metal enrichment in ebb water due to 908×10^6 liters per day of effluent from a secondary treatment plant released at midbay.

Values in parentheses pertain to advanced wastewater treatment—denitrification and phosphate removal. For each trace metal, the lesser value in columns E and F of Table 3 was used. Conflict intensity = (summer + winter/2)/water quality standard.

Substance	Summer	Winter	Conflict intensity value	Conflict rank
Nutrients, μmole/l				
Ammonia - N	147* (14)	78* (7)	3.9	2
Nitrate & nitrite-N	1 (14)	0.6(7)		
Phosphate-P	10(6)	5(3)		
Trace metals, μg/l				
Arsenic	1	0.5	0.08	9
Cadmium	2#	1#	7.50	1
Chromium	0.5	0.3	0.04	10
Copper	19	4	1.15	4
Iron	53	28	--	--
Lead	10	5	0.75	7
Manganese	8	4	0.30	8
Mercury	0.1	0.1	1.00	5
Nickel	10##	5##	##	--
Silver	2#	1	1.50	3
Zinc	23#	12	0.88	6

*exceeds permissible level (Table 3, column B)

#exceeds minimal level of deleterious effects (Table 3, column C)

##not applicable, concentration in seawater equals level of deleterious effect.

water might reach toxic amounts (28.6 micromoles per liter). Even if advanced wastewater (tertiary) treatment were used, ammonia concentrations would be greater than the half-saturation constant for maximum algal uptake, which probably ranges from 1.3 to 10 micromoles per liter in eutropic marine communities.[22]

No federal standard has been proposed for phosphate, but 3 micromoles per liter, the smallest value in Table 4, might support an algal bloom. Trace metal concentrations would be at less than permissible levels, although silver and zinc might have deleterious effects (Table 3, columns B and C). At a midbay outfall, trace metals would, however, rank well below nutrients on the conflict scale, and we conclude that the control of nutrients, ammonia in particular, is a problem of paramount concern.

Pollutants from other sources, tidal mixing, and dilution outside the release area are beyond the scope of this article. We should keep in mind, however, that downbay the amount of mixed water moving seaward daily increases. Indeed better calculations show that steady-state nutrient concentrations due to a tertiary treatment plant operating at peak efficiency during average river flow might be well below half-saturation values. The costs, however, would seem to be substantial.

Gaps in our understanding of natural processes create additional problems. For example, good circumstantial evidence indicates that the phytoplankton in the Raritan do not achieve full photosynthetic potential.[23] If the inhibitor is a pollutant, would it be removed during sewage treatment? If so, what would the consequences be? We know that about half the total carbon in secondary effluent is humic material.[24] These complex molecules chelate substances, affecting algal growth.[25] Thus humics could make trace metabolites in sewage available for uptake, or they could scavenge inhibitory substances, acting indirectly as powerful stimulants for undesirable algal blooms. Advanced secondary treatment may all but eliminate humics from sewage effluents.

Before a plankton biologist could help to solve the many problems of coastal waters, detailed information is needed on the following:

1. The causes, nature, toxic severity, and consequences of algal blooms and red tides.
2. The dilution, uptake, and recycling of nutrients in polluted areas.
3. The disruptions of energy flow to herbivores caused by toxic substance and by the kinds of algal species that respond to nutrient enrichment.

In management there is an adage "Dilution is the solution to pollution." We may be able to prolong the old idea for awhile, but the time has come when a new way must be found. A plankton biologist must conclude that the need for such a new way far exceeds present efforts to find it.

REFERENCES

1. J. E. G. Raymont. 1963. *Plankton and Productivity of the Oceans*. Pergamon Press, New York, 600 pp.
2. G. A. Riley. 1955. "Review of the oceanography of Long Island Sound." *Deep-Sea Research, Supplement*, Vol. 3, pp. 224–238.
3. C. B. Jørgensen. 1966. *Biology of Suspension Feeding*. Pergamon Press, New York, 357 pp.
4. H. P. Jeffries. 1962. "Succession of two *Acartia* species in estuaries." *Limnology and Oceanography*, Vol. 7, pp. 354–364.
5. H. P. Jeffries. 1962. "Salinity–space distribution of the estuarine copepod genus *Eurytemora*." *Intern. Rev. Ges. Hydrobiol.*, Vol. 47, International Revue der Gesamten Hydrobiologie. pp. 291–300.
6. T S. Petipa, E. V. Pavlova, and G. N. Moronov. 1970. "The food web structure, utilization and transport of energy by trophic levels in the planktonic communities." *In* J. H. Steele, Ed., *Marine Food Chains*. University of California Press, Berkeley, California.
7. B. C. Patten. 1962. "Species diversity in net phytoplankton of Raritan Bay." *Journal of Marine Research*, Vol. 20, pp. 57–75.
8. T. J. Smayda. 1973. "A survey of phytoplankton dynamics in the coastal waters from Cape Hatteras to Nantucket." In *Coastal and Offshore Environmental Inventory, Cape Hatteras to Nantucket Shoals*. University of Rhode Island, Marine Publication Series No. 2, Kingston, Rhode Island, pp. 3–1 to 3–100.
9. H. P. Jeffries. 1964. "Comparative studies on estuarine zooplankton." *Limnology and Oceanography*, Vol. 9, pp. 348–358.
10. H. T. Odum, B. J. Copeland, and E. A. McMahan, Eds. 1969. *Coastal Ecological Systems of the United States*, Vols. I–III.
11. H. P. Jeffries. 1962. "Environmental characteristics of Raritan Bay, a polluted estuary." *Limnology and Oceanography*, Vol. 7, pp. 21–31.
12. B. H. Ketchum, A. C. Redfield, and J. C. Ayers. 1951. "The oceanography of the New York Bight." *Papers in Physical Oceanography and Meterology*, Vol. 12, pp. 3–46.
13. J. Coleman. Personal communication.
14. S. Nixon. Personal communication.
15. P. G. Brewer via S. Pietrowicz. Personal communication.
16. D. R. Kester and R. A. Courant. 1973. "A summary of chemical oceanographic conditions: Cape Hatteras to Nantucket Shoals." In *Coastal and Offshore Environmental Inventory, Cape Hatteras to Nantucket Shoals*. University of Rhode Island, Marine Publication Series No. 2, Kingston, Rhode Island, pp. 2–1 to 2–36.
17. U.S. Environmental Protection Agency. 1973. *Proposed Criteria for Water Quality*, Vols. I

and II. Washington, D.C., 589 pp. (mimeographed).

18. B. H. Ketchum. 1974. "Biological implications of global marine pollution." In S. F. Singer, Ed., *The Changing Global Environment*. Reidl Publishing Company, Dordrecht, Holland, pp. 311–328.

19. U. S. Department of the Interior. 1969. *The National Estuarine Pollution Study*, Vols. I–III. Report to the Congress by the Federal Water Pollution Control Administration, Washington, D.C.

20. J. M. Craddock. 1973. *Water and Sewage Works*, June, pp. 74–81.

21. See bottom, Table 3.

22. R. W. Eppley, J. N. Rogers, and J. J. McCarthy. 1969. "Half-saturation constants for uptake of nitrate and ammonium by marine phytoplankton" *Limnology and Oceanography*, Vol. 14 pp. 912–920.

23. J. H. Ryther and W. M. Dunstan. 1971. "Nitrogen, phosphorus and eutrophication in the coastal marine environments." *Science*, Vol. 171, pp. 1008–1013.

24. M. Rebhun and J. Manka. 1971. "Classification of organics in secondary effluents." *Environmental Science and Technology*, Vol. 5, pp. 606–609.

25. A. Prakash and M. A. Rashid. 1968. "Influence humic substances on the growth of marine phytoplankton: dinoflagellates." *Limnology and Oceanography*, Vol. 13, 598–606.

26. RADIOACTIVITY

J. P. Baptist
T. R. Rice
National Marine Fisheries Service
Beaufort, North Carolina

Man-made radioactivity in the coastal environment has originated from nuclear weapons fallout, nuclear power plants, and nuclear-powered ships and submarines, as well as from hospitals, industries, and research institutions that use radioisotopes. Coastal waters are natural collecting basins for fallout and radioactive wastes transported by rivers and estuaries from land drainage and from upstream power plants. From 1945 until the early 1960s, worldwide fallout from nuclear weapons was the major source of radioactivity, some of which still persists in the environment. After the Nuclear Weapons Test-Ban Treaty of 1963, fallout radioactivity gradually began to subside, and nuclear power has since become the principal source of radioactivity in coastal waters.

The basis of operation of a nuclear power plant is nuclear fission, the splitting of nuclei of uranium atoms to obtain heat. From that point on, electricity is generated in the same way as in a conventional fossil fuel power plant. The fragments resulting from nuclear fission, unfortunately, are radioactive elements (fission products) which increase in quantity as the uranium fuel is used up. After about 1 year of operation it becomes necessary to replace one-fifth to one-third of the "dirty" fuel with new fuel because the presence of fission products within the fuel cladding reduces the efficiency of reactor operation. Although the fission products remain within the Zircaloy-clad fuel rods, small amounts may escape through defective cladding into the primary coolant water. In addition to fission products, impurities in the coolant become transformed into radioactive elements such as zinc 65, iron 59, cobalt 60, and manganese 54; these are also called "activation products," and most of them are concentrated and solided before being shipped offsite to an approved disposal area.

Remaining small concentrations of radioactivity, which are either too costly or impracticable to remove, are routinely released into the environment by way of the condenser cooling water. Although more than 200 radionuclides are produced in a nuclear reactor,[1] a relatively small number enter the environment (Table 1). Most radionuclides are effectively prevented from reaching the environment because of their fast radioactive decay and removal through waste treatment. For these same reasons the quantities of radioactivity released to the aquatic environment also are small, considerably less than the legal limits established to protect public health (Table 2). In addition to the liquid wastes, thousands of curies of gaseous wastes per year, mostly radioisotopes of krypton and xenon, are vented to the atmosphere from most nuclear power plants.

Table 7.26.1   Radionuclides in liquid effluents discharged from nuclear power plants. Radionuclides having half-lives less than 8 days are not included.

Radionuclide	Half-life
Tritium	12 years
Chromium 51	28 days
Manganese 54*	312 days
Cobalt 57*	272 days
Cobalt 58*	71 days
Iron 59*	45 days
Cobalt 60*	5 years
Zinc 65*	243 days
Selenium 75	120 days
Strontium 89*	51 days
Strontium 90*	29 years
Zirconium 95	65 days
Niobium 95	35 days
Ruthenium 103*	40 days
Ruthenium 106*	1 year
Silver 110m	253 days
Antimony 124	60 days
Iodine 131*	8 days
Cesium 134*	2 years
Cesium 137*	30 years
Barium 140	13 days
Cerium 144*	285 days

*Probable ecological significance

The spent fuel elements from nuclear power plants are shipped to a fuel-reprocessing plant for the recovery of unused uranium and plutonium. Although there are only three commercial reprocessing plants in the United States, each one must dispose of thousands of curies of radioactive wastes removed from several hundred metric tons of spent fuel each year.[3] The first commercial fuel-reprocessing plant (Nuclear Fuel Services, West Valley, New York) has released in its liquid effluents some radionuclides not ordinarily released from the power plants themselves, namely, plutonium and uranium isotopes and antimony 125.[4] At present this plant is shut down and is being modified to upgrade its tech-

Table 7.26.2 Amounts of radioactivity in liquid effluents discharged from nuclear power plants during 1972 (SOURCE: Reference 2)

Mixed Fission and Activation Products

Facility	Curies released	Average concentration (uCi/ml)	Percent of limit
Boiling Water Reactors			
Oyster Creek	10.0	8.62×10^{-9}	32.3
Nine Mile Point	34.6	7.80×10^{-8}	3.18
Millstone 1	51.5	8.35×10^{-8}	7.04
Dresden 1	6.75	2.32×10^{-8}	23.2
Dresden 2, 3	22.1	1.49×10^{-8}	14.9
LaCrosse	48.5	1.46×10^{-7}	6.39
Monticello	2.90×10^{-6}	2.78×10^{-16}	2.05×10^{-8}
Big Rock Point	1.09	1.06×10^{-8}	0.88
Humboldt Bay	1.40	7.78×10^{-9}	0.11
*Pilgrim	1.45	5.58×10^{-8}	7.98
Quad Cities 1, 2	2.41	1.73×10^{-9}	1.73
*Vermont Yankee	No liquid discharges for the report period.		
Pressurized Water Reactors			
*Maine Yankee	0.0169	1.75×10^{-10}	0.0919
Palisades	6.81	8.50×10^{-9}	0.005
Yankee	0.0206	1.28×10^{-10}	0.0249
Indian Point 1	25.4	5.12×10^{-8}	2.88
R.E. Ginna	0.375	5.18×10^{-10}	0.00234
Connecticut Yankee	4.78	6.20×10^{-9}	0.233
H.B. Robinson	0.826	3.82×10^{-9}	3.82
San Onofre	30.3	5.22×10^{-8}	1.49
Point Beach 1, 2	1.53	3.11×10^{-9}	0.0052
*Surry 1	0.0252	1.83×10^{-10}	0.00395
Nonwater Reactors			
Peach Bottom 1	0.0209	1.57×10^{-9}	1.57
Fermi	0.222	9.54×10^{-9}	7.53

*Plants operated less than 1 year.

nology and increase its reprocessing capacity.[2] The other two commercial plants (the Mid-West Fuel Reprocessing Plant at Morris, Illinois, and the Barnwell Nuclear Fuel Plant, Barnwell County, South Carolina) are designed to release no liquid effluents, but essentially all of the tritium is released in the form of water vapor in gaseous effluents.[3]

The release of tritium from nuclear power plants in recent years has been one of the leading subjects of controversy over nuclear power. Tritium, a radioactive isotope of hydrogen which becomes part of the water molecule, cannot easily be removed from radioactive wastes. It accounts for more than 90 percent of the wastes released into the aquatic environment. Because it has a low energy, a relatively rapid biological turnover rate (12 days, the same as that of water), and a low specific activity when released (low ratio of tritium atoms to stable hydrogen atoms), tritium has a high maximum permissible concentration in man. The controversy concerns the possibility of tritium atoms being incorporated in the DNA molecule and causing genetic mutations in human beings. The route often mentioned, in addition to drinking water, for tritium to be incorporated in people is through the aquatic food chain. The effects of tritium on aquatic organisms, however, are not very well known. Because of the increasing number of disproportionately large releases of tritium into the environment and its long physical half-life (12 years), additional research is needed on the ecological and radiation effects of this radionuclide.

The environmental effects of radioactive discharges vary with the characteristics of the radionuclide involved. Krypton and xenon isotopes, which constitute the bulk of gaseous effluents, are biologically inert. Therefore any radiation exposure to living forms would be external, occurring only by direct contact and inhalation rather than by biological action. On the other hand, liquid wastes contain many radionuclides of ecological significance (Table 1), which have the potential for adverse environmental effects if present in sufficient quantities. When released into coastal waters, radioactive elements, like their stable counterparts, are cycled through the water, sediments, and biota. The pathways followed depend on the chemical–physical form of the element, the ecosystems involved, and the various environmental factors, such as temperature, salinity, hydrology, and stable element concentrations in the waters.

Plants and animals generally accumulate radioisotopes of biologically essential elements or nonessential elements with similar chemical characteristics. The extent to which these radionuclides are accumulated by organisms and passed through the food web depends in part on whether they are in soluble or particulate form or are converted to the soluble form to pass through biological membranes and be associated in the tissues of organisms. Radionuclides thus incorporated are transferred to higher trophic levels in the food web. The accumulation of particulate radionuclides, however, occurs by surface adsorption; and particulate radionuclides such as ruthenium 106 and cerium 144 are concentrated by plankton and sediments, which provide large surface-to-volume ratios for surface adsorption. Radionuclides thus adsorbed, however, are transferred only to about the second or third trophic level.

Administrative control of radioactive discharges in the United States is the mandate of the U.S. Nuclear Regulatory Commission, as prescribed in the Code of Federal Regulations, Title 10, Parts 20 and 50.[5] The standards for permissible limits of radioactivity in effluents to the environment (Part 20) were adopted from the International Commission on Radiological Protection and the National Council on Radiation Protection and Measurements. Maximum permissible concentrations (MPCs) of various radionuclides in radioactive effluents to unrestricted areas are based on drinking water and air intake, but provisions are included to limit the intake of radionuclides from foods as well. The latter provisions are intended to take into account the concentration of radionuclides by plants and animals and the transmission of radionuclides through the food chain to human beings. Although there are no similar standards for the protection of plants and animals, it is generally believed that discharges of radioactivity in conformance with the above MPCs are unlikely to produce sufficient radiation to harm plants and animals.[6]

Among the thousands of pollutants discharged into the environment by man, radioactivity is one of the few that has been investigated extensively, has been discharged under strict legal controls, and has been monitored regularly to protect the public.

REFERENCES

1. Samuel Glasstone and Alexander Sesonske. 1963. *Nuclear Reactor Engineering.* D. Van Nostrand Company, Princeton, New Jersey.

2. U.S. Atomic Energy Commission. 1973. *Report on Releases of Radioactivity in Effluents and Solid Waste from Nuclear Power Plants for 1972.*

3. U.S. Atomic Energy Commission. 1973. *The Safety of Nuclear Power Reactors (Light Water-Cooled) and Related Facilities.* WASH-1250.

4. P. Magno, T. Reavey, and J. Apidianakis, 1970. *Liquid Waste Effluents from a Nuclear Fuel Reprocessing Plant.* U.S. Public Health Service, Rockville, Maryland, BRH-NERHL 70-2.

5. *Code of Federal Regulations.* 1967 (with supplements to 1973). U.S. Atomic Energy Commission, Title 10, Parts 20 and 50. U.S. Government Printing Office, Washington, D.C.

6. W. L. Templeton, R. E. Nakatani, and E. Held. 1971. "Radiation effects." In *Radioactivity in the Marine Environment.* Prepared by the Panel on Radioactivity in the Marine Environment, Committee on Oceanography, National Research Council—National Academy of Sciences, Washington, D.C.

27. RED TIDES

Clarice M. Yentsch
Charles S. Yentsch
Bigelow Laboratory for Ocean Sciences
West Boothbay Harbor, Maine

Red tides are high concentrations of planktonic organisms that discolor seawater and often cause conditions toxic to marine life and to persons who consume affected animals. The causative organisms are dinoflagellates that produce a toxin. The cells are individually microscopic; but when they occur in sufficient quantities to discolor the water (Figure 1), the phenomenon is referred to as "red tide" or "red water." Such blooms of plankton organisms and resulting discolored water have been known since ancient times. The Red Sea was named for them, as was the Vermillion Sea, now renamed the Gulf of California.

Red tides are of two types. Bird kills are often the first alarm signals of *Gonyaulax* red tides. Fish kills are characteristic of *Gymnodinium* red tides. Medical reports of human respiratory malfunction and desensitization often follow.

A bloom is a natural phenomenon, and most blooms that do not cause economic stress go unnoticed. Blooms are an integral part of the seasonal sequence of primary production of food energy within the sea, and to the scientist the phenomenon is fascinating.

In many temperate waters blooms occur every spring and often in the fall. During this period microscopic marine plants may grow to some 10 to 15 times their normal concentration. The genesis and decline of blooms involve a series of factors: solar radiation, water temperature, vertical water motions, salinity, availability of nutrient sources (especially forms of nitrogen and phosphorus), and grazing by the animal populations. These and many other factors, such as vitamins, iron, organics, and chelators, have been implicated as causes of red tides. After much research no single factor has as yet been shown to be responsible for red tides; probably various factors are interrelated. Rapid growth and/or the accumulation of the dinoflagellates parallel meterological disturbances and hydrographic perturbations. Storms can result in excessive runoff from the land, which washes growth nutrients into the coastal waters. Storms can disrupt the entire water column, thus mixing nutrient-rich bottom water upwards. In other cases dinoflagellates may accumulate regularly because of existing oceanographic conditions.

The dinoflagellates, or "fire algae" as they are often called, are classified sometimes as plants and sometimes as animals, because they possess characteristics of both. Some species photosynthesize like plants, and others feed like animals; a third group does both. Reproduction is sexual and accomplished by fission, that is, the cells simply split. Some are bioluminescent, capable of giving off visible light by combining two chemicals produced inside their single-celled bodies. The flagellae, whip-like locomotion organs, are not obvious except when viewed through a microscope. During adverse survival conditions, many dinoflagellates form cysts, which are quite resistant to most external environmental factors.

Few geographic areas are spared the nuisance of a sudden outbreak of dinoflagellates. In North America red tides are caused by several species. Whereas *Gymnodinium* red tides have created public concern in Florida for decades, *Gonyaulax tamarensis,** which occurs in the coastal waters of the North Atlantic, has only recently been publicized. This

---

*A name change to *Gonyaulax excavata* was suggested by Loeblich and Loeblich in 1975.

Figure 7.27.1   New England red tide organism, *Gonyaulax*. (Photo by L. A. Loeblich and A. R. Loeblich, *Proceedings of the First International Conference on Toxic Dinoflagellate Blooms*, November 1974, Boston, Massachusetts.)

dinoflagellate, although often present in off-shore waters, is occasionally triggered into bloom. The yet undefined triggering factors are under intensive investigation. Light, warm water temperatures, lowered salinities, and nutrients are important for the rapid growth of this organism in culture. Apparently, the nutrient demands of this organism with regard to nitrogen and phosphorus are much lower than those of other plant plankton.

The results of a red tide outbreak of *Gonyaulax tamarensis* are airborne irritation to human eyes and respiratory function, massive bioluminescence in the water, and the poisoning of shellfish and persons who ingest them. Outbreaks of red tide in the Northeast have usually been confined to the late summer months, although shellfish may retain the toxin until the next outbreak, which may be a year or two later. Maine has a good monitoring program to warn of the presence of the toxin, as does Canada, and Massachusetts has recently developed a monitoring program.

Few organisms directly or indirectly consum-ing the dinoflagellates or the resulting toxin are spared negative physiological effects. The animals directly affected by *Gonyaulax tamarensis* are filter-feeding bivalve mollusks. These animals feed by filtering microscopic plants such as *tamarensis* from a stream of water pumped through the gills by ciliary action. A clam 2 inches long may filter as much as 4 gallons of water each day. With *tamarensis* in the water, the bivalves filter the cells, which are then digested in the stomach and the toxin is released. The toxin (paralytic shellfish poisoning agent, or PSP; also, saxitoxin) passes into the tissues, and the shellfish become toxic to other animals that ingest them. Carnivorous snails can become quite toxic. Some people in Canada have died from eating highly toxic whelks.

The degree to which the toxin is concentrated depends on the resistance of the animal's nerves to the toxin. Mussels are more resistant than clams; therefore live mussels can have higher concentrations of the toxin than live clams. On the other hand, some animals such as quahogs are very resistant to the toxin but do not concentrate it. The tissues of scallops contain the toxin, yet the adductor muscle, the part that is customarily eaten, contains only very low levels and therefore scallops remain safe to eat. Lobsters that have eaten clams with human-lethal levels of PSP have been demonstrated to be entirely free of the toxin and therefore edible. Cooking does denature the toxin somewhat; however, cooking toxic organisms will not render them safe.

The toxin acts to block the passage of sodium ions through the nerve membrane and thus causes the nerve to become insensitive; that is, it blocks minute pores in the nerve Unlike the toxin of *Gonyaulax* which is inside the cell wall, the toxin of *Gymnodinium* is confined to the surface outside the cell.
membrane in the same way that a cork blocks the neck of a bottle.

The northwestern coast of North America witnesses blooms of *Gonyaulax catanella* or *Gonyaulax acatanella*. Species classification is still uncertain, and some experts suspect the latter to be *Gonyaulax tamarensis* because the effects and the toxin are nearly identical. Although there is rarely sufficient growth to discolor water, bioluminescence is often noted, and butter clams, mussels, and to some extent oysters can become toxic.

The bloom dinoflagellate characteristic of the Pacific coast off the southern portion of California is often *Gonyaulax polyhedra*. This organism is considered nontoxic, or at least far less toxic than other species. Let us explain: the standard assay is to inject the toxin into a mouse and to calculate the potency of the toxin as a function of death time. Toxin from *polyhedra* will kill a mouse, but the death time is very slow. Although the toxicity is minimal, blooms are annoying and often discourage tourism. The occurrence along the California coast is usually in the fall and is termed "red water" instead of "red tide."

Coastal waters off the Gulf of Mexico and off eastern Florida are at times plagued with massive outbreaks of *Gymnodinium breve*. Masses of fish killed by this dinoflagellate regularly cover Florida's west coast beaches. Because *Gymnodinium* is naked—that is, it has no external plates, as do species of *Gonyaulax*.

Although there are some adverse effects of a bloom of *Gymnodinium breve* on human health (e.g., prolonged exposure can cause irritation to respiratory function), the most serious economic effects occur when the massive fish kills become public nuisances and discourage tourism as well as the sport and commercial fisheries. The decomposing fish also impose an unusual demand on the oxygen content of the water.

Observers in Florida often mention hot weather accompanying the *G. breve* bloom and a cold snap preceding the decline. Although no single month has been free of red tide in the Gulf area, most blooms have occurred in the fall. Blooms have been increasing in frequency in waters off Florida (or possibly they have been noted with increasing frequency), and parallels have been drawn with runoff due to heavy rainfall from phosphate-mined areas, as well as domestic sewage dumping.

The most thoroughly researched red tide organism is *G. breve*. Suggestions have been advanced for prevention, control, and alleviation; however, no suggestion made has been entirely satisfactory to date.

To what extent man's activity (manifested as sewage, nutrient runoff, etc.) along coastlines augments blooms of red tide is yet unknown. Without man's involvement red tides will come and go. However, if we desire to eat shellfish and enjoy recreation along coastlines, the causes of the red tide blooms must be discovered by further research. With adequate prediction, shellfish can be shipped to cooperative markets in areas contaminated with PSP with a minimum of public alarm. Beyond prediction lies control. The eventual methods may be biological, chemical, or physical.

REFERENCES

1. George A. Rounsefell and Walter R. Nelson. 1966. *Red Tide Research Summarized to 1964, Including an Annotated Bibliography.* U.S. Department of Interior, Fish and Wildlife Service, Special Scientific Report—Fisheries No. 535, Washington, D.C.

2. A. Prakash, J. C. Medcof, and A. D. Tenant. 1971. *Paralytic Shellfish Poisoning in Eastern*

Canada. Fisheries Research Board of Canada, Bulletin No. 177.

3. Edward Gilfillan and Clarice M. Yentsch. 1973. "A marine population explosion." *Aquasphere,* Vol. 7, pp. 8–11. New England Aquarium, Boston, Massachusetts.

4. Vincent R. LoCicero, Ed. *Proceedings of the First International Conference on Toxic Dinoflagellate Blooms.* Massachusetts Science and Technology Foundation, 10 Lakeside Office Park, Wakefield, Massachusetts.

28. SALINITY

Gordon Gunter
Gulf Coast Research Laboratory
Ocean Springs, Mississippi

Salinity denotes the salts dissolved in water. Seawater contains several salts. Inorganic salts are simple compounds formed by the action of acids on metals. In water the molecules ionize into positive and negative ions, making salt water an excellent conductor of electricity. In average ocean water the weight of salts is close to 3.5 percent or 35 ppt. In bays and estuaries, where the rivers drain fresh water from the land, the salinity is less.

The salts of the sea are in the same proportions as those of water from the deep earth released by vulcanism, and apparently the sea salts originated from this source. The salts in the rocks in the shallow earth are not in the same proportion as those in sea water, but more like those of briny, landlocked lakes. Apparently the erosion of land and the dissolving of its salts by precipitated water was not the process by which most salt got into the sea.

The eight most abundant salts in seawater are listed in Table 1 as kilograms found in 1 cubic meter of water. The first five make up a little more than 99.7 percent of the total. There are many other salts in seawater, but the proportions are so small as to be negligible. For instance, there is approximately 1 ton of gold in each cubic mile of seawater, this being about 1 pound of gold to 7.5 billion pounds of seawater. Ordinarily, however, we are concerned only with the compounds listed in Table 1.

Salinity determines or affects some of the most important physical and chemical characteristics of seawater. It causes variations in specific gravity, which affects the movements and flow of the vast ocean water masses, and thus it is of great importance in physical oceanography. Salinity also lowers the freezing point of seawater so that it remains liquid at subfreezing temperatures. By its osmotic properties seawater may limit or permit many varieties of life and determine what lives where. The chemical properties of the salts in seawater also affect the basic metabolism of organisms and, similarly, limit or permit life of various kinds. Thus the salinity of seawater determines the distribution of thousands of species of organisms.

Seawater salinity has been defined as "the total amount of solid material in grams in one kilogram of seawater, when all the carbonate has been converted to oxide, the bromine and iodine replaced by chlorine, and all the organic matter completely oxidized."[1] It is measured

Table 7.28.1   Main salts of seawater (per cubic meter of seawater of 35 percent salinity and at 20°C) (SOURCE: Reference 1; reprinted by permission of Prentice-Hall, Inc. Englewood Cliffs, New Jersey)

Sodium chloride	$NaCl$	28.14 kg
Magnesium chloride	$MgCl_2$	3.812
Magnesium sulphate	$MgSO_4$	1.752
Calcium sulphate	$CaSO_4$	1.283
Potassium sulphate	K_2SO_4	0.816
Calcium carbonate	$CaCO_3$	0.122
Potassium bromide	KBr	0.101
Strontium sulphate	$SrSO_4$	0.028

by the conductivity of an electric current, by determination of its specific gravity, or by titration of the chloride content with closely determined amounts of silver nitrate. The titration determination is most commonly used; it depends on the fact that the proportions of salts in seawater are extremely uniform even at varying salinities, being $1.805 + 0.03$ to the total chlorinity.

Hypersaline water is found occasionally in tide pools and salt flats, but extensively only in the Sivash Sea, which connects with the Black Sea, and in the Laguna Madre of south Texas and northern Mexico. These briny waters retain the general proportions of sea salts until they become so concentrated that differential precipitation of individual salts takes place. Rather pure table salt is made by the evaporation of seawater because sodium chloride is the last salt to be precipitated during evaporation and can be poured off from the other salts.

Marine waters of low salinity are more common than hypersaline waters. Most of the coast of eastern North America is made up of bay waters, which may range in salinity down to fresh water in the upper reaches.

Determination of the lower salinity limit of sea water has received considerable attention. The Venice Conference on this subject came to the conclusion that 0.5 ppt saline was the best limit. However, the proportions of salts in some bay waters may be the same as in seawater at 0.18 ppt, and it is only below this point that the proportion of chloride to other salts begins to change. Thus a more definitive limit between fresh water and seawater might be set at the salinity where the proportions of other salts to chloride change from 1.805. The limit will vary, depending on the type of water draining down from land. In areas where there is drainage of hard fresh water, the salinity at the point of change may be 0.8 ppt total salts. In other areas it may be near 0.18 ppt, which is equivalent to soft fresh water. Such low dilutions of seawater are characteristic of the areas off the Amazon River and parts of the northern Gulf of Mexico, particularly the Mississippi and Alabama coasts. On the other hand, west Florida waters have high carbonate and phosphate contents and high freshwater salinity.

In North America, far the greater part of the sea fisheries is supported by animals with nursery areas in fresh water (the anadromous species) and those with nurseries in the bays after being spawned at sea, plus the species that seldom or never leave the bays (the estuarine-dependent species). In the Gulf of Mexico, which now produces 40 percent of the commercial fisheries of the United States, 98 percent of the commercial catch is connected with the bays and estuaries, at least at some stage of life history.[2] The general life history of Middle and South Atlantic and Gulf coast fisheries species of the United States is that the parents migrate to high-salinity waters to spawn, and the young return to the bays and estuaries to grow up, moving again toward the sea as they mature.

The great estuarine area around the mouth of the Mississippi River produces 30 percent of the nation's total fishery products and has been called the "Fertile Fisheries Crescent."[3] With the decline of the Peruvian anchovy fisheries it is now the world's most productive fishery area. The Peruvian fishery is in high-salinity waters, whereas the Mississippi fisheries are tied to low salinities. The common denominator is the nutrient salts continuously provided by upwelling in one instance and river drainage in the other. Figure 1 shows nutrient content and other environmental factors, by monthly averages, in the east and west deltas of the lower Mississippi River. It should be noted that low salinity is not the cause of coastal fertility, but that it is an important factor affecting the life histories, distributions, and geographical limits of many marine organisms.

Organisms that are unable to withstand much salinity change are said to be "stenohaline" and these may, like the mackerel, live only in high-salinity waters or, like the American sunfish, live only in fresh water. Organisms that live in the bays and estuaries generally can withstand wide salinity changes and are termed "euryhaline." The catadromous fish, which live in fresh water but go to sea to spawn, such as eels, and the anadromous fish, which live in the sea but go into fresh water to spawn, can probably stand the greatest salinity changes. Many species that are said to be purely euryhaline (salinity

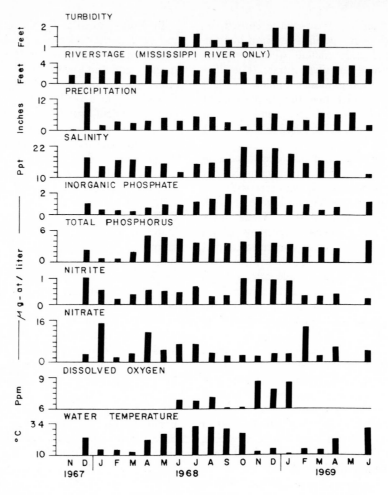

Figure 7.28.1 Environmental factors, Mississippi River delta. (SOURCE: Reference 4.)

toleraut) an can go back and forth from fresh water to salt water do so somewhat gradually and hence are not subjected to sudden great salinity changes.

Species that live in the estuaries are mostly osmoregulators over wide salinity ranges; that is, by processes of excretion and absorption of water and salts they maintain their body liquids at fairly stable salinities. More primitive species withstand changing salinities because they are osmolabile; that is, their body fluids change with the water of the environment, and their cellular components can withstand the change. The power of osmoregulation seems to improve from molluscs, to worms, to crustaceans, to fish. It should not be forgotten that a number of organisms adjust to wide

and sudden salinity changes by migrating or retreating into holes in the bay bottom, and sometimes by closing these holes, or simply by closing their shells. In spite of all methods of regulation and adjustment, most species of estuarine organisms have lower limits of salinity which they cannot withstand, and weakly motile species are eliminated by sustained low-salinity periods.

Salinity limits determine survival, spawning areas, optimum growth conditions, and even movements during life history stages. Some organisms are broadly tolerant of salinity changes, and some are narrowly tolerant. In general the kinds of organisms decline with lowering salinities, so that predators and diseases are low in number at low salinities. This gives a nursery ground advantage to the young marine animals that seek the low-salinity waters of the bays. Because they return to high salinity as they grow, there is a differential size distribution, and even a rather close relationship between increasing salinity and size, which has been noted by several workers, particularly in numerous organisms such as shrimp. Because of its multitudinous important effects, salinity has been termed a "master factor" of the environment by European zoologists.

The various fine distinctions occurring in the salinity relationships of organisms could not have developed in a short while. This means that vast estuaries have been present in North America for millions of years, and they are not transient phenomena, as some geologists have maintained.

REFERENCES

1. Gerhard Neumann and Willard J. Pierson, Jr. 1966. *Principles of Physical Oceanography.* Prentice-Hall, Englewood Cliffs, New Jersey, p. 40.
2. Gordon Gunter. 1967. "Some relationships of estuaries to the fisheries of the Gulf of Mexico. Part IX: Fisheries." In George H. Lauff, Ed., *Estuaries.* American Association for the Advancement of Science, Publication No. 83, Washington, D.C., pp. 621–638.
3. Gordon Gunter. 1963. "The fertile fisheries crescent." *Journal of the Mississippi Academy of Sciences,* Vol. 9, pp. 286–290.
4. Barney B. Barrett et al. 1971. *Cooperative Gulf of Mexico Estuarine Inventory and Study— Louisiana, Phase II: Hydrology, and Phase III: Sedimentology.* Louisiana Wild Life and Fisheries Commission, New Orleans, Louisiana.

29. SALT MARSHES

William A. Niering,
R. Scott Warren
The Connecticut Arboretum
Connecticut College
New London, Connecticut

Coastal salt marshes are tidal wetlands fringing the land–water interface of many temperate regions. They are part of a much larger marine system—the tidal marsh–estuarine ecosystem, which is recognized as one of the most biologically productive in the world. Chapman[1] describes nine different geographical salt-marsh regions throughout the world. In eastern North America salt marshes occur from Nova Scotia to southern Florida, where they are replaced by mangrove swamps. Because of the physiographical nature of the Pacific coast, marshes are much more limited in their distribution on the western shores of North America.

Geologically, tidal marshes are a relatively recent landform. Most appear to have originated about 3000 years ago, when the rise in sea level slowed sufficiently to favor marsh development. The ontogeny and dynamics of the Barnstable marshes on Cape Cod have been described by Redfield.[2,3] The formation of these marshes has occurred in conjunction with a barrier beach, which is apparently a common pattern.[4] Tidal marshes can also develop along and up the mouths of river estuaries. Deposition of silt, sand, and organic sediments is involved in the formation of marshes in either situation. Saltwater cordgrass (*Spartina alterniflora*) becomes established in the intertidal zone and further accelerates sediment accretion. Other species can also become established, and eventually peat deposits may accumulate to a considerable depth.

The vegetation pattern is influenced by a complex of environmental factors, including frequency and range of tides, salinity, microrelief, substrate, ice scouring, and storms. In addition, historical influences and more recent anthropic factors, including fires, cutting, diking, grazing, and ditching, also influence the distribution of species on salt marshes.

In many marshes a characteristic belting pattern occurs. In southern New England, Miller and Egler[5] recognize four major zones —the bay to upland sequence. As shown in Figure 1, *S. alterniflora* dominates the intertidal zone; salt meadow cordgrass (*Spartina patens*), the high marsh; black grass (*Juncus gerardi*), a rush, the lower border; and switch grass (*Panicum virgatum*), the upper border. However, within this pattern there is a mosaic of subtypes—stunted *S. alterniflora* pannes,

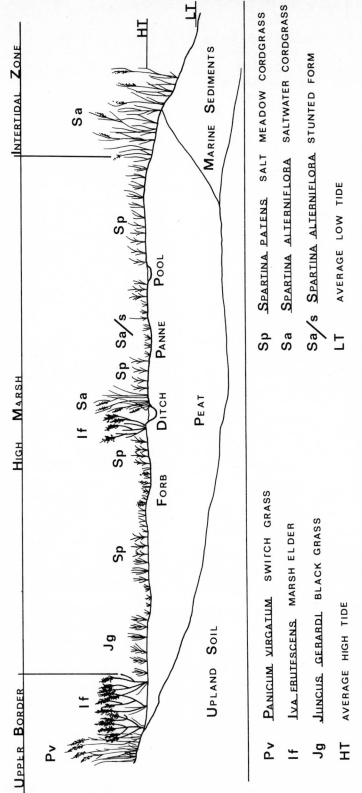

Figure 7.29.1 Typical vegetative "belting" pattern characteristic of New England salt marshes.

UPPER BORDER HIGH MARSH INTERTIDAL ZONE

Pv Jg If Sp Sp If Sa Sp Sp Sa/s Sa HT LT

FORB DITCH PANNE POOL

UPLAND SOIL PEAT MARINE SEDIMENTS

Pv PANICUM VIRGATUM SWITCH GRASS
If IVA FRUTESCENS MARSH ELDER
Jg JUNCUS GERARDI BLACK GRASS
HT AVERAGE HIGH TIDE

Sp SPARTINA PATENS SALT MEADOW CORDGRASS
Sa SPARTINA ALTERNIFLORA SALTWATER CORDGRASS
Sa/s SPARTINA ALTERNIFLORA STUNTED FORM
LT AVERAGE LOW TIDE

forb areas, algal pannes, and pools. Southward along the Atlantic coast, the width of the tall *S. alterniflora* belt increases dramatically, and *J. gerardi* is replaced by *J. roemerianus*. In southern California Purer[6] reports a lower littoral zone with *Spartina foliosa*, a middle littoral dominated by *Salicornia* spp., and an upper littoral with an admixture of *Frankenia grandifolia*, *Distichlis spicata*, *Atriplex watsonii*, and *Monanthochloe littoralis*.

A question that has long intrigued marsh ecologists is why or what ecological factors favor the development of various vegetation types. The results of other workers and findings from our research on New England marshes suggest some possible explanations. Johnson and York[7] in New York, Adams[8] in North Carolina, and others have suggested that the frequency of inundation, or the "hydroperiod," is very important in influencing species distribution. Adams also correlates the distribution of *S. alterniflora* in both the low and the high marsh with high concentration of soluble soil iron. The stunted form of *S. alterniflora* has been recognized as an ecotype in South Carolina[9] but as an ecophene in North Carolina[10] and in Connecticut.[11] Miller and Egler[5] suggest that high soil salt concentrations are the probable factor favoring this distributional pattern. Niering[12] reports higher soil salinities in *S. alterniflora* pannes than in other sites on the high marsh. Other factors that may be involved in influencing species distribution include nutrients, especially nitrogen,[13] and soil oxygen. Recent studies of Niering and Warren[14] on Connecticut marshes suggest that microrelief is also a relevant factor and that an undrained depression of less than 0.1 foot can result in a transition from the high marsh *S. patens* to stunted *S. alterniflora*. Such depressions may serve to collect and trap water, and with subsequent evaporation the soil salt increases. The distributions of other species, however, fail to show consistent relationship to microrelief differences. For example, *J. gerardi* occurs regularly at higher elevations along the lower border near the uplands, and not uncommonly on levees, but it also appears to persist in dense islands within the *S. patens* high marsh with no marked topographic differences.

The most ubiquitous marsh species is spike grass (*Distichlis spicata*), a typical halophyte, of exceptionally wide distribution in coastal and inland saline wetlands. It appears capable of persisting as an admixture of pure stands in almost every site on the marsh above mean high tide. Its extreme salt tolerance and vigorous rhizome system may favor this species as a pioneer and one that can resist the competition of adverse site conditions. A diversity of forbs lends an especially colorful aspect to the northeast Atlantic marshes. Sea lavender (*Limonium caroliniamum*), arrow grass (*Triglochin maritima*), seaside plantain (*Plantago maritima*), gerardia (*Gerardia maritima*), and aster (*Aster tenuifolius*) are among the most common and frequently are found in close association, sometimes in slight depressions or bare spots or even scattered within stands of the high marsh grasses. Seaside goldenrod (*Solidago sempervirens*) may also be an especially showy species on the high marsh. However, the often pure nature of the *S. patens* and *J. gerardi* stands does not tend to favor associates. In fact, it appears that competitive exclusion is a major factor operative in maintaining these relatively pure types. Areas bared of higher vascular vegetation frequently become dominated by the annual glassworts (*Salicornia* spp.) The most conspicuous shrub associated with the marsh is marsh elder (*Iva frutescens*). Although typical along the upper border, where it commonly seperates *P. virgatum* from *J. gerardi*, it may advance bayward on the elevated spoil along the mosquito ditches. Within the broad patterns described here, any given tidal marsh should be viewed as a constantly changing mosaic, continually being modied by subtle environmental influences. It should also be noted that over a long time frame the overall trend of coastal submergence is toward a landward movement of any bay-to-upland sequence of belts.

As one proceeds up the estuary, the increasingly fresh water favors a new spectrum of species such as cattail (*Typha angustifolia*), reed grass (*Phragmites communis*), and sedges (*Scirpus* spp.). These may ultimately replace the typical salt-marsh species previously mentioned. *Phragmites* is commonly associated with disturbed sites, especially where the normal saltwater flushing has been arrested.

The dominant animal populations found on

tidal marshes can be divided into those occurring in the intertidal zone and those restricted to the higher marsh, which is not inundated by each high tide. Studies on Connecticut marshes[15] reveal a high diversity of insects, for example, some seven orders and 40 families. Members of the Homoptera, Diptera (flies), and Hemiptera (true bugs) are most abundant. In the high marsh Homoptera of *S. patens* and *J. gerardi*, primarily leaf hoppers and plant hoppers, are the most abundant herbivorous grazers in Connecticut[16] and North Carolina.[17] The dominant detritus–algae feeders on the high marsh are the marsh snail (*Melampus bidentatus*), amphipods (*Orchestia* spp.), and the isopod *Philoscia vittata*. Spiders are the important invertebrate predators. In the intertidal *S. alterniflora* zone the leaf bug (*Trigonotylus* spp.), the fiddler crab (*Uca pugnax*), the ribbed mussel (*Modiolus demissus*), the rough periwinkle (*Littorina saxatilis*), and the mud snail (*Nassarius obsoletus*) are the most common. Other crustaceans found here include the marsh crab (*Sesarma reticulatum*) and green crab (*Carcinus maenas*).

Among the factors controlling the distribution of the invertebrates are food and protection, as well as elevation and frequency of tidal flooding.[15] Food and protection appear to be major factors controlling insects, whereas tidal effects seem paramount in determining the distributional pattern of the crustacea and mollusks.

Ecologically these marsh invertebrates are important as primary consumers, as enrichers of the grass production which is exported to the estuary, and as a vital part of the estuarine and terrestrial food chain.[16] In the Georgia marshes Teal[18] reports that 55 percent of the net production is dissipated by consumers. Respiration resulting from bacterial decomposition of the primary production accounts for 47 percent, whereas the primary consumers are responsible for only 7 percent and secondary consumers for approximately 17 percent. Since the high marsh is more widespread northward and herbivorous insects are abundant consumers in the high marsh, the figures for primary and secondary consumers may be somewhat higher in the northeast marshes. It is also of interest that most of the grass

production is enriched in amino acids by detritis feeders and bacteria before being flushed into the estuary.

In terms of wildlife productivity, the salt marshes play a major role along the Atlantic flyway by contributing food, shelter, and nesting sites for thousands of waterfowl. In addition to the wading birds, such as the herons and egrets, marsh hawks, ospreys, rails, marsh sparrows, and some 50 other species are part of the marsh avifauna. Among the reptiles the diamondback terrapin is unique to the tidal marshes. Muskrats are abundant and "harvested" for their fur; a variety of other mammals are frequent visitors and indirectly dependent on these wetlands.

As previously mentioned, tidal marshes are among the most productive ecosystems in the world. In the southern marshes, up to 10 tons of marsh grass may be produced annually. In the Northeast this figure ranges from 3 to 7 tons. The marsh grasses, mud algae, and phytoplankton of the tidal creeks comprise the three major units of primary production. As Pomeroy[19] has found in Georgia, the mud algae are especially well adapted to maximizing productivity by reaching their highest photosynthetic activity when the mud flats are sun-warmed and exposed in winter and when they are covered by the intertidal waters in summer.

The ribbed mussels embedded in the intertidal zone among the tall *S. alterniflora* grasses also play a major role in trapping phosphorus and keeping it in the estuarine system. The physical nature of the tidal marsh–estuarine system with its freshwater–saltwater interface tends also to act as a nutrient trap. In essence the marsh is the primary nutrient source for the highly productive finfish and shellfish resources in the contiguous estuarine waters. Marsh creeks also serve as nurseries and spawning grounds for coastal fish and other marine organisms.

Recently it has been documented that tidal wetlands are important pollution filters. Data from the Tinicum marshes near Philadelphia indicate 50 to 70 percent reductions in nitrate and phosphate levels several hours after the waters from sewage and effluent passed over a 500-acre tidal marsh.[20]

Although their high wildlife diversity has been mentioned, it should be stressed that these wetlands play a particularly significant role in our nation's waterfowl production. In the best years an estimated 200,000 waterfowl are produced on the eastern coastal marshes, and another 700,000 from marshes bordering 14 southern states.

Geologically too the marshes play a significant role. They act as sediment accretors or as depositories for sediments, thereby reducing the frequency of dredging for navigation. This in turn reduces the potential for smothering shellfish and other bottom organisms in the estuary, an indirect result of dredging. During severe storms the marshes exhibit resiliency and thereby act as buffers to protect the developed contiguous shoreline.

With man's attraction to the coastal region the salt marshes have suffered greatly from his activities. Filling, dredging, ditching, impounding, and draining, as well as polluting, have greatly reduced the total acreage. In Connecticut over 50 percent of the marshes have been destroyed, and somewhat similar trends have occurred in other highly populated coastal regions. Some of man's activities have actually obliterated the marshes; others have modified their biotic composition and productivity. Ditching has had a profound effect in reducing invertebrate productivity and modifying the vegetational pattern.[21] Impounding destroys the salt-marsh vegetation and results in fewer saline water bodies favoring waterfowl. Causeways constructed for highways and railroads restrict tidal flow, thereby modifying the vegetation and encouraging the less desirable *P. communis*. Tidal gates designed for flood protection also restrict tidal flushing and result in a conversion of the typical salt-marsh grasses to essentially pure *P. communis*. Development on barrier beaches that attempts to stabilize these normally dynamic land masses often results in restricting the tidal inlet to marsh systems. Only by developing a new wetland land-use ethic, will we begin to end these many subtle encroachments.

REFERENCES

1. V. J. Chapman. 1960. *Salt Marshes and Salt Deserts of the World*. Interscience Publishers, New York, 392 pp.

2. A. C. Redfield. 1965. "Ontogeny of a salt marsh estuary." *Science*, 147: 50–55.

3. A. C. Redfield. 1972. "Development of a New England salt marsh." *Ecological Monographs*, Vol. 43, pp. 201–237.

4. J. M. Teal and Mildren Teal. 1969. *Life and Death of the Salt Marsh*. Little, Brown and Company, Boston.

5. W. R. Miller and F. E. Egler. 1950. "Vegetation of the Wequetequock-Pawcatuck Tidal-Marshes, Connecticut." *Ecological Monographs*, Vol. 20, pp. 143–172.

6. A. Edith Purer. 1942. "Plant ecology of the coastal salt marshlands of San Diego County, California." *Ecological Monographs*, Vol. 12, pp. 81–111.

7. D. S. Johnson and H. H. York. 1915. *The Relation of Plants to Tide Levels*. Carnegie Institution of Washington, Publication No. 206, 162 pp.

8. D. A. Adams. 1963. "Factors influencing vascular plant zonation in North Carolina salt marshes." *Ecology*, Vol. 44, pp. 445–456.

9. R. Stalter and W. T. Batson. 1969. "Transplantation of salt marsh vegetation, Georgetown, South Carolina." *Ecology*, Vol. 50, pp. 1087–1089.

10. M. T. Mooring, A. W. Cooper, and E. D. Seneca. 1971. "Seed germination response and evidence for height ecophenes in *Spartina alterniflora* from North Carolina." *American Journal of Botany*, Vol. 58, pp. 48–55.

11. M. L. Shea, R. S. Warren, and W. A. Niering. 1975. "Biochemical and transplantation studies of the growth form of *Spartina alterniflora* on Connecticut salt marshes." *Ecology*, Vol. 56, pp. 461–666.

12. W. A. Niering. 1961. *Tidal Marshes: Their Use in Scientific Research*. Connecticut Arboretum, Bulletin No. 12, pp. 3–7.

13. I. Valiela, J. M. Teal, and W. Sass. 1973. "Nutrient retention in salt marsh plots experimentally fertilized with sewage sludge." In *Estuarine and Coastal Marine Science*, Vol. 1, pp. 261–269.

14. W. A. Niering and R. S. Warren. 1974. "Tidal marshes of Connecticut: vegetation, microrelief and environmental impacts." In W. A. Niering and R. S. Warren, Eds., *Tidal Wetlands of Connecticut: Vegetation and Associated Animal Populations*, Vol. 1. Department of Environmental Protection, State of Connecticut and Bureau of Sports Fisheries and Wildlife, U.S. Department of the Interior.

15. P. E. Pellegrino and A. T. Carroll. 1974. "The distribution of invertebrates in Connecticut salt marshes." In W. A. Niering and R. S. Warren, Eds., *Tidal Wetlands of Connecticut: Vegetation and Associated Animal Populations*, Vol. 1. Department of Environmental Protection, State of Connecticut, and Bureau of Sports Fisheries and Wildlife, U.S. Department of the Interior.

16. N. C. Olmstead and P. E. Fell. 1974. "The invertebrates of the Cottrell salt marsh in eastern Connecticut with an emphasis on the salt marsh snail, *Melampus bidentatus*." In W. A. Niering and R. S. Warren, Eds., *Tidal Wetlands of Connecticut: Vegetation and Associated Animal Populations*, Vol. 1. Department of Environmental Protection, State of Connecticut, and Bureau of Sports Fisheries and Wildlife, U.S. Department of the Interior.

17. L. V. Davis and I. E. Gray. 1966. "Zonal and seasonal distribution of insects in North Carolina marshes." *Ecological Monographs*, Vol. 36, pp. 275–295.

18. J. M. Teal. 1962. "Energy flow in the salt marsh ecosystem of Georgia." *Ecology*, Vol. 43, pp. 614–624.

19. L. R. Pomeroy. 1959. "Algal productivity in salt marshes of Georgia." *Limnology and Oceanography*, Vol. 4, pp. 386–397.

20. R. R. Grant, Jr., and Ruth Patrick. 1970. "Tinicum marsh as a water purifier." In *Two Studies of Tinicum Marsh*. The Conservation Foundation, Washington, D.C., pp. 105–123.

21. W. S. Bourn and C. Cottam. 1950. *Some Biological Effects of Ditching Tidewater Marshes*. U.S. Department of the Interior, Fish and Wildlife Service, Research Report No. 19, 30 pp.

30.   SEA GRASS BEDS

Joseph Zieman
Department of Environmental Sciences
University of Virginia
Charlottesville, Virginia

In recent years, as marine science has paid increasing attention to the living resources of the shallow coastal seas, the vast beds of submerged sea grasses bordering the temperate and tropical coastlines have been recognized as important resources. Although the significance of sea grasses was documented over 60 years ago, little further work on the ecological importance of these highly productive and easily studied areas followed until recently.

Sea grasses are unique among submerged marine and estuarine plants, as they are higher plants (Spermatophyta) that have returned to the sea, thus possessing an extensive root and rhizome system and reproducing by flowers fertilized by waterborne pollen. Because of this root and rhizome system within the sediments, coupled with high growth rates and dense leaf development, the sea grasses exert considerable influence over their environment. Wood. et al.[1] summarized the functions of sea grasses in estuarine and marine ecosystems as follows:

1. Seagrasses have a rapid rate of growth and high organic productivity, rivaling some of the most intensive agricultural crops.

2. They serve directly as food for only a limited number of organisms since the demise of the large, grazing sea turtles; but they supply large quantities of detrital material, which, along with its resident microbes, provide a major food pathway for the estuarine ecosystem.

3. The leaves support large numbers of epiphtic organisms, which, under favorable conditions, may be comparable in biomass to the sea grass leaf weight, and which are grazed extensively by fishes and invertebrates.

4. Sea grasses provide organic matter, which initiates sulfate reduction and maintains an active sulfur cycle in the estuarine sediments; this stimulates the rapid release of nutrients for increased plant growth.

5. The dense leaves reduce the current velocity near the sediment surface and promote sedimentation of organic and inorganic particles.

6. The roots and rhizomes bind the sediments and hinder erosion of the surface of the sediment.

Sea grasses are widely distributed throughout the shallow coastal seas from the Arctic to the southern tips of Africa and New Zealand. Den Hartog[2] recognizes 12 genera of sea grasses with 49 species. Of these, 7 genera are considered tropical and the rest are temperate in distribution. As is common with many marine groups, the highest diversity in the sea grasses is found in the Indo-West Pacific with a secondary center in the Caribbean area. In the North American and Central American–Caribbean areas, only two species are important, other than in localized situations.

In the cooler temperate waters, eelgrass, *Zostera marina*, is the dominant sea grass, forming broad meadows of luxurient beds, which support a diverse fauna; while in the Caribbean and the Gulf of Mexico, turtle grass, *Thalassia testudinum*, replaces *Zostera*. Both sea grasses are known to be highly productive with rates of net production of 2 to 10 grams carbon per square meter day. This exceptionally high productivity is supplemented in a sea grass community by epiphytes, algae, and associated benthic and planktonic microalgae, and is maintained by the action of decomposition in the sediments and the apparent ability of sea grasses not only to extract nutrients from either seawater or the sediments, but also to pump nutrients from the sediments into the water column. Because of this high productivity, and the shelter offered by the dense blades, sea grasses function as nurseries, important in the rearing and sheltering of small fish and invertebrates.

Although a few animals have been recorded as feeding directly on sea grasses, since the demise of the Caribbean green sea turtle there is little direct grazing pressure on the beds except in certain localized situations. *Zostera* is the primary food of the black brant (*Branta bernicla*) throughout much of its range, while sea urchins and parrotfish nibble and ingest *Thalassia* blades, and mullets selectively graze the epiflora. Nevertheless, most of the energy fixed by these plants, usually 95 percent or greater, is transfixed through the food via the detritus after the leaf dies and decays. In addition to supplying food for the detritus grazers associated with the beds, much material is tidally exported to provide communities further offshore with particulate and dissolved organic food sources.

Sea grass beds are especially vulnerable to degradation by human-induced stresses as they inhabit only the shallow marginal seas, because of a requirement for high light levels for photosynthesis, and it is in this zone that the activities of man are greatest. Moreover, because their mode of growth is unique for marine plants, the sea grasses are subject to damage from stresses or pollutants in the water column or in the sediments. Thus they are exceptionally susceptible to damage from man's activities in the coastal zone.

Eutrophication and dredging greatly increase the suspended particulate matter in seawater and decrease light penetration, thus reducing photosynthesis in sea grasses. In addition, by decreasing the speed of water flow over the grass beds, the blades promote rapid sedimentation of the particles, which can smother the beds. Studies have shown that the thermal pollution from power plants and the modication of the natural seasonal temperatures and salinity regime can be harmful to sea grass communities. When sea grass communities were subjected to thermal pollution in south Florida, *Thalassia* proved to be one of the most resistant organisms, although it too was severely damaged.

The ultimate impact of pollution or stresses that damage the sea grasses will be greatly magnified. Although many consider sea grass communities to be highly diverse, because of the richness of plants and animals therein, most of these are "second story" species that are totally reliant on the sea grasses. Hence the diverse epiphytic flora and fauna will totally disappear if the sea grasses are eliminated.

During the 1930s, the east coast of the United States and the coast of western Europe experienced a dramatic decline of *Zostera* due to the famous "wasting disease." In many areas over 30 years was required before the communities renewed. This protracted recovery time is not unusual in sea grasses. *Thalassia* is a robust plant and an active, rapid producer, yet when a bed is subjected to a relatively small cut from an outboard boat propeller, from 3 to 5 years can be required for the cut to repair itself after this seemingly superficial damage.

Because of the areas these plants cohabit with man, they are most susceptible to two particular forms of pollution: turbidity from dredging or poor land management, and modications in the natural temperature–salinity regime due to power plants and desalinization facilities. Frequently in the past, major industries or utilities were sited with no thought of the ecological effect of their effluents. Now there is an increase in laws to deter such ecological oversights, and they must be actively enforced.

Techniques such as sediment curtains are

available to greatly decrease the loss of sediments during dredging operations. Other techniques such as the use of sediment ponds and/or the application of straw to exposed soil can greatly reduce soil erosion and the subsequent waterborne sediment load.

Recognition by government of the importance of sea grass beds is slowly becoming a reality as the linkage between ecology and economy is recognized. The state of Florida has declared sea grass beds "preservation areas" where no development is permitted. An area that is highly dependent on its income from recreation, primarily water-oriented recreation, must maintain high water quality standards and esthetic values.

As important as this concern is to industrialized society, it is even more important to undeveloped areas, such as many tropical regions, where the local populace is dependent on subsistence fishing.

There are few examples in ecology where a single species dominates a community to the degree shown by the sea grasses. Thus extreme care must be used when evaluating the impact of man's activities in zones inhabited by these plants and their associated communities.

REFERENCES

1. E. J. F. Wood, W. E. Odum, and J. C. Zieman 1969. "Influence of sea grasses on the productivity of coastal lagoons." *Mem. Simp. Intern. Lagunas Costeras,* UNAM–UNESCO, pp. 495–502.

2. C. den Hartog. 1970. *The Sea-Grasses of the World.* North-Holland Publishing Company, Amsterdam, 275 pp.

31. SETTLEABLE ORGANIC WASTES

M. Waldichuk
Environment Canada
Fisheries and Marine Service
Pacific Environment Institute
West Vancouver, British Columbia

Settleable organic wastes are carbonaceous substances that enter the aquatic environ-

ment and eventually settle to the bottom. They may be heavier than water to start with and remain in suspension only because of the swift and turbulent flow of water bearing them, or they may become water-logged (saturated with water) and eventually sink to the bottom. Some waterborne organic wastes may float in fresh water by virtue of their colloidal properties, created by electrostatic characteristics, but they sink when they enter the sea because of the presence of electrolytes, which tend to neutralize the charges on the particles and cause flocculation. Other organic substances may float in seawater of high salinity, but will tend to sink, because of reduced buoyancy, once they are carried into the coastal zone, where the freshwater inflow is large and results in a comparatively low salinity.

Ocean dumping of solid wastes as a national problem, with some alternatives for solids disposal and recommendations for action, is discussed in a report to the President by the Council on Environmental Quality.[1] Also, a review of some of the biological problems involved in ocean disposal of solids, including organic wastes, is given by Pratt et al.[2], describing experimental studies conducted at the University of Rhode Island.

There is a variety of sources of organic wastes from our society, including domestic sewage and a whole host of industries. Sewage sludge is perhaps a major component of the total settleable organic solids released into the coastal environment from population centers. This enters receiving waters either through sewage outfalls of untreated domestic wastes, or through pipelines conveying sludge from primary treatment centers into the coastal environment for dispersal and/or barging it to disposal areas in the coastal seas. It was estimated that sewage sludge constituted 9 percent of the materials dumped into the ocean by the United States during 1968.[1] A simple treatment for raw sewage discharged into coastal waters has often been comminution, which is simply breaking down the larger solid fraction into finer fragments.

Agriculture contributes a great deal of organic matter from natural soil constituents and from organic fertilizers, because of continuous tilling of the soil, especially during heavy runoff. Irrigation contributes to runoff in the drier agricultural areas. Of the 75 percent of total soil discharge into coastal waters contributed by agriculture, a large proportion is organic. Barnyard manure, which is often distributed over agricultural land as fertilizer, may be partly washed into drainage systems by runoff, especially if the manure is spread over the land before the spring thaw of ice and snow. The modern trend toward feedlots for intensive feeding of livestock concentrated in large numbers within enclosures amplifies the problem of barnyard waste disposal. Some of this waste, including animal excrement, sawdust, hay, and straw, may escape into stream courses when proper management is not practiced. Being generally lighter than the inorganic fraction, the organic solids from agricultural runoff may be transported further seaward in the coastal zone.

Construction projects contribute soil through erosion during periods of rain and heavy runoff. Whether the construction is for a golf course or urban housing, the initial stages always involve disturbance of the ground cover, which contains a large proportion of organic material, arising from vegetation and litter. Later stages may contribute soil, uncombusted products from burning, and building refuse, including sawdust, chips, paper products, and plastic.

Dredge spoils from harbors, where there are or have been industries and/or domestic wastes have been discharged, usually contain a high concentration of organic solids in the top layer, arising from the runoff-borne litter from the drainage basin. Dredging for sand and gravel in the coastal zone will resuspend organic materials, at least in the initial stages of such operation.

A major contribution to settleable organic wastes from other industries includes logging and forest products manufacturing. Logging contributes bark, chips, leaves, and other wood wastes, both in the forest operations and in log booming and hauling in water.[3] It also provides organic matter from the soil overburden disturbed in road building and log hauling. In manufacturing, the sawmilling and pulp and paper industries[4] perhaps are principal contributors. Bark and sawdust are major components of wastes from the sawmilling industries. Although some of these residues are now recovered for paperboard manufacturing and hog fuel, a proportion still escapes into re-

ceiving waters. In addition to these waste products, the pulp and paper mills introduce tiny fibers ("fines") and other wood residues that are not recovered for commercial use at the present time.

Beverage and food processing industries contribute settleable organic solids to receiving waters, particularly where there is no waste treatment. These include breweries, distilleries, canneries of fruits, vegetables, meat and fish products, slaughterhouses, sugar refineries, reduction plants for oil, fish meal, and fish protein concentrate, potato processors, and cereals production. Tannery wastewaters contain animal hair, flesh, and other organic particles from rendering the hides. Textile mills, processing both natural and synthetic fibers, are a source of particulate organic solids in the waste waters. Woolen and cotton mills contribute a biochemical oxygen demand (BOD) not only from the dissolved constituents, but also from the fibers that escape into the waste stream.

Chemical industries may contribute organic substances that are heavier than water, although the tendency is to recover these for reuse as much as possible. Examples of such chemical wastes might occur in the plastics industries, where unusable small fragments may escape into the sewer and be discharged into receiving waters. Liquid organic chemicals characterized by immiscibility with water may be released into the sewer, and polymerize on exposure to the atmosphere and sunlight. These may eventually settle to the bottom, forming a rather persistent component of the bottom materials.

Various petroleum residues may be considerably heavier than water and eventually settle to the bottom. Bilge cleanings and residues from petroleum installations, including refineries, may be a source of this type of waste. It has been found that intensive mixing of surface waters by wind and tide can cause a substantial amount of heavy oil, such as Bunker C, to be dispersed in tiny droplets into the water column.

A contribution from the forest industries that is not normally considered as a settleable organic waste is driftwood. Either deliberately released into rivers (logs for pulp and paper are still transported by river through "log drives" in some areas), disposed of from coastal installations, or inadvertently released from log booms, wood can eventually become water-logged and settle to the bottom to form "deadheads" or the wood litter on the bottom of coastal environments. Deadheads are a major hazard for small craft, and wood litter affects the benthic environment for bottom organisms and becomes a detriment to underwater recreation. The same thing can happen, of course, to the flotsam and jetsam released from ships, which may eventually settle to the bottom. To some extent, this is the litter of the sea, which also includes such things as plastic bags and sheets, plastic ropes, and a variety of paper products that eventually settle to the bottom if they are not first washed ashore.

By their very nature settleable organic wastes are eventually deposited on the bottom or remain in a thin-slurry suspension just above the bottom of receiving waters. They may be readily resuspended through wave or current action. Depending on how rapidly and in what concentration these wastes are discharged, they may merely modify slightly the bottom characteristics, or they may totally destroy the natural benthic habitat and introduce a rapid silting-in process.

When there is only a slight addition of organic material to the bottom sediments, the organic solids, depending on their biodegradability, may be rapidly decomposed by bacteria or integrated into the sediments as a persistent component. The reworking by bottom organisms, particularly the worms, may modify and redistribute this sedimented material within the upper few centimeters. If the organic solids are added more rapidly than they can be assimilated into the bottom sediments, accumulation occurs and the bottom becomes blanketed by the organic materials.

In the latter situation, if the organic substances are biodegradable, decomposition takes place by the action of bacteria, dissolved oxygen is taken up from the water and sediments, and noxious gases may be produced. In coastal environments, if sludge banks are built up through the disposal of solid organic wastes, methane is one of the major gases produced.[5,6] However, depending on the presence of sulfates in the water, hydrogen sulfide, formed under the reducing conditions in the sediments,

may also be a significant component. Because of its extreme toxicity, hydrogen sulfide can render waters highly noxious to aquatic life. This is particularly apparent when dredging takes place and the bottom sediments, along with the gases of decomposition, are stirred up into the water column.

Organic solids dredged from harbors receiving solid organic wastes may have a high BOD and may have toxic hydrogen sulfide associated with them. When such dredge spoils are released into coastal waters frequented by fish, there can be a threat to their survival.[7] It is also the wood solids from pulp mills that contribute to sludge beds in quiescent coastal waters near pulp mill outfalls.[8,9]

Sewage solids in large concentration may have an unfavorable ecological effect on the coastal marine environment. Often these solids are digested in holding tanks before being discharged, so that their BOD is moderately low once they reach the bottom sediments. However, they may still contain large concentrations of bacteria and viruses originating from human sewage. Hence, in addition to modifying the bottom habitat for benthic organisms, they could conceivably contaminate some of the filter-feeders and, through them, persons eating raw or semiraw seafood. Microorganisms attached to sewage sludge are particularly resistant to destruction by environmental factors active in the sea.

In areas where large volumes of sewage sludge are discharged into comparatively quiescent waters, the blanketing of the bottom by the deposited organic material may markedly change the bottom characteristics and the bottom fauna. This appears to have been the case with the disposal of sludges off New York, where a variety of solid wastes are barged to some distance offshore.[10] Studies conducted in the New York Bight by Pearce[11] suggest that fish may have been affected by an increasing incidence of diseases such as fin rot, as well as lesions of a tumorous type. Similar fish studies off the coast of California,[12] including also bone deformities, asymmetry, and external parasites, showed a high incidence of fin erosion in demersal fish only in areas with high concentrations of wastewater constituents in the sediments.

Large volumes of sewage sludge have also

been discharged since about 1890 into the Thames estuary from Greater London in England, and so far no ecological damage has been identified.[13] It appears that the tidal currents and mixing are so intense that sewage sludge is widely dispersed without concentrating in any one area. Wood[13] suggests that it is essential to maintain a careful watch on the concentrations of pesticides, polychlorinated biphenyls, and mercury, and on other metals from the sludge in the bottom sediments and in the near-bottom seawater of the area. However, such nonconservative properties as dissolved oxygen content, which are normally affected by organic wastes, do not appear to have been altered. Turbulent mixing ensures that dissolved oxygen saturation occurs almost from top to bottom at all times in this estuarine area.

Under some circumstances, especially when there is a very finely divided organic waste, the particulate material settles near the bottom, where it remains in a soupy layer. Turbulence may help to maintain it in suspension. This condition is often found in the vicinity of pulp mills, where fine fibers may deposit as a slurry with just sufficient tidal mixing to keep it slightly stirred above the bottom.

Plastics contribute to the litter on the ocean bottom, along with other debris, such as bottles, tin cans, and rubber tires, which do not biodegrade rapidly. Although some of the firmer littering substances, including bottles and tires, provide a substrate for attachment by larvae of invertebrates, plastic film is generally unsuitable for the settlement of larvae because of its pliability and smooth surface. It has been found that storage of logs in sheltered coastal bays causes the most rapid degradation of bottom characteristics and fauna.[14] Bark and wood chips litter the bottom, smother bottom organisms, and prevent the settling of larvae on a suitable substrate. Moreover, leachates from the bark and wood can exert a BOD, reducing the dissolved oxygen in the bottom water and sediments, and they may be directly toxic.

Oily sludges from ship machinery and bilges tend to be heavier than sea water because of the presence of metallic and other inorganic residues. Therefore they sink to the bottom along with other settleable organic wastes. Depending on the depth and the temperature of the water where these kinds of wastes are released, there may be very slow degradation of the petroleum products. Because oil sludges, when released in sufficiently large amounts, blanket the bottom with a rather impervious seal, they prevent the exchange of oxygen between the water and sediments. This leads to an adverse effect on the benthos, particularly the burrowing organisms. Clams, cockles, and worms will be destroyed through suffocation, while sedentary organisms will be eliminated as a result of adverse alteration of the substrate for their attachment.

Degradation of organic solids by bacterial action tends to be highly temperature and pressure dependent. This was first demonstrated by an inadvertant deep-sea biodegradability experiment; a packed lunch was recovered virtually unchanged after 10 months on board the submersible Alvin, which accidentally sank in some 1540 meters of water in the Northeast Atlantic.[15] Since this observation was made, a number of controlled experiments have shown that the combined effect of high pressure and low temperature can, in fact, be extremely significant in preserving organic solids at the bottom of deep-sea areas.

Suspended organic particles, when present in adequately high concentration, can affect fish. Abrasive wood particles can damage the gills. Clearly, a stress from other pollutants renders a fish less capable of clearing its gills of any accumulated fibers, and effects on stressed or unhealthy fish are more acute than on healthy fish exposed to fibers alone. Fish exposed to high concentrations of wood fibers, particularly of certain wood species, have died in bioassay experiments using both fresh water and sea water.[16,17] However, it is uncertain how much of the adverse effect is due to fibers per se and how much stems from the leachates associated with the fibers.

Ideally, it would be best not to dispose of organic materials of the solid type into any coastal area where ecological damage might be done. Because of the technology and economics of solid waste disposal, however, a number of factors, such as large population centers adjacent to the coast, made coastal disposal and ocean dumping economically attractive before the environmental consequences were carefully examined. Waterborne organic solids, among other types of wastes, were considered in a workshop on requirements for research, sponsored by the National Academy of Sciences and National Academy of Engineering, held in Jackson Hole, Wyoming, during July 1969.[18] Some of the recommendations of this workshop for research and monitoring in coastal waste management were reported by the Secretary of the Interior to the United States Congress in 1970.[19] During the same year, hearings before a Subcommittee of the Committee on Government Operations in the U.S. House of Representatives reviewed specific coastal pollution problems in such areas as the Potomac River estuary and San Francisco Bay related to the Environmental Decade (Action Proposals for the 1970's).[20,21] Settleable organic solids in wastewaters have been considered in several state and federal studies developing criteria for water quality to protect aquatic life.[22-25]

The following recommendations are made for solid organic waste management

1. An effort should be made to prevent solid organic waste from entering the coastal environment, if at all possible, particularly if it is not waterborne and is merely a solid waste product of manufacturing (e.g., bark, sawdust, plastic residues). With the energy crisis at the present time, such solid wastes could be incinerated for profitable use of the heat they can provide.
2. Solids lost from product manufacturing and waterborne in the effluent, such as fibers from cotton and wood pulp, should be recovered as fully as possible for use in the product. In the pulp and paper industry the fine fibers tend to be lost during processing and sheet forming and enter the waste stream to be discharged into receiving waters. Various screening devices and save-alls help to recover these fibers from the wastewater and in some cases can make them available for the production of paper and other wood-pulp materials.
3. Wood wastes and other solid organic residues, which cannot be utilized for the prime product, should be recovered to the maximum extent possible from the waste stream by efficient processes of screening, flocculation, and clarification, and then suitably dewatered. These residues, when at least partially dried, can serve as combustible material for furnaces (e.g., hog fuel in pulp mills) to provide heating and other energy requirements.
4. Such solid residues as sewage sludge, which are difficult to dewater, should be retained on land, where possible, to be used ultimately for soil conditioning in agriculture and/or landscaping. This is the ideal form of recycling, wherein solids arising mainly from agriculture go back to the soil. As an alternative, they should be processed into commercial soil conditioner and fertilizer, as practised now in some sewage treatment plants. A by-product of sewage treatment and sludge digestion is methane gas, which is used as a fuel supplement in operating some treatment plants. Sewage sludge can also be incinerated for its energy value, but this seems a less economical use of such material.
5. Agricultural practices should ensure that "green strips" are retained around tilled soil so that particulate materials are captured by the turf and other vegetation and are prevented from entering receiving waters, during heavy precipitation and runoff. Some similar provision should be made before construction projects are begun in order to prevent the washout of debris into storm sewers and other drainage systems.
6. When it is impossible to recover solids from the waste stream, discharge should occur only into coastal waters that are rapidly replaced and vigorously stirred by tidal currents and wind-mixing action. This will provide a high degree of dilution and dispersion, allowing assimilation of the substances into the water and sediments without local buildup of the solid waste material and degradation products.
7. Disposal of sludge from sewage and other types of wastes by barging offshore should occur only in carefully selected, nonproductive areas, where ecological damage would be expected to be minimal.
8. Dredge spoils, depending on their composition with respect to organic material,

should receive as much precaution in disposal as sewage sludge. Dredge spoils of a
low organic content may have less potential for ecological damage and therefore
may require less control. However, even
inorganic materials, when present in large
enough amounts, can cover up bottom
habitats.

9. Disposal of persistent plastics, oily sludges,
and any type of wood debris, which float
and/or may become waterlogged, should
be avoided in coastal waters.

10. Research should be increased on the development of new ways for removing solid
organic substances from wastewater and
rendering them usable either for product
manufacturing or as energy sources, and
on the technology required for these new
techniques.

REFERENCES

1. Council on Environmental Quality. 1970. *Ocean Dumping: A National Policy.* A Report to the President. Washington, D.C., 45 pp.

2. S. D. Pratt, S. B. Saila, A. G. Gaines, Jr., and J. E. Krout. 1970. *Biological Effects of Ocean Disposal of Solid Waste.* Marine Experiment Station, Graduate School of Oceanography, Marine Technical Report Series No. 9, University of Rhode Island, Kingston, Rhode Island, 53 pp.

3. Pacific Northwest Pollution Control Council. 1971. *Log Storage and Rafting in Public Waters.* A Task Force Report. Seattle, Washington, 56 pp.

4. M. Waldichuk. 1962. "Some water pollution problems connected with the disposal of pulp mill wastes." *Canadian Fish Culturist,* No. 31, pp. 3–34.

5. A. E. Werner. 1968. "Gases from sediments in polluted coastal waters." *Pulp and Paper Magazine (Canada),* Vol. 69, No. 5, pp. 127–136.

6. A. E. Werner and W. F. Hyslop. 1968. *Data Record: Gases from Sediments in Polluted Coastal Waters of British Columbia, 1964–1966.* Fisheries Research Board of Canada, Manuscript Report Series No. 958, 81 pp.

7. J. A. Servizi, R. W. Gordon, and D. W. Martens. 1969. *Marine Disposal of Sediments from Bellingham Harbor as Related to Sockeye and Pink Salmon Fisheries.* International Pacific Salmon Fisheries Commission, Progress Report No. 23, 38 pp.

8. A. E. Werner. "Suspended solids from mill effluents." *Canadian Pulp and Paper Industry,* Vol. 17, pp. 4–9.

9. A. E. Werner and W. F. Hyslop. 1968. "Accumulation and composition of sediments from polluted waters off the British Columbia Coast, 1963–1966." Fisheries Research Board of Canada, Manuscript Report Series No. 963, 81 pp.

10. M. G. Gross, J. A. Black, R. J. Kalin, J. R. Schramel, and R. N. Smith. 1971. *Survey of Marine Waste Deposits, New York Metropolitan Region.* Marine Sciences Research Center, Technical Report No. 8, State University of New York, Stony Brook, New York.

11. J. B. Pearce. 1972. "The effects of solid waste disposal on benthic communities in the New York Bight." In M. Ruivo, Ed., *Marine Pollution and Sea Life.* Food and Agriculture Organization, Fishing News (Books), Ltd., London, England, pp. 404–411.

12. Southern California Coastal Water Research Project. 1973. "Coastal fish populations." Chapter 7 in *The Ecology of the Southern California Bight: Implications for Water Quality Management.* Report No. SCCWRP TR104C, El Segundo, California, 251 pp.

13. L. B. Wood. 1972. "Discussion: Disposal of sludge at sea." *Water Research,* Vol. 6, No. 4–5, pp. 573.

14. N. G. McDaniel. 1973. *A Survey of the Benthic Macroinvertebrate Fauna and Solid Pollutants in Howe Sound.* Fisheries Research Board of Canada, Technical Report No. 385, 64 pp.

15. H. W. Jannasch, K. Eimhjellen, C. O. Wirsen, and A. Farmanfarmaian. "Microbial degradation of organic matter in the deep sea." *Science,* Vol. 171, pp. 672–675.

16. J. C. MacLeod and L. L. Smith. 1966. "Effect of pulpwood fiber on oxygen consumption and swimming endurance of the fathead minnow." *Transactions of the American Fisheries Society,* Vol. 95, pp. 71–84.

17. A. E. Werner. *Effects of Groundwood and Kraft Pulpmill Fibers on Sockeye Salmon, Oncorhynchus nerka* (in preparation).

18. Committee on Oceanography, National Academy of Sciences–Committee on Ocean Engineering, National Academy of Engineering. 1970. "Wastes management concepts for the coastal zone. Requirements for Research and Investigation." Washington, D.C., 126 pp.

19. U.S. Department of the Interior. 1970. *The National Estuarine Pollution Study.* Report of

the Secretary of the Interior to the U.S. Congress, Pursuant to Public Law 89-753, The Clean Water Restoration Act of 1966. U.S. Government Printing Office, Washington, D.C., 633 pp.

20. U.S. Committee on Government Operations. 1970. *The Environmental Decade (Action Proposals for the 1970's)* Hearings before a Subcommittee on Government Operations. House of Representatives, 91st Congress, 2nd Session, Feb. 2-6, Mar. 13, and Apr. 3, 1970. U.S. Government Printing Office, Washington, D.C., 361 pp.

21. U.S. Committee on Government Operations. 1970. *Protecting America's Estuaries: The San Francisco Bay and Delta.* 31st Report of the Committee, 91st Congress, 2nd Session. U.S. Government Printing Office, Washington, D.C., 142 pp.

22. J. E. McKee and H. W. Wolfe, Eds. 1963. *Water Quality Criteria,* 2nd Ed. California State Water Quality Control Board, Publication No. 3-A, Sacramento, California, 548 pp.

23. Federal Water Pollution Control Administration. 1968. *Water Quality Criteria.* Report of the National Technical Advisory Committee to the Secretary of the Interior. Washington, D.C., 234 pp.

24. National Academy of Sciences–National Academy of Engineering. 1973. *Research Needs in Water Quality Criteria, 1972.* Report of the Committee on Water Quality Criteria to the Environmental Studies Board, at the request of and funded by the U.S. Environmental Protection Agency, Washington, D.C., 64 pp.

25. National Academy of Sciences–National Academy of Engineering. 1973. *Water Quality Criteria, 1972.* Report of the Committee on Water Quality Criteria to the Environmental Studies Board, at the request of and funded by the U.S. Environmental Protection Agency, Washington, D.C.

32. SHELLFISH BEDS

Arthur S. Merrill
John W. Ropes
Middle Atlantic Coastal
Fisheries Center
Oxford, Maryland

It is well known that many benthic molluscan shellfish species form specific and often unique ecological associations with various bottom substrata as a prerequisite to survival. Species such as hard and soft clams live burrowed into bottom sediments that vary in consistency from soft mud to sand and coarse sand and gravel which is often mixed with shell and sundry debris. Other species, such as oysters and mussels, live on the bottom surface, attached to shells, stones, or other solid objects. A third group of species, for example, scallops and whelks, are free living with some horizontal mobility and are associated with a much wider variety of bottom substrates.

Most commercial shellfish are of separate sexes and spawn during months when warm water temperatures prevail. Fertilization is usually external, and the developing larvae spend their early life in pelagic waters as part of the plankton. At the termination of the larval stage they undergo a critical metamorphosis and must find a suitable substrate on which to "set"; otherwise they perish. When conditions are optimal, commercial shellfish larvae are in the water column in untold numbers; and if suitable substrata are available, a "set" can produce a tremendous bed of clams.

The association of a dominant species with secondary biota, on or in a bottom type, is often referred to as a "community." Concentration of a species on a preferred substrate produces a shellfish "bed." A bed may have a practical implication for a fisherman when it consists largely of a single species that can be harvested for food. However, commercial exploitation depends on the extent of bed formation—the larger and denser the species aggregation, the easier it is to harvest them.

Marine biologists survey large areas of the estuarine and coastal ocean waters to assess the abundance and distribution of shellfish species and to determine the annual commercial potential and health of the stocks. Assessment studies are particularly relevant in molluscan fisheries, since the animals are mostly sessile and more accurate population data can be acquired for them than for highly mobile finfish species. By the same token, because the animals are sessile, they are extremely vulnerable to forces adversely affecting the shellfish beds.

Any change in the basic composition of the bottom can seriously affect the requirements for survival of benthic creatures. The destruction of shellfish beds by physically removing or depositing materials, such as silt, dredge spoils, sewage sludge, and industrial wastes, may result in direct loss of valuable food-producing areas. The bed may be destroyed by simple smothering when waste materials are dumped over it. Equally destructive may be silting and toxic materials transported by water currents over considerable distance. Such toxic substances from sewage sludge and industrial waste may include harmful bacteria and viruses, chemical ions, and many other deleterious materials. These slowly filter into the sediments over a large area. Thus repetitive dumping can cause a strong accumulation of foreign materials in the sediments, often far removed from the specific dump site. On the other hand, shellfish beds may be improved by proper management practice. For instance, oysters cannot "set" on soft bottoms; they must cement themselves to solid objects. Empty shells, termed "cultch," are commonly spread on the bottom by the oyster industry to enhance an established bed or to create new beds.

The activities of man in the coastal zone have had the greatest influence on shellfish stocks in recent years. The weakly motile larval forms are almost completely under the influence of tidal or wind-driven currents. Turbidity-producing materials, such as silt, may be both directly and indirectly detrimental to larval growth. Lowered larval survival and settlement can be expected in coastal water areas that are being dredged or are receiving chemicals mixed with rainwater flowing off the land, or from drainage of untreated municipal or industrial sewage systems. Even the hydraulic action of the soft clam escalator dredge used in Chesapeake Bay creates a waterborne silt load that may be deposited on oyster spat living close to the harvesting operation.[1,2] Mortalities of oysters and clams caused by physical smothering have been observed; although some states have restrictions on harvesting too close to shellfish beds.

Shellfish of commercial importance usually feed by ingesting fine food particles from the water column. Soluble molecules and minute particles suspended in the water, which may include inorganic and organic pollutants, are drawn into the mantle cavity surrounding the soft body parts of shellfish. A complex filter-feeding system sorts particles, which are either ingested or bound up for disposal as pseudofeces. Soluble molecules are ingested and concentrated in the soft body parts by poorly known mechanisms. Trace metals in the tissues of some shellfish have been investigated.[3-5] The highest levels of trace metals are reported for oysters from the natural environment. Recent studies in Chesapeake Bay relate increases of heavy metal concentrations in oysters and sediments to man's activities.[6] Oysters from highly industrialized areas are often contaminated. In laboratory studies copper imparted a green color to the tissues of oysters, did not affect growth, and only slightly affected mortality, but cadmium adversely affected growth and caused high mortalities.[3] Most heavy metal concentrations reported for clams from oceanic coastal waters were higher than those for clams from the surrounding seawater.[4] Iron, manganese, lead, and chromium were higher in ocean quahogs, and nickel was higher in surf clams than in oysters.

Experimental observations indicate that water quality is very important for the survival of larval mollusks. Detergents, variation in pH, pesticides, bactericides, herbicides, insecticides, heavy metals, oils, solvents, disinfectants, and turbidity-producing substances have been tested for beneficial or harmful effects during larval culture.[7-10] Some chemicals promoted larval growth by reducing bacteria in cultures, but solutions containing copper, mercury, silver, zinc, iron, some plastics, and detergents were definitely toxic.

Extensive tests of pesticides on mollusks from natural beds have shown that the effects of each pesticide must be evaluated on an individual basis.[11] Mollusk species are widely variable in concentrating pesticides and usually rid themselves of the chemicals after being transferred to clean water. Residues of pesticides in North American shellfish are not high enough to be a human health hazard, but their persistence in the aquatic environment may be producing chronic effects on longevity, growth, and disease resistance in some marine organisms.

Shellfish concentrate bacteria and have been

implicated in the transmission of viral infectious hepatitis to man.[4,12] Methods of cleansing clams have been developed to eliminate the possible health hazard presented by clams marketed from some polluted areas.[13] Although such methods may be applicable in some areas and for some shellfish, they increase the cost of the product and would be of little value for clams living in grossly polluted areas containing petroleum derivatives. The effects of a petroleum derivative have been identified in hard clams.[14] Clams from polluted water were characterized by a dark meat color, abnormal shells, smaller size, and kidneys plugged with a black substance, as well as abnormal biochemical conditions. The ecological and physiological significance of the findings is that the stress symptoms remained for at least a year after the clams were transferred to clean areas.

Shellfish stocks can decline from natural causes of mortality, but these are often of local short-term significance and are generally considered to be rare events.[15,16] Abrupt changes in temperature and salinity are rather natural phenomena and can cause mortalities. Seasonal oxygen deficiencies and toxic phytoplankton blooms due to eutrophication processes can also kill shellfish, and predation by various fish and invertebrates is known to reduce shellfish populations. Catastrophic events in the ocean, such as intense storms, may cause excessive bottom currents that effectively root clams from their burrows and cast them on beaches by the millions.[17] Such mortalities are very difficult, if not impossible, to control.

Some of the more important commercial shellfish native to the Atlantic coast recently have been reviewed.[18] They include the oyster, *Crassostrea virginica*; the hard clam, *Mercenaria mercenaria*; and the soft-shell clam, *Mya arenaria*—all well-known food sources since colonial days. Sea scallops, *Placopecten magellanicus*, became important after World War I. Within the past three decades the surf or sea clam, *Spisula solidissima*, has risen to major importance, although it may be unfamiliar because it rarely, if ever, reaches the consumer in the shell, but appears as sliced, chopped, or minced meat in canned products or institutional preparations. Several other species, such

as the bay scallop, *Argopecten irradians*, and the calico scallop, *Argopecten gibbus*, are of local significance; and a few species—for example, the blue mussel, *Mytilus edulis*; the razor clam, *Ensis directus*; the sunray venus clam, *Macrocallista nimbosa*; and the black or ocean quahog, *Arctica islandica*—are potential sources of food. Most are found in beds in estuarine or ocean shelf waters in sufficient abundance to be commercially important species.

Molluscan shellfish other than those of commercial importance also should be considered. The array of species inhabiting a coastal area often numbers several hundred, with only a fraction of these of potential commercial value. One authority estimates that there are about 50,000 living mollusk species worldwide;[19] of these, about 7500 are bivalves, and 37,500 are snails. Most of these species are not used for food because they are too small, or they occur in too few numbers, or they are presently considered latent resources. The inability to man to utilize such species, however, should not overshadow their probable importance in the ecology of the coastal zone; large and abundant species that are not used now may be important in the future. Throughout the world man has learned to utilize many fresh- and saltwater molluscan shellfish, and in 1967 the world catch amounted to 3.1 million metric tons.[20] Squid, cuttlefish, octopus, various species of oysters, clams, and snails are included in the catch. Japan led the world by catching the largest poundage and variety of molluscan shellfish, but the United States was first in the catch of bivalved mollusks such as oysters, clams, and scallops—some 654 thousand metric tons of these seafood delicacies were landed.

In the United States, bivalved molluscan resources are far greater on the Atlantic than on the Pacific coast. Landings of oysters and clams alone at Atlantic ports averaged 149.1 million pounds annually during 1970–1974; those at Pacific coast ports (including Alaskan scallops), about one-twelfth that amount. A more extensive continental shelf and many estuaries for shellfish bed formation contribute importantly to the higher landings along the Atlantic than Pacific United States coasts.

Most United States oysters and clams come

from the Middle Atlantic Bight. This area has a gently sloping, broad oceanic continental shelf and includes Chesapeake Bay, one of the largest and most productive estuaries in the world. Studies of the continental shelf show that the bottom is composed chiefly of sand and gravel with irregular patches of sandy silt.[21] Chesapeake Bay has an accumulation of fine-grained silts and clay through most of its extent.[22] Through geological time, molluscan shellfish have evolved successfully to inhabit these substrata. In 1974, 83 percent of the clams in the United States came from the Middle Atlantic continental shelf and almost half of the oysters from Chespeake Bay. Since surf clams from this area contribute very significantly to molluscan shellfish landings in the United States, these great fisheries are presently being studied in depth to develop more effective management.

Landing statistics on oysters and clams since World War II are a measure of the commercial importance of these resources. Oyster landings have steadily declined in the United States from a high annual average of 78.6 million pounds of meats during 1950–1954 to 49.6 million pounds during 1970–1974.[24] The value of the landings has been stabilized at about $30 million annually by increased demand. All species of clams landed in the United States increased from a low annual average of 37.1 million pounds during 1950–1954 to 99.5 million pounds during 1970–1974. Although the total value of clams has steadily increased from an annual average of $11.1 million in 1950–1954 to $32.0 million in 1970–1974, the average cost per pound has been relatively constant, except for the 1960–1964 period, when the surf clam fishery expanded rapidly. The development of the surf clam fishery during the past two decades is principally responsible for the increase in total clam landings.[23] Surf clams increased from 30.6 to 74.8 percent of the clam meats landed in the United States during successive 5-year periods since 1950 (Table 1).

Several complex conditions have been identified as causes for the decline in oyster production.[25] During the early history of the fishery in the eastern United States, the supply of oysters was very abundant on extensive natural beds. Annual landings as high as 170 million pounds of meats were recorded near the turn of the century. Since World War II, however, increases in human population and overburdened sanitary facilities, as well as navigational, industrial, and domestic changes in the headwaters of estuaries and throughout the coastal zone, have affected the quality of water adversely for oysters and clams. Difficulties in controlling predators and disease organisms, which pose an ever-present threat to oyster populations, have also reduced oyster production. Oyster drills (*Urosalpinx* and *Eupleura*) have caused heavy mortalities of young oysters in high-salinity waters.[26,27] The

Table 7.32.1 Landings and value of oysters and clams in the United States for various 5-year periods from 1950 to 1974 (SOURCE: Reference 24)

| 5-year period | Oysters | | | All Clams | | |
| | Average annual millions of | | Average cents/lb | Average annual millions of | | Average cents/lb |
	Pounds	Dollars		Pounds	Dollars	
1950–54	78.6	30.6	.40	37.1	11.1	.30
1955–59	71.1	30.1	.42	38.4	10.8	.28
1960–64	59.4	29.3	.49	56.4	12.9	.23
1965–69	56.0	29.4	.53	72.6	20.3	.28
1970–74	49.6	31.8	.64	99.5	32.0	.33

effects of a protozoan parasite (*Minchinia nelsoni*) crippled the oyster industry in Delaware and Chesapeake Bays during the late 1950s and 1960s,[28] although reported mortalities from the pathogen have been lower in recent years.[29] A fungus parasite, *Labyrinthomyxa marina*, seriously affected oysters in the Gulf of Mexico and is a continuing problem in the Chesapeake Bay.[28,30]

Since World War II extensive portions of estuarine coastal waters have been closed to shellfish harvesting, and an unprecedented closure of two coastal oceanic areas for surf clams was effected in 1970. Each area comprises about 120 square miles of bottom in the New York Bight and offshore of Delaware Bay. These areas are dump sites for huge quantities of industrial and domestic wastes. Warnings of the effects of such disposal have been given,[31] and visible evidence of mortalities of marine organisms in the New Jersey area has been reported by divers.[32] Repopulation of an estuarine area by bivalves and other benthic organisms has been observed after pollution abatement.[33] Clearly, then, one significant step in maintaining high levels of shellfish production is to reduce pollution throughout coastal waters.

Many of the marine resources seemed inexhaustible years ago, and the necessity for management was less acute than is apparent today. Man is currently demanding more and more of the products from the marine environment to feed skyrocketing populations, and the need for effective management has increased accordingly. Management of wild shellfish resources is difficult, partly because of greater areas and open waters of the marine coastal zone as compared to inland freshwater lakes and streams. The decline from high annual landings and reduction in acreage of oyster beds near the turn of the century occurred because management measures were relatively ineffective.[25] An enforced management practice today in the Chesapeake Bay oyster fishery is the use of antiquated, relatively inefficient equipment and methods, such as sailboats and hand tongs, as an effective conservation measure to prevent overfishing and to limit daily catches. Methods to reduce starfish and oyster drills are also used in the fishery to lessen predation mortalities to shellfish. Management measures related to disease problems include restrictions on transferring oysters from one area to another and planting in areas where disease organisms are inhibited.[34] Raising oysters and clams under controlled artificial conditions and developing disease-resistant stocks[35] are important in supplementing depleted beds and providing stocks with desirable genetic traits, including faster growth. These methods are important management tools for manipulating and controlling a part of the natural world.

As previously stated, ocean fisheries are less amenable to management because of the very large areas involved. Surf clams, for example, are taken commercially from near the beach zone to 25 fathoms along most of the Middle Atlantic coast.[36] Sea scallops occur from 10 to deeper than 40 fathoms[37] and ocean quahogs from 15 to 35 fathoms off the New England and Middle Atlantic coasts. A future management aim in the surf clam fishery will probably be to open and close areas inshore and offshore along the coast for harvesting seasonally to prevent overfishing in any one area. Some Middle Atlantic states have already enacted legislation to license surf clam vessels, restrict fishing in waters under their jurisdiction, and limit catch to large clams. These management measures, however, are not uniform for all states involved in the fishery. Other desirable practices in the surf clam fishery might be relocating nearshore clams offshore before they are washed ashore, or moving them from dense beds with poor growth potential to less dense beds.

Fortunately, impact statements are demanded for all environmental projects that may affect a fishery, such as channel and harbor dredging, power plant installations, offshore drilling operations, and ocean dumping of wastes near clam and oyster beds. The preparation of impact statements requires assessment information and accurate landing records on all species, data equally essential for management of the resources.

Vigorous research efforts by federal, state, university, and private industry investigators are directed toward gaining an understanding of the effects of man's activities on the shellfish in the coastal zone. Evaluation of current and proposed uses often requires the application of advanced and costly scientific technology. The work is very challenging in view of the complexity of the problems involved but is vitally needed to protect adequately such productive and valuable coastal zone resources.

REFERENCES

1. J. H. Manning. 1957. *The Maryland Soft Shell Clam Industry and Its Effects on Tidewater Resources.*" Maryland Department of Research and Education, Chesapeake Biological Laboratory, Resource Study Report No. 11, Solomons, Maryland, 25 p.

2. Robert W. Hanks. 1963. *The Soft-Shell Clam.* U.S. Fisheries and Wildlife Service, Circular 162, 16 p.

3. C. N. Shuster, Jr., and B. H. Pringle. 1969. "Trace mental accumulation by the American eastern oyster, *Crassostrea virginica.*" *Proceedings of the National Shellfisheries Association*, Vol. 59, pp. 91–103.

4. R. W. Buelow, 1968. "Ocean disposal of waste material." In *Transactions of the National Symposium on Ocean Science Engineering, Atlantic Shelf*, Philadelphia, Mar. 19–20, 1968, pp. 311–337.

5. F. C. Kopfler and J. Mayer. 1973. "Concentrations of five trace metals in the waters and oysters *(Crassostrea virginica)* of Mobile Bay, Alabama." *Proceedings of the National Shellfisheries Association*, Vol. 63, pp. 27–34.

6. M. E. Bender, R. J. Huggett, and H. D. Slone. 1972. "Heavy metals—an inventory of existing conditions." *Journal of the Washington Academy of Science*, Vol. 62, pp. 144–153.

7. A. Calabrese and H. C. Davis. 1970. "Tolerances and requirements of embryos and larvae of bivalve molluscs." *Helgolaender Wissenschaftliche Meeresuntersuchungen*, Vol. 20, pp. 553–564.

8. A. Calabrese. 1972. "How some pollutants affect embryos larvae of American oyster and hard-shell clam." *Marine Fisheries Review*, Vol. 34, No. 11–12, pp. 66–77.

9. A. Calabrese, R. S. Collier, D. A. Nelson, and J. R. MacInnes. 1973. "The toxicity of heavy metals to embryos of the American oyster *Crassostrea virginica.*" *Marine Biology (Berlin)*, Vol. 18, pp. 162–166.

10. H. C. Davis and H. Hidu. 1969. "Effects of turbidity-producing substances in sea water on eggs and larvae of three genera of bivalve mollusks." *Veliger*, Vol. 11, pp. 316–323.

11. P. A. Butler. 1971. "Influence of pesticides on marine ecosystems." *Proceedings of the Royal Society of London, B.*, Vol. 177, pp. 321–329.

12. M. E. Rindge, J. D. Clem, R. E. Linkner, and L. K. Sherman. n.d. A *Case Study on the Transmission of Infectious Hepatitis by Raw Clams.* U.S. Department of Health, Education and Welfare, Public Health Service, 36 p.

13. R. B. MacMillan and J. H. Redman. 1971. "Hard clam cleansing in New York." *Commercial Fisheries Review*, Vol. 33, No. 5, pp. 25–33.

14. H. P. Jeffries. 1972. "A stress syndrome in the hard clam, *Mercenaria mercenaria.*" *Journal of Invertebrate Pathology*, Vol. 20, pp. 242–251.

15. M. L. H. Thomas and G. N. White. 1969. "Mass mortality of estuarine fauna at Bideford, P. E. I., associated with abnormally low salinities." *Journal of the Fisheries Research Board of Canada*, Vol. 26, pp. 701–704.

16. W. N. Shaw and F. Hamons. 1974. "The present status of the soft-shell clam in Maryland." *Proceedings of the National Shellfisheries Association*, Vol. 64, pp. 38–44.

17. J. W. Ropes, J. L. Chamberlin, and A. S. Merrill. 1969. "Surf clam fishery." In F. R. Birth, Ed., *The Encyclopedia of Marine Resources.* Van Nostrand Reinhold Company, New York, pp. 118–125.

18. Arthur S. Merrill and Haskell S. Tubiash. 1970. "Molluscan resources of the Atlantic and Gulf coast of the United States." In *Proceedings of the Symposium on Mollusca*, Part III. Marine Biological Association. India, Mandapam Camp.

19. Kenneth J. Boss. 1971. *Critical Estimate of the Number of Recent Mollusca.* Museum of Comparative Zoology, Occasional Papers on Mollusks, No. 3, pp. 81–135, Harvard University, Cambridge, Massachusetts.

20. Food and Agricultural Organization. 1969. *Yearbook of Fishery Statistics, Catches and Landings, 1968*, Vol. 26.

21. J. Schlee. 1968. *Sand and Gravel on the Continental Shelf off the Northeastern United States.* U.S. Geological Survey, Circular 602, 9 p.

22. J. R. Schubel. 1972. The Physical and Chemical Conditions of Chesapeake Bay." *Journal of the Washington Academy of Science*, Vol. 62, pp. 56–87.

23. John W. Ropes. 1972. "The Atlantic coast surf clam fishery, 1965-69." *Marine Fisheries Review*, Vol. 34, No. 7-8, pp. 20-29.

24. Charles H. Lyles. 1969. *Historical Catch Statistics (Shellfish).* U.S. Fish and Wildlife Services, Current Fisheries Statistics No. 5007, 116 p.

25. James B. Engle. 1966. "The molluscan shellfish industry: Current status and trends." *Proceedings of the National Shellfisheries Association*, Vol. 56, pp. 13-21.

26. M. R. Carriker. 1955. *Critical Review of Biology and Control of Oyster Drills* Urosalpinx *and* Eupleura. U.S. Fish and Wildlife Service, Special Report—Fisheries, No. 148, 150 p.

27. C. L. MacKenzie, Jr. 1970. "Oyster culture in Long Island Sound, 1966-69." *Commercial Fisheries Review*, Vol. 32, No. 1, pp. 27-40.

28. Carl J. Sindermann and Aaron Rosenfield. 1967. "Principal diseases of commercially important marine bivalve Mollusca and Crustacea." *U.S. Fish and Wildlife Service Fishery Bulletin*, Vol. 66, pp. 335-385.

29. Susan E. Ford. 1973. "Recent trends in the epizootiology of *Minchinia nelsoni* (MSX) in Delaware Bay." *Proceedings of the National Shellfisheries Association*, Vol. 63, pp. 2-3 (abstract).

30. Sammy M. Ray. 1966. "Notes on the occurrence of *Dermocystidium marinum* on the Gulf of Mexico coast during 1961 and 1962." *Proceedings of the National Shellfisheries Association*, Vol. 54, pp. 45-54.

31. R. T. Norris. 1972. "The future of New England's marine resources." *Commercial Fisheries Review*, Vol. 34, No. 1-2, pp. 13-18.

32. L. Ogren and J. Chess. 1969. "A marine kill on New Jersey wrecks." *Underwater Naturalist*, Vol. 6, No. 2, pp. 4-12.

33. D. Dean and H. H. Haskin. 1964. "Benthic repopulation of the Raritan River estuary following pollution abatement." *Limnology and Oceanography*, Vol. 9, pp. 551-563.

34. Aaron Rosenfield. 1971. "Oyster diseases in North America and some methods for their control." In K. S. Price, Jr., and D. L. Maurer, Eds., *Proceedings of the Conference of Artificial Propagation of Commercially Valuable Shellfish—Oysters, 1969.* College of Marine Studies, University of Delaware, Newark, Delaware, pp. 67-78.

35. A. C. Longwell and S. S. Stiles. 1973. "Oyster genetics and the probable future role of genetics in aquaculture." In *American Malacological Union, Inc., Bulletin for 1972*, p. 36.

36. A. S. Merrill and J. W. Ropes. 1969. "The general distribution of the surf clam and ocean quahog." *Proceedings of the National Shellsheries Association*, Vol. 59, pp. 40-45.

37. A. S. Merrill. 1962. "Abundance and distribution of sea scallops off the middle Atlantic coast." *Proceedings of the National Shellfisheries Association*, Vol. 51, 74-80.

33. SHORELINE SITE PLANNING AND DESIGN

Roy Mann
Roy Mann Associates, Inc.
Cambridge, Massachusetts

The appearance of structures and other objects in relation to the visual character of shorelines has long been recognized as a matter of importance to users of the coastal zone. Extant descriptions of Pharos, the legendary lighthouse of ancient Alexandria, and of the entrances of Greek and Roman ports indicate that aesthetic embellishments were significant features of the functional structures of those ports. In Japan beautifully designed torii arches have been placed in shallow waters near shore, to achieve unique aesthetic effects. In Venice the aesthetic component of the waterfront is the city's chief asset. In New England early architectural traditions contributed the carefully rhythmic placement of peaked roofs, saltbox buildings, shed structures, and other port features that distinguished such harbor towns as Menemsha and Nantucket Town, Massachusetts, and Camden, Maine. In each instance architectural traditions were adapted by sensitive architects and artisans to the aesthetic characteristics of the shore.

The aesthetic quality of shore and coastal development of the nineteenth and twentieth centuries has generally been less memorable than that of the examples cited above. Five reasons other than social and economic root causes may be given:

1. Components of ports, industries, utilities, and depots may be exposed to view from or against scenic shorelines or may repre-

sent aesthetic incongruities to nonindustrial users of the shore zones.

2. Larger scales of residential construction are common.

3. Broad freedom in the architectural design of residential, commercial, and institutional buildings has become accepted, allowing the introduction of eclectic and sometimes disparate building styles adjacent to earlier-established architectural traditions.

4. Some mass-produced building materials are visually unsympathetic with nearby architecture or natural landscape features.

5. Poor use has been made of landscape design (i.e., the modification of earth, vegetational, and built forms) to screen or buffer edges of negative areas.

In addition to effects involving appearance, noise, odor, and crowding or congestion have been recognized as negative aesthetic impacts on the coastal zone.

Public dissatisfaction with the appearance of latter-day coastal development is manifested in the Coastal Zone Management Act of 1972, which finds that aesthetic resources are among the coastal resources that have been misused and that wise use and management of them is in the national interest. Anticipated effects of development on aesthetic resources are also a concern of the National Environmental Policy Act of 1969, which requires environmental assessments of proposed federal actions, and of other federal law governing scenic, recreational, and wilderness protection and management. Concern for scenic coastlines is also manifested in legislation in a number of states; in some local communities, police powers and other controls effectuate some degree of management of aesthetic resources and waterfront development.

The characteristics of shore aesthetic resources can be categorized according to form, surface qualities, and use suitabilities.

Landform is the prime determinant of the overall aesthetic character of coastal areas. Among the distinctive landforms of United States coastal regions are (1) the rocky headlands and islands of northern and southern New England, (2) the moraine bluffs of the north shore of Long Island, (3) the barrier beaches of the Atlantic and Gulf coasts, (4)

the dendritic tributaries and creeks of Chesapeake Bay, (5) the mangrove shores of Florida, (6) the long marshes and bayous of the central Gulf states, (7) the limestone and sandstone cliffs of Lake Superior, (8) the high bluffs and cliffs of the Pacific coast, (9) the steep volcanic slopes of Hawaii, and (10) the island cliffs and glaciers of Alaska. The degree of slope, horizontal curvature, texture (e.g., roughness) of the slope's mineral surface, coloration, and vegetative characteristics of the land form are among the primary determinants of the specific aesthetic quality of the shore and of the susceptibility of the shore to adverse impacts of development. Vegetation may be of particular importance; when slopes are well wooded, minor development may be partially masked.

Surface qualities include color, ridge line or bluff-crest curvature, compositional qualities, contrast between near and far landforms or vegetational forms, and other appearance characteristics.

Analysis of surface characteristics, as well as of form and use, may aid in determining whether a coastal landscape unit is aesthetically unique, typical of a valued class of landscape, or scenically commonplace. Analysis of the use compatibilities of existing or proposed development is possible upon determining the degree of congruity or complementarity, or the lack thereof, of the development of structures or of land, water, and vegetational modifications, with the forms and other characteristics of the natural site or existing development. Through analysis the aesthetic suitabilities of landscape units for preservation, recreational use, and development, by type and degree of intensity, can be defined.

Landscapes vary widely, and area-by-area analysis is necessary before the application of specific criteria or performance standards for proposed development. Some of the important parameters are setback, height, spacing, roof types, and exterior materials and colors.

Setback

Generally, the closer a structure stands to the shore, dune ridge, bluff crest, or other local horizon, the more prominent and potentially obtrusive the structure may be. Thus the greater the setback from such horizons employed for nonshore structures or groups of structures, the less is the likelihood of adverse aesthetic impact upon shore users (shore structures being defined as those serving a boating, fishing, shipping, or other intrinsically shore-related role).

Height

Generally, the higher the structure, the more prominent and obstrusive it may be. This is particularly true of structures with forms of rigid geometry (i.e., disharmonious with natural forms on the coast). True cylinders and Cartesian slabs, for example, such as can be seen in some water towers and apartment buildings, respectively, are not as harmonious with natural coastal forms as traditional lighthouses (tapered cylinders) and peaked-roof houses (the peaks being evocative of dune crests, tree crowns, and other rhythmic points along the shore).

Spacing

The more asymmetric the spacing and the greater the availability of spacing between houses along natural, rural, or recreational shorelines, the greater the degree of sympathy with natural forms and rhythms that can be achieved. Concentration of individual housing units in unrigid clusters is aesthetically desirable, provided that greater spacing is allowed nearby to compensate for the higher densities.

Roof Types

Ridges and slopes are highly desirable features of building roofs in shore areas, since the peak forms achieved create harmonies with dunes, hills, and other natural forms of the coast. Even when the latter are absent, the presence of peaked roofs introduces forms similar, rather than dissimilar, to those found in coastal nature.

Exterior Materials and Colors

Reflective metals are not harmonious with most natural coastal materials. Although they are sometimes unavoidable, they are not as desirable as dull-finished, painted, or coated metals. Similarly, reflective glass is not as sympathetic as tinted, low-reflective glass; and corrugated metal and Fiberglas components are not as harmonius as wood, masonry, rough-aggregate concrete, and other earth-related materials. Pastel and other color tints or hues not indigenous to the coast are less desirable than earth colors (brown, mustard, green, ochre, etc.) or marine colors (sea blue, white and gray; black and red appear in nature and in navigation aids). Dark, earth-related colors (e.g., forest green or blue–green) are more suitable for tall structures such as water towers or fuel tanks than are light or sky colors (e.g., sky blue, pale green) because the viewer interprets a recognizably earth-bound object as rational if it fits with the ground environment, but irrational if it is made to appear as part of the sky. Painted patterns and other camouflage, either subtle or bold, may constructively be used to treat tall structures, depending on site conditions and urban–nonurban context.

SITE LANDSCAPE

Natural or naturalized earth forms (mounds, dunes, berms) maintained in the foreground of low or "medium-rise" structures will tend to mask the structures, particularly to viewers at close range. Such forms maintained as background will also tend to harmonize structures, especially those that possess bulk forms and roof shapes harmonius with them. The actual effect will depend also on the existence of major landscape features with similar rhythms and forms in the near or far distance.

Existing dunes, marshes, bluffs, and other fragile or unique landscape features should be maintained to enhance site development, as well as for ecological considerations. Wood-frame housing, including multiple-unit groupings, can often be developed on open substructures (pilings, deep footings, etc.), permitting the retention of existing terrain and vegetation beneath.

Site layout of buildings within given property boundaries may be varied to permit the preservation of fragile shore features; site conditions should be carefully studied to determine optimum plan alternatives.

Shore vegetation should be retained for aesthetic, as well as ecological, protection. Housing and marine elements on open understructures may aid in partial retention of marsh vegetation, although sunlight penetration will be limited. Avoiding the clear-cutting of wooded frontage will aid in preventing undesirable exposure of shore development when housing is sited on bluff tops or slopes; building structures with low profiles that merge with earth forms can enhance the integration of development with the shore environment. The retention of existing trees and shrubs and the planting of others can also aid in harmonizing development. Sloping roof forms and rooftop plantings of shrubs and forbs can also serve to integrate buildings with site topography and vegetation, particularly when buildings are designed to merge with ground slopes.

Underground or partially below-grade construction of parking facilities, some utilities and commercial structures, and even housing is feasible in upland areas where depth to water table allows. The below-grade parking area at Stonehenge, England, has provided significant aesthetic protection for this major archaeological asset and its landscape setting.

HEIGHT–DENSITY RELATIONSHIPS

High-density, high-rise housing development is of greater visual impact than spread single-unit housing and requires less land utilization; on the other hand, low-profiled buildings and low density create less visual impact in natural, rural, and semiurban areas. This anomaly can sometimes be resolved by locating high-density developments at substantial distances behind the coastal edge. Loss of shore amenity advantages for occupants may be offset by providing shuttle-vehicle access to shore edges and by allowing partial emergence of building tops above treelines.

HAZARD ZONE CONSTRUCTION

Housing, marine, and other small-scale development may often be constructed on open-work substructures for protective purposes in flood hazard areas. Examples of raised resi-

dential construction may be found on dunes of barrier beaches, in or near wetlands, and on floodplains. Such structural emplacement creates less environmental impact than development on filled-in wetlands and floodplains or on truncated or otherwise modified sand dunes. Avoidance of construction in wetland and dune systems altogether is the most effective environmental planning measure. If construction cannot be avoided, however, siting raised structures in troughs and overwash areas in the lee of dune systems and on the upland edges of wetlands may be the desirable alternative. Sanitary code, other water quality, human safety, and wildlife protection constraints must also be taken into full account.

ACCESS

Large-scale facilities and concentrated development, whether utilities or residential structures, diminish the aesthetic value of a natural or rural coastal landscape. Significant setback from the shore is thus a recommended standard for most development, as stated above. To require such setback for shoreland property owners and shore users, adequate and efficient access should be demonstrated. For utilities, a setback of several miles, for aesthetic and ecological reasons, can be achieved simply with extended piping for cooling water and effluent and an easement for service access. For residential owners, setting housing development at a significant distance from the shore or behind the crest of the first major bluff or ridge may be compensated for by improvement of feeder drives to the shore or, preferably, by providing bike paths and minibuses, jitneys, and other communal vehicles.

REFERENCES

California Coastal Zone Conservation Commissions. 1975. *California Coastal Plan.* San Francisco, California.

Kenneth H. Craik. 1972. "Psychological factors in landscape appraisal." *Environment and Behavior,* Vol. 4, p. 3.

R. Burton Litton, Jr., Robert J. Tetlow, Jens Sorensen, and Russell A. Beatty. 1974. *Water and Landscape: An Aesthetic Overview of the Role* of *Water in the Landscape*. Water Information Center, Inc., Port Washington, New York.

Roy Mann Associates, Inc. 1975. *Aesthetic Resources of the Coastal Zone*. Prepared for the Office of Coastal Zone Management, National Oceanic and Atmospheric Administration, Washington, D.C.

Roy Mann Associates, Inc. 1975. *Shoreline Appearance and Design: A Planning Handbook*. Prepared for the New England River Basins Commission and the National Parks Service, Cambridge, Massachusetts.

E. H. Zube. 1973. "Scenery as a natural resource." *Landscape Architecture*, Vol. 63, p. 2.

34. STORM HAZARDS

N. Arthur Pore
Techniques Development Laboratory
National Weather Service
Silver Spring, Maryland

The major storms that affect coastal areas of the United States cause flooding, property destruction, erosion, and loss of life. They are of two general types—tropical cyclones (which originate in tropical latitudes), and extratropical cyclones (which form in middle or high latitudes).

Tropical cyclones go through various stages of development and are classified according to their intensity. The maximum wind speed of a tropical cyclone is commonly used for classification. If the wind speed is less than 38 mpg, the storm is called a "tropical depression." Storms with winds of 38 to 73 mph are termed "tropical storms," and those with winds of 74 mph or greater are classified as "hurricanes."

Tropical cyclones form only over ocean areas where warm moist air is available. This air flows into the cyclonic circulation, ascends, and cools to the saturation point. The heat released in the subsequent condensation process is added to the storm as energy. The amount of energy in a hurricane is extremely large. For example, it has been estimated that, if the heat released by a hurricane in 1 day were converted to electricity, it could supply electrical power to the United States for a 6-month period.[1]

Hurricanes that affect the east and Gulf coasts of the United States originate in the tropical Atlantic, the Caribbean, or the Gulf of Mexico. Hurricanes do form along the west coast of Mexico and Central America, but their effects seldom reach as far north as California.

Most of the North Atlantic and Gulf of Mexico tropical cyclones occur in the months of August through October. Table 1 shows the monthly occurrence of hurricanes and is based on data from 1901 through 1963.[2]

Extratropical cyclones are important to United States coastal areas mainly during the winter months. They develop along frontal zones separating major air masses of different origins. Most important are the storms that develop as waves along the polar front. Some of these waves develop into intense low-pressure systems and cause very severe coastal weather conditions. The wind blows counterclockwise around these low-pressure systems. There is generally a frontal system in such storms, which consists of a cold front in the rear of the storm, separating the polar air from the warmer tropical air of the southern portion, and a warm front, which generally extends from the storm center through the forward part of the storm. Mature extratropical storms generally have occluded fronts at the surface. The most common type occurs when then cold front overtakes the warm front near the center of the low and forces it to rise.

The tracks of extratropical cyclones affecting the United States coastal areas generally are over three main areas.[3] One group of storms progresses through the northeast part of the country, along the Great Lakes and St. Law-

Table 7.34.1   Percent frequencies of North Atlantic, Caribbean, and Gulf of Mexico tropical cyclones by month for the years 1901–1963

June	July	August	September	October	November through May	Total
6.6	7.4	22.6	34.6	22.0	6.8	100

SOURCE: Reference 2.

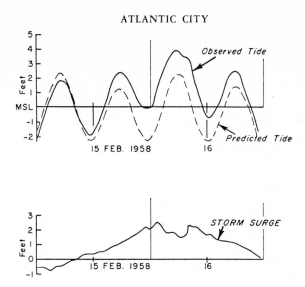

Figure 7.34.1 Example of tide data, showing the observed tide, the predicted tide, and the storm surge for a moderate winter storm.

rence Valley sections. Another major group forms over the southeast part of the country or the Gulf of Mexico and moves northeastward. Included in this group are storms that develop near the North Carolina and Virginia Capes area; these usually move rapidly toward the northeast. The third group consists of storms that move from the Aleutian Island area off the Pacific northwest coast.

The flooding and property destruction characteristics of coastal storms results mainly from abnormally high water levels and high wave conditions. The high storm tides consist of two components—the normal astronomical tide and the storm surge. "Storm surge" is defined as the meteorological effect on sea level and is computed as the algebraic difference between the observed tide and the normal astronomical tide. Figure 1 illustrates this definition with a 2-day length of tide record.

The principal factors involved in the generation and modification of storm surges are as follows:

1. The wind stress effect, which is the rise in water level caused by the force of the wind acting on the water. This effect on water height is greater for higher wind speeds and is inversely proportional to the water depth.

2. The reduction of atmospheric pressure, generally called the "inverted barometer effect," which causes an increase in sea level in areas of low pressure.

3. The transport of water by waves and swell in the shallow water area near shore.

4. The modifying effects of coastline configuration and offshore bottom topography. such as convergence or divergence in bays.

The time of occurrence of the storm surge with respect to the stage of the normal astronomical tide is important and can mean the difference between serious and minor flooding. Storm surges that occur at high tide result in higher and more damaging water levels.

As hurricanes approach or cross the coastline, they are often accompanied by storm surges of 4 to 10 feet. The peak surges generally occur to the right of the hurricane centers (facing the direction of storm movement), where the maximum onshore winds are experienced. Storm surges higher than 10 feet occasionally occur. For example, the famous Galveston hurricane of 1900, in which 6000 people lost their lives, had a storm tide of 14.5 feet above mean sea level. Hurricane Audrey of 1957, which claimed 350 lives, produced tide heights of over 12 feet above mean sea level at locations near Cameron, Louisiana.[4] Hurricane Camille of August 1969 was one of the most intense storms on record and caused the highest storm tides recorded along the United States coast.[5] Camille came inland from the Gulf of Mexico just east of Bay St. Louis, Mississippi. Wind gusts were estimated to be at least 190 mph at Bay St. Louis, and gusts of 150 mph were estimated to the east near Biloxi, Mississippi. The highest storm tide was measured as 24.6 feet above mean sea level near Pass Christian, Mississippi. Damage caused by Camille was estimated to exceed $1.4 billion. Major hurricanes have also affected the east coast of the United States. The September 1938 hurricane caused a maximum storm surge of over 14 feet on the south shore of Long Island. In 1954 hurricane Carol caused tides of 10 to 14 feet above mean sea level in the Narragansett Bay area.

Storm surges produced by extratropical storms are usually not as high as those caused by hurricanes, although some sections of the coast have experienced their highest water levels from extratropical storms. This is especially true in the New England area. Extratropical storm surges generally rise slower and stay up longer than those caused by hurricanes.

The high tides and waves generated by the storm of March 5–8, 1962, caused unprecedented damage to coastal areas from southern New England to Florida.[6] The persistent strong northeast winds over a large area off the east coast were responsible. An important factor was that the storm occurred at a time of exceptionally high astronomical tides.

Waves superimposed on the high storm tides cause much destruction of property. The height and length of the waves arriving at the shore are dependent on meterological conditions in the area of wave generation.[7] Wave height and length are determined by the wind speed, the length of the fetch (the distance the wind blows over the water in a relatively constant direction), and the length of time the wind blows over the fetch.

As the waves approach the shore, the shoaling effect of the shallow depth becomes quite important. The drag of the ocean bottom causes the waves to travel slower and become steeper. When the waves reach a depth of about 1.3 times the wave height, they become unstable and break.[8]

Another effect is that of refraction in depths of less than about half the length of the wave. Refraction is the bending of the waves caused by the friction of the bottom. This affects the speed in such a way that the parts of the wave in the shallowest water travel the slowest. Refraction causes the wave energy to converge on shore headlands and points and to diverge from concave shoreline recesses.

A different wave effect is of importance off the Pacific northwest coast of the United States. Waves and swell generated by extratropical storms in this area approach shore and cause very hazardous conditions in the vicinity of the bars in the mouth of the Columbia River and at the entrance to Yaquina Bay.[9] Lives are lost each year by boat operators attempting to cross these areas during adverse wave conditions. When wave conditions are especially severe, even large ships must wait for the situation to improve before crossing the treacherous bar area. An example of a severe storm in this area was that of November 3–6, 1969. At the Columbia River entrance 30-foot breakers were reported in the ship channel, and the bar pilots considered the bar closed to shipping for about 20 hours.[10]

In addition to damage to structures such as buildings and docks, these waves can cause severe beach erosion. The waves stir up the sand and tend to eat away the beaches. Then a current moving along shore, caused by the high, steep waves, transports the loosened sand along the shore. The damaging erosion is therefore caused by a combination of the high water levels, which let the erosion occur inland beyond the normal beach line, and the steep waves approaching the shore at a critical angle.

The detection and forecasting of tropical cyclones is the responsibility of the National Hurricane Center in Miami, Florida, and several National Weather Service Forecast Offices in coastal areas. The detection and monitoring of these storms is accomplished by a radar network that covers the east and Gulf coasts, by reconnaissance of civilian and military aircraft, by photographs from satellites, and by analysis of the hundreds of meterological observations available several times daily. Forecasting of the storm track and intensity is done by experienced personnel with some guidance from computerized models of storm processes. When such a storm moves within range to threaten a coast, a *hurricane watch* is announced for the threatened area. A *hurricane warning* is issued when a hurricane is forecast to reach a coastal area within 24 hours. The storm surges caused by tropical storms are forecast by putting storm forecast information into a computerized model of storm surge generation.[11] Data such as the intensity, speed, direction, and track of the storm are the input to the model. The forecast consists of the height of the storm surge along the open coast of the affected area.

Forecasting of extratropical storm conditions for coastal areas is done at National Weather Service Forecast Offices by considering the analysis of weather conditions at the surface and in the upper levels of the atmosphere and the numerical weather forecasts made by the National Meteorological Center in Suitland, Maryland. Forecasters estimate the storm surge by considering the offshore meteorological conditions such as the wind velocity and fetch length. Guidance for forecasting extratropical storm surge is obtained for the northeast coast of the United States from a computerized statistical model that relates the surge height to the offshore meteorological conditions.[12]

Meteorological and climatological conditions are so varied for different coastal areas that for planning purposes each segment of the coast should be studied separately in great detail. Climatological records of weathers, tide levels, wave conditions, and storm tracks should be considered. Estimates can be made of the most intense storm conditions that might affect a particular area. The most severe wave, storm surge, and flooding conditions that can be expected in the area can then be calculated.

REFERENCES

1. G. E. Dunn and B. I. Miller. 1964. *Atlantic Hurricanes.* Louisiana State University Press, Baton Rouge, Louisiana.
2. G. W. Cry. 1965. *Tropical Cyclones of the North Atlantic Ocean, Tracks and Frequencies of Hurricanes and Tropical Storms, 1871–1963,* U.S. Weather Bureau, Technical Paper No. 55, Washington, D.C.
3. W. H. Klein. 1957. *Principal Tracks and Mean Frequencies of Cyclones and Anticyclones in the Northern Hemisphere,* U.S. Weather Bureau, Research Paper No. 40, Washington, D.C.
4. D. L. Harris. 1958. *Hurricane Audrey Storm Tide.* National Hurricane Research Project, U.S. Weather Bureau, Report No. 23, Washington, D.C.
5. R. H. Simpson, A. L. Sugg, and Staff, 1970. "The Atlantic Hurricane Season of 1969." *Monthly Weather Review,* Vol. 98, No. 4, pp. 293–306 (April).
6. J. Q. Stewart. 1962. "The Great Atlantic Coast Tides of 5–8 March, 1962. *Weatherwise,* Vol. 15, pp. 116–120 (June).
7. W. Bascom. 1964. *Waves and Beaches.* Anchor Books. Doubleday and Company, Garden City, New York.
8. U.S. Army Coastal Engineering Research Center. 1966. *Shore Protection Planning and Design.* Technical Report No. 4, 3rd ed., Washington, D.C.
9. W. H. Quinn and D. B. Enfield. 1971. *The Development of Forecast Techniques for Wave and Surf Conditions Over the Bars in the Columbia River Mouth and at the Entrance to Yaquina Bay,* Oregon State University, Final Report, Contract No. E–225–69 (N), Corvallis, Oregon.
10. G. B. Burdwell. *An Outstanding Storm Off the Coast of Oregon and Washington, November 3–6, 1969.* Unpublished Weather Bureau Report.
11. C. P. Jelenianski. 1972. *SPLASH (Special Program to List Amplitudes of Surges from Hurricanes).* I: *Landfall Storms.* National Oceanic and Atmospheric Administration, Technical Memorandum No. NWS TDL–46, Silver Spring Maryland.
12. N. A. Pore. 1973. *Automated Forecasting of Extratropical Storm Surges for the Northeast Coast of the United States.* Fifth Annual Offshore Technology Conference, Paper No. OTC 1830, Houston, Texas, April 29–May 2.

35. STORMWATER DETENTION

David L. Taylor
Taylor, Wiseman and Taylor
Consulting Engineers
Mt. Laurel, New Jersey

In recent years, there has been a general increase in concern about flood problems along the rivers, streams, and coastal waters of the

United States. There are two primary causes of these flood problems; first, improperly located development that can be damaged by flooding within floodprone areas along streams, rivers, and coasts; and, second, the increased flood flows and heights that result from urban, suburban, and agricultural use of land.

In the past the tendency has been to wait until problems develop and then take care of them. Flood control dikes and dams along United States rivers attest to this approach. More recently, however, increasing emphasis has been placed on measures that will prevent flood problems. These measures primarily involve regulation and control of land use in flood hazard areas along coasts, streams, and rivers. They are evolving as a result of the National Flood Insurance Program at the federal level and numerous programs at state and local levels that delineate and regulate the use of land within flood hazard areas. To a lesser but significant extent, these measures also involve requirements, usually established at the local level, for retarding stormwater runoff from developed areas in order to offset the increase in peak flows caused by such development. Detention basins are one method of retarding and attenuating peak flows.

Probably the easiest way to understand what a detention basin does is to visualize a bathtub. Assume that the tub will hold 50 gallons, that it drains at the rate of 5 gallons per minute (gpm), and that the flow from the faucet into the tub is 10 gpm. Since the inflow rate is 5 gpm more than the outflow rate, the tub will fill at the rate of 5 gpm. Of course, the tub will overflow after 10 minutes and the outflow rate will then equal the inflow rate. However, during the 10-minute period the storage in the tub will reduce the outflow to 5 gpm from the 10-gpm rate that would prevail if there were no storage.

If we change our assumptions slightly and the faucet is opened gradually to provide an inflow that increases uniformly from 0 to 10 gpm over a 20-minute period and then is gradually closed so that flow decreases uniformly to zero during the succeeding 20 minutes, the flow into the tub will occur over a 40-minute period. During the first 10 minutes outflow will equal inflow, and no storage will occur. During the next 20 minutes

inflow will exceed outflow, and the excess will be stored. During the last 10 minutes the inflow will drop below the 5-gpm outflow, and as a result outflow will exceed inflow and the storage will start to empty. Outflow will continue to the 45th minute, at which time the tub will be empty.

This is roughly analogous to what happens in a detention basin for stormwater runoff except that, in most cases, the rate of outflow will not be constant. Rather, it will vary with the depth and thus with the amount of water stored in the basin. In simple terms, then, a detention basin is a device that receives runoff from a surface area on which rain falls, temporarily stores a portion of such runoff, and thereby causes the peak rate of outflow to be less than the peak rate of inflow. In most applications the primary reason for doing this is to reduce flooding problems in downstream areas. There are, however, other reasons or benefits.

When soils are sandy and the groundwater table is well below the bottom of the basin, a considerable amount of groundwater recharge can be accomplished. In some cases, where groundwater recharge is of paramount importance or no adequate outlet is available, the entire outflow is handled through seepage into the ground. This results in a relatively low outlet rate and hence, a relatively high storage requirement.

Another benefit of detention basins is that they cause sedimentation of at least a portion of the eroded soils that are suspended in the runoff entering the basin. As a result sedimentation and turbidity in downstream channels are reduced, and the adverse environmental effects thereof minimized. When sedimentation basins are required during construction, because of the excessive erosion that can occur at that time, detention basins can be effectively used for this purpose. A slight increase in the depth, to receive the sediment, and a temporary modification of the outlet arrangement, to ensure low water velocities through the basin, will usually suffice.

Another reason for or benefit of using a detention basin is reduction of the cost of downstream drainage facilities. Often replacement or enlargement of existing facilities can be avoided, or the size of a long outfall pipeline or channel can be significantly reduced. Such savings can far exceed the cost of the basin.

Finally, the basin area can serve other purposes unrelated to the quality or quantity of water flow. It can often be used as a playfield, a park area, or, with provision of additional depth, a permanent pond. In the last case temporary storage of runoff must be provided above the normal water level. Still another possible purpose is natural open space. Leaving it, or allowing it to grow, as natural woodland can be very desirable both visually and environmentally.

Detention basins are most often used in connection with new development when it is desirable to minimize or offset the increase in peak rates of runoff caused by such development. The increase in rate of runoff has two primary causes, namely, the change of a portion of the land surface from vegetation to roof and pavement, and the decrease in flow time from all of the points of the upstream drainage area due to construction of gutters, pipelines, and channels. In the case of an area covered by impervious surfaces, virtually the entire rainfall runs off, and the resulting peak rate and volume of runoff can be four or more times as great as those from the same area with mature vegetation. Although the effect of the decrease in flow time is not as signicant, it does reduce the storm duration necessary to cause peak rates. Peak flow rates, not volume, increase because of the higher rainfall intensity characteristic of the shorter-duration storm. In most cases detention basins provide only for the reduction of peak rates of downstream flow. Volume of flow is not reduced unless soils, water table, and outlet conditions are such that a significant amount of seepage will occur in the basin.

A typical situation in which a detention basin might be used is pictured in Figure 1. The area is to be developed, and a drainage system of pipes and channels will carry runoff to the low point of the area at A. The basic problem is to provide a detention basin at point A with enough storage to ensure that the postdevelopment peak rate of outflow does not exceed the predevelopment peak. In very general terms the steps in the design process would be as follows:

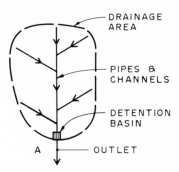

Figure 7.35.1   Typical basin area configuration.

1. Determine the predevelopment peak flow rate at point A. This will be the maximum outflow rate permitted from the basin.
2. Determine the inflow hydrograph that will require the maximum storage. A hydrograph is a curve that relates time with flow rate. The typical runoff hydrograph, resulting from rainfall, initially has a rising line, where the rate of runoff increases with time to a peak, and then a falling line, where the rate of runoff decreases with time. See Figure 2.
3. Using the inflow and outflow data, estimate the storage required. On the basis of the peak outflow permitted and the estimated storage, determine the basin dimensions and the hydraulic characteristics of the outflow structure.
5. Using the basin dimensions and hydraulics of the outflow structure, determine the storage–outflow relationship.
6. On the basis of the inflow hydrograph and the storage–outflow relationships, perform a flood routing through the basin and thereby determine the required storage, the outflow hydrograph, and the peak rate of outflow.
7. Compare the results in step 6 to the estimates made in previous steps. If they are not in close agreement, revise the estimates accordingly and repeat the procedure until the results of a subsequent flood routing are satisfactory.

The design procedure set forth is very general in nature, and the problem is, in fact, fairly complex. However, for basins serving small areas of up to a few hundred acres,

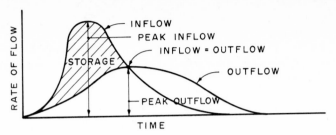

Figure 7.35.2   Stormwater flow at a detention basin.

simplifying assumptions can usually be made that will reduce the problem to workable dimensions. The most difficult aspect is determination of the inflow hydrograph. In the vast majority of cases this must be developed without stream gauging data. Derivation of the hydrograph must proceed from rainfall data or from local runoff formulas based on various characteristics of the drainage area to be served by the basin. Often rational formula theory is used as a basis for development of the hydrograph. In any case caution is needed because there are an infinite number of possible hydrographs, and it is necessary to pick the one that will give the most accurate picture of the peak storage required. In particular, it should be pointed out that the storm duration required to yield the peak flow/rate is shorter than that required to yield the peak storage. When rational formula theory is being used for hydrograph development, it is therefore necessary to consider storms of longer duration than the time of concentration for the basin drainage area. Various methods for hydrograph selection are used; the method chosen will depend to a great extent on the specific conditions at a site, including potential downstream flood damage.

Flood routing procedures are covered in any number of publications. They are based on the continuity equation, that is, inflow minus storage equals outflow. From the start of inflow to the end of outflow, at any point in time, the equation holds true for volumes to that time and for rates at that time.

Figure 2 shows the result of the process. In this case both inflow and outflow increase with time, but initially inflow exceeds outflow. The vertical difference between the two curves represents the rate of increase in storage, and the area difference the volume of storage. At the point of intersection of the curves, inflow equals outflow and the peak rate of outflow and the peak volume of storage are reached. The area between the two curves to the left of the intersection point represents the maximum storage required. At times to the right of the intersection point, outflow exceeds inflow, and the vertical difference between the two curves represents the rate of decrease in storage.

Probably the simplest form of detention basin is an earth bank with a pipe through it that limits flow. Water is temporarily stored on the upstream side of the bank. Often, however, this arrangement is not possible, and in such cases the basin is constructed by appropriate excavation and embankment over the entire basin area. In still other cases simple widening of a channel or the adjoining floodplain area will provide the needed storage, and the existing downstream channel or conduit will provide the flow limitation.

In the end analysis any measure that temporarily stores runoff and thereby reduces peak downstream rates of flow can be considered a detention basin. Such measures can include restriction of the capacity of roof drains and storm drainage inlet points on parking lots and streets. Depression of landscaped areas and limitation of outflow therefrom can also be helpful. Generally speaking, requirements covering storm drainage facilities in developed areas have tended toward increasing flow-carrying capacities. Although this increase reduces temporary flooding of pavements, roofs, and landscaped areas, in many cases it aggravates downstream flooding conditions. In determining design standards for such facilities, due consideration should be given to this problem, and wherever feasible the standards should provide for limiting rather than carrying peak flows.

In coastal areas there are many locations where the measures outlined here will have little or no effect on flood problems. In the oceans and in the rivers and bays proximate thereto, flooding is caused primarily by tides and winds; rainfall runoff is not a factor. However, on streams above the head of tide and often for considerable distances below the head of tide, the rate of runoff is the major or only factor. In portions of coastal areas where this is the case, detention basins can be used to advantage. When other advantages of such basins, such as groundwater recharge or sedimentation, are important, basins can be used even though downstream flow reduction is not important. In particular, groundwater recharge can be beneficial in coastal areas where saltwater intrusion is adversely affecting water supplies.

Under some circumstances the effect of a basin on downstream flooding may not be beneficial. If we consider the effect of a tributary stream on a river, it may be that the peak flow from the tributary normally occurs well ahead of that in the river. A basin placed on the tributary could delay the peak therefrom to a time when the river was reaching its crest and thus actually increase the tributary contribution to peak river flow and flooding. Such an occurrence would depend on the movement of storms, the relative sizes of tributary and river drainage areas, and other factors.

In cases where the purpose of a basin is to limit the flow contribution from the basin drainage area to a stream having a drainage area significantly larger than that of the basin, the outlet flow limitation should be based on the contribution to the stream at the time of peak flow in the stream rather than at the time of peak flow from the basin drainage area. When the area to be developed is adjacent to the stream to be protected, it is often possible to simply provide additional floodplain storage along the stream. When this is done, there can be no question about the efficacy of the storage provided.

Although under some conditions and circumstances a single basin can provide little benefit, it is the author's conviction that a number of basins, each serving a portion of a larger watershed, will be significantly beneficial. This is borne out to some extent by the fact that many formulas for determining peak flows include a factor or term for the percentage of ponds, lakes, or swamps. As the percentage of such areas increases, peak flows decrease.

The use of reasonable measures for stormwater detention is highly recommended.

REFERENCES

Herbert G. Poertner. *Practices in Detention of Urban Storm Water Runoff.* American Public Works Association, Special Report No. 43.

36. STORMWATER RUNOFF

Roy Burke III
Civil Engineering Department
University of Virginia
Charlottesville, Virginia

The natural system has always endured recurring periods of water excess and scarcity—floods and drought. Furthermore, over the ages the natural system has developed an interrelated and extremely efficient set of structures and processes for dealing with these excesses and scarcities. In fact, it can be strongly suggested that the natural system actually requires these periodic pulses as a necessary ingredient in its continuing existence. However, the point to be emphasized here is that the natural system provides examples of the most efficient ways (1) to manage excessive stormwater and, at the same time, (2) to extract benefits from this resource. For instance, broad, flat floodplains can regulate excessive stormflows and at the same time provide the opportunity for biological systems to extract nutrients and other valuable materials.

Man's activities, on the other hand, tend to conflict with these evolutionary structures and processes in the natural system. First, man prefers floodplain lands for his development purposes; this reduces natural storage space and establishes a potential for economic flood damages. Second, man constructs large areas of impervious surface that increase the volume of surface runoff and transport these larger volumes much more quickly to downstream receptors. And, third, man substantially alters the quality of overland flow from that which would naturally occur.

Impacts from these alterations in natural occurrences can be grouped into two broad categories: (1) impacts on man himself, and (2) impacts on the natural system. On man himself, one can identify impacts such as a reduction in recharge to subsurface water supplies, an increase in economic flood damages, and an impairment of waste treatment processes and the functioning of other water management facilities. On the natural system, the impacts are typical of those associated with pollution discharges in general and with other alterations of the natural hydrological regime.

Instead of perceiving stormwater as a valuable resource, man in his urban context has historically considered it to be a nuisance, something to be gotten out of the way as quickly as possible. With this in mind, he has developed a sophisticated array of facilities for removing efficiently large volumes of stormwater from urban areas, thus reducing its immediate nuisance potential.

In earlier days stormwater and urban wastewater were transported together in the same sewers, called "combined systems." However, storm flows can easily inundate waste treatment facilities and flush large volumes of raw pollution into receiving waters. This type of problem encouraged, in the 1950s and 1960s, a very expensive nationwide crusade to modify all urban combined systems so that wastewater and stormwater could be transported in separate, unconnected sewers, called "separate systems." Underlying this effort was the unquestioned rationale that urban surface runoff was merely rainwater, that is, clean water that should not be mixed with the dirty water—urban wastewater.

This rationale, however, misrepresented the nature of urban surface runoff, which, for this article, can be defined as the fraction of the total fainfall that does not return (soon) to the atmosphere or does not infiltrate into local groundwater systems. It has become clear through recent studies that apparently in-

nocuous stormwater carries a substantial source of water pollution created by the composite of man's total urban activities. Remaining paragraphs will thus (1) attempt to define the range of characteristics of stormwater as a pollutant, and (2) suggest management policies that can be applied to this nonpoint source of pollution.

If one takes a careful look around any urban area, the sources of storm runoff contamination will gradually become apparent. The problem is that each source by itself may appear inconsequential; however, when aggregated into a single storm washout, these separate small sources can add up to a substantial pollution loading. Although sources of contamination differ widely from area to area, depending on geography, climate, and land use, to name just a few factors, the following list illustrates their basic character:

1. *Rainfall itself.* Washout of particles, aerosols, and gases from the atmosphere.
2. *Street litter.* Material that accumulates on streets and parking lot surfaces.
3. *Yard refuse.* Leaves, grass, limbs, and so forth.
4. *Improper garbage handling.* Seepage from garbage cans and refuse piles.
5. *Stagnant water.* Water in depressions, containers, or, particularly, catch basins along each street.
6. *Car washings.* Soap and dirt from vehicle and other outdoor cleaning activities.
7. *Fuel and chemical spillage.* From bulk storage and handling.
8. *Lawn sprinkling.* Washdown of dirt, fertilizers, pesticides, and so forth.
9. *Vehicle drippings.* Gasoline, oil, brake fluid, and so forth from the periodic hosing down of service station areas.
10. *Commercial and industrial.* Exposure of potential contaminants to rainfall and seepage.
11. *Construction and maintenance.* Dirt piles, debris, erosion, and so forth.
12. *Areal spraying programs.* For mosquito control and the like.
13. *Illicit dumping.* Any foreign material dumped or poured into streets.
14. *Septic tanks, privies, inactive garbage dumps.* Seepage after rainfall

15. *Poorly paved or unpaved streets.* Disintegrated, washed out paving material, oil used for dust control on unpaved surfaces, and so forth.
16. *Animal droppings, dead animals.* Potential source of disease organisms.
17. *Snow and ice control.* Chemicals used for street clearance.

Usually street litter, direct erosion, and catch basin accumulations are identified as the primary sources of runoff pollution. But in addition there is an aggregation of surface-water pollutants from each person's individual activities. Thus good housekeeping is required at each point of origin to truly combat the contamination of urban surface runoff. It is not sufficient to focus attention only on the primary sources: litter, erosion, and catch basins.

Given these widespread, disjointed sources of potential contamination, any rainfall (or nonstorm flushing of urban surfaces) will combine and accumulate these materials as the surface flow moves through the urban drainage system. With this as the underlying process, one can readily see that the profile of urban runoff characteristics will be highly variable even within a single area. However, surveys[1-3] of localities throughout the country provide a generalized description of surface runoff that can be compared to that of typical raw domestic sewage. (See Table 1.)

It would not be appropriate, because of tremendous variations in the quality of both types of wastes, to make specific predictive statements about any given area; much more site-specific data would be required for this purpose. However, these generalized characteristics (Table 1) conform well to those of other contaminant profiles reported in the literature, and hence certain general statements about

Table 7.36.1   Comparison of contaminant profiles for urban surface runoff and raw domestic sewage

Constitutent*	Urban Surface Runoff	Raw Domestic Sewage
Suspended solids	250–300	150–250
Biochemical oxygen demand	10–250	300–350
Nutrients:		
(a) Total nitrogen	0.5–5.0	25–85
(b) Total phosphorus	0.5–5.0	2–15
Coliform bacteria, MPN/100 ml	10^4 to 10^6	10^6 or greater
Chlorides	20–200	15–75
Miscellaneous substances:		
(a) Oil and grease	yes	yes
(b) Heavy metals**	(10 to 100) times sewage concentration	traces
(c) Pesticides	yes	seldom
(d) Other toxins	potential exists	seldom

* All concentrations expressed as milligrams per liter, unless otherwise noted.

** Lead, zinc, copper, nickel, chromium, among others.

the quality of urban surface runoff can be made.

1. Solids contents in urban surface drainage approximate, and may even exceed, those in raw domestic sewage.
2. Biochemical oxygen demand (BOD) concentrations can reach high levels during storms. It would be reasonable to expect BOD concentrations of 0.1 to 0.2 of the BOD levels in typical raw domestic sewage. These concentrations more closely approximate those found in treated (secondary) sewage.
3. Stormwater should be considered to be an important source of nutrients, nitrogen, and phosphorus, when these substances are evaluated as potential pollutants.
4. Storm runoff contains fewer intestinal bacteria (coliforms) than raw sewage but many more organisms than would be permitted in "safe" public swimming waters, according to certain existing standards. Moreover, field studies have found organisms in surface runoff that would be pathogenic to man and other organisms not generally present in raw domestic sewage.
5. Oil and grease are not uncommon ingredients in surface runoff. The same can be said for chlorides, which approximate the levels of these chemicals reported for raw domestic sewage.
6. Urban storm drainage should be viewed as a potential source of various toxic materials, such as heavy metals, pesticides, and polychlorinated biphenyls. Observed concentrations have varied widely; however, these contaminants are not likely to be found in typical urban domestic sewage (unless industries discharge wastes to the sewers).

Hence urban storm drainage should be viewed as a source of water pollution contributing undesirable solids, organic material, nutrients, toxic substances, and other constituents. It confronts us as a pollutant only periodically, that is, during storms. However, because storms deposit huge volumes of water during relatively short intervals, the quick washoff or "shock load" effect often complicates our efforts to deal with runoff pollution: (1) shock loads may contain contaminant

levels that far exceed those given in Table 1, (2) huge pulses of water complicate the design of facilities that can more easily cope with continuous flow conditions, and (3) shock loads in both quantity and quality may overwhelm the absorptive capacities of natural receiving waters, which may likewise be capable of handling more uniform pollution loadings.

In general, the pollutant concentrations in storm runoff increase proportionally with the passage of time since the last rainfall. The longer the dry spells between storms, the more contaminants will accumulate. Thus a storm today will produce higher concentrations than a second or third storm tomorrow. Usually, though, it takes only about one relatively rainless week for enough materials to accumulate to restore potential contaminants to full strength.

In view of these factors and characteristics, the effective management of runoff pollution becomes an exceedingly complex problem. Nevertheless, certain reasoned steps can be taken to deal with this problem by (1) building on existing facilities and programs, and (2) demonstrating a willingness to implement different and more far-reaching management schemes.

First, however, any local management program will require the acquisition of a sound data base describing land use, potential sources of runoff pollution within each land-use type, existing drainage facilities, and so on. Since each land-use type (residential, agricultural, commercial, industrial, etc.) will generate its unique profile of runoff characteristics, this type of data will itself suggest certain management and control activities.

Within each land-use type a more detailed assessment should take the form of a source–constituent matrix, with sources as rows and constituents as columns (Figure 1). Each entry in the matrix should reflect the contribution of each activity or source to the aggregate runoff pollution potential. Given this broad inventory of information, along with the descriptions of existing drainage and control programs, planners and the public can begin to address the specific needs of more comprehensive management efforts.

For example, Table 2 summarizes the level of contaminant loadings observed at selected

Constituent	Solids			Organic Materials			Nutrients			Other		
Source	A	B	• • •	A	B	• • •	A	B	• • •	A	B	• • •
1. Rainfall												
2. Street litter												
3. Yard refuse												
4. Catch basins												
•												
•												
•												

Figure 7.36.1 A sample source-constituent matrix for use in urban runoff management. Each matrix describes a single homogeneous area or land-use activity.

locations in the United States.[5] These are averaged values but nonetheless represent (1) typical loadings to be expected for three different land-use categories (residential, industrial, commercial), and (2) the relationships among categories in terms of their contaminant potentials. The total pollution potential for storm runoff from a given urban area would be a "weighted" combination of these loadings, where the appropriate weights would include,

Table 7.36.2 Distribution of contaminant load (pounds per curb-mile per day) by land-use category*

Constituent	Residential	Industrial	Commercial
Total solids	590	1400	180
BOD	3.6	7.2	0.99
COD	20	81	5.7
Kjeldahl Nitrogen	0.60	1.2	0.12
Phosphates	0.37	1.1	0.10
Total heavy metals	1.2	1.6	0.34
Total coliforms**	60	150	120
Fecal coliforms**	5.8	1.6	18.0

*   Reference 5.

** Times 10^9, organisms per curb mile (no daily rate).

NOTE: These "daily" values do not reflect variations among locations in the effectiveness of street cleaning operations or the extent of rainfall and pollutant washout prior to data gathering.

at least, the relative areas (or curb-miles) associated with each land-use activity. To convert these dry loadings into pollutant concentrations would require site-specific data on local meteorology, hydrology, drainage system configurations, and the like and thus is beyond the scope of this article.

Management effort should be two-pronged, focusing on (1) control of each separate source, that is, decentralized, and (2) treatment–control of the aggregate storm flow, thus centralized. Both of these activities must be accompanied by information programs designed to educate and alert the public to the necessity for their participation, at the very least in terms of good housekeeping within the confines of each landholding.

Current decentralized activities include street sweeping, refuse collection, and other sanitation activities. Unfortunately, street sweeping removes only a small portion of the materials that eventually manifest themselves as runoff pollution. Hence the state of the art in decentralized approaches has not been well developed. In this context we can draw upon examples of runoff management provided by the natural system (mentioned at the beginning of this article). Such examples should be reflected in management programs by requiring "on-site" handling of runoff. Underlying this approach is the philosophy that each landholder should be required to manage his storm runoff in a way that minimizes damage to those outside his sphere of influences. Such on-site approaches might include:

1. Temporary ponding of rainwater on rooftops, parking lots, and especially prepared low areas, instead of rapid diversion to downstream receptors.
2. A reduction in the area of streets and other paved areas and/or the use of porous materials that would allow water to seep directly into soil and subsurface strata.
3. The maintenance and provision of vegetated open spaces and, in particular, vegetated waterways (in contrast to concrete gutters and sewers) that would capitalize on the natural system's ability to retard storm flow and to filter out contaminating substances.
4. Implementation of a forthcoming land-use program that would provide vegetated

open areas where needed and encourage a distribution of land uses more compatible with requirements for proper runoff control.
5. Encouragement of aggressive good housekeeping at each site, thereby eliminating much of the runoff pollution at its source.

Much more attention has been focused on the advancement of the state of the art in centralized approaches.[4] These include more sophisticated sewage systems, facilities for the temporary storage of large volumes of storm flow, a wide variety of physical, chemical, and biological treatment techniques, and computerized flow regulation systems, to mention just a few.

The point to be emphasized is that the effects of urban runoff can be managed only through a broadly based program of engineering design, land-use control, localized good housekeeping, on-site control activities, and public participation to alter our traditional perspectives on storm runoff.

These broadly based programs must focus on runoff quality and runoff quantity, including both decentralized and centralized managements procedures. Some examples include the following:

A. Management of runoff quantity
  1. Decentralized[2]on-site storage and slow release, reduction of impervious surfaces, on-site reuse of stormwater, use of porous pavement. . . .
  2. Centralized—sophisticated regulation of flows in sewage systems, in-system and/or off-system storage and slow release (storm standby basins, silos, etc.), diversion of storm flow for other uses, proper maintenance of facilities, control of infiltration. . . .
B. Management of runoff quality
  1. Decentralized—good housekeeping by each separate landholder, street cleaning, catch basin maintenance, proper sanitation and materials handling. . . .
  2. Centralized—treatment of runoff in conventional facilities, diversion of stormwater to crop irrigation or other benecial uses, treatment of storm flow at intermediate locations in the sewage system, regulation and slow release of runoff to receiving waters. . . .

In summary, urban runoff presents problems because of (1) high pulse flows and (2) surprisingly high pollutant concentrations. Thus management programs must deal with a double-edged problem. The basic rationale for handling high flows includes the exclusion of stormwater from sewage systems, the diversion of excess flows to other areas and uses, and/ or temporary storage followed by slow, more uniform release. The rationale for handling pollutants includes the initial prevention of contact between rainwater and potential contaminants, removal of pollutants by some type of "treatment," diversion of contaminated runoff to areas that can use the contaminants, and/or release of storm flow at a rate slow enough that pollutants can be effectively assimilated.

For any given area the "optimum" urban runoff management program will include some mixture of techniques, like those mentioned above. A wide variety of local site-specific factors will control the proper combination. For instance, it has been reported[4] that in some cases street sweeping can remove solid pollutants at a lower cost than conventional waste treatment ($25 to $30 per ton solids removed by street sweeping compared to $60 to $70 per ton solids removed by treatment plants). However, other local conditions may favor stormwater "treatment," even though street sweeping per se may be cheaper for solids removal. For example, street cleaning does not affect pulse flows, and for a particular area pulse flows may be the predominant problem.

Other articles[4,5] provide technical details on numerous management techniques (and combinations of techniques), including those presently in operation and others in developmental stages. However, in all cases, for a management program to be effective and successful it must be coordinated with broadly based public relations, including citizen involvement and education. Technological solutions by themselves will not be optimal or cost effective.

REFERENCES

1. Roy Burke III. 1971. *A Survey of Available Information Describing Expected Constituents in Urban Surface Runoff, with Special Emphasis on Gainesville, Florida.* An occasional paper prepared for Florida Defenders of the Environment, Inc., Gainesville, Florida.

2. James D. Sartor, Gail B. Boyd, and Franklin J. Agardy. "Water pollution aspects of street surface contaminants." *Journal of the Water Pollution Control Federation*, March 1974, pp. 458–467.

3. W. Whipple, J. V. Hunter, and S. L. Yu. "Unrecorded pollution from urban runoff." *Journal of the Water Pollution Control Federation*, May 1974, pp. 873–885 .

4. James D. Sartor and Gail B. Boyd. 1972. *Water Pollution Aspects of Street Surface Contaminants.* U.S. Environmental Protection Agency, Report No. EPA–R2–72–081, Washington, D.C., 236 pp.

5. Richard Field and Edmund J. Struzeski, Jr. "Management and control of combined sewer overflows." *Journal of the Water Pollution Control Federation*, June 1972, pp. 1393–1415.

37. THERMAL DISCHARGES

John Cairns, Jr.
Center for Environmental Studies
Virginia Polytechnic Institute and State University
Blacksburg, Virginia

Ecological problems associated with heated waste water discharges have been discussed by many authors,[1-4] and superb annual literature summaries have been prepared by Coutant (e.g., Reference 5). Four critical issues must be addressed in order to manage the ecological impact of heated wastewater and other steam electric power plant discharges:

1. The assimilative capacity of the particular ecosystem in the region of the proposed discharge.
2. The type and amount of ecological evidence that should be gathered before operations begin.
3. The type and amount of ecological evidence that should be gathered after operations begin.
4. The management plan to be followed if assimilative capacity or ecological limits are exceeded.

ECOSYSTEM ASSIMILATIVE CAPACITY

Assimilative capacity might be defined as the capacity of a specic ecosystem to receive waste discharges without deleterious alteration in either the structure or the function of that ecosystem. Unfortunately for standards setters, ecosystems are dynamic and constantly changing in biological, chemical, and physical characteristics. For example, replacement of one species by another is a recognized established characteristic of ecosystems. This replacement rate may be rapid for microbial species and considerably less rapid for fish and other vertebrates. Nevertheless, these changes do occur and are natural. Likewise, the chemical–physical characteristics are not constant but rather vary within certain limits and in certain patterns. However, the structure of an aquatic community is relatively constant despite the succession of species and may be used as an index of health.[6]

Assimilative capacity is the ability of a particular system at a particular time to receive wastes without degrading either the functioning or the structure of the system from the pattern characteristic of that locale. Since assimilative capacity is not constant, utilization of this characteristic is dependent on a constant flow of information about the system in question. The deficiency of fixed arbitrary standards for heated water and other waste discharges is that they do not take into consideration the varying vulnerabilities of a specific system at different seasons and thus either overprotect or underprotect it, depending on the particular assimilative capacity at the moment. Many ecologists, regulatory personnel, and legislators are reluctant to use assimilative capacity because of the difficulties of using it properly. They substitute zero discharge as a viable alternative despite the fact that zero discharge does not necessarily mean zero environmental impact. In fact, full treatment permitting complete recycling of water requires substantial additional energy, treatment facilities, and chemicals. These have to be produced somewhere, and presumably their production will ultimately have an environmental impact somewhere. Thus zero discharge does not eliminate environmental impact but merely changes the location and the nature of the impact. It is essential that ecologists, who are constantly stressing the interrelatedness and interdependence of natural systems, recognize the same qualities in industrial systems and

perceive that increasing the demand of an industrial plant upon industrial plants elsewhere (for energy or materials) will also ultimately increase the environmental impact elsewhere. In short, although reduction of impact is quite possible, absolute containment is impossible. The only real question is where and how assimilative capacity will be used.

PREOPERATIONAL ECOLOGICAL EVIDENCE

1. Evidence from an ecological generalist, on the site selection team, regarding the ecological vulnerabilities of the various sites being considered.
2. Bioassays[7] with important *local* organisms at different trophic levels to determine the effects of both thermal changes (including an abrupt drop in temperature if the plant shuts down in midwinter) and toxic chemicals (e.g., chlorine) present in discharges.
3. A complete preoperational "ecological physical" or assessment to establish the biological, chemical, and physical condition of the area that *might be affected* by plant operations, as well as one or two ecologically comparable reference or control areas well outside the area of influence.[8]
4 Establishment of a biological monitoring system with frequent regular information feedback about the biological condition of the ecosystem.[6,9] These monitoring units should be established in the same areas used for the detailed information gathering called for in item 3.

POSTOPERATIONAL ECOLOGICAL EVIDENCE

1. A complete postoperational ecological assessment to confirm that no damage has occurred because of plant operation or to delimit the extent of damage that has occurred. These complete surveys should be repeated whenever a major change in quality or quantity of plant discharges occurs or whenever the biological monitoring system indicates that something is wrong.

2. Continued operation of the biological monitoring system.
3. New bioassays whenever waste discharges change.

MANAGEMENT PLAN FOR COPING WITH DELETERIOUS ENVIRONMENTAL IMPACTS

Most regulatory agencies are organized to see that waste discharges meet certain standards and that the waste treatment system is adequate to accomplish this good under various operating conditions. Detailed protocols and plans are developed for meeting operational emergencies within power plants, but rarely is a comprehensive detailed set of protocols developed for meeting an environmental emergency such as a spill of toxic material or a sudden reduction of heated wastewater discharge in midwinter, when large numbers of fish may be congregated in the outfall plume. Such plans should include the type of evidence and data to be gathered during the emergency; reporting relationships, so that appropriate agencies and people are informed; a plan to immediately identify the cause of the kill; and plans to take immediate corrective action by scaling down plant operations or doing whatever else is required. Although neither environmental nor plant operational emergencies can be completely predicted, some types of emergencies have higher probabilities than others, and lack of plans for any kind of environmental emergency is evidence of inadequate management.

REFERENCES

1. John R. Clark. 1969. "Thermal pollution and aquatic life." *Scientific American*, Vol. 220, No. 3, pp. 19–27.
2. J. Cairns, Jr. 1970. "Ecological management problems caused by heated waste water discharge into the aquatic environment." *Water Resources Bulletin*, Vol. 6, No. 6, pp. 874–884.
3. J. Cairns, Jr. 1972. "Coping with heated waste water discharges from steam-electric power plants." *BioScience*, Vol. 22, No. 7, pp. 411–419.
4. P. A. Krenkel and F. L. Parker. 1969. *Biological Aspects of Thermal Pollution*. Vanderbilt University Press, Nashville, Tennessee.
5. C. C. Coutant. 1971. "Thermal pollution—biological effects: A review of the literature of 1970." *Journal of the Water Pollution Control Federation*, Vol. 43, pp. 1292–1334.
6. Ruth Patrick, M. H. Hohn, and J. H. Wallace. 1954. *A New Method for Determining the Pattern of the Diatom Flora*. Academy of Natural Sciences of Philadelphia, Notulae Natural, No. 259.
7. American Public Health Association, American Water Works Association, and Water Pollution Control Federation. 1971. *Standard Methods for the Examination of Water and Wastewater*, 13th ed., 874 pp.
8. J. Cairns, Jr. 1966. "Biological concepts and industrial waste disposal problems." In *Proceedings of the 20th Industrial Waste Conference*, Purdue University, Extension Series No. 118, pp. 49–59.
9. J. Cairns, Jr., Guy R. Lanza, Richard E. Sparks, and W. T. Waller. 1973. "Developing a biological information system for water quality management." *Water Resources Bulletin*, Vol. 9, No. 1, pp. 81–99.

38. TIDES

Dr. Edward P. Clancy
Department of Physics
Mount Holyoke College
South Hadley, Massachusetts

The earth and the moon constitute a single system revolving around a common center of gravity. The system is in equilibrium, because centrifugal forces exactly counterbalance the gravitational attraction between the two objects. The gravitational force acts as if all the mass of the moon were concentrated at its center, and that of the earth at its center.

But for objects not at the center of the two objects, this equilibrium does not exist. Although the amount of unbalance is not large, there do exist forces that, at certain regions of the earth's surface at certain times, tend to move objects toward or away from the moon. These are called "tidal forces." If the earth were free to deform under the action of these forces, it would become somewhat egg-shaped, with the long axis in the direction of the moon. Ocean water, relatively free to move under the influence of tidal forces, therefore forms two bulges, one on the side toward the moon, the other on the far side.

The earth turns under these bulges, and thus there arrive two tides a day, separated, however, not by 12 hours but by about 12 hours and 25 minutes, because while the earth is turning the moon is also pursuing its orbit around the earth. Open-ocean tides are small —perhaps 1 or 2 feet in height. Significant tidal range occurs only when local conditions produce it. These conditions involve resonant effects: the surging of water in enclosed areas, some of whose natural periods of vibration may be near the periodicities of the tidal forces.

The sun also produces tidal forces on the earth; it has a little less than half the effect of the moon. When the sun and moon forces cooperate, we have the situation every 2 weeks of *spring tides* with maximum range in height. When the sun's forces are at right angles to those of the moon, there occur *neap tides* of minimum range. Spring tides occur roughly at the times of full moon and new moon; neap tides, when the moon is in first and third quarters. It is typical that in a location where the average range of tides is 9 feet, say at Boston, the difference between the range at spring and at neap tides can be as much as 6 feet. In addition, there are yearly high and low average sea levels driven by yearly tidal cycles.

On most parts of the coast, tide is an important factor in the constant interaction between sea and land. If tidal range is considerable, on the less protected shores waves can unleash their energy over a wide stretch of beach. In bays and estuaries a large tide significantly modifies bottom configuration. It also alters the morphology of the shoreline and its nature as a biological habitat.

In locations where bars tend to form, a substantial range of tide often results in the formation of two sets of underwater ridges paralleling the shoreline. The tide is sinusoidal, so that sea level spends more time near the high and low marks that in between. Bars thus develop at two levels. On the beach itself, wave energy is dissipated over a wider area as a result of tidal action, and the equilibrium sand or shingle profile is affected. On rocky shores more than one abrasion platform may be formed, and the manner of carving marine cliffs is modified.

As sea level changes with the rhythm of the tides, currents are set in motion in and out of bays and estuaries. For a wide-mouthed bay the speed of tidal current is roughly 90 degrees out of phase with the ocean tidal curve (height of water as a function of time). For such a bay the maximum speed of the incoming current tends to occur about at midtide on a rising tide. For bays with narrow inlets, the phase relation between the ocean tidal curve and tidal current varies widely, depending on the width and depth of the inlet passage. The phase relation between ocean level and level in the bay will vary correspondingly. Furthermore, it follows that the average level of a tidal pond with a shallow entrance is considerably higher than the mean water level of the ocean.

The speed with which tide penetrates a river with few lateral constrictions depends largely on water depth. The advancing water mass is a true progressive wave. Clearly, the wave will not penetrate far into a river with appreciable gradient. In the Amazon, however, tide has been observed as much as 500 miles upstream. The part of a river giving tidal effects is called the "tide zone." The extent of this zone ordinarily varies markedly with river flow and hence with the seasons. At any time, however, the tidal curve of the river usually bears little resemblance to that in the ocean outside. For rivers the curve is unsymmetrical. Typically, the rise is faster and the fall slower.

As the tidal wave progresses up the river, it encounters shallower water and its profile changes. When the depth of the water is comparable to the amplitude of the wave, and the rate of rise is sufficient, parts of the wave crest go faster than water in the trough. The frontal slope becomes steeper, and finally the wave breaks. The result is a phenomenon called a "bore," which rushes upstream with a front that may be almost vertical. Few large-scale bores exist in the United States. There is one of moderate scale in the Peticodiac River in New Brunswick, however, and in a tributary of the Amazon a bore exists with a height of 16 feet.

River tides have an important environmental effect. They provide a large-scale flushing action of pollutants in the river,, since the net flow is seaward and the quantity of water available for flushing action is much larger than that of the freshwater flow alone.

Salt water entering a tidal river does not mix thoroughly with the fresh water upstream. Since the seawater is more dense, it tends to form a wedge moving up the river close to the bottom. If the natural flow of the river is large, there is usually a well-defined interface between the two water masses. In fact, further upstream there can result a freshwater tide, which has important economic consequences in parts of the world where rice growers must flood and drain their fields at intervals.

The reversing current in a tidal river results in an inherent instability of the river bed. In the normal course of its flow the usual river develops a well-defined channel, at least for short periods. This channel is determined by the laws of hydrodynamics for current moving in a certain direction in a bed of given configuration. But for a current entering an estuary the river channel is not a suitable one, and the inflow tends to create its own new channel. As a result unstable shoals and bars are formed, and maintenance of navigation is difficult.

The presence of tide in bays and rivers in the higher latitudes is important. Tidal rise and fall tends to break up ice formations, and the ice departs on the ebb tide. Thus New York Harbor is open throughout the winter, whereas regions further up the Hudson River, though filled with salt water, are entirely icebound.

Tidal currents can have great erosional power. They maintain tidal inlets, which are gaps originally produced by storm waves breaking over a barrier at high tide. Sandy sediment from littoral drift along the shore is carried through the inlet by an entering tide and forms a tidal delta. Much of the sediment is fine, however, and tends to be carried further, where it clots into small aggregates that then settle to the bottom of the bay or estuary. Since local organic mater is also ordinarily present, there results a layer rich in nutrients. After a time the sediments create in the bay

a system of mud flats, uncovered at low tide. Here marine plants take over and build up the level, and the area becomes a salt marsh. This is ordinarily partially flooded at every high tide and completely flooded at the time of spring tides. The salt marsh is interspersed with shallow tidal streams that provide twice-daily exchange of water with the ocean.

The salinity of estuaries, a direct function of tidal action, is important. The degree of salinity is a result of the interplay of three main factors: (1) salt contribution from the ocean (and perhaps from land), (2) evaporation, and (3) freshwater input from streams and from precipitation. In regions where tidal movement of water masses in large, the salinity of the estuary seldom differs significantly from that of the ocean. Changes in tidal flow due to alterations of the natural system of inlets and channels by the action of man, however, can have profound effects on the estuarine environment.

Reclamation of shallow tidal lands for agriculture has, since the dawn of civilization, been an important activity in many parts of the world. Reclamation regions tend to fall into two categories: open areas of mud, exposed only at low tide, and salt marshes, which usually have a rich underlying peat layer. In certain coastal regions, such as those of the Low Countries, a tideland may have a width of as much as 40 miles, making reclamation a highly rewarding activity. Dikes are built to enclose successive areas, and the water is gradually pumped out. As the pumping proceeds, salinity changes, and freshwater organisms replace saltwater life. With reclamation go a permanent loss in the estuarine environment and consequent declines in the food resources of the sea. Before reclamation proceeds, therefore, careful studies must ensure that the gain more than compensates for the losses in natural resources.

Coastal zone property lines sometimes become difficult to define in regions where extensive intertidal areas exist. Many states claim sovereignty up to the line of mean high water. However, since in many places the range of the level of high water from week to week is an appreciable fraction of the total rise and fall of the tide, this legal definition proves hard to apply precisely in practice. Furthermore, processes of accretion or erosion affect tidal penetration and hence alter a previously defined line. The title dilemma often leads to legal confrontations in determining the public interest.

The regular annual change in sea level may be most important; for example, in Florida, an increase of 6 or 8 inches above the yearly low has an appreciable effect on the inward extent of water penetration and on practical matters such as storm heights and property lines.

39. TIDEMARK BOUNDARIES

Joseph T. Bockrath
Dennis F. Polis
College of Marine Studies
University of Delaware
Newark, Delaware

The tidemark issue concerns the determination of the legal boundary or jurisdiction over tidal waters and their associated subaqueous lands. This article deals with the legal and scientific aspects of tidal boundary definitions but does not attempt to specify which rule of law will apply to any particular area.

Rapidly increasing property values in shoreline areas as a result of development, counterbalanced with pressures for the preservation of ecologically important wetlands, have made the tidemark question a crucial one for coastal zone managers. Tidal boundaries are always the lines of intersection of two surfaces—a horizontal tidal plane (e.g., mean high or low tide, or mean sea level) and the surface of terra firma. Along much of the Atlantic and Gulf coasts, the slope of the near shore areas is 1 : 500 or less, so that a difference of 1 inch in the tidal plane can result in a boundary displacement of 50 feet or more. Thus differences in tide level that are inconsequential for navigation purposes become crucial in boundary problems.

A portion of the legal difficulty attending the tidemark problem stems from the interchangeable use by various courts of such modifiers as "ordinary," "mean," and "usual" in reference to water marks. The National Bureau of Standards has regarded "ordinary" as the equivalent of "mean" in the tidal context, and this view is generally recognized as accurate by the courts. The term "mean or ordinary high-tide line or mark" does not refer to a visible line on the shore such as a line of foam or debris, but rather is a line ascertained from the mean rise of the tide outside the nearshore zone, where wave runup is appreciable, and projected horizontally therefrom to the shore, irrespective of the runup or wash of the waves.

Technically, the tides (see Article 38) are the variations in water level caused by astronomical forces. This fact is recognized in a number of state statutes, which explicitly exclude water level fluctuations due to other causes; however, sorting out the separate causes is not always possible in practice.

There is presently no means available for calculating the actual tides at any given point from first principles. Rather, they are predicted on the basis of past observations of *water level*. Apparent water level varies not only because of the tides, but also from other causes, including wind, barometric pressure, river discharge, wave runup, seawater density, ocean currents, long-term climatic changes, and geological processes.

In semi-enclosed areas, seiches, which are the resonant oscillations of water in a basin (typically with periods of the order of 1 hour or less), further confuse the record. The standard techniques of tidal analysis are able to separate the cyclic components of the astronomical tides from each other and from many, but not all, of the other causes of water level fluctuation.

The degree of separation possible depends on the length of record available to be analyzed. The tidal forces have several fundamental cyclic periods (namely, 24 hours, 27.32 days, 365.24 days, 8.85 years, 18.6 years, and 20,940 years) which combine to drive the tidal motions; records of 18.6 years or more provide the best practical data base for tidal analysis. Averages of tidal data over periods of 18.6 years (or integer multiples thereof) would be as close as possible to very long-term averages if only tidal and random forces were operative. Unfortunately, records of this duration are available for only a small number of stations. The large majority of tidal stations have only a few days of observations available. By comparing the observations at these stations with those for which long records exist, sufficient accuracy is obtained for navigation purposes, but errors on the order of 1 inch or more vertically may be expected at many of the more remote stations. It is especially difficult to extrapolate tidal plane data into estuaries, where basin configuration, wind, and river flow play a particularly large role in determining water levels. When any tidal plane other than mean sea level (e.g., mean high or low tide) is considered, even more difficulty is encountered, as these planes depend on the tidal range, which varies much more with location than does mean sea level.

The majority of courts that have dealt with the problem of what or where mean high tide is have based their decisions on the existence of the 18.6-year tidal cycle, and the Supreme Court of the United States has utilized this test on at least two occasions; however, some states have used 19 years. Recognizing that the needed data are not always available, a few courts have declared that the full cycle need be used only when possible, or that a considerable or reasonable period is adequate.

In a Texas case it was confirmed that mean high tide is the average of the high waters of each day in the averaging period, rather than the highest water each year over a number of years. When 19 years of daily readings are unavailable, one takes the daily local tide gauge readings for such periods as are available, provided that they are for not less than 1 year, and corrects them by comparison with the nearest gauge that affords a record for 19 years, the corrected result being a substantially accurate approximation of true mean high tide at the locality in question over the 19-year cycle.

California has developed a variation of the 18.6-year-cycle method in that it considers high tide to be the limit reached by the *neap tides*—the tides of small range that occur at a time midway between the full phase and change of the moon.

In another variant of the cyclical approach, necessitated by the presence of the seiche phenomenon, it has been held that high tide is the average between the highest limit reached by the combined seiche and tide, and the low point of high tide immediately before or after such high point.

A few courts, on the authority of cases dealing with nontidal water, have concluded that the ordinary high-tide line is the line that the water imposes on the land by covering it for sufficient periods to deprive the soil of upland vegetation and destroy its value for agricultural purposes. At least one court has utilized a test that combines the 18.6-year cycle and the vegetation test, but is concerned with the presence rather than the absence of vegetation of a certain type.

The title history of the property in question may be the determining factor as to which of the many tests is applied. Of particular importance may be the question of whether the title is traceable to a federal patent.

In light of these decisions it is important that mean sea level is not, as is commonly assumed, level in the sense of showing everywhere the same elevation as would a homogeneous, motionless fluid (a geodetic surface). For example, precise leveling has shown that sea level rises approximately 1 foot as one proceeds from Florida to Maine. Considerably greater slopes in mean water level are found locally, especially in estuaries. Nor is sea level constant in time. Analysis of long-term tidal data shows that sea level is rising along the east and Gulf coasts and Hawaii at a rate of 0.5 to 3.0 feet per century. Along the west coast, including Alaska, it is rising in some areas, while apparently falling relative to land in other areas.

The location of the tidal boundary line is further complicated by the fact that the land, which is the other surface forming a tidal boundary, is also changing as a result of erosion and accretion. The erosion or accretion of open coast at an average rate of 1 foot per year is quite common, but the rates for spits and headlands may be considerably greater. Cape Henlopen, Delaware, for example, is growing at about 80 feet per year. These average rates are often masked, however, by the much greater short-term effects of individual storms.

These difficulties serve to compound the problem inherent in a boundary that is generally not visible. Properly defined, the "mean" is constant within any given time frame. The exact value of the mean, however, will depend not only on the duration over which it is taken, but also on the exact times at which the period begins and ends. For New York, for example, the 19-year mean beginning in 1893 is 0.29 foot lower than that beginning in 1930. Under these conditions a mean properly describes the situation obtaining, not at the end of the period over which it is taken, but rather at a time approximately in the middle of that period.

It is possible to make a correction to approximate present conditions by adding to the mean an amount equal to the observed annual average increase in sea level times the number of years that have elapsed since the middle year of the averaging period. If a 18.6- or 19-year average is used, this will provide a well-defined but time-dependent meaning for any tidal plane.

In summary, it can be seen that the present situation is far from satisfactory. Eventually, the time dependence of tidemarks will have to be legally recognized. Until then, the view that three is a legal presumption that mean high tide is a constant may be the most workable one. This means that the burden of persuasion is placed on the party challenging a prior determination, if one has been made.

REFERENCES

1. Henry G. Avers. 1927. "A study of the variation of mean sea-level from a level surface." American Geophysical Union, Transactions, *National Research Council Bulletin*, No. 61, pp. 56–58.
2. Corker, 1968. "Where does the beach begin?" 42 *Washington Law Review* 33 (1968).
3. *City of Los Angeles vs. Borax Consolidated.* 1935. 296 U.S. 10
4. Steacy D. Hicks. 1973. *Trends and Variability of Yearly Mean Sea Level 1893–1971.* National Ocean Survey, National Oceanic and Atmospheric Administration, Technical Memorandum No. NOS. 12, U.S. Government Printing Office, Washington, D.C.
5. *Hughes v. State.* 1967. 410 p. 2d 20, 67 Wash. 2d 799; rev. o.g. 389 US. 290.
6. H. A. Marmer. 1951. *Tidal Datum Planes.* Coast and Geodetic Survey, Special Publication No. 135, U.S. Government Printing Office, Washington, D.C.
7. Aron L. Shalowitz. 1962, 1964. *Shore and Sea Boundaries* (2 vols.) Coast and Geodetic Survey, Publication 10–1, U.S. Government Printing Office, Washington, D.C.
8. *U.S. v. California.* 1965. 382 U.S. 448.

40. TOXIC SUBSTANCES

Jeffrey L. Lincer
National Wildlife Federation
Washington, D.C.

Toxic discharge is the transfer of toxic substances to coastal or other waters. These substances are termed "toxic" when, because of their physical or chemical properties, they interfere with normal biological functions. The interference can occur at any level, whether it be as subtle as pesticide-induced decreased growth in oysters or as gross as reproductive failure in bald eagles or mercury poisoning in human beings. There are naturally occurring toxic substances that include such things as the resin from certain plants and the toxin(s) associated with red tide organisms. By a wide margin, however, most deleterious substances find their origins with modern-day man and his efforts to promote "progress."

A logical breakdown of the toxic substances considered in this section is as follows:

1. Pesticides or biocides (any chemical that kills an organism identified as a "pest"; this would include insecticides, fungicides, piscicides, herbicides, miticides, etc.). *Insecticides* are commonly classified into three groups: (*a*) chlorinated hydrocarbons (organochlorines), like DDT, aldrin, dieldrin, heptachlor, and chlordane; (*b*) organophosphates, like malathion, parathion, diazinon, and guthion; and (*c*) carbamates, like Sevin and Zectran. *Fungicides* include such substances as dithiocarbamates (e.g., Ferbam and Ziram), nitrogen-containing compounds (e.g., phenylmercuric acetate), triazines, quinones, heterocyclics, and inorganics like the heavy metals. *Herbicides* are quite varied, the most common being the phenoxy

acids like 2,4-D and 2,4,5-T. Frequently used aquatic herbicides include endothal and diquat, often applied in combination with a surfactant (like a detergent).

2. "Industrial toxicants" is a catchall term that has been variously subdivided. *Polychlorinated biphenyls* (PCBs) are chlorinated compounds that find use in almost every sector of modern man's world and have recently come under close scrutiny.[1] They are used in such diverse products as printer's ink and the paint applied to swimming pools. *Phthalate esters* are industry-related toxicants that have even more recently been recognized as sources of potential harm. Pulp mill wastes and acids and other compounds from mining operations can also be considered in this group.

3. Heavy metals are given special attention here because, like the persistent organochlorine insecticides, they are extremely long lived and can be quite toxic. As a matter of fact, if not chemically bound in the estuarine environment so as to become unavailable to aquatic life, the heavy metals recycle through food chains indefinitely. These elements originate in a multitude of both man-produced and natural operations. Heavy metals are found in pesticide formulations, wastes from industrial and municipal sources, and wastes from earthmoving and mining activities. Superimposed on these sources is the constant, but significantly slower, recycling of heavy metals that has always taken place.

The man-oriented processes most commonly associated with toxic discharge include (1) agriculture, (2) land care, (3) water control (i.e., aquatic weed control), (4) mosquito and other disease vector control, and (5) municipal and industrial waste disposal. To a lesser extent, lumbering and power plants may also be associated with toxic discharges.

Agricultural practices, in order to supply the quantity and quality of produce demanded by the consumer, utilize a myriad of biocides. Pesticides, especially insecticides, nematocides, and fungicides, are applied at rates often exceeding recommended levels. More than 0.5 billion pounds of pesticides are used in agriculture in the United States each year.[2] In addi-

tion, aerial applications of toxicants are frequently inefficient, with as little as 50 percent hitting the target. The more persistent organochlorine compounds and those containing heavy metals will remain on the vegetation and in the soil for extended periods of time. Rains or irrigation efforts that move soil downstream take with them the biocides, which readily adsorb more to organic than to sandy soils. Being chemically more active, the loamy agricultural soil runoff is particularly capable of transferring these toxic substances to the coastal areas.

In a man-made landscape, dominated by exotic vegetation, commonly planted in endless monocultures, and depredated by imported pest species, chemical "control" is a major maintenance activity. Although most pesticide labels clearly spell out recommended application rates and target pest(s), homeowners are notorious for applying too much of the wrong chemical with great regularity. Coastal areas are highly prized for their development potential and, as such, often become large expanses of man-originated vegetation. Residential lawns and shrubs are maintained in a neatly manicured well-protected fashion that results in grass clippings, fertilizers, and pesticides finding their way to the coastal waters. Man finds that, after changing the landform adjacent to a waterway or estuary, he has to seawall his property so as not to lose any land. This philosophy of man-made landscaping is particularly confusing since the natural vegetation, like *Spartina*, *Juncus*, and mangroves, held the land quite adequately before it was removed in the name of "improvement." When seawalls replace the natural vegetation, not only do many forms of wildlife leave, but to make matters worse there is no "biological filter" left to keep toxicants from flowing, unaltered, into the coastal waters.

In an effort to create watercourses, control mosquito reproduction, or make the uplands more "usable" by drainage, man has often established unnatural bodies of water. Once introduced into these bodies of water, exotic vegetation like water hyacinths, *Hydrilla*, and *Elodea* become established and, lacking natural enemies (i.e., diseases, competitors, and grazers), require control, often in the form of herbicides applied with a surfactant. These

Table 7.40.1   United States production of major organochlorines (grams ×
10^9) (SOURCE: References 3 and 4)

Chemicals	DDT	Aldrin-^{t} Toxaphene	PCB
Period	1944-1968	1954-1968	1960-1971
Total	1,222	670	328
Yearly Ave.	49.0	44.7	26.4

t   Includes aldrin, chlordane, dieldrin, endrin, heptachlor, and
toxaphene.

chemicals are not as specific as the applicator is lead to believe, and nontarget organisms may be the ultimate recipients. Heavy metals are used to periodically manage blue–green algae blooms, but the perennial cause—land-originating nutrient runoff—is left unaltered. This situation is exacerbated if natural filters, like mangrove swamps and *Spartina* marshes, are replaced by inert bulkheads, or if meandering streams, which maximize the contact time between toxicant and degrader, are replaced by straight channels lined with denuded, ever-eroding sides of spoil.

Mosquitoes and other potential disease vectors are the targets for millions of pounds of pesticides, like DDT, in South America, India, and other underdeveloped countries. Similarly, although the health aspects may be stated and often overemphasized, the coastal areas of the United States are consistently sprayed with a variety of toxicants, primarily in response to pressure from homeowners and the tourist industry. If mosquitoes and other biting insects manage to reproduce, local pressures ensure biocidal control. The situation is, of course, intensified when dead-end canals provide still breeding waters for these skin-puncturing Culicidae. In addition, poor water quality, reduced habitat, or direct poisoning from pesticides prevent natural predators like the mosquito fish (*Gambusia*), and insectivorous birds and herps (frogs, salamanders, and lizards) from surviving and exerting their own control over their insect prey species.

The United States production of the major organochlorine pesticides and PCBs has been established (Table 1), and it is undeniable that the oceans are the recipients and ultimate accumulation sites for these persistent toxicants. For instance, approximately 25 percent of the DDT produced to date has been transferred to the sea.[5]

Of the organochlorine pesticides, DDE (a breakdown product of DDT) is probably the most widely distributed in fish and wildlife. Being lipophilic (i.e., "fat-loving"), DDE, like other organochlorines, is not very soluble in water and accumulates in the fat of organisms. Such chemicals are passed from prey to predator with little lost by way of excretion. This "biological magnification" with each transfer from one food level (i.e., trophic level) to the next results in animals at the tops of food chains acquiring inordinate amounts of these poisons.[6] Concentrations of DDE reached 1100 ppm (parts per million) in the fat from brown pelican eggs off California and 1000 ppm in the eggs of the white-tailed eagle in the Baltic.[7]

Organochlorine pesticides are readily accumulated by shellfish, and this characteristic has been utilized to estimate pesticide contamination. As part of a National Pesticide Monitoring Program,[8] shellfish were collected from coastal zones of the United States. Analyses of over 8000 samples for 15 persistent organochlorines showed that DDT-type residues were ubiquitous, with the maximum DDT level at approximately 5 ppm. Dieldrin was the second most commonly detected compound with a maximum of 0.23 ppm. Endrin, mirex, and toxaphene were occasionally found.

Although most organophosphate and carbamate pesticides are advertised as short-lived, there is ample evidence that some may not be. In an application of carbaryl (Sevin) at rates comparable to those used to control pests of oysters, the chemical could still be detected in the mud 42 days posttreatment.[9]

Organochlorine pesticides have been shown to interfere with almost every level of biological function tested in marine life. Levels of DDT as low as 0.001 ppm cause marked reduction in oyster growth,[10] and high levels of organochlorines have been associated with premature births in marine mammals.[11]

Some urea herbicides, like Diuron, significantly inhibit the growth of marine algae at levels as low as 1 ppb (parts per billion).[12] A few parts per million of DDT, dieldrin, or endrin are enough to reduce photosynthesis.[13,14]

Some organochlorine pesticides, like Mirex, a chemical commonly used to control the imported fire ant, *Solenopsis saevissima*, in the southern states, are particularly toxic to estuarine organisms. For example, juvenile shrimp and crabs died when exposed to *one* particle of mirex bait; and 1 ppb mirex in seawater killed 100 percent of the shrimp exposed.[15]

Although toxic to crustaceans, Sevin is fairly nontoxic to fish and mammals.[16] The sensitivity of a particular taxonomic group to any specific toxicant will vary appreciably. In very

general terms, Table 2 shows the relative toxicities of different pesticide groups to estuarine fauna.

In a toxicity test that included 12 insecticides and seven species of estuarine fish, the descending order of toxicity was as follows: endrin, DDT, dieldrin, aldrin, dioxathion, heptachlor, lindane, methoxychlor, Phosdrin, malathion, DDVP, and methyl parathion.[18]

Polychlorinated biphenyls are as widely distributed as DDT and have basically the same kinds of biological effects as many organochlorine pesticides because of similar molecule shape and composition. The physical and chemical properties of PCBs confer the same lipophilic property that allows biological accumulation and food chain magnification.

Estuarine organisms like fiddler crabs and shrimp readily pick up PCBs from the sediments,[19] and filter-feeding oysters accumulate these chemicals from the water.[20] It has been shown that PCBs significantly decrease oyster growth at levels as low as 5 ppb[20] and are lethal to shrimp at 1 ppb.[21] Like the organochlorine pesticides, PCBs accumulate to high levels in organisms representing the tops of food chains. Fat from the eggs of California brown pelicans contained 200 ppm PCBs, while similar samples from the Baltic white-tailed eagle contained 540 ppm.[7]

Detergents not only find their way into estuaries by way of municipal and industrial waste but also are applied directly to the environment to increase the effectiveness of pesticide applications and to disperse spilled oil. Detergents and detergent additives (NTA and

Table 7.40.2 Relative sensitivities of typical estuarine organisms to three major groups of pesticides; higher numbers reflect greater sensitivity (SOURCE: Reference 17)

Organism	Pesticide Type		
	Herbicide	Organophosphates	Organochlorines
Plankton	1	0.5	3
Shrimp	1	1,000	300
Crab	1	800	100
Oyster	1	1	100
Fish	1	2	500

Table 7.40.3   Production and potential ocean inputs of heavy metals (values in 10^6 tons per year) (SOURCE: Reference 26)

Heavy Metal	Source		
	Mining	River Transport	Atmospheric Washout
Lead	3	0.1	0.3
Copper	6	0.25	0.2
Nickel	0.5	0.01	0.03
Chromium	2	0.04	0.02
Cadmium	0.01	0.0005	0.01
Mercury	0.009	0.003	0.08
Zinc	5	0.7	?
Silver	0.01	0.01	?

EDTA, for example) are toxic to a variety of coastal organisms. In fact, studies show them to be even more toxic to fish and invertebrates when tested in seawater than in fresh water.[22] As with other toxicants, the young and larval stages of marine animals are generally more susceptible to detergents than the adults.[23] A test aimed at determining the toxicity of an oil dispersant revealed that larval shrimp were three to five times more sensitive to it than the adults. A similar bioassy with another invertebrate revealed the immature life stage to be 40 times more sensitive than the adults.

Waste disposal, whether in the form of the effluent from wastewater treatment plants or sanitary landfills or the vapors from waste incineration, can contribute toxic substances to the environment. Under most presently used systems of waste disposal, only a small fraction of the toxicants is removed before the effluent or vapors are returned to the waters or atmosphere, respectively.

Industrial wastes can be infinitely subdivided as to class of compound and source. It suffices to say that the total organic waste from water-using industries in the United States is estimated to have a pollution strength three

to four times greater than that of the domestic sewage treated by all municipal operations.[2] The kinds of industries that contribute to the total toxic discharge include (a) those that produce toxicants (e.g., pesticides of PCBs), and (b) industries that, because of their various processes, either inadvertently produce toxic waste materials (like heavy metals) or utilize biocides (like cleaning fluids or moth-proofing compounds) in their operations.

Interest in heavy metals in coastal and other waters is not a recent development,[24] nor is it restricted to the United States.[25] Exact data on the input of heavy metals into the coastal zones are not available. However, the amounts from a few sources have been estimated (see Table 3).

Pinpointing above-normal levels of heavy metals is difficult because of the complexities of natural variations in the coastal area.[27-30] Mercury concentrations in recently caught oceanic fish and in museum specimens of the same species seem to be comparable,[31,32] but mercury has been associated with some bizarre occurrences. For example, organic mercury has been repeatedly cited as the cause of the often-fatal "Minamata disease," which affects people who eat large quantities of seafood contaminated with mercury. Between 1956 and 1973 three outbreaks of Minamata hit Japan.[33]

It is becoming obvious that heavy metals do, in fact, precipitate out in the estuarine system. Investigators have found that when these metals were introduced upstream only small amounts could be identified in water leaving the estuary,[34] and others have reported that concentrations nearshore were higher than those further offshore.[35]

Heavy metals tend to be associated with the organic fraction of the estuarine bottom sediment[36] and seem to be concentrated to a greater degree in the surface layers than in the deeper sediments.[37] This supports the suspected role of recent input by modern man.[38]

Man-induced rates of metal mobilization exceed natural geological rates to varying degrees. For instance, man increases the production of silver and mercury (by mining efforts alone) by a factor of approximately 2. Iron, copper, zinc, and lead are increased by a factor of 10, phosphorus by 30, and tin by 100.[39]

Heavy metal concentrations in vegetation collected at increasing distances from smelting works indicate that airborne particulates can add to pollutant input by fallout.[40] Although not the direct source of heavy metals, the cooling water of a coal-fired electric plant was shown to react with metal-containing sediments to release those heavy metals into the water.[41]

Estuarine organisms readily accumulate heavy metals, whether they be seaweed,[42] shellfish,[43–45] finfish,[46] or fish-eating birds.[47,48] In particular, shellfish have the capacity to accumulate extraordinary levels. For example, oysters in the Patuxent estuary, Maryland, accumulated copper in excess of 1000 ppm, at which point the meat took on a green color and a bad taste.[49]

Natural concentrations of heavy metals in marine water may be minute when compared with those in dredge spoil. For instance, the concentration of cadmium is approximately 0.08 ppm in seawater but 130 ppm in dredge spoil. Concentrations toxic to marine life range between 0.01 and 10 ppm.[50] Heavy metal concentrations in sewage sludge can be

significant. For instance, copper and zinc may average approximately 600 and 2500 ppm, yet 0.1 and 10 ppm, respectively, are toxic to marine life.[50]

Levels of mercury in fish from unpolluted areas are generally less than 0.1 ppm (based on wet weight), whereas comparable samples from polluted areas have higher values.[51] Boon,[52] reporting on levels of heavy metals in commercial crabmeat, found an average of 21 ppm iron, 46 ppm zinc, 466 ppm magnesium, and approximately 15 ppm copper.

The biological effects of metals in the estuarine ecosystem are quite varied, depending on the particular metal, the organism, and such modifying factors as the presence of other toxicants, the environmental conditions, and the age or condition of the organism.[53]

In order of generally decreasing lethality to aquatic organisms, mercury, silver, and copper are at the top of the list, followed by cadmium, zinc, lead, chromium, nickel, and cobalt.[53] However, there has been considerable discussion over the toxicity of cadmium,[54] especially with respect to its teratogenic effects on mammals.[55]

There is evidence that levels of mercury equivalent to those already found in the sea will deleteriously affect plankton, the very base of many marine food chains.[56] The particular species of organism exposed to a toxic metal is important, and different species will vary significantly in their responses to the same metal.[57] Therefore, because of different sensitivities, the species composition in a particular area can be drastically changed.

As a matter of convenience and partly because of our lack of knowledge about the exact composition of effluent from industrial and municipal sewage and runoff, the last class to be considered will be termed "undifferentiated toxic discharge." Obviously it will contain many of the toxicants already discussed, but the original nonpoint source becomes more difficult to locate.

Organics represent a large group and are roughly divided into (1) soluble organics, which undergo biological oxidation and tend to reduce the oxygen available to aquatic organisms, and (2) organics that do not undergo biological oxidation and are the specific causes for such things as odor, color, foam, direct

Table 7.40.4 Domestic and industrial wastewater produced in the United States: 1963 (SOURCE: Reference 58)

Source	Volume (billions of gallons/year)
Chemical	3,700
Pulp and Paper	1,900
Petroleum and Coal	1,300
Primary Metals	4,300
Domestic Sewage	5,300
Other *	1,471

* Includes food processing, textile mills, transportation equipment, electrical, and other machinery and rubber and plastics.

toxicity, and, possibly, carcinogenic effects.[58]

As with most chemicals, the toxicity of any one organic compound varies from species to species, and its effect in the environment depends to a great extent on its availability. In the coastal zone, where natural and man-originating trace metals tend to accumulate from runoff, the interactions between organics and metals may affect toxicity in either direction. Of 21 identified sources of pollution, municipal sewerage systems emerged as the leading killer of fish in 1971. Of approximately 74 million fish reported in fish kills, agricultural operations were responsible for 1 million, industrial for 4.6 million, municipal for 24.8 million, transportation for 0.7 million, "other" for 7.3 million, and "unknown" for 35.3 million."[59]

An estimate of the amount of domestic and industrial wastewater produced in the United States in 1963 is given in Table 4.[58]

The chemical industry is vast, and, in general, it can be broken down into three divisions.[60] The first produces the basic chemicals, including inorganic chemicals, acids, alkalies, and salts. A second division manufactures intermediate chemicals, such as plastics, synthetic fibers, fats, and oils. The third group manufactures finished chemicals such as drugs, cosmetics, soaps, and pesticides. Obviously, each industry produces its own set of wastewater toxicants, which may be unique to that industry or shared with other ones. The toxicity of the individual toxicant or of a group of toxicants varies widely and depends on a multitude of factors. Each industry has to be approached independently in regard to the potential or proved effects of its waste water on the particular biotic community receiving its effluent.

The pulp and paper industry has the potential of contributing a variety of chemicals to coastal pollution loads. The kinds and amounts of toxicants vary with the particular process.[61] In addition to solid wastes and carbohydrates, which can reduce oxygen concentrations to toxic levels, heavy metals used as fungicides, acids and bases for treating pulp, chlorine for bleaching, and other chemicals are found in the wastes of this industry. What is disturbing is that, of the 1.9 trillion gallons of water discharged annually by the paper and allied products industry, only 34 percent undergoes any treatment to alleviate its effects on receiving waters.[61]

The petroleum industry produces the obvious oil and oil-coated solids. In addition, the electrical method of crude desalting produces wastewater containing sulfides, suspended solids, phenols, and ammonia—and all this commonly at an elevated temperature. Crude oil fractionation produces sulfides, chlorides, and phenols. The thermal cracking process, hydrotreating, lube oil finishing, and other operations produce wastewater containing phenols, oils, sulfur compounds, ammonia, and stable oil emulsions.[60]

Depen ling on its proximity to the coastal zone or to large rivers leading thereto, surface mining can contribute significantly to estuarine pollution. Some operations, obviously, contribute more than others. For instance, the Bureau of Mines estimates that for the period from 1960 to 1963 more solid waste was generated at copper mines in the United States than the total materials handled at any other type of metal mine.[60] The most serious type of pollution presented by surface mining is acid mine drainage. This is most commonly associated with the coal industry, where the sulfur-bearing coal mixes with the runoff water to produce toxic sulfuric acid. The salts of mined metals such as zinc, lead, copper, and aluminum represent another form of toxicant and are quite toxic to aquatic life even in small amounts. Still another category includes the slimy red or yellow iron precipitates from coal or metal mines.

The steel industry is plagued with an especially large wastewater problem; waste streams flow at rates of 10,000 to 25,000 gallons per minute. Waterborne wastes of this industry include suspended solids, oils, heated waters, acids, plating solutions, dissolved organics, soluble metals, emulsions, and coke plant chemicals.[60]

The toxicants actually or potentially associated with the operation and maintenance of nuclear power plants and cooling tower structures include the following:[62] acids, acrolein, arsenic compounds, ammonia and amine compounds, boron, carbonates, chlorine and bromine, chlorinated and/or phenylated phenols, chromates, cyanurates and cyanides, hydrazine compounds, hydroxides, metals and their salts, nitrates and nitrites, potassium compounds, phosphates, silicates, sulfates, sulfides, and fluorides. The toxicity of these compounds to aquatic life is reviewed in Reference 62. The impact of chlorine should not be underestimated, especially when it is found in company with amines and other compounds with which it can form more toxic and/or longer-lasting chlorine-based compounds.[63]

Combinations of toxicants have been tested for their effects on coastal organisms, resulting in more than additive effects. Such "synergistic" effects have been observed for combinations of heavy metals and for combinations of temperature and oxygen stress and mercury intoxication.[64,65] There are many such synergistic effects, involving combinations of pesticides, detergents, heavy metals, PCBs, pulp mill and sewage waste, petroleum products, radioactive substances, thermal pollution, and dredge-and-fill operations.

Disposing of DDT, PCBs, herbicides, and waste feedstock can be a real technological problem. Chlorinolysis has been reported to be a viable chemical treatment whereby these previously "undisposable" toxicants can be converted with high yields into valuable carbon tetrachloride.[66]

The United States pulp and paper industry produces about 60 million tons of product annually. The cost in terms of air and water has been estimated, and interim guidance limitations have been suggested. There are many uses to which the "wastes" of the pulp and paper industry can be put, rather than allowing them to enter the coastal zone or other waters.[67]

Information is readily available to administrators who are responsible for water quality control.[68] Of interest to those charged with wastewater management is a publication provided by the Department of Army Corps of Engineers, which assesses the effectiveness and effects of various land disposal methodologies.[69] Especially helpful to those responsible for waste management in the coastal zone is a publication produced jointly by the National Academy of Sciences and National Academy of Engineering.[70] A report specifically on the disposal of solid toxic wastes is available and provides information on a number of topics, including the proper way to handle sewage sludge and the pretreatment of solid toxic wastes.[71]

Although recent advances have been made in regard to industrial and municipal waste treatment and recycling,[72] too few decision-makers seem to have the insight or perhaps the courage to implement innovative ideas.

In 1956 the city of Miami installed a sewage disposal plant with the result that 30 to 50 million gallons of waste per day was discharged into the disposal plant instead of into northern Biscayne Bay. A study aimed at determining the biological effects of sewage pollution abatement revealed a variety of significant changes.[26] Soft-bottom (mud) communities were less affected by the pollution than were hard-bottom communities, and the latter responded dramatically to the sewage pollution abatement.

Runoff of toxicants from agricultural areas can be signicant. However, proper planting techniques can reduce the amount. Two watersheds planted to ridged corn (vs. surface-contoured corn) varied greatly as to the amount of atrazine, propachlor, and diazinon found in the runoff water.[73]

Historically, storm runoff and sewage systems have been intertwined to varying degrees. Recently, however, the trend has been toward separation of these systems, especially in suburban developments. The overriding philosophy seems to be that runoff is really quite clean and does not need treatment. This view may be quite erroneous and, in fact, may result in increased toxicants entering the coastal waters. Not only do organic materials, such as grass clippings and pet feces, find their way into receiving waters, but also toxicants like insecticides, herbicides, tar, oil, and other petroleum-based pollutants from cars and streets. Plans for on-site retention of such water should be the rule and not the exception, and environmental impact studies of potential runoff should precede site planning.

California seems to have taken the lead in 1963 in describing the presence and effects of toxicants relative to water quality criteria.[74] This action precipitated many studies and many questions. Perhaps the most important questions a coastal zone administrator ought to ask with reference to toxic discharges are, "How much should be allowed in our waters, and what chemicals should not be applied at all near estuaries?"

Attempts have been made to answer these and similar questions. In 1968 the National Technical Advisory Committee to the Secretary of the Interior targeted this problem and recommended that the following organochlorines *not* be applied near the marine habitat because of their extreme toxicity: aldrin, BHC, chlordane, endrin, heptachlor, lindane, DDT,

dieldrin, endosulfan, methoxychlor, perthane, TDE, and toxaphene.[75]

As mentioned previously, mirex has been shown to be exceptionally toxic to estuarine invertebrates like shrimp and should be included in this forbidden category. Similarly, hexachlorobenzene is particularly toxic to birds,[76] and its use around rookeries should be carefully monitored or prohibited. A similar list for organophosphates included coumophos, Fursban, Fenthion, Naled, Parathion, and Ronnel.

The organochlorines and organophosphates listed above are acutely toxic at concentrations of 5 milligrams per liter or less and should not be permitted to exceed 50 nanograms per liter. The next group discussed by the National Technical Advisory Committee is generally not quite as toxic but should not be allowed to exceed 10 milligrams per liter in estuarine waters. This group included arsenicals, botanicals, carbamates, 2,4-D compounds, 2,4,5-T compounds, phthalic acid compounds, triazine compounds, and substituted urea compounds.

This kind of information and guidance as to allowable levels of most common toxicants, including radionuclides, heavy metals, and PCBSs, was updated by the Environmental Protection Agency in 1974. The following guidance is recommended:[77]

1. Carry out baseline studies to establish biological community structure and existing toxicant levels.
2. Establish long-term monitoring programs to quantify levels of pollutants and states of health of biological systems, which can be compared with baseline studies.
3. Inventory the area to identify and classify potential pollution sources.
4. Provide educational programs and incentives that will encourage industries to recycle water and to make use of waste materials, rather than dumping them into coastal and other waters.
5. Investigate alternative approaches to pesticides.[78]
6. To avoid ecological disasters, insist on proper, high-quality impact statements complemented with innovative engineering efforts.[72]
7. For any particular operation require that

the decision-making process include a tabular display of benefits, costs (many of which are hidden), and alternatives.[79,80]

8. Encourage a multidisciplinary approach to land and coastal planning which will include both research and management input.

9. Insist that existing laws be enforced and that adequate funds be appropriated for their implementation.

REFERENCES

1. D. B. Peakall and J. L. Lincer. 1970. "Polychlorinated biphenyls, another longlife widespread chemical in the environment." *Bioscience*, Vol. 20, No. 17, pp. 958–964.

2. U.S. Council on Environmental Quality. 1970. *Environmental Quality, First Annual Report.* U.S. Government Printing Office, Washington, D.C.

3. E. D. Goldberg, et al. 1971. *Chlorinated Hydrocarbons in the Marine Environment.* National Academy of Science, Washington, D.C.

4. Monsanto Industrial Chemical Company. 1971. Press release, Nov. 30, by E. V. John, Public Relations Department.

5. Study Group on Critical Environmental Problems. 1970. *Man's Impact on the Global Environment.* The MIT Press, Cambridge, Massachusetts.

6. G. M. Woodwell, C. F. Wurster, and P. A. Isaacson. 1967. "DDT residues in an east coast estuary: A case of biological concentration of a persistent insecticide." *Science*, Vol. 156, pp. 821–824.

7. R. W. Risebrough, E. Huschenbenth, S. Jensen and J. E. Portmann, 1972. "Halogenated hydrocarbons." In E. G. Goldberg, Ed., *A Guide to Marine Pollution.* Gordon and Breach Science Publishers, New York/London/Paris.

8. P. A. Butler. 1973. "Organochlorine residues in estuarine mollusks, 1965–1972." National Pesticide Monitoring Program. *Pesticide Monitoring Journal*, Vol. 6, No. 4, pp. 238–362.

9. J. F. Karinen et al. 1967. "Persistence of carbaryl in the marine estuarine environment: Chemical and biological stability in aquarium systems." *Journal of Agricultural and Food Chemistry*, Vol. 15, No. 1, pp. 148–156.

10. P. A. Butler. 1966. "Pesticides in the marine environment." *Journal of Applied Ecology*, Vol. 3 (Supplement), pp. 253–259.

11. R. L. DeLong, W. G. Gilmartin, and J. G. Simpson. 1973. "Premature births in California sea lions: Association with high organochlorine pollution residue levels" *Science*, Vol. 181, pp. 1168–1169.

12. G. E. Walsh and T. E. Grow. 1971. "Depression of carbohydrate in marine algae by urea herbicides." *Weed Science*, Vol. 19, No. 5, pp. 568–570.

13. C. F. Wurster. 1968. "DDT reduces photosynthesis by marine phytoplankton." *Science*, Vol. 159, pp. 1474–1475.

14. D. W. Menzel, J. Anderson, and A. Randtke. 1970. "Marine phytoplankton vary in their response to chlorinated hydrocarbons." *Science*, Vol. 167, pp. 1724–1726.

15. J. I. Lowe et al. 1971. "Effects of Mirex on selected estuarine organisms." In *Transactions of 36th North American Wildlife and Natural Resources Conferences*, pp. 171–186.

16. J. I. Lowe. 1967. "Effects of prolonged exposure to Sevin on an estuarine fish, *Leiostomus xanthurus*." *Bulletin Environmental Contamination and Toxicology*, Vol. 2, pp. 147–155.

17. P. A. Butler, 1966. *The Problem of Pesticides in Estuaries.* American Fisheries Society, Special Publication No. 3, pp. 110–115.

18. R. Eisler. 1970. *Acute Toxicity of Organochlorine and Organophosphorus Insecticides to Estuarine Fishes.* Bureau of Sport Fishery and Wildlife, Technical Paper No. 46, pp. 3–11.

19. D. R. Nimmo et al. 1971. "Polychlorinated biphenyl adsorbed from sediments by fiddler crabs and pink shrimp." *Nature*, Vol. 231, No. 5297, pp. 50–52.

20. J. I. Lowe et al. 1972. "Effects of the polychlorinated biphenyl Aroclor 1254 on the American oyster *Crassostrea virginica*." *Marine Biology*, Vol. 17, pp. 209–214.

21. D. R. Nimmo et al. 1971. "Toxicity and distribution of Aroclor 1254 in the pink shrimp *Penaeus duorarum*." *Marine Biology*, Vol. 11, No. 3, pp. 191–197.

22. M. Jancovic and H. Mann. 1969. "Untersuchungen ueber die akute toxische Wirkung von Nitrilotriessigsaeure (NTA)." *Archiv fuer Fishereiwissenschaft*, Vol. 20, No. 2–3, pp. 178–181.

23. R. G. J. Shelton. 1971. "Effects of oil and oil dispersants on the marine environment." *Proceedings of the Royal Society of London*, B, Vol. 177, pp. 411–422.

24. P. S. Galtsoff. 1943. "Copper content of sea water." *Ecology*, Vol. 24, No. 2, pp. 263–265.

25. L. Newton. 1944. "Pollution of the rivers of

West Wales by lead and zinc mine effluent." *Annals of Applied Biology*, Vol. 31, No. 1, pp. 1–11.

26. J. K. McNulty. 1970. *Effects of Abatement of Domestic Sewage Pollution on Benthos, Volumes of Zooplankton, and the Fouling Organisms of Biscayne Bay, Florida.* University of Miami Press, Coral Gables, Florida.

27. R. C. Harriss, A. W. Andren, and E. Dion. 1971. *The Distribution of Mercury in Rivers and Estuaries of the Northern Gulf of Mexico.* Progress Report to the U.S. Environmental Protection Agency. Department of Oceanography, Florida State University, Tallahassee, Florida (unpublished).

28. R. C. Harriss, H. Mattraw, G. Horvath, and A. Andren. 1971. *Input, Cycling and Fate of Heavy Metals and Pesticides Pollutants in Estuaries of the Western Everglades.* Completion Report to U.S. Environmental Protection Agency. The Marine Laboratory, Florida State University, Tallahassee, Florida (unpublished).

29. D. A. Wolfe and T. R. Rice. 1972. "Cycling of elements in estuaries." *Fishery Bulletin*, Vol. 70, No. 3, pp. 959–972.

30. D. A. Wolfe, F. A. Cross, and C. D. Jennings. 1973 "The flux of Mn, Fe and Zn in an estuarine ecosystem." In *Radioactive Contamination of the Marine Environment.* International Atomic Energy Agency, Vienna, pp. 159–175.

31. H. E. Ganther et al. 1972. "Mercury concentrations in museum specimens of tuna and swordfish." *Science*, Vol. 175, pp. 1121–1124.

32. R. Barber, A. Vijayakumar, and F. Cross. 1972. "Mercury concentrations in recent and ninety year old benthopelagic fish." *Science*, Vol. 178, pp. 636–639.

33. Julian Josephson 1974. "How much metal is there in our waters?" *Environmental Science and Technology*, Vol. 8, No. 2, pp. 112–113.

34. K. K. Turkian. 1971. "Rivers, tributaries, and estuaries." In D. W. Hood, Ed., *Impingement of Man on the Oceans.* Wiley-Interscience, New York, pp. 9–73.

35. H. V. Weiss, S. Yamamoto, T. E. Crozier, and J. H. Mathewson. 1972. "Mercury: Vertical distribution at two locations in the eastern tropical Pacific Ocean." *Environmental Science and Technology*, Vol. 6, No. 7, pp. 644–645.

36. R. J. Huggett, M. E. Bender, and H. D. Slone. 1971. "Mercury in sediments from three Virginia estuaries" *Chesapeake Science*, Vol. 12, No. 4, pp. 280–282.

37. H. V. Weiss, M. Koide, and E. D. Goldberg. 1971. "Mercury in a Greenland ice sheet:

Evidence of recent input by man." *Science*, Vol. 174, No. 4010, pp. 692–694.

38. A. J. Pyzik and S. E. Sommer. 1972. "Geochemical profiles of Chesapeake Bay sediments: Upper Cretaceous to Recent." *Chesapeake Science*, Vol. 15, No. 1, pp. 39–44.

39. Study Group on Critical Environmental Problems. 1971. "Work group on ecological effects." In *Man's Impact on Terrestrial and Oceanic Ecosystems.* The MIT Press, Cambridge, Massachusetts.

40. A. Burkitt, P. Lester, and G. Nickless. 1972. "Distribution of heavy metals in the vicinity of an industrial complex." *Nature*, Vol. 238, pp. 327–328.

41. J. M. Hill and G. R. Hely. 1973. "Copper and zinc in estuarine waters near a coal-fired electric power plant—correlation with oyster greening." *Environmental Letters*, Vol. 5, No. 3, pp. 165–174.

42. A. Preston, D. F. Jeffries, J. W. R. Dutton, B. R. Harvey, and A K. Steel. 1972. "British Isles coastal waters: the concentrations of selected heavy metals in sea water, suspended matter and biological indicators (a pilot study)." *Environmental Pollution*, Vol. 3, No. 1, pp. 69–82.

43. P. S. Galtsoff. 1953. "Accumulation of manganese, iron, copper and zinc in the body of the American oyster *Crassostrea virginica.*" *Anatomical Record*, Vol. 117, No. 3, pp. 601–602.

44. P. A. Cunningham and M. R. Tripp. 1973. "Accumulation and depuration of mercury in the American oyster *Crassostrea virginica.*" *Marine Biology*, Vol. 20, pp. 14–19.

45. D. A. Wolfe. 1970. "Levels of stable zinc and [65]Zn in *Crassostrea virginica* from North Carolina." *Journal of the Fisheries Research Board of Canada*, Vol. 27, No. 1, pp. 47–57.

46. Anonymous. 1972. "Total and organic mercury in marine fish." *Bulletin Environmental Contamination and Toxicology*, Vol. 8, No. 5, pp. 257–266.

47. R. A. Faber, R. W. Risebrough, and H. M. Pratt. 1972. "Organochlorines and mercury in common egrets and great blue herons." *Environmental Pollution*, Vol. 3, No. 2, pp. 111–122.

48. A. A. Belisle et al. 1972. "Residues of organochlorine pesticides, polychlorinated biphenyls and mercury and autopsy data for bald eagles, 1969 and 1970." *Pesticide Monitoring Journal*, Vol. 6, No. 3, pp. 133–138.

49. W. H. Roosenburg. 1969. "Greening and copper accumulation in the American oyster, *Crassostrea virginica*, in the vicinity of a steam electric generating station." *Chesapeake Science*, Vol. 10, p. 241

50. E. H. Rabin and M. D. Schwartz. 1972. *The Pollution Crisis Official Documents*, Section IIB. Oceana Publications, New York.

51. D. Dryrssen, C. Patterson, J.Ui, and G. F. Werchart. 1972. "Inorganic chemicals." Chapter 3. in E. G. Goldberg, Ed., *A Guide to Marine Pollution*. Gordon and Breach Science Publishers, New York/London/Paris.

52. D. D. Boon. 1973. "Iron, zinc, magnesium and copper concentrations in body meat of the blue crab, *Callinectes sapidus*." *Chesapeake Science*, Vol. 14, No. 2, pp. 143–144.

53. G. W. Bryan. 1971. "The effects of heavy metals (other than mercury) on marine and estuarine organisms" *Proceedings of the Royal Society of London*, Vol. 177, No. 1048, pp. 389–410.

54. J. McCaull. 1971. "Building a shorter life." *Environment*, Vol. 13, No. 7, pp. 2–15.

55. N. Chernoff. 1973. "Teratogenic effects of cadmium in rats." *Teratology*, Vol. 8, No. 1, pp. 29–32.

56. R. Nuzzi. 1972. "Toxicity of mercury to phytoplankton." *Nature*, Vol. 237, pp. 38–40.

57. S. J. Erickson, N. Lackie, and T. E. Maloney. 1970. "A screening technique for estimating copper toxicity to estuarine phytoplankton." *Journal of the Water Pollution Control Federation*, Vol. 42, No. 8, pp. R270–R278.

58. S. D. Faust and J. V. Hunter. 1971. *Organic Compounds in Aquatic Environments*. Marcel Dekker, New York.

59. J. L. Lewis. 1972. *Fish Kills Caused by Pollution in 1971. U.S.* Environmental Protection Agency, Office of Air and Water Programs, Washington, D.C.

60. A. J. Van Tassel, Ed. 1970. *Environmental Side Effects of Rising Industrial Output*. Heath Lexington Books, Lexington, Mass.

61. L. Allen et al. 1972. *Pollution in the Pulp and Paper Industry*. The MIT Press, Cambridge, Massachusetts.

62. C. D. Becker and T. O. Thatcher. 1973. *Toxicity of Power Plant Chemicals to Aquatic Life*. U.S. Atomic Energy Commission, Washington, D.C.

63. W. A. Brungs. 1973. "Effects of residual chlorine on aquatic life." *Journal of the Water Pollution Control Federation*, Vol. 45, No. 10, pp. 2180–2193.

64. J. S. Gray and R. J. Ventilla. 1973. "Growth rates of a sediment-living marine protozoan as as a toxicity indicator of interacting heavy metals." *Ambio*, Vol. 2, No. 4, pp. 118–121.

65. W. B. Vernberg and J. Vernberg. 1972. "The synergistic effects of temperature, salinity and mercury on survival and metabolism of the adult fiddler crab, *Uca pugilator*." *Fishery Bulletin*, Vol. 70, No. 2, pp. 415–420.

66. Stanton S. Miller. 1974. "Emerging technology of chlorinolysis." *Environmental Science and Technology*, Vol. 8, No. 1, pp. 18–19.

67. Julian Josephson. 1974. "Cleaning up: Paper industry's mess." *Environmental Science and Technology*, Vol. 8, No. 1, pp. 22–24.

68. U.S. Environmental Protection Agency. 1971. *Digest of FY 1971. State Program Plans.* Water Quality Office, Washington, D.C.

69. U.S. Department of Army Corps of Engineers. 1972. *Assessment of the Effectiveness and Effects of Land Disposal: Methodologies of Wastewater Management*. Wastewater Management Report No. 72–1.

70. National Academy of Sciences–National Academy of Engineering. 1970. *Waste Management Concepts for the Coastal Zone*. Washington, D.C.

71. Ministry of Housing and Local Government, Scottish Development Department. 1970. *Disposal of Solid Toxic Wastes*. Her Majesty's Stationary Office, London.

72. G. F. Bennett. 1974. *Water–1973*. American Institute of Chemical Engineers, Symposium Series No. 136, Vol. 70, New York.

73. W. F. Ritter et al. 1974. "Atrazine, propachlor, and diazinon residues on small agricultural watersheds." *Environmental Science and Technology*, Vol. 8, No. 1, pp. 38–42.

74. McKee and Wolf. 1963. *Water Quality Criteria*. Resources Agency of California, State Water Quality Control Board, Publication No. 3–A.

75. National Technical Advisory Committee to the Secretary of the Interior. 1968. *Water Quality Criteria*. Federal Water Pollution Control Administration, Washington, D.C.

76. J. G. Vos, H. A. Breeman, and H. Penschap. 1968. "The occurrence of the fungicide hexachlorobenzene in wild birds and its toxicological importance" (a preliminary communication) *Med. Rijksfakuteit Landbouw-Wet. Gent*, Vol. 33, No. 3, pp. 1263–1268.

77. National Academy of Sciences–National Academy of Engineering. 1973. *Water Quality Criteria, 1972*. U.S. Environmental Protection Agency, Report No. EPA R3–73–033. Superintendent of Documents, U.S. Government Printing Office, Washington, D.C.

78. C. D. Reese, I. W. Dodson, V. Ulrich, D. L. Becker, and C. J. Kempter. 1972. *Pesticides in the Aquatic Environment*. U.S. Environmental Protection Agency, Washington, D.C.

79. B. H. Ketchum, Ed. 1972. "Contamination and coastal pollution through waste disposal practices." Chapter 7 in *The Water's Edge: Critical Problems of the Coastal Zone*. The MIT Press, Cambridge, Massachusetts.

80. W. H. Matthews, F. E. Smith, and E. D. Goldberg, Eds. 1971. *Man's Impact on Terrestrial and Oceanic Ecosystems* The MIT Press, Cambridge, Massachusetts.

41. ZONATION OF WETLANDS VEGETATION

John L. Gallagher
Marine Institute
University of Georgia
Sapelo Island, Georgia

In recent years pressure on the coastal zone for recreational purposes has increased dramatically. Second-home and vacation rental property demands have led developers to look to wetlands as cheap sites or, often, the only areas available to modify for use as house lots. Reacting to this pressure, conservationists, ecologists and watermen have effectively communicated to legislators the importance of these natural areas to the economic and ecological balance in the coastal zone. The resulting laws protecting these wetlands vary from state to state and prohibit development in certain plant species or marsh areas below one of several tidal datum points. Because of the great value of these wetlands in both the natural and the developed condition, it has become important to delineate public and private ownership boundaries, protected and unprotected marshland, and natural community boundaries. Since vegetation zonation occurs largely in response to tide level and since many of the laws regarding marshlands are written

in terms of the horizontal expression of various tide level points, much interest has developed in using vegetation zonation as an indicator of tide level.

Where a gradation of one or several environmental factors extends over an area, zones of vegetation are found. These zones may be either species zones or growth form zones of the same species. Examples of the zonation phenomenon can be found from the slopes of mountains to the rock shore of the coast.

In the rocky intertidal area the vegetative zonation is of various forms of algae, and these transition zones between the sea and terrestrial environment are often compressed into a few meters. On the other hand, marshland transitions of herbaceous seed plants develop on gentle sand, silt, and clay slopes and may extend for many kilometers. In Florida and on the Gulf coast of the United States mangrove swamps replace the marshland herbs to some extent as a barrier between fast ground and the sea. The marshes are the most extensive of these vegetated wetlands in the United States.

The dominant basic environmental gradient in the coastal marshes is the position of the plants in relation to tide level. Each geographic area has its own tidal peculiarities and tidal amplitudes, and periodicities vary widely. Tidal amplitudes range from several centimeters in some locations to several meters in others. In many areas where tidal amplitude is low, wind direction and velocity are the dominant factors in determining inundation of the wetlands. Some regions experience semidiurnal fluctuations, with two high and two low tides each tidal day, whereas others have diurnal tides, with one high and one low tide each tidal day. Still others experience mixed tides, with two unequal high and/or low tides each tidal day.

The tide has its effect on the plants through a number of physiological channels. These may be direct, or indirect, through the tidal water's influence on other components of a plant's environment. One direct effect of the tide is on the salinity regime to which the plants are exposed. The physiological effects may be the responses of plant processes either to osmotic stress or to specific ions.[1]

Some of the marsh plants are especially adapted to the saline conditions and have glands which excrete the salt that enters the plants (*Spartina alterniflora*, for example). Others have adapted by becoming succulent, thereby diluting the salt that is absorbed (*Salicornia virginica*, for example), while some must avoid the saline condition by living on the marsh fringes above the regular influence of the tides.

Plants living in the lower marsh are subjected to the tide daily, those in the marsh fringe are infrequently inundated, and those in the middle are flooded regularly, but not daily. The greatest ranges in salinity occur away from the creeks where evaporation may concentrate the salts in the water to several times the open-ocean sea water strength.

Other direct effects of the tidal waters on plant processes include nutrient supply, aeration of root zones, and possibly removal of wastes. In most natural situations these effects are complicated by the indirect effects of the tide and by environmental variations other than the tide.

Difference in soil texutre from one location to another may influence the uniformity of zonation because of the interaction of the tidal water and the soil. In coarse-textured soils percolation of rain water is rapid, and salt is removed from the surface. Soils rich in clay, in addition to having low percolation rates, also have higher cation exchange capacities and therefore retain sodium ions better. Aeration of the root depends on drainage, which in turn is determined by slope, soil texture, and the proximity of streams. Factors affecting salinity also affect aeration since sodium-saturated soils do not readily form structural units that promote the movement of air and water by increasing the porosity through the combination of individual sand, silt, clay, and organic particles. Zonation is further complicated by freshwater inflow from surface runoff from the adjacent high ground.[2] Nevertheless, inundation is the major factor in determining vegetation zonation by a given salinity regime within an estuary, although the patterns may be altered somewhat by other environmental influences.

The typical sequence of plants from the lower intertidal zone to the fast ground varies with the longitude, latitude, and salinity of the estuary. A few generalities, however, can be made. Sea grass beds may be found in the subtidal (submerged) zone adjacent to marshes. The most common plant in the low intertidal zone is *Spartina alterniflora*, which grows along the Atlantic and Gulf coasts. A zone of tall grass grows along the stream banks, while shorter plants are found at a somewhat higher elevation. *Spartina foliosa* is present in Pacific coast marshes. *Distichlis spicata*, *Spartina patens*, and various species of *Juncus* typically form zones above *S. alterniflora*. Several species of *Salicornia* are found in saline areas where the frequency of tidal inundation is relatively low and evaporation from the soil surface is high. The upper fringe of the marsh is frequently bordered by a number of shrubs of the genera *Iva*, *Baccahris*, and *Borrichia*. In mangrove swamps *Rhizophora* species usually occupy the lower regions of the intertidal zone, while *Avicennia* species are found on higher, better drained soils.[3] In rocky intertidal zones red algae typically dominate the lower levels, brown forms often occupy the next level, and green forms are below the blue–greens, which are located in the spray area. Extensive subtidal zones of brown algae are found on the northeastern and western coasts of the United States.[4] Figures 1 to 3 show characteristic zonation patterns in a number of typical wetlands. The tide level marks are only approximate and may vary somewhat from site to site.

In New Jersey[5] a good correlation between mean high tide and the boundary separating the tall and short forms of *Spartina alterniflora* has been found. The boundary is clearest where the slope of the marsh surface is greatest. In areas at the heads of creeks the problem of delineating boundaries is more severe, and less accurate determinations can be made.

In Georgia[6] good correlation was noted between the tall and short forms of *Spartina alterniflora* and the mean high-tide line in a pure stand. At another site, where *Juncus roemerianus* interfaced with *S. alterniflora*, the division was a good indicator of the mean high-tide line. Interest in using plant zonation as a means of approximating the horizontal position of tidal datum points is spurred by the need for rapid determination and the great difficulty in leveling in marshland. Tall, dense vegetation and a soft substrate, which is unsuitable as an instrument base, make leveling

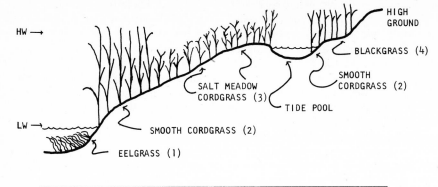

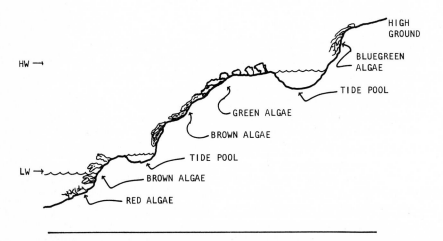

Figure 7.41.1   (Top) Northern Atlantic coast salt marsh: (1) *Zostera marina*; (2) *Spartina alterniflora*; (3) *Spartina patens*; (4) *Juncus geradi*. (Bottom) Rocky coast on either Atlantic or Pacific Ocean.

in the marsh a slow process and a difficult one to accomplish accurately. The approximate horizontal expression of the mean high-tide elevation in a Georgia salt marsh is shown in Figure 4.

Tides are extremely variable, and differences of several decimeters in mean high water may occur within a few miles. Tidal datum points cannot, therefore, be interpolated over very great distances along many shorelines. Tide stations must be closely spaced, and hence it

is very expensive to establish legal ownership and to identify protected marsh by leveling. A detailed analysis of vegetation zones between species and within species can readily be made from medium-scale aerial photographs (1:5000 to 1:24,000), and large acreages can be examined at a low cost per acre.[7,8] These remote sensing techniques are being used for wetlands management in some states but are not adaptable to all state laws.

Aerial photography of the marshlands gives

SOUTHERN ATLANTIC COAST SALT MARSH

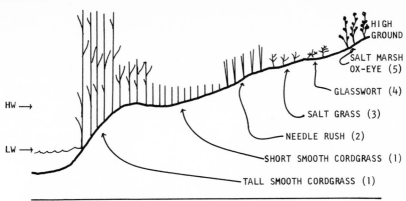

HIGH
GROUND

SALT MARSH
OX-EYE (5)

GLASSWORT (4)

SALT GRASS (3)

NEEDLE RUSH (2)

SHORT SMOOTH CORDGRASS (1)

TALL SMOOTH CORDGRASS (1)

HW →

LW →

SOUTHERN ATLANTIC COAST BRACKISH MARSH

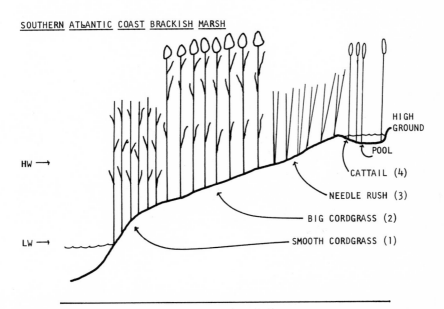

HIGH
GROUND

POOL

CATTAIL (4)

NEEDLE RUSH (3)

BIG CORDGRASS (2)

SMOOTH CORDGRASS (1)

HW →

LW →

Figure 7.41.2   (Top) Southern Atlantic coast salt marsh: (1) *Spartina alterniflora*; (2) *Juncus roemerianus*; (3) *Distichlis spicata*; (4) *Salicornia virginica*; (5) *Borrichia frutescens*. (Bottom) Southern Atlantic coast brackish marsh: (1) *Spartina alterniflora*; (2) *Spartina cynosuroides*; (3) *Juncus roemerianus*; (4) *Typha domingenis*.

a perspective of vegetation zonation over a large area that cannot be appreciated from ground level. The spatial relationships of the vegetation zones over a large area often enable the manager in charge to predict the consequence that altering one zone may have on another. For example, filling an area of short *Spartina alterniflora* may restrict spring tide-

water flow to a more productive tall *S. alterniflora* stand.

Photographs also provide a historical record of the vegetation conditions before and after an alteration is made. The response of a zone to fertilization, the extent of damage by construction, and the development of transplants on a previously barren mud flat can all be

NORTHERN PACIFIC COAST SALT MARSH

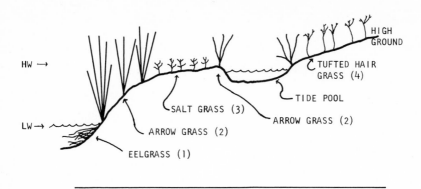

MANGROVE SWAMP

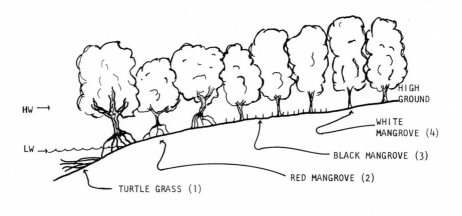

Figure 7.41.3 (Top) Northern Pacific coast salt marsh: (1) *Zostera marina*; (2) *Triglochium maritima*; (3) *Distichlis spicata*; (4) *Deschampsia caespitosa*. (Bottom) Mangrove swamp: (1) *Thallasia testudinum*; (2) *Rhizophora mangle*; (3) *Avicennia germinans*; (4) *Languncularia racemosa*.

documented and evaluated from aerial photography.

The importance of developing workable methods of delineating the boundaries between public and private ownership of wetlands and protecting those that are essential to the coastal environment cannot be overstated. In view of the higher cost of ground transportation associated with rising energy costs, water transportation will probably increase. The resulting need for docking facilities can be expected to cause additional demand for more and wiser wetlands management decisions. The zonation of vegetation in these areas provides the manager with several more or less discrete ecological units that simplify management procedures.

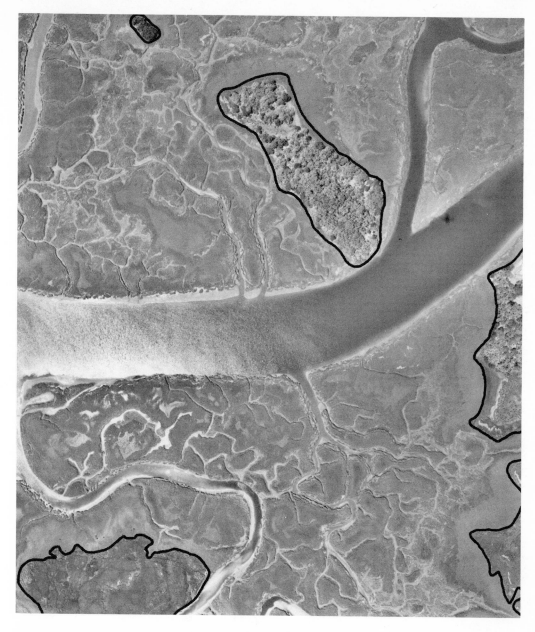

Figure 7.41.4 Approximate line of mean high water in a Georgia salt marsh. The areas in the lower left and right are stands of *Juncus roemerianus*. Two hammocks in the upper center are fringed with several species of plants, as is the edge of the hammock in the center right.

REFERENCES

1. D. S. Ranwell. 1972. *Ecology of Salt Marshes and Sand Dunes*. Chapman and Hall, London, 258 pp.
2. V. J. Chapman. 1960. *Salt Marshes and Salt Deserts of the World*. Interscience Publishers, New York, 392 pp.
3. B. G. Thom. 1967. "Mangrove ecology and deltaic geomorphology: Tabasco, Mexico." *Journal of Ecology*, Vol. 55, pp. 301–344.
4. E. Y. Dawson. 1966. *Marine Botany*. Holt, Rinehart and Winston, New York, 371 pp.
5. R. R. Anderson and F. J. Wobber. 1972. "Wetlands mapping in New Jersey." Pages 530–536 in W. J. Kosco, Chairman, *Proceedings of the 38th Annual Meeting, American Society of Photogrammetry*, Falls Church, Virginia, 636 pp.
6. A. O. Fornes and R. J. Reimold. 1973. "The estuarine environment: location of mean high water—its engineering, economic and ecological potential." Pages 938–978 in P. G. Teleki, Chairman, *Proceedings of the American Society of Photogrammetry*, Fall Convention, Falls Church, Virginia, 1055 p.
7. J. L. Gallagher, R. J. Reimold, and D. E. Thompson. 1973. "A comparison of four remote sensing media for assessing salt marsh primary production." Pages 1287–1295 in J. Cook, Chairman, *Eighth International Symposium on Remote Sensing of Environment*, Ann Arbor, Michigan, 1540 pp.
8. R. J. Reimold, J. L. Gallagher, and D. E. Thompson. 1973. "Remote sensing of tidal marsh." *Photogrammetry Engineering*, Vol. 39, pp. 477–478.

Appendices

The appendices present a variety of tabular, graphic, and textural matter to assist planners and managers in technical aspects of their programs.

I. Federal Policies, Programs, and Regulations

    1. Permits for Activities in Navigable Waters—U.S. Army Corps of Engineers
    2. Dredging and Fill Material Guidelines—U.S. Environmental Protection Agency
    3. Guidelines for Navigable Waters Work—U.S. Fish and Wildlife Service
    4. Oil and Gas Exploration and Development Guidelines—U.S. Fish and Wildlife Service
    5. Wetlands Policy—U.S. Environmental Protection Agency
    6. National Flood Insurance Program
    7. Coastal Zone Management Program Approval Regulations — National Oceanic and Atmospheric Administration

II. Technical Information

    1. Soil Texture and Structure
    2. Soil Texture Identification
    3. Soil Grain Sizes
    4. Soil Classification
    5. Soil Erosion, Transportation, and Deposition
    6. Settling Rates of Sediments
    7. Storm Runoff Rates
    8. Sediment Transport and Delivery
    9. Urban Runoff Rates
    10. Water Quality Parameters
    11. Solubility of Oxygen in Water
    12. Sewage System Removal Efficiencies
    13. Innovative Sewage Systems
    14. Industrial Waste Summary
    15. Industrial Waste Effects on Sewage Systems
    16. Shore Sediment Characteristics
    17 Shore Erosion and Protection Methods: Great Lakes
    18. Sample Nonconfroming Use Regulation
    19. Coastal State Regulatory Authority
    20. Land-Use Control Legislation
    21. Grass Channel Design and Specifications
    22. Dutch Drain Specifications
    23. Seepage Pit Specifications
    24. Detention Basin Specifications
    25. Porous Paving Slab Specifications
    26. Aerial Photograph Interpretation

III. Conversion Factors, Tables, and Graphs

    1. Conversion: Farenheit to Celsius
    2. Conversion: Meters to Feet
    3. Conversion: Salinity Units
    4. Conversion: Water Flow Units

Federal Policies, Programs, and Regulations

1. PERMITS FOR ACTIVITIES IN NAVIGABLE WATERS—U.S. ARMY CORPS OF ENGINEERS

Permits for activities in navigable waters or ocean waters.

SOURCE. *Federal Register*, Vol. 40, No. 144, Part IV (July 25, 1975).

Title 33—Navigation and Navigable Waters

CHAPTER II—CORPS OF ENGINEERS, DEPARTMENT OF THE ARMY

PART 209—ADMINISTRATIVE PROCEDURE

Permits for Activities in Navigable Waters or Ocean Waters

---

§ 209.120 **Permits for activities in Navigable Waters or Ocean Waters.**

(a) *Purpose.* This regulation prescribes the policy, practice, and procedure to be followed by all Corps of Engineers installations and activities in connection with applications for permits authorizing structures and work in or affecting navigable waters of the United States, the discharge of dredged or fill material into navigable waters, and the transportation of dredged material for the purpose of dumping it into ocean waters.

(d) Definitions. For the purpose of issuing or denying authorizations under this regulation.

(1) *"Navigable waters of the United States."* The term, "navigable waters of the United States," is administratively defined to mean waters that have been used in the past, are now used, or are susceptible to use as a means to transport interstate commerce landward to their ordinary high water mark and up to the head of navigation as determined by the Chief of Engineers, and also waters that are subject to the ebb and flow of the tide shoreward to their mean high water mark (mean higher high water mark on the Pacific Coast). See 33 CFR 209.260 (ER 1165-2-302) for a more definitive explanation of this term.

(2) *"Navigable waters".* (i) The term, "navigable waters," as used herein for purposes of Section 404 of the Federal Water Pollution Control Act, is administratively defined to mean waters of the United States including the territorial seas with respect to the disposal of fill material and excluding the territorial seas with respect to the disposal of dredged material and shall include the following waters:

(*a*) Coastal waters that are navigable waters of the United States subject to the ebb and flow of the tide, shoreward to their mean high water mark (mean higher high water mark on the Pacific coast);

(*b*) All coastal wetlands, mudflats, swamps, and similar areas that are contiguous or adjacent to other navigable waters. "Coastal wetlands" includes marshes and shallows and means those areas periodically inundated by saline or brackish waters and that are normally characterized by the prevalence of salt or brackish water vegetation capable of growth and reproduction;

(*c*) Rivers, lakes, streams, and artificial water bodies that are navigable waters of the United States up to their headwaters and landward to their ordinary high water mark;

(*d*) All artificially created channels and canals used for recreational or other navigational purposes that are connected to other navigable waters, landward to their ordinary high water mark;

(*e*) All tributaries of navigable waters of the United States up to their headwaters and landward to their ordinary high water mark;

(*f*) Interstate waters landward to their ordinary high water mark and up to their headwaters;

(*g*) Intrastate lakes, rivers and streams landward to their ordinary high water mark and up to their headwaters that are utilized:

(*1*) By interstate travelers for water-related recreational purposes;

(*2*) For the removal of fish that are sold in interstate commerce;

(*3*) For industrial purposes by industries in interstate commerce; or

(*4*) In the production of agricultural commodities sold or transported in interstate commerce;

(*h*) Freshwater wetlands including marshes, shallows, swamps and, similar areas that are contiguous or adjacent to other navigable waters and that support freshwater vegetation. "Freshwater wetlands" means those areas that are periodically inundated and that are normally characterized by the prevalence of vegetation that requires saturated soil conditions for growth and reproduction; and

(i) Those other waters which the District Engineer determines necessitate regulation for the protection of water quality as expressed in the guidelines (40 CFR 230). For example, in the case of intermittent rivers, streams, tributaries, and perched wetlands that are not contiguous or adjacent to navigable waters identified in paragraphs (a)–(h), a decision on jurisdiction shall be made by the District Engineer.

(ii) The following additional terms are defined as follows:

(a) *"Ordinary high water mark"* with respect to inland fresh water means the line on the shore established by analysis of all daily high waters. It is established as that point on the shore that is inundated 25% of the time and is derived by a flow-duration curve for the particular water body that is based on available water stage data. It may also be estimated by erosion or easily recognized charactertistics such as shelving, change in the character of the soil, destruction of terrestrial vegetation or its inability to grow, the presence of litter and debris, or other appropriate means that consider the characteristics of the surrounding area;

(b) *"Mean high water mark"* with respect to ocean and coastal waters means the line on the shore established by the average of all high tides (all higher high tides on the Pacific Coast). It is established by survey based on available tidal data (preferably averaged over a period of 18.6 years because of the variations in tide). In the absence of such data, less precise methods to determine the mean high water mark may be used, such as physical markings or comparison of the area in question with an area having similar physical characteristics for which tidal data are already available;

(c) *"Lakes"* means natural bodies of water greater than five acres in surface area and all bodies of standing water created by the impounding of navigable waters identified in paragraphs (a)–(h), above. Stock watering ponds and settling basins that are not created by such impoundments are not included;

(d) *"Headwaters"* means the point on the stream above which the flow is normally less than 5 cubic feet per second; *provided, however*, the volume of flow, point and nonpoint source discharge characteristics of the watershed, and other factors that may impact on the water quality of waters of the United States will be considered in determining this upstream limit; and

(e) *"Primary tributaries"* means the main stems of tributaries directly connecting to navigable waters of the United States up to their headwaters and does not include any additional tributaries extending off of the main stems of these tributaries.

(3) *"Ocean waters"*. The term "ocean waters," as defined in the Marine Protection, Research, and Sanctuaries Act of 1972 (P.L. 92–532, 86 Stat. 1052), means those waters of the open seas lying seaward of the base line from which the territorial sea is measured, as provided for in the Convention on the Territorial Sea and the Contiguous Zone (15 UST 1606; TIAS 5639).

(4) *"Dredged material"*. The term "dredged material" means material that is excavated or dredged from navigable waters. The term does not include material resulting from normal farming, silvaculture, and ranching activities, such as plowing, cultivating, seeding, and harvesting, for production of food, fiber, and forest products.

(5) *"Discharge of dredged material"*. The term "discharge of dredged material" means any addition of dredged material, in excess of one cubic yard when used in a single or incidental operation, into navigable waters. The term includes, without limitation, the addition of dredged material to a specified disposal site located in navigable waters and the runoff or overflow from a contained land or water disposal area. Discharges of pollutants into navigable waters resulting from the onshore subsequent processing of dredged material that is extracted for any commercial use (other than fill) are not included within this term and are subject to section 402 of the Federal Water Pollution Control Act even though the extraction of such material may require a permit from the Corps of Engineers under section 10 of the River and Harbor Act of 1899.

(6) *"Fill material."* The term "fill material" means any pollutant used to create fill in the traditional sense of replacing an aquatic area with dry land or of changing the bottom elevation of a water body for any purpose. "Fill material" does not include the following:

(i) Material resulting from normal farming, silvaculture, and ranching activities, such as plowing, cultivating, seeding, and harvesting, for the production of food, fiber, and forest products;

(ii) Material placed for the purpose of maintenance, including emergency reconstruction of recently damaged parts of currently serviceable structures such as dikes, dams, levees, groins, riprap, breakwaters, causeways, and bridge abutments or approaches, and transportation structures.

(iii) Additions to these categories of activities that are not "fill" will be considered periodically and these regulations amended accordingly.

(7) *"Discharge of fill material."* The

term "discharge of fill material" means the addition of fill material into navigable waters for the purpose of creating fastlands, elevations of land beneath navigable waters, or for impoundments of water. The term generally includes, without limitation, the following activities: placement of fill that is necessary to the construction of any structure in a navigable water; the building of any structure or impoundment requiring rock, sand, dirt, or other pollutants for its construction; site-development fills for recreational, industrial, commercial, residential, and other uses; causeways or road fills; dams and dikes; artificial islands, property protection and/or reclamation devices such as riprap, groins, seawalls, breakwalls, and bulkheads and fills; beach nourishment; levees; sanitary landfills; fill for structures such as sewage treatment facilities, intake and outfall pipes associated with power plants, and subaqueous utility lines; and artificial reefs.

(8) *"Person"*. The term "person" means any individual, corporation, partnership, association, State, municipality, commission, or political subdivision of a State, any interstate body, or any agency or instrumentality of the Federal Government, other than the Corps of Engineers (see 33 CFR 209.145 for procedures for Corps projects).

(9) *"Coastal zone."* The term "coastal zone" means the coastal waters and adjacent shorelands designated by a State as being included in its approved coastal zone management program under the Coastal Zone Management Act of 1972.

(e) *Activities Requiring Authorizations.* (1) Structures or work in navigable waters of the United States. Department of the Army authorizations are required under the River and Harbor Act of 1899 (See paragraph (b) of this section) for all structures or work in navigable waters of the United States except for bridges and causeways (see Appendix A), the placement of aids to navigation by the U.S. Coast Guard, structures constructed in artificial canals within principally residential developments where the canal has been connected to a navigable water of the United States (see paragraph (g)(11) below), and activities that were commenced or completed shoreward of established harbor lines before May 27, 1970 (see 33 CFR § 209.150) other than those activities involving the discharge of dredged or fill material in navigable waters after October 18, 1972.

(i) Structures or work are in the navigable waters of the United States if they are within limits defined in 33 CFR 209.260. Structures or work outside these limits are subject to the provisions of law cited in paragraph (b) of this section if those structures or work affect the course, location, or condition of the water body in such a manner as to significantly impact on the navigable capacity of the water body. A tunnel or other structure under a navigable water of the United States is considered to have a significant impact on the navigable capacity of the water body.

(ii) Structures or work licensed under the Federal Power Act of 1920 do not require Department of the Army authorizations under the River and Harbor Act of 1899 (see paragraphs (b) and (c) of this section); provided, however, that any part of such structures or work that involves the discharge of dredged or fill material into navigable waters or the transportation of dredged material for the purpose of dumping it into ocean waters will require Department of the Army authorization under Section 404 of the Federal Water Pollution Control Act and Section 103 of the Marine Protection, Research, and Sanctuaries Act, as appropriate.

(2) *Discharges of dredged material or of fill material into navigable waters.* (i) Except as provided in subparagraphs (ii) and (iii) below, Department of the Army permits will be required for the discharge of dredged material or of fill material into navigable waters in accordance with the following phased schedule:

(a) *Phase I:* After the effective date of this regulation, discharges of dredged material or of fill material into coastal waters and coastal wetlands contiguous or adjacent thereto or into inland navigable waters of the United States and freshwater wetlands contiguous or adjacent thereto are subject to the procedures of this regulation.

(b) *Phase II:* After July 1, 1976, discharges of dredged material or of fill material into primary tributaries, freshwater wetlands contiguous or adjacent to primary tributaries, and lakes are subject to the procedures of this regulation.

(c) *Phase III:* After July 1, 1977, discharges of dredged material or of fill material into any navigable water are subject to the procedures of this regulation.

(ii) All other discharges of dredged or fill material that occur before the dates specified in subparagraphs (i) (b) and (c) above, are hereby permitted for purposes of Section 404 of the Federal Water Pollution Control Act without further processing under this regulation; *provided, however,* That the procedures of this regulation including those pertaining to individual and general permits (see paragraph (i)(2)(ix), below) shall apply to any discharge(s) of dredged or fill material if the District Engineer determines that the water quality concerns as expressed in the guidelines (see 40 CFR 230) indicate the need for such action; and *further provided,* That the following conditions are met:

(a) That a water-quality certification.

under section 401 of the Federal Water Pollution Control Act (see paragraph (c)(1) of this section) is obtained before the discharge is commenced or the State has waived its right to so certify;

(b) That a certification of compliance with a State's approved coastal zone management program pursuant to section 307(c)(3) of the Coastal Zone Management Act (see paragraph (c)(2), above), is furnished, if applicable, before the discharge is commenced;

(c) That the discharge will not be located in the proximity of a public water supply intake;

(d) That the discharge will not contain unacceptable levels of pathogenic organisms in areas used for sports involving physical contact with the water;

(e) That the discharge will not occur in areas of concentrated shellfish production; and

(f) That the discharge will not destroy or endanger the critical habitat of a threatened or endangered species, as identified under the Endangered Species Act.

(iii) Discharges of dredged or fill material in waters other than navigable waters of the United States that have been completed by the effective date of this regulation and discharges of dredged or fill material of less than 500 cubic yards into waters other than navigable waters of the United States that are part of an activity that was commenced before the publication of this regulation, that will be completed within six months of the publication of this regulation, and that involves a single and complete project and not a number of projects associated with complete development plans are hereby authorized for purposes of Section 404 of the Federal Water Pollution Control Act without further processing under this regulation; *provided, however,* That the exemption of these types of activities from the requirements of this regulation shall not be construed as a waiver of the requirement to obtain a State water-quality certification under section 401 of the Federal Water Pollution Control Act or a certification of compliance with a State's approved coastal zone management program pursuant to section 307(c)(3) of the Coastal Zone Management Act in those cases where the discharge of dredged or fill material has not been completed by the date of this regulation; and *further provided,* That the procedures of this regulation shall apply to any activity involving the discharge of dredged or fill material commenced before the date of this regulation if the District Engineer determines that the interests of water quality as expressed in the guidelines (see 40 CFR Part 230) so require. The term "commenced" as used herein shall be satisfied if there has been, before the date of this regulation, some discharge of dredged or fill material into the navigable water

as a part of the above activity or an entering into of a written contractual obligation to have the dredged or fill material discharged at a designated disposal site by a contractor.

(iv) All bulkhead and fill activities involving discharges of dredged material or of fill material in navigable waters other than navigable waters of the United States that are less than 500 feet in length, are constructed for property protection, and involve less than an average of one cubic yard per running foot are hereby permitted for purposes of section 404 of the Federal Water Pollution Control Act without further processing under this regulation; *provided, however,* That the procedures of this regulation including those pertaining to individual and general permits (see paragraph (l)(2)(ix), below) shall apply to any discharge(s) of dredged or fill material if the District Engineer determines that the water-quality concerns as expressed in the guidelines (see 40 CFR 230) indicate the need for such action; and *further provided,* That the conditions specified in subparagraph (ii)(a)-(f) are met.

(3) *Transportation of dredged material for the purpose of dumping it in ocean waters and construction of artificial islands and fixed structures on the outer continental shelf.* Department of the Army authorizations are required for the transportation of dredged material for the purpose of dumping it in ocean waters and construction of artificial islands and fixed structures on the outer continental shelf pursuant to Section 103 of the Marine Protection, Research, and Sanctuaries Act of 1972 and Section 4(f) of the Outer Continental Shelf Lands Act, respectively.

(f) *General Policies for Evaluating Permit Applications.* (1) The decision whether to issue a permit will be based on an evaluation of the probable impact of the proposed structure or work and its intended use on the public interest. Evaluation of the probable impact that the proposed structure or work may have on the public interest requires a careful weighing of all those factors that become relevant in each particular case. The benefit that reasonably may be expected to accrue from the proposal must be balanced against its reasonably foreseeable detriments. The decision whether to authorize a proposal and, if authorized, the conditions under which it will be allowed to occur, are therefore determined by the outcome of the general balancing process (e.g., see § 209.400, Guidelines for Assessment of Economic, Social and Environmental Effects of Civil Works Projects). That decision should reflect the national concern for both protection and utilization of important resources. All factors that may be relevant to the proposal must be considered; among those factors are conservation, economics, aesthetics, general environmental concerns, historic values, fish and wildlife values, flood-damage prevention, land-use classifications, navigation, recreation, water supply, water quality, and, in general, the needs and welfare of the people. No permit will be granted unless its issuance is found to be in the public interest.

(2) The following general criteria will be considered in the evaluation of every application:

(i) The relative extent of the public and private need for the proposed structure or work.

(ii) The desirability of using appropriate alternative locations and methods to accomplish the objective of the proposed structure or work.

(iii) The extent and permanence of the beneficial and/or detrimental effects that the proposed structure or work may have on the public and private uses to which the area is suited.

(iv) The probable impact of each proposal in relation to the cumulative effect created by other existing and anticipated structures or work in the general area.

(3) Permits will not be issued where certification or authorization of the proposed work is required by Federal, State, and/or local law and that certification or authorization has been denied. Initial processing of an application for a Department of the Army permit will proceed until definitive action has been taken by the responsible State agency to grant or deny the required certification and/or authorization. Where the required State certification and/or authorization has been denied and procedures for reconsideration exist, reasonable time not to exceed 90 days will be allowed for the applicant to attempt to resolve the problem and/or obtain reconsideration of the denial. If the State denial of authorization cannot be thus resolved, the application will be denied in accordance with paragraph (p) of this section.

(i) Where officially adopted State, regional, or local land-use classifications, determinations, or policies are applicable to the land or water areas under consideration, they shall be presumed to reflect local factors of the public interest and shall be considered in addition with the other national factors of the public interest identified in paragraph (f)(1), above.

(g) *Policies on particular factors of consideration.* In applying the general policies cited above to the evaluation of a permit application, Corps of Engineers officials will also consider the following policies when they are applicable to the specific application:

(3) *Effect on wetlands.* (i) Wetlands are those land and water areas subject to regular inundation by tidal, riverine, or lacustrine flowage. Generally included are inland and coastal shallows, marshes, mudflats, estuaries, swamps, and similar areas in coastal and inland navigable waters. Many such areas serve important purposes relating to fish and wildlife, recreation, and other elements of the general public interest. As environmentally vital areas, they constitute a productive and valuable public resource, the unnecessary alteration or destruction of which should be discouraged as contrary to the public interest.

(ii) Wetlands considered to perform functions important to the public interest include:

(a) Wetlands which serve important natural biological functions, including food chain production, general habitat, and nesting, spawning, rearing and resting sites for aquatic or land species;

(b) Wetlands set aside for study of the aquatic environment or as sanctuaries or refuges;

(c) Wetlands contiguous to areas listed in paragraph (g)(3)(ii)(a) and (b) of this section, the destruction or alteration of which would affect detrimentally the natural drainage characteristics, sedimentation patterns, salinity distribution, flushing characteristics, current patterns, or other environmental characteristics of the above areas;

(d) Wetlands which are significant in shielding other areas from wave action, erosion, or storm damage. Such wetlands often include barrier beaches, islands, reefs and bars;

(e) Wetlands which serve as valuable storage areas for storm and flood waters; and

(f) Wetlands which are prime natural recharge areas. Prime recharge areas are locations where surface and ground water are directly interconnected.

(iii) Although a particular alteration of wetlands may constitute a minor change, the cumulative effect of numerous such piecemeal changes often results in a major impairment of the wetland resources. Thus, the particular wetland site for which an application is made will be evaluated with the recognition that it is part of a complete and interrelated wetland area. In addition, the District Engineer may undertake reviews of particular wetland areas, in response to new applications, and in consultation with the appropriate Regional Director of the Bureau of Sport Fisheries and Wildlife, the Regional Director of the National Marine Fisheries Service of the National Oceanic and Atmospheric Administration, the Regional Administrator of the Environmental Protection Agency, the local representative of the Soil Conservation Service of the Department of Agriculture, and the head of the appropriate State agency to assess the cumulative effect of activities in such areas.

(iv) Unless the public interest requires otherwise, no permit shall be granted for work in wetlands identified as important by subparagraph (ii), above, unless the District Engineer concludes, on the basis of the analysis required in paragraph (f) of this section, that the benefits of the proposed alteration outweigh the damage to the wetlands resource and the proposed alteration is necessary to realize those benefits.

(a) In evaluating whether a particular alteration is necessary, the District Engineer shall primarily consider whether the proposed activity is dependent upon the wetland resources and environment and whether feasible alternative sites are available.

(b) The applicant must provide sufficient data on the basis of which the availability of feasible alternative sites can be evaluated.

(v) In accordance with the policy expressed in paragraph (f)(3) of this section, and with the Congressional policy expressed in the Estuary Protection Act, PL 90–454, state regulatory laws or programs for classification and protection of wetlands will be given great weight. (See also paragraph (g)(18) of this section).

(4) *Fish and wildlife.* (i) In accordance with the Fish and Wildlife Coordination Act (see paragraph (c)(5) of this section) Corps of Engineers officials will in all permit cases, consult with the Regional Director, U.S. Fish and Wildlife Service, the Regional Director, National Marine Fisheries Service, and the head of the agency responsible for fish and wildlife for the state in which the work is to be performed, with a view to the conservation of wildlife resources by prevention of their loss and damage due to the work or structures proposed in a permit application (see paragraphs (i)(1)(ii) and (j)(2) of this section). They will give great weight to these views on fish and wildlife considerations in evaluating the application. The applicant will be urged to modify his proposal to eliminate or mitigate any damage to such resources, and in appropriate cases the permit may be conditioned to accomplish this purpose.

---

(5) *Water quality.* (i) Applications for permits for activities which may affect the quality of navigable waters will be evaluated with a view toward compliance with applicable effluent limitations and water quality standards during both the construction and operation of the proposed activity. Certification of compliance with applicable effluent limitations and water quality standards required under provisions of Section 401 of the Federal Water Pollution Control Act will be considered conclusive with respect to

water quality considerations unless the Regional Administrator, Environmental Protection Agency (EPA), advises of other water quality aspects to be taken into consideration. If the certification provided is to the effect that no effluent limitation and water quality standards have been established as applicable to the proposed activity, or if certification is not required for the proposed activity, the advice of the Regional Administrator, EPA, on water quality aspects will be given great weight in evaluating the permit application. Any permit issued may be conditioned to implement water quality protection measures.

(ii) If the Regional Administrator, EPA, objects to the issuance of a permit on the basis of water quality considerations and the objection is not resolved by the applicant or the District Engineer, and the District Engineer would otherwise issue the permit, the application will be forwarded through channels to the Chief of Engineers for further coordination with the Administrator, EPA, and decision. (See also paragraphs (b)(7) and (b)(8), above, and (g)(17) and (i)(2)(i) of this section.)

(6) *Historic, scenic, and recreational values.* (i) Applications for permits covered by this regulation may involve areas which possess recognized historic, cultural, scenic, conservation, recreational or similar values. Full evaluation of the general public interest requires that due consideration be given to the effect which the proposed structure or activity may have on the enhancement, preservation, or development of such values. Recognition of those values is often reflected by State, regional, or local land use classifications (see paragraph (f)(3) of this section), or by similar Federal controls or policies. In both cases, action on permit applications should, insofar as possible, be consistent with, and avoid adverse effect on, the values or purposes for which those classifications, controls, or policies were established.

---

(7) *Structures for small boats.* As a matter of policy, in the absence of overriding public interest, favorable consideration will be generally be given to applications from riparian proprietors for permits for piers, boat docks, moorings, platforms and similar structures for small boats. Particular attention will be given to the location and general design of such structures to prevent possible obstructions to navigation with respect to both the public's use of the waterway and the neighboring proprietors' access to the waterway. Obstructions can result from both the existence of the structure, particularly in conjunction with other similar facilities in the immediate vicinity, and from its inability to withstand wave action or other forces which can be expected. District Engineers will inform

applicants of the hazards involved and encourage safety in location, design and operation. Corps of Engineers officials will also encourage cooperative or group use facilities in lieu of individual proprietor use facilities.

---

(11) *Canals and other artificial waterways connected to navigable waters.* (i) A canal or similar artificial waterway is subject to the regulatory authorities discussed in paragraph (b) (2) of this section if it constitutes a navigable water of the United States, or if it is connected to navigable waters of the United States in a manner which affects their course, condition, or capacity. In all cases the connection to navigable waters of the United States requires a permit. Where the canal itself constitutes a navigable water of the United States, evaluation of the permit application and further exercise of regulatory authority will be in accordance with the standard procedures of this regulation. For all other canals the exercise of regulatory authority is restricted to those activities which affect the course, condition, or capacity of the navigable waters of the United States. Examples of the latter may include the length and depth of the canal; the currents circulation, quality and turbidity of its waters, especially as they affect fish and wildlife values; and modifications or extensions of its configuration.

(ii) The proponent of canal work should submit his application for a permit, including a proposed plan of the entire development, and the location and description of anticipated docks, piers and other similar structures which will be placed in the canal, to the District Engineer before commencing any form of work. If the connection to navigable waters of the United States has already been made without a permit, the District Engineer will proceed in accordance with paragraph (g)(12)(i) of this section. Where a connection has not yet occurred, but canal construction is planned or has already begun, the District Engineer will, in writing, advise the proponent of the need for a permit to connect the canals to navigable waters of the United States. He will also ask the proponent if he intends to make such a connection and will request the immediate submission of the plans and permit application if it is so intended. The District Engineer will also advise the proponent that any work is done at the risk that, if a permit is required, it may not be issued, and that the existence of partially-completed excavation work will not be allowed to weigh favorably in evaluation of the permit application.

---

(17) *Discharge of dredged or fill material in navigable waters or dumping of dredged material in ocean waters.* (i) Applications for permits for the discharge of dredged or fill material into navigable waters at specific disposal sites will be reviewed in accordance with guidelines promulgated by the Administrator, EPA, under authority of section 404(b) of the Federal Water Pollution Control Act. If the EPA guidelines alone prohibit the designation of a proposed disposal site, the economic impact on navigation and anchorage of the failure to authorize the use of the proposed disposal site in navigable waters will also be considered in evaluating whether or not the proposed discharge is in the public interest.

(ii) Applications for permits for the transporting of dredged material for the purpose of dumping it into ocean waters will be evaluated to determine that the proposed dumping will not unreasonably degrade or endanger human health, welfare, or amenities, or the marine environment, ecological systems, or economic potentialities. In making the evaluation, Corps of Engineers officials will apply criteria established by the Administrator, EPA, under authority of section 102 (a) of the Marine Protection, Research and Sanctuaries Act of 1972, and will specify the dumping sites, using the recommendations of the Administrator, pursuant to section 102(c) of the Act, to the extent feasible. (See 40 CFR Part 220). In evaluating the need for the dumping as required by paragraph (f) (2) (i) of this section, Corps of Engineers officials will consider the potential effect of a permit denial on navigation, economic and industrial development, and foreign and domestic commerce of the United States.

(iii) Sites previously designated for use as disposal sites for discharge or dumping of dredged material will be specified to the maximum practicable extent in permits for the discharge or dumping of dredged material in navigable waters or ocean waters unless restricted by the Administrator, EPA, in accordance with section 404(c) of the Federal Water Pollution Control Act or section 102(c) of the Marine Protection, Research, and Sanctuaries Act of 1972.

(iv) Prior to actual issuance of permits for the discharge or dumping of dredged or fill material in navigable or ocean waters, Corps of Engineers officials will advise appropriate Regional Administrators, EPA, of the intent to so issue permits. If the Regional Administrator advises, within fifteen days of the advice of the intent to issue, that he objects to the issuance of the permits, the case will be forwarded to the Chief of Engineers in accordance with paragraph (s), below, for further coordination with the Administrator, EPA, and decision. The report forwarding the case will contain an analysis for a determination by the Secretary of the Army that there is no economically feasible method or site available other than that to which the Regional Administrator objects. (See also paragraphs (b)(7) and (b)(8) of this section.)

(18) *Activities in coastal zones and marine sanctuaries.* (i) Applications for Department of the Army authorizations for activities in the coastal zones of those States having a coastal zone management program approved by the Secretary of Commerce will be evaluated with respect to compliance with that program. No permit will be issued until the applicant has certified that his proposed activity complies with the coastal zone management program and the appropriate State agency has concurred with the certification or has waived its right to do so (see paragraph (i)(2)(ii) of this section); however, a permit may be issued if the Secretary of Commerce, on his own initiative or upon appeal by the applicant, finds that the proposed activity is consistent with the objectives of the Coastal Zone Management Act of 1972 or is otherwise necessary in the interest of national security.

(ii) Applications for Department of the Army authorization for activities in a marine sanctuary established by the Secretary of Commerce under authority of section 302 of the Marine Protection, Research, and Sanctuaries Act of 1972 will be evaluated for impact on the marine sanctuary. No permit will be issued until the applicant provides a certification from the Secretary of Commerce that the proposed activity is consistent with the purposes of Title III of the Marine Protection, Research and Sanctuaries Act of 1972 and can be carried out within the regulations promulgated by the Secretary of Commerce to control activities within the marine sanctuary. Authorizations so issued will contain such special conditions as may be required by the Secretary of Commerce in connection with his certification.

2. DREDGING AND FILL MATERIAL GUIDELINES—U.S. ENVIRONMENTAL PROTECTION AGENCY

Discharge of dredged or fill material in navigable waters. See also Appendix I-1.

SOURCE. *Federal Register*, Vol. 40, No. 173, Part II (September 5, 1975).

Title 40—Protection of the Environment
CHAPTER I—ENVIRONMENTAL PROTECTION AGENCY
[FRL 421–1]
PART 230—NAVIGABLE WATERS
Discharge of Dredged or Fill Material

§ 230.3   Evaluation procedures.

(a) All proposed discharges of dredged or fill material will be processed and evaluated in accordance with these guidelines and with applicable Corps of Engineers regulations (33 CFR 209.120 and 33 CFR 209.145).

(b) Upon issuance of the public notice required by 33 CFR 209.120(j) and 209.-145(g) the District Engineer shall send a copy of the public notice to the Regional Administrator.

(c) The role of the Regional Administrator shall include consultation with the District Engineer on the interpretation of the guidelines, review and comment to the District Engineer on permit applications, and implementation of section 404(c) in appropriate cases.

(d) The District Engineer shall utilize these guidelines by making an ecological evaluation following the guidance in § 230.4, including technical evaluation where appropriate, in conjunction with the evaluation considerations specified in § 230.5. This evaluation shall be utilized by the District Engineer in making one of the following determinations pursuant to section 404(b)(1) of the Act:

(1) Allowing the proposed discharge with appropriate discharge conditions to minimize unacceptable effects on the aquatic environment;

(2) Denying the proposed discharge when the discharge will have an unacceptable effect on the aquatic environment;

(3) Requesting additional information where necessary to ensure a sound decision.

§ 230.4   General approaches for technical evaluation.

The effects of discharges of dredged or fill material on aquatic organisms and human uses of navigable waters may range from insignificant disruption to irreversible change at the disposal site. Section 230.4–1 describes the types of ecological effects that may result from the discharge of dredged or fill material and technical approaches to evaluate such effects. Ecological impact from dredged or fill material discharges can be divided into two main categories: (a) physical effects; and (b) chemical-biological interactive effects.

§ 230.4–1   Physical and chemical-biological interactive effects and approaches for evaluation.

No single test or approach can be applied in all cases to evaluate the effects of proposed discharges of dredged or fill material. Evaluation of the significance of physical effects often may be made without laboratory tests by examining the character of the dredged or fill material proposed for discharge and the discharge area with particular emphasis on the principles given in § 230.5. The chemical changes in water quality may best be simulated by use of an elutriate test. To the extent permitted by the state of the art, expected effects such as toxicity, stimulation, inhibition or bioaccumulation may best be estimated by appropriate bioassays. Suitability of the proposed disposal sites may be evaluated by the use, where appropriate, of sediment analysis or bioevaluation. In order to avoid unreasonable burdens on applicants in regard to the amounts and types of data to be provided, consideration will be given by the District Engineer to the economic cost of performing the evaluation, the utility of the data to be provided, and the nature and magnitude of any potential environmental effect. EPA in conjunction with the Corps of Engineers will publish a procedures manual that will cover summary and description of tests, definitions, sample collection and preservation, procedures, calculations, and references. Interim guidance to applicants concerning the applicability of specific approaches or procedures will be furnished by the District Engineer.

(a) *Physical Effects.* Physical effects on the aquatic environment include the potential destruction of wetlands, impairment of the water column, and the covering of benthic communities. Other physical effects include changes in bottom geometry and substrate composition that cause subsequent alterations in water circulation, salinity gradients and the exchange of constituents between sediments and overlying water with subsequent alterations of biological communities. (See § 230.5 of these guidelines.)

(1) From a national perspective, the degradation or destruction of aquatic resources by filling operations in wetlands is considered the most severe environmental impact covered by these guidelines. Evaluation procedures for determining the environmental effects of fill operations in wetlands are relatively straight forward. The guiding principle should be that destruction of highly productive wetlands may represent an irreversible loss of a valuable aquatic resource. (See 33 CFR 209.120(g)(3) and 230.5 of these guidelines.) Wetlands considered to perform important functions include but are not limited to the following:

(i) Wetlands that serve important natural biological functions, including food chain production, general habitat, and nesting, spawning, rearing and resting sites for aquatic or land species;

(ii) Wetlands set aside for study of the aquatic environment or as sanctuaries of refuges;

(iii) Wetlands contiguous to areas listed in paragraphs (a)(1)(i) and (ii) of this section, the destruction or alteration of which would affect detrimentally the natural drainage characteristics, sedimentation patterns, salinity distribution, flushing characteristics, current patterns, or other environmental characteristics of the above areas;

(iv) Wetlands that are significant in shielding other areas from wave action, erosion or storm damage. Such wetlands often include barrier beaches, islands, reefs and bars;

(v) Wetlands that serve as valuable storage areas for storm and flood waters; and

(vi) Wetlands that are prime natural recharge areas. Prime recharge areas are locations where surface and ground water are directly interconnected.

(2) Effects on the water column are principally those associated with a reduction in light transmission, aesthetic values, and direct destructive effects on nektonic and planktonic populations. The significance of water column physical effects are not readily predicted by current technical approaches.

(3) The effect on benthos is essentially the covering of benthic communities with a subsequent change in community structure or function. It has been noted that the benthic community often will reestablish, although sometimes of a somewhat different ecological structure. Evaluation of the significance of the effect on the benthic community can be estimated prior to the discharge activity from a knowledge of the hydrodynamics of the disposal site, mode of discharge, volume of materials, particle size distribution and types of dredged or fill material, and from a knowledge of the benthic community.

(b) Chemical-biological interactive effects. Ecological perturbation caused by chemical-biological interactive effects resulting from discharges of dredged or fill material is very difficult to predict. Research performed to date has not clearly demonstrated the extent of chemical-biological interactive effects resulting from contaminants present in the dredged or fill material. The principal concerns of open water discharge of dredged or fill material that contain chemical contaminants are the potential effects on the water column or on benthic communities.

(1) *Evaluation of chemical-biological interactive effects.* Dredged or fill material may be excluded from the evaluation procedures specified in paragraphs (b)(2) and (3) of this section if any of the conditions specified in paragraphs (b)(1)(i), (ii) or (iii) of this section are determined to exist, unless the District Engineer, after evaluating and considering any comments received from the Regional Administrator, determines that these approaches and procedures are necessary. The Regional Administrator may require, on a case-by-case basis, testing approaches and procedures by stating what additional information is needed through further analyses and how the results of the analysis will be of value in evaluating potential environmental effects. Dredged or fill material may be excluded from this evaluation, if:

(i) Dredged or fill material is composed predominantly of sand, gravel, or any other naturally occurring sedimentary material with particle sizes larger than silt, characteristic of and generally found in areas of high current or wave energy such as streams with large bed loads or coastal areas with shifting bars and channels;

(ii) Dredged or fill material is for beach nourishment or restoration and is composed predominantly of sand, gravel or shell with particle sizes compatible with material on receiving shores; or

(iii) When:

(*a*) The material proposed for discharge is substantially the same as the substrate at the proposed disposal site; and

(*b*) The site from which the material proposed for discharge is to be taken is sufficiently removed from sources of pollution to provide reasonable assurance that such material has not been contaminated by such pollution; and

(*c*) Adequate terms and conditions are imposed on the discharge of dredged or fill material to provide reasonable assurance that the material proposed for discharge will not be moved by currents or otherwise in a manner that is damaging to the environment outside the disposal site.

(2) *Water column effects.* Sediments normally contain constituents that exist in different chemical forms and are found in various concentrations in several locations within the sediment. The potentially bioavailable fraction of a sediment is dissolved in the sediment interstitial water or in a loosely bound form that is present in the sediment. In order to predict the effect on water quality due to release of contaminants from the sediment to the water column, an elutriate test may be used. The elutriate is the supernatant resulting from the vigorous 30-minute shaking of one part bottom sediment from the dredging site with four parts water (vol./vol.) collected from the dredging site followed by one-hour settling time and appropriate centrifugation and a 0.45u filtration. Major constituents to be analyzed in the elutriate are those deemed critical by the District Engineer, after evaluating and considering any comments received from the Regional Administrator, and considering known sources of discharges in the area and known characteristics of the extraction and disposal sites. Elutriate concentrations should be used in conjunction with the same constituents in disposal site water and other data which describe the volume and rate of the intended discharge, the type of discharge, the hydrodynamic regime at the disposal site, and other available information that

aids in the evaluation of impact on water quality (see § 230.5 of these guidelines). The District Engineer may specify bioassays when he determines that such procedures will be of value. In reaching this determination, dilution and dispersion effects subsequent to the discharge at the disposal site will be considered.

(3) *Effects on benthos.* Evaluation of the significance of chemical-biological interactive effects on benthic organisms resulting from the discharge of dredged or fill material is extremely complex and demands procedures which are at the forefront of the current state of the art. Although research has shown that benthic species can ingest contaminated sediment particles, it has not been determined to what degree the contaminants are dissociated from the sediment and incorporated into benthic body tissues thereby gaining entry to the food web. The District Engineer may use an appropriate benthic bioassay when such procedures will be of value in assessing ecological effect and in establishing discharge conditions.

(c) *Procedure for comparison of sites.*

(1) When an inventory of the total concentration of chemical constituents deemed critical by the District Engineer would be of value in comparing sediment at the dredging site with sediment at the disposal site, he may require a total sediment chemical analysis. Total sediment analysis is accomplished by concentrated strong acid digestion or solvent extraction for inorganic and organic constituents respectively. Markedly different concentrations of critical constituents between the excavation and disposal sites may aid in making an environmental assessment of the proposed disposal operation.

(2) When an analysis of biological community structure will be of value to assess the potential for adverse environmental impact at the proposed disposal site, a comparison of the biological characteristics between the excavation and disposal sites may be required by the District Engineer. Biological indicator species may be useful in evaluating the existing degree of stress at both sites. Sensitive species representing community components colonizing various substrate types within the sites should be identified as possible bioassay organisms if tests for toxicity are required. Community structure studies are expensive and time consuming, and therefore should be performed only when they will be of value in determining discharge conditions. This is particularly applicable to large quantities of dredged material known to contain adverse quantities of toxic ma-

terials. Community studies should include benthic organisms such as microbiota and harvestable shellfish and finfish. Abundance, diversity, and distribution should be documented and correlated with substrate type and other appropriate physical and chemical environmental characteristics.

§ 230.4–2 Water quality considerations.

After application of the approaches presented in § 230.4, the District Engineer will compare the concentrations of appropriate constituents to applicable narrative and numerical guidance contained in such water quality standards as are applicable by law. In the event that such discharge would cause a violation of such appropriate and legally applicable standards at the perimeter of the disposal site after consideration of the mixing zone (see § 230.5(e)) discharge shall be prohibited.

§ 230.5 Selection of disposal sites and conditioning of discharges of dredged or fill material.

(a) *General considerations and objectives.* In evaluating whether to permit a proposed discharge of dredged or fill material into navigable waters, consideration shall be given to the need for the proposed activity (see 33 CFR 209,120 and 33 CFR 209.145), the availability of alternate sites and methods of disposal that are less damaging to the environment, and such water quality standards as are appropriate and applicable by law. The following objectives shall be considered in making a determination on any proposed discharge:

(1) Avoid discharge activities that significantly disrupt the chemical, physical and biological integrity of the aquatic ecosystem, of which aquatic biota, the substrate, and the normal fluctuations of water level are integral components;

(2) Avoid discharge activities that significantly disrupt the food chain including alterations or decrease in diversity of plant and animal species;

(3) Avoid discharge activities that inhibit the movement of fauna especially their movement into and out of feeding, spawning, breeding and nursery areas;

(4) Avoid discharge activities that will destroy wetland areas having significant functions in maintenance of water quality;

(5) Recognize that discharge activities might destroy or isolate areas that serve the function of retaining natural high waters or flood waters;

(6) Minimize, where practicable, adverse turbidity levels resulting from the discharge of material;

(7) Minimize discharge activities that will degrade aesthetic, recreational, and economic values;

(8) Avoid degradation of water quality as determined through application of § 230.4, 230.5 (c) and (d).

(b) *Considerations relating to degradation of water uses at proposed disposal sites*—(1) *Municipal water supply intakes.* No disposal site may be designated in the proximity of a public water supply intake. The District Engineer and the Regional Administrator will determine the acceptable location of the disposal site in such cases.

(2) *Shellfish.* (i) Disposal sites for dredged or fill material shall not be designated in areas of concentrated shellfish production. In the case of widely dispersed shellfish populations where it is demonstrated by the applicant that the avoidance of shellfish population areas is impossible the disposal site may be located within such areas, but should be situated so as to cause the least impact on the shellfish population with particular reference to the burial of living forms and maintenance of a suitable substrate.

(ii) Disposal sites should be located to minimize or prevent the possible movement of pollutants by currents or wave action into productive shellfish beds.

(iii) Banks formed by dredged or fill material should be located and oriented to prevent undesirable changes in current patterns, salinity patterns and flushing rates which may affect shellfish.

(iv) The disposal operation should be scheduled to avoid interference with reproductive processes and avoid undue stress to juvenile forms of shellfish.

(3) *Fisheries.* (i) Significant disruptions of fish spawning and nursery areas should be avoided.

(ii) Dredging and disposal operations should be scheduled to avoid interference with fish spawning cycles and to minimize interference with migration patterns and routes.

(iii) Consideration shall be given to preservation of submersed and emergent vegetation.

(4) *Wildlife.* Disposal sites will be designated so as to minimize the impact on habitat, the food chain, community structures of wildlife, and marine or aquatic sanctuaries.

(5) *Recreation activities.* In evaluating proposed discharges of dredged or fill material in or near recreational areas, the following factors should be considered:

(i) Reasonable methods should be employed to minimize any increase in amount and duration of turbidity which would reduce the numbers and diversity of fish or cause a significant aesthetically displeasing change in the color, taste, or odor of the water.

(ii) Release of nutrients from dredged or fill material should be minimized in or to prevent eutrophication, the degradation of aesthetic values, and impairment of recreation uses.

(iii) No material that will result in unacceptable levels of pathogenic organisms shall be discharged in areas used for recreation involving physical contact with the water.

(iv) No material shall be discharged which will release oil and grease in harmful quantities as defined in 40 CFR 110.

(6) *Threatened and endangered species.* No discharge will be allowed 'that will jeopardize the continued existence of threatened or endangered species or destroy or modify the habitat of those species determined critical in accordance with the Endangered Species Act.

(7) *Benthic life.* Disposal sites should be areas where benthic life which might be damaged by the discharge is minimal recognizing that enhancement may also occur. Use of existing disposal sites is generally desirable.

(8) *Wetlands.* (i) Discharge of dredged material in wetlands may be permitted only when it can be demonstrated that the site selected is the least environmentally damaging alternative; provided, however, that the wetlands disposal site may be permitted if the applicant is able to demonstrate that other alternatives are not practicable and that the wetlands disposal will not have an unacceptable adverse impact on the aquatic resources. Where the discharge is part of an approved Federal program which will protect or enhance the value of the wetlands to the ecosystem, the site may be permitted.

(ii) Discharge of fill material in wetlands shall not be permitted unless the applicant clearly demonstrates the following:

(*a*) the activity associated with the fill must have direct access or proximity to, or be located in, the water resources in order to fulfill its basic purpose, or that other site or construction alternatives are not practicable; and

(*b*) that the proposed fill and the activity associated with it will not cause a permanent unacceptable disruption to the beneficial water quality uses of the affected aquatic ecosystem, or that the discharge is part of an approved Federal program which will protect or enhance the value of the wetlands to the ecosystem.

(9) *Submersed Vegetation.* Disposal sites shall be located to minimize the impact on submersed grassflats (for example *Thalassia* and *Zostera* beds) and other areas containing submersed vegetation of significant biological productivity.

(10) *Size of disposal site.* The specified disposal site shall be confined to the smallest practicable area consistent with the type of dispersion determined to be appropriate by the application of these guidelines. Although the impact of the particular discharge may constitute a minor change, the cumulative effect of numerous such piecemeal changes often results in a major impairment of the water resource and interferes with the productivity and water quality processes of existing environmental systems. Thus, the particular disposal site will be evaluated with the recognition that it is part of a complete and interrelated ecosystem. The District Engineer may undertake reviews of particular areas in response to new applications, and in consultation with the appropriate Regional Director of the Fish and Wildlife Service, the Regional Director of the National Marine Fisheries Service of the National Oceanic and Atmospheric Administration, the Regional Administrator of the Environmental Protection Agency, the State Conservationist of the Soil Conservation Service of the Department of Agriculture, and the head of the appropriate State agencies, including the State Director of an approved Coastal Zone Management Program, to assess the cumulative effect of activities in such areas.

(c) The following may also be considered in determining the site and disposal conditions to minimize the possibility of harmful effects:

(1) Appropriate scientific literature, such as the National Water Quality Criteria developed by the Administrator, pursuant to section 304(a)(1) of the Act;

(2) Alternatives to open water disposal such as upland or confined disposal;

(3) Disposal sites where physical environmental characteristics are most amenable to the type of dispersion desired;

(4) Disposal seaward of the baseline of the territorial sea;

(5) Covering contaminated dredged material with cleaner material;

(6) Conditions to minimize the effect of runoff from confined areas on the aquatic environment; and

(7) The Regional Administrator may

specify appropriate monitoring conditions in proximity of disposal sites where necessary to control and minimize water quality degradation, pursuant to Section 308 of the Act.

(d) *Contaminated fill material restrictions*. The discharge of fill material originating from a land source shall not be allowed when the District Engineer determines that the material contains unacceptable quantities, concentrations or forms of the constituents deemed critical by the District Engineer or the Regional Administrator for the proposed disposal site, unless such material is effectively confined to prevent the discharge, leaching, or erosion of the material outside the confined area. Appropriate approaches in 230.4 may be used in making this determination.

(e) *Mixing zone determination*. The mixing zone shall be the smallest practicable mixing zone within each specified disposal site, consistent with the objectives of these guidelines, in which desired concentrations of constituents must be achieved.

The District Engineer and the Regional Administrator shall consider the following factors in determining the acceptability of a proposed mixing zone:

(1) Surface area, shape and volume of the discharge site;

(2) Current velocity, direction and consistency at the discharge site;

(3) Degree of turbulence;

(4) Stratification attributable to causes which include without limitation salinity, obstructions, and specific gravity;

(5) Any on-site studies or mathematical models which have been developed with respect to mixing patterns at the discharge site; and

(6) Such other factors prevailing at the discharge site that affect rates and patterns of mixing.

————————

DEFINITIONS FROM 33 CFR 209.120, "PERMITS FOR WORK IN NAVIGABLE WATERS OR OCEAN WATERS"

3. GUIDELINES FOR NAVIGABLE WATERS WORK—U.S. FISH AND WILDLIFE SERVICE

Guidelines for review of fish and wildlife aspects of proposals in or affecting navigable waters.

SOURCE. *Federal Register*, Vol. 40, No. 231, Part IV (December 1, 1975).

DEPARTMENT OF THE INTERIOR
Fish and Wildlife Service
REVIEW OF FISH AND WILDLIFE ASPECTS OF PROPOSALS IN OR AFFECTING NAVIGABLE WATERS
Adoption of Guidelines

2. *Objectives and policies.*
2.1 *Objectives* of the Department and Service in relation to dredge and fill and other water-related activities are to protect and preserve fish and wildlife habitat, conserve fish and wildlife resources, and protect public trust rights of use and enjoyment in and associated with navigable and other waters of the United States.

A. The Service strives to meet these objectives by encouraging developers to use every possible means, method, and alternative (including non-development) to prevent harmful environmental impacts and degradations, to restore habitat, and increase opportunities for public use through proper development and land use control.

B. The Service also assists, within the limits of its resources, the programs of other agencies, and especially those of other Interior bureaus dedicated to the public interest in man's environment.

C. More specifically the Service, through taking of every appropriate, useful action, has the following long-range objectives or goals:

(1) Respecting navigable waters, their tributaries and related wetlands of the United States:

(a) Stopping and remedying all illegal activities which are damaging or posing a threat of damage to the naturally functioning aquatic and wetland ecosystems or the dependent human uses and satisfaction, and assisting the actions of other bureaus in protection of environmental resources, values, and uses for which they and the Department of the Interior have responsibilities, including natural, cultural, and general recreational resources, values, and' uses, and the water quality aspects of such values and uses.

(b) Ensuring that all authorized works, structures, and activities are (1) judged to be the least ecologically damaging alternative or combination of alternatives (e.g., all appropriate means have been adopted to minimize environmental losses and degradations) and (2) in the public's interest in safeguarding the environment from loss and degradation. Water dependency of a work, structure, or activity will be considered when criterion (1) above has not been met.

In determining whether criteria (1) and (2) have been met, the Service will always consider: (a) The long-term effects of the proposed work, structure, or activity; (b) its cumulative effects when viewed in the context of other already existing or forseeable works, structures, or activities of the same kind; and/or (c) its cumulative effects, when viewed in the context of other already existing or forseeable works, structures, or activities of different kinds.

(2) Respecting all other waters and wetlands of the Nation not determined to be navigable waters in the context of Federal law, particularly with respect to proposals, activities, and sanctioning actions of the Federal Government and where the concerned resources involve a national interest: long-range objectives or goals are identical to those abovestated for navigable waters, insofar as legally possible.

2.2 *Policies.* A. The Service exercises and encourages all efforts to preserve, restore, and improve the fish, wildlife, and naturally functioning aquatic and wetland ecosystems and assists in the preservation of other environmental resources of the Nation, for the benefit of man.

(1) The Service reviews, investigates, and cooperates fully in providing ecological advice on formulation of Federal and federally permitted, assisted, and sanctioned plans for activities and developments in the Nation's waters and wetlands under provisions of the Fish and Wildlife Coordination Act, App. D-2e.

(2) The Service prepares comments and recommendations on proposals for Federal and federally permitted, assisted, and sanctioned activities and developments in the Nation's waters and wetlands.

(3) The Service provides technical guidance and assistance to government agencies and concerned citizens on environmental aspects of management of waters and wetlands. It encourages development and adoption of comprehensive regional and statewide plans for the management of such waters and lands as anticipated by the Water Resources Planning Act, the Estuary Protection Act, the Coastal Zone Management Act of 1972, as provided by certain State and local zoning actions, and as may be provided by any comprehensive national land-use act.

(4) The Service encourages and provides technical guidance and assistance to local and State programs, symposia, and other organized efforts designed to further public education and awareness of environmental values and actions to abate threats to waters and wetlands of the Nation.

(5) The Service assists all Federal agencies involved in planning construction or permitting and licensing activities in the Nation's waters and wetlands to meet their responsibilities under Section 7 of the Endangered Species Act of 1973. This includes helping to ensure that the continued existence of an endangered or threatened species is not further jeopardized nor will the actions to be taken result in the destruction or modification of such species habitat that is determined critical. Such assistance should enable these agencies to avoid initiation of proposals which could place such species or their critical habitat in jeopardy.

(6) The Service assists particularly other bureaus of the Department of the Interior in meeting their special responsibilities for the Nation's environmental values, including cultural and natural values, general recreation values, and water quality, among others.

B. The Service actively discourges activities and developments in or affecting the Nation's waters and wetlands which would individually or cumulatively with other developments on a waterway or group of related waterways unnecessarily destroy, damage, or degrade fish, wildlife, naturally functioning aquatic and wetland ecosystems, and/or the dependent human satisfactions. In this, the Service assists other Interior bureaus and seeks their aid in protecting all environmental resources under the purview of the Department of the Interior.

(1) The Service considers navigable waters to include all waters, water bodies, and wetlands subject to Federal jurisdiction under provisions of the River and Harbor Act of 1899 and the Federal Water Pollution Control Act Amendments of 1972, as clarified by Federal regulations and court decisions or as modified by Federal law.

(a) For nonwater-dependent works, particularly where biologically productive wetlands are involved and alternative upland sites are available (as may be suggested from field appraisal—see Sec. 4.1A—by a Service biologist), the Service usually recommends denial of a permit unless the public interest requires further consideration. Further consideration may be indicated by an approved land use plan (see Sec. 5.2A(2)) or in the absence of such a master plan, from the determination made by the responsible Federal regulatory agency after carefully weighing all factors relevant to the public interest and reflecting the national concerns for both protection and utilization of important resources (see paragraphs (f) and (g)(3) of 33 CFR 209.120, App. D-4a(2)).

(b) For water-dependent works, the Service discourages the occupation and destruction of biologically productive wetlands and shallows. The Service usually recommends that the site occupied involve the least loss of area on the least valuable of the alternative sites; that avoidable loss or damage to such productive wetlands and shallows, their fish and wildlife, and their human uses be prevented; and that any damages or losses of such resources, proved unavoidable, be reasonably mitigated or compensated.

(2) The Service places special emphasis on vegetated and other productive shallow waters and wetlands and on fish and wildlife species for which the Secretary of the Interior has delegated and specifically mandated responsibilities:

(a) Wetlands as described in "Wetlands of the United States," Circular 39 of the U.S. Fish and Wildlife Service, published in 1956, republished in 1971.

(b) Estuarine and Great Lakes areas as defined in the Estuary Protection Act, the Coastal Zone Management Act of 1972, and Sec. 104(n) of the Federal Water Pollution Control Act, App. D–2o, D–2v, and D–2s.

(c) Migratory birds, anadromous and Great Lakes fishes, and endangered species as defined respectively in the Migratory Bird Treaty Act, Anadromous Fish Conservation Act and the Endangered Species Act of 1973, App. D–2b, D–2l, and D–2q.

5.3 *Detailed policy guidelines.* Service personnel will observe additional detailed guidelines in screening and reviewing permit applications and Federal proposals as indicated below for particular types of projects (Note that where excavation of fill or deposition of spoil are involved in a proposal, the guidelines of items I or J are applicable in addition to the guidelines listed for the specific main proposed works or activity):

A. *Docks, moorages, piers, and platform structures.* (1) In crowed areas, individual single-purpose docks will be discouraged, and multiple-use facilities common to several property interests providing common pollution control works and minimizing occupation of public waters will be actively encouraged.

(2) Joint-use moorage facilities will be encouraged for subdivisions, motels, and multiple dwellings in preference to individual moorage.

(3) The size of docks and piers and their extension beyond the normal high water line will be recommended to be restricted to that required for the intended use.

(4) Anchor buoys will be encouraged in preference to docks.

(5) Piers or catwalks will be encouraged in preference to fills to provide needed access to navigable water.

(6) Dry storage on upland will be encouraged for small boats in preference to water moorage in crowded areas.

(7) Removal of docks, piers, or platform structures in existence without a Federal permit will be recommended where practicable and especially where the particular structure is found to interfere with or preclude preservation, management, or utilization of fish and wildlife resources and other environmental values.

(8) Removal will also be recommended of all piers and similar structures receiving little use, in a state of disrepair, and/or serving no demonstrated public purpose.

(9) Overwater location of apartments, shops, restaurants, and other nonwater-dependent facilities on pile structures or fills will generally be viewed by the Service as destructure intrusions upon the aquatic environment. Denial of a permit for a structure intended solely for such uses will be recommended unless it is clearly shown that the particular structure is required in the public interest (see Sec. 2.2B(1)(a) and Sec. 5.2A) and no alternative site mutually acceptable to the Service and the applicant is available.

(10) Permits for docks, piers, and other overwater structures will be recommended to be conditioned to require removal once the structure no longer serves the purpose for which it was originally permitted.

(11) Houseboat anchorage and moorage in public waters outside of publicly established harbor areas for more than 30 days will be discouraged.

(12) Service review of applications for the repair or replacement of previously permitted docks, piers, and moorages will be expedited.

B. *Marinas and port facilities.* (1) Designs that minimize disruption of currents, restriction of the tidal prism, excavation in shallow waters and wetlands, removal of barrier beaches, and filling of shallow waters and wetlands that do not occupy waters with poor flushing characteristics or sites with high siltation rates; and that preserve environmental values in general will be strongly encouraged.

(2) Facilities for the proper handling of boat and site-generated sewage, litter, other wastes and refuse, petroleum products, and precipitation runoff will be insisted upon with all marina and port proposals, including modifications to existing facilities, insofar as required by law.

(3) Regional and statewide planning for balanced land use and specifically to locate suitable spoil disposal sites, reduce unneeded dredging, and properly locate any new or expanded port, other necessary navigation and other water-dependent facilities will be encouraged. Shipping and support facilities including marine railways and launching ramps will be encouraged to make full utilization of developed areas to forestall disturbing new areas of high environmental value.

C. *Bulkheads and seawalls.* (1) Bulkheads and seawalls generally will be acceptable in areas having unstable shorelines, but their construction will be discouraged where marsh, mangrove, or other naturally protective and productive areas would be disturbed. In the latter situations, any necessary bulkhead should not reflect wave energy so as to destroy productive wetlands. In rapidly eroding situations where natural, protective vegetation or other controls are inadequate, bulkheads placed in navigable waters may be acceptable if properly designed to mitigate but not aggravate natural forces and processes.

(2) In extensively developed areas, rip-rap and/or designs utilizing natural vegetation will be encouraged in lieu of bulkheads of wood, concrete, or metal. Bulkheads will be acceptable that esthetically and/or ecologically enhance the aquatic environment.

(3) On barrier and sand islands and sand beaches, bulkheads which would adversely affect the littoral drift and natural deposition of sand materials will not be acceptable.

D. *Cables, pipelines, transmission lines, bridges and causeways.* (1) The Service will encourage the establishment of transportation-utility access corridors crossing navigable and other waters and wetlands at sites that localize and minimize environmental impact by limiting the encroachments to least valuable and productive areas.

(2) To be acceptable, aerial or submerged cables, pipelines, and transmission lines must be located and designed for maximum compatibility with the environment. In assessing environmental compatibility, Service personnel will give particular emphasis to the provisions made to protect water quality, fish and wildlife resources (notably, interference with migration routes) and to prevent interference with fishing and other public uses. Where unique natural areas, cultural sites, or significant impacts on scenic beauty or public access appear to be involved, Service personnel will alert and cooperate with concerned Interior bureaus and other agencies.

(3) Alteration of the natural water flow circulation patterns or salinity regimes through improper design or alignment will be discouraged.

(4) Enhancement of public access by the installation of fishermen catwalks, boat launching ramps, or other structural features will be encouraged.

(5) Bridge approaches required to be located in wetland areas will be recommended to be placed on pilings rather than constructed as solid fill causeways.

E. *Jetties, groins, and breakwaters.* Jetties, groins, and breakwaters that do not interfere with or, preferably, that enhance public access, and do not create adverse sand transportation patterns or unduly disturb the aquatic ecosystem will be acceptable. Service personnel will place particular emphasis on preventing project-related erosion and other harmful impacts caused by the installation—such as destruction of sand dunes and beaches and filling of shallows and tidal wetlands due to changes in littoral currents and drift—as well as on protecting fish and wildlife resources and uses.

F. *Lagoons and impoundments.* Lagoons or impoundments for waste treatment, cooling, or aquaculture which would occupy or damage significant wetlands or other ecologically productive areas in navigable waters will be unacceptable to the Service and denial of permit normally will be recommended. (A NPDES permit is required to discharge from these; see EPA's wetlands policy, App. F–2a, b, and c.)

G. *Navigation channels and access canals.* (1) Construction or extension of canals primarily to obtain fill material will be discouraged or opposed as appropriate.

(2) Designs and alignments should adequately serve the needs of commercial and sport fisheries and other water recreation as well as other demonstrated public needs.

(3) Designs should not create pockets, interior channels, or other hydraulic conditions which would cause stagnant water problems.

(4) Designs should not create or aggravate shoreline erosion problems or interfere with natural processes of beach nourishment.

(5) Channel alignments and spoil sites should avoid shellfish grounds, eelgrass beds, beds of other productive aquatic vegetation, coral reefs, fish spawning and nursery areas, fish and wildlife feeding areas, and other shallow water and wetland areas of value to fish and wildlife resources and uses.

(6) Alignments should make maximum use of natural or existing deep water channels.

(7) Designs should include temporary dams or plugs in the seaward ends of canals or waterways and competent confining dikes around spoiling sites to serve until excavation has been completed and all sediment has settled out.

(8) Designs should not alter tidal circulation patterns adversely, create change in salinity regimes, or change related nutrient and aquatic life distribution patterns.

(9) Construction should be conducted in a manner that minimizes turbidity and dispersal of dredged material into productive areas and on schedules that minimize interference with fish and wildlife migrations, spawning, nesting, or human uses.

(10) In addition, the Service will recomend that the applicant or permittee be required to supply the Service with a schedule of the dredging anticipated during the life of the permit (frequency, duration, type of dredge, amounts of material, etc.) and where appropriate give a two-week notification prior to the commencement of work at each location or phase of construction. Recommendation also will be made to require Service notification when work is completed and the amount of materials removed. Similar advice and notice will be requested for previously coordinated Federal projects.

H. *Drainage canals and ditches.* Construction of canals and ditches that would drain or facilitate drainage of any of the wetland types identified in the Fish and Wildlife Service's Circular 39, "Wetlands of the United States," will be discouraged, and denial of permit usually will be recommended by the Service. Channels draining such wetlands will be acceptable to the Service only where the following situation has been conclusively demonstrated: Insect vector control or some other public health, safety, or welfare measure is required as a public necessity and drainage would be the least damaging or only practicable means of accomplishment. But in these instances, the quantity and quality of any discharged waters should be controlled as required by the FWPCA and so as not to adversely affect the aquatic ecosystem unduly (a NPDES permit covering such discharges may be required).

I. *Excavation of fill material.* (1) Excavation and dredging in shallow waters and wetlands will be discouraged and any permits issued or Federal work approved will be recommended to be conditioned to prohibitt activities in fish and wildlife nursery areas and during periods of migration, spawning, and nesting activity.

(2) Whenever the excavation of fill materials from productive submerged or intertidal wetland areas or from wetland types identified in Circular 39 (see Sec. 2.2B(2)) is considered detrimental to fish and wildlife resources and unacceptable, permit denial for such work will be recommended by the Service.

(3) Uncontrolled stockpiling of dredged material in shallow water or on wetlands to achieve full bucket loads will not be acceptable. Unloading barges should be employed wherever possible to avoid such stockpiling of materials. Where stockpiling is required, the use of competently diked upland areas us-

ually will be recommended.

(4) Excavations should not create stagnant sumps or cul de sacs that trap and kill aquatic life.

(5) Dredging operations should be conducted so as to prevent petroleum spill, deposit of refuse, and avoidable dispersal of silt or other fines or other discharges of harmful materials (a NPDES permit may be required).

J. *Filling and deposition of spoil and refuse, materials.* (1) Filling in navigable waters generally will be discouraged and will be strongly objected to where the proposed development is nonwater dependent or would not serve a demonstrated public need.

(2) Whenever the filling of waters and wetlands is considered detrimental to fish and wildlife resources and unacceptable, permit denial for such work will be recommended by the Service.

(3) Spoil confinement works should be properly designed, constructed, and maintained to avoid discharge of fines, other particulates, or harmful material to natural waters and be located on dry upland. The location of outlets and other means of control of the effluent from the spoil retention area should yield water quality that will preserve the aquatic ecosystem (a NPDES permit may be required).

(4) Toxic, oxidizable organic, and other highly harmful materials must be disposed on dry upland areas behind impervious dikes or by other safe and environmentally-protective means.

(5) Dikes should be vegetated immediately to prevent erosion.

(6) In-bay, open-water, and deepwater disposal generally will be considered acceptable by the Service only after all upland and other alternative disposal sites have been explored and rejected for good cause. Deep-water disposal will be acceptable only at sites designated under State or Federal regulations or at sites specifically selected, including those selected for deposit of clean material for habitat improvement, where agreed upon by all concerned agencies.

(7) Sediment and/or effluent analysis will be recommended to be required in cases where there is suspected contamination by heavy metals or other toxicants. In cases where contaminant levels are high, the Service will either urge disposal on fully confined impervious upland sites or by other safe and approved means, or recommend denial of permit application.

(8) Turbidity and dispersal of dredged material will be recommended to be controlled in relation to open water dredg-

ing and disposal by means of fine-meshed curtains or other effective means.

(9) The foregoing guidelines on spoil deposition are also particularly applicable to Federal channel excavation and maintenance.

K. *Mineral exploration and development, territorial waters.* (1) To be acceptable, blanket permits issued for mineral exploration and development (including oil, gravel, sand, fossil shell, phosphates, sulfur, salt, placer metals, etc.) must be limited to the shortest time period essential to the work proposed and should provide by explicit conditions of the permits for such of the following that can be utilized to minimize environmental degradation: Areal exclusions; special exploration and development procedures (e.g. slant drilling); use of special equipment (e.g. use of shallow draft barges and low-impact swamp vehicles on wetlands); and limitations on dredging, filling, and spoiling (i.e. use of existing channels wherever possible rather than new ones, avoidance of productive wetlands and shallows for filling and spoiling, etc.).

(2) To be acceptable, proposed activities and works must be described as fully as possible in the original permit application, and to the extent that these cannot be described for the entire extent of the work and period of the permit, the undescribed extension and modifications when known and proposed must be subject to provision of adequate notice and opportunity for on-site assessment of potential environmental impact by the Service or its designee, and the permit must be further conditioned as may be required to protect environmental resources on the basis of such recommendations as the Service may make.

(3) To be acceptable, proposals must meet the applicable general and detailed guidelines set out hereinabove for other particular activities and works involved in the proposed mineral exploration and development.

(4) To be acceptable, proposals must make adequate provisions to keep environmental degradation to the minimum, particularly that from spillage of oil; release of refuse including polluting substances and solid wastes; spoiling on productive wetlands; dredging of productive shallows; and alteration of current patterns, tidal exchanges, freshwater outflow, erosion and sedimentation.

L. *Mineral and other developments, including rights of way, on public lands.* (1) As discussed more fully in Section 1, Interior bureaus and other Federal land management agencies are involved variously in leasing lands and granting permits for rights of way, mineral exploration and development, hydroelectric power development, and other activities on public lands of the United States. To the extent that these activities would involve identifiable effects on navigable waters they also require a permit from the Corps or Coast Guard under the 1899 Act and/or the Federal Water Pollution Control Act Amendments of 1972, and in certain cases a NPDES permit from EPA or the State.

(2) These guidelines do not cover procedures for the intra-Interior review of outer continental shelf and other public lands, mineral leases, and permits nor rights-of-way permits, but it is expected that Service personnel will apply any of the pertinent policy guidelines of this handbook as are appropriate.

(3) Corps, Coast Guard, and EPA permit applications covering such activities should be reviewed in the field for potential site-specific impacts as with any other permit, keeping in mind, however, that general protective conditions are included in the Interior permits which are deemed adequate for all known situations and contingencies and that known highly damageable areas have been excluded from the lease offers and use permits for lands of the Territories.

(4) If a particular case appears to the reviewing biologist to involve substantial impacts of a nature not certainly covered by conditions of the Interior permit, he should initiate action to so notify the district or regional office of the concerned regulatory agency and the responsible office of the concerned Interior bureau or for the Territory. If the responsible local Interior office cannot satisfy the Service concern, the matter should be referred to the Central Office for resolution and the district or regional office of the regulatory agency should be so apprised.

M. *Log handling, moorage, and storage.* (1) Log handling, moorage, and storage sites proposed to be located on salmon-spawning and other fish productive streams, shellfish grounds, or shallow water and wetland areas of value to fish and wildlife resources and uses will not be acceptable to the Service.

(2) Log handling, moorage, and storage in public waters will be discouraged, particularly where such activities would obstruct or impede public access, fishing, hunting, and other legitimate public uses of the water body; degrade and destroy fish and wildlife resources; or otherwise degrade environmental values.

(3) Environmentally sound practices of log handling will be encouraged through

recommendations for conditioning of any required Federal permit or contract and otherwise, as follows:

(a) Use of positive controls over bark, other debris, and leachates, including proper confinement, collection and disposal of all floatable, soluble, and settleable refuse. Rapidly flowing water, steep shores or other sites must be avoided for log dumping where positive controls cannot be effected.

(b) Use of easy let-down devices for placing logs in water to avoid safety and environmental hazards of violent free-fall dumping.

(c) Limiting the quantity of logs and the duration of their moorage and storage in public waters to the minimum required for efficiency.

(d) Use of upland sites for bundling of logs and disassembling the bundles.

N. *Steam electric powerplants and other facilities using navigable waters for cooling.* Although these facilities will be treated in detail in a separate Steam Electric Powerplant and Cooling Facilities Handbook, broad, general guidelines are included here:

(1) As a general rule, once-through cooling systems will be discouraged and closed-cycle cooling will be encouraged where the facility is proposed to be sited on or so as to affect biologically productive navigable waters. In particular, any facility will be strongly discouraged which would significantly change the environment and values of an estuarine area or other biologically productive navigable water by withdrawal and discharge of large volumes of water—thereby depleting aquatic life by entrainment and impingement; altering the natural or existing regime of salinity, temperature, and dissolved oxygen and the patterns of water currents, tidal exchange, volume, tidal excursion, and freshwater flow; disturbing the populations, dynamics, and distribution of aquatic life; scouring productive water bottoms or otherwise endangering the viability and productivity of the ecosystem; and lessening the human satisfactions dependent thereon.

(2) A facility to divert water from and release heated water to navigable waters where proposed to be sited so as to affect harmfully salmonid spawning, rearing, or migration waters or any water or wetland supporting highly sensitive and/or highly valued species of fish or wildlife will not be acceptable to the Service unless such facility is fitted with a closed-cycle cooling system and otherwise incorporates protective features that insure against any significant harm to such species at all times and under all foreseeable conditions.

(3) To be acceptable any facility incorporating once-through cooling involving navigable waters must:

(a) Be sited where wetland destruction, other habitat damage, interference with fish and wildlife and their uses, and overall environmental harm will be at the minimum compared to other possible sites in the region;

(b) Involve a plan layout based on preoperational baseline studies defining current, temperature, salinity, tidal, migratory fish or wildlife, and other patterns sufficient to select the smallest and most desirable heat mixing zone, providing adequate zone of passage, and other plan arrangements, including those of the transmission lines and other appurtenant facilities, that will minimize harmful impacts on fish and wildlife, their habitats and uses as well as overall environmental damages;

(c) Incorporate design features and operating programs and rules to avoid all avoidable harm to fish and wildlife, habitats, and uses as well as other environmental resources and uses; specifically:

(i) Incorporate a cooling system design employing the best available technology and combination of facilities to minimize harmful effects on the environment, including: Mechanical rather than chemical scale and algae controls; intake-outlet arrangements which minimize impingement, and entrainment, and damage to productive bottoms; fish bypasses and other saving devices as well as screens at intakes;

(ii) Schedule shutdowns to avoid harm to aquatic life as fully as possible;

(iii) Meet all applicable water quality requirements and goals; and

(iv) Adequately monitor the operations to satisfy the burden of proof upon the permittee or licensee that the foregoing and other appropriate environmental standards are met.

6. *Coordination, liaison, and negotiation.* It is difficult to overemphasize the value of taking steps at the earliest possible time to gain participation in the planning process to permit offering suggestions of modifications and alternatives and discouraging selection of naturally productive sites or harmful methods of development. This is difficult with piecemeal private developments, but even with these, publicizing Service concerns in the media, assisting concerned citizens who responsibly involve themselves in surveillance, accepting speaking engagements, arranging symposia, educating local planning, zoning,

and administrative boards, and other means can be of help in the long run.

With Federal activities close liaison by the Division Field Supervisor with the Federal planning agencies usually leads to early notice of actions and invitation to informal consultation during formula-tion of plans. This early consultation can be the most productive effort made by Division personnel in relation to Federal activities. If possible the consultation should be between the Division biologist and the lead agency planner assigned to the specific survey or project.

4. OIL AND GAS EXPLORATION AND DEVELOPMENT GUIDELINES—U.S. FISH AND WILDLIFE SERVICE

Guidelines for oil and gas exploration and development activities in territorial and inland waters and wetlands.

SOURCE. *Federal Register*, Vol. 40, No. 231, Part III (December 1, 1975).

DEPARTMENT OF THE INTERIOR

Fish and Wildlife Service

OIL AND GAS EXPLORATION AND DEVELOPMENT ACTIVITIES IN TERRITORIAL AND INLAND NAVIGABLE WATERS AND WETLANDS

Adoption of Guidelines

1. *Introduction.* 1.1 The U.S. Fish and Wildlife Service recognizes that an adequate and dependable supply of petroleum products is essential to meet the economic and standard of living needs of this Nation. The Service also recognizes the need for a strong, uniform policy for planning, evaluating, and reporting on oil and gas exploration and production activities affecting navigable waters and related natural resources. This pamphlet is directed toward meeting and satisfying the Nation's environmental and energy needs by presenting the Service's guidelines for geophysical, drilling and completion operations, pipeline construction, onshore facilities, and other associated exploration and development activities. These guidelines discourage the exploitation of one resource at the expense of another and encourage the use of environmentally sound planning criteria. Basically, these guidelines focus on the conservation, development, and improvement of fish and wildlife, their habitats, naturally functioning ecosystems, other environmental values, and related human uses of the Nation's waters and wetlands.

2. *Basis.* 2.1A. Federal permits are required for works proposed in the Nation's navigable waters and associated wetlands. Placing of any structure in or over such waters and wetland areas or excavating from or depositing material in such areas is unlawful unless a permit has been issued by the Department of the Army, Corps of Engineers, under authority of Section 10 of the River and Harbor Act of March 3, 1899 (33 U.S.C. 403). The U.S. Coast Guard, Department of Transportation, has special authority to regulate the location and clearances of bridges and causeways over navigable waters of the United States under Section 9 of the 1899 Act (33 U.S.C. 401) and the Department of Transportation Act (49 U.S.C. 1653).

B. Permits issued by the Environmental Protection Agency (EPA) or by a State agency under EPA overview also are required under Section 402 of the Federal Water Pollution Control Act Amendments of 1972 (33 U.S.C. 1251) for pollutant discharges into navigable waters. This Act also provides for certification by EPA or the State, that activities otherwise federally permitted will not abridge water quality requirements (Section 401), for permitting by the Corps of Engineers (Corps) of the placement of dredged and fill materials in defined disposal areas (Section 404), and for regulation by EPA of the disposal of sewage sludge which would result in pollutants entering navigable waters (Section 405).

C. Applications for permits described in the preceding paragraphs are made, as appropriate, to the District Engineer, Corps of Engineers; the District Commander, U.S. Coast Guard; or the Regional Administrator, Environmental Protection Agency (or the State water quality agency) for the District or Region in which the work or activity is proposed. *All persons or other entities, including Federal and other government agencies, are required to obtain the appropriate permits prior to commencing any construction or other activity in navigable waters.*

D. All of the above described Federal regulatory programs are subject to the provisions of the Fish and Wildlife Coordination Act (16 U.S.C. 661) and the National Environmental Policy Act of

1969 (42 U.S.C. 4321) which mandate, respectively, full consideration of fish and wildlife and environmental values in weighing the balance of the public interest in deciding whether a permit should be issued for a proposed activity.

3. *Authorities and responsibilities of the Department of the Interior.* 3.1A. The Secretary of the Interior, acting through the Bureau of Land Management, the U.S. Geological Survey, the Bureau of Indian Affairs, the U.S. Fish and Wildlife Service, the National Park Service, and the Bureau of Outdoor Recreation, has broad authority in the administration of public lands, reservations, and the mineral resources of such lands held in trust, and in providing consultation and advice on the protection of the Nation's fish, wildlife, scenic, natural, historic, recreational, and other environmental resources.

B. One such law administered for the Department of the Interior by the U.S. Fish and Wildlife Service is the Fish and Wildlife Coordination Act. This Act specifically requires (16 U.S.C. 662): "* * * *whenever the waters of any stream or body of water are proposed or authorized to be* impounded, diverted, the channel deepened, or the stream or other body of water otherwise *controlled or modified for any purpose whatever,* including navigation and drainage, by any department or agency of the United States, *or by any public or private agency under Federal permit or license, such department or agency first shall consult with the United States Fish and Wildlife Service,* Department of the Interior, and *with the head of the agency exercising administration over the wildlife resources of the particular State* * * * with a view to the conservation of wildlife resources by preventing loss of and damage to such resources as well as providing for the development and improvement thereof * * *."[1] (Similar responsibilities under the Fish and Wildlife Coordination Act are administered by the National Marine Fisheries Service for the Department of Commerce.)

4. *Objectives and policies of the Fish and Wildlife Service concerning the usage and development of the Nation's waters and wetlands.* 4.1 The following outline presents the overall objectives and polices of the Fish and Wildlife Service in its advisory, consultive, and

review role regarding works and activities in the Nation's waters and associated wetlands.

4.2 *Objectives.* 4.2A. The objectives of the U.S. Fish and Wildlife Service in relation to oil and gas exploration, development, and production activities are to prevent or minimize damages to fish and wildlife resources, their associated habitat, and other environmental resources, and to preserve public trust rights of use and enjoyment of such resources in and associated with navigable and other waters of the United States. The Service strives to meet these objectives by encouraging the industry to use every practical means, method, and alternative to prevent harmful environmental impacts and degradations.

B. More specifically the Service has the following long-range objectives respecting navigable waters, their tributaries, and related wetlands:

(1) Providing assistance to other Federal agencies in their enforcement of regulatory programs to prevent unauthorized activities from occurring, damaging, or posing a threat of damage to the naturally functioning aquatic and wetland ecosystems and other environmental resources, values, and uses.

(2) Ensuring that all authorized works, structures, and activities are (a) judged to be the least ecologically damaging alternative or combination of alternatives (e.g., all appropriate means have been adopted to minimize environmental losses and degradations) and (b) in the public's interest in safeguarding the environment from loss and degradation. Water dependency of a work, structure, or activity will be considered when criterion (a) above has not been met.

In determining whether criteria (a) and (b) have been met, the Service will always consider: (1) The long-term effects of the proposed work, structure, or activity; (2) its cumulative effects, when viewed in the context of other already existing or foreseeable works, structures, or activities of the same kind; and/or (3) its cumulative effects, when viewed in the context of other already existing or foreseeable works, structures, or activities of different kinds.

4.3A. *Policies.* (1) The U.S. Fish and Wildlife Service exercises and encourages all efforts to preserve, restore, and improve fish and wildlife resources and associated aquatic and wetland ecosystems, and supports State actions designed to protect areas of special biological significance.

(2) The Service opposes activities

[1] Wildlife and wildlife resources are defined by the Act to include: "birds, fishes, mammals, and all other classes of wild animals and all types of aquatic and land vegetation upon which wildlife is dependent."

and developments in or affecting the Nation's waters and wetlands which would individually, or cumulatively with other developments on a waterway or group of related waterways, needlessly destroy, damage, or degrade fish and wildlife resources, associated aquatic and wetland ecosystems, and the human satisfactions dependent thereon.

(3) The Service places special emphasis on the protection of vegetated and other productive shallow waters and wetlands and on fish and wildlife species for which the Secretary of the Interior has delegated and specifically mandated responsibilities.

---

7. *General guidelines.* 7.1A. Permits issued for oil and gas exploration and development operations in territorial waters and wetlands should be limited to a reasonable time period essential to the work proposed. These permits also should provide such explicit conditions as will minimize damages to fish and wildlife resources.

B. Proposals for other associated activities and works involved in mineral exploration and developments should meet the applicable general provisions to minimize environmental degradation particularly from: The spillage of oil; release of refuse including polluting substances and solid wastes; spoiling on productive wetlands; dredging of productive shallows; alteration of current patterns, tidal exchanges, and freshwater outflow, and erosion and sedimentation.

C. The U.S. Fish and Wildlife Service will consider the following criteria to ascertain if works requiring a Federal permit in shallow waters and wetlands can be implemented without significant damages to fish, wildlife, and the environment:

(1) In instances where proposed structures, facilities, or activities will utilize land fill procedures which involve the adverse alteration or destruction of estuarine or wetland areas, the applicant should demonstrate that practicable alternate upland sites are not available for proposed works.

(2) Permit applications for an unauthorized existing excavation, fill, structure, facility, or building will be examined on an individual basis. The condition, present use, and future potential of a particular work, and alternatives to its continued existence will be considered in determining whether or not to recommend denial of the permit, removal of the unauthorized work, and possible restoration.

D. This Service will recommend denial of Federal permits for proposed projects as follows:

(1) Projects which needlessly degrade or destroy wetland types identified in the Fish and Wildlife Service's Circular 39, Wetlands of the United States, published 1956, republished 1971. The decision whether a project needlessly degrades or destroys wetland types will be made with reference to the three criteria set forth in item 4.2B.(2).

(2) Projects not designed to prevent or minimize significant fish, wildlife and environmental damages.

(3) Projects which do not utilize practicable, suitable, and available upland sites as alternatives to wetland areas.

(4) Projects located on upland which do not assure the protection of adjacent wetland areas.

8. *Specific project guidelines.* 8.1A. The Service will utilize the following specific project guidelines when reviewing permit applications:

(1) *Geophysical operations.* (a) Gas or airguns, sparkers, vibrators, and other electromechanical and mechanical transducers should be used where practicable.

(b) When explosive charges must be used, the smallest charge consistent with acceptable recording should be used.

(c) Use of explosives should be avoided in important fish and wildlife spawning, nesting, nursery, and rearing areas during periods of high concentration or intense activity by the fish and/or wildlife of concern.

(d) All explosive charges should be fired in compliance with applicable State and Federal regulations.

(2) *Docks and piers.* (a) The size and extension of a dock or pier should be limited to that required for the intended use.

(b) Project proposals should include transfer facilities for the proper handling of litter, wastes, refuse, spoil drilling mud, and petroleum products.

(c) Piers and catwalks will be encouraged in preference to solid fills to provide needed access across biologically productive shallows and marshes to navigable water.

(3) *Bulkheads or seawalls.* Construction of bulkheads, seawalls, or the use of riprapping generally will be acceptable in areas having unstable shorelines. Except in special circumstances such as eroding shorelines, structures should be located no further waterward than the mean or normal high water line, and designated so that reflected wave energy does not destroy stable marine bottoms

or constitute a safety hazard. In areas which have undergone extensive development, applications for bulkheads will be acceptable that esthetically and/or ecologically enhance the aquatic environment.

However, denial of permits for the construction of bulkheads on barrier and sand islands, where such will adversely affect the natural transport and deposition of sand materials, will normally be recommended.

(4) *Cables and transmission lines.* Installation of aerial or submerged cables and transmission lines located and designed to provide maximum compatibility with the environment will be acceptable. Particular emphasis will be placed on measures to protect fish and wildlife resources, esthetics, and unique natural areas. In operational areas, routes should make maximum use of existing rights-of-ways.

(5) *Access roads.* (a) Existing roadways should be utilized.

(b) Timber, other matting, or special low impact vehicles should be utilized where possible when temporary access is required in shallows and wetlands.

(c) When access roads to a drilling site must be constructed, the roads should be minimal in size and number.

(d) Selection of location and design of proposed roadways should be based on wet-season conditions to minimize disruption of normal sheetflow, waterflow, and drainage patterns or systems.

(e) Adequate culverts must be placed in all roadways to minimize disruption of natural sheetflow, waterflow, and drainage patterns or systems.

(f) Shoulder and slope surfaces should be stabilized with natural vegetation plantings or by seeding of native species, where possible, or by riprapping.

(g) Upon abandonment of a project site, temporary access roads will be evaluated for their wildlife potential and will be recommended for their retention or removal.

(6) *Bridges.* (a) Designs and alignments should minimize disruption of sheetflow, waterflow, and drainage patterns or systems.

(b) Approaches to permanent structures in wetland areas should be located, to the maximum extent possible, on pilings rather than solid fill causeways.

(7) *Jetties, groins, and breakwaters.* Jetties, groins, and breakwaters that do not create adverse sand transportation patterns or unduly disturb the aquatic ecosystem will be acceptable.

(8) *Levees and dikes.* (a) Designs and alignments should minimize disruption of natural sheetflow, waterflow, and drainage patterns or systems.

(b) Shoulder and slope surface should be stabilized following construction with natural vegetation plantings or by seeding of native species, where possible, or by riprapping.

(c) Upon abandonment of a project site, levees and dikes will be evaluated for their wildlife potential and will be recommended for their retention or removal.

(9) *Lagoons, impoundments, waste pits, and emergency pits.* (a) Construction should minimize disruption of natural sheetflow, waterflow, and drainage patterns or systems.

(b) Areas should be excavated to an impermeable soil formation at the time of construction, or lined or sealed.

(c) Operation and use must be in strict compliance with applicable local, State, and Federal regulations.

(10) *Navigation channels and access canals.* (a) Designs and alignments should minimize disruption or natural sheetflow, waterflow, and drainage patterns or systems.

(b) Designs should meet demonstrated navigational needs.

(c) Designs should prevent the creation of pockets or other hydraulic conditions which would cause stagnant water problems.

(d) Designs should minimize shoreline or other erosion problems and interference with natural sand and sediment transport processes.

(e) Designs, where recommended, should use temporary dams or plugs in the seaward ends of canals or waterways until excavation has been completed.

(f) Designs should minimize changes in tidal circulation patterns, salinity regimes, or related nutrient and aquatic life distribution patterns.

(g) Alignments will be recommended by the Service that avoid or minimize damages to shellfish grounds, beds of productive aquatic vegetation, coral reefs, and other shallow water and wetland areas of value to fish and wildlife resources.

(h) Alignments should make maximum use of existing natural channels.

(i) Construction should be conducted in a manner that minimizes turbidity and dispersal of dredged material.

(j) Construction should follow schedules, which may be recommended by the Service. These schedules will aim at minimizing interference with fish and wildlife migrations, spawning, and nesting or the public's enjoyment and utilization of these resources.

(11) *Excavation of fill material.* Excavation and dredging in shallow waters and wetlands will be discouraged and the Service will recommend that any permit issued contains conditions to minimize adverse effects and activities in important fish and wildlife spawning, nesting, nursery, and rearing areas, and prohibit construction during critical periods of migration, spawning, and nesting activity.

(12) *Disposal of spoil and refuse material.* In-bay, open-water, and deep-water disposal generally will be considered acceptable by the Service only after all upland and other alternative disposal sites have been explored and rejected for good cause. Deep-water disposal will be acceptable only at sites specifically selected, including those selected for deposit of suitable material for habitat improvement, where agreed upon by all concerned agencies.

(13) *Drilling and injection wells, and production facilities.* (a) Directional drilling techniques should be used where practicable.

(b) Drilling and production facilities should utilize equipment that prevents or controls, to the maximum extent practicable, the discharge of pollutants.

(c) All drilling muds should be stored in tanks or diked non-wetland areas.

(d) Upon abandonment of a project site, pertinent facilities will be evaluated for their wildlife potential and will be recommended for retention or removal.

(14) *Pipelines.* (a) Pipeline routes that avoid or minimize damages to important spawning, nesting, nursery, or rearing areas will be encouraged by the Service.

(b) In established operational areas, pipeline routes should make maximum use of existing rights-of-way.

(c) In all areas, pipelines should be confined to areas which will minimize environmental impact; special care should be taken in unaltered areas.

(d) Where recommended, pipeline access canals should be immediately plugged at the seaward end and subsequently maintained to prevent freshwater or saltwater intrusion.

(e) Where recommended, bulkheads, plugs, or dams should be installed and maintained at all stream, bay, lake, or other waterway or water body crossings.

(f) Pipeline placement should be designed with a wide margin of safety against breakage from mud slides, currents, earthquakes, or other causes. In areas of high natural seismic activity, pipelines should be designed and situated, to the maximum extent possible, to be "earthquake proof."

(g) Pipeline placement by the push method in marshlands will be encouraged.

9. *Assistantce to applicants and prospective applicants.* 9.1A. All applications for works or activities subject to Federal jurisdiction over navigable waters will be considered within the framework of foregoing policies and guidelines. It is the position of the Service that these guidelines, if followed, will facilitate the orderly review of permit applications for oil and gas exploration and development activities. Protection is a national responsibility that cannot be shirked or comprised if future generations are to enjoy a satisfying and healthy environment. The Service considers that adherance to these guidelines is requisite to this national responsibility and the Nation's goal of environmental quality.

B. The Service stands ready at all times to assist permit applicants in formulating environmentally sound proposals and in avoiding unnecessary delays in developing environmentally compatible plans. Contacts should be made through the appropriate Regional Office of the Fish and Wildlife Service. The addresses and telephone numbers of the Service's Regional Offices and a map of the States each Region covers are contained, respectively, in Appendices 1 and 2 below.

Regional directors' addresses and phone numbers

Region	Address	Phone No.
1	Fish and Wildlife Service, Department of the Interior, P.O. Box 3737, Portland, Oreg. 97208.	503-234-4050
2	Fish and Wildlife Service, Department of the Interior, P.O. Box 1306, Albuquerque, N. Mex. 87103.	505-766-2321
3	Fish and Wildlife Service, Department of the Interior, Federal Bldg., Fort Snelling, Twin Cities, Minn. 55111.	612-725-2500
4	Fish and Wildlife Service, Department of the Interior, Executive Park Dr. NE., Atlanta, Ga. 30329.	404-526-4671
5	Fish and Wildlife Service, Department of the Interior, John W. McCormack Post Office and Courthouse, Boston, Mass. 02109.	617-223-2961
6	Fish and Wildlife Service, Department of the Interior, P.O. Box 25486, Denver Federal Center, Denver, Colo. 80225.	303-234-2209
Alaska	Fish and Wildlife Service, Department of the Interior, 813 D St., Anchorage, Alaska 99501.	907-265-4864

5. WETLANDS POLICY—U.S. ENVIRONMENTAL PROTECTION AGENCY

Protection of the nation's wetlands.

SOURCE.   *Federal Register*, Vol. 38, No. 84 (May 2, 1973).

ENVIRONMENTAL PROTECTION AGENCY

PROTECTION OF NATION'S WETLANDS
Policy Statement

Purpose.—The purpose of this statement is to establish EPA policy to preserve the wetland ecosystems and to protect them from destruction through waste water or nonpoint source discharges and their treatment or control or the development and construction of waste water treatment facilities or by other physical, chemical, or biological means.

The wetland resource.—a. Wetlands represent an ecosystem of unique and major importance to the citizens of this Nation and, as a result, they require extraordinary protection. Comparable destructive forces would be expected to inflict more lasting damage to them than to other ecosystems. Through this policy statement, EPA establishes appropriate safeguards for the preservation and protection of the wetland resources.

b. The Nation's wetlands, including marshes, swamps, bogs, and other lowlying areas, which during some period of the year will be covered in part by natural nonflood waters, are a unique, valuable, irreplaceable water resource. They serve as a habitat for important f-r-bearing mammals, many species of fish, and waterfowl. Such areas moderate extremes in waterflow, aid in the natural purification of water, and maintain and recharge the ground water resource. They are the nursery areas for a great number of wildlife and aquatic species and serve at times as the source of valuable harvestable timber. They are unique recreational areas, high in aesthetic value, that contain delicate and irreplaceable specimens of fauna and flora and support fishing, as well as wildfowl and other hunting.

c. Fresh-water wetlands support the adjacent or downstream aquatic ecosystem in addition to the complex web of life that has developed within the wetland environment. The relationship of the fresh-water wetland to the subsurface environment is symbiotic, intricate, and fragile. In the tidal wetland areas the tides tend to redistribute the nutrients and sediments throughout the tidal marsh and these in turn form a substrate for the life supported by the tidal marsh. These marshes produce large quantities of plant life that are the source of much of the organic matter consumed by shellfish and other aquatic life in associated estuaries.

d. Protection of wetland areas requires the proper placement and management of any construction activities and controls of nonpoint sources to prevent disturbing significantly the terrain and impairing the quality of the wetland area. Alteration in quantity or quality of the natural flow of water, which nourishes the ecosystem, should be minimized. The addition of harmful waste waters or nutrients contained in such waters should be kept below a level that will alter the natural, physical, chemical, or biological integrity of the wetland area and that will insure no significant increase in nuisance organisms through biostimulation.

Policy.—a. In its decision processes, it shall be the Agency's policy to give particular cognizance and consideration to any proposal that has the potential to damage wetlands, to recognize the irreplaceable value and man's dependence on them to maintain an environment acceptable to society, and to preserve and protect them from damaging misuses.

b. It shall be the Agency's policy to minimize alterations in the quantity or quality of the natural flow of water that nourishes wetlands and to protect wetlands from adverse dredging or filling practices, solid waste management practices, siltation or the addition of pesticides, salts, or toxic materials arising from nonpoint source wastes and through construction activities, and to prevent violation of applicable water quality standards from such environmental insults.

c. In compliance with the National Environmental Policy Act of 1969, it shall be the policy of this Agency not to grant

Federal funds for the construction of municipal waste water treatment facilities or other waste-treatment-associated appurtenances which may interfere with the existing wetland ecosystem, except where no other alternative of lesser environmental damage is found to be feasible. In the application for such Federal funds where there is reason to believe that wetlands will be damaged, an assessment will be requested from the applicant that delineates the various alternatives that have been investigated for the control or treatment of the waste water, including the reasons for rejecting those alternatives not used. A cost-benefit appraisal should be included where appropriate.

d. To promote the most environmentally protective measures, it shall be the EPA policy to advise those applicants who install waste treatment facilities under a Federal grant program or as a result of a Federal permit that the selection of the most environmentally protective alternative should be made. The Department of the Interior and the Department of Commerce will be consulted to aid in the determination of the probable impact of the pollution abatement program on the pertinent fish and wildlife resources of wetlands. In the event of projected significant adverse environmental impact, a public hearing on the wetlands issue may be held to aid in the selection of the most appropriate action, and EPA may recommend against the issuance of a section 10 Corps of Engineers permit.

Implementation.—EPA will apply this policy to the extent of its authorities in conducting all program activities, including regulatory activities, research, development and demonstration, technical assistance, control of pollution from Federal institutions, and the administration of the construction and demonstration grants, State program grants, and planning grants programs.

WILLIAM D. RUCKELSHAUS,
Administrator.

MARCH 20, 1973.

[FR Doc.73-8579 Filed 5-1-73;8:45 am]

6. NATIONAL FLOOD INSURANCE PROGRAM

Proposed criteria of National Flood Insurance Program.

SOURCE. *Federal Register*, Vol. 40, No. 59, Part II
(March 26, 1975).

DEPARTMENT OF HOUSING AND URBAN DEVELOPMENT

Federal Insurance Administration

[24 CFR Parts 1909, 1910, 1911, 1914, 1915, 1917]

[Docket No. R–75–324]

NATIONAL FLOOD INSURANCE PROGRAM

Proposed Criteria

Section 1361 of the National Flood Insurance Act of 1968 requires the Federal Insurance Administrator to develop comprehensive criteria designed to encourage, where necessary, the adoption of adequate state and local measures' which, to the maximum extent feasible will: (1) Constrict the development of land which is exposed to flood damage where appropriate, (2) guide the development of proposed construction away from locations which are threatened by flood hazard, (3) assist in reducing damage caused by floods, and (4) otherwise improve the long-range land management and use of flood-prone areas, and he shall work closely with and provide any necessary technical assistance to State, interstate, and local governmental agencies, to encourage the application of such criteria and the adoption and enforcement of such measures.

A. BACKGROUND

1. Description of program and program limits. (a) The National Flood Insurance Program was enacted by the Congress in 1968 as a means of making flood insurance, which was previously unavailable from the private insurance industry, available at reasonable rates through a joint Government-industry program, within communities that meet eligibility requirements by adopting certain flood plain management regulations, consistent with Federal criteria, to reduce or avoid flooding in connection with future construction in their flood plains.

(b) The program is highly subsidized and seeks in its early stages to assure wiser future flood plain management rather than to obtain adequate premiums for the coverage provided. However, flood insurance for buildings constructed within identified special flood hazard areas after December 31, 1974 (or the effective date of the initial Flood Insurance Rate Map, whichever is later), can only be made available at actuarial rather than the subsidized premium rates. Such rates can be prohibitively expensive unless the buildings are properly elevated or floodproofed to lessen flood damage.

(c) Communities entering the National Flood Insurance Program generally do so in two phases. They first become eligible for the sale of flood insurance in the Emergency Program, under which only half of the program's total limits of coverage are available and all such insurance is sold at subsidized premium rates. After the flood insurance rate study has been completed, a community enters the Regular Program under which full limits of coverage are available.

(d) Under the Regular Program, buildings constructed on or before December 31, 1974 (or the effective date of the initial rate map, if later) as well as those located outside of the special flood hazard areas, remain eligible for the first half of available coverage (known as "first layer" coverage) at either subsidized rates or actuarial rates, whichever are cheaper. All other buildings can only be insured at actuarial rates on both layers of coverage.

(e) Regardless of date of construction, actuarial rates are always required for the second layer of coverage.

(f) Present limits of coverage under the Emergency Program (except in Alaska, Hawaii, the Virgin Islands and Guam) are $35,000 on single family dwellings and $100,000 on all other types of buildings, with $10,000 per unit available for residential contents, and $10,000 per building available for nonresidential contents. In Alaska, Hawaii, the Virgin Islands, and Guam, limits on residential structure coverage under the Emergency Program are $50,000 on single-family dwellings and $150,000 on buildings containing more than one unit.

(g) Present limits of coverage under the Regular Program are double those indicated in paragraph (f) for the Emergency Program.

(h) The regulations governing the National Flood Insurance Program are set forth in title 24 of the Code of Federal Regulations, Chapter 10, Subchapter B, commencing at Part 1909. Specific information on insurance coverage and rates is set forth in 24 CFR Part 1911, as amended.

2. Community eligibility and special flood hazard area identifications. (a) Once a community has met eligibility requirements for the Emergency Program and has submitted a copy of its preliminary flood plain management regulations, the Federal Insurance Administration arranges for the sale of flood insurance within the community in less than two weeks (normally, within 6 working days).

PART 1910—CRITERIA FOR LAND MANAGEMENT AND USE

SUBPART A—REQUIREMENTS FOR FLOOD PLAIN MANAGEMENT REGULATIONS

Section 1910.1 *Purpose of subpart.* This section remains substantially the same.

Section 1910.3 *Required flood plain management regulations for flood-prone areas.* New additions include the following:

1. In accordance with § 1910.3(b)(3), prior to the time that the Administrator has formally determined 100-year flood elevations for a particular community, a community must consider and utilize any available 100-year flood elevation data as criteria for administering the flood plain management regulations adopted by the community.

2. In accordance with § 1910.3(c)(6), the standards contained within specified sections of the U.S. Army Corps of Engineers publication entitled "Flood-Proofing Regulations" must be required by a community for the floodproofing of new construction and substantial improvements of non-residential structures located within special flood hazard areas. Furthermore, pursuant to § 1910.3(c)(7), a community must require, for each structure which is floodproofed, a certification by a registered professional engineer or architect attesting that the floodproofing methods utilized are reasonably adequate for the structure to withstand the 100-year flood, and all such certificates must be kept on file by the community in order that the structure

may be the subject of a lower actuarial flood insurance rate.

3. In accordance with §§ 1910.3(c)(9) and 1910.3(c)(10), a distinction is made between new and existing mobile home parks located within special flood hazard areas. For new parks, specific standards are required for elevation of mobile homes to the 100-year flood level. For mobile homes moving into existing parks where concrete pads, streets and utility connections are in existence, elevation of mobile homes is not required, but full disclosure must be given to all new mobile home purchasers that the mobile home is being located in a special flood hazard area, and an evacuation plan must be filed with Disaster Preparedness Authorities. Furthermore, pursuant to §§1910.3(d)(7) and 1910.3(e)(6), the location of any new mobile home park is prohibited within any designated floodway and coastal high hazard area.

4. In accordance with §§1910.3(b)(5) and 1910.3(c)(12), riverine communities must submit to the Administrator evidence of coordination with concerned communities if any development, fill, encroachments or alteration or relocation of a watercourse may adversely affect such upstream, downstream, or adjacent communities.

5. In accordance with § 1910.3(e)(5), the use of fill for structural support is prohibited within any designated coastal high hazard area.

Section 1910.4 *Required flood plain management regulations for mudslide (i.e., mudflow) areas.* This section has been revised to add specific standards with respect to new development within mudslide (i.e., mudflow) areas, in order to replace the reliance within the existing section on the provisions of the Uniform Building Code.

Section 1910.5 *Required flood plain management regulations for flood related erosion areas.* This section completely revises present § 1910.5, the substance of which is now included in § 1910.6. The new section adds specific standards with respect to new development within flood-related erosion areas. The primary standard is a setback requirement permitting suitable open space uses within identified special flood-related erosion hazard areas.

PART 1909—GENERAL PROVISIONS

Subpart A—General

§ 1909.1 [Amended]

1. By revising § 1909.1 by amending certain definitions and adding in alpha-

betical sequence certain new definitions
as follows:

As used in this subchapter—

"Area of special flood-related erosion hazard" is the land within a community which is most likely to be subject to severe flood-related erosion losses. Under the Emergency Program, it may be designated as Zone E on the Flood Hazard Boundary Map (FHBM). After the detailed evaluation of the special flood-related erosion hazard area, in preparation for publication of the Flood Insurance Rate Map (FIRM), Zone E may be further refined. Under the Regular program, no new construction or substantial improvement can be insured in the special flood-related erosion hazard area at other than actuarial rates for both layers of flood insurance available.

"Area of special flood hazard" is the land within a community in the flood plain, which is subject to a one percent chance of flooding annually. Under the Emergency Program, it is usually designated as Zone A on the Flood Hazard Boundary Map (FHBM). After the detailed "Flood elevation study" of the special flood hazard area has been completed in preparation for publication of the Flood Insurance Rate Map (FIRM), Zone A may be segmented by refinement into Zones A, AO, A1–30, and V (V1–V30). Under the Regular program no new construction or substantial improvement can be insured in the special flood hazard area at other than actuarial rates for both layers of flood insurance available.

"Coastal high hazard area" means the portion of a flood plain having special flood hazards that is subject to high velocity waters, including hurricane wave wash and tsunamis.

"Erosion" means the collapse or subsidence of land along the shore of a lake or other body of water as result of undermining caused by waves or currents of water exceeding anticipated cyclical levels or suddenly caused by an unusually high water level in a natural body of water, accompanied by a severe storm, or by an unanticipated force of nature, such as a flash flood or an abnormal tidal surge, or by some similarly unusual and unforeseeable event which results in flooding. Therefore; the use of the word "erosion" within this subchapter shall mean flood-related erosion.

"Erosion area" or "erosion prone area" means a land area adjoining the shore of a lake or other body of water, which due to the composition of the shoreline or bank and high water levels or wind-driven currents, is likely to suffer flood-related erosion damage.

"Flood elevation determination" means a determination by the Administrator of the level of the 100-year flood; that is, the level of flooding that has a one percent chance of occurring during any given year.

"Flood elevation study" or "Flood Insurance Study" means a scientific examination, evaluation and determination of flood hazards and corresponding water surface elevations, or a scientific examination, evaluation and determination of mudslide (i.e., mudflow) and/or flood-related erosion hazards.

"Flood Hazard Boundary Map" (FHBM) means an official map or plat of a community, issued or approved by the Administrator, on which the boundaries of the flood plain, mudslide (i.e., mudflow) and/or flood-related erosion areas having special hazards have been drawn.

"Flood insurance" means the insurance coverage provided under the program.

"Flood Insurance Rate Map" (FIRM) means an official map of a community, on which the Administrator has delineated the area in which flood insurance may be sold under the regular flood insurance program and the actuarial rate zones applicable to such area.

"Flood plain" or "flood-prone area" means any normally dry land area that is susceptible to being inundated by water from any source (see definition of flooding).

"Flood plain area having special flood hazards" means that maximum area of the flood plain that, on the average, is likely to be flooded once every 100-years (i.e., that has a 1-percent chance of flood occurrence in any given year).

"Flood plain management" means the operation of an overall program of corrective and preventive measures for reducing flood damage, including but not limited to emergency preparedness plans, flood control works, and flood plain management regulations.

"Flood plain management regulations" means zoning ordinances, subdivision regulations, building codes, health regulations, special purpose ordinances such as a flood plain ordinance, grading ordinance and erosion control ordinance, and other applications and extensions of the normal police power. The term describes such legally-enforceable regulations, in any combination thereof, which provide standards for the control of the use and occupancy of flood-prone, mudslide (i.e., mudflow)-prone and/or flood-related erosion-prone areas.

"Floodproofing" means any combination of structural and non-structural additions, changes, or adjustments to properties and structures which reduce or eliminate flood damage to lands, water and sanitary facilities, structures, and contents of buildings.

"Floodway" means the channel of a river or other watercourse and the adjacent land areas that must be reserved in order to discharge the 100-year flood without cumulatively increasing the water-surface elevation more than one foot at any point.

"Floodway encroachment lines" means the lines marking the limits of floodways on official Federal, State, and local flood plain maps.

"Habitable Floor" means any floor used for living, which includes working, sleeping, eating, cooking or recreation, or combination thereof. A floor used only for storage purposes is not a Habitable Floor.

"Mean sea level" means the average height of the sea for all stages of the tide over a nineteen year period, usually determined from hourly height observations on an open coast or in adjacent waters having free access to the sea.

"100-year flood" means a flood event having a one percent chance of occurrence in any given year.

PART 1910—CRITERIA FOR LAND MANAGEMENT AND USE

Subpart A—Requirements for Flood Plain Management Regulations

---

§ 1910.3 **Required flood plain management regulations for flood-prone areas.**

The Administrator generally will provide the data upon which flood plain management regulations must be based. If the Administrator has not provided sufficient data to furnish a basis for these regulations in a particular community, the community may initially use hydrologic and other technical data obtained from other Federal or State agencies or from consulting services, pending receipt of data from the Administrator. How-

ever, when special hazard area designations and water surface elevations have been furnished by the Administrator, they shall apply. In all cases the minimum requirements governing the adequacy of the flood plain management regulations for flood-prone areas adopted by a particular community depend on the amount of technical data formally provided to the community by the administrator. Minimum standards for communities are as follows:

(a) When the Administrator has not defined the special flood hazard areas within a community, has not provided water surface elevation data, and has not provided sufficient data to identify the floodway or coastal high hazard area, the community must—

*   *   *   *   *

(3) Review subdivision proposals and other proposed new developments to assure that (i) all such proposals are consistent with the need to minimize flood damage, (ii) all public utilities and facilities, such as sewer, gas, electrical, and water systems are located and constructed to minimize or eliminate flood damage, and (iii) adequate drainage is provided so as to reduce exposure to flood hazards; and

*   *   *   *   *

(b) When the Administrator has identified the flood plain area having special flood hazards by the publication of a Flood Hazard Boundary Map (FHBM), but has neither produced water surface elevation data nor identified a floodway or coastal high hazard area, the community:

(1) Must require building permits for all proposed construction or other improvements in the flood plain area having special flood hazards;

(2) Must require the standards of paragraphs (a) (2), (3) and (4) of this section within the identified flood plain areas having special flood hazards;

(3) Must take reasonable measures to consider and utilize any 100-year flood elevation data available from a Federal, State or other source as criteria for administering the standards of paragraphs (a)(2), (3) and (4) of this section within the identified flood plain areas having special flood hazards and within any areas not identified as flood plain areas having special flood hazards, and;

(4) Must (i) obtain information, at the time a building permit is issued for a new structure or substantial improvement located within the identified flood plain areas having special flood hazards, concerning the elevation (in relation to

mean sea level) of the lowest floor (including basement) of the structure and, where the lowest floor is below grade on one or more sides, the elevation of the floor immediately above, and' (ii) maintain a record of all such information with the official designated by the community under § 1909.22(13)(ii);

(5) Must in rivering situations, submit to the Administrator evidence of coordination with upstream, downstream or adjacent communities adversely affected by any development, fill, encroachment, or alteration or relocation of a watercourse;

(6) [Reserved]

(7) [Reserved]

(8) [Reserved]

(c) When the Administrator has identified the flood plain area having special flood hazards by the notice of a final flood elevation determination which provides water surface elevations for the 100-year flood within certain areas of special flood hazards, but the Administrator has not identified a floodway or coastal high hazard area, the community:

(1) Must require building permits for all proposed construction of other improvements in the flood plain area having special flood hazards;

(2) Must require the review of building permit applications for new construction or substantial improvements within the flood plain area having special flood hazards to assure that the proposed construction (including prefabricated homes) is designed (or modified) and anchored to prevent flotation, collapse or lateral movement of the structure;

(3) Must require the review of the subdivision proposals and other proposed new developments within the flood plain area having special flood hazards to assure that (i) all such proposals are consistent with the need to minimize flood damage, (ii) all public utilities and facilities, such as sewer, gas, electrical and water systems are located and constructed to minimize or eliminate flood damage; and (iii) adequate drainage is provided so as to reduce exposure to flood hazards;

(4) Must require new or replacement water supply systems and sanitary sewage systems within the flood plain area having special flood hazards to be designed to minimize or eliminate infiltration of flood waters into the systems and discharges from the system into flood waters, and require on-site waste disposal systems to be located so as to avoid impairment of them or contamination from them during or subsequent to flooding;

(5) Must require new construction and substantial improvements of residential structures within the area of special flood hazards for which base flood elevations have been provided to have the lowest floor (including basement) elevated to or above the level of the 100-year flood, unless the community is granted an exception for the allowance of basements and/or storm cellars in accordance with § 1910.6(b)(2);

(6) Must require new construction and substantial improvements of non-residential structures within the area of special flood hazards for which base flood elevations have been provided to have the lowest floor (including basement) elevated to or above the level of the 100-year flood, or together with attendant utility and sanitary facilities to be flood-proofed to or above the level of the 100-year flood in accordance with the standards for completely flood-proofed structures contained within sections 210.2.1 FP1 or 210.2.2 FP2 of the U.S. Army Corps of Engineers Publication entitled "Flood-Proofing Regulations," June 1972, GPO:19730–505–026 Edition or any subsequent edition thereto;

(7) Must provide that where flood-proofing is utilized for a particular structure in accordance with paragraphs (c)(6) of this section or (b)(2) of § 1910.6, a registered professional engineer or architect shall certify that the floodproofing methods are reasonably adequate to withstand the flood depths, pressures, velocities, impact and uplift forces and other factors associated with the 100-year flood, and a record of such certificates shall be maintained with the official designated by the community under § 1909.22(13)(ii);

(8) Must (i) obtain information, at the time a building permit is issued for a new structure or substantial improvement located within the identified flood plain areas having special flood hazards, concerning the elevation (in relation to mean sea level) of the lowest floor (including basement) of the structure, and where the lowest floor is below grade on one or more sides, the elevation of the floor immediately above, and (ii) maintain a record of all such information with the official designated by the community under § 1909.22(13)(ii);

(9) Must require within the area of special flood hazards for new mobile home parks for expansions to existing mobile home parks, and for new mobile homes not in a mobile home park and for existing mobile home parks where the repair, reconstruction or improvement of

streets, utilities and pads equals or exceeds 50 percent of the value of the streets, utilities and pads before the repair, reconstruction or improvement has commenced, that (i) ground anchors for tie downs are required in accordance with the Mobile Home Manufacturers Association standards or standards determined by the Administrator, (ii) stands or lots are elevated on compacted fill or on piers within areas of special flood hazards for which base flood elevations have been provided, so that the lowest floor of the home will be at or above the 100-year flood level, (iii) adequate surface drainage and easy access for a hauler is provided, and (iv) in the instance of elevation on piers, lots are large enough to permit steps, pier foundations are placed on stable soil no more than 10 feet apart and steel reinforcement is provided for piers more than 6 feet high;

(10) Must require within the area of special flood hazards for mobile homes moving into existing mobile home parks where concrete pads for the placement of mobile homes are in existence and where streets and utility connections are in existence that (i) ground anchors for tie downs are required in accordance with the Mobile Home Manufacturers Association standards or standards determined by the Administrator, (ii) the fact that the mobile home is being located in a flood plain area having special flood hazards is disclosed to the mobile home and/or lot purchaser or lessee in the purchase contract, deed or lease, and (iii) an evacuation plan indicating alternate vehicular access and escape routes is filed with Disaster Preparedness Authorities;

(11) Must require the standards of paragraph (b) of this section within any flood plain area having special flood hazards for which base flood elevations have not been provided;

(12) Must, in riverine situations, submit to the Administrator evidence of coordination with upstream, downstream, or adjacent communities adversely affected by any development, fill, encroachment, or alteration or relocation of a watercourse;

(13) Must require in riverine situations, that until a floodway has been designated, no use, including land fill, may be permitted within the flood plain area having special flood hazards for which base flood elevations have been provided unless it is demonstrated that the cumulative effect of the proposed use, when combined with all other existing and reasonably anticipated uses of a similar nature, will not increase the water surface elevation of the 100-year flood more than 1 foot at any point within the community;

(d) When the Administrator has identified the flood plain area having special flood hazards by the notice of a final flood elevation determination which provides water surface elevations for the 100-year flood within certain areas of special flood hazards, and the Administrator has provided floodway data, the community:

(1) Must meet the requirements of paragraphs (c)(1) through (c)(12) of this section;

(2) [Reserved]

(3) [Reserved]

* * * * *

(5) [Reserved]

(6) Must prohibit, within the designated floodway, fill, encroachments, and new construction and substantial improvements of existing structures, which would result in any increase in flood heights within the community during the recurrence of the 100-year flood discharge;

(7) Must prohibit, within the designated floodway, the location of any portion of a new mobile home park, of any expansion to an existing mobile home park, and of any new mobile home not in a mobile home park.

(e) When the Administrator has identified the flood plain area having special flood hazards by the notice of a final flood elevation determination which provides water surface elevations for the 100-year flood within certain areas of special flood hazards, and the Administrator has identified a coastal high hazard area, the community:

(1) Must meet the requirements of paragraphs (c)(1) through (c)(12) of this section;

(2) Must provide that all new construction or substantial improvements within the designated coastal high hazard area be located landward of the reach of the mean high tide;

(3) Must provide that all new construction and substantial improvements within the designated coastal high hazard area be elevated on adequately anchored piles or columns to a lowest floor level (including basement) at or above the 100-year flood level and securely anchored to such piles or columns;

(4) Must provide that all new construction and substantial improvements within the designated coastal high hazard area have the space below the lowest floor free of obstructions or are con-

structed with "breakaway walls" intended to collapse under stress without jeopardizing the structural support of the building so that the impact on the building of abnormally high tides or wind-driven water is minimized. Such temporarily enclosed space shall not be used for human habitation;

(5) Must prohibit, within the designated coastal high hazard area, the use of fill for structural support;

(6) Must prohibit, within the designated coastal high hazard area, the location of any portion of a new mobile home park, expansion to an existing mobile home park, and any new mobile home not in a mobile home park.

10. By revising § 1910.4 in part, to read as follows:

§ 1910.4   Required flood plain management regulations for mudslide (i.e., mudflow) areas.

The Administrator generally will provide the data upon which flood plain management regulations must be based. If the Administrator has not provided sufficient data to furnish a basis for these regulations in a particular community, the community may initially use geologic and other data obtained from other Federal or State agencies or from consulting services, pending receipt of data from the Administrator. However, when special hazard area designations have been furnished by the Administrator, they shall apply. In all cases the minimum requirements governing the adequacy of the flood plain management regulations for mudslide (i.e., mudflow)-prone areas adopted by a particular community depend on the amount of technical data formally provided to the community by the Administrator. Minimum standards for communities are as follows:

(a) When the Administrator has not yet identified any area within the community as an area having special mudslide (i.e., mudflow) hazards, the community must—

*   *   *   *   *

(2) Require review of each permit application to determine whether the proposed site and improvements will be reasonably safe from mudslides (i.e., mudflows). Factors to be considered in making such a determination should include but not be limited to (i) the type and quality of soils, (ii) any evidence of ground water or surface water problems, (iii) the thickness and quality of any fill, (iv) the overall slope of the site, and (v) the weight that any proposed structure will impose on the slope;

(3) Require, if a proposed site and improvements are in a location that may have mudslide (i.e., mudflow) hazards, that (i) a site investigation and further review be made by persons qualified in geology and soils engineering, (ii) the proposed grading, excavations, new construction or substantial improvements are adequately designed and protected against mudslide (i.e., mudflow) damages, (iii) the proposed grading, excavations, new construction or substantial improvements do not aggravate the existing hazard by creating either on-site or off-site disturbances, and (iv) drainage, planting, watering, and maintenance be such as not to endanger slope stability.

(b) When the Administrator has delineated the areas having special mudslide (i.e., mudflow) hazards within a community, the community must:

(1) Meet the requirements of paragraph (a) of this section; and

(2) Adopt and enforce a grading ordinance in accordance with data supplied by the Administrator which (i) regulates the location of foundation systems and utility systems of new construction and substantial improvements, (ii) regulates the location, drainage and maintenance of all excavations, cuts and fills and planted slopes, (iii) provides special requirements for protective measures including but not necessarily limited to retaining walls, buttress fills, sub-drains, diverter terraces, benchings, etc., and (iv) requires engineering drawings and specifications to be submitted for all corrective measures, accompanied by supporting soils engineering and geology reports. Guidance may be obtained from the provisions of the 1970 edition and any subsequent edition thereto of the Uniform Building Code, sections 7001 through 7006, and 7008 through 7015. The Uniform Building Code is published by the International Conference of Building Officials, 50 South Los Robles, Pasadena, California 91101.

11. By revising § 1910.5 to read as follows:

§ 1910.5   Required flood plain management regulations for flood-related erosion areas.

The Administrator generally will provide the data upon which flood plain management regulations for flood-related erosion-prone areas must be based. If the Administrator has not provided sufficient data to furnish a basis for these regulations in a particular community, the community may initially use geologic and other data obtained from other Federal or State agencies or from consulting services, pending receipt of data from the Administrator. However, when special hazard area designations have been furnished by the Administrator, they shall apply. In all cases the minimum requirements governing the adequacy of the flood plain management regulations for flood-related erosion-prone areas adopted by a particular community depend on the amount of technical data formally provided to the community by the Administrator. Minimum standards for communities are as follows:

(a) When the Administrator has not yet identified any area within the community as having special flood-related erosion hazards, the community must:

(1) Require the issuance of a permit for any grading, fill, dredging excavation or construction in the area of flood-related erosion hazard, as it is known to the community;

(2) Require review of each permit application to determine whether the proposed site alterations and improvements will be reasonably safe from flood-related erosion and will not cause any changes in barrier beaches, sanddunes, natural drainage, channels, soil infiltration capacity, or otherwise aggravate the existing erosion hazard; and

(3) If a proposed improvement is found to be in the path of flood-related erosion or to increase the erosion hazard, require the improvement to be relocated or adequate protective measures to be taken which will not aggravate the existing erosion hazard.

(b) When the Administrator has delineated the areas having special flood-related erosion hazards within a community, the community must:

(1) Meet the requirements of paragraph (a) of this section; and

(2) Require a setback for all new development from the ocean, lake or riverfront, to create a safety buffer consisting of a natural vegetative or contour strip. This buffer will be designated by the Administrator according to the flood-related erosion hazard and erosion rate, in conjunction with the anticipated "useful life" of structures, and depending upon the geologic, hydrologic, topographic and climatic characteristics of the community's land. The buffer may be used for suitable open space purposes, such as for picnic, agricultural, forestry, outdoor recreation and wildlife habitat areas, and for other activities using temporary and portable structures only.

12. § 1910.6 is completely revised to read as follows:

§ 1910.22 State and local development goals.

State and local flood plain management regulations should contribute to social and economic development goals by:

(a) Diverting unwarranted and unwise development away from flood-prone, mudslide (i.e., mudflow)-prone, and flood-related erosion-prone areas;

(b) Encouraging flood, mudslide (i.e., mudflow) and flood-related erosion control and damage abatement efforts through public and private means;

(c) Deterring the unnecessary or improper installation of public utilities and public facilities in flood-prone, mudslide (i.e., mudflow)-prone and flood-related erosion-prone areas;

(d) Requiring construction and land use practices that will reduce flooding resulting from surface runoff, improper drainage, or inadequate storm sewers, and reduce the potential for mudslides (i.e., mudflow) flood-related erosion.

By revising § 1910.23, in part, to read as follows:

§ 1910.23 Planning considerations for flood-prone areas.

(a) The goals of the flood plain management regulations adopted by a community for flood-prone areas should be—

(1) To encourage only that development of flood-prone areas which (i) is appropriate in light of the probability of flood damage and the need to reduce flood losses, (ii) is an acceptable social and economic use of the land in relation to the hazards involved, and (iii) does not increase the danger to human life;

(2) To discourage all other development.

(b) In formulating community development goals and in adopting flood plain management regulations, each community should consider at least the following factors—

(1) Human Safety;

(2) Importance of diverting future development to areas not exposed to flooding;

(3) Possible reservation of flood-prone areas for open space purposes;

(4) Possible adverse effects of flood plain development on other flood-prone areas;

(5) Need to encourage floodproofing to reduce the flood hazard;

(6) Need for flood warning and emergency preparedness plans;

(7) Need to provide alternative vehic-

ular access and escape routes to be utilized when normal routes are blocked or destroyed by flooding;

(8) Need to establish minimum floodproofing and access requirements for schools, hospitals, nursing homes, penal institutions, fire stations, police stations, communications centers, water and sewage pumping stations, and other public or quasi-public institutions already located in the flood-prone area to enable them to withstand flood damage, and to facilitate emergency operations;

(9) Need to improve local drainage and to control any increased runoff that might increase the danger of flooding elsewhere in the area;

(10) Need to coordinate local plans with neighboring flood plain area management and conservation programs;

(11) Possibilities of acquiring land or land development rights for public purposes consistent with effective flood plain management;

(12) State and local water pollution control requirements;

(13) For riverine areas, the need for requiring subdividers to furnish delineations of limits of floodways before approving a subdivision;

(14) For coastal areas, the need for preserving natural barriers to flooding, such as sand dunes, wetlands and vegetation;

(15) Need to prohibit any drainage, alteration or relocation of a watercourse, except as part of an overall drainage basin plan.

(16) Need to assure consistency between state, areawide and local comprehensive plans (particularly the land use element thereof) and flood plain area management and conservation programs.

----

§ 1910.26 State coordination.

(a) State participation in furthering the objectives of this part should include—

(1) Encouraging and assisting communities in qualifying for participation in the program;

(2) Enacting flood plain management regulations which regulate flood plains, mudslide (i.e., mudflow) areas and flood-related erosion areas;

(3) Enacting where necessary, legislation to enable counties and municipalities to regulate flood plain, mudslide (i.e., mudflow) areas and flood-related erosion area development;

(4) Designating an agency of the State government to be responsible for coordinating Federal, State, and local aspects of flood plain, mudslide (i.e., mudflow)

area and Flood-Related erosion area management activities in the State;

(5) Assisting in the delineation of flood-related erosion area, mudslide (i.e., mudflow) areas, riverine floodways, and coastal high hazard areas and providing all relevant technical data to the Administrator;

(6) Establishing minimum State flood plain, mudslide (i.e., mudflow) and flood-related erosion regulatory standards consistent with those established in this part;

(7) Guiding and assisting municipal and county public bodies and agencies in developing flood plain, mudslide (i.e., mudflow) and flood-related erosion area management plans and flood plain management regulations;

(8) Recommending priorities for rate-making studies among those communities of the State which qualify for such studies;

(9) Communicating flood plain, mudslide (i.e., mudflow) and flood-related erosion area information to local governments and to the general public;

(10) Participating in flood, mudslide (i.e., mudflow) and flood-related erosion warning and emergency preparedness programs;

(11) Assisting communities in disseminating information on minimum elevations for structures permitted in flood plain areas having special hazards, and in disseminating other information relating to mudslide (i.e., mudflow) and flood-related erosion areas having special hazards;

(12) Advising public and private agencies (particularly those whose activities or projects might obstruct drainage or the flow of rivers or streams or increase slope instability) on the avoidance of unnecessary aggravation of flood, mudslide (i.e., mudflow) and flood-related erosion hazards;

(13) Requiring that proposed uses of flood plain, mudslide (i.e., mudflow) and flood-related erosion areas conform to standards established by State environmental and water pollution control agencies to assure that proper safeguards are being provided to prevent pollution;

(14) Providing local communities with information on the program, with particular emphasis on the coordination of State and Federal requirements pertaining to the management of flood-prone, mudslide (i.e., mudflow)-prone, and flood-related erosion-prone areas;

(15) Assuring coordination and consistency of flood plain management and planning with comprehensive planning at the state, areawide and local levels (par-

ticularly the land use element thereof).

(b) For States whose flood plain, mudslide (i.e., mudflow) area and flood-related erosion area management program substantially encompass the activities described in paragraph (a) of this section, the Administrator will—

(1) Give special consideration to State priority recommendations before selecting communities for ratemaking studies from the register described in § 1909.23 of this subchapter;

(2) Seek State approval of local flood plain management regulations before finally accepting such regulations as meeting the requirements of this part.

§ 1914.2 Flood insurance maps.

(a) The following maps may be prepared for use by the Administrator and the eligible community in connection with the sale of flood insurance:

(1) [Reserved]

(2) *Flood Insurance Rate Map* (*FIRM*). This map is prepared after the ratemaking study for the community has been completed and actuarial rates have been established, and enables the Administrator to authorize the sale of flood insurance under the regular program. It indicates the actuarial rate zones applicable to the community. The symbols used to designate these zones are as follows:

Zone symbol:	*Category*
A	Area of special flood hazards and without base flood elevations determined.
A1–A30	Area of special flood hazards with base flood elevations. Zones are assigned according to flood hazard factors.
AO	Area of special flood hazards that have shallow base flood elevation depths and/or unpredictable flow paths.

V (V1–V30)	Area of special flood hazards, with velocity, that are inundated by tidal floods. Zones are assigned according to flood hazard factors.
B	Area of moderate flood hazards.
C	Area of minimal hazards.
D	Area of undetermined but possible, flood hazards.
M	Area of special mudslide (i.e., mudflow) hazards.
N	Area of moderate mudslide (i.e., mudflow) hazards.
P	Area of undetermined, but possible, mudslide hazards.
E	Area of special flood-related erosion hazards.

Areas identified as subject to more than one hazard; i.e., flood, mudslide (i.e., mudflow), flood-related erosion, will be designated by use of the proper symbols in combination. Areas subject to only one hazard or where more than one hazard is minimal will be identified by only one symbol.

(3) *Flood Hazard Boundary Map* (*FHBM*). This map is issued and approved by the Administrator for use in determining whether individual properties are within or without the flood plain area having special flood hazards, the mudslide (i.e., mudflow) area having special mudslide hazards or the flood-related erosion area having special erosion hazards. Notice of the issuance or approval of new Flood Hazard Boundary Maps is given in Part 1915 of this subchapter.

(b) The Flood Hazard Boundary Map (FHBM) and the Flood Insurance Rate Map (FIRM) shall be maintained for public inspection....

7. COASTAL ZONE MANAGEMENT PROGRAM APPROVAL REGULATIONS —NATIONAL OCEANIC AND ATMOSPHERIC ADMINISTRATION

Regulations for approval of state coastal zone management programs.

Title 15—Commerce and Foreign Trade

CHAPTER IX—NATIONAL OCEANIC AND ATMOSPHERIC ADMINISTRATION

PART 923—COASTAL ZONE MANAGE-MENT PROGRAM APPROVAL REGULA-TIONS

§ 923.3 Submission of management programs.

(a) Upon completion of the development of its management program, a State shall submit the program to the Secretary for review and final approval in accordance with the provisions of these regulations. A program submitted for final approval must comply with all of the provisions set forth in Subparts A–E of this part, including, in particular, Subpart C, which requires that certain authorities and plans of organization be in effect at the time of the submission.

(b) Optionally, the State may submit for the preliminary approval of the Secretary a program complying with the substantive requirements of this part, but for which the proposed authorities and organization complying with the provisions of Subpart C are not yet legally effective. In reviewing a program submitted for preliminary approval, the Secretary may grant such approval subject to establishment of a legal regime providing the authorities and organization called for in the program. If the State elects this option, it shall continue to be eligible for funding under Section 305 but it shall not yet be eligible for funding under Section 306 of the Act until such time as its program is finally approved. Upon a showing by the State that authorities and organization necessary to implement the program which has received preliminary approval are in effect, final approval shall be granted.

Comment. The purpose of the optional procedure is to provide a State with an opportunity for Secretarial review of its program before State legislation is enacted to put the program into legal effect. Some States may prefer not to utilize the optional procedure, especially those which have legislative authority enabling the coastal zone agency of the State to put the program into effect by administrative action. In any event, the Office of Coastal Zone Management will be available for consultation during all phases of development of the program.

(c) States completing the requirements set forth in Subpart B—Land and Water Uses, and Subpart D—Coordination, will be deemed to have fulfilled the statutory requirements associated with each criteria. If, however, a State chooses to adopt alternative methods and procedures, which are at least as comprehensive as the procedures set forth below, for fulfilling those statutory requirements contained in Subparts B and D, they may do so upon prior written approval of the Secretary. The States are encouraged to consult with the Office of Coastal Zone Management as early as possible.

Comment. The thrust of the Act is to encourage coastal States to exercise their full authority over the lands and waters in the coastal zone by developing land and water use programs for the zone, including unified policies, criteria, standards, methods and processes for dealing with land and water uses of more than local significance. While the Act mandates a State to meet specific statutory requirements in order for the State to be eligible for administrative grants, it does not require the State to follow specific processes in meeting those requirements. The Secretary will review any State management program that meets the requirements contained in Subparts B and D in addition to the other subparts contained herein.

§ 923.4 Evaluation of management programs—general.

(a) In reviewing management programs submitted by a coastal State pursuant to § 923.3, the Secretary will evaluate not only all of the individual program elements required by the Act and set forth in Subparts B–E of this part.

but the objectives and policies of the State program as well to assure that they are consistent with national policies declared in Section 303 of the Act.

(b) Each program submitted for approval shall contain a statement of problems and issues, and objectives and policies. The statements shall address:

(1) Major problems and issues, both within and affecting the State's coastal zone;

(2) Objectives to be attained in interagency and intergovernmental cooperation, coordination and institutional arrangements; and enhancing management capability involving issues and problem identification, conflict resolution, regulation and administrative efficiency at the State and local level;

(3) Objectives of the program in preservation, protection, development, restoration and enhancement of the State's coastal zone;

(4) Policies for the protection and conservation of coastal zone natural systems, cultural, historic and scenic areas, renewable and non-renewable resources, and the preservation, restoration and economic development of selected coastal zone areas.

(c) The Secretary will review the management program for the adequacy of State procedures utilized in its development and will consider the extent to which its various elements have been integrated into a balanced and comprehensive program designed to achieve the above objectives and policies.

Comment. Evaluation of the statutory requirements established in this subpart will concentrate primarily upon the adequacy of State processes in dealing with key coastal problems and issues. It will not, in general, deal with the wisdom of specific land and water use decisions, but rather with a determination that in addressing those problems and issues, the State is aware of the full range of present and potential needs and uses of the coastal zone, and has developed procedures, based upon scientific knowledge, public participation and unified governmental policies, for making reasoned choices and decisions.

Management programs will be evaluated in the light of the Congressional findings and policies as contained in Sections 302 and 303 of the Act. These sections make it clear that Congress, in enacting the legislation, was concerned about the environmental degradation, damage to natural and scenic areas, loss of living marine resources and wildlife, decreasing open space for public use and shoreline erosion being brought about by population growth and economic development. The Act thus has a strong environmental thrust, stressing the "urgent need to protect and to give high priority to natural systems in the coastal zone." A close working relationship

between the agency responsible for the coastal zone management program and the agencies responsible for environmental protection is vital in carrying out this legislative intent. States are encouraged by the Act to take into account ecological, cultural, historic and esthetic values as well as the need for economic development in preparing and implementing management programs through which the States, with the participation of all affected interests and levels of government, exercise their full authority over coastal lands and waters.

Further assistance in meeting the intent of the Act may be found in the Congressional Committee Reports associated with the passage of the legislation (Senate Report 92–753 and House Report 92–1049). It is clear from these reports that Congress intended management programs to be comprehensive and that a State must consider all subject areas which are pertinent to the particular circumstances which prevail in the State. A comprehensive program should have considered at least the following representative elements:

(1) Present laws, regulations, and applicable programs for attainment of air and water quality standards, on land and water uses, and on environmental management by all levels of government;

(2) Present ownership patterns of the land and water resources, including administration of publicly owned properties;

(3) Present populations and future trends, including assessments of the impact of population growth on the coastal zone and estuarine environments;

(4) Present uses, known proposals for changes and long-term requirements of the coastal zone;

(5) Energy generation and transmission;

(6) Estuarine habitats of fish, shellfish and wildlife;

(7) Industrial needs;

(8) Housing requirements;

(9) Recreation, including beaches, parks, wildlife preserves, sport fishing, swimming and pleasure boating;

(10) Open space, including educational and natural preserves, scenic beauty, and public access, both visual and physical, to coastlines and coastal estuarine areas;

(11) Mineral resources requirements;

(12) Transportation and navigation needs;

(13) Floods and flood damage prevention, erosion (including the effect of tides and currents upon beaches and other shoreline areas), land stability, climatology and meteorology;

(14) Communication facilities;

(15) Commercial fishing; and

(16) Requirements for protecting water quality and other important natural resources.

The list of considerations is not meant to be exclusive, nor does it mean that each consideration must be given equal weight. State initiative to determine other relevant factors and consider them in the program is essential to the management of the coastal zone as envisioned by Congress.

In assessing programs submitted for approval, the Secretary, in consultation with other concerned Federal agencies, will examine such programs to determine that the full range of public problems and issues affecting the coastal zone have been identified and considered. In this connection, developments outside the coastal zone may often have a significant impact within the coastal zone and create a range of public problems and issues which must be dealt with in the coastal zone management program.

The Secretary encourages the States to develop objectives toward which progress can be measured and will review program submissions in this light. While it is recognized that many essential coastal zone management objectives are not quantifiable (e.g. public aspirations, "quality of life"), others are, and should be set forth in measurable terms where feasible (e.g. shore erosion, beach access, recreational demand, energy facility requirements). Identifying and analyzing problems and issues in measurable terms during the program development phase will facilitate the formulation of measurable objectives as part of the approval submission.

§ 923.5 Environmental impact assessment.

Individual environmental impact statements will be prepared and circulated by NOAA as an integral part of the review and approval process for State coastal zone management programs pursuant to the National Environmental Policy Act (Pub. L. 91-190, 42 USC 4321 et seq) and its implementing regulations. The Administrator of NOAA will circulate an environmental impact statement prepared primarily on the basis of an environmental impact assessment and other relevant data submitted by the individual applicant States.

Subpart B—Land and Water Uses

§ 923.10 General.

(a) This subpart deals with land and water uses in the coastal zone which are subject to the management program.

(b) In order to provide a relatively simple framework upon which discussion of the specific requirements associated with this subpart may proceed, it may be helpful to categorize the various types of land and water uses which the Act envisions.

(1) The statutory definition of the landward portion of the coastal zone states that it "extends inland from the shorelines only to the extent necessary to control shorelands, the uses of which have a direct and significant impact on the coastal waters." Thus, the coastal zone will include those lands and only those lands where any existing, projected or potential use will have a "direct and significant impact on the coastal waters." Any such use will be subject to

the terms of the management program, pursuant to Section 305(b)(2).

(2) There may well be uses of certain lands included within the coastal zone which will not have such "direct and significant impact." Such uses may be subject to regulation by local units of government within the framework of the management program.

(3) The Act also requires that management programs contain a method of assuring that "local land and water use regulations within the coastal zone do not unreasonably restrict or exclude land and water uses of regional benefit." This requirement is described more fully in § 923.17.

(c) As part of the State's management program, it must address and exercise authority over the following:

(1) *Land and water uses which have a direct and significant impact upon coastal waters.* These uses are described more fully in § 923.12.

(2) *Areas of particular concern.* Section 305(b)(3) specifies that the management program include an inventory and designation of areas of particular concern within the coastal zone. Section 923.13 deals more thoroughly with this statutory requirement. Such areas must be considered of Statewide concern and must be addressed in the management program.

(3) *Siting of facilities necessary to meet requirements which are other than local in nature.* The management program must take "adequate consideration of the national interest involved in the siting of facilities necessary to meet requirements which are other than local in nature" (Section 306(c)(8)). This requirement is more fully discussed in § 923.15.

§ 923.11 Boundaries of the coastal zone.

(a) *Requirement.* In order to fulfill the requirement contained in Section 305(b)(1), the management program must show evidence that the State has developed and applied a procedure for identifying the boundary of the State's coastal zone meeting the statutory definition of the coastal zone contained in Section 304(a). At a minimum this procedure should result in:

(1) A determination of the inland boundary required to control, through the management program, shorelands the uses of which have direct and significant impacts upon coastal waters,

(2) A determination of the extent of the territorial sea, or where applicable, of State waters in the Great Lakes,

(3) An identification of transitional

and intertidal areas, salt marshes, wetlands and beaches.

(4) An identification of all Federally owned lands, or lands which are held in trust by the Federal government, its officers and agents in the coastal zone and over which a State does not exercise any control as to use.

(b) *Comment.* Statutory citation: Section 305(b)(1):

Such management program shall include • • • an identification of the boundaries of the coastal zone subject to the management programs.

Useful background information concerning this requirement appears in Part 920.11, which is incorporated into this part by reference.

(1) The key to successful completion of this requirement lies in the development and use of a procedure designed to identify the landward extent of the coastal zone. Included in this procedure must be a method for determining those "shorelands, the uses of which have a direct and significant impact upon the coastal waters." These uses shall be considered the same as the "land and water uses" described in § 923.12, reflecting the requirements of Section 305(b)(2) of the Act regardless of whether those uses are found, upon analysis, to be "permissible." The coastal zone must include within it those lands which have any existing, projected or potential uses which have a direct and significant impact upon the coastal waters and over which the terms of the management program will be exercised. In some States, existing regulations controlling shoreland uses apply only in a strip of land of uniform depth (e.g. 250 feet, 1,000 yards, etc.) behind the shoreline. Such a boundary will be acceptable if it approximates a boundary developed according to the procedure outlined above and extends inland sufficiently for the management program to control lands the uses of which have a direct and significant impact upon coastal waters. States may wish, for administrative convenience, to designate political boundaries, cultural features, property lines or existing designated planning and environmental control areas, as boundaries of the coastal zone. While the Secretary will take into account the desirability of identifying a coastal zone which is easily regulated as a whole, the selection of the boundaries of the coastal zone must bear a reasonable relationship to the statutory requirement. Nothing in this part shall preclude a State from exercising the terms of the management program in a landward area

more extensive than the coastal zone called for in this part. If such a course is selected, the boundaries of the coastal zone must nevertheless be identified as above and the provisions of the Act will be exercised only in the defined coastal zone. It should be borne in mind that the boundary should include lands and waters which are subject to the management program. This means that the policies, objectives and controls called for in the management program must be capable of being applied consistently within the area. The area must not be so extensive that a fair application of the management program becomes difficult or capricious, nor so limited that lands strongly influenced by coastal waters and over which the management program should reasonably apply, are excluded.

(2) Inasmuch as the seaward boundary of the coastal zone is established in the Act, the States will be required to utilize the statutory boundary, i.e. in the Great Lakes, the international boundary between the United States and Canada, and elsewhere the outer limits of the United States territorial sea. At present, this limit is three nautical miles from the appropriate baselines recognized by international law and defined precisely by the United States. In the event of a statutory change in the boundary of the territorial sea, the question of whether a corresponding change in coastal zone boundaries must be made, or will be made by operation of law, will depend on the specific terms of the statutory change and cannot be resolved in advance. In the waters of Lake Michigan, the boundary shall extend to the recognized boundaries with adjacent States.

(3) A State's coastal zone must include transitional and intertidal areas, salt marshes, wetlands and beaches. Hence the boundary determination procedure must include a method of identifying such coastal features. In no case, however, will a State's landward coastal zone boundary include only such areas in the absence of application of the procedure called for herein or in § 923.43.

(4) Since the coastal zone excludes lands the use of which is by law subject solely to the discretion of, or which is held in trust by the Federal government, its officers and agents, the coastal zone boundary must identify such lands which are excluded from the coastal zone. In order to complete this requirement, the State should indicate those Federally owned lands, or lands held in trust by the Federal government, *and* over which the State does not exercise jurisdiction as to

use. In the event that a State fails to identify lands held by an agency of the Federal government as excluded lands, and the agency, after review of the program under Section 307(b), is of the opinion that such lands should be excluded, the disagreement will be subject to the mediation process set forth in said section.

§ 923.12 Permissible land and water uses.

(a) *Requirement.* In order to fulfill the requirements contained in Section 305(b)(2), the management must show evidence that the State has developed and applied a procedure for defining "permissible land and water uses within the coastal zone which have a direct and significant impact upon the coastal waters," which includes, at a minimum:

(1) a method for relating various specific land and water uses to impact upon coastal waters, including utilization of an operational definition of "direct and significant impact,"

(2) an inventory of natural and man-made coastal resources,

(3) an analysis or establishment of a method for analysis of the capability and suitability for each type of resource and application to existing, projected or potential uses.

(4) an analysis or establishment of a method for analysis of the environmental impact of reasonable resource utilizations.

(b) *Comment.* Statutory citation: Section 305(b)(2):

Such management program shall include • • • a definition of what shall constitute permissible land and water uses within the coastal zone which have a direct and significant impact upon the coastal waters.

Useful background information concerning this requirement appears in 15 CFR 920.12, which is incorporated into this part by reference. Completion of this requirement should be divided into two distinct elements: a determination of those land and water uses having a direct and significant impact upon coastal waters, and an identification of such uses which the State deems permissible.

(1) *Section 305(b)(4).* In identifying those uses which have a "direct and significant impact," the State should define that phrase in operational terms that can be applied uniformly and consistently, and should develop a method for relating various uses to impacts upon coastal waters. Existing, projected and potential uses should be analyzed as to the level and extent of their impact, be it adverse, benign or beneficial, intra-

state or interstate. These impacts should then be assessed to determine whether they meet the definition of "direct and significant impact upon coastal waters." (These are the ones by which the boundaries of the coastal zone are defined.) Those uses meeting that definition are automatically subject to control by the management program.

(2) In determining which land and water uses may be deemed permissible, a State should develop a method for assuring that such decisions are made in an objective manner, based upon evaluation of the best available information concerning land and water capability and suitability. This method should include at a minimum:

(i) An inventory of significant natural and man-made coastal resources, including but not limited to, shorelands, beaches, dunes, wetlands, uplands, barrier islands, waters, bays, estuaries, harbors and their associated facilities. This should not be construed as requiring long-term, continuing research and baseline studies, but rather as providing the basic information and data critical to successful completion of a number of required management program elements. States are encouraged, however, to continue research and studies as necessary to detect early warnings of changes to coastal zone resources. It is recognized that in some States a complete and detailed inventory of such resources may be expensive and time consuming in relation to the value of information gathered in the development of the management program. Much information, of course, already exists and should be integrated into the inventory. The Secretary, in reviewing this particular requirement, will take into account the nature and extent of the State's coastline, the funding available and existing data sources.

(ii) An analysis or establishment of a method for analysis of the capabilities of each resource for supporting various types of uses (including the capability for sustained and undiminished yield of renewable resources), as well as of the suitability for such resource utilization when evaluated in conjunction with other local, regional and State resources and uses. Resource capability analysis should include physical, biological and chemical parameters as necessary.

(iii) An analysis or establishment of a method for analysis of the impact of various resource uses upon the natural environment (air, land and water). Based upon these analyses and applicable Federal, State and local policies and standards, the State should define permissible uses as those which can be reasonably and safely supported by the resource, which are compatible with surrounding resource utilization and which will have a tolerable impact upon the environment. These analyses, in part, will be provided through existing information on environmental protection programs, and should be supplemented to the extent necessary for determining the relationship between land uses and environmental quality. Where a State prohibits a use within the coastal zone, or a portion thereof, it should identify the reasons for the prohibition, citing evidence developed in the above analyses. It should be pointed out that uses which may have a direct and significant impact on coastal waters when conducted close to the shoreline may not have a direct and significant impact when conducted further inland. Similarly, uses which may be permissible in a highly industrialized area may not be permissible in a pristine marshland. Accordingly, the definition may also be correlated with the nature (including current uses) and location of the land on which the use is to take place. The analyses which the State will undertake pursuant to this section should also be useful in satisfying the requirements of § 923.13 through § 923.17.

§ 923.13 Areas of particular concern.

(a) *Requirement.* In order to fulfill the requirements contained in Section 305 (b)(3), the management program must show evidence that the State has made an inventory and designation of areas of particular concern within the coastal zone. Such designations shall be based upon a review of natural and man-made coastal zone resources and uses, and upon consideration of State-established criteria which include, at a minimum, those factors contained in 15 CFR 920.13, namely:

(1) Areas of unique, scarce, fragile or vulnerable natural habitat, physical feature, historical significance, cultural value and scenic importance;

(2) Areas of high natural productivity or essential habitat for living resources, including fish, wildlife and the various trophic levels in the food web critical to their well-being;

(3) Areas of substantial recreational value and/or opportunity;

(4) Areas where developments and facilities are dependent upon the utilization of, or access to, coastal waters;

(5) Areas of unique geologic or topographic significance to industrial or commercial development;

(6) Areas of urban concentration where shoreline utilization and water uses are highly competitive;

(7) Areas of significant hazard if developed, due to storms, slides, floods, erosion, settlement, etc.; and

(8) Areas needed to protect, maintain or replenish coastal lands or resources, including coastal flood plains, aquifer recharge areas, sand dunes, coral and other reefs, beaches, offshore sand deposits and mangrove stands.

(b) *Comment.* Statutory citation: Section 305(b)(3).

Such management program shall include * * * an inventory and designation of areas of particular concern within the coastal zone. Useful background information concerning the requirement appears in 15 CFR 920.13, which is incorporated here by reference. It should be emphasized that the basic purpose of inventorying and designating areas of particular concern within the coastal zone is to express some measure of Statewide concern about them and to include them within the purview of the management program. Therefore, particular attention in reviewing the management program will be directed toward development by the State of implementing policies or actions to manage the designated areas of particular concern.

§ 923.14 Guidelines on priority of uses.

(a) *Requirement.* The management program shall include broad policies or guidelines governing the relative priorities which will be accorded in particular areas to at least those permissible land and water uses identified pursuant to § 923.12. The priorities will be based upon an analysis of State and local needs as well as the effect of the uses on the area. Uses of lowest priority will be specifically stated for each type of area.

(b) *Comment.* Statutory citation: Section 305(b)(5)

Such management program shall include * * * broad guidelines on priority of uses in particular areas, including specifically those uses of lowest priority.

As pointed out in 15 CFR 920.15, the priority guidelines will set forth the degree of State interest in the preservation, conservation and orderly development of specific areas including at least those areas of particular concern identified in § 923.13 within the coastal zone, and thus provide the basis for regulating land and water uses in the coastal zone, as well as a common reference point for resolving conflicts. Such priority guidelines will be the core of a successful management program since they will provide a framework within which the State, its agencies, local governments and regional bodies can deal with specific proposals for development activities in various areas of the coastal zone. In order to develop such broad guidelines, the management program shall indicate that a method has been developed and applied for (1) analyzing State needs which can be met most effectively and efficiently through land and water uses in the coastal zone, and (2) determining the capability and suitability of meeting these needs in specific locations in the coastal zone. In analyzing the States' needs, there should be a determination made of those requirements and uses which have Statewide, as opposed to local, significance. Section 302(h) of the Act states in part that land and water use programs for the coastal zone should include "unified policies, criteria, standards, methods and processes for dealing with land and water use decisions of more than local significance." The inventory and analyses of coastal resources and uses called for in § 923.12 will provide the State with most of the basic data needed to determine the specific locations where coastal resources are capable and suitable for meeting State-wide needs. In addition, these analyses should permit the State to determine possible constraints on development which may be applied by particular uses. The program should establish special procedures for evaluating land use decisions, such as the siting of regional energy facilities, which may have a substantial impact on the environment. In such cases, the program should make provision for the consideration of available alternative sites which will serve the need with a minimum adverse impact. The identifying and ordering of use priorities in specific coastal areas should lead to the development and adoption of State policies or guidelines on land and water use in the coastal zone. Such policies or guidelines should be part of the management program as submitted by the State and should be consistent with the State's specified management program objectives. Particular attention should be given by the State to applying these guidelines on use priorities within those "areas of particular concern" designated pursuant to § 923.13. In addition, States shall indicate within the management program uses of lowest priority in particular areas, including guidelines associated with such uses.

§ 923.15   National interest in the siting of facilities.

(a) *Requirement.* A management program which integrates (through development of a body of information relating to the national interest involved in such siting through consultation with cognizant Federal and regional bodies, as well as adjacent and nearby States) the siting of facilities meeting requirements which are of greater than local concern into the determination of uses and areas of Statewide concern, will meet the requirements of Section 306(c)(8).

(b) *Comment.* Statutory citation: Section 306(c)(8):

Prior to granting approval of a management program submitted by a coastal State, the Secretary shall find that * * * the management program provides for adequate consideration of the national interest involved in the siting of facilities necessary to meet requirements which are other than local in nature.

This policy requirement is intended to assure that national concerns over facility siting are expressed and dealt with in the development and implementation of State coastal zone management programs. The requirement should not be construed as compelling the States to propose a program which accommodates certain types of facilities, but to assure that such national concerns are included at an early stage in the State's planning activities and that such facilities not be arbitrarily excluded or unreasonably restricted in the management program without good and sufficient reasons. It is recognized that there may or may not be a national interest associated with the siting of facilities necessary to meet requirements which are other than local in nature. Requirements which are other than local in nature shall be considered those requirements which, when fulfilled, result in the establishment of facilities designed clearly to serve more than one locality (generally, the lowest unit of local, general-purpose government, excluding situations such as with cities and counties which exercise concurrent jurisdiction for the same geographic areas). In order to provide assistance to the States in completing this requirement, a listing is presented below which identifies those requirements which are both (1) other than local in nature, and (2) possess siting characteristics in which, in the opinion of the Secretary, there may be a clear national interest. For each such need, there is a listing of associated facilities. In addition, the principal cognizant Federal agencies concerned with these facilities are also listed. This list must not be considered inclusive, but the State should consider each requirement and facility type in the development of its management program. Consideration of these requirements and facilities need not be seen as a separate and distinct element of the management program, and the listing is provided to assure that the siting of such facilities is not overlooked or ignored. As part of its determination of permissible uses in the coastal zone (§ 923.12), as well as of priority of uses (§ 923.14), the State will have developed a procedure for inventorying coastal resources and identifying their existing or potential utilization for various purposes based upon capability, suitability and impact analyses. The process for responding to the requirements of Section 306(c)(8) should be identical to, and part of, the same procedure. No separate national interest "test" need be applied and submitted other than evidence that the listed national interest facilities have been considered in a manner similar to all other uses, and that appropriate consultation with the Federal agencies listed has been conducted. As a preliminary to adequate consideration of the national interest, the State must determine the needs for such facilities. Management programs must recognize the need of local as well as regional and national populations for goods and services which can be supplied only through the use of facilities in the coastal zone in order to make reasonable provision for such

facilities in light of the size and population of the State, the length and characteristics of its coast and the contribution such State is already making to regional and national needs. This will require the State to enter into discussions with appropriate Federal agencies and agencies of other States in the region, a process which should begin early in the development of the management program so that the full dimensions of the national interest may be considered as the State develops its program (§ 923.31 and §923.32). The management program should make reference to the views of cognizant Federal agencies as to how these national needs may be met in the coastal zone of that particular State. States should actively seek such guidance from these Federal agencies, particularly in view of the fact that all management programs will be reviewed with the opportunity for full comment by all affected Federal agencies prior to approval. It is recognized that Federal agencies will differ markedly in their abilities to articulate policies regarding utilization of individual State's coastal zones. NOAA's Office of Coastal Zone Management will encourage Federal agencies to develop policy statements regarding their perception of the national interest in the coastal zone and make these available to the States. The States should also consult with adjacent and nearby States which share similar or common coastal resources or with re-

Requirements which are other than local in nature and in the siting of which there may be a clear national interest (with associated facilities and cognizant Federal agencies)

Requirements	Associated facilities	Cognizant Federal Agencies
1. Energy production and transmission.	Oil and gas wells; storage and distribution facilities; refineries; nuclear, conventional, and hydroelectric powerplants; deepwater ports.	Federal Energy Administration, Federal Power Commission, Bureau of Land Management, Atomic Energy Commission, Maritime Administration, Geological Survey, Department of Transportation, Corps of Engineers.
2. Recreation (of an interstate nature)..	National seashores; parks, forests; large and outstanding beaches and recreational waterfronts; wildlife reserves.	National Park Service, Forest Service, Bureau of Outdoor Recreation.
3. Interstate transportation...........	Interstate highways, airports, aids to navigation; ports and harbors, railroads.	Federal Highway Administration, Federal Aviation Administration, Coast Guard, Corps of Engineers, Maritime Administration, Interstate Commerce Commission.
4. Production of food and fiber........	Prime agricultural land and facilities; forests; mariculture facilities; fisheries.	Soil Conservation Service, Forest Service, Fish and Wildlife Service, National Marine Fisheries Service.
5. Preservation of life and property....	Flood and storm protection facilities; disaster warning facilities.	Corps of Engineers, Federal Insurance Administration, NOAA, Soil Conservation Service.
6. National defense and aerospace......	Military installations; defense manufacturing facilities; aerospace launching and tracking facilities.	Department of Defense, NASA.
7. Historic, cultural, esthetic and conservation values.	Historic sites; natural areas; areas of unique cultural significance; wildlife refuges; areas of species and habitat preservation.	National Register of Historic Places, National Park Service, Fish and Wildlife Service, National Marine Fisheries Service.
8. Mineral resources..................	Mineral extraction facilities needed to directly support activity.	Bureau of Mines, Geological Survey.

gional interstate bodies to determine how regional needs may be met in siting facilities. Specific arrangements of "trade-offs" of coastal resource utilization should be documented with appropriate supporting evidence. The importance of this type of interstate consultation and cooperation in planning cannot be overemphasized for it offers the States the opportunity of resolving significant national problems on a regional scale without Federal intervention.

§ 923.16 Area designation for preservation and restoration.

(a) *Requirement*. In order to fulfill the requirement contained in Section 306(c) (9), the management program must show evidence that the State has developed and applied standards and criteria for the designation of areas of conservation, recreational, ecological or esthetic values for the purpose of preserving and restoring them.

(b) *Comment*. Statutory citation: Section 306(c) (9):

> Prior to granting approval of a management program submitted by a coastal State, the Secretary shall find that * * * the management program makes provision for procedures whereby specific areas may be designated for the purpose of preserving or restoring them for their conservation, recreation, ecological or esthetic values.

(1) This requirement is closely linked to that contained in § 923.13, dealing with designation of areas of particular concern. Unless the State can make a compelling case to the contrary, all areas designated according to the methods called for in this part shall also be considered as areas of particular concern.

(2) This requirement is reasonably self-explanatory. The State must develop procedures for the designation of areas with certain characteristics. The State, in doing so, must:

(i) Establish standards and criteria for the possible designation of coastal areas intended for preservation or restoration because of their conservation, recreational, ecological or esthetic values, and

(ii) Apply those standards and criteria to the State's coastal resources. (In this, the inventory associated with the requirement of § 923.13 will be most helpful.)

(3) The requirement of the statute goes to the procedures rather than substance; the fact that a State may be unable to move rapidly ahead with a program of preservation or restoration will not prevent the program from being approved. The State should also rank in order of relative priority areas of its

coastal zone which have been designated for the purposes set forth in this section. As funds become available, such a ranking will provide a set of priorities for selecting areas to be preserved or restored.

§ 923.17 Local regulations and uses of regional benefit.

(a) *Requirement*. In order to fulfill the requirement contained in Section 306(e) (2), the management program must show evidence that the State has developed and applied a method for determining uses of regional benefit, and that it has established a method for assuring that local land and water use controls in the coastal zone do not unreasonably or arbitrarily restrict or exclude those uses of regional benefit.

(b) *Comment*. Statutory citation: Section 306(e) (2):

> Prior to granting approval, the Secretary shall also find that the program provides * * * for a method of assuring that local land and water use regulations within the coastal zone do not unreasonably restrict or exclude land and water uses of regional benefit.

This requirement is intended to prevent local land and water use decisions from arbitrarily excluding certain land and water uses which are deemed of importance to more than a single unit of local government. For the purposes of this requirement, a use of regional benefit will be one which provides services or other benefits to citizens of more than one unit of local, general-purpose government (excluding situations such as in cities and counties which exercise jurisdiction over the same geographic areas). In order to assure that arbitrary exclusion does not occur, the State must first identify those uses which it perceives will affect or produce some regional benefit. This designation would normally be derived from the inventory and analysis of the uses contained in § 923.12. In any event, however, these uses should include those contained in the table of § 923.15. In addition, the State may determine that certain land and water uses may be of regional benefit under certain sets of circumstances; the State should then establish standards and criteria for determining when such conditions exist. There should be no blanket exclusion or restrictions of these uses in areas of the coastal zone by local regulation unless it can be shown that the exclusion or restriction is based upon reasonable considerations of the suitability of the area for the uses or the carrying capacity of the area. The requirement of this section does not exclude the possibility that in specific areas certain uses of regional benefit may be prohibited. However, such exclusions may not be capricious. The method by which the management program will assure that such unreasonable restrictions or exclusion not occur in local land and water use decisions will, of course, be up to the State, but it should include the preparation of standards and criteria relating to State interpretation of "unreasonable restriction or exclusion", as well as the establishment of a continuing mechanisms for such determination.

Technical Information

1. SOIL TEXTURE AND STRUCTURE

A characterization of soil texture and structure with special attention to mineral components, bulk soil density, total soil space, and porosity.

SOURCE. T. Ewald Maki, North Carolina University, Raleigh, North Carolina, 1975.

Soil texture refers to a very important physical property of soils, namely, the size of the mineral particles comprising the inorganic part of the soil profile. *Texture* refers specifically to the relative proportion of various size groups in a given soil. Together with *soil structure* (which concerns the arrangement of soil particles into aggregates), these two properties determine to an important degree the moisture and aeration interrelationships, as well as the nutrient-supplying ability of soil solids to sustain plant life.

Within the average life expectancy of man, the soil processes are incapable of appreciably altering the size of the individual *mineral* particles in the soil. Thus a sandy soil remains sandy, and a clay soil, six to seven decades hence, is still apt to be a clay. Soil texture, therefore, is a basic property that man cannot alter. The land manager can proceed in decision-making confident in the knowledge that the textural classes determining the soil types on his land are stable, and that he is stuck with them for the duration of his life.

To characterize the texture of a given soil, it is necessary, or at least desirable, to separate the ingredients of a soil sample into convenient groups according to size as determined by the range of particle diameters within groups. The relative amount of each soil size group is then used to describe the textural class of a soil, such as sand, sandy loam, or sandy clay loam. These soil classes convey some indication of the soil's physical properties and its behavior under tillage practices such as site preparation. Three broad classes are recognized: sands, loams, and clays.

In contrast to *soil texture*, which is altered through comminution (essentially on a geological time scale), *soil structure* is a very important physical property that may be altered significantly during a single site preparation or logging operation. "Soil structure" refers to the particular type of particle grouping that predominates in any part of the soil profile; it is a descriptive term designating the overall aggregation or arrangement of soil solids.

Structure is important because it influences (*a*) bulk density, (*b*) porosity, (*c*) water movement, (*d*) heat transfer, (*e*) aeration, and the like. It is at once clear that important physical changes wrought by the forester in logging, thinning, site preparation, and related operations are structural rather than textural.

Two physical changes in the context of soil structure deserve additional emphasis here. The first is *bulk density*. It happens that individual soil mineral particles have densities that vary within narrow limits of about 2.60 to 2.75. This narrow range reflects the dominance of quartz, feldspars, and silicates, which have densities falling within the range indicated above and which also make up the major portion of most mineral soils. When the parent material from which a given soil is derived or formed contains unusually large amounts of heavy minerals such as magnetite, garnet, epidote, zircon, tourmaline, and hornblende, the particle density may exceed 2.75, but for most soils we may assume 2.65 to be an acceptable working average. Obviously, an abundance of organic matter in a soil substantially reduces the average particle density of a given mass of soil. In contrast to particle density, *total soil space*, which includes not only the solid particles but also the pore spaces, is referred to as *bulk density*; this can be defined as the mass (weight) of a unit volume of dry soil. Symbolically, it can be expressed as follows:

$$BD = \frac{W_s}{V_s}$$

where BD = bulk density, W_s = weight of dry soil, and V_s = volume of the soil. Any activity that increases the weight of a given volume of soil obviously also increases its bulk density. In many forest soils bulk density may range from as low as 0.7 in loose surface horizons to as high as 1.8 in compacted or deep subsurface horizons. These ratios merely mean that dry soil weighs from 0.7 to 1.8 times an equal volume of water.

The second physical change is *porosity* or *pore space*, which defines the portion of the soil occupied by air and water. The amount of pore space is determined to an important degree by the soil structure which develops from two possible nonstructural states, namely, *single-grained* and *massive*. Loose sand is a good example of a single-grained soil in which each solid particle functions as an individual. Add organic matter or a little clay to it, and the single grains may coalesce into weak aggregates.

Between the extremes of single-grained and massive are seven structural types which may occur singly or in some combination within a given profile. These common seven structures are (*a*) *platy*, (*b*) *columnar*, (*c*) *prismatic*, (*d*) *blocky*, (*e*) *nutlike*, (*f*) *granular*, and (*g*) *crumb*. Obviously, it is easier and quicker to destroy a given structure than to create or recreate it. The mechanics of structure formation are complex and are influenced by many factors, such as climate, geologic origin, organic matter, and soluble salts.

For practical purposes, porosity can be thought of as being of two types, based on the diameters of the interstices. *Micropores* (often referred to as "capillary pores" in the past) are those with diameters less than 0.1 millimeter. *Macropores* are those with diameters larger than 0.1 millimeter, and they play an exceedingly important role in *detention* storage of water, allowing ready movement of both air and water. In micropores air movement is impeded, and water movement is largely restricted to the slow capillary transmission.

The total porosity of a soil can be readily determined if the particle density and bulk density are known. Percent pore space is simply equated as

$$P\% = (1 - \frac{BD)}{PD}100$$

where BD = bulk density, and PD = particle density. If, for example, $BD = 1.2$ and PD is 2.65, the percent pore space is

$$(1 - \frac{1.2}{2.65})100 = (1 - 0.45)\,100 = 55\%.$$

2. SOIL TEXTURE IDENTIFICATION

A dichotomous key for the identification of
soil texture on forest lands.

SOURCE. T. Ewald Maki, North Carolina State
University, Raleigh, North Carolina, 1975.

A. SOIL, WHEN PINCHED BETWEEN THE THUMB AND FINGER, CRUMBLES, WILL FORM
NO 'RIBBON'.

B. SOIL, SQUEEZED IN HAND WHEN DRY, FALLS APART READILY: SQUEEZED
WHEN MOIST, FORMS A CAST THAT BREAKS IF NOT HANDLED VERY CAREFULLY.
INDIVIDUAL SAND GRAINS CAN BE READILY SEEN AND FELT..... <u>SANDY LOAM</u>

B. SOIL, SQUEEZED IN HAND WHEN DRY, FORMS CAST THAT BEARS CAREFUL
HANDLING: SQUEEZED WHEN MOIST, FORMS A CAST THAT CAN BE HANDLED
QUITE FREELY WITHOUT BREAKING. SOIL SMOOTH, AND SAND GRAINS NOT
READILY EVIDENT.

C. Soil slightly plastic when moist, but not greasy. Gritty when
dry, not floury. (Colors tend to range from brown to dark
gray)... <u>LOAM</u>

C. Soil greasy when moist, floury when dry. On wetting it runs
together and puddles. (Color may be light gray to nearly
white) ....<u>SILT LOAM</u>

A. SOIL, WHEN PINCHED BETWEEN THE THUMB AND FINGER, FORMS A 'RIBBON',
AT LEAST BARELY SUSTAINING ITS OWN WEIGHT.

D. RIBBON BREAKS EASILY, BARELY SUSTAINS OWN WEIGHT.

E. Individual sand grains can be seen and felt readily. Moist
soil friable. (Color usually brownish yellow to brownish
red) .... <u>SANDY CLAY LOAM</u>

E. Soil smooth, sand grains not evident. Moist soil somewhat
plastic.

F. Soil heavy and greasy when moist.(Color dull gray, sometimes containing iron concretions) .... <u>SILTY CLAY LOAM</u>
F. Soil mellow and loose when moist. (Color usually yellowish
brown to reddish brown) .... <u>CLAY LOAM</u>

D. RIBBON IS LONG AND FLEXIBLE, STRONG.

G. Individual sand grains can readily be seen and felt. Moist soil
somewhat friable. (Color usually bright red or yellow)...<u>SANDY CLAY</u>

G. Sand not evident. Moist soil plastic.

H. Color usually gray, sometimes containing iron concretions
<u>SILTY CLAY</u>
H. Color usually dark red, often mottled with gray or yellow. In
wet situations essentially solid gray to blue gray ..... <u>CLAY</u>

3. SOIL GRAIN SIZES

A grain size scale for soil classification.

SOURCE. U.S. Army Corps of Engineers, *Shore Protection Manual*, Vol. I, Coastal Engineering Research Center, Vicksburg, Mississippi, 1973.

Wentworth Scale (Size Description)		Phi Units ϕ*	Grain Diameter d (mm)	U.S. Standard Sieve Size	Unified Soil Classification (USC)		
Boulder		−8	256		Cobble		
Cobble			76.2	3 in.			
		−6	64.0		Coarse		Gravel
Pebble			19.0	¾ in.	Fine		
			4.76	No. 4			
		−2	4.0		Coarse		
Granule		−1	2.0	No. 10			
Sand	Very Coarse	0	1.0		Medium		Sand
	Coarse	1	0.5				
	Medium		0.42	No. 40			
		2	0.25		Fine		
	Fine	3	0.125				
	Very Fine		0.074	No. 200			
		4	0.0625				
Silt		8	0.00391		Silt or Clay		
Clay							
Colloid		12	0.00024				

* $\phi = -\log_2$ d (mm)

4. SOIL CLASSIFICATION

The mechanical composition of the principal soil classes.

SOURCE. R. E. Davis and H. H. Bennett, *Grouping of Soils on the Basis of Mechanical Analysis*, U.S. Department of Agriculture, Circular No. 419, 1927.

Soil class	Per cent		
	Sand	Silt	Clay
Sand.....................	80–100	0–20	0–20
Sandy loam...............	50–80	0–50	0–20
Silt loam..................	0–50	50–100	0–20
Loam.....................	30–50	30–50	0–20
Silty clay loam.............	0–30	50–80	20–30
Sandy clay loam...........	50–80	0–30	20–30
Clay loam.................	20–50	20–50	20–30
Silty clay.................	0–20	50–70	30–50
Sandy clay...............	50–70	0–20	30–50
Clay.....................	0–50	0–50	30–100

5. SOIL EROSION, TRANSPORTATION, AND DEPOSITION

Erosion, transportation, and deposition velocities *versus* grain size of sediment.

SOURCE.   D. E. Bassi and D. R. Basco, *Field Study of an Unconfined Spoil Disposal Area of the Gulf Intracoastal Waterway in Galveston Bay, Texas,* Texas A&M University, Sea Grant Program Publication No. TAMU-SG-74-208, January 1974.

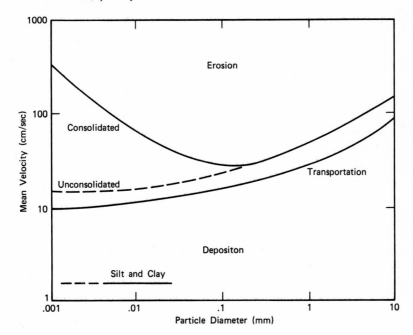

6. SETTLING RATES OF SEDIMENTS

The rates of settlement of sediment particles
in still water at 50°F (10°C).

SOURCE.   T. Merriman and T. H. Wiggin, *American Civil Engineer's Handbook*, 5th Ed.,
John Wiley, New York, 1949.

Kind of Material	Diameter of Particles in mm	Rate of Settlement, mm Per Second
Coarse sand	1	100
	0.20	21
Fine sand	0.10	8
	0.06	3.8
	0.04	2.1
	0.02	0.6
Silt	0.01	0.15
Coarse clay	0.001	0.0015
Fine clay	0.0001	0.000015

7. STORM RUNOFF RATES

Runoff curve numbers for selected agricultural, suburban, and urban land use. Average runoff potential as estimated by 5-day antecedent rainfall.

SOURCE. Soil Conservation Service, U.S. Department of Agriculture, *Urban Hydrology for Small Watersheds*, Technical Release No. 55, January 1975.

LAND USE DESCRIPTION	HYDROLOGIC SOIL GROUP			
	A	B	C	D
Cultivated land[1]/: without conservation treatment	72	81	88	91
: with conservation treatment	62	71	78	81
Pasture or range land: poor condition	68	79	86	89
good condition	39	61	74	80
Meadow: good condition	30	58	71	78
Wood or Forest land: thin stand, poor cover, no mulch	45	66	77	83
good cover[2]/	25	55	70	77
Open Spaces, lawns, parks, golf courses, cemeteries, etc.				
good condition: grass cover on 75% or more of the area	39	61	74	80
fair condition: grass cover on 50% to 75% of the area	49	69	79	84
Commercial and business areas (85% impervious)	89	92	94	95
Industrial districts (72% impervious).	81	88	91	93

LAND USE DESCRIPTION		HYDROLOGIC SOIL GROUP			
		A	B	C	D
Residential:[3]					
Average lot size Average % Impervious[4]					
1/8 acre or less 65		77	85	90	92
1/4 acre 38		61	75	83	87
1/3 acre 30		57	72	81	86
1/2 acre 25		54	70	80	85
1 acre 20		51	68	79	84
Paved parking lots, roofs, driveways, etc.[5]		98	98	98	98
Streets and roads:					
paved with curbs and storm sewers[5]		98	98	98	98
gravel		76	85	89	91
dirt		72	82	87	89

[1] For a more detailed description of agricultural land use curve numbers refer to National Engineering Handbook, Section 4, Hydrology, Chapter 9, Aug. 1972.

[2] Good cover is protected from grazing and litter and brush cover soil.

[3] Curve numbers are computed assuming the runoff from the house and driveway is directed towards the street with a minimum of roof water directed to lawns where additional infiltration could occur.

[4] The remaining pervious areas (lawn) are considered to be in good pasture condition for these curve numbers.

[5] In some warmer climates of the country a curve number of 95 may be used.

Peak rate of discharge *versus* drainage area (in acres) for moderate slope (4 percent) and varying amounts of 24-hour rainfall.

SOURCE.   Soil Conservation Service, *Minimizing Erosion in Urbanizing Areas*, U.S. Department of Agriculture, Madison, Wisconsin, 1972.

Runoff Curve Number—65
Moderate runoff conditions—low density development with moderate soil infiltration.

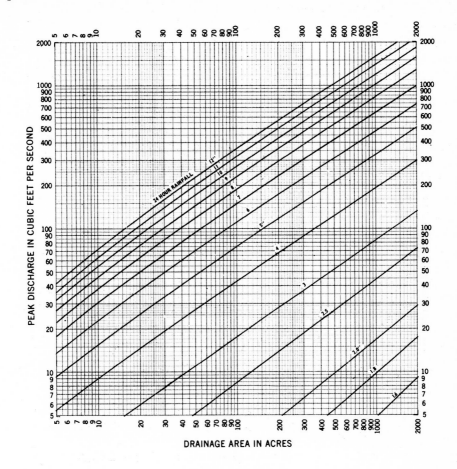

Runoff Curve Number—85

High runoff conditions—high density residential development with poor soil infiltration.

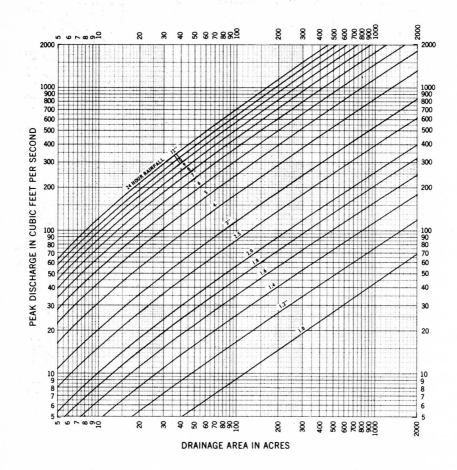

DRAINAGE AREA IN ACRES

8. SEDIMENT TRANSPORT AND DELIVERY

Sediment delivery ratio (percent of gross erosion that is transported out of drainage area) *versus* size of drainage area.

SOURCE.   U.S. Environmental Protection Agency, *Methods for Identifying and Evaluating the Nature and Extent of Non-point Sources of Pollutants*, Washington, D.C., 1973.

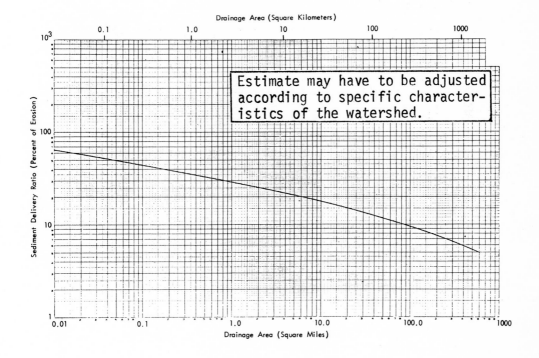

9. URBAN RUNOFF RATES

Runoff generation and sediment yields for various land-use characteristics.

SOURCE.   Joachim Tourbier and Richard Westmacott, *Water Resources Protection Measures in Land Development—A Handbook*. Water Resources as a Basis for Comprehensive Planning and Development of the Christina River Basin; a Prototype Project, Phase II. Water Resources Center, University of Delaware, Newark, Delaware, 1974.

Land Use Intensity	Gross Percentage of Impermeable Cover (1)					Permeable Surfaces		Assumed Runoff Generation (Increase in Mean Annual Flood)					
	Total (2)	Roofs	Roads	Parking	Other	% Perm. Surface Mowed Grass	% Perm. Surface Wood, Pasture or Abandoned	% Area Served by Storm Sewers (3,6)					
								0	20	40	60	80	100
1	0-2½	<1	<2½	<1	–	<25	>75	1.0	1.1	1.1	1.1	1.1	1.1
2	2½-5	1-1½	1-2½	½-1	–	25-50	50-75	1.1	1.2	1.2	1.2	1.2	1.2
3	5-10	1½-3½	2½-5	1-1½	–	50-80	10-50	1.2	1.3	1.4	1.4	1.4	1.4
4	10-20	3½-7	5-10	1½-3	–	100	0	1.3	1.4	1.7	2.0	2.1	2.1
5	20-33	7-10	10-16	3-7	–	100	0	1.4	1.8	2.0	2.4	2.5	2.5
6	33-50	10-17	16-23	7-10	–	100	0	1.5	2.2	2.4	2.7	2.8	3.0
7	50-75	17-25	23-25	10-20	0-5	100	0	1.8	2.5	3.0	3.8	4.0	4.2
8	75-100	25	25	>20	5-15	100	0	2.5	3.0	4.2	5.0	5.4	6.0

Land Use Intensity	Assumed Sedi. Ylds t/sq mi/yr		Average Assumed Residential User Characteristics								
	During Construction (5)	After Construction (4)	Gross Lot Size (Acres)	Gross Land-Use Intensity (7)	Persons Per Gross Acre (8)	Sewage Generation Gal Per Day (9)	Water Usage GPD (10)	Lgth of Utility Lines per Acre	Lgth of Utility Line per DU	Assumed Sewerage	Assumed Water
1	400	400	>5	-	<1	<100	<125	200	1000	-	-
2	600	600	2-5	-	1- 2	100- 200	125- 250	200	750	-	-
3	1000	750	1-2	-	2- 4	200- 400	250- 500	200	300	-	✓
4	2500	1000	½-1	-	4- 6	400- 800	500-1000	200	150	-	✓
5	5000	1250	¼-½	-	6-12	800-1600	1000-2000	145	55	✓	✓
6	10000	1500	⅛-¼	3.5	12-24	1600-3200	2000-4000	145	30	✓	✓
7	20000	1750	1/16-1/8	4.5	24-40	3200-6400	4000-8000	140	15	✓	✓
8	50000	2000	<1/16	-	>40	>6400	>8000	140	<15	✓	✓

(1) This includes collector roads, streets, etc.
(2) This is a low estimation of % impermeable cover for lot sizes shown based on Leopold's references in Hydrologic Data for Land Planners, 1968, p.2.
(3) Squares indicate most usual combination of % impermeable cover and % storm sewers. Data from Leopold, 1968.
(4) Figures for the higher land uses are largely due to increased streambank erosion caused by increased runoff.
(5) Figures estimated from references quoted by Leopold, 1968.
(6) DRBC Compact report (April 1971) estimates increase for 20% cover and 20% storm sewer = 2, and increase due to 50% cover and 50% storm sewer = 5.
(7) Land-Use Intensity Index as used by the Urban Land Institute in the Community Builders Handbook for a dwelling size of 1089 sq ft.
(8) Four persons per unit assumed for lower densities; 2.5 persons per unit for high densities.
(9) Based on New Castle County (DE) Design Flow Standards.
(10) Based on 125 gallons per day per person; Urban Land Institute, Community Builders Handbook.

10. WATER QUALITY PARAMETERS

Water quality parameters for surface water
and bottom sediment analyses.

SOURCE. Interstate Commission on the Potomac
River Basin, Potomac River Basin Water
Quality Status and Trend.

Because of its abundance and life-giving properties, water is one of the most important resources on earth. In a given volume of water, dissolved oxygen (DO) is 30 times less abundant than in air, and nitrogen, which comprises 79 percent of the atmosphere, is present only in minute quantities. Thus, many of the constituents of air that influence terrestrial life are limiting factors on the growth of organisms in water.

Water, the universal *solvent*, is composed of two atoms of hydrogen attached at 105° angles to one atom of oxygen (H_2O). In liquid form, a molecule establishes hydrogen bonds with its neighbors to form long branching chains. On the surface layer these bonds extend sideways and downward to form an elastic film. Water is 775 times more dense than air, and attains its greatest density at a temperature of 3.94° *centigrade* (C) at a pressure of one atmosphere (760 millimeters of mercury-pressure at sea level).

The amounts and kinds of materials found in water effect temperature (stored thermal energy), *density*, rate of evaporation and light reflectance. For example, although the greatest density of water occurs at about 4°C, negligible amounts of dissolved solids will change its density. *Sea* (salt) *water* containing 35 *parts per thousand*

(ppt) or 35,000 *parts per million* (ppm) (= milligrams per liter (mg/l)) dissolved solids (principally sodium chloride) has a density of 1.02822.

Increasing salinity lowers the solubility of gases in water. Also, increasing salinity lowers the temperature of maximum density, because each increase of 1.0 ppt salinity decreases the point of maximum density by 0.2°C. Thus sea water has maximum density at −3.52°C. The density of water has great importance for the maintenance of *planktonic organisms*, floating plants and animals that are tied through the food chain to the productivity of higher animals such as fish, *shellfish*, and other commercial seafood. The addition of extraneous materials to water may upset the equilibrium to which the organisms have adapted over thousands of years, endangering their continued existence.

Although the kinds and amounts of complex wastes discharged into the waters of the Potomac basin are varied, they generally fit one of the following categories: inorganic salts, acids, and alkalis, organic matter, suspended and dissolved solids, floating solids and liquids, heated water, color, toxic substances, microorganisms and foam producing matter. This water quality trend analysis traces the following parameters that reflect most, but not all, of the kinds of pollution found in the basin.

Parameter (Unit)	Abbreviation	STORET No.	Reflects
Chemical:			
Alkalinity, Calcium Carbonate (mg/l) . . . . . $CaCO_3$		00410	Buffering capacity of the water
Ammonia Nitrogen (mg/l) . . . . NH_3^{-N}		00610	Common nitrogen form in STP effluents, released by decomposition of organic matter
Chloride (mg/l) Cl		00940	Amount of sodium chloride in water
Dissolved Oxygen (mg/l) . . . . DO		00300	Weight/volume of DO in water: increases with photosynthesis and decreases with exertion of organic decomposable wastes and respiration.
Dissolved Oxygen percent saturation . . . . −		00301	An expression of DO in relation to the maximum possible under ambient conditions
Hydrogen Ion Activity (Standard Unit) . . . . pH SU		00400	Acids & alkalis (acidity)
Kjeldahl Nitrogen, Total (mg/l) . . . . TKN		00625	Organic nitrogen (found in plant cells) and NH_3^{-N}

Parameter (Unit)	Abbreviation	STORET No.	Reflects
Nitrate Nitrogen (mg/l) . . . . $NO_3{}^{-N}$		00620	Completely oxidized form of nitrogen in STP Effluents utilized by plants as nutrients and by bacteria
Nitrite Nitrogen (mg/l) . . . . $NO_2{}^{-N}$		00615	Oxidized form of nitrate nitrogen; low concentrations in natural water
Phenols (mg/l). . . . . −		32730	Hydroxyl derivatives of benzene in industrial & domestic wastewaters
Phosphorus, Total (mg/l) . . . . TP		00665	All phosphorus in water expressed in the elemental form
Phosphate, Total as PO_4 (mg/l) . . . . . TPO_4		00650	All phosphates in water expressed as PO_4
Microbiologic:			
Biochemical Oxygen Demand (mg/l) BOD–5		00310	Oxygen demand by microbes in decomposition of organic wastes during 5 days
Coliform, Fecal (MPN/100 ml) . . . . −		31615	Number of coliform bacteria of fecal origin from warm blooded animals
Coliform, Total (MPN/100 ml) . . . . . −		31505	All coliform bacteria in water including those in soil and plants as well as warm-blooded animals
Physical:			
Flow (cfs) . . . . −		00060	Volume of water (cubic feet) passing a point in one second
Solids, Dissolved (mg/l) . . . . DS		00515	Salts of metals, pigments and other substances passing through a glass fiber filter
Solids, Suspended (mg/l) . . . . SS		00530	Organic & inorganic coarse materials retained on a glass fiber filter
Solids, Total (mg/l) . . . . TS		00500	All dissolved and undissolved solid substances
Temperature (°C). . . . . −		00010	Ambient heat content of water
Turbidity (Jackson Units) . . . . JTU		00070	Material in water affecting light transparency

Trace metals such as copper, zinc, mercury, oils, radioactivity and pesticides were not measured routinely prior to 1973. However, the revised Baseline Water Quality Monitoring Network (1974) conducted jointly by state water quality control agencies incorporates these and other parameters for surface water and bottom sediment analyses.

The brief overview that follows presents several parameters and a rationale for their use.

Alkalinity

Total alkalinity measures the amount of acid required to dissociate bound carbon dioxide (CO_2), bicarbonate (HCO_3^-), carbonate ($CO_3^=$), and hydroxide ions (OH^-) in in the water. These anions (positive charged ions) and cations (negatively charged ions) tend to balance one another. At low pH values (<6.3) free CO_2 is abundant. For pH of 6.3 to 10, most of the CO_2 is found as HCO_3^-.

Above pH 10, most of the CO_2 is found as $CO_3^=$. Both high and low free CO_2 (low pH) in the aquatic system is toxic to aquatic life. Moderate $CaCO_3$ alkalinity usually lies between 40-200 mg/l.

Bacteriological Indicators

The coliform bacteria include all of the aerobic (utilizing oxygen) and facultative anaerobic (may live either with or without oxygen) bacteria. They are gram-negative (do not stain), non-sporeforming (spores are not formed in reproduction), rod-shaped (long straight bacteria) and ferment lactose and form gas within 48 hours at 35°C. Coliform bacteria are found in the soil, on plants, as well as in the excreta of mammals, insects and poultry.

Fecal coliform bacteria, although harmless to man, are found in excreta of warm blooded animals along with pathogenic bacteria, and because they are easier to detect than pathogenic organisms, they are used to indicate water likely to cause illness. Since pathogenic organisms can cause dysentery and other diseases, close monitoring of them is a major concern to the public. In nutritive media, fecal coliform bacteria produce gas at 44.5°C.

Fecal streptococci have been found in the excreta of birds and mammals. The proportion of fecal streptococci and fecal coliform to the feces weight differs with animals. For example in man, fecal coliforms number 13 million/gram, and fecal streptococci number 3 million/gram of feces, whereas in pigs the former number 3 million/gram while fecal streptococci number 84 million/gram. In chickens, fecal coliforms number 1.3 million/gram whereas fecal streptococci number 3.4 million/gram.

In waters designated for recreation, where the whole body may be submerged completely, or where a significant probability of ingestion exists, the maximum acceptable limit for fecal coliform bacteria is the log mean 200 most probable number (MPN)/100 ml of water sample. See Table 2—Water Quality Standards, for definitions of coliform standards.

Two primary methods are utilized to obtain coliform density estimates: multiple tube fermentation and membrane filter. In the first method, the formation of gas is observed in tubes containing five dilutions of the sample, usually .01, .1, 1, 10, and 100 ml, each dilution with five duplicates. Based on the number of positive tubes (gas production), for each dilution the most probable number *(MPN)* index code is obtained. A MPN table is consulted giving the probable true densities for the series along with a range of expected values at a particular confidence limit, i.e., if the chance of an event occurring is 19 times out of 20, a 95% confidence limit is established. Thus, multiple tube counts are derived estimates and not necessarily the actual bacterial densities. This is a partial answer to the varying counts that are sometimes encountered.

The membrane filter technique utilizes the retention of bacteria on a small (47 mm diameter) filter pad with .45 micron openings. After the sample is filtered, the pad is placed on a similar pad with nutrient, incubated for 2 hours at 35°C in 100 percent humidity and then transferred to nutrient medium and held at 35°C for 20-22 hours. Coliform colonies have a characteristic dark green metallic sheen and when counted are expressed in numbers per 100 ml of sample (e.g., 300/100 ml). Since the pores of the filter may become clogged by the fine clay particles found in the waters of the Potomac basin, the multiple tube technique is more widely used.

The relationship between the levels of total and fecal coliform and pathogenic organisms in water supplies is not clearly understood. However, studies have shown that there is a certain risk involved anytime coliform bacteria are present. For example, if total coliform levels are near 200,000 MPN/100 ml (1973 maximum counts in the Potomac estuary) and a person while swimming injests 10 ml of water every day for 90 days, the chance of contacting a single *Salmonella typhus* (causing typhoid

fever) would be 1:1,000. Total coliform levels of 5,000 MPN/100 ml (a general goal for recreational water) presents a risk of 1:100,000. Although the current standards appear strict, caution in raising the limits will probably be practiced until more evidence is gathered on the risk of illness at higher coliform levels. Also, the maximum coliform levels often greatly exceed the log mean counts which may present a greater risk of illness than the log mean of several estimates might indicate.

Biochemical Oxygen Demand (BOD-5)

BOD is an empirical microbiological measurement of the oxygen consumed (in mg/l) by native bacteria. Success and precision of the measurement depends upon the controlled incubation of the water sample for a period of 5 days (BOD-5) at 20°C and a suitable bacterial "seed" used to innoculate the water to begin the decomposition process. Generally, BOD-5 values greater than 5 mg/l indicate polluted water.

Chloride

Chloride in waters may originate from several sources, including leaching from salt bearing deposits, industrial wastes and in the effluent discharge of sewage treatment plants (70-500 mg/l). The Chloride salinity of sea water is about 19,000 mg/l or 19 parts per thousand (ppt) and comprises 1.9 percent of the total 3.5 percent (35ppt) salinity. "Freshwater" contains less than 100 mg/l chloride, "brackish water" 100-1,000 mg/l and "sea water" over 1,000 mg/l.

Dissolved Oxygen (DO)

DO depletion in waters caused by pollution can place stress on aquatic animals and reduce their ability to meet the demands of their environment, and in extreme cases cause death by oxygen starvation. The amount of DO in the water depends upon the atmospheric pressure and temperature, i.e., cold water in low altitudes retains more DO than warm water in high altitudes.

Fish occupying a habitat well saturated with oxygen during daylight hours may be subjected to stress conditions in the early morning hours when the demand for oxygen exhausts photosynthetic reserves. Generally, waters with DO concentrations less than 5.0 mg/l will not support good fisheries.

A change in temperature, barometric pressure and/or contamination could change the oxygen percent saturation. The best conditions vary for each species of fish, e.g., the critical level of saturation for brook trout is 75 percent of the possible saturation at ambient conditions, whereas catfish can survive at 45 percent saturation.

Dissolved Solids (DS)

Dissolved solids (DS) is the general term that describes the concentration of dissolved substances (filterable residue) in water. The more conspicuous constituents in natural surface water include the carbonates, sulfates, chlorides, phosphates, and nitrates. Ions occur in combination with metallic ions such as calcium, sodium, potassium, magnesium, and iron ionizable salts. The quantity and quality of dissolved solids are major factors determining the variety and abundance of plant and animal life in the aquatic system.

Hydrogen Ion Activity (pH)

The pH is a measure of acidity. It is found by taking the log of the reciprocal of the hydrogen ion concentration. When the quantity of hydrogen ions exceeds 10^{-7} gram-atoms per liter, the solution is acid, when equal to 10^7, the solution is neutral (pH 7), and when less than 10^7, the solution is basic. Acidic water can exert stress conditions or kill aquatic life and basic conditions (pH above 8.5) begin to decrease reproduction in many aquatic species.

Nutrients

Nutrients such as *carbon, phosphorus* and *nitrogen* limit the growth of plants. Excessive nutrient loads result in *eutrophication*. Under natural conditions, bodies of water age by filling with debris from the surrounding land areas and by internal biological processes. This aging process is usually slow in nutrient poor (oligotrophic) waters and progressively increases in speed as nutrient rich (eutrophic) conditions are reached. In the latter stages of filling, the body of water progresses through a marsh stage and finally becomes entirely terrestrial. In lakes, soluble phosphorus values exceeding 0.01 mg/l (10 μg/l) and inorganic nitrogen values of 0.30 mg/l are sufficient to trigger nuisance algal blooms. Total phosphorus concentrations in streams exceeding 0.1 mg/l for extended periods are likely to cause algal blooms.

Forms of Phosphorus:

1. Total Phosphorus (P) — all phosphorus in a sample
   A. Orthophosphate (P, ortho) — inorganic phosphorus
   B. Hydrolyzable phosphorus (P, hydro) — sometimes called "polyphosphates" measured by acid digestion
   C. Organic phosphorus (P, organic) — phosphorus minus A. and B.

2. Dissolved Phosphorus (P, D) — phosphorus present in the filtrate of a sample passed through a .45 micron filter
   A. Dissolved orthophosphate
   B. Dissolved hydrolyzable phosphorus
   C. Dissolved organic phosphorus

3. Insoluble phosphorus — forms as above.

Forms of Nitrogen:

1. Inorganic Nitrogen

   A. Nitrate Nitrogen (NO_3^{-N})
   B. Nitrite Nitrogen (NO_2^{-N})
   C. Ammonia Nitrogen (NH_3^{-N})

2. Total Kjeldahl Nitrogen (TKN) — the sum of the NH_3^{-N} and organic nitrogen compounds

3. Organic Kjeldahl Nitrogen — organic nitrogen minus NH_3^{-N}

4. Total Nitrogen — $(NO_2^{-N}) + (NO_3^{-N}) + (TKN)$

Parameters and Eutrophic Classification

	Oligotrophic	Mesotrophic	Eutrophic
Total Phosphorus (mg/l)	$\leq .01$	.01-.6	$\geq .6$
Phosphorus loading gm/m²•year	$< .5$	.5-2	≥ 2
Nitrate-Nitrogen (mg/l)	$\leq .2$	.2-.5	$\geq .5$
Chlorophyll a (mg/m³)	≤ 3	3-20	≥ 20

Suspended Solids

Suspended solids (SS) include both inorganic (sand and clay) and organic (particulate material, bacteria, and plankton) substances in the water that are retained on a glass fiber filter. Suspended matter inhibits light penetration, can restrict the zone of primary (plant) production and influences temperature patterns as well. Agricultural runoff, construction activities, industrial operations, storm sewers, and municipal wastes are the principal sources of SS in bodies of water. Finely divided SS may kill fish directly by interfering with respiration, inhibit growth or egg and larval development, interfere with natural movements, reduce the availability of food, and prevent successful reproduction by blanketing spawning sites. Suspended particles also serve as a transport mechanism for pesticides and other toxic substances readily adsorbed onto fine clay particles.

Concentrations of SS less than 25 mg/l usually have no harmful effect on fisheries. Waters containing concentrations of 25 to 80 mg/l should be capable of supporting good to moderate fisheries. Where concentrations exceed 80 mg/l, good freshwater fisheries are unlikely.

Temperature

To a great extent in water, temperature governs changes in the physiology of aquatic life. The temperature of the surface layer of water usually corresponds more closely to the ambient air temperature than do the lower layers of water, and thermal gradients occur naturally from the surface to the bottom layer. Aquatic organisms have upper and lower thermal tolerance limits and optimum temperatures for growth. They seek out preferred temperatures for growth and reproduction.

Temperature also affects the physical environment of the aquatic medium, (e.g., viscosity, degree of ice cover, and oxygen capacity). Therefore, the composition of aquatic communities depends largely on temperature characteristics of the environment. Even slight changes in temperature in an aquatic ecosystem may be detrimental to certain species, but other species may benefit from slightly altered thermal characteristics.

Turbidity

Turbidity is a measure of the amount of light transmitted through water. If the water transmits one candle power of light 72.9 centimeters (cm), the turbidity is 25 scale units. Turbidity is an indirect measure of the suspended particulate matter, including aquatic life, in the water.

Heat absorbs rapidly near the surface in turbid waters, creating density stratification which may interfere with vertical mixing and heat and oxygen transfer. Research suggests that water with an average turbidity over 130 units usually has diminished fish productivity.

11. SOLUBILITY OF OXYGEN IN WATER

Nomograph relating the solubility of oxygen in water (B) to temperature (A) and salinity (C). Example: For water at 5 parts per thousand (‰) salinity and 20°C the solubility of O_2 is 8.95 milligrams per liter.

SOURCE. Milo C. Bell, *Fisheries Handbook of Engineering Requirements and Biological Criteria*, U.S. Army Corps of Engineers, Fisheries-Engineering Research Program, Portland, Oregon, February 1973.

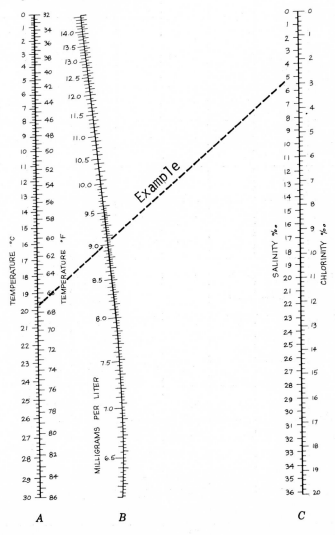

12. SEWAGE SYSTEM REMOVAL EFFICIENCIES

Removal efficiencies, costs, and energy requirements for municipal wastewater treatment methods.

SOURCE. The Conservation Foundation, *Water Quality Training Institute Manual*, Washington, D.C., 1972.

Type of Treatment	Required Pretreatment	Removal Rates [1] BOD Theor.	BOD Act.	COD Theor.	COD Act.	NITROGEN Theor.	NITROGEN Act.	PHOSPHORUS Theor.	PHOSPHORUS Act.
SEPTIC TANKS	None	80	20-50						
PRIMARY	None	60-80	20-65	5-20		0-5	0-5	25	0-25
SECONDARY	Usually Primary	70-95	85-90	50-70	65	0-15	5-10	30-50	30-50
Activated Sludge		70-95	85			0-15	5-10	30-50	30-50
Trickling Filter		70-95	65-85	70-95	65-85	Virtually 0		Virtually 0	
Lagoon		95	65-70						
LAND TREATMENT	Usually Secondary								
Spray Irrigation		100	90-100	100	99.9	80-90	50-90	80-99	80-99
Rapid Infiltration		100	90-99	90-100	95	0-80	0-80	70-95	70-95
Overland Runoff		80-99	80-99	80-99	80-99	70-90	50-90	80	50-60
AWT	Secondary	95-100	97		96		90	100	99.5
Ammonia Stripping [2]		N/A	N/A	N/A	N/A	25-90	47-89	N/A	N/A
Breakpoint Chlorination		N/A	N/A	N/A	N/A	99	95-99	N/A	N/A
Nitrification-Denitrification		N/A	N/A	N/A	N/A	90-97	?	N/A	N/A
Lime Coagulation		99	85-98					80-99	98
Activated Carbon		100	99.5	95-99	95.5				
Mixed Media Filtration			96					90	90
PHYSICAL CHEMICAL TREATMENT	Primary	95-100		90-100		80-85		90-100	

Type of Treatment	Capital Cost (1000 gal.)	Operating Cost (1000 gal.)	Chemical Input (per 1,000,000 gal.)	Energy Input [2] (per 1,000,000 gal.)
SEPTIC TANKS	$1000-1500			
PRIMARY	14¢	8.5¢	None	55 KWH electricity 187,000 Btu total
SECONDARY	$.90-1.00 [3] per gal.		150 lbs. chlorine	1570 KWH, [4] 29,100 Btu, 27,600 cu.ft. natural gas
Activated Sludge	20.9¢	13.7¢	210 lbs. metal salts or polymer	
Trickling Filter	18.9¢	9.7¢	None	
Lagoon			None	
LAND TREATMENT				
Spray Irrigation	10.1¢ [5]	5.5¢-9¢	None	Solar Energy
Rapid Infiltration	5.3¢ [5]	2.5¢	None	Solar Energy
Overland Runoff	9.5¢ [5]	5.5¢	None	Solar Energy
AWT	$.90-1.00 [6] per gal.			
Ammonia Stripping [7]	7.1¢		1600 lbs. makeup lime [8] 6400 lbs. total lime	456 KWH, stripping tower; 135 KWH, recarbonation and lime sludge collection
Breakpoint Chlorination	6.8¢	.5¢ [9]	1250 lbs. chlorine	
Nitrification-Denitrification	.03¢	[11]	375 lbs. methanol	87 KWH
Lime Coagulation			1600 lbs. makeup lime; 6400 lbs. total lime	57 KWH for lime 172 KWH for lime recovery and recalcining; 40,800 cu. ft. natural gas
Activated Carbon		2¢ [9]	31 lbs. makeup carbon; 207 lbs. total carbon	552 KWH; [10] 100 cu. ft. natural gas
Mixed Media Filtration			340 lbs. Alum	560 KWH
PHYSICAL CHEMICAL TREATMENT	$.65-1.50 estimated	26-30¢ estimated		

1. Figures given represent removal by all previous treatment in addition to the present one.
2. Antonucci, 1973.[1] Figures are given for the 7.5-mgd AWT plant at South Lake Tahoe; data in Antonucci's report are from South Tahoe Public Utility District, 1971.
3. Covers construction costs for primary–secondary treatment plants. Friend, 1973a, p. 2.[2]
4. Includes activated sludge aeration, solids incineration, and final chlorination at 7.5-mgd plant.
5. Average prices assume average land value at $500 per acre.

6. Preliminary EPA estimate; see Friend, 1973a, p. 2.[2]
7. South Lake Tahoe plant.
8. Required only if lime coagulation does not precede stripping.
9. Does not include cost of chemicals.
10. Includes energy for activated carbon pumps and carbon regeneration.
11. Depends on the cost of methanol, which is in very short supply.

[1]Antonucci, David C. 1973. "Environmental Effects of Advanced Wastewater Treatment at South Tahoe." Department of Civil Engineering, Oregon State University, Corvallis, Oregon.

[2]Friend, Edward. 1973. "Dollars Down the Drain: An Economic Critique of the Montgomery County Advanced Waste Treatment Study."

13. INNOVATIVE SEWAGE SYSTEMS

Characteristics of innovative wastewater
treatment technologies.

SOURCE.   Water Purification Associates and Process
Research, Inc., *Innovative Technology
Study prepared for the National Commission on Water Quality*, August 1975, p.
361.

	Technology	Technology Capability	Residuals	Cost
Membrane Technologies	Reverse Osmosis	Removes dissolved materials of all sorts	Concentrated solutions about 2%	Medium to Low
	Ultrafiltration	Removes large dissolved molecules, colloidal and suspended solids	Concentrated suspension, or solution	Medium
	Electrodialysis (including other electromembrane processes)	Removes dissolved ionic species only	Concentrated solution, usually about 2%, can be up to 20%	Low
	Adsorption (mainly ion exchange)	Removes dissolved salts & other dissolved compounds	For ion exchange concentrated solution about 12%	Low
	Evaporation (including vapor compression)	Removes nonvolatile contaminants	Highly concentrated solution or slurry	Medium
	High Gradient Magnetic Separation	Removes suspended material, preferably magnetic material	Concentrated slurry or sludge	Low
	Filter-Coalescence	Removes oil	Concentrated oil	Low
	Wet Oxidation	Destroys COD, phenols, cyanides, etc.	As vapor, as hot suspension	High
	Ozonation	Destroys COD, disinfects	None	Low
	Land Treatment	Removes biodegradable solids, BOD and nutrients	None	Low

	Technology	Energy & Other Requirements	State of Development
Membrane Technologies	Reverse Osmosis	~ 8 kwh/1000 gal	Demonstration, semi-commercial
	Ultrafiltration	~ 8 kwh/1000 gal	Demonstration, semi-commercial
	Electrodialysis (including other electromembrane processes)	~ 10 kwh/1000 gal	Commercial for potable water, demonstration for wastewater
	Adsorption (mainly ion exchange)	~ 1/3 of the cost is chemicals	Commercial for potable water & boiler feed; demonstration for wastewater
	Evaporation (including vapor compression)	400-1700 Btu/gal[+] 62-87 kwh/1000 gal (for vapor compression)	Commercial
	High Gradient Magnetic Separation	~ 0.7 kwh/1000 gal (depends on size)	Laboratory
	Filter-Coalescence	~ 0.1 kwh/1000 gal	Demonstration
	Wet Oxidation	Depends on COD removal, ~ 0.34 kwh/lb COD	Commercial
	Ozonation	~ 9 kwh/1000 gal	Commercial for potable water, demonstration for wastewater
	Land Treatment	Large land areas 0.5-0.8 kwh/1000 gal[#]	Full scale, very site specific

* High > $7/1000 gal
  Medium = $1-7/1000 gal
  Low < $1/1000 gal

+ This amount of energy would, at 40% efficiency, be used to generate 47-200 kwh/1000 gal.

For spray irrigation; other methods have lower requirements.

14. INDUSTRIAL WASTE SUMMARY

Origin, character, and treatment of industrial wastes.

SOURCE. Albert E. Millar, Jr., Ed., *Clean Water: Affluence, Influence, Effluents*, Old Dominion University, Norfolk, Virginia, 1971.

Industries producing wastes	Origin of major wastes	Major characteristics	Major treatment and disposal methods
Food and Drugs Canned Goods	Trimming. culling. juicing. and blanching of fruits and vegetables	High in suspended solids. colloidal and dissolved organic matter	Screening. lagooning. soil absorption or spray irrigation
Dairy products	Dilutions of whole milk. separated milk. buttermilk. and whey	High in dissolved organic matter. mainly protein. fat. and lactose	Biological treatment. aeration. trickling filtration. activated sludge
Brewed and distilled beverages	Steeping and pressing of grain. residue from distillation of alcohol. condensate from stillage evaporation	High in dissolved organic solids. containing nitrogen and fermented starches or their products	Recovery. concentration by centrifugation and evaporation. trickling filtration: use in feeds
Meat and poultry products	Stockyards. slaughtering of animals. rendering of bones and fats. residues in condensates. grease and wash water. picking of chickens	High in dissolved and suspended organic matter. blood. other proteins. and fats	Screening. settling and/or flotation. trickling filtration
Beet sugar	Transfer. screening and juicing waters. drainings from lime sludge. condensates after evaporator. juice. extracted sugar	High in dissolved and suspended organic matter. containing sugar and protein	Reuse of wastes. coagulation. and lagooning
Pharmaceutical products	Mycelium. spent filtrate. and wash waters	High in suspended and dissolved organic matter. including vitamins	Evaporation and drying; feeds
Yeast	Residue from yeast filtration	High in solids (mainly organic) and BOD	Anaerobic digestion. trickling filtration
Pickles	Lime water. brine. alum and tumeric. syrup. seeds and pieces of cucumber	Variable pH. high suspended solids. color and organic matter	Good housekeeping. screening equalization
Coffee	Pulping and fermenting of coffee bean	High BOD and suspended solids	Screening. settling. and trickling filtration
Fish	Rejects from centrifuge. pressed fish. evaporator and other wash water wastes	Very high BOD. total organic solids. and odor	Evaporation of total waste. barge remainder to sea
Rice	Soaking. cooking. and washing of rice	High in BOD. total and suspended solids. (mainly starch)	Lime coagulation. digestion
Soft drinks	Bottle washing. floor and equipment cleaning. syrup-storage-tank drains	High pH. suspended solids and BOD	Screening. plus discharge to municipal sewer
Apparel Textiles	Cooking of fibers. desizing of fabric	Highly alkaline. colored. high BOD and temperature. high suspended solids	Neutralization. chemical precipitation. biological treatment. aeration and/or trickling filtration
Leather goods	Unhairing. soaking. deliming and bating of hides	High total solids. hardness. salt. sulfides. chromium. pH. precipitated lime and BOD	Equalization. sedimentation. and biological treatment
Laundry trades	Washing of fabrics	High turbidity. alkalinity. and organic solids	Screening. chemical precipitation. flotation. and absorption

Industries producing wastes	Origin of major wastes	Major characteristics	Major treatment and disposal methods
Chemicals Acids	Dilute wash waters: many varied dilute acids	Low pH. low organic content	Upflow or straight neutralization. burning when some organic matter is present
Detergents	Washing and purifying soaps and detergents	High in BOD and saponified soaps	Flotation and skimming, precipitation with CaCl
Cornstarch	Evaporator condensate. syrup from final washes. wastes from "bottling up" process	High BOD and dissolved organic matter: mainly starch and related material	Equalization. biological filtration
Explosives	Washing TNT and guncotton for purification. washing and pickling of cartridges	TNT. colored. acid. odorous. and contains organic acids and alcohol from powder and cotton. metals. acid. oils and soaps	Flotation. chemical precipitation. biological treatment. aeration. chlorination of TNT. neutralization
Insecticides	Washing and purification products such as 2.4D and DDT	High organic matter. benzene ring structure. toxic to bacteria and fish. acid	Dilution. storage. activated carbon absorption. alkaline chlorination
Phosphate and phosphorous	Washing. screening. floating rock. condenser bleed-off from phosphate reduction plant	Clays. slimes and tall oils. low pH. high suspended solids. phosphorous. silica and flouride	Lagooning. mechanical clarification. coagulation and settling of refined waste
Formaldehyde	Residues from manufacturing snythetic resins. and from dyeing snythetic fibers	Normally has high BOD and HCHO. toxic to bacteria in high concentrations	Trickling filtration. absorption on activated charcoal
Materials Pulp and paper	Cooking. refining. washing of fibers. screening of paper pulp	High or low pH: colored; high suspended. colloidal. and dissolved solids; inorganic fillers	Settling. lagooning. biological treatment. aeration. recovery of by-products
Photographic products	Spent solutions of developer and fixer	Alkaline. contains various organic and inorganic reducing agents	Recovery of silver. plus discharge of wastes into municipal sewer
Steel	Coking of coal. washing of blast-furnace flue gases. and pickling of steel	Low PH. acids. cyanogen. phenol. ore. coke. limestone. alkali. oils. mill scale. and fine suspended solids	Neutralization. recovery and reuse. chemical coagulation
Metal-plated products	Stripping of oxides. cleaning and plating of metals	Acid. metals. toxic. low volume. mainly mineral matter	Alkaline chlorination of cyanide. reduction and precipitation of chromium. and lime precipitation of other metals
Iron-foundry products	Wasting of used sand by hydraulic discharge	High suspended solids. mainly sand: some clay and coal	Selective screening. drying of reclaimed sand
Oil	Drilling muds. salt. oil and some natural gas. acid sludges and miscellaneous oils from refining	High dissolved salts from field. high BOD. odor. phenol. and sulphur compounds from refinery	Diversion. recovery. injection of salts: acidification and burning of alkaline sludges
Rubber	Washing of latex. coagulated rubber. exuded impurities from crude rubber	High BOD and odor. high suspended solids. variable pH. high chlorides	Aeration. chlorination. sulfonation. biological treatment
Glass	Polishing and cleaning of glass	Red color. alkaline non-settleable suspended solids	Calcium chloride precipitation
Naval stores	Washing of stumps. drop solution. solvent recovery. and oil recovery water	Acid. high BOD	By-product recovery. equalization. recirculation and reuse. trickling filtration

Industries producing wastes	Origin of major wastes	Major characteristics	Major treatment and disposal methods
Energy Steam power	Cooling water boiler blow-down, coal dr age	Hot, high volume, high inorganic and dissolved solids	Cooling by aeration, storage of ashes, neutralization of excess acid wastes
Coal processing	Cleaning and classification of coal, leaching of sulphur strata with water	High suspended solids, mainly coal; low pH, high H_2SO_4 and $FeSO_4$	Settling, froth flotation, draining control, and sealing of mines
Nuclear power and radioactive materials	Processing ores, laundering of contaminated clothes, research-lab wastes, processing of fuel, power-plant cooling waters.	Radioactive elements, can be very acid and "hot"	Concentration and containing, or dilution and dispersion

SOURCE: Nemerow. N.L. 1963. Theories and Practices of Industrial
Waste Treatment. Addison-Wesley. pp. 270-274.

15. INDUSTRIAL WASTE EFFECTS ON SEWAGE SYSTEMS

Concentrations of industrial pollutants that inhibit biological sewage treatment.

SOURCE. U.S. Environmental Protection Agency, *Pretreatment of Pollutants Introduced into Publicly Owned Treatment Works,* Washington, D.C., October 1973.

Pollutant	Concentration[1], mg/L		
	Aerobic Processes	Anaerobic Digestion	Nitrification
Copper	1.0	1.0	0.5
Zinc	5.0	5.0	0.5
Chromium (Hexavalent)	2.0	5.0	2.0
Chromium (Trivalent)	2.0	2000[2]	*
Total Chromium	5.0	5.0	*
Nickel	1.0	2.0	0.5
Lead	0.1	*	0.5
Boron	1.0	*	*
Cadmium	*	0.02[2]	*
Silver	0.03	*	*
Vanadium	10	*	*
Sulfides (S)	*	100[2]	*
Sulfates (SO$_4$)	*	500	*
Ammonia	*	1500[2]	*
Sodium (Na)	*	3500	*
Potassium (K)	*	2500	*
Calcium (Ca)	*	2500	*
Magnesium (Mg)	*	1000	*
Acrylonitrite	*	5.0[2]	*
Benzene	*	50[2]	*
Carbon Tetrachloride	*	10[2]	*
Chloroform	18.0	0.1[2]	*
Methylene Chloride	*	1.0	*
Peintachlorophenol	*	0.4[2]	*
1,1,1-Trichloroethane	*	1.0[2]	*
Trichlorofluoromethane	*	0.7	*
Trichlorotrifluoroethane	*	5.0[2]	*
Cyanide (HCN)	*	1.0	2.0
Total oil (Petroleum origin)	50	50	50

* Insufficient data

[1] Concentrations refer to those present in raw wastewater unless otherwise indicated.

[2] Concentrations apply to the digester influent only. Lower values may be required for protection of other treatment process units.

[3] Petroleum-based oil concentration measured according to the API Method 733-58 for determing volatile and non-volatile oily materials. The inhibitory level does not apply to oil of direct animal or vegetable origin.

16. SHORE SEDIMENT CHARACTERISTICS

Sand sources, sinks, and corrective processes in the littoral zone.

SOURCE. U.S. Army Corps of Engineers, *Shore Protection Manual*, Vol. I, Coastal Engineering Research Center, Ft. Belvoir, Virginia, 1973.

Sources	
Rivers and streams	The major source in the limited areas where rivers carry sand to the littoral zone. In affected areas notable floods may contribute several times Q_g.
Cliff, dune and backshore erosion	Generally the major source where rivers are absent. 1 to 4 cu.yd./yr./ft.
Transport from offshore	Quantity uncertain.
Wind transport	Not generally important as a source.
CaCO₃ production	Significant in tropical climate. The value of 0.25 cu.yd./yr./ft. seems reasonable upper limit on temperate beach.
Beach replenishment	Varies from 0 to greater than Q_g.

Sinks	
Inlets and lagoons	May remove from 5 to 25 percent of Q_g per inlet. Depends on number of inlets, inlet size, tidal flow characteristics, and inlet age.
Overwash	Less than 1 cu.yd./yr./ft. at most, and limited to low barrier islands.
Beach storage	Temporary, but possibly large, depending on beach condition when budget is made. (See Table 4-5, pages 4-72, 4-73.)
Offshore slopes	Uncertain quantity. May receive much fine material, some coarse material.
Submarine canyons	Where present, may intercept up to 80 percent of Q_g.
Deflation	Usually less than 2 cu.yd./yr./ft. of beach front, but may range up to 10 cu.yd./yr./ft.
CaCO₃ loss	Not known to be important.
Mining and dredging	May equal or exceed Q_g in some localities.

Convective Processes	
Longshore transport (waves)	May result in accretion of Q_g, erosion of Q_n, or no change depending on conditions of equilibrium.
Tidal Currents	May be important at mouth of inlet and vicinity, and on irregular coasts with high tidal range.
Winds	Longshore winds are probably not important, except in limited regions.

17. SHORE EROSION AND PROTECTION METHODS: GREAT LAKES

SOURCE.   U.S. Army Corps of Engineers, *Help Yourself*, Chicago, Illinois.

The beach profile is a relatively small physiographic feature whose limits are defined by the effects of waves. As waves approach the shore they react in special ways; they reflect, diffract, and refract. The beach then acts as a natural defense against the attack from waves. The first defense against the waves is the sloping near shore bottom which dissipates the energy or weakens the force of the deepwater waves.

The shoreline erodes from the force of wave action. The erosive energy of a wave is a function of wave height and the depth of water in which the wave acts. Wave energy is strongest in deep water but it's effect is greatest thru the surf zone, from the start of breaking waves to the limit of run up.

The amount of erosive energy delivered to the beach depends on the level of the lake and the storm set up or storm induced temporary rise in lake stage. The offshore depth is the most important parameter in the design of shore protection structures. During high lake levels the typical shore becomes a narrow unstable beach at the foot of a steep bluff or dune. Waves attack the toe of the bluff undercutting its face which falls on the beach. Waves wash out the fine bluff material, carry it offshore to deep water, or move it along the shore by littoral currents.

The high lake levels change the effects that waves have on the beach profile as shown below. The natural beaches are submerged and waves act directly on the highly erodible backshore. The increased wave action on the beach increases the rate of erosion of the bluff. In the new balance, a beach will reform its equilibrium slope, but the foreshore would be moved landward. During high lake levels beaches may exhibit a steep and rather uniformly sloping profile and the effects of storm waves are greatly increased.

Material is moved and redistributed along the beach by the waves and wave generated currents. Long flat waves pick the sand up, move it forward, and deposit it on the beach berm. Short steep waves

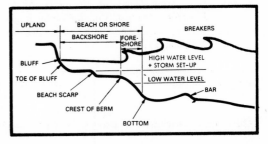

acting on the beach carry the sand lakeward. The direction of littoral drift depends on the direction of the wave generated energy which impinges on a shore.

Short period fluctuations of the lakes (Storm set up) result from meteorological disturbances and may last from a few hours to a few days. Wind and barometric pressure cause the lake surface to tilt as shown below. The amount of storm set up depends on local conditions. The storm set up values are added to the projected lake levels to determine the design water

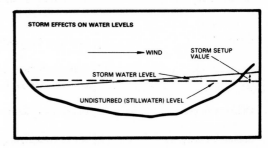

surface for the protective works described here

The Great Lakes act similar to a system of reservoirs, but their size makes them unique. When the net supply to one of the lakes exceeds the outflow, its level rises. When the net supply is less than the outflow its level falls. The lake levels are now approaching record highs because the precipitation, in recent years, (supply) over the Great Lakes Basin exceeded the basin averages. The probable maximum levels for the summer of 1973 are given in the following tabulation.

1973	Lake Superior	Lakes Michigan- Huron	Lake St. Clair	Lake Erie	Lake Ontario
Maximum Monthly Elevation (Mid-Summer)	601.7	581.2	576.1	573.1	247.9
February	600.4	579.9	575.4	572.5	246.3
Low Water Datum	600.0	576.8	571.7	568.6	242.8

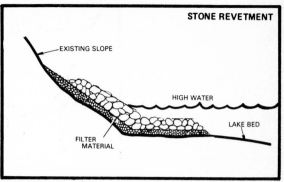

STONE REVETMENT

ADVANTAGES

Most effective structure for absorbing wave energy.

Flexible — not weakened by slight movements.

Natural rough surface reduces wave runup.

Lends itself to stage construction.

Easily repaired — low maintenance cost.

The preferred method of protection when rock is readily available at a low cost.

DISADVANTAGES

Heavy equipment required for construction.

Subject to flanking and moderate scour.

Limits access to beach.

Moderately high first cost.

Difficult construction where access is limited.

COST/LIN. FT. — $28 to $100

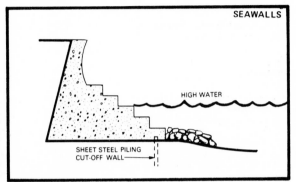

SEAWALLS

ADVANTAGES

Provides protection both from wave action and stabilizes the backshore.

Low maintenance cost.

Readily lends itself to concrete steps to beach.

Stabilizes the backshore.

DISADVANTAGES

Extremely high first cost.

Subject to full wave forces, fail from scour, flanking of foundation.

Not easily repaired.

Complex design and construction problem. Qualified engineer is essential.

Slope design is most important.

More subject to catastrophic failure unless positive toe protection is provided.

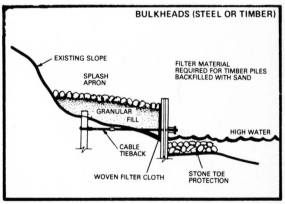

BULKHEADS (STEEL OR TIMBER)

ADVANTAGES

Provides positive protection.

Maintains shoreline in fixed position.

Low maintenance cost.

Materials are available locally.

DISADVANTAGES

Vertical walls induce severe beach scouring. Adequate toe protection required.

High first cost.

Subject to flanking; bulkheads must be tied back securely.

Pile driving requires special skill and heavy construction equipment.

Complex engineering design problem.

Limits access to beach.

COST/LIN. FT. — $57 to $105 (TIMBER)
— $200 to $300 (STEEL)

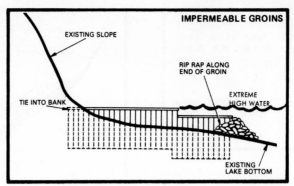

ADVANTAGES

Resulting beach protects upland areas and provides recreational benefit.

Moderate first cost and low maintenance cost.

DISADVANTAGES

Extremely complex coastal engineering design problem. Qualified coastal engineering services are essential. Groins rarely function as intended.

Areas downdrift will probably experience rapid erosion.

Unsuitable in areas of low littoral drift.

Subject to flanking, must be securely tied into bluff.

COST/LIN. FT. — $125 to $150

18. SAMPLE NONCONFORMING USE REGULATION

Model code for definition of a state of nonconformance for a use or structure.

SOURCE. U.S. Army Corps of Engineers, *Flood-Proofing Regulations,* Washington, D.C., June 1972.

Sec. 201.2 NONCONFORMING USE: A structure or the use of a structure or premises which was lawful before the passage or amendment of the ordinance but which is not in conformity with the provisions of these Regulations may be continued subject to the following conditions:

(1) No such use shall be expanded, changed, enlarged or altered in a way which increases its nonconformity.

(2) No structural alteration, addition, or repair to any conforming structure over the life of the structure shall exceed _____ per cent of its value at the time of its becoming a nonconforming use, unless the structure is permanently changed to a conforming use.

(3) If such use is discontinued for _____ consecutive months, any future use of the building premises shall conform to these Regulations. The assessor shall notify the zoning administrator in writing of instances of nonconforming uses which have been discontinued for a period of _____ months.

(4) If any nonconforming use or structure is destroyed by any means, including floods, to an extent of _____ per cent or more of its _____ value it shall not be reconstructed except in conformance with the provisions of these Regulations; provided, the Board of Adjustment may permit reconstruction if the use or structure is located outside the floodway and is adequately and safely flood-proofed, elevated, or otherwise protected in conformance with these Regulations.

(5) Uses or adjuncts thereof which are or become nuisances shall not be entitled to continue as nonconforming uses.

(6) Except as provided in "The Building Code," any use which has been permitted as a special exception shall not be deemed a nonconforming use but shall be considered a conforming use.

(7) Any alteration, addition, or repair to any nonconforming structure which would result in substantially increasing its flood damage or flood hazard potential shall be protected as required by these Regulations.

(8) The Building Official shall maintain a list of nonconforming uses including the date of becoming nonconforming, assessed value at the time of its becoming a nonconforming use, and the nature and extend of nonconformity. This list shall be brought up-to-date annually.

(9) The Building Official shall prepare a list of those nonconforming uses which have been flood-proofed or otherwise protected in conformance with these Regulations. He shall present such list to the Board of Adjustment which may issue a certificate to the owner stating that such uses, as a result of these corrective measures, are in conformance with these Regulations.

19. COASTAL STATE REGULATORY AUTHORITY

Areas of regulatory authority for environmental protection in coastal state governments.

SOURCE. H. Crane Miller, *Management Techniques in the Coastal Zone, A Report to the Nassau–Suffolk Regional Planning Board*, August 1975.

Key

1. State authority and enforcement.
2. State authority to act if local government fails to act.
3. State enabling legislation.
4. State enabling legislation; local administration.
5. Mandatory state building code.
6. Model state building code; local option to adopt code.
7. State enabling legislation; local option to adopt building code.
8. State building code for public and nonresidential buildings; local option to cover private buildings.
9. Mandatory planning prior to zoning or subdivision controls.
10. Discretionary planning prior to zoning or subdivision controls.

	Land Use Policy	Water Quality	Water Supply	Air Quality	Solid Waste Mgmt	Utility Siting	Dredge/ Fill Permits	Open Space Acqu'n	Envir'l Impact Assess't
Alabama	–	1	1	1	4	1	1,4	3	1
Alaska	–	1	1	1	4	1	1,4	3	–
California	–	1	1	1	1	1	1,4	3	1
Connecticut	–	1	1	1	1	1	1,4	3	1
Delaware	–	1	1	1	1	1	1,4	3	1
Florida	4	1	1	1	1,2	1	1,4	3	1
Georgia	–	1	1	1	1	–	1,4	3	–
Hawaii	4,2	1	1	1	1	1	1,4	3	1
Illinois	–	1	1	1	1	–	1,4	3	–
Indiana	–	1	1	1	4	–	1,4	3	1
Louisiana	–	1	1	1	4	–	1,4	3	–
Maine	4,1	1	1	1	4	1	1,4	3	–
Maryland	–	1	1	1	4	1	1,4	3	1
Massachusetts	–	1	1	1	4	1	1,4	3	1
Michigan	–	1	1	1	1	–	1,4	3	1
Minnesota	4	1	1	1	1	1	1,4	3	1
Mississippi	–	1	1	1	4	–	1,4	3	1
New Hampshire	–	1	1	1	4	1	1,4	3	1
New Jersey	–	1	1	1	1	1	1,4	3	1
New York	–	1	1	1	1	1	1,4	3	1
North Carolina	4	1	1	1	1	–	1,4	3	1
Ohio	–	1	1	1	1	1	1,4	3	–
Oregon	4	1	1	1	4	1	1,4	3	–
Pennsylvania	–	1	1	1	1	–	1,4	3	–
Rhode Island	–	1	1	1	4	–	1,4	3	1
South Carolina	–	1	1	1	1	–	1,4	3	–
Texas	–	1	1	1	1,4	–	1,4	3	–
Virginia	–	1	1	1	1,4	–	1,4	3	1
Washington	–	1	1	1	2	1	1,4	3	1
Wisconsin	–	1	1	1	1	–	1,4	3	1
Total States	6	30	30	30	30	17	30	30	20

	Zoning	Sub-division Controls	State/Other Building Code	State Flood-Plain Regs.	Coast/Lake-shore	Tidal Wet-lands	In-land Wet-lands	Plan-ing/Zon-ing	Plan-ing/Sub-div'n
Alabama	4	4	8	–	1	–	–	9	9
Alaska	4	4	7	–	–	–	–	9	10
California	4	4	5	4	1	–	–	9	9
Connecticut	4	4	5	1	–	1	2	9	9
Delaware	4	4	7	–	1	1	–	9	10
Florida	4	4	5	4,2	4,2	–	–	9	9
Georgia	4	4	6	–	–	1	–	9	9
Hawaii	4	4	7	4	1	–	–	9	10
Illinois	4	4	7	1	–	–	–	9	9
Indiana	4	4	8	1	–	–	–	10	9
Louisiana	4	4	7	–	–	–	–	9	10
Maine	4	4	7	–	1	1	–	9	9
Maryland	4	4	6	1	–	1	–	9	9
Massachusetts	4	4	5	1	–	1	1	10	10
Michigan	4	4	6	1	1	–	1	9	9
Minnesota	4	4	5	4	4	–	–	9	10
Mississippi	4	4	7	–	–	1	–	9	10
New Hampshire	4	4	7	–	–	1	–	9	10
New Jersey	4	4	6	4	–	1	–	9	10
New York	4	4	6	2	–	1	1	9	9
North Carolina	4	4	6	–	1	1	–	9	10
Ohio	4	4	8	–	–	–	–	9	9
Oregon	4	4	6	–	1	–	–	9	9
Pennsylvania	4	4	7	1	–	–	–	9	10
Rhode Island	4	4	5	–	1	1	1	9	10
South Carolina	4	4	5	–	–	–	–	9	9
Texas	4	4	7	–	–	–	–	9	9
Virginia	4	4	5	–	–	1	–	10	10
Washington	4	4	5	1,4	1	–	–	9	10
Wisconsin	4	4	8	2	2,4	–	–	9	9
Total States	30	30	30	14	13	13	5	27	17

20. LAND-USE CONTROL LEGISLATION

Purposes of coastal zone land-use control legislation in selected states.

SOURCE. Steven Zwicky and John Clark, "Environmental protection motivation in coastal zone land-use legislation," *Coastal Zone Management Journal*, Vol. I, No. 1, pp. 103–108 (Fall, 1973).

	1. Protect wildlife, fisheries	2. Protect ecosystems	3. Control development	4. Enhance aesthetics	5. Protect life, property	6. Enhance public recreation	7. Protect water resources	8. Conserve soil resources	9. Promote commerce	10. Protect navigability	11. Public access	12. Develop resource use
California	X	X	X	X	X	X		X			X	
Connecticut	X	X		X	X	X			X	X		
Delaware	X	X	X	X		X	X	X	X	X	X	
Georgia	X	X	X			X	X	X	X	X		
Maine	X		X	X	X		X					
Maryland	X	X	X	X	X	X				X		
Massachusetts	X				X							
Michigan	X	X	X			X		X				
Minnesota		X	X	X	X	X	X	X	X			X
Mississippi		X		X		X	X		X			
New Hampshire	X							X				
New Jersey	X	X	X	X	X		X		X			
North Carolina	X				X		X	X				
Rhode Island		X	X		X							X
Virginia	X	X	X	X	X	X	X	X	X	X		
Washington	X	X	X	X		X					X	
Wisconsin	X		X	X			X	X				
	14	12	12	11	10	10	9	9	7	5	3	2

21. GRASS CHANNEL DESIGN AND SPECIFICATIONS

Plans for grass channels to stabilize drainageways in order to prevent channel erosion (tables and figures are selected, not continuous).

SOURCE. Joachim Tourbier and Richard Westmacott, *Water Resources Protection Measures in Land Development—A Handbook*. Water Resources as a Basis for Comprehensive Planning and Development of the Christina River Basin; a Prototype Project, Phase II. Water Resources Center, University of Delaware, Newark, Delaware, 1974.

PURPOSE

For velocities of up to 8 fps, runoff can be handled by grass channels, if correctly graded and stabilized.

SITE CHARACTERISTICS & APPLICATION

May be used on any site where flow velocities make the use of grass swales feasible. On steep sites the use of grass swales will be limited by the difficulty of keeping within the limits for hydraulic gradient of swales. On highly erodible soils a lower design velocity must be used as shown in the table below. Natural channels can often be improved by regrading and grassing.

ADVANTAGES

1. Grass-lined channels are cheaper than those lined with concrete or stabilized by a 'bio-technical' measure (see Spec. 2:16).
2. Grass will delay runoff and considerably reduce the energy and consequently the erosive capacity of runoff.
3. Grass channels are visually much more acceptable than those lined with concrete.
4. The vegetated waterway maximizes the loss of surface runoff through infiltration, where the lined waterway allows no infiltration to occur.

DISADVANTAGES

1. Very careful design and a good maintenance program are necessary if channels stabilized with grass are to be effective without gully erosion.
2. The installation of new areas of impermeable surface in the area drained by a grass channel may increase runoff velocities and exceed the capacity of the channel. This must be considered.
3. Vegetated channels should not be constructed for maximum flow velocities since in practice vegetation is rarely maintained well enough to take such flows.

REFERENCES

1. USDA, Soil Conservation Service. Engineering Field Manual for Conservation Practices. 1969.
2. Minnesota Department of Highways, Conservation Div. Erosion Prevention and Turf Establishment Manual. 1970.

DESIGN CRITERIA & OUTLINE SPECIFICATIONS

<u>Cross Section</u>. Grassed waterways may be built in parabolic, trapezoidal, or V-shaped cross sections. Parabolic cross sections are most commonly found in nature and have proven the most satisfactory. Waterways constructed with trapezoidal sections tend to revert to a parabolic shape. Side slopes should not exceed 3:1 to enable channel to be mowed.

<u>Location</u>. Waterways should be located at areas of suitable grade where soil moisture conditions are favorable to vegetative growth. Natural swales should be favored, if possible.

<u>Design Criteria</u>. Size and location of grass waterways will depend on estimated runoff, gradient, the space allowable for the waterways and soil erodibility. Flow velocities on well-established soil of good quality generally do not exceed 5-6 fps except for special situations. Most waterways are constructed to accommodate the peak flow expected from a storm of at least 10-year frequency before overbank flow occurs. The flow-retarding factor of different vegetation should be considered in the design.

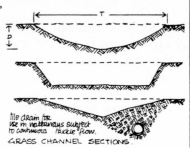

GRASS CHANNEL SECTIONS.

Grass Varieties and Permissible Velocities for Varying Situations			
		Permissible Velocity fps	
Cover Type	Slope %	Resistant Soil	Erodible Soil
Bermuda Grass	0-5	8	6
	5-10	7	5
	Over 10	6	4
Bahia Buffalo Kentucky blue grass Smooth brome Blue grama Tall fescue	0-5 5-10 Over 10	7 6 5	5 4 3
Grass mixtures Reed canarygrass	0-5 5-10	5 4	4 3
Lespedeza sericea Weeping lovegrass Yellow bluestem Redtop Alfalfa Red fescue	0-5	3.5	2.5
Common lespedeza Sudangrass	0-5	3.5	2.5

<u>Construction</u>. It is important to avoid excessive compaction during construction by earth-moving machinery which will result in an inferior grass sward. Between the time of seeding the cover and the actual establishment, the waterway will be unprotected and subject to damage. Provisions should be made to divert flows during this period. Vegetated waterways should not be subject to continuous flows of water nor be kept wet, since this will destroy good turf. A tile drain can help to offset this problem. Tiles should be laid parallel to the center line of the waterway but offset from the center by at least 1/4 its top width. This will prevent washout of the backfill material for the tile system (see diagram above.)

DESIGN OF GRASS CHANNELS

Grass-Lined Channels

Grass-lined channels are the cheapest and the least obtrusive
method of conveying runoff. However, unless the channel is properly designed and maintained, gulley erosion will result. Channels
must be capable of withstanding the abrasive action of water without damage. Generally, grass channels have slopes of between
1-10%, and are rarely used to drain areas of more than 150 acres.
Where the velocity or the slope is found to be too great for the
use of a grass lining, the slope may be reduced by the introduction of spillways which will effectively reduce the gradient
between spillways and make grass lining in these sections feasible. This may be aesthetically more desirable than lining the
channel with concrete, gabion mattress, etc. In exceptional cases
the 'safe' velocity of flow in grass channels may be increased by
reinforcing the sward with nylon netting or lattice concrete
blocks, and/or by introducing fiberglass erosion checks at regular intervals. In cases where grass channels are permanently wet,
install a tile drain beneath the channel.

Design Criteria

The design criteria of grass channels is less precise than for
storm sewers due to the difficulty of assessing accurately 'n',
the coefficient of roughness, and the retarding effect of the
grass lining. It is important to remember that continuing efficiency of a channel depends on maintaining a high quality sward
and this is made easier by maximum side slopes of 4:1. It is also
important to keep erosion in the drainage area to a minimum
because silt deposits in grass channels will reduce their efficiency.

Channel Section

Channel shapes may be parabolic, triangular, or trapezoidal. Parabolic sections approximate to that of natural channels and look
good but are difficult to build. Trapezoidal sections tend to take
up a parabolic shape in time. Side slopes of 4:1 allow easy crossing for vehicles and mowing machines.

Velocity

Permissible velocities for various types of grass and soil erodibility are shown on Table 7. Note that the range is between 2-6
with velocities of 7 or 8 only used where sward is of the highest
quality.

Roughness Coefficient

For most methods of designing grass channels, the roughness coefficient (Manning's 'n' as used in the design of storm sewers) is

converted into 'retardance' which depends also on the velocity and
hydraulic radius (see 7-12 SCS, Engineering Field Manual for Conservation Practices). A guide to the retardance for various types
of vegetation can be found on Table 6. However, this is only used
for Method 3 and for the simplified Methods 1 and 2. It may be
assumed that the 'coefficient of roughness' for grass channels is
0.04.

Capacity

The capacity of the channel must be sufficient to carry the peak
design storm discharge from the drainage area. This peak discharge
is calculated in the normal way by the rational formula Q = CiA
(where Q = discharge in cfs, C = runoff coefficient, i = intensity
of rainfall, and A = drainage area-acres). For very long channels
it may be necessary to estimate the flow for different reaches.

Location

Try to locate channels in natural swales and keep to a sweeping
alignment. Take particular care either to locate the outlet in an
area of well-established vegetation, or protect the outlet to prevent erosion.

Calculation of Channel Size, Method A

The discharge capacity of a channel (Q in cfs) is determined from
V, the velocity in the channel (in fps) and a, the end area of the
channel (sq. ft.) by the formula

$$Q = Va \ . \ : \ . \ . \ . \ . \ . \ . \ . \ . \ . \ . \ . \ . \ . \ . \ . \ . \ . \ \text{Equation 1}$$

V varies according to the 'coefficient of roughness', n, of the
channel which is normally 0.04 for grass-lined channels,
the hydraulic radius, r, (end area, a, divided by wetted
perimeter p) and the slope or gradient of channel, s. This relationship is expressed by the formula

$$V = \frac{1.486}{n} \ r^{2/3} \ s^{1/2} \ . \ . \ . \ . \ . \ . \ . \ . \ . \ . \ . \ . \ \text{Equation 2}$$

Substituting V in Equation 1

$$V = \frac{1.486}{n} \ r^{2/3} \ s^{1/2} \ a \ . \ . \ . \ . \ . \ . \ . \ . \ . \ . \ \text{Equation 3}$$

The selection of channel size using the above equations is a trial-and-error process of selecting an ideal location and cross section
for a channel, checking whether its velocity is within the safety
limits for the type of grass lining (Table 7) and whether the cross
section is sufficient for the discharge of runoff from the area
drained.

Example A1. Select a channel alignment and cross section to drain an
area with a peak discharge, Q, of 160 cfs (determined by the rational
formula Q = CiA). An ideal alignment for the channel has a slope, s,
of 0.03 and it is decided that the side slopes should be a maximum

No. R	.00	.01	.02	.03	.04	.05	.06	.07	.08	.09
0.0	0.000	0.046	0.065	0.074	0.097	0.136	0.153	0.170	0.186	0.201
0.1	0.215	0.229	0.243	0.256	0.269	0.282	0.295	0.307	0.319	0.331
0.2	0.342	0.353	0.364	0.375	0.386	0.397	0.407	0.418	0.428	0.438
0.3	0.448	0.458	0.468	0.477	0.487	0.497	0.506	0.515	0.525	0.534
0.4	0.543	0.552	0.561	0.570	0.578	0.587	0.596	0.604	0.613	0.622
0.5	0.630	0.638	0.647	0.655	0.663	0.671	0.679	0.687	0.695	0.703
0.6	0.711	0.719	0.727	0.735	0.743	0.750	0.758	0.765	0.773	0.781
0.7	0.788	0.796	0.803	0.811	0.818	0.825	0.832	0.840	0.847	0.855
0.8	0.862	0.869	0.876	0.883	0.890	0.897	0.904	0.911	0.918	0.925
0.9	0.932	0.939	0.946	0.953	0.960	0.966	0.973	0.980	0.987	0.993
1.0	1.000	1.007	1.013	1.020	1.027	1.033	1.040	1.046	1.053	1.059
1.1	1.065	1.072	1.078	1.085	1.091	1.097	1.104	1.110	1.117	1.123
1.2	1.129	1.136	1.142	1.148	1.154	1.160	1.167	1.173	1.179	1.185
1.3	1.191	1.197	1.203	1.209	1.215	1.221	1.227	1.233	1.239	1.245
1.4	1.251	1.257	1.263	1.269	1.275	1.281	1.287	1.293	1.299	1.305
1.5	1.310	1.316	1.322	1.328	1.334	1.339	1.345	1.351	1.357	1.362
1.6	1.368	1.374	1.379	1.385	1.391	1.396	1.402	1.408	1.413	1.419
1.7	1.424	1.430	1.436	1.441	1.447	1.452	1.458	1.463	1.469	1.474
1.8	1.480	1.485	1.491	1.496	1.502	1.507	1.513	1.518	1.523	1.529
1.9	1.534	1.539	1.545	1.550	1.556	1.561	1.566	1.571	1.577	1.582
2.0	1.587	1.593	1.598	1.603	1.608	1.613	1.619	1.624	1.629	1.634
2.1	1.639	1.645	1.650	1.655	1.660	1.665	1.671	1.676	1.681	1.686
2.2	1.691	1.697	1.702	1.707	1.712	1.717	1.722	1.727	1.732	1.737
2.3	1.742	1.747	1.752	1.757	1.762	1.767	1.772	1.777	1.782	1.787
2.4	1.792	1.797	1.802	1.807	1.812	1.817	1.822	1.827	1.832	1.837
2.5	1.842	1.847	1.852	1.857	1.862	1.867	1.871	1.876	1.881	1.886
2.6	1.891	1.896	1.900	1.905	1.910	1.915	1.920	1.925	1.929	1.934
2.7	1.939	1.944	1.949	1.953	1.958	1.963	1.968	1.972	1.977	1.982
2.8	1.987	1.992	1.996	2.001	2.006	2.010	2.015	2.020	2.024	2.029
2.9	2.034	2.038	2.043	2.048	2.052	2.057	2.062	2.066	2.071	2.075

TABLE 2. SOLUTION OF $r^{2/3}$ IN MANNING FORMULA FOR GRASS SWALES.

No. S	+0	+1	+2	+3	+4	+5	+6	+7	+8	+9
0.001	0.03162	0.03317	0.03464	0.03606	0.03742	0.03873	0.04000	0.04123	0.04243	0.04359
0.002	0.04472	0.04583	0.04690	0.04796	0.04899	0.05000	0.05099	0.05196	0.05292	0.05385
0.003	0.05477	0.05568	0.05657	0.05745	0.05831	0.05916	0.06000	0.06083	0.06164	0.06245
0.004	0.06325	0.06403	0.06481	0.06557	0.06633	0.06708	0.06782	0.06856	0.06928	0.07000
0.005	0.07071	0.07141	0.07211	0.07280	0.07348	0.07416	0.07483	0.07550	0.07616	0.07681
0.006	0.07746	0.07810	0.07874	0.07937	0.08000	0.08062	0.08124	0.08185	0.08246	0.08307
0.007	0.08367	0.08426	0.08485	0.08544	0.08602	0.08660	0.08718	0.08775	0.08832	0.08888
0.008	0.08944	0.09000	0.09055	0.09110	0.09165	0.09220	0.09274	0.09327	0.09381	0.09434
0.009	0.09487	0.09539	0.09592	0.09644	0.09695	0.09747	0.09798	0.09849	0.09899	0.09950
0.010	0.10000	0.10050	0.10100	0.10149	0.10198	0.10247	0.10296	0.10344	0.10392	0.10440
0.01	0.1000	0.1049	0.1095	0.1140	0.1183	0.1225	0.1265	0.1304	0.1342	0.1378
0.02	0.1414	0.1449	0.1483	0.1517	0.1549	0.1581	0.1612	0.1643	0.1673	0.1703
0.03	0.1732	0.1761	0.1789	0.1817	0.1844	0.1871	0.1897	0.1924	0.1949	0.1975
0.04	0.2000	0.2025	0.2049	0.2074	0.2098	0.2121	0.2145	0.2168	0.2191	0.2214
0.05	0.2236	0.2258	0.2280	0.2302	0.2324	0.2345	0.2366	0.2387	0.2408	0.2429
0.06	0.2449	0.2470	0.2490	0.2510	0.2530	0.2550	0.2569	0.2588	0.2608	0.2627
0.07	0.2646	0.2665	0.2683	0.2702	0.2720	0.2739	0.2757	0.2775	0.2793	0.2811
0.08	0.2828	0.2846	0.2864	0.2881	0.2898	0.2915	0.2933	0.2950	0.2966	0.2983
0.09	0.3000	0.3017	0.3033	0.3050	0.3066	0.3082	0.3098	0.3114	0.3130	0.3146
0.10	0.3162	0.3178	0.3194	0.3209	0.3225	0.3240	0.3256	0.3271	0.3286	0.3302

TABLE 3. SOLUTION OF $S^{1/2}$ IN MANNING FORMULA FOR GRASS SWALES.

of 4:1 to allow high speed maintenance by mowing. Soil conditions are very good and it is anticipated that the quality of turf will allow a maximum velocity, V, of 6 fps.

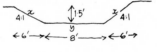

Step i) Select ideal channel section (for ease of calculation, this is trapezoidal).

Step ii) Calculate area of section a = 21 ft.^{2}

Step iii) Calculate hydraulic radius

$r = a \div p$ $p = y + 2x = 8 + 2\sqrt{6^2 + 1.5^2} = 20.18$

∴ $r = 21 \div 20.18 = \underline{1.03}$

Step iv) Calculate discharge capacity of channel

$Q = \dfrac{1.486}{n} r^{2/3} s^{1/2} a$ ($r^{2/3}$ & $s^{1/2}$ from Tables 3 & 4). Equation 3

$Q = \dfrac{1.486}{0.04} \times 1.02 \times 0.1732 \times 21 = 137.8$ cfs.

This is not sufficient to carry the peak discharge of 160 cfs.

Step v) Select a larger cross section

Note that both a deeper or a wider channel will increase capacity but a deeper channel will result in a higher velocity of flow.

a = 27 ft.^{2}

r = 27 ÷ 24.36 = 1.11

∴ $Q = \dfrac{1.486}{0.04} \times 1.072 \times 0.1732 \times 27 = 186$ cfs

This is sufficient with a safety margin to take 160 cfs discharge.

Step vi)   Check that the velocity of flow will not be too great
           for the grass lining.

$$V = \frac{Q}{a} \quad \ldots \ldots \ldots \ldots \ldots \ldots \text{Equation } ①$$

$$\therefore V = \frac{186}{27} = \underline{6.8 \text{ fps}}$$

         But this is too great (the maximum velocity decided
on was 6 fps). One could argue that peak discharge is 160 cfs.
Maximum design velocity = $\frac{160}{27}$ = $\underline{5.9 \text{ fps}}$ and is $\therefore$ O.K.
However, if not considered safe, then:

Step vii) If velocity is too great, make the channel <u>wider</u> but
           <u>shallower</u>.

           a = 28 ft.^{2}

           r = $\frac{28}{32.24}$ = 0.87

$$\therefore Q = \frac{1.486}{0.04} \times 0.911 \times 0.1732 \times 28 = \frac{6.411}{0.04} = \underline{164.1 \text{ cfs}}$$

         Channel is just sufficient to take discharge of 160 cfs.

Step viii) Check that <u>velocity of flow in channel (step vii) is not
           too great</u>.

$$V = \frac{Q}{a} \quad \ldots \ldots \ldots \ldots \ldots \ldots \text{Equation } ①$$

$$\therefore V = \frac{160.3}{28} = \underline{5.7} \text{ fps which is O.K.}$$

The same technique may be applied to a parabolic or 'V' shaped section; this just makes the calculation slightly more complex.

Note: One could have done this example a different way. For instance
if space were very tight, one could start by finding the minimum
cross section for a velocity of 6 fps to take a discharge of 160 cfs
thus:

$$a = \frac{Q}{V} \quad \ldots \ldots \ldots \ldots \ldots \ldots \text{Equation } ①$$

$$\therefore a = \frac{160}{6} = 26.7 \text{ sq. ft.}$$

Say, then, that only 24' is available; we know from Steps v and vi
above that a 24' channel width will give too great a velocity. Therefore, the gradient must be decreased. Note that if the gradient is
the same but the side slopes are increased, it effectively increases
(a) but also Q, and therefore is not advisable.

Note: About 10% should be added to width and 0.5' to depth for
freeboard in permanent channels.

Example A2

Design a channel with a maximum velocity, V, of 3 fps and a slope, s, of 0.05 with a peak discharge Q of 30 cfs. On Table 5 enter the chart on line reading 30 cfs, follow to right in column reading 5% (0.05) slope. For a velocity of 3 fps, top width is 45' and depth is 0.4' (add 4' to width and 0.5' to depth for freeboard in permanent channels).

Note: The dimensions given in this example are for a parabolic section for a Manning's coefficient of 0.04. If the maximum allowable velocity had been 4 fps, the width could be reduced to 23' and depth increased to 0.5'; and if 5 fps, a 13' width and 0.7' depth would have been permissible.

Using Method A for the above example,

$$r = a \div p = 10.5 \div 23.1 = \underline{0.45}$$

$$Q = \frac{1.486}{0.04} \times 0.587 \times 0.2236 \times 10.5 = \frac{2.0475}{0.04}$$

$$Q = 51.198 \text{ cfs}$$

$$V = \frac{50.1}{10.5} = 4.876 - \text{too high, but if}$$

$$Q = 30 \text{ cfs} \quad V = \frac{30}{10.5} = 2.9 \text{ fps (O.K.)}$$

N.T.S.

TABLE 5 GRASS WATERCOURSE DIMENSION CHART

— EXPLANATIONS —

The first column on the left is the runoff in cubic feet per second. The top line across the page shows the percent slope of the watercourse. The second line gives a choice of three different design velocities – 3 s.f. ; 4 s.f. and 5 s.f. The third line gives the depth in feet at center of the watercourse and is read under desired velocity. The figures in the body of the chart are top width in feet.

— NOTE —

For slopes less than 0.5 percent use size shown for 0.5 percent slope, or use diversion design chart.
Special designs may be requested from Engineer.

Calculation of Channel Size, Method B

For the design of grass channels in critical situations, use this technique.

Example B1. (From Engineering Field Manual for Conservation Practices, 1971). Determine the safe velocity and dimensions for a grass waterway with a parabolic cross section.

> Maximum discharge from drainage area = 55 cfs
> Gradient of channel = 5% or 0.05
> Vegetable cover = Bluegrass
> Condition of vegetation = (Good stand, mowed 3-4").
> Soil type = Easily erodible

Step i)   Determine retardance for Bluegrass (Table 6) = D.

Step ii) Determine permissible velocity for soil/vegetation type (Table 7) = 4.0 fps.

Step iii) Using Table 8, determine the channel dimensions; enter the chart on line reading 55 cfs. Follow to the right to column V_1 = 4.0. Find T (top width of channel) 32.6' D (depth) 0.75', V_2 (velocity when vegetation is long instead of short) 3.33 fps.

TABLE 6.   CLASSIFICATION OF VEGETATION COVER AS TO DEGREE OF RETARDANCE.

	Cover	Condition
A	Reed canarygrass	Excel. stand, tall (average 36")
	Yellow bluestem Ischaemum	Excel. stand, tall (average 36")
B	Smooth bromegrass	Good stand, mowed (average 12-15")
	Bermuda grass	Good stand, tall (average 12")
	Native grass mixture (little bluestem, blue grama, and other long and short midwest grasses)	Good stand, unmowed
	Tall fescue	Good stand, unmowed (average 18")
	Lespedeza sericea	Good stand, not woody, tall (average 19")
	Grass-Legume mixture--Timothy, smooth bromegrass, or orchard grass	Good stand, uncut (average 20")
	Reed canarygrass	Good stand, mowed (average 12-15")
	Tall fescue, with bird's foot trefoil or lodino	Good stand, uncut (average 18")
	Blue grama	Good stand, uncut (average 13")
C	Bahia	Good stand, uncut (6-8")
	Bermuda grass	Good stand, mowed (average 6")
	Redtop	Good stand, headed (15-20")
	Grass-Legume mixture--summer (Orchard grass, redtop, Italian ryegrass, and common lespedeza)	Good stand, uncut (6-8")
	Centipede grass	Very dense cover (average 6")
	Kentucky bluegrass	Good stand, headed (6-12")
D	Bermuda grass	Good stand, cut to 2.5" height
	Red fescue	Good stand, headed (12-18")
	Buffalo grass	Good stand, uncut (3-6")
	Grass-Legume mixture--fall, spring (Orchard grass, redtop, Italian ryegrass, and common lespedeza)	Good stand, uncut (4-5")
	Lespedeza sericea	After cutting to 2" height. Very good stand before cutting.
E	Bermuda grass	Good stand, cut to 1.5" height
	Bermuda grass	Burned stubble

TABLE 7. PERMISSIBLE VELOCITIES FOR CHANNELS LINED WITH VEGETATION

Cover	Slope range [2] (percent)	Permissible velocity [1]	
		Erosion resistant soils (fps)	Easily eroded soils (fps)
Bermuda grass	0-5 5-10 over 10	8 7 6	6 5 4
Bahia Buffalo grass Kentucky bluegrass Smooth brome Blue grama Tall fescue	0-5 5-10 over 10	7 6 5	5 4 3
Grass mixtures Reed canarygrass	[2] 0-5 5-10	5 4	4 3
Lespedeza sericea Weeping lovegrass Yellow bluestem Redtop Alfalfa Red fescue	[3] 0-5	3.5	2.5
Common lespedeza [4] Sudangrass [4]	[5] 0-5	3.5	2.5

[1] Use velocities exceeding 5 fps only where good covers and proper maintenance can be obtained.

[2] Do not use on slopes steeper than 10% except for vegetated side slopes in combination with a stone, concrete, or highly resistant vegetative center section.

[3] Do not use on slopes steeper than 5% except for vegetated side slopes in combination with a stone, concrete, or highly resistant vegetative center section.

[4] Annuals--use on mild slopes or as temporary protection until permanent covers are established.

[5] Use on slopes steeper than 5% is not recommended.

v_1 for RETARDANCE "D". Top Width (T), Depth (D) and v_2 for RETARDANCE "C".

Grade 5.0 Percent

Q cfs	$v_1=2.0$			$v_1=2.5$			$v_1=3.0$			$v_1=3.5$			$v_1=4.0$			$v_1=4.5$			$v_1=5.0$			$v_1=5.5$			$v_1=6.0$		
	T	D	v_2	T	D	v_2	T	D	v_2	T	D	v_2	T	D	v_2	T	D	v_2	T	D	v_2	T	D	v_2	T	D	v_2
15	29.3	0.57	1.33	21.1	0.60	1.74	15.0	0.66	2.23	12.2	0.70	2.58	9.0	0.75	3.25	7.2	0.83	3.70	5.8	0.93	4.09	4.6	0.99	4.81	5.3	1.06	5.21
20	39.0	0.57	1.33	28.1	0.61	1.74	19.9	0.66	2.26	16.2	0.70	2.62	12.0	0.75	3.26	9.5	0.81	3.84	7.6	0.89	4.35	6.1	0.97	4.95	6.5	1.02	5.56
25	48.6	0.57	1.34	35.1	0.61	1.73	24.8	0.65	2.28	20.3	0.70	2.59	15.0	0.75	3.27	11.9	0.89	3.82	9.5	0.89	4.37	7.6	0.96	5.03	7.8	1.01	5.59
30	58.1	0.57	1.34	42.0	0.61	1.74	29.7	0.66	2.28	24.3	0.70	2.61	18.0	0.76	3.26	14.2	0.80	3.89	11.3	0.87	4.49	9.1	0.96	5.08	9.1	1.01	5.60
35	67.6	0.57	1.35	48.8	0.61	1.75	34.6	0.66	2.28	28.2	0.70	2.64	20.9	0.75	3.30	16.6	0.81	3.86	13.2	0.88	4.47	10.5	0.94	5.26	10.3	0.99	5.77
40	77.0	0.57	1.35	55.7	0.61	1.75	39.5	0.66	2.28	32.2	0.70	2.64	23.9	0.75	3.29	18.9	0.80	3.90	15.0	0.88	4.46	12.0	0.94	5.26	11.6	1.00	5.75
45	86.4	0.57	1.35	62.5	0.61	1.75	44.3	0.66	2.29	36.1	0.70	2.65	26.8	0.75	3.31	21.3	0.81	3.87	16.9	0.87	4.52	13.5	0.94	5.25	12.9	1.00	5.73
50	95.7	0.57	1.36	69.2	0.61	1.76	49.1	0.66	2.30	40.1	0.70	2.64	29.7	0.75	3.32	23.6	0.81	3.89	18.8	0.88	4.50	15.0	0.94	5.25	14.1	1.00	5.84
55	105.0	0.57	1.36	75.9	0.61	1.77	53.9	0.66	2.30	44.0	0.70	2.65	32.6	0.75	3.33	25.9	0.81	3.90	20.6	0.87	4.54	16.5	0.94	5.24	15.4	0.99	5.81
60	114.2	0.57	1.36	82.6	0.61	1.77	58.7	0.66	2.30	47.9	0.70	2.56	35.5	0.75	3.34	28.2	0.81	3.92	22.4	0.87	4.57	17.9	0.93	5.32	16.5	0.99	5.78
65	123.4	0.57	1.35	89.3	0.61	1.77	63.4	0.66	2.31	51.8	0.70	2.66	38.4	0.75	3.34	30.5	0.81	3.92	24.3	0.87	4.54	19.4	0.94	5.30	16.7	1.00	5.85
70	132.4	0.57	1.37	95.9	0.61	1.77	68.2	0.66	2.31	55.6	0.70	2.67	41.3	0.75	3.34	32.8	0.81	3.93	26.1	0.87	4.56	20.8	0.93	5.36	17.9	0.99	5.82
75	141.5	0.57	1.37	102.4	0.61	1.78	72.9	0.66	2.31	59.4	0.70	2.68	44.1	0.75	3.36	35.1	0.81	3.93	27.9	0.87	4.58	22.3	0.94	5.34	19.2	1.00	5.88
80	150.5	0.57	1.37	109.0	0.61	1.78	77.5	0.65	2.32	63.3	0.70	2.68	47.0	0.75	3.36	37.4	0.81	3.92	29.7	0.87	4.60	23.8	0.94	5.32	20.4	0.99	5.91
90	168.8	0.57	1.38	122.3	0.61	1.79	87.0	0.66	2.33	71.0	0.70	2.69	52.8	0.75	3.36	42.0	0.81	3.93	33.4	0.87	4.59	26.7	0.94	5.35	22.9	0.99	5.86
100	187.0	0.57	1.38	135.5	0.61	1.79	96.5	0.66	2.33	78.7	0.70	2.70	58.5	0.75	3.37	46.5	0.81	3.96	37.0	0.87	4.62	29.5	0.93	5.38	25.5	0.99	5.88
110	205.1	0.57	1.38	148.7	0.61	1.79	105.9	0.66	2.33	86.4	0.70	2.70	64.3	0.75	3.37	51.1	0.81	3.96	40.7	0.87	4.61	32.5	0.93	5.39	28.0	0.99	5.89
120	223.1	0.57	1.39	161.8	0.61	1.80	115.3	0.65	2.33	94.1	0.70	2.70	70.0	0.75	3.38	55.7	0.81	3.96	44.3	0.87	4.62	35.4	0.93	5.41	30.5	0.99	5.90
130	240.9	0.57	1.39	174.8	0.61	1.80	124.6	0.66	2.34	101.7	0.70	2.71	75.7	0.76	3.38	60.2	0.81	3.97	47.9	0.87	4.64	38.3	0.93	5.41	33.0	0.99	5.91
140	258.7	0.57	1.40	187.7	0.61	1.81	133.9	0.66	2.34	109.3	0.70	2.71	81.3	0.75	3.39	64.7	0.81	3.98	51.5	0.87	4.64	41.2	0.93	5.42	35.5	0.99	5.91
150	276.4	0.58	1.40	200.6	0.61	1.81	143.1	0.66	2.35	116.8	0.70	2.72	87.0	0.76	3.39	69.3	0.81	3.97	55.1	0.87	4.65	44.1	0.93	5.42	37.9	0.99	5.96
160	293.9	0.58	1.40	213.4	0.61	1.81	152.3	0.66	2.35	124.3	0.70	2.72	92.6	0.76	3.40	73.7	0.81	3.99	58.7	0.87	4.65	47.0	0.94	5.42	40.4	0.99	5.95
170	311.4	0.58	1.40	226.1	0.61	1.82	161.5	0.66	2.35	131.8	0.70	2.73	98.2	0.76	3.41	78.2	0.81	3.99	62.3	0.87	4.65	49.9	0.94	5.41	42.9	0.99	5.95
180	328.7	0.58	1.41	238.8	0.61	1.82	170.6	0.65	2.36	139.2	0.70	2.73	103.8	0.76	3.41	82.7	0.81	3.99	65.9	0.87	4.67	52.7	0.93	5.44	45.4	0.99	5.94
190	346.0	0.58	1.41	251.4	0.61	1.83	179.7	0.67	2.36	146.6	0.70	2.74	109.4	0.76	3.41	87.1	0.81	4.00	69.4	0.87	4.66	55.6	0.94	5.43	47.8	0.99	5.97
200	363.1	0.58	1.42	263.9	0.61	1.83	188.7	0.67	2.37	154.0	0.70	2.74	114.9	0.76	3.42	91.6	0.81	4.00	73.0	0.87	4.68	58.4	0.94	5.45	50.3	0.99	5.96
220	398.3	0.58	1.42	289.6	0.62	1.83	207.1	0.67	2.37	169.0	0.70	2.75	126.1	0.76	3.43	100.6	0.81	4.00	80.1	0.87	4.68	64.1	0.94	5.45	55.2	0.99	5.99
240	433.2	0.58	1.42	315.0	0.62	1.84	225.4	0.67	2.37	184.0	0.70	2.75	137.4	0.76	3.43	109.5	0.81	4.01	87.3	0.87	4.68	69.9	0.94	5.46	60.2	0.99	5.98
260	467.9	0.58	1.43	340.4	0.62	1.84	243.7	0.67	2.38	198.9	0.70	2.76	148.5	0.76	3.44	118.5	0.81	4.01	94.4	0.87	4.69	75.6	0.94	5.47	65.1	0.99	5.99
280	502.5	0.58	1.43	365.6	0.62	1.84	261.8	0.67	2.38	213.7	0.70	2.76	159.7	0.76	3.44	127.4	0.81	4.02	101.5	0.87	4.70	81.4	0.94	5.46	70.0	0.99	6.01
300	536.7	0.58	1.43	390.7	0.62	1.85	279.9	0.67	2.38	228.5	0.71	2.77	170.7	0.76	3.45	136.2	0.81	4.03	108.6	0.87	4.70	87.0	0.94	5.48	74.9	0.99	6.01

Table 8   Parabolic Waterway Design
Retardance "D" and "C"

NOTE that there are different charts for various gradients and retardance. This example is included for explanatory purposes only, and designers should refer to SCS Engineering Field Manual of Conservation Practices (Chapter 7) for other values of retardance and gradient. Note also that the above dimensions make no allowance for freeboard.

22. DUTCH DRAIN SPECIFICATIONS

Plans for Dutch drains to increase rainwater infiltration in order to reduce runoff volume.

SOURCE. Joachim Tourbier and Richard Westmacott, *Water Resources Protection Measures in Land Development—A Handbook.* Water Resources as a Basis for Comprehensive Planning and Development of the Christina River Basin; a Prototype Project, Phase II. Water Resources Center, University of Delaware, Newark, Delaware, 1974.

PURPOSE

To reduce the volume of storm runoff and to reduce flood peaks by increasing ground infiltration. Dutch drains intercept 'sheet' runoff prior to concentration as compared to infiltration ditches.

SITE CHARACTERISTICS & APPLICATION

May be used on any site class where permeability of soil is sufficient or where seasonably high water tables are not anticipated. Minimum soil porosity 0.12 ft/day (all except D,F,M,W). These drains may either accommodate the maximum flow for 24-hour flood and thus avoid the need for a storm-drain system or they may be designed to take less runoff, in which case, they will act only as retarding devices as far as reduction of flood peaks is concerned.

ADVANTAGES

1. Reduces the total volume of runoff and can reduce 'peaking' effect of local floods.
2. Enhance ground-water supply.
3. Improve quality of vegetation on site by increasing available water in the ground.
4. Will result in a reduction in the size of storm drains required downslope of the facility.

DISADVANTAGES

1. Unless 'at source' seepage facilities are either designed for large storms or incorporate some method of controlled runoff release, they may not effectively reduce flood peaks when one storm follows another so closely that all facilities are full. The drains should, if possible, be designed to overflow before their capacity is reached during intensive storms.
2. Dutch drains are subject to clogging.
3. Dutch drains do not eliminate the need for a storm system downslope to take overflow from exceptional storms. They do, however, significantly decrease the necessary size of this system.

REFERENCES

Product Information: Metropolitan Brick, Negley, Ohio. (Photo Credit 2:6)

DESIGN CRITERIA & OUTLINE SPECIFICATIONS

Suggested locations for the use of Dutch drains are as follows:
1. To collect roof runoff for roofs without gutters. Drains run the whole length
   of the eaves. Runoff falls directly onto the surface of the Dutch drain which
   may be bare gravel, grass or occasionally porous paving. A combination
   Dutch and French drain could also be used to ease the problem of
   maintenance. Sidewalks running alongside may also discharge into
   Dutch drains.
2. Dividing strips between areas of impermeable paving to collect
   sheet runoff. These will usually be paved so as not to hinder
   the passage of traffic. Alternatives are shown below.

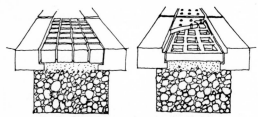

Note that a thin
layer of porous
asphalt could
also be used.

2:1 Granite, brick or concrete   2:2 Perforated concrete slab 2 1/2"   2:3 Grass and 6-8"
    blocks set on 4" of sand   set on 'web', or lattice concrete   course sand set on
                                           slab & 2" of sand   a crushed stone base

Note: Tile drains set at the base of Dutch drains and discharging into an overflow storm system will more
      effectively reduce flood peaks during intensive storms. Similarly, if the surface of Dutch drains have
      a longitudinal fall allowing runoff during excessively heavy rain, peaks will be lower.

23. SEEPAGE PIT SPECIFICATIONS

Plans for seepage pits to store runoff in order
to reduce flood peaks.

SOURCE. Joachim Tourbier and Richard Westmacott, *Water Resources Protection Measures in Land Development—A Handbook.* Water Resources as a Basis for Comprehensive Planning and Development of the Christina River Basin; a Prototype Project, Phase II. Water Resources Center, University of Delaware, Newark, Delaware, 1974.

PURPOSE

Seepage pits collect runoff and store
it until it percolates into the soil,
but unlike Dutch drains, seepage pits
do not conduct water along their
length when filled.

SITE CHARACTERISTICS & APPLICATION

May be used on all sites where permeability of soil is sufficient (over 0.15
ft/day) and where seasonably high water tables are not anticipated (all
except D,W,F,M). Seepage pits may be designed to accommodate a maximum
design frequency 24-hour storm, or they may be designed at least to allow
infiltration of runoff at predevelopment level. In this case a supplementary system of storm drains will be necessary to accommodate overflows.

ADVANTAGES

1. If properly designed, seepage pits may reduce local
   flood peaks.
2. Enhance ground-water supply.
3. In some cases they may eliminate the need for storm
   drains or reduce the size of storm drains necessary.

DISADVANTAGES

A seepage pit will, provided the soil permeability is
sufficient, accomplish the aim of increasing infiltration. However, unless very large (equivalent to at least
5" over all impermeable surfaces drained), it may not
result in a reduction of flood peaks (see schematic hydrographs for Dutch drains). Seepage pits are more liable
than Dutch drains to clogging by sediment, as runoff has
more chance to collect solids before reaching the pit.

REFERENCES

Chow, Ven Te. Handbook of Applied Hydrology. Section 9, p 46, 1964.

DESIGN CRITERIA & OUTLINE SPECIFICATIONS

Unless the seepage pit is designed to take the total amount of anticipated runoff for a design storm, some provision for overflow must be made. In order to have the maximum benefit in reducing flood peaks, the pit should, in fact, overflow during intense storms before its capacity is reached.

Alternatives for achieving this are:
1. Downpipes: Where down pipes discharge into seepage pits, they can incorporate a simple overflow to function during intense storms.

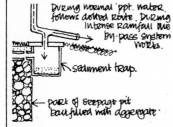

2. Small seepage pits with a relatively low porosity capping in the overland drainage channel.

3. In informal areas where a gravel-filled seepage hole is a more appropriate term, this may be situated in a depression, but with a porous section leading to the overflow channel.

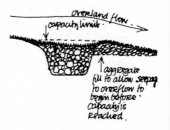

In a paved channel, seepage pits may be surfaced with porous asphalt or modular blocks set on sand. The gradient & porosity of the surface of the pit will determine the point at which runoff starts to bypass the pits.

This system is likely to prolong the life of the pit as the sediment trap will not function effectively with full flow.

Porosity: Soil should have a minimum porosity of 0.1 ft. per day. (Note the range for septic tank is 0.134 - 0.402 ft. per day. Minimum for porous paving is 0.042 ft. per day.

24. DETENTION BASIN SPECIFICATIONS

Plans for detention basins to collect runoff in order to catch sediments.

SOURCE.   Joachim Tourbier and Richard Westmacott, *Water Resources Protection Measures in Land Development—A Handbook*. Water Resources as a Basis for Comprehensive Planning and Development of the Christina River Basin; a Prototype Project, Phase II. Water Resources Center, University of Delaware, Newark, Delaware, 1974.

PURPOSE

To retain or detain runoff in order to increase the time of concentration or to reduce the maximum discharge rate of runoff from an urban area.

SITE CHARACTERISTICS & APPLICATION

A detention basin is the most effective technique for reducing the peak flow at a point immediately downstream of the impoundment, and should be used where frequent flooding in the area immediately downstream is intolerable. Some detention ponds have a retention capacity (a small permanent pool), but although retention of the design storm for periods longer than the time of concentration can depress hydrograph, retention ponds should only be used where recreational or water supply advantages are required.

ADVANTAGES

1. A detention pond can be designed to catch a large proportion of suspended solids of more than 10μ in diameter.
2. A detention pond with a large freeboard for detention may have some recreational and aesthetic benefits if runoff is not carrying heavy sediment loads.
3. May allow significant reduction in the size of storm drainage structures, etc.

DISADVANTAGES

1. A detention pond for maximum runoff control will have very little recreational or aesthetic value.
2. Detention basins that empty out completely can have an unslightly nature that can be a detriment in urban developments.

REFERENCES

DESIGN CRITERIA & OUTLINE SPECIFICATIONS

A single-purpose runoff control pond will clearly have very different design criteria from one that is also
required to have some recreational, aesthetic, or sediment control value. Spec. 2:7 shows that a single-purpose
runoff control pond could be effective in settling out a large proportion of the sediment above 10µ in size, especially if the spillway design was modified during the construction period.

1:1 Detention Ponds. The most effective reduction in peak discharge per unit of storage from a given drainage area
is given by a detention basin. The aim may be to reduce the peak to predevelopment levels or to reduce the peak
to a level at which it will not damage or overflow a facility (bridge, culvert, etc.) immediately downstream.
A detailed method for preliminary sizing of basins is given in Appendix 1:10. This method assumes that the discharge from the drainage area will rise constantly until a maximum discharge (for a storm of that intensity) is
reached at the 'time of concentration' (B) [Figure 1]. At this point, the discharge is assumed to remain constant until the storm ceases (C), at which point the discharge will decrease at a constant rate over a period
equal to the time of concentration. The maximum discharge rate is plotted on the descending limb of the hydrograph at which point (D) the pond would be full. It is assumed that the spillway (usually a perforated vertical
riser or simple pipe spillway) would discharge water at a constantly increasing rate until a maximum is reached
when the pond is full and the 'head' largest (Line AD). The total required storage capacity of the pond is
represented by the area ABCD. The volume of water discharged during the period of inflow into the pond is represented by the area ADE and the volume of water discharged from storage by the area DEF. (Note that DEF = ABCD
and ABCE = ADF.) The selection of a duration of a storm varies. In the example in Appendix 1:10, it was shown
that the required volume of storage reached a maximum for storms of duration of 90 minutes and then dropped off
again. As the intensity of rainfall decreases with longer duration storms, the discharge in cfs gradually drops
to below predevelopment maximum discharge rate from a storm with a duration equal to the time of concentration.
In reality, of course, the inflow hydrograph would not be a simple trapezium and will depend on basin characteristics, nor does the drainage from the spillway increase constantly as shown. This technique, however, gives a
sufficiently accurate estimate for most purposes. A simple pipe spillway will require slightly less storage
capacity than a perforated spillway as it will overflow more rapidly during the early stages of the storm. This

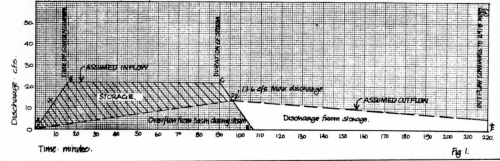

Fig 1.

25. POROUS PAVING SLAB SPECIFICATIONS

Plans for porous paving slabs to allow infiltration in order to decrease stormwater runoff.

SOURCE.   Joachim Tourbier and Richard Westmacott, *Water Resources Protection Measures in Land Development—A Handbook*. Water Resources as a Basis for Comprehensive Planning and Development of the Christina River Basin; a Prototype Project, Phase II. Water Resources Center, University of Delaware, Newark, Delaware, 1974.

PURPOSE

There are various types of precast paving slabs which provide a hard surface and yet are porous to varying degrees.

SITE CHARACTERISTICS & APPLICATION

Porous paving can only be used where soil is sufficiently porous to allow rapid drainage (all site classes except W,M,F,D). These materials may be used in a wide variety of ways. Perforated slabs on a honeycomb base may be used to cover Dutch drains between areas of impermeable paving (making a lattice of permeable paving throughout a parking area). Brick strips incorporating tree pits may be used in similar ways.

ADVANTAGES

1. In case of lattice blocks, grass can substantially cover the site.
2. They are flexible and can withstand a certain amount of movement.
3. When used as strips between asphalt, sections can be lifted to plant trees, place street signs, etc., or to maintain utility lines beneath.

DISADVANTAGES

1. Most of these materials are not as useful as <u>porous asphalt</u> paving for following reasons:
   1:1 Expensive and difficult to lay.
   1:2 Permeability not as good as asphalt.
   1:3 Only perforated slabs on a honeycomb give a good walking surface.

   Thus, they tend to be used in situations where <u>porous asphalt</u> is not suitable which may include:
   (1) Very formal 'hard' areas
   (2) Unstable areas subject to subsidence or heave.
   (3) Areas where a grass covered surface is desired.

REFERENCES

1. Modular pavers available from Cold Springs Granite Co., Minn., 56320. Photo Reference.
2. Lattice concrete blocks available from Peitz Industries, Inc., P. O. Box 89, Ridgefield Park, N. J. 07660
3. The Franklin Institute Research Labs, Investigations of Porous Pavements for Urban Runoff Control. U.S. Environmental Protection Agency, Water Pollution Control, Spr. 11034 DUY 03, 1972.
4. KNR Concrete Products, Ltd., Georgetown, Ont. Photo Reference.

DESIGN CRITERIA & OUTLINE SPECIFICATIONS

1. Lattice concrete blocks. These are concrete pavers made to a variety of different shapes and specifications (2).

Ref 2.

Length ins.	Width ins.	Depth ins.	Compressive Strength psi.	Units/ sq. yd.	Lbs/ Unit
24	16	4	6,400	3.35	73

Use: For parking areas where an 'informal' grass surface is required but sufficiently hard wearing to withstand regular use. For lining grass swales to provide protection from erosion and for grass ramps. Where a surface of high porosity is required (parking areas, etc.), blocks should be laid on a bed of gravel or crushed aggregate to give a sufficient capacity for the design storm (see porous asphalt specification) and a 2" layer of fines and gravel. Interstices of blocks should be filled by screening with coarse sand. Where erosion control only is desired, blocks may be laid directly on soil and screened with topsoil. Where used for a driveway under a lawn, blocks may be covered in an inch of topsoil.

1:1 AUTO DRIVEWAY. SOIL. BLOCKS 4" SAND. 1"

1:2. TRUCK DRIVEWAY. BLOCKS 4" SAND 1" CRUSHED STONE 2"-5"

1:3. ROADS UNDER LAWN. 2" SOIL BLOCKS 4" 1" SAND. 2-5" CRUSHED STONE

2. Modular pavers. Perforated bricks or bricks with lugs to control spacing. Brick or concrete pavers made to a variety of specifications depending on use, usually with a compressive strength of between 7,500 - 10,000 psi for use in areas where more wear is expected than for lattice blocks.

Use: Interstices and perforations are usually kept free from vegetation. This paving type is used in more formal areas than lattice blocks for paving around trees, for dividing strips between impermeable paved surfaces, etc. Generally, not a comfortable walking surface.

Installation: Lay on a bed of gravel topped with coarse sand (2"). The depth of the gravel will depend on the required storm water storage capacity.

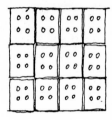 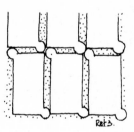
Ref 3.

26. AERIAL PHOTOGRAPH INTERPRETATION

Scale conversions for vertical aerial photographs.

SOURCE.   T. Eugene Avery, *Forester's Guide to Aerial Photo Interpretation*, U.S. Department of Agriculture, Forest Service, Washington, D.C., October 1966.

Representative fraction (scale)	Feet per inch	Chains per inch	Inches per mile	Acres per square inch	Square miles per square inch
(1)	(2)	(3)	(4)	(5)	(6)
1:7,920	660.00	10.00	8.00	10.00	0.0156
1:8,000	666.67	10.10	7.92	10.20	.0159
1:8,400	700.00	10.61	7.54	11.25	.0176
1:9,000	750.00	11.36	7.04	12.91	.0202
1:9,600	800.00	12.12	6.60	14.69	.0230
1:10,000	833.33	12.63	6.34	15.94	.0249
1:10,800	900.00	13.64	5.87	18.60	.0291
1:12,000	1,000.00	15.15	5.28	22.96	.0359
1:13,200	1,100.00	16.67	4.80	27.78	.0434
1:14,400	1,200.00	18.18	4.40	33.06	.0517
1:15,000	1,250.00	18.94	4.22	35.87	.0560
1:15,600	1,300.00	19.70	4.06	38.80	.0606
1:15,840	1,320.00	20.00	4.00	40.00	.0625
1:16,000	1,333.33	20.20	3.96	40.81	.0638
1:16,800	1,400.00	21.21	3.77	45.00	.0703
1:18,000	1,500.00	22.73	3.52	51.65	.0807
1:19,200	1,600.00	24.24	3.30	58.77	.0918
1:20,000	1,666.67	25.25	3.17	63.77	.0996
1:20,400	1,700.00	25.76	3.11	66.34	.1037
1:21,120	1,760.00	26.67	3.00	71.11	.1111
1:21,600	1,800.00	27.27	2.93	74.38	.1162
1:22,800	1,900.00	28.79	2.78	82.87	.1295
1:24,000	2,000.00	30.30	2.64	91.83	.1435
1:25,000	2,083.33	31.57	2.53	99.64	.1557
1:31,680	2,640.00	40.00	2.00	160.00	.2500
Method of calculation	$\dfrac{RFD}{12}$	$\dfrac{RFD}{792}$	$\dfrac{63,360}{RFD}$	$\dfrac{(RFD)^2}{6,272,640}$	$\dfrac{Acres/sq. in.}{640}$

[1] Conversions for scales not shown can be made from the relationships listed at the bottom of each column.   With the scale of 1:7,920 as an example (column 1, line 1), the number of feet per inch is computed by dividing the representative fraction denominator (RFD) by 12 (number of inches per foot).   Thus, 7,920÷12=660 feet per inch (column 2).   By dividing the RFD by 792 (inches per chain), the number of chains per inch is derived (column 3).   Other calculations can be made similarly.   Under column 4, the figure 63,360 represents the number of inches in one mile; in column 5, the figure 6,272,640 is the number of square inches in one acre; and in column 6, the number 640 is acres per square mile.

Actual crown widths of trees for various photo-crown widths and photo scales.

Note: May be used to estimate size for any object.

Photo crown width (thousandths of an inch)	1:10,000 or 833 ft./in.	1:12,000 or 1,000 ft./in.	1:15,840 or 1,320 ft./in.	1:18,000 or 1,500 ft./in.	1:20,000 or 1,667 ft./in.	1:24,000 or 2,000 ft./in.
	Feet	*Feet*	*Feet*	*Feet*	*Feet*	*Feet*
2.5	2	3	3	4	4	5
5.0	4	5	7	8	8	10
7.5	6	8	10	11	13	15
10.0	8	10	13	15	17	20
12.5	10	13	17	19	21	25
15.0	12	15	20	23	25	30
17.5	15	18	23	26	29	35
20.0	17	20	26	30	33	40
22.5	19	23	30	34	38	45
25.0	21	25	33	38	42	50
27.5	23	28	36	41	46	55
30.0	25	30	40	45	50	60
32.5	27	33	43	49	54	------
35.0	29	35	46	53	58	------
37.5	31	38	50	56	63	------
40.0	33	40	53	60	67	------
42.5	35	43	56	------	------	------
45.0	37	45	59	------	------	------
47.5	40	48	63	------	------	------
50.0	42	50	66	------	------	------

Conversion Factors, Tables, and Graphs

1. CONVERSION: FARENHEIT TO CELSIUS

Table for converting temperature from Farenheit to Celsius degrees. Degrees Farenheit expressed in left vertical column and top horizontal row; corresponding degrees Celsius in body of table.

	0	0.1	0.2	0.3	0.4	0.5	0.6	0.7	0.8	0.9
+30	-01.1	-01.1	-01.0	-00.9	-00.9	-00.8	-00.8	-00.7	-00.7	-00.6
31	-00.6	-00.5	-00.4	-00.4	-00.3	-00.3	-00.2	-00.2	-00.1	-00.1
32	00.0	00.1	00.1	00.2	00.2	00.3	00.3	00.4	00.4	00.5
33	00.6	00.6	00.7	00.7	00.8	00.8	00.9	00.9	01.0	01.1
34	01.1	01.2	01.2	01.3	01.3	01.4	01.4	01.5	01.6	01.6
35	01.7	01.7	01.8	01.8	01.9	01.9	02.0	02.1	02.1	02.2
36	02.2	02.3	02.3	02.4	02.4	02.5	02.6	02.6	02.7	02.7
37	02.8	02.8	02.9	02.9	03.0	03.1	03.1	03.2	03.2	03.3
38	03.3	03.4	03.4	03.5	03.6	03.6	03.7	03.7	03.8	03.8
39	03.9	03.9	04.0	04.1	04.1	04.2	04.2	04.3	04.3	04.4
40	04.4	04.5	04.6	04.6	04.7	04.7	04.8	04.8	04.9	04.9
41	05.0	05.1	05.1	05.2	05.2	05.3	05.3	05.4	05.4	05.5
42	05.6	05.6	05.7	05.7	05.8	05.8	05.9	05.9	06.0	06.1
43	06.1	06.2	06.2	06.3	06.3	06.4	06.4	06.5	06.6	06.6
44	06.7	06.7	06.8	06.8	06.9	06.9	07.0	07.1	07.1	07.2
45	07.2	07.3	07.3	07.4	07.4	07.5	07.6	07.6	07.7	07.8
46	07.8	07.8	07.9	07.9	08.0	08.1	08.1	08.2	08.2	08.3
47	08.3	08.4	08.4	08.5	08.6	08.6	08.7	08.7	08.8	08.8
48	08.9	08.9	09.0	09.1	09.1	09.2	09.2	09.3	09.3	09.4
49	09.4	09.5	09.6	09.6	09.7	09.7	09.8	09.8	09.9	09.9
50	10.0	10.1	10.1	10.2	10.2	10.3	10.3	10.4	10.4	10.5
51	10.6	10.6	10.7	10.7	10.8	10.8	10.9	10.9	11.0	11.1
52	11.1	11.2	11.2	11.3	11.3	11.4	11.4	11.5	11.6	11.6
53	11.7	11.7	11.8	11.8	11.9	11.9	12.0	12.1	12.1	12.2
54	12.2	12.3	12.3	12.4	12.4	12.5	12.6	12.6	12.7	12.7
55	12.8	12.8	12.9	12.9	13.0	13.1	13.1	13.2	13.2	13.3
56	13.3	13.4	13.4	13.5	13.6	13.6	13.7	13.7	13.8	13.8
57	13.9	13.9	14.0	14.1	14.1	14.2	14.2	14.3	14.3	14.4
58	14.4	14.5	14.6	14.6	14.7	14.7	14.8	14.8	14.9	14.9
59	15.0	15.1	15.1	15.2	15.2	15.3	15.3	15.4	15.4	15.5
60	15.6	15.6	15.7	15.7	15.8	15.8	15.9	15.9	16.0	16.1
61	16.1	16.2	16.2	16.3	16.3	16.4	16.4	16.5	16.6	16.6
62	16.7	16.7	16.8	16.8	16.9	16.9	17.0	17.1	17.1	17.2
63	17.2	17.3	17.3	17.4	17.4	17.5	17.6	17.6	17.7	17.7
64	17.8	17.8	17.9	17.9	18.0	18.1	18.1	18.2	18.2	18.3

Degrees Farenheit expressed in left vertical
column and top horizontal row; corresponding degrees Celsius in body of table.

	0	0.1	0.2	0.3	0.4	0.5	0.6	0.7	0.8	0.9
65	18.3	18.4	18.4	18.5	18.6	18.6	18.7	18.7	18.8	18.8
66	18.9	18.9	19.0	19.1	19.1	19.2	19.2	19.3	19.3	19.4
67	19.4	19.5	19.6	19.6	19.7	19.7	19.8	19.8	19.9	19.9
68	20.0	20.1	20.1	20.2	20.2	20.3	20.3	20.4	20.4	20.5
69	20.6	20.6	20.7	20.7	20.8	20.8	20.9	20.9	21.0	21.1
70	21.1	21.2	21.2	21.3	21.3	21.4	21.4	21.5	21.6	21.6
71	21.7	21.7	21.8	21.8	21.9	21.9	22.0	22.1	22.1	22.2
72	22.2	22.3	22.3	22.4	22.4	22.5	22.6	22.6	22.7	22.7
73	22.8	22.8	22.9	22.9	23.0	23.1	23.1	23.2	23.2	23.3
74	23.3	23.4	23.4	23.5	23.6	23.6	23.7	23.7	23.8	23.8
75	23.9	23.9	24.0	24.1	24.1	24.2	24.2	24.3	24.3	24.4
76	24.4	24.5	24.6	24.6	24.7	24.7	24.8	24.8	24.9	24.9
77	25.0	25.1	25.1	25.2	25.2	25.2	25.3	25.4	25.4	25.5
78	25.6	25.6	25.7	25.7	25.8	25.8	25.9	25.9	26.0	26.1
79	26.1	26.2	26.2	26.3	26.3	26.4	26.4	26.5	26.6	26.6
80	26.7	26.7	26.8	26.8	26.9	26.9	27.0	27.1	27.1	27.2
81	27.2	27.3	27.3	27.4	27.4	27.5	27.6	27.6	27.7	27.7
82	27.8	27.8	27.9	27.9	28.0	28.1	28.1	28.2	28.2	28.3
83	28.3	28.4	28.4	28.5	28.6	28.6	28.7	28.7	28.8	28.8
84	28.9	28.9	29.0	29.1	29.1	29.2	29.2	29.3	29.3	29.4
85	29.4	29.5	29.6	29.6	29.7	29.7	29.8	29.8	29.9	29.9
86	30.0	30.1	30.1	30.2	30.2	30.3	30.3	30.4	30.4	30.5
87	30.6	30.6	30.7	30.7	30.8	30.8	30.9	30.9	31.0	31.1
88	31.1	31.2	31.2	31.3	31.3	31.4	31.4	31.5	31.6	31.6
89	31.7	31.7	31.8	31.8	31.9	31.9	32.0	32.1	32.1	32.2
90	32.2	32.3	32.3	32.4	32.4	32.5	32.6	32.6	32.7	32.7
91	32.8	32.8	32.9	32.9	33.0	33.1	33.1	33.2	33.2	33.3
92	33.3	33.4	33.4	33.5	33.6	33.6	33.7	33.7	33.8	33.8
93	33.9	33.9	34.0	34.1	34.1	34.2	34.2	34.3	34.3	34.4
94	34.4	34.5	34.6	34.6	34.7	34.7	34.8	34.8	34.9	34.9
95	35.0	35.1	35.1	35.2	35.2	35.3	35.3	35.4	35.4	35.5
96	35.6	35.6	35.7	35.7	35.8	35.8	35.9	35.9	36.0	36.1
97	36.1	36.2	36.2	36.3	36.3	36.4	36.4	36.5	36.6	36.6
98	36.7	36.7	36.8	36.8	36.9	36.9	37.0	37.1	37.1	37.2
99	37.2	37.3	37.3	37.4	37.4	37.5	37.6	37.6	37.7	37.7
100	37.8	37.8	37.9	37.9	38.0	38.1	38.1	38.2	38.2	38.3
101	38.3	38.4	38.4	38.5	38.6	38.6	38.7	38.7	38.8	38.8
102	38.9	38.9	39.0	39.1	39.1	39.2	39.2	39.3	39.3	39.4
103	39.4	39.5	39.6	39.6	39.7	39.7	39.8	39.8	39.9	39.9
104	40.0	40.1	40.1	40.2	40.2	40.3	40.3	40.4	40.4	40.5

2. CONVERSION: METERS TO FEET

Table for converting distance from meters to feet. Length in meters expressed in left vertical column and in top horizontal row; corresponding lengths in feet in body of table.

Meters	0	1	2	3	4	5	6	7	8	9
0	0.00	3.28	6.56	9.84	13.12	16.40	19.69	22.97	26.25	29.53
10	32.81	36.09	39.37	42.65	45.93	49.21	52.49	55.78	59.06	62.34
20	65.62	68.90	72.18	75.46	78.74	82.02	85.30	88.58	91.87	95.15
30	98.43	101.71	104.99	108.27	111.55	114.83	118.11	121.39	124.67	127.96
40	131.24	134.52	137.80	141.08	144.36	147.64	150.92	154.20	157.48	160.76
50	164.04	167.33	170.61	173.89	177.17	180.45	183.73	187.01	190.29	193.57
60	196.85	200.13	203.42	206.70	209.98	213.26	216.54	219.82	223.10	226.38
70	229.66	232.94	236.22	239.51	242.79	246.07	249.35	252.63	255.91	259.19
80	262.47	265.75	269.03	272.31	275.60	278.88	282.16	285.44	288.72	292.00
90	295.28	298.56	391.84	305.12	308.40	311.69	314.97	318.25	321.53	324.81
100	328.09	331.37	334.65	337.93	341.21	344.49	347.78	351.06	354.34	357.62

3. CONVERSION: SALINITY UNITS

Conversion of several methods of expressing
salinity. Read across. For example, a specific
conductance of 8.6 millimhos per centimeter
is equivalent to 16 percent sea strength.

SOURCE.   Soil Conservation Service, *Louisiana Gulf
Coast Marsh Handbook*, U.S. Department
of Agriculture, Alexandria, Louisiana, November 1966.

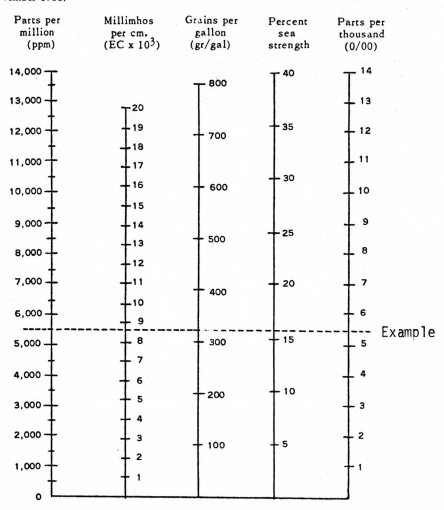

4. CONVERSION: WATER FLOW UNITS

Conversion of several methods of expressing water flow. Read across.

SOURCE. J. H. Feth, *Water Facts and Figures for Planners and Managers*, Geological Survey Circular No. 601-1, Washington, D.C., 1973.

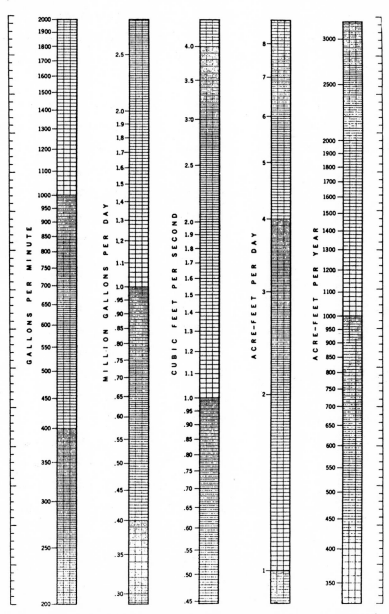

5. CONVERSION: HYDROLOGICAL UNITS OF MEASUREMENT

Conversion of basic measures used in hydrology.

Multiply	By	To Obtain
Acre feet	43,560	Cubic feet
" "	325,851	Gallons
" "	1233.49	Cubic meters
" "	12.10	Cubic feet/second hours
" "	0.01875	Inches depth on 1 square mile
" " per day	0.5042	Cubic feet/second
" " per square mile	0.01875	Inches depth
Centimeters/second	0.03281	Feet/second
" "	0.036	Kilometers/hour
" "	0.02237	Miles/hour
Cubic centimeters	3.531×10^{-5}	Cubic feet
" "	6.102×10^{-2}	Cubic inches
" "	2.642×10^{-4}	Gallons
" "	10^{-3}	Liters
Cubic feet	1728	Cubic inches
" "	0.02832	Cubic meters
" "	0.03704	Cubic yards
" "	7.48052	Gallons
" "	28.32	Liters
Cubic feet/minute	472.0	Cubic cms./sec.
Cubic feet/second	1.983	Acre feet per day
" " "	724.0	Acre feet per year
" " "	448.8	U.S. gallons per min.
" " "	0.6463	Million U.S. gallons per day

Multiply	By	To Obtain
Cubic feet/second days	1.983	Acre feet
" " "	0.03719	Inches depth on 1
		square mile
Cubic feet/second/sq. mi.	13.57	Inches depth per year
		(365 days)
Cubic inches	16.39	Cubic centimeters
" "	5.787×10^{-4}	Cubic feet
" "	4.329×10^{-3}	Gallons
Cubic meters	35.31	Cubic feet
" "	264.2	Gallons
" "	10^{3}	Liters
Cubic yards	0.7646	Cubic meters
Gallons U.S.	0.1337	Cubic feet
" "	231	Cubic inches
" "	3.785	Liters
" "	0.83267	Imperial gallons
Gallons, water	8.3453	Pounds of water
Gallons/min.	2.228×10^{-3}	Cubic feet/sec.
" "	0.06308	Liters/sec.
" "	8.0208	Cubic feet/hr.
Imperial gallons	1.200	U.S. gallons
Inches per hour	645.3	csm
" "	1.008	cfs per acre
Inches depth	53.33	AF per square mile
Liters	0.03531	Cubic feet
"	61.02	Cubic inches
"	0.2642	Gallons

Multiply	By	To Obtain
Liters/min.	5.886×10^{-4}	Cubic feet/second
Million U.S. gallons per day	1.547	Cubic feet/second
" " "	3.069	Acre feet
Ounces (fluid)	1.805	Cubic inches
" "	0.02957	Liters

6. CONVERSION: BRITISH AND METRIC UNITS OF MEASUREMENT

Conversion factors for basic British and metric units.

Note: Figures in bold type are exact measurements.

	Multiply number of	by	to obtain equivalent number of	Multiply number of	by	to obtain equivalent number of
Length	Inches (in)	**25·4**	millimetres (mm)	Millimetres	0·03937	inches
		2·54	centimetres (cm)	Centimetres	0·3937	inches
	Feet (ft)	**30·48**	centimetres			
		0·3048	metres (m)	Metres	39·3701	inches
	Yards (yd)	**0·9144**	metres		3·2808	feet
	Fathoms (6ft)	**1·8288**	metres		1·0936	yards
					0·54681	fathoms
	Miles (land: 5,280 ft)	**1·609344**	kilometres (km)	Kilometres	0·62137	miles (land)
	Miles (UK sea: 6,080 ft)	**1·853184**			0·53961	miles (UK sea)
	Miles, international nautical	**1·852**			0·53996	miles, international nautical
Area	Sq. inches (in²)	**645·16**	sq. millimetres (mm²)	Sq. millimetres	0·00155	sq. inches
		6·4516	sq. centimetres (cm²)	Sq. centimetres	0·1550	sq. inches
	Sq. feet (ft²)	**929·0304**	sq. centimetres			
		0·092903	sq. metres (m²)	Sq. metres	10·7639	sq. feet
	Sq. yards (yd²)	0·836127	sq. metres		1·19599	sq. yards
		4,046·86	sq. metres	Hectares	2·47105	acres
	Acres	0·404686	hectares (ha)			
		0·004047	sq. kilometres (km²)	Sq. kilometres	247·105	acres
	Sq. miles	2·58999	sq. kilometres		0·3861	sq. miles
Volume and capacity	Cu. inches (in³)	**16·387064**	cu. centimetres (cm³)	Cu. centimetres	0·06102	cu. inches
	UK pints	34·6774	cu. inches			
	UK pints	0·568		Litres	61·024	cu. inches
	UK gallons	4·546	litres (l)		0·0353	cu. feet
	US gallons	3·785			0·2642	US gallons
	Cu. feet (ft³)	28·317			0·2200	UK gallons
	Cu. feet	0·028317	cu. metres (m³)		26·417	US gallons
	UK bushels	0·3637	hectolitres (hl)	Hectolitres	21·997	UK gallons
	US bushels	0·3524			2·838	US bushels
	UK gallons	1·20095	US gallons		2·750	UK bushels
	US gallons	0·832674	UK gallons		35·3147	cu. feet
		36	UK gallons	Cu. metres	1·30795	cu. yards
	UK bulk barrels	43·2342	US gallons		264·172	US gallons
		0·1637	cu. metres		219·969	UK gallons
					6·11025	UK bulk barrels
Weight (mass)	Grains (gr)	**64·79891**	milligrams (mg)	Milligrams	0·01543	grains
	Ounces, avoirdupois (oz)	28·3495	grams (g)	Grams	0·03527	ounces, avoirdupois
	Ounces, troy (oz tr)	31·1035			0·03215	ounces, troy
	Ounces, avoirdupois	0·9115	ounces, troy	Kilograms	2·20462	pounds, avoirdupois
	Pounds, avoirdupois (lb)	**453·59237**	grams	Metric quintals	220·462	
		0·45359	kilograms (kg)	Tonnes	2,204·62	pounds, avoirdupois
	Hundredweights (cwt) (112 lb)	**0·05**	long tons		1·10231	short tons
		0·508023	metric quintals (q)		0·984207	long tons
	Short tons (2,000 lb)	0·892857	long tons			
		0·907185	tonnes (t)			
	Long tons (2,240 lb)	**1·12**	short tons			
		1·01605	tonnes			

Sources of Technical Assistance

1. U.S. ENVIRONMENTAL PROTECTION AGENCY

Regional Offices	States covered
EPA Region I John F. Kennedy Building Boston, Massachusetts 02203 (617)223-7223	Connecticut, Maine, Massa- chusetts, New Hampshire, Rhode Island, Vermont
EPA Region II 26 Federal Plaza New York, New York 10007 (212)264-2515	New Jersey, New York, Puerto Rico, Virgin Islands
EPA Region III 6th & Walnut Streets Philadelphia, Pennsylvania 19106 (215)597-9904	Delaware, Maryland, Pennsyl- vania, Virginia, West Virginia, D.C.
EPA Region IV 1421 Peachtree Street, N.E. Atlanta, Georgia 30309 (404)526-9904	Alabama, Florida, Georgia, Kentucky, Mississippi, North Carolina, South Carolina, Tennessee
EPA Region V One North Wacker Drive Chicago, Illinois 60606 (312)353-1478	Illinois, Indiana, Michigan, Minnesota, Ohio, Wisconsin
EPA Region VI 1600 Patterson Street Dallas, Texas 75201 (214)749-1151	Arkansas, Louisiana, New Mexico, Oklahoma, Texas
EPA Region IX 100 California Street San Francisco, California 94111 (415)556-6266	Arizona, California, Hawaii, Nevada, American Samoa, Trust Territories of the acific, Wake Island
EPA Region X 1200 Sixth Avenue Seattle, Washington 98101 (206)442-1203	Alaska, Idaho, Oregon, Washington

2. U.S. ARMY CORPS OF ENGINEERS

Office, Chief of Engineers
Department of the Army
Washington, D.C. 20314

Districts:
U.S. Army Engineer District, **Memphis**
668 Federal Office Building
Memphis, Tennessee 38103

U.S. Army Engineer District, **New Orleans**
P.O. Box 60267
New Orleans, Louisiana 70160

U.S. Army Engineer District, **St. Louis**
210 North 12th Street
St. Louis, Missouri 63101

U.S. Army Engineer District, **Vicksburg**
P.O. Box 60
Vicksburg, Mississippi 39180

U.S. Army Engineer District, **Kansas City**
700 Federal Building
601 East 12th Street
Kansas City, Missouri 64106

U.S. Army Engineer District, **Omaha**
6014 U.S. Post Office and Court House
215 N. 17th Street
Omaha, Nebraska 68102

U.S. Army Engineer Division, **New England**
424 Trapelo Road
Waltham, Massachusetts 02154

U.S. Army Engineer District, **Baltimore**
P.O. Box 1715
Baltimore, Maryland 21203

U.S. Army Engineer District, **New York**
26 Federal Plaza
New York, New York 10007

U.S. Army Engineer District, **Norfolk**
803 Front Street
Norfolk, Virginia 23510

U.S. Army Engineer District, **Philadelphia**
U.S. Custom House
2d and Chestnut Streets
Philadelphia, Pennsylvania 19106

U.S. Army Engineer District, **Buffalo**
1776 Niagara Street
Buffalo, New York 14207

U.S. Army Engineer District, **Chicago**
219 S. Dearborn Street
Chicago, Illinois 60604

U.S. Army Engineer District, **Detroit**
P.O. Box 1027
Detroit, Michigan 48231

U.S. Army Engineer District, **Rock Island**
Clock Tower Building
Rock Island, Illinois 61201

U.S. Army Engineer District, **St. Paul**
1210 U.S. Post Office and Custom House
St. Paul, Minnesota 55101

U.S. Army Engineer District, **Alaska**
P.O. Box 7002
Anchorage, Alaska 99510

U.S. Army Engineer District, **Portland**
P.O. Box 2946
Portland, Oregon 97208

U.S. Army Engineer District, **Seattle**
1519 Alaskan Way, South
Seattle, Washington 98134

U.S. Army Engineer District, **Walla Walla**
Building 602
City-County Airport
Walla Walla, Washington 99362

U.S. Army Engineer District, **Huntington**
P.O. Box 2127
Huntington, West Virginia 25721

U.S. Army Engineer District, **Louisville**
P.O. Box 59
Louisville, Kentucky 40201

U.S. Army Engineer District, **Nashville**
P.O. Box 1070
Nashville, Tennessee 37202

U.S. Army Engineer District, **Pittsburgh**
Federal Building
1000 Liberty Avenue
Pittsburgh, Pennsylvania 15222

U.S. Army Engineer District, **Charleston**
P.O. Box 919
Charleston, South Carolina 29402

U.S. Army Engineer District, **Jacksonville**
P.O. Box 4970
Jacksonville, Florida 32201

U.S. Army Engineer District, **Mobile**
P.O. Box 2288
Mobile, Alabama 36628

U.S. Army Engineer District, **Savannah**
P.O. Box 889
Savannah, Georgia 31402

U.S. Army Engineer District, **Wilmington**
P.O. Box 1890
Wilmington, North Carolina 28401

U.S. Army Engineer Division, **Pacific Ocean**
Building 96
Fort Armstrong
Honolulu, Hawaii 96813

U.S. Army Engineer District, **Los Angeles**
P.O. Box 2711
Los Angeles, California 90053

U.S. Army Engineer District, **Sacramento**
650 Capitol Mall
Sacramento, California 95814

U.S. Army Engineer District, **San Francisco**
100 McAllister Street
San Francisco, California 94102

U.S. Army Engineer District, **Albuquerque**
P.O. Box 1580
Albuquerque, New Mexico 87103

U.S. Army Engineer District, **Galveston**
P.O. Box 1229
Galveston, Texas 77550

U.S. Army Engineer District, **Little Rock**
P.O. Box 867
Little Rock, Arkansas 72203

U.S. Army Engineer District, **Forth Worth**
P.O. Box 17300
Fort Worth, Texas 76102

U.S. Army Engineer District, **Tulsa**
P.O. Box 61
Tulsa, Oklahoma 74101

3. U.S. SOIL CONSERVATION SERVICE: STATE OFFICES

Wright Building
138 South Gay Street
P.O. Box 311
ALABAMA, Auburn 36830

204 East Fifth Avenue
Room 217
ALASKA, Anchorage 99501

2828 Chiles Road
P.O. Box 1019
CALIFORNIA, Davis 95616

Mansfield Professional Park
Route 44A
CONNECTICUT, Storrs 06268

Treadway Towers, Suite 2-4
9 East Loockerman Street
DELAWARE, Dover 19901

Federal Building
P.O. Box 1208
FLORIDA, Gainesville

Federal Building
355 E. Hancock Avenue
P.O. Box 832
GEORGIA, Athens 30601

440 Alexander Young Bldg.
HAWAII, Honolulu 96813

Federal Building
200 W. Church Street
P.O. Box 678
ILLINOIS, Champaign 61820

Atkinson Square-West
Suite 2200
5610 Crawfordsville Road
INDIANA, Indianapolis 46224

3737 Government Street
P.O. Box 1630
LOUISIANA, Alexandria 71301

USDA Building
University of Maine
MAINE, Orono 04473

Room 522, Hartwick Building
4321 Hartwick Road
MARYLAND, College Park 20740

29 Cottage Street
MASSACHUSETTS, Amherst 01002

1405 Harrison Road
MICHIGAN, East Lansing 48823

200 Federal Bldg. and
U.S. Courthouse
316 North Robert Street
MINNESOTA, St. Paul 55101

Milner Building, Room 590
P.O. Box 610
MISSISSIPPI, Jackson 39205

Federal Building
NEW HAMPSHIRE, Durham 03824

1370 Hamilton Street
P.O. Box 219
NEW JERSEY, Somerset 08873

Midtown Plaza - Room 400
700 East Water Street
NEW YORK, Syracuse 13210

Federal Office Building
310 New Bern Avenue
Fifth Floor - P.O. Box 27307
NORTH CAROLINA, Raleigh 27611

311 Old Federal Building
3rd & State Streets
OHIO, Columbus   43215

Washington Building
1218 S.W. Washington Street
OREGON, Portland 97205

Caribbean Area
1409 Ponce de Leon Avenue
Stop 20
PUERTO RICO, Santurce   00907
Mailing address:
   GPO Box 4868
   PUERTO RICO, San Juan
      00936

222 Quaker Lane
RHODE ISLAND, West Warwick
   02893

Federal Building
901 Sumter Street
SOUTH CAROLINA, Columbia
   29201

16-20 South Main Street
P.O. Box 648
TEXAS, Temple 76501

Federal Bldg., Room 9201
400 N. 8th Street
P.O. Box 10026
VIRGINIA, Richmond 23240

360 U.S. Courthouse
W. 920 Riverside Avenue
WASHINGTON, Spokane 99201

4601 Hammersley Road
P.O. Box 4248
WISCONSIN, Madison 53711

4. U.S. DEPARTMENT OF HOUSING AND URBAN DEVELOPMENT FLOOD INSURANCE ADMINISTRATION

REGION I (For Connecticut, Maine, Massachusetts, New Hampshire, Rhode Island, Vermont):
    John F. Kennedy Building
    Room 405A
    Boston, Massachusetts 02203

REGION II (For New Jersey, New York, Puerto Rico):
    26 Federal Plaza
    New York, New York 10007

REGION III (For Delaware, District of Columbia, Maryland, Pennsylvania, Virginia, West Virginia):
    Curtis Building
    Sixth and Walnut Streets
    Philadelphia, Pennsylvania 19106

REGION IV (For Alabama, Florida, Georgia, Kentucky, Mississippi, North Carolina, South Carolina, Tennesse):
    1371 Peachtree Street, N.E.
    Atlanta, Georgia 30309

REGION V (For Illinois, Indiana, Michigan, Minnesota, Ohio, Wisconsin):
    300 South Wacker Drive
    Chicago, Illinois 60606

REGION VI (For Arkansas, Louisiana, New Mexico, Oklahoma, Texas):
    New Federal Building
    1100 Commerce Street
    Dallas, Texas 75202

REGION IX (For Arizona, California, Hawaii, Nevada):
    450 Golden-Gate Avenue
    P.O. Box 36003
    San Francisco, California 94102

REGION X (For Alaska, Idaho, Oregon, Washington):
    Room 3068 Arcade Plaza Building
    1321 Second Avenue
    Seattle, Washington 98101

5. U.S. GEOLOGICAL SURVEY:
FIELD OFFICES

Alabama

    P.O. Box V
    Rm. 202 Oil & Gas Board Bldg
    Univ. of Alabama
    Tuscaloosa, AL 35486

Alaska

    Skyline Bldg
    218 E Street
    Anchorage, AK 99501

California

    855 Oak Grove Avenue
    Menlo Park, CA 94025

Connecticut

    P.O. Box 715
    Hartford, CT 06101

Delaware

    300 S. New Street
    Federal Bldg, Rm. 1201
    Dover, DE 19901

Florida

    Suite F240
    325 John Knox Road
    Tallahassee, FL 32303

Georgia

    6481 Peachtree Industrial
        Blvd.
    Suite B
    Doraville, GA 30340

Hawaii

    1833 Kalakuau Avenue
    Honolulu, HI 96815

Illinois

    P.O. Box 1026
    605 N. Neil Street
    Champaign, IL 61820

Indiana

    1819 N. Meridian Street
    Indianapolis, IN 46202

Louisiana

    Rm. 215 Prudential Bldg.
    P.O. Box 66492
    Baton Rouge, LA 70806

Maine

    State House Annex
    Capitol Shopping Center
    Augusta, ME 04330

Maryland

    8809 Satyr Hill Rd.
    Parkville, MD 21234

Massachusetts

    150 Causeway Street
    Suite 101
    Boston, MA 02114

Michigan

    2400 Science Parkway
    Red Cedar Research Park
    Okemas, MI 48864

Minnesota

    Rm. 1033, P.O. Bldg
    St. Paul, MN 55101

Mississippi

    430 Bounds Street
    Jackson, MS 39206

Missouri

    P.O. Box 340
    103 West Tenth Street
    Rolla, MO 65401

New Hampshire

    Rm. 307 Federal Bldg.
    55 Pleasant Street
    Concord, NH 03301

New Jersey

    P.O. Box 1238
    Rm. 420 Federal Bldg
    402 E. State Street
    Trenton, NJ 08607

New York

    P.O. Box 1350
    Rm. 343, US Post Office &
      Court House
    Albany, NY 12201

North Carolina

    P.O. Box 2857
    Raleigh, NC 27602

Ohio

    975 West Third Avenue
    Columbus, OH 43212

Oregon

    P.O. Box 3202
    830 N.E. Holladay St.
    Portland, OR 97208

Pennsylvania

    P.O. Box 1107
    Federal Bldg
    328 Walnut Street
    Harrisburg, PA 17108

Puerto Rico

    P.O. Box 34168, Bldg. 652
    Fort Buchanan
    San Juan, PR 00934

Rhode Island

    Rm. 314 Federal Bldg &
      Post Office
    Providence, RI 02903

South Carolina

    Suite 200
    2001 Assembly Street
    Columbia, SC 29201

Texas

    Rm. 630 Federal Bldg
    300 East 8th Street
    Austin, TX 78701

Virginia

    Rm 304
    200 West Grace Street
    Richmond, VA 23220

6. NATIONAL AUDUBON SOCIETY:
REGIONAL OFFICES

NEW YORK
514 St. Lawrence Avenue
Bronx, New York 10473

CENTRAL MIDWEST
Mauckport, Indiana 47142

MID-ATLANTIC STATES
P.O. Box 4181
Harrisburg, Pennsylvania 17111

NORTHEAST
P.O. Box 151
Stephentown, New York 12168

NORTH MIDWEST
R.R. 4, Roving Hills
Red Wing, Minnesota 55066

SOUTHEAST
P.O. Box 28191
Atlanta, Georgia 30328

SOUTHWEST
2507 Rogge Lane
Austin, Texas 78723

WEST
555 Audubon Place
Sacramento, California 95825

SOUTHEASTERN FLORIDA
7615 S.W. 62 Avenue
South Miami, Florida 33143

7. NATIONAL WILDLIFE FEDERATION: STATE OFFICES

ALABAMA WILDLIFE FEDERATION
660 Adams Avenue
Montgomery, AL 36 04

ALASKA WILDLIFE FEDERATION
& SPORTSMEN'S COUNCIL
Box 3072, Rt. 3
Juneau, AK 99801

CALIFORNIA NATURAL RESOURCES
FEDERATION
451 Parkfair Dr., Suite 2
Sacramento, CA 95825

CONNECTICUT WILDLIFE FEDERATION,
INC.
P.O. Box 7 (438 Main Street0
Middletown, CT 06457

DELAWARE WILDLIFE FEDERATION
26 Brookside Drive
Wilmington, DE 19804

FLORIDA WILDLIFE FEDERATION
4080 N. Haverhill Road
West Palm Beach, FL 33407

GEORGIA WILDLIFE FEDERATION
4019 Woburn Drive
Tucker, GA 30084

GUAM SCIENCE TEACHERS ASSOCIATION
INC.
P.O. Box 2872
Agana, Guam 96910

HAWAII CONSERVATION COUNCIL
P.O. Box 2923
Honolulu, HI 96802

ILLINOIS WILDLIFE FEDERATION
Box 116 (13005 S. Western Avenue)
Blue Island, IL 60406

INDIANA CONSERVATION COUNCIL, INC.
2245 Parkview Place
South Bend, IN 46616

LOUISIANA WILDLIFE FEDERATION
Box 16089 LSU
(6936 Renoir)
Baton Rouge, LA 70803

NATURAL RESOURCES COUNCIL OF
MAINE
20 Willow Street
Augusta, ME 04330

MARYLAND WILDLIFE FEDERATION
P.O. Box 343
Baltimore, MD 21218

MASSACHUSETTS WILDLIFE FEDERATION
P.O. Box 343
Natick, MA 01760

MICHIGAN UNITED CONSERVATION CLUBS
Box 2235 (2101 Wood Street)
Lansing, MI 38911

MINNESOTA CONSERVATION FEDERATION
Room 218 C, 790 Cleveland Avenue
St. Paul, MN 55116

MISSISSIPPI WILDLIFE FEDERATION
Box 1814
Jackson, MS 39205

NEW HAMPSHIRE WILDLIFE FEDERATION
116 Hazelton Avenue
Manchester, NH 03103

NEW JERSEY STATE FEDERATION OF
  SPORTSMEN'S CLUBS
P.O. Box 488
Freehold, NJ 07728

NEW YORK STATE CONSERVATION
  COUNCIL, INC.
5 Broadway, Room 505
Troy, NY 12180

NORTH CAROLINA WILDLIFE FEDERATION
P.O. Box 10626
(2209 Century Drive, Suite 402)
Raleigh, NC 27605

LEAGUE OF OHIO SPORTSMEN
2404 Cleveland Avenue
Columbus, OH 43211

OREGON WILDLIFE FEDERATION
P.O. Box 12438
Portland, OR 97212

NATURAL HISTORY SOCIETY OF
  PUERTO RICO, INC.
P.O. Box 1393
Hato Rey, Puerto Rico 00919

ENVIRONMENT COUNCIL OF RHODE
  ISLAND, INC.
40 Bowen Street
Providence, RI 02903

SOUTH CAROLINA WILDLIFE FEDERATION
5205 Trenholm Road
Columbia, SC 29206

SPORTSMEN'S CLUBS OF TEXAS, INC.
311 Vaugn Building
Austin, TX 78701

VIRGINIA WILDLIFE FEDERATION
5608 Waycross Drive
Alexandria, Virginia 22310

VIRGIN ISLANDS CONSERVATION
  SOCIETY
Box 4187
St. Thomas, Virgin Islands 00801

WASHINGTON STATE SPORTSMEN'S
  COUNCIL
P.O. Box 569
Vancouver, WA 98660

WISCONSIN WILDLIFE FEDERATION
Rt. 3, Box 896 A
Burlington, WI 53105

8. SIERRA CLUB

National Sierra Club
1050 Mills Tower
200 Bush Street
San Francisco, CA 94104

Chapters

Alaska
P.O. Box 2025
Anchorage, AK 99501

Angelese
2410 W. Bererly Blvd.
Suite 2
Los Angeles, CA 90057

Atlantic
50 West 40th Street
New York, NY 10018

Chattahoochee
P.O. Box 19574
Station N
Atlanta, GA 30325

Connecticut
Hartford Environ. Serv. Cen.
60 Washington Street
Suite 611
Hartford, CT 06106

Delta
111 S. Hennessey Street
New Orleans, LA 70119

Florida
c/o Entwistle
2036 Sussex Road
Winter Park, FL 32789

Great Lakes
53 West Jackson, Suite 1064
Chicago, IL 60604

Hawaii
c/o Bishop Museum
P.O. Box 6037
Honolulu, HI 96818

John Muir
444 West Main Street
Madison, WI 53703

Joseph LeConte
c/o Easton
818 Henley Place
Charlotte, NC 28207

Kern-Kaweah
c/o Ludeke
2632 Century Drive
Bakersfield, CA 93306

Loma Prieta
1176 Emerson Street
Palo Alto, CA 94301

Lone Star
c/o Walden
1507 Newfield Lane
Austin, TX 78703

Los Padres
P.O. Box 30222
Santa Barbara, CA 93105

Mackinac
409 Seymour Street
Lansing, MI 49833

Mother Lode
P.O. Box 1335
Sacramento, CA   95806

New England
14 Beacon Street
Rm. 719
Boston, MA   02108

New Jersey
360 Nassau Street
Princeton, NJ   08540

North Star
807 Midland Bank Bldg.
Minneapolis, MN   55401

Ohio
c/o Tybout
324 Pingree Drive
Worthington, OH   43085

Pacific Northwest
4534 1/2 University Way NE
Seattle, WA   98105

Potomac
c/o Denham
826 Glen Allen Drive
Baltimore, MD   21229

Rocky Mountain
c/o Sorenson
Rt. 2
7 Spruce Canyon Circle
Golden, CO   80401

San Diego
1549 El Prado
San Diego, CA   92101

San Francisco Bay
5608 College Avenue
Oakland, CA   94618

San Gorgonio
c/o Cleaver
1183 E. 28th Street
San Bernardino, CA   02404

Santa Lucia
c/o Bracken
765 Highland Drive
Los Osos, CA   93402

Tehipite
P.O. Box 5396
Fresno, CA   93755

Toiyabe
P.O. Box 8096
University Station
Reno, NV   98507

Ventana
c/o Vandevere
93 Via Ventura
Monterey, CA   93940

9. STATE COASTAL ZONE MANAGEMENT CONTACT OFFICES (NOAA)

ALABAMA
Alabama Development Office
State Office Building
Montgomery, Alabama 36104

ALASKA
Office of the Governor
Division of Policy Development and Planning
Pouch AD
Juneau, Alaska 99801

CALIFORNIA
Executive Director
California Coastal Zone Conservation Commission
1540 Market Street
San Francisco, California 94102

CONNECTICUT
Department of Environmental Protection
71 Capitol Avenue
Hartford, Connecticut 06115

DELAWARE
State Planning Office
Thomas Collins Building
530 South Dupont Highway
Dover, Delaware 19901

FLORIDA
Coastal Coordinating Council
309 Office Plaza
Tallahassee, Florida 32301

GEORGIA
Office of Planning and Budget
270 Washington Street, SW
Atlanta, Georgia 30334

GUAM
Director, Bureau of Budget and Management
Office of the Governor
Agana, Guam 96910

HAWAII
State Planning Division
250 South King Street
Honolulu, Hawaii 96813

ILLINOIS
Department of Transportation
2300 South Dirksen Parkway
Springfield, Illinois 62706

INDIANA
143 West Market Street
Indianapolis, Indiana 46204

LOUISIANA
State Planning Office
P.O. Box 44425
Baton Rouge, Louisiana 70804

MAINE
State Planning Office
Coastal Planning Group
184 State Street
Augusta, Maine 04330

MARYLAND
Coastal Zone Program
Tawes State Office Building
Annapolis, Maryland 21401

MASSACHUSETTS
Executive Office of Environmental Affairs
18 Tremont Street
Boston, Massachusetts 02108

MICHIGAN
Department of Natural Resources
Stevens T. Mason Building
Lansing, Michigan 48926

MINNESOTA
Coastal Zone Program
State Planning Agency
440 Cedar Street
St. Paul, Minnesota 55101

MISSISSIPPI
Coastal Zone Coordinator
P.O. Box 497
Long Beach, Mississippi 39560

NEW HAMPSHIRE
Office of Comprehensive Planning
State House Annex
Concord, New Hampshire 03301

NEW JERSEY
Department of Environmental Protection
Office of Public Information
P.O. Box 1390
Trenton, New Jersey 08046

NEW YORK
Office of Planning Services
488 Broadway
Albany, New York 12207

NORTH CAROLINA
Department of Natural and Economic Resources
P.O. Box 27687
Raleigh, North Carolina 27611

OHIO
Department of Natural Resources
Shoreland Management Section
Fountain Square Building E
Columbus, Ohio 43224

OREGON
Land Conservation and Development Commission
1175 Court Street
Salem, Oregon 97310

PENNSYLVANIA
Department of Environmental Resources
P.O. Box 1467
Harrisburg, Pennsylvania 17120

PUERTO RICO
Department of Natural Resources
P.O. Box 5887
Puerto de Tierra, Puerto Rico 00906

RHODE ISLAND
Marine Advisory Service
University of Rhode Island
Kingston, Rhode Island 02881

SOUTH CAROLINA
Coastal Zone Planning Office
Marine Resources Center
P.O. Box 12559
Charleston, South Carolina 29412

TEXAS
Coastal Management Program
General Land Office
State Office Building
Austin, Texas 78701

VIRGINIA
Division of State Planning and Community Affairs
1010 Madison Building
Richmond, Virginia 23219

VIRGIN ISLANDS
Director of Planning
Virgin Islands Planning Office
P.O. Box 2606
Charlotte Amalie
St. Thomas, Virgin Islands 00801

WASHINGTON
Department of Ecology
State of Washington
Olympia, Washington 98504

WISCONSIN
State Planning Office
B-130, One West Wilson Street
Madison, Wisconsin 53702

Artificial Dune Case Study

Artificially elevated dunes—the North Carolina experience.

SOURCE. Adapted from the following three sources:
1. Robert Dolan, Paul J. Godfrey, and William E. Odum. 1973. "Man's impact on the barrier islands of North Carolina: A case study of the implications of large-scale manipulation of the natural environment." *American Scientist*, Vol. 61 (March–April).
2. Robert Dolan and Paul J. Godfrey. 1972. *Dune Stabilization and Beach Erosion, Cape Hatteras National Seashore, North Carolina.* Dune Stabilization Study, Natural Resource Report No. 5, U.S. Department of the Interior, National Park Service, Washington, D.C.
3. Robert Dolan. 1972. *Man's Impact on the Outer Banks of North Carolina.* Dune Stabilization Study, Natural Resource Report No. 3, U.S. Department of the Interior, National Park Service, Washington, D.C.

From a geological point of view, the Outer Banks of North Carolina constitute one of the most dynamic areas under the jurisdiction of the National Park Service. The barrier islands that comprise the region undergo continual changes in position. Since oceanic overwash plays an essential role in this process, an unbalanced situation is developing wherever an artificial barrier dune has been built or encouraged. Moreover, the false impression of safety and stability offered by the barrier dune has encouraged further human development in the fragile barrier island area. Numerous structures, including restaurants, beach cottages, park facilities, and a United States naval station at Cape Hatteras, have been built immediately behind the barrier dune in the mistaken belief that it would provide permanent protection from encroachment by the sea. Instead, the beach has steadily narrowed, and the barrier dune has subsequently eroded away, leaving these structures with little protection from extreme storms.

The frequency of destructive storms along coastal North Carolina, with accompanying oceanic overwash, precluded the establish-

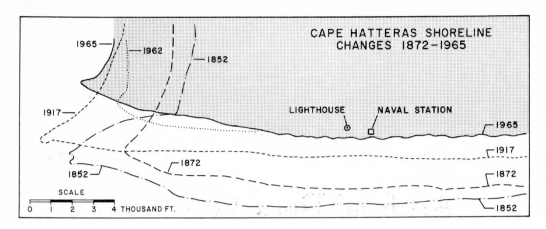

ment of a permanent road network until the 1930s. It was decided at that time to construct a protective dune system between the proposed road and the beach. In the period between 1936 and 1940, the Civilian Conservation Corps and the Works Progress Administration, under the direction of the National Park Service, erected almost 3 million feet of sand fencing to create a continuous barrier dune along the Outer Banks.

Because of steadily rising sea level—3 inches in 10 years (1973 data)—the beaches have receded in most places, resulting in overwash and build-up in the interior sand flats and the marshes. The net effect of this process has been a gradual westward movement of the islands.

Combined with the presence of a permanent dune structure, this beach-narrowing process has created a situation in which high wave energy is concentrated in an increasingly steeper beach profile. Because of the resultant increased turbulence, breakers have tended to grind the beach sand into finer pieces and then wash it away. The net effect is further erosion and narrowing of the beach (see figure). Ultimately the beach may disappear above the high-water mark; the wave uprush will then strike directly upon the stabilized dune. This has occurred in several places within the Cape Hatteras National Seashore and has resulted in a gradual undercutting of the dunefront, with

eventual destruction of the dune system and endangering of man-made structures behind the dunes.

Interference with the overwash process and inlet dynamics cannot help but decrease the productivity of the sounds behind the barrier islands. In the past, new marsh areas have grown up on sand deposited in the sounds through temporary inlets, and marsh grasses have invaded overwash sediment carried across the islands into the sounds. Marshes normally grow vertically by organic accumulation, but cannot now expand into the sounds because the supply of overwash sand, the basis for gradual lateral growth, has been cut off. Without the foundation for further growth the marsh edges become scarped and eroded.

Another problem associated with dune stabilization is the flooding and erosion of the barrier islands that occur when northeast storms pile the water of Pamlico Sound up against the islands. In the past the surge water simply flowed out between the dunes and over the beach to the sea, but now the water cannot drain off readily and vast areas of land are submerged at times. Hurricane winds from the southeast also force surplus waters into the sounds. When the storm moves off the coast, the winds shift to the northwest, resulting in a rapid reversal in flow which cuts into the island as it returns to the ocean. Wherever there are large barrier dunes, a hurricane results in severe beach erosion on the ocean side and floods on the sound side.

The natural opening and closing of inlets, together with oceanic overwash, creates serious problems in maintaining a permanent highway down the center of the Outer Banks. It is frequently necessary to clear the highways of sand deposited by overwash. On several occasions the highways have had to be rerouted when erosion destroyed the neighboring dunes and threatened the roadway. In other cases inlet formation has destroyed sections of the highway. The Ash Wednesday storm of 1962, for example, opened a new inlet between Buxton and Avon that required $700,000 to close, in addition to almost $1 million to rebuild the dune system and replace the roadway. The same storm destroyed segments of over 20 kilometers of the artificial barrier dune system, which also had to be rebuilt.

Although the present system is undependable, endangered, and expensive to maintain, proposed alternatives are even less economical and have questionable value in preventing additional destruction. One suggested approach is to attempt to maintain the beaches by constructing groins at right angles to them. The cost of groin fields commonly runs into millions of dollars, and yet they have not been very effective on the Outer Banks at Hatteras Lighthouse. Dredging and beach nourishment may cost $700,000 per kilometer and in most cases is also only a temporary measure.

A third suggestion has been to build a reinforced dune system at critical sites by forming seawalls of sand bags and filling the center with loose sand. Even a structure such as this, estimated to cost about $3 million per kilometer, will not stop heavy surf action for very long. A better solution, and one clearly more desirable from both an ecological and a geological standpoint, would be to construct an elevated highway on the sound side of the islands, allowing natural processes to take place with little resultant damage.

Survival of the natural beach environment along coastal North Carolina requires a strategy of submission and rebuilding. Man has attempted to draw a line and prevent the sea from passing. The results have been unexpected and negative. Because the Cape Hatteras portion of the Outer Banks has already been developed to the point where it would be virtually impossible to remove the highway, it must be maintained. However, as the system continues to narrow, new instances of overwash, erosion of the artificial barrier dunes, and inlet formation can be forecast. Many of the structures that have been built in the proximity of the beach will be lost, and the highway will require relocation in several places within a few years.

The Cape Lookout section of the Outer Banks presents an entirely different situation. The islands from Portsmouth Island south to Cape Lookout and then west along Shackleford Bank are undeveloped. There are no highways, utilities, and permanent settlements to protect. Placement of a permanent roadway down the island would require a continuous artificial dune system for protection and stabilization.

Indicator Plant Species
of Coastal Wetlands

Descriptions of selected plants that may be helpful in locating coastal marsh vegetation zones.

SOURCE. Plates A-H: Merrin F. Roberts and Mary Lohman, *Tidal Marshes of Connecticut— A Primer of Wetland Plants*, The Connecticut Arboretum, Reprint Series No. 1, New London, Connecticut, May 1971. Plates I-K: William Hammond, Lee County, Florida, Schools, Environmental Education Center, Fort Myers, Florida.

Key to the Mangroves

Note: Mangroves are trees or shrubs generally found growing on the shores of rivers, bays, estuaries, and protected beaches. They can tolerate salinities that range from Gulf access waters to freshwater creeks.
1. If the tree or seedling has no prop roots, go to number 2.
1. If the tree or seedling has prop roots extending from the trunk, it is a red mangrove (*Rhizophora mangle*), Plate I.
2. If the tree or shrub has leaves with a dark green upper surface and a gray–green, slightly hairy underside, go to number 3.
2. If the tree or shrub has leaves with a waxy green surface on both upper and lower surfaces, go to number 4.
3. If the tree has ridged or scaly bark, has leaves waxy on both surfaces, and lacks fingerlike projections or has only a few small ones, go to number 4.
3. If the trunk is dark brown to black and has fingerlike growths around its base (pneumatophores), the tree is a black mangrove (*Avicennia nitida*), Plate J.
4. If the leaves are opposite, are oval with a notch in the apex, and have a small lump on the petiole at the base of the leaf blade, the tree is a white mangrove (*Laguncularia racemosa*), Plate K.
4. If the leaves are pointed and alternate, the tree is a buttonwood (false mangrove) (*Conocarpus erectus*), Plate K.

894

SUNFLOWER family

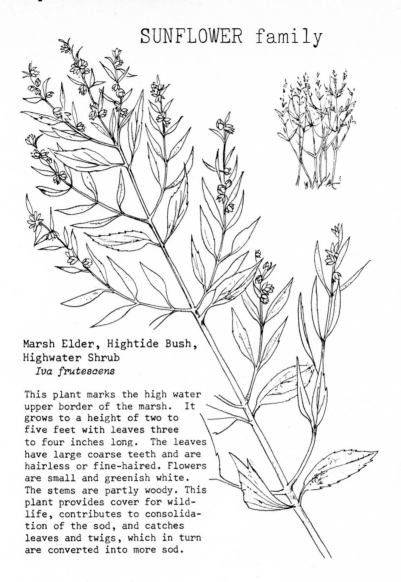

Marsh Elder, Hightide Bush,
Highwater Shrub
  Iva frutescens

This plant marks the high water
upper border of the marsh. It
grows to a height of two to
five feet with leaves three
to four inches long. The leaves
have large coarse teeth and are
hairless or fine-haired. Flowers
are small and greenish white.
The stems are partly woody. This
plant provides cover for wildlife, contributes to consolidation of the sod, and catches
leaves and twigs, which in turn
are converted into more sod.

Plate A

Common Reed-grass
Phragmites communis

Found on upper slope and exceptional high tide levels of the
marsh. Stalks five to fifteen
feet tall; from long horizontal
root stocks. The flower cluster is six inches to a foot or
more long and looks feathery.
Found in wetlands throughout
Connecticut where swamps and
marshes have been disturbed for
one reason or another. Small
stands occur on Great Island
and in Lieutenant River estuary - generally on the higher
ground where dredged river bottoms have been dumped. The
north end of Calves Island has
a classic example of this.
The plant has very little food
value for wildlife but serves
as an important stabilizer of
the marsh and hiding places
for wildlife. Esthetically it
has great appeal, but the fish
and wildlife people consider
it undesirable for waterfowl
production and are trying to
control its spread.

GRASS family

Plate B

GRASS family

Saltmeadow Grass
Spartina patens

This is the smaller and the finer
of the two saltmeadow grasses.
The larger species is known as
saltwater grass, Spartina alterniflora. This grass is easily recognized because the small flowers
and fruits are produced along one
side of the stalks. The smooth
stalks are one to two feet high.
There is a lot of it on Great
Island and interestingly, it will
grow both on salt meadows and on
sandy beaches which are wet by
the tides. This, and blackgrass
furnish most of the salt hay along
the Atlantic Coast. The seeds are
an important food for the black
duck. Geese and muskrat eat the
rootstocks. Jersey cows eat the
leaves and stems.

Plate C

Smooth Cordgrass, Saltwater
Grass, Saltmarsh Grass
Spartina alterniflora

Stalks are erect and smooth growing in height from one to nine
feet. Unfortunately for amateur
botanists, this plant is very variable in its forms but generally it
can be recognized by comparison
with this drawing if it is mature,
and if it is growing on the lower
border of a tidal marsh. As in
saltmeadow grass on the preceding
page, flowers are borne along one
side of the stalks. Brant, ducks
and geese eat the rootstock and
seeds and muskrats eat just the
rootstocks.

GRASS family

Plate D

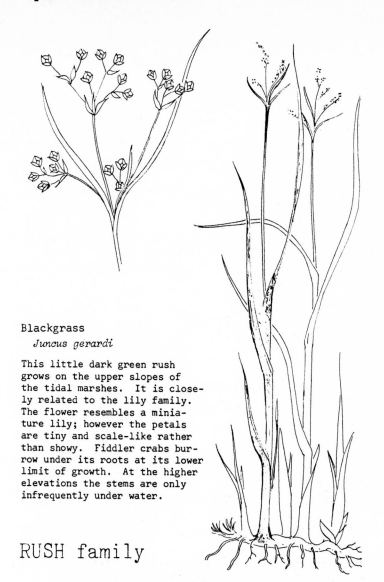

Blackgrass
  Juncus gerardi

This little dark green rush
grows on the upper slopes of
the tidal marshes. It is closely related to the lily family.
The flower resembles a minia-
ture lily; however the petals
are tiny and scale-like rather
than showy. Fiddler crabs burrow under its roots at its lower
limit of growth. At the higher
elevations the stems are only
infrequently under water.

RUSH family

Plate E

GRASS
family

Spikegrass, Saltgrass
Distichlis spicata

This plant is found in a variety of places on the
salt marshes. It is hairless throughout, and the
stems (from three inches to two feet tall) rise
from a horizontal rootstock. The flower clusters are pale green, dense, and spike-like. It
grows in dense colonies and provides nesting
cover for waterfowl. Black-ducks and teal eat
the seedheads, plants and rootstocks. Like black
grass it is a plant of the salty wetlands.

Plate F

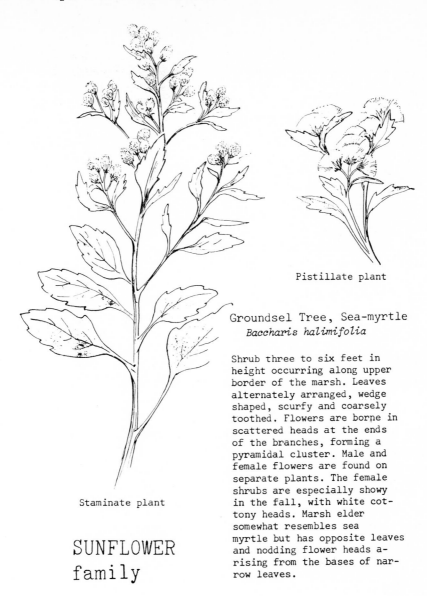

Pistillate plant

Staminate plant

SUNFLOWER family

Groundsel Tree, Sea-myrtle
Baccharis halimifolia

Shrub three to six feet in height occurring along upper border of the marsh. Leaves alternately arranged, wedge shaped, scurfy and coarsely toothed. Flowers are borne in scattered heads at the ends of the branches, forming a pyramidal cluster. Male and female flowers are found on separate plants. The female shrubs are especially showy in the fall, with white cottony heads. Marsh elder somewhat resembles sea myrtle but has opposite leaves and nodding flower heads arising from the bases of narrow leaves.

Plate G

GOOSEFOOT family

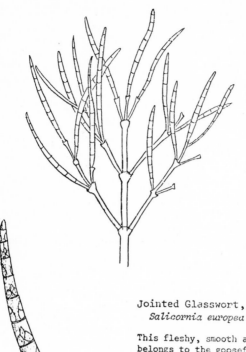

Jointed Glasswort, Saltwort
Salicornia europea

This fleshy, smooth annual plant
belongs to the goosefoot family.
This saltwort is the most common
one of several species. It grows
four to twenty inches high and
its outstanding feature is that
it often turns bright red in the
autumn. It grows in saltmarshes,
especially invading bare spots
where the usual wetland vegetation
has been disturbed by exceptionally high tides or by man. Geese
eat the branches; pintails and
scaup eat the seeds.

Plate H

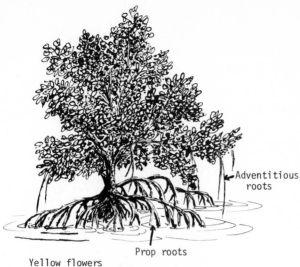

Adventitious
roots

Prop roots

Yellow flowers

Opposite leaves

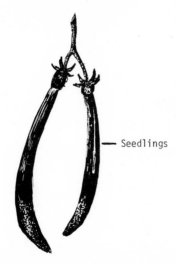

Seedlings

RED MANGROVE   Mangrove Family
                    (Rhizophoraceae)

Rhizophora mangle

Pioneer tree - Red Mangrove
grows into bays, tidal creeks
and estuaries. The trees in Lee
County often reach a height of
more than twenty feet in old
stands.

The tree has shiny, waxy
leaves, dark green on both surfaces and leathery, simple and
opposite. The leaves often excrete salt on both upper and
lower leaf surfaces (touch your
tongue to the leaf surfaces).

Trees have small yellow
4-petal flowers throughout most
of the year. Flowers develop
into a brown cone-shaped berry.
The new seedling grows out of
the center of this berry and
forms a pencil-like green seedling 6-10 inches long, which then
drops into the water, floating
first horizontally then vertically
until it reaches shallows where
it wedges itself into the mud to
begin a new colony. They have
extensive prop roots and adventitious roots which support them
while forming new colonies.

Red Mangroves in Lee County
are primary producers on which
many food chains depend, including
man.

Plate I

Pneumatophores

White flower cluster

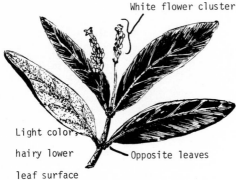

Light color,

hairy lower

leaf surface

Opposite leaves

BLACK MANGROVE   Verbena Family
                       (Verbenacea)

Avicennia nitida

Black Mangrove is closely associated with Red Mangrove stands on the
shoreward borders.

Black Mangrove has opposite ob-
long to elliptical green leaves that
are a lighter color and hairy underneath. It has small white flower
terminal clusters with four-lobed
flowers.

The seed pod resembles a large
lima bean about an inch in diameter.

Black Mangrove is very efficient
at excreting salt through its upper
leaf surface. In India and Asia this
sometimes is used as a source for salt.

The Black Mangroves generally
have a surrounding carpet of pencil or
finger-like projections called pneumatophores sticking up from the soil
surrounding the tree. Their function
is thought to be related to support
and respiration. In any event, they
form ideal habitat for juvenile fish
to hide, feed and mature safe from
large predatory fish.

The Black and Red Mangrove provide the primary habitat for marine
and bird life up to, and slightly
above, the mean high tide line.

There are many Black Mangroves
in Lee County 30 feet or more in
height and 10 or more inches in
diameter

Lima bean-like seed

Plate J

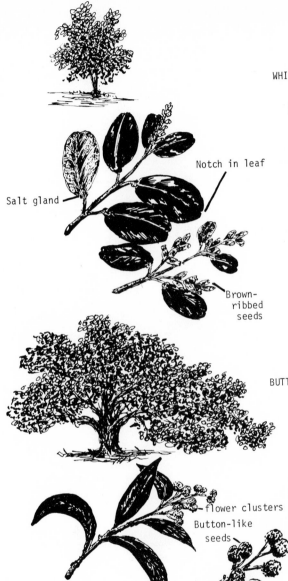

WHITE MANGROVE   Combretum Family
                       (Combretaceae)

Laguncularia racemosa

Generally a shrub-like tree
rarely reaching the mature sizes
of the Red and Black Mangroves in
Lee County.
Has simple, opposite leaves
with a rounded or notched apex,
reddish petioles and a pair of salt
excretion glands on the petiole at
the leaf blade base.
The flowers are greenish white
and grow on a spike. The fruit are
small, brown, ribbed, round, and
leathery.
The White Mangroves are common
on ground between the mean high tide
line and the upland transition zone
washed by storm tides. They also
often replace the Red Mangrove on
fresh water stream banks. This tree
is not as ecologically important as
the Red and Black Mangrove.

Salt gland

Notch in leaf

Brown-
ribbed
seeds

BUTTONWOOD, BUTTON-MANGROVE Combretum Family
                             (Combretaceae)

Conocarpus erectus

The Buttonwoods generally live
in the high, but sometimes wet, ground
bordering salt water, in groves inland
or on low islands. The leaves are
simple. alternate, green on both surfaces with smooth edges and a pointed
apex.
The flowers are in berry-like
heads which are composed of reddish
fruits in the tightly packed cone-like
spheres. The flower heads develop into mature brown button-like spheres.
The Buttonwoods were a primary
source for wood used by Indians and
early settlers for smoking and preserving fish and meats.
They also provide a habitat for
a wide variety of Bromeliads and orchids,
particularly where they grow in groves. A valuable tree as wildlife habitat.

flower clusters

Button-like
seeds

Plate K

Outer Continental Shelf Activities

A description of offshore oil exploration, development, and production.

SOURCE. American Petroleum Institute, Washington, D.C.

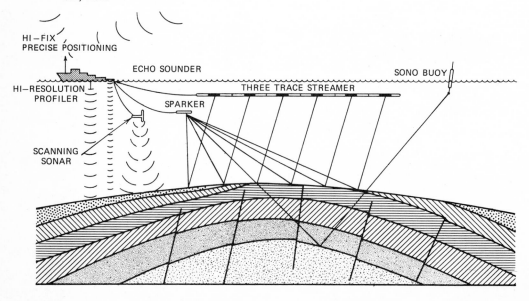

During the exploratory phase, three types of drilling rig
supports are likely to be encountered.

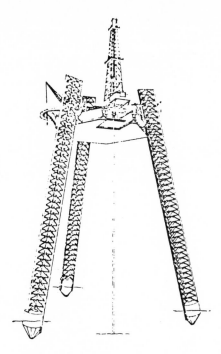

The jack-up rig is
the most popular rig afloat.
It is floated to location, its
elevating legs are positioned
solidly into the bottom, and
the platform surface is jacked-
up above the effect of sea storm
waves, to approximately 80 feet.

This rig is normally limited
to water depths of 50 fathoms.
Within this range, jack-up rigs
are considered very stable.

Supply boats of all shapes and sizes will run back and forth. . .
from shore facilities to rigs and back again to shore.

A second type of drilling
rig is the semi-submersible,
which can work in water from
20 to 50 fathoms. Older
models had to be towed to
the various drilling sites
while more modern rigs are
self-propelled. Once on the
site, they are partially
submerged and held in place
by anchors.

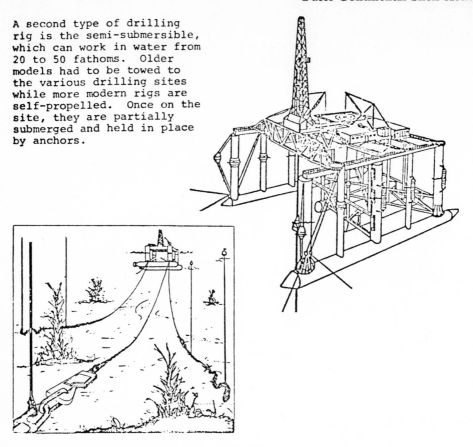

Since semi-submersibles will probably not be stationed within
50 miles of shore, runs will be long for the vessels bringing
supplies and crew members out to the rig.

The third type of drilling rig is a drilling ship which is used to operate in deep ocean water at great distances from land. They are self-propelled, require no assistance to move to most locations, and they are equipped with thrusters to maintain position dynamically. They require less support from supply vessels, because they are built to be self-sustained for at least a month at a time.

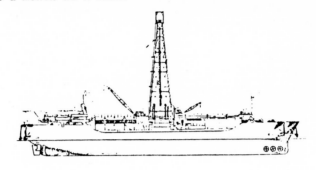

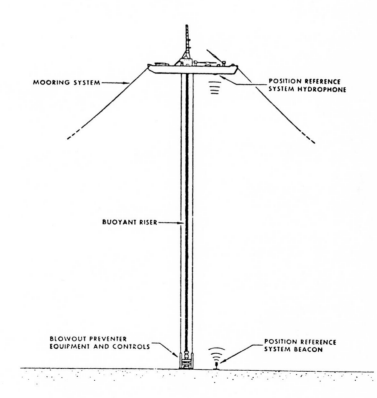

After enough oil or gas has
been discovered in one area to
make it profitable to develop
a field, production platforms
are constructed ashore and
floated to site. When on site,
the framework is flooded slowly
and ballasted down toward vertical position with floating cranes
controlling the rate of descent.

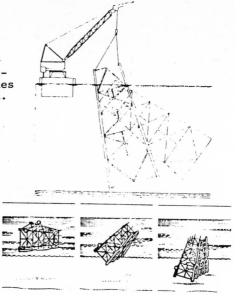

The platform is craned over its
precise location, oriented vertically, and eased onto the
bottom.

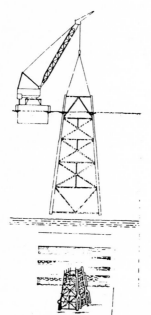

Piles are driven through
the legs of the framework
to anchor the platform firmly
to the bottom.

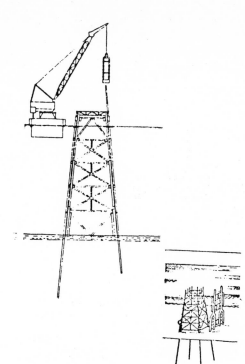

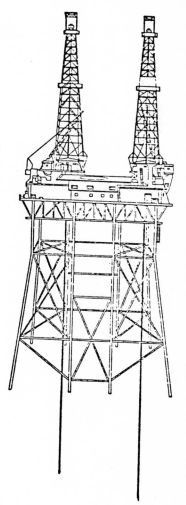

Drilling rigs are mounted on
the platform. These can drill
up to 30 wells from a single
platform and location. Wells
may slant up to 45° and extend
a mile beyond the platform.
After development drilling is
completed, rigs are removed and
the platform is used for production.

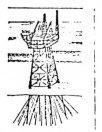

Depending upon the size of the field, a number of
platforms may be interconnected by pipelines. Oil and gas
produced from that area are sent through a single collecting
platform which monitors the volume of product before it is
(transported) sent ashore.

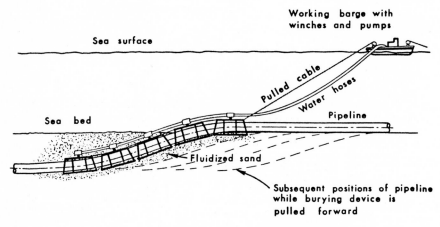

TRAIN OF SLEDGES DURING BURYING PROCEDURE

Glossary

Adverse effect

An adverse reaction of an ecosystem to a disturbance.

Agitation dredging

A method of dredging that involves overboard discharge of spoil with a high induced rate of dispersal.

Anadromous

Oceanic or estuarine fish species that enter fresh waters to spawn.

Areas of environmental concern

Areas which, because of their environmental significance, require special management considerations.

Aquifer

A geologic stratum that contains water that can be economically removed and used for human purposes.

Back dune

A stable dune behind the shifting frontal beach dune, often characterized by heavier vegetation.

Barrier islands

Elongate seafront islands of sand formed by the action of the sea.

Bay

A large estuary with a relatively high degree of flushing.

Benthos

The community of bottom-dwelling life.

Berm

A formation of sand deposited as a ridge on the shore just above the normal high water mark by wave action.

Biochemical oxygen demand (BOD)

A measure of the amount of dissolved oxygen required in biochemical processes to oxidize wastes in water (impounds).

Biocide

A chemical preparation used for the control or eradication of a pest or a plant, including insecticides, herbicides, fungicides, and rodenticides.

Biomass

The total mass of living matter in a given space.

Biological magnification

A process through which toxins become concentrated as they are passed up the food chain.

Biota

The plant and animal assemblage of a biologic community.

Brackish water

Fresh water diluted with a small amount of salt water.

Buffer area

A limited use area separating a developed area from a protected area.

Carrying capacity

The limit to the amount of life that can be supported by any given habitat; specifically, the number of individuals of any particular species that can be supported by a habitat. In another sense, the reasonable limits of human occupancy or use of a resource.

Characteristics

The qualities that give each coastal water basin its distinctiveness, such as the species mix, the general water condition, or the visual appearance of the basin.

Circulation

The pattern of water movement in a coastal basin.

Climax state

The final equilibrium community reached in the process of botanical succession.

Closed cycle

A self-contained steam-condenser cooling system for electric power plants that requires water input only to replace evaporative losses and to dilute residues.

Coastal

Of or pertaining to the seacoast; specifically, the waters, margins, or shorelands of estuarine basins, and the nearshore ocean.

Coastal upwelling

A process by which water moves shoreward along the bottom of a water basin into the shore zone; a reaction usually caused by wind forcing surface waters offshore.

Coastal waters

As a management definition, territorial or interior waters that contain a measurable quantity or percentage of seawater (e.g., more than 0.5 parts per thousand).

Coastal watershed

A drainage basin that drains directly into coastal waters; excludes drainage basins that drain wholly into freshwater channels tributary to coastal waters.

Community

The plants and/or animals of a particular habitat.

Confinement

The degree of closure of a coastal water basin; "confined" indicates shoreline length three times width of opening.

Consumers

Plant-eating animals (herbivores).

Contouring

The practice of planting or preparing a field according to the contour of the land.

Decomposers

Bacteria that reduce dead matter to basic minerals.

Detritus

Particles of plant matter in varying stages of decomposition.

Disturbance

A disruption, or perturbation, of an ecoystem resulting from human activity.

Diversity

The variety of species present in a biological community.

Diversity index

A measure of diversity.

Drainage basin

The entire area of shorelands drained by a single watercourse and its tributaries.

Drainageway

A pathway for watershed drainage characterized by wet soil vegetation; often intermittent in flow.

Dunes

Accumulations of sand in ridges or mounds landward of the beach berm formed by natural processes and usually parallel to the shoreline.

Ecologic effect

The reaction of an ecosystem to an ecologic disturbance.

Ecology

The science that relates living forms to their environment.

Ecosystem

The complete ecological system operating in a given geographic unit, including the biological community and the physical environment.

Ecotone

The transition area, or border area, between two ecological communities, as between a marsh system and a forest system.

Eddy

A water current moving contrary to the direction of the main current, especially in a circular motion.

Embayment

A relatively small and shallow estuary with rather restricted flushing (differs from lagoon by having significant freshwater inflow).

Endemic

A species of limited geographic extent, confined to or indigenous to a region.

Entrainment

Removal of suspended life from an aquatic ecosystem by withdrawal of water.

Environmental impact

An environmental change that affects human needs (cf. ecologic effect).

Erosion

The weathering and displacement of rock and soil by the force of moving water, wind, and gravity.

Estuary

A confined coastal water body with an open connection to the sea and a measurable quantity of salt in its waters.

Eutrophication

Nutrient overenrichment of water that leads to excessive growth of aquatic plants.

Evapotranspiration

A collective term for the processes of evaporation and plant transpiration by which water is returned to the atmosphere.

Fauna

A collective term for the animal species present in an ecosystem.

Features

The fixed physical objects, such as coral reefs, mud flats, or grass beds of a coastal ecosystem.

Fertilizer

Any material or mixture used to supply one or more of the essential plant nutrient elements.

Filling

Artificial elevation of land by deposit of soil or sediment.

Flocculation

The process by which clay and colloidal particles are aggregated into small groups or masses, called "flocs," which settle from liquid suspension.

Floodplain

The area of shorelands extending inland from the normal yearly maximum stormwater level to the highest expected stormwater level in a given period of time (i.e., 5,50,100 years).

Flora

A collective term for the plant species present in an ecosystem.

Flushing rate

The rate at which the water of an estuary is replaced (usually expressed as the time for one complete replacement).

Food chain

The step-by-step transfer of food energy and materials, by consumption, from the primary source in plants through to increasingly higher forms of fauna.

Food web

The network of feeding relationships in a biological community; a system of interlocking food chains in a biological community.

Foragers

Animals that feed on consumers.

Frontal dune

A shifting dune lying directly behind the berm, usually parallel to the shoreline, formed by natural processes.

Groin

A structure perpendicular to the shore which serves to stabilize the shoreline by trapping littoral drift.

Gut

A narrow, deep channel characterized by rapid currents.

Habitat

The place of residence of an animal species or a community of species.

Impact assessment

The evaluation of ecological effects to determine their impact on human needs.

Indicator species

A species chosen to represent a particular environmental condition.

Intertidal area

The area between high and low tide levels.

Jackson Turbidity Unit (JTU)

The standard unit used in measuring the turbidity of a water sample; defined in terms of the depth of water to which a candle flame can be clearly distinguished. The Jackson candle turbidimeter is the standard measuring instrument which compares the amount of light penetrating a given water sample with that penetrating a standard sample.

Lagoon

A relatively shallow estuary with very restricted exchange with the sea and no significant freshwater inflow.

Leach

The dissolution and removal of substances (usually contaminated) by water flow.

Littoral

Of or pertaining to the shore, especially of the sea; coastal.

Littoral drift

The movement of sand by littoral (longshore) currents in a direction parallel to the beach along the shore.

Littoral zone

The part of the ocean immediately adjacent to the shore.

Longshore current

A current, created by waves, which moves parallel to and against the shore, particularly in shallow water, and which is most noticeable in the surf or breaker zone; littoral current.

Mangrove stand

An assemblage of subtropical trees of the genus Rhezaphora forming dense thickets which extend into coastal waters.

Modulators

The variable factors that limit the carrying capacity of the coastal ecosystem on a short-term (often day-to-day) basis. These include temperature, available mineral nutrients, dissolved gas concentration, and presence of toxic chemicals.

Nursery area

A place where larval, juvenile, or young stages of aquatic life concentrate for feeding or refuge.

Pathogenic

Capable of causing disease.

Percolation rate

The rate of seepage of water or liquid effluent downward through the soil.

Performance standard

A specific measure for control of a human activity.

Perviousness

Related to the size and continuity of void spaces in soils; related to a soil's permeability.

Photosynthesis

The manufacture by plants of carbohydrate food from carbon dioxide and water in the presence of chlorophyll, by utilizing light energy and releasing oxygen.

Phytoplankton

The plant component of the plankton.

Plankton

Small suspended aquatic plants or animals that passively drift or swim weakly.

Porosity

The soil's capacity to pass water.

Predators

Animals that feed primarily on foragers.

Primary productivity

The amount of organic matter produced by photosynthesis.

Processes

The energy flows that "drive" the coastal ecosystem; the flow rates that limit the productivity of the system.

Producers

Green plants, photosynthesizers.

Pump-storage plant

A hydroelectric generating facility operated by gravity flow of artificially elevated water.

Resuspension

The return of settled, deposited sediment to a state of suspension in the water body.

Rookery

A communal breeding site of shore birds or seals.

Salinity

A measure of the quantity of dissolved salts in sea water, in ppt., parts per thousand of water.

Salt front

The inland limit of measurable salt (0.5 parts per thousand) in an estuary at any given time.

Salt marsh

A tidal wetland supporting salt-tolerant vegetation.

Saltwater intrusion

A movement of salt water inland through soils into freshwater aquifers.

Sanitary landfill

A disposal area wherein solid wastes are spread in layers, compacted, and covered with soil each working day.

Sediment

Material (such as clay, silt, sand, gravel, organic matter, and debris) deposited by water, wind, or glaciers.

Sedimentation

A process involving the settling or deposition of particles of material such as eroded soils that are suspended in water or being moved by it.

Septic tank

A buried receptacle that receives and treats sewage from individual dwelling units.

Shearing strength

Resistance to shearing; a measure of the ability of soil particles to resist displacement relative to one another.

Shoaling

Reduction of depth of a water basin.

Shorelands

The terrain of the coastal watershed down to the upper margin of the wetlands (lower margin of coastal floodplain).

Sidecast disposal

The simplest technique for overboard disposal of dredged material whereby the spoil is discharged directly to the water.

Silt

Fine particulate matter suspended in water.

Sludge

A dewatered semiliquid mass of settled solids deposited from sewage.

Spoil

Materials dredged from water basins.

Standing crop

The number of a species in a specified area at a given time; also the mass of a species, or numbers or mass of all species.

Storage

Capability of a biological system to store energy supplies in one or more of its components.

Stratified estuary

An estuary with a surface freshwater layer flowing out and a heavier saltwater flowing in.

Submerged sill

A raised, horizontal formation along the bottom of an estuary mouth separating the estuarine basin from the ocean; the "lower lip" of the estuary mouth.

Subsidence

Downward local mass movement of the earth surface; often caused by excessive groundwater removal or by settling of fill.

Substrate

The base or surface upon which an organism lives.

Succession

The sequential, systematic, replacement of species by other species in a biological system.

Surfacing

Installation of impervious material over the land.

Suspended solids

Particles of material suspended in water, including plankton, organic detritus, and sediment.

Swale

A low-lying area frequently moist or marshy; an intermittent drainageway; a slough.

Tideflat

An unvegetated intertidal area.

Tide rip

A shearing of two adjacent currents causing a noticeable surface discontinuity.

Trophic

Of or pertaining to food or feeding.

Tsunami

A great sea wave produced by submarine earth movement or volcanic eruption.

Turbidity

Reduced water clarity resulting from the presence of suspended matter.

Vital area

A physical component, or feature, of such extreme importance to the functioning of an ecosystem that it should not be altered.

Waterfowl

Of the family Anatidae; includes swans, geese, ducks, brant; the "game birds."

Wetlands

Wet vegetated areas. *Coastal*. Naturally vegetated areas between mean high water and the yearly normal maximum flood water level.

Zooplankton

The animal component of the plankton.

Index